Fro

D0353769

WILEY
John Wiley and Sons, Inc.

Contents

1 **1 The Best of Great Britain**
2 Our Favorite Moments
4 The Most Picturesque Villages
5 Favorite Small Cities & Towns
6 The Greatest Historic Houses
7 The Best Palaces
8 The Best Museums
9 Britain's Finest Art Collections
10 The Best of Ancient Britain
11 The Best of Modern Britain
12 The Best Cathedrals & Abbeys
13 The Best Literary Experiences
14 *Spotlight: Britain Goes to the Movies*
16 The Best of Natural Britain
17 Our Favorite Romantic Getaways
18 Our Favorite Hotels & Inns
19 Most Memorable Dining Experiences
20 The Best Pubs
21 The Best Places to Enjoy the Arts

22 **2 The Best All-Britain Itineraries**
24 The Best of Great Britain in 1 Week
28 Highlights of Great Britain in 2 Weeks
32 Britain at Its Scenic Best
36 British Houses & Gardens
40 Royal Britain

44 **3 London**
46 Our Favorite London Moments
50 The Best of London in 1 Day
56 The Best of London in 2 Days
60 The Best of London in 3 Days
64 Victoria and Albert Museum
68 The British Museum
72 Royal London
76 Hampton Court Palace
80 London with Kids
84 Hyde Park
88 Regent's Park
90 *Spotlight: Up in Smoke*
92 Mayfair

96 Chelsea
100 Whitehall
102 London Shopping Best Bets
103 London Shopping A to Z
110 London Restaurant Best Bets
111 London Restaurants A to Z
118 London Hotel Best Bets
119 London Hotels A to Z
126 London Nightlife & Entertainment Best Bets
127 London Nightlife & Entertainment A to Z
134 Windsor & Eton
137 Fast Facts

140 **4 Kent & Sussex**
142 Favorite Kent & Sussex Moments
144 The Best of Kent & Sussex in 3 Days
148 The Best of Kent & Sussex in 5 Days
152 Great Houses & Gardens
160 *Spotlight: Mad, Bad & Dangerous to Know*
162 Dover
166 Canterbury
171 Where to Stay & Dine
172 Brighton
176 Where to Stay & Dine
178 Rye & Battle
181 Where to Stay & Dine
182 Chichester
184 Fast Facts

186 **5 South-Central England**
188 Favorite Moments
190 Best of South-Central England in 3 Days
193 Where to Stay & Dine
194 The Hampshire & Dorset Coast
197 Where to Stay & Dine
198 Ancient Sites in Wiltshire & Dorset
201 Where to Stay & Dine
202 Great Houses & Gardens of Wiltshire
208 *Spotlight: A Passion for Gardening*
210 Salisbury
213 Where to Stay & Dine
214 Winchester
218 Fast Facts

PAGE 83

PAGE 173

PAGE 212

PAGE 266

PAGE 311

PAGE 354

220 **6 The West Country**
222 Our Favorite West Country Moments
224 The Best of the West Country in 3 Days
228 The Best of the West Country in 1 Week
235 Where to Stay & Dine
236 Discovering the Southwest Coast
243 Where to Stay & Dine
244 Great Houses of the West Country
250 Great Gardens of the West Country
255 Where to Stay & Dine
256 Dartmoor National Park
259 Where to Stay & Dine
260 Somerset
263 Where to Stay & Dine
264 *Spotlight: Miniskirts & Millinery*
266 Bath
271 Where to Stay & Dine
272 Bristol
275 Where to Stay & Dine
276 Exeter
279 Where to Stay & Dine
280 Penzance
283 Where to Stay & Dine
284 St. Ives
287 Where to Stay & Dine
288 Fast Facts

290 **7 The Cotswolds**
292 Our Favorite Cotswolds Moments
294 The Best of the Cotswolds in 3 Days
298 The Best of the Cotswolds in 5 Days
302 The Cotswolds Wool Villages
309 Where to Stay & Dine
310 Gardens & Great Houses
314 Cirencester
317 Where to Stay & Dine
318 Cheltenham
320 Fast Facts

322 **8 Oxford & The Heart of England**
324 Favorite Moments
326 The Best of Oxford & the Heart of England in 3 Days
330 The Best of Oxford & the Heart of England in 5 Days

337 Where to Stay & Dine
338 *Spotlight: Whodunit?*
340 Great Houses & Gardens
346 Outdoors in the West Midlands
354 Charming Towns & Villages of the West Midlands
359 Where to Stay & Dine
360 Oxford
365 Where to Stay & Dine
366 Stratford-upon-Avon
371 Where to Stay & Dine
372 Fast Facts

374 **9 Cambridge & East Anglia**
376 Our Favorite East Anglia Moments
378 The Best of Cambridge & East Anglia in 3 Days
381 Where to Stay & Dine
382 The Best of Cambridge & East Anglia in 5 Days
385 Where to Stay & Dine
386 Historic Homes of East Anglia
390 Broads, Fens & Coastal Wonders
394 Norwich
397 Where to Stay & Dine
398 Cambridge
402 Where to Stay & Dine
403 Fast Facts

404 **10 The Northwest & the Lake District**
406 Favorite Northwest Moments
408 The Best of the Northwest in 3 Days
412 The Northwest in 1 Week
416 Off the Beaten Path in the Northwest
420 The Lake District
427 Where to Stay & Dine
428 Chester
431 Where to Stay & Dine
432 *Spotlight: R-O-C-K in the U.K.*
434 Liverpool
439 Where to Stay & Dine
440 Manchester
447 Where to Stay & Dine
448 An Excursion to the East Midlands
457 Where to Stay & Dine
458 Fast Facts

PAGE 396

PAGE 408

PAGE 456

PAGE 477

460 **11 Yorkshire & the Northeast**
462 Favorite Yorkshire & the Northeast Moments
464 Best of Yorkshire & the Northeast in 3 Days
468 Best of Yorkshire & the Northeast in 1 Week
473 Where to Stay & Dine
474 National Parks of Yorkshire
477 Where to Stay & Dine
478 Cathedrals, Monasteries & a Holy Island
482 *Spotlight: They Came, They Saw, They Conquered*
484 York
489 Where to Stay & Dine
490 Leeds
492 Fast Facts

494 **12 Edinburgh**
496 Our Favorite Edinburgh Moments
500 Best of Edinburgh in 1 Day
504 The Best of Edinburgh in 2 Days
508 Historic & Literary Edinburgh
514 Leith
518 Edinburgh Shopping A to Z
523 Edinburgh Restaurants A to Z
526 Edinburgh Hotels A to Z
531 Edinburgh Nightlife & Entertainment A to Z
535 Fast Facts

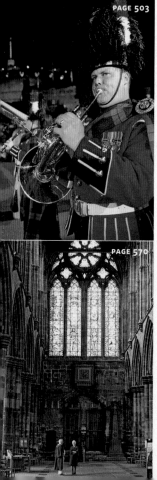

PAGE 503

536 **13 Glasgow & the Lowlands**
538 Our Favorite Glasgow & the Lowlands Moments
540 Best of Glasgow & the Lowlands in 1 Week
544 The Best of the Borders & Galloway
551 Where to Stay & Dine
552 The Best of the West Coast
556 Where to Stay
557 Where to Dine
558 *Spotlight: Golf*
560 The Best of the Central Belt
565 Where to Stay & Dine
566 Glasgow & the Lowlands for Architecture Buffs
570 Glasgow
578 Glasgow Shopping A to Z
579 Glasgow Restaurants A to Z
582 Glasgow Hotels A to Z
583 Glasgow Nightlife & Entertainment A to Z
586 Fast Facts

PAGE 570

588 14 Scottish Highlands & Islands
590 Favorite Highlands & Islands Moments
592 Best of the Highlands & Islands in 1 Week
596 Best of the Highlands & Islands in 2 Weeks
600 Best of North Argyll to Lochaber
605 Where to Stay & Dine
606 Best of the Trossachs to Balmoral
611 Where to Stay & Dine
612 *Spotlight: The Scottish Clans*
614 Best of the Northwest Highlands
619 Where to Stay & Dine
620 Best of the Hebrides
625 Where to Stay & Dine
626 Fast Facts

628 15 Cardiff & South Wales
630 Our Favorite South Wales Moments
632 The Best of South Wales in 3 Days
636 The Best of South Wales in 1 Week
642 Cardiff
645 Where to Stay & Dine
646 *Spotlight: British Castles*
648 The Brecon Beacons
651 Where to Stay & Dine
652 The Gower Peninsula
654 Pembrokeshire
658 Where to Stay & Dine
659 Fast Facts

662 16 North Wales
664 Our Favorite North Wales Moments
666 The Best of North Wales in 3 Days
670 The Best of North Wales in 1 Week
678 Snowdonia
681 Where to Stay & Dine
682 Anglesey & the Northwest Coast
685 Where to Stay & Dine
686 Conwy

688 17 Great Britain's History & Culture
690 Britain's 10 Greatest Cultural Hits
692 *Spotlight: Bombs and Blackouts*
694 A Timeline of British History
696 A Brief History of Great Britain

PAGE 603

PAGE 652

PAGE 672

PAGE 708

703 Britain's Architectural Evolution

706 British Art

706 British Music

707 Great British Fiction

708 British Theater

709 British Television

710 British Film

711 British Food & Drink

714 **18 The Best Special Interest Trips**

716 Short Jaunts

716 Multi-Activity Outfitters

716 Outdoor Activities A to Z

718 Special Interest Trips A to Z

720 **19 The Savvy Traveler**

722 Before You Go

726 Getting There

728 Getting Around

731 Tips on Accommodations

732 Fast Facts

739 **Index**

755 Photo Credits

PAGE 712

PAGE 716

PUBLISHED BY

John Wiley & Sons, Inc.

111 River St., Hoboken, NJ 07030-5774

ISBN 978-0-470-64869-8

Frommer's®

Editorial by Frommer's

EDITOR
Naomi P. Kraus

PHOTO EDITOR
Cherie Cincilla

CARTOGRAPHER
Andrew Murphy

CAPTIONS
Donald Strachan

COVER PHOTO EDITOR
Richard Fox

COVER DESIGN
Paul Dinovo

Produced by Sideshow Media

PUBLISHER
Dan Tucker

MANAGING EDITOR
Megan McFarland

PROJECT EDITOR
Kathryn Williams

PHOTO EDITOR
John Martin

PHOTO RESEARCHER
Tessa Perliss

DESIGN
Kevin Smith, And Smith LLC

SPOTLIGHT FEATURE DESIGN
Em Dash Design LLC

For information on our other products and services or to obtain technical support, please contact our Customer Care Department within the U.S. at 800/762-2974, outside the U.S. at 317/572-3993 or fax 317/572-4002.

Wiley also publishes its books in a variety of electronic formats. Some content that appears in print may not be available in electronic formats.

MANUFACTURED IN CHINA

5 4 3 2 1

How to Use This Guide

The Day by Day guides present a series of itineraries that take you from place to place. The itineraries are organized by time (The Best of London in 1 Day), by region (Kent & Sussex), by town (Bath), and by special interest (Historic & Literary Edinburgh). You can follow these itineraries to the letter, or customize your own based on the information we provide. Within the tours, we suggest cafes, bars, or restaurants where you can take a break. Each of these stops is marked with a coffee-cup icon ☕. In each chapter, we provide detailed hotel and restaurant reviews so you can select the places that are right for you.

The hotels, restaurants, and attractions listed in this guide have been ranked for quality, value, service, amenities, and special features using a star-rating system. Hotels, restaurants, attractions, shopping, and nightlife are rated on a scale of zero stars (recommended) to three stars (exceptional). In addition to the star-rating system, we also use a kids icon **kids** to point out the best bets for families.

The following **abbreviations** are used for credit cards:

AE American Express   **MC** MasterCard
DC Diners Club   **V** Visa
DISC Discover

A Note on Prices

Frommer's lists exact prices in local currency. Currency conversions fluctuate, so before departing consult a currency exchange website such as **www.oanda.com/currency/converter** to check up-to-the-minute conversion rates.

How to Contact Us

In researching this book, we discovered many wonderful places—hotels, restaurants, shops, and more. We're sure you'll find others. Please tell us about them, so we can share the information with your fellow travelers in upcoming editions. If you were disappointed with a recommendation, we'd love to know that, too. Please email us at frommersfeed back@wiley.com or write to:

Frommer's Great Britain Day by Day, 1st Edition
John Wiley & Sons, Inc.
111 River Street
Hoboken, NJ 07030-5774

Travel Resources at Frommers.com

Frommer's travel resources don't end with this guide. **Frommers.com** has travel information on more than 4,000 destinations. We update features regularly, giving you access to the most current trip-planning information and the best airfare, lodging, and car-rental bargains. You can also listen to podcasts, connect with other Frommers.com members through our active reader forums, share your travel photos, read blogs from guidebook editors and fellow travelers, and much more.

Advisory & Disclaimer

Travel information can change quickly and unexpectedly, and we strongly advise you to confirm important details locally before traveling, including information on visas, health and safety, traffic and transport, accommodations, shopping, and eating out. We also encourage you to stay alert while traveling and to remain aware of your surroundings. Avoid civil disturbances, and keep a close eye on cameras, purses, wallets, and other valuables.

About the Authors

Stephen Brewer (chapters 1, 2, 4, 7, 10 & 17-19) is a writer and editor who has worked in magazines, books, radio, and corporate communications for more than 30 years. He is the author of *Frommer's Best Day Trips from London, Frommer's Venice Day By Day,* and coauthor of *Frommer's Italy Day by Day* and *Frommer's Greece Day by Day.*

Novelist, playwright, and travel writer **Donald Olson** (chapters 3, 5, 6, 8, 9 & 11) has written several guidebooks for Frommer's, including *Germany Day by Day,* and has contributed travel stories to *The New York Times* and many other publications. His plays have been produced in the U.S. and Europe, and his novels appear under the pen name Swan Adamson.

Barry Shelby (chapters 12-14) recently completed his 10th title for Wiley and is the author of several guides to Edinburgh and Glasgow and of *Scotland for Dummies.* He is active in small-scale horticultural advocacy and is a crofter on the Isle of Lewis in Scotland's Outer Hebrides, raising vegetable crops, hens, pigs, and sheep. www.earshadercroft.com.

Donald Strachan (chapters 15 & 16) is a London-based journalist, writer, and editor who has contributed to newspapers worldwide, including the *Sydney Morning Herald,* the *Independent* on Sunday, and the U.K. *Sunday Telegraph.* He has authored or coauthored several guidebooks, including *Frommer's England 2012* and *Florence and Tuscany Day by Day.*

About the Photographers

Hamburg-based **Anne Ackermann** enjoys personal projects and assignment work for national and international medias, such as GEO, chrismon plus, and Caritas. www.anneackermann.com.

After deciding graphic design was not for him, Wales-based **Neil Beer** figured a career travelling around the world as a photographer seemed a plan. www.neilbeer.com.

Elisabeth Blanchet is a French London-based freelance photographer who works for *Time Out London* and contributes regularly to U.K., French, Belgian, and Swiss publications.

Alice Carfrae is a freelance photographer in the southwest of England. She photographs for a number of charities and runs workshops with young people and vulnerable adults.

Central American-based **Thornton Cohen** has photographed more than 40 countries for international travel publications and regional media outlets. www.thorntoncohen.com.

Scottish photographer **Kieran Dodds'** humanitarian and natural history work has been recognized by World Press Photo and the U.K. Picture Editor's Guild. www.kierandodds.com.

Jenny Hardy is a freelance British photographer. She has worked for the BBC, *Countryfile Magazine,* and the national press and lives in Bristol.

Paul Harris is a Europe-based advertising, documentary, and travel photographer.

Nic Holman is a photographer and cinematographer based in London. He divides his time working for major U.K. TV channels and companies and on personal documentary projects.

Widely traveled, **Gavin Parsons** photographs for a range of clients including Greenpeace and International Animal Rescue. He is also known for underwater and wildlife imagery.

Tim Smith is a photographer, writer, and researcher based in northern England. His projects have been showcased in dozens of exhibitions and 11 books. www.timsmithphotos.com.

With over 20 years of experience, **John Stroud** has had images grace the covers and pages of countless books, magazines, and other publications. www.jonstroudmedia.com.

Chiara Tocci is an Italian photographer living in the U.K. Her work has been exhibited and published internationally. www.chiaratocci.com.

1
The Best of Great Britain

Our Favorite Britain Moments

Standing in the middle of the Thames on the Millennium Bridge. London is a city that successfully meshes old and new, a truism that comes to the fore on this crossing that spans not just the river but the centuries, with St. Paul's Cathedral on one side, the Tate Modern on the other. The city views from the bridge are among London's best. See p. 54, **8**.

Wandering around Sissinghurst. The British love to garden, and this 1930s horticultural tour de force consists of a series of outdoor "rooms" that never fails to charm. See p. 156, **5**.

Circling Stonehenge. These imposing stones have been standing above the Salisbury Plain for 4,000 years; their purpose unknown, the great monoliths are an enigmatic and stunning presence. See p. 199, **2**.

Sitting in front of a fire with a glass of whisky at a Cotswolds inn. A sip of whisky in one of the region's atmospheric inns will hit just the right spot after a day spent exploring the picture-perfect Cotswolds countryside. See p. 309.

Strolling through the water meadows in Oxford. The water meadows alongside the River Cherwell serve practical functions such as grazing livestock, but they also make for lovely strolling—a natural enhancement to the architectural and artistic sights in Oxford. See p. 363, **6**.

Visiting the Shakespeare sites in Stratford-upon-Avon. Top off a tour of the literary shrines commemorating the greatest writer in the English language with a Shakespeare play at the newly refurbished Royal Shakespeare Theatre. See p. 366.

Hearing Evensong at Cambridge's King's College Chapel. The magnificent chapel at King's College in Cambridge seems most magical during Evensong services sung by the chapel's internationally famous choir, always a divine experience. See "The Voice of Evensong," p. 400.

Boating and walking in the Lake District. The picturesque peaks of the Lake District rise high above lakes, crags, forests, and meadows—a landscape that, according to William Wordsworth, is the "loveliest spot that man hath ever known." See p. 420.

Following the canals through Castlefield. The network of canals (and the warehouses and factories alongside it) that fueled Manchester's rise to power during the Industrial Revolution is now a well-preserved historic district. See p. 443, **7**.

Exploring the remains of Hadrian's Wall. Soldiers from all corners of the Roman Empire once patrolled this 73-mile defensive bulwark, started in A.D. 122 on the order of Emperor Hadrian and, for the most part, amazingly well preserved. See p. 472, **7**.

Admiring medieval York. The city's walls make an excellent vantage point for taking in the half-timbered houses and merchant halls that line the city's narrow lanes. See p. 484.

Strolling Edinburgh's Old Town. Begin atop Calton Hill to enjoy Robert Louis Stevenson's favorite view of the city; then follow the city's famed Royal Mile from Edinburgh Castle through the Old Town, exploring the many alleys that jut off this historic street. See p. 500.

Hiking in the Scottish Highlands. Britain's highest peaks are undoubtedly dramatic, with sheer cliffs rising from the sea, rugged countryside, and green, green hills surrounding secluded lochs. See p. 592.

Island hopping in the Hebrides. Getting around Scotland's Hebridean Islands is part of the fun, and once you arrive, you'll find yourself on the windswept northwest fringes of Europe: rich in Gaelic culture, prehistory, wildlife, sandy beaches, rugged moors, and lots and lots of water. See p. 620.

Standing on Yr Wyddfa. From Mount Snowdon's 1,085m (3,560-ft.) peak, the spectacular view extends over the Snowdonia range into all of the British Isles. You'll fall easily for the myths that dragons and King Arthur have made their homes in the wrinkles and folds of the mountain's flanks. See p. 678, **1**.

> PREVIOUS PAGE Windsor Castle is just a short
train ride from London. THIS PAGE Hadrian's Wall,
in Northumberland, may have once marked the
northern limit of the Roman Empire.

The Most Picturesque Villages

> *The beautiful Cotswold village of Bibury is known for its rows of traditional English stone cottages.*

Clovelly. Tiny, whitewashed cottages climb along a pebbled main street so steep that donkeys and sledges are used to haul goods up from this village's 14th-century quay. See p. 242, ⓭.

St. Ives. A compact village, now a famous seaside resort, faces the honey-colored sands and soft, shimmering sea—a setting that has inspired the many artists who have settled here. See p. 284.

Broadway. This lovely village of mellow golden stone has long been a popular escape of urban sophisticates; as one of them, expatriate American novelist Henry James, once said, "It's delicious to be in Broadway." See p. 305, ❹.

Bibury. No less an expert than William Morris, founder of the Arts and Crafts Movement, proclaimed Bibury the "most beautiful village in England." Thanks to its string of stone, pitch-roofed cottages alongside a gurgling stream, we'd be hard-pressed to argue with him. See p. 308, ❾.

Lavenham. Time melts away as you contemplate the charms of this picture-perfect Suffolk village, chockablock with half-timbered Tudor and Elizabethan houses with distinctive pink facades. See p. 383, ❸.

Hawkshead. This Lake District village of 17th- and 18th-century houses is not only attractive, but still resonates with the memories of its two most famous inhabitants, Beatrix Potter and William Wordsworth. See p. 422, ❷.

Kirkcudbright. The appeal of this thriving late-19th- and early-20th-century artist colony remains, thanks to its small, colorful cottages, wee lanes, and many galleries. See p. 549, ❽.

Plockton. Palm-like trees sway above the crescent-shaped main street of this most attractive village of the Scottish Highlands (and arguably the country), which faces the sheltered bay of Loch Carron. See p. 614, ❶.

Portmeirion Village. Designed to evoke the feel of an Italian village, this tourist magnet has inspired many an artist—it starred as "The Village" in TV's *The Prisoner*—and maintains its charming character thanks to a fanciful mix of architecture and gardens. See p. 675, ❺.

Favorite Small Cities & Towns

Rye. Step back in time as you walk past the Tudor, Elizabethan, and Georgian houses that line the cobblestoned streets of this beautiful old town, an inspiration to many a writer. See p. 178.

Winchester. This Hampshire city, one of England's prettiest and best preserved, boasts a magnificent cathedral, several historic buildings, and a picturesque location alongside the River Itchen. See p. 214.

Wells. A largely ignored gem, England's smallest cathedral city is also one of its most charming, thanks to a superb cathedral and the array of remarkably preserved medieval buildings that surround it. See p. 261, **5**.

Bath. The Romans, followed by 18th-century ladies and dandies, created England's most elegant and beautiful spa city—an attractive assemblage of Regency architecture sprinkled with ancient history. See p. 266.

Ludlow. Half-timbered "black-and-whites" share this Shropshire village's stage with elegant Georgian mansions, churches, and a mighty ruined castle. See p. 357, **7**.

Norwich. In this atmospheric and intriguing old city—the capital of East Anglia and a lively market city—picturesque medieval lanes wind around an ancient castle and beautiful cathedral. See p. 394.

York. This well-preserved medieval city's maze of ancient streets and hidden alleyways are encircled by walls and surround its crowning gem—the Gothic York Minster. See p. 484.

Conwy. A mighty fortress built for Edward I sits high above a pint-sized and atmospheric Welsh market town that for all its picturesque quaintness was a crucial 12th-century garrison and thriving 19th-century trading center. See p. 686.

> Rye was a member of the historic maritime confederation known as the "Cinque Ports."

The Greatest Historic Houses

> *The grandeur of Chatsworth makes it a worthy home for the Duke of Devonshire, but visitors are welcome to wander through some of its splendid rooms.*

Ightham Mote, Kent. This 14th-century moated manor house, nestled in a hidden valley, has seemingly remained untouched by the outside world for the past 700 years and sheds light on Tudor and Jacobean domestic life. See p. 153, ❸.

Hever Castle, Kent. Two wives of Henry VIII and the Astor family have called this medieval stone fantasy home; the moat and stunning gardens are icing on the cake. See p. 158, ❽.

Cotehele, Cornwall. One of the least altered medieval houses in England, built of granite and slate on the steep, wooded slopes of the River Tamar, is filled with a wonderful collection of ancient oak furniture, pewter, armor, and tapestries. See p. 247, ❹.

Saltram House, Devon. A largely undiscovered gem, this is one of England's finest examples of an intact Georgian-era house; stately rooms reflect the Age of Elegance with exquisite furnishings and elaborate plasterwork. See p. 247, ❺.

Owlpen Manor, Gloucestershire. One of England's most romantic houses, this lovely stone manor set in a secluded valley has been renovated several times since it was built around 1200 and even claims its own resident ghost. See p. 312, ❺.

Rodmarton Manor, Gloucestershire. One of the last manor houses to be built in England; the extensive gardens that surround it are a monument to early-20th-century Arts and Crafts design. See p. 313, ❻.

Holkham Hall, Norfolk. A first-rate Palladian manse is set amidst acres of parkland and filled with ancient Roman statues, Flemish tapestries, and important paintings. See p. 389, ❼.

Chatsworth, Derbyshire. Technically a country house (arguably, Britain's best), but probably more accurately described as a palace, this baroque beauty lives up to its nickname, "the Second Versailles." See p. 451, ❺.

Castle Howard, Yorkshire. One of the largest houses in the realm is known for its elegant architectural details, a beautiful cupola, superb rooms, and a 400-hectare (1,000-acre) park—and as a shooting location for popular films and television programs. See p. 466, ❷.

Harewood House, Yorkshire. An all-star line-up of 18th-century domestic architecture (John Carr), interior design (Robert Adams and Thomas Chippendale), and landscape design ("Capability" Brown) teamed up to create this superb neoclassical mansion and its gardens. See p. 473, ⓫.

The Best Palaces

> *Buckingham Palace has served as the official home of Britain's monarch since Queen Victoria.*

Buckingham Palace, London. Buck House, the queen's famous 500-room abode in the capital, is filled with treasures (this gilded cage of English royalty can be viewed by the public in July & Aug), and its State Rooms remain largely unchanged from the early 19th century. See p. 72, ❶.

Hampton Court Palace, near London. This Tudor masterpiece built by Cardinal Thomas Wolsey in 1514 was snatched up by Henry VIII, and its well-preserved staterooms, apartments, and gardens served as a suitably grandiose royal residence for 2 centuries. All told, Hampton Court is hard to beat for historic ambience. See p. 76.

Royal Pavilion, Brighton. You might think you're in India when you get your first look at this profusion of onion domes and minarets, commissioned in the early 19th century by George IV back in his Prince Regent days. The prince gave John Nash full license, and the result is an ornate fantasy, both inside and out. See p. 172, ❷.

Palace of Holyroodhouse, Edinburgh. You can tour the current queen's digs (okay...her State Rooms) in Edinburgh when she isn't in town, but the ruling attraction of this palace is the old wing associated with Mary, Queen of Scots, who lived here in the 16th century. See p. 512, ⓬.

Scone Palace, Perthshire. Some of Scotland's earliest monarchs called this palace home (the last coronation took place here in 1651). Though it's most associated with the country's hallowed Stone of Scone (which now resides in Edinburgh Castle; p. 510, ❹), there's a noteworthy collection of furniture and porcelain worth seeing. See p. 609, ❺.

The Best Museums

> A glass roof—added in 2000—soars over the British Museum's 150-year-old Great Court.

Victoria and Albert Museum, London. The world's greatest collection of decorative arts encompasses millions of objects in fields ranging from silver and sculpture to fashion and photography. See p. 64.

The British Museum, London. London's famous repository of priceless treasures—including the Rosetta Stone and the infamous "Elgin Marbles"—testify to the power the British Empire once exerted over the farthest reaches of the globe. See p. 68.

The Natural History Museum, London. Behind a famous façade adorned with statues of beasts are animatronic dinosaur displays, an interactive rainforest, and top-notch gem, mineral, and meteorite exhibits. See p. 80, ❷.

Roman Baths Museum, Bath. Navigate your way through fascinating exhibits showing the steaming rooms and saunas where Roman legionnaires once soaked and sweated. See p. 266, ❷.

SS *Great Britain,* Bristol. The world's first iron, propeller-driven, transatlantic steamship has been fully restored to its original 1843 appearance to provide a fascinating glimpse into ocean travel in the Victorian era. See p. 272, ❶.

Ironbridge Gorge, Heart of England. A fascinating assortment of museums housed in 18th- and 19th-century factories and warehouses details the birth of the Industrial Revolution in England. See p. 333, ❽.

Merseyside Maritime Museum, Liverpool. Galleries filled with lifejackets, photos, and other artifacts tell the stories of three great early-20th-century ocean liners: the RMS *Titanic,* the RMS *Lusitania,* and the RMS *Empress of Ireland.* See p. 434, ❷.

National Railway Museum, Yorkshire. An absolute must for train buffs shows off vintage locomotives and railway cars, including those from the royal trains. See p. 488, ❽.

Royal Armouries Museum, Leeds. This first-rate showcase for the remarkable collection of historic arms and armor from the Tower of London includes jousting sticks and elephant armor as well as medieval helmets, ancient hunting guns, and hand revolvers. See p. 490, ❶.

National Slate Museum, North Wales. A courtyard and vast halls that once echoed with the industrial din of slate production today chronicle the methods, machinery, and men that dug 90,000 tons of the rock annually from the surrounding mountainsides. The quarrymen's cottages are especially evocative. See p. 679, ❷.

Britain's Finest Art Collections

> *Pallant House Gallery, on the Sussex coast, offers a crash course in modern British art and an exciting schedule of temporary shows.*

Tate Britain, London. For an overview of British art from the 16th century to the dawn of the 20th century (including an unparalleled collection of works by renowned landscape artist J. M. W. Turner), you can't do much better than this prestigious museum. See p. 58, **7**.

National Gallery, London. More than 2,000 works representing the world's major artistic periods from 1250 to 1900 call this world-renowned museum home. See p. 62, **7**.

Pallant House Gallery, Chichester. One of Britain's most noted museums of modern art showcases works by Barbara Hepworth, Graham Sutherland, Henry Moore, Ben Nicholson, and other well-known 20th-century artists. See p. 182, **2**.

Barbara Hepworth Museum and Sculpture Garden, St. Ives. Dame Barbara Hepworth, one of the great sculptors of the 20th century, lived and worked here from 1949 until her death in 1975, creating the beautiful works on display. See p. 285, **2**.

Sainsbury Centre for Visual Arts, Norwich. This eclectic collection spans several thousand years, and you'll find works by such major English artists as Henry Moore and Francis Bacon sharing space with pieces by Picasso and Degas. See p. 397, **12**.

The Walker Art Gallery, Liverpool. Stroll the long galleries of the so-called "National Gallery of the North," and you'll find yourself standing in front of Dutch and Italian masterpieces, Pre-Raphaelite paintings, and the masterworks of Thomas Gainsborough and other British artists. See p. 436, **8**.

Manchester Art Gallery, Manchester. The Pre-Raphaelites take center stage at one of Britain's finest collections of painting and decorative arts, but don't skip the excellent textile and silver displays. See p. 441, **2**.

National Gallery of Scotland, Edinburgh. A classic Victorian exhibition hall shows off Scottish art from the 18th and early 19th centuries, along with Renaissance and Impressionist masterpieces. See p. 502, **7**.

The Best of Ancient Britain

Fishbourne Roman Palace, Chichester. The largest Roman residence in Britain, built around A.D. 50, features 20 magnificent mosaic floors, an underground heating system, and an elaborate bath. See p. 183, ❸.

Stonehenge, Wiltshire. This giant stone circle of pillars and lintels is Britain's most famous prehistoric monument, though how and why the stones were put here remains one of history's great unsolved mysteries. See p. 199, ❷.

Avebury, Wiltshire. An entire village is contained within the largest stone circle in the world, dating from 2500 to 2200 B.C.; you won't encounter any of the crowds that mob Stonehenge, and at Avebury you can get up close and personal with the mysterious sarsen stones. See p. 199, ❸.

Old Sarum, Salisbury. Earthwork ramparts, constructed around 500 B.C., still surround the remains of a city the Romans built on the site of an even older Iron Age settlement. William the Conqueror evidently approved of the workmanship—he set up shop here around 1070. See p. 212, ❿.

Chedworth Roman Villa, Cirencester. Eleven rooms of a large villa, one of the many Roman farming estates that surrounded Roman Corinium, are outfitted with elaborate mosaics, baths, and other signs of the ancient version of the good life. See p. 316, ❼.

Roman walls and amphitheater, Chester. Britain's largest circuit of walls, almost 2 miles in length, hails from the days when the city was a Roman fort, Deva Victrix. The enormous amphitheater was an assembly point for troops and possibly a base from which to invade Ireland. See p. 430, ❺ & ❻.

Callanish Standing Stones, Outer Hebrides. This circle- and cross-shaped formation of large standing stones atop a flat hill by the sea, a testament to a little-understood prehistoric community, was erected sometime around 3000–2500 B.C. See p. 624, ⓫.

> *The bluestone megaliths at Stonehenge were erected millennia before there even was a Great Britain.*

The Best of Modern Britain

London Eye, London. This glass-and-steel Ferris wheel (the tallest of its kind in Europe) solemnly rotates at one revolution per half-hour, and has become a London icon, much loved by even the most hardened London traditionalists. See p. 54, **7**.

Tate Modern, London. Britain's premier modern art museum is housed in the former Bankside Power Station and displays works from 1900 onward. You'll find works by Dalí, Matisse, Picasso, Giacometti, Mondrian, and other ground-breaking artists of the past century. See p. 58, **6**.

Thermae Bath Spa, Bath. In a striking mix of historic architecture and contemporary design just a few steps from Bath's ancient Roman Baths, you can soak, swim, and be pampered with all manner of modern spa treatments. See "Bathing in Bath," p. 268.

Albert Dock, Liverpool. The most advanced shipping complex in the world when completed in 1841, Albert Dock's magnificent brick warehouses have been beautifully restored for the modern era and now house shops, restaurants, museums, and other attractions. See p. 434, **1**.

Imperial War Museum North, Manchester. Renowned architect Daniel Libeskind designed the award-winning (and super modern) glass and steel shell that houses this adjunct of the Imperial War Museum in London; the building is meant to portray the earth shattering into shards representing earth, water, and air. See p. 444, **12**.

Cardiff Bay, Cardiff. One of Britain's most appealing contemporary districts follows the redeveloped docklands along Cardiff's waterfront, with a modern boardwalk, the copper oxide-treated steel shell of the Wales Millennium Centre, and the Senedd building, a testament to sustainable architecture and home of the Welsh Assembly. See p. 644, **4**.

> *Cardiff Bay, one of the most architecturally exciting waterfront developments of recent years, is frequented by locals and visiting families.*

The Best Cathedrals & Abbeys

> *Famed for its stained glass, York Minster is the most imposing cathedral in northern England.*

Westminster Abbey, London. Technically, it's not really a cathedral because it's under the direct jurisdiction of the reigning monarch instead of a bishop—but nearly every English sovereign since 1066 has been crowned in this stunning English Gothic edifice. Many of them are buried here as well. See p. 50, ❶.

Canterbury Cathedral, Canterbury. The first cathedral in England to be built in the Gothic style is most famously associated with St. Thomas Becket, who was murdered here by knights of Henry II in 1170. Pilgrims have flocked to this graceful assemblage of soft gray stone and medieval stained glass for centuries. See p. 166, ❸.

Winchester Cathedral. Britain's longest medieval cathedral was begun in the 11th century, and the Perpedicular nave is a stunning masterpiece. The cathedral is famously the final resting place of 12 Saxon kings, as well as a literary queen—Jane Austen. See p. 214, ❶.

Wells Cathedral. A facade with six tiers of medieval sculptures, and 14th-century remnants that include ornate stained glass, beautiful inverted arches, and a chapter house, make this a stunning example of Early English Gothic architecture. See p. 261, ❺.

Exeter Cathedral. Its clock reportedly inspired "Hickory Dickory Dock," but the main reason to visit this cathedral is England's largest surviving array of 14th-century sculpture and the longest fan-vaulted roof in the world. See p. 276, ❶.

Rievaulx Abbey, Yorkshire. The enormous ruins of this once rich and powerful monastic complex include a triple-arched nave, a three-tiered presbytery, and a chapter house—all romantically littering a wooded valley. See p. 480, ❹.

Durham Cathedral. This cathedral's spectacular setting high above the River Wear enhances the mighty effects achieved by Norman architects of the 11th century. See p. 481, ❻.

York Minster. Stand inside this former missionary teaching church, England's largest Gothic cathedral, and watch as diffused light streams divinely through half of all the stained glass in England. See p. 484, ❶.

Glasgow Cathedral. Mainland Scotland's only intact medieval cathedral rises above a vaulted Gothic-style crypt that houses the tomb of St. Mungo (d. 614), patron saint of the city. See p. 570, ❷.

The Best Literary Experiences

British Museum Reading Room, London. Follow in the footsteps of the many famous writers—Karl Marx, Rudyard Kipling, and H.G. Wells, just to name a few—who've spent time in this auspicious library while seeking inspiration and knowledge. See p. 68, ❷.

Monk's House, Rodmell. Novelist Virginia Woolf (who's buried here) and her publisher husband Leonard often retreated to this small and unassuming white clapboard house to relax and recharge their literary batteries. See p. 157, ❻.

Lamb House, Rye. Henry James, the expatriate American novelist, lived in this handsome, brick-fronted 18th-century dwelling from 1898 to 1916, followed by novelist-humorist E.F. Benson. See p. 178, ❶.

Hardy's Cottage and Max Gate, Dorchester. Fans can visit the thatched-roof cottage where the great Thomas Hardy was born and Max Gate, his Dorchester home, where he wrote *Tess of the d'Urbervilles, The Mayor of Casterbridge*, and other works. See p. 193, ❼.

Jane Austen's House Museum, Chawton. The famed novelist lived in this Georgian home during her most creative period from 1809 until 1817, and you can examine precious manuscripts and other Austen memorabilia. See "For Jane Austen Fans," p. 217.

Stratford-upon-Avon. Even the clamor of commercialism can't detract from the spirit of the greatest writer in the English language, and touring Shakespeare's Birthplace and other shrines to the Bard is a moving experience. See p. 366.

Dove Cottage and Wordsworth's Grave, Grasmere. Do pay your respects to the famous Romantic poet William Wordsworth at his gravesite, but no site associated with him in the Lake District is as moving as the simple and cramped cottage where he wrote his now-famous works in front of the hearth. See p. 425, ❻.

> Shakespeare's grave, inside Holy Trinity Church, is a popular Stratford stop for lovers of the Bard.

Brontë Parsonage Museum, Haworth. Literary sisters Charlotte, Emily, and Anne lived and did the majority of their writing in this home; it looks much as it did in their lifetime and contains a museum full of manuscripts and memorabilia. See p. 472, ❾.

BRITAIN GOES TO THE MOVIES

A Tradition of Cinematic Excellence BY STEPHEN BREWER

SOME OF THE WORLD'S FIRST MOVIES WERE SHOWN IN ENGLAND IN 1889, when moving images were first captured on celluloid film and projected onto the wall of a London workshop. The British cinema has been breaking new ground and enthralling audiences ever since, capturing the country at its finest and worst moments. *In Which We Serve* (1942) and other films captured the nation at war; *A Taste of Honey* (1961) and similarly gritty "kitchen sink dramas" portrayed working class life; and *Monty Python and the Holy Grail* (1975) showed off the twisted sense of humor lurking beneath the famous British reserve. Whether you're watching Alec Guinness' zany antics to inherit a dukedom in *Kind Hearts and Coronets* (1949) or being seduced by Highlands charm in *Local Hero* (1983), the region's classic films offer viewers a window into British life.

The Great Stars

RICHARD BURTON
(1925–84)

Captivated the public with two marriages to Elizabeth Taylor, his melodious Welsh accent, and brilliant performances in *Becket, Who's Afraid of Virginia Woolf?, Equus,* and other blockbusters.

COLIN FIRTH
(b. 1960)
The definitive cinematic Mr. Darcy graces the screen with quiet charm, whether he's bumbling his way through *Love Actually* or overcoming a disability in *The King's Speech.*

DEBORAH KERR
(1921–2007)

Delighted with her gentle Scotch lilt and remarkable versatility in tearjerkers (*An Affair to Remember*), musicals (*The King and I*), and drama (*Separate Tables*).

LAURENCE OLIVIER
(1907–89)

The revered actor, arguably the greatest of his era, appeared in almost 60 films, endearing audiences to a brooding Heathcliff in *Wuthering Heights* and transforming Shakespearean classics into Hollywood hits.

MAGGIE SMITH
(b. 1934)

One of Britain's greatest actresses won renown as a school teacher on the edge in *The Prime of Miss Jean Brodie,* and excels at polished portrayals of snobbish aristocrats (*A Room with a View* and *Gosford Park*).

The 21st Century and Beyond

Britain has not rested on its cinematic laurels. British studios, such as famed Pinewood, still produce many of the world's greatest hits, and British films in the 21st century continue to rack up worldwide acclaim and box-office treasure. Be it classic, award-winning period

dramas (*The King's Speech*); the latest slick James Bond thriller (*Quantum of Solace*); musicals (*Mamma Mia!*); major blockbusters (the *Harry Potter* series); or modern romantic comedies (*Bridget Jones's Diary*), British cinema continues to exercise a wide-reaching influence on the global film scene.

The Great Directors

DAVID LEAN The king of the big-screen epic, Lean (1908–91) captivated moviegoers with such award-winning classics as *Great Expectations, Lawrence of Arabia,* and *Dr. Zhivago.*

ALFRED HITCHCOCK The greatest British director of all time and a master of cinematic suspense, Hitchcock (1899–1980) demonstrated with *The 39 Steps, Psycho,* and other scary classics how a psychological thriller should be done.

The Best of Natural Britain

> *Within easy reach of many of Britain's most visited cities, you'll find peace, quiet, and wonderful scenery in South Wales.*

The White Cliffs of Dover, Kent. These iconic natural landmarks are composed of chalk and flint; a clifftop walk provides encounters with the many species of birds that inhabit the headlands, heady doses of bracing sea air, and stunning views of the Channel below. See p. 163, ❷.

Jurassic Coast, Dorset. You can't get a better lesson in coastal geography than hiking this 95-mile stretch, littered with prehistoric fossils and graced with coves, arches, and such beautiful strands as Chesil Beach. See p. 196.

Dartmoor National Park, West Country. One of England's last unspoiled landscapes consists of high, open moorland covered with colorful flowers and windswept granite outcroppings called tors. See p. 256.

The Malvern Hills, Heart of England. More than 100 miles of scenic hiking trails crisscross this ridge, which rises suddenly and spectacularly from the Severn plain and is home to a number of peaks with a bird's-eye view of the surrounding countryside. See p. 351.

Wicken Fen National Nature Preserve, East Anglia. Boardwalk nature trails wind through this 280-hectare (700-acre) nature preserve, revealing the unique characteristics of the now mostly vanished fenland ecosystem. See p. 393, ⑫.

Lake District. The hauntingly beautiful scenery here includes craggy peaks, bracken-covered hillsides, shimmering waters carved out by glaciers eons ago, and green forests. See p. 420.

Peak District National Park, East Midlands. England's oldest national park is a haven for hikers and climbers thanks to its protected, picture-perfect heathland, dales, hills, caves, and green fields. See p. 453.

Isle of Skye, Scotland. This misty isle, where the steep, sharp heights of the Cuillin Hills are a dramatic backdrop, enchants legions of visitors. See p. 596, ❶.

Gower Peninsula, South Wales. This lovely stretch of Welsh coastline, popular with outdoor enthusiasts, was the first location in Britain to be officially recognized for its outstanding natural beauty. See p. 635, ❸.

Mount Snowdon, North Wales. The stunning views of Snowdonia National Park from the summit of Wales's highest mountain are hard to beat for sheer natural beauty; your best bet for an ascent is to hike the scenic Llanberis Path. See p. 678, ❶.

Our Favorite Romantic Getaways

Gidleigh Park, near Chagford. For old-fashioned English romance and a dose of luxurious service, splurge on a stay (and dinner in the restaurant) at this wonderful country-house hotel, set on 18 hectares (45 acres) of beautifully landscaped gardens. See p. 259.

Cotswold House, Chipping Campden. The Cottage Rooms in this beautifully restored 17th-century house are your best choice for romance, thanks to the hot tubs and fireplaces; the first-rate spa enhances the mood, too. See p. 309.

Lygon Arms, Broadway. Frequented by the rich and royal over the centuries, some of the rooms in this luxury hotel date back to 1532, and there's historic atmosphere galore (as well as pretty much any amenity you can ask for). See p. 309.

Linthwaite House, Bowness-on-Windermere. This country house's quiet hilltop setting above Lake Windermere affords stunning views of the lake and surrounding countryside; luxurious rooms and gracious service do justice to the setting. See p. 427.

Miller Howe Hotel, Windermere. Relax in front of a cozy fire or take in the stunning views from the balcony of a lakeview room at this gracious mansion, set amid 2.2 hectares (5½ acres) of lush hillside gardens off the shores of Lake Windermere. See p. 427.

The Grange, York. Full of classic Regency charm, this antiques-filled house provides the expected comforts in a location just a few minutes' walk from atmospheric York Minster. See p. 489.

Middlethorpe Hall, York. Step back into the 18th century (with 21st-century luxury) when you enter this stunningly restored hotel, whose beautiful rooms are matched by equally lovely gardens. See p. 489.

Ardanaiseig Hotel, Kilchrenan. A romantic retreat on the shores of Loch Awe near

> *The panoramic terrace at Miller Howe, in Windermere.*

Argyll provides plenty of luxury and soothing views of gardens and the loch. See p. 605.

Tan-y-Foel, Betws-y-Coed. This secluded inn/restaurant with stunning views of the Welsh countryside and a no-kids policy ensures a romantic retreat. See p. 681.

Our Favorite Hotels & Inns

Durrants Hotel, London. This quintessentially English hotel dates back to the 18th century and boasts large rooms, a solid sense of comfort, and a great location. See p. 122.

The Cranley on Bina Gardens, London. Plenty of gorgeous period details, along with a rooftop terrace, high ceilings, and comfortable furnishings, add up to one of London's most restful getaways. See p. 122.

The DeVere Grand, Brighton. This dazzling Victorian seafront resort is one of England's best. If you can swing it, opt for a seaview room with a balcony. See p. 176.

Jeake's House, Rye. This atmospheric B&B with a pedigree—it dates back to the 17th century and is the former home of American poet Conrad Aiken—is a wonderfully cozy place to settle in for the night. See p. 181.

The Swan, Lavenham. An eccentric floor plan and distinctive architecture lend atmospheric credence to this well-preserved 15th-century inn, which adeptly mixes old and new while providing lots of cozy comfort. See p. 263.

The Abbey, Penzance. Set above Penzance's harbor, this small but elegant hotel will make you feel as if you're staying in a beautifully decorated private home; a lovely garden is an added bonus. See p. 283.

Albright Hussey Hotel, Shrewsbury. Dating back to Tudor times, this charming hotel and restaurant is a winner when it comes to period atmosphere combined with modern convenience. See p. 359.

By Appointment, Norwich. This elegant boutique B&B, located right in the heart of Norwich, is filled with antiques that enhance the 15th-century charm. See p. 397.

The Lowry, Manchester. Stylish minimalism rules at this sleek, luxury hotspot, a favorite of celebs and set on the banks of the River Irwell. See p. 447.

Balmoral, Edinburgh. This legendary city landmark overflows with Scottish flavor, from the kilted doormen at the entrance to the magnificent guest rooms with views of Edinburgh Castle. See p. 526.

Gleneagles, Auchterarder. This swanky resort provides no end of luxury (especially in the suites), along with some of the world's finest golfing. See p. 611.

> *The elegant drawing room at the Abbey, Penzance.*

Most Memorable Dining Experiences

> *An alfresco family lunch at the Seafood Cabin, Skipness.*

Rules, London. Founded in the 18th century, the oldest restaurant in London is a must if you yearn to dine on classic British cuisine (Yorkshire pudding, etc.) in an appropriately venerable setting. See p. 117.

English's of Brighton. The dining room is cramped, but the fresh seafood (opt for the Dover sole) at this family-owned restaurant is worth the modest inconvenience. See p. 176.

Jamie's Italian, Bath. Famed "Naked Chef" Jamie Oliver's fresh take on Italian cuisine attracts hordes to his Bath restaurant, but you won't mind that wait for a table once you start eating. See p. 271.

Michael Caines, Exeter. An impressive array of sophisticated cuisine comes out of the kitchen at this classy hotel restaurant, whose celeb chef makes wonderful use of local produce. See p. 279.

Abbey Restaurant, Penzance. A modern European menu of fresh local fish, meat, and produce mixes with lovely harbor views and a stylish dining room to produce a top-notch dining experience. See p. 283.

Anthony's Restaurant, Leeds. Chef Anthony James Flinn is a devotee of molecular gastronomy, and his forward-thinking dishes are both winning and ambitious. See p. 491.

Seafood Cabin, Skipness. On a sunny day, you can't do much better than picnicking on this summer-only operation's fresh seafood with views of the Isle of Arran in the distance. See p. 557.

Restaurant Andrew Fairlie, Auchterarder. The undisputed champ of Scotland's restaurant scene is a good place to splurge; the Scottish take on French cuisine is both creative and superb. See p. 611.

The Best Pubs

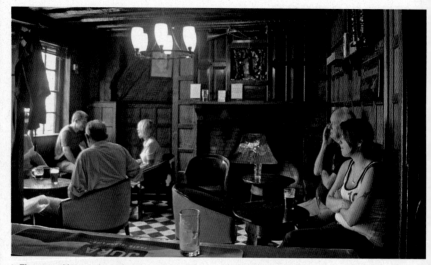

> *The warrenlike, wood-paneled interior of Salisbury's Haunch of Venison.*

Cittie of York, London. This Bloomsbury gathering spot has Britain's longest bar, a church-like interior (thanks to the enormously high ceilings), enormous wine vats, an historic pedigree, and real ale. See p. 133.

Basketmakers Arms, Brighton. It's a trifle cluttered, but this cozy retreat boasts a warm and friendly atmosphere and some of the best ales in town. See p. 176.

Haunch of Venison, Salisbury. This atmospheric but tiny 14th-century pub is reportedly haunted, and the service can be slow, but that doesn't scare off fans of its well-prepared meals. See p. 213.

The Ship Inn, Exeter. Set off a narrow lane, this ancient lair was reportedly the favorite of Sir Francis Drake and still retains a bit of maritime flavor. See p. 279.

The Turf Tavern, Oxford. A favorite of Oxford students and the fictional Inspector Morse, this 13th-century watering hole is a bit hard to find but worth seeking out for its convivial atmosphere and variety of drinking options. See p. 365.

Hole in t'Wall, Bowness-on-Windermere. A fire warms these 17th-century rooms, a local favorite, in winter; in summer, you can drink out in the garden. Either way, you'll get a friendly welcome and a choice of good ales. See p. 427.

The Philharmonic, Liverpool. A beautiful Victorian interior coupled with a great selection of ales and pub grub makes this place—once a favorite of John Lennon's—a must-do Liverpool experience. See p. 439.

Peveril of the Peak, Manchester. A friendly atmosphere pervades this popular and unpretentious pub, which mixes a traditional interior with a very distinct green-tiled exterior. The selection of food and drink is great. See p. 447.

Café Royal Circle Bar, Edinburgh. This institution is a longtime local favorite, boasting lots of atmosphere and Victorian trappings. It's a reliably comfortable place to grab a drink. See p. 531.

The Best Places to Enjoy the Arts

> *At the modern replica of Elizabethan London's Shakespeare's Globe Theatre, you can watch open-air theater much as they did in the 1600s.*

Shakespeare's Globe Theatre, London. The Bard himself would feel right at home in this meticulous replica of the Elizabethan original; to really get into the spirit, get a "groundling" ticket that lets you stand and watch a play much as they did back in the day. See p. 58, **5**.

Royal Opera House, London. This impressive and brilliantly restored 19th-century venue hosts both the Royal Ballet and the Royal Opera; it's beautifully decorated and has marvelous acoustics. See p. 130.

London Coliseum, London. This splendid Edwardian venue is totally suited to its role as the home of the English National Opera. See p. 130.

Royal National Theatre, London. Three separate stages at this acclaimed venue—the Olivier, Lyttleton, and Cottesloe—present some of the world's best theater productions in a variety of genres. See p. 133.

Chichester Festival Theatre. Locals wanted a swimming pool but got this renowned venue instead (a pretty good deal) that has played host to a who's who of British acting for the last half-century. See p. 183.

The Minack Theatre, Penzance. First used in the 1930s, this dramatic outdoor theater hosts touring companies from all over England every summer. The ocean views match the drama of the productions. See p. 241, **9**.

Theatre Royal Bath, Bath. This Georgian-style theatre is one of Britain's most beautiful theatrical venues and hosts a bevy of festivals as well as a series of touring companies throughout the year. See p. 268, **5**.

Royal Shakespeare Theatre, Stratford-upon-Avon. Few theatrical experiences beat watching the incredible actors of the Royal Shakespeare Company stage a great play in their Stratford home. See p. 370, **6**.

Usher Hall, Edinburgh. This Beaux Arts beauty is one of the principal venues for the famed Edinburgh International Festival and is highly prized by musical artists for its great acoustics. See p. 533.

2
The Best All-Britain Itineraries

The Best of Great Britain in 1 Week

If you only have a week to get to know Britain, then it's best and most efficiently spent in England. First explore the vast riches of London, one of the world's most fascinating cities. Then venture out to see other landmarks so iconic of British life—the great cathedral at Canterbury, the medieval university at Cambridge, the shrines to Shakespeare in Stratford-upon-Avon, and even a mighty castle at Warwick. You'll get a hearty taste of England, and an appetite for more.

START **Fly into London (p. 137). Check into your hotel for 5 nights.**

1 **London.** Though 3 days in the capital are hardly enough time to take in the full scope of this complex and fascinating city, they are just enough to whet your appetite and to see some of the abundance of sights and cityscapes. What better place to begin than **Westminster Abbey** (p. 50, **1**), the iconic place of worship where most of England's royalty has been crowned and where many monarchs have been married and/or been laid to rest. In your ramblings,

> PREVIOUS PAGE *A hike in the Brecon Beacons.* THIS PAGE *Canterbury Cathedral, long a place of Christian pilgrimage.*

don't overlook Poets' Corner, filled with dozens of memorials to England's writers and poets, and the beautiful Chapter House.

Just to the east are **Big Ben** (p. 50, **2**), the iconic clock tower whose chimes send a chill up the spine of even jaded lifelong Londoners, and the splendid Gothic Revival **Houses of Parliament** (p. 52, **3**), home of the House of Commons and the House of Lords. You'll get memorable views of these two landmarks from **Westminster Bridge** (p. 52, **5**), and on the other side of the River Thames rises one of London's newest and most popular landmarks, the **London Eye** (p. 54, **7**). This huge Ferris wheel solemnly rotates at one revolution per half-hour, affording views across the sprawling city.

You can't really experience London without a ride on its famous Underground (aka "the Tube"), so use it to get to **St. Paul's Cathedral** (p. 54, **9**), Sir Christopher Wren's stunning

1 London
2 Canterbury
3 Cambridge
4 Stratford-upon-Avon
5 Warwick Castle

NORTH SEA

CHESHIRE • Manchester ✈ • Peak District National Park • Sheffield • Market Rasen

Crewe • Buxton • Chesterfield • Lincoln

Matlock • DERBYSHIRE • Newark-on-Trent • LINCOLNSHIRE • Skegness

M6 • Stoke-on-Trent • Derby • Nottingham • Grantham • Boston • The Wash • Hunstanton • Cromer • North Walsham

STAFFORD-SHIRE • Stafford • East Midlands ✈ • West Bridgford • Loughborough • Spalding • King's Lynn • Norwich • The Broads National Park • Great Yarmouth

Glenfield • Oakham • RUTLAND • Stamford • Wisbech • NORFOLK • Lowestoft

Wolverhampton • WEST MIDLANDS • Leicester • LEICESTERSHIRE • Peterborough • March • Thetford • Diss • Southwold

Birmingham ✈ Birmingham • Coventry • Corby • CAMBRIDGESHIRE • Ely • Bury St. Edmunds • SUFFOLK

Kidderminster • Rugby • Northampton • A1(M) • Huntingdon • Cambridge • Stowmarket • Ipswich

WORCESTER-SHIRE • 5 Warwick • WARWICKSHIRE • M1 • Bedford • Saffron Walden • Sudbury • Felixstowe

Worcester • 4 Stratford-upon-Avon • Banbury • Milton Keynes • BEDFORD-SHIRE • Bishop's Stortford • Stansted ✈ • Colchester • Harwich • Walton-on-the-Naze

Great Malvern • Buckingham • Leighton Buzzard • Luton ✈ Luton • Hertford • ESSEX • Maldon • Clacton-on-Sea

M50 • Tewkesbury • Cheltenham • Cotswolds • Witney • Oxford • Aylesbury • Watford • Chelmsford • Billericay • Burnham-on-Crouch

Gloucester • GLOUCESTERSHIRE • Cirencester • OXFORDSHIRE • High Wycombe • BUCKINGHAMSHIRE • HERTFORDSHIRE • M25 • Southend-on-Sea

M5 • Malmesbury • Swindon • Thames • Slough • Windsor • 1 LONDON • London City • Dartford • Sheerness

Bath • Avebury • M4 • Reading • Heathrow ✈ • GREATER LONDON • Gillingham • Chatham • Margate

Hungerford • Devizes • Newbury • BERKSHIRE • M25 • Sevenoaks • Canterbury 2 • Ramsgate

Trowbridge • Basingstoke • M3 • SURREY • Maidstone • KENT • Deal

WILTSHIRE • Andover • Aldershot • Guildford • Gatwick ✈ • Tonbridge • Ashford • M20 • Dover

Salisbury • HAMPSHIRE • Winchester • Crawley • Royal Tunbridge Wells • Folkestone • Strait of Dover • Calais

Blandford Forum • Eastleigh • South Downs National Park • WEST SUSSEX • Haywards Heath • Lewes • EAST SUSSEX • Battle • Rye • FRANCE

DORSET • Southampton • New Forest National Park • Chichester • Arundel • Brighton • Pevensey • Hastings

Poole • Portsmouth • Newport • Bognor Regis • Newhaven • Eastbourne

Dorchester • Bournemouth • ISLE OF WIGHT • Shanklin • Ventnor • English Channel

Weymouth • Swanage • Isle of Portland

0 — 30 mi / 0 — 30 km

17th-century masterpiece, which survived bombardment during World War II. From there, it's a pleasant walk or quick Tube ride to the **British Museum** (p. 68), a treasure house filled with eclectic holdings from every corner of the British Empire.

Spend the next morning at the **Tower of London** (p. 56, ❶), part of which dates back to the days of William the Conqueror. Successive monarchs have put their own stamp on it, and the Tower has been the site of many a power struggle, execution, and murder. The city's most important historical site is home to the famed (and priceless) **Crown Jewels** (including the world's largest diamond); **Tower Green,** where some of history's greats lost their heads; and a number of ravens (kept prisoner here because legend says the kingdom will fall if they ever leave the grounds). Bid the Tower farewell and head across the Thames on the ornate, neo-Gothic **Tower Bridge** (p. 57, ❸), where you can ascend to the bridge's top level for a bird's-eye view of the Thames.

A short walk west along the riverside promenade brings you to **Shakespeare's Globe Theatre** (p. 58, ❺), the painstakingly accurate reconstruction of the theater where the Bard's comedies and tragedies were first performed—and still are. A little farther west along the river is the **Tate Modern** (p. 58, ❻), Britain's premier modern art museum; some of the world's most

> Technically, the job of the Beefeaters is to guard prisoners in the Tower of London, but they'll be just as happy to give you a tour.

important and exciting art of the past century is here. Board a boat for the prestigious **Tate Britain** (p. 58, ⑦), which houses an exceptional collection of British art from the 16th century to the dawn of the 20th century; the star of the gallery is landscape artist J. M. W. Turner, who bequeathed most of his paintings to the museum.

Spend Day 3 discovering London's many other charms, notably the city's parks and museums. Begin at **Buckingham Palace** (p. 72, ①), the queen's famous abode in London. You can witness the pageantry of the **Changing of the Guard** (every other day in winter and every day in summer at 11am) before escaping the crowds with a stroll through **St. James's Park** (p. 61, ④), London's prettiest patch of greenery. Tip your hat to the lions guarding iconic **Trafalgar Square** (p. 62, ⑥), and then view the paintings of such renowned artists as Botticelli and Van Gogh at the **National Gallery** (p. 62, ⑦), Britain's best art museum and the home of some 2,000 works spanning nearly 650 years. For a look at some of those who've shaped Britain politically, socially, and culturally, head next door to the **National Portrait Gallery** (p. 62, ⑧). Finish up your tour of

London with a stop at **Covent Garden** (p. 62, ⑩), a lively arcade filled with shopping, dining, and impromptu street performances. If you want to finish your stay with a more polished performance, head to one of London's famed theaters for a night of drama or music. ⊙ 3 days. See chapter 3.

On Day 4, venture south on a day trip to Canterbury. Trains leave from Victoria and Charing Cross Stations about every 30 min. The trip takes from 1½ to 2 hr.

② **Canterbury.** A trip down to Canterbury introduces you to one of England's most atmospheric medieval towns and most beautiful cathedrals. Visitors have been wending their way to this walled city since medieval pilgrims came to pay homage to St. Thomas Becket, who was murdered in the cathedral by knights of Henry II in 1170. Cobblestone streets pass such landmarks as **Eastbridge Hospital** (p. 166, ②), a hostel for pilgrims. Among the remains of the town's even earlier past are **St. Augustine's Abbey** (p. 168, ④), founded by the saint in 597, and the **Roman Museum** (p. 170, ⑥), showing artifacts from the settlement founded by legions of Emperor Claudius in A.D. 43. You'll soon find your way to the massive and magnificent Gothic-style **Canterbury Cathedral** (p. 166, ❸). Top off your visit by attending Evensong, when the transporting voices of the choir blend with the mellow hues of soft gray stone and late light streams through the medieval stained glass. ⏱ 1 day. See p. 166.

Return to London for the evening. Day 5 takes you on another excursion, this time to Cambridge in East Anglia. Trains leave from King's Cross Station as often as every 15 min. The trip takes from 45 min. to 1 hr.

❸ **Cambridge.** Follow in the footsteps of such luminaries as Sir Isaac Newton, Ralph Vaughan Williams, and C.S. Lewis, and spend the day exploring this pleasant and pedestrian-friendly medieval university city, built around bustling **Market Square** (p. 398, ❶). You can visit a few of its legendary colleges and admire them from the Backs, the acres of greenery behind the colleges along the River Cam. Cambridge also has some notable collections, including the Egyptian and Greek antiquities at the **Fitzwilliam Museum** (p. 402, ❾) and the 20th-century artwork and decorative objects at **Kettle's Yard** (p. 401, ❽). Before heading back to London, attend Evensong in the beautiful **King's College Chapel** (p. 400, ❹). ⏱ 1 day. See p. 398.

Spend a final night in London. Depart on the morning of Day 6 for an overnight in Stratford-upon-Avon. Trains for the 2-hr. journey leave about every 1½ hr. from London's Marylebone Station.

❹ **Stratford-upon-Avon.** After checking into your hotel, spend your afternoon paying homage to the Bard, visiting the main literary shrines: **Shakespeare's Birthplace** (p. 366, ❶); the gardens of **New Place** (p. 366, ❷), where he retired; **Hall's Croft** (p. 368, ❸), where his daughter Susanna lived; and **Holy Trinity Church** (p. 368, ❹), where Shakespeare is buried with his wife Anne and daughter Susanna. It's an easy 1-mile walk to **Anne Hathaway's Cottage** (p. 370, ❼), where Shakespeare's wife was raised and where the couple courted. Seeing a Shakespeare play performed at the newly refurbished **Royal Shakespeare Theatre** (p. 370, ❻) is a memorable way to end your evening.

> *A "royal weekend party" is re-created in wax in the rooms of Warwick Castle.*

⏱ 1 day. See p. 366.

On the morning of Day 7, take a Stagecoach bus to Warwick Castle, 9 miles northeast of Stratford-upon-Avon.

❺ **Warwick Castle.** The intriguing old streets of the ancient county town of Warwick are worth a stroll, but the main reason you're here is to visit mighty Warwick Castle, dramatically sited above the River Avon. The medieval fortress has been adapted over the centuries to reflect its inhabitants' tastes and ambitions, and includes comfortable Victorian and 20th-century apartments (inhabited by wax figures) that demonstrate what life was like inside the castle. Take some time to stroll through the beautiful parkland and gardens. ⏱ Half-day. See p. 342, ❷.

In the afternoon, head back to Stratford and catch a train back to London.

Highlights of Great Britain in 2 Weeks

You'll see many guises of Britain in these 2 weeks, including its three capital cities: London, Cardiff, and Edinburgh. Stops in between show off cathedrals, great houses, and the remnants of the many peoples who have influenced the realm, from Romans to Saxons to medieval traders. More than just presenting historic landmarks, this jaunt around Britain will also introduce you to animated street scenes, lively marketplaces and cozy lanes, and a distinctly British approach to life. You will make this trip entirely by train, so we recommend you equip yourself with a 2-week BritRail pass (see p. 728).

> *Salisbury Cathedral, here viewed from the water meadows surrounding the city, was a favorite subject for English painter John Constable.*

START Fly into London and check into your hotel for 3 nights.

1 London. ⏱ 3 days. See p. 24. **1**.

On Day 4, head to Salisbury. Trains run from London's Waterloo Station about every 30 min. The trip takes about 1½ hr.

2 Salisbury. Graceful **Salisbury Cathedral** (p. 212, **9**), a Gothic masterpiece topped with the country's tallest spire, dominates this lovely Wiltshire town. One of the finest landmarks is **Mompesson House** (p. 202, **1**), a Queen Anne–period town house tucked away in the Cathedral Close. Outlying **Old Sarum** (p. 212, **10**) is the site of "Old Salisbury," an enormous Iron Age hill fort that was later used by the Romans and Saxons. ⏱ Half-day. See p. 210.

Make an afternoon trip out to Stonehenge. Stonehenge Tour buses depart from the Salisbury train and bus station about every 30 min. to 1 hr. throughout the year.

③ Stonehenge. Built some 4,000 years ago on the Salisbury Plain, this giant stone circle of pillars and lintels is mysteriously aligned with the summer equinox. Whatever the reason for the presence of these great monoliths—the circle may have been intended in part as an astronomical observatory—seeing one of the world's most famous ancient monuments is a chilling experience (even if it is often crowded). ⏲ Half-day. See p. 199, ②.

Return to Salisbury for the night. On Day 5, move on to Bath. Trains run every 30 min. to 1 hr. throughout the day, and the trip takes about 55 min.

④ Bath. The Regency architecture that characterizes Bath is so unique that UNESCO has designated the entire city a World Heritage Site. Spend a day exploring such landmarks as the **Circus** (p. 268, ⑦), **the Royal Crescent** (p. 269, ⑨), **Pulteney Bridge** (p. 268, ④), and the **Assembly Rooms** (p. 269, ⑧), where ladies (such as one-time resident Jane Austen) and dandies gambled and danced the night away. The **Roman Baths Museum** (p. 266, ②) preserves the ancient bath

> *Stately Castle Howard is a spectacular example of English baroque architecture.*

complex where legionnaires once soaked. ⏱1 day. See p. 266.

Day 6 takes you to Cardiff, the capital of Wales. Trains run roughly every hour, and the trip takes a little over an hour.

5 Cardiff. Your first stop should be Norman **Cardiff Castle** (p. 642, **1**), where you can admire the 19th-century Gothic Revival renovations. The **National Museum** (p. 642, **2**), a short walk away, houses some of Britain's most significant portrait and landscape painters as well as one of the world's most important collections of French Impressionism. Then hop on an Aquabus out of Bute Park for a trip down the River Taff into **Cardiff Bay** (p. 644, **4**), where a bold new architectural renaissance is shaping the city's waterfront. Back on terra firma, take a walk around Cardiff Bay to see the restaurants and shops and to check out such architectural standouts as the very modern Senedd building, seat of Wales's government. ⏱1 day. See p. 642.

On Day 7, travel west to Oxford. Trains run roughly every 30 min. The trip takes about 1 hr. 45 min.

6 Oxford. Get an early start so you have the late morning and early afternoon to explore this esteemed university city, one of the world's great centers of learning. Thanks to its lively atmosphere, cobbled lanes, and riverside walks, Oxford also happens to be one of England's most appealing cities. A number of Oxford's 39 colleges open at least part of their premises to visitors. You can also visit such landmarks as the **Sheldonian Theatre** (p. 363,

9), designed in the style of a Roman theater (unlike many of the Gothic structures built at the time), and the **Ashmolean Museum** (p. 364, **12**), the oldest public museum in England, with a vast collection of art and archaeology. ⏱ Half-day. See p. 360.

Make the 30-min. trip out to Blenheim on bus no. 20 from the Oxford train station.

7 Blenheim Palace. Spend the rest of the afternoon touring this enormous baroque country estate, the only non-royal home grand enough to be labeled a palace. The home of the Dukes of Marlborough, it was the birthplace of Sir Winston Churchill and has memorabilia related to the former prime minister. Blenheim is imposing, but don't spend all of your time exploring the house; the lovely and extensive grounds were designed in part by the great Lancelot "Capability" Brown. ⏱ Half-day. See p. 340, **1**.

Return to Oxford for the evening. On the morning of Day 8, board one of the hourly trains that connect Oxford and Stratford-upon-Avon. The trip requires a change in Banbury and takes about 1½ hr.

8 Stratford-upon-Avon. ⏱1 day. See p. 27, **4**.

On Day 9, move on to Chester. The trip takes at least 3 hr. and requires a change or two en route, so check train schedules to arrange the fastest travel times.

9 Chester. You'll have a full afternoon and evening to enjoy this city where Romans established a fort back in the 1st century A.D. Chester is still surrounded by the fortifications the legions built, Britain's longest and most intact circuit of **city walls** (p. 430, **⑤**). Later inhabitants left such landmarks as the **Rows** (p. 428, **①**), a Tudor-era shopping arcade; and a landmark medieval cathedral (p. 429, **③**). ⊙ Half-day. See p. 428.

Rise early on Day 10 and head north to York, where you'll settle in for 2 days. Trains run as frequently as every 30 min., and the trip takes about 2½ hr.; a change en route is usually required in Manchester.

⑩ York. After a late-morning arrival, make your first stop mighty **York Minster** (p. 484, **①**); stand inside this mammoth cathedral and soak in the spectacle of medieval stone awash in the colorful light streaming through 128 stained-glass windows. A walk on the Roman and medieval walls will give you sweeping views of this fascinating city, which you'll explore on narrow alleys and lanes lined with such medieval landmarks as the 14th-century **Merchant Adventurers' Hall** (p. 486, **⑤**). The **JORVIK Viking Centre** (p. 487, **⑥**) recalls the days of Viking settlement, and the **National Railway Museum** (p. 488, **⑧**) evokes the power of train travel with such treasures as the carriages used by Queens Victoria and Elizabeth II. ⊙ 1½ days. See p. 484.

On the afternoon of Day 11, make a leisurely excursion from York to Castle Howard, 15 miles north and easily reached by direct bus from York.

⑪ Castle Howard. One of the largest houses in England is stunning both inside and out and crowned with a cupola. Works by Rubens, Reynolds, and other masters hang in the galleries and staterooms, and the 400-hectare (1,000-acre) park is landscaped with lakes and gardens. If the grandiose surroundings seem familiar, you probably saw Castle Howard in the television and film versions of Evelyn Waugh's novel *Brideshead Revisited;* in both, the house steals the show. ⊙ Half-day. See p. 466, **②**.

Return to York for the evening; then get an early start on Day 12, as you'll be heading into Scotland. Trains run from York to Edinburgh about every 30 min., and the trip takes 2½ hr.

⑫ Edinburgh. You'll spend most of your time in Scotland's capital city in medieval Old Town

(where Edinburgh sprang up) and the 18th-century New Town, the largest historical conservation area in Great Britain. Your tour will take in such landmarks as the **Princes Street Gardens** (p. 500, **①**), one of the most picturesque parks in Europe; the **Royal Mile** (p. 502, **③**), certainly the most famous street in Scotland; **Edinburgh Castle** (p. 510, **④**); and a wealth of museums that include the **Museum of Scotland** (p. 502, **⑥**) and the **National Gallery of Scotland and Royal Scottish Academy** (p. 502, **⑦**). ⊙ 2 days. See p. 496.

Take a train from Waverley Station to Glasgow; trains run every 15 min., and the trip takes about 45 min. Leave your luggage at the train station.

⑬ Glasgow. You only have time for a quick look at this cosmopolitan city, which successfully blends Victorian architecture and modernity. Take one of **City Sightseeing Glasgow's** (p. 570, **①** tours to get an overview; then follow that up with one of the city's major sites—perhaps the **Burrell Collection** (p. 574, **⑦**) or the **Mackintosh Trail** (p. 574, **⑤**), before heading off to Glasgow International Airport. ⊙ Half-day. See p. 570.

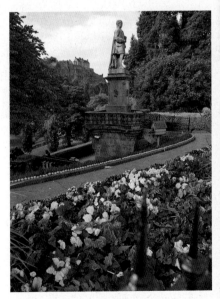

> *Where once stood an open sewer serving medieval Edinburgh, you'll now find the lawns and flower beds of Princes Street Gardens.*

Britain at Its Scenic Best

For all its cities, monuments, and industrial might, Britain is also deeply rural, with spectacular sweeps of hills, pastureland, mountainsides, and coastlines. You can take in a generous swath of Britain's most scenic places in a 2-week driving tour that begins at the southwestern reaches of Cornwall and ends in the northern Highlands and Hebrides.

> Land's End, at the furthest reach of the county of Cornwall, is mainland Britain's most southwesterly point.

START Fly into London, rent a car there, and make the 300-mile drive down to St. Ives in Cornwall; check into a hotel for 2 nights.

1 St. Ives. Artists have been flocking to St. Ives for decades, and you can see some of their work in the **Tate St. Ives** (p. 284, **1**) and the **Barbara Hepworth Museum and Sculpture Garden** (p. 285, **2**). The warren of narrow lanes and side-by-side stone fisherman's cottages are wildly popular with non-artists as well, as are the shimmering sands and magnificent seascapes. ⏱ 1 day. See p. 284.

In the afternoon, drive 17 miles southwest on the A30 and B3311 to

2 Land's End. In the days of ship travel, this tip of land was hallowed ground, the first or last bit of English land sighted from sea. Its sanctity and rugged beauty has been marred by a tacky shopping center, but it's easy to escape the intrusion with a walk along the cliffside path that follows the rocky coastline. ⏱ 2 hr. See p. 241, **10**.

Return to St. Ives. On Day 2, make the scenic 9-mile trip across the Penwith Peninsula to

3 St. Michael's Mount. An imposing castle atop an offshore island began life as a 12th-century Benedictine monastery and was later turned into a fortress, and finally, for the past 350 years, the home of the St. Aubyn family. When high tide floods the causeway, you'll be ferried over to the island by boatmen known as hobblers—a colorful introduction to this remarkable assemblage of 12th-century chambers, plush 19th-century drawing rooms, and medieval chapels. And the views of the bay are stunning. ⏱ Half-day. See p. 249, **9**.

On Day 3, leave St. Ives and follow the A30 and A39 for 72 miles northeast along the Cornish coast to

4 Tintagel. The ruins of this castle perched on the side of a rocky cliff are said to be the birthplace of King Arthur. It's easy to see how the spectacular setting overlooking the thundering waves of the Atlantic inspires such romantic tales, but in reality, the Earls of Cornwall built the castle in the 13th century on the site of a 6th-century Celtic monastery. ⏱ 1 hr. See p. 226, **4**.

From Tintagel, follow the A39 about 20 miles east into

5 Dartmoor National Park. These 368 square miles of high, open moorland (often carpeted in flowers in spring)—a rare pristine landscape

> *The woodland trails of the Fforest Fawr can get boggy after rain, but on a sunny day, they are sublime.*

in England—are covered with heather and granite outcroppings and green valleys. You might spot wild ponies and other wildlife roaming the moors. Enjoy a brief hike or follow well-marked roads for a scenic jaunt through the park. ⏱ 2 hr. See p. 256.

Follow the A386 north from the park for 20 miles to

6 Clovelly. One of the most picturesque hamlets in England clings to an oceanside cliff and is a welcoming place to spend the night. One steep, stone-set path called Up-along (or Down-along, depending on which way you're going) zig-zags past tiny stone cottages to the ancient quay far below. ⏱ 1 evening. See p. 242, **13**.

Early on the morning of Day 4, a 100-mile drive along the A361, M5, and A371 brings you to

7 Cheddar Gorge. Towering limestone cliffs line the length of this scenic, 2-mile-long cleft in the Somerset hills. You can ascend the 274 steps of Jacob's Ladder, cut into the side of the gorge, for a walk along the clifftops and panoramic views of the countryside. ⏱ 2 hr. See p. 230, **2**.

Slip into Wales via the M5 and M4 to Cardiff (about 60 miles), and then follow the A470 north for 45 miles into Brecon Beacons National Park; the drive will take at least 2 hr. Settle into an inn (p. 651) for 2 nights.

8 Brecon Beacons National Park. The Beacons, distinctive flat-headed sandstone outcroppings, are the highest points in southern Britain. The park's varied landscapes include the Black Mountains, a peaceful, rural idyll of narrow valleys, and the Fforest Fawr, with beautiful rock formations and waterfalls. A network of hiking paths crisscrosses the pleasant terrain. ⏱ 1 day. See p. 634, **2**.

On the morning of Day 6, retrace your steps to Cardiff and drive east on the M4 and M48 (crossing the lovely Severn Bridge) into England. Follow the M5 north to Cheltenham, then the A429 to Chipping Campden. The drive covers 100 miles and takes at least 2 hr.

9 The Cotswolds. The better part of 2 days in the Cotswolds introduces you to one of the most scenic corners of England. Settle into the attractive old wool village of **Chipping Campden** (p. 304, **3**) for 2 nights and wander at will through this compact region of rolling hills and pastureland. A short list of must-sees would include **Hidcote Manor Garden** (p. 310, **1**), where a series of outdoor rooms incorporates acres of rare plantings, pools, and long vistas, and a clutch of picturesque villages of mellow golden stone. ⏱ 2 days. See p. 292.

Day 8 begins with a scenic, 30-mile drive on the B4035 and A4104 from Chipping Campden to

10 Great Malvern. This Victorian spa, famed for its mineral waters, is one of many attractive little towns scattered on the slopes of the Malvern Hills and is the starting point for many scenic walks in the area. ⏱ 1 hr. See p. 350, **7**.

Head west on the A4013 through rolling countryside for 21 miles to

11 Hereford. Apple orchards and lush pasturelands where white-faced Hereford cattle graze surround the county capital of Herefordshire. This is some of the most bucolic countryside in England, and this quiet, unassuming country town built around a sturdy cathedral begun in 1080 is one of the country's most attractive. ⏱ 1 hr. See p. 357, **8**.

Continue north on the A49 through the Severn Valley for 23 miles to

> *The Lake District is one of Britain's most visited beauty spots, but you can still plot a route away from the crowds.*

12 Ludlow. This small, picture-perfect Shropshire town, set amid impossibly green rolling hills, is a delight to explore. Streets are lined with half-timbered and elegant Georgian houses that huddle beneath the atmospheric ruins of Ludlow Castle. ⏱ 1 hr. See p. 357, **7**.

Continue north on the A49 for 28 miles to

13 Shrewsbury. Spend the night in the loveliest town in Shropshire, tucked onto a peninsula created by a loop in the Severn River. Timber-framed Queen Anne and Georgian houses hang over narrow medieval lanes and passageways, and a fine medieval Market Hall recalls the days when the town made its fortunes trading in wool. ⏱ 1 evening. See p. 355, **2**.

On the morning of Day 9, follow the A5 and the M6 for 135 miles to Windermere, at least a 3-hr. drive.

14 The Lake District. This small but stunning section of northwest England is filled with hills, secluded valleys, and lakes—a veritable feast of natural beauty. Base yourself in or around **Windermere and Bowness-on-Windermere** (p. 420, **1**), two adjoining towns. From there, set out to explore such places as **Grasmere** (p. 425, **6**), where the poet William Wordsworth spent his life, and **Castlerigg Stone Circle** (p. 425, **8**), one of the most impressive prehistoric sites in England. Much of the appeal here, of course, has to do with natural beauty rather than human enterprise, and your best moments in the Lake District will be spent cruising across **Coniston Water** (p. 423, **3**), hiking through unspoiled countryside to Aira Force waterfall, and soaking up the scenery. ⏱ 2 days. See p. 420.

On Day 11, a drive of 140 miles north on the M6 and the M74 will take you to Glasgow, and from there north another 30 miles on the A82 to the shores of Loch Lomond; the trip will take at least 3 hr.

15 The Scottish Highlands and Islands. Even a brief foray into the Scottish Highlands and the Hebrides will be memorable, and **Loch Lomond** (p. 606, **1**), Britain's largest inland body of water, is a sparkling introduction. Settle in for the evening, and then set out to explore more of the region the next morning. A 60-mile drive will take you through **Inveraray** (p. 594, **2**) to **Loch Awe** (p. 594, **3**), where the well preserved ruins of **Kilchurn Castle** (p. 602, **3**) stand at the edge of the cold, deep waters surrounded by wild, remote scenery, then on to the port of **Oban** (p. 594, **4**). Get the ferry to the **Isle of Mull** (p. 594, **5**) and the pastel-colored seaside town of **Tobermory** (p. 622, **4**). Another ferry trip brings you to **Iona** (p. 595, **6**), a tiny Hebridean island settled by Christian pilgrims from Ireland. You'll also want to visit 13th-century **Iona Abbey** (p. 621, **2**), but the real pleasure of being on the isle is the sense of getting away from it all. ⏱ 3 days. See Chapter 14.

British Houses & Gardens

The infamously moist British climate is a blessing for gardeners, who have nurtured native plants, imported exotic species, and pushed landscape design to new heights. Enjoy their creations on this 1-week tour of south and central England; you'll be able to engage in indoor pursuits as well, touring some of England's most fascinating country houses. Note that many of these properties are open only from April through October and that gardens usually look their best in spring. To get the best bang for your buck, you may want to equip yourself with a money-saving pass from the National Trust (p. 726), which administers many of these properties.

> *The finest example of English 18th-century landscaping, the gardens at Stourhead are especially enticing in summer, when the rhododendrons bloom.*

START Fly into London's Gatwick Airport (p. 137), rent a car, and follow the A25 18 miles east to

❶ Knole. This aristocratic and immense manor has a room for every day of the year, spooky galleries filled with priceless paintings and furnishings, and the largest private garden in England. ⊙ 2 hr. See p. 153, ❷.

Follow the A21 and A262 24 miles southwest to

❷ Sissinghurst. One of Britain's most cherished gardens was a labor of love by the writer Vita Sackville-West (well-known for her newspaper gardening columns) and her husband Harold Nicolson. Planted in the 1930s, its 10 "outdoor rooms" are separated by hedge walls. ⊙ 2 hr. See p. 156, ❺.

1. Knole
2. Sissinghurst
3. Brighton
4. Monk's House
5. Charleston
6. Wilton House
7. Longleat
8. Stourhead
9. Lanhydrock
10. The Lost Gardens of Heligan
11. Cotehele
12. Hidcote Manor Garden
13. Owlpen Manor
14. Rodmarton Manor
15. Chatsworth
16. Hardwick Hall

Cross the Kent countryside on A229 and the A27 for 35 miles to

3 Brighton. One of Britain's favorite seaside getaways serves up sea views, medieval lanes, and gleaming white rows of Regency-era houses. Arrive in time for a tour of the **Royal Pavilion** (see p. 172, ❷), the garish palace of fun-loving King George IV, and then stroll along the seaside promenade and walk out to the end of the brightly lit amusement pier. Brighton is notorious for its nightlife, but don't get too carried away because you need to rise early the next morning. ⏱ 1 evening. See p. 172.

Get an early start and follow the A27 8 miles northeast through the town of Lewes to a turnoff to the village of Rodmell.

4 Monk's House. A look at more modest though no less intriguing English living, courtesy of novelist Virginia Woolf and her husband Leonard. The unassuming home is perfectly preserved and loaded with cozy, literary charm. ⏱ 2 hr. See p. 157, ❻.

Backtrack through Lewes and continue east another 7 miles on the A27. You'll see a turnoff to Charleston on the right side of the road, between the villages of Firle and Selmeston.

5 Charleston. More than a half century's worth of artistic creativity marks this rambling farmhouse, decorated by the designers Vanessa and Clive Bell with artwork, fabrics of their own design, and distinctive paint work. The Mediterranean-inspired garden is certainly muse-worthy. ⏱ 2 hr. See p. 157, ❼.

In the afternoon, drive 90 miles west from Lewes on the A27 and the M27 to Salisbury (p. 210). Spend the night there; then rise early if you want to check out the city's Mompesson House (p. 202, ❶), a fine example of Queen Anne domestic architecture, before driving west on the A36 for 3 miles to

6 Wilton House. The country estate of the Earls of Pembroke is a showcase of the architectural and design genius of Inigo Jones, Hans Holbein the Younger (allegedly), and James Wyatt. The works of many artists, from Rubens to Sir Joshua Reynolds, line the magnificent staterooms. ⏱ 1 hr. See p. 203, ❷.

Drive 22 miles northwest on the A36 to

7 Longleat. The magnificent 16th-century Elizabethan manse designed by Robert Smythson is home to the Marquess of Bath and decorated in lavish Italianate taste. Even the

> *The Italian opera master Rossini once performed for King George IV in the stunning Music Room in Brighton's Royal Pavilion.*

grounds, landscaped by "Capability" Brown in the 18th century, have flair and are home to an assortment of exotic beasts. ⏱ At least 2 hr. See p. 204, ❸.

Head 5 miles west of Longleat on the A36 and A303 to

❽ **Stourhead.** Though the Palladian-style villa here is lovely, it's of less interest than the world-famous 18th-century landscape gardens, where small temples, monuments, rare trees, flowering shrubs, and plants surround a beautiful lake. ⏱ 2 hr. See p. 205, ❹.

Giving yourself enough time to avoid driving in the dark, depart Stourhead and head 140 miles west on the A303 and the A30 to Fowey (p. 233, ❾), a picturesque little port town (pronounced foy) where you'll spend 2 nights. On the morning of Day 4, drive 10 miles north of Fowey on the B3269 to

❾ **Lanhydrock.** One of the grandest homes in Cornwall is set in woodland gardens overlooking the valley of the Fowey River. Many of the 50 rooms are lavishly decorated in Victorian finery, but the kitchens, sculleries, and larders are especially interesting. ⏱ 2 hr. See p. 249, ❻.

Return to Fowey and continue 8 miles west on the A3082 to

❿ **Lost Gardens of Heligan.** Not only are the exotic plantings, jungle-like wetlands, and acres of flowers here a pleasure to behold, but the 400-hectare (1,000-acre) Heligan estate has a fascinating history. Seat of the Tremayne family for more than 400 years, the estate fell into disrepair after World War I and the grounds went wild. A vast restoration project begun in the 1990s is ongoing, so these fascinating landscapes are a work in progress. ⏱ 2 hr. See p. 251, ❸.

Backtrack through Fowey and follow the A38 and A390 32 miles east to

⓫ **Cotehele.** Few houses evoke the Middle Ages as readily as this sturdy manor of granite and slate, beautifully preserved with its original furnishings and so authentic to the period that electricity has never been installed. Exotic plants bloom in the terraced gardens. ⏱ 1 hr. See p. 247, ❹.

Return to Fowey for the night. On Day 5, drive northeast to the Cotswolds via the A30 to Exeter, followed by the M5 to Tewkesbury, and then the A46 to Chipping Campden. The 200-mile trip takes about 4 hr. After checking into a hotel, pay a visit to Hidcote Manor, 4 miles northeast of Chipping Campden on a well-marked lane.

12 Hidcote Manor Garden. One of the world's most inventive and influential 20th-century gardens comprises 4 hectares (10 acres) of outdoor rooms, separated from each other by walls, hedges, and terraces, and fragrant with native plantings and exotic flowers. The gardens are laced with walkways, fountains, ponds, and many quiet nooks. ⏱ 1 hr. See p. 310, **1**.

On the morning of Day 6, follow the A44 and A419 south about 45 miles to

13 Owlpen Manor. This exceptionally romantic house, tucked away in a secluded valley, came into being during the medieval era but underwent subsequent renovations and restorations during Tudor times and the 1930s. The stone manor, surrounded by magnificent gardens and shaded by ancient yews, is allegedly haunted by the ghost of Queen Margaret of Anjou. ⏱ 1 hr. See p. 312, **5**.

Follow the A4135 and A433 8 miles east to

14 Rodmarton Manor. One of England's greatest monuments to early-20th-century design took 20 years to complete, and all of its construction adhered to the principles of Arts and Crafts design. The same care went into the extensive gardens, laced with walls and walls of Cotswolds stone. ⏱ 1 hr. See p. 313, **6**.

A trip of about 70 miles north on the M5 and M6 brings you to Stoke-on-Trent, where you can switch over to the A53 for the 20-mile trip east to Buxton, a faded spa town in the middle of Peak District National Park that is a good overnight stop before heading into the East Midlands. On the morning of Day 7, drive 16 miles east to

15 Chatsworth. Fit for a queen (Mary, Queen of Scots was held prisoner here), this stunner often tops the lists of Britain's best country houses, and little wonder: painted ceilings depict the Triumphs of Caesar, and rooms are filled with numerous artistic treasures. The Great Conservatory, a palace of glass, rises from the vast park and gardens. ⏱ 2 hr. See p. 451, **5**.

Return to Buxton and drive 35 miles southeast to

16 Hardwick Hall. The most perfectly preserved "pure" Elizabethan house in England is renowned for its high ceilings and huge windows (filling the galleries and State Rooms with light), as well as a magnificent collection of textiles. The 12 hectares (30 acres) of gardens and orchards are also prime examples of Elizabethan splendor. ⏱ 1 hr. See p. 454, **9**.

You can zip back down to London, about 150 miles south, on the M1.

> *The garden at Hidcote Manor, designed by Paris-born American Lawrence Johnston, was hugely influential on later 20th-century landscapers.*

Royal Britain

Britain's history is richly evoked in castles and palaces across the realm, and this tour lets you follow in the footsteps of many a famous monarch. You'll travel through centuries of royal British history as you visit mighty fortresses (the Tower of London), famous royal residences (Buckingham Palace), and historic houses (Leeds Castle).

> *The Crown Jewels form the glittering centerpiece of the collection at the Tower of London.*

START Fly into London; check into a hotel for 3 nights.

❶ London. Spend a day soaking in Royal London. Your first stop is Britain's most famous fortress/castle, the **Tower of London** (p. 56, ❶). The tower was the first undertaking of William the Conqueror soon after he came to power in 1066; it's subsequently served as a home to several monarchs, a prison for others, and today is best known for housing the Crown Jewels. Your next stop is **Buckingham Palace** (p. 72, ❶), the official London residence of the monarch since the days of George III. In August and September you can

tour some of the treasure-filled State Rooms, though there is plenty to interest you the rest of year as well. The **Royal Mews** (p. 73, ❹) house the Queen's privileged horses, as well as some stunning ceremonial carriages. The nearby **Queen's Gallery** (p. 72, ❷) shows off highlights of the monarchy's priceless private collection; exhibits rotate as works are circulated around the various royal residences and lent to museums, but you can almost always count on seeing a clutch of magnificent Old Masters, along with furniture and objets d'art. **Kensington Palace** (p. 74, ❼) exudes a more livable air, though there's plenty of gilt, murals, and finery around to suggest a royal presence.

1	London
2	Hampton Court Palace
3	Windsor Castle
4	Hever Castle
5	Leeds Castle
6	Battle
7	Dover Castle
8	Royal Pavilion
9	Edinburgh

Residents have included William and Mary, Queen Victoria, and most recently Princess Diana. ⏱ 1 day. See p. 70, **1** .

On Day 2, make the 13-mile trip by train from Waterloo Station to

2 Hampton Court Palace. For royal atmosphere, it's hard to top this historic landmark, which has served as a home to monarchs from the Tudor to the Hanoverian eras. Walk through the staterooms of Henry VIII (the ghost of the executed Queen Catherine Howard reportedly walks the halls), and tour the private apartments of Queen Caroline, wife of George II. The fascinating Tudor kitchens

bespeak the labor required to feed a royal household that could number in the thousands, and the gardens are endowed with ponds and the famous (or infamous) Hedge Maze. ⏱ 1 day. See p. 76.

On Day 3, make a day trip to Windsor Castle; trains leave from Paddington for the 20-mile trip.

3 Windsor Castle. The largest inhabited castle in the world (and the current queen's favorite abode), with a skyline of towers and battlements, was built by William the Conqueror and is the final resting place of 10 English monarchs (entombed in St. George's

> *Hever Castle, in Kent, was the childhood home of Anne Boleyn, second wife of Henry VIII.*

Chapel, one of the finest medieval buildings in England). Within walking distance of the castle is Eton College, founded by Henry VI and the alma mater of numerous heirs to the throne. ⏲ 1 day. See p. 134, ❷.

On Day 4, take a train to Gatwick Airport and rent a car there, avoiding city traffic. Drive 20 miles east via the B2028 and B2026 to

❹ **Hever Castle.** Anne Boleyn, the unfortunate young second wife of Henry VIII who helped launch the English Reformation, was raised at this lovely castle, which has a collection of memorabilia related to the doomed queen. Henry's fourth queen, Anne of Cleves, proved more astute than some of her predecessors and gladly granted the king a desired divorce... and got the castle as part of her settlement. But it is royalty of a different sort that has had the most influence on Hever; American fur magnate William Waldorf Astor restored the castle in the early 20th century with exquisite taste and laid out lavish Italian gardens. ⏲ 2 hr. See p. 158, ❽.

Drive 30 miles east via the A26 and M20 to

❺ **Leeds Castle.** Royalty associated with this castle—a picture-perfect combination of turrets, towers, and light gray stone—include Edward I and Eleanor of Castile; Joan of Navarre; Anne of Bohemia; Henry VIII and Catherine of Aragon; and Elizabeth I. A walk through the castle involves time travel into dungeons, the 15th-century bathroom of Catherine de Valois (the wife of Henry V), and a medieval banquet hall. Ironically, the castle survived the English Civil War because its inhabitants at the time sided against the Royalists. ⏲ 3 hr. See p. 154, ❹.

Follow the M20 and A2070 35 miles southeast to Rye, an appealing town of Tudor, Elizabethan, and Georgian houses, and check into a hotel for the night. On the morning of Day 5, head 15 miles west of Rye via the B2089 and A2100 to

❻ **Battle.** On October 14, 1066, upon this hallowed ground, the Battle of Hastings changed the course of British history (and the monarchy) when Duke William of Normandy (later William the Conqueror) defeated Harold II, the Saxon king of England, and brought the country under unified Norman rule. The grassy battlefield spreads down a hillside topped with the ruins of the monastic complex that William built to honor his conquered foe. ⏲ 1 hr. See p. 180.

Drive 55 miles south on the A28 and M20 to

❼ **Dover Castle.** You'll get a sense of the longstanding importance of Britain's oldest fortifications as you walk this castle's circuit of walls and overlook the Roman lighthouse, Saxon church, a magnificent keep, and other remnants of the vast compound. Much of what you see is the work of Henry II, who in the 12th century built the imposing Keep and Great Tower and reinforced the walls to make Dover one of the mightiest fortresses in Europe (helping secure his reign—and England—from French invasion). Follow a visit with a bracing walk along the top of the **White Cliffs** (p. 163, ❷), where the chilly sea lanes of the English Channel wash against the white coastline. ⏲ 3 hr. See p. 162, ❶.

Drive west 100 miles on the M20 and M23 to Brighton (p. 172) and settle in for the night.

> *Hampton Court Palace was originally built for Thomas Wolsey, a powerful cardinal who fell out of favor with Henry VIII.*

Spend a couple of hours on the morning of Day 6 taking in the breezy promenades, garish amusement pier, quaint medieval lanes, and other quirky and faded charms of Britain's favorite seaside playground. There's one royal stop here that's a must.

8 Royal Pavilion. For sheer royal excess, it's hard to top Brighton's exotic Royal Pavilion, a 19th-century building so decidedly avant-garde that Queen Victoria unloaded the palace from the roster of royal residences. The fun-loving Prince Regent (the future George IV) had the cash to indulge his outlandish taste and an architect, John Nash, who was more than willing to accommodate the prince's fantastical ideas. The result is an Oriental and Indian-influenced wonder that's loaded with oodles of gilt, velvet, elaborate carvings, and the best chinoiserie work in Britain. You may well agree with Victoria's appraisal of the palace as vulgar, but you won't soon see anything like it. ⏱ 1 hr. See p. 172, **2**.

Return to Gatwick in the early afternoon, a quick trip of about 30 miles on the A23 and M23. With a mid- to late afternoon train departure from Kings Cross Station, you can be in Edinburgh in time for a late dinner.

9 Edinburgh. On Day 7, head to imposing hilltop **Edinburgh Castle** (p. 510, **4**), begun in the 11th century as a royal residence by Malcolm III and now the home of the legendary Stone of Scone, upon which Scottish rulers were crowned. The Scottish Crown jewels are also on display, but the real attraction here is the view of the city and surrounding countryside from the lofty ramparts. The Royal Mile, Edinburgh's most famous thoroughfare, follows a ridge for a mile from the castle to the **Palace of Holyroodhouse** (p. 512, **12**), favored home of Scottish royalty after the middle of the 16th century, when James IV commissioned the palace near the site of a now-ruined abbey from 1128. Tours take in the second-floor apartments of Mary, Queen of Scots and the reception rooms still used by Queen Elizabeth II, who stays at Holyrood whenever she's in town. ⏱ 1 day. See p. 508.

3
London

Our Favorite London Moments

"When a man is tired of London, he is tired of Life; for there is in London all that Life can afford." Dr. Samuel Johnson may have been exaggerating a bit, but boredom with London may indeed be a sign of depression. On the rare occasions I become weary of this marvelous city, the experiences outlined in this section are my mood-elevating prescriptions. Side effects may include euphoria, infatuation, and a sudden loss of pounds (sterling, that is).

> PREVIOUS PAGE For many, the Palace of Westminster represents the pinnacle of Victorian Gothic architecture. THIS PAGE Long-running musicals are the staple diet of West End theatergoers.

❶ **Taking photos from the top of the London Eye.** The top of this Ferris wheel is the best place to get a picture-perfect shot of London's far-reaching landscape. Any time is a good moment to take this "flight," but for a truly breathtaking photo op, jump aboard on a late afternoon as the sun starts sinking and the lights come on across the city. See p. 54, ❼.

❷ **Chatting with Sir Walter Raleigh, William the Conqueror, and other historical figures at the Tower of London.** The Tower's entertaining actors have their characters' life stories down pat, and are walking, talking history. Don't be shy; they love to interact with visitors and answer questions. They may even approach you in a friendly, if archaic, manner ("What ho, my good lady? Methinks thou art in need of a boon companion") as you wander around. See p. 56, ❶.

❸ **Eating ice cream at the intermission of a West End production** as a well-deserved splurge for having gotten a half-price ticket for a very good seat at one of London's many famous theaters. If ice cream's not your thing, order drinks before your play starts and pick them up during the "interval." See p. 132.

❹ **Drinking champagne and digging the music** (classical or jazz) at the Late View at the V&A, held under the museum's thrilling Dale Chihuly glass chandelier on Friday evenings. Several of the renowned museum's galleries are open for exploring, and the relaxed atmosphere makes for a leisurely and seductive visit. See "The V&A: Practical Matters," p. 66.

The Millennium Bridge was the subject of national ridicule when it opened in 2000, being quickly nicknamed the "Wobbly Bridge."

Crisscrossing the scenic Serpentine in a paddle boat on a sunny morning as ducks and geese wheel overhead and quack alongside. The little island on the north side is reputed to be local resident J. M. Barrie's inspiration for the island of the Lost Boys in *Peter Pan*. Bring a camera and your energy, or opt for a rowboat and let your companion do the work. See p. 86, **6**.

Haggling for a bargain at Portobello Road Market, either at the open-air stalls or in the warrens of indoor arcades. You may get 10% to 15% off the asking price (which everyone involved knows is set just for that probability). Saturday's the big day for this famous antiques market, and part of the fun is sharing the street with seething crowds of bargain hunters and loiterers. See p. 109.

Listening to Big Ben strike the hour, an event that thrills even Londoners. It's the bell itself that's named Big Ben, though most assign that name to the whole clock tower. Though the bell has a crack in it and can't sound an E note, its chimed aria from Handel's *Messiah* is the undisputed aural symbol of London. See p. 50, **2**.

8 Standing in the middle of the Thames on the Millennium Bridge, which spans not just the river, but the centuries, with St. Paul's Cathedral on one side and the Tate Modern on the other. The views of the cityscape are impressive, especially at sunrise and sunset. See p. 54, **8**.

9 Stuffing yourself with a full afternoon tea at one of the many deluxe hotels (the Goring is a good option) that rise to the task of impressing visitors with an array of tea sandwiches, scones, clotted cream, and desserts—all washed down with a strong cuppa. Make no dinner plans—you won't be hungry. See p. 122.

10 Exploring the breadth of the old Empire at the British Museum, where priceless treasures acquired from all parts of the globe (including the Rosetta Stone and the Parthenon Sculptures) testify to the power that Britain once exerted—and give insight into just how greedy its adventurers were. If your interests tend more toward the literary, there are few better places in the world to soak up the power of the written word than the museum's famous Reading Room. See p. 68.

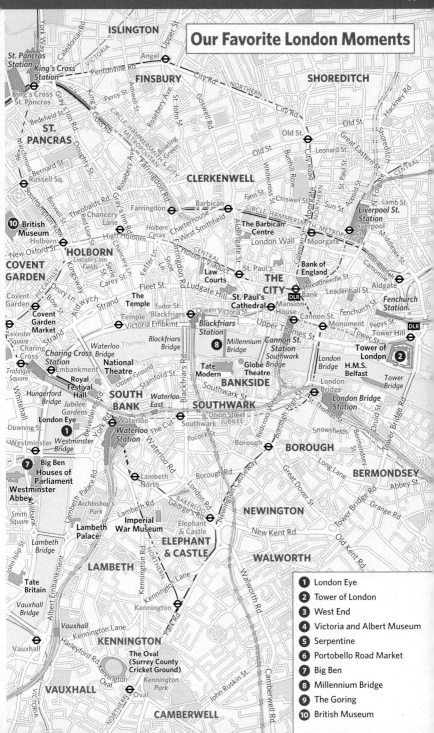

Our Favorite London Moments

1. London Eye
2. Tower of London
3. West End
4. Victoria and Albert Museum
5. Serpentine
6. Portobello Road Market
7. Big Ben
8. Millennium Bridge
9. The Goring
10. British Museum

The Best of London in 1 Day

With London's abundance of sights, how much can you manage to see in just 1 day? Plenty. In this tour, you'll visit the oldest (Westminster Abbey); the newest (the London Eye); and one of the world's oldest and greatest museums. Throw in classic London cityscapes viewed from some of the famous bridges that span the Thames River, and you've got yourself a great 1-day jaunt that won't leave you feeling exhausted.

START Westminster Tube Station.

SITE GUIDE PAGE 53

① ★★★ Westminster Abbey. Though inside it's a mixture of styles, Westminster Abbey is considered one of the finest examples of Early English Gothic architecture in Europe. Since 1066, when William the Conqueror became the first English monarch to be crowned here, every successive British sovereign except for two (Edward V and Edward VIII) has been crowned in the Abbey, and many of them laid to rest here, along with some of the most important figures in England's political, military, and cultural life. There are hundreds of tombs, memorials, and architectural details to explore.

② ★★★ Big Ben. The iconic Clock Tower at the eastern end of the Palace of Westminster has come to be known as Big Ben, though that appellation really refers to the largest bell in the clock's chime. The 14-ton bell, installed in 1858, is believed to have been named for the commissioner of public works at the time—Sir Benjamin Hall—although some historians insist it was named for a famous boxer of the era, Benjamin Caunt. Brits can make the ascent up the tower's 334 spiral steps by special guided tour, but non-U.K. citizens have to content themselves with a must-have snapshot. British citizens should contact their local MP to apply for permission to tour the clock tower. ⏱ 5 min. Near St. Stephen's Entrance of Westminster Palace, Old Palace Yard. Tube: Westminster.

> Although commonly used to mean the entire clock tower, "Big Ben" is in fact the 14-ton bell inside.

1 Westminster Abbey
2 Big Ben
3 Houses of Parliament
4 The Jewel Tower
5 Westminster Bridge
6 Café Manga
7 London Eye
8 Millenium Bridge
9 St. Paul's Cathedral
10 The British Museum

> *The first literary figure to be buried in Poets' Corner was Geoffrey Chaucer, author of the 14th-century Canterbury Tales.*

❸ ★★ **Houses of Parliament.** A royal palace was built on this site in the 11th century and functioned as the London home of a number of kings before it burned down; its palatial 16th-century replacement was given over to Parliament instead. Today's immense 3-hectare (7½-acre) Palace of Westminster (aka The New Palace), a splendid example of Gothic Revival architecture, dates back to 1840 (the Old Palace was all but destroyed by fire in 1834). The iconic landmark is the home of the 650-member House of Commons (where elected officials do their legislating) and the 780-plus-member House of Lords (a number the 2010 coalition government pledged to reduce). You may observe debates for free from the Stranger's Galleries in both houses, but the long entry lines make this spot better for a quick photo op than a lengthy visit. The only exception: U.K. citizens can take worthwhile guided tours of the premises on select days throughout the year; non-U.K. citizens can take a guided tour only during Parliament's summer break. ⏱5 min. Old Palace Yard. ☎0207/219-3000 House of Commons; ☎0207/219-3107 House of Lords. www.parliament.uk. Free admission. Mon–Wed 2:30–10:30pm; Thurs 11:30am–7:30pm; Fri 9:30am–3pm. Closed Easter week. Guided tours (£15 adults, £6 kids 16 & under) offered Aug–Sept (check website or call for exact tour times). Tube: Westminster.

❹ ★ **The Jewel Tower.** This medieval structure (not to be confused with the structure of the same name in the Tower of London) was one of only two buildings to survive an 1834 fire that destroyed the original Palace of Westminster. The tower dates back to 1365 and was originally used to house Edward III's wardrobe and treasures. Today, it's home to a very informative exhibit, "Parliament Past & Present," which details the inner workings of the British government. Look carefully at the building's exterior as you enter, and you'll spot the remains of a moat. ⏱25 min. Abingdon St. ☎0207/222-2219. www.english-heritage.org.uk. Admission £3.20 adults, £1.60 kids 12 & under. Daily 10am–5pm (Nov–Mar until 4pm). Closed Dec 24–26 & Jan 1.

❺ **Westminster Bridge.** From the center of this bridge, completed in 1862 and restored most recently in 2007, you can enjoy a sweeping view of the Houses of Parliament and Big Ben—one of the most familiar and beloved cityscapes in the world. Note the bridge's green color, which corresponds to the color of the benches in the House of Commons, the occupant of the Palace of Westminster closest to the bridge (nearby Lambeth Bridge is red in keeping with the color of the seats in the House of Lords). ⏱10 min. Tube: Westminster.

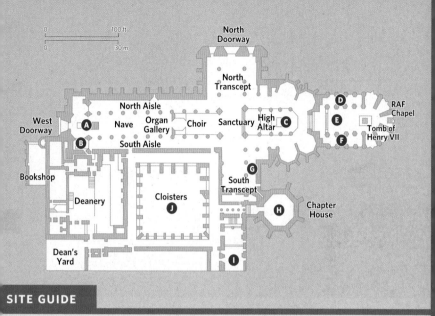

North Doorway

North Transcept

North Aisle

Nave

Organ Gallery

Choir

Sanctuary

High Altar

C

D

RAF Chapel

E

Tomb of Henry VII

F

West Doorway

A

B

South Aisle

G

South Transcept

H

Chapter House

Bookshop

Deanery

Cloisters

J

Dean's Yard

I

0   100 ft
0   30 m

SITE GUIDE

① Westminster Abbey

As you enter the French Gothic nave of the cathedral, completed in 1519, you first come to the **A** **Tomb of the Unknown Warrior** and the **Memorial to Winston Churchill** (Britain's wartime prime minister), and **B** **St. George's Chapel**—all of which commemorate Britain's sacrifices in World Wars I and II. **C** **The Chapel of St. Edward the Confessor** contains the hallowed and decidedly unglamorous **Coronation Chair** in which England's monarchs are crowned. Next, have a look at the magnificent carving in the medieval-style **D** **Henry VII's Lady Chapel,** consecrated in 1519 and one of the prettiest in Europe. Inside the chapel you'll find the **E** **Tomb of Elizabeth I**—the face of the royal effigy atop it was taken from the celebrated queen's death mask—and of her half-sister, Mary I (aka Bloody Mary). The **F** **Tomb of Mary, Queen of Scots,** who was beheaded in 1587 by order of her cousin, Elizabeth I, was erected by her son James I soon after his accession to the throne in 1612. **G** **Poets' Corner** contains dozens of memorials to England's writers and poets, including Chaucer, Austen, Dickens, Thomas Hardy, and (as of 1995) Oscar Wilde. The **H** **Chapter House,** a beautiful octagonal

building with a vaulted ceiling and stunning stained-glass windows, displays rare examples of medieval English sculpture and wall paintings, while the **I** **Undercroft Museum** contains the 11th-century **Pyx Chamber,** with a display of church silver. You can also wander (free of charge) in the serene **J** **Cloisters,** dating from the 13th to the 15th century. ⏱ At least 1 hr.; arrive before 9:30am to avoid lines. 20 Dean's Yard. ☎ 0207/222-5152. www.westminster-abbey.org. Admission £16 adults, £13 seniors, £6 kids 11–18, £32 families; free admission to services. Mon–Fri 9:30am–4:30pm (Wed until 7pm); Sat 9:30am–2:30pm; closed Sun. Tube: Westminster.

> *The London Eye Ferris wheel is the tallest, most expensive, and one of the most memorable of the South Bank's attractions.*

⑥ 🍽 ★ **Café Manga,** located in County Hall, has outdoor seating behind the London Eye. It's a Japanese anime-themed joint, but don't let that put you off: They serve plenty of good food and drinks, and the people-watching opportunities are endless. Westminster Bridge Rd. ☎ 0207/928-5047. Menu items £4–£10.

❼ ★★★ kids **London Eye.** This huge Ferris wheel, a London icon, solemnly rotates at one revolution per half-hour and is visible from as far away as Hyde Park. It's much loved by even the most hardened London traditionalists. Although it was originally planned for only a 5-year stint, there's no way the London Tourist Board will let it go. You are encouraged to buy your timed ticket well in advance, which can end up in disappointment if you get a gray and rainy day. You may, however, be able to buy same-day tickets during the off season, which can eliminate the guesswork about the weather. Show up 30 minutes before your scheduled departure time (15 if you have a Fast Track ticket). Don't forget your camera. ⏱ 1 hr., from lining up through half-hour ride. **South Bank (at Westminster Bridge).**

☎ 0870/500-0600. www.londoneye.com. Admission £18.50 adults, £15 seniors, £9.50 kids 4–15. Book Fast Track tickets via the website or in person for double the price. Book through the website for a 10% discount. Daily 9:30am–8pm (July–Aug until 10pm). Closed bank holidays & 3 weeks in Jan. Tube: Westminster.

❽ ★★★ kids **Millennium Bridge.** This gorgeous sliver of a footbridge connecting Bankside to the City and its attractions is an efficient way to cross the river and a wonderful spot from which to take photos of the surrounding landmarks. When it first opened in 2000, the 325m (1,066-ft.) steel suspension bridge swayed and had to be shut down (locals nicknamed it "the Wobbly Bridge" after it made some pedestrians seasick), but it has since been stabilized. ⏱ 10 min. Tube: Southwark or Blackfriars.

❾ ★★★ kids **St. Paul's Cathedral.** For centuries, the Dome of St. Paul's had no competition in the skyline of London; it was the highest and most impressive building in town. Though it has since been dwarfed by the skyscrapers in the financial district, none of them inspires

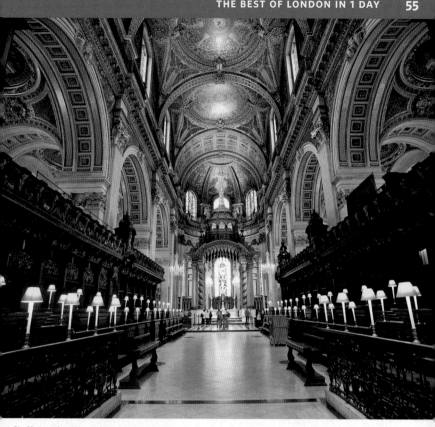

> Sir Christopher Wren's baroque masterpiece, St. Paul's, was built to replace a previous cathedral swept away by the Great Fire of London.

the same awe as this masterpiece by Sir Christopher Wren (1632–1723), built after the Great Fire of 1666. That it still exists today is something of a miracle—it was twice struck by bombs during World War II's Blitz and had a few other close calls. The cathedral is the culmination of Wren's unique and much-acclaimed fusion of classical (the exterior Greek-style columns) and baroque (the ornate interior decorations) architecture. The Whispering Gallery is a miracle of engineering, in which you can hear the murmurs of another person from across a large gallery. The 530 stairs to the top are demanding, but you'll be rewarded with a magnificent view, not only of London, but of the marvel of the cathedral. Wren—who is buried in the church's crypt alongside several scientific notables (penicillin discoverer Sir Alexander Fleming, for

one), artists (Sir Joshua Reynolds and J.M.W. Turner, who are interred next to each other), and politicians (Sir Winston Churchill)—considered it his ultimate achievement and most demanding effort. Indeed, Wren's tomb famously notes, "If you seek his monument, look around you." There are guided tours at 11am, 11:30am, 1:30pm, and 2pm. If you visit in spring, when the roses are in full bloom, the cathedral's garden makes for a lovely stroll. ⏱ 30 min. Ludgate Hill, EC4 (at Paternoster Sq.). ☎ 0207/236-4128. www.stpauls.co.uk. Admission £14.50 adults, £13.50 seniors, £5.50 kids 6–18. Mon–Sat 8:30am–4:30pm. Tube: St. Paul's.

🔟 ★★★ kids **The British Museum.** You could spend days in this fabulous treasure trove and may want to return for more at a later date. ⏱ At least 1 hr. See p. 68.

The Best of London in 2 Days

On your second day in London, you will travel back in time, then fast-forward back to the here and now. Even blasé Londoners get excited by the cauldron of history that is the Tower of London, the view from the top of the Monument, and the iconoclastic art of the 20th and 21st centuries on display at the Tate Modern. As a bonus, you get to see Shakespeare's Globe Theatre and traverse the Thames by boat.

> *Tower Bridge still opens to allow ships to pass below, causing traffic congestion on both sides of the River Thames.*

SITE GUIDE
PAGE 59

START Tower Hill Tube Station.

1 ★★★ kids **Tower of London.** The Tower of London is the city's best-known and oldest historic site. Built by William the Conqueror in 1066 and added to by subsequent generations of kings and queens, this fortress has a bloody past marked by power struggles, executions, and cruelty. It is an incomparable collection of buildings that reflect the range of England's architectural styles over the past 900 years.

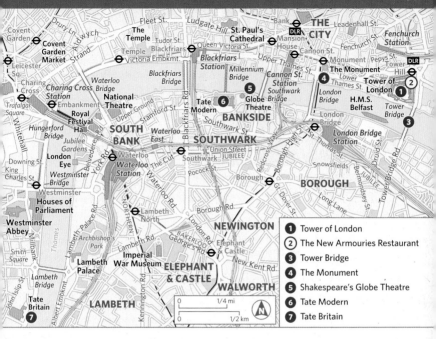

1 Tower of London
2 The New Armouries Restaurant
3 Tower Bridge
4 The Monument
5 Shakespeare's Globe Theatre
6 Tate Modern
7 Tate Britain

2 🍴 ★★ **The New Armouries Restaurant,** inside the Tower of London, is clean and pleasant, though not hugely atmospheric. Buy take-away sandwiches and drinks for an outdoor picnic, or settle in for a hot lunch of shepherd's pie, soup, Yorkshire pudding, or whatever you fancy. There are also snack shops scattered here and there around the Tower. Inside the Tower of London. ☎ 0870/756-6000. Snacks £4–£8.

3 ★★ kids **Tower Bridge.** This Neo-Gothic bascule bridge—a term derived from the French for "seesaw"—has spanned the Thames since 1894. Its skeleton of steel girders is clothed with ornate masonry designed to harmonize elegantly with the neighboring Tower of London. Its lower span opens and closes through hydraulics and behemoth machinery—details that even engineering-challenged visitors will find fascinating on the "Tower Bridge Exhibition" tour. Tour participants can also ascend to the bridge's top level for a bird's-eye view of the Tower of London and the Thames, 43m (141 ft.) below. ⏱ 1 hr. Tower Bridge. ☎ 0207/403-3761. www.towerbridge.org.uk. £7 adults, £5 seniors, £3 kids 5–15. Ticket office is on northwest side of bridge. Daily 9:30am–6pm. Tube: Tower Hill.

4 ★ kids **The Monument.** Sir Christopher Wren and Robert Hooke designed this 62m-high (203-ft.) Doric stone column topped with a copper flame to commemorate the Great Fire of 1666, a tragic disaster that started inside the house of a baker on Pudding Lane and destroyed more than 13,000 houses and 87 churches. If you're reluctant to climb the

Tower Ghosts

The Tower of London, said to be the most haunted spot in England, overflows with supernatural manifestations of tormented souls. The restless ghost of Queen Anne Boleyn (executed in 1536) is the most frequently spotted spirit. The tragic shades of the Little Princes (the two sons of Edward IV)—allegedly murdered by Richard III in 1483—have been spied in the Bloody Tower. Ghostly reenactments of the Tower Green beheading of the Countess of Salisbury—who was hacked to death by her inept executioner in 1541—have been seen on its anniversary. The ghostly screams of Guy Fawkes, who named his co-conspirators in the Gunpowder Plot after suffering unspeakable torture, reputedly still echo around the grounds.

> *Rossetti's* Dante's Vision of Rachel and Leah *in the Tate Britain's Pre-Raphaelite collection.*

311 steps to the top, you can see live views beamed down from on high in the Monument's new visitor center. ⏱ 50 min. Monument St. ☎ 0207/626-2717. www.themonument.info. Admission £3 adults, £2 seniors, £1 kids. Daily 9:30am–5:30pm. Tube: Monument.

⑤ ★★ 🅺🅸🅳🆂 **Shakespeare's Globe Theatre.** Even if you don't have tickets to a play (p. 133), this painstakingly accurate reconstruction of the Globe (only tools authentic to the original time period were used to build it) is a fascinating place to visit. It was at the Globe in the late 1500s and early 1600s that Shakespeare's comedies and tragedies were performed in daylight (as they are now) to delight the nobility (who sat in the tiers) as well as the rabble (who stood before the stage). Changing exhibits focus on related topics such as the frost fairs of medieval London, or the juicy history of nearby Southwark, once a haven for prostitutes, thieves, and

Tate to Tate by Boat

The Tate boat ferry service between the two Tate museums on opposite banks of the Thames is one of London's better tourist creations. The 18-minute ride runs from the Tate Britain to the Tate Modern and also makes a stop at the London Eye (p. 54, ⑦).One-way ferry tickets cost £5 adults, £2.50 kids 5 to 15. If you have a London Travelcard (p. 138), you get a good discount. Tickets for the ferry can be bought online or at the Tate Britain or Tate Modern. The boat runs daily every 40 minutes (more often in high season) between 10am and 6pm. For precise boat times, call ☎ 0207/887-3959, or check www.tate.org.uk/tatetotate.

actors. ⏱ 1 hr. 21 New Globe Walk. ☎ 0207/902-1500 exhibition; 0207/401-9919 box office. www.shakespeares-globe.org. Admission to museum & exhibits £11.50 adults, £10 seniors, £7 kids 5-15, £32 families (2 adults & 3 kids). Daily 10am–5pm (closed during afternoon theater matinees—call for schedules). Tube: London Bridge.

⑥ ★★★ 🅺🅸🅳🆂 **Tate Modern.** Britain's premier modern art museum, an offshoot of the Tate Britain, is housed in a gargantuan shell that was once a power station, and part of the fun of a visit here are the reminders of the building's utilitarian past—especially the immense Turbine Hall you see upon entering. The museum's curators have admirably risen to the challenge of filling the enormous space with exhibits, gigantic sculptures, and art installations. Collections here are displayed thematically instead of by period. Some of the world's most important and exciting art is here, with works by Dalí, Matisse, Picasso, Bonnard, Duchamp, Giacometti, Diego Rivera, Mondrian, Klee, Margaret Bourke White, David Hockney—think of the most groundbreaking artists of the past century, and you will likely find something of their work somewhere in this gargantuan cathedral of modern art. Do use their brilliant website to plan your visit if you can. ⏱ At least 2 hr. Take a free guided theme tour or an audioguide highlights tour (£3) to make the best use of your time. Bankside. ☎ 0207/887-8000. www.tate.org.uk. Free admission except for temporary exhibits. Daily 10am–6pm. Tube: Blackfriars.

⑦ ★★ 🅺🅸🅳🆂 **Tate Britain.** The Tate Britain, set on the former Thames-side site of the Millbank Prison, opened to the public in 1897 thanks to generous donations of money and art from sugar mogul Sir Henry Tate (1819–99). One of England's most prestigious art museums, the Tate features a collection consisting chiefly of British art from the 16th century to the dawn of the 20th century. The museum has an unparalleled collection of works by renowned landscape artist J. M. W. Turner, who bequeathed most of his paintings to the museum. Other notable British artists whose works adorn the walls include satirist William Hogarth, portraitist Thomas Gainsborough, traditionalist Joshua Reynolds, and pre-Raphaelite painter Dante Gabriel Rossetti. ⏱ 2 hr. Millbank. ☎ 0207/887-8008. www.tate.org.uk. Free admission, except for temporary exhibits. Daily 10am–6pm. Tube: Pimlico.

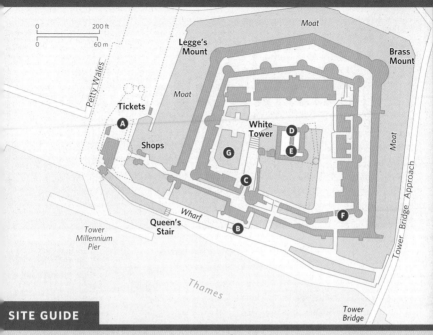

Legge's Mount

Brass Mount

Petty Wales

Moat

Moat

Moat

Tickets

A

Shops

White Tower

D

E

G

C

Wharf

Queen's Stair

Tower Millennium Pier

B

F

Tower Bridge Approach

Thames

Tower Bridge

SITE GUIDE

① Tower of London

In the **A Forecourt** you can join one of the Yeoman Warders, or Beefeaters, for an entertaining tour. Doomed prisoners entered the Tower by boat via the ominous **B Traitor's Gate** (upon which their severed heads were displayed). The **C Bloody Tower** (pictured right) was where, according to Shakespeare, the two little princes, sons of Edward IV, were murdered by henchmen of their uncle Richard III. With its four turrets and central location, you can't miss the Norman-style **D White Tower,** built in 1078 by William the Conqueror and for hundreds of years the seat of absolute power. Inside the White Tower, the **E Royal Armouries** exhibition "Fit for a King" displays 500 years of royal armor, offering an insight into the personalities and physical size of England's monarchs (Charles I's gilt get-up is particularly impressive). The priceless Crown Jewels displayed in the **F Jewel Tower** include the 530-carat Star of Africa (in the Sceptre with the Cross) and the famed Black Prince's Ruby (in the Imperial State Crown). Executions at the Tower—including those of Anne Boleyn, Catherine Howard, Lady Jane Grey, and Sir Thomas More—took place on

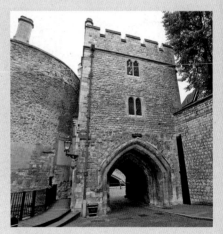

G Tower Green, where a "private" beheading away from the gaping crowds was a privilege of high rank. ⏱ 3 hr. Buy your tickets online and arrive before 9am to avoid the long line. Tower Hill. ☎ 0870/756-6000. www.hrp.org.uk. Admission £19.80 adults, £17.05 seniors, £10.45 kids 5–15; save 10% by booking online. Daily 9am–5:30pm (Nov–Feb until 4:30pm). Tube: Tower Hill.

The Best of London in 3 Days

This tour reveals London's great charms and artistic treasures. I follow this route when I'm feeling out of sorts, and by the time I hit St. James's Park, I've fallen in love with London all over again. From the glory of Hyde Park Corner's monuments, to the incomparable art in the National Gallery, to the street crazies and entertainers of Covent Garden, this is the London that even crabby cabbies quietly relish as they go about their business.

> Sitting atop one of the lions that guard Nelson's Column in Trafalgar Square is a classic London photo op.

START Hyde Park Corner Tube Station.

❶ ★ Hyde Park Corner. The busiest traffic circle in London is one of the city's most central locations, with Piccadilly, Knightsbridge, Park Lane, Constitution Hill, and Grosvenor Place radiating from its axis. It's the perfect place to get great morning photos of the majestic statue of *Winged Victory*, which replaced the statue of the Duke of Wellington in 1912

as a topper to the Wellington Arch. The arch itself was built in the 1820s to celebrate the British victory over the French. The underground walkways beneath the circle will save you from the treacherous crosswalks above and feature an interesting pictorial history of the Duke of Wellington, who orchestrated the crushing of Napoleon at Waterloo and remains one of Britain's most celebrated military heroes. ⊙ 10 min. Tube: Hyde Park Corner.

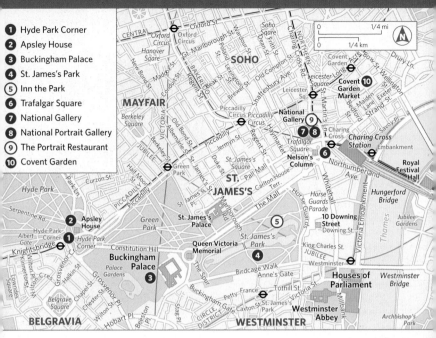

1. Hyde Park Corner
2. Apsley House
3. Buckingham Palace
4. St. James's Park
5. Inn the Park
6. Trafalgar Square
7. National Gallery
8. National Portrait Gallery
9. The Portrait Restaurant
10. Covent Garden

2 ★★ **Apsley House.** Designed by famed architect Robert Adam (1728–92), this neo-classical mansion was purchased by Arthur Wellesley, first Duke of Wellington (1769–1852), following his victories in the Napoleonic Wars. Its location, just past the old Knights-bridge tollgate, gave it the city's most grandiose address at the time: Number One London. The residence houses a renowned collection of decorative arts (many of the pieces bestowed upon the duke by grateful European monarchs), historic weaponry, numerous Old Masters, and a towering nude statue of his enemy Napoleon (with a strategic fig leaf). ⏱ 30 min. 149 Piccadilly. ☎ 0207/499-5676. www.english-heritage.org.uk. Admission £6.30 adults, £5.70 seniors, £3.80 kids 5–15. Tues-Sun 10am–5pm. Tube: Hyde Park Corner.

3 ★★ **Buckingham Palace.** Buck House, the queen's famous abode in London, is the setting for the pageantry of the Changing of the Guard, a London tradition that attracts a nightmarish mass of crowds in the summer. A better place to see all the queen's horses and all the queen's men in action is the **Horse Guards Parade** (p. 100, **3**). But if you're determined to see the guards change here, arrive

a half-hour early to get a spot by the statue of Victoria in front of the palace; it offers a reasonably good view. The ritual takes place every other day in winter and every day in summer at 11am in the forecourt of the palace. ⏱ 30 min. See p. 72, **1**.

4 ★★ kids **St. James's Park.** Arguably London's prettiest park, St. James's has an interesting history. The former swamp was tidied up in the 18th century, and evolved into a popular and notorious scene where prostitutes conducted business, laundresses brought their loads to dry on bushes, and drunken rakes took unsteady aim at dueling opponents. Now, however, it's very respectable, with a duck and pelican pond, weeping willows, and numerous paths lined with flower beds. The benches at the eastern end of the park offer a peaceful view of London's landmarks. ⏱ 30 min. Tube: St. James's Park.

5 ♨ ★ kids **Inn the Park**. At the northeast end of St. James's Park is this combination cafe and restaurant. Skip the expensive restaurant, where the food is overpriced; the same chefs supply the less-expensive cafeteria-style eatery, which features picturesque views of the London Eye and Whitehall. **In St. James's Park (by Pall Mall). ☎ 0207/451-9999. Snacks £3.50–£7.**

❻ Trafalgar Square. While you were once able to identify this landmark in front of the National Gallery by its staggering population of pigeons, the practice of feeding them was outlawed (as were cars, to create a useful pedestrian area). This famous square with its enormous fountain is named after Britain's most revered naval hero, Horatio Viscount Nelson (1758–1805), who fell at the Battle of Trafalgar (the most pivotal naval battle of the Napoleonic Wars), and whose statue stands on top of a 44m (144-ft.) pillar of granite guarded by kingly lions at the base. Street lamps at the Pall Mall end of the square are decorated with small replicas of the ships he commanded. The square is the scene of many rallies, demonstrations, and celebrations, and it's perfect for people-watching. ⏱ 15 min. **Tube: Charing Cross.**

❼ ★★★ National Gallery. This revered museum dominating Trafalgar Square sits roughly where the stables of King Henry VIII used to be. Founded in 1824 with a collection of 38 paintings bought by the British government, the National is now home to some 2,000 works representing the world's major artistic periods from 1250 to 1900. It's London's best museum for anyone interested in the arts.

❽ ★★ kids National Portrait Gallery. Adjacent to the National Gallery, the NPG is the best place to put a face to the names of those who have shaped Britain politically, socially, and culturally. The gallery displays about 60% of its 10,000-plus portraits at a given time, ranging from King Harold II (b. 1022) to actress Keira Knightley (b. 1985). Familiar faces include Judi Dench, Richard Branson, Vivienne Westwood, Diana Rigg, David Bowie, Simon Cowell, Julie Christie, Michael Caine, and other less celebrated Brits, such as the psycho Kray brothers and their mum. Start at the top and work your way down. ⏱ 1 hr. **2 St. Martin's Lane. ☎ 0207/306-0055. www.npg.org.uk. Free admission, except for temporary exhibits. Sat–Wed 10am–6pm; Thurs–Fri 10am–9pm. Tube: Leicester Sq.**

> *The soldiers who take part in the Changing of the Guard are photographed more than most British celebrities.*

❾ 🍽 ★★★ The Portrait Restaurant, on the top floor of the NPG, commands the most spectacular views over Trafalgar Square. The lounge area, serving salads, light meals, and afternoon tea, is your best bet for a quick bite. **National Portrait Gallery, 2 St. Martin's Lane. ☎ 0207/312-2490. Entrees £7–£24.**

❿ ★★★ kids Covent Garden. This famous marketplace—first laid out in the 17th century—is a good spot to end your day of cultural explorations. At its heart is the Inigo Jones–designed arcade now filled with upscale shops and uninspired cafes. **Jubilee Market,** with inexpensive whatnots and cheap clothing, is set on the southern side of the arcade; at the western end you'll find stalls that, depending on the day, offer antiques, handmade crafts, or flea market goods. This area offers busking at its best; be it an opera singer from the adjacent **Royal Opera House** (p. 130), a tattooed man juggling knives, or a chamber music quartet, you'll always find real talent in Covent Garden's street entertainment. ⏱ At least 1 hr. **Tube: Covent Garden.**

SITE GUIDE PAGE 63

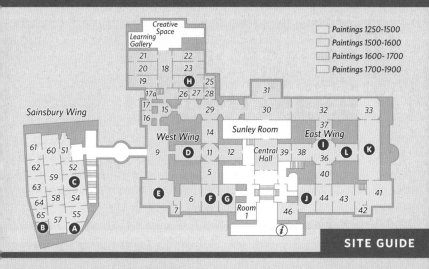

Paintings 1250-1500
Paintings 1500-1600
Paintings 1600-1700
Paintings 1700-1900

SITE GUIDE

7 National Gallery

Over 2,300 masterpieces are on display, but you can see a good representative selection in one visit. Start in the **A Sainsbury Wing's Room 56,** where you'll find familiar early European works, including Jan van Eyck's haunting *Arnolfini Portrait.* For a contrast in mood, go to **B Room 66** for Botticelli's *Venus and Mars* (above), a voluptuous allegory. In **C Room 53,** you'll find the heavenly 14th-century *Wilton Diptych,* a two-paneled altarpiece depicting Richard II, the Virgin and Child, and a number of saints. The **D ★★★ West Wing's Room 10** holds Titian's *Bacchus and Ariadne,* in colors still vibrant after 500 years; in **E Room 8** is an ethereal Raphael painting of *The Madonna of the Pinks.* *The Ambassadors,* by Hans Holbein the Younger, is in **F Room 4;** the skull in the foreground was painted using a geometrical process called anamorphosis, distorting the image unless you look at it from an angle. Pay your respects to Michelangelo and Da Vinci in **G Room 2,** where you'll

find Leonardo's *The Virgin of the Rocks,* whose sister painting in the Louvre featured in the book *The Da Vinci Code.* In **H Room 24** you'll find Rembrandt's confident *Self-Portrait at the Age of 34.* The **I East Wing** displays world-famous works by Impressionists Van Gogh, Monet, and Seurat, among others. A highlight in **J Room 45** is Van Gogh's radiant *Sunflowers.* Several notable English paintings hang in **K Room 34,** including Turner's *The Fighting Temeraire,* voted Britain's greatest painting; John Constable's *The Hay Wain,* one of his gorgeous East Anglian landscapes; and George Stubbs's 1762 portrait of the horse *Whistlejacket.* In **L Room 35** have a look at Gainsborough's charming *Mr. and Mrs. Andrews,* a portrait of a well-to-do couple in the mid-18th century. ⏱ 2 hr. Trafalgar Sq. (at St. Martin's Lane). ☎ 0207/747-2285. www. nationalgallery.org.uk. Free admission, except for temporary exhibits. Thurs–Tues 10am–6pm; Wed 10am–9pm. Tube: Leicester Sq.

Victoria and Albert Museum

This museum's 8 miles of corridors are resplendent with the world's greatest collection of decorative arts. Opened in 1852 by Prince Albert, this treasure-trove, known as the V&A, is home to millions of pieces of priceless arts and crafts spanning nearly 5 millennia of history. A massive refurbishment has polished to perfection its glorious displays of paintings, furniture, glass, ceramics, silver, and fashion.

> Exactly how many people have slept in the Great Bed of Ware, built for an inn in 1596, isn't recorded.

START South Kensington Tube Station, then follow the signs to the museum.

① ★ Chihuly Glass Chandelier. Renowned glass artist Dale Chihuly created this serpentine green and blue masterpiece specifically for the V&A in 2001, when an exhibition of his work was staged in the museum's outdoor courtyard. It's 8m (26 ft.) long, and made up of thousands of exquisite hand-blown glass baubles. Despite its airy effect, it weighs 1,724 kg (3,800 lb.). ⏱ 3 min. Foyer.

② ★★★ kids The British Galleries. This stellar example of 21st-century curatorship features some of England's greatest cultural treasures. The big draw is the Great Bed of Ware (Room 57), a masterpiece of woodcarving (built in 1596 for an inn, it's covered in I WAS HERE graffiti and wax seals left by centuries of visitors). Another highlight is the *Portrait of Margaret Laton* (Room 56); the painting is rather ordinary, but the jacket displayed alongside it is the very one worn in the portrait. My favorite

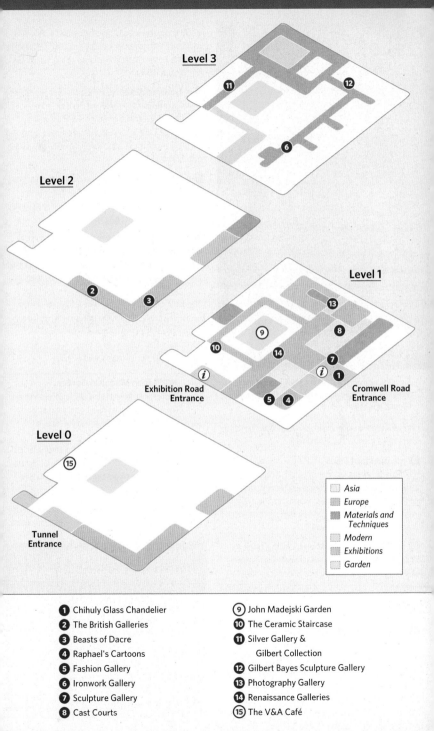

Level 3

⑪ Silver Gallery & Gilbert Collection
⑫ Gilbert Bayes Sculpture Gallery
⑥ Ironwork Gallery

Level 2

② The British Galleries
③ Beasts of Dacre

Level 1

⑬ Photography Gallery
⑧ Cast Courts
⑨ John Madejski Garden
⑩ The Ceramic Staircase
⑭ Renaissance Galleries
⑦ Sculpture Gallery
① Chihuly Glass Chandelier
ⓘ
ⓘ
⑤ Fashion Gallery
④ Raphael's Cartoons

Exhibition Road Entrance

Cromwell Road Entrance

Level 0

⑮ The V&A Café

Tunnel Entrance

Asia
Europe
Materials and Techniques
Modern
Exhibitions
Garden

❶ Chihuly Glass Chandelier
❷ The British Galleries
❸ Beasts of Dacre
❹ Raphael's Cartoons
❺ Fashion Gallery
❻ Ironwork Gallery
❼ Sculpture Gallery
❽ Cast Courts

❾ John Madejski Garden
❿ The Ceramic Staircase
⓫ Silver Gallery & Gilbert Collection
⓬ Gilbert Bayes Sculpture Gallery
⓭ Photography Gallery
⓮ Renaissance Galleries
⓯ The V&A Café

> *Even the entrance hall at the V&A contains a masterpiece of the decorative arts, the Chihuly Glass Chandelier.*

display allows you to design your own heraldic crest on a computer. ⏱ 30 min.

③ ★★ Beasts of Dacre. These four carved heraldic animals (gryphon, bull, dolphin, and ram) were carved for the Dacres, one of northern England's most important families, in 1520. Their weird whimsy has a wondrous dignity. ⏱ 5 min. Stairway C.

④ ★★★ Raphael's Cartoons. Dating back to 1521, these immense and expertly rendered drawings were used by the artist Raphael to plot a set of tapestries originally intended to hang in the Vatican's Sistine Chapel. ⏱ 10 min. Room 48a.

⑤ ★★ Fashion Gallery. From a ludicrous 18th-century, 1.2m-wide (4-ft.) skirt to vertiginous platform shoes by Vivienne Westwood, this gallery is proof positive that every age has its share of fashion victims. The collection, one of the world's largest, reopened in 2012 after a major 2-year renovation that unfortunately

resulted in the loss of the museum's beloved musical instruments gallery—music fans were outraged even as fashionistas rejoiced. ⏱ 15 min. Room 40.

⑥ ★ Ironwork Gallery. This gallery's highlight is the stupendous Hereford Screen, a masterpiece of Victorian ironwork designed by Sir George Gilbert Scott, the architect who devised the Albert Memorial (p. 74, ⑥). ⏱ 10 min. Room 114.

⑦ ★★ Sculpture Gallery. Sarcophagi, marble founts, and alabaster busts of great beauty are just some of the treasures you'll find in this gallery. ⏱ 15 min. Room 50a.

⑧ ★ Cast Courts. These two popular rooms used to be more colorfully titled "Fakes and Forgeries." Among the exceptionally executed imitations, you'll find a plaster cast of the statue of David (whose nudity so shocked Queen Victoria that she had a fig leaf made for it—it's now displayed behind the statue), a copy of Ghiberti's famous bronze doors for Florence's Baptistery, and an entire church facade. ⏱ 10 min. Rooms 46a & 46b.

⑨ 🍴 kids John Madejski Garden. For a quick outdoor snack, grab a table or recline on the lush lawns of this courtyard space. The fountain is great fun for kids, and on a sunny day, you may not want to go back into the museum. The sandwiches and teatime treats are plentiful and well-priced. Inner Courtyard. Snacks £4–£7.

⑩ ★ The Ceramic Staircase. The V&A's first director, Henry Cole, designed these stairs, intending to doll up all the museum's staircases

The V&A: Practical Matters

The Victoria and Albert Museum (☎ 0207/ 942-2000; www.vam.ac.uk) is located on Cromwell Road, off Exhibition Road. Admission is free, except to special exhibits. The museum is open daily from 10am to 5:45pm. On Friday, the V&A stays open until 10pm for the Late View, when live music, guided tours, and lectures are offered (it's best for adults). On weekends and school holidays, there are special activities for kids of all ages.

> *Highlights of the Gilbert Collection include a number of ornate snuff boxes.*

in this ceramics-gone-mad style. For better or worse, when the costs for the staircase spiraled out of control in 1870, the project was quietly dropped. ⏱ 10 min. Staircase I.

11 ★★★ **Silver Gallery & Gilbert Collection.** Possibly the museum's most impressive collection, these rooms shimmer with a jaw-dropping array of over 10,000 silver objects, ranging from baby rattles to candelabras to bath-sized punch bowls. Highlights include a 19th-century, gem-encrusted cup made by the architect and designer William Burges (1827–81) ; a rare, engraved 17th-century silver flask that belonged to the illegitimate son of Charles II and his mistress, actress Nell Gwyn; and a modern blouse made of silver mesh. Also jaw-dropping is the adjacent world-class Gilbert Collection of micro-mosaics and gold snuffboxes, including several jewel-encrusted beauties that belonged to Frederick II (the Great) of Prussia. ⏱ 25 min. Rooms 65–73.

12 ★★ **Gilbert Bayes Sculpture Gallery.** This gallery of small European sculpture in every imaginable medium gives you a treetop view of the Cast Courts, allowing you to inspect the dramatic details on top of the stone church facade below. ⏱ 20 min. Room 111.

13 ★★★ **Photography Gallery.** The V&A's vast and outstanding collection of some 300,000 images was started in 1852. Works from as far back as 1839 are shown on a rotating basis. You might see prints by noted British shutterbugs Julia Cameron and Bill Brandt, or early daguerreotypes. ⏱ 15 min. Room 38a.

14 ★★★ **Renaissance Galleries.** A mélange of mediums from the creatively fertile Renaissance era (1200–1650) is on display here, including tapestries, stained glass, statuary, glass, and metalwork. Notable items include a 15th-c. Murano glass goblet and a stained-glass panel of Holy Roman Emperor Maximilian I (ca. 1500) that originally hung in Bruges's Chapel of the Holy Blood. ⏱ 30 min. Rooms 21–25.

15 🍽 **The V&A Café** is a splendid cafeteria, overlooked by Arts and Crafts stained glass and ornate ceramics and tiles. The food includes traditional hot English fare, plus sandwiches and salads—delicious dining at cafeteria prices. Ground Level. Items £4–£7.

The British Museum

The British Museum, started with a donation by collector Sir Hans Sloane in 1753, opened at a time when the expansion of the British Empire into just about every corner of the earth ensured that its collection would be as eclectic as it was priceless. Note the frieze above the entrance—it signifies the museum's intention to encompass all the branches of science and art.

> *Authors like Karl Marx, Charles Dickens, and Charles Darwin researched and wrote in the famous, old Reading Room.*

START Holborn, Tottenham Court Road, or Russell Square Tube Stations.

❶ ★★★ **Great Court.** In December 2000, the museum's Great Court reopened with a marvelous glass-and-steel roof designed by Lord Norman Foster (b. 1935). Inaccessible to the general public for 150 years, the Great Court is now the museum's central axis and information center. ⏱ 5 min.

❷ ★ **The Reading Room.** This hallowed circular room with its gilt-and-azure dome has been restored to its 1857 grandeur. On either side of the entrance doors you'll see a list

of the authors (Dickens, Marx, Tennyson, Kipling, and Darwin, among others) who sat in this room to think and to research and write what would become some of the world's most important and influential scientific, political, historical, and literary works. A free multimedia database here allows you to search the museum's vast collections. ⏱ 5 min.

❸ ★★★ **Rosetta Stone.** One of the museum's most highly prized artifacts is an ancient text engraved on a tablet in three scripts (hieroglyphic, demotic, and Greek) and two languages (Greek and Egyptian) that enumerates the virtues of 13-year-old pharaoh Ptolemy V,

1 Great Court
2 The Reading Room
3 Rosetta Stone
4 The Parthenon Sculptures
  ("Elgin Marbles")
5 Statues of the
  Nereid Monument
6 Mausoleum of
  Halikarnassos
7 The Gallery Café
8 Lindow Man
9 Treasures of Sutton Hoo
10 Clocks and Watches
11 Egyptian Rooms
12 Asia Galleries
13 Enlightenment Gallery

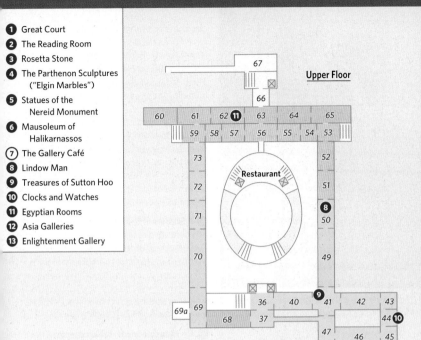

Upper Floor

67

66

60   61   62 ⑪   63   64   65
59   58   57   56   55   54   53

73   52

72   **Restaurant**   51

71   ⑧
                                      50

70   49

69a 69   36   40   41   42   43
     68   37   44 ⑩
                    47   46   45
                    48

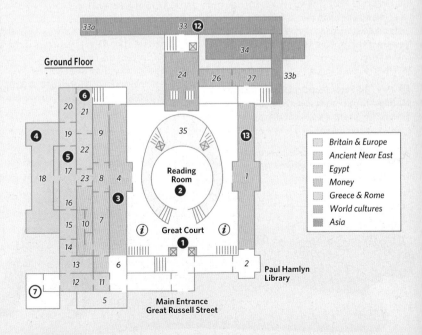

33a   33 ⑫
                          34

Ground Floor   24   26   27   33b

        20   ⑥
    ④   19   21   9   35   ⑬
    ⑤   17   22   1
18   23   8   4   **Reading**
        16   ③   7   **Room**
        15   10   ②
        14   13
    ⑦   12   11   ⓘ **Great Court** ⓘ
              6   ①
              5   **Main Entrance**   **Paul Hamlyn**
                   Great Russell Street   **Library**
                                          2

Britain & Europe
Ancient Near East
Egypt
Money
Greece & Rome
World cultures
Asia

> *The Rosetta Stone was the key to unlocking the mysteries of the Ancient Egyptian language.*

who lived in 196 B.C. The tablet was found in 1799 by Napoleon's troops and handed over to the British Army as part of the Treaty of Alexandria of 1801. The text was deciphered in 1822, a breakthrough that allowed archaeologists and historians to decode ancient Middle Eastern hieroglyphics and that proved that these symbols represented a spoken language. ⏲ 5 min. Room 4.

4 ★★★ **The Parthenon Sculptures ("Elgin Marbles").** The Greek government has been fighting for 2 centuries to get these detailed classical sculptures and artifacts—often referred to as the Elgin Marbles because they were taken from the Parthenon by Lord Elgin between 1801 and 1805—returned to Athens. The B.M. argues that it has provided a safe home for these carvings (including 75m/247 ft. of the original temple frieze), which would otherwise have been chipped away by vandals or degraded by remaining in the open air. The marbles may yet be returned to the Parthenon (a disastrous precedent for the museum, filled as it is with the booty of the world), but don't expect them to depart the B.M. any time soon. ⏲ 20 min. Room 18.

5 ★ **Statues of the Nereid Monument.** This 4th-century B.C. Lycian tomb from southwest Turkey arrived at the museum with the Elgin Marbles in 1816, and its lifelike statuary is almost surreal. Even without their heads, the daughters of the sea god Nereus (aka Nereids) look as graceful as the ocean waves they are meant to personify. ⏲ 5 min. Room 17.

6 ★★ **Mausoleum of Halikarnassos.** These are the remains of one of the Seven Wonders of the Ancient World—the breathtaking Ionian Greek tomb built for King Maussollos in about 350 B.C. ⏲ 5 min. Room 21.

7 ☕ ★★ kids **The Gallery Café** is a relaxed, cafeteria-style eatery decorated with the 1801 casts of the Elgin Marbles. The hot meals, sandwiches, and desserts are all reasonably priced. Off Room 12. ☎ 0207/323-8990. Items £4–£9.

> *The Parthenon Sculptures remain at the center of an interminable ownership wrangle between the museum and the Greek government.*

8 ★★ **Lindow Man.** The preserved remains of the 2,000-year-old "Bog Man," found preserved in a peat bog in Lindow Moss, Cheshire, in 1984, indicate that he was struck on the head, garroted, knifed, and then put head-first into the bog as part of some gruesome Druidic sacrifice. ⏱ 5 min. End of Room 50, on your right.

9 ★★★ **Treasures of Sutton Hoo.** When this 7th-century Anglo-Saxon ship tomb was excavated in 1939, its contents included exquisitely designed musical instruments, glassware, armor, and even Byzantine articles. The cache shattered previous beliefs about the inferior arts and crafts of England's Dark Ages. ⏱ 10 min. Room 41.

10 ★★ **Clocks and Watches.** The museum's outstanding collection of timepieces features the mind-blowing mechanical Galleon Clock, built in Germany around 1585, which used to roll along a table announcing dinnertime to guests by playing music, beating drums, and even firing tiny cannons. ⏱ 10 min. Room 39.

11 ★★★ **Egyptian Rooms.** It's said that the ghost of one of the 3,000-year-old mummies on display roams these rooms. Room 62 has a mummified cat, while Room 63 is filled with coffins, funerary objects, and a papyrus page from the Book of the Dead illustrating the necessary steps to a peaceful afterlife. In Room 64 you will usually find the 5,000-year-old carcass of a man the museum calls "Ginger," whose body dried out naturally in the desert. (His preserved red hair earned him the nickname.) ⏱ 20 min.

12 ★★ **Asia Galleries.** Room 33 is an oasis of calm that lures you with the serenity of meditating Buddhas and the grace of the "Dancing Shiva," a bronze sculpture depicting Shiva as Nataraja, the lord of the dance—one of India's most famous images. The intricate frieze of the Great Stupa (Room 33a) carved in India in the 3rd century B.C. so closely resembles the Elgin Marbles that you'll wonder about the artistic zeitgeist that seems to pass through borders and cultures. There are statues of bodhisattvas, Buddhist archetypes, in every medium—from porcelain to metal. As you exit through Room 33b, be sure to look at the Chinese jade carvings (some are over 4,000 years old). ⏱ 20 min.

> The museum holds one of the world's best collections of Egyptian mummies.

13 ★ **Enlightenment Gallery.** "Discovering the World in the 18th Century" is the permanent exhibit located in the restored King's Library, designed for George III by Sir Robert Smirke (1780–1867) and regarded as the finest neoclassical interior hall in London. The exhibit demonstrates the far-reaching, eclectic passions of an 18th-century Enlightenment scholar—the kind of person who made the British Museum possible. ⏱ 15 min.

Practical Matters

The British Museum (☎ 0207/636-1555; www.britishmuseum.org) is located on Great Russell Street. Admission is free, except to temporary special exhibits. The museum is open daily from 10am to 5:30pm; on Thursday and Friday, select galleries remain open until 8:30pm. A variety of specialty tours of the museum are offered, ranging from self-guided audio tours for families to free, 50-minute introductory tours; check the website for details or inquire at the Information Desk in the museum's Great Court. The website's "Compass" database offers access to data on thousands of the museum's objects.

Royal London

The various justifications for keeping the institution of the
English monarchy inevitably come down to the entertainment of tourists, who can't get enough of the wealth, history, and gossip that have always defined royalty. This full-day tour serves up some of the city's royal highlights and offers a glimpse into the London lives of royals past and present.

> The immense Gold State Coach, used at every British coronation since George IV, is stored in the Royal Mews when not in use.

START Green Park Tube Station.

❶ ★★ **Buckingham Palace.** The main draw of Queen Elizabeth II's official residence—a magnificent 500-room house that Queen Victoria despaired of ever making livable—is its exclusivity: It's open only in August and September, when the queen is not at home. The palace was originally built for the Duke of Buckingham and sold to King George III (who needed the room for his 15 kids) in 1761. George IV had it remodeled by famed architect John Nash in the 1820s, and the grandiose State Rooms you tour today remain virtually unchanged from his time. As an attraction, the treasure-laden palace has an

aloofness that may cause you to question its cost and effort, but it can't be beat for a look at one of the gilded cages of English royalty. ⏱ 2 hr. Book the earliest timed tour possible via the website to avoid the worst of the lines. Buckingham Palace Rd. ☎ 0207/766-7300. www.royal collection.org.uk. Admission (includes self-guided audio tour) £17.50 adults, £16 seniors, £10 kids 5–16, £46 family. Daily Aug–Sept 9:45am–5:30pm. Tube: Green Park.

❷ ★★ **Queen's Gallery.** This well-curated museum answers the question of how one furnishes and decorates a palace or two. Priceless treasures from the queen's private

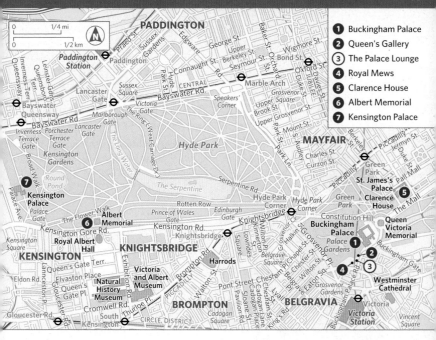

1 Buckingham Palace
2 Queen's Gallery
3 The Palace Lounge
4 Royal Mews
5 Clarence House
6 Albert Memorial
7 Kensington Palace

collection of paintings, jewelry, furniture, and bibelots are displayed in sumptuous Georgian-style surroundings. The exhibits rotate (the queen's holdings include, among other items, 10,000 Old Masters and enough objets d'art to fill several palaces—which they do when they aren't here), but whatever is on display will be top-notch. A highlight on my last visit to the gallery was an 18th-century silver vanity table—imagine having to polish that. You'll also find the city's best gift shop for royalty-related items, both cheap and dear. ⏱ 1½ hr. Buckingham Gate. ☎ 0207/766-7301. www.royalcollection.org.uk. Timed tickets necessary in summer. Admission £9 adults, £8.20 seniors, £4.50 kids 5–16, £22.50 families. Daily 10am–4:30pm. Tube: Green Park.

③ 🍽 **The Palace Lounge,** overlooking the entrance to the Royal Mews, is an atmospheric spot to grab a cup of tea or a tasty light meal. Lucky visitors may get a glimpse of deliveries being made to Buckingham Palace in old-fashioned wagons. In the Rubens at the Palace, 39 Buckingham Palace Rd. ☎ 0207/834-6600. Light meals £5–£18.

④ ★ kids **Royal Mews.** This oddly affecting royal experience is a great diversion on its own, or if you're waiting for your timed entry to Buckingham Palace. Even if you're not into horses, you'll be fascinated by this peek into the lives of the queen's privileged equines. The stalls at this working stable are roomy, the tack is pristine, and the ceremonial carriages (including the ornate Gold State Coach and the coach Princess Diana rode in to her wedding to Prince Charles) are eye-popping. A small exhibit tells you about the role the queen's horses have played in the past and present; old sepia-toned pictures show various royals and their four-footed friends. ⏱ 45 min. Buckingham Gate. ☎ 0207/766-7302. www.royalcollection.org.uk. Admission £8 adults, £7.25 seniors, £5 kids 5–16, £21.25 families. March-July & Oct Sat-Thurs 11am-4pm; Aug-Sept daily 10am-5pm. Tube: Green Park.

⑤ ★ **Clarence House.** Set in St. James's Park between the Mall and Pall Mall, this is another working palace that provides us lowly commoners with a glimpse of the royal lifestyle (like Buckingham Palace, it's only open in Aug and Sept, when the residents are hard at work in another royal residence). From 1953

> The over-the-top decoration of the Albert Memorial seems a mismatch for its somber role—to remember Queen Victoria's beloved husband.

including her collection of outstanding 20th-century paintings. Superb examples of Fabergé, English porcelain, and silver, particularly pieces relating to the Bowes-Lyon family, are also on display. ⏱ 30 min. St. James's Palace, St. James's Park. ☎ 0207/766-7303. Admission £8.50 adults, £4.50 kids under 17. Daily Aug–Sept 10am–4pm. Tube: St. James's Park.

6 ★ kids **Albert Memorial.** An inconsolable Queen Victoria spent an obscene amount of public money on this 55m-tall (180-ft.) shrine to her husband Albert, who died of typhoid fever in 1861. Designed by Sir George Gilbert Scott (1811–78), the project (completed in 1876) didn't go down too well with many of her ministers, but Victoria was not a woman to whom one said no. The excessively ornate mass of gilt, marble, statuary, and mosaics set in Kensington Gardens was restored (to the tune of millions of pounds) in the 1990s, and now stands in all its dubious glory across the street from the equally fabulous (and somewhat more useful) **Royal Albert Hall** (p. 130). That book Albert is holding is a catalogue from the Great Exhibition of which he was patron, and which formed the basis for the great museums of South Kensington (once called Albertopolis). ⏱ 10 min. Kensington Gardens (west of Exhibition Rd.). Free admission. Daily dawn–dusk. Tube: Kensington High Street.

SITE GUIDE
PAGE 75

7 ★★ kids **Kensington Palace.** Once the 17th-century country refuge of monarchs William III and Mary II, this former home of Queen Victoria and Princess Diana is more satisfying to visit than Buckingham Palace (and it's open year-round). Please note that until June 5, 2012, the palace will be undergoing a raft of changes meant to make it more accessible and appealing to the general public. The historic State Apartments remain open and have been fitted out with art and fashion installations that will remain in place until the palace officially reopens on the Queen's Diamond Jubilee. The rooms highlighted in the minitour below will all then be re-opened and become part of a new interactive reinterpretation in which stories of the seven queens and princesses who lived in the palace will be told in the rooms where they lived.

to 2002, Clarence House was the home of Queen Elizabeth, the Queen Mother; today it serves as the official residence of HRH the Prince of Wales and the Duchess of Cornwall (aka Prince Charles and his second wife, the former Camilla Parker-Bowles) and the home of the Princes William and Harry. Visitors are guided around the five ground-floor rooms where the royal residents undertake official engagements and receive guests from around the world. The arrangement of the rooms and the grouping of their contents remain much as they were in the late Queen Mum's time,

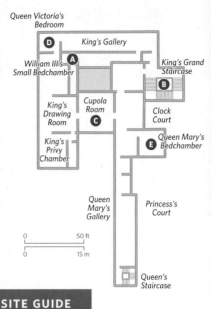

Queen Victoria's Bedroom

King's Gallery

William III's Small Bedchamber

A

D

King's Grand Staircase

B

King's Drawing Room

Cupola Room

C

Clock Court

King's Privy Chamber

E Queen Mary's Bedchamber

Queen Mary's Gallery

Princess's Court

0   50 ft
0   15 m

Queen's Staircase

SITE GUIDE

7 Kensington Palace

The palace is smaller, has more personality, and is more manageable to tour than Buckingham, with a number of pleasing architectural details that span the years from Jacobean England to the early 19th century. The front of the palace, now completely relandscaped as part of the new refurbishment scheme, was heaped high with floral tributes from London citizens following the 1997 death of Diana, the "People's Princess," in a car crash. **A William III's Small Bedchamber**, the first room you enter, is home to the Royal Ceremonial Dress Collection, which features gowns worn by both the queen and Diana. The **B ★ King's Grand Staircase** has a magnificent wrought-iron balustrade; the elaborate 16th-century-style Italianate murals on the walls and ceiling were commissioned by George I in 1725. The lavishly decorated **C ★★ Cupola Room,** where Victoria was baptized, features elaborately carved chandeliers, a breathtaking gilt clock, and a magnificent painted ceiling. **D ★ Queen Victoria's Bedroom,** hung with artwork commissioned by Victoria and Albert, is where the young princess and her mother slept until the teenager ascended the throne in

1837. **E ★ Queen Mary's Bedchamber** (pictured above) was likely the room where Mary II died of smallpox in 1694; the bed, however, probably belonged to James II. ⏱ 2 hr. The Broad Walk, Kensington Gardens. ☎ 0844/482-7777. www.hrp.org.uk. Admission (includes self-guided audio tour) £13 adults, £11 seniors, £6.25 kids 5-15, £34 families. Daily 10am–6pm. Tube: Kensington High Street.

Hampton Court Palace

This Tudor masterpiece was built by Cardinal Thomas Wolsey in 1514, only to be snatched up by Henry VIII (1491–1547). It served as a royal residence from 1528 to 1737, and few places in England exude as much historic atmosphere. Tread the same paths as Elizabeth I (1533–1603), William III (1650–1702), and George II (1683–1760) as you learn about life at court through the centuries.

START Take a train from London's Waterloo Station to Hampton Court Station, a 10-min. walk from the palace.

1 Base Court. Monarchs arrived at Hampton Court via the Thames and entered through the gardens, but visitors today pass through a gatehouse built by Henry VIII for the common folk, and into the Tudor-style courtyard, which is almost exactly as it was when Cardinal Wolsey first built it around 1515. Be sure to examine the turrets surrounding the courtyard, which sport the insignia of Henry VIII and Elizabeth I (who both resided here). ⏱ 5 min.

2 ★★ Clock Court. From the Base Court, pass through the Anne Boleyn Gatehouse (built in the 19th c., long after the beheaded queen's death) and into the Clock Court, which encompasses several architectural styles, ranging from Tudor (the north side) to 18th-century Gothic (the east side). The major attraction is the elaborate Astronomical Clock, built for Henry VIII (note the sun revolving around the earth—the clock was built before Galileo and Copernicus debunked that myth). ⏱ 5 min.

> The Astronomical Clock in Clock Court was made for King Henry VIII but still functions today.

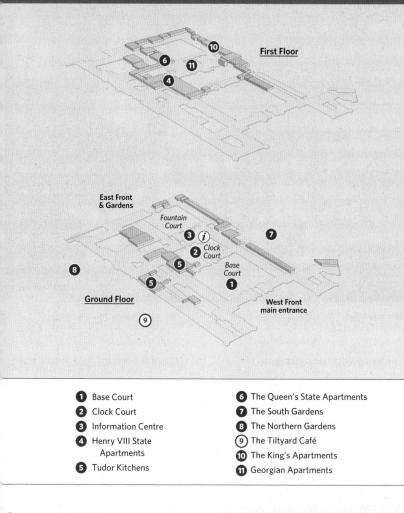

First Floor

East Front
& Gardens

Fountain Court

Clock Court

Base Court

Ground Floor

West Front
main entrance

1 Base Court
2 Clock Court
3 Information Centre
4 Henry VIII State Apartments
5 Tudor Kitchens
6 The Queen's State Apartments
7 The South Gardens
8 The Northern Gardens
9 The Tiltyard Café
10 The King's Apartments
11 Georgian Apartments

3 ★★★ kids **Guided Tour.** Stop in at the Information Centre inside the baroque colonnade on the south side of the Clock Court and book a spot on one of the day's costumed guided tours (included with your admission fee). The guides here are knowledgeable and entertaining and dispense juicy historical tidbits. Kids especially enjoy the experience. You must book in person; do so as soon as you get to the palace. If you have a choice, opt for the tour of the Henry VIII State Apartments or the King's Apartments. Self-guided palace audio tours are also available (and free). ⏱10 min.

Practical Matters

Hampton Court Palace (☎ 0844/482-7777; www.hrp.org.uk) is located in Molesey, Surrey, 13 miles west of London. Admission to the palace and gardens costs £16 adults, £13.20 seniors and students, £8 kids, and £42.50 families. Booking your tickets online gives you a discounted rate. The palace is open daily 10am to 6pm (Nov–Mar until 4:30pm). The gardens are open 7am until dusk. Closed December 24, 25, and 26. Arrive at opening time to beat the crowds.

> *Before splitting with the Catholic Church, Henry VIII heard Mass in the magnificent Chapel Royal at Hampton Court Palace.*

4 ★★★ **Henry VIII State Apartments.** Even though Sir Christopher Wren modified some of them, these rooms represent the best examples of Tudor style in England. Don't miss the elaborately gilded ceiling of the **Chapel Royal,** a still-functioning church where Henry was informed of the "misconduct" of his adulterous fifth wife, Catherine Howard, and later married wife number six, Catherine Parr. Right off the chapel is the **Haunted Gallery,** where Howard's ghost reportedly still pleads for her life. The **Watching Chamber,** where senior courtiers would dine, is the only one of Henry VIII's many English estate rooms in something close to its original form (the fireplace and stained glass are not originals). Also impressive is the **Great Hall,** with a set of tapestries (real gold and silver thread) that cost Henry as much as his naval fleet. ⏱ 30 min.

5 ★★ **Tudor Kitchens.** At its peak, Hampton Court's kitchen staff catered two meals a day to a household of 800. The enormity of the labor needed to feed the household here is best experienced in the **Great Kitchens,** restored to the way they looked in the days of Henry VIII. In a small hatchway just outside them are the intriguing **Dressers,** where servants would "dress" and garnish platters sent up to the senior courtiers (check out the marzipan on the table—it's been painted with real gold). ⏱ 5 min.

6 ★ **The Queen's State Apartments.** The rooms in this section of the palace generally appear as they were when used by Queen Caroline, wife of George II, from 1716 to 1737. Most impressive is the ornate **State Bedchamber,** one of the only rooms with all of its original furnishings and tapestries (including the heavily draped 18th-c. bed). ⏱ 10 min.

7 ★★★ **The South Gardens.** The palace's most impressive gardens are home to William III's **Privy Garden,** with its elaborate baroque ironwork screen; the box-hedged **Knot Garden,** which resembles a traditional Tudor garden; and the lovely sunken **Pond Gardens,** which were originally ponds where the palace's fish were kept before delivery to the kitchens. Don't skip Andrea Mantegna's *Triumphs of Caesar,* a series of nine paintings housed in the Lower Orangery (a re-creation of the Palazzo San Sebastiano in Mantua), which are among the most important works of the Italian Renaissance. ⏱ 40 min.

8 ★★ kids **The Northern Gardens.** Renowned for their spring bulbs, the Northern Gardens are also where you'll find the palace's famous **Hedge Maze,** whose labyrinthine paths cover nearly a half-mile. Planted in 1702, the maze has trapped many a visitor in its clutches. When you do escape, stroll the adjacent **Tiltyard,** where you'll find several smaller gardens, as well as the only surviving tiltyard tower (used to seat spectators at tournaments) built by Henry VIII. ⏱ 30 min.

9 🍽 ★ **The Tiltyard Café** offers well-priced sandwiches, salads, afternoon teas, and light meals in a slightly upscale setting. If the weather's good, try to sit on the outdoor terrace. You can also picnic on the grass around the cafe, or on the benches in the Clock Court. Items £3–£8.

10 ★★★ **The King's Apartments.** These baroque rooms (among the finest of their kind) were designed by Sir Christopher Wren for William III, who did more to shape the palace than any other monarch, though he died shortly after moving in. The apartments were badly damaged in a 1986 fire (you can still see scorch marks on the ceiling in the **Privy Chamber**), but have been fully restored. All the rooms in this wing are impressive, but a few are particularly noteworthy. The **Guard Chamber** features a spectacular collection of nearly 3,000 weapons; the **Presence Chamber** has an exquisite rock-crystal chandelier; the **Private Dining Room** has a reproduction of the king's gold-plated dining service (strictly for show); and the **Great Bedchamber** (ceremonial only—the king slept elsewhere) is loaded with gilded furniture, priceless tapestries, and a magnificent red velvet canopy bed. ⏱ 30 min.

11 ★★ **Georgian Apartments.** The private apartments of George II and Queen Caroline still look as they did in 1737, when Caroline died and the royal court left the palace behind forever. The **Presence Chamber** of the 10-year-old Duke of Cumberland (the king's second son) is the only room at the palace that's fully paneled, gilded, and painted. Only a portion of the ceiling of the **Wolsey Closet** is from the Tudor era, though the ceiling is decorated in the Renaissance style. The state bed in the **Queen's Bedchamber** is a reproduction. If the king and queen wanted to sleep together in privacy (which was no mean feat for the royal couple), it was to this room they retired, thanks to a rather sophisticated door lock. ⏱ 30 min.

> *The Tudor Kitchens were responsible both for cooking the food and for making it look "fit for a king."*

London with Kids

London is one of Europe's best playgrounds for kids.
Nearly all the city's major museums have developed well-thought-out activities to entertain and inspire kids; one of the greatest London city parks has always been a kids' favorite; and of course there is, for better or for worse, Madame Tussaud's. Whether you make it to all the venues on this tour obviously depends on the amount of time you have (to see all the sights listed you'll need at least 2, preferably 3 days), and the temperaments and ages of your children.

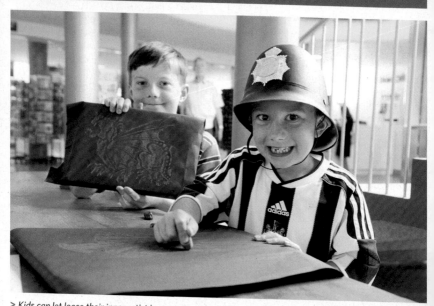

> Kids can let loose their inner artist in any get-up they'd like at the London Brass Rubbing Centre.

START South Kensington Tube Station.

① ★★★ kids **Science Museum.** Designed to appeal to children of all ages, this great institution offers consistently arresting exhibits with fun features, including the Garden, an interactive play area for 3- to 6-year-olds on the Lower Ground Floor. Its seven levels of displays succeed in getting both kids and adults to understand the place of science in everyday life, even as they provide hours of amusement. Highlights include "Launchpad" (hands-on chemistry and physics fun), Foucault's Pendulum, the *Apollo 10* command module, and an

IMAX theater (which charges a fee—buy your tickets as soon as you arrive). The gift shop is almost as interesting as the exhibits. ⏱ 2 hr. Come on weekdays to avoid throngs. Exhibition Rd. ☎ 0870/870-4868. www.sciencemuseum.org.uk. Free admission, except for special exhibits. Daily 10am–6pm. Tube: South Kensington.

② ★★★ kids **The Natural History Museum.** This museum's building alone is worth a look. Statues of beasts have been incorporated into its facade, and in the lobby, you'll find charming stained-glass windows. Although not as edgy and modern as the Science Museum

1 Science Museum
2 The Natural History Museum
3 Kensington Gardens
4 London Brass Rubbing Centre
5 Café in the Crypt
6 London's Transport Museum
7 Madame Tussauds
8 SEA LIFE London Aquarium
9 London Eye

> *The animatronic dinosaurs at the Natural History Museum may be a little too realistic for very young kids, but they are a hit with everyone else.*

next door, this museum is no fossil. Its exhibits include modern dinosaur displays and an interactive rainforest. The gem, mineral, and meteorite exhibits are all top-notch. The old animal dioramas are still around, but the new Darwin Wing (a £70-million project years in the making) has left them in the dust; its highlights include ongoing events with naturalists, photographers, and explorers (not to mention its 28 million insects and 6 million plant specimens). ⏱ 1½ hr. Cromwell Rd., off Exhibition Rd. ☎ 0207/942-5000. www.nhm.ac.uk. Free admission, except for temporary exhibits. Daily 10am–6pm. Tube: South Kensington.

❸ ★★ **kids Kensington Gardens.** Kensington Gardens adjoins Hyde Park west of the lake known as the Serpentine. Children especially love the famous bronze statue of **Peter Pan,** located north of the Serpentine Bridge. Commissioned in 1912 by Peter Pan's creator, J. M. Barrie, the statue marks the spot where, in the book *Peter Pan in Kensington Gardens,* Peter enters the gardens to get to his home on Serpentine Island. From spring through summer, you can rent paddleboats and paddle around the Serpentine Lake. The **Princess Diana Memorial Playground** in the northwest corner of the park is full of exercise equipment and fun attractions for toddlers and kids up to age 6. ⏱ At least 1 hr. See p. 86, **❿**.

❹ ★★★ **kids London Brass Rubbing Centre.** Located inside the basement crypt of **St. Martin-in-the-Fields,** a historic 18th-century church in Trafalgar Square, are 88 bronze plates of medieval subjects that kids (and adults) can reproduce by rubbing a waxy crayon over a piece of paper affixed to the plate. Admission is free, but rubbings start at £4.50 for a small drawing (a life-size knight will set you back £20). Kids love how they can produce impressive works of art with just a little effort. The Centre also sells great souvenirs. ⏱ 1 hr. St. Martin-in-the-Fields, Trafalgar Sq. ☎ 0207/766-1122. Free admission; rubbings from £4.50. Mon–Wed 10am–6pm; Thurs–Sat 10am–9pm; Sun noon–6pm. Tube: Charing Cross.

⑤ 🍽 ★ **Café in the Crypt,** also located in the basement of St. Martin-in-the-Fields, is a handy, no-fuss cafe that serves hot lunches, snacks, sweets, and drinks. St. Martin-in-the-Fields, Trafalgar Sq. ☎ 0207/839-4342. Items £6–£9.

⑥ ★★★ kids **London's Transport Museum.** If only the real London transport system were as up-to-date and well-maintained as this museum. Climb aboard a stagecoach, a double-decker omnibus, or an early underground train. The rest of the exhibits don't neglect other modes of transport in this huge city: Bicycles, motorcycles, and taxis all get their close-ups at this fascinating museum. There's plenty of interactive fun as you trace the evolution of London's public transport through photos, films, old vehicles, and more. 🕐 1½ hr. Covent Garden Piazza. ☎ 0207/379-6344. www.ltmuseum.co.uk. Admission £13.50 adults, £10 seniors. Sat–Thurs 10am–6pm; Fri 11am–9pm. Tube: Covent Garden.

⑦ kids **Madame Tussauds.** Madame Tussauds wax museum is a world-famous tourist attraction and a fun spot for older kids. The question is: Do you want to pay the exorbitant admission price? The original moldings of members of the French court (Madame Tussaud rose to fame by making molds of their heads after they were guillotined during the French Revolution) are undeniably fascinating. Animatronic gadgetry makes the Spirit of London theme ride fun, but Chamber Live (formerly called the Chamber of Horrors) is definitely for the ghoulish and unsuitable for kids under 12. The A-List exhibit features screen favorites like Daniel Radcliffe of the *Harry Potter* series and sport faves like David Beckham and his fashion-designer wife Victoria. But the cast of waxwork worthies on display is changing all the time, so you'll assuredly run into at least one celebrity *du jour*. Marylebone Rd. ☎ 020/7935-6861 or 0870/400-3000 for advance reservations with credit card. www.madametussauds.com. Admission £29 adults, £25 kids under 16, £90 families; children under 4 not admitted. Daily 9am–6pm. Tube: Baker Street.

⑧ kids **SEA LIFE London Aquarium.** You'd expect a bit more for your money at one of Europe's top aquariums, but when it comes

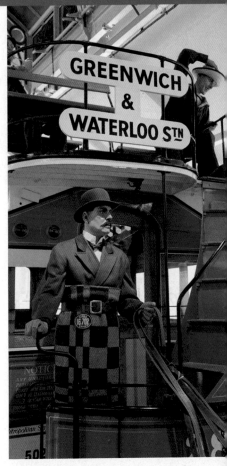

> *London's Transport Museum, in Covent Garden, gives kids plenty of opportunities to interact with the exhibits.*

down to it, kids adore this place. There's a petting tank of manta rays, a simulated coral reef with sea horses, and appropriately scary shark tanks. 🕐 1 hr. County Hall, Westminster Bridge Rd. ☎ 0207/967-8000. www.londonaquarium.co.uk. Admission £18 adults; £17 seniors, students & kids 15–17 (bring ID); £13 kids 3–14; £55 families. 25% discount for purchasing tickets online. Daily 10am–6pm. Tube: Westminster.

⑨ **London Eye.** London's famous observation wheel is a brilliant way to end your kids' tour of London. The ride is exciting (but stable) and provides unparalleled views of London. 🕐 1 hr. See p. 54, ⑦.

Hyde Park

Since 1536, when Henry VIII appropriated the land from the monks of Westminster Abbey for hunting, 142-hectare (351-acre) Hyde Park has been the scene of duels, highway robbery, and sport. Today this Royal Park, the site of London's Great Exhibition of 1851, is a beloved oasis of green in the midst of the city, a great place for horseback riding in London, and the best seat in town for viewing Londoners at play.

> June, when the blooms are at their best, is the ideal month to visit the Rose Garden.

START Hyde Park Corner Tube Station.

❶ ★★ **Hyde Park Corner Screen.** Erected in 1828, this imposing park entrance (one of six park entryways) was designed by Decimus Burton (1800–81), the noted architect responsible for much of Hyde Park's layout. The triple-arched screen is composed of Ionic columns, bronzed ironwork, and carved friezes inspired by the **Elgin Marbles** (p. 70, **❹**). Unfortunately, it's being degraded by air pollution at this busy traffic circle. ⏲ 10 min.

❷ ★ **Speakers' Corner.** A unique London institution for over 150 years, Speaker's Corner is dedicated to the ideal of free speech for all citizens. On Sunday mornings, anyone who wants to speak, on any topic or issue, can do so for 10 minutes at this spot. Whether anyone listens or not is another matter. ⏲ 10 min.

❸ ★★ **kids** **Rose Garden.** From the Rose Garden, a riot of color in the early summer, you can admire the back of **Apsley House** (p. 61, **❷**) and, to the east, Wellington Arch's majestic statue, *Winged Victory* (erected to commemorate the Duke of Wellington's war triumphs; p. 60, **❶**). The garden is filled with fountains and climbing rose trellises, both much loved by kids. Its central fountain is ringed with benches where you can sit with a picnic lunch, as hopeful (and picturesque) sparrows flutter around. ⏲ 15 min.

❹ ★★ **kids** **Rotten Row.** In the late 1680s, William III ordered 300 lamps to be hung from trees along this 1.5-mile riding path—whose name may be an English corruption of its original appellation, *Route de Roi* (King's Road)—in a vain attempt to stop the plague of highwaymen active in the park. Nowadays, it's where

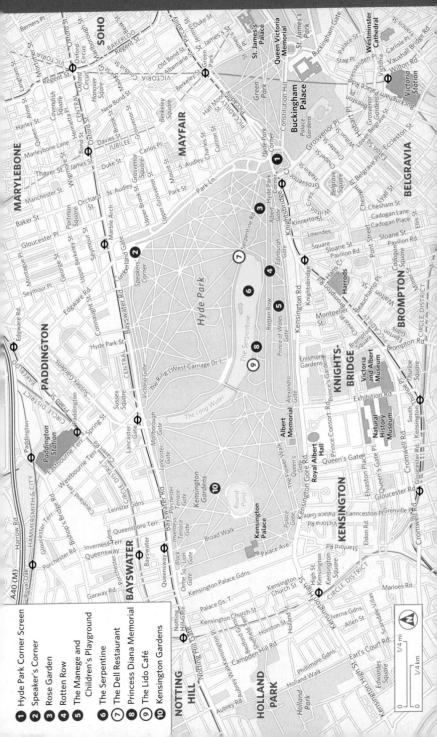

1 Hyde Park Corner Screen
2 Speaker's Corner
3 Rose Garden
4 Rotten Row
5 The Manege and
   Children's Playground
6 The Serpentine
7 The Dell Restaurant
8 Princess Diana Memorial
9 The Lido Café
10 Kensington Gardens

> A few pounds buy you an hour to see the Serpentine by pedal power.

horses carrying riders through the park often decide it's time to canter, possibly sensing the echoes of the wild and dangerous carriage races that took place here over a century ago. If you want to give it a try, the best horses in the park are at the **Ross Nye Stables,** 8 Bathurst Mews (☎ 0207/262-3791). ⏱ 1 hr. On the southern boundary of the park. 1-hr. rides start at £40.

⑤ ★ kids The Manege and Children's Playground. At the Manege, a special riding arena for royal steeds, you may be lucky enough to see all the queen's men exercising all the queen's horses or practicing for a ceremonial event. The adjacent playground has all the equipment a kid might want, plus a nice view of the riding ring. ⏱ 15 min. Off S. Carriage Dr.

⑥ ★★★ kids The Serpentine. Queen Caroline, wife of George II, had the Westbourne River dammed in 1730 to create the Serpentine Lake, upon which she moored two royal yachts. This lovely lake is now the premier boating spot in London for the masses. Should you venture out on the water, your yacht will

be a tad less splendid than the queen's—you can choose from among 110 paddle boats and rowboats at the Boat House. If you want to sit out an adventure on the high seas, you can entertain yourself watching the in-line skaters who love this stretch of the park. ⏱ 1 hr. Bluebird Boats Ltd., Serpentine Rd. ☎ 0207/262-1330. Hourly rentals £6 adults, £2.50 kids, £15 families. Mar–Oct 10am–5pm.

⑦ 🍽 kids The Dell Restaurant has the best view of the Serpentine in the park, and serves hot meals, sandwiches, and drinks (wine included) that are a cut above the usual park cafeteria cuisine. You're welcome to picnic on the tables outside. **Eastern side of the Serpentine.** ☎ 0207/706-0464. Snacks £3.50–£7.

⑧ ★ kids Princess Diana Memorial. This contemporary granite fountain, across the Serpentine from the Boat House, was opened by the queen in July 2004. No less dogged by controversy than the woman who inspired it, the 700-ton, £6.5-million fountain has suffered from flooding, closures, and a slippery bottom. The water doesn't shoot up, it cascades and flows along an oblong channel around a central green space. Children, who were meant to splash around happily in its cascading waters, are now restricted to toe-dipping by the omnipresent security guards. ⏱ 10 min. Near the Lido, south of the Serpentine.

⑨ 🍽 kids The Lido Café offers blah food but is a good spot for a bathroom break, a cuppa, and good views. Sitting on the outdoor terrace, you may see people swimming in the adjacent Lido Pool, unfazed by the geese droppings. **South side of the Serpentine Terrace.** ☎ 0207/706-7098. Snacks £2.50–£7.

SITE GUIDE PAGE 87

⑩ ★★★ kids Kensington Gardens. Originally a part of Hyde Park, the 111-hectare (274-acre) Kensington Gardens were partitioned into an exclusive preserve of royalty in the 18th century, and were opened to the public only in the early 1800s. Originally laid out in Dutch style (emphasizing water, avenues, and topiaries), the attractive gardens are especially popular with families.

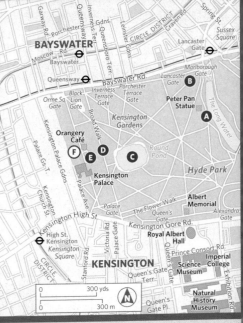

🔟 Kensington Gardens

The bronze Ⓐ ★★ kids **Peter Pan Statue** was sculpted in 1912 by Sir George Frampton (1860–1928) at the behest of author J. M. Barrie (1860–1937)—whose *Peter Pan in Kensington Gardens,* a prelude to the character's more famous adventures in Neverland, was set here—and is the most visited landmark in the park. A short walk north and you'll arrive at the Ⓑ ★★ kids **Italian Gardens,** whose fountains and classical statuary echoed the rage for all things Italian when it was built in 1861 by order of Prince Albert. Generations of children have plied model boats at the Ⓒ ★★★ kids **Round Pond,** created in 1728 at the behest of Queen Caroline. Today you'll also find adults trying out more sophisticated models. West of the pond is the Ⓓ **Broad Walk.** Nineteenth-century ladies and gentlemen promenaded along this tree-lined path past Kensington Palace and flirted by the nearby bandstand. Peek through the front gates of Kensington Palace at the Ⓔ ★★★ kids **Sunken Garden,** which was planted in 1908 and inspired by the Tudor gardens at Hampton Court Palace. End your tour at the exquisite Ⓕ ★★★ kids **Orangery Café,** where a very good tea (£14) is offered and the atmosphere is airy and refined. 🕐 At least 1 hr. ☎ 0203/166-6112. www.hrp.org.uk. Tube: Kensington High Street, Queensway, or Lancaster Gate.

Regent's Park

This 197-hectare (487-acre) gem started out as a hunting ground for Henry VIII, who liked to gallop here from Whitehall for the exercise. The park's ambitious design by John Nash (1752–1835) followed the romantic ideal of rus in urbe (country in the city). It's more urbe than rus with its civilized decorative features and activities and sophisticated flower beds, and the leafy paths are lined with benches good for conversations, sunning, or people-watching.

> *The open spaces of Regent's Park are easily accessed on foot from both the West End and Camden Town.*

START Camden Town Station.

1 ★★ kids **Grand Union Canal/Regent's Canal.** Londoners once traveled the city by boat when Regent's Park was in its infancy, and this is your chance to follow in their wake. The Grand Union Canal, opened in 1814, now covers 137 miles of waterways connecting the River Thames and the Chiltern Hills in Oxfordshire. Water buses now ply the scenic Regent's Canal section (opened in 1820) and will take you from Camden Lock's markets through the neighborhoods of colorful houseboats and grand Victorian houses on either side of the canal path in Little Venice—an area whose name is more wishful than accurate (there's just the one canal). Your final destination is the **London Zoo** (**3**), for which you can buy slightly discounted combo tickets before getting on the boat. ⏱ 50 min. Camden Lock. ☎ 0207/482-2660. www.londonwaterbus.com.

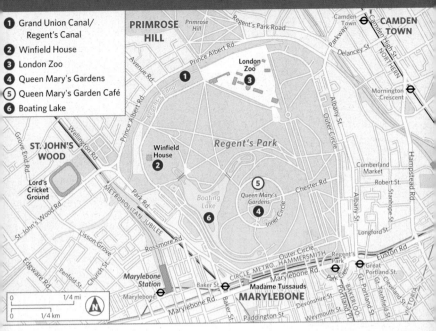

1. Grand Union Canal/
   Regent's Canal
2. Winfield House
3. London Zoo
4. Queen Mary's Gardens
5. Queen Mary's Garden Café
6. Boating Lake

One-way tickets £6 adults, £4.30 kids 3–15. Year-round, depending on the weather.

2 Winfield House. Woolworth heiress Barbara Hutton built this Georgian mansion in 1936, adding extensive gardens and trees. A year after World War II, Hutton donated the antiques-filled home to the American government for use as the official residence of the U.S. ambassador. Unfortunately, you have to be an invited guest to enter, so just give it a glance as you sail by.

3 ★★★ kids London Zoo. When this former zoology center opened to the public in 1847, many of its captives, such as Jumbo the Elephant (later bought by P. T. Barnum and shipped off to the U.S.), were celebrities. Visitors who complain about the high price of admission might feel differently about this venerable institution if they know that roughly one-sixth of its 650 species (about 5,000 animals reside here) are endangered—and that the zoo's world-renowned breeding program is the only thing preventing their extinction. I'm particularly fond of the reptile house and the gorillas and other simians. ⏱ 2 hr.; longer for families. Outer Circle, Regent's Park. ☎ 0207/722-3333. www.zsl.org. Admission £20

adults, £18.30 seniors, £16 kids 3–15; 10% online discount for families. Daily 10am–5:30pm (Nov–Feb until 4pm).

4 ★★★ kids Queen Mary's Gardens. Laid out in the 1930s, these regal gardens lie at the heart of the park's Inner Circle and are a place of enchanting colors, fragrances, and watery vistas. The fabulous and carefully tended Rose Gardens are especially beautiful in spring. ⏱ 15 min. Inner Circle.

5 🍽 ★ Queen Mary's Garden Café is a less informal alternative to the food kiosks scattered around Regent's Park. Here you can choose from a good variety of salads and sandwiches, as well as wine and beer, and enjoy a light meal on a lovely terrace. Queen Mary's Garden, adjacent to Rose Garden. ☎ 0207/935-5729. Snacks £3.50—£8.

6 ★★ kids Boating Lake. Operating on a schedule that changes with the weather and day of the week, Park Boats rents paddle boats and rowboats you can take out on this picturesque lake. Be sure to call ahead. ⏱ 1 hr. ☎ 0207/724-4069. Hourly rentals £6.50 adults, £4.40 kids, £20 families. Daily Mar–Oct 10:30am–4:30pm (extended hours in summer—call ahead).

UP IN SMOKE

How the Great Fire Changed London BY DONALD OLSON

SHORTLY AFTER MIDNIGHT ON SEPTEMBER 2, 1666, a spark from an oven set fire to the thatched roof of the house of King Charles II's baker, touching off a 4-day conflagration that would reduce the City of London to a heap of smoking rubble and change its character forever. London was still a medieval city, with closely packed houses made of wood, plaster, and thatch, so the fire had plenty of fuel as it leapt from house to house, fanned by the dry September winds. Panic-stricken Londoners fled to boats on the Thames and out to Hampstead Heath as the roaring flames created heat so intense that it melted the lead roof on old St. Paul's Cathedral. When the fire was finally spent, 13,000 houses and 89 churches had been destroyed. Amazingly, only six people died. And the fire may actually have saved lives in the long run; plague was running rampant in London, and the fire destroyed most of the rats carrying the disease.

Christopher Wren Rebuilds London

In 1669, King Charles II appointed the Oxford-trained architect Sir Christopher Wren (1632–1723) as Surveyor of Works, responsible for planning and rebuilding London after the fire. Wren—a brilliant astronomer, mathematician, and scientist, as well as an architect— immediately went to work, and thanks to him, a new London emerged from the ashes of the Great Fire. Sturdy, elegant, classically-inspired buildings of brick and stone replaced the timber structures of medieval London. Wren, who personally designed 51 churches in the City of London, is buried under the dome of his masterpiece, St. Paul's Cathedral (p.54, **9**).

The Monument

Designed by Sir Christopher Wren to commemorate the Great Fire of 1666, the Monument (p. 57, **4**) rises like a giant candle at the intersection of Fish Street and Monument Hill in the City of London. The total height of the column (61.6m/202 ft.) is equal to its distance east of the site to the baker's house in Pudding Lane where the fire began. Wren submitted several schemes for the Monument, including one with copper flames protruding from the sides and a giant phoenix rising from the top (to symbolize a London newly arisen from the fire), before the present Roman Doric design was accepted in 1671. Capped by an urn of copper flames, the Monument is the tallest isolated stone column in the world. Inside, a spiral staircase of 311 steps leads to a wonderful viewing platform, or you can see live images beamed down from on high in the Visitor Center.

> "I saw a fire as one entire arch of fire above a mile long: it made me weep to see it. The churches, houses are all on fire and flaming at once, and a horrid noise the flames made and the cracking of the houses."
>
> (FROM THE DIARY OF SAMUEL PEPYS, SEPTEMBER 2, 1666.)

Mayfair

For over 3 centuries, Mayfair has been an exclusive neighbor- hood of the aristocracy, who used to live in grand style inside elegant mansions run by armies of servants. Most of these urban palaces have been destroyed over the years, but enough survive to make a walk through Mayfair a fascinating glimpse into how London's rich lived—and often still live. This walk focuses on the southern part of Mayfair.

> *Many of the buildings in Mayfair, like this one in Berkeley Square, are built from distinctive Victorian red brick.*

START Green Park Tube Station.

1 ★ Berkeley Square. Immortalized in song and associated with nightingales (nowhere to be found today), this square was once the most aristocratic spot in London. Notables who've called the square home include Prime Ministers Winston Churchill (who lived at no. 48 as a boy) and George Canning (who resided briefly at no. 50; see **2**). Its modern east side, loaded with undistinguished office buildings, doesn't bear looking at. Keep your eyes on the lovely old houses on the west side. (Lansdowne House on the southwest corner was designed by famed Scottish architect Robert Adam (1728–92).) And check out the maple-like plane trees that surround the square; they were planted in 1789 and are among the oldest in the city.

2 ★★ 50 Berkeley Square. This Georgian-style building (now home to a respectable bookshop) was known as the "most haunted house in London" in the 19th century, when sightings of a bewigged man and sounds of an unearthly nature kept the house untenanted. Though strange happenings here have been reported in recent years by visitors, the worst of the haunting seems to have taken place in Victorian days, when an evil presence in what was known as the "haunted room" so terrified a visitor that he threw himself out the window and was impaled on the railings below.

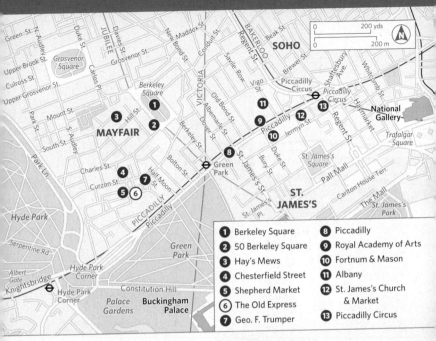

➊ Berkeley Square	➑ Piccadilly
➋ 50 Berkeley Square	➒ Royal Academy of Arts
➌ Hay's Mews	➓ Fortnum & Mason
➍ Chesterfield Street	⑪ Albany
➎ Shepherd Market	⑫ St. James's Church & Market
➏ The Old Express	⑬ Piccadilly Circus
➐ Geo. F. Trumper	

➌ ★ **Hay's Mews.** There were once mews—garages with carriages and horses on the lower floor, and living quarters for the groom and coachmen upstairs—like this one found throughout London. Today, most mews have been converted into expensive homes, but some lucky owners still use them for their cars. **To the left of the Coach & Horses Pub on Hays Mews.**

➍ ★★ **Chesterfield Street.** This is the least altered Georgian street in Mayfair and a great place to soak up the neighborhood's atmosphere. Its former inhabitants include historians Edward Gibbon and Edmund Burke. As you stroll along its sidewalks, you'll see plaques identifying the former homes of Regency dandy Beau Brummell and writer Somerset Maugham.

➎ ★★★ **Shepherd Market.** In the mid–18th century, developer Edward Shepherd bought the land on which the riotous May Fair (the neighborhood's namesake) took place each spring. Subsequent development put an end to that often-outlawed orgy. The result was much what you see now: charming yet humble buildings from the days when the market was the hub of the servant classes in Mayfair.

> *George F. Trumper has been the place to get a proper shave in Mayfair since 1875.*

> *Piccadilly Circus is the brash, neon counterpoint to genteel, dignified Mayfair.*

Where once you would find useful emporia selling meat and groceries, today you'll find upscale chocolate shops and jewelry stores.

⑥ ★★ The Old Express, a favorite with the locals, serves great traditional English food such as fish and chips, sausage and mash, and cottage pie. **30 Shepherd Market. ☎ 0207/499-1299. Lunch entrees £7–£18.**

⑦ ★★ Geo. F. Trumper. Where else can you get a shave with a straight razor and shaving brush these days? This English institution opened in 1875, and is so authentically old-fashioned that you half expect to be told not to touch anything. Even if you don't need a shave or toiletries, do have a look at this wonderful shop. **9 Curzon St. ☎ 0207/499-1850. www. trumpers.com.**

⑧ ★★ Piccadilly. The name Piccadilly is said to have come from the word "picadil," a stiff collar manufactured by a tailor of the early 17th century who bought a great parcel of land on which he built a grand home. Lest the upstart forget his beginnings, it was sneeringly referred to as "Piccadilly Hall." In the 18th and 19th centuries, many great mansions were built along the street facing Green Park. Head east on Piccadilly so you can admire the elaborate gates surrounding Green Park and the carved classical-style heads on the Parisian-inspired facade of the Ritz Hotel.

⑨ ★★★ Royal Academy of Arts. Burlington House, built in the 1660s, was a magnificent estate purchased by the government in 1854 to house England's oldest arts society. The Royal Academy mounts popular exhibitions in this small but lovely space. The permanent collection includes one of only four Michelangelo sculptures found outside of Italy. **Burlington House, Piccadilly. ☎ 0207/300-8000. www.royalacademy.org.uk.**

⑩ ★★ Fortnum & Mason. This famous partnership began in 1705, when shop owner Hugh Mason let a room to William Fortnum, a footman for Queen Anne at the Palace of St.

James. The enterprising Fortnum "recycled" candle ends from the palace (the Queen required fresh candles nightly), and sold them to Mason. From this humble beginning, Fortnum & Mason grew to rule Britannia (or at least, Piccadilly) with one of the earliest of globally recognized brand names. For an authentic (and pricey) afternoon tea, try the St. James Restaurant on the fourth floor. 181 Piccadilly. ☎ 0207/734-8040. www.fortnumandmason.com.

⑪ ★★ **Albany.** Built in the 1770s by architect William Chambers for Lord Melbourne, this grand Georgian building was turned into a residence for gentlemen in 1802. Since then, many poets (Lord Byron), authors (Graham Greene), and playwrights have all called this prime Piccadilly patch home. At Albany Court off Piccadilly.

⑫ ★★ **St. James's Church & Market.** This unprepossessing red brick church is one of Christopher Wren's simplest, said by Charles Dickens to be "not one of the master's happiest efforts." The poet William Blake was baptized here, as was William Pitt, the first Earl of Chatham, who became England's youngest prime minister at age 24. You are welcome to enter and sit in its quiet interior, or enjoy the free (donations desperately needed) lunchtime recitals. There's a market in the forecourt Tuesday through Saturday, featuring crafts, clothes, and collectibles. 197 Piccadilly. ☎ 0207/734-4511. www.st-james-piccadilly.org.

⑬ ★★ **Piccadilly Circus.** London's answer to New York's Times Square was the first place in the city to sport electrical signage, and it still dazzles the eye at night. The word "circus" refers to a circular juncture at an intersection of streets, and the plaza was built in 1819 to connect two of London's major shopping streets: Regent Street and Piccadilly. The statue of Eros on the central island of Piccadilly Circus is a favorite meeting place and hangout. Officially, it's called the Shaftesbury Memorial Fountain, designed in 1893 by Alfred Gilbert in memory of the seventh Earl of Shaftesbury, a venerable Victorian philanthropist. It was supposed to be a statue of the Angel of Christian Charity, but has always been known as Eros.

Licensed to Kill

Mayfair is not only a haunt of the rich and famous, but a surprising hotbed of international espionage as well. KGB agents often exchanged messages with their handlers in Mayfair's parks during the height of the Cold War. More recently, one of the modern era's most notorious assassinations occurred here. In 2006, former Russian spy Alexander Litvinenko, a noted critic of Russia's Putin administration, was poisoned using radioactive polonium-210 (allegedly dropped into a cup of tea at a local sushi restaurant) after meeting up with some ex-KGB agents in Mayfair. The crime caused a worldwide scandal and remains unpunished, as Russia has refused to extradite the main suspect—now a member of Russia's Duma—to England.

But perhaps the neighborhood's greatest claim to fame when it comes to matters of espionage is as the birthplace of author Ian Fleming (1908–64), creator of Britain's iconic secret agent, James Bond. Fleming was born inside his family home at 27 Green St., in the heart of Mayfair, and went on to serve in British Naval Intelligence in World War II, drawing on his wartime experiences and favored local haunts while penning his novels about the British Secret Service's famously suave operative (and Fleming's alter ego). The best place to soak up Mayfair's 007 vibe is the bar at **Dukes Hotel,** 35 St. James's Place (☎ 0207/491-4840), a favorite watering hole of Fleming's and where Sean Connery reportedly celebrated when he won the role of Bond in *Dr. No.* Do remember to dress up in your Bond best and to get that martini "shaken, not stirred" (the famous phrase originated right here in the hotel).

Chelsea

Since the 16th century, when Henry VIII and Thomas More built country manors on its bucolic Thames riverbanks, Chelsea has had a long tradition of eccentricity, aristocracy, and artisanship. Home to some of the most picturesque buildings in London, this posh district is one of my favorite spots for a stroll. Keep an eye peeled for blue plaques affixed to the local houses; they tell the story of the many leading figures of English culture who once called this neighborhood home.

> *Like many after him, Thomas More started as friend and confidant to Henry VIII, but ended on the chopping block.*

START Sloane Square Tube Station.

❶ ★★ Sloane Square. Physician Sir Hans Sloane (1660–1753), who helped found the British Museum and at one point owned most of Chelsea, is the namesake of this attractive square. In addition to his educational and medical achievements, Sloane discovered the chocolate recipe that became the basis of the Cadbury empire. **Intersection of Sloane St. & King's Rd.**

❷ ★★ Royal Court Theatre. This restored theater, originally built in 1888, is famous for showcasing playwrights such as George Bernard Shaw and Harold Pinter, as well as today's cutting-edgers. A few steps to the right of the Sloane Sq. Tube exit. ☎ 0207/565-5000. www.royalcourttheatre.com.

❸ ★★★ King's Road. Chelsea's main road was once an exclusive royal passage used by Charles II to go from Whitehall to Hampton Court. It was also a favorite route of highwaymen looking to "liberate" some royal goods. An echo of these King's Road robbers can be found in the extortionate prices of the chichi stores that now line this shopping-focused thoroughfare. The area is a favorite of the young and free-spending members of London's upper social strata. **Runs from Sloane Sq. southwest to Putney Bridge.**

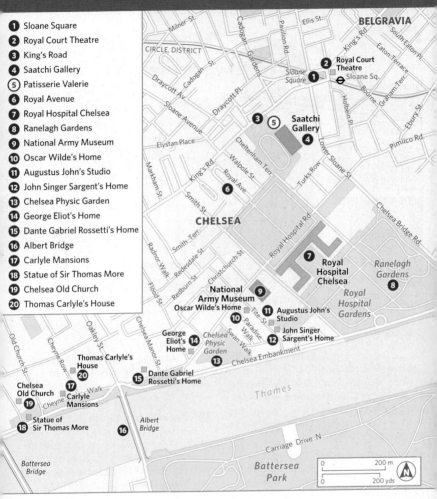

1. Sloane Square
2. Royal Court Theatre
3. King's Road
4. Saatchi Gallery
5. Patisserie Valerie
6. Royal Avenue
7. Royal Hospital Chelsea
8. Ranelagh Gardens
9. National Army Museum
10. Oscar Wilde's Home
11. Augustus John's Studio
12. John Singer Sargent's Home
13. Chelsea Physic Garden
14. George Eliot's Home
15. Dante Gabriel Rossetti's Home
16. Albert Bridge
17. Carlyle Mansions
18. Statue of Sir Thomas More
19. Chelsea Old Church
20. Thomas Carlyle's House

4 **Saatchi Gallery.** Ex-adman Charles Saatchi has amassed one of the world's largest independent collections of contemporary British and international art. His gallery shows pieces from the permanent collection, as well as changing international exhibits. There's a savvy cafe on the premises, as well as a bookstore. ⏱ 30 min. Duke of York's HQ, Sloane Sq. ☎ 0207/825-2363. www.saatchi-gallery.co.uk. Free admission. Daily 10am–6pm.

5 🍴 ★ **Patisserie Valerie** is one of several good dining spots in Duke of York Square, but you can't go wrong here. Hot dishes, salads, and sandwiches are reliably good, and the desserts are killer. 81 Duke of York Sq. (off King's Rd.). 0207/245-6161. Items £3–£7.

6 ★ **Royal Avenue.** This small, picturesque road was intended to extend all the way from nearby Chelsea Royal Hospital to Kensington Palace when it was laid out in 1682 by Sir Christopher Wren, but construction was cut short upon the death of its commissioner, Charles II. Btw. St. Leonard's Terrace & King's Rd.

7 ★★★ **Royal Hospital Chelsea.** This Christopher Wren masterpiece, commissioned by Charles II in 1692 as a retirement estate for injured and old soldiers, is home to 400-plus pensioners who still dress in traditional uniforms and offer informative tours of the

> *Until 2009, only men could become Chelsea Pensioners—that is, residents at the Royal Hospital veterans' retirement home.*

historic grounds and chapel. It's the site of the **Chelsea Flower Show,** held on the hospital grounds every May since 1912. Royal Hospital Rd. ☎ 0207/881-0161. Free admission. Guided tours by prior arrangement only. Mon–Sat 10am–noon, 2–4pm; Sun 2–4pm. Church services open to public, Sun 10:30am.

⑧ ★★ Ranelagh Gardens. These gardens, some of the prettiest in London, were a favorite of 18th-century socialites, who were occasionally entertained here by a young Mozart. At Chelsea Royal Hospital. Free admission. Mon–Sat 10am–noon, 2–4pm; Sun 2–4pm.

⑨ ★★ National Army Museum. Home of the Duke of Wellington's shaving mirror and Florence Nightingale's lamp, this museum follows the history of Britain's fighting forces from the Middle Ages to the present. Royal Hospital Rd. ☎ 0207/730-0717. www.national-army-museum.ac.uk. Free admission. Daily 10am–5:30pm.

⑩ ★★ Oscar Wilde's Home. The eccentricities of Oscar Wilde (1854–1900) and his wife Constance (they lived here from 1885 to 1895) were well known to neighbors, who would often see them on the street dressed in velvet (him) and a huge Gainsborough hat (her). Street boys would shout, "'Ere comes 'Amlet and Ophelia!" The house is not open to the public. 34 Tite St.

⑪ ★ Augustus John's Studio. A renowned Welsh painter (1878–1961), John was one of Chelsea's most illustrious artists. His insightful portraits and landscapes made him famous, while his bohemian lifestyle and love affairs earned him notoriety. 33 Tite St.

⑫ ★★ John Singer Sargent's Home. The renowned American portraitist of the high and mighty lived and worked at this address (the former abode of the equally famous artist James Abbott McNeill Whistler) from 1901 until his death in 1925. 31 Tite St.

⑬ ★★ Chelsea Physic Garden. This garden was established in 1673 by the Apothecaries' Company to cultivate medicinal plants and herbs. Cotton seeds from the garden were sent to America in 1732, and slavery became their eventual harvest. 66 Royal Hospital Rd. ☎ 0207/352-5646. www.chelseaphysicgarden.co.uk. Admission £8 adults, £5 kids 5–15. Mid-Mar to Nov Wed–Fri noon–5pm, Sun noon–6pm. See website for special events.

14 ★ George Eliot's Home. The famous Victorian novelist, born Mary Ann Evans in 1819, moved into this house with her new and much younger husband, John Cross, only a few months before her death in December 1880. 4 Cheyne Walk.

15 ★ Dante Gabriel Rossetti's Home. The eccentric pre-Raphaelite poet and painter (1828–82) moved here in 1862 after the death of his wife. He kept a menagerie of many exotic animals, including kangaroos, a white bull, peacocks, and a wombat that inspired his friend, Lewis Carroll, to create the Dormouse in *Alice in Wonderland.* 16 Cheyne Walk.

16 ★ Albert Bridge. Designed by R. M. Ordish (1824–86), this picturesque suspension bridge linking Battersea and Chelsea was completed in 1873. In 1973, the cast-iron structure had new supports installed so it could cope with the rigors of modern traffic.

17 ★ Carlyle Mansions. Henry James, the great American novelist *(Portrait of a Lady),* was sick in bed inside his riverview flat when he was honored for his work (and for taking British citizenship) with the Order of the British Empire. Only a few weeks later, the writer drew his last breath here in this beautiful and chic apartment house. **Cheyne Walk.**

18 ★★ Statue of Sir Thomas More. Despite his long friendship with Henry VIII, Lord Chancellor Thomas More (1478–1535) refused to accept Henry as head of the Church of England after the king's notorious break with the Roman Catholic Church. More paid for his religious convictions with his life—he was tried and subsequently beheaded for treason in 1535. In 1935, the Roman Catholic Church canonized him as Saint Thomas More, the patron saint of lawyers and politicians. **Old Church St.**

19 ★ Chelsea Old Church. Though the structure suffered serious damage during the Blitz, it has since been rebuilt and restored. Sir Thomas More worshiped here (he built the South Chapel in 1528), and it was also the setting of Henry VIII's secret marriage to third wife, Jane Seymour, in 1536. **64 Cheyne Walk.** ☎ 0207/795-1019. www.chelseaoldchurch.org.uk.

> In the 1700s, the Chelsea Physic Garden started a seed exchange program that survives to this day.

20 ★★★ Thomas Carlyle's House. The famous Scottish historian (1795–1881) and his wife, Jane, entertained friends Charles Dickens and Frédéric Chopin in this remarkably well-preserved Victorian home. It was here that the "Sage of Chelsea" finished his important *History of the French Revolution.* **24 Cheyne Row.** ☎ 0207/352-7087. www.nationaltrust.org.uk. Admission £5.10 adults, £2.60 kids 5–16. Apr-Oct Wed-Fri 2–5pm, Sat-Sun 11am-5pm.

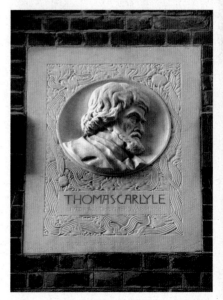

> Thomas Carlyle hosted many of the leading lights of the Victorian arts scene at his home in Chelsea.

Whitehall

Once the site of the vast Palace of Whitehall—London's chief royal residence from 1530 to 1698—this area is now a dignified neighborhood of government buildings whose grand architecture confers a certain beauty to the dull business of bureaucracy. If the United Kingdom has a political center, then Whitehall is it.

> Horse Guards Parade is a better spot to view the Changing of the Guard than Buckingham Palace.

START Westminster Tube Station. This tour is best in the morning; time your arrival at Horse Guards Parade to the 11am Changing of the Guard.

❶ ★★ **Boadicea Statue.** A tall and ferocious queen of the Iceni tribe of East Anglia, Boadicea (or Boudicca) waged battle against Britain's 1st-century Roman invaders until being defeated by the Roman army. The queen became a heroic figure of Victorian England, and this statue by Thomas Thornycroft (1815–85) was erected in 1902. Bridge St. & Victoria Embankment.

❷ ★★ **Churchill Museum & Cabinet War Rooms.** Winston Churchill directed World War II from this underground shelter as German bombs rained down on London. The basements of the Civil Service buildings along King Charles Street were converted in 1938 in order to house offices, a hospital, a cafeteria, sleeping quarters, and even a shooting range. After the war, the area was locked and left untouched until Churchill's quarters were turned into a museum in 1981. It's a fascinating time capsule that history buffs won't want to miss. ☻ 45 min. Clive Steps, King Charles St. ☎ 0207/930-6961. http://cwr.iwm.org.uk. Admission £16 adults, £12.80 seniors. Daily 9:30am–6pm.

❸ ★★ kids **Horse Guards Parade.** London's largest open space dates back to 1745 and is best known as the site for the annual Trooping the Colour ceremony. Every day at 11am (10am on Sun) there's a much mellower (and less crowded) Changing of the Guard than you'll find at Buckingham Palace (p. 61, ❸). Horseguards Rd.

❹ ★★ **The Mall.** This thoroughfare—running west from Buckingham Palace (see p. 72, ❶) to Trafalgar Square (p. 62, ❻)—was created in 1660 as an annex to St. James's Park for the gallants to play the popular game of paille-maille (a precursor to croquet), and was redesigned in 1903 as a processional route for royal occasions. Btw. Buckingham Palace & Admiralty Arch.

❺ ★ **Admiralty Arch.** Built in 1910, this quintuple-arched building looks west to the grand statue of Queen Victoria in front of Buckingham Palace. The central gates are for ceremonial use, opening only to let a royal procession pass.

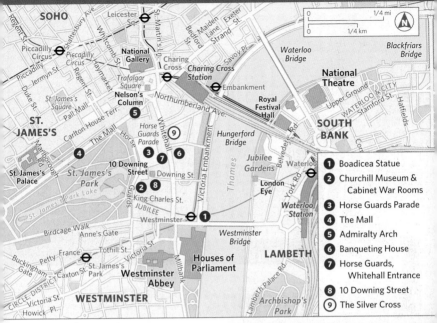

❶	Boadicea Statue
❷	Churchill Museum & Cabinet War Rooms
❸	Horse Guards Parade
❹	The Mall
❺	Admiralty Arch
❻	Banqueting House
❼	Horse Guards, Whitehall Entrance
❽	10 Downing Street
❾	The Silver Cross

❻ ★★★ **Banqueting House.** All that remains of Whitehall Palace is this hall, completed in 1622 by Inigo Jones (1573–1652). The city's first Renaissance-style construction is best known for its glorious Rubens-painted ceiling commissioned by Charles I (1600–49), who was beheaded just outside the hall. ⏱ 20 min. ☎ 0844/482-7777. www.hrp.org.uk. Admission £5 adults, £4 seniors. Mon–Sat 10am–5pm.

❼ **Horse Guards, Whitehall Entrance.** Just across from the Banqueting House is another entrance to Horse Guards Parade guarded by two mounted soldiers in ceremonial garb, who appear to do nothing but provide good photo ops for visitors.

❽ ★ **10 Downing Street.** The home address of Britain's prime minister since 1732 is set in a quiet cul-de-sac blocked off by iron gates for security reasons. There's not much to see now except a lot of security guards giving you the evil eye.

❾ 🍴 **The Silver Cross** is genuinely old, despite its faux "ye olde England" decor (it was granted a brothel license in 1674). It also offers good fish and chips, lots of seating, and its own ghost—a young girl in Tudor dress. 33 Whitehall. ☎ 0207/ 930-8350. Items £5–£9.

> Rubens's painted ceiling inside the Banqueting House is rich in allegory relating to the divine right of Stuart dynasty kings.

London Shopping Best Bets

Best Time to Shop
During the August and January citywide, month-long sales

Best Shot at Last Season's Designer Threads
Pandora 16–22 Cheval Place (p. 106)

Best Fun & Vintage Jewelry
Hirst Antiques 59 Pembridge Rd. (p. 108)

Best Important Jewelry
Ritz Fine Jewellery 150 Piccadilly (p. 108)

Best Sugar Rush
The Chocolate Society 36 Elizabeth St. (p. 107)

Best Children's Toy Store
Honey Jam 267 Portobello Rd. (p. 109)

Best Foot Forward
The Natural Shoe Store 21 Neal St. (p. 106)

Best Historic Bookstore
Hatchards 187 Piccadilly (p. 103)

Best Weekend Browsing
Portobello Road Market Portobello Rd. (p. 109)

Best Everything
Selfridges 400 Oxford St. (p. 107)

Best Museum Shop
Victoria and Albert Museum Cromwell Rd. (p. 109)

Best Place to Score Stuff from Other People's Attics
Grays Antique Market 58 Davies St. (p. 103)

Best Hot-Date Lingerie
Agent Provocateur 6 Broadwick St. (p. 108)

Best Art Supplies
Print Gallery Art Shop 22 Pembridge Rd. (p. 103)

Best Bed Linens
Cologne & Cotton 88 Marylebone High St. (p. 103)

Best Posh Stationery You'll Never Use
Smythson of Bond Street 40 New Bond St. (p. 106)

Best Affordable Street Fashion
Topshop 216 Oxford St. (p. 106)

Best Over-the-Top Food Hall
Harrods Food Halls 87–135 Brompton Rd. (p. 107)

Best Tartans and Woolens
Pringle of Scotland 141 Sloane St. (p. 109)

> *The stores and stalls of Portobello Road are known for their eclectic stock.*

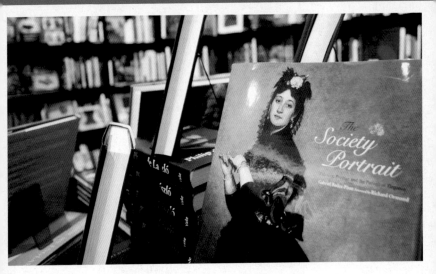

London Shopping A to Z

Antiques

★★★ Grays Antique Market MAYFAIR

Stalls here sell everything from Art Deco paperweights to antique jewelry to vintage Edwardian toys. 58 Davies St. ☎ 0207/629-7034. www.graysantiques.com. Some dealers take credit cards. Tube: Bond St., Marble Arch.

Arts & Crafts Supplies

★★★ kids The Print Gallery Art Shop

KENSINGTON   For creative kids and grownups, this is one of the most crammed-full arts and crafts shops in London and is sourced from all over Europe. Stock up on craft kits and materials for rainy afternoons. 22 Pembridge Rd. ☎ 0207/221-8885. AE, DC, MC, V. Tube: Notting Hill Gate.

Beauty Products

★★ Geo. F. Trumper MAYFAIR

An essential shop for the well-groomed man, the woman who wants a great gift for her guy, or anyone interested in high-quality toiletries and accessories. 9 Curzon St. ☎ 0207/499-1850. www.trumpers.com. AE, MC, V. Tube: Gloucester Rd.

> *Hatchards, on Piccadilly, stocks a broad range of signed editions.*

★★ Miller Harris MAYFAIR

Trained in Grasse, France, Lyn Harris has created a global brand of sexy and elegant scents of the finest quality. 21 Bruton St. ☎ 0207/629-7750. www.millerharris.com. AE, DC, MC, V. Tube: Green Park.

Bed Linens

★★ Cologne & Cotton MARYLEBONE

Stock up here on elegant bed clothes of pure linen and cotton sheets in soothing colors and simple designs. The pillowcases are gorgeous and come in all sizes. 88 Marylebone High St. ☎ 0207/486-0595. www.cologneandcotton. com. AE, MC, V. Tube: Baker St.

Books & Stationery

★★★ Daunt Books MARYLEBONE

One of the few independent bookshops left in London, with an excellent travel section and the latest U.K. fiction. 183 Marylebone High St. ☎ 0207/224-2295. www.dauntbooks.co.uk. MC, V. Tube: Baker St.

★★★ Hatchards PICCADILLY

This home for discerning bibliophiles has been in business since 1797. 187 Piccadilly. ☎ 0207/439-9921. www.hatchards.co.uk. AE, DC, MC, V. Tube: Green Park.

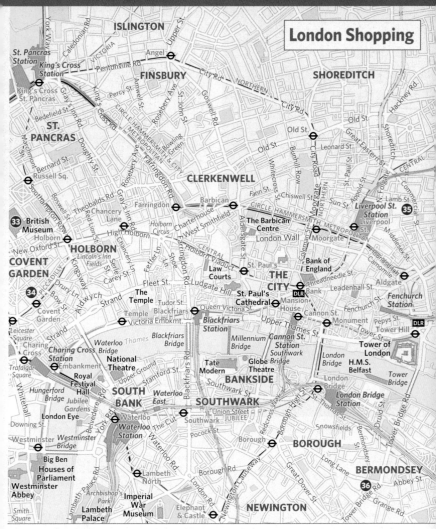

London Shopping

Agent Provocateur 28

Bermondsey (New Caledonian) Market 36

British Museum 33

Browns 20

Catwalk 17

The Chocolate Society 5

Cologne & Cotton 16

The Conran Shop 2

Daunt Books 15

Fortnum & Mason 31

The General Trading Company 3

Grays Antique Market 19

Geo. F. Trumper 29

Hamleys 27

Harrods 8

Harrods Food Halls 9

Hatchards 32

Hirst Antiques 13

Honey Jam 14

John Lewis 21

La Senza 24

Marks & Spencer 18

Miller Harris 25

The Natural Shoe Store 34

Pandora 6

Portobello Road Market 10

Pringle of Scotland 4

The Print Gallery Art Shop 11

Rigby & Peller 7

Ritz Fine Jewellery 30

Selfridges 22

Smythson of Bond Street 26

Spitalfields Market 35

Summerill & Bishop 12

Topshop 23

Victoria and Albert Museum 1

> *It's a common misconception that Harrods is London's best department store.*

> *Antique jewelry on display at Grays.*

★★★ Smythson of Bond Street MAYFAIR
This expensive and exclusive stationer caters to generations of posh Londoners, who would feel naked without a Smythson appointment diary. 40 New Bond St. ☎ 0207/629-8558. www.smythson.com. AE, DC, MC, V. Tube: Bond St.

Clothing & Shoes
★★ Browns MAYFAIR
The best place in town for up-to-the-minute fashions, including a discriminating collection of hip designers. 23–27 S. Moulton St. ☎ 0207/514-0000. www.brownsfashion.com. AE, MC, V. Tube: Bond St.

★★ Catwalk MARYLEBONE
There's always an excellent chance of getting some designer clothes and shoes at this "nearly new" shop, crammed with top labels that are priced to move. 52 Blandford St. ☎ 0207/935-1052. MC, V. Tube: Baker St.

★★ The Natural Shoe Store COVENT GARDEN
Come here for the best of Birkenstock, Ecco, Arche, and other comfortable hippie styles now totally in vogue. 21 Neal St. ☎ 0207/836-5254. www.thenaturalshoestore.com. AE, DC, MC, V. Tube: Covent Garden.

★★★ Pandora KNIGHTSBRIDGE
A big, well-organized shop featuring lots of designer names, shoes, and accessories left on consignment by frightfully fashionable Knightsbridge clotheshorses. 16–22 Cheval Place. ☎ 0207/589-5289. www.pandoradressagency.com. AE, MC, V. Tube: Knightsbridge.

★★★ Topshop MARYLEBONE
An absolute must-go for the younger generation, but even older women find something to love in this mecca of street fashion at decent prices. The flagship shop on Oxford Circus is a madhouse but has the most variety. 216 Oxford St. ☎ 0207/636-7700. www.topshop.com. AE, MC, V. Tube: Oxford Circus.

Department Stores
★ Harrods KNIGHTSBRIDGE
From its food halls to its home entertainment centers, Harrods is a London institution—as well as an overhyped and overpriced bore. 87–135 Brompton Rd. ☎ 0207/730-1234. www.harrods.com. AE, DC, MC, V. Tube: Knightsbridge.

> *There's more to Fortnum & Mason than just its fabulous Food Hall.*

★★★ John Lewis MARYLEBONE
This is *the* place to find homey necessities such as sewing notions, fabrics, and kitchenware. 278–306 Oxford St. ☎ 0207/629-7711. www.johnlewis.co.uk. AE, DC, MC, V. Tube: Oxford Circus.

★ Marks & Spencer MARYLEBONE
This beloved, reliable outlet is a nationwide fave for comfy cotton underwear for men and women, reasonably priced food halls, and sturdy but up-to-date clothing for all ages. 458 Oxford St. ☎ 0207/935-7954. www.marksandspencer.com. AE, DC, MC, V. Tube: Marble Arch.

★★★ Selfridges MARYLEBONE
Inside and out, this grand old department store is the best in town. 400 Oxford St. ☎ 0870/837-7377. www.selfridges.com. AE, DC, MC, V. Tube: Marble Arch.

Food & Chocolates
★★★ The Chocolate Society PIMLICO
With its amazing variations on a theme of cocoa beans, this shop offers creatively killer chocolate for grown-up tastes. 36 Elizabeth St. ☎ 0207/259-9222. www.chocolate.co.uk. MC, V. Tube: Victoria or Sloane Sq.

★★ Fortnum & Mason MAYFAIR
The city's ultimate grocer features goodies fit for the queen—or friends back home—plus gourmet picnic fare and specialty teas. 181

Piccadilly. ☎ 0207/734-8040. www.fortnumandmason.com. AE, DC, MC, V. Tube: Green Park.

★ Harrods Food Halls KNIGHTSBRIDGE
Harrods sells loads of edible gifts branded with its famous name. 87–135 Brompton Rd. ☎ 0207/730-1234. www.harrods.com. AE, DC, MC, V. Tube: Knightsbridge.

Home Decor
★★ The Conran Shop SOUTH KENSINGTON
Your best bets among the large and varied selection of high-priced merchandise here are the kitchenware and bath items. Michelin House, 81 Fulham Rd. ☎ 0207/589-7401. www.conranshop.co.uk. AE, MC, V. Tube: S. Kensington.

★★★ The General Trading Company CHELSEA
Started in the 1920s, this shop sells useful as well as merely charming household goods and clever knickknacks from all over the world. 2 Symons St. ☎ 0207/730-0411. www.generaltrading.co.uk. AE, MC, V. Tube: Sloane Sq.

★★★ Summerill & Bishop HOLLAND PARK
Shop here for a sumptuous collection of French housewares, from efficient, humble radiator dusters to the finest table settings and cookery. 100 Portland St. ☎ 0207/221-4566. www.summerillandbishop.com. AE, MC, V. Tube: Holland Park.

> *Spitalfields Market has been going since the 1600s.*

Jewelry

★★ Hirst Antiques NOTTING HILL
Something of a jewelry museum. You'll find extravagant vintage costume baubles from European catwalks of yore, and some interesting new gems as well. 59 Pembridge Rd. ☎ 0207/727-9364. www.hirstantiques.co.uk. MC, V. Tube: Notting Hill Gate.

★★★ Ritz Fine Jewellery ST. JAMES
Arguably the best hotel jewelry shop in the world, thanks to its collections of well-set semiprecious gems and serious rocks. Of course, when the hotel is the Ritz, it had better be the best. 150 Piccadilly. ☎ 0207/409-1312. www.ritzfinejewellery.com. AE, MC, V. Tube: Green Park.

Lingerie

★★ Agent Provocateur SOHO
Provocative, indeed! This store's sexy underclothes are works of art. 6 Broadwick St. ☎ 0207/439-0229. www.agentprovocateur.com. AE, DC, MC, V. Tube: Piccadilly Circus.

★★ La Senza FITZROVIA
Come here for classy, well-priced lingerie; some of the bras are almost too beautiful to hide beneath clothing. 162 Oxford St. ☎ 0207/580-3559. www.lasenza.com. AE, DC, MC, V. Tube: Oxford Circus.

★ Rigby & Peller KNIGHTSBRIDGE
The corsetiere to the queen specializes in classy underwear, bathing suits (ask for "swimming costumes"), and finely engineered brassieres. 2 Hans Rd. ☎ 0207/589-9293. www.rigbyandpeller.com. AE, DC, MC, V. Tube: Knightsbridge.

Markets

★ Bermondsey (New Caledonian) Market BERMONDSEY
If you're up at 4am on a Friday, join the crush of dealers fighting over the estate goods and antiques sold here. Stalls are pretty much all packed up and gone by 9am. Corner of Bermondsey St. & Long Lane. ☎ 0207/969-1500. Some dealers take credit cards. Tube: Bermondsey.

> *Paddington, the quintessential fictional English bear on sale here at Hamleys, was named after a London railway station.*

★★★ Portobello Road Market NOTTING HILL

Saturday is the best day to join the throngs at Portobello's famous antiques market, although you can do some weekday shopping as well. Bring cash. Portobello Rd. (from Notting Hill end to Ladbroke Grove). www.portobelloroad.co.uk. Some dealers take credit cards. Tube: Notting Hill.

★★ Spitalfields Market SHOREDITCH

Head to Spitalfields's huge market on Sunday for organic produce, ethnic clothes, knick-knacks, and handmade crafts. Commercial St. ☎ 0207/247-8556. www.visitspitalfields.com. Most dealers take cash only. Tube: Liverpool St.

Museum Shops

★ kids British Museum BLOOMSBURY

The B.M. sells inexpensive key chains, children's toys, fine reproductions, gorgeous scarves, and great T-shirts themed to its collections. Great Russell St. ☎ 0207/636-1555. www.britishmuseum.org. AE, DC, MC, V. Tube: Russell Sq.

★★★ kids Victoria and Albert Museum SOUTH KENSINGTON

This must-stop shop sells everything from postcards to jewelry. Cool finds include hand-painted tools and nostalgic toys. Cromwell Rd. ☎ 0207/942-2000. www.vam. ac.uk. AE, DC, MC, V. Tube: S. Kensington.

Toys

★ kids Hamleys PICCADILLY

A kid-thrilling selection of more than 35,000 toys and games spread over seven floors. 189–196 Regent St. ☎ 0870/333-2455. www.hamleys.com. AE, DC, MC, V. Tube: Piccadilly Circus.

★★★ kids Honey Jam NOTTING HILL

Created by two mums, this fabulously fun and on-target toy shop sells fine toys from Europe and crazy little gimcracks for party bags. There's also a small selection of adorable clothes. 267 Portobello Rd. ☎ 0207/243-0449. www.honeyjam.co.uk. MC, V. Tube: Ladbroke Grove.

Woolens

★★ Pringle of Scotland CHELSEA

Putting its rep for cornball golf cardigans behind it, this luxury retailer now sells an assortment of dressy casual wear and woolens that are very much up to the minute. 141 Sloane St. ☎ 0207/259-1660. www.pringlescotland.com. AE, DC, MC, V. Tube: Sloane Sq.

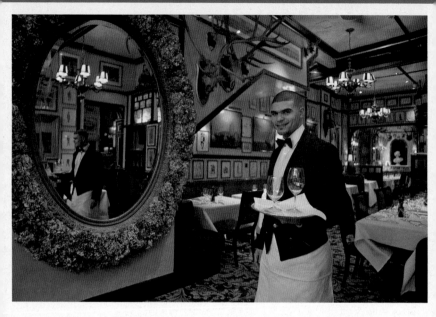

London Restaurant Best Bets

Best Vegetarian
Mildred's 45 Lexington St. (p. 115)

Best Self-service or Take-away
Whole Foods Market Dining Halls 63–97 Kensington High St. (p. 117)

Best Neighborhood Italian
The Ark 122 Palace Gardens Terrace (p. 111)

Best Afternoon Tea
Goring Hotel Beeston Place (p. 114)

Best Fish and Chips
Geale's 2 Farmer St. (p. 114)

Best Olde England Vibe
Rules 35 Maiden Lane (p. 117)

Best View
OXO Tower Brasserie OXO Tower Wharf, Bargehouse St. (p. 116)

Best Thai
Nahm Halkin Hotel, Halkin St. (p. 115)

Best French
Le Gavroche 43 Upper Brook St. (p. 115)

Best Indian
Tamarind 20 Queen St. (p. 117)

Most Romantic
Corrigan's Mayfair 28 Upper Grosvenor St. (p. 111)

Best American Diner Food
Automat American Brasserie 33 Dover St. (p. 111)

Best Lebanese
Fakhreldine 85 Piccadilly (p. 114)

Best Place for an Argentinian Steak
Gaucho Piccadilly 19 Swallow St. (p. 114)

Best Place for Hungarian Cherry Soup
The Gay Hussar 2 Greek St. (p. 114)

Best Spot for Spicy Moroccan *Tajines*
Momo 25 Heddon St. (p. 115)

Best Breakfast
The Providores and Tapa Room 109 Marylebone High St. (p. 116)

> *For traditional English cuisine such as pies and game, it's hard to beat Rules, near Covent Garden.*

London Restaurants A to Z

★★★ **The Ark** KENSINGTON *ITALIAN*
A modest building houses one of the best Italian restaurants in London. Everything in this longtime favorite is made on the premises, from the fresh pasta to the tiramisu; the latter is an experience in itself. 122 Palace Gardens Terrace. ☎ 0207/229-4024. www.ark-restaurant.com. Entrees £13–£35. AE, MC, V. Lunch Tues–Sat, dinner Mon–Sat. Tube: Notting Hill Gate.

★★★ **kids Automat American Brasserie** MAYFAIR *AMERICAN* This elegantly appointed re-creation of a classic diner offers good old Yankee meals for the well-heeled Londoner, and is a little piece of the U.S.A. for homesick visitors. 33 Dover St. ☎ 0207/499-3033. www.automat-london.com. Entrees £12–£30. AE, DC, MC, V. Breakfast, lunch & dinner daily. Tube: Green Park.

★★ **Bibendum** SOUTH KENSINGTON *MODERN EUROPEAN* Reliably good food with an emphasis on fresh fish and an airy location in the stylish Art Nouveau Michelin Building make this restaurant an old favorite. 81 Fulham Rd. ☎ 0207/581-5817. www.bibendum.co.uk. Entrees £20–£35. AE, DC, MC, V. Lunch & dinner daily. Tube: S. Kensington.

★★★ **Brasserie St. Quentin** KNIGHTSBRIDGE *CLASSIC FRENCH* This classy, friendly Paris-style brasserie shines with simple but delicious cuisine. 243 Brompton Rd. ☎ 0207/589-8005. Entrees £13–£25. AE, DC, MC, V. Lunch & dinner daily. Tube: Knightsbridge.

★ **Busaba Eathai** SOHO *THAI*
This cheerful branch of a small London chain serves clever and affordable Thai dishes at communal tables to a convivial mix of locals and tourists. 106-110 Wardour St. ☎ 020/7255 8686. www.busaba.com. Entrees £5–£12. AE, MC, V. Lunch & dinner daily. Tube: Tottenham Court Rd.

★★★ **Corrigan's Mayfair** MAYFAIR *MODERN BRITISH* Richard Corrigan, one of London's most inventive chefs, uses French and Irish techniques to create English culinary wonders in a beautiful contemporary dining room.

> *The terrace at the OXO Tower Brasserie, on the South Bank.*

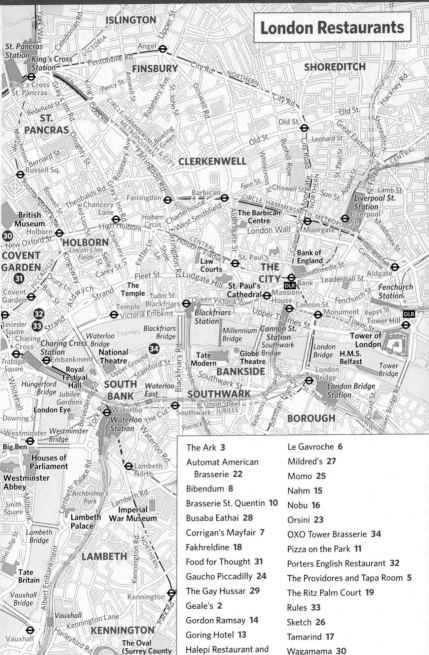

London Restaurants

The Ark **3**

Automat American Brasserie **22**

Bibendum **8**

Brasserie St. Quentin **10**

Busaba Eathai **28**

Corrigan's Mayfair **7**

Fakhreldine **18**

Food for Thought **31**

Gaucho Piccadilly **24**

The Gay Hussar **29**

Geale's **2**

Gordon Ramsay **14**

Goring Hotel **13**

Halepi Restaurant and Kebab House **4**

Itsu **9**

Langan's Brasserie **21**

La Poule au Pot **12**

Le Gavroche **6**

Mildred's **27**

Momo **25**

Nahm **15**

Nobu **16**

Orsini **23**

OXO Tower Brasserie **34**

Pizza on the Park **11**

Porters English Restaurant **32**

The Providores and Tapa Room **5**

The Ritz Palm Court **19**

Rules **33**

Sketch **26**

Tamarind **17**

Wagamama **30**

Whole Foods Market Dining Halls **1**

The Wolseley Café Restaurant **20**

> *Dishes are prepared with precision at Corrigan's Mayfair.*

28 Upper Grosvenor St. ☎ 0207/499-9943. www.corrigansmayfair.com. Lunch entrees £12–£23; set dinner menu £58–£70. AE, DC, MC, V. Lunch & dinner daily. Tube: Piccadilly Circus.

★★★ kids **Fakhreldine** MAYFAIR *LEBANESE* London's best Lebanese restaurant, thanks to its traditional menu, solid service, and fine views of Green Park. 85 Piccadilly. ☎ 0207/493-3424. www.fakhreldine.co.uk. Entrees £13–£23. AE, MC, V. Lunch & dinner daily; Sun brunch. Tube: Green Park.

★★ kids **Food for Thought** COVENT GARDEN *VEGETARIAN* Since 1974, this tiny spot has been an underground favorite. The food is fresh, vegetarian, imaginative, and very healthy. 31 Neal St. ☎ 0207/836-0239. Entrees £5–£8. No credit cards. Breakfast, lunch & dinner Mon–Sat; lunch Sun. Tube: Covent Garden.

★★★ kids **Gaucho Piccadilly** WEST END *ARGENTINIAN* The best Argentinian dining in Europe, with an emphasis on grilled beef. There's also a small selection of South American wines. 19 Swallow St. ☎ 0207/734-4040. www.gauchorestaurants.co.uk. Entrees £14–£39. AE, DC, MC, V. Lunch & dinner daily. Tube: Piccadilly Circus.

★★ **The Gay Hussar** SOHO *HUNGARIAN* Since 1953, this tiny dining room has served tasty goulashes, potato pancakes, blini, and other comfort foods to locals and tourists. Try the wild cherry soup. 2 Greek St. ☎ 0207/437-0973. www.gayhussar.co.uk. Entrees £10–£17. MC, V. Lunch & dinner daily. Tube: Tottenham Court Rd.

★★★ **Geale's** KENSINGTON *FISH* Yes, it's got caviar, fresh flowers, linen table cloths, and other posh touches, but go for the humble fish and chips, among the best in London. The sticky toffee pudding is another classic done well at this popular restaurant. 2 Farmer St. ☎ 0207/727-7528. Entrees £10–£16. AE, MC, V. Lunch & dinner daily. Tube: Notting Hill Gate.

★★★ **Gordon Ramsay** CHELSEA *FRENCH* Its three Michelin stars are no joke: This is serious haute cuisine at its best, and dedicated gastronomes find it worth every pound. 68 Royal Hospital Rd. ☎ 0207/352-4441. www.gordonramsay.com. Set lunch £45, dinner £90. AE, DC, MC, V. Lunch & dinner Mon–Fri. Tube: Sloane Sq.

★★★ **Goring Hotel** VICTORIA *BRITISH* Mutton broth, steak and kidney pie, grilled liver, fish galore, and crumble: You can't get more English than the menu at the Goring (p. 122), a hotel whose dining room and garden recall Edwardian elegance at its finest. Afternoon tea is done just right. Beeston Place. ☎ 0207/396-9000. www.goringhotel.co.uk. Breakfast £20, set lunch £35, dinner £48, afternoon tea £35. AE, DC, MC, V. Breakfast, lunch & dinner daily. Tube: Victoria.

★★★ kids **Halepi Restaurant and Kebab House** BAYSWATER *GREEK* Bring the whole family to share classic home-style Greek dishes and simple Mediterranean-grilled fish and meat. The baklava is the best around. 18 Leinster Terrace. ☎ 0207/262-1070. www.halepi.co.uk. Entrees £10–£23. MC, V. Lunch & dinner daily. Tube: Bayswater.

> Geale's serves some of the best traditional fish and chips in London.

★★ kids **Itsu** SOUTH KENSINGTON *ASIAN*
A fun place where diners choose from an excellent selection of small but pricey dishes that roll by on a conveyor belt. 118 Draycott Ave. ☎ 0207/590-2400. www.itsu.com. Entrees £5–£10. MC, V. Lunch & dinner daily. Tube: S. Kensington.

★★ kids **Langan's Brasserie** ST. JAMES *BRASSERIE* A big upscale brasserie with two noisy floors of dining, serving everything from spinach soufflé to fish and chips. Stratton St. ☎ 0207/491-8822. www.langansrestaurants. co.uk. Entrees £14–£22. AE, DC, MC, V. Lunch & dinner Mon–Fri; dinner Sat. Tube: Green Park.

★★ **La Poule au Pot** CHELSEA *FRENCH*
This chic retro French bistro, much-loved by Londoners, brings a slice of rural France to Chelsea. The cozy atmosphere, friendly staff, and classic dishes always make eating here a joyous occasion. Ask for a large carafe of the house wine to complete the festive experience. 231 Ebury St. ☎ 0207/730-7763. Entrees £15–£23. AE, MC, V. Lunch & dinner daily. Tube: Sloane Sq.

★★★ **Le Gavroche** MAYFAIR *FRENCH*
Internationally renowned chef Michel Roux, Jr., oversees the kitchen at this Michelin three-star extravaganza serving classic French haute cuisine in a clubby, elegant dining room. 43 Upper Brook St. ☎ 0207/408-0881. www. le-gavroche.co.uk. Prix-fixe lunch £48, tasting menu £95. AE, DC, MC, V. Lunch & dinner Mon–Fri; dinner Sat. Tube: Marble Arch.

★★★ **Mildred's** SOHO *VEGETARIAN*
The best vegetarian/vegan restaurant in London serves well-priced health food faves such as stir-fries, veggie burgers, salads, and juices. Don't skip the tasty desserts. 45 Lexington St. ☎ 0207/494-1634. www.mildreds.co.uk. Entrees £7–£12. MC, V. Lunch & dinner daily. Tube: Piccadilly Circus.

★★★ kids **Momo** MAYFAIR *MOROCCAN*
Decorated in Arabian Nights splendor, this West End success story is a wonderful place for a taste of exotic and fantastic *tajines* (Moroccan spiced stews). 25 Heddon St. ☎ 0207/434-4040. www.momoresto.com. Entrees £11–£20. AE, DC, MC, V. Lunch, dinner & afternoon tea daily. Tube: Oxford Circus.

★★★ **Nahm** BELGRAVIA *THAI*
This chicly appointed Thai restaurant in the Halkin Hotel has been going strong for years,

> *The Tapa Room, in Marylebone.*

thanks to impeccable service and wizardry in the kitchen. A favorite among gourmands. Halkin St. ☎ 0207/333-1234. www.halkin.como. bz/eat-and-drink/nahm. Entrees £12–£18. AE, DC, MC, V. Lunch & dinner daily. Tube: Hyde Park Corner.

★★★ **Nobu** MAYFAIR *JAPANESE/FUSION* Famous for its glamour, its staggering tabs, and its creative sushi. Metropolitan Hotel, 19 Old Park Lane. ☎ 0207/376-5650. www.nobu restaurants.com. Entrees £15–£28. AE, MC, V. Lunch & dinner Mon–Fri; dinner Sat–Sun. Tube: Hyde Park Corner.

★★★ kids **Orsini** SOUTH KENSINGTON *ITALIAN* Opposite the V&A, this cafe right out of Naples features great daily specials, perfectly prepared pastas, and great cappuccino. 8a Thurloe Place. ☎ 0207/581-5553. www.orsini ristorante.com. Entrees £7–£14. AE, MC, V. Breakfast, lunch & dinner daily. Tube: S. Kensington.

★★ **OXO Tower Brasserie** SOUTHBANK *GLOBAL FUSION* Get the best river views in London while dining on a somewhat pricey menu of dishes that combine Mediterranean, French, and Asian ingredients. The 1930s-style dining room is quite chic, but you should dine on the balcony in summer. OXO Tower Wharf, Bargehouse St. ☎ 0207/803-3888. www.

harveynichols.com/restaurants/oxo-tower-london. Entrees £17–£34. AE, DC, MC, V. Lunch & dinner daily. Tube: Blackfriars.

★★ kids **Pizza on the Park** KNIGHTSBRIDGE *PIZZA/ITALIAN* Live jazz makes this pizza joint more attractive than all its brethren in the city. 11–13 Knightsbridge. ☎ 0207/235-5273. www. pizzaexpress.co.uk. Entrees £8–£15. AE, DC, MC, V. Breakfast, lunch & dinner daily. Tube: Hyde Park Corner.

★ kids **Porters English Restaurant** COVENT GARDEN *TRADITIONAL BRITISH* The Earl of Bradford's eatery serves simple and traditional English food in the heart of Theaterland. The comfortable two-story restaurant is family-friendly, informal, and lively. Check the website for theater- or attractions-and-dinner deals. 17 Henrietta St. ☎ 0207/836-6466. www. porters.uk.com. Entrees £10–£16. AE, MC, V. Lunch & dinner daily. Tube: Charing Cross.

★★ kids **The Providores and Tapa Room** MARYLEBONE *GLOBAL* The Tapa Room features savory breakfasts; head upstairs to the restaurant for interesting twists on global favorites. 109 Marylebone High St. ☎ 0207/935-6175. www.theprovidores.co.uk. Entrees £8–£17. AE, MC, V. Tapa Room: Breakfast, lunch & dinner daily. Restaurant: Lunch & dinner daily. Tube: Bond St.

> *Indian meals, such as this* thali *of traditional dishes, are a popular choice among London diners.*

★★★ **The Ritz Palm Court** WEST END *ENGLISH TEA* Women, wear your best dress to this very deluxe (and pricey!) tea, served in a Versailles-like setting. Book way ahead. 150 Piccadilly. ☎ 0207/493-8181. www.theritzhotel. co.uk. £40 per person. AE, DC, MC, V. Afternoon tea daily. Tube: Green Park.

★★ **Rules** COVENT GARDEN *TRADITIONAL ENGLISH* The most traditional Olde English restaurant in London, Rules dates back to 1798, and is a must for Anglophiles and lovers of roast beef and Yorkshire pudding. 35 Maiden Lane. ☎ 0207/836-5314. www.rules.co.uk. Entrees £14–£30. AE, MC, V. Lunch & dinner daily. Tube: Charing Cross.

★★ **Sketch** MAYFAIR *FRENCH/MODERN BRITISH* Sketch is a must-see place thanks to its beyond-quirky artful decor and its variety of eating venues. The Lecture Room, with Michelin-starred chef Pierre Gagnaire, is where the serious gastronomy goes on; for less money, go for tea at the Parlour or lunch at the Glade. 9 Conduit St. ☎ 0870/777-4488. www. sketch.uk.com. Entrees £12–£100. AE, DC, MC, V. Lunch & dinner daily. Tube: Oxford Circus.

★★ **Tamarind** MAYFAIR *INDIAN* Diners ranging from business execs to couples appreciate this spot's elegant decor and the imaginative menu that goes beyond the usual curries. 20 Queen St. ☎ 0207/629-3561. www. tamarindrestaurant.com. Entrees £14–£22. AE, DC, MC, V. Lunch & dinner daily. Tube: Green Park.

★ kids **Wagamama** BLOOMSBURY *JAPANESE* You sit at large cafeteria-like tables where the noise level is considerable, but this popular Tokyo-style noodle chain is tops for reasonably priced Asian food. 4a Streatham St. ☎ 0207/323-9223. www.wagamama.com. Entrees £6–£15. AE, MC, V. Lunch & dinner daily. Tube: Tottenham Court Rd.

★★ kids **Whole Foods Market Dining Halls** KENSINGTON *GLOBAL* You'll love the wealth of options and reasonable prices at the top of the Whole Foods Market building. Excellent takeout and treats to bring back to your hotel room. 63–97 Kensington High St. ☎ 0207/368-4500. www.wholefoodsmarket.com. Entrees £4–£15. AE, MC, V. Breakfast, lunch & dinner daily. Tube: Kensington High St.

★★★ **The Wolseley Café Restaurant** ST. JAMES *ENGLISH* This hugely popular restaurant on Piccadilly has a high-ceilinged Art Deco dining room, dishes out celeb sightings, and has an extensive menu offering decent value. And it serves breakfast! 160 Piccadilly. ☎ 0207/499-6996. www.thewolseley.com. Entrees £10–£30. AE, DC, MC, V. Breakfast, lunch & dinner daily. Tube: Green Park.

London Hotel Best Bets

Best Historic Hotel
Hazlitt's 6 Frith St. (p. 122)

Best Self-catering Rooms
Astons Apartments 31 Rosary Gardens (p. 119)

Best Luxury Hotel
Claridge's Brook St. (p. 119)

Best Base for South Kensington Museum-hopping
The Gallery Hotel 8-10 Queensberry Place (p. 122)

Best Base for British Museum
The Montague on the Gardens 15 Montague St. (p. 124)

Best Hotel in Earls Court
Twenty Nevern Square 20 Nevern Sq. (p. 125)

Best Value
The Mowbray Court Hotel 28-32 Penywern Rd. (p. 124)

Best Boutique Hotel
The Haymarket Hotel 1 Suffolk Place (p. 122)

Best Family Hotel
Lord Jim Hotel 23-25 Penywern St. (p. 123)

Most Romantic Hotel
San Domenico House 29-31 Draycott Place (p. 125)

Best Bathrooms
The Dorchester 53 Park Lane (p. 122)

Best Business Hotel
The Chamberlain Hotel 130-135 Minories (p. 119)

Best for Theater Buffs
Thistle Piccadilly Coventry St. (p. 125)

Best Traditional English Hotel
Durrants Hotel George St. (p. 122)

Most Convenient to Covent Garden
Covent Garden Hotel 10 Monmouth St. (p. 122)

Best South Bank Hotel
Park Plaza County Hall Hotel 1 Addington St. (p. 124)

> *The Jonathan Swift room at Hazlitt's.*

London Hotels A to Z

★★ kids **Abbey Court** NOTTING HILL
This four-floor Victorian town house has considerable charms, if you can get along without an elevator. 20 Pembridge Gardens. ☎ 0207/221-7518. www.abbeycourthotel.co.uk. 22 units. Doubles £110–£140 w/breakfast. AE, DC, MC, V. Tube: Notting Hill Gate.

★ kids **Astons Apartments** SOUTH KENSINGTON
One of London's best and most budget-conscious self-catering options, Astons offers studio rooms with compact kitchens. 31 Rosary Gardens. ☎ 0207/7590-6000. www.astons-apartments.com. 54 units. Doubles £105–£111. AE, MC, V. Tube: Gloucester Rd.

★★ kids **The Chamberlain Hotel** THE CITY
Business travelers love the easy access to the City, and Tower of London lovers couldn't be happier with the location of this modern hotel in an old Georgian building. 130–135 Minories. ☎ 0207/373-3232. www.fullershotels.com. 64 units. Doubles £185–£260. AE, DC, MC, V. Tube: Tower Hill.

★★ kids **The Cherry Court Hotel** PIMLICO
They don't come much cheaper than this pleasant hotel, at least not with the same degree of cleanliness and comfort. 23 Hugh St. ☎ 0207/828-2840. www.cherrycourthotel.co.uk. 12 units. Doubles £60–£85 w/breakfast. Add 5% for credit cards. AE, MC, V. Tube: Victoria.

★★★ kids **Claridge's** MAYFAIR
This redoubtable London institution, close to Bond Street's shopping, has been the final word in elegance for decades. Rooms are spacious and service is impeccable. Brook St. ☎ 0207/629-8860. www.claridges.co.uk. 203 units. Doubles £299–£800. AE, DC, MC, V. Tube: Bond St.

★★★ **The Connaught** MAYFAIR
With all the stately grandeur of an old-style gentlemen's club, this grand old hotel is as gloriously dignified as the neighborhood around it but still offers all the necessary modern touches. Go for tea if you can't afford the steep rates. 16 Carlos Place. ☎ 0207/499-7070.

> The swank pool at the Haymarket Hotel.

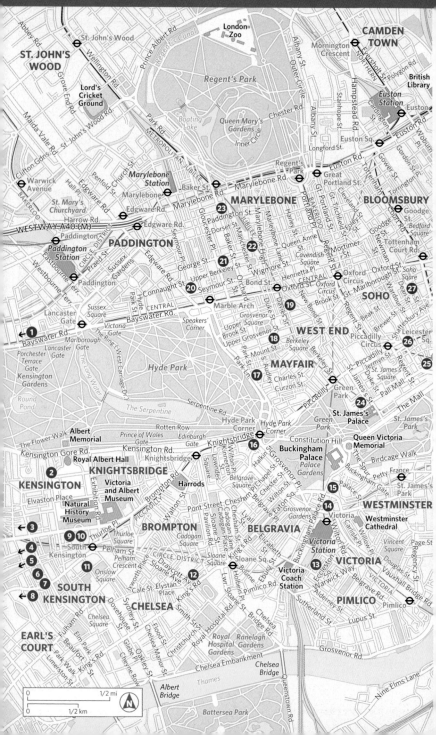

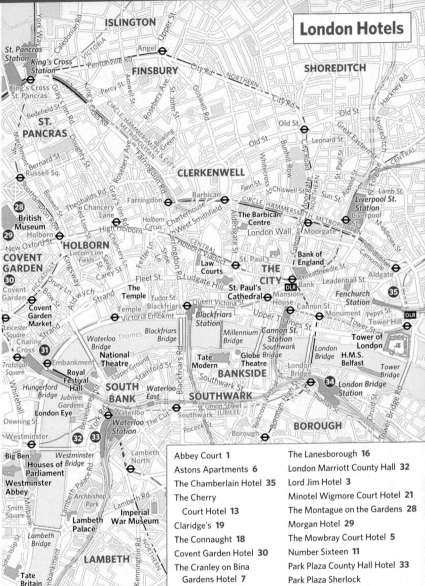

London Hotels

Abbey Court **1**

Astons Apartments **6**

The Chamberlain Hotel **35**

The Cherry
  Court Hotel **13**

Claridge's **19**

The Connaught **18**

Covent Garden Hotel **30**

The Cranley on Bina
  Gardens Hotel **7**

The Dorchester **17**

Durrants Hotel **22**

The Gainsborough **10**

The Gallery Hotel **9**

The Gore **2**

The Goring **14**

Haymarket Hotel **25**

Hazlitt's **27**

K + K Hotel George **8**

The Lanesborough **16**

London Marriott County Hall **32**

Lord Jim Hotel **3**

Minotel Wigmore Court Hotel **21**

The Montague on the Gardens **28**

Morgan Hotel **29**

The Mowbray Court Hotel **5**

Number Sixteen **11**

Park Plaza County Hall Hotel **33**

Park Plaza Sherlock
  Holmes Hotel **23**

The Rembrandt Hotel **34**

Royal Adelphi Hotel **31**

The Rubens at the Palace **15**

San Domenico House **12**

The Stafford Hotel **24**

Sumner Hotel **20**

Thistle Piccadilly **26**

Twenty Nevern Square **4**

www.the-connaught.co.uk. 123 units. Doubles £339–£725. AE, DC, MC, V. Tube: Bond St.

★★★ kids Covent Garden Hotel COVENT GARDEN

Big beds, relatively large rooms, and a deft English decor make this popular hotel one of the best in the neighborhood. The downside: The neighborhood gets a bit rowdy at night and is touristy during the day. 10 Monmouth St. ☎ 0207/806-1000. www.firmdale.com. 50 units. Doubles £240–£340. AE, DC, MC, V. Tube: Covent Garden.

★★★ kids The Cranley on Bina Gardens Hotel

SOUTH KENSINGTON Very romantic (the classic decor is laid over gorgeous period details), this hotel boasts a rooftop terrace, high ceilings, and Zen-brand toiletries—all in a quiet but convenient location. 10–12 Bina Gardens. ☎ 0207/373-0123. www.thecranley.com. 39 units. Doubles £170–£275. AE, MC, V. Tube: Gloucester Rd.

★★★ The Dorchester MAYFAIR

This opulent gem welcomes kings and commoners with equal panache. Elegant decor, first-rate amenities, and to-die-for bathrooms. 53 Park Lane. ☎ 800/727-9820 in the U.S.; 0207/629-8888. www.dorchesterhotel.com. 250 units. Doubles £330–£525. AE, DC, MC, V. Tube: Hyde Park Corner.

> The lobby of the Lanesborough.

★★ kids Durrants Hotel MARYLEBONE

This clubby hotel offers good value and a great location close to Oxford Street's shopping and the Wallace Collection. George St. ☎ 0207/935-8131. www.durrantshotel.co.uk. 92 units. Doubles £235–£275. AE, MC, V. Tube: Bond St.

★★ kids The Gainsborough SOUTH KENSINGTON

A stone's throw from the Natural History Museum, this traditional hotel offers well-appointed rooms at a decent price. 7–11 Queensberry Place. ☎ 0207/838-1700. www. eeh.co.uk/hotel_gainsborough. 49 units. Doubles £125–£160 w/breakfast. AE, DC, MC, V. Tube: S. Kensington.

★★ kids The Gallery Hotel SOUTH KENSINGTON

This Victorian hotel's pluses include small but comfortable rooms with attractive marble bathrooms, and a great breakfast. 8–10 Queensberry Place. ☎ 0207/970-1805. www. eeh.co.uk/hotel_gallery. 37 units. Doubles £165–£185 w/breakfast. AE, DC, MC, V. Tube: S. Kensington.

★★ kids The Gore SOUTH KENSINGTON

Every room inside this gorgeous re-creation of an early Victorian hotel is individually decorated with fine antiques. 189 Queen's Gate. ☎ 0207/584-6601. www.gorehotel.co.uk. 48 units. Doubles £260–£300. AE, DC, MC, V. Tube: Gloucester Rd.

★★★ kids The Goring PIMLICO

A stone's throw from Victoria Station, this hotel has the feel of a country house, with a big walled garden, charming public spaces, and excellent afternoon teas. Beeston Place. ☎ 0207/396-9000. www.goringhotel.co.uk. 71 units. Doubles £375–£525. AE, DC, MC, V. Tube: Victoria.

★★★ kids Haymarket Hotel WEST END

The Haymarket's location is perfect for West End fun, and the decor is worth dropping by to gawk at. It's not cheap, but neither is putting a fabulous pool in central London. 1 Suffolk Place. ☎ 0207/470-4004. www.firmdale.com. 50 units. Doubles £285–£390. AE, MC, V. Tube: Piccadilly Circus.

★★★ Hazlitt's SOHO

Favored by the literary set, the 18th-century-flavored Hazlitt's feels more like a boarding

> *A room at the Covent Garden Hotel.*

house than a hotel. There's no elevator. 6 Frith St. ☎ 0207/434-1771. www.hazlittshotel.com. 23 units. Doubles £220–£360. AE, DC, MC, V. Tube: Tottenham Court Rd.

★★ kids **The Bloomsbury Hotel** BLOOMSBURY Excellent access to the British Museum, Oxford Street shopping, and the West End. Congenial staff and pleasant decor make it a solid if unexciting home away from home. 16–22 Great Russell St. ☎ 0207/347-1000. www.doylecollection.com. 170 units. Doubles £120–£295. AE, DC, MC, V. Tube: Tottenham Court Rd.

★★★ kids **K + K Hotel George** KENSINGTON Part of a popular European chain, this is a good bet for elegance and convenience at an affordable rate (depending on season). Enjoy the garden when weather permits. 1–15 Templeton Place. ☎ 0207/598-8700. www.kkhotels.com. 154 units. Doubles £155–£275. AE, DC, MC, V. Tube: Earl's Court.

★★★ kids **The Lanesborough** KNIGHTSBRIDGE Housed in a former hospital building, this grand Regency-style hotel features state-of-the-art amenities—and your very own butler. Hyde Park Corner. ☎ 0207/259-5599. www. lanesborough.com. 95 units. Doubles £395–£650. AE, DC, MC, V. Tube: Hyde Park Corner.

★★ kids **London Marriott County Hall** SOUTH BANK You can't beat the views of Big Ben and Parliament from this historic hotel's rooms, though you'll pay dearly for the privilege. County Hall. ☎ 0207/928-5200. www.marriotthotels.com. 186 units. Doubles £300–£395. AE, DC, MC, V. Tube: Waterloo.

★★ kids **Lord Jim Hotel** EARLS COURT Known for its attractive package deals, this budget hotel offers plainly but pleasantly decorated rooms; families will fit easily in the bigger rooms. 23–25 Penywern St. ☎ 0207/370-6071. www.thelordsgroup.co.uk. 50 units. Doubles £85–£100 w/breakfast. AE, DC, MC, V. Tube: Earl's Court.

★ kids **Minotel Wigmore Court Hotel** MARYLEBONE Clean, friendly, and well located, the Wigmore Court is a favorite of the budget-conscious and is well suited to families and groups. 23 Gloucester Place. ☎ 0207/935-0928. www.wigmore-hotel.co.uk. 16 units. Doubles £70–£89 w/breakfast. MC, V. Tube: Marble Arch.

> *Refreshments in the Terrace Bar at the Montague.*

★★ kids **The Montague on the Gardens**

BLOOMSBURY In the shadow of the British Museum, this deluxe, country-style hotel has a lovely garden and a ton of amenities. 15 Montague St. ☎ 0207/637-1001. www.montague hotel.com. 100 units. Doubles £290–£325. AE, DC, MC, V. Tube: Russell Sq.

★★ kids **Morgan Hotel** BLOOMSBURY

The family-run Morgan features well-kept Georgian-style rooms. It's an old favorite of Anglophiles who can't get enough of the nearby British Museum. 24 Bloomsbury St. ☎ 0207/636-3735. www.morganhotel.co.uk. 21 units. Doubles £115–£170 w/breakfast. MC, V. Tube: Tottenham Court Rd.

★★ kids **The Mowbray Court Hotel** EARLS COURT

This spotless budget hotel, run by a friendly Irish family, features basic rooms, some without private bathrooms. 28–32 Penywern Rd. ☎ 0207/370-2316. www.mowbraycourthotel. co.uk. 90 units. Doubles £76–£86 w/breakfast. AE, DC, MC, V. Tube: Earl's Court.

★★ kids **Number Sixteen** SOUTH KENSINGTON

This modernized Victorian town-house hotel is popular with Americans, quiet, and in a fun neighborhood. 16 Sumner Place. ☎ 0207/589-5232. www.numbersixteenhotel.co.uk. 42 units. Doubles £165–£280. AE, DC, MC, V. Tube: S. Kensington.

★★ kids **Park Plaza County Hall Hotel** WATERLOO

Can't beat this hotel on the Thames for price, views, and amenities. The rooms are good-sized, too. 1 Addington St. ☎ 0207/034-4820. www.parkplazacountyhall.com. 398 units. Doubles £155–£200. AE, DC, MC, V. Tube: Baker St.

★★ kids **Park Plaza Sherlock Holmes Hotel**

MARYLEBONE This modern boutique hotel with large rooms is close to Regent's Park and Oxford Street but hardly Sherlockian in decor. 108 Baker St. ☎ 0207/486-6161. www.park plazasherlockholmes.com. 119 units. Doubles £160–£190. AE, DC, MC, V. Tube: Baker St.

★★ kids **The Rembrandt Hotel** SOUTH KENSINGTON

A solid tourist hotel across from the V&A; it's popular with groups because of its package deals and many rooms. 11 Thurloe Place. ☎ 0207/589-8100. www.sarova.com/ rembrandt. 195 units. Doubles £255–£275 w/ breakfast. AE, DC, MC, V. Tube: S. Kensington.

> *A junior suite at the boutique San Domenico House.*

★ kids **Royal Adelphi Hotel** WEST END
It's a bit like a college dorm, with small, spartan rooms and no elevator, but what it lacks in charm it makes up for in value. 21 Villiers St. ☎ 0207/930-8764. 47 units. Doubles £80–£100 w/breakfast. AE, DC, MC, V. Tube: Embankment.

★★★ kids **The Rubens at the Palace** VICTORIA
Traditional English hospitality combined with the latest in creature comforts. The Royal Rooms have the most atmosphere. 39 Buckingham Palace Rd. ☎ 877/955-1515 in the U.S.; 0207/834-6600. www.rubenshotel.com. 161 units. Doubles £300–£375. AE, DC, MC, V. Tube: Victoria.

★★★ **San Domenico House** CHELSEA
An exquisite hotel delivering divine Italian luxury at its most romantic and English-accented. 29–31 Draycott Place. ☎ 0207/581-5757. www.sandomenicohouse.com. 16 units. Doubles £255–£330. AE, DC, MC, V. Tube: Sloane Sq.

★★★ kids **The Stafford Hotel** MAYFAIR
This gorgeous 18th-century hotel, set in a grand old neighborhood, combines English country style with modern amenities. St. James's Place. ☎ 0207/493-0111. www.thestaffordhotel.co.uk. 81 units. Doubles £360–£490. AE, DC, MC, V. Tube: Green Park.

★★★ **Sumner Hotel** MARBLE ARCH
One of London's best small, reasonably priced hotels, the Sumner is well-loved by clued-in visitors. 54 Upper Berkeley St. ☎ 0207/723-2244. www.thesumner.com. 20 units. Doubles £160–£195 w/breakfast. AE, DC, MC, V. Tube: S. Kensington.

★★ kids **Thistle Piccadilly** PICCADILLY
There's no better location for those who want to hit the theaters, clubs, and restaurants of the West End. Check the website for packages and promotions. Coventry St. ☎ 0870/333-9118. www.thistle.com. 92 units. Doubles £295–£397 w/breakfast. AE, DC, MC, V. Tube: Piccadilly Circus.

★★ **Twenty Nevern Square** EARLS COURT
An elegant European-Asian decor, a full range of amenities, and a garden make this one of the more sumptuous B&Bs in London. 20 Nevern Sq. ☎ 0207/565-9555. www.twentynevernsquare.co.uk. 20 units. Doubles £100–£200 w/breakfast. AE, DC, MC, V. Tube: Earl's Court.

London Nightlife & Entertainment Best Bets

Best for Blues
Ain't Nothin But 20 Kingly St. (p. 127)

Most Diverse Entertainment
Madame JoJo's 8–10 Brewer St. (p. 131)

Most Wacky Decor
Beach Blanket Babylon 45 Ledbury Rd. (p. 127)

Best Club to Wear Your Bathing Suit To
Club Aquarium 256 Old St. (p. 131)

Most Unpretentious
Plastic People 147–149 Curtain Rd. (p. 132)

Best Views
Vertigo 42 Tower 42, 25 Old Broad St. (p. 130)

Best for a Laugh
Comedy Cafe 66–68 Rivington St. (p. 130)

Best for Opera
Royal Opera House Covent Garden (p. 131)

Best Free Live-Music Performances
St. James's Piccadilly 197 Piccadilly (p. 130)

Best Dance Club
Fabric 77a Charterhouse St. (p. 131)

Best Jazz Club
Ronnie Scott's, 47 Frith St. (p. 132)

Most Elegant Pub/Bar
The Audley 41 Mount St. (p. 133)

Best Gay Bar
The Edge 11 Soho Sq. (p. 130)

Best Hotel Bar
The Library Lanesborough Hotel, 1 Lanesborough Place (p. 130)

Best Baroque Concerts
St. Martin-in-the-Fields Evening Candlelight Concerts Trafalgar Sq. (p. 130)

Best Classical Music Festival
The Proms, Royal Albert Hall Kensington Gore (p. 130)

Best Outdoor Performances
Open Air Theatre Inner Circle, Regent's Park (p. 133)

Best Spot for a Belgian Beer
Abbaye 102 Old Brompton Rd. (p. 127)

> *Covent Garden's Royal Opera House is one of the world's most prestigious performing arts venues.*

London Nightlife & Entertainment A to Z

Bars

★★ Abbaye SOUTH KENSINGTON
A mellow atmosphere and some truly out-standing beers make this European brasserie and bar a great hangout. Wash down some mussels with the great Belgian suds. 102 Old Brompton Rd. ☎ 0207/373-2403. Tube: Gloucester Rd.

★★ Ain't Nothin But SOHO
A blues joint plucked straight from the bayou; it may not be Bourbon Street, but there's good jambalaya, funky tables, and live blues every night of the week. Be prepared to wait in line on weekends. 20 Kingly St. ☎ 0207/287-0514. www.aintnothinbut.co.uk. Tube: Piccadilly Circus.

★★★ BBar VICTORIA
This super-trendy bar with African-inspired decor serves more than 60 cocktails. There's a vast wine cellar and a fusion menu of appe-tizing noshes. 43 Buckingham Palace Rd. ☎ 0207/958-7000. www.bbarlondon.com. Tube: Victoria.

★ Beach Blanket Babylon KENSINGTON
Truly wacko decor (a fireplace shaped like a tiger's mouth, a gangplank, and other kitschy excesses) will bring a smile to your lips that the often lousy service won't entirely wipe off. 45 Ledbury Rd. ☎ 0207/229-2907. www.beach blanket.co.uk. Tube: Notting Hill Gate.

★★ Blue Bar KNIGHTSBRIDGE
In the lovely Berkeley Hotel, this tiny (50-person) and, yes, blue (Luytens Blue, to be exact) bar serves 50 varieties of whisky and tapas-type snacks to a very upscale crowd. Wilton Place. ☎ 0207/235-6000. www.the-berkeley.co.uk. Tube: Hyde Park Corner.

★★★ Dorchester Bar MAYFAIR
The mega-expensive hotel's bar is awash in lacquered mahogany and velvet, red glass stalagmites, and mirrored tables. The vast selection of spirits and cocktails boasts more vermouth than any other bar in the U.K. 53 Park Lane. ☎ 0207/629-8888. www.the dorchester.com. Tube: Hyde Park Corner.

> *Heaven hosts London's biggest gay and gay-friendly club nights.*

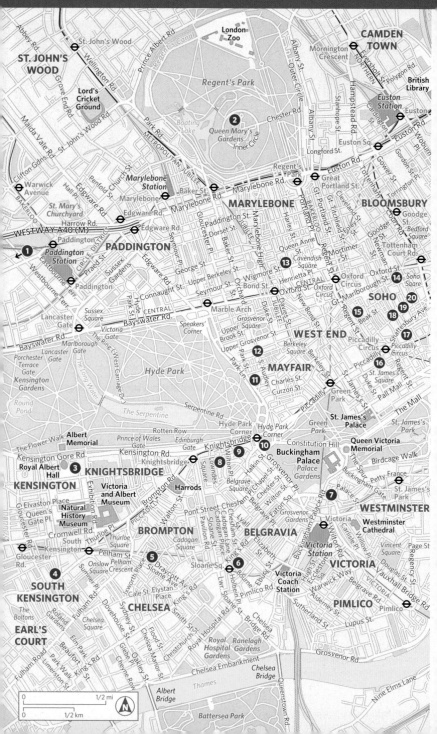

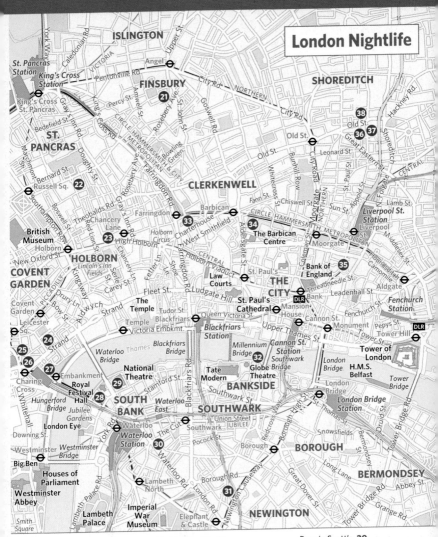

London Nightlife

Abbaye **4**
Admiral Codrington **5**
Admiral Duncan **19**
Ain't Nothin But **15**
The Audley **12**
Bar Rumba **17**
Barbican Centre **34**
BBar **7**
Beach Blanket Babylon **1**
Blue Bar **9**
Cittie of York **23**
Club Aquarium **38**
Comedy Cafe **37**

Dorchester Bar **11**
The Edge **14**
Fabric **33**
Heaven **27**
The Lamb **22**
The Library **10**
London Coliseum **25**
Madame JoJo's **18**
Ministry of Sound **31**
Nags Head **8**
Old Vic Theatre Southbank **30**
Open Air Theatre **2**
Plastic People **36**

Ronnie Scott's **20**
Royal Albert Hall **3**
Royal Court Theatre **6**
Royal Festival Hall **28**
Royal National Theatre **29**
Royal Opera House **24**
Sadler's Wells **21**
St. James's Piccadilly **16**
St. Martin-in-the-Fields **26**
Shakespeare's
   Globe Theatre **32**
Vertigo 42 **35**
Wigmore Hall **13**

★★★ The Edge SOHO

This four-floor gay and lesbian club caters to a diverse crowd with a cafe, piano bar, lounge, dance floor, and plenty of colorful characters. 11 Soho Sq. ☎ 0207/439-1313. Tube: Tottenham Court Rd.

★★★ G-A-Y Bar SOHO

In the center of Old Compton Street's "Gaysville," three floors filled with video screens and pop music cater to people of every sexual persuasion looking for fun. 30 Old Compton St. ☎ 0207/494-2756. www.g-a-y.co.uk. Tube: Leicester Sq.

★★★ The Library KNIGHTSBRIDGE

Lots of business execs on expense accounts sip cocktails and cognac at this sophisticated and atmospheric bar in the Lanesborough (p. 123). A roaring fire and tinkling piano keys complete the picture. 1 Lanesborough Place. ☎ 0207/259-5599. Tube: Hyde Park Corner.

★★★ Vertigo 42 THE CITY

On the 42nd floor of a skyscraper, this bar is the highest in England and features splendid (and rare for London) views. It's the perfect place to sip a cocktail at sunset. Tower 42, 25 Old Broad St. ☎ 0207/877-7842. www.vertigo 42.co.uk. Tube: Liverpool St.

Classical Music

★★★ Barbican Centre THE CITY

A gargantuan modern venue whose acoustics make it the best place for hearing music in the U.K. It's home to the first-class London Symphony Orchestra, which plays some 90 concerts here every year. Silk St. ☎ 0207/638-8891. www.barbican.org.uk. Tickets £10–£80. Tube: Barbican.

★★ London Coliseum WEST END

Converted into an opera house in 1968, London's largest theater is home to the English National Opera. Productions range from Gilbert and Sullivan to more challenging modern fare; most are staged in English. St. Martin's Lane. ☎ 0207/632-8300. www.eno.org. Tickets £10–£75. Tube: Charing Cross.

★★★ Royal Albert Hall KENSINGTON

This splendid Victorian pleasure palace is best known as the home of the city's annual Henry Wood Promenade Concerts (the Proms) in summer, when you'll hear orchestral classics and chamber music. Kensington Gore. ☎ 0207/589-8212. www.royalalberthall.com. Tickets £10–£80. Tube: Kensington High St.

★★★ Royal Festival Hall SOUTH BANK

More than 150,000 hours of music have been performed at this acoustically exceptional complex since it opened in 1951. The hall's many free and low-priced concerts make it a great bet for those on a budget. Belvedere Rd. ☎ 0870/401-8181. www.southbankcentre.co.uk. Tickets £10–£75. Tube: Waterloo.

★★★ Royal Opera House COVENT GARDEN

The brilliantly restored 19th-century ROH is one of the top opera stages in the world, featuring internationally known singers and top-caliber productions. Covent Garden. ☎ 0207/304-4000. www.roh.org.uk. Tickets £10–£200. Tube: Covent Garden.

★★ St. James's Piccadilly ST. JAMES

This gorgeous, old, Wren-designed church hosts 50-minute lunchtime classical recitals (Mon, Wed & Fri 1pm; £3 donation suggested) and evening concerts as well. 197 Piccadilly. ☎ 0207/381-0441. www.st-james-piccadilly.org. Tickets free–£19. Tube: Piccadilly Circus.

★★★ St. Martin-in-the-Fields WEST END

Follow (allegedly) in Mozart's footsteps, and attend a concert at this atmospheric, newly refurbished church. Admission to its popular lunchtime concerts (Mon, Tues & Fri 1pm) is by suggested donation (£3.50). The candlelit evening musicales are one of London's best deals. Trafalgar Sq. ☎ 0207/839-8362. www.stmartin-in-the-fields.org. Tickets £6–£30. Tube: Charing Cross.

★★★ Wigmore Hall MARYLEBONE

Bechstein Pianos built this grand Renaissance-style recital hall—one of the world's finest—in 1901. The greatest names in classical music have taken advantage of this venue's fabulous acoustics. 36 Wigmore St. ☎ 0207/935-2141. www.wigmore-hall.org.uk. Tickets £8–£30. Tube: Bond St.

Comedy

★★★ Comedy Cafe EAST END

Crowded tables and exposed brick walls provide an appropriate setting for raw comedy and plenty of heckling. There's a happy hour from 6 to 7pm. Closed Sunday to Tuesday.

> *There's always something going on, across a whole range of the arts, at the Royal Festival Hall.*

66–68 Rivington St. ☎ 0207/739-5706. www. comedycafe.co.uk. Tickets £8–£15. Tube: Old St.

Dance

★★★ Royal Opera House COVENT GARDEN

The brilliantly restored 19th-century ROH houses the even more brilliant Royal Ballet, a company on par with the world's best. You can catch any number of classics, such as *Giselle* or *Sleeping Beauty,* but you'll pay for the privilege. Covent Garden. ☎ 0207/304-4000. www. royaloperahouse.org. Tickets £10–£165. Tube: Covent Garden.

★★★ Sadler's Wells ISLINGTON

The best dance troupes in the world—from cutting edge to classical—are delighted to perform at this chic theater, where they are assured of modern facilities and an appreciative audience. Rosebery Ave. ☎ 0207/863-8198. www.sadlerswells.com. Tickets £10–£38. Tube: Angel.

Dance Clubs & Live Music/Entertainment

★★★ Bar Rumba SOHO

An intimate basement venue with mood lighting and leather couches. The versatile club has drum and bass, R&B, hip-hop, salsa, and comedy nights. 36 Shaftesbury Ave. ☎ 0207/287-6933. www.barrumba.co.uk. £3–£12 cover after 9pm. Tube: Leicester Sq.

★★★ Club Aquarium EAST END

This crazy but popular nightclub offers you the chance to doff your clothes and jump in a pool with strangers. Germaphobes may want to stick to the fully clothed drinking and dancing. 256 Old St. ☎ 0207/251-6136. www.club aquarium.co.uk. £8–£15 cover. Tube: Old St.

★★★ Fabric EAST END

A favorite with London's committed weekend partygoers and hot-off-the-press vinyl lovers. Dance till 5am to the drum and bass, electro, and techno beats on the "bodysonic" dance floor, where you can feel the music's vibrations through your feet. 77a Charterhouse St. ☎ 0207/336-8898. www.fabriclondon.com. Tube: Farringdon.

★★★ Heaven COVENT GARDEN

Proving no one does clubs better than gay revelers, this London landmark has 25 years of partying under its belt, and it's growing old disgracefully. Under the Arches, Villiers St. ☎ 0207/930-2020. www.heaven-london.com. £6–£15 cover. Tube: Embankment.

★★★ Madame JoJo's SOHO

This unpretentiously cool spot has a well-earned reputation as one of Soho's most fun clubs, with decent drink prices and a good dance floor. The nightly offerings range from live music to comedy to Saturday-night drag queens. 8–10 Brewer St. ☎ 0207/734-3040. www.madamejojos.com. £5–£15 cover. Tube: Piccadilly Circus.

> Soho's number one jazz venue, Ronnie Scott's.

★★★ Ministry of Sound ELEPHANT & CASTLE

Housed in a converted warehouse with four bars, MOS has three huge dance floors (including the Box, which is painted black from floor to ceiling), flatscreen TVs, and a hefty sound system playing techno, hip-hop, funk, house, and garage. E-mail ahead to get on the guest list and skip the lengthy queue outside. 103 Gaunt St. ☎ 0207/378-6562. www.ministryofsound.com. £15–£20 cover. Tube: Elephant & Castle.

★★★ Plastic People EAST END

For true music aficionados, the decidedly unpretentious Plastic People offers live jazz, Latin, techno, soul, hip-hop, house, and funk. Ironically named, it attracts a casual, jovial crowd. 147–149 Curtain Rd. ☎ 0207/739-6471. www.plastic people.co.uk. £8–£15 cover. Tube: Old St.

★★★ Ronnie Scott's SOHO

Open since 1959, this granddaddy of London's jazz clubs fully deserves its legendary reputation. The best jazz musicians in the world play this classy but relaxed venue every night. 47 Frith St. ☎ 0207/439-0747. www.ronniescotts. co.uk. £20–£25 cover. Tube: Leicester Sq.

Pubs

★★ Admiral Codrington CHELSEA

This pub has modern British cuisine, a friendly staff, a well-heeled crowd from neighboring Chelsea and South Kensington, and a nice atmosphere, with a retractable glass roof. Outdoor tables handle overflow on warm evenings. 17 Mossop St. ☎ 0207/581-0005. Tube: S. Kensington.

Buying Theater Tickets

You can buy advance tickets for most of London's entertainment venues through the theaters' websites or through **Ticket-master** (www.ticketmaster.co.uk). Expect to pay a booking fee as high as £3.50 per ticket. Some concierges can set aside theater tickets for hotel guests, so ask when booking your room.

For same-day, half-price tickets, your best bet is the **TKTS booth** (www.officiallondon theatre.co.uk) in the Clock Tower on the south side of Leicester Square, which opens at noon. Two boards list the day's available West End shows. The blockbusters will probably be MIA, but decent seats at all the longer-running productions should be available. Many theaters sell their own half-price standby tickets at the box office about an hour before curtain time.

Last Minute (www.lastminute.com) has scads of good deals on theater-dinner packages, but read the fine print carefully—some may have restrictions and booking fees that add up to more than £10.

> *The three stages at the National Theatre host the city's best drama.*

★★ **Admiral Duncan** SOHO
This popular gay bar weathered a homophobe's bomb in 1999 and today offers bargain shots, cocktails, and a selection of wines. Gay or straight, it's a friendly place to drink. 54 Old Compton St. ☎ 0207/437-5300. Tube: Leicester Sq.

★★★ **The Audley** MAYFAIR
One of London's more beautiful old-school pubs, evocative of a Victorian-era gentlemen's club (it was built in the 1880s). Slip into a booth beneath the original chandeliers and sample the traditional English grub. 41 Mount St. ☎ 0207/499-1843. Tube: Green Park.

★★★ **Cittie of York** BLOOMSBURY
There's been a pub on this site since 1430, and though the current building dates back "only" to the 1890s, there's still an old-world (faux) vibe and (real) ale. Closed Sunday. 22 High Holborn. ☎ 0207/242-7670. Tube: Chancery Lane.

★★ **The Lamb** BLOOMSBURY
You'll find one of the city's few remaining "snob screens"—used to protect drinkers from prying eyes—at this Victorian pub. Those who've enjoyed the anonymity here include the Bloomsbury Group and Charles Dickens. 98 Lamb's Conduit St. ☎ 0207/405-0713. Tube: Russell Sq.

★★★ **Nags Head** BELGRAVIA
This rarity, an independently owned pub, was built in the early 19th century for the posh area's working stiffs. A "no cellphones" rule attempts to keep the 21st century from intruding. 53 Kinnerton St. ☎ 0207/235-1135. Tube: Knightsbridge.

Theater

★★★ **Old Vic Theatre Southbank** SOUTHBANK
Except for a few wartime interruptions, this venerable theater has been in continuous operation since 1818. The repertory troupe at "the actors' theatre" has included a veritable who's who of thespians over the years, including Sir Laurence Olivier, Dame Maggie Smith, and the Redgrave clan. The Cut. ☎ 0870/060-6628. www.oldvictheatre.com. Tickets £15–£50. Tube: Waterloo.

★★★ **Open Air Theatre** MARYLEBONE
The setting is idyllic, and the seating and acoustics are excellent at this Regent's Park venue. Presentations are mainly of Shakespeare's plays, usually in period costume. The season runs from June to mid-September. Inner Circle, Regent's Park. ☎ 0870/060-1811. www.openairtheatre.org. Tickets £10–£40. Tube: Baker St.

★★★ **Royal Court Theatre** CHELSEA
This leader in provocative, cutting-edge theater is home to the English Stage Company, which was formed to promote serious drama. Sloane Sq. ☎ 0207/565-5000. www.royalcourttheatre.com. Tickets £10–£30. Tube: Sloane Sq.

★★★ **Royal National Theatre** SOUTH BANK
Home to one of the world's greatest stage companies, the Royal National presents the finest in world theater, from classic drama to award-winning new plays, comedies, and musicals. South Bank. ☎ 0207/452-3000. www.nationaltheatre.org.uk. Tickets £10–£60. Tube: Waterloo or Charing Cross.

★★★ **Shakespeare's Globe Theatre** SOUTH BANK
This outdoor theater is a replica of the Elizabethan original, with wooden benches (you can rent a cushion) and thatched galleries. It's the perfect spot to watch the Bard's works. New Globe Walk, Bankside. ☎ 0207/902-1400. www.shakespeares-globe.org. Tickets £5 groundlings, £12–£40 gallery seats. Tube: Blackfriars.

Windsor & Eton

Located in Windsor, Berkshire, 20 miles from London, Windsor Castle is the second-most-visited historic building in England (after the Tower of London) and one of the queen's three official residences (reputedly, her favorite). Eton, a town right across the Thames from Windsor, is the site of Eton College, one of the most exclusive boys' schools in the world. Give yourself at least a half-day for this day trip.

> Although Windsor Castle is still used as a royal residence, you can view its interiors on a self-guided tour.

START Trains from London Paddington arrive at Windsor Central Station (change at Slough); direct trains from London's Waterloo Station arrive at Windsor and Eton Riverside Station. Trip time is 1 hr. Both stations in Windsor are a 10-min. walk from the castle.

1 The Royal Windsor Information Centre provides detailed information about Windsor, Eton, and other nearby attractions. Old

Booking Hall, Royal Windsor Station, Thames St. ☎ 01753/743-900. www.windsor.gov.uk. Oct-Apr Mon–Sat 10am–5pm, Sun 11am–4pm; May-Sept Mon–Sat 9:30am–5:30pm, Sun 10am–4pm.

2 ★★★ Windsor Castle. Built some 900 years ago by William the Conqueror, this imposing castle, with its skyline of towers and battlements, rises from the center of the 1,940-hectare (4,800-acre) Great Park. Windsor is the largest inhabited castle in the world and

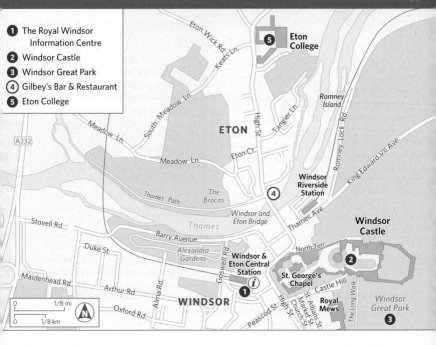

1. The Royal Windsor Information Centre
2. Windsor Castle
3. Windsor Great Park
4. Gilbey's Bar & Restaurant
5. Eton College

the oldest in continuous occupation. When the queen is in residence, the Royal Standard flies from the Round Tower (at all other times you will see the Union Flag). On a self-guided tour you can visit the ★★★ **State Apartments,** from the intimate chambers of Charles II to the enormous Waterloo Chamber, built to commemorate the victory over Napoleon in 1815. All are furnished with important works of art from the Royal Collection. The ★★ **Semi-State Rooms,** created by George IV in the 1820s as part of a new series of Royal Apartments for his personal occupation, continue to be used by the queen for official entertaining. In a separate area of the castle, you'll find ★★ **Queen Mary's Dollhouse,** a marvelous miniature palace designed by the architect Sir Edwin Lutyens as a present for

Queen Mary (wife of King George V) in 1924. It took nearly 1,500 artists and craftsmen 3 years to create and is full of incredible detailing, such as moving elevators and running water. ★★★ **St. George's Chapel,** also part of the Windsor Castle complex, is one of the finest medieval ecclesiastical buildings in England and the final resting place of 10 English monarchs, including Edward IV; Henry VIII and his third (and favorite) wife, Jane Seymour; Charles I; George V and his wife, Queen Mary; and George VI. Elizabeth,

Getting Around

Walking is the best way to see Windsor and Eton, but **City Sightseeing** (☎ 01708/ 865-656; www.city-sightseeing.com) offers a hop-on/hop-off bus service that makes a 45-minute circuit of all the main sights. A 24-hour ticket is £8 adults, £7 seniors, £4 kids 5–15.

Changing of the Guard

The ★★★ **Changing of the Guard** is as much of an event at Windsor as it is at Buckingham Palace, and the guards here are often accompanied by a band. You can watch the guards as they march up High Street (be there no later than 10:50am) and into the castle, but to see the actual ceremony, you need to be inside the castle (admission required). The half-hour ceremony takes place Monday to Saturday at 11 am from April through July, and on alternate days (except Sun) from August through March.

the Queen Mother, and Princess Margaret are also buried here. The **Albert Memorial Chapel,** just beyond St. George's Chapel, was converted by Queen Victoria into a memorial to her husband, Prince Albert, who died in 1861. ⏱ 1 hr. ☎ 01753/831-118. www.royal.gov.uk. Admission £16.50 adults, £15 seniors, £10 kids under 17. Daily Nov–Feb 9:45am–4:15pm (last entry 3pm); Mar–Oct 9:45am–5:30pm (last entry 4pm). Closed Mar 28, June 16 & Dec 25–26. Visiting hours subject to change at short notice, especially in June.

❸ ★★★ Windsor Great Park. Long Walk, a pedestrian walkway, winds through this 1,940-hectare (4,800-acre) oasis. The current contours of the park, once a favored hunting spot for Saxon kings, were established in the 1360s. The park today is a perfect place for picnics, walking, and cycling. ⏱ At least 30 min. for a stroll. Year-round dawn–dusk.

④ 🍷 Gilbey's Bar & Restaurant, with its delicious and reasonably priced bar menu and garden seating, is a great place to enjoy a drink, lunch, or a snack. 82–83 High St., Eton. ☎ 01753/854-921. Entrees £8–£10.

❺ ★ Eton College. This famous school was founded in 1440 by the 18-year-old King Henry VI to provide free education to poor scholars who would go on to study at King's College, Cambridge. Over the centuries, the student body has expanded to about 1,280 boys, ages 13 to 18, who are admitted by competitive examination. One of the most exclusive schools in the world, Eton has graduated 18 former British

Runnymede

★ Located on the banks of the Thames, with magnificent views across the Thames Valley, **Runnymede,** 3 miles southeast of Windsor on the A308 (free admission; open daily dawn–dusk), is the famous meadow where King John sealed the Magna Carta in 1215, establishing the principle of the constitutional monarchy and affirming the individual's right to justice and liberty. In 1957 the American Bar Association erected a memorial here to commemorate the fact that the American Constitution is based on the Magna Carta. From May to September, **French Brothers** (☎ 01735/851-900; www.boat-trips.co.uk) provides boat service from Windsor to Runnymede at 4pm on Wednesday and Friday through Sunday. The one-way fare is £8.60 for adults, £4.30 for kids.

prime ministers (including the Duke of Wellington), numerous heirs to the throne (Prince William studied here), and leading literary figures (from George Orwell to Ian Fleming). The cloisters, the chapel (note the 15th-c. artwork and reconstructed fan vaulting), the oldest classroom in the college, and the Museum of Eton Life are all open to visitors during school holidays by guided tour only. ⏱ 1 hr. High St. ☎ 01753/671-177. www.etoncollege.com. Admission £6.50 adults, £5.50 kids 8–13. Tours daily late Mar to mid-Apr & June–Sept 10:30am–4:30pm.

> *Several prime ministers and royals have received the finest education money can buy at Eton College.*

Fast Facts

Accommodation Services

You can get help reserving a hotel room by phone, online, or in person at the **Britain & London Visitor Centre,** 1 Lower Regent St. (hotel-booking line ☎ 08701/566-366; www.visitlondon.com; Tube: Piccadilly Circus), open weekdays 9am to 6:30pm and Saturday to Sunday 10am–4pm. The **British Hotel Reservation Centre** (☎ 020/7092-3055; www.bhrconline.com) provides free reservations and discounted rates at all the leading hotels and has reservations desks in the airports and major London train stations.

Arriving

BY PLANE **Heathrow** (☎ 0870/000-0123; www.baa.co.uk), about 15 miles west of Central London, is the largest of London's five airports and serves flights from around the globe. You have several options for getting into the city. The **London Underground** (the "Tube") is the cheapest mode of public transportation (fare £4) and takes about 45 minutes to reach Central London. All five terminals link up with the Tube system. The buses operated by **National Express Airport** (☎ 08701/781-8181; www.nationalexpress.com) may be a better alternative if you have lots of heavy luggage; the trip from the airport to Victoria Coach Station takes between 45 and 75 minutes and costs as little as £5 if you purchase your ticket online in advance. Fastest and most convenient is the **Heathrow Express** (☎ 0845/600-1515; www.heathrowexpress.co.uk), a dedicated train line running from all Heathrow terminals to London's Paddington Station in only 15 minutes. Fares vary according to seat class and age; they run £7 to £26. A **taxi** (£55–£85) is cost-effective if four or five people are traveling together. You can order one at the Taxi Information booths.

Gatwick (☎ 0870/000-2468; www.baa.co.uk), about 28 miles south of Central London, is considerably smaller than Heathrow but basically provides the same services and handles national and international flights. Your quickest way of getting into Central London is the convenient **Gatwick Express** train (☎ 0845/850-1530; www.gatwickexpress.com), which

> *Although classic Routemaster buses have been mostly phased out, they still ply a couple of "heritage routes" through the center.*

leaves from the South Terminal and takes about 30 minutes to reach Victoria Station (one-way fare is £17 adults, £8.45 kids under 10). **National Express Airport** buses (☎ 08705/808-080; www.nationalexpress.com) provide service to Victoria Coach Station in Central London for as little as £4.50 (advance purchase online). For 24-hour taxi service (avg. fare is £95) between Gatwick and Central London, call **Barker's Plus** (☎ 01293/562-291).

Stansted (☎ 0870/000-0303; www.stanstedairport.com), about 50 miles northeast of Central London, is a single-terminal airport used for national and

European flights. The **Stansted Express** train (☎ 0845/600-7245) to Liverpool Street Station takes 45 minutes (one-way ticket costs £18–£30).

London City Airport (☎ 020/7646-000; www.londoncityairport.com), only 6 miles east of the city center, services New York and several European destinations. An extension of the **Docklands Light Railway (DLR)** travels from the airport to Bank Street, in Central London, in 22 minutes. **BY TRAIN** If you're coming from the Continent via train and ferry, you cross the English Channel and disembark at one of the United Kingdom's Channel ports (travelers on Eurostar trains crossing via the Chunnel do not disembark). The ports closest to London are Dover, Folkestone, and Ramsgate to the east and Newhaven, Portsmouth, and Southampton to the south. Trains connecting with ferries on the U.K. side of the Channel generally go to Liverpool Street Station, Victoria Station, or Waterloo International. Eurostar Chunnel trains from Paris and Brussels arrive at King's Cross/St. Pancras International Station. All London stations link to the Underground system.

Dentists & Doctors

Dental Emergency Care Service, Guy's Hospital, St. Thomas St. (☎ 020/7188-7188; Tube: London Bridge), is open Monday to Friday 8:45am to 3:30pm for walk-in patients. **24 Hour Emergency Dental Treatment,** 102 Baker St. (☎ 0207/955-2186; www.24houremergencydentist.co.uk; Tube: Baker Street), delivers just what its name promises.

Most hotels have physicians on call. **Medical Express,** 117A Harley St. (☎ 020/7499-1991; www.medicalexpressclinic.com; Tube: Regent's Park), is a private clinic with walk-in medical service Monday to Friday 9am to 6pm, and Saturday 10am to 2pm. **Doctorcall,** 121 Harley St. (☎ 0844/257-9507; www.doctorcall.co.uk) makes house calls.

Emergencies

Call ☎ 999 for accidents and dire medical emergencies free of charge from any phone. Hospitals with emergency rooms in Central London include **Charing Cross Hospital,** Fulham Palace Rd., Hammersmith (☎ 0208/846-1234), and **Chelsea & Westminster Hospital,** Fulham Rd., Chelsea (☎ 0208/746-8000).

Getting Around

Do not even think about using a car while in London; your best bets for getting around are your own two feet or public transportation. For 24-hour information on London's Underground, buses, and ferries, call ☎ 020/7222-1234 or go to the Transport for London website at www.tfl.gov.uk. **BY UNDERGROUND** London's Underground (or Tube) system is usually the quickest way to get around the city. All Tube stations are clearly marked with a red circle and blue crossbar. Routes are color-coded. The Tube runs daily from 5:30am to 12:30am (until 11:30pm Sun), after which you must take a night bus or taxi. Fares are based on zones and start at £4 for a single journey within Zones 1 through 6 (the ones most frequented by travelers). Several special passes are available that dramatically reduce the cost of traveling by Tube. Using a prepaid **Oyster Card** (www.oystercard.com) is one money-saving option; you pay a one-time charge of £3 for the plastic card, but you'll save that on your first few trips with the Oyster Card's discounted fares (£1.50 for a one-way, off-peak trip in Zones 1 and 2). London Transport's **Travelcards** offer unlimited use of buses, Underground, and British Rail services in Greater London for one price. The **1-day Travelcard** costs £6.70, £2 kids; a **3-day Travelcard** costs £20 adults, £6 kids 5 to 15. You can buy Travelcards and Oyster Cards at ticket windows or at machines in Underground stations. **BY BUS** London's bus system costs half as much as the Tube, and you get better views of the city. Route maps are available at major Underground stations (Euston, Victoria, and Piccadilly Circus, to name a few) or online at www.tfl.gov.uk. Fares start at £2 for Zones 1 and 2, with prices rising the farther out you travel from Central London. Oyster Cards and Travelcards are valid on buses. (A single bus fare using the Oyster Card is only 90p peak time.) A 1-day bus pass costs £3.50, a 7-day is £13, and a booklet of Bus Saver tickets costs £6 for six single trips. Kids 15 and under ride free, but a photo bus pass is required for 14- and 15-year-olds. Most Central London buses require that you buy your bus ticket from a ticket machine at a bus stop before boarding; these machines take exact change only. If there is no machine at your bus stop, you can pay the driver or conductor in cash (use small bills or coins only). **Night buses** are the only way to get around by public transport after the Tube stops operating. Be sure that there is an "N" bus listed on your bus stop's route, or you'll wait in vain until morning. **BY TAXI** All airport and train stations have well-marked areas for taxis. You can hail a taxi anywhere, on any street, except in certain no-stopping zones marked by white zigzag lines along the curb. Available taxis will have a lit sign on top of the cab. Only black cabs, whose drivers have undergone rigorous training known as "the Knowledge," are allowed to cruise the streets for fares. Don't get into cruising minicabs, which can legally pick up only those passengers who have booked them by telephone. Black cabs have metered fares (minimum fare is £2.20), and surcharges are assessed after 8pm and on weekends. Minicab charges should be negotiated in advance. Taxis can also be requested by phone, but you will pay more. To book a black cab, call **Radio Taxis** (☎ 0207/272-0272) or **Dial-a-Cab** (☎ 0207/253-5000). For a minicab, call **Addison Lee** (☎0207/387-8888).

Internet Access

Wi-Fi or dial-up Internet service is available at hotels throughout London, sometimes for free but more often for a daily or hourly fee. Cybercafes were once ubiquitous but are now becoming as scarce as pay phones. Try the following: **easyinternet Café,** Whiteley's Shopping Centre, 2nd floor, Bayswater (no phone); **coffee@Bermondsey St.,** 163 Bermondsey St. (no phone); **coffee@Brick Lane,** 154 Brick Lane (no phone); **Global Net,** 22 Great Windmill St. (☎ 020/7434-4484); and **Rex Lounge,** 33 Woburn Place (☎ 020/7637-4545).

Pharmacies

The leading drugstore chain in the U.K., **Boots the Chemist** (www.boots.com), has branches all over London. One late-night pharmacy (open until midnight) is **Bliss Chemist,** 5–6 Marble Arch (☎ 0207/723-6116; Tube: Marble Arch). An all-night chemist is **Zafash Pharmacy,** 233–235 Old Brompton Rd., Earls Court (☎ 0207/373-2798; Tube: West Brompton).

Post Office

The **Main Post Office,** 24 William IV St. (☎ 020/7930-9580; Tube: Charing Cross) is open Monday to Saturday 9:30am to 5:30pm. Other post offices and sub-post offices (windows in the backs of news agents) are open Monday to Friday 9am to 5:30pm, Saturday 9am to 12:30pm. For general post office information, go to www.royalmail.com.

Safety

London has its share of violent crime, just as any other major city does—its biggest crime-related problems are public intoxication, muggings, and sexual assault—but it is usually quite safe for visitors as long as you take common-sense precautions when you're in a crowded public area or walking alone at night. The area around Euston Station has more purse snatchings than anywhere else in London.

Telephones

London's city code is **020,** but you don't need to dial it within city limits; just dial the eight-digit number. To call London from the rest of the U.K., you must dial the 020 followed by the number. When calling London from abroad, dial the international code (011 from North America; 0011 from Australia; and 00 from New Zealand), followed by 44 (England's country code), followed by 20, and then the eight-digit number.

Toilets

Clean, city-maintained public toilets can be found in shopping areas, parks, and tourist zones. Some are free, and some charge either 20p or 50p for use. Pubs and hotels don't get too fussy if you discreetly nip in to use the loo (especially if you buy a drink first). Department stores have public restrooms, usually stashed on high floors to discourage traffic.

Visitor Information

The **Britain & London Visitor Centre,** 1 Regent St., Piccadilly Circus (☎ 0870/156-6366; Tube: Piccadilly Circus), provides tourist information to walk-in visitors Monday to Friday 9:30am to 6:30pm, Saturday and Sunday 10am to 4pm. There's another Tourist Information Centre in the Arrivals Hall of Waterloo International Terminal (daily 8:30am–10pm). For more information, check the London Visitor Centre website at www. visitlondon.com.

4
**Kent &
Sussex**

Favorite Kent & Sussex Moments

The counties of Kent and Sussex, tucked into the southeast corner of England, are jam-packed with relics of the kingdom's rich past—Battle, where William the Conqueror defeated the Saxons in 1066; Canterbury Cathedral, where Thomas Becket was slain; Dover Castle, where Henry II built the mightiest medieval keep in the realm; and Brighton, where George IV built the most outlandish palace in the land, just for starters. Few places offer as much to see and do.

> PREVIOUS PAGE *Meadows abloom at Sissinghurst.* THIS PAGE *Piers, like this one at Brighton, were traditionally the epicenter of seaside resort fun.*

1 **Poking around Knole.** One of England's largest and grandest houses is no one's vision of home sweet home—with 365 rooms, to quote the novelist Virginia Woolf, the place is "a town rather than a house." The paneled rooms and spooky galleries, filled with priceless paintings and furnishings, provide a memorable look at how the other half once lived. See p. 153, **2**.

2 **Walking around Chichester.** This pretty little town is packed with treasures: A Norman cathedral rises above the rooftops of Georgian houses, one of Britain's finest galleries of 20th-century art is tucked away on a medieval lane, and the Romans left behind exquisite mosaics at outlying Fishbourne. See p. 182.

3 **Witnessing the Battle of Hastings unfold.** Events of that fateful day in 1066 come alive as you cross the rolling hills where Duke William of Normandy defeated Saxon King Harold and took control of England. See p. 180.

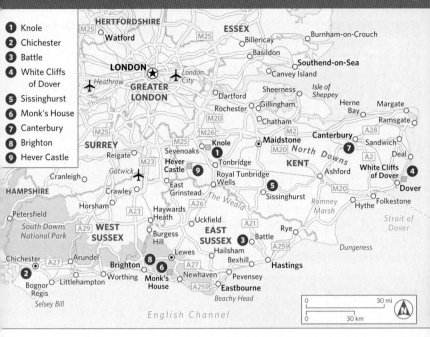

1 Knole
2 Chichester
3 Battle
4 White Cliffs of Dover
5 Sissinghurst
6 Monk's House
7 Canterbury
8 Brighton
9 Hever Castle

4 Ambling atop the White Cliffs of Dover.
The bracing sea air, the white cliffs stretching down the coast, ships plying the sea lanes of the English Channel below, and the mighty castle crowning the heights—the exhilarating and iconic British experience of a walk along the famous cliffs brings to mind the sentiment, "There will always be an England." See p. 163, **2**.

5 Wandering around Sissinghurst. The gardens planted in the 1930s by poet, novelist, and gardening writer Vita Sackville-West and her husband, the diplomat and writer Harold Nicolson, are horticulture heaven. As you step in and out of the 10 outdoor rooms, you'll discover that each has a look, feel, and charm all its own. See p. 156, **5**.

6 Getting into the spirit of Monk's House. At the unassuming Sussex home where novelist Virginia Woolf and her publisher husband Leonard often retreated, you'll see why the couple's greatest pleasure was to "sit, eat, play the gramophone, prop our feet up on the side of the fire and read endless books." You'll wish you could do the same. See p. 157, **6**.

7 Attending Evensong at Canterbury Cathedral. England's greatest Gothic-style cathedral will move you whenever you visit, but the experience is especially transporting when voices soar to the high vaults and magnificent medieval stained glass bathes the soft gray stone from French quarries in gentle light. See p. 166, **3**.

8 Having a good time in Brighton. The seaside retreat has been England's "fun city" ever since "Prinny," the Prince Regent who became George IV, came to town with his mistresses in the 1820s and built the Royal Pavilion in an exotic Indian style. An amusement pier, bars, and other diversions still fuel a light-hearted mood. See p. 172.

9 Getting into a millionaire's lifestyle at Hever. You can't step beyond the velvet ropes, but it's still easy to imagine how nice it would be to sip a cocktail in front of the fire in one of William Astor's early-20th-century drawing rooms or to have the Italian Gardens all to yourself. If medieval sobriety is more your style, there's plenty of that at Hever, too. See p. 158, **8**.

The Best of Kent & Sussex in 3 Days

Like Chaucer's pilgrims, who from "every shire's end of England to Canterbury do wend," first find your way to Canterbury, the famous medieval cathedral city on the River Stour. From there move on to Dover, where one of the mightiest fortresses in the realm stands sentinel atop the famous White Cliffs; Rye, a beautiful coastal town that claims to shelter more historic buildings than any other town in Britain; and Brighton, England's most popular seaside resort. Distances are short and train travel in the region is easy, leaving plenty of time to take in the sights.

> Canterbury has been settled since at least Roman times.

START Canterbury, 62 miles southeast of London. Trains from London's St. Pancras Station run every half-hour or so; the trip takes about an hour.

❶ **Canterbury.** Bell Harry, the cathedral's graceful bell tower, has led visitors across the fields and orchards of Kent since the end of the 11th century, and will make an appearance as you approach the city, too.

Canterbury became England's most popular pilgrimage site after knights of King Henry II slew Thomas Becket in the cathedral in 1170. Becket was canonized a saint three years later, and the penitent king erected a shrine that became a mecca for pilgrims seeking miracles and adventure—until 1538, when another king, Henry VIII, had the shrine destroyed after he broke with the Catholic Church. As the seat of the Archbishop of Canterbury, head of the Anglican Church, **Canterbury Cathedral** (p. 166, ❸) is one of England's most venerable monuments. As you wend your way through medieval lanes that were once thronged with pilgrims, you'll also come upon vestiges of a past that put the town on the map long before the Middle Ages. The Romans settled the outpost of Durovernum Cantiacorum here, and their presence is evoked in the **Roman Museum** (p. 170, ❻). In their wake, St. Augustine arrived in Canterbury in A.D. 597 to bring Christianity to England, and founded a monastic community that flourished to become **St. Augustine's Abbey** (p. 168, ❹), one of Europe's great centers of learning.

1 Canterbury
2 Dover
3 Rye
4 Brighton

As you wander through this delightful, age-old city, find your way to the cathedral at 5:30pm (5:15pm on Sun) for Evensong, when the transporting voices of the choir blend with the mellow hues of gray stone and late light streaming through the stained glass. ⏱ 1 day. See p. 166.

On Day 2, leave Canterbury East Station on one of the trains that run about every half-hour for the 20-min. trip to Dover Priory Station. Leave your bags at the station and walk or take Bus 15X or 593 from the adjacent bus station to the castle.

2 **Dover.** As you explore **Dover Castle** (p. 162, **1**), you will again be immersed in the scope of British history, this time while enjoying one of England's most iconic views over the White Cliffs of Dover. Britain's oldest and most important fortification encompasses a Roman lighthouse, a Saxon church, a magnificent keep at the heart of the medieval defenses of Henry II, underground soldiers' barracks put in place when an invasion by Napoleon seemed inevitable, and a massive network of tunnels used as a hospital, communications center, and bomb shelter during World War II. You'll get a sense of the

> For centuries Dover Castle has guarded the shortest sea route between England and France.

> *The cobblestones of Mermaid Street, like much of the rest of Rye, seem frozen in time.*

strategic importance of these mighty defenses when you walk the circuit of walls and take in the sweeping views of the English Channel and the long stretch of coastline.

Before you leave, take a bracing walk along the top of the **White Cliffs** (p. 163, ❷). There will not be, as the song promises, "bluebirds over the White Cliffs of Dover" (England is not one their habitats), but you will see many other nesting sea birds as well as the vast stretch of blue water meeting the white coastline. ⏱ Half-day. See p. 162.

Trains for Rye leave Dover Priory Station about every 45 min.; the trip takes about 1½ hr. and requires a change at Ashford.

❸ **Rye.** You will feel as though you've entered a time warp as you walk up the cobblestones of Mermaid Street and the other lanes of this beautiful old town, full of secret passageways, quaint corners, and Tudor, Elizabethan, and Georgian houses. The town's charms have proven irresistible to a weighty roster of writers, including American expatriate Henry James, who lived here in **Lamb House** (p. 178, ❶) the last 18 years of his life. British poet Patric Dickinson (1914–94) rhapsodized that "Rye is like an old beautifully jeweled brooch worn at South-England's throat," and you may well feel the same way after spending the afternoon and evening soaking in Rye's appealing atmosphere. ⏱ Half-day. See p. 178.

On Day 3, hourly trains will take you from Rye to Brighton in a little under 1½ hr.

❹ **Brighton.** While you've encountered venerable monuments in Canterbury and Dover and rarefied English town life in Rye, Brighton introduces you to another side of England. One of the nation's favorite seaside getaways since the early 19th century, when the future George IV, then Prince Regent, built the extravagantly ornate **Royal Pavilion** (p. 172, ❷), Brighton is these days a bit frayed. Even so, the town of seaside promenades, crescents and terraces of bright-white Regency and Georgian houses, and medieval lanes still exudes an air of fun. There's even a bit of the decadence that the closest seaside resort to London has long promised city dwellers getting away for a few days. Aside from the Pavilion, arcade-lined **Brighton Pier** (p. 172, ❶), beaches, and other attractions will keep you busy. Brighton also hosts a sizable gay and lesbian presence, ensuring a lively nightlife scene. ⏱ 1 day. See p. 172.

The Cinque Ports

In Dover and Rye you will notice mention of the Cinque Ports, a prestigious medieval alliance of towns on the coast of Kent and Sussex. Dover, Hastings, Hythe, Romney, and Sandwich were the five principal ports, and Rye and Winchelsea were attached as so-called Ancient Towns. Beginning in the 11th century, the monarchy exempted the Cinque Ports from taxation and turned a blind eye to smuggling in return for their being at the ready to ward off pirates and an invasion from the Continent. A Lord Warden of the Cinque Ports was appointed by the monarch and given a residence at Walmer Castle in Deal, 7 miles north of Dover. As early as the 15th century, the Cinque Ports had lost much of their prominence as shifting sands rendered some former ports inland towns, the sea washed away others, and new shipbuilding techniques and sophisticated dockyards elsewhere made the old towns obsolete. The alliance is now powerless but still prestigious, and Lord Wardens of recent years have included Winston Churchill and Queen Elizabeth, the Queen Mother.

Kings, Saints, and Sinners

On even a brief foray into Kent and Sussex, you will meet some of the most colorful figures of British history.

Canterbury was the scene of one of the great medieval melodramas: the power struggle between Henry II (1133–89) and Thomas Becket (1118–70). The two were once allies, and the king named Becket, the son of a prosperous merchant, Archbishop of Canterbury in 1162—even though Becket was not a priest. Becket held his own on several issues, including the Church's right to try its own clerics, and refused to honor the king's orders to reverse the excommunication of two bishops. Knights heard the monarch pout, "What sluggards, what cowards have I brought up in my court, who care nothing for their allegiance to their lord? Who will rid me of this meddlesome priest?" That was all it took to set them in motion: They went to Canterbury and slew Becket in the cathedral. The archbishop was soon canonized, Henry repented for the murder of a man who "in happier times had been a friend," and **Canterbury Cathedral** (p. 166, ❸) became one of medieval Europe's most popular pilgrimage sites.

You'll encounter Henry II again at **Dover Castle** (p. 162, ❶). Henry saw the strategic importance of the stronghold against invasion from the Continent, reinforcing the walls and building the mighty Great Tower. Dover became the largest and grandest of England's medieval castles, designed as a symbol that Dover was the gateway to the realm and to impress visitors arriving in England by sea.

In Brighton you'll meet another monarch, George IV (1762–1830; pictured above). The fun-loving dandy served as Prince Regent when his father, George III, slipped into insanity and started addressing his court as "my lords and peacocks." The younger George kept the tongues of gossips wagging with his many affairs and extravagant spending; the **Royal Pavilion** (p. 172, ❷), the palace he built near the Brighton seafront, gave plenty of reason to question the king's taste and sense of fiscal responsibility. His marriage to Maria Fitzherbert, a Catholic, was declared illegal because he could not ascend the throne with a Catholic wife, and his marriage to Caroline of Brunswick was so unhappy that she soon exiled herself to the Italian lakes. Cultured and stylish, George was often called the "First Gentleman of England," though it was also said of him that he would always prefer "a girl and a bottle to politics and a sermon."

The Best of Kent & Sussex in 5 Days

As you travel across the rolling countryside and chalky downs of Kent and Sussex, you will soon come to appreciate why kings, nobles, writers, artists, and ordinary folks have taken such pleasure in some of England's most appealing landscapes. You'll come upon the White Cliffs and other swaths of coastline, castles and country houses, medieval cathedrals, beautiful gardens, and quaint towns and seaside resorts. Travel by car to get the most out of this trip, but be prepared: As you maneuver the narrow twisting lanes, you may recall the words of the writer G.K. Chesterton: "Before the Roman came to Rye or out to Severn strode, the rolling English drunkard made the rolling English road."

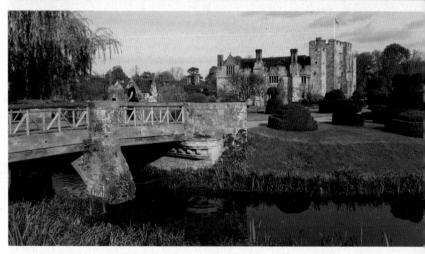

> Anne Boleyn, second wife of Henry VIII, spent her childhood at Hever—and her final days in the Tower of London.

START Knole, in Sevenoaks. From London, take the train to Gatwick Airport and pick up a car there; Sevenoaks is 18 miles east of Gatwick off A25. **TRIP LENGTH** 190 miles.

❶ **Knole.** One of England's largest and grandest houses, spreading across 1.8 hectares (4½ acres), is overwhelming, to say the least, with 365 rooms, a courtyard for every day of the week, and a staircase for every week of the year. The 15th-century manor, whose owners have included Henry VIII and Thomas

Sackville (1536–1608), a cousin of Elizabeth I, is filled with priceless furnishings and a museum's worth of paintings. It's the sheer size of Knole, however, that will make the greatest impression on you, as it did the novelist Virginia Woolf (1882–1941), who used to visit the poet Vita Sackville-West (1892–1962) at Knole. Woolf set part of her novel *Orlando* at Knole, and wrote, "It looked a town rather than a house... Courts and buildings, grey, red, plum colour, lay orderly and symmetrical... the

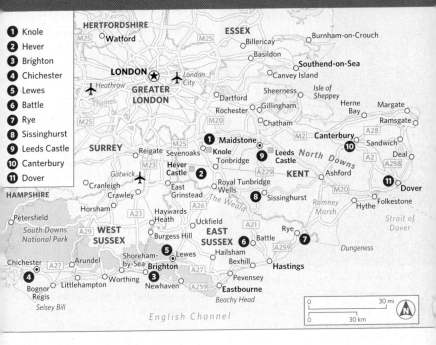

1	Knole
2	Hever
3	Brighton
4	Chichester
5	Lewes
6	Battle
7	Rye
8	Sissinghurst
9	Leeds Castle
10	Canterbury
11	Dover

buildings were some of them low, some pointed; here was chapel, there a belfry… while smoke from innumerable chimneys curled perpetually into the air." ⏱ 3 hr. See p. 153, **2**.

From Knole, follow B2042 10 miles south to

2 kids **Hever Castle.** The aura of the Middle Ages pervades this lovely castle of time-mellowed stone, with towers, moat, and a drawbridge. Hever has a colorful provenance as well. Anne Boleyn (1507–36), the unfortunate young second wife of Henry VIII, was raised at Hever, and the house later passed to Anne of Cleves (1515–57), Henry's fourth wife; the Long Gallery is peopled with mannequins of the monarch's six wives, and as the nursery rhyme tells us, "two beheaded, two divorced, one died, and one survived." Some of the most alluring aspects of Hever are from the early 20th century, when William Waldorf Astor (1848–1919), heir to an American fur-trading fortune, bought the castle, decorated the ground floor rooms in opulent Edwardian taste, and laid out lavish Italian gardens surrounding a 14-hectare (35-acre) lake that took 800 laborers 2 years to create. ⏱ 2 hr. See p. 158, **8**.

From Hever, follow B2026 and A22 35 miles south to

3 **Brighton.** Much of the glitter of Brighton's fashionable, 19th-century heyday has faded, but England's most popular seaside town is still an appealing mix of beaches, medieval lanes, and gleaming white rows of Regency-era houses. Arrive in time to enjoy the last of the afternoon sun while strolling on the seaside promenade. Brighton's nightlife is popular with Londoners who come down for some fun, and is fueled in part by a large gay and lesbian community. An evening constitutional out to arcade-lined **Brighton Pier** (p. 172, **1**), aglow with twinkling lights, has been a popular pastime since the late 19th century.

Start your explorations on Day 2 at the **Royal Pavilion** (p. 172, **2**), one of the most extravagant palaces in Europe, an Indian fantasy of turrets and minarets built for George IV in the early 19th century. ⏱ 1 day. See p. 172.

On the afternoon of Day 2, head 30 miles west on the A27 to

> A market cross, like this one in Chichester, was a common feature of medieval English towns.

4 Chichester. This handsome town is home to the most intact Norman cathedral (p. 182, **1**) in England, which rises above the rooftops of Georgian houses. Tucked away on the surrounding medieval lanes is **Pallant House** (p. 182, **6**), one of Britain's finest galleries of 20th-century art; outlying **Fishbourne Roman Palace** (p. 183, **3**) is a massive domestic complex with extensive mosaics. Before returning to Brighton you may want to see what's on stage at the renowned **Chichester Festival Theatre** (p. 183), founded under the directorship of Sir Laurence Olivier in 1962. ⏲ Half-day. See p. 182.

Spend the evening in Brighton; on Day 3 drive 8 miles northeast to Lewes, off the A22.

5 Lewes. An attractive country town, Lewes was home to Anne of Cleves after her divorce from Henry VIII (you can tour her house, p. 175) and to Thomas Paine (1737–1809), who became a fiery American patriot. Paine debated many of the principles that would appear in his pamphlet *Common Sense,* and later in the Declaration of Independence, in the bar of the White Hart Hotel on High Street, where you can still enjoy a pint of good ale.

The countryside around Lewes, known as the Sussex Downs, became popular in the early 20th century with the writers, artists, and intellectuals of the Bloomsbury Group; you can visit the homes of two of them—Virginia Woolf's **Monk's House** (p. 157, **6**), and **Charleston** (p. 157, **7**), the farmhouse her sister, Vanessa Bell, shared with her husband, the designer Clive Bell, and lover, the artist Duncan Grant. ⏲ Half-day. See p. 175.

Take A27 and A271 27 miles east to

6 Battle. In the 1066 Battle of Hastings, Duke William of Normandy (later known as William the Conqueror) defeated Saxon King Harold and took control of England. The battle took place not in Hastings but on the site of this pleasant town 6 miles north. The ruins of Battle Abbey, built by William to atone for the bloodshed and later destroyed by Henry VIII, stand at the entrance to the battlefield. Events of that fateful day unfold as you follow a clever self-guided audio tour across the rolling hills where an estimated 7,000 soldiers of each side squared off with swords, lances, and arrows. ⏲ 2 hr. See p. 180.

Take B2089 15 miles east to

7 Rye. End Day 3 in this appealing old town, where fine Georgian houses line cobbled lanes. One of them, **Lamb House** (p. 178, **1**), was home to American expatriate novelist Henry James. Like him and many other writers who have settled in Rye, you'll probably be taken with the town's many quaint corners, views over the surrounding marshes, and colorful remnants of a seafaring past. ⏲ Half-day. See p. 178.

After a walk around Rye and into Romney Marsh on the morning of Day 4, head 21 miles north of Rye via the A268 and A229 to

8 Sissinghurst. One of England's favorite gardens was the creation of poet, novelist, and gardening writer Vita Sackville-West and her husband, the diplomat and writer Harold Nicolson (1886–1968). You encountered Vita earlier in this itinerary at Knole, the estate where she was raised (p. 153, **2**). As a woman she was not able to inherit her beloved ancestral home, so at Sissinghurst, on the remains of a ruined Elizabethan estate, she created another kind of splendor—10 outdoor rooms that have become the model for gardens around the world. ⏲ 2 hr. See p. 156, **5**.

Drive 9 miles northeast of Sissinghurst via the A274 to

9 kids **Leeds Castle.** The so-called "loveliest castle in the world" is a vision of turrets, towers, and light gray stone that seems to float in the middle of a swan-filled lake. Leeds traces its roots to the 9th century, and its stone walls have housed a remarkable roster of tenants. Residents who've left their mark in the storied rooms include Edward I; Queen Joan, whose stepson, Henry V, imprisoned her on charges of witchcraft at Leeds; Henry VIII and his first queen, Catherine of Aragon; Lord Culpeper, colonial governor of Virginia; and Olive, Lady Baillie, a wealthy Anglo-American heiress who made Leeds her home in 1926. Thanks to beautiful gardens and stream-crossed lawns, Leeds is also a pleasure to explore. ⏱ Half-day. See p. 154, **4**.

End Day 4 in Canterbury, about 21 miles east of Leeds Castle via A20 and A22.

10 **Canterbury.** As you pull into Canterbury, you will be following in the footsteps of the medieval pilgrims who walked across England and Europe to reach this old cathedral city. If you settle in by late afternoon, make your way to the cathedral for Evensong (p. 166, **3**). Spend the morning of Day 5 exploring the city's venerable past at the **Roman Museum** (p. 170, **6**) and the ruins of **St. Augustine's Abbey** (p. 168, **4**), a great medieval center of learning. And do spend some time simply taking in the mellow atmosphere of one of England's most venerable and appealing cities. ⏱ Half-day. See p. 166.

After spending the morning in Canterbury, continue 15 miles southeast of Canterbury on the A2 to

11 **Dover.** Your itinerary comes to an end at two of the greatest sights in England—the **White Cliffs** (p. 163, **2**) that are the natural gateway to the realm, and **Dover Castle** (p. 162, **1**), one of the oldest, largest, and mightiest fortifications in the land. Spend the rest of Day 5 exploring the castle and enjoying a walk along the top of the cliffs. ⏱ Half-day. See p. 162.

> *Leeds Castle is an ideal spot to take both history buffs and inquisitive kids.*

Great Houses & Gardens

Some of England's finest houses are tucked into the rolling hills of Kent and Sussex, and they are easily reached on leisurely drives through fields, orchards, pastoral villages, and chalky downs. As you visit these country manors and castles, you'll encounter such notable figures as Winston Churchill, Anne Boleyn, Virginia Woolf and the Bloomsbury Group, and Henry VIII.

> *Ightham Mote is one of England's few remaining 14th-century moated manor houses.*

START Chartwell, outside Edenbridge, about 10 miles east of Gatwick Airport off A25.

TRIP LENGTH 4 days, covering 170 miles.

1 ★★ Chartwell. Sir Winston Churchill (1874–1965), England's wartime prime minister, and Lady Churchill moved into this brick manor overlooking rolling hills in 1924 and made it their home for the next 40 years. The rooms are still furnished as the Churchills left them and seem to resound with activity. The

couple entertained many of the great statesmen of the 20th century in the five reception rooms, and Sir Winston wrote his *History of the English-Speaking Peoples* and many other books in the study, where he wore out the carpet as he walked back and forth while dictating through the night. The couple planted gardens and transformed the 32 hectares (80 acres) of grounds with ponds and a swimming pool. Many of Sir Winston's paintings hang in the studio, where he often retreated; the wall he

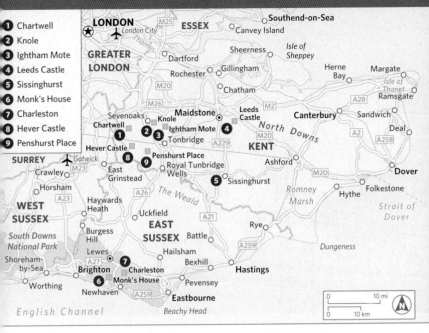

built around the kitchen garden still stands; and the roses Lady Churchill planted bloom through much of the summer. ⏱ 2 hr. Maple-ton Rd., Westerham. ☎ 01732/868-381. www.nationaltrust.org.uk. Admission £12 adults, £6 kids under 16, £30 families. Mid-Mar to early July & late Aug-Oct Wed-Sun 11am-5pm; early July-late Aug Tues-Sun 11am-5pm.

Follow A25 east 8 miles to Sevenoaks.

SITE GUIDE PAGE 155

② ★★ Knole. One of Britain's largest houses was built for Thomas Bouchier, Archbishop of Canterbury, in 1456. Henry VIII took a liking to the house and seized it a century later. Henry's daughter, Elizabeth I, gave Knole to her cousin, Thomas Sackville, the 1st Earl of Dorset, and the Sackvilles have lived here ever since.

One of the most appreciative residents was Vita Sackville-West, the 20th-century novelist who grew up at Knole and once wrote of footmen being stationed during dinner at the edge of carpets to keep them from float-ing up in drafts. Knole's 365 rooms are filled with Stuart furniture, textiles, and portraits by such masters as Anthony van Dyck, Thomas

Gainsborough, and Sir Joshua Reynolds. Sackville-West described the estate as a "very old woman who has always been beautiful, who has had many lovers and seen many generations come and go." As you walk across the 400-hectare (1,000-acre) Deer Park and look back at the manor, you might also think of Vita's friend and sometime lover Virginia Woolf, who described the vast assemblage of roofs and chimneys as "a town rather than a house."

Continue 6 miles east on A25 to Ivy Hatch. From there follow well-marked country lanes for about 2½ miles to Ightham Mote.

③ ★★ Ightham Mote. One of the best-preserved medieval residences in England, this moated manor house—dating back to the early 14th century—seems to have remained nestled in its hidden valley without being touched by the outside world. ("Mote" is an old word for meet, and the house once served as a gathering spot for local landowners.) The Great Hall, drawing room, billiards room, and family chapels evoke centuries' worth of do-mestic life, with Tudor hearths and Jacobean staircases. Woodland trails crisscross the extensive grounds. ⏱ 1 hr. Mote Rd., Ivy Hatch.

> *Many of the rooms at Leeds Castle were decorated and furnished in the 1920s by Lady Baillie, an Anglo-American heiress.*

☎ 01732/810-378. www.nationaltrust.org.uk. Admission £11.50 adults, £5.75 kids under 16, £29 families. Mid-Mar to Oct Mon, Thurs–Sun 11am–5pm; Nov–late Dec Thurs–Sun 11am–3pm.

Make your way south to Rye and settle in for 2 nights. The fastest route takes you back through Sevenoaks, then south on A21 to Rye. Total distance is about 21 miles. Set out from Rye on Day 2 to visit two more houses and gardens. First follow A268 25 miles north to the junction of the M20, and the well-marked turnoff for Leeds Castle from there.

❹ ★★★ kids Leeds Castle. The so-called "loveliest castle in the world" is a vision of turrets, towers, and light gray stone that seems to float in the middle of a swan-filled lake. Leeds traces its roots to the 9th century, when Leed, a minister of the king of Kent, built a wooden fortress on two islands in the River Len; it was transformed into a royal palace for Edward I in 1278. King Henry V (1387–1422) imprisoned his stepmother, Queen Joan, at Leeds on charges of witchcraft, then turned the castle over to his wife, Catherine de Valois, who, being French, installed a surprisingly well

equipped and luxurious bathroom. Henry VIII made substantial improvements to Leeds for his first queen, Catherine of Aragon (1485–1536). The Norman cellars, Henry VIII's Banqueting Room, and other medieval quarters retain many of their original fittings, including the limewood carved panels and four paintings by the late-14th-century Florentine Niccolò di Pietro Gerini (1340–1414) in the Chapel that depict the Passion of Christ.

The castle was later the country seat of Lord Culpeper (1635–89), colonial governor of Virginia. A wealthy Anglo-American heiress, Olive, Lady Baillie, purchased Leeds in 1926 and amassed many of the furnishings and paintings that are on view in the rooms she restored with great taste and an eye to 20th-century comfort.

On the extensive and manicured grounds, streams bubble through the Wood Garden and Duckery, and flowers bloom in English and Mediterranean gardens. A maze of 1,000 yew trees surrounds the entrance to a secret tunnel and an underground grotto. The castle's vineyard, still yielding grapes from which a white wine is made, is listed in the

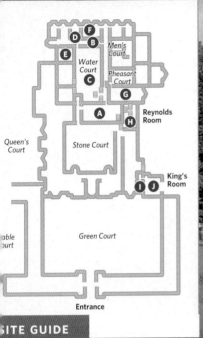

SITE GUIDE

② Knole

Most of Knole remains the private domain of the Sackville family, and public visits are confined to 13 rooms. You'll enter through the **A Great Hall,** where residents once dined while an orchestra played from the gallery above. The Great Staircase, embellished with carvings and murals, climbs to the first-floor staterooms, comprising long galleries, bedchambers, and dressing rooms. **B Lady Betty Germain's China Closet** houses a notable collection of Delftware and looks into the half-timbered **C Water Court,** one of 52 courtyards at Knole. In the nearby **D Leicester Gallery** (named for the Earl of Leicester, a 16th-century owner of Knole who was a favorite of Elizabeth I), James I is pictured sitting on an X-framed chair exactly like the one beneath the painting. In the **E Venetian Ambassador's Room** is the bed in which King James II awoke at Whitehall on December 18, 1688, the day William of Orange took the crown and forced him into exile. The 17th-century bed in the **F Spangle Bedroom** is covered with thousands of silver panels intended to sparkle in the sunlight. A van Dyck

portrait of a teenaged Frances Cranfield, who married a 17th-century owner of Knole, is in the **G Ballroom,** and a collection of paintings by Sir Joshua Reynolds hangs in the **H Reynolds Room.** In the **I King's Closet** is what is euphemistically called a "seat of easement" used by Charles II or James II, and the **J King's Room** shows off a grandiose bed made for Charles, as well as a set of rare silver furniture. ⏱ 3 hr. Sevenoaks. ☎ 01732/462-100. www.nationaltrust. org.uk. Admission £11.50 adults, £5.75 kids under 16, £29 families. Mid-Mar to mid-Oct Wed–Sun noon–4pm.

> *The Long Library is one of only two rooms you can visit inside Sissinghurst.*

11th-century Domesday Book. ⏱ **Half-day.** Outside Bearsted. ☎ 01622/765-400. www. leeds-castle.com. Admission £18.50 adults, £16 seniors, £11 kids 4–15. Daily 10:30am–5:30pm (Oct–Mar until 5pm).

Follow B2163 and A274 south to Headcorn, and from there follow the signs to Sissinghurst. The drive is about 10 miles.

➎ ★★★ **Sissinghurst.** In 1930, poet, novelist, and gardening writer Vita Sackville-West and her husband, the diplomat and writer Harold Nicolson, bought the nearly ruined remains of a grand Elizabethan house and fashioned living quarters out of the gatehouse, stables, tower, and other buildings across the estate. You can visit just two rooms, the Long Library and Vita's study in the Tower. Most notably the couple turned their attention to the gardens, now some of the most famous in England. They were inspired by Britain's best-known garden designers of the early 20th century, Sir Edwin Lutyens (1869–1944) and Gertrude Jekyll (1843–1932), in stressing color, texture, and the overall experience of

being in a garden; and by Lawrence Johnston (1871–1958), the American-born heir who created a series of roomlike gardens at **Hidcote Manor** (p. 310, ➊), his estate in the Cotswolds. Vita's childhood home was **Knole,** one of the largest houses in England (p. 153, ➋), and with the gardens at Sissinghurst she and Harold sought to re-create outside the feeling of a grand English house.

Vita and Harold laid out 10 outdoor rooms, each with a distinct look and feel, separated by hedges and walls, and each having plants of different appearance and color. One is planted almost entirely in whites and grays, another in bright reds and oranges. The key to appreciating Sissinghurst is simply to walk randomly through the gardens, slipping through a gate or opening in a hedge to discover another room. ⏱ 2 hr. Sissinghurst, near Cranbrook. ☎ 01580/710-700. www.nationaltrust.org.uk. Admission £11 adults, £5.50 kids under 16, £27.50 families. Mid-Mar to Oct Mon–Tues & Fri–Sun 11am–6:30pm.

Follow A268 10 miles south back to Rye. After another night there, on Day 3 take A259 20 miles east to Lewes (p. 175), your

jumping-off point for Monk's House and Charleston. Plan on spending the night there or in nearby Brighton (p. 172), 8 miles southwest. Monk's House is in the village of Rodmell, 4½ miles west of Lewes off A27.

6 ★★★ **Monk's House.** In the years between the world wars, novelist Virginia Woolf and her publisher husband Leonard often retreated to this small and unassuming white clapboard house. They frequently entertained many of the great intellectuals of their day, including the biographer Lytton Strachey, economist John Maynard Keynes, and the poet T.S. Eliot, but the luxury the Woolfs valued most was the leisure to do what they wanted—she to write such profoundly influential, groundbreaking novels as *Mrs. Dalloway* and *Orlando*; he to run the small, literary Hogarth Press that published such writers as E. M. Forster, and to garden. It's quite easy to imagine the couple in the sitting room where, Virginia wrote, "We sit, eat, play the gramophone, prop our feet up on the side of the fire and read endless books." The house is filled with paintings by members of their circle, the Bloomsbury Group, as well as furniture painted by Virginia's sister, Vanessa Bell (1879-1961).

In 1941, Virginia walked from Monk's House to the nearby River Ouse, put stones in her pockets, and drowned herself. Her ashes are buried in the garden. Leonard remained at Monk's House until his death in 1969, and the house has been in the hands of the National Trust ever since. As a result, almost nothing has changed since these two literary giants of the 20th century inhabited its small rooms. Virginia wrote in a rustic structure at the far end of the garden known as the Lodge, where apples from the large orchard were stored throughout the winter. The orchard still bears fruit, and if you visit in the autumn, you can get into the spirit of Monk's House by picking some to take with you. ☉ 2 hr. Rodmell. ☎ 01323/870-001. www.nationaltrust.org.uk. Admission £4 adults, £2 kids under 16, £10 families. Early Apr-Oct Wed & Sat 2-5:30pm.

To reach Charleston from Monk's House, follow A27 back through Lewes and continue east another 7 miles. You'll see a turnoff to Charleston on the right side of the road, between the villages of Firle and Selmeston.

> *When the Bloomsbury Group wanted to decamp to the country, they came to Monk's House, home of author Virginia Woolf.*

7 ★★ **Charleston.** Virginia Woolf discovered this rambling old farmhouse in the 1920s and told her sister, the painter Vanessa Bell, "If you lived here you would make it absolutely divine." Vanessa, her husband, Clive Bell (1881-1964), and her friend and sometime lover Duncan Grant (1885-1978) took Virginia's advice and made Charleston their home until their deaths many years later. Vanessa and Duncan were both painters and decorative artists, and they created designs for many of the leading fabric and ceramics producers of the time. Their designs appear on upholstery, draperies, and tile work throughout the house. They also brought a personal style to Charleston by painting their distinctive geometric patterns on walls, window frames, mantelpieces, and just about every other surface. The sense of design extends to the small walled garden just outside Vanessa's bedroom, where the hedges, gravel pathways, pond, and statuary are distinctly Mediterranean in feel. Entry is by guided, one-hour tour (unguided on Sun), and the knowledgeable docents' tours take visitors through the dining room, bedrooms, sitting room, and studio. The

> *Wander the grounds at Hever Castle, and you'll find gardens inspired by classical and Italian architecture.*

Charleston Tour (Thurs–Fri in July–Aug) tells the story of Vanessa Bell, Duncan Grant, and their lives at the house; *Bloomsbury in Sussex* (Wed & Sat Apr–Oct) links the house with the Bloomsbury Group and is a nice complement to a tour of Monk's House, also open on these 2 days. The Friday tour (Apr–Oct) focuses on collecting or another aspect of life at Charleston. ⏱ 2 hr. Near Firle. ☎ 01323/811-265. www. charleston.org.uk. Admission £9 adults, £5 kids 6–16. Apr–June & Sept–Oct Wed–Sun 1–6pm; July–Aug Wed–Sat noon–6pm.

From Lewes, follow A26 north, then the B2026 east for about 15 miles to Hever Castle.

❽ ★★★ **kids Hever Castle.** Anne Boleyn, the second wife of Henry VIII, spent her childhood in this squat, stone fantasy of turrets and crenellations surrounded by a moat. Henry later gave the house to his fourth wife, Anne of Cleves, as part of the couple's divorce settlement, and by the early 20th century Hever had fallen into near ruin. In stepped William Waldorf Astor, heir to an American fur-trading fortune, who restored the castle, created the property's stunning classical and natural gardens, and built a mock Tudor village alongside the moat to house his staff. The Long Gallery and 13th-century Gatehouse reflect the castle's medieval history, while the drawing room, library, and other ground-floor rooms where William Astor fashioned his living quarters are lavishly furnished in exquisite early-20th-century taste. Hever remained in private hands until 1983 and was for many years the home of William Astor's son, John Jacob Astor (1886–1971), who served in the British Parliament, owned London's *The Times* newspaper, and was named the 1st Baron Astor of Hever in 1956; he and his wife, Violet Astor, are buried on the grounds.

Some 1,800 workers toiled for more than 4 years creating the castle's gardens, among the finest in England and ablaze in color from late winter well into the fall. The Italian Gardens contain a stunning collection of classical sculpture and surround a 14-hectare (35-acre) lake that a crew of 800 laborers dug out over a 2-year period. The Yew Maze and the Water Maze are especially popular with young visitors. ⏱ 2 hr. Hever, near Edenbridge. ☎ 01732/865-224. www.hevercastle.co.uk. Admission £14 adults, £12 seniors, £8 kids 5–15, £36 families. Mar Wed–Sun gardens 10:30am–4pm, castle noon–4pm; Apr–Oct daily gardens 10:30am–6pm, castle noon–6pm.

From Hever, follow the well-marked country lane (B2176) to the village of Penshurst. For a pleasant and scenic excursion, you can walk from Hever to Penshurst on well-maintained footpaths. From the gates of Hever it's about 1½ miles to Chiddingstone, a charming village of half-timbered houses, and from there another 3 miles onto Penshurst. Ask for directions since the network of paths can be confusing.

❾ ★★ **Penshurst Place.** This remarkably intact medieval manor house dates from the 13th century, and has been embellished many times since then. At the manor's heart is the stone-floored Baron's Hall, which has a chestnut-paneled ceiling, massive octagonal hearth, and minstrels' gallery, and is considered to be one of the finest interiors remaining from the Middle Ages. It is easy to imagine the servants and estate workers gathered around the fire and sleeping on mats on the floor. Many of the grander staterooms and the Long Gallery date from the 16th century, when King Edward VI (1537–53) presented the house to the Sidney family, who have lived at Penshurst ever since. Sir Philip Sidney (1554–86), soldier, courtier, poet, and personification of an Elizabethan gentleman, was born at Penshurst. The walled and terraced gardens are a gracious retreat from which to admire the solid stone exterior and battlements. ⏱ 1 hr. Penshurst. ☎ 01892/870-307. www. penshurstplace.co.uk. Admission £9.80 adults, £6.20 kids 5–16, £26 families. Mar Sat–Sun noon–4pm; Apr–Oct daily noon–4pm.

> *In its day, the impressive Penshurst, home to courtier and poet Sir Philip Sidney, attracted medieval literati such as Ben Jonson.*

HENRY VIII
1491–1547

▶ "Good King Harry" executed wife Anne Boleyn on trumped-up adultery charges (in order to secure himself a son with Jane Seymour); divorced Anne of Cleves (calling her "a cow"); and forced daughter Mary I to acknowledge herself a bastard (she wasn't), starting her down a path of serious neurosis.

▶ The "Defender of the Faith" dumped Rome and formed the Anglican Church (with himself, naturally, as Supreme Head) when the pope refused to grant him a divorce from Catherine of Aragon.

▶ Used the Reformation as an excuse for the Dissolution of the Monasteries and filled the depleted treasury (thanks to royally profligate spending) with assets seized from the Catholic Church.

MAD, BAD & DANGEROUS TO KNOW

A Few of Britain's Most Notorious Monarchs

BY NAOMI P. KRAUS

IT'S GOOD TO BE THE KING (OR QUEEN)—especially if you're a self-indulgent megalomaniac. The British monarchy has seen more than its fair share of tabloid-worthy behavior since as far back as the days of William the Conqueror. Take a close look at the rap sheet of some of the region's best-known rulers, and you'll find depressives and despots indulging in murder, mayhem, and outright madness (inherited and otherwise).

JOHN I
1166–1216

▶ The favored youngest son of Henry II inherited no land at his birth (earning the nickname John Lackland), so dad tried to make him king of Ireland; alas, John's fits of rage and cruelty led the Irish to rebel and throw him out.

▶ Unsuccessfully attempted to kill his father and overthrow his brother Richard the Lionheart; did, however, succeed in murdering nephew Arthur of Brittany.

▶ Heavily taxed the nobility to fight a series of dismally unsuccessful wars; they revolted and forced him to sign the Magna Carta, curtailing royal power.

RICHARD III
1452–85

▶ Likely murdered Henry VI on May 22, 1471, in order to ensure the ascendancy of the House of York under his brother Edward IV.

▶ Definitely usurped the throne of his nephew Edward V, and then (most historians think he's guilty) murdered Edward and his brother, the so-called "Princes of the Tower," in order to keep it.

"BLOODY" MARY TUDOR (MARY I)
1516–58

▶ Outraged England when she married Philip II, heir to the throne of archrival Spain; he promptly lost England's last Continental territories while sinking Mary's reputation.

▶ Determined to reunify England with the Roman Catholic Church, Mary burned more than 300 prominent Protestants (including the Archbishop of Canterbury) at the stake for heresy.

JAMES VI OF SCOTLAND (JAMES I OF ENGLAND)
1566–1625

▶ Obsessed with witchcraft, James wrote an anti-witchcraft guide, *Daemonologie*, and personally supervised the torture of suspected witches.

▶ An extravagant spender with a belief in his own divine right (and a serious sense of paranoia), James strongly suppressed religious dissension, promoted a host of inept (and costly) gay lovers at court, let his mother be executed without much protest, and was deemed by peers "the wisest fool in Christendom."

"MAD" GEORGE III
1738–1820

▶ "Farmer George's" preference for agriculture over politics helped spark the colonial unrest that led to the American Revolutionary War.

▶ Went mad due to hereditary porphyria (or possibly its treatment at the time—arsenic). At various times, he attacked son George IV, claimed Queen Charlotte was not his wife, declared himself dead, and once famously addressed his court as "my lords and peacocks."

Dover

Dover has been an important stronghold ever since the Roman occupation, facing the English Channel at a point where only 17 miles of sea lie between England and France. The Dover docks are England's main port for ferries and freighters to and from the Continent, and one of England's mightiest fortifications faces the Channel from atop the famous White Cliffs. Exploring Dover brings you face to face with a huge swath of English history, intriguing landmarks, and some magnificent views.

> *The mighty chalk cliffs around Dover are the first landmark visible from the deck of a ferry from France.*

START Dover Castle. Dover is 72 miles southeast of London.

SITE GUIDE PAGE 165

❶ ★★★ kids Dover Castle. Romans, medieval kings, and World War II troops all appreciated the strategic importance of this outpost high above the English Channel, one of England's most importance defenses for much of its 2,000-year history. In fact, Dover is known as the "Key to England," because an army that took it would have easy access to the rest of the island.

When France invaded England in 1216, London fell to Louis VIII, the French Dauphin, but Dover held out and became the marshalling point for the English troops that managed to overthrow the invaders. When Henry VIII feared a European invasion after his excommunication from the Catholic Church in 1539, he thought war with the Continent was inevitable and came to Dover for reassurance that the castle could keep invading navies at bay. When Britain evacuated 340,000 forces from Dunkirk in 1940 during the early stages of World War II, Dover

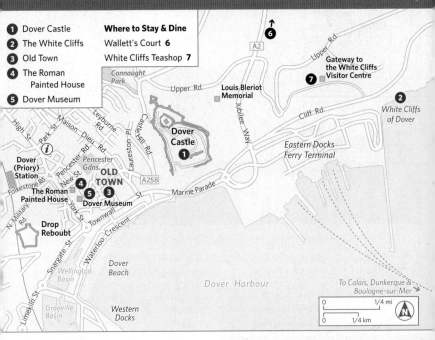

1. Dover Castle
2. The White Cliffs
3. Old Town
4. The Roman Painted House
5. Dover Museum

Where to Stay & Dine

Wallett's Court **6**

White Cliffs Teashop **7**

---

became the headquarters for the massive operation. As it turned out, it was determined during the Cold War years that the castle and the labyrinth of tunnels that ran beneath it could not provide protection against a nuclear blast, since radiation would seep through the underlying chalk soil. Even so, the 28-hectare (70-acre) castle enclosed within 2 miles of walls is a formidable sight.

2 ★★★ kids **The White Cliffs.** A trail that begins about a quarter of a mile north of the castle entrance follows the famed White Cliffs of Dover for about 2.5 miles. The cliffs are the closest point in Britain to the coast of Continental Europe, just 17 miles across the Strait of Dover. Keen-eyed observers can see the gleaming white cliffs from the French coast on a clear day, and many travelers crossing the Channel over the centuries have gazed sentimentally upon the cliffs as their first or last sight of Britain. The National Trust's **clifftop walk** provides encounters with the many species of birds that inhabit the cliffs, heady doses of bracing sea air, and stunning views of the busy shipping lanes in the Channel below and the mighty castle at the edge of the cliffs. Another clifftop landmark is the **South**

> *The first shore-to-ship radio transmission was broadcast from South Foreland Lighthouse.*

Foreland Lighthouse, from which Guglielmo Marconi (1874–1937) made his first shore-to-ship radio transmissions in 1898. ⏱ 1 hr. Lighthouse: Admission £2 adults, £1 kids under 16, £5 families. Mar–June Thurs–Mon 11am–5:30pm; July–Aug daily 11am–5:30pm.

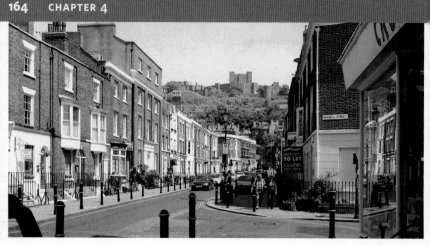

> *Despite extensive bombing damage to the city during World War II, Dover still has some quaint corners.*

❸ ★ Old Town. Dover was more or less blown to smithereens during World War II, and rebuilding was geared more to efficiency than beauty. A few old landmarks remain in the small city center. The **Maison Dieu,** in the Town Hall complex, Biggin St. (open only some Sun and select days during summer), was built in 1221 as a hostel for pilgrims traveling from the Continent to Canterbury.

❹ ★ The Roman Painted House. This lodging built around A.D. 200 for Roman officials traveling across the Channel is decorated with colorful frescoes and equipped with an underground heating system. ⏱ 30 min. New St. ☎ 01304/203-279. Admission £3 adults, £2 seniors & kids. Tues–Sat May 10am–5pm (June to mid-Sept also Sun 1–5pm).

❺ ★★ Dover Museum. A 3,000-year-old wooden boat on display here is the world's oldest seagoing vessel. The craft, of which about 9m (30 ft.) of the original 13.7m-length (45-ft.) remains, was probably used to ferry cargo, livestock, and passengers across the Channel and was discovered during road work between Dover and Folkestone in 1992. ⏱ 30 min. Market Sq. ☎ 01304/201-066. www.doverdc.co.uk/museum. Admission £3 adults, £2 seniors & kids. Mon–Sat 10am–5:30pm Sept–Mar. (Apr–Aug also Sun noon–5pm).

Staying the Night near Dover

A manor house that dates to the Norman Conquest, at the edge of the White Cliffs about 10 miles outside Dover, ★★★ **Wallett's Court** is a distinctive and comfortable base for exploring the region. Stylish rooms are in the manor house and converted barns, and the in-house restaurant is excellent and serves delicious and fresh local seafood. Westcliffe, St. Margaret's-at-Cliffe. ☎ 01304/852-424. www.wallettscourthotelspa.com. Doubles £120–£140. AE, MC, DC.

★ **White Cliffs Teashop,** in a handsome glass pavilion at the entrance to the National Trust's White Cliffs walk (p. 163, ❷), is a delightful place for a simple snack or light meal. Sandwiches, a few hot dishes, desserts, and beverages can be enjoyed in the airy dining room or on the terrace. White Cliff Visitors Centre. ☎ 01304/202-754. Most items £4–£8. DC, MC, V. Lunch & afternoon tea daily.

Dover from the Water

Boat tours through **Dover White Cliff Tours** (☎ 01303/271-388; www.doverwhiteclifftours.com) provide a dramatic view of the castle and the White Cliffs, along with a look at the extensive docks of Britain's busiest Channel port. Tours leave from the western end of Dover promenade and cost £8 for adults, £4 for kids, and £20 for families. Tours run daily in summer at noon, 2pm, and 4pm.

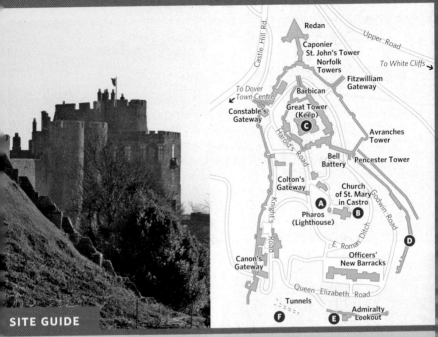

Redan
Upper Road
Caponier
St. John's Tower
Norfolk
Towers
To White Cliffs →
Fitzwilliam
Gateway
Barbican
To Dover
Town Centre ←
Constable's
Gateway
Great Tower
(Keep)
C
Avranches
Tower
Harold's Road
Bell
Battery
Pencester Tower
Colton's
Gateway
Church
of St. Mary
in Castro
A
B
Godwin Road
Pharos
(Lighthouse)
Knight's Road
E. Roman Ditch
D
Officers'
New Barracks
Canon's
Gateway
Queen Elizabeth Road
Tunnels
F
Admiralty
Lookout
E

SITE GUIDE

1 Dover Castle

On the highest point of the castle grounds, a stone **A** *pharos* (lighthouse), one of two the Romans built to guide their ships across the Channel, still stands next to the humble **B Church of St. Mary in Castro,** a remnant of a fortified Saxon settlement from around 600. The **C Great Tower** or Keep, 25m (83 ft.) tall with walls 6.5m (21 ft.) thick, is the work of Henry II. Between 1160 and 1180, Henry and his architect, Maurice the Engineer, transformed the stockade of timbers and earthworks commissioned by William the Conqueror shortly after his victory in 1066 into one of Europe's mightiest fortresses. In addition to its military importance, the Keep was a palace where Henry could entertain guests in the Great Hall. Many were pilgrims traveling to the shrine of St. Thomas Becket in Canterbury, who was slaughtered by Henry's knights in 1170. A repentant Henry built a chapel to Becket within the Keep. He also reinforced the circuit of **D walls** that enclose the compound, adding many of the defensive towers. As you walk the walls, at **E Admiralty Lookout** and other viewpoints high above the

Channel, you can appreciate the castle's strategic importance. The walls were fortified again during the Napoleonic Wars of the late 18th century, and a network of **F tunnels** (pictured above)was dug to house as many as 2,000 troops. The tunnels came into use again during World War II, when they served as a military command center, a hub to facilitate communication with ships in the Strait of Dover, a hospital, and a virtually unassailable bomb shelter. ⏱ Half-day. Eastern edge of Dover, atop the White Cliffs. ☎ 01304/201-628; www.english-heritage.org.uk. Admission £16 adults, £14.40 seniors, £9.60 kids, £41.60 families. Daily 10am–6pm (Oct until 5pm; Nov–Mar until 4pm).

Canterbury

Pilgrims have made their way across the fields and orchards of Kent to Canterbury for centuries, setting their sights on Bell Harry, the famous bell tower of Canterbury Cathedral. The great cathedral began to rise in 1070, knights of Henry II murdered Archbishop of Canterbury Thomas Becket 100 years later, and pilgrims were soon flooding the town to pay homage at Becket's shrine, as Chaucer so famously recounted in his 14th-century *Canterbury Tales*. Long before that, St. Augustine made Canterbury a famous center of learning when he founded a monastery in the 6th century to spread Christianity. You'll encounter all this fascinating history as you follow in the pilgrims' footsteps through this delightful medieval city.

> *The Gothic cathedral gate has been worked on over the centuries by generations of master stonemasons.*

START West Gate, in town walls. Canterbury is 60 miles southeast of London.

❶ ★ West Gate. At the city walls, the road to and from London becomes St. Peter's Street, crosses the River Stour, and enters the city beneath this 600-year-old gate under which hundreds of thousands of medieval pilgrims passed on their way to visit Thomas Becket's shrine. A spiral access stair leads up to the battlements for a panoramic view of the city and its cathedral. Next to the gate, beautiful gardens line the banks of the River Stour. ⏱ 15 min. Tower: Admission £1.30 adults, £.80 seniors & students, £3 families. Mon–Sat 11am–12:30pm & 1:30–3:30pm.

❷ ★ Eastbridge Hospital. Medieval pilgrims visiting the shrine of Thomas Becket were offered straw mats in the undercroft of these hospitable surroundings. Amenities were minimal, but the pilgrims were treated to services in the Pilgrim's Chapel and a meal in a refectory decorated with murals, a few fragments of which remain. ⏱ 15 min. High St. ☎ 01227/471-688. Admission £1 adults, £.75 kids & seniors. Mon–Sat 10am–4:45pm.

SITE GUIDE PAGE 169

❸ ★★★ kids Canterbury Cathedral. The origins of this massive and magnificent structure date back to A.D. 597, when St. Augustine arrived in Canterbury from Rome and was the first to assume the title Archbishop of Canterbury.

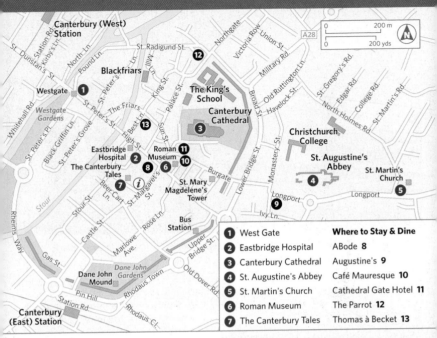

		Where to Stay & Dine
1	West Gate	ABode **8**
2	Eastbridge Hospital	Augustine's **9**
3	Canterbury Cathedral	Café Mauresque **10**
4	St. Augustine's Abbey	Cathedral Gate Hotel **11**
5	St. Martin's Church	The Parrot **12**
6	Roman Museum	Thomas à Becket **13**
7	The Canterbury Tales	

He founded what has come to be known as St. Augustine's Abbey (p. 168, **4**) and established a church on the site of today's soaring monument, begun in 1070 and the first cathedral in England to be built in the Gothic style. The massive building, constructed of soft gray stone from French quarries, is bathed in gentle light from the magnificent medieval

Markets in Canterbury

At the **Canterbury Goods Shed Daily Farmers Market** (www.thegoodsshed. net), farmers and other local suppliers sell produce and an enticing range of breads and cakes, local meats, and seafood. It's in the refurbished Victorian goods shed just outside Canterbury West train station (Tues–Sat 9am–7pm, Sun 10am–4pm). An adjacent restaurant, the **Goods Shed** (01227/459-153; lunch & dinner Tues–Fri, lunch Sun), serves a menu that changes twice daily to reflect the best seasonal fare available at the market. A market selling general goods, from clothes to baked goods, winds through the city center Wednesday and Friday, 8am to 4pm.

> *Pilgrims visiting the shrine of murdered archbishop Thomas Becket slept overnight at the Eastbridge Hospital.*

> *St. Augustine of Canterbury founded the monastery here and was Canterbury's first archbishop.*

Canterbury Tours

Guided walks of the city (☎ 01227/459-779; www.canterbury-walks.co.uk) leave from the Tourist Information Centre on Sun Street and explore the cathedral precincts, medieval lanes, weavers' houses, St. Augustine's Abbey, and other landmarks. The cost is £6 adults, £5.50 seniors and students, £4.25 kids under 12, and £16 families. Tours run June to September daily at 11:30am and 2pm, and in other months daily at 2pm.

Canterbury Historic River Tours (☎ 07790/534-744; www.canterburyrivertours.co.uk) provides half-hour boat trips on the River Stour with commentary on the history of the buildings you pass. Tours leave from the Weaver's House, 1 St. Peter's St., and cost £7.50 adults, £6.50 seniors and students, £5 kids 12 to 16, and £4.50 kids under 12. Tours run April to October, river conditions permitting, every 15 or 20 minutes from 10am to 5pm.

The **Canterbury River Navigation Company** (☎ 01227/760-869; www.crnc.co.uk) offers punt trips along the River Stour, including an hour-long punt showing off the city sights. Trips leave from Westgate Gardens and cost £14 adults, £6 kids. Tours run Easter to late September or early October, weather permitting.

stained-glass windows that depict the miracles of Christ. Enormous bells ring out the time from a central bell tower (nicknamed Bell Harry for Prior Henry of Eastry, who oversaw its completion in 1510) that for centuries has guided pilgrims across the Kent countryside to Canterbury.

The cathedral is most famously associated with Saint Thomas Becket, murdered in the cathedral in 1170 by knights of Henry II when they heard their king cry, "Who will rid me of this meddlesome priest?"—not an execution order, the penitent king later claimed, but frustration over Becket's fierce defense of the Church against encroachment by the State.

❹ ★★★ St. Augustine's Abbey. St. Augustine (not to be confused with the Church Father St. Augustine of Hippo, who wrote the *Confessions*) founded a monastic community here in A.D. 597, when he was sent from Rome to England to spread Christianity. The community flourished, and by 1500 the abbey was one of Europe's great centers of learning, with a scriptorium and 2,000-volume library. Henry VIII ordered the destruction of the abbey when he broke with the Church in the mid-16th century and commissioned a palace to be built on the grounds as a gift for Anne of Cleves, arriving from France to become his fourth wife. (The marriage was short-lived and soon annulled; Anne was given Hever Castle (p. 158, ❽) as part of her settlement). The

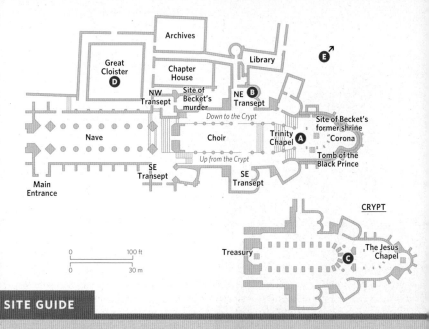

SITE GUIDE

③ Canterbury Cathedral

Thomas Becket was canonized three years after his death, and pilgrims from all over Europe came to Canterbury to pay homage to the fallen martyr (their offerings paying for the cathedral's upkeep). The cathedral is today, as it has been for centuries, the seat of the Archbishop of Canterbury and the mother church of Anglicanism. The stone floor where Becket's shrine once stood in the **A Trinity Chapel,** at the end of the longest choir in Europe, is worn with the grooves made by pilgrims crawling past on their knees. Even in death Becket ran afoul of another king, Henry VIII, who had the shrine destroyed in his campaign to diminish the power of the Church. Puritans ransacked the church during the English Civil War in the 1640s and destroyed the vibrant paintings that once covered the walls, sparing a **B fragment** that depicts St. Paul and the viper in the northeast corner. The cathedral houses the medieval royal tombs of Henry IV (1367–1413) and Edward, the Black Prince (1330–76), but most stirring is the **C crypt,** supported by columns embellished with a beautiful bestiary, where Becket is buried; as penance for killing the priest, Henry walked

through the streets of Canterbury as 80 cathedral monks flogged him and then spent the night on the floor of the crypt next to Becket's tomb. A vast and beautiful **D cloister** lies just beyond the northwest transept, and within the close is **E The King's School,** the oldest public school in England founded by Henry VIII in a 7th-century monastery; dramatist and poet Christopher Marlowe (1564–93), the novelist and short story writer Somerset Maugham (1874–1965), and many other noted Britons were educated at King's. ⏱ 2 hr. The Precincts. ☎ 01227/762-862. www.canterbury-cathedral. org. Admission for those not attending a service £9 adults, £8 seniors, £6 kids 17 & under. Daily Mar–Oct 9am–5pm (Nov–Feb until 4:30pm).

> A little Disney-esque but entertaining, the ani-matronic exhibit at the Canterbury Tales brings Chaucer's Middle English manuscript to life.

⑤ ★ St. Martin's Church. The oldest parish church in England in continuous use was already in existence when Augustine arrived from Rome to convert the Anglo-Saxon natives. The tiny church is built partly of Roman bricks and tiles and is named for the Bishop of Tours; it was presented to Queen Bertha (539–612), the French (Christian) wife of (pagan) 6th-century Saxon King Ethelbert of Kent (560–616), as part of her marriage contract. The church, along with Canterbury Cathedral and St. Augustine's Abbey, is a designated World Heritage Site. ⏱ 15 min. North Holmes Rd. ☎ 01227/768-072. Free admission. Mon–Wed 10am–noon & services Sun.

⑥ ★ kids Roman Museum. Romans lived in Canterbury for almost 400 years. They established the town of Durovernum Cantiacorum as the legions of the Emperor Claudius (10 B.C.–A.D. 54) began to fan out across southeast England in A.D. 43. Their daily lives are chronicled in a working archaeological site of the Roman city beneath street level near the cathedral. On view are excavations of a Roman house, reconstructions of the marketplace, video presentations, and mosaics and other artifacts. ⏱ 45 min. Butchery Lane. ☎ 01227/785-575. Admission £3.10 adults; £2.10 seniors, students & kids; £8 families. Nov–May Mon–Sat 10am–4pm (June–Oct also Sun 1:30–4pm).

⑦ ★ kids The Canterbury Tales. The medieval Church of St. Margaret is now filled with scenes from Geoffrey Chaucer's spirited and sometimes bawdy stories about a group of medieval pilgrims on their way to visit Becket's shrine at Canterbury Cathedral. Animatronic figures bring the lusty Wife of Bath, the chivalrous Knight, uncouth Miller, and several other pilgrims to life in a series of well-executed tableaux, accompanied by an animated audio tour that retells the tales and presents the historical context of the pilgrimage to Canterbury. The theatrics are informative and entertaining, but visitors who prefer to absorb history by the touch of old stone might choose to spend their time exploring the cathedral and other medieval monuments just outside the door. ⏱ 1 hr. 23 St. Margaret's St. ☎ 01227/454-888. www.canterburytales.org.uk. Admission £7.75 adults, £6.75 seniors & students, £5.75 kids 5–15. Daily July–Aug 9:30am–5pm; Sept–Oct & Mar–June 10am–5pm; Nov–Feb 10am–4:30pm.

extensive ruins of the abbey church, which once rivaled the cathedral in size, as well as the cloister, refectory, and Tudor palace, are set within a spacious park. An intelligent audio tour offers insights into the extensive and complex history of the place, and carvings and other remains from the abbey are housed in a small museum onsite. ⏱ 45 min. Lower Chantry Lane & Longport Rd. ☎ 01227/767-345. www.english-heritage.org.uk. Admission £4.50 adults, £3.80 seniors & students, £2.30 kids under 16. Apr–June Wed–Sun 10am–5pm; July–Aug daily 10am–6pm; Sept–Mar Sun 11am–5pm.

Where to Stay & Dine

★★ ABode CITY CENTER
A complete renovation has infused the comfy old 17th-century County Hotel with contemporary chic. Guest rooms are attractive and comfortable, with hand-crafted furnishings and state-of-the-art bathrooms. The newly revamped public rooms include a snug tavern, a bar-lounge facing High Street through leaded windows, and the excellent **Michael Caines** restaurant. High St. ☎ 01227/766-266. www.abodehotels.co.uk. 72 units. Doubles £100–£170. AE, DC, MC, V.

★★★ Augustine's CITY CENTER *MODERN BRITISH*
A Georgian building just outside the gates of St. Augustine's Abbey houses an informal restaurant where innovative dishes using fresh, local ingredients are served in an atmosphere of wood-plank floors, blond furnishings, and homey earth hues. 1 & 2 Longport. ☎ 01227/453-063. Entrees £12–£25. MC, V. Lunch & dinner Tues–Sat, lunch Sun. Closed Jan.

★ Café Mauresque CITY CENTER *MOROCCAN*
An escape to the exotic provides a nice break from the quaint medievaldom that pervades much of Canterbury. Couscous and tapas are served amid Moroccan tiles and furnishings, atmospherically candlelit. 8 Butchery Lane. ☎ 01227/464-300. Entrees £9–£13. MC, V. Lunch & dinner daily.

★★ Cathedral Gate Hotel CITY CENTER
You might feel like a pilgrim of yore as you bed down in the shadows of the cathedral in this homey inn from 1438. Sloping floors, massive oak beams, and winding corridors add plenty of historic ambience. With the cheapest rooms, you'll be sharing a bathroom. 36 Burgate. ☎ 01227/464-381. www.cathgate.co.uk. 25 units. Doubles w/o bathroom £60–£72 w/ breakfast, doubles w/bathroom £100 w/breakfast. AE, DC, MC, V.

★★ The Parrot CITY CENTER *PUB FARE*
The oldest pub in Canterbury occupies one of the oldest structures in town, built in 1370 on Roman foundations. A large selection of local beers and ales accompany fish and chips, steak and ale pie, and other homey fare served in a series of fire-warmed rooms and a garden.

> *The Cathedral Gate Hotel, almost 600 years old and still offering great value in the city center.*

1–9 Church Lane. ☎ 01227/762-355. Entrees £4.50–£7.50. MC, V. Lunch & dinner daily.

★★ Thomas à Becket CITY CENTER *PUB FARE*
This cozy beamed room is a popular local gathering spot and a fine place to enjoy a pint and some nicely prepared traditional English fare, such as lamb shank, bacon and liver casserole, or lamb and apple pie. 21 Best Lane. ☎ 01227/464-383. Entrees £5–£9. AE, DC, MC, V. Lunch & dinner daily.

Brighton

Brighton has been one of England's most famous seaside getaways ever since fun-loving King George IV had the Royal Pavilion built in the 1820s, when he was still the Prince Regent. A fashionable set followed and took up residency in the white Regency houses that are still a gleaming presence next to the sea. Victorians came for the sea air, and the world-weary and fun-seeking have set their sights on Brighton ever since. An amusement pier, miles of sandy beaches (London's nearest sea experience), George's exotic palace, medieval lanes lined with shops, and a sizable gay and lesbian presence are among this seaside Babylon's many attractions.

> *Brighton's half-mile-long pier is packed with attractions for the kids.*

START Brighton Pier. Brighton is 52 miles south of London.

1 ★★ **kids** **Brighton Pier.** Brighton's most famous attraction reaches ⅓ of a mile into the English Channel—a long, garish swath of arcades, shops, and amusement rides. The biggest thrill of all is stopping about two-thirds of the way out, where the neon-lit arcades come to an end and the pier is open on both sides to the sea. Here you can turn your back on all the noise and lights, take in a deep breath of sea air, and look up and down the coast. ⏱ 1 hr. Seafront. Free admission; charges vary for games and rides. Daily 10am–midnight.

2 ★★★ **kids** **Royal Pavilion.** George IV, womanizing, gambling, heavy-drinking Prince Regent and son of the insane George III, let his tastes run wild when he asked the architect John

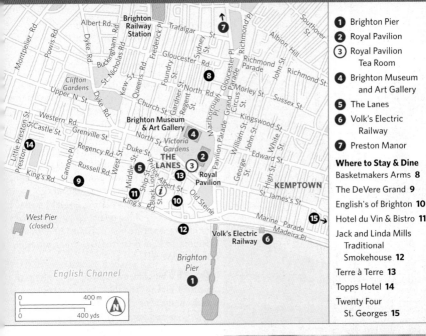

1. Brighton Pier
2. Royal Pavilion
3. Royal Pavilion Tea Room
4. Brighton Museum and Art Gallery
5. The Lanes
6. Volk's Electric Railway
7. Preston Manor

Where to Stay & Dine

Basketmakers Arms **8**

The DeVere Grand **9**

English's of Brighton **10**

Hotel du Vin & Bistro **11**

Jack and Linda Mills Traditional Smokehouse **12**

Terre à Terre **13**

Topps Hotel **14**

Twenty Four St. Georges **15**

Nash to build this palace in the early 19th century. With a profusion of onion domes and minarets, the palace looks like it belongs in a palm-shaded garden in India rather than in Brighton. The interior is just as exotic, filled with chinoiserie, carvings of dragons and other whimsical creatures, and masses of Regency furniture and fine china and crystal. The music room is especially ornate, a fantasy of red wall paintings depicting Chinese scenes beneath a domed ceiling encrusted with gilded shells; and the royal apartments where George lived with his mistress, Lady Conyngham, are awash in gilt and velvet. Even the kitchen is exotic, with a high ceiling supported by sculptural palm trees. Queen Victoria thought the palace was vulgar and sold it for £1 in 1850 to the city of Brighton, which in recent years has taken great care to restore the structure to its former splendor. The adjoining Dome, built at the same time as the palace as a riding school and stables, is now home to the Brighton Philharmonic Orchestra. ⏱ 1 hr. Pavilion Parade. ☎ 01273/290-900. www.royalpavilion.org.uk. Admission £9.80 adults, £7.80 seniors & students, £5.60 kids 5–15, £15–£25.40 families. Daily Apr–Sept 9:30am–5:45pm; Oct–Mar 10am–5:15pm.

> Architect John Nash, best known for his restrained Regency London terraces, really let rip with the Royal Pavilion.

> *The Lanes and North Laine are where you'll find Brighton's quirkiest and best shopping.*

③ 🍽 **Royal Pavilion Tea Room.** In a sunny room with a balcony overlooking the Pavilion gardens you can enjoy Regency snacks (which include spiced lamb with chutney and deviled kidneys). Sandwiches and cakes are also available. In the Royal Pavilion. ☎ 01273/290-900. www.royalpavilion.org.uk. Items £5–£15.

❹ ★ **Brighton Museum and Art Gallery.** King George's elaborate stables to one side of the gardens surrounding the Royal Pavilion now house an eclectic and engaging collection of Art Deco furniture, Lalique figurines, and period costumes, including regal attire from George's coronation. Many of the items were purchased by Henry Willett, a 19th-century Brighton brewer and social reformer. ⏱ 1 hr. Royal Pavilion Gardens. ☎ 03000/290-900. www.brighton-hove-rpml.org.uk. Free admission. Tues–Sun 10am–5pm.

❺ ★★ **The Lanes.** A quarter of twisting alleyways just off the seafront is the remnant of the days when Brighton was a small fishing village. The name refers not to the small streets but to the fishing lines the residents used to lay out along the cobblestones to dry. In fact, many of the streets in the old quarter are not lanes at all, but "catcreeps" and "twittens" (a catcreep is a flight of stairs connecting one lane to another; a twitten is a narrow, alleylike passageway). Many of the quaint houses on these various byways are now occupied by antique dealers. ⏱ 30 min. Off the waterfront, btw. Old Steine & West sts.

❻ ★ 🧒 **Volk's Electric Railway.** Britain's first electric railway (and the world's first operational public electric railway) has been hauling passengers up and down the Brighton seafront in open-air cars since 1883. Volk also outlined the Brighton Pavilion in electric lights, and the spectacle can still be witnessed nightly. ⏱ 30 min. www.whitstablepier.com/volks. For full route from Aquarium to Black Rock: £1.80 one-way, £2.80 round-trip adults; 80p one-way, £1.40 round-trip kids 13 & under. Trains run Easter–Sept Mon–Fri 11am–5pm, Sat–Sun until 6pm.

From the train station and elsewhere in the town center, take bus no. 5 to Preston Manor.

❼ ★★ **Preston Manor.** This handsome residence, built in 1738 on medieval foundations and extensively enlarged in 1903, reflects the style and tastes of the Edwardian era, with furniture, paintings, and table settings in place as they were a hundred years ago. The entire house is open to visitors, from the basement kitchens to the attic nurseries, so you get a glimpse at how an upper-class Edwardian family would have lived; you might feel you've stepped onto the set of *Upstairs, Downstairs*. ⏱ 1 hr. Preston Drove, 2 miles north of the city center. 03000/290-900. www.brighton-hove-rpml.org.uk. Admission £5.50 adults, £4.50 seniors, £3.10 kids under 16, £8.60–£14.10 families. Apr–Sept Tues–Sat 10:15am–4:15pm (45-min. escorted tours begin every 15 min.).

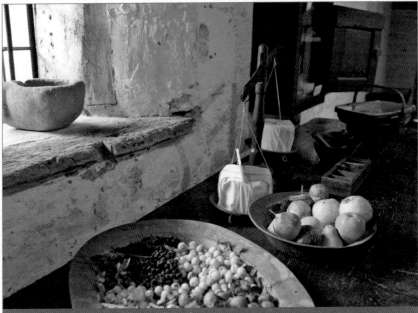

A Side Trip to Lewes: Town of Zealots

This quiet country seat of medieval lanes and handsome brick Georgian houses has a reputation for rebellion. When "Bloody" Queen Mary I (reigned 1553–58) tried to reinstate Catholicism to England after her father, Henry VIII, broke from the Church, Lewes remained Protestant and 17 citizens were burned at the stake. The town takes revenge every November 5 with England's most boisterous celebration commemorating the thwarting of Guy Fawkes, the Roman Catholic rebel who tried to blow up Parliament for its unjust treatment of Catholics under James I (reigned 1603–25).

Ruined, hilltop **Lewes Castle,** High St. (www.sussexpast.co.uk; £6 adults, £3 kids 5–15, £16 families), dates to the days of the Norman Conquest and was built to secure William the Conqueror's stronghold in Sussex. You'll understand the strategic value of the hilltop when you look across the Sussex Downs from the ramparts. From the castle, it is a steep downhill walk of about 10 minutes to the **Anne of Cleves House** (pictured above), Southover High St. (☎ 01273/405-732; www. sussexpast.co.uk; £4.20 adults, £2.10 kids 5–15, £11 families), a modest half-timbered cottage that Henry VIII presented to his fourth queen when he amicably divorced her in 1541. Discounted tickets are available if you visit both sites.

As you wander around Lewes, step into the dark, beamed bar room of the **White Hart Hotel,** 55 High St. (☎ 01273/476-694; items £4–£8), for a pint and a bit of history—American patriot Thomas Paine (1736–1809), who argued for American independence in his pamphlet *Common Sense,* used to debate politics here. Half-timbered Bull House on High Street was once his home. If possible, you may want to time your visit to coincide with a performance at **Glyndebourne** (☎ 01273/813-813; www.glyndebourne.com). The glass and steel opera house outside Lewes is the setting for the six operatic performances of the annual **Glyndebourne Festival,** one of England's most highly acclaimed musical events. Performances bring droves of formally attired aficionados to Glyndebourne, 2 miles east of Lewes, from May to August. You would do well to order tickets far in advance.

Lewes is 8 miles northeast of Brighton. Trains run about every 10 minutes throughout the day; if you prefer to drive, you can get there by car in less than 15 minutes on the A27.

Where to Stay & Dine

> The bar at Brighton's Hotel du Vin.

★ **Basketmakers Arms** THE LANES *PUB FARE*
A wander through the Lanes will bring you to this atmospheric old pub, where beams, posts, and walls are crammed with prints and photos. Many locals say the selection of real ales and the fish and chips are the best in town; the steak sandwiches and other pub grub are well done, too. 39 Cheltenham Pl. ☎ 01273/689-006. Entrees £5–£9. MC, V. Lunch & dinner daily.

★★★ **The DeVere Grand** SEAFRONT
A gleaming white presence on the seafront since 1864 is still the grandest hostelry in town, and one of the finest in England. Gorgeous guest rooms are enormous, and the many amenities include an indoor swimming pool. Kings Rd. ☎ 01273/224-300. www.devere. co.uk. 200 units. Doubles £130–£300 w/ breakfast. AE, DC, MC, V.

★★ **English's of Brighton** THE LANES *SEAFOOD*
One of England's most venerable seafood houses occupies three fishermen's cottages in the Lanes. Dining is out front in good weather, but a meal on the plush banquettes in the cramped dining room is a memorable experience. Oysters and Dover sole, prepared seven different ways, top the extensive menu. 29-31 East St. ☎ 01273/327-980. www.englishs. co.uk. Entrees £15–£30. AE, MC, V. Lunch & dinner daily.

★★★ **Hotel du Vin & Bistro** THE LANES
This member of a group of distinctive inns around Britain occupies Gothic revival buildings just off the seafront in the Lanes. Stylish and supremely comfortable rooms are equipped with deep soaking tubs and other luxuries, and downstairs in paneled and beamed salons are an excellent bistro and a wine bar that opens onto a delightful patio. Ship St. ☎ 01273/718-588. www.hotelduvin. com. 49 units. Doubles £145–£250 w/breakfast. AE, DC, MC, V.

★ **Jack and Linda Mills Traditional Smokehouse** SEAFRONT *SEAFOOD* Fresh seafood is smoked, grilled, and fried in the arches under the seaside promenade. You can buy smoked fish to take with you, or order a hot mackerel or crab sandwich or cup of fish soup and enjoy it at one of the outdoor tables. 167 King's Arches. No phone. Entrees £3–£6. Cash only. Lunch daily.

★★★ **Terre à Terre** CITY CENTER *VEGETARIAN*
Many diners come to Brighton primarily to enjoy a meal in this bright restaurant with rough-hewn floors and blond furnishings. The offerings are exclusively vegetarian, widely regarded as some of the finest such fare in Britain. The Terre à Tapas is an excellent introduction to what the kitchen can do. 73 East St. ☎ 01273/729-051. www.terreaterre. co.uk. Entrees £12–£15. MC, V. Lunch & dinner Tues-Sun.

★★ **Topps Hotel** CITY CENTER

Two adjoining houses on a Regency crescent near the sea offer commodious, high-ceilinged accommodations. Many face the sea, and all are done up handsomely, with handcrafted bedsteads, polished wood floors, and cushy reading chairs and other comforts. Many of the large, windowed bathrooms have soaking tubs and rocking chairs. 17 Regency Sq. ☎ 01273/729-334. www.toppshotel.com. 14 units. Doubles £125–£150 w/breakfast. AE, DC, MC, V.

★★ **Twenty Four St. Georges** CITY CENTER

MODERN BRITISH Brighton's lively Kemp Town neighborhood is the setting for an excellent meal in simple yet chic surroundings. The emphasis is on Sussex lamb, fresh fish, and other local bounty, beautifully prepared and nicely presented without a hint of pretense. 24-25 St. Georges Rd. ☎ 01273/626-060. www.24stgeorges.co.uk. Entrees £10–£18. MC, V. Lunch Tues-Sun; dinner Sat.

> The Victorian DeVere Grand is a star of the Brighton seafront.

Brighton at Night

Brighton has a well-deserved reputation for fun, with venues that range from pubs to stages. *What's On*, a magazine distributed for free around town, will keep you up to date on what's happening. Brighton's large gay and lesbian community is outshone only by the scene in London; *G-Scene* magazine, free around town, keeps up with gay clubs and events.

The well regarded **Theatre Royal,** New Rd. (☎ 01273/328-488; www.ambassador tickets.com), hosts traveling companies for short runs and London-bound shows doing tryouts. Almost every British actor of note has performed on the stage of this multi-tiered, Regency playhouse. **The Dome,** Pavilion Buildings, Castle Square (☎ 01273/ 290-131; www.brightondome.org), occupies part of George IV's stable block and retains the Art Deco interior of a 1935 revamping; the hall is home to the Brighton Philharmonic

and hosts many visiting classical and popular artists and companies.

One of the liveliest nightlife scenes outside of London includes **Cricketer's,** Black Lion St. (☎ 01273/329-472), Brighton's oldest pub, founded in 1549, and still one of its most popular. **Oceana Brighton,** West St. (☎ 01273/732-627), is the city's big dance venue for straight clientele, with several floors and Europe's largest illuminated dance floor.

Gay Brighton is concentrated east of St. James Street. **Legends,** 31-32 Marine Parade (☎ 01273/624-462), in the gay-friendly hotel of the same name, was the first gay bar in town and hosts much-attended cabaret shows. **Club Revenge,** 32-34 Old Steine (☎ 01273/606-064), spreads over two floors and seems to draw every gay visitor to Brighton, and **Marlborough,** 4 Princes St. (☎ 01273/570-028), is a traditional pub popular with lesbians.

Rye & Battle

For many centuries this lovely town on the Sussex coast fended off pirates and invading navies and harbored smugglers and fishing fleets. Even though Rye's prominence as a seaport ended when the harbor began silting up in the 15th century, the old cobblestone lanes reflect this maritime past, and few English towns are more picturesque or more inviting to explore. Rye is also within easy reach of Battle, scene of the most decisive event in British history, the Battle of Hastings in 1066.

> Rye's St. Mary's Church is closing in on its 1,000th birthday, though its lovely stained-glass windows are a 19th-century addition.

START Lamb House. Rye is 60 miles southeast of London.

❶ ★★ Lamb House. One of the finest homes in Rye became celebrated almost as soon as it was completed for James Lamb, mayor of Rye, in 1723, when a storm forced King George I to come ashore and take shelter. Henry James (1843–1916), the expatriate American novelist, lived in Lamb House from 1898 to 1916 and wrote *The Golden Bowl, The Wings of the Dove,* and *The Ambassadors* while living here. H.G. Wells, Rudyard Kipling, and Edith Wharton

were among his many distinguished guests. Some of the paneled rooms are still filled with his belongings, and his beloved walled garden is much as he left it. Novelist and humorist E.F. Benson (1867–1940) took up residence in Lamb House in 1918 and remained until his death in 1940. He set his humorous Mapp and Lucia novels in Rye, which appears as the fictional town of Tilling, and the house figures prominently. ⏱ 1 hr. Admission £4 adults, £2.10 kids, £10 families. Mid-Mar to late Oct Thurs & Sat 2–6pm.

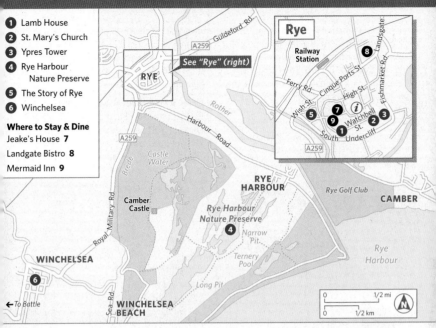

1 Lamb House
2 St. Mary's Church
3 Ypres Tower
4 Rye Harbour
   Nature Preserve
5 The Story of Rye
6 Winchelsea

Where to Stay & Dine
Jeake's House 7
Landgate Bistro 8
Mermaid Inn 9

2 ★ St. Mary's Church. For almost 900 years, pirate attacks, fires, and the other ups and downs of Rye's colorful history have swirled around this solid church, standing on the highest point of land in town. French looters took the bells off to France in 1377, but a rescue party from Rye retrieved them a year later. The giant bells continue to toll the hour, but a more recent set, the Quarter Boys, chime every quarter hour and are a boisterous presence in Rye. An enormous 1561 pendulum clock on the turret is said to be the oldest in England that still works and is said to have inspired the nursery rhyme "Hickory Dickory Dock." The stained-glass windows are relatively recent and include one by Sir Edward Burne-Jones (1833–98), the pre-Raphaelite painter. A climb to the tower is rewarded with views across the salt marshes that surround Rye to the sea. ⏱ 30 min. Church St. ☎ 01797/224-935. Admission £2 adults, £1 kids. Daily 9am–6pm (Sept–May until 4pm).

3 ★ Ypres Tower. Built in 1249 and known locally as "Wipers," the survivor of numerous attacks over the centuries is what remains of Rye Castle. Over the years the tower has served as a fortification, a residence (the tower is named for its 15th-century inhabitant

> Ypres Tower is all that remains of Rye's once mighty castle.

John Ypres), a mortuary, and a prison. Today the stone-walled rooms are filled with medieval pottery, old maps, and other memorabilia of the Rye Castle Museum. The Gungarden is a pleasant park beneath the tower, and the main galleries of the museum are across East Street in a former bottling factory just beyond; they house paintings of Rye and items related to the town's past as a port and infamous smugglers' lair. ⏱ 1 hr. 3 East St. ☎ 01797/226-728. www.ryemuseum.co.uk. Admission to tower: £2.50 adults, £2 students & seniors. Admission to tower and East St. museum: £5 adults, £4 students & seniors. Tower: Daily 10:30am–5pm (Nov–Mar until 3:30pm). East St. Museum: Apr–Oct Sat–Sun 10:30am–5pm.

❹ ★★ **Rye Harbour Nature Preserve.** These 326 hectares (806 acres) are part of Romney Marsh, a vast salty shingle formed as the sea has receded from present-day Rye. Viewpoints overlook the marshes that are home to

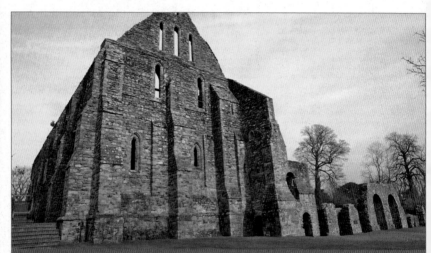

A Side Trip to Battle: Stepping Back to 1066

The Battle of Hastings, a most decisive event in British history, took place not in Hastings but 8 miles away in rolling countryside outside what is now the pleasant country town of ★★★ **Battle.** Here, on October 14, 1066, Duke William of Normandy slew Harold, the Saxon king of England. The duke, who would become known as William the Conqueror, was crowned on Christmas Day of that year and brought some degree of unity to England. To atone for the bloodshed that brought him to the throne, William imported stone from his native Caen, across the channel in France, to build a monastic complex on the spot where Harold supposedly fell, shot through the eye. Henry VIII later had the monastery destroyed, and a medieval gatehouse and the Dorter Range, a dormitory for the monks, are all that still stand among the ruins.

A video, exhibit, and self-guided audio tour bring the most famous date in English history vividly to life. At marked spots along the path visitors stop to listen to fictional firsthand accounts of the battle from the perspective of Aelfric, a Saxon soldier; Henri, a Norman knight; and Edith, mistress of Harold. Before or after visiting the abbey and battlefield, stroll through the medieval market town to the Church of St. Mary the Virgin, built in 1115 and decorated in part with 14th-century frescoes.

Battle is 15 miles west of Rye on a route that follows the B2089 to the A2100. Admission to the **Battlefield** and **Abbey** (☎ 01424/773-792; www.english-heritage.org.uk) costs £7.30 adults, £6.60 seniors, £4.40 kids, and £19 families. They are both open April to September 10am to 6pm, October to March 10am to 4pm. Plan on spending 2 hours exploring all of the sights.

50 or so species of terns, oystercatchers, and plovers, and trails lead to windswept beaches. ⏱ 1 hr. Off Harbour Rd., about 2 miles southwest of town. Daily dawn–dusk.

⑤ ★ The Story of Rye. An old sail loft near the harbor houses the Rye Tourist Office and the Rye Heritage Centre, filled with mementoes of the town's past. A small theater presents *The Story of Rye,* a sound and light show in which events are depicted on an elaborate scale model of the town. ⏱ 20 min. Strand Quay. ☎ 01797/226-696. www.visitrye.co.uk. Free admission; admission to the show is £3 adults, £1.50 seniors & students, £1.50 kids, £7 families. Daily 10am–5pm (Nov, Dec & Mar until 4pm; Jan–Feb until 3pm).

Winchelsea is about 2.5 miles south of Rye off A259.

⑥ ★ Winchelsea. Once directly on the sea and part of the Cinque Port defense network (p. 146), Winchelsea was fortified in the 13th century against constant French invasions and laid out in a tidy grid pattern, the first such example of town planning in England. Today, handsome houses lining quiet lanes overlook the sea and coast from a pleasing distance. Outlying **Smallhythe Place,** Tenterden (☎ 01580/762-334; £6.40 adults, £3.50 kids under 16, £16 families), was built in the early 16th century and in the early 20th century was the country house of Dame Ellen Terry (1847–1928), the famous Shakespearean actress. The low-ceilinged, beamed rooms are filled with playbills, costumes, and other fascinating mementoes of her colorful life in the theater, and tucked into the orchard and rose garden is the Elizabethan barn that was converted to a theater shortly after the actress's death. ⏱ 2 hr.

Where to Stay & Dine

★★★ Jeake's House RYE
The former home of American poet Conrad Aiken (1889–1973) is one of England's most highly acclaimed bed and breakfasts, with lovely guest quarters and book-lined, fire-warmed lounges. Mermaid St. ☎ 01797/222-828. www.jeakeshouse.com. 12 units. Doubles £90–£130 w/breakfast. MC, V.

★★ Landgate Bistro RYE *MODERN BRITISH*
Fresh seafood and local produce show up in excellent, straightforward preparations in plain, bright rooms occupying what were once Georgian shops. The homemade bread alone will transport you, as will lamb fed on the grasses of Romney Marsh just outside of town. 5-6 Landgate. ☎ 01797/222-829. Entrees £9–£14; set menus £15–£18. MC, V. Lunch & dinner Tues-Sat, dinner Sun.

★ Mermaid Inn RYE
One of the oldest inns in England has plenty of creaking timbers and secret passages, as well as a ghost or two, to satisfy a yearning for character. Accommodations vary in size and decor, but all are charmingly comfortable. Among the public rooms are a fine dining

> *The vine-clad exterior of Jeake's House, one of southern England's best B&Bs.*

room and cozy bar. Mermaid St. ☎ 01797/223-065. www.mermaidinn.com. 31 units. Doubles £160–240 w/breakfast. AE, DC, MC, V.

Chichester

Georgian houses line the streets of this lovely town near the Sussex coast, and above their roofs rises a beautiful Norman cathedral. Enticingly medieval and Georgian as Chichester is, the town traces its origins to the Romans, who left behind the walls that still partially enclose the city, as well as a magnificent villa on its outskirts.

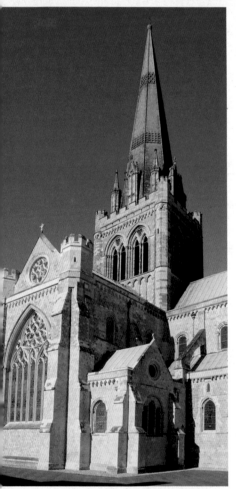

> *Chichester's 11th-century cathedral is a supremely harmonious example of Norman architecture.*

START **Chichester Cathedral. Chichester is 70 miles south of London.**

❶ ★★★ Chichester Cathedral. This mighty church was begun on the remains of a Roman shrine in 1076 and completed a mere 40 years later, a rarity in terms of medieval cathedral building. As a result, the structure is a magnificent assemblage of Norman architecture in which the arches, vaulting, and stained glass work in perfect harmony. Some Roman mosaics are visible beneath glass panels in the floor, and two sculptures near the choir, depicting Lazarus rising from the dead and Christ arriving at Bethany, are considered to be some of the world's finest works of Romanesque sculpture. Not all the treasures are from the distant past: a window by painter Marc Chagall visualizes Psalm 150, and a painting by 20th-century British artist Graham Sutherland depicts Christ appearing to Mary Magdalene. ⏱ 45 min. West St. ☎ 01243/812-482. www.chichestercathedral.co.uk. Free admission. Daily 7:15am–7pm (Oct–Apr until 6pm); free 45-min. guided tours Mon–Sat 11:15am & 2:30pm.

❷ ★★★ Pallant House Gallery. In one of Britain's most noted showcases for modern art, works by Barbara Hepworth, Graham Sutherland, Henry Moore, Ben Nicholson, and other well-known 20th-century British artists hang in bright, airy galleries. The collections also include 18th-century porcelain from London's famous Bow Factory. ⏱ 1 hr. North Pallant St. ☎ 01243/774-557. www.pallant.org.uk. Admission £7.50 adults, £2.30 kids 6–16; half-price Tues & on Thurs evenings. Tues–Wed & Fri–Sun 10am–5pm; Thurs 10am–8pm.

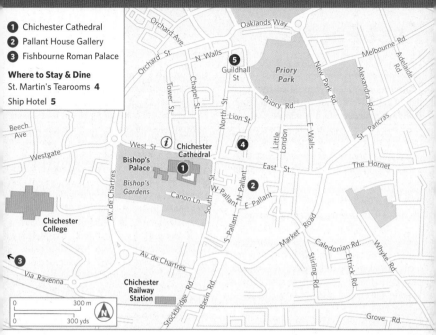

Map Legend:

1. Chichester Cathedral
2. Pallant House Gallery
3. Fishbourne Roman Palace

Where to Stay & Dine
St. Martin's Tearooms **4**

Ship Hotel **5**

❸ ★★★ kids Fishbourne Roman Palace. The largest Roman residence unearthed in Britain, built around A.D. 50, is a palace as lavish as those in Rome. The magnificent mosaic floors, 20 of which are beautifully preserved, include a colorful depiction of Cupid riding on the back of a dolphin. Excavations have also uncovered an underground heating system and an elaborate bath, and the garden has been planted as it would have been in Roman times. A country path leads from Chichester center to Fishbourne. ⏱ 1 hr. Salthill Rd., Fishbourne, 1 mile west of Chichester, off A259. ☎ 01243/785-859. www.sussexpast.co.uk/fishbourne. Admission £8 adults, £7 seniors & students, £4.20 kids, £21 families. Jan Sat-Sun 10am-4pm; Feb & Nov-Dec daily 10am-4pm; Mar-July & Sept-Oct daily 10am-5pm; Aug daily 10am-6pm.

Staying the Night in Chichester

At the almost mandatory stop of ★★★ **St. Martin's Tearooms,** sandwiches, a few hot dishes, cakes, and tea are served in beamed, hearth-roomed rooms and a lovely garden. 3 St. Martin's St. ☎ 01243/786-715. www.organictearooms.co.uk. Entrees £4-£8. MC, V. Lunch & tea Mon-Sat.

An old world ambiance, including a sweeping staircase, pervades ★★ **Ship Hotel,** located in a gracious Georgian home, built for an admiral in 1790 and now the only hotel in the old city. Guest rooms are soothingly furnished in a comfortable contemporary style, and the ground floor bar and excellent brasserie are among Chichester's most pleasant gathering spots. North St. ☎ 01243/778-000. www.theship hotel.net. 36 units. Doubles £99-£125. AE, DC, MC, V.

See the Stars

Alan Bates, Julie Christie, John Gielgud, Derek Jacobi, and just about every leading British actor of note of the past 50 years has performed at the **Chichester Festival Theatre** North St. (☎ 01243/784-437; www.cft.org.uk; tickets £10-£55), founded in 1962 by Sir Lawrence Olivier. The Festival stages its own award-winning productions from April through September and hosts visiting companies the rest of the year.

Fast Facts

Accommodations Booking Services
A good source for character-filled accommodation in Kent and Sussex is **National Trust Holiday Cottages,** P.O. Box 536, Melksham, Wiltshire (☎ 0844/800-2070; www.national trustcottages.co.uk); the National Trust offers accommodations in more than 350 historic properties around Britain, many in Kent and Sussex.

Arriving & Getting Around
BY TRAIN If you're only planning on visiting a few cities and towns in Kent and Sussex, taking the train is definitely the way to go; it will probably be less expensive than renting a car and spare you the stress of driving and parking. Extensive train service runs between London and cities and towns throughout the region; most trains leave from Charing Cross and Victoria Stations. For example, more than 40 trains a day run between Victoria and Brighton; about 30 a day between Victoria and Charing Cross and Dover, and the same number between Victoria and Charing Cross and Canterbury. It's also quite easy to travel by train between major towns in Kent and Sussex, though service may require a change of trains at Ashford or another major hub. To reach some small towns, such as Hever, you will need to transfer to local trains, which sometimes do not run with great frequency and are often not staffed with ticket takers—be sure to have all the information you need before you board. For schedules and information, contact **National Rail Enquiries** (☎ 08457/484-950; www.nationalrail.co.uk).
BY CAR The M23 leads south from London to Brighton, the A21 toward Battle and Rye, and the A2 toward Dover and Canterbury. Most places in Kent and Sussex are no more than an hour away from London by car. If you are renting a car to visit the region, do so at Gatwick Airport, at the northern edge of Kent, which is easy to reach from central London by train (see p. 137). Renting a car there will spare you the hassle of driving in central London, and you will be within minutes of many of the places you want to see in the region, such as Knole (p. 153, ❷) and Hever (p. 158, ❽). Drive slowly when following the many narrow and twisting back lanes of Kent and Sussex, best negotiated by light of day. Driving in and out of Brighton and other larger towns is relatively easy on well-marked routes, and signs lead to municipally-run parking lots. BY BUS Buses run hourly between London's Victoria Coach Station and Brighton (trip time: about 1 hr.) and almost as frequently to other towns in Kent and Sussex; for schedules and information, contact **National Express** (☎ 0871/781-8181; www.nationalexpress.co.uk). A number of bus companies service the region. Brighton, Canterbury, and Dover are among major hubs with many connections to other towns, villages, and outlying sights. For service information and schedules for the region, contact **Traveline** (☎ 0871/200-2233; www.traveline.org.uk). If you arrive at a station on the outskirts of town, you can usually take a local bus to the town center. Taxis are also usually available, or they are on call and their numbers are posted at the station.

Emergencies
Call ☎ 999 for police and fire emergencies, and to summon an ambulance. Most hotels will be able to refer you to a local doctor or dentist. Brighton is especially well equipped for medical care.

Internet Access
Many hotels are now equipped with Wi-Fi, and many have a public terminal as well. Ironically, connections are usually free in less expensive hotels and can be quite costly in more expensive hotels. Internet cafes, where you can log on for about £1 an hour, are common in major towns, and public libraries are often Wi-Fi equipped or have terminals you can use for free.

Pharmacies
Pharmacies (also known as "chemists") are often quite helpful, especially in rural areas, where the pharmacist often acts as a local health care provider. By U.K. regulations, pharmacies are only permitted to fill prescriptions issued by physicians licensed in the U.K. Pharmacies are usually open 9am–7pm, though at least one in a region stays open 24 hours on a rotating basis.

Post Office

Post offices are generally open from Monday to Friday 8am to 5pm, and some on Saturday mornings. **BRIGHTON** You'll find a large post office in the center of town at 62 North Rd. (☎ 0845/774-0740). **CANTERBURY** 29 High St. (☎ 0845/722-3344).

Safety

Like the rest of England, Kent and Sussex is by and large safe, with relatively little crime. In Brighton, often crowded with day-trippers from London looking for a day at the beach, you might encounter pickpockets, so use standard precautions.

Visitor Information

You'll find tourist offices in almost any town and village of any size in Kent and Sussex. All dispense advice and maps and will help you book accommodations in the area. Call ahead or check the websites for the most up-to-date hours of operation (seasonal variations are common in smaller towns). **BRIGHTON** Royal Pavilion Shop, 4–5 Pavilion Buildings (☎ 0906/711-2255; www.visitbrighton.com). **CANTERBURY** Tourist Information Centre, 12–13 Sun St., opposite Christchurch Gate entrance to the cathedral precincts (☎ 01227/378-100). **CHICHESTER** Tourist Information Centre, 29a South St. (☎ 01243-775-888; www.visit chichester.org). **DOVER** Old Town Gaol, Biggin St. (☎ 01304/205-108; www.whitecliffs country.org.uk). **RYE** Tourist Information Centre, High St. (☎ 01797/226-696; www. visitrye.co.uk).

Festivals & Events

You'll find many events throughout Kent and Sussex, especially in the summer, and if your visit coincides with the following you may want to go out of your way to attend. The **Brighton Fringe Festival** (☎ 01273/292-950; www.brightonfestivalfringe.org.uk) in May is one of England's best-known arts festivals, with a wide array of drama, literature, visual arts, dance, and concert programs. In July of every third year, Chichester (p. 182) hosts the **Southern Cathedrals Festival** (www. southerncathedralsfestival.org.uk) with the choirs of Chichester, Winchester, and Salisbury cathedrals. **Hever Castle** (p. 158, ❽; ☎ 01732/865-224; www.hevercastle.co.uk) celebrates its beautiful gardens with Spring Garden Week in March, Rose Week in June, and Autumn Color Week. **Leeds Castle** (p. 154, ❹; ☎ 01622/765-400; www.leeds-castle.com) hosts concerts, fireworks, jousting tournaments, a Christmas tournament, and other events throughout the year. The **Rye Arts Festival** (www.ryefestival.co.uk) in September presents concerts and other performances, and the town celebrates Guy Fawkes Night on November 5 with the **Rye Bonfire Weekend.** Glyndebourne, just outside Lewes, presents opera from mid-May to late August during the **Glyndebourne Festival** (p. 175; ☎ 01273/813-813; www.glyndebourne.com).

5
South-Central England

Favorite Moments

South-Central England, which includes the counties of Wiltshire, Dorset, and Hampshire, offers a rich and surprisingly varied menu of delights. The lovely towns of Winchester and Salisbury are home to two of the most historically and architecturally important cathedrals in the country. In the Hampshire village of Chawton you can visit the home where Jane Austen lived and worked, and in the Wiltshire countryside you can ponder the ancient and mysterious stone circles of Stonehenge and Avebury. Along the south-central coast, you can climb aboard famous vessels at the Historic Dockyard in Portsmouth, visit the seaside town of Lyme Regis, and explore the wonders of the Jurassic Coast.

> PREVIOUS PAGE *Stonehenge's original purpose remains shrouded in mystery.* THIS PAGE *The banks of the Itchen, in Winchester, make a good route for a gentle walk.*

1 Wandering around Winchester. There's nothing more pleasant than walking around Winchester, one of the loveliest towns in England, and visiting its 900-year-old cathedral, once more important than Westminster Abbey in London. See p. 214, **1**.

2 Snooping around Jane Austen's House Museum. The famed novelist arrived at this house in Chawton at the age of 33 and wrote or revised some of her greatest novels here. Family artifacts and handwritten letters by the author herself are among the treasures you'll find here. See p. 217.

3 Marveling at the stone circle at Stonehenge. The megaliths of Stonehenge—Britain's most famous prehistoric monument—have been standing for some 4 millennia, but their secrets continue to elude scientists, scholars, and archaeologists. Maybe you'll come up with a theory of your own. See p. 199, **2**.

4 Allowing the imagination to run wild at Avebury. It's not as famous as Stonehenge, or as complete (many of the megaliths were destroyed to eliminate traces of paganism or reused as building material), but the remnants of this giant stone circle are just as enigmatic—and a whole lot less crowded. See p. 199, **3**.

5 Surveying the swans at Abbotsbury Swannery. For hundreds of years, the lagoon that separates Chesil Beach from the mainland has been a protected swannery and one of the best places to see these elegant birds nesting, fighting, and rearing their young. See p. 197, **6**.

6 Sailing back into history at the Historic Dockyard in Portsmouth. Though modern

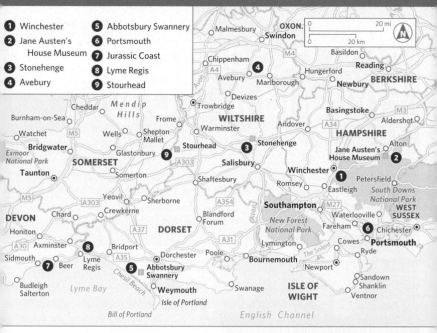

1. Winchester
2. Jane Austen's House Museum
3. Stonehenge
4. Avebury
5. Abbotsbury Swannery
6. Portsmouth
7. Jurassic Coast
8. Lyme Regis
9. Stourhead

Portsmouth isn't all that compelling, it's a thrill to climb aboard Lord Nelson's ship, the HMS *Victory,* and the other painstakingly restored historic vessels berthed in the city's Historic Dockyard. See p. 194, **1**.

7 Journeying along the Jurassic Coast. Traveling along this stretch of coastline in Hampshire and Dorset, rich in fossils and archaeological finds, is a sublimely rewarding experience and a living lesson in coastal geology. See p. 196.

8 Lingering in Lyme Regis. If you don't want to walk out onto the windy Cobb and stare moodily out to sea, as Meryl Streep did in *The French Lieutenant's Woman,* you can visit the fascinating museums dedicated to the dinosaur fossils found along this section of the Dorset coast. Or simply enjoy the cozy Georgian ambiance of this seaside gem. See p. 197, **5**.

9 Enjoying the follies of Stourhead. This magnificent garden marks a watershed in English garden design. It has miles of paths for strolling and admiring its 18th-century follies and viewpoints and its magnificent plantings. See p. 205, **4**.

> *The HMS* Victory *saw Admiral Lord Nelson's greatest military victory and was the place he drew his last breath.*

Best of South-Central England in 3 Days

The counties of Wiltshire, Hampshire, and Dorset cover
a portion of south-central England that has been inhabited for thousands of years—Wiltshire, after all, is where the stones of Stonehenge have been standing for some 4,000 years. This itinerary introduces you to two of England's greatest cathedral towns, one of its most ancient monuments, a grand country house, and two very different cities on the south coast, one a naval base and the other a holiday resort.

> *Half-timbered buildings and architectural remnants of medieval England are part of the scenery in the center of Salisbury.*

START Winchester is 68 miles west of London, about a 1½-hr. drive on the M3. By train, the trip from London's Waterloo Station takes about an hour. **TRIP LENGTH** 215 miles.

① ★★★ **Winchester.** Spend your first day and night in this historic Hampshire town, home of the Norman **Winchester Cathedral** (p. 214, **①**), which was in danger of collapse due to waterlogged foundations until it was restored in the early 20th century by divers forced to

work underwater. On an easy 2-hour stroll you can see the **Jane Austen House** (p. 216, **⑤**); the ruins of **Wolvesey Castle** (p. 216, **⑦**); and the **Great Hall** (p. 217, **⑬**), where the legendary (if not real) Round Table of King Arthur and his knights hangs. **Jane Austen's House Museum** (p. 217) in nearby Chawton is a must for Austen aficionados and an easy day trip from Winchester. ⏱ 1 day. See p. 214.

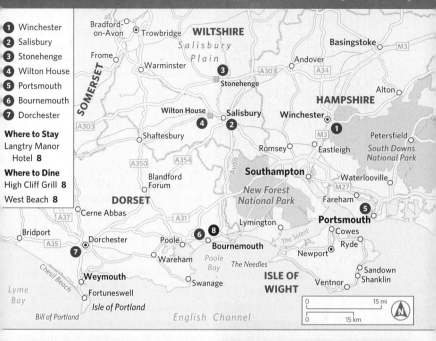

1 Winchester
2 Salisbury
3 Stonehenge
4 Wilton House
5 Portsmouth
6 Bournemouth
7 Dorchester

Where to Stay
Langtry Manor
Hotel **8**

Where to Dine
High Cliff Grill **8**
West Beach **8**

Travel Tip

On this itinerary, having a car makes getting from place to place faster and lets you see more of the countryside. Your best option is to take the train to Winchester and rent a car there.

On Day 2, head 25 miles (45 min.) west on the A30 to

2 ★★ **Salisbury.** The most graceful Gothic cathedral in England, with the country's tallest spire, dominates the lovely, lively Wiltshire town that is your second overnight stop. Head first to sublime **Salisbury Cathedral** (p. 212, 9), and then explore the **Cathedral Close** (p. 211, 5) and elegant **Mompesson House** (p. 202, 1), a beautifully preserved home with stunning plasterwork. **Old Sarum** (p. 212, 10) was the site of "Old Salisbury" before the town relocated to the area around the cathedral in the 13th century. ⏱ Half-day. See p. 210.

On the afternoon of Day 2, head 10 miles (20 min.) north of Salisbury on the A360 to

3 ★★★ **Stonehenge.** Built some 4,000 years ago on the Salisbury Plain, Stonehenge is one of the most famous ancient monuments in

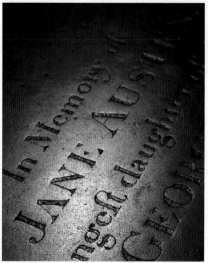

> Jane Austen's gravestone, inside Winchester Cathedral, makes no mention of her prodigious writing talent.

the world. Archaeologists have uncovered some of the secrets of these giant standing stones, but their essential mystery remains to tantalize your imagination. ⏱ At least 1 hr. See p. 199, 2.

> One of the viewing decks at the top of the Spin-
naker Tower has Europe's largest glass floor.

After visiting Stonehenge, continue 9 miles
(15 min.) south on the A360 to

④ ★★ **Wilton House.** The stateliest of Wiltshire's stately homes, Wilton House was designed by 17th-century superstar Inigo Jones
(1573–1652) in a cool, classical style. The
art-filled house served as a top-secret Allied
headquarters during World War II. ◷ At least 1
hr. See p. 203, ②.

From Wilton House return to Salisbury for
your overnight. Get an early start on Day 3,
and drive 43 miles (1 hr.) southeast on the
A36 and M27 to

⑤ kids **Portsmouth.** Though this home port
of the Royal Navy isn't a very attractive city,
it has several memorable (and kid-friendly)
attractions worth a couple of hours of your

time, including **Portsmouth Historic Dockyard,** where you can see Lord Nelson's ship
HMS *Victory;* the **Spinnaker Tower,** with its
far-reaching views and a striking design that
resembles a spinnaker being inflated by wind;
and the **Blue Reef Aquarium,** which is home
to a number of exhibits, including an "underwater" tunnel from which visitors can observe
aquatic life on a coral reef**.** ◷ At least 2 hr. See
p. 194, ①.

**Continue 52 miles (1 hr.) west on the M27,
A31, and A338 to Bournemouth. On this
segment you'll pass through the New Forest.**

⑥ **Bournemouth.** Culturally and historically,
there's not much to see in this seaside holiday
town in Dorset, but if you need a place to stay
for the night, it's a good option. Bournemouth
sprang to life when sea-bathing became all
the rage in the Victorian era, and there is a
famous 7-mile-long ★★ **beach** where holidaymakers head (you can rent cabanas, umbrel-
las, deck chairs, and wind screens), as well
as two entertainment **piers**: Bournemouth
and Boscombe. The city's newest attraction
is the **Boscombe Artificial Reef,** just east of
Boscombe Pier, where surfable 2.4m (8-ft.)
waves are artificially created. The city's famous ★ **Pleasure Gardens** extend northwest
from the seafront for 1½ miles and are lined
with distinctive, sharp-sided valleys called
chines. If you like Victorian paintings and Victoriana, breeze through the ★ **Russell-Cotes
Art Gallery & Museum,** Russell-Cotes Rd.
(☎ 01202/451-858; admission by donation),
a substantial Victorian mansion that displays
19th-century British art. Kids will enjoy the

Double-Decker History

Double-decker buses operated by **Stonehenge Tour** buses (☎ 01983/827-005;
www.thestonehengetour.info) depart from
the Salisbury train and bus station daily
throughout the year and take visitors to
Old Sarum (p. 212, ⑩) and on to **Stonehenge** (p. 199, ②), while a guide provides
commentary on the sites. This is an excellent and easy way to explore the region's
lengthy history. The cost is £11 for adults,
£5 for kids (£18 or £9 with admission to
Stonehenge).

Oceanarium, West Promenade (☎ 01202/311-933; www.oceanarium.co.uk; £8.95 adults, £6.40 kids), with its fish-filled ocean and river habitats (including those from the Amazon, Mediterranean, and Africa). You can also make Bournemouth your base for exploring more of the south coast (see p. 194). ⏱ 2 hr.

If you have extra time and are a fan of Thomas Hardy, you can make an easy side trip to Dorchester, 29 miles west of Bournemouth, about an hour's drive on the A35.

7 ★ **Dorchester.** This attractive Dorset town is closely associated with the novelist and poet Thomas Hardy (1840–1928), and many visitors use it as a base to explore the Jurassic Coast (see p. 196). Founded by the Romans in the 1st century A.D., Dorchester today is mostly Georgian and Victorian in character, with stone-fronted houses and shops along High Street and South Street, the town's principal thoroughfares. You can easily stroll through the town in an hour. **Hardy's Cottage,** the author's birthplace in Higher Bockhampton (☎ 01305/262-366; £4 adults), is a thatched-roof cottage with a pretty garden 3 miles northwest of Dorchester. Trained as an architect, Hardy built and lived in **Max Gate,** Allington Ave. (☎ 01305/262-538; £3 adults, £1.50 kids), for 43 years, writing *Tess of the D'Urbervilles, Jude the Obscure, The Mayor of Casterbridge,* and much of his poetry. The world's largest collection of Hardy manuscripts and memorabilia, including his reconstructed study from Max Gate, is to be found at the ★ **Dorset County Museum,** High West St. (☎ 01305/262-735; www.dorsetcounty museum.org; £6.50 adults), which also has fossils collected from the nearby Jurassic Coast. ⏱ At least 1 hr.

Where to Stay & Dine

★ **Highcliff Grill** BOURNEMOUTH *TRADITIONAL BRITISH/SEAFOOD* Fresh seafood, grilled steaks, and local produce are the specialties at this upscale brasserie and bar. **Bournemouth Highcliff Marriott Hotel, 105 St. Michael's Rd.** ☎ 01202/557-702. Entrees £15–£24. AE, MC, V. Lunch & dinner daily.

★★ **Langtry Manor Hotel** BOURNEMOUTH The opulent home built for Lillie Langtry (1853–1929), mistress of Edward VII, is the setting for this charmingly atmospheric hotel noted for its personal service. **26 Derby Rd.** ☎ 01202/553-887. www.langtrymanor.co.uk. 27 units. Doubles £105–£195 w/breakfast. AE, MC V.

★ **West Beach** BOURNEMOUTH *SEAFOOD* The sands of Bournemouth Beach come right up to the door of this foodie favorite with the best panoramic views in town. **West Promenade.** ☎ 01202/587-785. Entrees £18–£21. AE, MC, V. Lunch & dinner daily.

> Live like a king, or at least the mistress of one, at the Langtry Manor Hotel.

The Hampshire & Dorset Coast

This region of England is home to some of the most spectacular coastal scenery in the country—so special, in fact, that parts of it have been designated a UNESCO World Heritage Site. But before you embark on the scenic route, you'll pay a visit to Portsmouth and Southampton, major harbors that have long served as home base for the Royal Navy and ports of call and departure for ocean liners, passenger ferries, and cargo ships.

> Poole and Bournemouth have southern England's best stretches of sand—but expect crowds on a sunny weekend.

START Portsmouth is **75 miles southwest of London,** about 1 hr. 35 min. by train from London's Waterloo Station.

TRIP LENGTH 3 days, 130 total miles.

1 kids **Portsmouth.** England's naval power has been concentrated in this city, home port of the Royal Navy, since the 16th century. Its old buildings were mostly destroyed by German bombs during World War II, and the postwar

city isn't what you'd call picturesque, but there are several attractions that make a visit to Portsmouth memorable. Spend at least 2 hours visiting the three historic vessels and museum berthed at the ★★★ **Portsmouth Historic Dockyard,** Victory Gate, HM Naval Base (☎ 023/9283-9766; www.historicdockyard.co.uk; combined ticket to all attractions £22 adults, £16 kids, £62 families): The HMS *Victory,* Lord Nelson's 104-gun warship, was

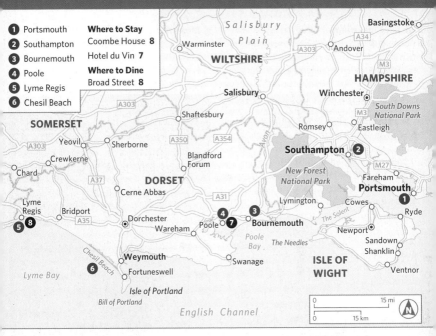

① Portsmouth
② Southampton
③ Bournemouth
④ Poole
⑤ Lyme Regis
⑥ Chesil Beach

Where to Stay
Coombe House **8**
Hotel du Vin **7**
Where to Dine
Broad Street **8**

launched in 1765 and saw action in 1805 at the pivotal Battle of Trafalgar; the Tudor-era *Mary Rose,* Henry VIII's favorite ship, sank in 1545 and was raised from the seabed in 1982 (note that the ship hull is closed for refurbishment until 2012, but the adjacent *Mary Rose* Museum is open); and the HMS *Warrior,* built in 1860, is fitted out just as it was in the Victorian era. A 40-minute **boat tour** of **Portsmouth Harbor,** Historic Dockyard (☎ 023/9772-8060), is part of the all-inclusive ticket. Whiz up on the elevator or trek up the stairs to see the fantastic views from Portsmouth's newest landmark and tourist attraction, the ★★ **Spinnaker Tower,** Gunwharf Quays (☎ 023/9285-7539; www.spinnakertower.co.uk; £8 adults, £6.30 kids), at 170m (558 ft.) the tallest publicly accessible structure in the U.K. If you have kids in tow, they'll enjoy the

Travel Tip

Portsmouth, Southampton, and Bournemouth can all be easily reached by train from London, but a car is necessary if you want to explore the most beautiful parts of the coast. You can rent a car in Bournemouth for that part of the itinerary.

> *Portsmouth has been the home of Britain's Royal Navy since the 16th century.*

Blue Reef Aquarium at Clarence Esplanade, Southsea (☎ 023/9287-5222; www.bluereef aquarium.co.uk; £9.25 adults, £7.20, £31 families), with its walk-through ocean habitats. ⏱ At least 2 hr.

On the afternoon of Day 1, take the train 1 hr. to

② Southampton. Like Portsmouth, Southampton is an ancient port city that was heavily bombed during World War II and rebuilt in a modern, no-nonsense, not-particularly-attractive way. The *Titanic* is the most famous of the giant ocean liners that once set sail from Southampton, and the *Queen Mary 2* still docks here, but Southampton is now primarily a commercial harbor and transportation hub with a big university and a couple of interesting attractions to keep things lively. You can still see a glimmer of medieval Southampton with its imposing ramparts, half-timbered houses, and stone entrance gates in the **Old Town** area. The city's oldest building is **St. Michael's Church,** St. Michael's Square, identified by its needle-thin Gothic stone spire built atop an 11th-century Norman tower. A quick sail through the **Maritime Museum,** Wool House, Town Quay Rd. (☎ 023/8022-3941; £2.50 adults, £1.50 kids), will clue you in on Southampton's long maritime history and tell you about the ill-fated *Titanic,* which left Southampton on April 10, 1912, on her maiden voyage to New York. The **Southampton City Art Gallery** at the Civic Centre, Commercial Rd. (☎ 023/8083-2277; free admission), displays works by major British painters, including Turner, Gainsborough, and Stanley Spencer. ⏱ 2 hr.

Take a 50-min. train ride to

③ Bournemouth. Bournemouth, your overnight stop for Day 1, was built for pleasure. And for health, too, since bathing in sea water and smelling its salty tang was considered a tonic by the Victorians, who left their sturdy architectural imprint on this seaside resort. It's a place to unwind and fool around. If the weather's good, have a walk on the sands of **Bournemouth Beach** or go for a bracing sea swim, and then stroll through the lush **Pleasure Gardens,** where something is in bloom every month of the year. Other attractions include the **Russell-Cotes Art Gallery**

& Museum, which displays Victorian art in an imposing mansion, and the **Oceanarium,** with its fishy exhibits. ⏱ 2 hr. See p. 192, **⑥**.

Jurassic Coast World Heritage Site

An array of classic coastal landforms and a rich prehistoric fossil record from the Mesozoic era led UNESCO to designate a 95-mile stretch of the Dorset and Devon coast between Exmouth and Swanage a World Heritage Site in 2001. In addition to the important Jurassic-era fossils that have been found here, the Jurassic Coast showcases classic coastal landforms, such as coves, arches, and a tombolo (Chesil Beach; p. 197, **⑥**). Lyme Regis (p. 197, **⑤**) and Dorchester (p. 193, **⑦**) are good bases for exploring this natural national treasure.

Spend the morning of Day 2 relaxing in Bournemouth. In the afternoon, pick up your rental car and head for Poole, 5 miles west of Bournemouth, a 20-min. drive on the A35.

4 Poole. This old port overlooking Poole Bay is a good place to have lunch. It lies just north of Sandbanks, a beach community with some of the most highly priced real estate in the world. After lunch, give yourself an hour to a stroll along Poole's restored and revitalized **harbor** area, through **Old Town** with its 18th-century buildings, and to visit the ★ **Poole Museum,** 4 High St. (☎ 01202/262-600; free admission) for a look at a preserved Iron Age log boat dredged up from Poole Harbor. If you're interested in a coastal day trip from Poole, **Brownsea Island Ferries** (☎ 01929/462-383; www.brownseaferries.com) offers seasonal trips to the nature preserve on nearby **Brownsea Island** and on to Sandbanks, with its clean, popular beaches. ⏱ 2 hr.

Continue on to Lyme Regis, 49 miles (1 hr. 10 min.) west of Poole on the A35 and B3162, your overnight stop.

5 Lyme Regis. In the annals of fossil-hunting, the little seaside resort of Lyme Regis has a distinguished history dating back to the early 19th century when paleontologist Mary Anning (1799–1847) found the first complete Ichthyosaurus skeleton in a nearby cliff. You can see dozens of the fossilized dinosaurs and other prehistoric creatures found in the Jurassic rocks around Lyme Regis at the ★ **Lyme Regis Museum,** Bridge St. (☎ 01297/443-370; www.lymeregismuseum.co.uk; £3 adults),

built on the site of Mary Anning's home, and at ★ **Dinosaurland Fossil Museum,** Coombe St. (☎ 01297/443-541; www.dinosaurland.co.uk; £4.50 adults, £3.50 kids), where the fossilized treasures include T. rex eggs and a 73-kg (163-lb.) lump of dino dung. But it's not all fossils and fossil-hunting in Lyme Regis. There's a clean, white-sand beach to enjoy, a causeway-jetty called the **Cobb** (where Meryl Streep gazed out to sea in *The French Lieutenant's Woman*), and the town itself, full of whitewashed Georgian buildings. This is a good place to headquarter yourself if you want to further explore this gorgeous section of England's south-central coast. ⏱ 2 hr.

Spend the morning of Day 3 enjoying the charms of Lyme Regis. In the afternoon, head over to Chesil Beach, 24 miles west of Lyme Regis, about an hour's drive on the A35 and B3157. This section of Dorset coastline is part of the Jurassic Coast World Heritage Site.

6 ★★ Chesil Beach. A uniquely beautiful geologic landform called a tombolo, this narrow, 18-mile-long strip of pebbly beach is separated from the mainland by the Fleet Lagoon. The lagoon is the site of the amazing ★★ **Abbotsbury Swannery,** New Barn Rd. (☎ 01305/871-858; www.abbotsbury-tourism.co.uk; £9.95 adults, £7 kids), founded by Benedictine monks from nearby Abbotsbury some 600 years ago and still attracting hundreds of nesting pairs of black and white swans (who get fed by hand daily). ⏱ 2 hr. Chesil Beach Visitors Centre, Portland Beach Rd., Portland. ☎ 01305/760579. www.chesilbeach.org.

Where to Stay & Dine

★ **Broad Street** LYME REGIS *MODERN BRITISH*
A sophisticated little spot with an inventive menu that makes use of local ingredients. 57 Broad St. ☎ 01297/445-792. Fixed-price menu £28. MC, V. Dinner June–Sept Wed–Sun; Oct–Mar Thurs–Sun.

★ **Coombe House** LYME REGIS
An affordable, well-run B&B with comfortable, airy rooms in an old stone house that's a 1-minute walk from the sea. Coombe St.

☎ 01297/443-849. www.coombe-house.co.uk. 3 units. Doubles £52–£58 w/breakfast. MC, V.

★★ **Hotel du Vin** POOLE
This luxuriously appointed boutique hotel offers balcony rooms with panoramic sea views and a top-notch French bistro. Thames St., The Quay. ☎ 01202/785-570. www.hotelduvin.com. 38 units. Doubles £170–£245 w/breakfast. AE, MC, V.

Ancient Sites in Wiltshire & Dorset

Evidence suggests that Britain has been inhabited for at least 700,000 years, but it wasn't until about 4000 B.C., when Neolithic peoples from Europe migrated to such places as Salisbury Plain, that a substantial archaeological record begins. This itinerary introduces you to that fascinating and mysterious record of ancient, pre-Roman life, taking you to the stone circles, burial mounds, and forts that were homes and places of ritual and worship for people thousands of years ago.

> Giant, ancient standing stones surround the quaint "modern" village of Avebury.

START Salisbury is 92 miles west of London, a 1½-hr. train trip from London's Waterloo Station.

TRIP LENGTH 3 days, 135 total miles.

1 ★★ **Salisbury.** Salisbury makes a good base for exploring the ancient sites in Wiltshire. You'll want to see superlative **Salisbury Cathedral** (p. 212, **9**), even though it's a 13th-century Gothic building, but if you really want to peel away the centuries, visit **Old Sarum** (p. 212, **10**), where you can see the remains of an enormous Iron Age hill fort that was later taken over by the Romans and then the Saxons. Strategically placed at the junction of two trade routes and the River Avon, the oval-shaped fort was 400m (1,300 ft.) long and 360 (1,180 ft.) wide, with an external bank and a ditch with an entrance on the eastern side. ⏱ 3 hr. See p. 210.

On the afternoon of Day 1, pick up your rental car and head 10 miles (20 min.) north of Salisbury on the A360 to

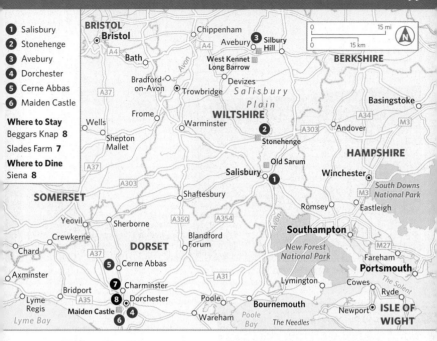

1 Salisbury
2 Stonehenge
3 Avebury
4 Dorchester
5 Cerne Abbas
6 Maiden Castle

Where to Stay
Beggars Knap **8**
Slades Farm **7**
Where to Dine
Siena **8**

2 ★★★ **Stonehenge.** This giant stone circle of pillars and lintels was erected on Salisbury Plain almost 4,000 years ago. Why these stones are here or what they signify is not known, but the complex was obviously a meeting place and a ceremonial center of great significance. Given the stones' alignment with the summer equinox, the monument may have been intended in part as an astronomical observatory. Stonehenge also seems to have served at times as a burial ground. Whatever the reason for the presence of these great monoliths, getting the stones to this site was a herculean task that involved cutting huge slabs from the Prescelly Mountains in Wales, 240 miles southwest, and Marlborough Downs, 20 miles north, and then dragging them overland on roller and sledge and floating them over the sea and down rivers. To fully appreciate the site and get into the spirit of its enigmatic mysteries, turn your back on the nearby parking lot and concession stands and follow the self-guided audio tour along the walkway that encircles one of the world's most famous ancient monuments. ⏱ At least 1 hr. ☎ 01980/624-715. www.english-heritage. org.uk. Admission £7.50 adults, £6.80 seniors, £4.50 kids 5–15, £19.50 families. Daily Mar 16–

May 9:30am–6pm; June–Aug 9am–7pm; Sept–Oct 15 9:30am–6pm; Oct 16–Mar 15 9:30am–5pm.

Return to Salisbury for the night. On Day 2, drive 29 miles (1 hr.) north on the A345 to

3 ★★ **Avebury.** The entire village of Avebury is contained within the largest Neolithic ★★ **stone circle** (free admission) in the world, dating from 2500 to 2200 B.C., and within this huge circle there are smaller stone circles. As at Stonehenge, the stones used at Avebury weighed up to 20 tons and were hauled great distances, cut, and placed upright in painstakingly exact alignments. Only a handful of the stones remain standing today, tantalizing reminders of a vanished culture that may have used stone circles to anticipate and celebrate the movement of the sun and stars. The giant stone circle at Avebury is divided into quadrants by the modern roads leading into the

Travel Tip

The ancient sites included in this itinerary are in the country, and you'll need a car to reach most of them. Take the train from London to Salisbury and rent a car there.

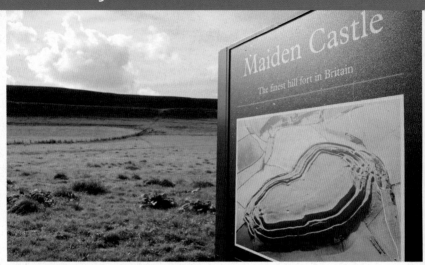

> *Archaeological finds from the Iron Age fort of Maiden Castle can be seen at the nearby Dorset County Museum.*

More Ancient Sites Around Avebury

The area around Avebury is rich in prehistoric sites, and with a full day and a sturdy pair of shoes, you can walk to many of them. Located 1½ miles northwest of Avebury, a 20-minute walk on a signposted footpath or a 5-minute drive on the A436, the Neolithic camp at **Windmill Hill** (free admission) dates back to 3700 B.C. and is part of the Avebury UNESCO World Heritage Site. Large quantities of animal bones found in this enclosure indicate that feasting, animal trading, or religious rituals (or all three) took place here. Rising above the fields about 2 miles southwest of Avebury, a 5-minute drive on the A4361 and the A4, **Silbury Hill** (no public access, view from the parking lot on the A4) is the largest constructed mound in Europe, built for unknown reasons around 2500 B.C. A signposted, 1¼-mile footpath just east of Silbury Hill follows the A4 and then turns south to ★ **West Kennet Long Barrow** (free admission), a 5,500-year-old stone-sided and stone-roofed burial chamber. If you're a dedicated hiker and want to walk on one of the oldest trails in the world, the **Ridgeway National Trail** (www.nationaltrail.co.uk/ridgeway) follows an 87-mile track used by prehistoric peoples over open downland and through secluded valleys and woods.

village. You'll gain some sense of the size of the circle if you begin at High Street and walk around the site; give yourself at least an hour. You won't encounter any of the crowds that mob Stonehenge, and at Avebury you can get up close and personal with the mysterious sarsen (a form of sandstone) stones used to build the monument. Finds from the site and an interactive model of the prehistoric landscape are housed in the 17th-century threshing barn and stables of the **Alexander Keiller Museum,** Avebury Manor (☎ 01672/539-250; £4.40 adults, £2.20 kids, £12.20 families), located on the grounds of the manor where marmalade heir and Avebury enthusiast Keiller (1889–1955) lived. ⏱ At least 1 hr. Avebury Tourist Information Centre, Chapel Centre, Green St. ☎ 01380/734-669. www.visitwiltshire.co.uk.

Drive 69 miles (2 hr.) southwest on the A354 to Dorchester. Check into a hotel for the night.

❹ ★ **Dorchester.** Thomas Hardy, this attractive town's most famous resident, was fascinated by the prehistoric and Roman past of the region. He used Stonehenge as a setting in *Tess of the d'Urbervilles,* and evoked Roman Britain in *The Mayor of Casterbridge.* If you're a fan of the great novelist, you can visit the **Thomas Hardy Cottage,** where he was born, and **Max Gate,** his home in Dorchester. ⏱ 2 hr. See p. 193, ❼.

On Day 3, head 8 miles north (20 min.) on the A352 to

⑤ ★ Cerne Abbas. This lovely Dorset village lined with 16th-century half-timbered houses and a fine 12th-century church is overshadowed by the ★ **Cerne Abbas Giant,** a 55m-high (180-ft.) outline of a naked man with an erect phallus wielding a club, carved into a chalky hillside at the edge of town. Nobody is quite sure when the figure was carved, or why. A mound below the giant's left hand may be the sculpted remnant of a severed head that he once clutched, a common ancient Celtic religious symbol. Or is he perhaps meant to represent the Roman hero Hercules, who was often depicted naked with a club in his right hand? Or is he a 17th-century satirical rebuff to Oliver Cromwell and his Puritans? There are several footpaths around the village for walks up to the Cerne Abbas Giant. If you want to learn more about the area, the village store serves as a tourist information point. ⊙ 1 hr.

> *Villages around the Cerne Abbas Giant, which may be an ancient fertility symbol, have the highest birth rates in England.*

Drive 9½ miles (25 min.) south on the A352 to

⑥ Maiden Castle. This is the largest and most complex Iron Age hill fort in Britain (its name is allegedly derived from the Gaelic for "great hill"), laid out in 600 B.C. over an earlier Neolithic settlement. Extended with multiple ramparts over the following centuries, the fort eventually enclosed 19 hectares (47 acres) and was home to several hundred people. In A.D. 43, it was taken by the Roman army and its inhabitants moved to the new town of Durnovaria, modern Dorchester. Access to the site is by a short but steep trail to the right of the parking lot, which leads you through the original Iron Age entrance to the hill fort. ⊙ 1 hr. Free admission. Daily dawn–dusk.

Where to Stay & Dine

★ Beggars Knap DORCHESTER
The decor in this luxuriously comfortable guesthouse is flamboyantly Victorian, and the level of personal service is high. 2 Weymouth Ave. ☎ 01305/268-191. www.beggarsknap. co.uk. Doubles £65–£75 w/breakfast. MC, V.

Siena DORCHESTER *MODERN EUROPEAN*
A little bistro with some big pan-European flavors and a menu of local specialties such as Dorset lamb. 36 High West St. ☎ 01305/

250-022. Fixed-price meals £20–£31. MC, V. Lunch & dinner Tues-Sat.

★ Slades Farm CHARMINSTER
A beautifully converted stone-and-flint barn 2 miles north of Dorchester on the road to Cerne Abbas provides delightful accommodations and home-cooked breakfasts. North St. ☎ 01305/264-032. 2 units. www.bandbdorset. org.uk. Doubles £70–£80 w/breakfast (2-night min). No credit cards.

Great Houses & Gardens of Wiltshire

This itinerary takes you to several of Wiltshire's historic architectural and garden treasures. From the Elizabethan grandeur of Longleat, with its distinctly un-Elizabethan wildlife safari park and fun-fair attractions, to the gracefully modest urbanity of the Queen Anne-style Mompesson House in Salisbury's lovely Cathedral Close, this tour offers a fascinating compendium of styles and stories. Some of England's best-known architects—including Inigo Jones, Lancelot "Capability" Brown, and John Nash—left their imprint on these houses and the magnificent gardens that surround them.

> In 1946, Longleat became the first British stately home to open to the public.

START Salisbury is 92 miles west of London, a 1½-hour train ride from London's Waterloo Station.

TRIP LENGTH 3½ days, 111 total miles.

❶ ★★ **Mompesson House.** On Day 1, after you've checked into your hotel and visited glorious **Salisbury Cathedral** (p. 212, ❾), pass through the 18th-century wrought-iron gateway of this house, located in the tranquil confines of the Cathedral Close, and explore this lovely example of Queen Anne domestic architecture. The coat of arms of Charles Mompesson, who completed the house in 1701 (it was begun by his father early in the 17th century), is carved above the front door. Mompesson House, which had a starring role in the 1995 movie version of Jane Austen's *Sense and Sensibility,* is famous for its magnificent Baroque **plasterwork ceilings,** graceful period furniture, and an elegant **oak staircase**

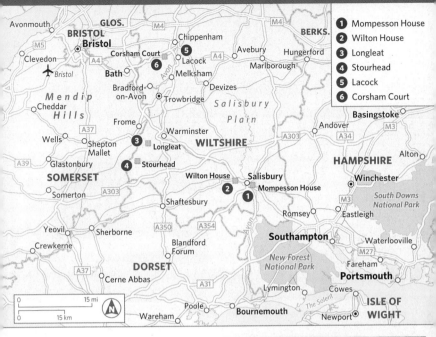

1. Mompesson House
2. Wilton House
3. Longleat
4. Stourhead
5. Lacock
6. Corsham Court

constructed at the back of the house in 1740. A remarkable collection of English drinking glasses from 1700 is displayed in the Drawing Room and Little Drawing Room. ⏱ 1 hr. Cathedral Close, Salisbury. ☎ 01722/335659. www. nationaltrust.org.uk. Admission £5.20 adults, £2.60 kids. Mid-Mar to Oct Sat–Wed 11am–5pm.

On the afternoon of Day 1, head out to Wilton House, 3 miles west of Salisbury. You can easily reach the house on bus no. 60 or 61 from the Salisbury bus station.

② ★★ **Wilton House.** The country estate of the Earls of Pembroke has gone through many architectural changes since it was built in 1551. Fire, changing tastes and fortunes, and a succession of architects—including Inigo Jones

Travel Tip

This itinerary is set up as a series of day trips from Salisbury (p. 210) and Lacock (p. 206, ⑤). Except for Day 1, you'll need a car to reach the destinations on this itinerary. Take the train from London to Salisbury and rent a car there (it'll save you the expense of a day's car rental and some time as well).

> *Mompesson House feels like a miniature version of a Queen Anne stately home marooned in the center of Salisbury.*

> *Over the centuries, Wilton House has hosted dignitaries ranging from writers Daniel Defoe and Charles Dickens to General Eisenhower.*

and, reputedly, Hans Holbein the Younger (1498–1543)—have all played a role in how the house looks today. The exterior was primarily Palladian until the 19th century, when James Wyatt (1746–1813) gave it a neo-Gothic makeover. The Neoclassical sensibility of the 17th century is most evident inside, in the **Double Cube Room,** used as a stand-in for Windsor Castle in many a movie, including, most recently, *The Young Victoria.* In 1944 General Dwight D. Eisenhower planned the logistical support for the D-Day Landings in this room, when Wilton was a top-secret operations center. Paintings by Van Dyck, Rubens, Pieter Bruegel, Sir Joshua Reynolds, and other masters hang in a succession of magnificent **staterooms.** One of the most striking treasures is the elegant Chippendale bookcase in the **Large Smoking Room.** The River Avon, spanned by a Palladian bridge, flows through the lawns and gardens (home to giant cedars of Lebanon, planted here in 1630). ⏱ At least 2 hr. Wilton, Wiltshire. ☎ 01722/746720. www.wiltonhouse.com. Admission £12 adults, £9.75 seniors, £6.50 kids, £30 families. House: Apr–Aug daily 11:30am–4:30pm. Grounds: May–Aug daily 11am–5pm (Sept Sat–Sun).

Return to Salisbury for your overnight. On the morning of Day 2, rent a car. Plan on spending most of the day at Longleat, 26 miles northwest of Salisbury, a 45-min. drive on the A36.

❸ ★★★ kids **Longleat.** It's probably a good idea to schedule a full day for your visit to Longleat, especially if you have kids in tow, because there are so many attractions—including a narrow-gauge railway, a butterfly garden, and a drive-through wildlife safari park—that the place can be as time-consuming as an adventure park. If you just want to tour the house and gardens, give yourself at least 2 hours. The magnificent 16th-century Longleat, designed by Robert Smythson (1535–1614) and built in 1580 for Sir John Thynne (whose descendant, the Marquess of Bath, still lives there), is an enormous Elizabethan manse with three tiers of windows set in an elegant facade of honey-colored stone. Several rooms on the ground floor were remodeled in the 19th century to reflect the Italianate tastes of the 4th Marquess. The **Great Hall** is notable for its hammerbeam ceiling, and the **Ante-Library** for its Italian furniture and marble door frames. Italian Renaissance *palazzi*

> *Classically inspired statuary and follies chime with a garden landscaped in the 18th century at magical Stourhead.*

Lacock Abbey and the Birth of Photography

The history of photography began at Lacock Abbey in 1834 when William Henry Fox Talbot experimented with a process he called photogenic drawing. After coating drawing paper with a salt solution and silver nitrate, he placed a leaf, fern, or piece of lace on the paper's surface and exposed it to the sun, obtaining an image. In 1835, Talbot made the earliest known surviving photographic negative using a camera. A copy of this small photogenic drawing of the latticed window in the south gallery of Lacock Abbey can be seen in the room where it was taken.

nspired the decor of the **Red Library** with ts *trompe l'oeil* panels, and the **Lower Dining Room** with its coffered gilded ceiling. Upstairs, the walls of the Elizabethan-era **State Dining Room** are covered with Cordoba leather, and a portrait of Henry VIII hangs over the fireplace in the **Prince of Wales bedroom.** Have a look at the Victorian **kitchens** and the collection of curios and whatnots in the stable block. In 1946, Longleat became the first stately home in England to open its doors to the public; its famous **Safari Park,** also the first of its kind, opened in 1966. A considerable menagerie of animals, including lions, hippos, Indian elephants, tigers, camels, and white rhinos, roam grounds originally landscaped by Lancelot "Capability" Brown (1716–83) in the 18th century. ⏱ 1 day. Off the A36 btw. Bath and Salisbury. ☎ 01985/844-400. www.longleat. co.uk. Passport ticket for house, safari park, and all attractions £26 adults, £21 seniors, £18.50 kids. House: daily 10am–5pm. Safari park and other attractions: Apr–Nov daily 10am–4pm.

Return to Salisbury for your second overnight. Your first stop on Day 3 is Stourhead, 30 miles west of Salisbury, a 45-min. drive on the A36 and A303.

❹ ★★★ **Stourhead.** Built in 1722 for Henry Hoare I, a merchant banker, the Palladian-style villa at Stourhead, with its early

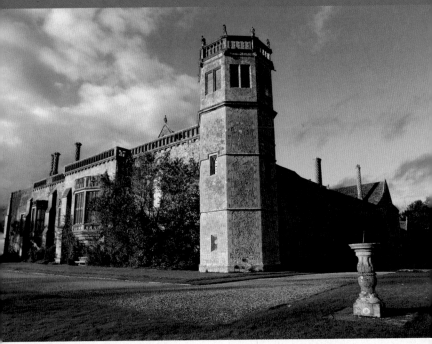

> Lacock Abbey was where the first recorded photographic prints were made, in 1834.

Chippendale furniture and art treasures, is of less interest than the world-famous 18th-century landscape gardens. Laid out in 1741 by Henry's son, the gardens represent a dramatic change in English garden design. Until the early 18th century, English gardens generally followed the formal, geometrical French style. At Stourhead, the landscape was fashioned to look more natural and more picturesque, with small temples, monuments, rare trees, flowering shrubs, and plants set around a beautiful lake. With its tranquil walks and long vistas, Stourhead is pleasant to visit any time of year, but the grounds explode into blossom in May and June. You can make a 2-mile circuit of the grounds and around the lake to the **Temple of Apollo,** or take a longer 3½-mile trek from near the **Pantheon** to have a gander at the view from the 50m-high (164-ft.) folly known as **King Alfred's Tower** (www.alfredstower.info), designed by noted Palladian architect Henry Flitcroft (1697–1769) and allegedly inspired by St. Mark's Tower in Venice. ☺ 2 hr. Stourton, Warminster, Wiltshire.

☎ 01747/841152. www.nationaltrust.org.uk. Admission to house and garden £13.40 adults, £6.70 kids, £32 families; King Alfred's Tower £3.20 adults, £1.70 kids, £7.20 families. Garden: daily 9am–6pm. House and King Alfred's Tower: mid-Mar to Oct Fri–Tues 11am–5pm.

Continue on to Lacock, 29 miles north of Stourhead, an hour's drive on the A350. On the way to Lacock, your overnight stop for Day 3, you'll pass through some of the prettiest countryside in Wiltshire.

❺ ★★ **Lacock.** This idyllic Wiltshire village has been used as a setting in many films, including *Pride and Prejudice, Moll Flanders,* and the Harry Potter blockbusters. Spend an hour exploring its picturesque streets, lined with a collection of cottages, shops, and buildings, some of which date back to the 15th century; owned and preserved by the National Trust, Lacock is blissfully free of modern intrusions like power poles and car traffic. Spend another hour visiting ★ **Lacock Abbey,** founded in the early 13th century as an Augustinian nunnery.

> *Since 1998, a sustained restoration plan has revitalized the pastoral landscape of Corsham Park.*

Following the Dissolution of the Monasteries in the 16th century, it was sold and converted into a house. Many additions were made over the centuries, giving the house a Renaissance-style tower and a Gothic Revival entrance hall. The house is most strongly associated with the scientist and inventor William Henry Fox Talbot (1800–77), whose pioneering work in the field of photography is chronicled in the ★★ **Fox Talbot Museum of Photography** located in the former cloisters. ⏱ At least 1 hr. Lacock Abbey and Fox Talbot Museum: High St. ☎ 01249/730459. www.nationaltrust.org.uk. Admission to abbey, grounds & museum £11.50 adults, £5.70 kids. Nov to mid-Feb Sat–Sun 11am–4pm; mid-Feb to Oct daily 11am–5pm.

Day 4 is an easy one, with only one stop. Corsham Court is 5 miles northwest of Lacock, a 10-min. drive on the A4.

❻ ★★ **Corsham Court.** Built in 1582 for Thomas Smythe, this Elizabethan house was bought by Paul Methuen in the mid-18th century to house a collection of 16th- and 17th- century Italian and Flemish master paintings and statuary. Over the centuries, several architects were called in to modify, enlarge, or rebuild portions of the house. Capability Brown, known primarily for his landscape designs, worked on the house in the 1760s, John Nash (1752–1835) in 1800, and Thomas Bellamy (1798–1876) in the 1840s. Some of the greatest works—by Caravaggio, Tintoretto, Veronese, Rubens, and Van Dyck—hang in the elegant **Picture Gallery.** Two other famous works worth seeking out are Fra Filippo Lippi's *Annunciation* in the **Cabinet Room** and Michaelangelo's *Sleeping Cupid* in the **Octagon Room.** Family portraits by Sir Joshua Reynolds hang in the **Dining Room.** The **gardens,** designed by Capability Brown and his landscaping successor Humphry Repton (1752–1818), contain herbaceous borders, secluded gardens, lawns, a rose garden, a lily pool, and a stone bath house. ⏱ 2 hr. Corsham, Wiltshire. ☎ 01249/712-214. www.corshamcourt.co.uk. Admission to house and gardens £7 adults, £6 seniors, £3 kids. Mid-Mar to Sept Sat–Sun, Tues–Thurs 2–5:30pm; Oct to mid-Mar Sat–Sun 2–4:30pm.

Staying the Night in Lacock

The B&B rooms at **King John's Hunting Lodge,** located in Lacock's oldest building, are old-fashioned and comfortable. The tearoom serves equally old-fashioned delights, such as meat-and-cheese pies and pastries. 21 Church St. ☎ 01249/730-313. 4 units. Doubles £90–£140 w/breakfast. Lunch & afternoon tea daily. Menu items £5–£8. MC, V.

Atmosphere abounds at **Sign of the Angel,** a 15th-century inn with antiques-laden B&B rooms and a good restaurant that serves decidedly non-trendy classics. 6 Church St. ☎ 01249/730-230. www.lacock.co.uk. 6 units. Doubles £120–£145 w/breakfast. Lunch & dinner daily. Entrees £14–£20. MC, V.

A PASSION FOR GARDENING

The Best of British Horticulture

BY STEPHEN BREWER

BRITISH GARDENERS have been inspiring the rest of the world with their ingenuity and inventiveness almost since Roman colonists laid out hedges and gravel paths at Fishbourne Roman Palace (p. 183, ❸). The herb and produce plots medieval monks planted at monasteries across Britain gave rise to English Cottage-style gardens that are still the pride of households from Manchester to Minneapolis. On a larger scale, the sweeping lawns and woodlands (the prototypical "English Garden") that Capability Brown created in the 18th century for many a great house have been the model for parks and gardens around the world. You'll encounter Britain's gardening legacy just about anywhere you travel, from Sissinghurst (p. 156, ❺) in Kent, to the enormous and high-tech Great Glasshouse at the National Botanic Garden of Wales (p. 639, ❽) at Llanarthne, to a Mediterranean-inspired landscape in a most unlikely spot, Inverewe Garden (p. 616, ❹) in the Scottish Highlands.

Highlights of British Gardening

1ST CENTURY A.D.
Garden at Fishbourne Roman Palace is the first in Britain to feature a topiary.

c.1180
A stained-glass window in Canterbury Cathedral depicting Adam with a spade is the first-known image of garden implements.

1520s
Henry VIII fashions elaborate gardens at Hampton Court.

1621
Botanic Garden, the first in Britain, is established at Oxford University.

1830s–40s
The lawnmower replaces the scythe to give British lawns a tidy appearance.

1935–45
British lawns are dug up to grow produce; by 1941, a million acres of potatoes are planted.

2000–PRESENT
Millennium Seed Bank at Wakehurst Place in Sussex conserves more than 24,000 plant species from around the world.

Gardening Greats

LANCELOT "CAPABILITY" BROWN (1716–83)
Britain's most influential landscape architect was often called "the greatest English gardener." Brown graced more than 170 landscapes with his telltale lakes, lawns, and copses. Some of his best work can be found at Blenheim Palace and Warwick Castle.

GERTRUDE JEKYLL (1843–1932)
This garden architect, artist, and author was a major advocate of the popular herbaceous border. She planted over 500 gardens worldwide that are awash in radiant color, creating living canvases that evoke Impressionist paintings. Her prolific writings continue to influence gardeners today.

Best in Show

Flower shows enjoy almost royal status in Britain. The queen of the calendar is late May's **Chelsea Flower Show,** one of the world's greatest horticultural events, a theatrical showing of gardens and floral displays.

Blame It on the Weather

Britain's two major preoccupations—gardening and the weather—are intricately linked. The North Atlantic Drift travels north from the Gulf of Mexico to deliver a moist, mild climate to much of the British Isles, where palms grow at latitudes inhabited by polar bears in North America.

Salisbury

In this beautiful Wiltshire cathedral city, half-timbered inns and houses line medieval lanes surrounding a lively marketplace, the tallest church spire in England pierces the sky, and the Avon and Nadder rivers course through water meadows made famous in the paintings of John Constable. The compact city is easy to get around and makes a good base for explorations of the surrounding region.

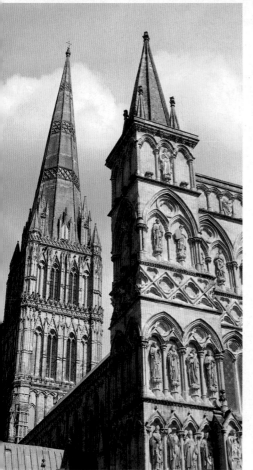

> *Because Salisbury Cathedral took just 38 years to complete, it is a uniquely harmonious example of the Early English Gothic.*

START Salisbury is 92 miles west of London, about a 2-hr. drive on the A4 and M4, or a 1½-hr. train ride from London's Waterloo Station. The marketplace is at the north end of the city center, about a 15-min. walk from the train station.

❶ ★ **Marketplace.** Vendors have congregated here, in the heart of the city, since 1227, and continue to do so every Tuesday and Saturday. ⏲ 15 min.

❷ **Poultry Cross.** This medieval stone cross rising above the market stalls once marked the poultry section of the market (other crosses marking the sales of such items as cheese and wool didn't survive the ravages of time). The names of the narrow medieval lanes surrounding the cross—Fish Street, Silver Street, Butcher Row—are reminders of the trades that once held sway here. ⏲ 5 min.

❸ ★ **St. Thomas Church.** Step inside this 700-year-old church to see the terrifying medieval painting hanging over the chancel arch. Believed to have been painted by a religious pilgrim in the 15th century, this Doom painting depicts men and women rising from their graves and marching toward heaven or hell. ⏲ 5 min. 5 St. Thomas's Sq. ☎ 01722/322537. www.stthomassalisbury.co.uk. Daily 8am–6pm.

④ 🍴 **Reeve the Baker.** Stop in this popular spot for a sandwich, a piece of quiche, or a delicious pastry. 2 Butcher Row. ☎ 01722/320367. Menu items £1.50–£5.

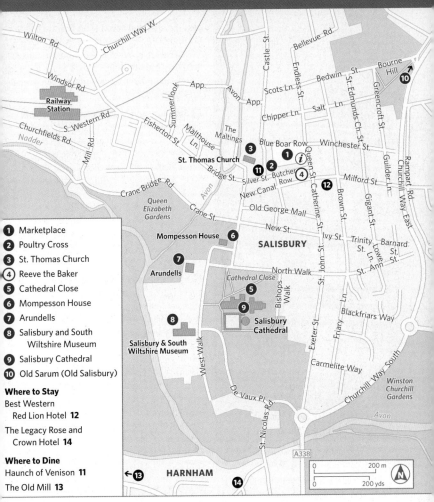

1 Marketplace
2 Poultry Cross
3 St. Thomas Church
4 Reeve the Baker
5 Cathedral Close
6 Mompesson House
7 Arundells
8 Salisbury and South
   Wiltshire Museum
9 Salisbury Cathedral
10 Old Sarum (Old Salisbury)

Where to Stay
Best Western
   Red Lion Hotel **12**
The Legacy Rose and
   Crown Hotel **14**

Where to Dine
Haunch of Venison **11**
The Old Mill **13**

5 ★★ **Cathedral Close.** The area around the cathedral is a small city, protected by walls constructed of stone taken from the Norman cathedral at Old Sarum (p. 212, 10) and entered through four gates. From High Street, you'll pass through the 14th-century **High Street Gate,** with elaborate stonework above its archway. The entrance from Queen Street is through **St. Anne's Gate,** where George Frideric Handel (1685–1759) reputedly gave his first public recital in England in a room over the gatehouse. When the cathedral was built in the 13th century, the Close was planned as a sort of medieval housing development in which persons attached to the cathedral

would live, and over the following centuries, various deacons and officers were allocated about half a hectare (1½ acres) on which to build their homes. The large Close comprises approximately 75 buildings, including some of Salisbury's finest houses. ⏱ 20 min. www.salisburycathedral.org.uk.

6 ★★ **Mompesson House.** If you love historic houses, then you'll enjoy exploring this Queen Anne-style beauty, completed in 1701. It retains its original plasterwork, paneling, and furnishings, including an astonishing collection of 18th-century glassware. ⏱ 30 min. See p. 202, 1.

> *Salisbury is easily reached by road and rail and is well located for exploring rural southern Wiltshire.*

7 **Arundells.** West Walk, where the houses back onto the River Avon, is the most desirable part of the Close, and where you can visit the art-filled home of Sir Edward Heath (1916–2005), Prime Minister from 1970 to 1974. ⏱ 20 min. West Walk, Cathedral Close. ☎ 01722/326546. Admission to house & garden £8. 45-min. guided tours Apr–Oct Mon–Wed & Sat 12:30–5:30pm.

8 **Salisbury and South Wiltshire Museum.** This local history museum occupies a magnificent house (known as the King's House—James I was a visitor in the 17th century), on West Walk in the Cathedral Close. Flints and other archaeological artifacts from the Stonehenge site are on display, as well as Stone Age and Roman finds from around Salisbury. ⏱ 30 min. 65 The Close. ☎ 01722/332151. www.salisburymuseum.org.uk. Admission £6 adults, £4 seniors, £2 kids. Mon–Sat 10am–5pm (June–Sept also Sun noon–5pm).

9 ★★★ **Salisbury Cathedral.** Because it was built in just 38 years, from 1220 to 1258, and because this graceful and soaring structure doesn't bear the influence of other centuries, Salisbury Cathedral (whose official name is actually the Cathedral of St. Mary) is thoroughly Gothic and has the tallest **spire** (123m/404 ft) and largest **cloisters** in England. The **mechanical clock** in the north aisle is one of the oldest pieces of working machinery in the world, telling time since 1386 (note the lack of a face—clocks back then were designed to ring on the hour). The octagonal **Chapter House** is remarkable for its 13th-century stone friezes that tell Old Testament stories, and for possessing one of four copies of the Magna Carta, housed here since 1225. To learn more about the cathedral's history and details of its construction, take one of the **free guided tours** offered throughout the day. ⏱ At least 30 min.; 45 min. for guided tour. ☎ 01722/555120. www.salisburycathedral.org.uk. Admission £5.50 adults, £4.50 seniors, £3 kids. Cathedral: daily 7:15am–6:15pm. Chapter House: Mon–Sat 9:30am–5:30pm; Sun 12:45–5:30pm (Nov–Mar until 4:30pm).

10 ★★ **Old Sarum (Old Salisbury).** In the 2nd century A.D., on a plain 2 miles north of present-day Salisbury, the Romans built a town where an even older Iron Age settlement had stood. Earthwork ramparts, constructed around 500 B.C., still surround the remains of a city where William the Conqueror

Aspiring to the Spire

On 90-minute ★★★ **Tower Tours** (£8 adults, £6 seniors & kids; Nov–Feb Mon–Sat 2:15pm; Mar–Sept Mon–Sat 11:15am, 2:15pm, 3:15pm; May–Sept also Sun 2:15pm and 4:15pm), you can climb into the tower of Salisbury Cathedral via 332 winding steps, past medieval scaffolding, to enjoy magnificent views.

(1028–87) took up residence around 1070 and that, by the 13th century, had become one of the most important centers in England. Old Sarum was abandoned later in the 13th century when Salisbury Cathedral was constructed and a new town took root around the walls of its close. The moody ruins of the Norman castle (built for Henry I), cathedral, and Bishop's Palace attest to what an important place this once was. ⏱ 1 hr. Castle Rd. ☎ 01722/335398. www.english-heritage.org.uk. Admission £3.70 adults, £3.30 seniors, £2.20 kids. Daily Apr–June, Sept 10am–5pm; July–Aug 9am–6pm; Oct, Feb–Mar 10am–4pm; Nov–Jan 11am–3pm. Take the well-marked footpaths along the River Avon or bus nos. 4, 5/6 & 69.

> *You may recognize the rooms of Mompesson House from the 1995 film adaptation of* Sense and Sensibility.

Where to Stay & Dine

Best Western Red Lion Hotel CITY CENTER Atmosphere fills every nook and cranny of this 750-year-old coaching inn, where the cozy lounge is a popular spot for tea and some of the guest rooms come with fireplaces and four-poster beds. Milford St. ☎ 01722/323334. www.the-redlion.co.uk. 51 units. Doubles £130–£140. AE, DC, MC, V.

★ **Haunch of Venison** CITY CENTER *MODERN BRITISH* Salisbury's oldest and most atmospheric pub dates from 1320 and serves meals in a tiny barroom downstairs and beamed dining rooms above. The menu ranges from burgers to adept preparations of fish and meat. 1 Minster St. ☎ 01722/411313. Entrees £7.50–£18. AE, MC, V. Lunch & dinner daily.

★ **The Legacy Rose and Crown Hotel** OUTSIDE CITY CENTER If it's atmosphere you're after, book a room in the older section of this 13th-century inn on the River Avon, about a 10-minute walk to the center of town and featuring lovely cathedral views across the water meadows. Harnham Rd. ☎ 0844/411-9046. www.legacy-hotels.co.uk. 28 units. Doubles £75–£145 w/breakfast. AE, MC, V.

The Old Mill OUTSIDE CITY CENTER *PUB FARE* The riverside garden of this pub, housed in a lovely flint-and-stone building that was

> *The tiny, traditional bar at the Haunch of Venison, in the center.*

England's first paper mill, is a nice spot for a sandwich or light meal. The mill is about a 10-minute walk across the water meadows from the cathedral, near the outlying hamlet of Harnham. Town path, Harnham. ☎ 01722/327517 Pub fare £5–£8. No credit cards. Lunch & dinner daily.

Winchester

The county seat of Hampshire is one of the best-kept and prettiest small cities in England, with one of the country's most magnificent cathedrals. Winchester was an important Roman military headquarters, and then became capital of the ancient kingdom of Wessex and the most important city in England up until the time of the Norman Conquest. Give yourself at least half a day to explore Winchester's charming streets, historic buildings, and picturesque surroundings along the banks of the River Itchen. The literary-minded will revel in the fact that Winchester is the final resting place of Jane Austen, who wrote and lived in nearby Chawton.

> *The Deanery once functioned as the house of the Prior of St. Swithun.*

START Winchester is 68 miles west of London, about a 1½-hr. drive on the M3. By train, the trip from London's Waterloo Station takes about an hour.

❶ ★★★ Winchester Cathedral. One of Europe's greatest cathedrals, the 900-year-old structure, begun in 1079, is graced with the longest **nave** of any church in Europe, and is the repository of many historic treasures, including chests containing the remains of 12 Saxon kings. **Jane Austen's grave** is a simple stone marker in the north aisle, near a 12th-century **font** made of Tournai marble carved with stories of St. Nicholas, the patron saint of pawnbrokers long before he became known as Old Saint Nick. The beautiful **choir stalls** were carved in about 1308. The famous Winchester Bible, a 12th-century illuminated manuscript, is displayed in the **library.** ⊕ 30 min; 1 hr. with tour. ☎ 01962/857-200. www.winchester-cathedral.org.uk. Admission £6.50 adults, £5 seniors. Daily 9am–5pm; free 1-hr. tours hourly Mon–Sat 10am–3pm.

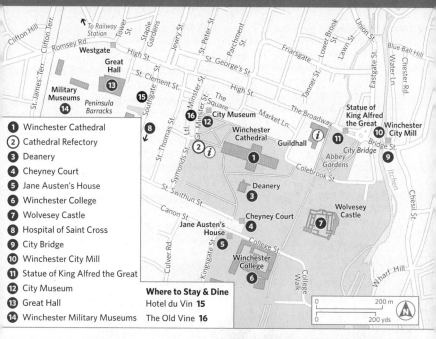

1. Winchester Cathedral
2. Cathedral Refectory
3. Deanery
4. Cheyney Court
5. Jane Austen's House
6. Winchester College
7. Wolvesey Castle
8. Hospital of Saint Cross
9. City Bridge
10. Winchester City Mill
11. Statue of King Alfred the Great
12. City Museum
13. Great Hall
14. Winchester Military Museums

Where to Stay & Dine
Hotel du Vin 15
The Old Vine 16

② 🍽 **Cathedral Refectory,** located behind a medieval wall next to the cathedral, is an appealing spot that specializes in desserts, Hampshire cream teas, and meals made from fresh local ingredients. Inner Close, Cathedral. ☎ 01962/853-224. Items £4–£10.

❸ **Deanery.** This building (not open to the public) adjacent to the cathedral was formed from 13th-century buildings that belonged to the Priory of St. Swithun, which stood here before Henry VIII dissolved all the monasteries in 1539.

❹ **Cheyney Court.** This picturesque half-timbered porter's lodge (not open to the public) beside the ancient priory gate was formerly the courthouse of the powerful bishops of Winchester. One of them, William of Wykeham (1324–1404), founded New College at Oxford and Winchester College, part of the cathedral compound.

Getting Around

The center of town is about a half-mile from the train station, an easy 10-minute walk, or hop on a Park and Ride bus from the rank outside the station.

> *Intricate stained glass is just one among the many art and architectural treasures of Winchester Cathedral.*

5 Jane Austen's House. Identified by a plaque, this house is where Jane Austen died on July 18, 1817, at the age of 42. The ailing writer came to Winchester from her home in the nearby village of Chawton (p. 217) so she could be close to her doctor. She is buried in Winchester Cathedral. 8 College St.

6 ★ Winchester College. Heavy doors guard the entrance to the oldest public school in England, founded in 1382 by William of Wykeham, bishop of Winchester and Chancellor of England. The chapel, cloister, scholars' dining room, and a 17th-century schoolroom are open to the public on excellent 45-minute guided tours. ⏱ 45 min. Queen St. ☎ 01962/621-209. Admission £4. Tours Mon, Wed, Fri-Sat 10:45am, noon, 2:15pm, 3:30pm; Tues, Thurs 10:45am, noon; Sun 2:15pm, 3:30pm.

7 Wolvesey Castle. Now nothing more than evocative ruins, this 12th-century palace was home to the bishops of Winchester until it was destroyed in 1646, during the English Civil War (1642–51). "Bloody Mary" Tudor and Philip I of Spain held their wedding breakfast here in 1554 after marrying in Winchester Cathedral. ⏱ 10 min. Free admission. Apr-Sept daily 10am-5pm.

8 ★ Hospital of Saint Cross. Henry de Blois (1101-71), a grandson of William the Conqueror, founded this almshouse between 1132 and 1136 as a resting place for pilgrims making their way to the cathedral and to house crusaders on their way to the Holy Land. Mixing medieval and Tudor architecture, this structure is now the oldest continuously operating almshouse in England. The resident brothers will show you the kitchen, Brethren's Hall, and garden—and serve you a small chunk of bread, a symbolic link to their almost 900 years of service to wayfarers. ⏱ 30 min. St. Cross Rd. ☎ 01962/851-375. www.stcrosshospital.co.uk. Admission £3.50 adults, £3 seniors, £1.50 kids. Apr-Oct Mon-Sat 9:30am-5pm, Sun 1-5pm; Nov-Mar Mon-Sat 10:30am-3:30pm.

9 City Bridge. This bridge is an 1813 reconstruction of a Saxon span built 1,000 years earlier.

10 Winchester City Mill. Stop in to have a look at the mill's 18th-century machinery (still operational), an exhibition on the history of milling (and some flour-making demonstrations), and a pretty island garden that's home to kingfishers, otters, and water voles. ⏱ 10 min. Bridge St. ☎ 01962/870-057. www.national trust.org.uk. Admission £3.60 adults, £1.80 kids. Wed-Sun 11am-5pm.

11 Statue of King Alfred the Great. This bronze statue, erected in 1899, commemorates the Saxon king (849-99) who made Winchester the capital of his southern England kingdom,

> *King Alfred's statue gazes down the high street over the city from where he ruled the Kingdom of Wessex.*

Wessex. What made Alfred so "great?" Probably that he was an enlightened man (statesman and scholar) in the Dark Ages, and drove off the marauding Danes. **Bridge St.**

⑫ **City Museum.** The most interesting room in this small, attractive museum is devoted to Roman Winchester and contains a fine Roman mosaic centerpiece. ⊙ 15 min. The Square. ☎ 01962/863-064. Free admission. Mon–Sat 10am–5pm; Sun noon–5pm (Nov–Mar until 4pm, closed Mon).

⑬ ★ **Great Hall.** Accessed through Westgate, a fortified medieval gateway, this enormous stone hall is all that remains of once-mighty Winchester Castle, and is famous for displaying what is called the Round Table of King Arthur and his knights. The table is indeed old (Henry VIII commissioned the paintwork), but

Staying the Night in Winchester

A converted Georgian house in the city center is the setting for ★★ **Hotel du Vin** (pictured above), a stylish hotel with handsomely decorated rooms and an excellent bistro serving hearty French fare. Southgate St. ☎ 01962/841-414. www.hotelduvin.com. 24 units. Doubles £140–£200 w/breakfast. AE, MC, V.

★ **The Old Vine,** a woody pub with a garden just outside the cathedral precincts, is a relaxing place to enjoy a pint and a salad, sandwich, innovative curries, or more substantial fish and meat dishes. 8 Great Minster St. ☎ 01962/854-616. Menu items £5–£14. MC, V. Lunch & dinner daily.

For Jane Austen Fans

If you're a Jane Austen fan, you might enjoy a visit to ★★ **Jane Austen's House Museum,** Chawton, Alton (☎ 01420/83262; www.jane-austens-house-museum.org.uk; £7 adults, £2 kids), about 17 miles northeast of Winchester. The witty novelist lived in this sturdy red brick Georgian house with her mother and her sister, Cassandra, from 1809 until 1817, revising her novels *Pride and Prejudice* and *Sense and Sensibility* and writing *Mansfield Park* and *Emma*. Creatively, this was where she spent the most productive years of her life. Austen family memorabilia is spread throughout the house.

It's easy to get there by bus. **Stagecoach Hampshire Bus** (☎ 01256/464-501) routes no. 64 and X64 leave from Winchester bus station to Chawton. Ask the driver to drop you at the Alton Butts stop, the one closest to the Austen house. From the bus stop, walk toward the railway bridge, cross the very busy road, and continue straight on, passing a brown tourist sign and following the road beneath the underpass; the walk from the bus stop to the museum takes about 15 minutes. If you're driving from Winchester, take the A31 northeast; you'll see a signed turnoff to the house from the roundabout junction with A32.

not old enough to have served 6th-century Arthur (himself probably legendary). However, it has hung here and been called that for some 600 years, thereby attaining legendary status. ⊙ 10 min. Castle Ave. ☎ 01962/846-476. Admission by donation. Daily 10am–5pm (Sat–Sun until 4pm in winter).

⑭ **Winchester Military Museums.** Collections honoring various British regiments include dioramas and artifacts that pay tribute to Nepalese troops in the **Gurkha Museum;** a vivid re-creation of World War I trench warfare in the **King's Royal Hussars Museum;** and a dramatic diorama depicting the Battle of Waterloo in the **Royal Green Jackets Museum.** ⊙ 15 min. Peninsula Barracks, Romsey Rd. ☎ 01962/877-826. http://winchestermilitarymuseums.co.uk. Admission Gurkha Museum £2 adults, £1 seniors; Royal Green Jackets Museum £3 adults, £2 seniors, £1.50 kids; other museums free. Tues–Sat 10am–4pm; Sun noon–4pm.

Fast Facts

> *The boom in mobile phone ownership has made finding a working public telephone box harder than it once was.*

Arriving & Getting Around

BY CAR You can get to all the major cities in this chapter on the train, but you'll need a car to see the countryside and the coastline. You can fly into London, rent a car there, and then drive into the region (it's 1½ hr. on the M3 to Winchester); alternatively, you can take the train to Salisbury, Winchester, Portsmouth, Southampton, or Bournemouth and rent a car there. If you drive, you'll need a detailed road atlas: The best are the large-format maps produced by the Automobile Association (AA), Collins, Ordnance Survey, and Royal Automobile Club (RAC). **BY TRAIN** Fast intercity trains leave London's Waterloo Station for the 1-hour trip to Winchester, the approximately 1½-hour trip to Salisbury and Portsmouth, and the 2-hour trip to Bournemouth. For train schedules and information, contact **National Rail Enquiries** (☎ 08457/484-950; www.nationalrail. co.uk). **BY PLANE** The closest airport to the cities in this chapter is **Southampton International Airport** (☎ 0844/481-7777; www.southamptonairport.com), with links to cities in the U.K. and Europe. All of the major car rental agencies have desks at the airport. **BY BUS National Express** (☎ 0990/808-080; www.nationalexpress.com) serves the major towns and cities in Wiltshire, Hampshire, and Dorset, but if you are traveling from London and intent on keeping a schedule, taking the bus is not a good idea because of the time involved. Tourist offices can provide you with local and regional bus information.

Emergencies

To call for emergency help anywhere in England, dial ☎ 999 or ☎ 112; these are free calls from public phones. If you have a medical emergency, ask your concierge or B&B proprietor for help in locating a doctor or dentist. **Salisbury District Hospital,** 2 miles south of Salisbury on Oldstock Road (☎ 01722/336262; www.salisbury.nhs.uk), serves Wiltshire, Hampshire, and Dorset.

Internet Access

Wi-Fi or dial-up Internet service is available at hotels throughout Wiltshire, Hampshire, and Dorset, either in-room or at a computer reserved for guests; you may not find Internet access at smaller B&Bs. You can check e-mail at the Salisbury Library, Market Place; in Portsmouth at Online Cafe, 163 Elm Grove; and at the Bournemouth Library, 22 The Triangle.

Pharmacies

Cities and larger towns in Wiltshire, Hampshire, and Dorset have at least one pharmacy ("chemist"). Boots (www.boots.com), the most common, has a branch in Salisbury at 41–51 Silver St. (☎ 01722/333233), and in Winchester at 35–39 High St. (☎ 01962/852-020).

Post Office

You'll find them in every city and small town, identified by a red box labeled ROYAL MAIL. In smaller towns, the post office may be in a local store rather than a post office building. SALISBURY The main post office is near Castle Street and Chipper Lane. WINCHESTER On Middle Brook Street. PORTSMOUTH On Palmerston Road, Southsea. The post offices are open Monday to Saturday 9am to 5:30pm.

Safety

If you take common sense precautions, it's unlikely you'll encounter any problems with crime in Wiltshire, Hampshire, and Dorset. If you're driving through the countryside, be aware that some of the local roads are quite narrow; you may have to pull off to the side to let another car or truck pass. If you're leaving your car in a parking lot or visiting a sight in the country, always make sure that your car is locked and your valuables are stowed in the trunk.

Visitor Information

The local tourist offices in Salisbury, Winchester, Portsmouth, Southampton, and Bournemouth are your best sources for up-to-date information and assistance in booking accommodations. For general region-wide

> Post boxes are usually labeled with the time of that day's last postal collection.

information that includes Dorset and Wiltshire, visit the website for the **South West Tourist Board** (www.visitsouthwest.com), the **Hampshire Tourist Board** (www.visithampshire.co.uk), and the **Wiltshire Tourist Board** (www.visitwiltshire.co.uk).

Local tourist offices include: BOURNEMOUTH Bournemouth Tourist Information Office, Westover Rd. (☎ 08450/511-701; www.bournemouth.co.uk). DORCHESTER Dorchester Tourist Information Centre, Antelope Walk (☎ 01305/267-992; www.westdorset.com). LYME REGIS Lyme Regis Tourist Information Centre, Guildhall Cottage, Church St. (☎ 01297/442-138; www.lymeregis.org). POOLE Bournemouth and Poole Tourist Information Centre, Westover Rd., Bournemouth (☎ 08450/511-701; www.bournemouthandpoole.co.uk). PORTSMOUTH Portsmouth Tourist Information Centre, The Yard (☎ 023/9282-6722; www.visitportsmouth.co.uk). SALISBURY Salisbury Information Centre, Fish Row (☎ 01722/334956; www.visitwiltshire.co.uk/Salisbury). SOUTHAMPTON Southampton Tourist Information Centre, 9 Civic Centre Rd. (☎ 023/8083-3333; www.visit-southampton.co.uk). WINCHESTER Winchester Tourist Information Centre, Guildhall, High St. (☎ 01962/840-500; www.visitwinchester.co.uk).

6
The West Country

Our Favorite West Country Moments

An air of myth and mystery pervades Devon, Cornwall, and Somerset, the counties that make up England's beloved West Country. Notable for its dramatic coastline, dotted with sites such as ancient Tintagel and medieval St. Michael's Mount, the West Country is also home to the splendid cathedral towns of Exeter and Wells and the seaside resort of St. Ives. The Regency spa town of Bath, as popular today as it was in Jane Austen's day, is close to big-city Bristol and the fabled Cheddar Gorge. The West Country is also prime recreation country, with countless hiking paths, a national park to explore, and, in Devon and Cornwall, plenty of sandy "Blue Flag" beaches (a designation for the cleanest shore and water).

> PREVIOUS PAGE *St. Ives was the home and inspiration of sculptor Barbara Hepworth.* THIS PAGE *The architecture of Exeter Cathedral incorporates elements from both the Norman and Gothic periods.*

1 Enjoying Exeter Cathedral. It's the chief reason to visit the city, and its west front boasts the most magnificent array of 14th-century sculpture in England. See p. 276, **1**.

2 Moseying through St. Michael's Mount. A must-see attraction in Cornwall, this island fortress-castle-home is a fascinating historical and architectural treasure. Cross the causeway by foot (or boat, if the tide is in) and climb the steps hewn into the rock to the entrance of this remarkable structure. See p. 249, **9**.

3 Stepping into Barbara Hepworth's studio in St. Ives. The great English sculptor lived for years in St. Ives, and her home and studio are now open as a museum. You'll get an intimate

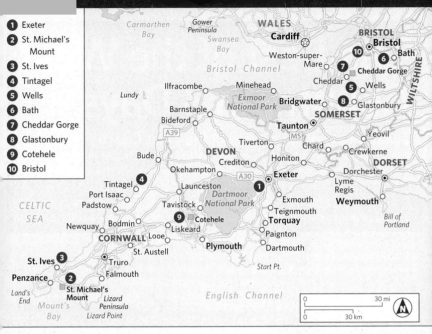

1. Exeter
2. St. Michael's Mount
3. St. Ives
4. Tintagel
5. Wells
6. Bath
7. Cheddar Gorge
8. Glastonbury
9. Cotehele
10. Bristol

glimpse of where Hepworth spent her days, and the sculptures on display in her garden constitute a major collection of her work. See p. 285, **2**.

4 **Traipsing up to Tintagel.** The climb there is arduous, but the oceanside ruins of Tintagel Castle are remarkably dramatic and steeped in Arthurian legend. See p. 226, **4**.

5 **Wandering through Wells.** England's smallest cathedral city is also one of its prettiest, with a superb cathedral and an array of remarkably preserved medieval buildings around it. Overflowing with charm, and relatively undiscovered by tourists, compact Wells invites strolling and dreaming. See p. 261, **5**.

6 **Visiting the Roman Baths Museum in Bath.** It's so well done, so interesting, and so historic, that it never fails to fascinate. As you wander through the rooms where Roman soldiers bathed and exercised, you'll truly be soaking up the atmosphere of Roman Britain. See p. 266, **2**.

7 **Caving in the Cheddar Gorge.** Beneath the towering limestone cliffs of the Cheddar Gorge are a series of caves that are fun to visit

and reveal the geological and human history of Somerset. See p. 230, **2**.

8 **Going New Age at Glastonbury.** This town in Somerset attracts all kinds of New Age practitioners who come to see the legend-filled ruins of Glastonbury Abbey and Glastonbury Tor. The annual Glastonbury Festival is one of England's most popular pop-rock events and turns the town into a crowded carnival for 4 days every June. See p. 262, **6**.

9 **Pretending to be medieval at Cotehele.** The rooms in this remarkable medieval manor remain virtually unchanged, which means they're dark and ever so atmospheric. See p. 247, **4**.

10 **Stepping up the gangplank of the SS *Great Britain* in Bristol.** This immaculately restored 1843 vessel, the first steam-powered transatlantic ocean liner, presents a vivid picture of what it was like to sail the high seas 150 years ago. The iron-clad ship and the famous Clifton Suspension Bridge, both designed by 19th-century engineering genius Isambard Brunel, are among the many attractions to be found in and around the city of Bristol. See p. 272, **1**.

The Best of the West Country in 3 Days

The diversity of landscapes of the West Country—which includes Devon, Cornwall, and Somerset counties—is matched by the variety of the towns and cities you'll find there. This itinerary is meant to give you a taste of the best of both, taking in the ancient cathedral cities of Exeter and Wells, the picturesque fishing village-*cum*-beachside resort of St. Ives, dramatic ruins associated with King Arthur, and the beautifully preserved Regency spa town of Bath.

> More than just a pretty place, St. Ives is known for its beaches, seafood dining, and artists' colony.

START Exeter is 197 miles west of London, about a 3½-hr. drive on M4 and M5, or a 2 hr. 15-min. train ride from London's Paddington Station. **TRIP LENGTH** 3 days. Total distance is 339 miles.

❶ ★★ Exeter. Start your 3-day West Country tour by spending a couple of hours exploring this small, lively city in Devon. Exeter's centerpiece and most important building is twin-spired **Exeter Cathedral** (p. 276, **❶**), begun

in Norman times and notable for the gallery of 14th-century sculpted kings, bishops, and angels decorating its west front. After you've spent a half-hour visiting the cathedral, head over to the **Royal Albert Memorial Museum** (p. 278, **❹**) for a look at the paintings, glassware, and Roman artifacts. The local history exhibits in the **Quay House Visitor Centre** (p. 278, **❸**), housed in a restored warehouse in Exeter's old port area, are also worth a brief visit. If you'd like to extend your stay an hour

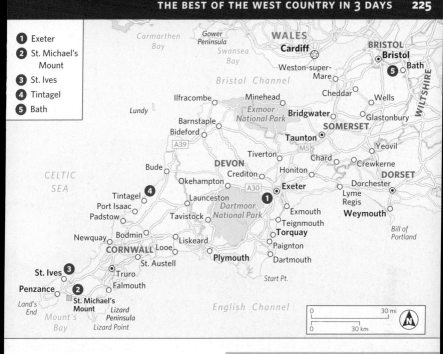

1. Exeter
2. St. Michael's Mount
3. St. Ives
4. Tintagel
5. Bath

longer, the **Underground Passages** (p. 278, 5) tour takes you into a warren of medieval tunnels dug to channel water into the city. ⏱ 4 hr. See p. 276.

Your first stop on Day 2 is St. Michael's Mount, 108 miles southwest of Exeter, about a 2-hr. drive on the A30.

2 ★★★ **St. Michael's Mount.** The imposing castle atop the scenic offshore island looks like the stuff of legend, but it began life as a 12th-century Benedictine monastery and was later turned into a fortress and finally a family home. Plan to spend at least 2 hours exploring the castle, which has been the home of the St. Aubyn family for some 350 years. If the tide is in, boatmen will ferry you across to the island;

Travel Tip

You can easily get to the major towns in this itinerary—Exeter, Penzance (for St. Michael's Mount), St. Ives, and Bath—by train. But to see Tintagel and part of the Cornish coast, you'll need a car. Your best option is to travel by train to Exeter, where the itinerary begins, and rent a car there, returning it in Bath at the end of the tour.

> The architecture of St. Michael's Mount reflects its history as monastery, fort, and family home.

> *The romantic ruins at Tintagel are steeped in Arthurian legend.*

once there, be prepared for some steep stairs, narrow passageways, and fabulous views over Mount's Bay. ⏱ 2 hr. See p. 249, **❾**.

St. Ives is 9 miles north of St. Michael's Mount, about a 20-min. drive on the B3311.

Princely Perks: The Duchy of Cornwall

In his redistribution of English lands, William the Conqueror gave Cornwall to one of his relatives. In the 14th century, Edward III created the Duchy of Cornwall as an estate for the eldest son of the monarch. Cornwall, through 24 dukes, has remained a duchy ever since. Prince Charles, the oldest son of Queen Elizabeth II, is the present Duke of Cornwall (and his wife, Camilla Parker-Bowles, is the Duchess). Income from the Duchy of Cornwall, in leased lands and estates, amounts to tens of millions of pounds every year and is a "nice little earner" for Charlie.

❸ ★★ St. Ives. This erstwhile fishing village on the north coast of Cornwall is your overnight stop on Day 2. St. Ives was discovered about a century ago by artists who were mesmerized by the shimmering shades of sea and sand. Their work can be seen in the ★★ **Tate St. Ives** (p. 284, **❶**) art museum and at the ★★★ **Barbara Hepworth Museum and Sculpture Garden** (p. 285, **❷**), located in the home and studio of one of England's greatest sculptors. Today, St. Ives is one of Cornwall's busiest summer resorts, its old fisherman's cottages converted into restaurants, shops, and galleries. ⏱ 3 hr. See p. 284.

Get an early start on your third day, which begins with a drive up the rocky, windswept north coast of Cornwall to Tintagel, 58 miles northeast of St. Ives, a 1½-hr. drive on the A30 and A39.

❹ ★★ Tintagel. The sites associated with King Arthur are legion, but none are quite so dramatic or romantic as the ruins of Tintagel Castle. A stronghold of the Earls of Cornwall,

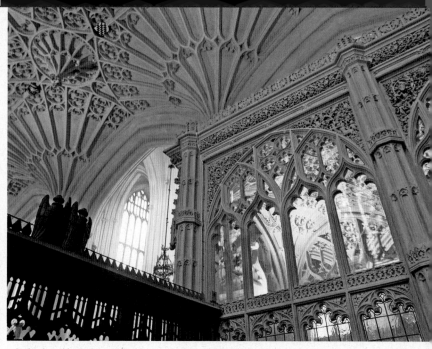

> Bath is famed for its Georgian buildings, but at Bath Abbey, a medieval architectural heritage is much in evidence.

the castle was built in the 13th century on the site of a 6th-century Celţic monastery, right on the edge of a cliff, with the Atlantic thundering below. Tintagel Castle has long been associated with romantic stories of King Arthur—some say he was born here, which is perhaps true if you regard Arthur as a legend. The cliffside castle ruins require some steep stair-climbing if you want to fully explore them. The surrounding area is rich in flora and fauna and provides a breeding ground for sea birds, lizards, and butterflies. ⏱ 1 hr. ☎ 01840/770-328. www.english-heritage.org.uk. Admission £5.20 adults, £4.40 seniors, £2.60 kids. Daily 10am–5pm (Nov–Mar until 4pm).

From the Cornish coast you'll be moving inland into Somerset to Bath, 162 miles northeast of Tintagel, about a 2½-hr. drive on the A30 and M5.

❺ ★★★ **Bath.** The Regency architecture that characterizes Bath is so unique that UNESCO has designated the entire city a World Heritage Site. Spend your third day and night exploring late-18th-century urban landmarks like the **Circus** (p. 268, ❼), the **Royal Crescent** (p. 269, ❾), and **Pulteney Bridge** (p. 268, ❹), modeled on the Ponte Vecchio in Florence, Italy. The heady social whirl of Regency-era Bath is exemplified by the **Assembly Rooms** (p. 269, ❽), where ladies and dandies flirted, gambled, and danced the night away, wearing the elaborate gowns and frock-coats now on display in the **Fashion Museum** (p. 269, ❽). The **Jane Austen Centre** (p. 268, ❻) is dedicated to Bath's most famous resident, who cast her acerbic eye on its social-climbing denizens. Spend a few minutes in **Bath Abbey** (p. 266, ❶), famed for its medieval fan vaulting, but allot at least an hour to tour the adjacent **Roman Baths Museum** (p. 266, ❷), the site of an ancient Roman bath complex. You can taste the mineral-laden waters that made Bath the pre-eminent spa resort of the Regency era in the adjoining **Pump Room** (p. 266, ❷). ⏱ 4 hr. See p. 266.

The Best of the West Country in 1 Week

This itinerary expands on the shorter 3-day version and introduces you to more of the fascinating historic and scenic pleasures found in the West Country. Stately homes, lush gardens, tiny fishing villages, limestone caves, legendary Arthurian sites—you can see all of them in a week's time.

> *Six tiers of Gothic sculptures embellish the magnificent West Front of Wells's Gothic cathedral.*

START Bath, 115 miles west of London, about a 2½-hr. drive on the M4, or a 1½-hr. train ride from London's Waterloo Station. **TRIP LENGTH** 1 week. Total distance is 291 miles.

1 ★★★ **Bath.** With its enchanting mixture of crescents, circuses, colonnades, promenades, assembly rooms, and flower-bedecked parks and squares (p. 227, **5**), Bath is the Regency spa city *par excellence* and the perfect place to spend the first 2 days of your West Country tour. In addition to enjoying Bath's gems of Regency architecture, be sure to visit the fascinating **Roman Baths Museum** (p. 266, **2**), where Roman soldiers soaked in Bath's thermal waters 1,600 years before the city became the most famous spa in Regency England; **No. 1 Royal Crescent** (p. 270, **10**), a Regency town house; and the **Fashion Museum** (p. 268, **8**), one of the world's great collections of historic and contemporary fashion. ⊕ 2 days. See p. 266.

Travel Tip

Many of the places on this itinerary are in the country; so you'll need a car if you want to see all of them. Your best option is to take a train to Bath, where the itinerary begins, and rent a car there.

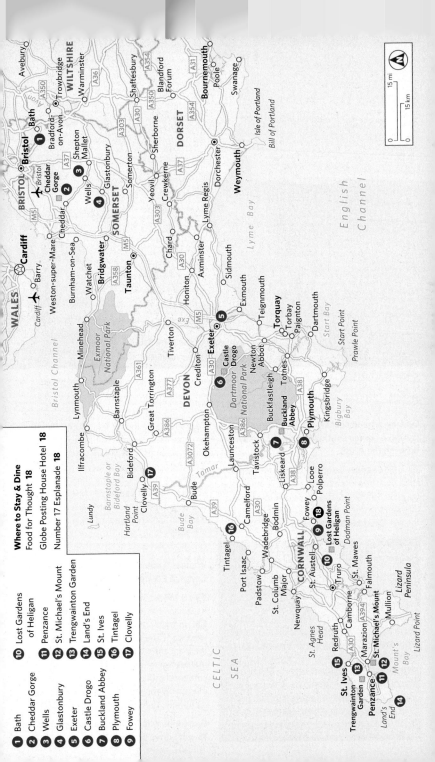

Where to Stay & Dine
Food for Thought **18**
Globe Posting House Hotel **18**
Number 17 Esplanade **18**

1 Bath
2 Cheddar Gorge
3 Wells
4 Glastonbury
5 Exeter
6 Castle Drogo
7 Buckland Abbey
8 Plymouth
9 Fowey
10 Lost Gardens of Heligan
11 Penzance
12 St. Michael's Mount
13 Trengwainton Garden
14 Land's End
15 St. Ives
16 Tintagel
17 Clovelly

> *The limestone below Cheddar Gorge is riddled with caves long used to age the famous local cheese.*

On Day 3, head southwest to the Cheddar Gorge, 24 miles southwest of Bath, a 45-min. drive on the A368.

② ★ **kids** **Cheddar Gorge.** Towering limestone cliffs line the length of this scenic, 2-mile-long gorge in Somerset. You may want to drive through to admire the scenery, or stop to visit the ★★ **Cheddar Gorge Caves** (☎ 01934/

Cheddar Man

The limestone caves in the Cheddar Gorge were inhabited by prehistoric peoples as long ago as 20000 B.C. In 1903, the 9,000-year-old skeleton of a Stone Age hunter was uncovered in one of the caves and dubbed "Cheddar Man." Recent genetic tests on Cheddar Man and the local population have established that some of his modern descendants still live in this part of Somerset. The story of Cheddar Man is told in the **Museum of Prehistory,** which is part of the Cheddar Gorge Caves complex and included in the price of your ticket.

742-343; £17 adults, £11 kids, £45 families) and marvel at the mineral-tinted stalactites and stalagmites that adorn Cox's Cave and Gough's Cave. Allow at least a half-hour to visit each. If you're feeling energetic, the 274 steps of **Jacob's Ladder,** cut into the side of the gorge, lead up to marvelous panoramic views of Somerset and a 3-mile circular ★★ **walk** along the clifftops of the Cheddar Gorge. ⏱ At least 1 hr. to visit one cave.

Wells is 9 miles northwest of the Cheddar Gorge, a 20-min. drive on the A371.

③ ★★ **Wells.** Stop in this diminutive city to have a look at its glorious **cathedral** (p. 261, **⑤**), famed for the beauty of its sculpted west front and the unique inverted arches in the transept crossing, and the atmospheric mélange of medieval buildings found in the cathedral precincts. The charms of Wells are many, and you may decide to spend your third night here. ⏱ At least 1 hr. See p. 261, **⑤**.

Glastonbury is 6 miles southwest of Wells, a 15-min. drive on the A39.

4 ★ **Glastonbury.** Another good choice for your third overnight, Glastonbury is associated with legends of the Holy Grail and King Arthur, and draws all kinds of New Age practitioners and believers. The major sights are the ruins of **Glastonbury Abbey,** and the giant hill known as **Glastonbury Tor.** ⏱ 2 hr. See p. 262, **6** .

On Day 4, drive to Exeter, 60 miles southwest of Glastonbury, about a 75-min. drive on the M5, or 65 miles southwest of Wells, a 1½-hr. drive on the A39 and M5.

5 ★★ **Exeter.** A lively regional hub of Devon and the West Country, ancient Exeter with its splendid **cathedral** (p. 276, **1**) is a good

> *Exeter Cathedral is another of southern England's masterpieces of Gothic stonemasonry.*

Rockin' Out in Glastonbury

The **Glastonbury Festival of Contemporary Performing Arts** (known almost universally as "Glastonbury") is the world's largest open-air music festival and takes place annually on the last weekend in June. Though it stages dance, comedy, and other artistic performances, it's primarily renowned for its contemporary and indie-rock music. The first festival in the early 1970s featured only a couple of acts and attracted 1,500; today, the festival features hundreds of live performances and attendees number around 175,000. Performers over the years have included Kings of Leon, Midlake, and The Killers (with an occasional big-name headliner like Jay-Z or Coldplay). For up-to-date information on the festival and getting tickets (which often sell out less than 24 hours after going on sale), see www.glastonbury festivals.co.uk. Do note that there will be no festival in 2012 because of the Summer Olympic Games in London.

overnight choice for Day 4. You can see the main sights in a couple of hours. Make your first stop the cathedral, admiring its twin Norman spires and Decorated Gothic interior; then have a look at the **Guildhall** (p. 276, **2**), one of the oldest municipal buildings in England. The collections in the **Royal Albert Memorial Museum** (p. 278, **4**) include paintings and glassware, and local history is chronicled in exhibits at the **Quay House Visitor Centre** (p. 278, **3**), housed in an old warehouse in Exeter's revamped port area. If you have kids in tow, they'll love the guided **Underground Passages** (p. 278, **5**) tour through Exeter's medieval water tunnels. ⏱ 2 hr. See p. 276.

Castle Drogo is 16 miles west of Exeter, about a half-hour drive on the A30. This drive takes you into the northeastern section of Dartmoor National Park (p. 256).

> *Castle Drogo is set dramatically in Dartmoor National Park.*

6 ★★ **Castle Drogo.** The last castle to be built in England, Castle Drogo was designed by the famous English architect Sir Edward Lutyens and built between 1910 and 1930 on a scenic spot in what is now Dartmoor National Park. The home of a self-made shipping tycoon, the castle was fitted out with all the modern conveniences of the early 20th century and presents a unique time capsule of a vanished era of affluence and elegance. Give yourself about an hour to tour the house and its lovely gardens. ⏱ 1 hr. See p. 246, **2**.

Buckland Abbey is 26 miles southwest of Castle Drogo, about a 50-min. drive on the B3212, which cuts diagonally through Dartmoor National Park.

7 ★ **Buckland Abbey.** Two famous Elizabethan seafarers, Sir Richard Grenville and Sir Francis Drake, are associated with this manor house tucked into a secluded valley on the fringes of Dartmoor near Plymouth. Portions of the house were part of a 12th-century monastery dissolved by Henry VIII; the **Great Barn** used by the monks still exists. You can see the house, the barn, and the grounds in about an hour. ⏱ 1 hr. See p. 246, **3**.

Plymouth is 10 miles southwest of Buckland Abbey, a 25-min. drive on A386.

The Saint's Way

This part of Cornwall is great walking country. The 26-mile-long **Saint's Way** begins at Padstow on the north coast, crosses the moors of central Cornwall, and ends at Fowey. During the Bronze and Iron Ages, Saint's Way was a coast-to-coast trading route that avoided the treacherous waters off Land's End. Later, Saint's Way became the route for missionaries and pilgrims crossing from Ireland to take ships from Fowey to France and on to Rome or Santiago de Compostela in Spain. You can see hill forts, granite Celtic crosses, holy wells, and ancient churches all along the route.

> With a population of just over 2,000, Fowey is the quintessential Cornish harbor town and also serves as a good base for coastal exploring.

8 Plymouth. The old port of Plymouth, where the Elizabethan seafarer Sir Francis Drake set sail in 1577 for his 3-year circumnavigation of the globe and where the Pilgrims left for the New World in 1620, was gutted by German bombs in World War II and has sadly lost much of its medieval character. It's not an important stop in your exploration of the West Country, but you may want to spend a couple of hours looking at the old ramparts and citadel known as **the Hoe** and the modest **Mayflower Steps** memorial. You may also want to visit the **National Marine Aquarium,** which chronicles the aquatic life in Devon's rivers and streams, or you may want to take a **boat tour** of Plymouth Sound. ⏱ 2 hr. See p. 238, **2**.

Fowey is 38 miles west of Plymouth, about an hour's drive on A38 and A390.

9 ★ Fowey. Located about midway between Plymouth and Penzance, Fowey (pronounced foy) is a small, scenic harbor town that stretches along the green, wooded banks of the River Fowey, a shipping channel that empties into St. Austell Bay. The river is a favorite spot for pleasure boats of all kinds. A car-ferry service runs between Fowey to Bodinnick, on the east side of the river. Daphne du Maurier (1907–89), who used Cornwall as a setting for her most famous novel, *Rebecca*, grew up in Bodinnick. Fowey is a pleasant spot to get out of the car and spend half an hour strolling along the picturesque streets and the river, or you can make it your overnight stop for Day 4. ⏱ 30 min.

On Day 5, make your first stop the Lost Gardens of Heligan, 14 miles west of Fowey, a half-hour's drive on the A3082 and B3273.

10 ★★ Lost Gardens of Heligan. Cornwall has many magnificent gardens, but the gardens at Heligan have a poignant history that makes them quite unique. If you're a garden-lover, plan to spend at least 3 hours discovering the past and exploring the present at this special place. ⏱ 2 hr. See p. 251, **3**.

Head next to Penzance, 41 miles southwest of the Lost Gardens of Heligan, about an hour's drive on the A30.

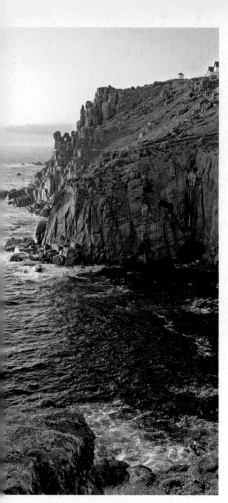

> *The Atlantic Ocean first hits the British mainland at Land's End, the southwestern tip of Cornwall.*

⑪ Penzance. Busy, bustling Penzance is your overnight stop for Day 5. The most westerly city in England, this holiday town overlooking Mount's Bay is close to several popular spots on and around the tip of Cornwall. In the afternoon, drive the short distance to **St. Michael's Mount** and/or **Trengwainton Garden.** In town, you can stroll along **Chapel Street,** the historic center of Penzance, and enjoy a meal at one of Penzance's many good restaurants. ⏲ At least 1 hr. See p. 280.

St. Michael's Mount is 3½ miles east of Penzance, a 10-min. drive on the A30.

⑫ ★★★ St. Michael's Mount. No tour of Cornwall would be complete without a visit to the island-castle of St. Michael's Mount, an easy half-day trip from Penzance. ⏲ 2 hr. See p. 249, ⑨.

Trengwainton Garden is 2½ miles northwest of Penzance, a 10-min. drive on Boscathnoe Lane.

⑬ ★★ Trengwainton Garden. Another easy half-day excursion from Penzance, the luxurious gardens at Trengwainton date back to the 18th century and are famed for their rhododendrons, some of which were the first specimens to flower outside their native habitats. The gardens are a year-round treasure. ⏲ 1 hr. See p. 255, ⑩.

Cornish coastal explorations are on the roster for Day 6. Start by driving to Land's End, 9 miles southwest of Penzance, a 15-min. drive on the A30.

⑭ Land's End. In the days of ship travel, the southwesternmost tip of Cornwall was the last hallowed bit of England that immigrants and passengers on ocean liners saw as they left England. The rocky coastline remains intact, and you can just have a look at the view or, if the place intrigues you, spend a pleasant hour walking along the cliffs, but to get to the overlook and pathways you have to pass through a cheesy collection of fun-fair "attractions." ⏲ 15 min. for overlook. See p. 241, ⑩.

St. Ives is 18 miles northeast of Land's End, a half-hour drive on the A30 and B3311.

⑮ ★★ St. Ives. Spend your sixth day and night in St. Ives, where the honey-colored sands and soft, shimmering colors of the sea have attracted artists for over a century. A compact and close-knit fishing village before it spread out and became one of Cornwall's most famous seaside resorts, St. Ives still enchants with its warren of narrow lanes and side-by-side stone fisherman's cottages, now converted into galleries, restaurants, and shops. The town makes a great base for exploring the tip of Cornwall and draws visitors to its clean, family-friendly **beaches** and two major attractions: the **Tate St. Ives** (p. 284, ❶), a museum that displays the works of artists who lived in or visited St. Ives, and the **Barbara Hepworth Museum and Sculpture Garden** (p. 285, ❷), the home and studio of the great sculptor Barbara Hepworth. ⏱ 4 hr. See p. 284.

On Day 7, you'll continue up the Cornish coast to Tintagel, 72 miles northeast of St. Ives, a 1½-hr. drive on the A30 and A39.

⑯ ★★ **Tintagel.** The atmospheric ruins that add such a romantic and mysterious allure to this beauty spot on the northern Cornish coast are thought to have been part of an ancient monastery and have mythical associations with the legend of King Arthur. Several British scribes, including poet Alfred, Lord Tennyson in his famed *Idylls of the King,* have declared Tintagel as the legendary king's birthplace. Spend an hour exploring this spectacular site overlooking the thundering waves of the Atlantic, but be prepared for a fairly steep set of stairs. ⏱ 1 hr. See p. 226, ❹.

Clovelly is 33 miles north of Tintagel, an hour's drive on B3263 and B39.

⑰ ★ **Clovelly.** One of the most charming, unusual, and picturesque hamlets in Cornwall, this former fishing village clings to the side of an oceanside cliff and has one steep, stone-set path called **Up-along** (or Down-along, depending on which way you're going) that zig-zags down from the **Visitor Centre** to the ancient **quay** far below. Spend a couple of hours exploring this collection of tiny stone cottages with their pocket gardens; if you're snagged by Clovelly's charm, you can spend the night. ⏱ 1½ hr. See p. 242, ⑬.

> The streets of Clovelly are so small and steep, donkeys are required to haul goods up from the sea.

Where to Stay & Dine

★ **Food for Thought** FOWEY *FRENCH*
A French bistro atmosphere, an outdoor patio next to the river, and a great fixed-price menu make this friendly restaurant a smart choice for lunch or dinner. 4 Town Quay. ☎ 01726/832-221. www.foodforthought.fowey.com. Entrees lunch £9–£12, dinner £16–£25, fixed-price menu £20. MC, V. Lunch & dinner Mon–Sat, brunch Sun.

Globe Posting House Hotel FOWEY
The rooms in this 16th-century cottage near the quay are small, snug, and simple; an on-site restaurant serves lunch and dinner daily during the summer. 19 Fore St. ☎ 01726/833-322. 3 units. Doubles £50–£70 w/breakfast. MC, V.

★ **Number 17 Esplanade** FOWEY
Lovely rooms, most of them overlooking the Fowey River, and a fine-dining restaurant, make this small hotel a charming place to spend the night. Esplanade. ☎ 01726/833-315. www.number17esplanadefowey.co.uk. 12 units. Doubles £144–£248 w/breakfast. AE, MC, V.

Discovering the Southwest Coast

From sheltered, balmy bays and beaches of tawny sand to wild, windswept cliffs and rocky headlands pummeled by thundering waves, the coastline of Devon and Cornwall in southwest England has something for everyone. This 3-day itinerary takes you to places where fishermen and explorers set out to sea, pirates plundered, and smugglers traded contraband and eluded the authorities.

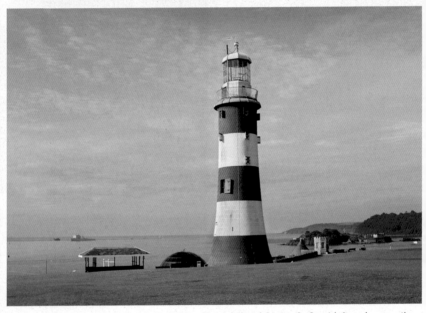

> *Plymouth Hoe was where Sir Francis Drake played bowls before defeating the Spanish Armada—or so the legend goes.*

START Torquay, 216 miles west of London, a 4-hr. drive on the M4 and M5 or a 3- to 4-hr. train trip from London's Paddington Station.
TRIP LENGTH 3 days; 252 miles.

❶ Torquay. Torquay (pronounced tor-*key*) lies on sheltered **Tor Bay,** an inlet of the English Channel, in an area known as the **English Riviera** because of its mild temperatures and easy access to the sea. Though it's a bit dull

Travel Tip

You can easily get to Torquay, Plymouth, Penzance, and St. Ives—the major cities and towns on this 3-day itinerary—by train from London, but to explore the coast of Devon and Cornwall you need a car. Your best option is to take the train to Torquay, the start of the tour, and rent a car there.

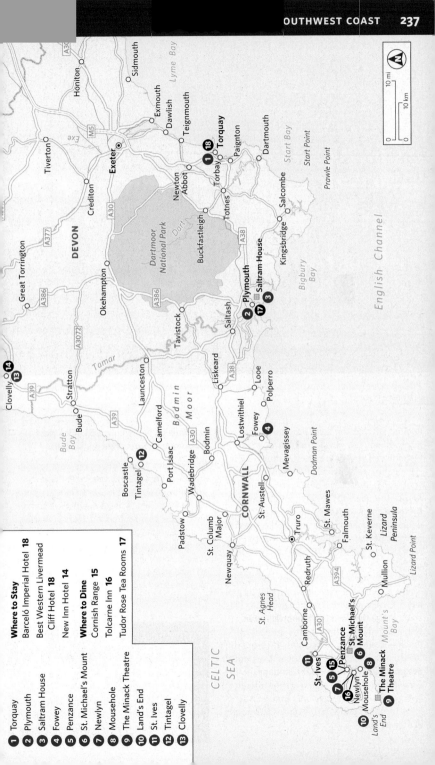

Sidmouth
Lyme Bay
Honiton
Exmouth
Tiverton
Dawlish
Teignmouth
Torquay
1 **18**
Exeter
Torbay Paignton
Crediton
Newton Abbot
Dartmouth
Start Bay
Start Point

DEVON

Totnes
Salcombe
Prawle Point

Great Torrington

Dartmoor National Park

Buckfastleigh
Kingsbridge
Okehampton

Saltram House
Plymouth **2** **17** **3**
Bigbury Bay
English Channel
Saltash
Tavistock

Stratton
Tamar
Launceston
Liskeard
Looe
Polperro

Clovelly **14** **13**

Bude Bay
Bude
Camelford
Bodmin Moor
Lostwithiel
Fowey **4**
Mevagissey
Dodman Point

Boscastle
Tintagel **12**
Port Isaac
Bodmin
Wadebridge
St. Austell

CORNWALL

Padstow
St. Columb Major
St. Mawes
Falmouth
St. Keverne
Lizard Peninsula

Newquay
Truro
Redruth
Mullion
Lizard Point

St. Agnes Head
Camborne
Mount's Bay

CELTIC SEA
St. Ives **11** **15**
Penzance
St. Michael's Mount **6**
5 **8**
7 **16**
Newlyn
Mousehole
The Minack Theatre 9
10
Land's End

Where to Stay
18 Barceló Imperial Hotel **18**
Best Western Livermead Cliff Hotel **18**
New Inn Hotel **14**

Where to Dine
Cornish Range **15**
Tolcarne Inn **16**
Tudor Rose Tea Rooms **17**

1 Torquay
2 Plymouth
3 Saltram House
4 Fowey
5 Penzance
6 St. Michael's Mount
7 Newlyn
8 Mousehole
9 The Minack Theatre
10 Land's End
11 St. Ives
12 Tintagel
13 Clovelly

10 mi
10 km

> *The beaches and attractions of Torquay and surrounding towns make up what's ambitiously dubbed the "English Riviera."*

and has seen better days, Torquay makes for a convenient, low-key overnight stop at the beginning of your coastal explorations. Victorian health-seekers made the town a popular spot, and it remained a popular resort until the 1970s. Torquay and the neighboring towns of **Brixham** and **Paignton** form **Torbay,** a cluster of resorts with sandy beaches, parks, seaside promenades, and gardens. **Torre Abbey** (The King's Drive; ☎ 01803/293-593; £5.75 adults, £4.80 seniors, £2.45 kids), a 12th-century abbey later converted to a luxurious residence, is now a municipal museum with painting galleries, furnished period rooms, ancient cellars, and the **Agatha Christie Memorial Room** displaying manuscripts and memorabilia of the famous mystery writer, born in Torquay in 1890. From May through October, **Dartmouth Steam Railway & Riverboat Company,** Totnes Quay (☎ 01803/555-872; www.dartmouth railriver.co.uk), runs daily boat excursions from Torquay up the Dart River to Dartmouth. ⏱ At least 1 hr.

Continue on to Plymouth, 31 miles west of Torquay, an hour's drive on the A38.

❷ Plymouth. Many Americans want to visit Plymouth because the *Mayflower* Pilgrims set sail from this port in Devon in 1620, but if you're expecting to find a quaint Elizabethan town you'll be disappointed. During World War II, German bombs gutted the ancient town, and the way it's been rebuilt isn't what you would call picturesque. If you want to stop off here, give yourself a couple of hours to explore the area around Plymouth Harbour. **The Barbican,** a small segment of the Elizabethan

Plymouth: Departure Point for the U.S.

During the 19th century, more emigrant ships bound for the United States left from Plymouth than from anywhere else in Europe. Small wonder that more than 100 towns in New England are named after places in Devon.

town reconstructed around the harbor, is Plymouth's primary tourist area. Today's mall-like atmosphere makes it difficult to imagine Plymouth when it was one of England's greatest ports. Sir Francis Drake, who lived at **Buckland Abbey** (p. 246, ❸), became Plymouth's mayor after he made his famous 3-year round-the-world voyage (1577–80) on the *Golden Hind.* South of the Barbican is **the Hoe,** a promontory with ramparts, a citadel, and an 18th-century lighthouse overlooking **Plymouth Sound,** an inlet of the English Channel. The River Tamar, the age-old boundary between Devon and Cornwall and a Royal Navy anchorage for more than 400 years, flows into the sound from the west. To the east, you can see the River Plym, from which Plymouth takes its name. The **Mayflower Steps** (West Pier, Barbican), actually a small commemorative venue with a rather unimposing neoclassical archway erected in 1934, mark the spot from which the *Mayflower* sailed for the New World. The popular and well-designed **National Marine Aquarium,** Rope Walk, Coxside (☎ 01752/600-301; www.national-aquarium.co.uk; £11 adults, £9 seniors, £6.50 kids, £30 families), gives insight into the lives of the sealife that inhabit the rivers of Devon and the waters of Plymouth Sound. **Plymouth Boat Cruises,** Phoenix Wharf (☎ 01752/671-166; £6.25 adults, £3 kids), offers a 1-hour cruise of Plymouth Sound. ⏱ At least 1 hr.

Your next stop is Saltram House, 3½ miles west of Plymouth, a 15-min. drive on the A379.

Exploring the Penwith Peninsula

On a leisurely half-day tour from Penzance, you can explore the Penwith Peninsula and see more of the Cornish coastline. B3315 follows the peninsula's southern coastline past small fishing villages to famous Land's End, where you can pick up the fast A30 back to Penzance or St. Ives. The distances here aren't great; driving this loop without stopping takes about an hour. You may prefer to skip the peninsula portion of the itinerary and head directly to St. Ives (⓫ and p. 284), an 8-mile, 20-minute drive north of Penzance on the B3311.

> *Scotsman Robert Adam, who designed Saltram House, pictured, was one of 18th-century Britain's foremost architects.*

❸ ★★ **Saltram House.** This Georgian-era mansion with interiors by the 18th-century master-designer Robert Adam is one of the best-preserved houses of the Age of Elegance and well worth at least an hour of your time. ⏱ 1 hr. See p. 247, ❺.

Your last stop on Day 1 is Fowey, 38 miles west of Plymouth, an hour's drive on the A38 and A390.

❹ ★ **Fowey.** This picturesque town with its quay on the Fowey River makes a romantic spot for an overnight stay. ⏱ 30 min. to stroll through town. See p. 233, ❾.

On the morning of Day 2, you'll head for Penzance, 55 miles southwest of Fowey, a 75-min. drive on the A30.

❺ **Penzance.** With its assortment of hotels and restaurants and proximity to the Penwith Peninsula and Land's End, St. Michael's Mount, and Trengwainton Garden, this small city overlooking Mount's Bay on the south coast of Cornwall is a good place to spend the second night of your coastal journey. ⏱ 1 hr. to explore the town. See p. 280.

> *Like so many Cornish seaside settlements, Mousehole was frequented by smugglers in centuries past.*

St. Michael's Mount is 3½ miles east of Penzance, a 10-min. drive on A30.

6 ★★★ **kids** **St. Michael's Mount.** The St. Aubyn family has called this island-castle home for some 350 years. In the 16th and 17th centuries, St. Michael's Mount was a coastal fortress, and back in the 12th century the island was a monastery. Today, this history-laden castle atop a sea-girt island is one of the most popular attractions in Cornwall, and on a 2-hour visit you'll see why. ⏱ **2 hr. See p. 249, 9 .**

The first stop on the Penwith Peninsula is Newlyn, 1½ miles south of Penzance on the B3315.

7 **Newlyn.** Chances are that any fresh fish or lobster you eat in Penzance or St. Ives was caught in the waters near Newlyn, home of England's second-largest fishing fleet. Because of overfishing, however, the pilchard (mature sardines) fishing industry, which was the mainstay of Cornwall's coastal villages from the medieval era until the early part of

the 20th century, is now a tiny fragment of what it once was. **The Pilchard Works Museum and Factory,** Fore St. (☎ 07809/609-545), the last remaining salt pilchard factory in England, has a small adjunct museum that explains the process of curing pilchards. The seascapes and the quality of light along this part of the Cornish coast lured several artists to the area in the late Victorian era. **The Newlyn Art Gallery,** Newlyn Green (☎ 01736/363-715; free admission), has a small collection of the distinctive Arts and Crafts copper work that was produced in Newlyn from 1890 to 1950. ⏱ 30 min.

Mousehole is 1½ miles south of Newlyn, a 5-min. drive on the B3315 and Mousehole Lane.

8 **Mousehole.** With its curving quay, small protected harbor, and quaint stone cottages, the former fishing village of Mousehole (pronounced *muz*-zle) is a pretty place. The town attracts many tourists who come for lunch or tea and a look around. ⏱ 30 min.

The Minack Theatre is 8½ miles southwest of Mousehole on B3315.

9 The Minack Theatre. Carved out of a rocky hillside, the Minack is legendary because of its outdoor stage overlooking the ocean, where theater companies from all over England stage performances of everything from Shakespeare to musical comedies, a tradition dating to 1932. The Visitor Centre has information on the theater's history. ⏱ 15 min. Porchcurno. ☎ 01736/810-694. www.minack.com. Visitor Centre: admission £3.50 adults, £1.40 kids. Performances: May to mid-Sept Mon–Fri 8pm, Wed & Fri also 2pm. Visitor Centre: daily Apr–Sept 9:30am–5:30pm, Oct–Mar 10am–4pm.

Land's End is 3½ miles northwest of the Minack Theatre, a 10-min. drive on the B3315.

10 Land's End. Atlantic-facing Land's End, where high granite cliffs plunge down to the roaring sea, is one of the country's most famous and dramatic landmarks. But a theme park development that you have to pass through to reach the headland mars the grandeur of this windy point, the westernmost point in England. A well-marked path leads out to an **observation point,** and you can follow other coastal paths. The British-owned Isles of Scilly are 28 miles out to sea; otherwise, nothing lies between England and the eastern coast of North America. ⏱ 15 min.

On Day 3, drive the short distance to St. Ives, 17 miles northeast of Land's End, a half-hour drive on the A30.

11 ★★ St. Ives. When you see the shimmering cerulean sea around St. Ives, you'll understand why, a century ago, this erstwhile fishing village became an artists' colony and was then discovered by sun-starved Brits. But long before fishermen hauled in their catches of cod, crab, and herring; before painters reveled in the warm, clear light; and before holidaymakers played on the beaches of golden sand, the area around St. Ives was home to prehistoric peoples whose mysterious stone circles, tombs, and villages still dot the countryside.

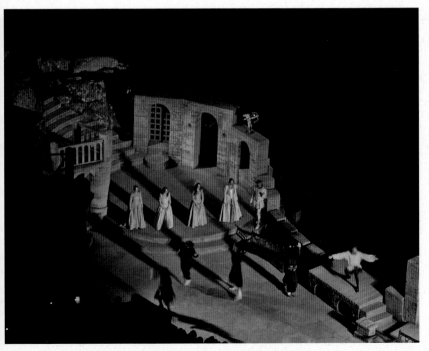

> The outdoor Minack Theatre is surely Britain's most dramatically sited stage.

> *The picturesque seaside towns of Cornwall, such as St. Ives, pictured, fill quickly during the peak summer season.*

St. Ives is artsy and sophisticated, with no lack of galleries and upscale boutiques, but it still remains a sunny summer resort town with lots of buzz and some of the busiest beaches in Cornwall. ⏱ 2 hr. See p. 284.

From St. Ives, head up the northern coast of Cornwall to Tintagel, 72 miles northeast of St. Ives, a 1½-hr. drive on A30 and A39.

⑫ ★★ **Tintagel.** The magic and majesty of Cornwall, a land where ancient legends never seem to die, springs to life in the ruins of Tintagel, a castle dramatically sited on a cliff overlooking the sea. ⏱ 30 min. See p. 226, ❹.

Clovelly is 33 miles north of Tintagel, an hour's drive on the B3263 and B39, about 12 miles west of Bideford; turn off the main road at Clovelly Cross roundabout and follow the signs to the Visitor Centre.

⑬ ★★ **Clovelly.** Your recommended overnight stop for Day 3, Clovelly on Cornwall's north coast, is absolutely unique: a privately owned Devon fishing village built along one main street that is so steep donkeys and sledges are used to haul goods up and down (cars are not allowed and wouldn't fit). The street, intricately cobbled with pebbles from the beach below, is called "Up-along" if you're panting your way up it, or "Down-along" if you're heading downhill to the harbor. Clovelly's impressive **quay** dates from the 14th century, as do many of the tiny, whitewashed cottages lining Up-along/Down-along. There are some pretty clifftop walks in the vicinity, but otherwise not a lot to do except poke around in secretive little alleys and enjoy the views and overall charm. If you're a gardener, you may want to stop in to visit **Clovelly Court Gardens** (50p), where Victorian greenhouses shelter tender plants and fruits and the herbaceous borders are ablaze with color all summer. All visitors to Clovelly must park at the **Visitor Centre** (☎ 01237/131-781; www.clovelly. co.uk), which is a large and somewhat tacky souvenir and food shop with a video about the town's history. Day visitors must pay to visit the town (£5.95 adults, £3.75 kids, £16 families); if you're staying overnight, you can pass through free of charge. ⏱ 1½ hr.

Where to Stay & Dine

> *A guest room at the New Inn Hotel, Clovelly.*

★★ **kids** **Barceló Imperial Hotel** TORQUAY
Grand in all senses of the word, this old-fashioned hotel with modern amenities overlooks Tor Bay and is the dowager empress of Torquay luxury resort hotels. **1 Park Hill Rd.** ☎ 01803/294-301. www.barcelo-hotels.co.uk. 152 units. Doubles £120–£230 w/breakfast. AE, MC, V.

★ **kids** **Best Western Livermead Cliff Hotel** TORQUAY This hotel sits right on the water's edge, with steps down to a beach, and offers comfortable rooms with sea views. **Sea Front.** ☎ 01803/299-666. www.livermeadcliff.co.uk. 67 units. Doubles £120–£140 w/breakfast. AE, MC, V.

★ **Cornish Range** MOUSEHOLE *SEAFOOD*
Fish soup, crab Florentine, roast cod, and mullet are staples on the menu of this good seafood restaurant, which also rents out three comfortable and attractive guest rooms. **6 Chapel St.** ☎ 01736/731-488. 3 units. Doubles £80–£110 w/breakfast. Lunch & dinner daily summer, Wed–Sat winter. Entrees £12–£19. MC, V.

New Inn Hotel CLOVELLY
The town's best hotel offers cozy, quiet rooms, the town's best restaurant, and special deals that include bed, breakfast, and dinner. **High St. (another name for Up-along/Down-along).** ☎ 01237/431-303. www.clovelly.co.uk. 8 units. Doubles £104–£114 w/breakfast. MC, V.

Tolcarne Inn NEWLYN *FISH & CHIPS/PUB FARE*
If the sea air has you feeling peckish, this pub-restaurant is the best place in town for fish and chips, fresh crab, and Newlyn fish pie. **Tolcarne Place.** ☎ 01736/365-074. Entrees £6–£16. MC, V. Lunch & dinner daily.

Tudor Rose Tea Rooms PLYMOUTH *TEA/LIGHT FARE* This convenient and inexpensive little tearoom and lunch spot, close to the Mayflower Steps but away from the crowds on the quay, dates from 1640 and has an outdoor garden. **36 New St.** ☎ 01752/255-502). Menu items £5–£7. No credit cards. Lunch & afternoon tea Tues–Sat.

Great Houses of the West Country

The varied landscapes of Devon and Cornwall are dotted with a wonderful assortment of stately homes, from medieval manors to modern mansions built in the early 20th century. This itinerary takes you to the best of them, following a trail that runs from Exeter to Penzance. You'll best enjoy these magnificent reminders of times gone by if you don't try to see more than two of them in one day.

> One of the Blue Drawing Rooms in the castle on St. Michael's Mount.

START Exeter, 197 miles southwest of London, a 3½-hr. drive on M4 and M5, or a 2½-hr. train ride from London's Waterloo Station. **TRIP LENGTH** 4 days. Total distance is 175 miles.

1 ★★ **Exeter.** This small, busy cathedral city in Devon is a good place to begin your house tour of the West Country. After you arrive by car or train, spend a couple of hours exploring the majestic **cathedral** (p. 276, **1**), looking at the paintings and artifacts in the **Royal Albert Memorial Museum** (p. 278, **4**), and perusing the local history exhibits at the **Quay House Visitor Centre** (p. 278, **3**). You can easily visit **Castle Drogo** (**2**) as a half-day trip on your first day. ⊙ At least 2 hr. See p. 276.

On your first afternoon, take a trip to Castle Drogo, 16 miles west of Exeter, a half-hour drive on the A30.

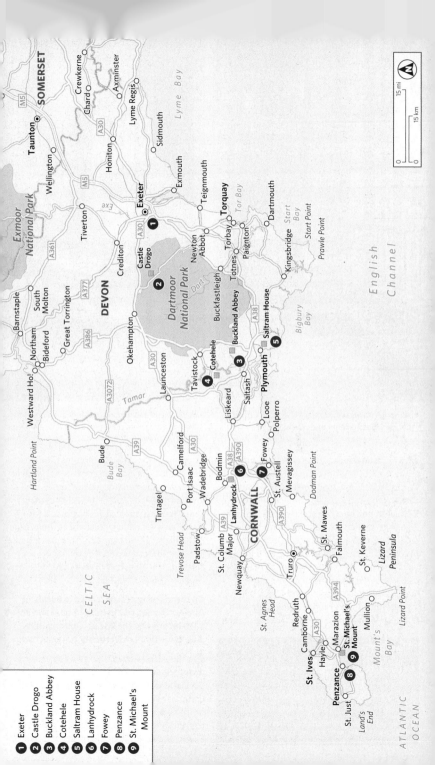

> *Although it was only completed in 1930, Castle Drogo exudes an aura of centuries past.*

> *Buckland, like so many monasteries and abbeys, was converted into a private manor house during the reign of Henry VIII.*

❷ ★★ Castle Drogo. The architect Sir Edwin Lutyens (1869–1944) designed this granite castle for a self-made millionaire, Julius Drewe, who had it built between 1910 and 1930. Perched on a rocky cliff above the Teign River, the castle commands panoramic views of Fingle Gorge and Dartmoor. Drewe wanted his dream house—the last castle built in England—to combine the grandeur of a medieval castle with the comforts of 20th-century life. Designed for easy, elegant living, the interior includes a grand drawing room with family memorabilia, a kitchen, a scullery, and elaborately appointed bathrooms. The extensive grounds include terraced formal gardens with roses and herbaceous borders as well as lovely woodlands. ⏱ 2 hr. to visit house & gardens. Drewsteignton, near Chagford. ☎ 01647/433-306. www.nationaltrust.org.uk. Admission £9.10 adults, £4.60 kids, £22.70 families. House: mid-Mar to Oct daily 11am–5pm; rest of year Sat–Sun 11am–4pm (call to verify opening times). Garden: daily 8:30am–5pm.

On the morning of Day 2, head to Buckland Abbey, 41 miles southwest of Exeter and about a 1½-hr. drive on the B3212. This drive cuts diagonally through Dartmoor National Park.

❸ ★ Buckland Abbey. Tucked away in its own secluded valley above the River Tavy, Buckland was originally a small but influential Cistercian monastery. Parts of the abbey date from the 13th century, but the main part of the house was built in the 16th century, when Sir Richard Grenville remodeled the dissolved

> *The elegant surrounds of Saltram House offer an escape from the high-season seaside crowds.*

abbey into a manor house. The tower over the church's crossing and many other original features of Buckland Abbey are still visible. The great Elizabethan navigator Sir Francis Drake bought Buckland in 1581, shortly after circumnavigating the world. The house displays memorabilia of Drake and Grenville. Behind the house lies the magnificent ★★ **Great Barn,** a monastic tithe barn where the monks stored the food farmers were required to give them. There are some delightful woodland walks on the estate grounds. ⏱ 1 hr. South of Yelverton. ☎ 01822/853-607. www.nationaltrust.org.uk. Admission £9 adults, £4.50 kids, £22.50 families. Mid-Mar to Oct daily 10:30am–5:30pm; other months check website for open hours.

Cotehele, the next great house on the itinerary, is 12 miles southwest of Buckland Abbey, a half-hour drive on the B3257.

❹ ★★ **Cotehele.** One of the least altered medieval houses in England, and noteworthy for its magnificent gardens, Cotehele (pronounced co-*teel*) was built of granite and slate on the steep, wooded slopes of the River Tamar and blends in beautifully with the landscape. The rooms inside, unlit by electricity (some so dim you may have trouble finding your way), display a wonderful collection of ancient oak furniture, pewter, armor, and tapestries. The chapel contains the oldest working domestic clock in England, still in its original place. Formal gardens, terraces, and a daffodil meadow surround the house, situated near the top of the valley. The steep valley gardens below contain many species of exotic plants that thrive in Cornwall's mild climate. A good restaurant is in the nearby medieval barn. ⏱ 1 hr. St. Dominick, near Saltash. ☎ 01579/351-346. www.nationaltrust.org.uk. Admission £10 adults, £5 kids, £25 families. House: mid-Mar to Oct Sat–Thurs 11am–4:30pm. Garden: daily 10am–dusk.

After visiting Buckland Abbey, you may want to call it a day and make your way to a hotel in Dartmoor National Park (for hotel recommendations in Dartmoor, see p. 259) or Plymouth, 16 miles south on the A38, about a 40-min. drive from Cotehele (see p. 238, ❷, for more on Plymouth, and p. 243 for hotel recommendations). On the morning of Day 3, head for Saltram House, 3½ miles west of Plymouth, about a 15-min. drive on the A79.

❺ ★★ **Saltram House.** Even though it's one of England's finest examples of an intact Georgian-era house, Saltram remains largely undiscovered by the public, which makes a visit here all that much more enjoyable. Originally a Tudor manor owned by the Earls of

> *The Great Hall at Cotehele is largely unaltered since Tudor times.*

Morley, Saltram eventually became the home of the Parker family, who lived in it for over 300 years. When a fire in the mid-18th century destroyed part of the Tudor mansion, John Parker II hired his friend, the painter Sir Joshua Reynolds (1723–92), the architect-designer Robert Adam (1728–92), the furniture designer Thomas Chippendale (1718–79), and the painter Angelica Kauffmann (1741–1807) to help with the new house. Working together, this illustrious quartet created a wonderfully elegant home, inside and out. The interiors, with their original decor, furnishings, and plasterwork, represent what many believe to be Robert Adam's finest work. Particularly impressive are the **Saloon** (main drawing room) and the **Western Apartments,** only recently opened to visitors. The house was used as the setting for the 1995 film version of Jane Austen's *Sense and Sensibility*. The lovely park surrounding the house contains a small castle folly with a view of Plymouth Sound and a neoclassical amphitheatre. ⏱ 1 hr. Plympton, near Plymouth. ☎ 01752/333-500. www.nationaltrust.org.uk. Admission £10.10 adults, £5 kids, £25.10 families. Mid-Mar to Oct Sat–Thurs noon–4:30pm.

Your second great house of the day is Lanhydrock, 34 miles west of Saltram House, about an hour's drive on the A38.

❻ ★★ Lanhydrock. Set in a beautiful landscape overlooking the valley of the Fowey River, Lanhydrock (lan-*hi*-druck) is one of the grandest homes in Cornwall. The magnificent **Long Gallery,** with its 17th-century plaster ceiling depicting scenes from the Old Testament, is one of the few rooms that survived a disastrous fire in 1881, after which the house was rebuilt in a High Victorian style with all the modern conveniences available at the time. You can view approximately 50 rooms that reflect the organization and lifestyles of a rich Victorian household, which depended on servants (and lots of them) to keep it running. In the kitchens, sculleries, and larders where the staff toiled long hours, Lanhydrock reveals the other side of grand living. And that's part of what makes this place so fascinating. Different kinds of gardens—from Victorian parterres to woodland gardens with camellias, magnolias, and rhododendrons—surround the house. An avenue of ancient beech and sycamore trees runs from the 17th-century gatehouse down to a medieval bridge across the Fowey. ⏱ 2 hr. Southeast of Bodmin. ☎ 01218/265-950. www.nationaltrust.org.uk. Admission £11.50 adults, £5.70 kids, £29 families. House: Apr–Oct Tues–Sun 11am–5:30pm (Oct until 5pm). Garden: daily 10am–6pm.

Fowey is 10 miles south of Lanhydrock, about a 20-min. drive on the B3269.

❼ ★ Fowey. This small town stretched along the Fowey River is one good option for spending your third night before continuing your great houses tour. ⏱ 30 min. See p. 233, ❾.

On Day 4, head to Penzance, 55 miles southwest of Fowey, a drive of about 1 hr. 15 min. on the A30.

❽ Penzance. The number of good hotels and restaurants in Penzance, and its proximity to St. Michael's Mount, make it a good overnight choice. ⏱ 1 hr. to explore town. See p. 280.

St. Michael's Mount is 3½ miles east of Penzance, a 10-min. drive on the A30. If you don't want to drive, take bus no. 20 or 22 from Penzance to Marazion, the town opposite St. Michael's Mount.

❾ ★★★ St. Michael's Mount. For nearly 350 years, this amazing island-castle in Mount's Bay has been the home of the St. Aubyn family. Connected to the mainland by a 152m-long (500-ft.) causeway (if the tide is in, boatmen known as hobblers can ferry you over or back), the castle incorporates parts of an earlier 12th-century Benedictine priory that was founded as the daughter house of Mont St. Michel in Normandy. Later, in the 16th and 17th centuries, St. Michael's Mount was an important fortress to protect the coastline from foreign attack. (The beacon on top of the church tower was lit to warn of the approach of the Spanish Armada in 1588.) A royalist stronghold during the Civil War, the fort was forced to surrender after a long siege. The **Entrance Hall,** altered in the 19th century, was the living area for the Captain of the Mount in the 16th and 17th centuries. The little adjacent chamber, known as **Sir John's Room,** is the owner's private sitting room. Sporting weapons and war memorabilia hang in the **Armoury.** The snug **Library** is in the oldest (12th-century) part of the castle, as is the **Dining Room,** which served as the monks' refectory. The **Priory Church** on the island's summit has beautiful rose windows. In a newer section of the castle, you can see the elegant rococo-style **Blue Drawing Rooms.** Be aware that you have to climb many stairs to reach the castle. If you need some nourishment after all those stairs, you can have lunch or tea at one of two restaurants on the island (menu items £4–£8; Apr–Oct same hours as house). ⏱ 2 hr. Mount's Bay, Marazion. ☎ 01736/710-507. www.stmichaelsmount.co.uk. Castle and garden: admission £8.75 adults, £4.25 kids, £22 families. Apr–Oct Sun–Fri 10:30am–5pm (July–Aug until 5:30pm).

If you have extra time, from Penzance you can also easily reach the famed garden at Trengwainton (p. 255, ❿) or continue on to St. Ives (p. 284).

Great Gardens of the West Country

Plants flourish in the mild climate and sheltered valleys of Devon and Cornwall, so it's not surprising that these two southwestern counties have some truly magnificent gardens filled with a variety of species, many of them exotics collected from Asia, Africa, and the Americas during the heyday of British plant collecting in the early to mid–19th century. This itinerary takes you to some of the most enchanting and beautiful places in England, created with enormous skill, foresight, and patience, and filled with year-round color.

> You can make significant savings by buying Eden Project tickets online before visiting.

START Fowey, 38 miles west of Plymouth, an hour's drive on the A38 and A390. **TRIP LENGTH** 3 days. Total distance is 157 miles.

❶ ★ Fowey. This charming town on the Fowey River makes a good starting point and overnight stop for the first day of your garden tour of Devon and Cornwall. ⏱ 30 min. to stroll through the town. See p. 233, **❾**.

Your first garden stop is Eden Project, 6½ miles west of Fowey, a 20-min. drive on the A3082.

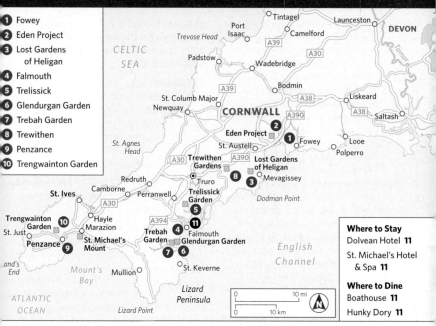

1. Fowey
2. Eden Project
3. Lost Gardens of Heligan
4. Falmouth
5. Trelissick
6. Glendurgan Garden
7. Trebah Garden
8. Trewithen
9. Penzance
10. Trengwainton Garden

Where to Stay
Dolvean Hotel **11**
St. Michael's Hotel & Spa **11**

Where to Dine
Boathouse **11**
Hunky Dory **11**

---

2 ★ kids **Eden Project.** Eden Project, overlooking St. Austell Bay, is both an educational resource and an environmental showcase. The site, which opened in 2001, comprises two gigantic geodesic conservatories (biodomes), one devoted to the rainforest and the other to the fruits and flowers of the Mediterranean, South Africa, and California. Sunflowers, lavender, and hemp are among the plants that grow outside on the acres of landscaped grounds. This intriguing project grows specimens from all sorts of different terrains in microhabitats—a fun way to introduce kids to plants and environmental issues. There are several cafes and restaurants on the grounds offering everything from Cornish cream teas to Mediterranean pasta dishes. ⏰ At least 2 hr. Bodelva, St. Austell. ☎ 01726/811-911. www.edenproject.com. Admission £20 adults, £14 seniors, £7.50 kids 5–16. Jan–Aug Fri–Mon 9:30am–6pm, Tues–Thurs 9:30am–8pm; Sept–Oct daily 9:30am–6pm; Nov–Dec Mon–Thurs 9:30am–3pm, Fri–Sat 9:30am–9pm, Sun 9:30am–6pm. Hours change yearly; call to verify.

Next, drive to The Lost Gardens of Heligan, 11 miles west of Eden Project, about a half-hour drive on the B3273.

3 ★★★ **Lost Gardens of Heligan.** The 400-hectare (1,000-acre) Heligan estate was the seat of the Tremayne family for more than 400 years, and by the late 19th century had reached its peak of productivity and ornamental beauty. World War I changed the fortunes of the family and the fate of the garden; by 1914 many of the staff had been enlisted to fight in the Great War and never returned. Over the next 70 years, as nature pursued its course, greenhouses and garden walls collapsed, the vegetable gardens went wild, and the entire estate became virtually lost beneath ivy and weeds. It wasn't rediscovered until the 1990s when ex-record producer Tim

Travel Tip

A car is necessary for this itinerary, which moves in a southwesterly direction from Devon into Cornwall. In some cases you can see two gardens in one day, but it would be unwise to try to see more than that. With a maximum of two gardens per day, you can linger a bit longer in the ones that really catch your fancy. If you're starting out in London, you may want to take the train to Plymouth and rent a car there.

Smit—who spearheaded the Eden Project (②)—decided to restore the gardens to their Victorian glory and to honor the hard-working gardeners who had made Heligan what it was. Today, 80 hectares (200 acres) have been restored. The **Northern Gardens** contain a walled **Flower Garden** and the **Victorian Production Gardens,** where 200 varieties of heritage fruit and vegetables are grown and supplied to the **Heligan Teahouse** (menu items £3.50–£7; same hours as garden). Exotic plants and romantic follies embellish the **Pleasure Grounds,** first laid out over 2 centuries ago. A boardwalk meanders through the **Jungle,** with its four ponds, giant rhubarb plants, banana plantations, and palm trees. In the **Wider Estate,** you can explore ancient pastures, woodlands, wetlands, ponds, and lakes all sustainably managed to maximize the biodiversity of habitats. ⏱ At least 1 hr. Pentewan, St. Austell. ☎ 01726/845-100. www. heligan.com. Admission £10 adults, £9 seniors, £6 kids, £27 families. Daily 10am–6pm (Oct–Mar until 5pm).

Return to Fowey for your first overnight. On the morning of Day 2, head to Falmouth, 33 miles southeast of Fowey and about an hour's drive on the A390.

④ **Falmouth.** A bustling port city overlooking the third-deepest natural harbor in the world makes a good place to stop for the second night of your garden tour. ⏱ 1 hr. to stroll through town. Falmouth Tourist Information Office, 11 Market Strand. ☎ 01326/312-300. www. discoverfalmouth.co.uk.

Your first garden visit on Day 2 is Trelissick, 11 miles northeast of Falmouth, a 25-min. drive on the A39.

⑤ ★ **Trelissick.** This beautiful garden at the head of the Fal estuary overlooking the Fal River was first planted over 200 years ago, and has evolved into one of the most beautiful landscape gardens in Cornwall. A pathway runs from the main garden, where magnolias, rhododendrons, camellias, flowering cherries, hydrangeas, and exotics such as gingkos and palms cover several tiered terraces down

> *The Victorian gardens at Heligan were rescued from the brink of oblivion in the 1990s.*

to what was once the private beach of the Copeland estate. As managing director of the Spode china factory in Stoke-on-Trent, Ronald Copeland was instrumental in having the flowers grown at Trelissick used as models for those painted on Spode china. Trelissick Garden is the home of the National Plant Collections of photinias and azaras. ⏱ At least 1 hr. Feock, near Truro. ☎ 01872/862-090. www.nationaltrust.org.uk. Admission £7.40 adults, £3.70 kids, £18 families. Daily Nov to mid-Feb 11am–4pm; mid-Feb to Oct 10am–5:30pm.

Head next to Glendurgan Garden, 5 miles southwest of Falmouth, a 15-min. drive on Carlidnack Rd.

❻ ★ kids **Glendurgan Garden.** Back in the 1820s and 1830s, when this sublime subtropical garden was first planted, finding new non-native plants was a major undertaking. Luckily, the family of Alfred Fox (1794–1874), the first owner-gardener of Glendurgan, had a shipping business, and their boats sailing into nearby Falmouth estuary carried with them trees, shrubs, and plants from Asia, Africa, and the Americas that thrived in the mild Cornish climate. Set in a wooded valley above the Helford River and Fal estuary, Glendurgan, with its serpentine paths and lush plantings, reflects the early Victorian taste for things romantic and picturesque. The garden has been added to over succeeding generations by other gardeners in the Fox family, and today is packed with plants from all over the world providing color and variety throughout the year. One of its most unique features, much loved by kids, is the laurel maze, planted in 1833. In the spring you'll see shows of bluebells, Lent lilies, columbines, and primroses, followed by rhododendrons, magnolias, and camellias. The winding garden paths gradually descend down the valley and lead to the tiny fishing village of Durgan. ⏱ At least 1 hr. Mawnan Smith, near Falmouth. ☎ 01326/252-020. www.nationaltrust.org.uk. Admission £7 adults, £3.60 kids, £17.50 families. Mid-Feb to Oct Tues–Sat 10:30am–5:30pm (Aug Mon also).

You can make an exception to the "two gardens a day" recommendation by visiting adjacent Trebah Garden, a half-mile southwest of Glendurgan Garden and a 2-min. drive on a signposted road.

> *Several non-native species flourish at Trelissick.*

❼ ★ **Trebah Garden.** The Fox family of Falmouth (the same family responsible for Glendurgan Garden, just to the west), acquired the ancient estate of Trebah (Gaelic for "the House on the Bay") in 1831. Alfred Fox's brother Charles (1797–1878), who first laid out Trebah as an 11-hectare (26-acre) pleasure garden, paid meticulous attention to the exact positioning of every tree. The garden was further embellished when Fox's daughter, Juliet Backhouse, acquired a huge collection of exotic plants and trees from all over the world, including many rare rhododendrons. Purchased in 1907, the garden continued to develop over the next 32 years. In 1944, however, the beach along the Helford River was covered in concrete, the rocks dynamited to allow access for tanks and vehicles (a memorial commemorates the regiment of U.S. infantry that

> *Giant* Gunnera *plants, here at Trebah Garden, are large enough for little visitors to hide beneath.*

8 ★★ **Trewithen.** The huge and spectacular flowering magnolia trees for which this 90-hectare (230-acre) woodland garden is justly famous were all grown from seeds collected in Asia between 1919 and 1932 and cultivated at Trewithen with infinite care and patience—the trees are frost-sensitive and can take 20 years before they begin to flower. These spectacular beauties, some of them now 20m (65 ft.) tall and considered the finest specimens in the U.K., explode in clouds of white, pink, and carmine-purple blooms in spring, as do the spectacular collections of tree rhododendrons and huge camellias, also propagated from wild seed obtained during the First World War. From the main lawn behind the 18th-century house, you are enticed into the woods down a network of grass and gravel paths that meander through thickets and glades where the magnolias share space with tree ferns, maples, Asiatic birches, azaleas, and camellias. Raised viewing platforms allow you to get closer to the flowers. The garden boasts 24 Champion Trees, all of which are either the tallest or the widest of their respective species in the U.K. A **camera obscura,** a device that projects an image from outside onto a table inside, is housed in a wooden hut high in the canopy of the trees. The **Sycamore Avenue,** one of the original parts of the garden, is planted with Cornish-bred varieties of daffodils, crocuses, and scillas to create a beautiful spring display. A small

embarked from Trebah for the D-Day assault on Omaha Beach in Normandy), and the garden used as an ammunition dump. In the postwar years, new owners introduced massive hydrangea plantings, and the concrete was removed from the beach. But it wasn't until 1981 that new owners Tony and Eira Hibbert began to reclaim the once-famous garden, which they reopened to the public in 1987. The **Planter's Café** (menu items £3.50–£7; daily 10am–4:30pm) is a good place for tea or a sandwich before or after your tour of Trebah. ◔ At least 1 hr. Mawnan Smith, near Falmouth. ☎ 01326/252-200. www.trebahgardens.co.uk. Admission Apr–Oct £7.50 adults, £6.50 seniors, £2.50 kids; Nov–Mar £3 adults, £2.50 seniors, £1.50 kids. Daily 10am–6:30pm (last entry 4:30pm).

Return to Falmouth for your overnight and start Day 3 with a visit to Trewithen, 18 miles northeast of Falmouth, a 40-min. drive on the A39 and A390.

Climate Change and Changing Gardens

Adapting to climate change is one of the biggest challenges facing gardens in Cornwall and throughout Great Britain. The changing climatic conditions are the equivalent of the U.K. moving southward by 16 miles every 5 years. Gardeners at Trewithen report higher temperatures, less rainfall, more light intensity in summer, fewer autumn frosts (which means less leaf color), and more wind storms and torrential rains in winter. The long-term effects on Trewithen's famous magnolias remain to be seen, but they are now flowering a month earlier than a century ago, with some varieties starting as early as December.

museum in the house chronicles the history of the plant hunters who are responsible for the superlative trees and rare shrubs you can see at Trewithen today. ⏲ At least 1 hr. Grampound, near Truro. ☎ 01726/883-647. www.trewithen gardens.co.uk. Admission £7.50 ages 12 & up. Mar–Sept Mon–Sat 10am–4:30pm (Mar–May Sun also).

Continue on to Penzance, 35 miles southwest of Trewithen, an hour's drive on the A30.

⑨ Penzance. Fine restaurants, good hotels, and close proximity to the final garden on this itinerary make Penzance a good choice for an overnight stay on Day 3. See p. 280.

Your second garden tour on Day 3 is Trengwainton Garden, 2 miles west of Penzance, a 5-min. drive on the B3312. To get to Trengwainton by bus from Penzance, take the First Western National (www.firstgroup.com) bus no. 10/A to St. Just and ask the driver to let you off at the stop nearest Trengwainton.

⑩ ★★ Trengwainton Garden. Nowhere else on mainland Britain is there a garden with plants as exotic as the ones grown here. Trengwainton (pronounced as it's spelled, treng-*wain*-ton), which means the "House of the Springs" in Cornish, is set in the granite hills behind Penzance, and commands panoramic views of Mount's Bay and the Lizard Peninsula. The first walled gardens were constructed in the 18th century, but the plantings didn't

> *The spectacular magnolia trees at Trewithen were all grown onsite from seeds.*

really flourish until the late 1920s, under Sir Edward Bolitho (1882–1969). Several species of rhododendrons, which Bolitho planted from seeds collected in Asia, flowered for the first time outside their native habitat in this garden. From camellias and magnolias in early spring to acres of blue hydrangea in late summer, Trengwainton is colorful year-round. You can have lunch or a Cornish cream tea in the teahouse. ⏲ At least 1 hr. Madron, near Penzance. ☎ 01736/363-148. www.national trust.org.uk. Admission £6.50 adults, £3.20 kids, £16.20 families. Mid-Feb to Oct Mon–Thurs & Sun 10:30am–5pm.

Where to Stay & Dine

★ Boathouse FALMOUTH *MODERN BRITISH*
This popular gastropub is a great place to enjoy a pint or a well-prepared meal of local seafood and Cornish produce. Trevethan Hill. ☎ 01326/315-425. Entrees £6–£11. MC, V. Lunch & dinner daily.

★ kids Dolvean Hotel FALMOUTH
The Victorian decor may be a bit too frilly and fussy for some, but this is one of Falmouth's top B&Bs and a comfy place to stay. 50 Melville Rd. ☎ 01326/313-658. www.dolvean.co.uk. 10 units. Doubles £75–£96 w/breakfast. MC, V.

★★ Hunky Dory FALMOUTH *SEAFOOD/ MODERN EUROPEAN* Enjoy freshly caught seafood and local Cornish specialties at this tony but casual and highly regarded restaurant. 46 Arewenack St. ☎ 01326/212-997. Entrees £12–£26. MC, V. Dinner nightly.

★★ St. Michael's Hotel & Spa FALMOUTH
A sunny, contemporary "coastal style" of decor, great ocean views, a full-service spa, and a fine restaurant make this upscale hotel a good choice. Gyllyngvase Beach. ☎ 01326/312-707. www.stmichaelshotel.co.uk. 30 units. Doubles £120–£210 w/breakfast. AE, MC, V.

Dartmoor National Park

A protected national park since 1951, Dartmoor encompasses some 368 square miles of high, open moorland covered with yellow-flowering gorse, purple heather, and windswept granite outcroppings called tors. Moorland rivers and their many small waterfalls rush down green wooded valleys. The last unspoiled landscape in England, Dartmoor is home to wild ponies, among many other kinds of wildlife. Although a national park, the land in Dartmoor is privately owned, and about 33,000 people live and work in the area. Scattered throughout Dartmoor are grand country hotels, cozy village inns, and countryside B&Bs.

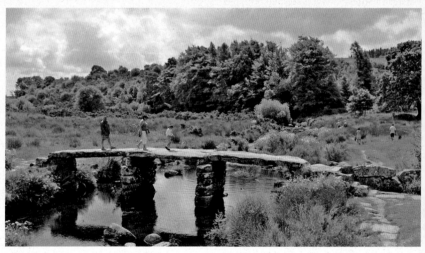

> Dartmoor boasts more than 500 miles of public footpaths.

START Exeter, 197 miles west of London, is about a 3½-hr. drive on the M4 and M5, or a 2 hr. 15-min. train ride from London's Waterloo Station. TRIP LENGTH 2 days. Total distance is 44 miles.

❶ ★★ **Exeter.** The nearest large city to the park, Exeter is a good starting point for exploring Dartmoor. After picking up your rental car, spend an hour visiting **Exeter Cathedral** (p. 276, ❶) and strolling through the town. See p. 276.

From Exeter, head into Dartmoor to visit Castle Drogo, 15 miles west of Exeter, a half-hour's drive on the A30.

❷ ★★ **Castle Drogo.** The last castle to be built in England, designed by Sir Edwin Lutyens and completed in 1930, sits high above a wooded valley amidst acres of gardens in what is now Dartmoor National Park. ⊙ 1 hr. See p. 246, ❷.

Chagford is 4 miles southwest of Castle Drogo, a 10-min. drive on the B3206.

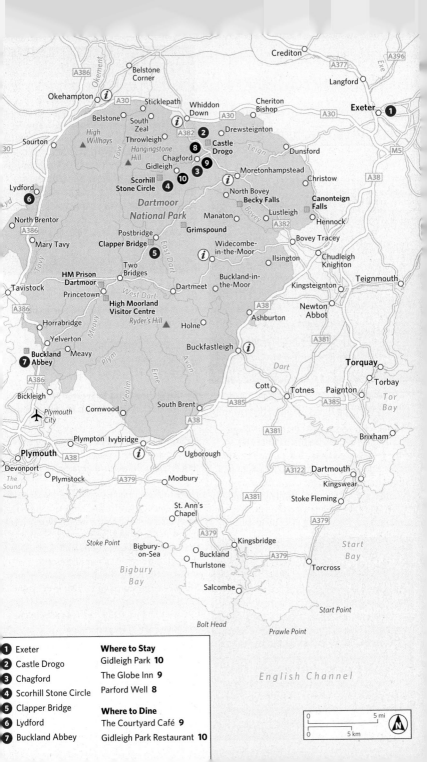

Crediton
Langford
A396
A377
Exeter **1**

Belstone
Corner
A386
Okehampton *i*
A30
Sticklepath
Whiddon
Down
A30
Cheriton
Bishop
A30
Belstone
South
Zeal
i
A382
Castle
Drogo **2**
Drewsteignton
Dunsford
M5

High
Willhays
Throwleigh
Hangingstone
Hill
Gidleigh
Chagford
8 Castle
Drogo
9
3
10
Moretonhampstead
Christow
A38

Sourton
30
Scorhill
Stone Circle
4
i
North Bovey
Becky Falls
Canonteign
Falls

Lydford
6
Dartmoor
National Park
Manaton
Lustleigh
A382
Hennock

North Brentor
A386
Mary Tavy
Postbridge
Grimspound
Bovey Tracey
Chudleigh
Knighton

Clapper Bridge
5
Widecombe-
in-the-Moor
i
Ilsington
Kingsteignton
Teignmouth

Tavistock
A386
HM Prison
Dartmoor
Two
Bridges
West Dart
Dartmeet
Buckland-in-
the-Moor
A38
Newton
Abbot

Horrabridge
Princetown
High Moorland
Visitor Centre
Ryder's Hill
Holne
Ashburton
A381

Yelverton
Meavy
Buckfastleigh
i
Dart
Torquay

Buckland
Abbey
7
A386
Plym
Erne
Torbay

Bickleigh
Plymouth
City
Cornwood
South Brent
A385
Cott
Totnes
Paignton
A385
Tor
Bay

Plympton Ivybridge
i
Ugborough
A381
Brixham

Plymouth
A38
Devonport
Plymstock
A379
Modbury
A3122
Dartmouth
Kingswear

The
Sound
St. Ann's
Chapel
A379
A381
Kingsbridge
Stoke Fleming
A379

Stoke Point
Bigbury-
on-Sea
Buckland
Thurlstone
A379
Torcross
Start
Bay

Bigbury
Bay
Salcombe
Start Point

Bolt Head
Prawle Point
English Channel

0   5 mi
0   5 km

1 Exeter
2 Castle Drogo
3 Chagford
4 Scorhill Stone Circle
5 Clapper Bridge
6 Lydford
7 Buckland Abbey

Where to Stay
Gidleigh Park **10**
The Globe Inn **9**
Parford Well **8**

Where to Dine
The Courtyard Café **9**
Gidleigh Park Restaurant **10**

> The Scorhil Stone Circle, near Gidleigh, is Dartmoor's eeriest sight.

❸ Chagford. The ancient moorland village of Chagford, with its traditional thatched stone cottages and fine 15th-century church, makes a good base for touring Dartmoor and is your overnight stop for Day 1. Open moors with high granite tors and remnants of prehistoric settlement surround the town, which overlooks the River Teign in its deep valley.

Chagford is one of the original four Stannary towns established in 1305. Miners brought their tin there to be weighed and stamped. Oddly enough, it was the first town west of London to get electric lights. Today it serves as a center for backpackers and outdoor enthusiasts. ⏱ 1 hr. to explore town.

On Day 2, head first to Scorhill Stone Circle, 3 miles west of Chagford, a 10-min. drive on Mill St.

❹ Scorhill Stone Circle. It's not Stonehenge, but this prehistoric site consists of 23 standing and 11 fallen stones forming a circle 27m (88 ft.) in diameter. Estimates suggest that the circle originally had 60 or 70 stones. Scorhill dominates the landscape, but there are also several prehistoric cairns nearby. A recurrent theme in the legends surrounding Scorhill is that horses or livestock often refuse to be led through the circle. A short distance to the south by the North Teign River is the **Tolmen Stone,** a large stone with a hole in it; legend has it that passing through the hole will cure various ailments. ⏱ 30 min. Free admission. Site open 24 hr. daily year-round.

The Clapper Bridge is 9 miles south of Chagford, a 20-min. drive on the B3212.

❺ Clapper Bridge. This so-called clapper bridge—a giant slab of flat rock spanning the East Dart River near the village of Postbridge—is a legacy of Dartmoor's medieval past. ⏱ 10 min. Near Postbridge.

Lydford is 19 miles west of Postbridge, about a 40-min. drive on B3357 and A386.

6 ★ Lydford. This attractive moorland village on the River Lyd dates back to Saxon times, when Lydford Castle, now in ruins, was first built as a military outpost (free admission; site open daily). Stroll through town and visit 13th-century Lydford Church (no phone; daily 9am–4pm), with its stone belltower and intricate wood carvings on the backs of the pews. ⏱ 1 hr. www.lydford.co.uk.

The final stop on your Dartmoor tour is Buckland Abbey, 19 miles south of Lydford, a half-hour drive on the A386.

7 ★ Buckland Abbey. When he returned from his 3-year circumnavigation of the globe, the great English navigator Sir Francis Drake settled at this country estate in a secluded valley near Plymouth, just outside the boundaries of today's Dartmoor National Park. ⏱ 1 hr. See p. 246, 3.

> *It looks like the monastery it once was, but Buckland Abbey was converted into a private home in the 16th century.*

Where to Stay & Dine

The Courtyard Café CHAGFORD *VEGETARIAN* Part of a local store dedicated to all things organic and sustainable, this cafe makes a good spot for a vegetarian lunch or a nice tea. 76 The Square. ☎ 01647/432-571. Entrees £4–£7. No credit cards. Lunch & afternoon tea Mon–Sat.

★★★ Gidleigh Park NEAR CHAGFORD Staying at this marvelous country-house hotel, built in 1929 on 18 hectares (45 acres) of beautifully landscaped gardens, is an unforgettable splurge. The enormous guest rooms have fine marble baths and a wonderfully old-fashioned English ambience, and the restaurant (below) is famous throughout the West Country for its cuisine. Gidleigh Rd. ☎ 01647/432-367. www.gidleigh.com. 15 units. Doubles £310–£650 w/breakfast, tea & dinner. MC, V.

★★★ Gidleigh Park Restaurant NEAR CHAGFORD *MODERN BRITISH* Even if you're not overnighting at Gidleigh Park (above), you may want to consider eating there, because it's one of the best restaurants in the West Country,

acknowledged with two Michelin stars. You can choose from various fixed-price menus at lunch and dinner; nothing will disappoint you. Gidleigh Rd. ☎ 01647/432-367. www.gidleigh.com. Reservations essential. Fixed-price dinner £85–£95; fixed-price lunch £35–£45. AE, MC, V. Lunch & dinner daily.

The Globe Inn CHAGFORD This 16th-century stone inn in the center of charming Chagford has nicely furnished guest rooms and a good restaurant that serves traditional English dishes. High St. ☎ 01647/433-485. www.globeinnchagford.co.uk. 7 units. Doubles £75–£90 w/breakfast. V.

★ Parford Well NEAR CHAGFORD This very charming B&B in a modern house set within a walled garden offers three comfortable, cozy guest rooms decorated with an understated English elegance. Sandy Park. ☎ 01647/433-353. www.parfordwell.co.uk. 3 units. Doubles £75–£95 w/breakfast. No credit cards.

Somerset

Hidden within the peaceful, pastoral landscapes of Somerset are English gems such as the Regency-era city of Bath; the ancient town of Wells, with its magnificent cathedral; and legend-laden Glastonbury, as well as natural wonders such as the Cheddar Gorge, with its limestone caves, and the big port city of Bristol. This itinerary takes you to all of them, showing off the beauties of this ancient county in the west of England.

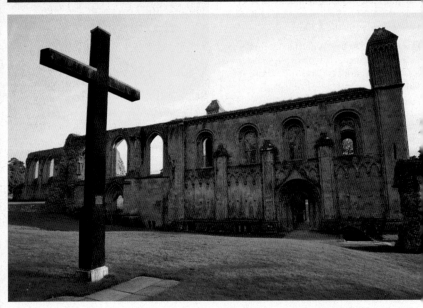

> *Its Arthurian links may be apocryphal, but what is certain is that now-ruined Glastonbury Abbey is one of Britain's oldest Christian sites.*

START **Bath,** 115 miles west of London, about a 2 hr. 15-min. drive on M4, or a 1½-hr. train journey from London's Paddington Station TRIP LENGTH 3 days. Total distance is 119 miles.

① ★★★ **Bath.** This almost perfectly preserved Regency-era spa town has been declared a World Heritage Site by UNESCO, and makes an excellent base for exploring the rest of Somerset. ⏲ 1 day. See p. 266.

On the morning of Day 2, head to Bradford-on-Avon, 8 miles southeast of Bath, a 20-min. drive on the A363.

② ★★ **Bradford-on-Avon.** This picturesque village, one of the prettiest in the region (just across the Somerset border in west Wiltshire) is an easy side trip from Bath and a lovely place to have lunch or tea. Houses built of local cream-colored limestone in the 17th and 18th centuries, when the village was a prosperous wool center, rise up the hillside from the Avon River, spanned by a bridge constructed in 1610 with a chapel on one end. The ★★ **Church of St. Laurence,** 15a Church St. (☎ 01225/868-282; free admission), a rare Saxon church dating from the 7th or 8th

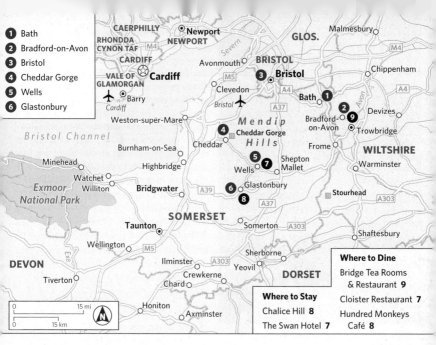

1. Bath
2. Bradford-on-Avon
3. Bristol
4. Cheddar Gorge
5. Wells
6. Glastonbury

Where to Dine

Bridge Tea Rooms & Restaurant **9**

Cloister Restaurant **7**

Hundred Monkeys Café **8**

Where to Stay

Chalice Hill **8**

The Swan Hotel **7**

century, is noteworthy for its steeply pitched roof and blind arcading (arches applied to walls as an ornamental feature). Also worth visiting is the giant stone ★ **tithe barn,** a half-mile south of the town center off the B3109 (free admission), with its magnificent wooden roof dating from the early 14th century. ⏱ 1 hr.

Continue on to Bristol, 27 miles northwest of Bradford-upon-Avon, a half-hour drive on the M4.

3 Bristol. A long process of gentrification has brought new life and vitality to the largest city in western England. On a 3- or 4-hour sweep you can see all the major attractions. ⏱ 3 hr. See p. 272.

Return to Bath, 13 miles southeast of Bristol on the A4, for your second overnight. On the morning of Day 3, make your first stop the

Travel Tip

You can easily get to Bath and Bristol on fast trains from London, but you'll want a car for the rest of this itinerary. You may want to take the train to Bath and rent a car there.

Cheddar Gorge, 23 miles southwest of Bath, a 40-min. drive on the A368.

4 ★ kids Cheddar Gorge. Inaccessible to all but rock climbers until the 19th century, the Cheddar Gorge is today one of the most popular tourist attractions in the West Country. Be prepared during the summer months for long lines at the ★★ **Cheddar Gorge Caves,** formed some 350 million years ago and filled with glistening underground wonders. The cool limestone caves found in the gorge were once used to store and ripen cheese (yes, including cheddar). You can climb to the top of the cliffs for a panoramic view of the nearby Mendip Hills. ⏱ At least 1 hr. See p. 230, **2**.

Continue on to Wells, 9 miles southeast of the Cheddar Gorge, a 20-min. drive on the A371.

5 ★★ Wells. Wells, your suggested overnight stop for Day 3, is England's smallest cathedral city, but what it lacks in size it more than makes up for in picturesque charm. Dominating the town is ★★★ **Wells Cathedral** (☎ 10749/674-483; free admission but suggested £5.50 donation), a stunning example of Early English Gothic architecture, its facade decorated with six tiers of medieval

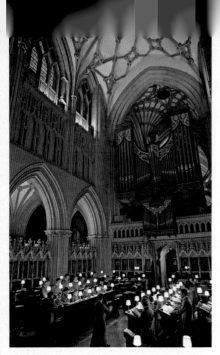

> *Wells Cathedral's famous boys' choir sings evensong daily.*

sculptures. The interior is notable for its 14th-century stained glass; for the unique and striking beauty of its inverted arches, built in the 14th century to help support the weight of the central tower; and for its beautiful 14th-century **chapter house.** Give yourself at least a half-hour to visit the cathedral, and try to time your visit (or return later) so you can hear its famous choir singing Choral Evensong (Mon–Sat 5:15pm, Sun 3pm). After visiting the cathedral, spend some time exploring the **cathedral precincts,** where you'll find the ★ **Vicar's Close,** a medieval street of houses constructed for the canons and choristers, and rows of ancient almshouses built to shelter the poor and elderly. You can also stroll through the grounds of the ★ **Bishop's Palace,** surrounded by a moat where swans glide and ring a bell when they want to be fed, and visit the wells (natural springs) that gave Wells its name. On Wednesdays and Saturdays, Wells's venerable **marketplace** springs to life just as it has for the last 900 years. ⏱ 1 hr.

Round out your third day in Somerset by visiting Glastonbury, 6 miles south of Wells, a 15-min. drive on the A39.

❻ ★ **Glastonbury.** Over the past 3 decades, this small town in Somerset has become the New Age capital of England, attracting everyone from "Angel Therapy Practitioners" to necromancers, mediums, aura readers, and modern-day druids. They are drawn to Glastonbury because of the ancient Christian and Arthurian legends surrounding Glastonbury Tor and Glastonbury Abbey. On a 2- or 3-hour stopover, you can visit these two icons and explore the commercial side of New Age life along **Magdalen Street** and **High Street,** with their picturesque assortment of 15th- to 19th-century inns, shops, and houses. The monumental ruins of ★★ **Glastonbury Abbey,** Magdalene St. (☎ 01458/832-267; www.glastonburyabbey.com; £6 adults, £4 kids), bear witness to its past as one of the richest and most influential Benedictine monasteries in England until the Dissolution of 1539. In the 12th century, two skeletons identified by the monks as belonging to King Arthur and Queen Guinevere were discovered in a tomb on the abbey grounds and reburied in front of the high altar, a claim that draws Arthurian enthusiasts to this day. Legend also has it that after being slain by his nephew Mordred, King Arthur was brought to the Isle of Avalon, long identified with ★★ **Glastonbury Tor,** the 159m-high (521-ft.) hill on the outskirts of town. It takes about 45 minutes to hike up to the summit, crowned by the ruined 14th-century spire of St. Michael, but you'll be rewarded by marvelous far-ranging views of the countryside. An even earlier myth has it that Joseph of Arimathea traveled to Avalon with the Holy Grail (the chalice used at the Last Supper) and buried it there. The **Glastonbury Thorn,** a famous tree on the grounds of Glastonbury Abbey that bloomed at Christmas and Easter, and supposedly grew from Joseph's staff, was destroyed by vandals in 2010. That the marshy area around Glastonbury was the site of an ancient civilization is no myth. On display at the **Lake Village Museum,** the Tribunal, High St. (☎ 01458/832-954; £2.50 adults, £1 kids), are artifacts unearthed from a nearby Iron Age village. Country life in 19th-century Somerset is the focus of displays at the **Somerset Rural Life Museum,** Abbey Farm, Chikwell St. (☎ 01458/831-197; free admission). ⏱ 2 hr.

Where to Stay & Dine

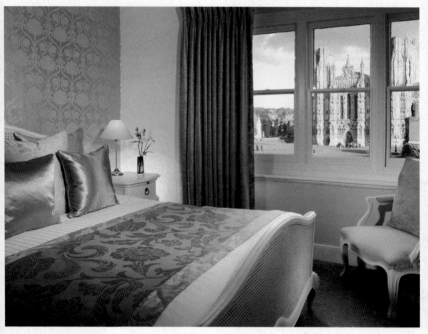

> Some rooms at the Swan Hotel have a view of Wells Cathedral's glorious West Front.

★ **Bridge Tea Rooms & Restaurant** BRADFORD-ON-AVON *TEA/TRADITIONAL BRITISH* Servers wearing Victorian garb dole out delicious cream teas in this atmospheric, award-winning tea room that becomes a restaurant serving traditional English meals at night. 24a Bridge St. ☎ 01225/865-537. Menu items £4–£15. MC, V. Breakfast, lunch & tea daily; dinner Mon–Sat (Nov–Easter Fri–Sat).

★ **Chalice Hill** GLASTONBURY
A Georgian manor house set in leafy grounds 5 minutes from the center of town, this boutique B&B is one of the most charming, elegant, and comfortable in Glastonbury. Dod Lane. ☎ 01458/830-828. www.chalicehill.co.uk. 3 units. Doubles £100 w/breakfast. MC, V.

★ **Cloister Restaurant** WELLS *MODERN EUROPEAN* This bistro in the ancient atmospheric cloisters of Wells Cathedral serves surprisingly good pastas, plenty of updated English favorites, and yummy cakes for your tea-time delight. Wells Cathedral. ☎ 01749/676-543. Menu items £4–£8. MC, V. Lunch & tea daily (closed Sun Nov–Mar).

Hundred Monkeys Café GLASTONBURY *MODERN EUROPEAN* The daily specials listed on the blackboard at this pleasant, casual cafe usually include fresh pastas, salads, and entrees made from local ingredients and produce. 52 High St. ☎ 01458/833-386. Entrees £5–£11. MC, V. Lunch Mon–Wed, lunch & dinner Thurs–Sat, brunch Sun.

★ **The Swan Hotel** WELLS
This Best Western property backing onto the grounds of the cathedral was originally a 15th-century coaching inn, and now offers inviting, atmospheric rooms and a fine-dining restaurant. 11 Sadler St. ☎ 01749/836-300. www.swanhotelwells.co.uk. Doubles £116–£186 w/breakfast. AE, MC, V.

MINISKIRTS & MILLINERY

The Highs & Lows of London Fashion

DONALD OLSON

LONDON HAS BEEN A CENTER OF FASHION FOR CENTURIES, but fashion in the sense of individual style didn't appear until the late 18th century with the advent of manufacturing techniques that made cloth more affordable for an emerging middle class. The earliest trendsetters were the kings and queens and their courtiers, for whom clothes defined social status and wealth. Over the centuries, London fashion followed the economic and political fortunes of court and country. The ornate costumes of the Elizabethan era were followed by the severe black garb of the Puritans, which in turn gave way to the ruffles and mile-high wigs of the Restoration period and the brightly dressed dandies of the Regency. Conservative styles ruled from the late Victorian era up to the 1960s, when youth-oriented designers permanently altered the face of London fashion.

London Punk

When the punk movement emerged in the mid-1970s, London quickly became one of its fashion hot spots. A desire to shock, outrage, and flout middle-class norms motivated punk fashion, which employed highly theatrical clothing, spiked and dyed Mohawk hairstyles, bizarre makeup, tattoos, spiked jewelry, and body modification to make its aesthetic point—which was, perhaps, that there was no point.

Trend-setting British Designers

STELLA MCCARTNEY (b. 1971) Sir Paul's daughter is known for eschewing animal-derived fabrics in her signature line of pantsuits, vintage-inspired dresses, and casualwear.

ALEXANDER MCQUEEN (1969–2010) The bad boy of British fashion courted controversy and accusations of promoting gore, violence, and misogyny before he committed suicide in 2010.

MARY QUANT (b. 1934) Her famous signature look included the miniskirt (which she originated), lace-up white patent-leather boots, skinny rib sweaters, and short plastic raincoats.

PAUL SMITH (b. 1946) This Nottingham native developed a distinctive, idiosyncratic look combining traditional English fabrics and tailoring with unusual or witty prints.

PHILIP TREACY (b. 1967) Hat-loving ladies love the glam headwear created by this award-winning darling of English millinery.

VIVIENNE WESTWOOD (b. 1941) This household name has no formal training, but has become a fashion industry icon thanks to her challenging punk creations.

The Swinging Sixties

Bolstered by the recovery of the British economy and an eagerness to shake off the austerities of postwar Britain, London's youthful Swinging Sixties movement would define fashion for an entire generation. Launched in 1955 by Mary Quant, it hit full swing by the early 1960s, when the Beatles burst onto the scene wearing peg-leg trousers, narrow-collared jackets, and pointed-toe shoes. The decade eventually became synonymous with colorful Mod fashion, the miniskirt, and models like stick-thin Twiggy. The swingingest shopping streets were the King's Road in Chelsea and Carnaby Street in the West End.

Bath

The Romans channeled Bath's hot, sulfurous waters into elaborate thermal pools some 2,000 years ago, but it was 18th-century ladies and dandies who created one of England's most elegant and beautiful spa cities when they began coming to Bath to take the waters and enjoy "the season." Among those who found themselves amid the city's swirling social milieu was Jane Austen, who lived here in the early 19th century. These days, millions of visitors come to this gracious, mellow city—designated by UNESCO as a World Heritage Site—not to take the waters (although that can be done) but simply to enjoy Bath's unique beauty.

> Bath Abbey has been rebuilt several times over the centuries, most recently under the reign of Elizabeth I.

START Bath Abbey, a 15-min. signposted walk from Bath Spa train station. **TRIP LENGTH** At least 1 day.

❶ ★ **Bath Abbey.** This airy cathedral was established in the 8th century and was the site of the coronation of the first English king, Edgar, in 973. The Normans tore down the original and built their own massive cathedral here, but it was in ruins by 1499, when a new church was begun. That edifice succumbed to Henry VIII's Dissolution of the Monasteries in the mid-16th century, but Elizabeth I ordered it restored and the abbey was promptly rebuilt in the Gothic Perpendicular style, with a graceful fan-vaulted ceiling and large expanses of stained glass that fill the church with light. It's little wonder the cathedral is nicknamed the "Lantern of the West." ◷ 15 min. Abbey Church Yard. ☎ 01225/422-462. Admission £2.50; hourly tours £5. Mon–Sat 9am–6pm (until 4pm in winter); Sun 1–2:30pm & 4:30–5:30pm.

❷ ★★★ kids **Roman Baths Museum and Pump Room.** In A.D. 75, the Romans channeled Bath's hot mineral springs into a luxurious bathing complex that rivaled any of the baths in Rome. Today, a viewing platform overlooks the large pool where legionnaires once soaked

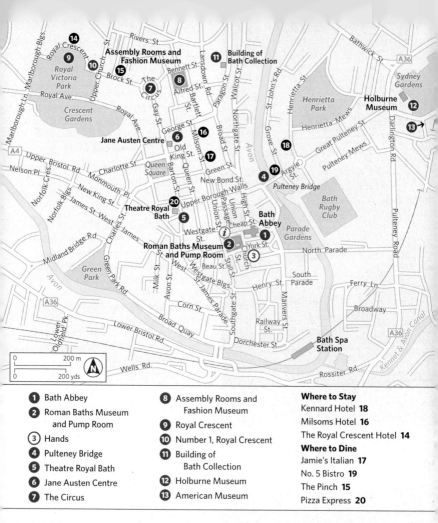

1. Bath Abbey
2. Roman Baths Museum and Pump Room
3. Hands
4. Pulteney Bridge
5. Theatre Royal Bath
6. Jane Austen Centre
7. The Circus

8. Assembly Rooms and Fashion Museum
9. Royal Crescent
10. Number 1, Royal Crescent
11. Building of Bath Collection
12. Holburne Museum
13. American Museum

Where to Stay
Kennard Hotel 18
Milsoms Hotel 16
The Royal Crescent Hotel 14

Where to Dine
Jamie's Italian 17
No. 5 Bistro 19
The Pinch 15
Pizza Express 20

in waters that continue to bubble forth at 116°F (47°C), at the rate of about 240,000 gallons a day. In a maze of subterranean chambers, which you navigate with the aid of excellent self-guided audio commentary, are the remains of steaming pools and saunas, surrounded by elaborate paving. The tour is augmented by intriguing videos showing ancient construction techniques and a ghostly projection of Roman bathers beside one of the pools. You can sample the famous waters in the adjacent 18th-century **Pump Room** (free with admission ticket), though you may opt to sip coffee or enjoy a civilized afternoon tea instead. ⊕ At least 1 hr. Abbey Church Yard.

☎ 01225/477-785. www.romanbaths.co.uk. Admission £12.50 adults, £10.50 seniors, £7.80 kids, £34 families. Combined ticket with Fashion Museum (p. 269, ⑧) £15.50 adults, £13.30

Getting Around

The center of Bath is compact and easy to get around on foot. City Sightseeing (www.city-sightseeing.com) offers a 1-hour open-top bus tour with audio commentary that departs from the bus station every 15 minutes in summer, hourly the rest of the year; tickets are valid all day, and you can get off and on to explore places along the route.

> The spa waters at Bath were first popularized in Roman times, as artifacts at the Roman Baths Museum testify.

Bathing in Bath

Visitors to Bath can once again soak in the city's famous warm, mineral-laden waters. The recently opened **Thermae Bath Spa,** Hot Bath St. (☎ 0844/888-0844; www.thermaebathspa.com), offers spa sessions in the New Royal Bath, a striking mixture of historic architecture and contemporary design just a few steps from the ancient Roman baths. You can soak and swim in the Minerva Bath, a large open-air pool on the roof with views over the city, or in the Cross Bath, a smaller open-air pool where a 1½-hour soak costs £14 and no reservation is required. All manner of other spa treatments are available, from Vichy showers to facials.

seniors, £9.30 kids, £44 families. Daily Jan–Feb & Nov–Dec 9:30am–5:30pm; Mar–June & Sept–Oct 9am–6pm; July–Aug 9am–10pm.

③ 🍴 **Hands.** These bright, airy rooms next to Bath Abbey are popular for morning coffee, afternoon tea, and light lunches. Abbey St. ☎ 01225/463-928. Lunch £4.50–£8; cream teas £4–£8.

❹ ★ **Pulteney Bridge.** This 18th-century span over the Avon River is modeled on the Ponte Vecchio in Florence—and, like its Italian counterpart, lined with shops.

❺ ★ **Theatre Royal Bath.** Built in 1805, this is one of Britain's oldest working theaters and today accommodates three stages. The exterior doesn't give much away, but backstage tours let you see the ornate interior. The house next to the theater was once the home of Richard "Beau" Nash (1674–1762), an 18th-century arbiter of taste and a high-living gambler who is credited with putting Bath on the map as a fashionable watering hole. Sawclose. ☎ 01225/448-844. www.theatreroyal.org.uk. Tours first Wed & Sat of the month at 1pm.

❻ **Jane Austen Centre.** A rather dull but informative collection of text-heavy displays honors the life and work of the ever-popular novelist. Austen visited Bath twice in the late 18th century and lived there from 1801 to 1806, drawing from her experiences for her novels *Persuasion* and *Northanger Abbey*. The most satisfying part of a visit is the gossipy introductory lecture where you'll learn that the author came to loathe Bath, where she and her mother and sister fell upon hard times. You can enjoy tea in the center's Regency Tea Rooms. ⏱ 30 min. 40 Gay St., Queen Sq. ☎ 01225/443-000. www.janeausten.co.uk. Admission £7.45 adults, £6 seniors, £4.25 kids, £19.50 families. Summer daily 9:45am–5:30pm (until 7pm Thurs–Sat July–Aug); winter Sun–Fri 11am–4:30pm, Sat 9:45am–5:30pm.

❼ ★ **The Circus.** The Circus—where three semicircular terraces of Regency town houses surround a circular park—was designed in the prevalent neoclassical style by noted architect John Wood the Elder (1704–54), the man responsible for much of Bath's 18th-century

> *This 18th-century dress is part of a 2,000-strong collection at the Fashion Museum.*

development. Note the symmetry and classical columns reminiscent of Imperial Rome.

⑧ ★ Assembly Rooms and Fashion Museum.
If the Assembly Rooms are not being used for a private function, you can stroll through the four elegant rooms that were the center of 18th-century Bath's social life, in which balls, card-playing, and gossip ranked high among life's priorities. Downstairs, and open daily, is the **Fashion Museum,** where you can view the finery in which a lady or dandy of

Jane Austen's Bath

The Jane Austen Centre offers walking tours that take you to the houses where Austen lived and the places she frequented and wrote about. The tours are offered year-round on Saturday and Sunday at 11am with additional tours in July and August on Friday and Saturday afternoons at 4pm. Tours begin outside the Bath Tourist Information Centre in Abbey Churchyard and cost £4.

> *The Royal Crescent is Bath's most recognizable landmark and a towering achievement of Georgian architecture.*

the time would have flirted and danced away an evening. This is one of the world's leading collections of fashion (about 2,000 pieces are on display), and includes creations by Versace, Armani, and other contemporary designers. ⏱ 45 min. Bennett St. ☎ 01225/477-789. www.fashionmuseum.co.uk. Admission to both venues £7.25 adults, £6.50 seniors, £5.25 kids, £20 families. Combined ticket with Roman Baths Museum (❷) available. Daily 10:30am–4:30pm (Mar–Oct until 5:30pm).

⑨ ★★★ Royal Crescent. This amazing architectural creation—a semicircle of elegant neoclassical town houses built by John Wood the

> *A tapestry depicting the restoration of Charles II to the throne of England is one of the many decorative objects found in the Holburne Museum.*

Younger (1728–82) from 1767 to 1774—is one of the most distinctive examples of Georgian architecture in the world. **Royal Crescent.**

⑩ ★★★ Number 1, Royal Crescent. This spacious, three-story corner town house (whose tenants included, in 1776, the Duke of York, second son of George III) has been restored using only paint, wallpapers, fabrics, and othermaterials available in the 18th century, and furnished with a superlative collection of period antiques. ⊕ 20 min. 1 Royal Crescent. ☎ 01225/428-126. www. bath-preservation-trust.org.uk. Admission £6 adults, £5 seniors, £2.50 kids, £12 families. Mid-Feb to mid-Dec Tues–Sun 10:30am–5pm (Nov to mid-Dec until 4pm).

⑪ ★ Building of Bath Collection. Exhibits in this museum, which examines the city's Georgian and Regency architecture and interiors, detail the crafts used in the course of construction and introduce the architects who contributed to Bath's remarkable development. ⊕ 30 min. The Countess of Huntingdon's Chapel, The Vineyard (off Paragon St.). ☎ 01225/333-895. www. bath-preservation-trust.org.uk. Admission £4 adults, £3.50 seniors & students, £2 kids 6–16. Mid-Feb to Nov Sat–Mon 10:30am–5pm.

⑫ ★ Holburne Museum. When this mansion was Bath's finest hotel, Jane Austen kept an eye on the fashionable clientele from her house nearby. Now the elegant rooms house silver, glass, and other decorative objects, as well as paintings by Joseph Turner, Thomas Gainsborough, and other masters, collected by 19th-century Bath resident Sir William Holburne. *Note:* At press time the museum was closed for a major refurbishment; it is scheduled to reopen on May 14, 2011. **Great Pulteney St.** ☎ 0125/466669. www.holburne.org.

⑬ ★★ American Museum. On display at 19th-century Claverton Manor are quilts, folk art, Shaker pieces, and the other holdings of Britain's only museum devoted to Americana. Nearly 50 hectares (125 acres) of gardens, including a replica of the one at Mount Vernon, spill down the hillside. The museum is closed most of the winter, except from mid-November to mid-December, when the rooms are decorated for Christmas. ⊕ 30 min. Off The Avenue, Bathwick Hill. ☎ 01225/460-503. www. americanmuseum.org. Admission £8 adults, £7 seniors, £4.50 kids. Mid-Mar to Oct & mid-Nov to mid-Dec Tues–Sun noon–5pm. Bus: no. 18 to the museum from the train station.

Where to Stay & Dine

★★ Jamie's Italian *ITALIAN*
At his hot-spot restaurant, celebrity chef Jamie Oliver uses fresh, regional ingredients whenever possible in an Italian-inspired menu of pastas, salads, grilled meats, and fish. 10 Milson Place. ☎ 01225/510-051. www.jamies italian.com. Entrees £8–£12. AE, MC, V. Lunch & dinner daily.

★★ Kennard Hotel NEAR CITY CENTER
Just across the Pulteney Bridge from the city center, this handsome town house was built as lodgings in 1794 and still treats guests to tidy and comfortable accommodations, an attractive breakfast room, and a gracious welcome. 11 Henrietta St. ☎ 01225/310-472. www.kennard. co.uk. Doubles £98–£140 w/breakfast. MC, V.

★ Milsoms Hotel CITY CENTER
Milsoms offers a great location, good value, and a unique charm with individually decorated rooms. Be aware that the reception area is up a fairly steep flight of stairs, and there is no elevator. The **Loch Fyne** restaurant, located below the hotel, is a nice choice for dinner, serving some of the city's freshest and most adeptly prepared fish. 24 Milsom St. ☎ 01225/750-128. www.milsomshotel.co.uk. 9 units. Doubles £85–£115 w/breakfast. AE, DC, MC, V.

★ No. 5 Bistro *FRENCH*
Typical offerings from the small but appealing menu of simple French bistro-style preparations include pan-fried pepper steak, Provençal fish soup, chargrilled loin of lamb, and vegetarian dishes such as roast stuffed peppers and vegetable gratin. 5 Argyle St. ☎ 01225/444-499. Entrees £14–£17. AE, MC, V. Lunch & dinner daily.

★ The Pinch *MODERN FRENCH*
Bath's only French brasserie offers about a dozen dishes each day based on traditional French and European cafe cooking (steak frites, coq au vin, and boeuf bourguignon). You can stop in for a morning espresso and croissant or drop by for a leisurely lunch or dinner with a glass of wine. 11 Margarets Buildings (off Brock St.). ☎ 01225/421-251. www.thepinch.biz. Entrees £10–£18. MC, V. Lunch & dinner Wed–Sat, dinner Tues.

> The dining room at Jamie's Italian.

★ kids Pizza Express *PIZZA/PASTA*
The service is relaxed and friendly, kids are given crayons and paper, and the pizzas are great. There's nothing spectacular or showy on the menu, but the food is consistently good. 1–3 Barton St. ☎ 01225/420-119. Entrees £7–£13. AE, MC, V. Lunch & dinner daily.

★★★ The Royal Crescent Hotel CITY CENTER
These elegant, interconnected town houses not only boast the best address in town (right in the center of the Royal Crescent) but provide elegant and lavishly appointed accommodations as well as a delightful garden and a beautiful pool and spa. 16 Royal Crescent. ☎ 01225/823-333. www.royalcrescent.co.uk. 45 units. Doubles £195–£430. AE, MC, V.

Bristol

The largest city in western England is located just across the Bristol Channel from Wales and has a long history as a port (by the Middle Ages it was England's second city after London) and engineering center. German bombs destroyed the old core of the city in World War II, and postwar rebuilding didn't add much in the way of charm or architectural character, though some wonderful old churches and buildings still dot the urban fabric. After years of industrial decline, the city—like Leeds and Sheffield—has bounced back by transforming its neglected warehouses and harborside areas into shops, restaurants, and clubs. If you want to stay in a city, Bristol makes a good base for exploring Somerset and other parts of the West Country.

> The SS *Great Britain*, *pictured, made her maiden voyage between Liverpool and New York.*

START SS *Great Britain,* 1½ miles west of Bristol Temple Meads train station on York Rd. and Cumberland Rd., a 5-min. drive or taxi ride or a half-hour walk.

1 ★★★ **kids** SS *Great Britain* **and Maritime Heritage Centre.** If you have time to see only one attraction in Bristol, it should be the SS *Great Britain,* the world's first iron, propeller-driven,

transatlantic steamship, now fully restored to its original 1843 appearance. Designed by the Victorian engineering genius Isambard Kingdom Brunel (1806–59), who also designed the famous **Clifton Suspension Bridge** (p. 275, **8**), the 98 m (322-ft.) ship served as a luxury liner and cargo vessel for 43 years and was rescued from rusting into oblivion in 1970 and hauled back to her original dry dock. The

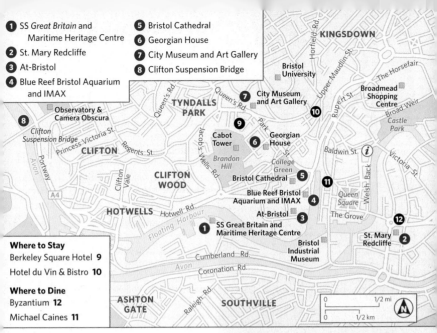

1 SS *Great Britain* and Maritime Heritage Centre
2 St. Mary Redcliffe
3 At-Bristol
4 Blue Reef Bristol Aquarium and IMAX
5 Bristol Cathedral
6 Georgian House
7 City Museum and Art Gallery
8 Clifton Suspension Bridge

KINGSDOWN

Bristol University

Broadmead Shopping Centre

Castle Park

TYNDALLS PARK

City Museum and Art Gallery 7

Observatory & Camera Obscura

8 Clifton Suspension Bridge

CLIFTON

9 Cabot Tower

Brandon Hill

6 Georgian House

College Green

Baldwin St.

CLIFTON WOOD

Bristol Cathedral 5

Queen Square

HOTWELLS

Hotwell Rd.

Blue Reef Bristol Aquarium and IMAX 4

At-Bristol 3

The Grove

12

Floating Harbour

1 SS Great Britain and Maritime Heritage Centre

St. Mary Redcliffe 2

Bristol Industrial Museum

Cumberland Rd.

Coronation Rd.

Avon

ASHTON GATE

SOUTHVILLE

Raleigh Rd.

0   1/2 mi
0   1/2 km

N

Where to Stay
Berkeley Square Hotel 9
Hotel du Vin & Bistro 10

Where to Dine
Byzantium 12
Michael Caines 11

interior provides a fascinating glimpse into transatlantic travel in the Victorian era. The ship's history and Bristol's role in shipbuilding is chronicled in the adjacent Maritime Heritage Centre. ⏱ 2 hr. Great Western Dockyard. ☎ 01179/260-680. www.ssgreatbritain.org. Admission £12.50 adults, £10 seniors, £6.25 kids, £33.50 families. Daily 10am–5:30pm (Nov–Mar until 4:30pm). Bus: no. 500 from Temple Meads train station.

2 ★ **St. Mary Redcliffe.** When she visited Bristol in 1574, Queen Elizabeth I praised the graceful Gothic church of St. Mary Redcliffe as the "fairest, goodliest, and most famous parish church in England." Perhaps that's why a rare late-16th-century wooden likeness of the

Getting Around

Bristol Temple Meads train station is in the city center, and you can easily get around on foot or by using city buses. You can see the main sights on a 3- to 4-hour walking tour. From mid-March through October, City Sightseeing (www.citysightseeing.co.uk) offers a hop-on/hop-off bus tour of all the major sights listed below.

> The fan vaults and pointed arches of St. Mary Redcliffe are typical of the Gothic style.

> *Opened in 2009, Bristol's aquarium is a favorite with visiting children.*

queen graces the **St. John the Baptist Chapel.** The church is a wonderful example of Gothic architecture as it evolved from the Early English to Perpendicular style. The 90m (295-ft.) tower, added in 1872, is a city landmark. ⏱ 15 min. 12 Colston Parade. ☎ 01179/291-487. Free admission, donations suggested. Mon–Sat Apr–Oct 8:30am–5pm, Nov–Mar 9am–4pm; Sun year-round 8am–7:30pm.

❸ ★ kids **At-Bristol.** Bristol's decade-old science museum is hands-on and highly interactive, and will thrill the kids. In zones devoted to space, technology, and the human brain, they can spin on a human gyroscope, walk through a tornado, and strum a stringless harp, among other things. ⏱ 1 hr. Anchor Rd., Harbourside. ☎ 01179/155-000. www.at-bristol.org.uk. Admission £12.50 adults, £10.50 seniors, £8 kids, £35.50 families. Mon–Fri 10am–5pm; Sat–Sun 10am–6pm.

❹ ★ kids **Blue Reef Bristol Aquarium and IMAX.** Bristol's newest attraction opened in 2009 and offers an underwater tour that takes you from the British coastline to more exotic tropical reefs and watery habitats around the globe. In 40 recreated marine environments and walk-through tanks, you'll encounter everything from giant sharks to tiny seahorses. Nature-related films play on the giant IMAX screen. ⏱ 1 hr. Anchor Rd., Harbourside. ☎ 01779/298-929. www.bluereefaquarium. co.uk. Admission (including IMAX films) £14 adults, £12 seniors, £9.20 kids, £43 families. Mon–Fri 10am–5pm; Sat–Sun 10am–6pm.

❺ **Bristol Cathedral.** The gatehouse and chapterhouse date from the 12th century, when construction began on what was originally an Augustinian abbey, with a crenellated and pinnacled tower added in 1466. When the monasteries were abolished in 1539, the unfinished nave was demolished and the building became a cathedral church. In the 19th century the nave was rebuilt according to the original plan, with chancel and aisles of the same height, a unique example of a medieval hall church. Look for the expressively carved misericords in the **choir,** charming stone carvings in the **Elder Lady Chapel,** the colorful medieval wall painting in the **East Lady Chapel,** and, in the east transept, the Harrowing of Hell, a 1,000-year-old carved coffin lid. ⏱ 15 min. College Green. ☎ 01179/264-879. Free admission, £3 donation suggested. Daily 8am–6pm.

❻ ★★ **Georgian House.** This handsome and impeccably restored late-18th-century house provides a glimpse of what domestic life was like for a wealthy Georgian-era gentleman. Restrained and elegant in design, the house was built for merchant and sugar planter John Pinney, who carefully oversaw every detail of its construction and furnishing. In the basement, near the service rooms, is the cold-water plunge pool that Pinney used every day. ⏱ 30 min. 7 Great George St. ☎ 01179/211-362. Free admission. Easter–Oct Wed–Sun 10am–4pm.

❼ **City Museum and Art Gallery.** There's a bit of everything at this browsable museum, housed in an imposing Edwardian neo-Baroque building: 19th- and 20th-century

British paintings; collections of locally produced silver, glass, and pottery; Assyrian and Egyptian antiquities; costume jewelry; and wings devoted to local archaeology and geology. ⏲ 1 hr. Queen's Rd. ☎ 01179/223-571. Free admission. Daily 10am–5pm.

To reach the elegant 18th-century suburb of Clifton, about 3 miles west of the city center, take bus no. 8 or 9 from St. Augustine's Parade; the ride takes about 10 min.

❽ ★★★ **Clifton Suspension Bridge.** This iconic landmark spanning the Avon Gorge in Clifton was designed in 1831 by 24-year-old Isambard Kingdom Brunel, who won the job in a competition that jumpstarted his career as one of England's pre-eminent engineers. Construction of the elegant stone and iron bridge began in 1836, but was dogged by financial and political problems and not completed until 1864, after Brunel's death. Rising 75m (245 ft.) above the Avon, the span was designed for pedestrians and horse-drawn carriages to cross over to Leigh Woods in northern Somerset, but today is used by cars. ⏲ At least 1 hr. to walk across and back. Bridge Rd. www.cliftonbridge.org. uk. Free admission. Bridge: daily 24 hr. Visitor information point at Leigh Woods side: daily 10am–5pm.

Where to Stay & Dine

★★ **Berkeley Square Hotel** CITY CENTER
A Georgian town house is the setting for this hip boutique hotel, which plays with unconventional decor but provides uncompromisingly comfy accommodation. 15 Berkeley Sq. ☎ 01179/254-000. www.cliftonhotels.com. 42 units. Doubles £115–£180 w/breakfast. AE, MC, V.

★ **Byzantium** MODERN EUROPEAN
The exotic interior of this trend-setting restaurant almost overshadows the food, which has a Mediterranean bias but utilizes as many fresh local products as possible. Portwall Lane. ☎ 01179/221-883. www.byzantium.co.uk. Entrees £13–£20. MC, V. Dinner Mon–Sat.

★★ **Hotel du Vin & Bistro** WATERFRONT
Housed in several imaginatively recycled sugar-refining warehouses, this hotel offers stylish, comfortable rooms (some are lofts) and a popular restaurant that serves modern French and European cuisine. The Sugar House, Narrow Lewis Mead. ☎ 01179/255-577. www.hotelduvin.com. 40 units. Doubles £145–£195. AE, MC, V.

★★ **Michael Caines** MODERN BRITISH
Celebrity chef Michael Caines's signature restaurant enjoys a classy setting in the Bristol Marriott Royal and serves up wonderfully prepared cuisine using the freshest of local

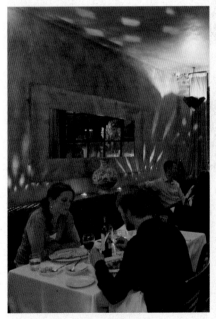

> *Dining on modern European flavors at Byzantium.*

ingredients; dress up if you're going to dine here. Bristol Marriott Royal Hotel, King St. ☎ 01179/105-309. www.michaelcaines.com. Entrees £18–£32. AE, MC, V. Lunch & dinner daily.

Exeter

Exeter began as the most westerly outpost of the Roman Empire and, by the time of the Norman Conquest, was one of England's largest towns. Sustained by the English wool trade until the 18th century, it was a center for silverwork well into the 19th century. German bombing raids during World War II gutted much of Exeter's medieval core but luckily spared the city's greatest treasure, its magnificent Norman cathedral. Exeter is a good overnight choice, close to Dartmoor National Park, Castle Drogo, and Buckland Abbey.

> Gothic sculpture adorns the West Front of Exeter Cathedral.

START Exeter Cathedral, ½ mile from Exeter Central Station, a 10-min. walk.

❶ ★★★ Exeter Cathedral. The cathedral's twin towers are of Norman origin, built in the 12th century. The west front has the largest surviving array of 14th-century sculpture in England. The original Norman interior was remodeled in the 13th century in a soaring Decorated Gothic style. The remarkable fan-vaulted roof is the longest of its kind in the world, stretching some 91m (300 ft.), with brightly colored and gilded corbels decorating the intersections of the vaulting. Make sure to have a look at the choir stalls, incorporating the oldest surviving misericords in England (carved between 1260 and 1280), and the splendidly carved bishop's throne dating from 1312. The cathedral's astronomical clock is reputedly the source of the "Hickory Dickory Dock" nursery rhyme. The cathedral sits in the center of the diamond-shaped cathedral close with the red sandstone bishop's palace to the east; it's surrounded by an assortment of fine 17th- to 19th-century homes and the remains of Exeter's old city wall. ⏱ 30 min. 1 The Cloisters. ☎ 01392/255-573. Free admission; suggested donation £5. Daily 9:30am–5:30pm. Guided tours Mar–Oct Mon–Fri 11am, 12:30 & 2:30pm; Sat 11am & 12:30pm; Sun 1:30pm.

❷ Exeter Guildhall. One of England's oldest municipal buildings, the Guildhall was referred to in surviving documents as far back

Getting Around

You can see the noteworthy sights of Exeter in a couple of hours on foot.

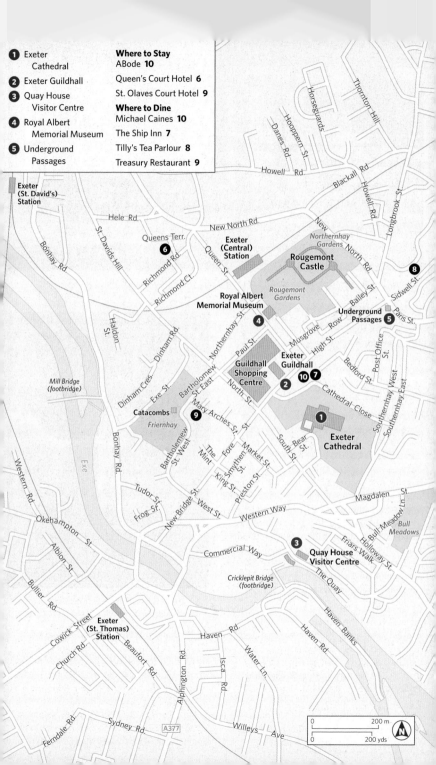

1 Exeter Cathedral
2 Exeter Guildhall
3 Quay House Visitor Centre
4 Royal Albert Memorial Museum
5 Underground Passages

Where to Stay
ABode **10**
Queen's Court Hotel **6**
St. Olaves Court Hotel **9**

Where to Dine
Michael Caines **10**
The Ship Inn **7**
Tilly's Tea Parlour **8**
Treasury Restaurant **9**

Exeter (St. David's) Station

Hele Rd.
Bonhay Rd.
St. Davids Hill
Queens Terr.
New North Rd.
Richmond Rd.
Richmond Ct.
Queen St.
Exeter (Central) Station
Howell Rd.
Howell Rd.
Hoopern St.
Danes Rd.
Horseguards
Thornton Hill
Blackall Rd.
Longbrook St.
North Rd.
New
Northernhay Gardens
Rougemont Castle
Rougemont Gardens
Bailey St.
Sidwell St.
Paris St.
Haldon St.
Dinham Rd.
Northernhay St.
Royal Albert Memorial Museum
Musgrove Row
High St.
Underground Passages
Post Office
Bedford St.
Southernhay West
Southernhay East
Paul St.
Guildhall Shopping Centre
Exeter Guildhall
Mill Bridge (footbridge)
Dinham Cres.
Exe St.
Bartholomew St. East
North St.
Mary Arches St.
Catacombs
Friernhay
Bartholomew St. West
Cathedral Close
Exeter Cathedral
Bear St.
South St.
The Mint
Fore St.
Smythen St.
Market St.
King St.
Preston St.
Exe
Bonhay Rd.
Western Rd.
Okehampton St.
Albion St.
Bulller Rd.
Tudor St.
Frog St.
New Bridge St.
West St.
Western Way
Magdalen St.
Bull Meadow Ln.
Bull Meadows
Holloway St.
Friars Walk
Commercial Way
Quay House Visitor Centre
The Quay
Cricklepit Bridge (footbridge)
Haven Banks
Exeter (St. Thomas) Station
Cowick Street
Church Rd.
Beaufort Rd.
Alphington Rd.
Isca Rd.
Haven Rd.
Water Ln.
Haven Rd.
Ferndale Rd.
Sydney Rd.
A377
Willeys Ave.

0 — 200 m
0 — 200 yds
N

> *Exeter's regenerated Quayside area abuts the River Exe.*

as 1160. Its colonnaded front is a Tudor addition of 1593. Inside, there's a display of silver representative of Exeter's silvermaking past. This is a working building and may be closed without notice; call first to verify opening. High St. ☎ 01392/265-500. Free admission. Mon–Fri 10:30am–1pm, 2–4pm.

❸ Quay House Visitor Centre. The Visitor Centre in Exeter's revamped Quayside area is housed in a 17th-century stone building that was used to store wool during the city's heyday as a wool center. Originally it had an overhanging roof so that the cloth would remain dry as it was loaded onto the oceangoing ships that arrived and departed by means of a 5½-mile-long canal dug in the 16th century. An audiovisual program in the visitor center fills you in on key events in Exeter's 2,000-year history. ⏱ 10 min. Quayside. ☎ 01392/265-213. Free admission. Easter–Oct daily 10am–5pm; Nov–Easter Sat–Sun 11am–4pm.

❹ Royal Albert Memorial Museum. The city's large Victorian-era museum, set to reopen in late 2011 after a major refurbishment, has collections of paintings, local glassware, clocks and watches, silver, and Roman artifacts. The Royal Albert also administers **St. Nicholas Priory,** off Fore St., the guest wing of a 700-year-old Benedictine Priory that later became an Elizabethan merchant's home. ⏱ 30 min. Queen St. ☎ 01392/665-858. www.rammuseum.org.uk. Free admission. Mon–Sat 10am–5pm.

> *As long as you don't mind enclosed spaces, the tour of the tunnels below central Exeter is great fun.*

❺ kids Underground Passages. This labyrinth of vaulted underground tunnels was dug beneath High Street during the medieval era to bring fresh water to the city. Kids love the tour, which includes an introductory video and a guided tour that explores the ancient tunnels. ⏱ 1 hr. 2 Paris St. ☎ 01392/265-887. Admission £5 adults, £3 kids. Mon–Sat 9:30am–5:30pm; Sun 10:30am–4pm (closed Mon Oct–May).

Where to Stay & Dine

> A pint at the Ship Inn, the oldest pub in Exeter.

★★ ABode CITY CENTER
This Georgian-era hotel opposite the cathedral was transformed into one of the most stylish and innovative boutique hotels in the region. Michael Caines, the hotel restaurant, is one of Exeter's top dining spots (below). **Cathedral Yard. ☎ 01392/319-955. www.abodehotels.co.uk. 56 units. Doubles £110–£150 w/breakfast. AE, DC, MC, V.**

★ kids Michael Caines MODERN BRITISH
This classy hotel restaurant and an adjacent cafe use local, organically grown products and cook up fresh local fish, lamb, and venison. The restaurant has a special kids' menu, and kids under 5 eat free. **ABode Hotel, Cathedral Yard. ☎ 01392/310-031. Reservations recommended. Entrees: restaurant £16–£22, cafe £8–£17. AE, DC, MC, V. Lunch & dinner daily.**

★ Queen's Court Hotel CITY CENTER
Located on a quiet square just a few minutes' stroll from High Street and the cathedral, this hotel has freshly redecorated rooms, an attentive staff, and the onsite Olive Tree restaurant. **6-8 Bystock Terrace. ☎ 01392/272-709. www.queenscourt-hotel.co.uk. 18 units. Doubles £110–£150 w/breakfast. AE, MC, V.**

★ St. Olaves Court Hotel CITY CENTER
Set in its own walled garden close to the cathedral, this intimate hotel was created from an 1827 town house. You can dine on excellent gourmet cuisine in the hotel's Treasury Restaurant (below). **Mary Arches St. (off High St.). ☎ 01392/217-736. www.olaves.co.uk. 15 units. £115–£125. AE, DC, MC, V.**

The Ship Inn TRADITIONAL ENGLISH/PUB
For an atmospheric, inexpensive pub lunch, try the oldest pub in Exeter. Sir Francis Drake and Sir Walter Raleigh frequented the place more than 400 years ago. **St. Martin's Lane. ☎ 01392/272-040. Entrees £6.25–£9. MC, V. Lunch daily, dinner Tues–Sat.**

Tilly's Tea Parlour TEAS/LIGHT FARE
Pop into Tilly's for breakfast, lunch, or an old-fashioned cream tea with rich Devonshire cream and home-baked scones. **48 Sidwell St. ☎ 01392/213-633. Entrees £3–£6. No credit cards. Breakfast, lunch & tea daily.**

Treasury Restaurant CONTINENTAL
At this Georgian town house-hotel restaurant, all the ingredients are sourced in the West Country, including local seasonal lamb, filet steak, fresh fish, and duck. **St. Olaves Court Hotel, Mary Arches St. ☎ 01392/217-736. Reservations recommended. Entrees £15–£25. AE, DC, MC, V. Breakfast, lunch & dinner daily.**

Penzance

The most westerly town in England, Penzance overlooks

Mount's Bay and enjoys a climate temperate enough to grow palm trees and subtropical plants. The town has survived several major calamities over the centuries—raids by Barbary pirates, burning by Spaniards in the 16th century, partial destruction by Cromwell's troops in the 17th-century Civil War, and German bombs in the 1940s—so it tends to be a hodge-podge of architectural styles. Except for its excellent hotels and restaurants, Penzance doesn't offer much in the way of tourist attractions, but is an excellent base for exploring western Cornwall. It's an unusually friendly place, and may be the only town in England where you'll hear yourself addressed as "my love."

> Penzance is the jumping-off point for family-friendly boat trips around Mount's Bay.

START Chapel St., a 10-min. walk southwest from the train station.

❶ Chapel Street. Running north-south from St. Mary's Church near the waterfront up to Parade Street, Chapel Street is the most architecturally significant street in Penzance. Strolling the length of it takes only a few minutes, and doing so gives you a glimpse of the Penzance of yore. Chapel Street has always been a mixture of residential and commercial buildings. Facades that look Georgian (from the late 18th and early 19th centuries) often hide much older buildings. Two hundred years ago, the **Union Hotel,** 1 Chapel St., with its assembly rooms, was the center of the town's social activities. Across the road is

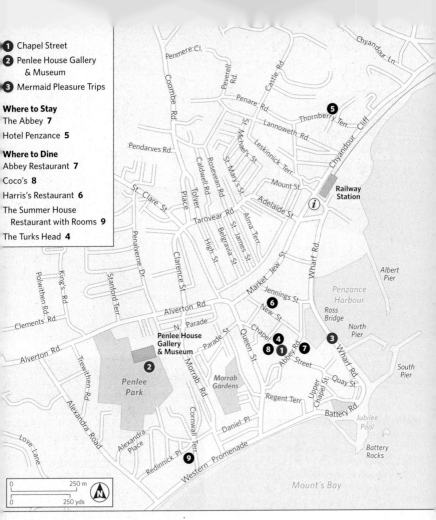

1 Chapel Street

2 Penlee House Gallery
& Museum

3 Mermaid Pleasure Trips

Where to Stay

The Abbey **7**

Hotel Penzance **5**

Where to Dine

Abbey Restaurant **7**

Coco's **8**

Harris's Restaurant **6**

The Summer House
  Restaurant with Rooms **9**

The Turks Head **4**

the **Egyptian House,** 6–7 Chapel St., built in 1835 with Egyptian motifs and ornamentation. Other houses on the street belonged to mayors, mariners, and traders. The interior of the **Old Custom House,** 53 Chapel St., retains many original 18th-century features. Farther down is the **Turks Head,** 49 Chapel St. (p. 283), which claims to be the oldest inn in Penzance. The austere **Wesleyan Chapel** (unnumbered) of 1814 is situated across from the Turks Head. The nearby house marked by a blue plaque was the home of Maria Branwell, the beloved "Aunt Branwell" who moved to Yorkshire to raise Charlotte, Emily, Anne, and Branwell Brontë after their mother died. Chapel Street's most impressive building is

St. Mary's Church, the Vicarage, Chapel St., rebuilt in the 1830s on the site of an earlier medieval chapel. ☉ **30 min.**

Honoring Dame Daphne

Daphne du Maurier, whose famous novel Rebecca is set in Cornwall, lived in Bodinnick in nearby Fowey (p. 233, **9**). Every year in May, Penzance sponsors the Daphne du Maurier Festival of Arts and Literature, featuring all kinds of performers and events. For information, call the box office at ☎ 01726/223-535, or check out the website, www.dumaurierfestival.co.uk.

> *Penlee House houses local photography and archaeology exhibits, as well as paintings by the Newlyn School.*

2 Penlee House Gallery & Museum. Built as a private residence in 1865, Penlee House now serves as Penzance's art gallery and museum. The painting collection focuses on the Newlyn School of artists, mostly landscape painters active in the area between 1880 and 1930. The museum has exhibits ranging from Stone Age to the present day. The Orangery Café is a nice spot for tea or a light lunch. ⏱ **20 min.** Morrab Rd. ☎ 01736/363-625. www.penlee house.org.uk. Admission £4.50 adults, £3 seniors. Mon–Sat May–Sept 10am–5pm; Oct–Apr 10:30am–4:30pm.

3 ★★ kids Mermaid Pleasure Trips. A cruise around Mount's Bay, passing St. Michael's Mount and local coastal beauty spots where you may see seals or dolphins, makes for a fun excursion and lets you see Penzance from the water. ⏱ **2 hr.** Ross Bridge, Wharf Rd. ☎ 07901/731-201. www.cornwallboattrips.co.uk. Reservations recommended. Cruises £12 adults, £10 kids 5–12, £5 kids 2–4. Departures summer 1 & 3pm, rest of the year 3pm.

An Art Deco Dip

Though the coastal beaches in Devon and Cornwall are lovely, swimming in the sometimes rough sea is not for everyone. In Penzance, however, you can swim to your heart's content and enjoy a scenic seaside setting at the Jubilee Pool (☎ 01736/334-832; www.jubileepool.co.uk; adults £4, kids £2.70, half-price after 3:30pm), an Art Deco gem located at the eastern end of the city's 19th-century promenade. Opened to great fanfare in 1935, the triangular-shaped pool (called a "lido" at the time) was designed to protect bathers and sun-worshippers from the often-ferocious Cornish seas and coastal winds. By the early 1990s this popular pool had become so derelict that it was in danger of being closed. Citizens rallied to restore it to its former grandeur, and today it ranks as one of the most interesting icons of the Art Deco period. Sun loungers and deck chairs are provided free, and there's a small kids' pool set within the main pool. A poolside cafe offers snacks, light refreshments, lunch, and dinner. One note of caution: Though the water in the pool is calm, it is also fresh—meaning unheated.

Where to Stay & Dine

★★ **The Abbey** HARBOR AREA
The Abbey, in a 17th-century building overlooking the harbor, is the most stylish guesthouse in Penzance, using bold colors and antiques to convey an atmosphere of overstuffed, old-fashioned, and very comfortable English elegance. The original building dates from 1660, but was rebuilt in 1820 in a Georgian Gothic style. Since 1979 the hotel has been owned by Jean Shrimpton, one of the first internationally famous fashion models, and is today managed by her son. Abbey St. ☎ 01736/366-906. www.theabbeyonline.co.uk. 9 units. Doubles £105–£210 w/breakfast. AE, DC, MC, V.

★★★ **Abbey Restaurant** MODERN EUROPEAN
This stylish restaurant has a luscious red bar-lounge, an airy dining room with views out over Penzance harbor, and a Michelin-starred menu (it's the only Michelin-starred restaurant in all of Cornwall) that makes use of fresh local fish, meat, and produce. Abbey St. ☎ 01736/330-680. Entrees £18–£20. MC, V. Dinner Tues–Sat, lunch Fri–Sat.

★ kids **Coco's** INTERNATIONAL
With big windows looking out on Chapel Street, this hip and friendly bar-restaurant-bistro is a nice place to relax and enjoy a relatively inexpensive meal, a snack, a glass of wine, or just a good latte. The menu features daily specials, vegetarian options, and a kids' menu. 12–13 Chapel St. ☎ 01736/350-222. Entrees £10–£12. MC, V. Lunch & dinner daily.

★★★ **Harris's Restaurant** MODERN BRITISH/FRENCH This restaurant, which has been in the Harris family for over 30 years, is one of Penzance's best and most highly regarded. The cooking emphasizes fresh, local produce and seafood, offering both a lighter brasserie menu (try the fish platter with locally smoked salmon, white crab from nearby Newlyn, and prawns) and an a la carte dinner menu that features fish, lamb, steak, and venison. 46 New St. ☎ 01736/364-408. Entrees £20–£30. AE, MC, V. Lunch & dinner Tues–Sat.

★ kids **Hotel Penzance** NEAR CITY CENTER
This impeccably maintained hotel overlooking

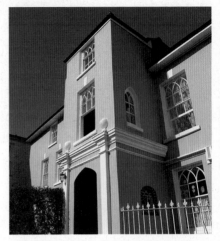

> The Abbey, Penzance's lodging for the fashion conscious.

Mount's Bay and the town features comfortable rooms with sea views and a pool. There's also a very good on-site restaurant that serves fresh, seasonal dishes. Britons Hill. ☎ 01736/363-117. www.hotelpenzance.com. 24 units. Doubles £155–£195 w/breakfast. AE, MC, V.

★★ **The Summer House Restaurant with Rooms**
ITALIAN Head to this restaurant-inn in a Regency-era house if you're in the mood for innovative Mediterranean-style food served in a beautiful walled garden. Five large, stylishly furnished rooms with private bathrooms are available. Cornwall Terrace. ☎ 01736/363-744. www.summerhouse-cornwall.com. Doubles £120–£150 w/breakfast. Hotel closed Dec–Feb. Dinner Mar–Nov Tues–Sun. Reservations required. Fixed-price dinner £30. MC, V.

The Turks Head INTERNATIONAL/PUB FARE
The atmospheric, low-ceilinged Turks Head claims to be the oldest tavern in town because an inn on this spot has been welcoming travelers since the 13th century. The menu features everything from fisherman's pie and seafood platters to ratatouille and chicken tikka masala. 49 Chapel St. ☎ 01736/363-093. www.turksheadpenzance.co.uk. Entrees £6–£11. MC, V. Lunch & dinner daily.

St. Ives

It's easy to understand why this former fishing village on the north coast of Cornwall attracts artists: The sea at St. Ives changes color like a jewel shimmering in the sunlight, and the town's whitewashed stone cottages and painted stucco villas stretch along rocky coves and a long, curving bay with golden sand beaches. St. Ives is a relaxing and picturesque place to stay beside the sea, with a major museum, dozens of small galleries, nearby beaches, and plenty of good hotels and restaurants. It also makes a good base for exploring the rest of Cornwall.

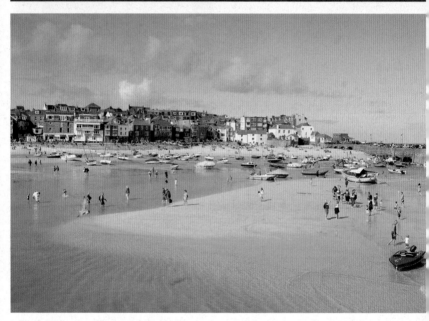

> *The Cornish resort of St. Ives is famed for its crystal waters and sweeping sands.*

START Tate St. Ives, a 10-min. walk south on Wharf Rd. from the train station.

1 ★★ **Tate St. Ives.** When it opened in 1993, this branch of the Tate Museum quickly became the biggest attraction in St. Ives. The museum is devoted exclusively to modern art, and particularly to the works of artists who lived in Cornwall. St. Ives itself has been an artists' colony since 1928. The museum has no permanent collection but presents changing exhibitions four times a year; the paintings, sculptures, and ceramics on display are chosen from works in the Tate's vast collection (the British National Collection of Modern Art). The museum cafe is a pleasant spot for lunch or a snack. ⏱ 1 hr. Porthmeor Beach. ☎ 01736/796-226. Admission £6.25 adults, £3.75 seniors; combined ticket with Barbara Hepworth Museum £9.75 adults, £5.25 seniors. Mar–Oct daily 10am–5pm; Nov–Feb Tues–Sun 10am–4pm.

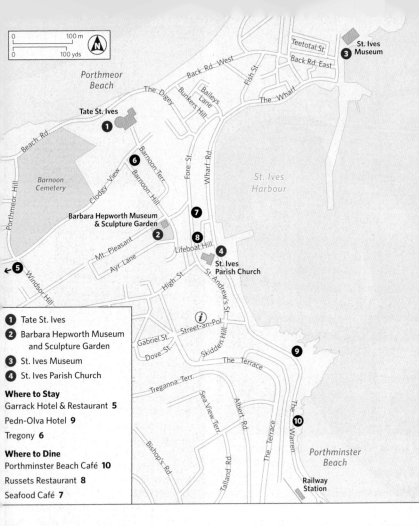

Map labels:

Porthmeor Beach

The Digey

Back Rd. West

Baileys Lane

Bunkers Hill

Teetotal St.

Back Rd. East

Fish St.

St. Ives Museum **3**

The Wharf

Tate St. Ives **1**

Beach Rd.

Barnoon Terr.

Barnoon Hill

Clodgy View

Fore St.

Wharf Rd.

St. Ives Harbour

6

Porthmeor Hill

Barnoon Cemetery

Barbara Hepworth Museum & Sculpture Garden **2**

7

8

Mt. Pleasant

Ayr Lane

Lifeboat Hill

4 St. Ives Parish Church

5

Windsor Hill

High St.

St. Andrew's St.

i

Street-an-Pol

Gabriel St.

Dove St.

Skidden Hill

The Terrace

9

Treganna Terr.

Sea View Terr.

Albert Rd.

The Warren

10

Porthminster Beach

Bishop's Rd.

Talland Rd.

The Terrace

Railway Station

Legend:

1 Tate St. Ives
2 Barbara Hepworth Museum and Sculpture Garden
3 St. Ives Museum
4 St. Ives Parish Church

Where to Stay
Garrack Hotel & Restaurant **5**
Pedn-Olva Hotel **9**
Tregony **6**

Where to Dine
Porthminster Beach Café **10**
Russets Restaurant **8**
Seafood Café **7**

0   100 m
0   100 yds

2 ★★★ **Barbara Hepworth Museum and Sculpture Garden.** This wonderful adjunct of the Tate St. Ives (just a couple of minutes' walk from that museum) gives remarkable insight into the work of Dame Barbara Hepworth (1903–75), one of the great sculptors of the 20th century, and is housed in Hepworth's studio, where she lived from 1949 until her death at age 72. On the lower level there's an informative exhibit on her life and career; upstairs is a marvelous living area, and from there you can walk out into the sculpture garden. On display throughout are about 47 sculptures and drawings from 1928 to 1974, as well as photos, working tools, and Hepworth memorabilia. ⏱ 45 min. Barnoon Hill. ☎ 01736/ 796-226. Admission £5.25 adults, £3 seniors; combined ticket with Tate St. Ives £9.75 adults, £5.25 seniors. Mar–Oct daily 10am–5pm; Nov–Feb Tues–Sun 10am–4pm.

Getting Around

The narrow lanes in the center of the old fishing village are for pedestrians only, so park in one of the nearby lots and walk in. You can walk everywhere within the main part of town, but you'll need a car to explore the surrounding area.

> *Barbara Hepworth, whose sculpture garden is open to the public, was a leading figure in British Modernism.*

③ St. Ives Museum. Located in the old fishing quarter of town overlooking St. Ives Bay, and housed in a heritage building once used to pack pilchards, this small and somewhat dull local history museum has exhibits and artifacts relating to blacksmithing, fishing, and shipwrecks. ⏱ 20 min. Wheal Dream. ☎ 01736/796-005, Admission £1.50 adults, 50p kids. Apr–Oct Mon–Fri 10am–5pm, Sat 10am–4pm.

④ ★ St. Ives Parish Church. Distinguished by its pinnacled granite tower, this 15th-century church by the harbor is interesting for the wagon roof of the nave, carved bench ends, and Barbara Hepworth's 1953 *Mother and Child* sculpture in the Lady Chapel. St. Andrew's St. ☎ 01736/796-404. Daily 8am–5pm.

Prehistoric Sites around St. Ives

Cornwall is full of prehistoric sites, although nothing as grand as Stonehenge. There are three ancient sites near St. Ives that you may want to visit, but check with the Tourist Information Centre for more exact directions before you set out. At **Chysauster** (key-sis-ter), 15 miles east of St. Ives on the B3311 (£3.20 adults, £1.60 kids), you can see the remains of a remarkable Iron Age village with four pairs of oval houses, each fronting a village street and with a stone-fenced back garden. **Lanyon Quoit** (above), 11 miles west of St. Ives on the B3306 to the signposted turnoff just before Morvah (free admission), a huge granite slab resting on three upright stones, is all that remains of a Neolithic tomb. **Zennor Quoit** (also called Mulfra Quoit) is an unusual Early Bronze Age megalithic tomb of a type that originated in Brittany and is found throughout the Penwith area of Cornwall. It's 5 miles west of St. Ives on the B3306 to the signposted turnoff; be prepared for a 15-minute walk on a path that's often wet and overgrown.

Where to Stay & Dine

> The Porthminster Beach Café is known for its seafood—and an idyllic location overlooking the sea.

★★ **kids** **Garrack Hotel & Restaurant** NEAR TOWN CENTER Located in a traffic-free area of St. Ives with views looking out over the gardens to the sea, this hotel with swimming pool offers rooms in a traditional house, as well as in a modern annex and separate cottage. The romantic seaview restaurant serves fresh fish and lobster from Newlyn; organic beef, lamb, and venison; and produce from its own garden. Burthallan Lane. ☎ 01736/796-199. www.garrack.com. 18 units. Doubles £128–£196 w/breakfast. AE, DC, MC, V.

★★ **Pedn-Olva Hotel** OCEANFRONT Located on the edge of a cliff, this bright, airy hotel has smallish rooms with the best sea views in St. Ives, a fine restaurant, sunny terraces, and a pool. Porthminster Beach. ☎ 01736/796-222. Fax: 01736-797-710. www.pednolva.co.uk. 30 units. Doubles £130–£290 w/breakfast. AE, DC, MC, V.

★ **Porthminster Beach Café** MODERN BRITISH/INTERNATIONAL The offerings at this relaxed cafe on Porthminster Beach overlooking St. Ives Bay emphasize fresh fish, but vegetarian options are always on the menu. Porthminster Beach. ☎ 01736/795-352. Entrees £9–£19. MC, V. Lunch & dinner daily Apr–Oct.

★ **Russets Restaurant** SEAFOOD/INTERNATIONAL A favorite with both locals and visitors, this intimate restaurant specializes in fresh seafood, including crab soup, fish stew with aioli, or your choice of duck, chicken, or lamb. 18A Fore St. ☎ 01736/794-700. Entrees £7–£15. AE, DC, MC, V. Lunch & dinner daily (closed Mon Nov–Mar).

★ **kids** **Seafood Café** SEAFOOD/INTERNATIONAL This popular cafe specializes in local seafood, with several choices daily. Select your local fish or shellfish from the display case, and it's cooked to order with whatever sauce, potatoes, or vegetables you want. They've also got good fish soup, fish skewers, and salads. 54 Fore St. ☎ 01736/794-004. Entrees £13–£18. AE, MC, V. Lunch & dinner daily.

kids **Tregony** TOWN CENTER This well-maintained B&B in a pretty, bay-fronted Victorian house with comfortable rooms sits just above the Tate St. Ives and Porthmeor Beach and welcomes families with kids. 1 Clodgy View. ☎ 01736/795-884. www.tregony.com. 5 units. £70–£80 w/breakfast. MC, V.

Fast Facts

Arriving & Getting Around

BY PLANE Most international travelers arrive in London. **Bristol International Airport** (☎ 0871/334-4344; www.bristolairport.co.uk) handles regional flights within the U.K. and direct flights from European cities, as does **Exeter International Airport** (☎ 01392/367-433; www.exeter-airport.co.uk). **BY TRAIN** There is fast, frequent train service from London's Paddington Station to all the major towns and cities in the West Country: Bath (1½ hr.), Bristol (1½ hr.), Exeter (2 hr.), Plymouth (3 hr.), and Penzance (5 hr.). Contact **National Rail Enquiries** (☎ 08457/484-950; www.nationalrail.co.uk) for information and schedules. **BY CAR** A car is the best way to follow the itineraries in this chapter. You can easily rent a car in London (there are car rental agencies at all the major airports; p. 137). Alternatively, you can take a train to Bath, Exeter, Plymouth, Penzance, or Bristol and rent a car there for local exploration. If you drive, you'll need a detailed road atlas; the best are the large-format maps produced by the Automobile Association (AA), Collins, Ordnance Survey, and Royal Automobile Club (RAC). In some cities you cannot park in the center of town; look for "Park and Pay" signs to guide you to the closest lot. **BY BUS National Express** (☎ 0990/808-080; www.nationalexpress.com) offers daily express bus service from London's Victoria Coach Station to all of the towns in the West Country.

Emergencies

To call for emergency help anywhere in England, dial ☎ 999 or ☎ 112; these are free calls from public phones. For a general phone link to police stations throughout the region, dial ☎ 0845/456-7000. **BATH** The police station is located on Manvers Street. **BRISTOL** On Nelson Street. **PLYMOUTH** On Charles Cross.

If you have a medical emergency, ask your concierge or B&B proprietor for help in locating a doctor. **BATH** You can get medical assistance at Royal United Hospital, Combe Park, ☎ 01225/428-331. **BRISTOL** At Bristol Royal Infirmary, 2 Marlborough St. (☎ 01179/230-000). **EXETER** At Royal Devon & Exeter Hospital, Barrack Rd. (☎ 01392/411-611).

Internet Access

Wi-Fi and Internet service is available at hotels throughout the West Country. **BATH** Internet access is available at Retailer Internet, 3 Manvers St. (☎ 01225/443-181). **BRISTOL** Bristol Central Library, College Green (☎ 01179/037-200). **EXETER** Exeter Central Library, Castle Street (☎ 01392/384-200). **PENZANCE** At the public library, Morrab Road (☎ 01736/363-954). **PLYMOUTH** Plymouth Central Library, Drake Circus (☎ 01752/305-923).

Pharmacies

Cities and larger towns throughout the West Country have at least one pharmacy ("chemist"); Boots (www.boots.com) is the most common and there is a branch in Bath at 25 Westgate St. (☎ 01225/482-069). Ask at your hotel or the tourist office for options in other towns.

Post Office

You'll find them in every city and small town, identified by a red box labeled royal mail. In smaller towns, the post office may be in a local store rather than a post office building. **BRISTOL** You'll find a post office on Baldwin Street (☎ 0845/722-3344). **EXETER** On Bedford Street (☎ 01392/223-344).

Safety

It's unlikely you'll encounter any problems with crime in the West Country; in Bristol, avoid walking at night in unlit areas. If you're driving, always make sure that your car is locked and your valuables are stowed in the trunk.

Visitor Information

Local tourist information offices in the region dispense information and maps, and can help you book accommodations. Call ahead or check the websites for the most up-to-date hours of operation (seasonal variations are common in smaller towns). **BATH** The **Bath Tourist Information Centre** is at Abbey Church Yard (☎ 01225/477-101; www.visitbath.co.uk). **Bath Quarterly,** at www.bathquarterly.com, and **What's On,** at www.whatsonbath.co.uk, are good sites to find out what's

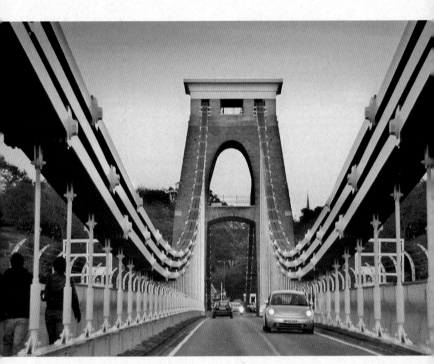

> *Designed by Isambard Kingdom Brunel, the Clifton Suspension Bridge is an icon of Victorian engineering.*

going on in ever-popular Bath. **BRADFORD** The **Bradford-on-Avon Tourist Information Centre** is at 34 Silver St. (☎ 01225/ 865-767; www.bradfordonavon.co.uk). **BRISTOL** The **Bristol Tourist Information Centre** is at The Annexe, Wildscreen Walk, Harbourside (☎ 0906/711-2191; www.visitbristol.co.uk). For general information and events in Bristol, check out www.whatsonbristol.co.uk and www.venue.co.uk. **DARTMOOR NATIONAL PARK** The **Dartmoor National Park High Moorland Visitor Centre** is at Tavistock Rd., Princetown, Yelverton (☎ 01822/890-414). For more information on the park and locations of other visitor centers, go to www.dartmoor-npa.gov.uk, the website of the Dartmoor National Park Authority. **EXETER** The **Exeter Tourist Information Centre** is at Civic Centre, Paris St. (☎ 01392/265-700; www.exeter.gov.uk). **FOWEY** The **Fowey Tourist Information Centre,** the Ticket Shop, is at 4 Custom House Hill

(☎ 01726/833-616). **GLASTONBURY** The **Glastonbury Tourist Information Centre** is at the Tribunal, High St. (☎ 01458/832-954; www.glastonburytic.co.uk). **PENZANCE** The **Penzance Tourist Information Centre** is at Station Rd. (☎ 01736/362-207; www.penzance.co.uk). **PLYMOUTH** The **Plymouth Tourist Information Centre** is at Island House, the Barbican (☎ 17 52/306-330; www.visitplymouth.co.uk). **ST. IVES** The **St. Ives Tourist Information Centre** is at the Guildhall, Street-an-Pol (☎ 01736/ 796-297; www.stives-cornwall.co.uk). **TORQUAY** The Torquay Tourist Information Centre is at Vaughan Parade (☎ 01803/297-428). **WELLS** The **Wells Tourist Information Centre** is at Town Hall, Market Place (☎ 01749/672-552).

For regional information on the Web, check out the following: www.visitsomerset.co.uk or www.visitcornwall.co.uk.

Our Favorite Cotswolds Moments

Even for the British, the Cotswolds Hills, known simply as the Cotswolds, capture rural England as we all like to imagine it to be—gentle landscapes of green hillsides, cozy villages of golden stone, sheep grazing in the meadows. These scenes do indeed unfold along the country lanes, but be prepared for much more as you explore this compact but rich region. You'll also discover considerable remnants of a Roman presence, a great deal of medieval might, exquisite gardens, and the refined influence of the 20th-century Arts and Crafts Movement.

> PREVIOUS PAGE *Bibury's picturesque stone cottages help make it a shining example of a Cotswolds village.* THIS PAGE *The Cotswold hills are crisscrossed by paths suited to walkers of any ability.*

❶ Walking alongside the River Coln in Bibury. The clear rushing waters, the green of the water meadows, and a row of stone, thatched-roof cottages present a picture-perfect scene of rural England. See p. 308, **❾**.

❷ Viewing the mosaics at Chedworth Roman Villa. The intricate designs of the still-glistening tiles pay homage to the Romans who enjoyed the good life at the far edges of the empire. See p. 316, **❼**.

❸ Touring Rodmarton. One of the last great manor houses to be built in England provides a rare look into early-20th-century artistry. The simplicity and harmony of the surroundings, the beautiful handcrafted furniture, and the attention to every detail show off the Arts and Crafts Movement at its finest. See p. 313, **❻**.

❹ Finding a bench in a quiet corner of Hidcote. Hedges and walls create a series of outdoor rooms, and it's easy to find yourself alone next

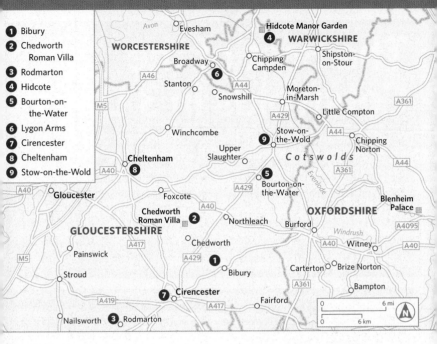

1. Bibury
2. Chedworth Roman Villa
3. Rodmarton
4. Hidcote
5. Bourton-on-the-Water
6. Lygon Arms
7. Cirencester
8. Cheltenham
9. Stow-on-the-Wold

to a bubbling fountain amid the scent of color-ful plantings. If you're looking for a subject to contemplate, consider the beauty of a British garden. See p. 310, **1**.

5 Escaping the crowds in Bourton-on-the-Water. When crowds make it hard to appreci-ate the beauty of the River Windrush sprinting through the village center beneath a string of low bridges, just follow a well-marked path, the Warden's Way, toward the Slaughters. You'll soon find yourself in open countryside on your way to much more bucolic territory. See p. 306, **6**.

6 Sitting in front of a fire with a glass of whisky at the Lygon Arms. It's a favorite form of relaxation at just about any Cotswolds inn, and well deserved after a day of walking and exploring. See p. 309.

7 Visiting a Saxon Princess in Cirencester. Ro-mans steal the show at the excellent Corinium Museum, but "Mrs. Getty" also deserves a visit—the Anglo-Saxon princess is so-called because of the loot with which she was buried. See p. 315, **4**.

8 Strolling through the Imperial Gardens to Montpellier Parade in Cheltenham. It's easy to get into the spirit of this town frozen in time and imagine yourself as a 19th-century fashion plate—or not. You may just want to enjoy the shaded paths, lawns, and plantings; the elegant Regency architecture; and such remnants of the spa's heyday as the caryatids adorning the storefronts. See p. 318, **1**.

9 Walking along the Cotswold Way past a field of bleating sheep. The 102-mile route takes you deep into a countryside of rolling green hills and cozy valleys. Stone manor houses, thatched-roof cottages, and stands of beech trees dot the landscapes, as do grazing flocks of the gentle creatures that made the region rich in the Middle Ages. See p. 296.

10 Following narrow alleyways to the market-place in Stow-on-the-Wold. The stone village evokes sturdy medieval wealth and com-merce, and the view over the Vale of Eversham below captures the meaning of the word "wold"—Old English for "God's high open land." See p. 306, **5**.

The Best of the Cotswolds in 3 Days

A 3-day meander through the old Cotswolds introduces you to a slice of England that is almost picture-perfect—grassy hills studded with sheep, stands of magnificent beeches, thatched-roofed cottages and handsome stone manor houses. Even on a short visit you'll have time to see several of the region's most attractive medieval wool villages, where traders once came from as far away as Florence to buy wool, along with Hidcote, one of England's finest gardens, and Snowshill, one of the many fine manor houses in the region. One of the greatest pleasures of being in the Cotswolds is to soak in the endless prospects of rolling hills, woodlands, and highland plateaus.

> Stone cottages line the unusually wide High Street after which Broadway was named.

START Moreton-in-Marsh, 81 miles northwest of London. **TRIP LENGTH** Total distance covered is 30 miles.

❶ Moreton-in-Marsh. This pretty village of handsome 17th- and 18th-century houses straddles the Fosse Way, historically a major route for Roman legions and, in the days before the steam engine, coach passengers traveling between the west of England and London. If you are in Moreton on Tuesday, you'll find yourself in the middle of a lively market that surrounds the elaborate **Redesdale Market Hall**—designed by noted English architect Sir Ernest George (1839-1922) and built in 1887 by the first Baron Redesdale—and the Norman-style **Curfew Tower,**

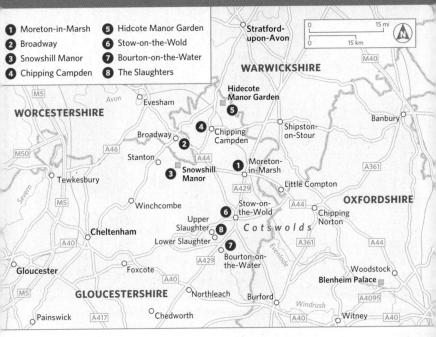

1 Moreton-in-Marsh   **5** Hidcote Manor Garden
2 Broadway   **6** Stow-on-the-Wold
3 Snowshill Manor   **7** Bourton-on-the-Water
4 Chipping Campden   **8** The Slaughters

whose tolling bells (they date back to the 17th century) once alerted residents to extinguish their fires.

The surrounding Cotswolds Hills are laced with footpaths, and you can get a nice sense of the countryside on a trek of only a mile or so on a well-marked route to the pretty country village of **Bourton-on-the-Hill,** returning through **Batsford Arboretum,** where Japanese maples and bamboo thrive on the grounds of a former estate. The total excursion is about 3 miles round-trip. ⏱ **1 day.** See p. 320, **2**.

Travel Tip

Moreton-in-Marsh is one of the few villages in the Cotswolds served by train, with service to and from London's Paddington Station, usually leaving hourly (sometimes every 1½ hr.; the trip takes about 2 hr.). Buses link Moreton-in-Marsh with many other Cotswolds villages, and public transportation and your own two feet are the best way to do this itinerary. For more on transportation within the region, see p. 304.

> *The weekly Tuesday market at Moreton-in-Marsh is the best place to buy local produce.*

After a night in Moreton-in-Marsh, set out by bus on Day 2 on bus no. 21 for Broadway, just 8 miles northwest. Beginning at 7am, the bus departs about every hour from the train station in Moreton-in-Marsh, and the trip takes about 20 min.

> *Snowshill Manor is a veritable treasure box, stuffed with collectibles dating from the first half of the 20th century.*

Walking through the Cotswolds

The Cotswolds hills are laced with footpaths. Some popular short walks are those from Moreton-in-Marsh to Bourton-on-the-Hill, with a side trip through **Batsford Arboretum** (p. 303, ❷); the hike up to Broadway Tower from Broadway (p. 305, ❹); the walk on Warden's Way between Bourton-on-the-Water (p. 306, ❻) and the Slaughters; and the trek between Chipping Campden and Broadway on the **Cotswold Way,** the 102-mile-long walking route that originates in Bath (p. 266) and traverses the region before terminating in Chipping Campden. A walk on most of this path requires only moderate exertion, and you get some wonderful views in return. Pubs, tea shops, and inns in the many villages along the route are welcoming rest stops. For organized trips on the Cotswold Way, see p. 718. Tourist offices (p. 321) throughout the region offer walking maps and other information on walking in the Cotswolds, as does the website for the **Cotswold Way National Trail** (www.nationaltrail.co.uk/cotswold).

❷ **Broadway.** This lovely village of mellow golden stone dates back to the 16th century and has been popular with visitors since the late 19th century, when artist-craftsman William Morris (1834–96) began spending weekends nearby and extolling the rural virtues to his sophisticated London crowd. It's still easy to agree with expatriate American novelist Henry James, who once said, "It's delicious to be in Broadway." The village takes its name from the width of its High Street, once lined with inns (some of which, such as the venerable **Lygon Arms**, remain; p. 309) that did a brisk business providing rest to horses and travelers readying for the steep climb up Fish Hill, the escarpment that looms over the village. The hill is topped by the 18th-century Gothic **Broadway Tower,** which rises 17m (55 ft.) and is a popular Cotswolds viewpoint. You can take a taxi up to the tower, or follow a well-marked footpath; the trip up and back on foot is a little over 2 hours. ⏱ 3 hr. See p. 305, ❹.

Snowshill Manor is an easy walk of about 2 miles southwest of Broadway. Alternatively, you can take a taxi from any of the hotels on High St.

3 Snowshill Manor. This manor house of Cotswold stone once belonged to Catherine Parr, the last wife of Henry VIII, but the most recent occupant made the place the fascinating jumble it is. Craftsman and architect Charles Paget Wade bought the house in 1919 and filled it with bicycles, toys, suits of armor, and other objects—22,000 pieces in all—that he spent his lifetime collecting. Wade also oversaw the design of the beautiful terraced gardens. The property was donated to the National Trust in 1951. ⏱ 4 hr. See p. 311, **2**.

Continue by bus no. 22 or a taxi from Broadway to Chipping Campden, just 4 miles west. If you're feeling energetic, you can also walk between the two villages on the Cotswolds Way.

4 Chipping Campden. This beautiful village of 14th- to 17th-century houses owes its substantial air of prosperity to its centuries-long prominence in the wool trade (the word "chipping" means "marketplace" in Old English). Sheep still graze the verdant Vale of Evesham below the village, and the fine 14th-century **Woolstaplers Hall** and **Church of St. James** (p. 298, **1**) were built from the proceeds of "white gold." ⏱ 1 hr. See p. 304, **3**.

From Chipping Campden, take a short taxi ride to

5 Hidcote Manor Garden. One of England's most beautiful gardens is just outside Chipping Campden. Lawrence Waterbury Johnston, son of the wealthy American heiress Gertrude Winthrop, lived at Hidcote for nearly 40 years, creating a series of outdoor rooms that incorporate acres of rare plantings, topiaries, lush borders, pools, lawns, and long vistas. The gardens are said to have inspired

generations of landscape designers and influenced the poet Vita Sackville-West and diplomat and writer Harold Nicolson in their designs for **Sissinghurst** (p. 156, **5**), their famous garden in Kent. ⏱ 2 hr. See p. 310, **1**.

Return to Moreton-in-Marsh for another night. On Day 3, set out on bus no. 855 to Stow-on-the-Wold, about 4 miles to the south. Service runs roughly every 1–1½ hr. throughout the day.

6 Stow-on-the-Wold. It's said that in Stow "the wind blows cold," a meteorological reality attributed to the fact that Stow is one of the highest of the Cotswold villages (it sits atop a 245m/800 ft. hill). Norman noblemen didn't seem to mind the cold and, taking advantage of a location easily accessed by a number of major roads, founded the town in the early 14th century as a marketplace. ⏱ 1 hr. See p. 306, **5**.

Continue another 5 miles to Bourton-on-the-Water by bus no. 855. Service runs roughly every 1–1½ hr. throughout the day.

7 Bourton-on-the-Water. This oft-visited village owes much of its appeal to the River Windrush gurgling a course through the center of town beneath a string of incredibly picturesque bridges. Bourton-on-the-Water has expanded upon its natural attributes with many commercial attractions, including a model village, bird park, and motoring and toy museum, making the town especially popular with young travelers. ⏱ 1 hr. See p. 306, **6**.

A comfortable walk on a well-marked footpath of 2 miles brings you to the more serene and rural atmosphere of Lower and Upper Slaughter.

8 The Slaughters. These two villages of limestone cottages are quaintly and quietly nestled along the banks of the River Eye. The surroundings, with thatched roofs, an old mill, and ducks floating in millponds beside the gentle river, seem like a painting—and inspire many artists and photographers. ⏱ 1 hr. See p. 307, **7**.

Cotswolds Bus Info

For schedules and other information on bus service from Moreton-in-Marsh north to Chipping Campden and Broadway, contact **Johnsons Coach and Bus Travel** (☎ 01564/797-000). A single source for service information and schedules throughout the region is **Traveline** (☎ 0871/200-2233; www.traveline.org.uk).

The Best of the Cotswolds in 5 Days

In 5 days you can see most of the Cotswolds, with stops at one beautiful stone wool village after another and some of England's most distinguished homes and gardens. You can also catch a glimpse of British history dating from the Roman legions to the early-20th-century Arts and Crafts Movement that took root in the Cotswolds, enjoy centuries-old inns, and walk through some of England's most beautiful countryside.

> *There are few villages more quintessentially English than Bibury.*

START Chipping Campden, 93 miles northwest of London. **TRIP LENGTH** Total distance is about 120 miles.

① **Chipping Campden.** Plan on spending 2 nights in this handsome village at the northern edge of the Cotswolds. A short walk will take you past thatched-roof cottages, Tudor and Elizabethan houses, and such landmarks as the **Woolstaplers Hall,** built in 1314 as a major wool exchange (merchants from as far as Italy flocked here), and the 15th-century **Church of St. James** (☎ 01386/841-927;

suggested donation £1), a prime example of a "wool church" built in the Perpendicular style and housing notable brasses and some finely carved tombs. Most pleasant of all is the prospect of observing sheep grazing below the village in the Vale of Evesham. See p. 304, **③**.

Follow the B4632 northeast of Chipping Campden to Mickelton; Hidcote is just outside the village.

② **Hidcote Manor Garden.** These beautiful gardens, owned by the National Trust since 1947, are some of England's finest and

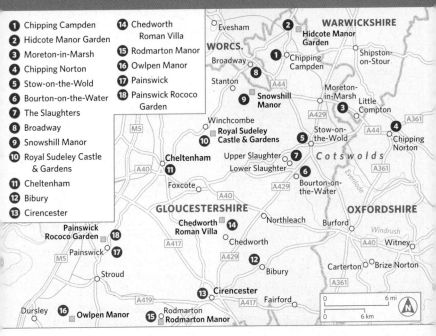

1. Chipping Campden
2. Hidcote Manor Garden
3. Moreton-in-Marsh
4. Chipping Norton
5. Stow-on-the-Wold
6. Bourton-on-the-Water
7. The Slaughters
8. Broadway
9. Snowshill Manor
10. Royal Sudeley Castle & Gardens
11. Cheltenham
12. Bibury
13. Cirencester
14. Chedworth Roman Villa
15. Rodmarton Manor
16. Owlpen Manor
17. Painswick
18. Painswick Rococo Garden

a superb example of 20th-century garden design, in which hedges and walls suggest a series of outdoor rooms. See p. 310, **1**.

Day 2 takes you to a string of beautiful villages. Begin by following the A44 for 6 miles east to

3 Moreton-in-Marsh. This market town was granted its charter way back in 1227, though it's functioned as a magnet for travelers for close to 1,800 years. Today, it's most renowned for the lovely 17th- and 18th-century houses strung out along the route of the Fosse Way, an ancient Roman road through the region. Stretch your legs with a walk of about a mile or so on a well-marked footpath up to the hilltop hamlet of Bourton-on-the-Hill, returning through Batsford Arboretum. See p. 303, **2**.

Follow the A44 for another 6 miles east to

4 Chipping Norton. Less visited than many villages in the region, Chipping Norton is home to a wealth of medieval buildings, including one of the Cotswolds' great medieval monuments, **St. Mary's.** See p. 302, **1**.

Now head west again via the A44 and A436 for 12 miles to

5 Stow-on-the-Wold. Stow's fine stone buildings seem to huddle around the marketplace at the center of the village. The old stones have witnessed some momentous events—not only were sheep once rounded up here for sale, but in 1646 so were royalist troops captured by Oliver Cromwell during the English Civil War. See p. 306, **5**.

Follow the A429 south for 5 miles to

6 Bourton-on-the-Water. One of the prettiest Cotswolds villages, Bourton-on-the-Water is known as the "Venice of the Cotswolds," thanks to the many low bridges that cross the clear, rippling water of the River Windrush as it passes through the town. See p. 306, **6**.

From the village green, follow a well-marked footpath, Warden's Way, to

7 The Slaughters. You can take in the sheer prettiness of these two villages by following the banks of the River Eye for a mile or so from Lower Slaughter to Upper Slaughter, passing centuries-old cottages, stands of willows, and sheep-filled meadows. See p. 307, **7**.

Return to Chipping Campden by following the A429 north to Moreton-in-Marsh and the A44 and B84479 west and north from there. The

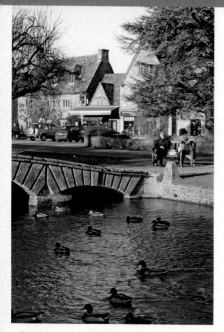

> *Pretty Bourton-on-the-Water, the so-called "Venice of the Cotswolds," can get very busy on a sunny summer weekend.*

trip is about 15 miles. Begin Day 3 by following the B84479 and A44 south and west for just 6 miles to Broadway.

8 Broadway. A visit to this lovely village of stone houses and centuries-old coaching inns can include a climb or drive up Fish Hill (medieval monks allegedly stored fish here). The summit is made even higher by Broadway Tower, an 18th-century folly built by the Earl of Coventry for his wife, who wanted to see the beacon from her home in Worcester (yes, it was visible). Today the tower houses exhibits on local history and the surrounding region. See p. 305, **4**.

Travel Tip

A car is a must for this itinerary. If you are coming from London, consider renting a car at Heathrow and continuing west through Oxford; Chipping Campden is 93 miles west of London and 36 miles west of Oxford. The route will take you west on the M4 and M40 to Oxford, then northwest on the A44 to Chipping Campden.

Snowshill is 2½ miles southwest of Broadway off the A44.

9 Snowshill Manor. This storied stone house traces its origins to the 16th century, but much of the estate's appeal, including the lavish gardens, are the 20th-century innovations made by its final owner, the theatrical architect Charles Paget Wade. See p. 311, **2**.

Return to Broadway and from there follow the B4632 about 4 miles south to

10 Royal Sudeley Castle & Gardens. This Elizabethan castle (it was mentioned in the 11th-century Domesday Book, but most of the current structure is from the 16th century) is one of the few in England that still functions as a private residence. The gardens, Banqueting Hall, and galleries have witnessed the comings and goings of many great figures of English history. See p. 312, **3**.

Follow the B4632 8 miles south to Cheltenham. Plan on spending the night in this gracious old spa town.

11 Cheltenham. A spa town for much of the 18th and 19th centuries, it still retains an air of elegance, with lovely gardens, terraces of Regency town houses, and the **Pittville Pump Room** (p. 319, **3**), where Britain's only natural consumable alkaline waters are channeled into a marble fountain. **Cheltenham Art Gallery and Museum** (p. 318, **2**) celebrates the Arts and Crafts Movement that flourished in the Cotswolds in the early 20th century. See p. 318.

Begin Day 4 with a drive across the southern Cotswolds, following the A40 and A33 east for 21 miles to

12 Bibury. You'll get a firm fix on the charm of one of England's most beautiful villages with a stroll past **Arlington Row,** where honey-colored stone cottages rise alongside a gurgling stream and a water meadow. See p. 308, **9**.

Take the B4425 and A429 for 10 miles west to Cirencester. Plan on spending the night in this old Roman city.

13 Cirencester. The second-largest Roman settlement in Britain and the center of the Cotswold wool industry in the Middle Ages, Cirencester retains much of its remarkable past in a Roman amphitheater and in the fascinating relics on display at the **Corinium Museum** (p. 315, ❹). See p. 314.

Make a short excursion to Chedworth Roman Villa, about 8 miles north of Circencester off the A429.

⓮ Chedworth Roman Villa. Most evocative of the Roman presence in the Cotswolds are the mosaics, baths, and these other ruins that have been unearthed in the countryside outside Cirencester. See p. 316, ❼.

Begin Day 5 by following A433 about 5 miles southwest to

⓯ Rodmarton Manor. The last great manor house to be built in England is a showplace of Arts and Crafts-inspired stonework, metalwork, and furniture. The 3.2 hectares (8 acres) of gardens, designed as a series of outdoor rooms, are a good place to spot birds and butterflies in summer. See p. 313, ❻.

Follow the A433 about 6 miles south to Tetbury, and from there the B4066 another 6 miles to

⓰ Owlpen Manor. One of England's most romantic country houses dates from around 1200 (its name is derived from the Old English for "Olla's enclosure") and was beautifully renovated in the 1930s. Should you encounter a spirit as you explore the halls and gardens, it may be that of Queen Margaret of Anjou, a 15th-century guest who, it is said, never left. See p. 312, ❺.

Continue north about 10 miles on the B4066 through Stroud to

⓱ Painswick. It's only fitting that the last Cotswold village you'll explore is also one of the most beautiful, where 15th-century limestone mansions line the lanes and 99 yew trees grow in the churchyard. See p. 308, ❿.

Painswick House is at the edge of Painswick, half a mile outside the village on the B4073.

⓲ Painswick Rococo Garden. A hidden valley behind Painswick House has been transformed into a pleasure garden complete with a statue of Pan and a pavilion devoted to Venus; in late winter/early spring it is literally carpeted with snowdrops. See p. 312, ❹.

> *Like its more famous neighbor Bath, Cheltenham was a spa town frequented by royalty and known for its Regency architecture.*

The Arts and Crafts Movement in the Cotswolds

Among the many admirers of the Cotswolds were practitioners of the late-19th-century and early-20th-century Arts and Crafts Movement (stressing handcrafted work, simplicity of design, and medieval ornamentation), who were drawn to the region's attractive landscapes and tradition of craftsmanship. Many were followers of textile designer and artist William Morris, who spent his summers in the Cotswolds. In his wake, craftsmen such as furniture maker Gordon Russell established studios in Broadway and other towns, and others built and restored manor houses, including Owlpen (p. 312, ❺) and Rodmarton (p. 313, ❻).

The Cotswolds Wool Villages

In the Cotswolds, lovely villages of soft golden stone rise from gentle landscapes of woodlands and open plateaus known as "wolds." Throughout the Middle Ages, these villages made their fortunes from "white gold" (aka wool), and sturdy stone market halls and elaborate churches attest to the region's one-time prosperity. Touring these handsome stone villages, surrounded by fields and woods, introduces you to British country life as you probably imagined it to be.

> Stow-on-the-Wold hosted one of Middle Age England's most important sheep fairs, where buyers would meet sellers from across the Cotswolds.

START Chipping Norton, 78 miles northwest of London. **TRIP LENGTH** 3 days. Total distance covered is about 85 miles.

1 ★★ **Chipping Norton.** In hilltop Chipping Norton, the highest town in the Cotswolds, handsome stone houses crowd around the Market Square, where the Guildhall and other landmarks show off the town's medieval prosperity as a center of the wool trade (Chipping means "market" in Old English). **St. Mary's** (www.stmaryscnorton.com) is one of the great Cotswolds wool churches, begun as early as the 12th century, though its exterior was redone in the Perpendicular style in the 15th century and its lovely interior is more Victorian. The town's great monument, however, belongs to ancient people who 3,500 years ago erected the **Rollright Stones,** 4 miles north of Chipping Norton off the A3400 (www.rollrightstones.co.uk; £1 adults, 50p kids over 7; daily sunrise–sunset). According to folklore, the 77 slabs that form

1. Chipping Norton
2. Moreton-in-Marsh
3. Chipping Campden
4. Broadway
5. Stow-on-the-Wold
6. Bourton-on-the-Water
7. The Slaughters
8. Burford
9. Bibury
10. Painswick
11. Tewkesbury

Where to Stay & Dine

Cardynham House 12
Cotswold House 13
Lygon Arms 14
Mill House Hotel 15
Royalist Hotel 16
The Swan 17

a circle about 30m (100 ft.) in diameter are the petrified remains of a king and his knights who come alive at midnight to dance and drink from a nearby spring. It's said that anyone who sees them will die or go mad—which explains why there are no witnesses to the nocturnal event. The stones most likely served as a meeting place or ceremonial ground. ☺1 hr.

Follow the A44 for 6 miles west to

❷ ★★ **Moreton-in-Marsh.** Moreton-in-Marsh hosts the Cotswolds' largest market, where more than 200 vendors gather every Tuesday to sell everything from antiques to produce. A mile-long string of stone houses set amid pretty gardens follows the Fosse Way, the Roman road that extended from Norfolk to Cornwall (p. 316) and is known as High Street as it passes through town. The origins

Travel Tip

A car is a must for this itinerary. If you are coming from London, consider renting a car at Heathrow and continuing west through Oxford. Chipping Norton is 78 miles northwest of London and 22 miles west of Oxford. The route will take you west on the M4 and M40 to Oxford, then northwest on the A44 to Chipping Campden.

> *The gardens at Hidcote Manor, just a short drive from Chipping Campden, took over 3 decades to landscape.*

of Moreton's name are up for grabs: Some say marsh derives from "henmarsh," a medieval term for marshy land, and others from "march," for boundary; the **Four Shires Stone** 1½ miles east of town marks the convergence of Gloucestershire, Worcestershire, Oxfordshire, and Warwickshire counties.

The town's 17th-century **Curfew Tower** is so-called for the bell that was rung to tell residents to extinguish their fires for the night and to help them find their way home in the fog. In 1644, not long after the first bell rang out and the English Civil War had begun, King Charles I took shelter in the **White Hart Royal,** a manor house on High Street that is now a hotel. A 19th-century resident—Algernon Bertram Freeman-Mitford, first Baron Redesdale (1837-1916)—erected **Redesdale Market Hall** and planted **Batsford Arboretum,** 1 mile west of Moreton-in-Marsh off the A44 (☎ 01386/701-441; www.batsarb. co.uk; £6 adults, £2.50 kids 4-16), gathering specimens in China and Japan to create one of England's largest collections of rare trees.

Lord Redesdale is best known, though, for his granddaughters, the stylish and controversial Mitford sisters, who were raised in a nearby manor house and later gained individual fame as writers and political activists. ⏱ 2 hr., including a visit to Batsford Arboretum.

Continue west on the A44, then north on the B4081 to Chipping Campden; total distance is about 9 miles. Plan on spending the night in Chipping Campden.

❸ ★★★ **Chipping Campden.** The historian G. M. Trevelyan observed early in the 20th century that Chipping Campden's High Street "is the most beautiful village street now left in the island," and its curving row of golden-stone houses continues to epitomize the beauty and charm of the Cotswolds. Among the town's handsome landmarks are the **Church of St. James, Woolstaplers Hall,** and almshouses bequeathed by the town's wealthy wool merchants. Chipping Campden was home to highly acclaimed novelist Graham Greene (1904-91), and also to Charles Robert Ashbee (1863-1942), a designer in the Arts and Crafts

Movement who relocated his furniture and metalworking studios to the town in 1905.

Every May, the town hosts the Cotswolds Olympic Games, founded in 1612 to promote physical exercise and to bring the social classes together—an unpopular notion that kept aristocratic participation to a minimum. Current events include equestrian contests, shin-kicking (contestants are allowed to stuff straw down their trousers), dwile flonking (in which dancers try to avoid a beer-soaked rag thrown at them), and Morris dancing, performed by handkerchief-waving men. **Hidcote Manor Garden** (p. 310, ❶), one of England's most beautiful gardens, is 4 miles northeast of Chipping Campden off the B4632. ⏱ **3 hr., including a visit to Hidcote.**

On the morning of Day 2, take the B4081 back to A44 and follow that west for about 5 miles to

❹ ★★★ **Broadway.** When Broadway was a stop on the busy post road between London and Worcester, travelers alighted at the **Lygon Arms** (p. 309) and more than 30 other inns along High Street, the width of which gives the village its name. After a change of horses, they made the steep climb up Fish Hill, an escarpment looming over the Vale of Eversham that is topped by **Broadway Tower,** a mock Saxon castle built at the end of the 18th century for the Earl of Coventry (☎ 01386/852-390; www.broadwaytower.co.uk; £4.50 adults, £2.50 kids 4–14, £12 families). You can follow a well-worn footpath from the village up to the tower; the round trip takes a little over 2 hours.

Artist and craftsman William Morris made the beautiful, bucolic town popular with sophisticated urbanites in the 19th century. Among the great names who found inspiration in this quintessential English village of mellow, honey-colored stone were J.M. Barrie (1860–1937), creator of Peter Pan; the American painter John Singer Sargent (1856–1925); and composers Edward Elgar (1857–1934) and Ralph Vaughan Williams (1872–1958). Henry James, the expatriate American novelist, summed up the town's appeal: "Broadway and much of the land around it are in short the perfection of the old English rural tradition." Hordes of travelers still share the sentiment, and those looking to get away from the crush

> Saxon castle meets gentleman's folly at Broadway Tower, built in the 18th century to crown Fish Hill.

on High Street can follow the footsteps of Sir Gordon Russell (1892–1982), designer of Arts and Crafts-inspired furniture, to the workshops he established in Broadway. They now house the **Gordon Russell Museum** on Russell Square (☎ 01386/854-695; www.gordonrussellmuseum.org; £3.50 adults, £3 seniors, £1 kids 12–16), filled with the early-20th-century radio cabinets and other pieces that more than 200 craftsmen once produced. Another distinguished resident, connoisseur Charles Paget Wade, left his fascinating collection behind at Snowshill Manor (p. 311, ❷), 2½ miles southwest of Broadway off the A44. ⏱ **3 hr., including a visit to Snowshill Manor.**

Take the A424 south for about 10 miles from Broadway to

5 ★★ **Stow-on-the-Wold.** Set high atop a hill above rolling grazing lands, this was once one of the most important market towns in England, famous in the Middle Ages for its sheep fairs. The convergence of several roads (including the Fosse Way; see p. 316) ensured a steady stream of traffic, bringing buyers and sellers to the large square in the center of town. Sheep were herded between the stone houses along narrow alleyways (known as "tures"), and as many as 20,000 animals would change hands during the busy trading. Stow-on-the-Wold is still known for an autumn horse fair, but most of the time this handsome collection of stone houses is spared the crowds that overrun many Cotswolds towns. It may be the famous couplet often used to describe the town that keeps visitors at bay, for Stow is where "the wind blows cold and the cooks can't roast their dinners." ⏱ 1 hr.

Follow the A429 south for 5 miles to Bourton-on-the-Water. After visiting Bourton-on-the-Water, plan on returning to Chipping Campden (only 20 miles north) for the evening.

6 kids ★★ **Bourton-on-the-Water.** The River Windrush darts through Bourton-on-the-Water, spanned by several low bridges and lined with greenery and handsome stone houses. But even the enchanting, ever-present gurgle of the river can't dispel the dispiriting commercialism that overruns the once-quiet lanes. The village is especially popular with young travelers, who enjoy such attractions as the **Model Village,** High St. (☎ 01451/820-467; www.theoldnewinn.co.uk; £3 adults, £2 kids), a one-ninth scale replica of Bourton crafted from local stone in 1937. A comfortable walk on a well-marked footpath of 2 miles brings you to more bucolic surroundings in Lower Slaughter (**7**). ⏱ At least a half-day, including a walk to the Slaughters.

From the green in Bourton-on-the-Water, you can follow a well-worn footpath known as the Warden's Way for 1½ miles to Lower Slaughter, and from there continue another mile to Upper Slaughter. The path crosses lovely countryside, following the route of the Roman road, the Fosse Way (see p. 316).

> *Lambswool was a source of Cotswold prosperity throughout the Middle Ages.*

> *A quaint footpath follows the River Eye between Lower and Upper Slaughter.*

7 ★★★ **The Slaughters.** The Slaughters (the name comes from the Old English "slohtre," for muddy place) nestle alongside the gentle River Eye. As befits the quiet surroundings, the most popular activity is following the riverbanks past Lower Slaughter's old mill for a mile or so to Upper Slaughter, alongside water fowl and sheep grazing in the meadows. The prettiness of Upper Slaughter is not entirely uncontrived. Sir Edwin Lutyens (1869–1944), the architect of many English country houses and monuments, reconstructed the quaint stone and timbered cottages that surround the village square in 1906.

The next morning, follow the A429 5 miles south to the A40 and take that east for 10 miles to

8 ★ **Burford.** This animated market town has seen more history than the gentle prospect of High Street sloping down to the willow-lined banks of the River Windrush suggests. In 1649, during the Civil War, Cromwell's troops rounded up former royalist troops known as the Burford Levellers and imprisoned them in the 12th-century **Burford Church** (www.burfordchurch.org), where the stones are still etched with the initials and graffiti they carved. Some 900 years earlier, in 752,

Kids in the Cotswolds

Young travelers can enjoy a day on the town in **Bourton-on-the-Water.** Pelicans, toucans, and penguins are among the 500 colorful inhabitants of **Birdland,** Rissington Rd. (☎ 01451/820-480; www.birdland.co.uk; £6.50 adults, £4.25 kids 3–15, £20 families). The **Cotswolds Motoring Museum and Toy Collection,** Old Mill (☎ 01451/821-255; www.cotswold-motor-museum.com; £4.10 adults, £2.70 kids 4–15, £12 families), houses a collection of old cars, along with historic toys and pedal cars. At the **Bourton Model Railway,** High St. (☎ 01451/820-686; www.bourtonmodelrailway.co.uk; £2.50 adults, £7.50 families), vintage stock rolls over more than 500 feet of track.

> *If you're approaching the region from Oxford, the Cotswolds begin at Burford.*

Cuthred, king of the West Saxons, slaughtered the troops of King Aethelbald of Mercia near the banks of the Windrush in Burford; the enormous stone sarcophagus of Athelhum, a giant who served as Aethelbald's standard-bearer and carried a mighty flag emblazoned with a golden dragon, rests in the churchyard. The slate-roofed houses of golden stone that line High Street overlook the humble structure that enriched their residents—the 12th-century **Tolsey** served as a market and as a collection booth for tolls extracted from sheep farmers who came to town to sell their wool. ⏱ 1 hr.

Follow the B4425 9 miles west to

⑨ ★★★ **Bibury.** Victorian poet, artist, and founder of the Arts and Crafts Movement William Morris described Bibury as the "most beautiful village in England," a claim that could well still hold true. **Arlington Row,** a string of 16th-century pitch-roofed stone cottages alongside a gurgling stream, is certainly one of the most scenic sights in the realm, so alluring that Henry Ford once tried to buy the quaint assemblage in its entirety and ship the houses stone by stone back to Detroit. Just on the other side of a water meadow known as Rack Isle is **Arlington Mill,** a 17th-century remnant of the wool industry that once made the town prosperous. Much of that good fortune was channeled into embellishing the **Church of St. Mary's,** where some 8th-century Saxon stone work is still in evidence. ⏱ 1 hr.

Take the B4425 and A429 for 10 miles west to Cirencester (p. 314), then the A419 for 15 miles to Stroud, and from there continue on the A46 for 3 miles to

⑩ ★★★ **Painswick.** The misnamed New Street in the so-called "Queen of the Cotswolds" is lined with 15th-century limestone mansions, and the entire village is immersed in legends—many surrounding the parish **Church of St. Mary.** It's said that exactly 99 yew trees, some 300 years old, grow in the churchyard, because no one has ever been able to grow the 100th, killed by the devil himself. On the Sunday nearest September 19, villagers dance in a "clypping" circle around the church, re-enacting a Saxon rite that once ended in drunkenness and debauchery—shops in town sell china figurines of puppies standing atop a pie, harking back to the days when innkeepers met medieval revelers' demand for food with "puppy dog pies." The wonderfully romantic **Painswick Rococo Garden** (p. 312, ④) is half a mile outside the village on the B4073. ⏱ 2 hr.

Follow the A46 and M5 18 miles north to

⑪ **Tewkesbury.** Though Tewkesbury is not geographically in the Cotswolds, this medieval market town at the confluence of the Avon and Severn Rivers is as beautiful as its neighbors. A warren of narrow lanes and half-timbered Tudor houses surround 12th-century **Tewkesbury Abbey,** Church St. (www.tewkesburyabbey.org.uk), topped by what is claimed to be the tallest Norman tower in England. ⏱ 1 hr.

Dining Tip

Many of the best restaurants in the Cotswolds are those of inns.

Where to Stay & Dine

★★ **Cardynham House** PAINSWICK
Plenty of exposed beams and antiques lend no end of character to this 15th-century house in the center of town. The in-house restaurant, the **Bistro,** is Painswick's finest. Tibbiwell St. ☎ 01452/814-006. www.cardynham.co.uk. 9 units. Doubles £80–£210 w/breakfast. Bistro: Lunch Tues–Sat, dinner Tues–Sun. Entrees £10–20. AE, MC, V.

★★★ **Cotswold House** CHIPPING CAMPDEN
A 17th-century house in the center of Chipping Campden has been beautifully and distinctively restored, combining traditional comfort and contemporary flair. Cottage rooms, in stone buildings set in the gardens, are especially stylish and equipped with such amenities as hot tubs and fireplaces. The excellent in-house restaurant, **Hick's Brasserie,** serves innovative dishes based on fresh produce and other local ingredients in a relaxed setting. The Square. ☎ 01386/840-330. www.cotswold house.com. 30 units. Doubles £150–£195 w/breakfast. Hick's: Breakfast, lunch & dinner daily. Entrees £11–25. AE, DC, MC, V.

★★ **The Lygon Arms** BROADWAY
This 16th-century coaching inn sheltered both Oliver Cromwell and King Charles I. It provides character-filled accommodation in a paneled and beamed original structure and comfortable, slightly less colorful ambience in new wings. Gardens sprawl over many acres, and hearths blaze in the bars, sitting rooms, and baronial dining room. High St. ☎ 01386/852-255. www.barcelo-hotels.co.uk. 83 units. Doubles £145–£230 w/breakfast. AE, DC, MC, V.

★★ **Mill House Hotel** OUTSIDE CHIPPING NORTON
A converted stone mill house next to a gurgling brook is a relaxed country retreat, with extremely comfortable, traditionally furnished rooms and an excellent restaurant, the **Mill Brook Room,** where meals begin with a drink in the cozy bar. Kingham, Oxfordshire. ☎ 01608/658-188. www.millhousehotel.co.uk. 23 units. Doubles £160–£200 w/breakfast. Mill Brook Room: Lunch & dinner daily. Entrees £16–£18. AE, DC, MC, V.

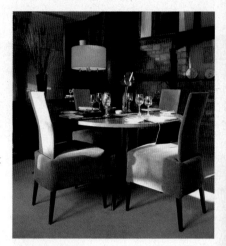

> *The Eagle and Child, inside the Royalist Hotel, Stow-on-the-Wold.*

★★ **Royalist Hotel** STOW-ON-THE-WOLD
A 10th-century inn, the oldest in England, is now one of the Cotswolds' most distinctive hideaways, where stylish furnishings are accented with wood beams, stone walls, rough-hewn floors, and the patina of ages. Two in-house restaurants are among the best in the region: the casual **Eagle and Child Pub** and the more serious **947 AD** restaurant. Digbeth St. ☎ 01451/830-870. www.theroyalist hotel.com. 14 units. Doubles £120–£150 w/breakfast. Eagle and Child Pub: Lunch & dinner daily. Entrees £9–£13. 947 AD: Lunch & dinner Tues–Sun. Entrees £17–£20. AE, DC, MC, V.

★★ **The Swan** BIBURY
All the rooms here are large and distinctively furnished, but those in the front of the house face one of the most picturesque scenes in England, the River Colm meandering through water meadows past a row of stone cottages. The hotel's formal dining room and informal cafe face the same scenery, and the gardens run down to the river banks. Several self-contained cottages are tucked away on the grounds. Village center. ☎ 01285/740-695. www.cotswold-inns-hotels.co.uk. Doubles £155–£235 w/breakfast. AE, DC, MC, V.

Gardens & Great Houses

The gentle Cotswolds hills and broad valleys, blessed with a temperate climate, have provided fertile ground for some of Britain's most beautiful gardens. Several, such as those at Royal Sudeley Castle and Owlpen Manor, surround some of the country's most distinguished homes; others, such as Hidcote Manor Garden, are landmarks in themselves.

> The gardens at Hidcote Manor are arranged like a series of outdoor rooms, each individually designed by Lawrence Waterbury Johnston.

START Hidcote Manor Garden is 4 miles northeast of Chipping Campden, which is 90 miles northwest of London. **TRIP LENGTH** Allow at least 2 days to properly enjoy the houses and gardens. Total distance covered is only about 50 miles.

❶ ★★★ Hidcote Manor Garden. One of the most influential and inventive gardens of the 20th century was created by Lawrence Waterbury Johnston (1871–1958), son of the American heiress Gertrude Winthrop. Starting in 1907, Johnston landscaped 4 hectares (10 acres) over the course of some 30 years into a series of outdoor rooms, separated from each other by walls, hedges, and terraces. Each room is small and unique, with its own planting scheme and atmosphere; the Fuschia Garden, White Garden, and other rooms are fragrant with native plantings and exotic varieties Johnston gathered from Africa, Asia, and South Africa. The gardens are laced with walkways, fountains, and many quiet nooks, and the great variety of borders and rare trees ensures that something is usually in bloom. Poet Vita Sackville-West wrote of Hidcote, "This place is a jungle of beauty. I cannot hope to describe it in words, for indeed it is an impossible thing to reproduce the shape, colour, depth and design of such a garden through the poor medium of prose." ⏱ 2 hr. Hidcote Bartrim, 4 miles northeast of Chipping Campden off the B4632. ☎ 01386/438-333. www.nationaltrust.org.uk. Admission £10 adults, £5 kids, £25 families. Mid-Mar to June & Sept Sat–Wed 10am–6pm; July–Aug daily 10am–6pm; Oct Sat–Wed 10am–5pm; Nov to mid-Dec Sat–Sun 10am–5pm.

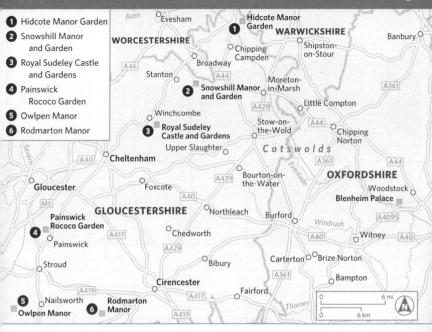

1 Hidcote Manor Garden
2 Snowshill Manor and Garden
3 Royal Sudeley Castle and Gardens
4 Painswick Rococo Garden
5 Owlpen Manor
6 Rodmarton Manor

From Chipping Campden, follow the A44 4 miles west to Broadway and Snowshill.

2 ★ **Snowshill Manor and Garden.** In the 8th century, Snowshill Manor was part of the vast holdings of Winchcombe Abbey, capital of the Anglo-Saxon kingdom of Mercia. Henry VIII confiscated Snowshill during the Dissolution of the Monasteries in 1539 and presented it to his last queen, Catherine Parr (1512–48); the estate eventually came into the hands of Charles Paget Wade (1883–1956) in 1919. An architect, craftsman, and collector, Wade began amassing furniture, clothing, armor, and paintings at the age of 7, and by the time of his death, he had accumulated more than 22,000 items, many of which are on display in the stone manor house. The elaborate gardens show off Wade's fascination with color and scent. They were designed by architect Baillie Scott (1865–1945), a proponent of the Arts and Crafts Movement that proliferated in the Cotswolds in the early 20th century, and are arranged as mysterious and intriguing terraced rooms that essentially serve as an extension of the house. ⏱ 2 hr. 2½ miles southwest of Broadway off the A44. ☎ 01386/852-410. www.nationaltrust.co.uk. Admission £9.50 adults, £4.80 kids, £24 families. Mid-Mar to Oct Wed–Sun noon–5pm (garden 11am–5:30pm).

> Scent and color are recurring themes in the gardens that surround Snowshill Manor.

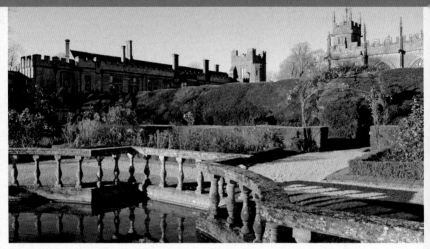

> *Royal Sudeley Castle is one of the only castles in Great Britain still used as a private residence.*

From Broadway, follow the B4632 about 4 miles south to Winchcombe.

3 ★★ **Royal Sudeley Castle and Gardens.** Queen Catherine Parr, the last wife of Henry VIII, lived out her days at Sudeley and is buried in the estate chapel (it's rumored that her ghost still walks the halls). Other distinguished royalty who've visited the castle over the centuries include Elizabeth I, Richard III, Charles I, and Lady Jane Grey. Sudeley lay in romantic ruin for almost 200 years until the Dents, a wealthy glove-making family from Worcester, began restoring the castle in the 19th century; their descendants still live on the grounds. More than 5 hectares (14 acres) of gardens bloom against a gentle backdrop of the Cotswolds Hills, and the kitchen wing, stables, and Banqueting Hall show off fine furnishings; paintings by Constable, Turner, and other masters; and letters and other keepsakes of Catherine Parr. The family's private apartments can be toured on select weekdays. ☺ Half-day. Near Winchcombe, about 8 miles east of Cheltenham, off the B4632. ☎ 01242/602-308. www.sudeleycastle.co.uk. Admission £7.20 adults, £6.20 seniors, £4.20 kids 5–15, £21 families. Apr–Oct daily 10:30am–5pm.

Continue south on the B4632 to Cheltenham, about 8 miles, and continue on the A46 another 10 miles to Painswick. Plan on spending the night in this beautiful village (p. 308, **10**). On the morning of Day 2, head for

4 ★ **Painswick Rococo Garden.** Painswick House was built in the 1730s by the asthmatic Charles Hyett (1675–1738), who soon succumbed to his ailment. His son Benjamin oversaw the design of the gardens, following the short-lived Georgian Rococo style to transform a hidden valley into a pleasure garden famous for its statue of Pan and a pavilion devoted to Venus. Such frivolity was not well received by the locals, one of whom observed, "You are taken to a pompous and gilded building, consecrated to Venus for no other purpose (than) that the squire riots here in vulgar love with a couple of orange wenches from the local play-house." These days the garden is especially noted for a profusion of snowdrops, which begin to carpet the beautifully planted slopes as early as February. ☺ At least 1 hr. Half a mile outside Painswick on the B4073. ☎ 01452/813-204. www.rococogarden.co.uk. Admission £6 adults, £5 seniors, £3 kids 5–16, £16 families. Jan 10–Oct 31 daily 11am–5pm.

Continue south about 10 miles on the B4066 to Owlpen.

5 ★★★ **Owlpen Manor.** One of the most romantic houses in England lies in a secluded valley at the edge of the Cotswolds. It was built around 1200, rebuilt during the 16th-century Tudor era, and then restored in the 1930s by Arts and Crafts architect Norman Jewson (1884–1975). When Jewson acquired

> *Like many great Cotswold houses, the history of Rodmarton Manor is intertwined with the Arts and Crafts movement.*

roam the upper floors in a fur-trimmed gown and veil. ⏱ At least 2 hr. Near Uley, about 10 miles south of Painswick, off B4066. ☎ 01453/860-261. www.owlpen.com. Admission £8 adults, £4 kids 5–15. May–Aug Mon, Wed–Thurs & Sat noon–5pm.

Follow the A4135 about 7 miles to Tetbury; then get on the A433 and drive another 7 miles to Rodmarton.

❻ ★★★ **Rodmarton Manor.** One of the last manor houses to be built in England was begun in 1909 and completed 20 years later. Craftsmen used local stone and timber, following designs by architect and furniture designers Ernest Barnsley (1863–1926) and Norman Jewson, noted proponents of Cotswolds crafts. Metalwork, furniture, brass, and other fittings were all made on the grounds or nearby using Arts and Crafts designs and techniques. As Jewson wrote, Rodmarton was "the last house of its size to be built in the old leisurely way, with all its timber grown from local woods, sawn on the pit and seasoned before use." The same care went into the extensive gardens, laced with walks and walls of Cotswolds stone, and the house and gardens are among England's greatest monuments to early-20th-century design. ⏱ At least 2 hr. Outside Cirencester, off the A433. ☎ 10285/841-253. www.rodmarton-manor.co.uk. Admission £8 adults, £4 kids 5–15. May–Aug Wed & Sat 2–5pm.

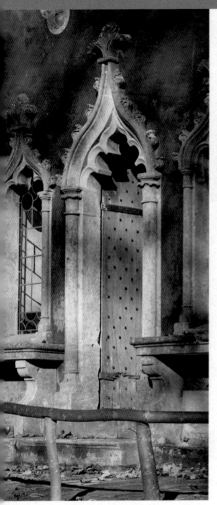

> *You'll find rococo detailing throughout the pleasure gardens at Painswick.*

Owlpen, the manor had lain in ivy-covered ruin for almost a century. With such a provenance, it is little wonder that the stone manor surrounded by magnificent gardens shaded by ancient yews is also said to be one of the most haunted houses in England. The most noted spirit is that of Queen Margaret of Anjou (1430–82), who spent her last happy night at Owlpen in 1471. Her Lancaster husband, King Henry VI (1421–71), and son, Prince Edward of Westminster (1453–71), were soon murdered by troops of the Yorkist Edward IV (1442–83), and she was exiled to France; she is said to

Cirencester

Cirencester (pronounced with the emphasis on the "ses," as in Siren-ses-ter) flourished 2,000 years ago as Corinium Dobunnorum, the second-largest Roman settlement in Britain. Even under the Romans the town was known for wool, and Cirencester became one of the great centers of the Cotswolds medieval wool industry. Today the largest town in the Cotswolds is pleasantly animated and, just as it was under the Roman legions, at the crossroads of many of the routes leading through the region.

> *The great Gothic wool church of St. John the Baptist dominates Cirencester's Market Place.*

START Cirencester is 89 miles west of London.

❶ ★ Market Place. Cirencester was recorded in the Domesday Book of 1086 as a marketplace for wool, and this broad expanse at the center of town, surrounding the 17th-century market hall, still fills with vendors on weekday mornings. The cathedral-like Church of St. John the Baptist, built in the 12th century and embellished by wealthy wool merchants over the centuries, overlooks the square, and handsome stone Cotswold houses fan out along High Street and surrounding lanes. The stalls

of a large market still spill across Market Place on Mondays and Fridays, selling produce, meats and cheeses, and household items. **Corn Hall,** on the Market Place, hosts an antiques market on Fridays and a crafts market on Saturdays. ⏱ 30 min.

❷ ★ Parish Church of St. John the Baptist. This elaborate medieval structure shows off Cirencester's prominence in the wool trade, the proceeds from which went into building this church. It was begun in 1117 at the behest of Henry I, though what you see today

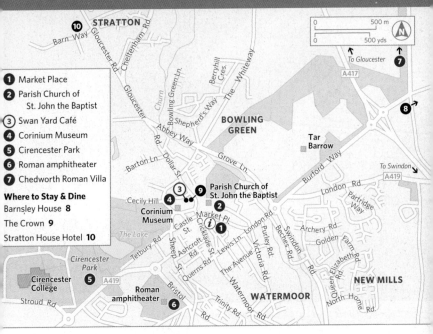

1 Market Place
2 Parish Church of
  St. John the Baptist
3 Swan Yard Café
4 Corinium Museum
5 Cirencester Park
6 Roman amphitheater
7 Chedworth Roman Villa

Where to Stay & Dine
Barnsley House 8
The Crown 9
Stratton House Hotel 10

---

dates mostly to the 16th-century Gothic era. A graceful Perpendicular-style porch faces the square, beneath a massive tower, and the overall effect is one of a cathedral (it's nickname is, in fact, "the Cathedral of the Cotswolds") rather than a mere parish church. Market Place. ☎ 01285/654-552. www.ciren parish.co.uk/parishchurch.htm. Free admission. Mon–Fri 10am–1pm.

③ 🍽 **Swan Yard Café.** Take your pick from a serve-yourself counter well stocked with a large selection of quiches, scones, and other light fare, enjoyed in a sunny room off Market Square. 6 SwanYard, West Market Place. ☎ 01285/641-300. Daily 8am–5pm. Items £4–£6.

④ ★★★ **Corinium Museum.** The fascinating relics of Cirencester's Roman past that come to light in these handsome galleries include mosaic tile floors, excavated under present-day Cirencester, as well as a re-creation of rooms, shops, and a Roman garden. A 6th-century Anglo-Saxon princess is laid out in her coffin, surrounded by replicas of some of the 500 grave goods found with her, giving her the moniker "Mrs. Getty" (a reference to the

wealthy American industrialist family). Medieval sculpture and architectural elements are from Cirencester Abbey, once the largest Augustinian community in Britain and destroyed during Henry VIII's Dissolution of the Monasteries in 1539. ⏱ 2 hr. Park St. ☎ 01285/655-611. www.cirencester.co.uk. Admission £4.50 adults, £3.75 seniors, £2.25 kids 5–15. Mon–Sat 10am–5pm; Sun 2–5pm.

⑤ ★ **Cirencester Park.** Just to the west of Market Square are the gates to the vast estate of the Earl of Batsford. The first Earl of Batsford and his friend, the poet and landscape designer Alexander Pope (1688–1744), laid out the geometric greens and gardens over 30 years in the first part of the 18th century, transforming 1,200 hectares (3,000 acres) into a manicured and gently wooded park that is 3 miles wide and 5 miles long. Among their plantings is a 12m-tall (40-ft.) yew hedge, an imposing presence as you look into the park from the town center. ⏱ 1 hr. Off Cecily Hill. Free admission. Daily 9am–5pm.

⑥ ★ **Roman amphitheater.** One of the largest amphitheaters in Roman Britain was enclosed in earthwork mounds, across which planks were laid for seating as many as 8,000

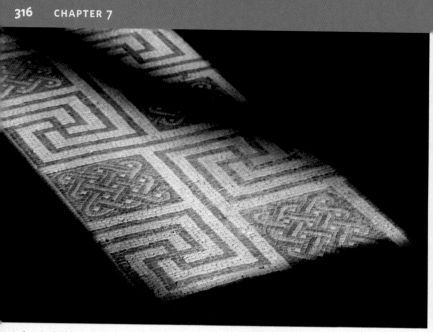

> A major highlight of Chedworth Roman Villa is its intact mosaic floors.

spectators for gladiatorial contests and other events. Saxons used the structure as a fort around the 8th century, and crowds gathered in the theater as recently as the 18th century to watch bull-baiting contests; even today the ruin is known as the Bull Ring. ⏱ 30 min. Off Bristol Rd. Free admission. Dawn to dusk.

Chedworth Roman Villa is about 8 miles north of Circencester off the A429.

❼ ★★★ Chedworth Roman Villa. A large villa, one of the many Roman farming estates that surrounded Roman Cirencester (Corinium), came to light in 1864, when a gameskeeper found some fragments of flooring and pottery while digging for a ferret. Excavations have unearthed the mosaics, baths, parts of hypocausts (a Roman system of underground heating), and latrines of what began as a simple farm dwelling in the 2nd century and by the 4th century had been enlarged and embellished as a fine residence. Eleven of the rooms surrounding the courtyard are floored with elaborate mosaics. ⏱ 1 hr. Yanworth. ☎ 01242/890-256. www.chedworthromanvilla.com. Admission £7 adults, £4 kids, £18 families. Mar–Oct Wed–Sun 10am–5pm (Mar until 4pm).

The Romans in the Cotswolds

The Romans built a fort near present-day Cirencester as early as A.D. 49, and enlisted the aid of the Dubonni, a local Celtic tribe, in defending their frontier and establishing a settlement. A century later, Corinium was a thriving town of 100 hectares (250 acres) enclosed in a massive wall (parts of which still stand), and by the 4th century A.D., Corinium was the capital of the Province of Britannia Prima and the second-largest city in Britain after London. The city stood at the intersection of the Fosse Way, which ran between present-day Exeter in the southwest and Lincoln in the Midlands; and Akeman Street, which served as a connector between the Fosse Way and St. Alban's, where it intersected another important Roman road, Watling Street. A large forum and basilica stood in the center of Corinium, now buried deep beneath modern Cirencester, and sheep-rearing for wool and other agricultural pursuits brought considerable wealth to the Romans, who remained in force until they retreated from Britain in the 5th century A.D.

Where to Stay & Dine

★★★ Barnsley House BARNSLEY
One of England's most stylish country inns occupies the former estate of garden designer Rosemary Verey (1918–2001) and her architectural historian husband, David (1913–84). Guest rooms offer such amenities as stone fireplaces and private gardens and are outfitted with stylish contemporary furnishings, soaking tubs, and other luxuries. The grounds are exquisite, and with the in-house spa and restaurant, you may find no need to leave them. 4 miles east of Cirencester off B4425. ☎ 01285/740-000. www.barnsleyhouse.com. 11 units. Doubles £275–£335 w/breakfast. AE, DC, MC, V.

> Barnsley House, unsurprisingly the former estate of a garden designer.

Antiques Hunting in Cirencester and the Cotswolds

Long past are the days when weekenders might discover a Chippendale highboy at a ridiculously low price in a quaint Cotswolds shop. In fact, the region is now one of England's prime antiques centers and home to many top dealers. Cirencester hosts a weekly antiques market in the Corn Hall, in Market Square, on Fridays from 9am to 3pm.

Among the town's well-known antiques dealers are **Rankine Taylor,** 34 Dollar St. (☎ 01285/652-529), and **William H. Stokes,** 68 Dollar St. (☎ 01285/653-907). Many dealers also do business in the region's small villages, and Stow-on-the-Wold (p. 306, ⑤) is especially well known for antiques. Shops on the village square and adjoining Church Street include **Anthony Preston** (☎ 01451/831-586); **Baggott Church Street** (☎ 01451/830-370); and **Huntington's** (☎ 01451/830-842). The **Cotswolds Art and Antique Dealers' Association (CADA)** provides a free brochure listing its 45 members, scattered throughout the region; to obtain it, contact CADA, Broadwell House, Sheep Street, Stow-on-the-Wold, Gloucestershire GL54 1JS (☎ 07789/968-319; www.cotswolds-antiques-art.com).

★ The Crown CITY CENTER *PUB*
Cirencester's favorite gathering spot for almost 400 years serves fish and chips and other pub favorites in woody, convivial surroundings. 17 W. Market Place. ☎ 02185/653-206. www.crownciren.com. Entrees £6–£10. MC, V. Lunch & dinner daily.

★★ Stratton House Hotel CITY CENTER
An 18th-century manor house has been added to many times over the centuries, creating a pleasant traditional ambience that extends to the modern wing, where most guest rooms are located. The extremely pleasant lounges, bar, and restaurant all have the feel of a country house, as do the beautiful lawns and gardens. Gloucester Rd. ☎ 01285/651-761. www.stratton househotel.co.uk. 40 units. Doubles £130–£145 w/breakfast. AE, DC, MC, V.

Cheltenham

Cheltenham solidly belongs to the Regency era—that brief period of the early 19th century marked by extravagance, pomp, and glamour and indulgences that included spending seasons at spas like those fueled by Cheltenham's healing waters. Beautiful parks and gardens, street after street of elegant houses, and a still-steady stream of alkaline waters are the legacy of the town's fashionable past.

> *Each March, elegant, sleepy Cheltenham is energized by the Cheltenham Festival, British national hunt horseracing's most important annual event.*

START Cheltenham is 100 miles northwest of London.

① ★ Imperial Gardens. Shaded paths and lawns were laid out near the town center in 1818 to provide spa patrons with an "ornamental pleasure ground" and a place to take healthful promenades. Today the gardens are ablaze with more than 25,000 colorful plantings that surround a statue of composer Gustav Holst (1874–1934), who was born in Cheltenham and is best known for his musical suite *The Planets.* Montpellier Parade flanks the western side of the gardens and is Cheltenham's most fashionable shopping street—as the classical statues adorning the storefronts suggest. ⏱1 hr. Off Montpellier Walk, town center.

② ★★ Cheltenham Art Gallery and Museum. The Arts and Crafts Movement flourished in the Cotswolds in the early 20th century (p. 301), and furniture, ceramics, textiles, and other work by William Morris and other local craftspeople fill these galleries. A small but excellent selection of paintings ranges from works of Dutch and Flemish masters to those by early-20th-century post-impressionist Stanley Spencer (1891–1959), who gives Cotswold village life a Biblical slant in *Village Gossips.* The Wilson room displays the snowsuit and other belongings of Cheltenham native Edward Wilson (1872–1912), who died on Captain Robert Scott's ill-fated journey to the South Pole in 1912. ⏱2 hr. Clarence St. ☎01242/262-334. www.cheltenhamartgallery.

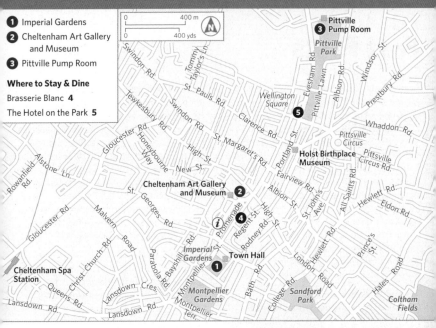

1 Imperial Gardens
2 Cheltenham Art Gallery and Museum
3 Pittville Pump Room

Where to Stay & Dine
Brasserie Blanc 4
The Hotel on the Park 5

org.uk. Free admission. Daily 10am–5pm (Nov–Mar until 4pm).

3 ★ **Pittville Pump Room.** Britain's only natural consumable alkaline waters are channeled into a marble fountain in an elegant oval gallery, where they can be enjoyed for their beneficial effects on digestion. A ground floor ballroom, the major social venue of 19th-century Cheltenham, is still the setting for concerts and dances. The streets and squares of the surrounding Pittville quarter are lined with Cheltenham's finest houses. ☺ 1 hr. Pittville Park. ☎ 01242-523-852. Free admission. Wed–Mon 10am–4pm.

> The town's Imperial Gardens were laid out during the Regency Era, at the peak of Cheltenham's spa boom.

Staying the Night in Cheltenham

★ **Brasserie Blanc,** a stylish bistro in the city center under the stewardship of re-nowned chef Raymond Blanc, serves hearty French favorites, including a rich boeuf bourguignon, as well as innovative lighter fare. In the Queen's Hotel, The Promenade. ☎ 01242/266-800. www.brasserieblanc.com/locations/cheltenham.html. Entrees £8–£25. Fixed price lunch from £12, fixed price dinner from £15. AE, DC, MC, V. Lunch & dinner daily.

No other Cheltenham hostelry so thoroughly captures the elegance of the town's bygone days than ★★★ **The Hotel on the Park.** The 1830s villa in Pittville has been lavishly restored, and guest rooms are furnished in traditional and luxurious comfort. The in-house restaurant, **Parkers,** serves modern British cuisine and is one of the best dining rooms in town. 38 Evesham Rd. ☎ 01242/518-898. www.thehoteluk.co.uk. 12 units. Doubles £150–£230 with breakfast. AE, MC, V.

Fast Facts

Accommodations Booking Services

A good source for character-filled accommodation is **National Trust Holiday Cottages,** P.O. Box 536, Melksham, Wiltshire (☎ 0844/800-2070; www.nationaltrustcottages.co.uk); the National Trust offers accommodation in more than 350 historic properties around Britain, many in the Cotswolds. **Sherpa Van Accommodation Service,** 29 The Green, Richmond, North Yorkshire (☎ 0871/5200-124; www.sherpavan.com) is geared to walkers and arranges accommodation on the Cotswold Way and other routes as well as luggage transport from inn to inn, allowing you to walk from one stop to another unencumbered.

Arriving & Getting Around

BY PLANE There is no airport that services the Cotswolds; you'll need to fly into London (p. 137). BY TRAIN You can reach the Cotswolds by train on service that runs more or less hourly from London's Paddington Station. The main stop for Cotswolds villages is Moreton-in-Marsh. Trains on this line also make a stop in Oxford en route. Travel time from London to Moreton-in-Marsh is a little over 1½ hours; Oxford is about 30 minutes from Moreton-in-Marsh. You can also reach the larger towns by train: Cheltenham is 2¼ hours from London Paddington, usually with a change in Bristol or Swindon, and the nearest train station to Cirencester is Kemble, which is 4 miles southwest; the trip from London Paddington takes about 80 minutes, often with a change in Swindon. For more information, contact **National Rail Enquiries** (☎ 08475/484-950; www.nationalrail.co.uk). BY CAR By car, the M40 leads west from London through Oxford, and from there the A40 leads into the Cotswolds. A car is definitely the best way to get around the region and see all of the sights in a timely manner. Roads are extremely well marked, and parking is well signposted at the edges of the villages. BY BUS Buses make as many as 10 daily trips between London's Victoria Coach Station and Cheltenham and Cirencester; for schedules and information, contact **National Express** (☎ 0871/781-8181; www.nationalexpress.co.uk). A number of bus companies service the Cotswolds. In general, you can reach even the smallest village with once-a-day service, and most major villages and towns are served more often than that. You can get around on public transport with a bit of planning, but a car is the easiest way to see this rural region. Moreton-in-Marsh, with its train connections, is a bus hub for the region. For service information and schedules for the region, contact **Traveline** (☎ 0871/200-2233; www.traveline.org.uk).

Dentists & Doctors

If you need non-urgent medical or dental care, hotels will be able to refer you to a local doctor or dentist. Cheltenham and Cirencester are the best equipped for medical care.

Emergencies

Call ☎ 999 for police and fire emergencies and to summon an ambulance. You can also ask at any local police station (there are offices in almost every village).

Internet Access

Many Cotswolds hotels are now equipped with Wi-Fi, and many have a public terminal as well. Ironically, connections are usually free in less expensive hotels and can be quite costly in more expensive hotels. Internet cafes, where you can log on for about £1 an hour, are common in major towns. Two popular venues for Internet access—each with its own Facebook page—are the community-owned **Blockley Village Shop and Café,** 4 miles west of Moreton-in-Marsh near Batsford Arboretum, the Old Coach House, Post Office Sq., Blockley (☎ 01386/701-411; http://blockley shop.com), which offers free Wi-Fi access, and **Butty's** in Chipping Campden (The Old Bakehouse, Lower High St.; ☎ 01386/840-401), a family-run sandwich shop and Internet cafe.

Additionally, all public libraries in the Cotswolds have at least one computer with Internet access. The **Cirencester library,** the Waterloo (☎ 0845/230-5420), not only has Wi-Fi, but is one of the branches in

Gloucestershire that features an Internet cafe; the Internet suite provides up to 2 hours of free access.

Pharmacies

Pharmacies (also known as "chemists") are often quite helpful, especially in rural areas like the Cotswolds, where the pharmacist often acts as a local health care provider. By U.K. regulations, pharmacies are only permitted to fill prescriptions issued by physicians licensed in the U.K. Pharmacies are usually open 9am to 6pm, though at least one in the region is open 24 hours on a rotating basis. There is a Boots pharmacy open daily in Cirencester at 49–43 Crickade St. (☎ 01285/653-019; www.boots.com).

Post Office

Local post offices are generally open from Monday to Friday 8am to 5pm, and some on Saturday mornings.

Safety

The Cotswolds are by and large safe, with very little crime. Bring plenty of water when hiking, and let an innkeeper or another party know of your intended whereabouts when setting out on a long trek.

Visitor Information

You'll find tourist offices in almost any Cotswolds village of any size; they all dispense information on sights and accommodations, as well as maps and other advice. Call ahead or check the websites for the most up-to-date hours of operation (seasonal variations are common in smaller towns, and some offices aren't open at all on Sunday). **BROADWAY** Broadway Tourist Information Centre, Russell Sq. (☎ 01386/852-937; www.beautiful broadway.com). **BURFORD** Burford Tourist Information Centre, Old Brewery, Sheep St. (☎ 01993/823-558). **CHELTENHAM** Visit Cheltenham, 77 The Promenade (☎ 01242/522-878; www.visitcheltenham.com). **CHIPPING CAMPDEN** Chipping Campden Information Centre, Old Police Station, High St. (☎ 01386/841-206; www.chippingcampdenonline.org). **CIRENCESTER** Cirencester Visitor Information

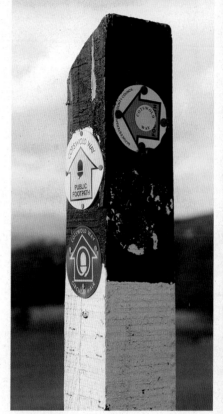

> The well-marked Cotswold Way follows a 100-mile path through the best of the region's outdoors.

Centre, Corinium Museum, Park St. (☎ 01285/654-180; www.cirencester.gov.uk). **PAINSWICK** Tourist Information Centre, Painswick Library, Stroud Rd. (☎ 01452/813-552). **STOW-ON-THE-WOLD** Tourist Information Centre, Hollis House, The Square (☎ 01451/831-082). **TEWKESBURY** Tourist Information Centre, 100 Chruch St. (☎ 01684/855-040).

Some helpful websites for visitors are www.cotswolds.com and www.cotswolds.info, as well as a website about the region's status as an "Area of Outstanding Natural Beauty" (AONB), www.cotswoldsaonb.org.uk.

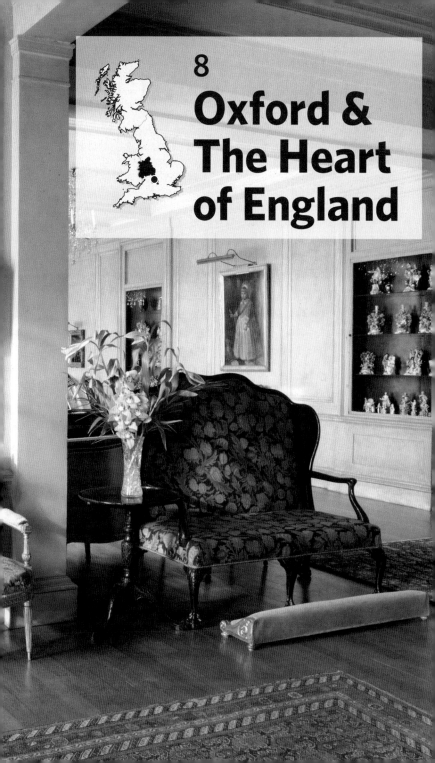

8

Oxford &
The Heart
of England

Favorite Moments

England's long-settled heartland of green hills and fertile farmland is watered by clear, flowing streams and dotted with medieval towns like Ludlow, with its rich heritage of half-timbered architecture, and Hereford, with its small, lovely cathedral. The country's mid-section—including Warwickshire, Oxfordshire, and the Midlands—is a region where you can enjoy Shakespeare plays in his hometown of Stratford-upon-Avon, explore the colleges and quads of Oxford, marvel at the might of Warwick Castle, and wander through Blenheim Palace, one of the largest homes in England. The Ironbridge Gorge, with its restored factories and foundries, provides a fascinating glimpse of England's industrial past.

> *PREVIOUS PAGE Upton House is famed for its extensive art collection. THIS PAGE Cycling is the preferred mode of transport on central Oxford's narrow streets.*

❶ Wandering through the water meadows in Oxford. There's much of architectural and artistic interest to enjoy in Oxford, but it's also a pleasure to stroll or bike through the quiet meadows beside the Cherwell River behind Magdalen College. See p. 363, ❻.

❷ Pondering the past at the Pitt Rivers Museum in Oxford. It's definitely old-fashioned and low-tech, but that's why the Victorian-era Pitt Rivers Museum is so delightfully intriguing. See p. 364, ❽.

❸ Perusing the paintings of Winston Churchill at Blenheim. The palace is a bloated paean to power, but the watercolors of Sir Winston Churchill are quiet, lovely, and reveal the human side of Britain's wartime prime minister. See p. 340, ❶.

❹ Attending a play at the Royal Shakespeare Theatre in Stratford-upon-Avon. What could be more memorable than to see great actors in a great play in the newly restored Royal Shakespeare Theatre? See p. 370, ❻.

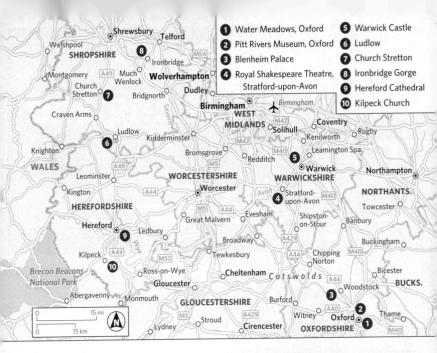

1	Water Meadows, Oxford	**5**	Warwick Castle
2	Pitt Rivers Museum, Oxford	**6**	Ludlow
3	Blenheim Palace	**7**	Church Stretton
4	Royal Shakespeare Theatre, Stratford-upon-Avon	**8**	Ironbridge Gorge
		9	Hereford Cathedral
		10	Kilpeck Church

5 Exploring the glory and gory at Warwick Castle. Lifelike wax figures of aristocrats attending a party at Warwick "people" the State Rooms, but there's also that horrible dungeon where earlier generations met their doom. See p. 342, **2**.

6 Loafing in Ludlow. It's hard not to be charmed by this ever-so-pretty Shropshire village, and even harder to leave it. See p. 357, **7**.

7 Hiking the hills around Church Stretton. The new "Walkers are Welcome" designation is an apt one, for this Shropshire village in an Area of Outstanding Natural Beauty is surrounded by hiking trails for all ages and abilities. See p. 348, **6**.

8 Contemplatng the "Iron Age" at Ironbridge Gorge. The birthplace of the Industrial Revolution is now a UNESCO World Heritage Site filled with a fascinating assortment of museums housed in original 18th- and 19th-century factories and warehouses. See p. 333, **8**.

9 Marveling at the Mappa Mundi in Hereford Cathedral. It's one of the oldest maps in the world, a historic treasure that's decidedly inaccurate, but looking at this 700-year-old

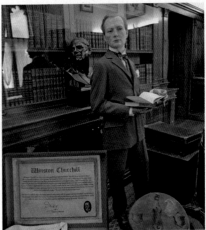

> Meet waxwork nobles in the State Rooms at Warwick Castle.

view of the world still sends a shiver of wonder down the spine. See p. 357, **8**.

10 Acknowledging the Norman at Kilpeck Church. The small Norman church in the village of Kilpeck is covered in a riot of 12th-century carving that's quite simply amazing. See p. 351, **9**.

Best of Oxford & the Heart of England in 3 Days

In addition to the major tourist magnets of Stratford-upon-Avon and Oxford, the heart of England includes grand estates, atmospheric cathedral towns, and a UNESCO World Heritage Site. You'll be introduced to all of them on this quick tour of the region.

> *Christ Church College, which has the largest quad in Oxford, has educated 13 British prime ministers over the centuries.*

START Oxford is 60 miles northwest of London, an hour's train ride from London's Paddington Station. TRIP LENGTH 200 miles.

1 ★★★ **Oxford.** Arrive in the morning, check into your hotel, and spend at least half a day exploring this ancient university city, which is also a good overnight destination. Visit some of Oxford's famous **colleges,** admire the city's architectural landmarks, discover the treasures of the **Ashmolean Museum** (p. 364, **12**), and take a **riverside walk** in the meadows beside the Thames and Cherwell rivers (p. 333). ◷ At least 3 hr. See p. 360.

Take the no. 20 bus from Oxford train station to Blenheim Palace's front gate (15 min.).

2 ★★ **Blenheim Palace.** On the afternoon of your first day, drive or take the bus from Oxford to this enormous baroque palace, birthplace of Sir Winston Churchill, Britain's wartime prime minister, and full of Churchill memorabilia. Blenheim was built for grandeur, not intimacy, as you'll see in the **Great Hall** and various state-rooms. ◷ At least 1 hr. See p. 340, **1**.

Return to Oxford for the evening. On Day 2, take an early-morning train (1½ hr.) to

1 Oxford
2 Blenheim Palace
3 Stratford-upon-Avon
4 Warwick Castle
5 Ironbridge Gorge
6 Worcester

Stratford-upon-Avon, 53 miles northwest of Oxford.

3 ★★★ Stratford-upon-Avon. Spend your second day and night in this Warwickshire town that has been given over—no way around it—to the commercialized memory of William Shakespeare, and at neighboring Warwick Castle. To make this work you need to get an early start. It will take you at least 3 hours to visit the four literary shrines in town: **Shakespeare's Birthplace;** the gardens of **New Place,** where he retired; **Hall's Croft,** where his daughter Susanna lived; and **Holy Trinity Church,** where Shakespeare is buried with his wife Anne and daughter Susanna. It's

an easy 1-mile walk to **Anne Hathaway's Cottage,** where Shakespeare's wife was raised and where the couple courted; and a short

Travel Tip

You don't need a car for most of this itinerary. From London you can easily get a train to Oxford, and a convenient local bus runs between Oxford and Blenheim Palace. Another train will get you from Oxford to Stratford-upon-Avon, Warwick Castle, and Worcester. Ironbridge, however, is best toured by car; rent one in Stratford and use it for a day trip to Ironbridge Gorge.

> Thatched Anne Hathaway's Cottage, where the Bard's wife was raised, is a gentle 1-mile walk from central Stratford.

drive or bus ride to **Mary Arden's House,** his mother's home. Seeing a Shakespeare play performed at the newly refurbished **Royal Shakespeare Theatre** is a memorable treat. ⏱ 3 hr. See p. 366.

In the afternoon of Day 2 you're off to Warwick Castle, 9 miles east of Stratford. Stagecoach (☎ 08456/001-314; www.stagecoach bus.com) provides direct bus service from Stratford to Warwick (15 min.), or you can take Chiltern Railways (☎ 08705/165-165), which runs direct trains from Stratford to Warwick (20 min.). The castle is a 15-min. walk from the train or bus station.

4 ★★★ [kids] **Warwick Castle.** You can explore some intriguing old streets in the ancient county town of Warwick (pronounced *war-ick*), but most visitors come here to visit mighty Warwick Castle, one of England's most popular tourist attractions. Dramatically sited above the river on the town's south side, the castle is a splendid example of a medieval fortress that's been adapted over the centuries to reflect its inhabitants' tastes and ambitions. Give yourself at least 2 hours to explore the castle complex, especially the **Private Apartments.** Several exhibitions use sound and light effects and wax figures to tell stories about the castle. Take some time to stroll through the beautiful parkland and **gardens** laid out by "Capability" Brown, one of the greatest landscape gardeners of 18th-century England. ⏱ 1½ hr. See p. 342, **2**.

Return to Stratford for the evening. On the morning of Day 3, rent a car and head for Ironbridge Gorge, 70 miles (1½ hr.) northwest of Stratford-upon-Avon on the M40, A464, and M54. Both the Ironbridge Gorge and Worcester are close enough to Stratford to be a day trip.

5 ★★★ **Ironbridge Gorge.** The verdant, forested Severn Valley in Shropshire is called the "birthplace of the Industrial Revolution" because it was here, about 300 years ago, that Abraham Darby perfected a method of smelting iron that changed the face of the world. Named for the famous iron bridge constructed across the Severn River in 1781, the gorge contains several historic sites (all signposted and easy to find) related to its industrial past, all of them housed in restored buildings of the period. Give yourself time to explore the major sites, including the **Museum of the Gorge,** the **Coalbrookdale Museum of Iron,** the **iron bridge,** and **Blists Hill Victorian Town,** a recreation of a Victorian iron-making town. ⏱ 3 hr. See p. 333, **8**.

From the Ironbridge Gorge, head over to Worcester, 38 miles (1 hr. 15 min.) south of Ironbridge on the A442 and A449.

6 ★ **Worcester.** One of England's least-explored cathedral cities, Worcester (*wooster*) has a quiet and rather elegant charm, but you have to ignore the modern architectural excrescences erected in the 1950s and 1960s and concentrate on the historic core around the cathedral. Majestic ★★★ **Worcester Cathedral,** College Yard (☎ 01905/732-900; www.worcestercathedral.co.uk; suggested donation £3), rising dramatically above the Severn River, is the city's major sight and chief glory. The mostly 14th-century cathedral sits atop an 11th-century Norman crypt, the largest in England, and features a lovely 12th-century octagonal chapter house, a 13th-century Lady Chapel, and the tomb of King John (1167–1216), one of England's worst monarchs but the one who signed (under duress) the Magna Carta. Attending **Evensong** (Mon–Wed & Fri–Sat 5:30pm, Sun 4pm) is a memorable experience.

Another monarch, Charles II (1630–85), used an impressive medieval building

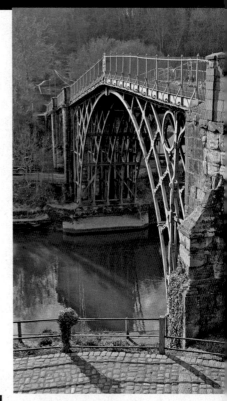

> *Ironbridge Gorge was named after the world's first cast iron bridge, raised in this former industrial area in 1781.*

On the Trail of Elgar

Worcester was the birthplace of **Edward Elgar** (1857–1934), the English composer whose best-known compositions include the *Enigma Variations* and *Pomp and Circumstance*. If you're an Elgar fan, and have a car, you might want to take the 40-mile circular loop called ★ **The Elgar Trail.** A 3-hour side trip from Worcester, the well-signposted trail begins at the **Edward Elgar Birthplace Museum,** Crown E. Lane, Lower Broadheath (☎ 01905/333-224; £6 adults, £5 seniors), a charming red brick, rose-bowered cottage filled with an assortment of Elgar memorabilia, and links all the houses and sites associated with Elgar in and around Worcester, the final stop being his gravesite in the churchyard of St. Wulstan's Roman Catholic Church in **Little Malvern.** The image of a violin is used on the trail's signposts. For more information visit the Elgar Society website at **www. elgar.org.**

called the ★ **Commandery,** 109 Sidbury St. (☎ 01905/361-821; £5.25 adults, £4 seniors & kids), as his headquarters during the Civil War. Now a local history museum, it has a special exhibition that chronicles the bloody era of England's Civil War (1642–51). Have a look at the 18th-century red brick **Guildhall** on High Street, now the tourist information center, and step into the **Greyfriars,** Friars St. (☎ 01905/23571; £4.15 adults, £2.05 kids), a 15th-century timber-framed merchant's house with a charming walled garden.

Worcester is known as the place where tangy Worcestershire sauce was first bottled in 1835, and where Royal Worcester Porcelain Factory was founded in 1751. You can learn more about the famous china and see how it is produced at the ★ **Worcester Porcelain Museum,** Severn St. (☎ 01905/21247; £5 adults, £4.25 seniors). ⏱ 2 hr.

Best of Oxford & the Heart of England in 5 Days

The heart of England includes tranquil English countryside; time-capsule villages full of black-and-white timber-framed houses; magnificent cathedrals, both old and new; and such major industrial cities as Birmingham and Coventry that you can't pretend are picturesque, but which offer some surprising cultural treats. This itinerary highlights the amazing contrasts waiting to be found in a relatively small area.

> The small border city of Hereford is a comfortable place to explore on foot, and has a fine cathedral.

START **Oxford is 60 miles northwest of London, a 1-hr. train trip from Paddington Station. TRIP LENGTH 393 miles.**

1 ★★★ **Oxford.** This intellectual and academic powerhouse, your first overnight stop, provides a lively and reflective introduction to your regional tour. Spend at least 3 hours visiting some of Oxford's ancient **colleges,** enjoying the architectural delights woven into the city's ancient urban fabric, and visit the bit-of-everything collections in the **Ashmolean Museum** (p. 364, **12**). Enjoy a stroll along the riverside meadows and, if the mood strikes, try your hand at punting. ◷ 3 hr. See p. 360.

In the afternoon, take the no. 20 bus to Blenheim Palace, 8 miles north of Oxford (buses leave on the half-hour and drop you off at Blenheim's front gate).

2 ★★ **Blenheim Palace.** Declared a World Heritage Site in 1987, this enormous palace is the home of the Dukes of Marlborough and the birthplace of Winston Churchill. It's best seen by guided tour. ◷ At least 1 hr. See p. 340, **1**.

On Day 2, head by direct train (1½ hr.) to Stratford-upon-Avon, 53 miles northwest of Oxford.

1 Oxford	**7** Birmingham	**Where to Stay**		
2 Blenheim Palace	**8** Ironbridge Gorge	Macdonald Burlington		
3 Stratford-upon-Avon	**9** Shrewsbury	Hotel **14**		
4 Warwick Castle	**10** Ludlow	Malmaison **15**		
5 Kenilworth Castle	**11** Worcester	**Where to Dine**		
6 Coventry	**12** Hereford	Al Frash **13**		
		Purnell's **16**		

3 ★★★ **Stratford-upon-Avon.** This shrine to the Bard of Avon is a good choice for your second overnight and makes a good all-round headquarters for touring the rest of the region. The major attractions are all related in one way or another to Shakespeare: his **birthplace** (p. 366, **1**); **Anne Hathaway's Cottage** (p. 370, **7**), the house where his wife was raised; the gardens of **New Place** (p. 366, **2**), the last house he owned; **Hall's Croft** (p. 368, **3**), where his daughter Susanna lived; and **Holy Trinity Church** (p. 368, **4**), where he is buried. To add to your enjoyment, book in advance to see a play performed by the Royal Shakespeare Company in its newly revamped theater (p. 370, **6**). See p. 366.

By headquartering in Stratford and renting a car on Day 3, you can easily visit Warwick Castle, Kenilworth Castle, and Coventry as a combined day trip. On the morning of Day 3, head first to Warwick, 9 miles northeast of Stratford-upon-Avon, a 20-min. drive on the M40. The castle is right in the center of Warwick.

Travel Tip

For this tour, I'd recommend that you take the train to Oxford and Stratford-upon-Avon, the first two destinations, and rent a car in Stratford for day trips.

> Coventry Cathedral, dedicated to St. Michael, is one of Britain's most important modernist buildings built after World War II.

4 ★★★ **Warwick Castle.** It's a major tourist attraction, but it's done well and has many intriguing attractions, both inside and out. The **Private Apartments,** filled with an assembly of historic figures created by Madame Tussauds, are where you want to head first. End your explorations with a stroll through the gardens and 18th-century landscaped park. ⏱ At least 2 hr. See p. 342, **2**.

Head next to nearby Kenilworth Castle, 6½ miles north of Warwick, a 15-min. drive on the A46.

5 ★★ **Kenilworth Castle.** Spend an hour discovering the evocative and less-frequented ruins of Kenilworth. An excellent audio tour guides you through the power trips and political treacheries that have been played out in the castle that inspired Sir Walter Scott's novel *Kenilworth.* ⏱ 30 min. See p. 342, **3**.

Your next stop is Coventry, 5½ miles northeast of Kenilworth, a 15-min. drive on the A429.

6 **Coventry.** In 1940, German bombers destroyed most of Coventry in an incendiary attack that left this old Warwickshire city a smoking heap of rubble. Postwar reconstruction did not create an attractive city, but it did result in one architectural masterpiece that makes the city worth a stop. ★★ **Coventry Cathedral,** Priory Row (☎ 024/7622-7597; suggested donation £3), designed by Sir Basil Spence (1907–76), was built adjacent to the bomb-gutted ruins of the old cathedral. Sir Jacob Epstein's (1880–1959) iconic sculpture of St. Michael conquering the devil stands outside; inside, the church is aglow with brilliant stained glass and features a giant tapestry by English artist Graham Sutherland (1903–80). If you are a car buff, you might want to take an additional hour to visit the ★ **Coventry Transport Museum,** Hales St. (☎ 024/7623-4270; free admission), a surprisingly vast collection of historic bicycles, cars, and trucks produced in Coventry before the war. ⏱ At least 1 hr.

Return to Stratford-upon-Avon. On Day 4, head for Birmingham, 38 miles northwest of Stratford-upon-Avon, a 45-min. drive on the M40 and M42.

7 ★ **Birmingham.** Postwar reconstruction created a metropolis hedged in by ring roads and swimming in concrete, but in the last decade, Birmingham has funneled enormous resources into making itself a cultural, shopping, and convention destination. Because of its array of hotels, restaurants, and nightlife options, it's a useful place to spend your fourth night. In terms of sightseeing, concentrate on the city's two major art collections.

The ★★ **Birmingham Museum and Art Gallery,** Chamberlain Sq. (☎ 0121/303-2834; free admission), is renowned for its collection of Pre-Raphaelite paintings and works by earlier English artists such as Gainsborough, Hogarth, and Constable. Old Masters dominate the collections of the ★★ **Barber Institute of Fine Arts,** University of Birmingham, near East Gate, 2½ miles from city center (☎ 0121/414-7333; www.barber.org.uk; free admission), with paintings by Bellini, Brueghel, and Rubens, but there's also an excellent

> *The collection at the Birmingham Museum and Art Gallery is fêted particularly for works by the 19th-century Pre-Raphaelite Brotherhood.*

Riverside Walks and Rides

For a quick escape into bucolic settings within Oxford, take a riverside walk: From St. Aldate's Street you'll find entrances to Christ Church Meadow and a network of paths that follow the Thames and Cherwell rivers. From Walton Road, northwest of the center, you can enter Port Meadow, where you may be joined by grazing livestock. For a leisurely afternoon, follow the Thameside path north from Port Meadow to two charming pubs: the **Perch** (☎ 01865/728-891) and the nearby **Trout** (☎ 01865/302-071); they are about a 2-mile walk from the center of Oxford and have delightful riverside gardens. You can also enjoy the rivers from a punt, rented by the hour from the **Cherwell Boathouse,** Banbury Rd. (☎ 01865/515-978), and from **Old Horse Ford,** off High St. under the Magdalen Bridge (☎ 01865/202-643). Both are open from mid-March to mid-October and charge £12 to £14 per hour, plus a damage and theft deposit fee.

group of Impressionist and Post-Impressionist works.

Birmingham has an extensive series of 18th- and 19th-century canals that provide an unusual and enjoyable way to tour the city. One-hour boat tours are offered by ★ **Sherborne Wharf Heritage Narrowboats,** Heritage Marina, near junction of Macclesfield and Trent & Mersey Canals in Scholar Green (☎ 0121/455-6163; www.sherbornewharf. co.uk; 1-hr. tour £6.50 adults, £5.50 seniors, £5 kids). ⏲ At least 2 hr.

Make an afternoon trip to the Ironbridge Gorge, 37 miles northwest of Birmingham, a 45-min. drive on the M6 and M54.

SITE GUIDE PAGE 334

❽ ★★★ **Ironbridge Gorge.** Ten historic sites collectively make up this UNESCO World Heritage Site. All of them are now museums housed in original 18th- and 19th-century buildings related to the Severn Valley's industrial heritage, which began in the early 18th century when a new method for smelting iron was discovered.

8 Ironbridge Gorge

Begin your tour at the **A ★ Museum of the Gorge Visitor Centre,** the first site you come to as you leave B4380 and head east on B4373 on the north bank of the Severn River. In this restored neo-Gothic warehouse by the water's edge, you'll get a good overview of the geology and human history of the Ironbridge Gorge and the personalities of the Darby family. Backtrack on B4380 and take A4169 north to the Coalbrookdale **B ★ Museum of Iron,** housed in another restored warehouse built in 1838 using (for the first time) cast-iron components. This museum fills you in on the history of iron-making and the founding of the Coalbrookdale Company by Abraham Darby. Nearby is the **C Darby Furnace,** where in 1709 Abraham Darby pioneered his new method of smelting iron using coke instead of charcoal, making it possible to mass-produce cast iron that could be used for railroad tracks, steam locomotives, and prefabricated building components. The Quaker Darbys lived not lavishly but in comfort at **D Rosehill House** (far right) and **Dale Cottage,** just northwest of their Coalbrookdale factory. You can visit both houses, which are filled with period furnishings. To see how the

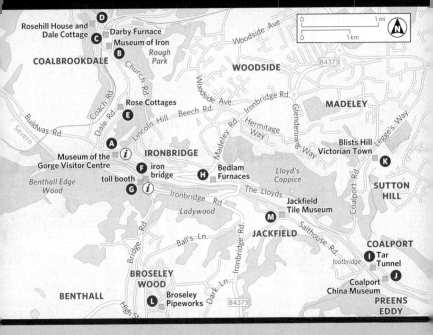

Rosehill House and Dale Cottage
Darby Furnace
Museum of Iron
Rough Park
COALBROOKDALE
WOODSIDE
Woodside Ave.
B4373
MADELEY
Rose Cottages
Blists Hill Victorian Town
IRONBRIDGE
Museum of the Gorge Visitor Centre
iron bridge
toll booth
Bedlam Furnaces
Lloyd's Coppice
SUTTON HILL
Benthall Edge Wood
The Lloyds
Jackfield Tile Museum
Ladywood
JACKFIELD
COALPORT
Tar Tunnel
footbridge
BROSELEY WOOD
Coalport China Museum
BENTHALL
Broseley Pipeworks
PREENS EDDY
B4373

factory workers lived, stop at **E** **Rose Cottages** on your way back south on A4169. Then continue east on B4373 to see and walk across the famous **F** ★★★ **iron bridge,** a marvel of engineering and material, created from cast-iron parts and opened in 1781. The **G** **toll booth** on the south side of the bridge serves as a tourist information center. A bit further to the east are the **H** **Bedlam Furnaces,** custom-built for smelting iron from coke, and the **I** **Tar Tunnel,** a water-irrigation tunnel that was closed when naturally occurring bitumen began oozing through the walls. Continuing east on A343, you reach the **J** ★★ **Coalport China Museum,** which celebrates the china that was produced in this factory from 1792 to 1926. Just to the north is **K** ★★ **Blists Hill Victorian Town,** an open-air museum that recreates a Victorian town replete with costumed interpreters and Victorian houses, shops, and pubs. Cross the bridge just to the east of the Bedlam Furnaces and you come to **L** **Broseley Pipeworks,** once one of the U.K.'s largest makers of pipes (the kind you smoke); its interior remains exactly as it was when the factory closed its doors in 1957. To the east is the **M** **Jackfield Tile Museum,** in Victorian

times a famous local industry that created the glazed tiles now on display in gaslit showrooms. ⏱ At least 2 hr. ☎ 01952/884-391. www.ironbridge.org.uk. Admission to all museums £22 adults, £18 seniors, £14 kids, £60 families (separate admission prices for each museum are available; consult the website). All museums daily 10am–5pm.

> *Half-timbered houses, pictured here in Ludlow, are called "black-and-whites" for the contrast between their dark wood frame and light plaster or clay nogging.*

Return to Birmingham. Early on the morning of Day 5, head first for Shrewsbury, 47 miles west of Birmingham, about an hour's drive on the M6 and M54.

❾ ★★ Shrewsbury. Shropshire has many picturesque towns, and Shrewsbury is at the top of the list. Wedged into a horseshoe-shaped bend above the River Severn, the old wool town casts an old-world spell with its ancient timber-framed houses, epitomized by **Ireland's Mansion,** and once-mighty **Shrewsbury Abbey,** built of local red sandstone. Wander through narrow medieval streets with names like **Fish Street** and **Grope Lane,** and pay a visit to the **Shrewsbury Museum and Art Gallery** and **St. Mary's Church,** with its medieval spire. ⏱ At least 1 hr. See p. 355, ❷.

Next head to Ludlow, 31 miles south of Shrewsbury, a 45-min. drive south on the A488.

❿ ★★ Ludlow. Ludlow is a small town with lots of historic cachet, as you'll discover when you wander among the atmospheric ruins of **Ludlow Castle** and visit **St. Laurence's Church,** one of the largest parish churches in England. Half-timbered houses called "black-and-whites" share the stage with elegant Georgian mansions on streets lined with antiques shops and small stores selling local food products. In the past decade, Ludlow has become a haunt of foodies all over the region. ⏱1 hr. See p. 357, **7**.

Continue on to Worcester, 30 miles southeast of Ludlow, a 45-min. drive on the A456 and A449.

11 ★ **Worcester.** A quick stop in this old cathedral town is enough to enjoy a leisurely stroll and see all the major sights. The great red sandstone **cathedral** rising majestically above the Severn is the town's chief attraction, followed by the **Worcester Porcelain Museum.** ⏱1 hr. See p. 329, **6**.

Round out Day 5 with a trip to Hereford, 30 miles southwest of Worcester, a 45-min. drive on A4103.

12 ★ **Hereford.** The bucolic charms of farms and orchards add a timeless serenity to this Herefordshire town graced by ★★ **Hereford Cathedral,** one of the oldest in England and proud owner of the 13th-century **Mappa Mundi.** Spend an hour strolling through the cathedral and wandering the streets of **High Town;** then refresh yourself with a visit to the ★ **Cider Museum and King Offa's Brandy Distillery.** ⏱1 hr. See p. 357, **8**.

Where to Stay & Dine

★ **Al Frash** BIRMINGHAM *KASHMIRI*
Birmingham is famous for *balti,* a Kashmiri style of fast-cooking meat and vegetables over a high flame, and this down-to-earth place is where you can sample the city's best. 186 Ladypool Rd., Sparkhill. ☎0121/753-3120. www.alfrash.com. Entrees £5.50–£8.25. MC, V. Dinner daily.

★ **Macdonald Burlington Hotel** BIRMINGHAM
This venerable classic is centrally located in the Burlington Arcade and has a mixed bag of room types and a good restaurant that serves continental cuisine. 126 New St., Burlington Arcade. ☎0844/8799-9019. www.burlington hotel.com. 115 units. Doubles £83–£195 w/ breakfast. AE, MC, V.

★★ **Malmaison** BIRMINGHAM
This trendy boutique hotel serves up stylish comfort and excellent French food in a central location. 1 Wharfside St. ☎0121/246-5000. www.malmaison.com. 189 units. Doubles 129–£180. AE, MC, V.

★★ **Purnell's** BIRMINGHAM *MODERN BRITISH*
Bold, innovative cooking using local ingredients (chef Glynn Purnell has a Michelin star) and international influences make this place a culinary stand-out. 55 Cornwall St. ☎0121/212-9799. www.purnellsrestaurant.com. Reservations required. Fixed-price lunch £7–£20, fixed-price dinner £34–£40. AE, MC, V. Lunch & dinner Tues–Fri, dinner Sat.

> *Purnell's, where you'll find Birmingham's finest dining.*

WHODUNIT?

A Lineup of the Queens and Kings of British Crime Writing

BY NAOMI P. KRAUS

	Wilkie Collins (1824–89)	**Sir Arthur Conan Doyle** (1859–1930)	**Agatha Christie** (1890–1976)	**Dorothy L. Sayers** (1893–1957)
CLAIM TO FAME	English author lauded as the creator of the first detective novel in the English language.	Scottish physician, spiritualist, and novelist; creator of the world's most famous fictional detective.	The prolific Queen of Crime is revered for her intricate plots and her very "English" characterization.	Poet and novelist known for incorporating literary, academic, and religious themes into her works.
A BIT OF BACKGROUND	The son of an accomplished artist, Collins was born in London and lived there for most of his life. He could often be found moving about the city with friends such as Charles Dickens.	Born to Irish parents in Edinburgh; a good deal of Holmes's character was influenced by Conan Doyle's medical school professors at the University of Edinburgh.	Born in Devon, where she set many of her novels (though fictional St. Mary Mead is likely in Kent); check out the Agatha Christie Memorial Room in Torquay (p. 236, ❶).	One of the first women to be awarded a degree from her native Oxford, Sayers worked in the '20s as an ad copywriter in London. She is buried in Soho's St. Anne's Church.
MOST MEMORABLE SLEUTH	Franklin Blake	Sherlock Holmes	Hercule Poirot; Jane Marple	Lord Peter Wimsey
MUST-READ WORK	*The Moonstone*	*The Complete Sherlock Holmes*	*The Murder of Roger Ackroyd*	*Murder Must Advertise*
SKELETONS IN THE CLOSET	Collins suffered from neuralgia and other health problems, leading to a lifelong problem with drug addiction.	Tired of Sherlock Holmes, Conan Doyle killed him off in "The Final Problem"; the public outcry was so great, he was forced to bring him back from the dead.	In 1926, after discovering her husband was having an affair, Christie mysteriously disappeared for 11 days—touching off a countrywide hunt for the missing writer.	Sayers allegedly found her Peter Wimsey so perfect, she fell hard for her fictional work and created a thinly veiled Harriet Vane in order to get her guy.

WITH THE EXCEPTION, perhaps, of the U.S., Britain has had more influence on the development of the mystery genre—be it the classic locked-room puzzle or the modern crime thriller—than any other country. Edgar Allan Poe may have introduced the first fictional detective, but it was the likes of Sir Arthur Conan Doyle (who introduced Sherlock Holmes in 1887) and Dame Agatha Christie (who headlined the Golden Age of Detective Fiction in the 1920s and '30s) who launched the whodunit into the stratosphere. And they are only just a couple of the usual suspects. Here's a small sampling of Britain's best planters of clues, red herrings, and plot twists.

Josephine Tey (1896–1952)	P.D. James (b. 1920)	Ruth Rendell (b. 1930)	Ian Rankin (b. 1960)
Scottish playwright and novelist best known for her characterization and penchant for breaking the conventions of the whodunit.	Master of the art of merging classical detection with modern literary sensibilities and psychology; works are often bleak.	Pioneer of the psychological crime novel, often credited with turning the "whodunit" into the "whydunit."	Scottish novelist whose gritty depiction of Edinburgh has made him the U.K.'s current bestselling crime writer.
The reclusive native of Inverness (born Elizabeth Mackintosh) trained as a phys-ed teacher before turning to writing. She died in London under yet another pseudonym, Gordon Daviot.	Born in Oxford but schooled in Cambridge (where she set *An Unsuitable Job for a Woman*), this former civil servant now sits in the House of Lords.	Born in London, she covered that city as a journalist before moving on to fiction; created the Baroness of Babergh in 1997, she regularly sits in the House of Lords.	Born in Edinburgh to a dock worker, Rankin still lives there; he sometimes has a pint at the Oxford Bar (p. 513, ⑮).
Inspector Alan Grant	Commander Adam Dalgliesh	Chief Inspector Reginald Wexford	Inspector John Rebus
The Daughter of Time	*Shroud for a Nightingale*	*A Judgment in Stone*	*Black & Blue*
Her controversial but captivating defense of Richard III in *The Daughter of Time* touched off a firestorm that still rages over the innocence/guilt of one of England's most notorious monarchs.	If there's a major scandal in James's closet, it's a mystery as yet unsolved.	Was fired from a reporting job when she penned a story about a dinner she skipped out on—ironically, missing the death of the featured speaker mid-speech.	A soused (and married) Rankin got caught with a young woman not his wife at the British Book Awards in 2008.

Great Houses & Gardens

The West Midlands, and especially the area around Stratford-upon-Avon, abounds in stately homes and mighty castles that have played pivotal roles in English history. This driving tour takes you to an all-star roster of magnificent mansions built (and rebuilt) in different eras and different styles—from Tudor to Art Deco—and the superlative gardens that surround them. Base yourself in Stratford-upon-Avon (p. 366) and visit the houses and gardens in this tour as day trips.

> Behind Upton House's handsome exterior are Art Deco interiors and a painting collection that includes Canaletto and Bosch.

START Blenheim Palace. Take the train to Stratford-upon-Avon, a 2-hr. trip from London's Marylebone Station. Headquarter in Stratford and rent a car for day trips to the houses and gardens. **TRIP LENGTH 4 days.** Total distance is 242 miles.

On the afternoon of Day 1, after checking into your hotel and picking up your rental car, head 32 miles southeast of Stratford on the A3400 (1 hr.) to

1 ★★ **Blenheim Palace.** This 18th-century baroque palace—one of the largest houses in England—is the home of the Dukes of Marlborough and was the birthplace of Sir Winston Churchill, Britain's wartime prime minister. Blenheim is imposing and a bit overwhelming, so it's best to take one of the free tours. Your guide will point out such details as the carvings by Grinling Gibbons in the **Great Hall** and the portraits by Sir Joshua Reynolds (1723–92)

1	Blenheim Palace
2	Warwick Castle
3	Kenilworth Castle
4	Ragley Hall
5	Coughton Court
6	Charlecote Park
7	Upton House & Gardens

and John Singer Sargent (1856–1925). Just as impressive as the house's considerable treasures are the small rooms where Sir Winston was born in 1874 and, in an exhibition devoted to him, several of the former prime minister's paintings are displayed. The grounds, designed in part by the great Lancelot "Capability" Brown (1716–83), are lavish and extensive. If your time is limited, don't bother with the 35-minute multimedia tour called "Blenheim Palace: The Untold Story"—it's not as interesting as it sounds. ⏱ At least 2 hr. Brighton Rd., Woodstock. ☎ 08700/602-080. www.blenheimpalace.com. Admission to palace and gardens £19 adults, £15 seniors & students, £10.50 kids, £50 families. Palace: daily mid-Feb

> A well-preserved example of the English baroque style, Blenheim Palace is matched by equally classic English landscaped gardens.

> *Warwick Castle is packed with attractions designed to appeal to history-minded children.*

to mid-Dec 10:30am–4:45pm (closed Mon–Tues Nov–Dec). Grounds: daily summer 9am–6pm; winter 9am–4pm.

Return to Stratford-upon-Avon. On Day 2, drive 9 miles northeast on the M40 (20 min.) to

❷ ★★★ kids Warwick Castle. Located in the town of Warwick, mighty Warwick Castle is one of the most popular tourist attractions in England. Dramatically sited above the River Avon, the castle is a splendid example of a medieval fortress that's been adapted to different uses and renovated in different styles over the centuries. Though the first fortifications were built on this site in 914, much of the external structure dates to the 14th century; the interiors, however, were renovated in the 18th century when the fortress was converted into a mansion for the Earl of Warwick. Scattered through the castle **apartments** (restored to the way they appeared in the late 19th century) are lifelike wax figures created by Madame Tussauds to represent famous figures who visited the castle, and the servants who kept the place running. There's also a gory **dungeon** (not recommended for kids under 10), an exhibition on the warlords who built the place, **battlements** to walk on, and **towers** to explore. The lovely **gardens** and parkland around the castle were also designed by the great "Capability" Brown. Throughout the year there are special events such as jousting tournaments and falconry displays. ⏱ At least 2 hr. Warwick. ☎ 0870/442-2000. www.warwick-castle.co.uk. Admission £29 adults, £26 seniors, £24 kids, £92 families (discounts in low season and if you book online). Daily 10am–6pm (Aug until 7pm; Oct–Mar until 5pm).

Head 6½ miles north of Warwick, a 15-min. drive on the A46, to

❸ ★★ Kenilworth Castle. Kenilworth Castle was founded in the 1120s by Geoffrey de Clinton (d. 1134), a favorite of Henry I, but it later became a royal possession and mostly remained in royal hands until Elizabeth I gave it to her favorite, Robert Dudley (1532–88), Earl of Leicester. Dudley transformed the castle to suit the tastes of Elizabeth, who visited him at Kenilworth several times. (One 19-day visit included an entourage of several hundred people, pageants, bear baiting, and lavish banquets—and cost Dudley the equivalent of £190,000 in today's currency, almost bankrupting him.) When Dudley died, the castle returned to the Crown and was stormed and looted by Parliamentarian troops during the English Civil War. More than 350 years later, Kenilworth became the property of English Heritage, which has restored its vast **Elizabethan gardens.** You can now wander through this sumptuous landscape as Queen Elizabeth I would have done herself. In the **Gatehouse,** which Dudley built for his queen, there is a noteworthy exhibit on Dudley and Elizabeth. ⏱ 1 hr. Castle Green, off Castle Rd., Kenilworth. ☎ 01926/852-078. www.english-heritage.org.uk. Admission £8 adults, £7.20 seniors, £4.80 kids, £21 families. Daily 10am–6pm (Sept–Oct until 5pm; Nov–Feb until 4pm).

> *Ragley Hall's South Staircase features* trompe l'oeil *painting on an oversized scale.*

Return to Stratford-upon-Avon. On Day 3, drive 10 miles west of Stratford-upon-Avon off the A46 to

4 ★ kids **Ragley Hall.** Like other stately homes in England, Ragley Hall is a family residence and a working estate that opens its doors and gardens to paying visitors. The gigantic portico you see on the front of this Palladian mansion, the home of the Marquess of Hertford, was added in 1780, a century after Robert Hooke (1635–1703) designed and built the house, one of the earliest Palladian-style houses in the country. Collections of art, porcelain, and furniture adorn the rooms. Of particular interest is the two-story **Great Hall,** with its superb Baroque plasterwork from 1750; the **South Staircase Hall,** with its *trompe l'oeil* ceiling painting of *The Temptation* (1969) by the artist Graham Rust; the **Red Saloon,** a drawing room with silk damask wall coverings and Louis XVI furniture that remains exactly as it was in 1780, when James Wyatt (1746–1813) designed it; and the impressive **State Dining Room.** The Prince Regent's bedroom,

music room, and library are wonderful examples of Regency design. Placed alongside a trail that threads through the 18th-century gardens and parkland laid out by "Capability" Brown are the contemporary sculptures that comprise the **Jerwood Sculpture Collection.** You can also visit the carriage collection in the **Stables,** and if you have kids in tow, take them to **Adventure Playground,** which includes a 3-D maze and climbing walls. The Lakeside Café is a nice place to stop for lunch or tea. ⏲ 2 hr. Near Alcester, Warwickshire. ☎ 01789/762-090. www.ragleyhall.com. Admission £6.50 per person, £25 families. House & gardens: noon–4pm (opening days vary; call or check website). Park & gardens only: Sat Mar–Oct 10am–5pm.

Head 3 miles north of Ragley Hall, a 5-min. drive on the A435, to

5 ★★ **Coughton Court.** In 2009, the Throckmortons—one of the oldest Catholic families in England—celebrated the 600th anniversary of their residence at Coughton (pronounced

> *The Victorian Morning Room at Charlecote Park still shows traces of the house's Tudor heritage.*

coat-un) Court, the estate at which they have lived since 1409 (they currently have a 300-year lease on the property from the National Trust, so it's unlikely they are leaving any time soon). The half-timbered house, with its flamboyant Elizabethan gatehouse, sits amidst 10 hectares (25 acres) of grounds. Coughton is one of the last remaining Roman Catholic houses in the country to retain its original family relics, including curiosities such as the chemise reputedly worn by the Catholic Mary, Queen of Scots (1542–87) when she was executed, and a bishop's cope with intricate needlework believed to have been worked upon by devout Catholic Catherine of Aragon (1485–1536). The award-winning **gardens** that surround the house were created in 1991 and include a walled rose garden, an orchard, riverside walks, and a bog garden. ⏲ At least 1 hr. Near Alcester, Warwickshire. ☎ 01789/762-435. www.nationaltrust.org.uk and www.coughtoncourt.co.uk. Admission £9.40 adults, £4.70 kids, £24 families. Opening times vary; consult the website or call ahead for the most up-to-date information.

Return to Stratford. On Day 4, drive 5½ miles east on the B4066 (15 min.) to

❻ ★★ Charlecote Park. The Throckmortons have lived at Coughton Court for 600 years, but the Lucys have lived at Charlecote Park for 700, and have owned the land around it since the 12th century. With its mellow stonework facade and ornate chimneys, and its approach guarded by a two-story gatehouse, Charlecote is the epitome of a grand Tudor mansion. Although the basic floor plan remains unchanged, the interior has been extensively remodeled over the centuries, and today is mostly Victorian. The **Great Hall,** with its barrel-vaulted ceiling made

Playwright and Poacher?

Was the Bard of Avon a poacher? For centuries, stories have circulated that a young Will Shakespeare poached deer in Charlecote Park. It adds a nice touch of romance to the history of Charlecote Park, but there's just one problem—apparently it wasn't a deer park in Shakespeare's time.

of plaster painted to look like timber, contains a collection of Lucy family portraits. Decorated plaster ceilings, wood paneling, period furniture, and paintings (including a portrait of Elizabeth I, who stayed in what is now the drawing room) are found throughout the house. The house is surrounded by 75 hectares (185 acres) of **garden and parkland** landscaped by "Capability" Brown in 1760 and backing on to the River Avon. You can stroll through a formal parterre and a sensory garden, and enjoy trails that thread through woodland and open parkland with views of the Avon and a long-established herd of fallow deer. ⊙ At least 2 hr. Wellesbourne, Warwickshire. ☎ 01789/470-277. www.national trust.org.uk. Admission £9.50 adults, £4.75 kids, £23.75 families. House: Fri–Tues Mar–Oct noon–4:30pm; May–Sept 11am–5pm. Gardens & park: daily 10am–5:30pm.

Continue 13 miles east, a 20-min. drive on the A429 and A422, to

❼ ★★ Upton House & Gardens. Here's your chance to leave all those Tudors, Elizabethans, and Victorians behind and see a fabulous 13-hectare (32-acre) country estate built in the 1930s. Oilman and philanthropist Walter Samuel (1882–1948), second Viscount Bearsted, was the Chairman of Shell Oil and son of the company's founder. In the 1920s, he took a 17th-century mansion and had it remodeled as a country retreat to house his art collection. The glamorous Art Deco interior, which looks like the setting for a Noel Coward play, features paintings by El Greco, Canaletto, Hogarth, Stubbs, and Hieronymus Bosch, and an impressive porcelain collection. The **gardens,** in use since the 12th century, were transformed in the 1920s and 1930s by Kitty Lloyd-Jones (1898–1978), a society landscape designer who gave them a quintessential English country house look—vast green lawns cascading down in a series of terraces with stone stairways, herbaceous borders, an old-fashioned rose garden, and a bog garden created on the marshy site of the medieval fish ponds. The gardens are home to the National Aster Collection. ⊙ At least 1 hr. Near Banbury, Warwickshire. ☎ 01295/670-266. www.national trust.org.uk. Admission £9.50 adults, £4.80 kids, £24 families. House: mid-Mar to Oct Fri–Wed noon–4pm; Nov to mid-Dec Sat–Sun noon–4pm. Gardens: Feb–Oct Fri–Wed 11am–5pm.

If You Have More Time...

If you have an extra day to spare, you can make an optional trip on Day 5 to ★ **Burford House & Gardens** in Tenbury Wells, Worcestershire (☎ 0584/810-777; www.burford.co.uk); it's 44 miles west of Stratford-upon-Avon (1hr. 20 min.) via the A443. This stop combines garden browsing with a retail opportunity if you feel so inclined. Burford House is a small, elegant Georgian house dating from 1728 that is now a showroom for all kinds of house and garden accessories. Along the banks of the River Teme are gardens created in 1958 by nurseryman John Treasure (1911–93), an expert on clematis cultivation. You can stroll through 2.8 hectares (7 acres) of lawns, borders, and a water garden. A Georgian turfed bridge (above) takes you across a brook to a woodland garden with wildflowers, trees, and meadows. But what makes the gardens quite special is that they contain the National Clematis Collection, with some 400 varieties in bloom from early spring through early autumn. If you're visiting in May (peak garden time), you'll also see a giant 50-year-old wisteria cascading its blue blossoms down the back of the house and perfuming the air. The riverside **cafe** is a lovely spot to stop for lunch or tea. Admission to the home and gardens is free, and it's open daily from 9am to 6pm (or dusk).

Outdoors in the West Midlands

For a long time, the area around Birmingham was called the Black Country because of the smoke and soot created by the industries concentrated in this part of England. Parts of the landscape presented quite a different picture from the rich farmland, fruit orchards, and woodlands you see today. This itinerary introduces you to some lesser-known gems and scenic beauties in the West Midlands, with suggestions for some walking tours.

> *The Shropshire hills around Church Stretton are littered with attractive trails for walkers of all abilities.*

START Stratford-upon-Avon is 91 miles northwest of London, 2¼ hr. by train from London Marylebone. **TRIP LENGTH** 4 days. Total distance is 230 miles.

❶ ★★★ Stratford-upon-Avon. The birthplace of William Shakespeare is a good place to start your trip and spend your first night. ⊙ At least a half-day. See p. 366.

On Day 2, pick up your rental car and head to Lichfield, 44 miles north of Stratford-upon-Avon, an hour's drive on the M42.

❷ ★ Lichfield. Shakespeare of Stratford turned the English language into poetry, and Samuel Johnson (1709–84) of Staffordshire codified it by creating the world's first dictionary. A statue of the great lexicographer stands in the **Market Place** of this pretty country town, across from the **Samuel Johnson Birthplace Museum,** Breadmarket St. (☎ 01543/264-972; www.samueljohnsonbirthplace.org.uk; free admission). The museum is worth a few minutes of your time, but the real star of Lichfield is beautiful **★★ Lichfield Cathedral** on the Close (☎ 01543/306-150; free admission), with its three spires and exquisitely carved west front showing the kings of England (from Edgar to Henry I). A Norman church with Gothic overlays, the cathedral displays an extremely rare 8th-century illustrated gospel

1	Stratford-upon-Avon
2	Lichfield
3	Ironbridge Gorge
4	Much Wenlock
5	Shrewsbury
6	Church Stretton
7	Great Malvern
8	Hereford
9	Kilpeck
10	Ross-on-Wye
11	Goodrich Castle
12	Symonds Yat Rock
13	Dean Heritage Centre

and contains 16th-century Flemish stained glass. The lovely **Cathedral Close,** ringed by 17th- and 18th-century houses, is also worth a stroll. ⏱ 1 hr.

The Ironbridge Gorge is 36 miles west of Lichfield, an hour's drive on the M6 and M54.

3 ★★★ kids **Ironbridge Gorge.** Abraham Darby fueled a worldwide industrial revolution when he invented a way to smelt iron using coke instead of charcoal. His iron-making factories in this wooded valley ushered in a 19th-century "Iron Age" and a boom in transportation (locomotives and tracks could be made of iron) and building (cast-iron was used for facades,

interior supports, and bridges). Several museums, housed in restored factories and foundries of the 18th and 19th centuries, make for a fascinating excursion into England's industrial past. ⏱ At least 2 hr. See p. 333, **8**.

Continue on to Much Wenlock, 6 miles southwest of Ironbridge Gorge, a 15-min. drive on the B4373 and B4376.

Travel Tip

Having a car is necessary for this countryside tour; your best option is to take the train to Stratford-upon-Avon and rent a car there.

4 Much Wenlock. Explore the picturesque welter of Tudor, Jacobean, and Georgian buildings that crowd the narrow streets of this gem of a Shropshire village. Have a look at the half-timbered **guildhall** and the fascinating ruins of ★ **Wenlock Priory** (☎ 01952/727-466; www.english-heritage.org.uk; admission £4 adult, £2.40 kids 5–15), founded by the Normans in the 12th century for an order of Cluniac monks. ⏱ At least 30 min.

Your last stop of the day is Shrewsbury, 13 miles northwest of Much Wenlock, a 20-min. drive on the A458.

Walking Wenlock Edge

The thickly wooded limestone escarpment of ★★ **Wenlock Edge,** stretching for 18 miles from Much Wenlock to the village of Craven Arms (see p. 357, **6**), is great for walking, and offers dramatic views of the Shropshire countryside immortalized by A. E. Housman in his poem cycle *A Shropshire Lad,* set to music (*On Wenlock Edge*) by Ralph Vaughan Williams. There are marked walking trails scattered along B4371. For more information visit **www.nationaltrust.org.uk**.

5 ★★ Shrewsbury. Built in a bend above the Severn River, the lovely town of Shrewsbury is a good place to stop for lunch or to spend the night on Day 2. You can explore the town with its narrow medieval streets, medieval **St. Mary's Church,** and host of half-timbered "black-and-whites" in less than 2 hours. See p. 355, **2**.

On Day 3, head first for Church Stretton, 16 miles south of Shrewsbury and a 20-min. drive on the A49.

6 Church Stretton. Set in an area of the Shropshire Hills designated an Area of Outstanding Natural Beauty (awarded to distinctive or beautiful landscapes of national importance), this centuries-old town offers a host of outdoor-oriented activities, including hot-air ballooning and paragliding (the Long Mynd has some of the best thermals in Europe). In 2008, Church Stretton became the first town in the West Midlands to receive the "Walkers are Welcome" designation, which means it has a diverse array of walks and pathways of varying lengths, at all levels, in and around the town. For information on activities, visit the **Church Stretton Visitor Information Centre** located next to the library (☎ 01694/723-133; www.churchstretton.co.uk).

> *The area around Coalbrookdale witnessed a revolution in the production of cast iron during the 18th century.*

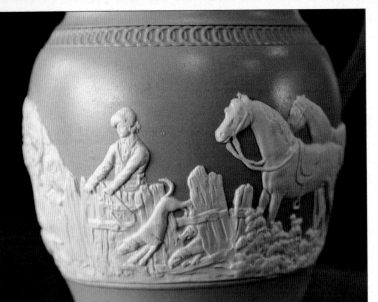

Pottering around the Potteries

Staffordshire, the West Midlands county wedged in between Birmingham and Manchester, is the china and pottery capital of Britain. The industry is centered in and around **Stoke-on-Trent,** 44 miles north of Lichfield, about an hour's drive on the M6 and M46. If you want to shop for top-quality china made in England, you can make a side trip from Lichfield to the **Potteries,** as the areas around Stoke-on-Trent are collectively called.

Stoke-on-Trent is made up of six areas: Tunstall, Burslem, Hanley, Stoke, Fenton, and Longton. It's not a particularly interesting place except for the potteries themselves and the two museums that chronicle the area's china-making history, each of them worth about a half-hour of your time. The **Gladstone Pottery Museum,** Uttoxeter Rd., Longton (☎ 01782/319-232; £5.95 adults, £4.95 seniors, £4.50 kids), housed in a restored Victorian pottery factory, provides a good introduction to Staffordshire pottery, with craftspeople explaining as they work and a collection of china (not just plates; one section is devoted to toilet bowls). One of the largest and finest ceramic collections in the world is on display at the **Potteries Museum and Art Gallery,** Bethesda St., Hanley (☎ 01782/232-323; free admission).

There are about 40 factories with gift shops and seconds shops, but the place that gets the lion's share of attention is the new ★ **Wedgwood Visitor Centre,** Barlaston (☎ 01782/371-911; www.wedgwood museum.org.uk; £6 adults, £5 seniors & kids), with its renowned collection of blue-and-white Jasperware pieces; a section on the company's founder, Josiah Wedgwood (1730–95); a studio where you can throw your own piece of pottery; and a very nice cafe—plus the shop, of course. Two other brand-name potteries worth visiting are **Spode,** Church St., Stoke-on-Trent (☎ 01782/744-011; www.spode.com; free admission to Visitor Centre; tours £4.50 adults, £4 seniors & kids), in business on the same site since 1770, and **Moorcroft Pottery,** Sandbach Rd., Burslem (☎ 01782/820-500; www.moorcroft.com; tours £4.50 adults, £3.50 seniors & kids), which began production in 1898. For information on the area, consult the Stoke-on-Trent Tourist Office, Victoria Hall, Bagnall St. (☎ 01782/236-000; www.visitstoke.co.uk).

Great Malvern is 50 miles south of Church Stretton, 1½ hr. on the A49 and A44.

7 ★ **Great Malvern.** Great Malvern, the principal town among a string of attractive little towns stretching along the slopes of the Malvern Hills and collectively known as the Malverns, is famed for its mineral waters, first used in the late 18th century. The Victorians flocked to Great Malvern for various "water cures," and today Malvern water is bottled and sold throughout the U.K. You can sample the water yourself at **St. Anne's Well,** located on the hill behind the town (signposted), and learn more about Malvern's history as a spa town in the small **Malvern Museum of Local History,** Abbey Rd. (☎ 01684/567-811; £2). Adjacent to the museum on Church Street is the town's other principal sight, **Great Malvern Priory** (☎ 01684/561-020; suggested donation £3), its interior adorned with stained-glass windows (including one in the north transept with a portrait of Arthur, Henry VII's oldest son and brother of Henry VIII) and hundreds of medieval tiles. At the turn of the 20th century, the

Winding Along Long Mynd

Designated a Site of Special Scientific Interest, the **Long Mynd** (Long Mountain) is excellent walking country. An ancient track called the Portway runs along the top of the 10-mile ridge that is home to a wide range of upland flora and fauna. For more information, check with the tourist office in Church Stretton (p. 348, **6**).

composer Edward Elgar lived in nearby **Malvern Link,** a 1½-mile walk north from the center of Great Malvern on Cockshot Road (see "On the Trail of Elgar," p. 329). ⏱ 30 min.

Continue on to Hereford, 21 miles west of Great Malvern, a 35-min. drive on the A4115.

8 Hereford. This lovely Herefordshire town on the border of Wales is a good place to spend your third night. Small and a little sleepy it may be today, but back in the 7th century Hereford was an important city and eventually became the capital of the ancient Saxon kingdom of Mercia, with its own mint. Later, it grew into an

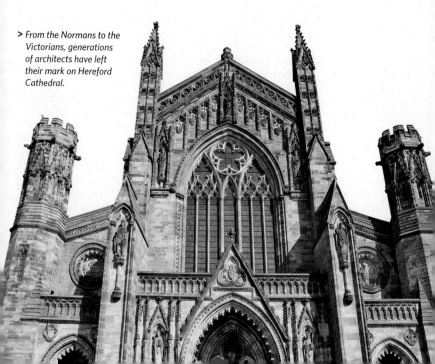

> From the Normans to the Victorians, generations of architects have left their mark on Hereford Cathedral.

> *A profusion of surviving timber housing makes Shrewsbury one of the most atmospheric towns along the England–Wales border.*

important agricultural center and market town. By the 12th century it had a **cathedral** (made of local red sandstone) and two chained libraries, one in the cathedral and the other in **All Saints Church,** High St. (☎ 01432/370-1414; free admission), a great distinction in an age when books were so rare they had to be tethered to their shelves. The town has many fine half-timbered buildings, and strolling here is a pleasure. ⏲ At least 1 hr. See p. 357, **8**.

On Day 4, your first stop is Kilpeck, 9 miles south of Hereford, 1 mile off A465, a 20-min. drive.

9 ★ **Kilpeck.** This hamlet tucked deep in the sleepy Herefordshire countryside is worth a stop to see ★★ **Kilpeck Church** (☎ 01981/570-315; free admission), a well-preserved Norman church covered with an amazing profusion of primitive and powerful 12th-century carvings, including beasts, gargoyles, and even a spread-legged Celtic fertility figure. ⏲ 10 min.

Walking in the Malverns

The **Malvern Hills,** a ridge that rises suddenly and spectacularly from the Severn plain and runs roughly north-south to the west of Great Malvern on the border between the counties of Worcestershire and Herefordshire, provide some of the loveliest walks in Worcestershire, if not all of England. The highest of the 18 named peaks is 425m (1,395-ft.) **Worcester Beacon.** Over 100 miles of hiking trails entice ramblers to the Malverns, which are dotted with dozens of fresh gushing springs. From Great Malvern it's possible to take any number of scenic day hikes into the Malvern Hills, including a 4½-hour loop to the remains of an Iron Age fort high on the ridge to the south of town. From the top you have a bird's-eye view of the surrounding countryside, with the plain to the east, the green Malvern hills all around you, and the Black Mountains of Wales to the west. The best place to start this walk is from Chase End Hill to the south, working your way north. The tourist offce in Great Malvern can provide you with information. For details on other walks in the area, including downloadable maps for portable GPS devices, visit **www.malverntrail.co.uk**.

(☎ 01432/260-675; free admission), and stop in the 700-year-old parish church of **St. Mary's** to have a look at the **tomb of William Rudhall.** His alabaster effigy is one of the last sculptures created in Nottingham by medieval masons whose alabaster tomb figures were coveted throughout Europe, and there are wonderful views from the church tower. A rare **plague cross** in the churchyard marks the place where hundreds of townspeople were buried in a mass grave during an outbreak of plague in 1637. If you want to linger longer, the tourist office has brochures describing local footpaths that wind down to the river and through the fields around town. Weston under Penyard, Herefordshire, is a small village which lies 2 miles east of Ross-on-Wye. Most travel there by road, but it is far nicer to walk the forest path. ⏱ 30 min.

Continue on to Goodrich Castle, 5 miles south of Ross-on-Wye, a 10-min. drive on the A40.

⓫ Goodrich Castle. Stop for a few minutes to admire the majestic view from this 12th-century castle overlooking the Wye River with the forests of Wales in the distance. The castle, a Royalist stronghold during the English Civil War of the 17th century, is mostly in ruins, but you can climb the ramparts and wander through passageways and the square

> *Plague crosses, like this one in Ross-on-Wye, mark the site of ancient mass graves.*

Continue on to Ross-on-Wye, 13 miles southeast of Kilpeck, 30 min. on the B4348 and A49. If you're a walker and have extra time to kill, take the 16-mile **Wye Valley Walk** through some lovely countryside; for information and directions visit www.wyevalleywalk.org.

⓾ Ross-on-Wye. This picturesque Herefordshire village sitting atop a bluff above the River Wye is a good place to stop before heading on into the Forest of Dean. It's a pleasingly proportioned place thanks to the efforts of John Kyrle, a 17th-century town-planning pioneer responsible for laying out the clifftop garden promenade called **The Prospect.** After a stroll in the Prospect, have a quick look around the **Ross-on-Wye Heritage Centre** housed in the 17th-century **Market Hall,** Market Place

The Ancient Forest of Dean

Stands of oak trees, silver birch, and ash cover the valleys between the Wye and Severn rivers, forming one of the oldest tracts of deciduous woodland in England. Although it was designated a royal forest by the Normans in the 11th century, the Forest of Dean you see today is the result of massive reclamation efforts that began in the 16th century. The forest was almost completely denuded as trees were felled to fuel charcoal-fired iron smelters, a process that was reversed only when Abraham Darby pioneered the use of coke instead of charcoal (p. 333, ❽). Replanting efforts took place under Henry VIII, Charles II, and in the early 19th century, and today the 43 square miles of forest are home to an estimated 20 million trees.

> *Wedged between the Severn and the Welsh border, the ancient Forest of Dean became Britain's first National Forest Park in 1938.*

Norman keep. ⊙ 15 min. Castle Lane, Goodrich. ☎ 01600/890-538. www.english-heritage. org.uk. Admission £5.50 adults, £4.70 seniors, £2.80 kids, £14 families. Daily 10am–6pm (Nov–Mar until 4pm).

Your next stop is Symonds Yat Rock, 3 miles south of Goodrich Castle, 5 min. via the B4432 and a signposted country lane.

⑫ ★ **Symonds Yat Rock.** Make a brief stop to admire the celebrated view from this landmark rock formation perched 120m (394 ft.) above the River Wye. Sightings of wildlife both above (peregrine falcons hunt and nest here in spring and summer) and below (deer and the occasional otter) are not out of the question if your timing is right. ⊙ 15 min.

The final stop on the tour is the Dean Heritage Centre, 11 miles east of Symonds Yat Rock, about 30 min. on the B4432 and B4226.

⑬ **Dean Heritage Centre.** This is a good place to begin your explorations of the Forest of Dean and to learn more about it. Easy hiking paths wind through 2 hectares (5 acres) of forest, and at the center you can obtain information about other trails in the forest. **Sudley,** near Cinderford. ☎ 01594/822-170. www. deanheritagemuseum.com. Admission £5.40 adult, £2.5 kids, £15 families. Daily 10am–5pm (Nov–Feb until 4pm).

Staying the Night in Hereford

Housed in a medieval church, **Café @ All Saints** is a coffee bar and vegetarian restaurant that makes for a great casual meal or snack. All Saints Church, High St. ☎ 01432/370-415. Menu items £5–£10. MC, V. Breakfast, lunch & dinner Mon–Sat.

A former bishop's residence in a Georgian townhouse, ★ **Castle House** is now Hereford's toniest little hotel, with a good restaurant and riverside dining. The rooms are large, quietly elegant, and individually decorated; some have garden views. Castle St. ☎ 01432/356-321. www.castlehse.co.uk. 17 units. Doubles £185 w/breakfast. MC, V.

Charming Towns & Villages of the West Midlands

The counties of West-Central England known collectively as the West Midlands include Warwickshire, Worcestershire, Staffordshire, Shropshire, and Herefordshire. This itinerary takes you to the gems of the region, some of them large enough to have a magnificent cathedral, others so small that you can walk through them in a few minutes. Many are market towns with histories that date back centuries. All of them are found in a verdant countryside of rolling hills, small rivers, and farmland, and characterize the green heart of England.

> Half-timbered houses still line some of the pleasant streets in central Shrewsbury.

START Worcester is 26 miles west of Stratford-upon-Avon (see p. 366) on the A3400 and A422; take a direct 2-hr. train from London Marylebone to Stratford and rent a car there. TRIP LENGTH 3 days. Total distance is 178 miles.

❶ ★ **Worcester.** Start your tour in this small and rather elegant cathedral city on the Severn River, and make 14th-century **Worcester Cathedral** your first priority. The city's Civil War history is chronicled at the **Commandery,** and you can get a glimpse of

1 Worcester
2 Shrewsbury
3 Church Stretton
4 Bishops Castle
5 Clun
6 Craven Arms
7 Ludlow
8 Hereford
9 Alcester

Where to Stay & Dine
Albright Hussey Hotel **10**
Feathers Hotel **12**
Mr. Underhill's Restaurant
with Rooms **11**

medieval Worcester at the **Greyfriars,** a 15th-century merchant's house. Also pay a visit to the **Worcester Porcelain Museum,** where you can see how the city's famous china is made. ⏱ 2 hr. See p. 329, **6**.

Continue on to Shrewsbury, 49 miles northwest of Worcester, 1½ hr. on the M5 and M54.

2 ★★ **Shrewsbury.** Considered by many to be the loveliest town in Shropshire, Shrewsbury is your overnight stop for Day 1. The town, which occupies a strategic point on the Welsh border, on a peninsula created by a loop in the Severn River, is loaded with timber-framed, Queen Anne and Georgian houses and narrow

medieval lanes and passageways called "shuts." For a quick overview of the city's history, stop in at the **Shrewsbury Museum and Art Gallery,** Music Hall (☎ 01743/361-196; free admission), which has a bit of everything local, from Roman finds to material on Charles Darwin, Shrewsbury's most famous son. Spend your afternoon strolling through the town, stopping to take a look at the 16th-century **Market Hall,** Claremont St., built during the heyday of the city's wood trade; **Ireland's Mansion,** High St., one of the city's finest black-and-white timber-framed buildings; atmospheric **Fish Street;** and the evocatively named **Grope Lane,** a narrow medieval thoroughfare with overhanging buildings. Stop in at ★ **St. Mary's Church,** St. Mary's St. (no phone), with its beautiful medieval spire and Jesse window (a window showing Christ's descent from Jesse) made of 14th-century stained glass. Cross graceful **English Bridge** over the Severn to reach ★ **Shrewsbury Abbey,** Abbey Foregate (☎ 01743/232-723; £2 adults, £1 kids), built in a mixture of Norman, Early English, and Victorian styles and containing a west window paned with 14th-century heraldic glass. ⏲ 2 hr.

Day 2 begins with a 20-min. drive to Church Stretton, 16 miles south of Shrewsbury on A49.

❸ **Church Stretton.** Nestled in a lovely wooded valley between the Stretton hills and the Long Mynd ridge, Church Stretton is the only market town in the relatively undiscovered South Shropshire Hills Area of Outstanding Natural Beauty. In the picturesque town center, you'll find traditional shops and tea-rooms. To experience what life was like on an upland farm a century ago, visit ★ **Acton Scott Historic Working Farm,** Acton Scott, 4 miles south of Church Stretton (☎ 01694/781-306; £6 adults, £5.50 seniors, £3.75 kids), where the land is still worked by heavy horses and there are daily demonstrations of period skills, providing a picture of rural life on a Victorian country estate. ⏲ 1 hr.

Head next to Bishop's Castle, 13 miles (20 min.) southwest of Church Stretton on the A489.

❹ ★ **Bishop's Castle.** This small medieval hamlet has been a market town since Welsh drovers first began bringing their livestock along the Kerry Ridgeway to sell at Bishop's Castle (of which there is almost nothing left today) some 800 years ago. It remains a working market town to this day, with regular sheep and cattle auctions and markets held in the **Town Hall** and **Market Square.** It's also a magnet for walkers who come to explore the Stiperstone and Long Mynd ridges to the northeast and Offa's Dyke, the 8th-century defensive earthwork that runs along the old border with Wales, to the west. As you stroll through the town, have a look at the clock on **St. John's Church:** it's one of the few one-handed clocks in England. Bishop's Castle also has two breweries, as well as good pubs and cafes. ⏲ At least 30 min. Bishop's Castle Visitor Information Point, Old Time, High St. ☎ 01588/636-467. www.bishopscastle.co.uk.

Your next stop is Clun, 7 miles (15 min.) south of Bishop's Castle on the A488.

❺ **Clun.** Surrounded by the green Shropshire hills, Clun was immortalized by the poet A. E. Housman as one of the "quietest places under the sun." The 600-year-old town is known for its medieval **stone bridge,** built for packhorses; the ruins of its **Norman castle;** and the fine walks on **Llanfair Hill,** the highest point on Offa's Dyke (www.offasdyke.demon.co.uk), and **Bury Ditches,** one of the finest Iron Age forts in Britain (4½ miles northeast of Clun on the B3468). ⏲ 15 min. in town. Visitor Information Point, Clun Garage, High St. www.clun.org.uk.

> *Ludlow was the first British town to be officially endorsed as a "Cittaslow."*

Continue on to Craven Arms, 9½ miles east of Clun, 20 min. on B4368.

6 Craven Arms. The town's a mix of modern and medieval with a couple of worthwhile attractions to keep you occupied for an hour. Start at the ★ **Shropshire Hills Discovery Centre,** School Rd. (☎ 01588/676-060; www. shropshirehillsdiscoverycentre.co.uk; free admission), which provides a good overview of the entire region, including a full-size reproduction of a woolly mammoth and the interior of an Iron Age roundhouse; there's also a good cafe for a cup of tea or a snack, as well as visitor information for the town. For a lovely view of the surrounding countryside, climb the tower of ★ **Stokesay Castle,** 1 mile south of the town center (☎ 01584/875-053; £5.50 adults, £4.70 seniors, £2.80 kids), a fortified medieval manor (the oldest in England—some parts date back to the 13th century) adjoining Stokesay Church. ⊕ At least 1 hr. www.shropshirehills.co.uk.

Ludlow, your overnight stop for Day 2, is 8 miles southeast of Craven Arms, a 10-min. drive on the A49.

7 ★★ Ludlow. This small, picture-perfect Shropshire town on the River Teme is a delight to explore, its streets lined with half-timbered Jacobean and elegant Georgian houses and dozens of shops selling antiques and locally produced foods. You can see everything on a leisurely 2-hour stroll. The main visitor attraction is ★ **Ludlow Castle,** Castle Sq. (☎ 01584/873-355; www.ludlowcastle.com; £4.50 adults, £4 seniors, £2.50 kids), built by the Normans in the 11th century to defend against the Welsh and remodeled into a palace in the 14th century. In 1501, Henry VIII's older brother, Arthur, Prince of Wales, honeymooned in the castle with Catherine of Aragon, and died there the following year (after which Henry married Catherine, the first of his eight wives). One of the country's largest parish churches, ★ **St. Laurence's Church,** King St. (☎ 01584/872-073; £2), was built in a transitional style between Norman and Early English, with later 15th-century additions and exquisitely carved misericords. To learn more about Ludlow's rich and fascinating history, spend a few minutes in **Ludlow Museum** on Castle Sq. (☎ 01584/813-666; free admission). ⊕ 2 hr.

> *Master woodcarvers decorated the interior of St. Laurence's Church, Ludlow.*

Start Day 3 by driving to Hereford, 24 miles (40 min.) south of Ludlow on the A49.

8 ★ Hereford. Surrounded by apple orchards and lush pasturelands where the famous white-faced Hereford cattle graze, the county capital of Herefordshire is a quiet, unassuming country town that epitomizes the rural nature of Shropshire. Straddling the River Wye, Hereford is small enough that you can see everything on foot in an hour or two. When the Welsh burned down Hereford's old cathedral, a new one was built of red sandstone. ★★ **Hereford Cathedral,** 5 College Cloisters (☎ 01432/374-200; suggested £4 donation), its cornerstone laid in 1080, is one of England's oldest and has, in addition to its Norman nave and 13th-century Lady Chapel, two historic treasures: an ancient **"chained" library,** where the books, some dating back to the 8th century, are literally chained to the shelves; and

> *Butter Street, in Alcester, has surviving rows of houses from the Tudor period.*

the ★★ **Mappa Mundi,** one of the oldest and rarest maps in the world, dating from 1290 and drawn showing Jerusalem as the center of the world. After strolling through the area known as **High Town,** a pedestrian-only area with a wealth of historic buildings, visit the ★ **Cider Museum and King Offa's Brandy Distillery,** 21 Ryelands St. (☎ 01432/354-207; £3.50 adults, £3 seniors), where you'll learn all about the local tradition of cider-making and be able to sample a few different kinds. ⏱ At least 1 hr.

Alcester, the last stop on the tour, is 46 miles east of Hereford, about 1 hr. 20 min. via the A4103 and A422

❾ Alcester. An old market town of Roman origin and later, in the 12th century, the site of an important Benedictine Abbey, Alcester (pronounced *al*-ster) sits at the junction of the Alne and Arrow rivers. You can easily see the town on foot in less than an hour. You may want to spend a few minutes in the **Roman Alcester Heritage Centre,** Globe House, Priory Rd. (☎ 01739/762-216; free admission), which displays locally found artifacts from the 1st

to the 4th century A.D., or simply have a look at the Tudor, Georgian, and Victorian houses found near **St. Nicholas' Church,** Butter St., with its 14th-century tower and unusually placed clock, and the early-17th-century **Town Hall,** High St. ⏱ 30 min.

If you have extra time, you may want to combine a visit to Alcester with a tour of one of the nearby stately homes: **Coughton Court (p. 343, ❺),** 2½ miles north on Birmingham Rd.; or **Ragley Hall (p. 343, ❹),** 1½ miles southwest via A422. **Stratford-upon-Avon (p. 366)** is 8 miles east of Alcester, a 10-min. drive on A46.

Walking the Heart of England Way

Alcester is one of the towns found along the 100-mile **Heart of England Way,** a long-distance walking path that follows a deeply rural route through Gloucestershire, Staffordshire, Warwickshire, and the West Midlands. For more information, visit **www.ldwa.org.uk,** the website of the Long Distance Walkers Association.

Where to Stay & Dine

> *Mr. Underhill's Restaurant with Rooms has delightful suites and one of the best restaurants in England.*

★★ **Albright Hussey Hotel** SHREWSBURY
Black swans swim in the moated garden of this 16th-century manor house that's been converted into a charming, character-filled hotel and restaurant. The individually decorated rooms are furnished with period reproduction furniture and have been updated to include modern bathrooms and amenities. Ellesmere Rd, Shrewsbury. ☎ 01939/290-571. www.albrighthussey.co.uk. 26 units. Doubles £95–£140 w/breakfast. AE, MC, V.

★★ **Feathers Hotel** LUDLOW
The intricate black-and-white timber-framed exterior of this Jacobean-era inn is something of a wonder; ask for a room in the original wing so you can enjoy the atmosphere within. The Bull Ring, Ludlow. ☎ 01584/875-261. www.feathersatludlow.co.uk. 40 units. Doubles £95–£205 w/breakfast. AE, MC, V.

★★★ **Mr. Underhill's Restaurant with Rooms**
LUDLOW *MODERN BRITISH* This Michelin-starred restaurant was voted the "Best All-Round U.K. Restaurant Outside of London" by Harden's Restaurant Guide in 2010. Not only can you eat superbly, you can rent a delightful room or a suite overlooking the river. Dinham, Ludlow. ☎ 01584/874-431. www.mr-underhills.co.uk. 8 units. Doubles £140–£300 w/breakfast. Dinner served daily. Fixed-price dinner £53–£60. MC, V.

Oxford

This "sweet city with her dreaming spires" (to quote the poet Matthew Arnold) is one of the world's great centers of learning, and also happens to be one of England's most appealing cities, with a lively street life, a wonderful urban core with architectural masterpieces, medieval cobbled lanes, snug pubs, and a lovely riverside walk. Most of Oxford's 39 colleges are hidden behind thick walls, but many of them open part of their premises to visitors. With its sophisticated array of hotels and restaurants, Oxford also makes a great base for exploring the heart of England.

START Oxford is 60 miles northwest of London, a 1K-hr. drive on the M40, or a 1-hr. train ride from London's Paddington Station.

1 ★ kids **Carfax Tower.** Climb up the spiral staircase of this tower, set at the crossroads of the town's busiest thoroughfares. As you look out over the surrounding streets and spires, you'll get a good sense of the layout of the university—the colleges sit behind high walls and are built around inner courtyards called "quads." The 23m (74-ft.) tower once rose above the 14th-century church of St. Martin (demolished in the late 19th century to ease traffic flow), and no building in central Oxford is permitted to exceed its height. ⏱ 15 min. Queen St. ☎ 01865/792-653. Admission £2. Daily Apr–Oct 10am–5pm; Nov–Mar 10:30am–3:30pm.

2 🍴 **Covered market.** To stock up on provisions for a picnic on the water meadows or simply to grab a quick bite, visit this location at the intersection of High and Cornmarket streets, where vendors and small cafes sell a variety of prepared meals and take-away provisions. Most shops are open daily 9am–5:30pm. ☎ 01865/250-133. www.oxfordcity.co.uk/shops/market.

> The bell in Christ Church College's Tom Tower sounds *101 times each night at 9:05pm.*

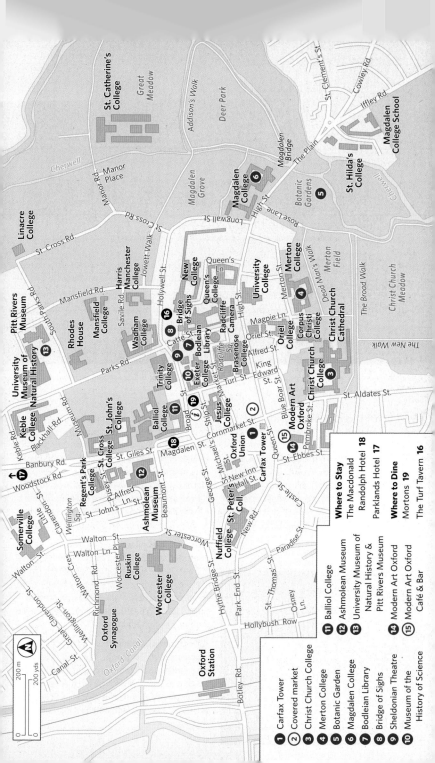

Where to Stay
The Macdonald
Randolph Hotel **18**
Parklands Hotel **17**

Where to Dine
Mortons **19**
The Turf Tavern **16**

1 Carfax Tower
2 Covered market
3 Christ Church College
4 Merton College
5 Botanic Garden
6 Magdalen College
7 Bodleian Library
8 Bridge of Sighs
9 Sheldonian Theatre
10 Museum of the
   History of Science

11 Balliol College
12 Ashmolean Museum
13 University Museum of
   Natural History &
   Pitt Rivers Museum
14 Modern Art Oxford
15 Modern Art Oxford
   Café & Bar

> *Magdalen College enjoys an enviable position on the eastern fringes of the city center, surrounded by the River Cherwell's water meadows.*

❸ ★★ **Christ Church College.** As you enter, you'll pass beneath Tom Tower, from which a bell (the loudest in Oxford) tolls 101 times nightly at 9:05pm, when the college gates are closed. Cardinal Thomas Wolsey (1471–1530), King Henry VIII's powerful chancellor, founded the college in 1525 and graced it with the largest quad in Oxford. Christ Church (once known as the 800-year-old **St. Frideswide**) claims a **Picture Gallery** graced with works by Sir Joshua Reynolds and William Gainsborough. William

Penn and John Wesley studied at Christ Church, as did many British prime ministers, and Charles Dodgson (better known as Lewis Carroll, author of *Alice in Wonderland),* taught mathematics here for many years. ⏱ 20 min St. Aldates. (☎ 01865/286-573. www.chch.ox.acuk. Admission £8 adults; £6.50 seniors, students & kids; £16 families. Mon–Sat 9am–5:30pm; Sun 2pm–5:30pm (Oct–Mar until 4:30pm).

❹ ★ **Merton College.** Dating from the 13th century and rich in medieval ambience, this is one of the earliest centers of learning in Oxford; the 14th-century **library** houses Geoffrey Chaucer's astrolabe. ⏱ 10 min. Merton St. ☎ 01865/276-310. Free admission. Mon–Fri 2–4pm; Sat–Sun 10am–4pm.

❺ ★ **Botanic Garden.** Founded in 1621 for the study of medicinal plants, it features a lovely rose garden that commemorates the Oxford researchers whose work paved the way for the discovery of penicillin. ⏱ 15 min. Rose Lane. ☎ 01865/276-920. Admission £3.80. Daily 9am–5pm.

Travel Tip

The opening times of Oxford's colleges vary widely; check the university website (www.ox.ac.uk/visitors) or visit the Oxford Information Centre (see p. 373) for hours. A good way to gain admittance to a selection of colleges is to take one of the **Oxford Guild of Guides** 2½-hour walking tours, offered daily at 11am and 2pm (additional walks on Sat at 10:30am and 1pm); the cost is £7 and you can buy tickets at the Visitor Information Centre.

6 ★ **Magdalen College.** The 15th-century bell tower of Magdalen (pronounced *maud*-lin), one of the city's most famous landmarks, rises above the Cherwell River and the most extensive grounds of any Oxford college—including a deer park and **water meadows** (once used as an irrigation system) along the river. Founded in 1458, Magdalen additionally boasts the oldest **botanical garden** in England. You can cross a small footbridge and stroll through the water meadows along the path known as **Addison's Walk,** named after essayist and Magdalen alumnus Joseph Addison (1672–1719). The college's **bell tower** is the center of Oxford's famous May Day celebrations—at dawn a choir climbs the tower to sing a hymn, and the sound of the voices floating over the city signals pubs to open and a day of raucous behavior to begin. Oscar Wilde studied at Magdalen, as did Sir Edward Gibbon, author of *The Decline and Fall of the Roman Empire,* who described his time here as "the most idle and unprofitable of my whole life." ⏱ 30 min. High St. ☎ 01865/276-000. Admission £3 adults, £2 seniors & kids. Daily July–Sept noon–6pm; Oct–May 1pm–dusk.

7 ★★★ **Bodleian Library.** One of the oldest libraries in Europe, with roots going back to about 1320, the Bodleian is also one of the largest, with more than 5 million volumes tucked away on its 80 miles of shelving. Students using the library still take an oath "not to bring into the library or kindle therein any fire or flame." This tradition stems from the not-so-long-ago days when the library was not lit or heated and scholars resorted to dangerous means of illumination and warmth. The Bodleian's main reading room is the domed and round **Radcliffe Camera.** Although this and other reading rooms are closed to the public, you can see the Divinity School; a 15th-century lecture hall; the Exhibition Room, which mounts rotating displays of rare volumes and prints; Duke Humfrey's Library, a collection of early manuscripts; and other parts of the library on guided tours. ⏱ 45 min. for tour. Radcliffe Square. ☎ 01865/277-224. Admission £6.50. Tours daily 10:30am, 11:30am, 2pm & 3pm.

8 ★ **Bridge of Sighs.** This landmark enclosed bridge connects Hertford College and New

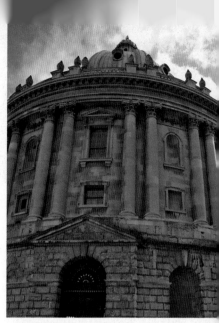

> *The circular Radcliffe Camera is used by university students as a place for study.*

College and is named for its resemblance to the Venetian Ponte Sospiri (Bridge of Sighs). It's not open to the public, but have a look as you pass by. New College Lane.

9 ★★ **Sheldonian Theatre.** This building was designed in the style of a Roman theater by Sir Christopher Wren (1632–1723), the famous architect of St. Paul's Cathedral in London. Wren was a professor of astronomy at Oxford, but his first major architectural commission was for the Pembroke Chapel at Cambridge, which was not begun until the Sheldonian

Getting Around

You can get anywhere you want to go in Oxford on foot. The train station is about a 10-minute walk west of the city center, off Park End Street, and the bus station is on the north side of the city center at Gloucester Green. **City Sightseeing** (www.citysightseeing.co.uk) offers a 1-hour bus tour (£9.50) with hop-on/hop-off service departing every 15 to 20 minutes daily from the train station starting at 9:30am and running until 5 or 6pm, depending on the season.

> *Arranged like an overstuffed treasure box of fascinating finds, the Pitt Rivers Museum has an old-fashioned charm of its own.*

was completed. The university holds its commencement exercises (in Latin) in the richly paneled hall, and you can step inside for a look. ⏱ 10 min. Broad St. ☎ 01865/277-299. Admission £2 adults, £1 kids. Mon–Sat 10am–12:30pm & 1–4:30pm.

🔟 ★ **Museum of the History of Science.** Early medical and scientific instruments and paraphernalia such as Albert Einstein's blackboard are on display in this 17th-century building, which once housed Elias Ashmole's Cabinet of Curiosities, the forerunner of the Ashmolean Museum (⑫). ⏱ 15 min. Broad St. 01865/277-280. Free admission. Tues–Sat noon–4pm; Sun 2–5pm.

⓫ ★ **Balliol College.** This famous college was founded in 1263. In the 16th century, bishops Hugh Latimer and Nicholas Ridley, and Thomas Cranmer, the Archbishop of Canterbury, were burned at the college entrance for heresy on the orders of "Bloody Mary" Tudor; the huge gates still bear scorch marks. The three men are also commemorated with the Martyrs Monument, just across St. Giles Street. ⏱ 10 min. Broad St. ☎ 01865/277-777. Admission £1. Daily 2–6pm.

⓬ ★★ **Ashmolean Museum.** This grand classical building, the oldest public museum in England, holds the university's vast collections of art and archaeology. Poke around the galleries and you'll come upon many treasures, from Paolo Uccello's *The Hunt in the Forest* to Chinese ceramics and antiquities from ancient Egypt, Greece, and Rome that reflect the bounty of the expeditions the university has sponsored over the years. ⏱ 45 min. Beaumont

St. ☎ 01865/278-000. www.ashmolean.org. Free admission. Tues–Sat 10am–5pm; Sun noon—5pm.

⓭ ★ **University Museum of Natural History & Pitt Rivers Museum.** Though somewhat off the main tourist track, these two side-by-side museums have an unexpected charm. The venerable Natural History Museum shows off a good collection of dinosaur skeletons and other curiosities in a marvelous glass-roofed Victorian hall. The Pitt Rivers Museum, entered from the Natural History Museum, contains more than half a million objects—including some 150 pieces collected during Captain James Cook's second Pacific voyage, from 1772 to 1775—crammed into old-fashioned cases in a dimly lit room. ⏱ 30 min. Museum of Natural History: Parks Rd. ☎ 01865/272-950. www.oum.ox.ac.uk. Free admission. Daily 10am–5pm. Pitt Rivers Museum: South Parks Rd. ☎ 01865/270-927. www.prm.ox.ac.uk. Free admission. Mon noon–4:30pm; Tues–Sun 10am–4:30pm.

⓮ ★ **Modern Art Oxford.** This leading center for contemporary visual arts holds ever-changing exhibitions of sculpture, architecture, photography, video, and other media. ⏱ 30 min. Pembroke St. ☎ 01865/722-733. www.modernartoxford.org.uk. Free admission. Tues–Sat 10am–5pm; Sun noon–5pm.

⓯ 🍽 **Modern Art Oxford Café & Bar** is a great and affordable place for lunch or a tea-time snack; if you like coffee, the cafe offers a delicious, specially selected artisan blend that is roasted in small batches. In Modern Art Oxford, Pembroke St. ☎ 01865/722-733. Menu items £5–£7.

Where to Stay & Dine

> The low-slung interior at the Turf Tavern, still a favorite haunt of university students.

Mortons CITY CENTER *SANDWICH SHOP*
If you don't want to spend a lot for lunch, stop in at Mortons for one of their delicious baguette sandwiches or a bowl of their daily soup. You can eat upstairs, in the back garden, or take your sandwich and picnic elsewhere. 22 Broad St. ☎ 01865/200-860. Sandwiches £3–£5. MC, V. Breakfast & lunch daily.

★ **The Turf Tavern** CITY CENTER *PUB FARE*
For good pub grub (salads, soups, sandwiches, beef pie, chili con carne) or a pint of beer, try this old favorite. Dating to the 13th century, the tavern has served the likes of Thomas Hardy, Richard Burton and Elizabeth Taylor, and Bill Clinton, who was a frequent visitor during his student days at Oxford. 4 Bath Place (accessed via St. Helen's Passage btw. Holywell St. & New College Lane). ☎ 01865/243-235. www.theturftavern.co.uk. Entrees £4–£9. MC, V. Lunch & dinner Mon–Sat.

★ **Parklands Hotel** OUTSIDE CITY CENTER
This large Victorian home, built for an Oxford don in a leafy residential neighborhood about a mile from the city center, now offers pleasant and quiet accommodations. 100 Banbury Rd. ☎ 01865/554-374. www.parklandsoxford. co.uk. Doubles £87–£135 w/breakfast. MC, V.

★★★ **The Macdonald Randolph Hotel** CITY CENTER This grand old Victorian hostelry is the best address in town. The most atmospheric rooms are the high-ceilinged ones in the front of the house, but all of the rooms are smartly furnished and have large marble bathrooms with tubs. The Morse Bar is a popular gathering spot. Beaumont St. ☎ 0870/400-8200. www.macdonaldhotels.co.uk. Doubles £180–£250 w/breakfast. AE, MC, V.

Stratford-upon-Avon

This market town on the River Avon is a shrine to the world's greatest playwright, William Shakespeare (1564–1616), who was born, lived much of his life, and is buried here. Stratford's formerly bucolic setting has changed to accommodate mass tourism, but you'll find plenty of quaint corners as you explore.

START Stratford-upon-Avon is 91 miles northwest of London; 2½ hr. by car on the M40 or 2¼ hr. by train from London Marylebone.

❶ ★★★ Shakespeare's Birthplace. You enter this literary shrine through the modern **★ Shakespeare Centre,** where exhibits illustrate the playwright's life and times. In the house, you can visit the bedroom where Shakespeare, son of a glover and wool merchant, was born on April 23, 1564, as well as the living room and a fully restored Tudor-style kitchen. Henley St. ☎ 01789/204-016. www.shakespeare.org.uk. Admission £12.50 adults, £11.50 seniors & students, £8 kids. Daily Apr–Oct 9am–5pm (July–Aug until 6pm); Nov–Mar 10am–4pm.

❷ New Place/Nash's House. The gardens at New House are all that remain of the Stratford house where a relatively prosperous Shakespeare retired in 1610 and died in 1616. The Bard bought the house for the then-astronomical sum of £60. Reverend Francis Gastrill, a mid-18th-century owner, allegedly tore the house down rather than continue paying taxes on a property where he couldn't

> Arguably the most influential writer in the history of the English language was born in this modest Tudor house in 1564.

Getting Around

Stratford is compact, and you can walk everywhere. The train and bus stations are less than a 15-minute walk from the town center. **City Sightseeing** (www.citysightseeing.co.uk) runs a hop-on/hop-off bus service to all the Shakespeare properties. The best guided tour of Stratford is the 2-hour **★★ Stratford Town Walk** (☎ 01789/292-478), which departs daily (Mon–Wed 11am, Thurs–Sun 2pm; £5 adults, £2 kids) from the Swan Fountain near the Royal Shakespeare Theatre.

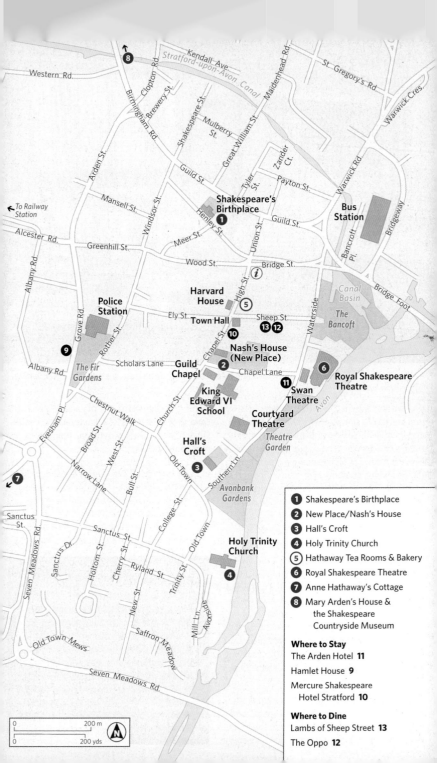

Stratford-upon-Avon

Kendall Ave.

Stratford-upon-Avon Canal

Western Rd.

Clopton Rd.

Brewery St.

St. Gregory's Rd.

Warwick Cres.

Birmingham Rd.

Shakespeare St.

Mulberry St.

Maidenhead Rd.

Warwick Rd.

Arden St.

Guild St.

Great William St.

Tyler St.

Zander Ct.

Payton St.

Bridgeway

Mansell St.

Windsor St.

Henley St.

Shakespeare's Birthplace ❶

Guild St.

Bus Station

Bancroft Pl.

Warwick Rd.

To Railway Station

Alcester Rd.

Meer St.

Union St.

Greenhill St.

Wood St.

Bridge St.

i

Bridge Foot

Albany Rd.

Grove Rd.

Police Station

Rother St.

Harvard House

High St.

Town Hall

❺

Ely St.

Sheep St. ❶❸ ❶❷

Waterside

Canal Basin

The Bancroft

Chapel St.

❶❿

Scholars Lane

Nash's House (New Place) ❷

Guild Chapel

Chapel Lane

❶❶

Royal Shakespeare Theatre ❻

Albany Rd.

The Fir Gardens

❾

Chestnut Walk

Broad St.

West St.

Church St.

King Edward VI School

Swan Theatre

Avon

Evesham Pl.

Narrow Lane

Bull St.

Old Town

Courtyard Theatre

❼

Hall's Croft ❸

Southern Ln.

Theatre Garden

Sanctus St.

Sanctus St.

College St.

Avonbank Gardens

Sanctus Dr.

Seven Meadows Rd.

Holtom St.

Cherry St.

Ryland St.

New St.

Trinity St.

Old Town

Mill Ln.

Avonside

Holy Trinity Church ❹

Old Town Mews

Saffron Meadow

Seven Meadows Rd.

0 ——— 200 m
0 ——— 200 yds

❶ Shakespeare's Birthplace

❷ New Place/Nash's House

❸ Hall's Croft

❹ Holy Trinity Church

❺ Hathaway Tea Rooms & Bakery

❻ Royal Shakespeare Theatre

❼ Anne Hathaway's Cottage

❽ Mary Arden's House & the Shakespeare Countryside Museum

Where to Stay

The Arden Hotel **11**

Hamlet House **9**

Mercure Shakespeare Hotel Stratford **10**

Where to Dine

Lambs of Sheep Street **13**

The Oppo **12**

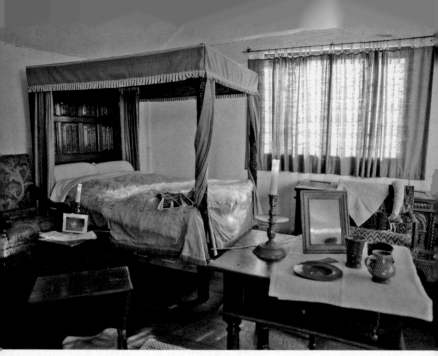

> *Hall's Croft, luxuriously furnished by 17th-century standards, is where Shakespeare's daughter lived with her physician husband.*

live peaceably because of the hordes of visitors coming to see where its famous past resident had lived. You enter the garden through Nash's House, which belonged to Thomas Nash, husband of Shakespeare's granddaughter, and which contains 16th-century period rooms and an exhibit illustrating the history of Stratford. Chapel St. ☎ 01789/204-016. www.shakespeare.org.uk. Admission £12.50 adults, £11.50 seniors & students, £8 kids. Daily Apr–Oct 10am–5pm; Nov–Mar 11am–4pm.

❸ ★★★ Hall's Croft. Shakespeare's daughter Susanna and her husband, Dr. John Hall, lived in this magnificent Tudor house. It's furnished in the style of a middle-class 17th-century home and has exhibits illustrating the theory and practice of medicine in Dr. Hall's time. Old Town. ☎ 01789/204-016. www.shakespeare.org.uk. Admission £12.50 adults, £11.50 seniors & students, £8 kids. Daily Apr–Oct 10am–5pm; Nov–Mar 11am–4pm.

❹ ★ Holy Trinity Church. Shakespeare died on his birthday, April 23, 1616, at age 52, and is buried in this small church beside the River Avon. A bust of the immortal Bard looks down on his gravesite in front of the altar. Southern Lane. ☎ 01789/266-316. Admission £1.50. Mon–Sat 8:30am–6pm (Nov–Feb 9am–4pm); Sun year-round 2–5pm.

❺ 🍵 Hathaway Tea Rooms & Bakery. Stop in here for a baked good to go, or enjoy tea or a snack in the tearoom on the second floor of a building that dates from 1610. 19 High St. ☎ 01789/292-404. Bakery items £1.50–£2.50; teas £5.75–£7.95.

Travel Tip

All of the Shakespeare properties keep basically the same hours, and one ticket gets you into the three Shakespeare town sites: Shakespeare's Birthplace, New Place/Nash's House, and Hall's Croft. You have to pay separate admissions for Anne Hathaway's Cottage and Mary Arden's House, both outside of the town center. Crowds are heaviest on weekends from June through mid-September. If you want to see a play at the **Royal Shakespeare Theatre** (p. 370, ❻), book ahead.

> The revamped Royal Shakespeare Theatre, which reopened after a £113-million restoration in 2010, can accommodate 1,000 spectators for performances.

Shakespeare's Kids

You may know a line or two from Shakespeare, but what do you know about Shakespeare's line? The Bard of Avon had three children. His oldest child, Susanna, was born in May 1583, 6 months after the 18-year-old Shakespeare married 26-year-old Anne Hathaway. Two years later, Anne gave birth to twins, a boy named Hamnet and a girl named Judith. Anne raised all of the children in Stratford, often on her own, as Shakespeare was frequently away, working at the Globe in London and in other playhouses and private palaces. Neither of Shakespeare's daughters learned to read or write. It seems likely that Hamnet was given some schooling, but the boy died at age 11, perhaps from the bubonic plague that periodically swept through Elizabethan England. In 1607, at age 24, Susanna wed Dr. John Hall, who had a prosperous medical practice, and settled with her husband at Hall's Croft (p. 368, ❸). Susanna gave birth to a baby girl, Elizabeth, 8 months after her wedding. Shakespeare, who approved of his daughter's marriage to one of Stratford's leading citizens, appointed Hall and Susanna executors of his will, and Susanna inherited the bulk of Shakespeare's estate. Susanna and her husband moved to New Place (p. 366, ❷), her father's house, after his death. Both Shakespeare and Anne, who died in 1623 at age 67, are buried side by side in Holy Trinity Church (p. 368, ❹).

In 1616, when she was 31, Judith, the youngest of Shakespeare's three children, married a 27-year-old Stratford vintner named Thomas Quiney. A Shakespearian scandal ensued when it was discovered that Quiney had made another girl pregnant and hadn't obtained the proper license for his marriage to Judith. Both Judith and Quiney were excommunicated, and Quiney was made to pay a fine. The couple had three children: Shakespeare, born in 1616, died in infancy; Richard, born in 1617, died at age 21, possibly from the plague; and Thomas, born in 1619, who died at age 19, the same month as his brother and probably also of the plague. Elizabeth, Shakespeare's only surviving grandchild, married twice. At 21 she wed Thomas Nash; after Nash's death 6 years later, she married Sir John Bernard (or Barnard). William Shakespeare's last direct descendant thus became Lady Elizabeth Bernard, who inherited her grandfather's estate. She never had children.

Swanning on the Avon

Avon Boating (☎ 01789/267-073) offers half-hour cruises on the River Avon in traditional Edwardian launches from Easter through October (daily 10am-dusk) from Swan's Nest Boatyard near the Royal Shakespeare Theatre. The cost is £4 adults, £3 seniors, £2.50 kids. Rowboats, punts, and canoes can be rented for £3 per hour.

6 ★★★ **Royal Shakespeare Theatre.** Closed for several years, the Stratford home of the Royal Shakespeare Company reopened in fall 2010, to celebrate its 75th anniversary. The theater has been made more accessible to the public, with a new visitor center, observation tower, exhibit, and cafe. Shakespearean plays are performed in the theater from November to September. Waterside. ☎ 01789/403-403. www.rsc.org.uk. Free admission to building and exhibit. Exhibit: daily 10am-4pm. Box office: Mon-Sat 9:30am-8pm.

7 ★★★ **Anne Hathaway's Cottage.** Anne Hathaway, who came from a family of yeomen farmers, lived in this thatched cottage until 1582, the year she married 18-year-old William Shakespeare (8 years her junior). Many original 16th-century furnishings are preserved inside the house, which was occupied by Anne's family until 1892. Before leaving, be sure to stroll through the beautiful garden and orchard. Cottage Lane, Shottery (1 mile south of Stratford via well-marked path from Evesham Place, or bus from Bridge St.). ☎ 01789/204-016. www.shakespeare.org.uk. Admission £7.50 adults, £6.50 seniors & students, £4.50 kids. Daily Apr-Oct 9am-5pm; Nov-Mar 10am-4pm.

8 ★ **Mary Arden's House & the Shakespeare Countryside Museum.** Dating from 1514, the girlhood home of Shakespeare's mother contains country furniture and domestic utensils; the extensive collection of farm implements in the barns and outbuildings illustrates life and work in the local countryside from Shakespeare's time to the present. Wilmcote (3½ miles north of Stratford on A34; drive or take City Sightseeing bus). ☎ 01789/204-016. www.shakespeare.org.uk. Admission £9.50 adults, £8.50 seniors & students, £5.50 kids. Daily 10am-5pm (Nov-Mar until 4pm).

> Shakespeare's wife, Anne Hathaway, was raised in simple surrounds, as her family cottage shows.

Where to Stay & Dine

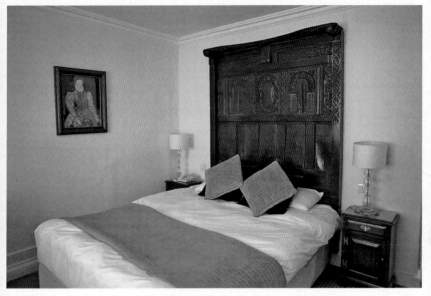

> *Rooms in the Mercure Shakespeare Hotel Stratford retain some "olde worlde" styling.*

★★★ **The Arden Hotel** NEAR RIVER
Completely refurbished and reopened in 2010, this hotel, located directly across from the Royal Shakespeare Theatre beside the River Avon, is Stratford's most sophisticated and up-to-date place to stay, with a waterside bar and a good brasserie. Waterside. ☎ 01789/ 298-682. www.theardenhotelstratford.com. 45 units. Doubles £125–£295 w/breakfast. AE, MC, V.

kids **Hamlet House** NEAR TRAIN STATION
This unpretentious, well-maintained B&B in a Victorian town house is a 3-minute walk from the train station and close to everything else in Stratford. The included breakfast is hearty. 52 Grove Rd. ☎ 01789/204-386. www. hamlethouse.com. 5 units. Doubles £50–£60 w/ breakfast. No credit cards.

★ **Lambs of Sheep Street** CITY CENTER MOD-ERN BRITISH Housed in one of Stratford's oldest buildings, Lambs serves up modern British cooking (saddle of lamb, ravioli with wild mushrooms) and is especially good for an atmospheric, pre-theater dinner. 12 Sheep St. ☎ 01789/292-554. www.lambsrestaurant.co.uk. Entrees £11–£20; fixed-price lunch £10–£15; fixed-price dinner £15–£20. MC,V. Lunch & dinner Tues–Sun, dinner Mon.

★★ **Mercure Shakespeare Hotel Stratford** CITY CENTER Parts of this centrally located hotel date from 1635 and preserve the original Tudor-era beams and stone floor, but all rooms have been updated in a comfortably elegant and traditional style. Chapel St. ☎ 0870/400-8182. www.mercure.com. 76 units. £90–£200 w/breakfast. AE, DC, MC, V.

★ **The Oppo** CITY CENTER BRITISH/INTER-NATIONAL A mix of traditional and Modern British cuisine with a few international choices (Italian pastas, Cajun chicken) is served up in this cozy, oak-beamed restaurant, housed in a 16th-century building. 13 Sheep St. ☎ 01789/ 269-980. www.theoppo.co.uk. Entrees £11–£15. Lunch & dinner daily. MC, V.

Fast Facts

Arriving & Getting Around

BY PLANE Most international travelers arrive in London (see p. 137). For information on getting from London to Oxford or Stratford-upon-Avon, see p. 360 and p. 366. **Birmingham International Airport** (☎ 0844/576-6000; www.birminghamairport.co.uk) handles direct flights from New York and many European cities and offers easy train access to the rest of the region and the entire country. **BY CAR** A car opens up the West Midlands countryside and makes it easier to follow most of the itineraries in this chapter. You can easily rent a car in London (there are car rental agencies at all the major airports). Alternatively, you can take a train from London to Oxford, Stratford-upon-Avon, or Birmingham and rent a car there for local exploration. If you drive, you'll need a detailed road atlas: the best are the large-format maps produced by the Automobile Association (AA), Collins, Ordnance Survey, and the Royal Automobile Club (RAC). In some cities you cannot park in the center of town; look for "Park and Pay" signs to guide you to the closest lot (expect to pay a minimum of £5 for 2-hour stopover). **BY TRAIN** Taking the train to the first stop on the tours in this chapter and renting a car upon arrival will save you the time and hassle of driving from London. Fast, direct trains to Stratford-upon-Avon leave from London's Marylebone Station and take about 2¼ hours. Trains for Oxford leave from London Paddington and take about an hour. Train service is available to all of the major towns in the West Midlands, including Birmingham, Worcester, Shrewsbury, Ludlow, and Hereford. Contact **National Rail Enquiries** (☎ 08457/484-950) or visit www.nationalrail.co.uk for information and schedules. **BY BUS National Express** (☎ 0990/808-080; www.nationalexpress.com) offers daily express bus service from London's Victoria Coach Station to all of the towns in the West Midlands; the trip to Stratford takes about 3 hours, to Oxford about an hour and 40 minutes. The bus is your cheapest option, but takes considerably longer than the train.

Emergencies

To call for emergency help anywhere in England, dial ☎ 999 or ☎ 112; these are free calls from public phones. If you have a medical emergency, ask your concierge or B&B proprietor for help in locating a doctor. In Oxford, you can get medical assistance at **John Radcliffe Hospital,** Headley Way (☎ 01865/741-166).

Internet Access

Wi-Fi and Internet service are available at hotels throughout the West Midlands. **BIRMINGHAM** Internet access is available at **Unis Internet Lounge,** Pavillons Shopping Centre (☎ 0121/632-6172). **OXFORD C-Works,** New Inn Hall Street (☎ 01865/722-044). **STRATFORD-UPON-AVON Cyber Junction,** 28 Greenhill St. (☎ 01789/263-400). Prices vary but expect to pay a rate of £1 per 20 minutes.

Pharmacies

Cities and larger towns throughout the West Midlands have at least one pharmacy ("chemist"); Boots (www.boots.com) is the most common, and there's a branch in Oxford at 151a Cowley Rd. (☎ 01865/243-633). Ask at your hotel or the local tourist office for other pharmacy locations.

Post Office

You'll find them in every city and small town, identified by a red box labeled "ROYAL MAIL." In smaller towns the post office may be in a local store rather than a post office building. In Oxford, the post office is at 102 St. Aldate's (☎ 0845/722-3344).

Safety

It's unlikely you'll encounter any problems with crime in the West Midlands; in Birmingham, avoid walking at night in unlit areas. If you're driving, always make sure that your car is locked and your valuables stowed in the trunk.

Visitor Information

The local tourist offices in each town are your best sources for local information and help in booking accommodations; call ahead or check the websites for the most up-to-date hours of

> *Flying into Birmingham International Airport is a convenient alternative to using the busier hubs around London.*

operation (seasonal variations are common in smaller towns). **BIRMINGHAM** Birmingham Convention & Visitor Bureau, 150 New St. (☎ 0870/225-0127; www.beinbirmingham.com). **CHURCH STRETTON** Visitor Information Centre, located next to the library (☎ 01694/723-133; www.churchstretton.co.uk). **COVENTRY** Coventry Tourist Office, St. Michael's Tower, Coventry Cathedral (☎ 024/7622-5616; www.visitcoventry.co.uk). **HEREFORD** Hereford Tourist Information Centre, King St. (☎ 01432/ 268-430; www.visitherefordshire.co.uk). **IRONBRIDGE GORGE** Ironbridge Tourist Office, Toll Booth (☎ 01952/884-391); the Visitor Centre is at Wharfage. **LICHFIELD** Lichfield Tourist Office, Lichfield Garrick, Castle Dyke (☎ 01543/412-112; www.visitlichfield.com). **LUDLOW** Ludlow Tourist Information Centre, Castle St. (☎ 01584/875-053; www.ludlow.org.uk). **THE MALVERNS** The Great Malvern Tourist Office, 21 Church St. (☎ 01684/892-289; www.malvernhills.gov.uk). **MUCH WENLOCK** Much Wenlock Tourist Office, The Square (☎ 01952/727-679). **OXFORD** The Oxford Information Centre, 15/16 Broad St. (☎ 01865/726-871; www.visitoxford.org). **ROSS-ON-WYE** Ross-on-Wye Tourist Office, at the corner of Edde Cross & High sts. (☎ 01989/562-768). **SHREWSBURY** Shrewsbury Tourist Office, Music Hall, The Square (☎ 01743/281-200; www.visitshrewsbury.com). **STRATFORD-UPON-AVON** Stratford Tourist Information Centre, Bridgefoot (☎ 0870/160-7930; www.shakespeare-country.co.uk). **WORCESTER** Worcester Tourist Information Centre, The Guildhall, High St. (☎ 01905/353-518; www.visitworcester.com).

The website www.visittheheartofengland.com has general information on the West Midlands; www.shakespeare-country.co.uk deals with Stratford and the surrounding area. For regional information, visit the following: www.visitworcestershire.org; www.visitherefordshire.co.uk; or www.shropshiretourism.info.

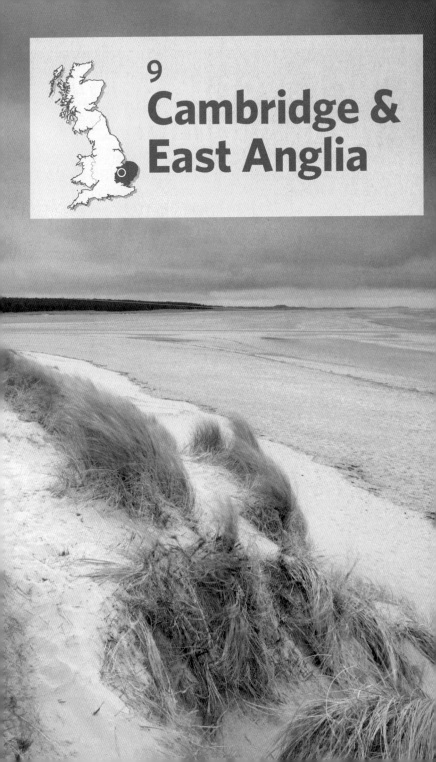

9
Cambridge & East Anglia

Our Favorite East Anglia Moments

If you've ever seen one of the landscape paintings by John Constable (1776–1837), you've seen something of East Anglia. Named for the ancient Anglo-Saxon Kingdom of the East Angles, and today consisting of Norfolk, Suffolk, and parts of Cambridgeshire and Essex, this flat, fertile region of eastern England has a rich heritage that dates back to Roman times. It includes the superbly preserved medieval village of Lavenham, sedate Bury St. Edmunds with its Georgian facades and imposing abbey ruins, delightful Norwich, and distinguished Cambridge. Atmospheric East Anglia, with its big skies, famous fens and Broads (a designated area of navigable rivers and lakes), and rich assortment of stately homes, is a delight to explore.

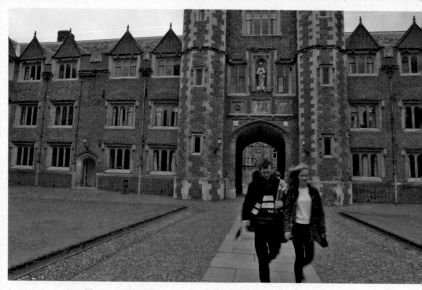

> PREVIOUS PAGE *The sands at Holkham, one of the most dramatic stretches of the Norfolk coast.* THIS PAGE *Cambridge University, the second-oldest university in Britain (just behind rival Oxford).*

1 Listening to Evensong at King's College Chapel, Cambridge. The magnificent chapel at King's College in Cambridge is the setting for free Evensong services sung by the chapel's internationally famous choir, and listening to them is an ethereal and unforgettable experience. See p. 400, **4**.

2 Exploring the colleges and Backs of Cambridge. The beautiful city of Cambridge is renowned for its colleges, many of them open to visitors, and its lovely Backs, an area behind the colleges along the river Cam that is eminently suited to strolling and dreaming. See p. 398.

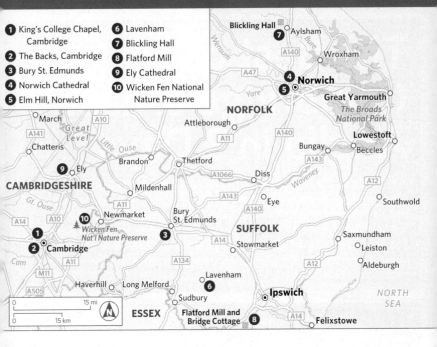

1 King's College Chapel, Cambridge
2 The Backs, Cambridge
3 Bury St. Edmunds
4 Norwich Cathedral
5 Elm Hill, Norwich
6 Lavenham
7 Blickling Hall
8 Flatford Mill
9 Ely Cathedral
10 Wicken Fen National Nature Preserve

3 Roaming among the ruins at Bury St. Edmunds. The ruins of the great abbey that dominated Bury St. Edmunds before Henry VIII dissolved the monasteries in 1539 cover several acres and provide an atmospheric backdrop to this small, charming town. See p. 378, **2**.

4 Marveling at marvelous Norwich Cathedral. One of the glories of East Anglia, Norwich Cathedral is a masterpiece of Anglo-Norman architecture and a good reason to visit this bustling city with its surprising assortment of architectural delights. See p. 394, **1**.

5 Exploring Elm Hill in Norwich. Sometimes you come across a street that is so untouched by time that it takes your breath away, and medieval Elm Hill is one of those streets. See p. 396, **9**.

6 Lollygagging in Lavenham. Time melts away as you contemplate the charms of this picture-perfect Suffolk village, chockablock with half-timbered Tudor and Elizabethan buildings with distinctive pink facades. See p. 383, **3**.

7 Peering at the plasterwork in Blickling Hall. There's much more to this grand Jacobean manor than its plasterwork, but those richly decorated plaster ceilings are extraordinary. See p. 389, **6**.

8 Seeing Constable's Flatford Mill in person. John Constable painted scenes throughout Sussex, including this famous mill, preserved exactly as it was when the painter immortalized it on canvas. See p. 391, **3**.

9 Enjoying Ely Cathedral. This medieval gem of a cathedral, with its amazing octagonal lantern spire rising above the fens, is an inspiring sight both outside and in. See p. 385, **10**.

10 Wandering through Wicken Fen National Nature Preserve. Though parts of East Anglia may look unchanged, human activities such as farming, peat digging, and land reclamation have erased most of the region's primeval landscape of bogs and fens. At Wicken Fen, however, you can explore several hundred acres of untouched fenland and see for yourself what ancient East Anglia really looked like. See p. 393, **12**.

The Best of Cambridge & East Anglia in 3 Days

East Anglia abounds with medieval memories from the time when it was one of the richest areas in England. Many treasures, both natural and man-made, are to be found in this flat landscape, with its rich farmland and long stretch of coastline. This tour introduces you to the major and most historical cities in East Anglia, including Cambridge; gives you a glimpse at the unique landscape of the Norfolk Broads; and ends with a visit to the queen's royal residence at Sandringham.

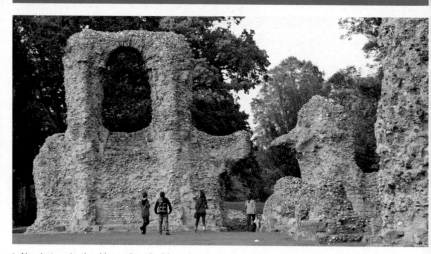

> Now just a ruin, the abbey at Bury St. Edmunds was once one of England's most powerful religious institutions.

START Cambridge is 55 miles north of London. **TRIP LENGTH** 147 miles.

1 ★★★ **Cambridge.** East Anglia's largest and most important city is your first overnight stop. Spend the day exploring the bountiful charms of this academic powerhouse, stepping into a few of its distinguished colleges and museums. ⏱ 1 day. See p. 398.

On Day 2, drive 29 miles east, about 40 min., on the A1305 and A14 to

2 ★ **Bury St. Edmunds.** Stop at this genteel and appealing Suffolk town to spend an hour or so visiting the **Abbey ruins and park,** Angel Hill (free admission), entered through the heavily fortified 14th-century **Great Gate.** The Abbey, one of the largest and most powerful religious houses in Christendom before Henry VIII confiscated and sold it, was dedicated to St. Edmund, a Saxon king venerated as a martyr after he was killed by the Danes in 870.

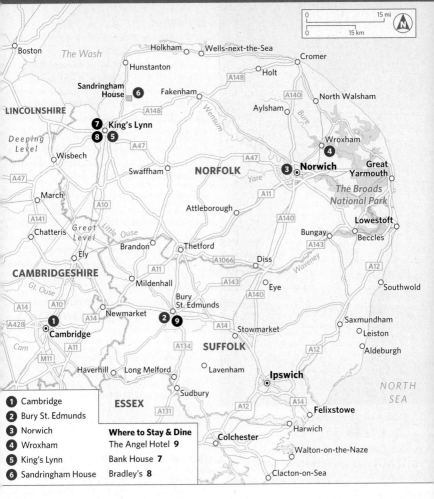

0   15 mi
0   15 km

Boston

The Wash

Holkham   Wells-next-the-Sea

Cromer

Hunstanton   Holt   A148

Sandringham House **6**   Fakenham   A140   North Walsham

LINCOLNSHIRE   A148   Aylsham   Bure   Wensum

Deeping Level   **7** King's Lynn   A47   Wroxham **4**

8 **5**   A47   Norwich **3**   Great Yarmouth

Wisbech   NORFOLK   *Yare*   A11   *The Broads National Park*

A47   Swaffham   Attleborough   A140   Lowestoft

March   A10   Bungay   Beccles

A141   *Great Level*   *Little Ouse*   Brandon   Thetford   A143

Chatteris   Diss   *Waveney*   A12

Ely   A11   A1066   Eye   Southwold

CAMBRIDGESHIRE   Mildenhall   A143   A140

Gt. Ouse   Newmarket   Bury St. Edmunds   A14   Saxmundham

A14   A10   **2** **9**   Stowmarket   Leiston

Cam   Cambridge **1**   A14   Aldeburgh

M11   A11   A134   SUFFOLK   A12

Haverhill   Long Melford   Lavenham   Ipswich   *NORTH SEA*

Sudbury   A12   A14   Felixstowe

ESSEX   Harwich

A131   Colchester   Walton-on-the-Naze

Clacton-on-Sea

1 Cambridge
2 Bury St. Edmunds
3 Norwich
4 Wroxham
5 King's Lynn
6 Sandringham House

Where to Stay & Dine
The Angel Hotel **9**
Bank House **7**
Bradley's **8**

The atmospheric ruins of this once massive edifice are scattered about the park grounds. Pay a quick visit to adjacent **St. Edmundsbury Cathedral,** Angel Hill (☎ 01284/748-720; www.stedscathedral.co.uk; admission by donation), built in the 16th century but with a tower completed only in 2005, and then stroll around the gracious and mostly Georgian town, laid out on its original 11th-century town grid. You might want to take a quick look at the **Greene King Brewery,** Crown St. (☎ 01284/714-297; tours £8), makers of one of the U.K's most popular beers and still housed in its Victorian-era brewery buildings; there's a free museum exhibition, or you can take a tour with tastings. You might also want to take a peek at the **Theatre Royal,** Westgate St. (☎ 01284/769-505; www.theatreroyal. org), one of England's loveliest Regency-era playhouses. ⏱ At least 1 hr.

Travel Tip

Though you can easily reach the cities and towns on this tour by train, a car opens up parts of the East Anglian landscape you might not otherwise see and makes visiting the Broads and Sandringham easier. Instead of driving from London (a 1-hour trip on the M11), you might want to take a train to Cambridge (1 hr.) and pick up a rental car there.

> *After Salisbury, the cathedral in Norwich has the tallest spire in England.*

Drive 44 miles northeast on the A134 and A11 (1 hr.) to Norwich. Check into a hotel for the night.

❸ ★★★ Norwich. Cambridge may be the busiest and most important city in East Anglia, but Norwich is the region's capital, and at one time it was second only to London in size and importance. That history is part and parcel of Norwich today, a city whose urban fabric includes magnificent **Norwich Cathedral** (p. 394, ❶), the hilltop **Norwich Castle** (p. 396, ⓫), and a rich mixture of medieval buildings, both religious and secular with a prim overlay of Victoriana. ⏱ At least 2 hr. See p. 394.

In the afternoon, drive northeast to Wroxham, a 20-min. journey on the A1151. This excursion will give you a glimpse of the Norfolk Broads, one of East Anglia's most distinctive landscapes.

❹ Wroxham. This hamlet on the River Bure is the unofficial capital of the Broads and one of the area's main boating and tourist centers. You can explore a stretch of the Broads by renting a boat from **Blakes** (☎ 0870/220-2498; www.blakes.co.uk), or you can arrange a 1½-hour boat tour through **Broads Tours** (☎ 01603/782-207; www.broads.co.uk; £7.50 adults, £6 kids age 6 & over). ⏱ At least 1 hr.

From Wroxham, backtrack to Norwich for the night. On Day 3, drive northwest for about an hour on the A47 to

❺ ★ King's Lynn. This town on the Great Ouse River at the mouth of the Wash is your overnight stop for Day 3. King's Lynn was founded in the 11th century and became a major port and member of the Hanseatic League. Avoid the newer part of the city, marred by banal constructions from the 1960s, and concentrate on the historic core, a picturesque area between the High Street and the quayside. Step into twin-spired **St. Margaret's Church** (☎ 01553/722-858; www.stmargaretskingslynn.org.uk), founded in 1101, to have a look at the elaborate brasses, the 14th-century carved screens, and a rare moondial.

Across from the church stands **Hanse House** (formerly **St. Margaret's House**), once a Hanseatic League warehouse. Spend a few minutes looking at the civic treasures, especially the ornate King John Cup from 1340, on

What Are the Broads?

The Norfolk Broads are 14 broad, shallow lakes lying along slow-moving rivers, fens, and marshes that form a unique habitat within the flat terrain of coastal Norfolk. The lakes were formed during the Middle Ages when the water level rose and flooded areas that had been given over to extensive peat harvesting. Today, with 125 miles of lockless and easily navigable waterways, the Broads are popular with boaters and wildlife watchers. The area is home to many plant, bird, and animal species found nowhere else in England, and has several conservancy areas and nature trails. For more information on the area, contact the **Broads Authority** (☎ 01603/610-734; www.broads-authority.gov.uk) or visit **www.norfolkbroads.com**.

> *Boating on the Broads, shown here at Wroxham, has for decades been the mainstay of Norfolk's tourist industry.*

display in the **Old Gaol House,** College Lane (☎ 01553/774-297; £3 adults, £2.20 kids). Adjacent is the flint-and-brick **Town Hall** from 1421 and the **Town House Museum,** Queen St. (☎ 01553/773-450; £3 adults, £1.75 kids), dedicated to local history. At **Purfleet Quay,** the town's principal harbor during its medieval heyday, stands the 17th-century **Custom House,** now the town's visitor center. Another treasure is **St. George's Guildhall,** King St. (☎ 01553/764-864), the largest surviving medieval guildhall in England, now converted into an arts center. ⏱ 2 hr.

Drive north 8½ miles from King's Lynn on the A1046 and A49, about a 20-min. trip, to

❻ ★ Sandringham House. Queen Elizabeth II's house in Norfolk sits amidst 8,000 hectares

(19,700 acres) of landscaped gardens, woodlands and lakes. Queen Victoria bought the place in 1862 for her son, the Prince of Wales (later Edward VII). When the Royal Family is not in residence, ordinary mortals can wander through the lavishly decorated rooms of the manse, ogle royal memorabilia and fancy carriages in a museum in the stables, and stroll through the grounds. There's also a restaurant and gift shop on the premises. ⏱ 2 hr. Sandringham. ☎ 01553/612-908. www.sandringhamestate.co.uk. Admission £11 adults, £9 seniors & students, £5.50 kids 5-15, £28 families. Daily late Apr–late July and Aug–Sept 11am–4:30pm.

Return to King's Lynn, 10 miles southwest of Sandringham, a 25-min. drive on the A149.

Where to Stay & Dine

★ The Angel Hotel BURY ST. EDMUNDS
If you're looking for a good lunch or a comfortable room, stop in at this historic coaching inn on the main square. Angel Hill, Bury St. Edmunds. ☎ 01284/714-000. www.theangel.co.uk. 70 units. Doubles £80–£140. Lunch entrees £8–£12. AE, MC, V.

★ Bank House KING'S LYNN
An 18th-century bank wonderfully situated on the waterfront houses this excellent B&B.

King's Staithe Sq. ☎ 01553/660-492. www.thebankhouse.co.uk. 5 units. Doubles £100–£120 w/breakfast. MC, V.

★ Bradley's KING'S LYNN *MODERN BRITISH*
You can eat in the elegant Georgian dining room or a secluded courtyard, or enjoy a small plate in the bar at this atmospheric riverside restaurant, the best in King's Lynn. 10 South Quay. ☎ 01553/819-888. www.bradleysbytheriver.co.uk. Entrees £13–£19, bar plates £8. MC, V.

The Best of Cambridge & East Anglia in 5 Days

This itinerary introduces you to the best that East Anglia has to offer—the stateliest of stately homes, remarkable cathedrals, marvelous medieval cities, and a flat, fertile landscape of farms and fens and ocean beaches. The rich diversity of the region, both natural and man-made, is on display at every stop in this 5-day itinerary.

> Norwich's Elm Hill district was narrowly saved from demolition in the 1950s.

START Hatfield House is 26 miles north of London on the A5, B510, and A1, about a 1-hr. drive. To get there from Cambridge, drive south on the A505 and A1; the 40-mile drive takes about an hour. **TRIP LENGTH** 215 miles.

❶ ★★ **Hatfield House.** Start your exploration of East Anglia at this historic Jacobean mansion built on the grounds of a palace where Elizabeth I spent her childhood. It contains

famous portraits of the Virgin Queen and even some of the garments she wore. ⏱ 1 hr. See p. 386, ❶.

❷ ★★★ **Cambridge.** There is plenty to see in this famous university town, which is your first overnight stop. Spend the afternoon visiting some of Cambridge's illustrious colleges and attend an Evensong service at **King's College Chapel** (p. 400, ❹). Round out your first day

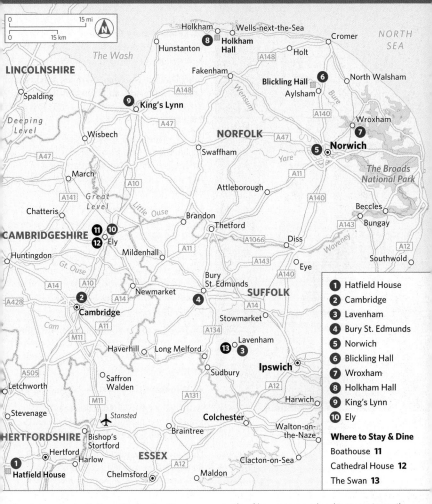

Map legend:
1. Hatfield House
2. Cambridge
3. Lavenham
4. Bury St. Edmunds
5. Norwich
6. Blickling Hall
7. Wroxham
8. Holkham Hall
9. King's Lynn
10. Ely

Where to Stay & Dine
Boathouse 11
Cathedral House 12
The Swan 13

with a leisurely stroll along the **Backs,** the riverside meadows behind the colleges, or try your hand at **punting** on the River Cam. Spend the morning of Day 2 visiting the eclectic art and artifact collections at **Kettle's Yard** (p. 401, ❽) and the **Fitzwilliam Museum** (p. 402, ❾). ⏱ Half-day. See p. 398.

On Day 2, drive to Lavenham, 40 miles east of Cambridge on the A14, about an hour's drive.

❸ ★★ **Lavenham.** An unrivalled collection of half-timbered medieval houses makes this Suffolk village the stuff of dreams—which is why it's a good place to spend your second night. Check into your hotel and then take a

couple of hours to wander down ancient village streets lined with immaculately preserved Tudor dwellings painted a distinctive "Suffolk pink." The early-16th-century **Corpus Christi Guildhall,** Market Place (☎ 01787/247-646; £4 adults, £1.65 kids), has a museum dedicated to the wool trade that made Lavenham so wealthy, and **Little Hall,** Market Place

Travel Tip

This itinerary is best done by car. If you're setting out from London, the first stop is less than an hour away. You could also take the train to Cambridge and rent a car there.

> *The Jacobean-style Blickling Hall.*

(☎ 01787/247-019; £2.50 adults), lets you see what the inside of a medieval wool merchant's house looked like. The impressive **Church of St. Peter and St. Paul,** Church St. (no phone; free admission), a "wool church" built in the Perpendicular style between 1485 and 1530, has a soaring spire, lofty windows, and a beautiful interior. ⏱ At least 1 hr.

In the afternoon, head to Bury St. Edmunds, 11 miles north of Lavenham on the A1141 and A134, about a 25-min. drive.

④ ★ Bury St. Edmunds. This genteel Suffolk town sits on its original 11th-century town grid, the first example of town planning in England since the Roman era. An enormous abbey was built to accommodate the hordes of pilgrims who once came to worship at the shrine of St. Edmund. Explore the **abbey ruins,** scattered around a lovely park, pay a quick visit to **St. Edmundsbury Cathedral,** stop in at the **Greene King Brewery** for a tasting tour, then just wander. ⏱ 2 hr. See p. 378, **②**.

Start Day 3 in Norwich, 44 miles northeast of Bury St. Edmunds, about an hour's drive on the A134 and A11. Check into a hotel here for the night.

⑤ ★★★ Norwich. Explore the lively, historic capital of East Anglia's medieval treasures, chief among them being **Norwich Cathedral** (p. 394, **①**), the Anglo-Norman **castle** (p. 396, **⑪**), and **Elm Hill** (p. 396, **⑨**), a remarkably intact medieval street. ⏱ Half-day. See p. 394.

Blickling Hall is 14 miles north of Norwich on the A40 and B1354, about a half-hour drive.

⑥ ★★ Blickling Hall. Spend the afternoon visiting this remarkable Jacobean house with its splendid plasterwork ceiling, restored servants' quarters, and lush gardens. ⏱ 1½ hr. See p. 389, **⑥**.

On Day 4, explore the unique habitat of the Broads (p. 380) by boat or by car. Wroxham is 8 miles northeast of Norwich, a 20-min. journey on the A1151.

⑦ Wroxham. ⏱ At least 1 hr. See p. 380, **④**.

You'll get a taste of Norfolk's coastal atmosphere on the 43-mile drive (1 hr. 15 min.) to Holkham Hall on the A149.

⑧ ★★★ Holkham Hall. This palatial Palladian manse set amidst acres of parkland was built in the mid–18th century and contains a splendid series of state rooms decorated with ancient statues, Flemish tapestries, and important paintings. ⏱ 1½ hr. See p. 389, **⑦**.

King's Lynn, your overnight stop for Day 4, is 27 miles southwest of Holkham Hall, about an hour's drive.

⑨ ★ King's Lynn. Spend a couple of hours exploring the old part of this once-powerful port. Worth visiting are 12th-century, twin-spired **St. Margaret's Church; Hanse House,** a medieval warehouse; the **Old Gaol House,** with its collection of civic treasures; the **Town House Museum,** dedicated to local history; and **St. George's Guildhall,** England's largest surviving medieval guildhall. ⏱ 2 hr. See p. 380, **⑤**.

Day 5 is spent in Ely, 29 miles south of King's Lynn via the A10, about an hour's drive.

10 ★★ **Ely.** This small and sleepily beautiful town basks in the glory of one of England's most remarkable cathedrals. The landmark 14th-century octagonal tower of ★★★ **Ely Cathedral** (☎ 01353/667-735; www.ely cathedral.org; £6.50 adults, £5.50 kids) rises so dramatically above the flat countryside that it's known as the "Ship of the Fens." Built in the 11th century atop an earlier 7th-century shrine to St. Etheldreda, the enormous cathedral has a Norman nave, a Perpendicular Lady Chapel, a painted wooden ceiling, and the amazing central Octagon Tower, constructed in the 14th century when the original Norman tower collapsed. Housed in the cathedral's triforium, the intriguing ★ **Stained Glass Museum** (www.stainedglassmuseum.com) explains how stained glass was manufactured in England and Europe. Exhibits in the **Oliver Cromwell House,** 29 St. Mary's Church (☎ 01353/662-062; £4 adults, £3.60 kids), tell the story of Ely's most famous resident, the 17th-century Puritan who became Lord Protector of England. If you're a local history buff, spend a few minutes browsing the contents of **Ely Museum,** in the Old Gaol on Market Street (☎ 01353/666-655; www.ely museum.org.uk; £3.50 adults, £2.50 kids). Ely also has a splendid array of historic buildings with a beautiful waterside area where you can enjoy a boat trip or riverside walk, or explore the many cafes and antiques shops. ☺ 1 day.

> *Ely's grand cathedral testifies to the former importance of this small, rural market town.*

Where to Stay & Dine

★ **Boathouse** ELY *MODERN BRITISH*
This gastropub housed in a converted boathouse on the River Ouse serves traditional and innovative dishes using local and regional ingredients. 3 Annesdale. ☎ 01353/664-388. www.theboathouseely.co.uk. Set meals £15–£23. AE, MC, V. Lunch & dinner daily.

★ **Cathedral House** ELY
This antiques-filled Georgian house with a walled garden and views of the cathedral is one of the most atmospheric B&Bs in East Anglia. 17 St. Mary's St. ☎ 01353/662-124. www. cathedralhouse.co.uk. 3 units. Doubles £75–£90 w/breakfast. No credit cards.

★★ **The Swan** LAVENHAM
This ancient half-timbered inn with creaking floors and a mystifying floor plan offers comfortable, modern rooms, lots of cozy corners, and a good restaurant that serves traditional English food. High St. ☎ 01787/247-477. www. theswanatlavenham.co.uk. Doubles £200–£260 w/breakfast & dinner. AE, MC, V.

Historic Homes of East Anglia

East Anglia abounds in stately homes, and touring these historic mansions provides visitors with an unfolding panorama of English political, architectural, social, and garden history. Notable for their sumptuously decorated rooms adorned with fine paintings, furniture, and art objects of all kinds, many of the houses have further broadened their appeal by opening up the "downstairs" areas where the staff toiled to keep the gigantic households running smoothly.

> Elizabeth I found out she had ascended to the English throne while at Hatfield House, her favorite childhood residence.

START Cambridge is 55 miles north of London. **TRIP LENGTH** 4 days; 394 total miles.

After picking up your car and checking into your hotel, drive south on the A505 and A1 to Hatfield House; the 40-mile drive takes about an hour.

❶ ★★★ **Hatfield House.** Elizabeth I (1533–1603) spent her youth in a palace that once stood on this site, but the house visitors see today was completed in 1611 by her secretary of state, Robert Cecil, first Earl of Salisbury (1563–1612). Inside, the oak carving on the **Grand Staircase** and the **stained glass** in the chapel are superb examples of Jacobean craftsmanship. Elizabeth's silk stockings, hat, and gloves are on display in the **Long Gallery;** her *Ermine Portrait* by Hilliard hangs in the **Marble Hall.** The **Gardens,** covering 17 hectares (42 acres), were laid out in the 17th century by naturalist John Tradescant the Elder (d. 1638), who was sent to Europe to collect trees and plants that had never previously been grown in England. ⏱ At least 1 hr. Hatfield, Hertfordshire. ☎ 01707/287-010. www.hatfield-house.co.uk. Admission £18.50 adults, £17.50 seniors, £11.50 kids. House: Apr–Sept Wed–Sun noon–4pm. Garden & park: Wed–Sun 11am–5pm.

Audley End is 35 miles northeast of Hatfield House, an hour's drive on the B1383.

❷ ★★ **Audley End House & Gardens.** In 1538, Sir Thomas Audley (1488–1544), Henry VIII's Lord Chancellor, was given a confiscated abbey and began to refashion its buildings into his personal mansion. In addition to the classically inspired **Great Drawing Room** and **Small Drawing Room,** both designed by Robert Adam in the 1720s, and the **Great Hall,** Audley End is interesting for its refurbished Victorian **Service Wing,** which provides an

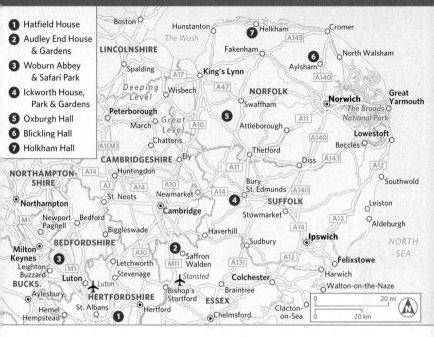

1 Hatfield House
2 Audley End House & Gardens
3 Woburn Abbey & Safari Park
4 Ickworth House, Park & Gardens
5 Oxburgh Hall
6 Blickling Hall
7 Holkham Hall

insight into the "below stairs" working of this privileged household during the 1880s. Audley End's delightful 18th-century **park**—designed, in part, by the great landscaper, Lancelot "Capability" Brown (1716–83—includes an artificial lake, a temple, and a formal parterre garden. The **Stable Block** is one of the grandest surviving stables of the early 17th century. ☺ At least 1 hr. Saffron Walden, Essex. ☎ 01799/522-399. www.english-heritage.org.uk. Admission £12.50 adults, £11.30 seniors, £7.50 kids, £32.50 families. House: Mar & Oct Thurs–Mon 10am–4pm; Apr–Sept Wed–Mon 11am–5pm. Grounds: daily 10am–5pm.

Return to Cambridge for the night. Start Day 2 at Woburn Abbey, 44 miles (1 hr. 15 min.)

Travel Tip

The best strategy for this itinerary is to base yourself in Cambridge (see p. 398) for 2 nights and Norwich (see p. 394) for 2 nights and visit the houses as day trips; every one of them has an on-site restaurant or cafe. Instead of driving from London (a 1-hour trip on the M11), you might want to take a train to Cambridge (1 hr.) and pick up a rental car there.

southwest of Cambridge via the A428 and A421.

3 ★★ kids **Woburn Abbey & Safari Park.** Woburn Abbey has been the home of the Dukes of Bedford for nearly 400 years. The sumptuously decorated **State Rooms,** dating from 1747, include **Queen Victoria's Bedroom,** with etchings done by the queen and Prince Albert, and **Queen Victoria's Dressing Room,** with its collection of 17th-century Dutch and Flemish paintings. A portrait by Van Dyck is displayed in the **State Dining Room** and a collection of Canalettos in the **Dining Room.** Two Rembrandts and the famous *Armada Portrait* of Elizabeth I hang in the **Library.** The grounds, designed in the 18th century by Henry Repton, encompass 12 hectares (30 acres) of formal and natural gardens and a 1,200-hectare (3,000-acre) **deer park,** home to nine species of deer. The **Woburn Safari Park** (☎ 01525/290-826; www.woburn.co.uk/safari), with a separate entrance 1 mile from the house, is a drive-through wildlife park with elephants, lions, zebras, bison, rhinos, and tigers. ☺ 1 hr. for house, 2 hr. for safari park. Near Woburn, Bedfordshire. Woburn Abbey: ☎ 01525/290-333. www.woburn.co.uk/abbey. Admission £13 adults, £11 seniors, £6

> *Kids will love animals like this Manchurian Sika Deer, at Woburn Safari Park.*

> *Ornate plasterwork ceilings are a feature of the interiors at Blickling Hall, north of Norwich.*

kids. Woburn Safari Park (separate admission): £20 adults, £17.50 seniors, £15 kids. Abbey & gardens: Apr–Sept daily 11am–4pm. Safari park: Mar–Oct daily 10am–5pm.

To reach Ickworth House from Woburn Abbey, drive east 71 miles (1½ hr.) on the A14.

④ ★★ Ickworth House, Park & Gardens. This extraordinary neoclassical structure topped by a giant rotunda was begun in 1795 for the eccentric fourth Earl of Bristol and sits in a park laid out by the famous "Capability" Brown. The pristine **State Rooms** house a superb collection of paintings and family portraits by Velázquez, Titian, Gainsborough, Reynolds, and Hogarth. It's also home to an exceptional collection of silver and Regency furniture. Extending beyond the wooded **Pleasure Grounds** and formal **Italianate Garden** are 320 hectares (800 acres) of park, vineyards, and woodland. ⏰ At least 1 hr. The Rotunda, Horringer, Bury St. Edmunds. ☎ 01284/735-270. www.nationaltrust.org.uk. Admission £10.60 adults, £4.60 kids, £25 families. Park: daily 8am–8pm. House: Mar–Oct Fri–Tues 11am–5pm. Gardens: Nov–Feb 11am–4pm; Mar–Oct 10am–5pm.

Return to Cambridge (29 miles west of Ickworth, a 40-min. drive via the A14) for

the night. On Day 3, head first to Oxburgh Hall, 44 miles (1 hr. 10 min.) northeast of Cambridge on the A14 and A1065.

5 ★★ **Oxburgh Hall.** As you cross the moat, pass through the gatehouse, and enter the courtyard of this Tudor house, you're entering what has been the home of the Bedingfeld family since 1482. Inside, the family's Catholic history is revealed, complete with a Tudor-era **priest's hole** where the Bedingfields' Catholic priest could hide if the house was raided. The hall is also notable for its needlework hangings by Mary, Queen of Scots. You can enjoy panoramic views from the gatehouse roof and wander through the gardens and woodlands. ⏱ 1 hr. Oxborough, Norfolk. ☎ 01366/328-258. www.nationaltrust.org.uk. Admission £8.20 adults, £4.10 kids, £20.50 families. Apr & Aug daily 11am–5pm; Mar, May–July & Sept Sat–Wed 11am–5pm; Oct Sat–Wed 11am–4pm. Garden open most weekends.

Blickling Hall is 45 miles (1 hr. 10 min.) southwest of Oxburgh Hall via the A1065 and B1354.

6 ★★ **Blickling Hall.** Massive 18th-century yew hedges line the main approach to the hall, begun in the 1620s by Sir Henry Hobart (1560–1625) and famed for its superb plasterwork ceiling in the **Long Gallery** and for the enormous tapestry, which hangs in the **Peter the Great Room.** The **library** contains one of the most historically significant collections of manuscripts and books in England. The beautiful and extensive **garden** at Blickling contains formal and informal gardens, woodlands, topiaries, and a treasure trove of romantic buildings. ⏱ At least 1 hr. Blickling, Norwich, Norfolk. ☎ 01263/738-030. www.nationaltrust.org.uk. Admission £10.75 adults, £5.25 kids, £29 families. May to mid-July & Sept–Oct Wed–Sun 11am–5pm; mid-July to mid-Sept Wed–Mon 11am–5pm.

Norwich (see p. 394), your overnight stop for Days 3 and 4, is 14 miles south of Blickling Hall, a 30-min. drive on the A140. Check into your hotel and spend the remainder of Day 3 exploring this lovely, historic city. On Day 4, head 35 miles north of Norwich, about an hour's drive on the A1067 and B1105, to

> *Holkham's Marble Hall is largely modeled from alabaster shipped in from rural Derbyshire.*

7 ★★★ **Holkham Hall.** This palatial Palladian mansion, seat of the Earls of Leicester and Coke, was designed by architect William Kent (1685–1748) in the mid-18th century. The **Marble Hall** features a 15m (50-ft.) ceiling modeled after the Pantheon in Rome, and the **Statue Gallery** contains a remarkable collection of original Roman statues from the 1st to the 3rd centuries. Rubens's *The Flight into Egypt* and Van Dyck's equestrian portrait of the Duc d'Arenberg hang in the opulent **Saloon.** The **Old Kitchen** was in use from 1757 up until World War II. Outside the house, the **Bygones Museum** is a nostalgic paean to the house and those who lived and worked there, and a **History of Farming Exhibition** chronicles the invention of modern agriculture by the Earls of Leicester and Coke. There's a good restaurant, too. ⏱ 2 hr. Wells-next-the-Sea, Norfolk. ☎ 01328/710-227. Admission £11 adults, £5.50 kids 5–16, £27 families; parking £2.50 per day. House: Apr–Oct Sun, Mon & Thurs noon–4pm. Bygones Museum, History of Farming Exhibition & Cafe: Apr–Oct daily 10am–5pm.

Broads, Fens & Coastal Wonders

East Anglia has over 250 miles of coastline characterized by cliffs, shingle spits, mudflats, salt marshes, and tidal estuaries teeming with birds and wildfowl. This driving tour takes you to historic coastal villages and ancient wool towns, passing through the Broads and the fens and rural areas that still look as they did when John Constable painted them 2 centuries ago.

> The countryside around Flatford Mill provided the backdrop for The Hay Wain, *John Constable's most famous painting, now in London's National Gallery.*

START Colchester is 60 miles northeast of London, 1 hr. 40 min. on the A12. You'll need a car for this tour. **TRIP LENGTH** 3 days; 255 total miles.

1 ★ **Colchester**. This ancient city in Essex sits on England's oldest (5th c. B.C.) inhabited site. The Romans arrived in A.D. 43 and established a military fort here—the first Roman settlement in England. The legendary warrior-queen Boudicca (p. 697) burned it down in A.D. 60, after which the **Roman walls and gate** (best seen from Balkerne Hill) were constructed. When the Normans conquered England in 1066, they built the largest military fort in England; on that site today you'll find **Colchester Castle,** Castle Park (☎ 01206/282-939;

admission £5.70 adults, £3.60 kids), with browsable exhibits on the city's past. Stop in at the **Tymperleys Clock Museum,** High St. (☎ 01206/282-939; free admission), which chronicles Colchester's clock-making past, and stroll through the **Dutch Quarter,** filled with Tudor-era houses where Huguenot weavers from Holland settled in the 16th century. Exhibits in the **Hollytrees Museum,** High St. (☎ 01206/282-940; free admission), focus on domestic life here since the 17th century. ⏱ 1 hr. Colchester Museums: ☎ 01206/282-939. www.colchestermuseums.org.uk.

Ipswich is 18 miles north of Colchester, a half-hour's drive on the A12.

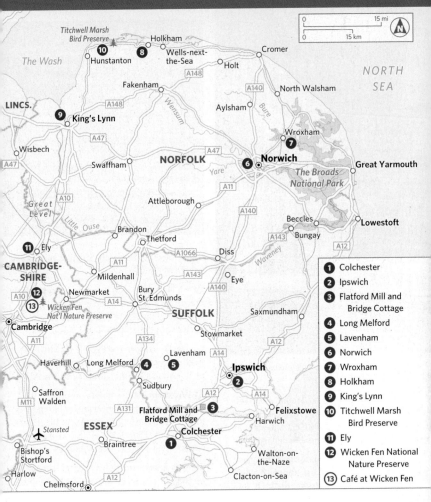

1. Colchester
2. Ipswich
3. Flatford Mill and Bridge Cottage
4. Long Melford
5. Lavenham
6. Norwich
7. Wroxham
8. Holkham
9. King's Lynn
10. Titchwell Marsh Bird Preserve
11. Ely
12. Wicken Fen National Nature Preserve
13. Café at Wicken Fen

2 Ipswich. With a port on the Orwell River founded over 1,300 years ago, the maritime history of this bustling city in Sussex runs deep indeed, but the town today is mostly Victorian and modern in character. Spend a half-hour in the ★ **Christchurch Mansion,** Soane St. (☎ 01473/433-554; free admission), viewing the collection of East Anglian landscape paintings by John Constable and Thomas Gainsborough (1727–88). Have a quick look at the elaborate 17th-century pargeting (stucco ornamentation) on the **Ancient House,** Buttermarket, and Lord Norman Foster's **Willis Corroon Building,** 16 Friars St., the first building from the 1970s to be listed as a protected monument. ⏱ 45 min.

The bucolic Sussex landscapes that inspired Constable and Gainsborough can still be seen in the Stour Valley. Flatford Mill is 11 miles southwest of Ipswich, a 25-min. drive on the A12 and B1070.

3 ★★ Flatford Mill and Bridge Cottage. Owned by Constable's father, this 16th-century thatched cottage and adjacent mill look exactly as they did when Constable painted them. Take a few minutes to stroll down the path beside the Stour River and into the heart of "Constable Country," then enjoy tea or a light lunch at the charming riverside tea room (May–Oct, teas £4–£6) next to the cottage. ⏱ 1 hr. Flatford, East Bergholt. ☎ 01206/298-260.

> *Norwich's Elm Hill district still retains much of its original medieval character.*

www.nationaltrust.org.uk. Grounds: Jan–Feb Sat–Sun 11am–3:30pm; Apr, Nov–Dec Wed–Sun 11am–5pm; May–Oct daily 10:30am–5:30pm. No public access to interior of buildings.

You'll see even more pastoral scenery as you drive to Long Melford, about 19 miles northwest of Flatford Bridge on the B1068 and A134, a 40-min. journey.

4 **Long Melford.** Park and spend a few minutes strolling the village's High Street, lined with pink half-timbered houses from the 16th and 17th centuries, and have a look at **Holy Trinity Church** (free admission), a great "wool church" built of stone and flint in the 15th century. ⏲ 30 min.

Lavenham is 5 miles northeast of Long Melford, a 15-min. drive on Lavenham Rd.

5 ★★ **Lavenham.** Stop and enjoy a leisurely stroll through this picture-perfect Sussex village with its half-timbered Tudor and Elizabethan-era buildings. ⏲ At least 1 hr. See p. 383, **3**.

Finding the Fens

The rich, flat farmland you see around Ely today was once part of a vast and very different wetlands environment. Watery marshes punctuated by clay hills (such as the one Ely was built on), the fens were home to people who caught eels (how Ely got its name) and cut reeds for thatching. After extensive peat-cutting in the Middle Ages, the fens flooded. Reclamation efforts using windmills designed by Dutch engineers actually shrank the land, and it wasn't until steam water pumps were introduced in the Victorian era that the fenland was reclaimed for agriculture.

Continue on to Norwich, 55 miles northeast of Lavenham (1½ hr.).

6 ★★ **Norwich.** With its beautiful **cathedral,** dramatic **castle,** and medieval streets, Norwich is a great city to explore and makes a good overnight stop for Day 1. See p. 394.

On Day 2, explore the Broads (p. 380) by boat or by car. Wroxham is 8 miles northeast of Norwich, a 20-min. journey on the A1151.

7 **Wroxham.** At this holiday center on the River Bure, you can rent boats or hire guides to show you the unique habitat of the Broads, a series of shallow lakes and slow-moving coastal rivers. ⏲ 2 hr. See p. 380, **4**.

Enjoy Norfolk's northern coastal landscape on the 75-min. drive to Holkham, 43 miles from Wroxham on the B1359.

8 ★★ **Holkham.** Stroll through the picturesque streets of this pretty Norfolk village, known for its stately home, ★★★ **Holkham Hall** (p. 389, **7**), and for the sandy, 3-mile sweep of **Holkham Beach** (parking access Lady Anne's Drive; £3.50), one of England's most dramatic ocean beaches and a favorite with walkers and outdoor enthusiasts. ⏲ At least 2 hr.

King's Lynn is 27 miles southwest of Holkham, about an hour's drive.

9 ★ **King's Lynn.** This ancient and once-powerful port town on the Great Ouse River near the Wash estuary is your overnight stop for Day 2. ⏲ 2 hr. See p. 380, **5**.

Start Day 3 by exploring the Wash, England's largest tidal estuary and one of the country's most important winter-feeding areas for wading birds and wildfowl. To see this coastal landscape of marshes and mudflats, head north from King's Lynn to Hunstanton, a 16-mile drive on the A149 to

⑩ ★★ Titchwell Marsh Bird Preserve. This popular bird-watching haunt has a visitor center with a restaurant and a path down to a sandy beach that runs past reed beds and shallow lagoons that are often full of birds, including the marsh harrier and avocet. ⏱ At least 1 hr. Near Hunstanton. www.rspb.org.uk. Admission £4 per car. Center: daily 9:30am-5pm.

Return to King's Lynn and continue on from there to Ely, 28 miles south via the A12, about an hour's drive. Make Ely your overnight stop for Day 3.

⑪ ★★ Ely. The 14th-century spire of **Ely Cathedral** rises like a beacon above the pancake-flat fens that characterize this part of East Anglia. Visit the magnificent cathedral, have a look at the historic **Oliver Cromwell House,** and browse the exhibits in the **Ely Museum;** then walk along the beautiful Great Ouse or go boating on the river, a popular local pastime. ⏱ 1½ hr. See p. 385, ⑩.

On the afternoon of Day 3, drive 9 miles south of Ely via the A10 and A123, a 15-min. drive, to

⑫ ★★ Wicken Fen National Nature Preserve. Boardwalk nature trails wind through this 280-hectare (700-acre) nature preserve, one of England's last remaining bits of natural fenland, revealing the unique characteristics of the now mostly vanished ecosystem. ⏱ 1 hr. Visitor Centre. ☎ 01353/720-274. www.wicken.org.uk. Admission £6 adults, £3 kids; parking £2. Daily 10am-5pm (closed Mon Mar & Nov-Dec).

⑬ ☕ Café at Wicken Fen. What better way to end your tour of East Anglia than by enjoying an afternoon tea overlooking the ancient fenland at Wicken Fen? Wicken Fen Visitor Centre. ☎ 01353/720-274. www.wicken.org.uk. Menu items £3-£6.

> *The design of Holkham Hall was heavily influenced by Palladian and classical styles.*

Norwich

Norwich (pronounced *nor*-itch), the county seat of Norfolk and capital of East Anglia, is an atmospheric and intriguing old city, with picturesque medieval lanes and churches crowned by an ancient castle and presided over by a beautiful cathedral. By the late 11th century, when the Normans conquered England, the Saxon settlement on the river Wensum had grown into one of the largest and most important towns in England, its wealth coming from the wool trade. Today it is a lively and bustling market town. Give yourself at least half a day explore the historic charms of this lovely city.

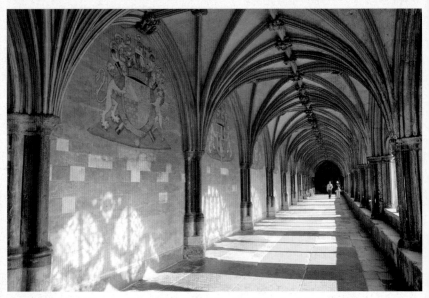

> The large vaulted cloisters at Norwich Cathedral exhibit all the hallmarks of the English Gothic architectural style.

START Norwich is 109 miles northeast of London.

① ★★★ **Norwich Cathedral.** The barbed spire of this magnificent Anglo-Norman cathedral, begun in 1096 and considered one of the architectural masterpieces of the Middle Ages, is second only to Salisbury's (p. 212, **⑨**) in height. The 1200 sculpted roof bosses in the enormous nave represent medieval stone carving at its best. The remarkable two-story **cloisters,** the largest in Europe, were built between 1297 and 1430 to serve a community of about 100 monks. ⏱ 30 min. The Close. ☎ 01603/218-300. www.cathedral.org.uk. Admission by donation. Daily 7am–7pm.

② 🍽 ★ **Norwich Market.** Produce and food vendors have been setting up their stalls here for 900 years, making it one of the oldest public markets in Europe. It's a good place to observe local life, pick up picnic supplies, or have a quick snack. Off Gentlemans Walk. www.norwich-market.co.uk. Mon–Sat 8am–5pm.

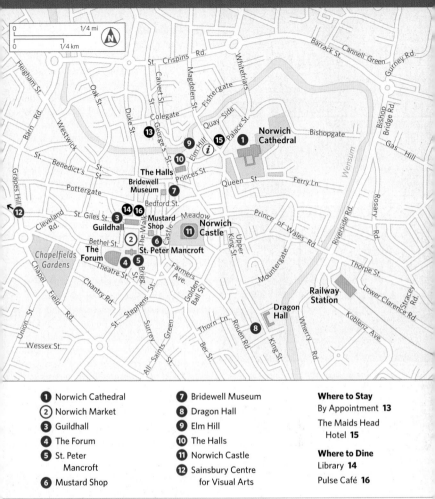

1 Norwich Cathedral
2 Norwich Market
3 Guildhall
4 The Forum
5 St. Peter Mancroft
6 Mustard Shop

7 Bridewell Museum
8 Dragon Hall
9 Elm Hill
10 The Halls
11 Norwich Castle
12 Sainsbury Centre for Visual Arts

Where to Stay
By Appointment 13
The Maids Head Hotel 15

Where to Dine
Library 14
Pulse Café 16

---

3 **Guildhall.** Built between 1407 and 1424, this is the most elaborate city hall outside of London and a reflection of Norwich's power and prominence in the Middle Ages. The checkered-flint building is still in use and not open to visitors. 43a Newmarket Rd.

4 ★ **The Forum.** This aggressively modern building complex, serving as a civic center and housing the Tourist Information Centre and library, was built in 2000 as part of the U.K.'s Millennium celebrations. ⏱ 5 min. Millennium Plain, Bethel St. ☎ 01603/727-920. Free admission. Daily 10am–5:15pm.

5 **St. Peter Mancroft.** Built in the Perpendicular style, Norwich's grandest parish church features a giant east window with medieval stained glass, a hammerbeam roof, and a 15th-century carved font. ⏱ 5 min. The Chantry. ☎ 01603/610-443. Free admission. Daily 8am–7pm.

Getting Around

The central area of Norwich is easily walkable. From the train station you can walk to Norwich cathedral. For visitor information, see p. 403.

> *Perhaps the most famous thing to come out of Norwich, Colman's Mustard is still sold from a museum-shop in the city center.*

❻ Mustard Shop. Housed in an elegant glass-roofed 19th-century shopping arcade, this small museum-shop tells the story of Colman's Mustard, a famous local product since the 19th century, and sells the same. ⏱ 5 min. 15a Royal Arcade. ☎ 01603/627-889. Free admission. Mon–Sat 9:30am–5pm.

❼ Bridewell Museum. In this museum, located in an old merchant's house, historic paraphernalia of all kinds is displayed within reconstructions of Norwich's principal stores and industries. ⏱ 15 min. Bridewell Alley. ☎ 01603/629-127. Admission £3.20 adults, £1.75 kids. Tues–Sat 10am–4:30pm.

❽ ★ Dragon Hall. Europe's only surviving medieval trading hall built by an individual takes its name from the carved dragons that once adorned the massive oak beams in the Great Hall; one of them still survives and is on display. ⏱ 10 min. King St. ☎ 01603/663-922. Admission £5 adults, £4.20 seniors, £3 kids. Mon–Fri 10am–5pm; Sun 11am–4pm.

❾ ★★★ Elm Hill. The city's most picturesque and intact medieval street was an overcrowded slum slated for demolition in the 1950s, but the residents raised such a fuss that Elm Hill was spared. Wander down this narrow cobbled thoroughfare with its crooked half-timbered buildings and you'll be transported back to medieval Norwich—except that today there are cafes and shops to entice the visitor. ⏱ 15 min.

❿ ★ The Halls. Another Elm Hill gem, this series of flint-stone buildings is the most complete medieval friary complex in England, built between 1307 and 1470, and today used for local events; the old cloister now hosts an antiques market. ⏱ 5 min. St. Andrew's Plain. ☎ 01603/628-477. www.standrewshall.co.uk. Free admission. Mon–Sat 10am–5pm.

⓫ ★★ kids Norwich Castle. This hilltop Norman stronghold overlooking the city is a fine example of Anglo-Norman military architecture and today houses a surprisingly interesting local history museum and an art gallery featuring the works of the 19th-century Norwich School of landscape painters. Grisly displays of the punishments meted out to medieval prisoners make the Keep a favorite spot for older kids. ⏱ 1 hr. Market Ave. ☎ 01603/493-636. www.museums.norfolk.gov.uk. Admission £6.60 adults, £4.80 kids. Mon–Fri 10am–4:30pm; Sat 10am–5pm; Sun 10am–5:30pm.

The Norwich 12

It may sound like the name of a gang, but the Norwich 12 is actually a dozen landmark buildings from many different eras of Norwich's long and colorful past. Many of the buildings are included in this itinerary; others are not open to the general public or have been converted to other uses, but you may want to check them out on your stroll through the city. Members of the 12 include the **Assembly House,** a Georgian-era entertainment venue; **St. James Mill,** a yarn factory built during the 1830s industrial revolution; and the Art Deco **City Hall** from the 1930s. You can get a free guide from the tourist office and find more information at **www.norwich12.co.uk.**

12 ★★ **Sainsbury Centre for Visual Arts.**
Works by major English artists such as Henry Moore and Francis Bacon share wall space with works by Picasso, Degas, and other artists from around the globe in this eclectic art collection. It was donated in 1973 by supermarket tycoon Sir Robert Sainsbury to the University of East Anglia and is displayed in a contemporary building designed by Lord Norman Foster (his first major public building) on the university's campus, a 15-minute bus ride from the city center. ⏱ 1 hr. **Earlham Rd., University of East Anglia (3 miles west of city center).** ☎ 01603/593-199. www.scva.org.uk. Free admission. Tues–Sun 10am–5pm. Take bus no. 25 or 35 from Castle Meadow or no. 22 from the train station.

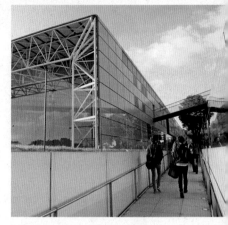

> *The Foster-designed Sainsbury's Centre for Visual Arts houses an eclectic painting collection that includes works by Picasso and Francis Bacon.*

Where to Stay & Dine

★★ **By Appointment** CITY CENTER
This charming and quietly elegant B&B occupies three 15th-century merchant houses and is loaded with creaky-floored charm; its restaurant serves excellent English fare. **25–29 St. George's St.** ☎ 01603/630-730. www.byappointmentnorwich.co.uk. 5 units. Doubles £70–£110 w/breakfast. MC, V.

★ **Library** CITY CENTER *BRASSERIE*
An old library is the setting for this well-liked brasserie with a wood-fired oven and a menu that concentrates on meat and fish. **Guildhall Hill.** ☎ 01603/616-606. Entrees £9–£14. MC, V. Lunch & dinner Mon–Sat, lunch Sun.

★ **The Maids Head Hotel** ELM HILL
England's oldest hotel has been in business since 1287 but features rooms with all the modern comforts you need, plus a cozy, old bar and restaurant. **Tombland.** ☎ 01603/209-955. www.maidsheadhotel.co.uk. 84 units. Doubles £150–£275 w/breakfast. AE, MC, V.

★ **Pulse Café** CITY CENTER *VEGETARIAN*
Housed in the former stables of an old fire station, this funky place offers an international menu of well-prepared vegetarian dishes. **Labour in Vain Yard.** ☎ 01603/765-562. Entrees £6–£10. MC, V. Lunch & dinner daily.

> *The refined interiors at By Appointment feature many antiques.*

Cambridge

Cambridge, which celebrated its 800th anniversary in 2009, is the largest (pop. 111,000) and most important city in East Anglia. To the Romans it was a place to ford the river Cam, and in the Middle Ages it attracted several religious orders, but for visitors today Cambridge is inextricably linked to its famous university, and it's the chance to step into the hallowed confines of a few of its 31 colleges that draws most people. But you can enjoy the city's appealing blend of busy shops, markets, medieval architecture, and riverside meadows (called the Backs) even if you don't visit any of the colleges.

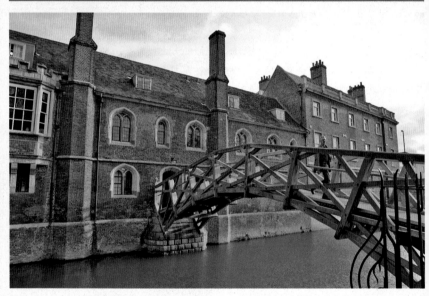

> *The Mathematical Bridge has been rebuilt twice since it was first constructed by architect James Essex in 1749.*

START Cambridge is 55 miles north of London.

❶ ★ **Market Square.** Busy and bustling Market Square sits in the center of Cambridge and is a great place to buy picnic provisions or browse an eclectic array of vendors' stalls. ⏱ 15 min. Mon–Sat 9:30am–4:30pm.

❷ ★★ **Queens' College.** Founded in 1448 and named for Margaret of Anjou (1430–82), the wife of Henry VI, and Elizabeth Woodville (1437–92), wife of Edward IV, the college straddles both banks of the River Cam, which you cross using the famous wooden **Mathematical Bridge,** named for the calculations needed to construct it without nails. Other architectural landmarks at Queens' College include the handsome 15th-century brick **President's Lodge** and the **Tower,** where the great scholar Erasmus (1466–1536) lived from 1510 to 1514. ⏱ 15 min. ☎ 01223/335-511. www. queens.cam.ac.uk. Admission £2.50. Daily mid-Mar to mid-May & July–Oct 10am–4:30pm; Nov to mid-March 2–4pm (call to verify).

1. Market Square
2. Queens' College
3. The Eagle
4. King's College
5. Trinity College
6. St. John's College
7. Jesus College
8. Kettle's Yard
9. The Fitzwilliam Museum
10. Scott Polar Research Institute

Where to Stay

De Vere University Arms 11

Hotel du Vin & Bistro 14

Where to Dine

The Anchor 13

Auntie's 12

Victoria Bridge

Chesterton Rd.

Jesus Green

Cam

0   200 m
0   200 yds

Castle Mound

Magdalene College

Kettle's Yard **8**

Park Parade

Midsummer Common

School of Pythagoras

Magdalen St.

Bridge St.

Portugal Pl.

Round Church St.

Park St.

Wesley House

Jesus College **7**

Victoria Ave.

Butts Green

St. John's College **6**

Bridge of Sighs

St. John's Bridge

Trinity Bridge

Jesus Lane

Maids Causeway

The Backs

Trinity College **5**

St. John's St.

Green St.

Sidney Sussex College

Sidney St.

Malcolm St.

Hobson St.

King St.

Willow Walk

New Sq.   Fitzroy St.

Garret Hostel Bridge

Market St.

Market Square **1**

Trinity St.

Clare Bridge

King's College Chapel

12

Petty Cury

St. Andrews St.

Christ's College

Christ's Pieces

Emmanuel Rd.

Clarendon St.

Eden St.

City Rd.

King's Bridge

King's College **4**

King's Parade

Benet St.

3

Corn Exchange

Drummer St.

Parker St.

Melbourne Pl.

Adam & Eve St.

East Rd.

Cam

Queen's Bridge

Queens' College **2**

13

Corpus Christi College

St. Catherine's College

Pembroke St.

Downing St.

Sedgwick Museum

Emmanuel St.

Emmanuel College

Park Terrace

11

Parkside

Peter's Field

Mill Rd.

Silver St.

Mill Ln.

Mathematical Bridge

Pembroke College

Downing Pl.

Parker's Piece

Gonville Pl.

Little St. Mary's Lane

Peterhouse College

Trumpington St.

Tennis Court Rd.

Downing College

Regent St.

Coe Fen

The Fitzwilliam Museum **9**

Hills Rd.

Gresham Rd.

Harvey Rd.

St. Paul's Rd.

Sheeps Green

The Fen Causeway

Lensfield Rd.

Scott Polar Research Institute **10**

To Railway Station

> The BBC broadcasts a famous carol concert each Christmas Eve from the magnificent Gothic surrounds of King's College Chapel.

The Voices of Evensong

The Evening Prayer service known as Evensong is a wonderful way to experience an ancient musical tradition in a magnificent setting. Held in the late afternoon or early evening in Anglican cathedrals and old university chapels throughout Britain, Evensong combines prayers, hymns, and readings from the Bible in a liturgical service that dates back to the 16th century, when the vespers and complines once sung by Catholic monks were refashioned for use by the Church of England. As the organ plays, the choir, led by priests, proceeds into the choir area and the half-hour service begins. Evensong always includes two canticles (hymns that celebrate the incarnation of Christ) sung by the priests and the choir. At the end of the service there is generally a hymn sung by the entire congregation. Listening to the ethereal voices of a choir singing Evensong is a wonderful way to end a day of sightseeing. The sung service is usually held 6 days a week and is free and open to the public.

③ 🍺 **The Eagle.** If you're thirsty, stop in for a pint of ale, a soft drink, or a cup of coffee at this pub-restaurant where airmen gathered during World War II and carved their names into the darkened ceiling of the back room. Benet St. ☎ 01223/505-020). Snacks £4–£8.

Getting Around

Cambridge is an easily walkable city. From the train station, located about 1 mile south of the city center, you can walk or take bus Citi 1, Citi 3, or Citi 7 (or a taxi) to Market Square.

④ ★★★ **King's College.** Founded by Henry VI (1421–71) in 1441, King's is noteworthy for its extraordinarily beautiful Gothic ★★★ **chapel** with its magnificent fan vaulting, stained-glass windows, Rubens's painting *The Adoration of the Magi,* and famous boys' choir. For a special experience, attend the sung Evensong service. 🕐 30 min. King's Parade. ☎ 01223/331-100. www.kings.cam.ac.uk. Admission £5 adults, £3.50 seniors & kids. During term Mon–Sat 9:30am–3:30pm (Sat until 3:15pm), Sun 1:15–2:15pm; Evensong Mon–Sat 5:30pm, Sun 10:30am & 3:30pm. Out of term Mon–Sat 9:30am–4:30pm; Sun 10am–5pm. Call to verify times; chapel closed Dec 26–Jan 1.

⑤ ★★★ **Trinity College.** The largest and wealthiest of Cambridge's colleges, Trinity was founded by Henry VIII (1491–1547) in 1546 and has produced 32 Nobel Laureates. Its long list of distinguished alumni includes Sir Isaac Newton, Lord Tennyson, Lord Byron, John Dryden, and Bertrand Russell. At just under 1 hectare (2 acres) in area, the **Great Court** is the largest enclosed courtyard in

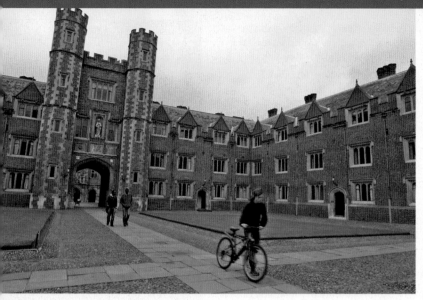

> *Students flock to the colleges of Cambridge University, often ranked by many as the best educational institution in the world.*

Europe. Pass through the hall at the west end of the court to **Nevile's Cloister** (where Sir Isaac Newton first calculated the speed of sound) and the impressive **Wren Library,** designed by Sir Christopher Wren (who also designed many of the furnishings in the library) and home to a treasure trove of priceless manuscripts. ⏰ 15 min. Trinity St. ☎ 01223/338-400. Admission to college £3; free admission to library. Daily 10am–5pm. Closed during exams, 1 week in June, all of Sept. Library: Mon–Fri noon–2pm; Sat 10:30am–12:30pm.

6 ★ **St. John's College.** A replica of Venice's Bridge of Sighs joins the **New Court,** a 19th-century neo-Gothic architectural fantasy of pinnacles and towers, with the older, authentically Tudor section of the college, founded by Lady Margaret Beaufort (1443–1509), the mother of Henry VII, in 1511. ⏰ 10 min. St. John's St. ☎ 01223/338-600. Admission £2.80 adults, £1.70 seniors & kids. Mar–Oct daily 10am–5:30pm; Nov & Feb Sat–Sun 10am–5:30pm.

7 ★ **Jesus College.** Founded in 1492 on the site of a nunnery, this college has some fine medieval buildings and a chapel enlivened by stained-glass windows designed by Edward Burne-Jones (1833–98) and a ceiling by

William Morris (1834–96); both were leaders in the 19th-century English Arts and Crafts Movement. The college has unpredictable opening hours, but you can admire the chapel during Evensong on Tuesday, Thursday, and Saturday at 6:30pm. ⏰ 10 min. Jesus Lane. ☎ 01223/339-339. Free admission. Call to verify opening times.

8 ★★ **Kettle's Yard.** This collection of artwork, furniture, and decorative objects is displayed in the former home of Jim Ede (1895–1990), an influential curator at the Tate (p. 58, **7**) during the 1920s and 1930s. Paintings by Ben Nicholson, Christopher Wood, and Alfred Wallis, and sculptures by Henry Moore, Henri Gaudier-Brzeska, Constantin Brâncuși, and Barbara Hepworth are on display. ⏰ At

least 30 min. Castle St. ☎ 01223/748-100. www.
kettlesyard.co.uk. Free admission. Tues–Sun
1:30–4:30pm (2–4pm in winter).

❾ ★★★ The Fitzwilliam Museum. This eclectic
treasure house shows off a horde of Egyptian
and Greek antiquities, Chinese jades and
bronzes, and the first draft of Keats's "Ode to a
Nightingale," as well as china, glass, majolica,
silver, and clocks. Its painting collection ranges
from medieval and Renaissance works to contemporary canvases and includes Titian's
Tarquin and Lucretia, Rubens's *The Death of Hip-
polytus,* etchings by Van Dyck, rare Hogarths,
and 25 Turners, as well as works by William
Blake, the Impressionists, and the more recent
artists Paul Nash and Sir Stanley Spencer. ⏱ At
least 1 hr. Trumpington St. ☎ 01223/332-900.
www.fitzmuseum.cam.ac.uk. Free admission.
Tues–Sat 10am–5pm; Sun 2:15–5pm.

❿ ★ Scott Polar Research Institute. One of
Cambridge's hidden gems of historical memo-
rabilia commemorates explorer Sir Robert
Falcon Scott (1868–1912) and his team, who
died at the South Pole in 1912. The gear, pho-
tos, and diaries of the doomed expedition are
haunting and fascinating. ⏱ 30 min. Lensfield
Rd. ☎ 01223/336-540. www.spri.cam.ac.uk.
Free admission. Tues–Fri 11am–1pm & 2–4pm;
Sat noon–4pm.

Punting on the Cam

Punting, or pole-boating, is a Cambridge
tradition and a fun experience that gives
you a special look at the river Cam and the
Backs. **Scudamore's Punting Company**
(☎ 01223/359-750; www.scudamores.
com) rents punts for £16 to £18 per hour
plus a refundable deposit, and offers
"chauffeured" punting tours of the college Backs. Punts are available at the **Mill
Lane punting station,** next to Silver Street
bridge; **Jesus Green,** near the Chesterton
Foot Bridge; **Magdalene Bridge;** and the
Main Boatyard, Mill Lane.

Where to Stay & Dine

★ The Anchor CITY CENTER *PUB*
Looking out on a raft of punts and the willow-
fringed river from a position opposite Queens'
College, the Anchor is loaded with atmo-
sphere and serves such traditional homemade
English pub grub as battered cod and lamb-
and-vegetable or leek-and-potato pies. Silver
St. ☎ 01223/353-554. Entrees £5–£11. MC, V.
Lunch & dinner Mon–Sat, Sun lunch.

★ Auntie's CITY CENTER *TEAROOM*
This tearoom is as much a tradition as the
nearby market. It dispenses sandwiches, soups,
full English breakfasts, teas, and pastries to an
interesting mix of town and gown. 1 St. Mary's
Passage, off Market Sq. ☎ 01223/315-641. Entrees
£5–£8. MC, V. Breakfast, lunch & dinner daily.

★★ De Vere University Arms CITY CENTER
This appealing hotel lies behind an unappeal-
ing modern entrance. The best guest rooms
are the high-ceilinged ones in the original
Victorian wing, but all accommodations are
comfortable and have well-equipped modern
bathrooms. Regent St. ☎ 01223/351-241. www.
devere.co.uk. Doubles £85–£170 w/breakfast.
AE, DC, MC, V.

★★★ Hotel du Vin & Bistro CITY CENTER
Located just down the street from the
Fitzwilliam Museum, Hotel du Vin offers
stylish accommodations and an excellent on-
site bistro. Trumpington St. ☎ 01223/227-330.
www.hotelduvin.com. Doubles £145–£220. AE,
MC, V.

Fast Facts

Arriving & Getting Around

BY AIR London (p. 137) is the closest and most convenient international hub. **Norwich International Airport** (☎ 0844/748-0112, www.norwichinternational.com) is 4 miles north of town and serves some European and U.K. destinations. **BY TRAIN** The major cities and larger towns in East Anglia can be easily reached by train from London, with stations that are either in or close to the centers. Trains depart from King's Cross Station for the 45-minute trip to Cambridge and the 70-minute trip to Ely; from Liverpool Street Station for the 2-hour trip to Norwich. For more information and schedules, call **National Rail Enquiries** (☎ 08457/484-950; www.nationalrail.co.uk). You can also get from one city to another within the region from the major railway hubs of Cambridge, Norwich, and Ely. **BY BUS** Departing from London's Victoria Coach Station, buses operated by **National Express** (☎ 08705/808-080; www.national express.com) serve all the cities and major towns in East Anglia. On the plus side, bus fares are cheaper than train fares; on the negative side, buses take much longer to reach the destination, making it difficult to follow a limited-time itinerary. **BY CAR** A car is the best way to see the region. You can easily rent a car in London or Cambridge, East Anglia's major city. If you drive, you'll need a detailed road atlas: the best are the large-format maps produced by the Automobile Association (AA), Collins, Ordnance Survey, and Royal Automobile Club (RAC). In some cities you cannot park in the center of town; look for "Park and Pay" signs to guide you to the closest lot.

Emergencies

To call for emergency help in England, dial ☎ 999 or ☎ 112; these are free calls from public phones. In Cambridge, you can contact the local police department at ☎ 01223/358-966.

If you have a medical emergency, ask your concierge or B&B proprietor for help in locating a doctor. **CAMBRIDGE** You can get medical assistance at **Addenbrooke's Hospital,** Hills Rd. (☎ 01223/245-151). **NORWICH** Go to **Norfolk & Norwich University Hospital,** Colney Lane (☎ 01603/286-286).

Internet Access

Wi-Fi or dial-up Internet service is available in hotels throughout East Anglia, either in-room or at a computer reserved for guests; you may not find Internet access at smaller B&Bs. **CAMBRIDGE Jaffa Internet Café,** 22 Mill Rd. (☎ 01223/308-180), is open daily 9am to 11pm. **NORWICH Battlenet,** 2a Queens Rd. (☎ 01603/765-595), is open 11am to 9pm.

Pharmacies

CAMBRIDGE At 28 Petty Cury (☎ 01223/350-213). **NORWICH** There's a Boots pharmacy at 19 Castle Mail (☎ 01603/767-970).

Post Office

You'll find them in every city and small town, identified by a red box labeled ROYAL MAIL. **CAMBRIDGE** The post office is at 9–11 St. Andrew St. (☎ 0871/266-8006). **NORWICH** At 84–85 Castle Mall (☎ 01603/761-635).

Visitor Information

The local tourist offices are your best sources for information and will also book accommodations; check the websites for the most up-to-date hours of operation. **BURY ST. EDMUNDS** Tourist Information Centre, 6 Angel Hill (☎ 01284/757-630; www.stedmundsbury.gov.uk). **COLCHESTER** Visit Colchester Information Centre, 1 Queen St. (☎ 01206/282-920; www.visitcolchester.com). **ELY** Ely & East Cambridgeshire Tourist Information Centre, Oliver Cromwell's House, 29 St. Mary's St. (☎ 01353/662-062; http://visitely.east cambs.gov.uk). **IPSWICH** Tourist Information Centre, St. Stephen's Church, St. Stephen's Lane (☎ 01473/258-070; www.visit-ipswich.com). **KING'S LYNN** Tourist Information Centre, Custom House, Purfleet Quay (☎ 01553/783-044; www.visitwestnorfolk.com). **LAVENHAM** Tourist Information Centre, Lady St. (☎ 01787/248-207; www.discoverlavenham.co.uk). **NORWICH** Tourist Information Centre, the Forum, Millennium Plain (☎ 01603/213-999; www.visitnorwich.co.uk).

For region-wide information, you can contact the **East of England Tourist Board** in Bury St. Edmunds (☎ 01284/727-470; www.visit eastofengland.com).

The Northwest & the Lake District

Favorite Northwest Moments

Not many parts of England are as beautiful as the Northwest, and not many are as evocative of the nation's 19th-century industrial might. You'll experience these extremes as you wander from gritty but fascinating Liverpool and bustling Manchester into the bucolic Lake District, rubbing elbows with Roman centurions, the Beatles, Victorians, and Romantic poets as you go.

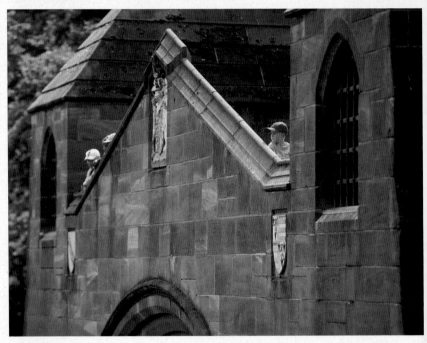

> *PREVIOUS PAGE The panoramas of the Lake District, like here at Derwentwater, inspired a whole generation of English Romantic poets. THIS PAGE The walls enclosing Chester are the most extensive in Britain.*

❶ Walking atop the Roman walls in Chester.
Not only do the sturdy fortifications commemorate the legionnaires who were stationed out here at the far reaches of the Empire, but also Saxons, Normans, Tudors, and all the others who shored up the old stones as they came and went from Chester over the millennia. **See p. 430, ❺**.

❷ Seeing the bright lights of Blackpool.
The north's favorite seaside getaway looks its garish best during the famous autumn Illuminations, but with amusement piers, roller coasters, a neon-etched tower, and all sorts of other attractions, this 7 miles of coastline washed by the Irish Sea puts on a pretty good show any time. **See p. 417, ❹**.

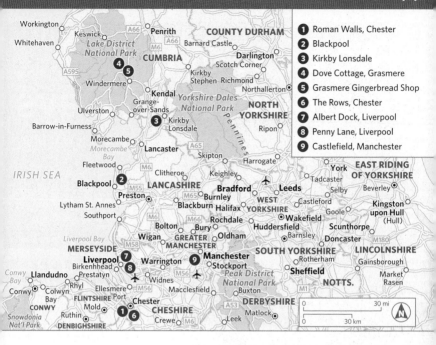

1. Roman Walls, Chester
2. Blackpool
3. Kirkby Lonsdale
4. Dove Cottage, Grasmere
5. Grasmere Gingerbread Shop
6. The Rows, Chester
7. Albert Dock, Liverpool
8. Penny Lane, Liverpool
9. Castlefield, Manchester

3 Taking in the Northwest's quiet beauty in Kirkby Lonsdale. A hilltop behind St. Mary's Church is the perfect perch from which to admire the placid valley of the River Lune, a scene that has inspired John Ruskin, J. M. W. Turner, and legions of unknown painters and photographers. See p. 419, 8.

4 Getting into the spirit of William Wordsworth at Dove Cottage. Plenty of places in the Lake District evoke the famous Romantic poet, but none are as moving as this simple cottage. He considered the village to be the "loveliest spot that man hath ever known," and wrote his now-famous works in front of the cottage's hearth and while pacing the garden. See p. 425, 6.

5 Stocking up on sweets at the Grasmere Gingerbread Shop. You can't live on natural beauty and poetry alone, so duck into a converted 17th-century schoolhouse for another Lake District specialty, an unforgettable treat made from a 150-year-old recipe. See p. 425, 7.

6 Shopping in the Rows in Chester. It's not what's on offer that matters—a trip to the mall

will never seem the same after you experience the half-timbered ambience of these long, shop-lined galleries dating to the Middle Ages. See p. 428, 1.

7 Exploring Liverpool's maritime history at Albert Dock. The wharves that once bustled with the commerce that made Liverpool one of the world's richest ports are a magnificent swath of brick and iron, evoking a colorful maritime past that comes alive at the Merseyside Maritime Museum. See p. 434, 1.

8 Remembering the Beatles in Liverpool. The Fab Four make an appearance all over the city, but the best ways to find them are on a memory-filled tour of their childhood homes, as well as Penny Lane and the other local sights they immortalized in their songs. See p. 437, 12.

9 Following the canals through Castlefield in Manchester. The warehouses, factories, docks, and locks look a lot spiffier than they did 150 years ago, but the old neighborhood still evokes the age when smoggy Manchester fueled the Industrial Revolution. See p. 443, 7.

The Best of the Northwest in 3 Days

Three days allows just enough time for a brief but rewarding foray into the Northwest. You can see Roman ruins in Chester, remnants of England's 19th-century industrial heritage and gleaming modern urbanity in Manchester, and the craggy peaks and deep, still waters of the Lake District that inspired William Wordsworth and other poets. Travel lightly and bring a good pair of walking shoes, as you'll be using various modes of transport and following some of England's most celebrated walking paths.

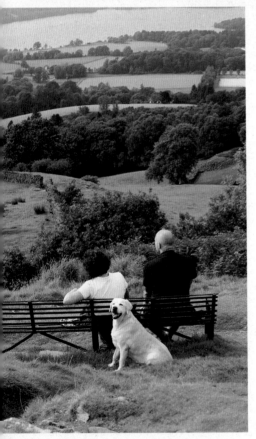

> Admiring the view, as here at Orrest Head, is one of the great pleasures of the English Lake District.

START **Chester, 205 miles northwest of London. Trains from London's Euston Station run about every 30 min.; the trip takes about 2 hr.**

❶ **Chester.** Your first stop will be this city where Romans established a fort, Deva Victrix, in A.D. 79. The outpost became one of the largest garrisons in Roman Britain, and the legions enclosed their camp within thick walls to keep out local tribes who greeted them with a less-than-friendly welcome. Saxons, Normans, and other inhabitants shored up the fortifications many times over the centuries, and Chester is still surrounded by Britain's longest and most intact circuit of **city walls.**

Part of your time in Chester will be spent following the footsteps of the legions, beginning at the **Chester Cross,** a medieval monument that marks the intersection of four Roman roads. The surrounding streets are lined with the half-timbered **Rows** (p. 428, ❶), an extraordinary, multilevel 13th-century shopping arcade that has been embellished many times over intervening centuries. Medieval **Chester Cathedral** (p. 429, ❸) is just to the north, tucked next to the walls; if you want some enlightenment and entertainment as you walk the 2-mile circuit, join a tour of the **Roman Walls** (p. 430, ❺) and other historic remnants, led by gladiators and

1 Chester
2 Manchester
3 The Lake District

other authentically clad Romans. To the south, the walls skirt the banks of the River Dee and pass the ruins of one of the largest **Roman amphitheaters** in Britain, an arena for military assemblies and gladiatorial contests (p. 431, 6). Helmets and other artifacts the soldiers left behind in this remote outpost of the Empire are preserved in the **Grosvenor Museum** (p. 428, 2). ⏱ 1 day. See p. 428.

Take a late-afternoon train to Manchester (a direct train runs as often as every 15 min.); the trip takes a little over 1 hr.

2 **Manchester.** An early evening arrival puts you in Manchester in time for a stroll through the city center, where Victorian and Edwardian landmarks are overshadowed by gleaming new office towers—showing off Manchester's prominence at the epicenter of the Industrial Revolution as well as the vibrant urban revival that is transforming the city in the wake of a devastating IRA bombing in 1996. The Gothic Revival-style **Town Hall** (p. 440, 1) is the proud emblem of Manchester's 19th-century might, though the city's industrial barons were savvy enough to turn a blind eye to the cynical murals that decorate the cavernous interior; depictions of an inventor of machinery fleeing

> *The Rows, in Chester, has been a popular shopping spot for over 700 years.*

from an angry mob and other scenes remind us that life for most of the 2 million working stiffs of so-called "Cottonopolis" was less than idyllic. The cotton mills and warehouses that once fueled the economy still line the lanes and canal-side quays of Chinatown and **Gay Village** (p. 444), though these days the sweat shops have given way to some of the city's liveliest nighttime scenes.

> *Manchester is the most prosperous city in the north of England and a major commercial center.*

Your wanderings on Day 2 won't take you too far afield from the city center. Begin at the **Manchester Art Gallery** (p. 441, **②**), housing one of Britain's finest collections of paintings and decorative arts, and from there set out for **Chetham's Library** (p. 442, **④**), the oldest library in the English-speaking world; **Manchester Cathedral** (p. 442, **⑤**), a sturdy remnant of the medieval city; and the **National Football Museum** (p. 442, **⑥**), a stunningly modern shrine to England's favorite pastime.

Manchester's prominence at the forefront of the 19th-century Industrial Revolution is much in evidence just south of the city center in **Castlefield** (p. 443, **⑦**), where canals and massive brick warehouses are preserved as an Urban Heritage Park. The world's first railway station now houses the **Museum of Science and Industry** (p. 443, **⑧**), filled with huge

turbines and other vestiges of the city's industrial past. ⏱ 1 day. See p. 440.

In the late afternoon of Day 2, take a train to Windermere (1 hr. 40 min.); the trains run hourly and the trip usually requires a change in Preston.

③ Lake District. Within an hour of leaving Manchester and the city's many vestiges of human enterprise, you will find yourself surrounded by a bounty of natural beauty. The compact Lake District is crammed with some of England's most spectacular scenery—craggy peaks, bracken-covered hillsides, and shimmering waters carved out by glaciers eons ago. Poets have been raving about the region for centuries, and paying homage at the haunts of the most beloved of them, William Wordsworth (1770–1850), is one of the

Industrialists and Romantics

To paraphrase Charles Dickens, the great chronicler of English life, the 19th century was the best of times and the worst of times for the Northwest of England. The Industrial Revolution was in full swing, and a system of canals, railroads, factories, and steam-powered machinery made the region the world's first great industrial hub. Fueling the enormous economic growth was the working class, who in Manchester and other smoggy, overcrowded cities worked 6 days a week and lived in squalid, unsanitary tenements. Their fate inspired Mark Twain to comment that he wanted to live in Manchester when he grew old because the transition to death would be unnoticeable; the conditions of the working classes also gave rise to trade unions and the works of the great 20th-century champions of workers, Karl Marx and Friedrich Engels, both of whom at one point lived in Manchester. Meanwhile, some 50 miles north amid the spectacular natural beauty of the Lake District, William Wordsworth and Samuel Taylor Coleridge were ushering in the age of English Romantic poetry, celebrating nature, beauty, and a return to innocence—all of which the Industrial Revolution was destroying at a terrifying pace. You will experience both extremes as you tour the Northwest.

> *Many of the most picturesque lakes in the Lake District offer organized sightseeing boat trips.*

pleasures of being in what he considered to be the "loveliest spot that man hath ever known."

You'll arrive in **Windermere and Bowness-on-Windermere** (p. 420, ❶), adjoining towns on Lake Windermere that have been the gateway to the Lake District ever since the railroad reached the region in the mid–19th century. The beauty of the surroundings will greet you like a clap on the back as soon as you find your way to the shores of Lake Windermere, England's largest, backed by the 239m (784-ft.) summit of Orrest Head; time permitting, make the easy walk to the top for memorable views of the lake, lakeshore villages, and surrounding hills.

Begin Day 3 with a cruise and walk by boarding a lake steamer in Windermere for Wray's Castle. From there, follow the beautiful lakeside path about 3½ miles to Far Sawrey and take the launch back to Bowness. William Wordsworth made the same crossing regularly when he was a schoolboy back in the late 18th century, and the 10-minute trip sets the tone for a Wordsworth pilgrimage in the afternoon.

Board a bus for the short ride north to **Grasmere** (p. 425, ❻), the pretty village of slate-roofed houses on Lake Grasmere where William Wordsworth spent most of his adult life. You can step into cramped little Dove Cottage, where the poet lived with his growing family and entertained fellow poet Samuel Taylor Coleridge and other guests, and then pore over original manuscripts and other memorabilia in the nearby Wordsworth Museum.

Fortify yourself with a piece of gingerbread or Kendal Mint Cake at the **Grasmere Gingerbread House** (p. 425, ❼) for the easy walk of about 2 miles through the bracken-covered hills to **Rydal Mount** (p. 424, ❺), where Wordsworth moved his family in 1813 and died in 1850. His attic study, flagstone-floored dining room, drawing room, and several bedrooms attest to a comfortable domestic life—proof, if you choose to look at it this way, that the artistic temperament can accommodate a bourgeois comfort or two. A country walk of another 2 miles brings you to Ambleside, where you can board a steamer and rest your feet for the half-hour cruise down the lake back to Windermere. ⏱ 1 day. See p. 420.

The Northwest in 1 Week

You can see the many sides of the Northwest in a week, from Roman walls in Chester and modern towers in Manchester to solid-brick 19th-century warehouses and docks in Liverpool and bracken-covered hillsides in the Lake District. Driving is the easiest way to cover the terrain, but distances are short, so you'll have plenty to time to explore stops on the route and discover that each has a distinct character that provides a rewarding glimpse into English life.

> The Albert Dock was the source of Liverpool's wealth—and is now the area where the city's regeneration is most apparent.

START Chester. From London, head north on the M1 and get onto the M6 near Coventry; follow that to the A54, which leads west to Chester. Allow about half a day for the drive of 205 miles. Alternatively, you might choose to take the train to Chester and rent a car there (though London rentals would be cheaper). If your travels in England are confined to the north, you can fly directly into Manchester and head from there to Chester.

1 Chester. Arrive in time to spend at least half a day and evening exploring this pleasant city, where you'll step through the ages, from the Roman occupation through the Middle Ages to the Tudor and Victorian eras. Britain's largest circuit of city walls, a Roman amphitheater, a medieval cathedral, and a wealth of half-timbered landmarks bear witness to these many centuries. So do a number of historic pubs where you may choose to begin and end the evening. ⊕ Half-day. See p. 428.

1 Chester
2 Liverpool
3 Manchester
4 Northwest Coast
5 The Lake District

On Day 2, drive 21 miles (40 min.) northeast to Liverpool on the M53 and A41.

2 Liverpool. You will have almost the full day to explore this famous old port city on the River Mersey. Begin your tour on the banks of the wide river, where from the 18th to mid–20th centuries wharfs bustled with commerce that made Liverpool one of the most important ports in the world. **Albert Dock** (p. 434, **1**), a miracle of 19th-century engineering, evokes this maritime past in restored brick, waterside warehouses that are the atmospheric setting for the **Merseyside Maritime Museum** (p. 434, **2**), the **International Slavery Museum** (p. 435, **3**), and the **Tate Liverpool** (p. 435, **4**). Farther north along the river are three other architectural landmarks of maritime Liverpool, a trio of handsome early-20th-century commercial buildings known as the **Three Graces** (p. 436, **6**).

Your next stops are inland. Follow Victoria Street through the city center to a formidable swath of municipal buildings on William Brown Street. Here, surrounded by fountains and statues, are the **Walker Art Gallery** (p. 436, **8**), where you can wander through galleries lined with European masterpieces,

> The half-timbered Rows meet at Chester Cross, the exact point at which the four streets of the old Roman city met.

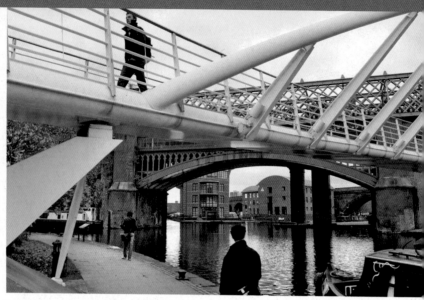

> *The quiet canals of Castlefield, in Manchester, were the arteries of the Industrial Revolution in the 19th century.*

and **World Museum Liverpool** (p. 436, **9**), a vast collection devoted to the natural world.

You can encounter Liverpool's greatest phenomenon of the 20th century, the Beatles, on a tour to the **childhood homes** (p. 437, **12**) of John Lennon and Paul McCartney or on a bus tour (p. 438). Then witness the city's determination to demonstrate its faith in two extravagant and extraordinary houses of worship, the futuristic **Roman Catholic Metropolitan Cathedral of Christ the King** (p. 437, **10**) and the vast, faux-Gothic **Anglican Cathedral Church of Christ** (p. 437, **11**); from the tower of the latter you can enjoy views over Liverpool, the Mersey, and the Welsh Hills. End the day paying homage to the Beatles in the **Cavern Club** (p. 438), where the Fab Four got their start. ⏱ 1 day. See p. 434.

On the morning of Day 3, drive 40 miles (40 min.) east on the M62 to

3 **Manchester.** Check into your hotel and spend the rest of Day 3 exploring another industrial city that fueled England's 19th-century commercial wealth, following the route set out on p. 409, **2**. Devote Day 4 to seeing a bit more of Manchester. First, head just south of the city to the campus of the University of Manchester to see two unexpected gems: the **Whitworth Art Gallery** (p. 443, **9**), with an outstanding collection of watercolors by British artists, and the **John Rylands Library** (p. 443, **10**), home of some of the world's rarest manuscripts.

The **Salford Quays** (p. 444, **11**), Manchester's docklands, is the setting for the **Imperial War Museum North** (p. 444, **12**) and the **Lowry** (p. 444, **11**), a visual and performing arts center; the nearby **Old Trafford Museum** (p. 446, **13**) commemorates one of the world's most famous soccer teams, Manchester United. ⏱ 2 days. See p. 440.

Begin Day 5 by following the M66 and A56 to Clitheroe; the 33-mile drive will take about 50 min.

4 **Northwest Coast.** On Day 5 you'll make the trip up to the Lake District, but take the trip slowly and explore some out-of-the-way backcountry following the drive laid out in "Off the Beaten Path in the Northwest" (p. 416). The route will take you through two quiet villages in the foothills of the Pennines, **Clitheroe** (p. 416, **1**) and **Slaidburn** (p. 416, **2**), then on to **Ribchester** (p. 417, **3**), a former Roman outpost. Just down the road, an entirely different sort of experience awaits you in **Blackpool** (p. 417, **4**), the resort on the Irish Sea where factory workers of the industrial north once enjoyed their vacations. It's not the Caribbean, but a good-time atmosphere still fills the salt air on the amusement piers and seaside promenades. The route next takes you to **Lancaster** (p. 418, **5**), the quiet capital of Lancashire that gave rise to the Tudor Dynasty, then **Carnforth** (p. 418, **6**), a little village with a railway station that film buffs will recognize from the film *Brief Encounter*. Once you reach **Kirkby Lonsdale** (p. 419, **8**), you'll be in the southern reaches of the Lake District. ⏱ 1 day.

Drive 21 miles (40 min.) northwest from Kirkby Lonsdale to Windermere on the A65 and A591 and settle in for two nights. Start driving well before nightfall so you don't have to negotiate country roads in the dark.

5 Lake District. On Day 6, begin your wanderings through the region as visitors have for centuries, in **Windermere and Bowness-on-Windermere** (p. 420, **1**), two adjoining towns above 11-mile-long Lake Windermere. Then set out to see more of the region, making the short crossing to the west side of the lake on the **Windermere Ferry** (p. 424) and continuing to **Hawkshead** (p. 422, **2**) to encounter two of the region's most famous inhabitants. William Wordsworth attended the **Old**

> *Poet William Wordsworth lived at Rydal Mount for 37 years, until his death in 1850.*

Grammar School in Hawkshead (where you can still see his desk) between 1779 and 1787, and Beatrix Potter (1866–1943), creator of *The Tale of Peter Rabbit* and other children's classics, settled at **Hill Top** just outside of town. You can visit her home, then see the sketches and watercolors she did for her books in town, in the **Beatrix Potter Gallery.**

A short drive west brings you to **Coniston** (p. 423, **3**), where you can sail across the lake on the steam yacht *Gondola,* a Victorian-era pleasure craft, and visit **Brantwood** (p. 423, **4**), home of another famous Lake District resident—poet, art and architecture critic, social reformer, and artist John Ruskin.

Devote the rest of the day to Wordsworth, visiting **Dove Cottage,** where he began raising his family; **Rydal Mount** (p. 424, **5**), the comfortable lakeside manor where he spent the last 35 years of his life; and the **Wordsworth Museum.**

Day 7 takes you into the northern reaches of the Lake District, first to **Keswick** (p. 425, **8**) and nearby **Castlerigg Stone Circle,** one of the most impressive prehistoric sites in England and beautifully set amid rolling green countryside. The final Lake District stop is **Ullswater** (p. 426, **9**), surrounded by vast tracts of unspoiled countryside. After the 3-mile hike to **Aira Force waterfall,** board the **Ullswater Steamers,** which sails the length of the lake from Glenridding. The trip takes a little over an hour, though many walkers get off at Howtown and follow the lakeside to Pooley Bridge, and return by boat to Glenridding. ⏱ 2 days. See p. 420.

The Lake District National Park

Much of the Lake District, 885 sq. miles, is protected as the **Lake District National Park.** Britain's largest national park, and certainly one of its most popular, encompasses England's highest mountain, **Scafell Peak;** deepest lake, **Wastwater;** and the beautiful landscapes that inspired William Wordsworth and Beatrix Potter. The **Lake District Visitor Centre** at Brockhole, 2 miles north of Windermere off the A591 (☎ 015394/46601; www.lakedistrict.gov. uk), is an attraction in itself. A mansion with terraced gardens on the shores of Lake Windermere, it is filled with exhibits on the history, geography, wildlife, and people of the Lake District, and provides extensive information on touring the region. The center is the starting point for many walks (some guided) and the launching point for kayaking and canoeing.

Off the Beaten Path in the Northwest

Moorlands, green Pennine Mountain foothills, and lush valleys will provide a welcome change of scenery from the industrial and commercial cities you've been visiting elsewhere in the Northwest, along with a breath of fresh air. Not all the attractions are natural, though—this leisurely drive takes you through several old villages and meets the sea at Blackpool, a lively resort since Victorian times. It makes for a great scenic day of driving if you're traveling north from Manchester to the Lake District.

> *The famous "hole in the wall" at Clitheroe Castle dates to a 1649 siege during the English Civil War.*

START Clitheroe, 33 miles north of Manchester via the M66 and A56. **TRIP LENGTH** 72 miles.

❶ ★ Clitheroe. This small village nestled in the Ribble Valley amid the rolling foothills of the Pennines makes two claims to fame. Clitheroe is said to be the village closest to the geographic center of Britain, and its 12th-century Norman castle has a gaping hole in one of its sides—said to have been created when the devil threw a large stone from Pendle Hill on the east side of town, but actually inflicted by Commonwealth troops in 1649

during the Civil War, when the keep sheltered Royalist troops. ⏱ 15 min.

Follow the B6478 north for 9 miles to

❷ ★★ Slaidburn. The moors and fells of the Forest of Bowland run right to the edge of quiet little Slaidburn. Stone weavers' cottages surround the 15th-century **Church of St. Andrew** (☎ 01200/446-238; free admission), a Perpendicular building with some fine interior details, and the **Hark to Bounty Inn** (www.harktobounty.co.uk). The inn was known

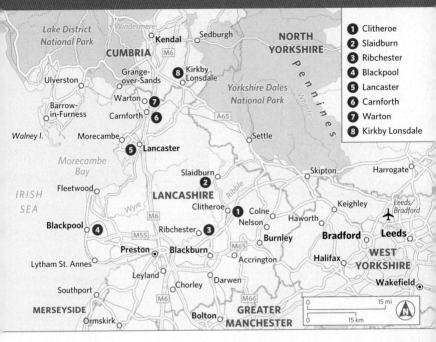

1. Clitheroe
2. Slaidburn
3. Ribchester
4. Blackpool
5. Lancaster
6. Carnforth
7. Warton
8. Kirkby Lonsdale

as the Dog until 1875, when the local rector stepped in for a drink, leaving his hounds outside. The pack began to bray, and the rector's favorite made himself most heard, to which he cried out, "Hark to Bounty." A well-marked path from the village makes an easy 4-mile circuit across the surrounding moors and fields, where great outcroppings of limestone burst through the grasses and wildflowers. ⏲ 30 min., including a short walk.

Backtrack 1 mile south to Newton, and then head south 10 miles on marked but unnumbered roads through Dunsop Bridge and Whitewell to

❸ ★★ **Ribchester.** The local Roman presence is much in evidence around Ribchester, where Bremetennacum, a fort from A.D. 79, once stood sentinel over the surrounding lands and a settlement grew up around it. Scant remains, including baths and a granary, have been excavated, and coins and other finds are in the **Ribchester Roman Museum,** Riverside (☎ 01245/878-261; www.ribchesterroman museum.org; £3 adults, £1.50 kids 6–16). The showiest artifacts from Bremetennacum are in the British Museum (p. 68) in London, where they are displayed as the Ribchester Hoard: a

two-piece parade helmet and other metalwork discovered by a schoolboy in 1796, after being placed beneath a barracks floor for storage some 16 centuries earlier. ⏲ 45 min.

Follow the B6245, B5269, and B5266 west for about 18 miles to

❹ ★★ **Blackpool.** Britain's largest seaside resort once provided workers in the North with a week of sand and fun during enforced holidays, when their mills shut down for annual maintenance. Blackpool continues to serve up a great abundance of both, with 7 miles of beaches washed by the chilly waters of the Irish Sea; three amusement piers; one of the world's tallest and most terrifying **roller coasters;** the **Opera House,** one of the largest theaters in Europe; and **Blackpool Tower,** a near cousin to the Eiffel Tower and for many years after its opening in 1894 the tallest structure in Britain. All these sights can be nicely surveyed from a ride on the Blackpool electric tramway (trams about every 5 min.; £1.50) that runs the length of the promenade. The town looks its garish best during Blackpool Illuminations on evenings in September and October when, as befits the first city in the world to be electrified, the promenade is illuminated with more than one million

> The tea rooms at Carnforth Station, where the Oscar-winning 1945 movie Brief Encounter was filmed.

Having Fun in Blackpool

You can partake in Blackpool's legacy of fun at **Pleasure Beach Amusement Park** (☎ 0871/222-1234; www.blackpool pleasurebeach.com; £25 adults, £20 kids 2–11), where attractions include dozens of roller coasters and other rides. An ascent up the **Blackpool Tower** (☎ 01253/622-242; www.theblackpooltower.co.uk; £14) affords views all the way to the Lake District, Manchester, and Liverpool, as well as a visit to the Victorian-era Tower Ballroom.

bulbs. At any time, this seaside town that has delighted generations of holiday makers puts on a pretty good show. ⏱ 2 hr. For other attractions in the city, see "Having Fun in Blackpool."

The A588 follows the coast north for about 20 miles to

⑤ ★ Lancaster. The past hangs heavily over the quiet capital of Lancashire. Supporters of the House of Lancaster, a branch of the Plantagenets, launched the Wars of the Roses between 1455 and 1485, and eventual victory for the Lancastrians (the "red" rose) gave rise to the Tudor Dynasty. The Tudor monarch Elizabeth I (1533–1603) enlarged **Lancaster Castle,** site of the infamous Pendle witchcraft trials in 1612 (after which nearly all the accused were hanged) and now a well-fortified prison. For much of the 18th century Lancaster was Britain's major port for trade with the American colonies, and the quays on the River Lune bustled with commerce. This past is captured in the **Lancaster Maritime Museum,** housed in the handsome Georgian Customs House, St. George's Quay (☎ 01524/382-264; www.lancashire.gov.uk/acs/sites/museums; £3 adults).

Next to the museum, the quay is lined with the warehouses of Dodshon Foster (1730–93), a Quaker slave trader whose ships *Barlborough* and *Bold* transported slaves from Africa to the Caribbean and returned to Lancaster laden with cotton, sugar, rum, and mahogany. ⏱ 1 hr.

It's only about 5 miles north on the M6 to

⑥ ★ Carnforth. Film buffs and outdoor enthusiasts find their way to this small market town on Morecambe Bay. The former come to visit the railway station, where David Lean filmed his classic *Brief Encounter;* the refreshment stand where most of the movie's action takes place has changed very little in the past 65 years and is kept in high polish. Hikers set out into the surrounding countryside on the towpaths of the Lancaster Canal, also navigable by small craft, and naturalists follow trails through the reeds, marshes, and woodlands of

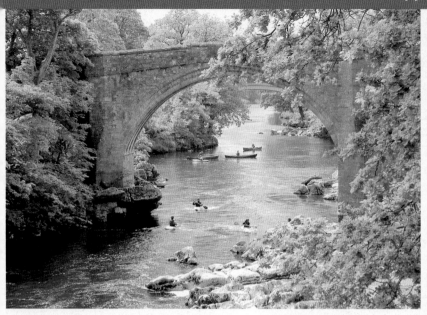

> *The Devil's Bridge spans the River Lune at Kirkby Lonsdale, a village with literary links to John Ruskin and the Brontës.*

Leighton Moss, 4 miles north of Carnforth off the A6 (☎ 01524/701-601; www.rspb.org.uk; £4.50 adults, £1 kids, £9 families), a protected habitat for many species of birds and other wildlife. ⏱ 1 hr. with visit to Leighton Moss.

Follow a marked country road 2 miles north to

❼ ★ Warton. A branch of the ancestral family of George Washington lived in Warton for centuries before their most famous descendant became the first president of the United States. The family coat of arms hangs in the slate-roofed **St. Oswald's Church,** Main St. (www.wartonstoswald.co.uk), and on close inspection you'll notice a familiar design of two stars and three stripes. Warton is also home to descendants of the famous Gillows family, England's leading cabinet makers for much of the 18th and 19th centuries. **Leighton Hall,** about 2 miles north of Warton on a marked road (☎ 01524/734-474; www.leightonhall.co.uk; £7.50 adults; £4.95 kids 5–12, £23 families), their Gothic-style manor house, is filled with fine furnishings of their making. More than 32 hectares (80 acres) of the grounds are laced with gardens and landscaped parkland. ⏱ 1 hr.

Follow marked country roads to Whittington, and from there continue on the B6254 to Kirkby Lonsdale. The total drive is about 9 miles.

❽ ★★ Kirkby Lonsdale. The 14th-century, three-arched Devil's Bridge (legend says Old Nick himself built the bridge) spans the River Lune in this small village, which has some formidable literary connections. Essayist John Ruskin (1819–1900) often wandered the surrounding countryside, and you can follow in his footsteps on a well-marked network of so-called Ruskin Walks. A hilltop behind St. Mary's Church overlooking the river valley and surrounding hills was his favorite perch on which to paint, and the same scene inspired J. M. W. Turner (1775–1851). From 1823 to 1825, Charlotte and Emily Brontë were sent from their father's parsonage in Haworth, Yorkshire (p. 472, ❾), to the nearby village of Cowan Bridge to attend the Clergy Daughters' School; Charlotte later drew on the less-than-nurturing experience for her depiction of the Lowood School in her novel *Jane Eyre.* ⏱ 30 min.

The Lake District

The bracken-covered peaks of the Lake District rise as high as almost 1,000m (3,200 ft.), and beneath them are meres, or lakes, that reflect the crags, forests, and meadows that run down to their shores. William Wordsworth, the romantic poet who spent his entire life in the region and captured the sublime beauty around him in his poetry, said that these landscapes "should be treasured by persons of good taste... with an eye to perceive and a heart to enjoy"—excellent advice as you explore this hauntingly beautiful corner of England.

> Wordsworth dubbed Grasmere "the loveliest spot that man hath ever known."

START Windermere, 275 miles northwest of London, 56 miles north of Liverpool.
TRIP LENGTH About 48 miles. Allow 3 days to explore the region by car, with time for walks and lake cruises. Spend your first day and evening in Windermere.

❶ ★★ Windermere and Bowness-on-Windermere. These two adjoining towns above Lake Windermere, with their tidy rows of slate-roofed cottages and modest Victorian houses, have been the gateway to the Lake District ever since the railroad arrived in the

mid–19th century. Windermere is about 1 mile from the lakeshore, while Bowness is right on the lake—England's largest, a remarkably beautiful and impressive body of water that is 11 miles long and half a mile wide. While this is not the place to experience the solitude William Wordsworth recounted when he wrote of wandering "lonely as a cloud that floats on high o'er vales and hills," it is easy to get away on foot or by water for some lovely **excursions** (see "Walks & Cruises from Windermere and Bowness," p. 424).

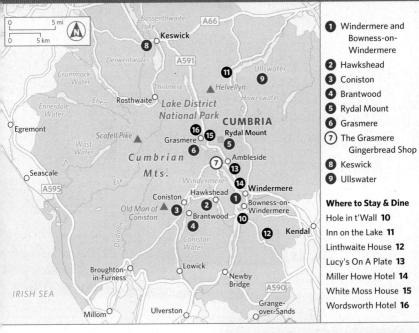

1. Windermere and Bowness-on-Windermere
2. Hawkshead
3. Coniston
4. Brantwood
5. Rydal Mount
6. Grasmere
7. The Grasmere Gingerbread Shop
8. Keswick
9. Ullswater

Where to Stay & Dine

Hole in t'Wall **10**
Inn on the Lake **11**
Linthwaite House **12**
Lucy's On A Plate **13**
Miller Howe Hotel **14**
White Moss House **15**
Wordsworth Hotel **16**

Children will enjoy an escape into the world of Peter Rabbit at the Lake District's most popular attraction, the **World of Beatrix Potter,** Old Laundry, Bowness-on-Windermere (☎ 015394/88444; www.hop-skip-jump.com; £6.75 adults, £3.50 kids), where colorfully animated tableaux re-create the famous stories of the longtime Lake District resident. Young visitors especially enjoy sipping tea in the Beatrix Potter Tea Room and wandering through the Peter Rabbit Garden, planted to replicate the vegetable patches and other greenery in the artist's enticing illustrations. Potter's well-heeled London family was among the many Victorians for whom the Lakes were a fashionable retreat. Many built homes on the lake shores, and one of the most beautiful is **Blackwell,** off the A5074 (☎ 015394/46139; www.blackwell.org.uk; £6.50 adults, £3.80 kids, £17 families), an Arts and Crafts mansion designed by Baillie Scott for Manchester brewer Sir Edward Holt on a hillside above Bowness-on-Windermere in 1897. The large, airy rooms look across the terraced grounds to the lake, and visitors are encouraged to lounge on the built-in window seats and take in the views. ⏱ 1 day.

> The Lakes is the place to indulge your romantic rowboat dreams, and many spots offer rentals by the hour.

> *Vast tracts of the scenic countryside around Hawkshead are owned by the National Trust.*

On Day 2, board the Windermere Ferry for the 20-min. trip across the lake to Far Sawrey on the western shore (£2 for cars). Once on the other side, follow the well-marked road about 10 miles to

② ★★ **Hawkshead.** This attractive village of 17th- and 18th-century houses still resonates with memories of its two most famous inhabitants. Beatrix Potter bought **Hill Top,** a farm with a lovely stone cottage located 2 miles south of town (☎ 015394/36269; www.nationaltrust.org.uk; £6.50 adults, £3.50 kids, £16 families), with the money she made from *The Tale of Peter Rabbit*—more than 30 million copies of which have been sold around the world since the classic appeared in 1902. Potter lived here until her death in 1943 and wrote her other famous children's tales in the cramped study. Hill Top is surrounded by vast tracts of Lake District land that Potter bought up over the years with the proceeds from her writings and deeded to the National Trust upon her death, helping ensure that the natural beauty of the Lake District will endure.

Note that only a limited number of visitors are allowed into the house at any one time, so you may be asked to wait in the garden.

The Hawkshead law office of Potter's husband, William Heelis, is the **Beatrix Potter Gallery,** Main St. (☎ 015394/36355; www.nationaltrust.org.uk; £4.40 adults, £2.10 kids, £11 families), which is filled with original sketches and watercolors that Potter did for her stories.

William Wordsworth attended the **Old Grammar School** (☎ 015394/36735; www.hawksheadgrammar.org.uk; £2 per person) between 1779 and 1787. You can make out his name carved into a battered old desk in the ground-floor classroom, and the headmaster's study upstairs displays Wordsworth mementoes, items relating to the founding of the school by the Archbishop of York in 1585, and some tankards and other bits and pieces that reveal that young William and his fellow pupils were allowed to smoke pipes and drink beer at school. ⏱ **2 hr.**

Follow the B1288 about 3 miles west to

3 ★★★ Coniston. Coniston Water is perhaps the most beautiful lake in the Lake District, with silent waters that slice through a deep valley and shimmer with the reflections of the surrounding fells. You can rent a rowboat at the **Coniston Boating Centre**, Lake Rd. (☎ 01539/44136), or cross the lake on the steam yacht *Gondola,* a Victorian-era pleasure craft that has been meticulously restored, from the upholstered salons to the polished wooden decks. The *Gondola* sails daily on 45-minute excursions from Coniston Pier (☎ 015394/41288; www.nationaltbrust.org. uk; £8.50 adults, £4.50 kids, £22 families) at 10:30am, 11:30am, 1:30pm, 2:30pm, and 3:30pm. Most boats call at Monk Coniston Jetty at the northern end of the lake, where passengers can get off for a 5-mile round-trip walk to Tarn Hows, a famous Victorian viewpoint. The beautiful little lake, or tarn, is fed by rushing streams and set amid heather-covered hills. Even the presence of many scenery-seekers doesn't detract from the rural beauty of the setting. ⏱ 2 hr.

Follow the well-marked road for about 1 mile south from Coniston along the east side of the lake to

4 ★★ Brantwood. This lakeside manor was the home of poet, art and architecture critic, social reformer, and artist John Ruskin (1819–1900) from 1872 until his death. Ruskin once famously said, "There is no wealth but life," and the furnishings, books, and paintings by J. M. W. Turner and the pre-Raphaelites, whose work Ruskin helped usher into popular acceptance, show how this intelligent and cultivated man embraced his dictum. Some of the most captivating pieces are Ruskin's own drawings and watercolors. Ruskin also laid out the gardens and plantings on the 100-hectare (250-acre estate), and walking paths lace the grounds. ⏱ 1 hr. Coniston. ☎ 015394-41396. www.brantwood.org.uk. Admission £6.30 adults, £5 students, £1.35 kids 5–15, £13.15 families. Mid-Mar to mid-Nov daily 11am–5:30pm; mid-Nov to mid-Mar Wed–Sun 11am–4:30pm.

> To see the best of the Lake District's panoramas, kit yourselves out for a day of fell walking.

> *William Wordsworth wrote some of his best known works seated by the fire in Dove Cottage, Grasmere.*

Follow the A593 northeast about 8 miles north to Ambleside and the A591 another 2½ miles northwest from there to

❺ ★★ **Rydal Mount.** In 1813, after enjoying some considerable success, Wordsworth moved his family to this large home on a verdant hillside above Rydal Water. He lived here until his death in 1850, writing in an attic study and fulfilling his largely honorary duties as Britain's Distributor of Stamps and, from 1843, Poet Laureate. Descendants of the poet still live in the house, though the flagstone-floored dining room, drawing room, several bedrooms, and study are preserved as domestic shrines to him. Wordsworth lovingly planted the gardens, including a patch he tended in memory of his daughter Dora, who died of tuberculosis at age 43. He wrote several poems to Dora, and in spring the garden blazes with daffodils, evoking his two most famous works. In "Daffodils," he writes: "When all at once I saw a crowd,/ A host, of golden daffodils;/ Beside the lake, beneath the trees,/ Fluttering and dancing in the breeze"; in "Intimations of Immortality" he opines, "Though nothing can buy back the hour/ Of splendour in the grass, of glory in the flower." ⏱ 1 hr. 2½ miles south of Grasmere off A591. ☎ 015394/33002. www.wordsworthlakes.co.uk. Admission £6.50 adults, £5.50 seniors, £3 kids. Wed–Mon Mar 1–Oct 31 9:30am–5pm; Nov 1–end of Feb 10am–4pm.

Continue 2½ miles on the A591 to Grasmere, where you should plan on spending the rest of Day 2 and the evening.

Walks & Cruises from Windermere and Bowness

If you're looking for an excursion in the area, an easy 2½-mile round-trip trail from the tourist office leads to 239m (784-ft.) Orrest Head for memorable views of the lake, lakeshore villages, and surrounding hills. Or, you can take the steamer from Windermere to Wray's Castle, follow the beautiful lakeside path from there to Far Sawrey, and take the launch from there back to Bowness.

Boat trips on Lake Windermere are available year-round. From piers at Bowness-on-Windermere, ferries make regular trips to Waterhead (near Ambleside) on the north shore and Lakeside on the southern end. November to early April, boats run roughly every hour in each direction, 10am to 3:35pm; early April to October, cruises run roughly every half hour in each direction, 9am to 6:30 pm. Fares for a round-trip between Bowness and Ambleside are £9.15 adults, £5.30 kids 5 to 15, and £26 families. A Walkers Special ticket, allowing you to get off the boat and hike along segments of the lakeshore path, is £8.40 adults, £4.80 kids ages 5 to 15, and £24 families. If you're staying around Lake Windermere, consider purchasing a Freedom of the Lake pass, which allows you to board a vessel any time you want in a 24-hour period and costs £17 adults, £8.25 kids, and £40 families. For more information, contact **Windermere Lake Cruises** (☎ 015395/43360; www.windermere-lakecruises.co.uk).

6 ★★★ **Grasmere.** William Wordsworth spent most of his adult life in this small village of slate houses and pretty gardens on Lake Grasmere, one of the smallest but most romantic of the lakes, overshadowed by craggy peaks. He referred to Grasmere as the "loveliest spot that man hath ever known." From 1799 to 1808, the poet lived in whitewashed **Dove Cottage** with his wife, Mary; sister, Dorothy; and several children. Cramped and primitive as the quarters were, Wordsworth wrote some of his greatest works seated in front of the fire or pacing the orchard and gardens. The nearby **Wordsworth Museum** in Grasmere Village (☎ 015394/ 35544; www.wordsworth.org.uk; £7.50 adults, £4.10 kids 6–15, £18 families) displays manuscripts, pictures, books, and memorabilia from the permanent collection of the Wordsworth Trust.

Wordsworth, his wife, sister, daughter Dora, and other children are buried in the churchyard of Grasmere's St. Oswald's Church, a somber stone structure from the 13th century. Wordsworth planted the eight yew trees that rise near the family plots. ⏱ 1 hr.

7 🏆 **The Grasmere Gingerbread Shop.** Do not even think of leaving Grasmere without tasting this tiny shop's famous gingerbread, made from Sarah Nelson's secret, 150-year-old recipe—so valuable it's kept in a bank vault. Also on offer are Kendal Mint Cakes, a Lake District specialty that Sir Edmund Hillary took with him for fortification during his 1953 ascent of Mount Everest. **Church Cottage, Grasmere.** ☎ 015394/35428. www.grasmeregingerbread.co.uk. Items from £2.

On Day 3, continue 10 miles north to

8 ★★ **Keswick.** The narrow streets lined with sturdy stone houses overlooking Derwentwater were home to the Lake District's two other famous poets, Robert Southey (1774–1843) and Samuel Taylor Coleridge (1772–1834). Though Southey preceded Wordsworth as Poet Laureate for 30 years, from 1813 to his death in 1843, he is best known for his children's tale *The Story of the Three Bears.* Coleridge, of course, is known for *The Rime of the Ancient Mariner* and *Kubla Khan,* as well as

> *The Castlerigg Stone Circle dates to around 3000 B.C.*

for his battles with depression and opium addiction. In happier times, the three would set out for long walks from Keswick, and the town is still a popular base for excursions.

An easy amble of 1½ miles (you can also drive along the A591) takes you east to **Castlerigg Stone Circle,** where 33 free-standing stones were erected around 3000 B.C., probably as a gathering spot for the early farmers who once occupied the region. Stand in the middle of the circle and you'll be afforded some great views of the surrounding mountains.

Graphite was discovered around Keswick in the early 16th century, providing a way for farmers to mark their sheep, and, more profitably, to mass-produce pencils. The **Cumberland Pencil Museum,** Southey Lane (☎ 017687/73626; www.pencilmuseum.co.uk; £3.75 adults, £2.50 kids 5–15, £10 families), documents the manufacture of the humble implement, still produced on the premises by Derwent, whose graphic and artists' pencils are for sale in a shop. ⏱ 2 hr., longer with lake cruise (see "Cruising Derwentwater," below).

Follow the A66 about 6 miles to the A591, and take that 4 miles south to the lakeshore road around

⑨ ★★★ **Ullswater.** One of the most rustic of the lakes is surrounded by 5,200 hectares (13,000 acres) of parkland administered by the National Trust. Tucked into the beautiful shoreline south of Pooley Bridge is **Aira Force,** a waterfall reached by an easy 3-mile walk through

a shady glen. The best way to explore the lake is from the deck of the **Ullswater Steamers** (☎ 017684/82229; www.ulswater-steamers. co.uk), which sails the length of the lake from Glenridding to Pooley Bridge. The trip takes a little over an hour, though many walkers get off at Howtown to continue the journey on a lakeside trail. Cruises operate year-round, and the charge for a full circuit of the lake is £10 adults, £5.15 kids, and £27 families. ⏱ 3 hr., with cruise and lakeshore walk.

More Walks in the Lake District

The Lake District is famous for ambling, with dozens of walks that range in length from a few miles to long treks on such routes as the Cumbria Way and the Coast to Coast Walk.

Keswick Rambles (☎ 017687-71302; www.keswickrambles.org.uk) leads walks of varying degrees of difficulty from the Moot Hall in Keswick into the spectacular countryside that surrounds the town. The organization leads a different walk every day, most starting at 10am and lasting a half or full day, and provides bus transportation to paths that are not easily accessible from the center of town. To join a walk, you need only show up at the Moot Hall; half-day walks are £6 adults and £2 kids, while full-day walks are £15 adults, £4 kids.

Britain's **Ramblers** (www.ramblers. org.uk) offers some 800 guided walks a year in the Lake District, and nonmembers are welcome to participate. The **Lake District National Park Authority** (www. lakedistrict.gov.uk) also leads walks in the region; for more information, check with the Lake District Visitor Centre at Brockhole (p. 459).

All the tourist centers in the region provide maps and other information for walks in the area, and shops are well stocked with maps and guidebooks to Lake District walks. John Dawson, a Lake District resident and avid walker, provides details and expert advice on some 40 walks in the region at www. lakedistrictwalks.com.

Cruising Derwentwater

You can make a circuit of 3-mile-long Derwentwater on small boats operated by **Keswick Launch;** the lake, studded with small islands and surrounded by craggy peaks, is one of the prettiest in the Lake District. Cruises operate year-round, with departures every half-hour, 10am to 6pm, late March to November 30, and every hour, 10:30am to 3:30pm, the rest of the year. Fares for round-the-lake cruises are £9 adults, £4.40 kids 5 to 16, £21 families of up to two adults and three kids. For more information, call ☎ 017687/77263 or go online to www.keswick-launch.co.uk.

Where to Stay & Dine

★ Hole in t'Wall BOWNESS-ON-WINDERMERE
PUB The dark, fire-warmed pub from 1612 is the favorite gathering spot for locals, who enjoy the Cumbrian ales on tap and the excellent pub fare that includes a good selection of daily specials. Lowside. ☎ 015394/43488. Entrees £7–£12. MC, V. Lunch & dinner daily.

★★ Inn on the Lake GLENRIDDING
A get-away-from-it-all atmosphere prevails at this old-fashioned hostelry on Ullswater. The lounges with blazing hearths; a lakeside terrace; comfortable, nicely furnished rooms; and a dining room provide an excellent base for walks amid some of the Lake District's most beautiful scenery. ☎ 017684/82444. www.lakedistricthotels.net/innonthelake. 35 units. Doubles £150–£240. AE, MC, V.

★★★ Linthwaite House BOWNESS-ON-WINDERMERE A fire greets you in the entryway of this gracious country house, where public rooms and accommodations are stylishly and comfortably decorated with traditional and contemporary flare. Airy public rooms look across the green hillsides to Lake Windermere, and the superb in-house restaurant is one of the best in the region. Crook Rd. ☎ 015394/86600. www.linthwaite.com. 405 units. Doubles £65–£125. AE, MC, V.

★ Lucy's on a Plate AMBLESIDE *MODERN EUROPEAN* Casual yet tasty meals are served (at times in an inexcusably lax fashion) in a pine-floored dining room and on a warm-weather patio. The freshest seafood and lamb are innovatively prepared, and an adjacent shop sells cheeses, cold cuts, bread, and other ingredients for a lakeside picnic. Church St. ☎ 0151394/31194. Entrees £7–£15. AE, MC, V. Breakfast, lunch & dinner daily.

★★★ Miller Howe Hotel WINDERMERE
A gracious mansion sits amid lush hillside gardens that cascade down to the lakeshore. Bedrooms are spacious and individually decorated with great style, while intimate public rooms are warmed by cozy fires and filled with deep arm chairs and couches. A six-course dinner,

> *A four-poster bedroom under the eaves at the Wordsworth Hotel, Grasmere.*

one of the Lake District's most noted gourmet experiences, is served in the candlelit dining room nightly. Rayrigg Rd. ☎ 015394/42536. www.millerhowe.com. 13 units. Doubles £210–£280 w/breakfast & dinner. AE, MC, V.

★★ White Moss House GRASMERE
A country house that was once home to the Wordsworth family is an atmospheric inn that still has the feel of a private home, with cozy guest rooms and lounges. Wonderful lakeside walks begin just outside the garden gate. Rydal Water, 2 miles south of Grasmere. ☎ 015394/35295. www.whitemoss.com. 7 units. Doubles £80–£200 w/breakfast. AE, MC, V.

★★ Wordsworth Hotel GRASMERE
A large stone house in the village center has the ambiance of a country estate, with impeccably decorated rooms that overlook gardens, an indoor pool and spa, and an excellent restaurant. ☎ 015394/355-92. www.thewordsworthhotel.co.uk. 38 units. Doubles £190–£210 w/breakfast & dinner for two. AE, DC, MC, V.

Chester

Romans founded an outpost, Deva Victrix, on the River Dee 2 millennia ago, and the city that has come to be known as Chester thrived well into the Victorian era as the riverside quays and markets bustled with trade. Remnants of this long and rich past are much in evidence in Chester, where half-timbered houses are enclosed within the longest circuit of intact city walls in Britain.

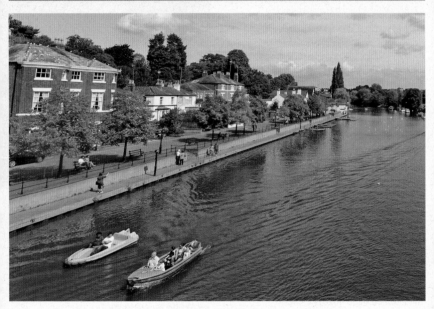

> A strategic location, on the banks of the River Dee, led the Romans to found Chester.

START Chester Cross. Chester is 207 miles north of London and 18 miles south of Liverpool.

1 ★★ The Rows. England's most extraordinary shopping center has a solid provenance, dating to the 13th century. In medieval times, shops and warehouses lined the ground floors, and living quarters, now shops, opened off a gallery above them. Upper floors were added in the 15th and 16th centuries, giving the Rows their Tudor, half-timbered facades and covered walkways that run a story above the four main streets of Chester. Long gone are the days when Sir Charles Napier (1782–1853)

complained that the Rows were filled with "all the rogues, and fools, and drunkards in the country," but the landmark is still pretty colorful without them (and you'll probably encounter one or two if you look hard enough). The Rows are next to **Chester Cross,** a medieval monument that marks the intersection of the four streets of Deva Victrix. ⏱ 30 min.

2 ★ Grosvenor Museum. Everyday life in Roman Chester comes alive in displays that re-create the routines of soldiers garrisoned in Deva Victrix, along with the day-to-day lives of women, children, and slaves. Among the artifacts are the many Roman tombstones that

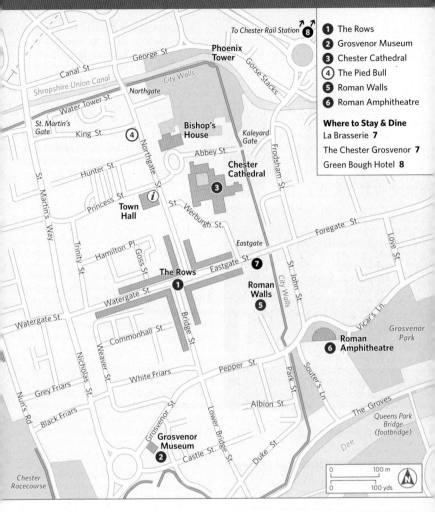

1 The Rows
2 Grosvenor Museum
3 Chester Cathedral
4 The Pied Bull
5 Roman Walls
6 Roman Amphitheatre

Where to Stay & Dine
La Brasserie 7
The Chester Grosvenor 7
Green Bough Hotel 8

To Chester Rail Station 8

Phoenix Tower

George St.

Canal St.

Shropshire Union Canal

Water Tower St.

Northgate

Gorse Stacks

City Walls

St. Martin's Gate

King St.

4

Hunter St.

Northgate St.

Bishop's House

Abbey St.

Kaleyard Gate

Chester Cathedral

3

Frodsham St.

St. Martin's Way

Princess St.

i

Town Hall

St. Werburgh St.

Foregate St.

Love St.

Trinity St.

Hamilton Pl.

Goss St.

Eastgate

Eastgate St.

7

St. John St.

Watergate St.

The Rows

1

Roman Walls

5

City Walls

Watergate St.

Commonhall St.

Bridge St.

Weaver St.

Nicholas St.

White Friars

Pepper St.

Park St.

Souter's Ln.

Vicar's Ln.

Grosvenor Park

Roman Amphitheatre

6

Grey Friars

Black Friars

Nun's Rd.

Grosvenor St.

Lower Bridge St.

Albion St.

Duke St.

The Groves

Queens Park Bridge (footbridge)

Grosvenor Museum

2

Castle St.

Dee

Chester Racecourse

0   100 m
0   100 yds

N

later generations embedded in the city walls. Later eras are re-created in a Stuart dining room, Victorian parlor, and Edwardian bathroom. ⏱ 1 hr. 27 Grosvenor St. ☎ 01244/402-033. www.cheshirewestandchester.gov.uk. Free admission. Mon–Sat 10:30am–5pm; Sun 1–4pm.

3 ★★ **Chester Cathedral.** The vast medieval landmark in the center of Chester dates to the 4th century, when a Christian chapel was built atop a Roman temple to Apollo. In 907, the remains of St. Werburgh, a Benedictine abbess, were brought to Chester to protect them from invading Vikings and placed in a church commissioned by Aethelflaed, the daughter

of King Alfred. A large Benedictine monastery was established around the church in 1092. The monastery and its shrine to St. Werburgh became one of the most important places of pilgrimage in northwest England, and for almost 4 centuries the monks devoted themselves to creating a cathedral to impress the devout. Carvings in the choir stalls provided visual entertainment when they were unveiled in the late 14th century; they depict many popular medieval tales, including that of Reynard the Fox, who lies still in the mud so birds alight on him and then snaps them in his jaws, and the Miracle of St. Werburgh (see "The Lady of the Geese," p. 430).

> The Eastgate Clock was a Victorian addition to a circuit of walls first laid down in Roman times.

The Lady of the Geese

The most famous miracle with which St. Werburgh (d. 700), Chester's patron, is associated concerns a flock of wild geese that were devouring cornfields. She bid servants to catch the geese and bring them to her; at her command they flew away and were never seen in the vicinity again. The servants had killed one of the geese for a meal, and when Werburgh learned this she resurrected the bird and bid it to fly off as well. St. Werburgh was influential even in death, and for centuries her casket was set atop Chester's town walls in times of war to fend off the invading Welsh. Legend has it that when Welsh King Gruffydd ap Llywelyn (1007–64) saw the casket he was struck blind.

The Gothic edifice that stands today was heavily restored in Victorian times but is still a supreme landmark of medieval architecture, surrounded by many of the original, 1,000-year-old monastery buildings. The monks' 13th-century refectory is now a cafe, serving snacks, lunch, and tea. ⏱ 30 min. Abbey Sq. ☎ 01244/324-756. www.chester cathedral.com. Admission (including excellent 45-min. audio tour) £5 adults, £4 seniors & students, £2.50 kids 15 & under. Mon–Sat 9am–5pm; Sun 1–4pm.

④   🍺 **The Pied Bull.** Before setting out for a circuit on the Roman Walls, step into the woodsy confines of this 18th-century coaching inn for a pint. 57 Northgate St. ☎ 01244/325-829. Beer £2.

❺ ★★★ **Roman Walls.** Chester is enclosed within Britain's largest circuit of walls, almost 2 miles in length. Many sections date from the days when Chester was a Roman fort, and the walls have been reinforced and extended many times over the centuries. Saxon Queen Aethelflaed had them reinforced in 907 to ward off raiding Vikings, Cromwell's forces knocked down huge sections during the British Civil War in 1650, and Victorians added the **Eastgate Clock,** the second largest time piece in Britain after Big Ben, to commemorate Queen Victoria's diamond jubilee in 1897. You can ponder the past 2 millennia as you walk the circuit, enjoying fantastic views over Chester and the surrounding countryside as you do so. Gladiators and other authentically clad Romans lead 1½-hour tours of the walls, amphitheater, and Chester's other ancient remnants. ⏱ 1½ hr. Start at the Visitor Information

When in Chester . . .

Chester is famous for its pubs, many dating from the 17th and 18th centuries. The **Old Custom House Inn,** 65 Watergate St. (☎ 01244/324-435) takes its name from the old custom house for the port of Chester across the street. **Ye Olde Boot Inn,** Eastgate St. (☎ 01244/324-435), and **Ye Olde King's Head,** 48 Lower Bridge St. (☎ 01244/324-855) are known for offering spirits, both in a glass and in the form of ghosts who waft through the upstairs rooms.

> *Chester is home to Britain's largest unearthed amphitheater, as well as the longest set of Roman walls in the region.*

Centre in Town Hall. ☎ 01244/402-111. www. visitchester.com. Tours £5 adults, £4 seniors, £13 families. Tues–Sat 3pm.

❻ ★ Roman amphitheater. The Romans built an enormous amphitheater in Chester in the 1st century, probably for military training and as an assembly point for troops. Seating for 8,000 spectators and a vast complex of subterranean dungeons suggests that the arena was also used for gladiatorial contests and other entertainment. The sheer size of the amphitheater, at 98m by 87m (322 ft. x 285 ft.) the largest in Britain, leads scholars to speculate that the Romans had plans to make their city a base from which to invade Ireland and eventually the capital of Roman Britain. The amphitheater fell into disuse in the 4th century and was not unearthed until 1929. ⏱ 15 min. Off Duke St. Free admission. Dawn to dusk.

Where to Stay & Dine

★★★ **La Brasserie** CITY CENTER *FRENCH/CONTINENTAL* Nosh on a burger or indulge in a steak in a homey room that evokes its Parisian namesakes, and does justice to them with flair. Chester Grosvenor, Eastgate. ☎ 01244/895-618. Entrees £8–£18. AE, MC, V. Breakfast, lunch & dinner daily.

★★ **Chester Grosvenor** CITY CENTER The finest hotel in town dates to Elizabethan times and provides extremely comfortable, spacious accommodations behind a half-timbered facade in the center of town. Amenities include a spa and several bars and restaurants, including Simon Radley at the Chester, one of the finest dining rooms in the Northwest. Eastgate. ☎ 01244/324-024. www.chestergrosvenor.co.uk. 80 units. Doubles £205–£325 w/breakfast. AE, DC, MC, V.

★★★ **Green Bough Hotel** CITY CENTER A commodious Victorian town house at the edge of the city center is a sophisticated getaway, with stylish rooms and suites, a fragrant garden, and an excellent in-house restaurant, the Olive Tree. A night here is a perfect end to a day spent wandering through Chester, all the more so since rates often include dinner. 60 Hoole Rd. ☎ 01244/326-241. www. chestergreenboughhotel.com. 15 units. Doubles £175–£195 w/breakfast. AE, DC, MC, V.

R-O-C-K IN THE U.K.
The British Invasion and Beyond

BY KATHLEEN WARNOCK

	BRITISH INVASION	HARD ROCK/METAL	PSYCHEDELIC/ PROG ROCK
THE SOUND	Jangly guitars, vocal harmonies, hook-laden lyrics	TURN IT UP TO 11, massive Marshall amp stacks, humongous drum kits	Comfortably numb, dense/mysterious lyrics, synthesizers, occasional strings/brass
LEADERS	The Beatles, Dusty Springfield, The Animals, The Rolling Stones, The Kinks, The Dave Clark Five, Herman's Hermits	The Who, Led Zeppelin, Black Sabbath, Def Leppard, The Jeff Beck Group, Deep Purple, Motör-head, Judas Priest	Pink Floyd, The Beatles, Traffic, Cream, Moody Blues, Jethro Tull, Emerson Lake & Palmer, Yes
INFLUENCES	Chuck Berry, The Everly Brothers, "skiffle" music, girl groups	American blues, garage rock, R&B	LSD, folk music, classical music, folklore, myth, J.R.R. Tolkien
CLASSIC SONG	"You Really Got Me," The Kinks	"White Room," Cream	"Lucy in the Sky with Diamonds," The Beatles
ICONIC ALBUM	*Help,* The Beatles	*Led Zeppelin,* Led Zeppelin	*The Dark Side of the Moon,* Pink Floyd
DEFINING MOMENT	Feb. 9, 1964: The Beatles conquer America on *The Ed Sullivan Show*	1974: Debut of British supergroup Bad Company	1979: Pink Floyd releases *The Wall,* a concept album that spawns live theatrical concerts and a film

Rock 'n' roll was born in the U.S.A. and returned to the Old Country via radio, television, and 45 rpm singles. Elvis Presley, Little Richard, and Chuck Berry were some of the artists whose work inspired the British Invasion of the early 1960s, which was followed by wave after wave of great rock and pop music, incorporating country, blues, garage rock, folk, the psychedelic scene, punk, and grunge. From "Love Me Do" to "Let it Bleed" and "London Calling" to "Bittersweet Symphony," British musicians have staked their claim and broken new ground in rock, punk, metal, and other genres that make up popular music.

GLAM/GLITTER	PUNK	NEW WAVE	BRITPOP
Raucous with guitars, drums, heavy bass, keyboards, saxophones	People who don't know how to play their instruments	Synthesizers, complex/ironic lyrics, driving vocals	Jangly guitars, drum machines
T. Rex, Gary Glitter, David Bowie, Queen, Elton John, Suzi Quatro, Bay City Rollers	The Sex Pistols, The Clash, The Damned, Siouxsie and the Banshees, The Slits, The Buzzcocks, X-Ray Spex	Elvis Costello, The Specials, Wham!, Duran Duran, Culture Club, Pretenders, The Police, Squeeze	Blur, Oasis, Coldplay, Bush, Elastica, The Verve, Radiohead, Suede, Pulp
Art rock, "camp," cabaret, theater, androgyny	The Ramones, garage rock, angry youth, beer, heroin	Art school, romantic poetry	Classic rock, grunge, pop/punk, alternative
"Bang a Gong," T. Rex	"I Fought the Law," The Clash	"Sweet Dreams (Are Made of This)," Eurythmics	"Wonderwall," Oasis
Goodbye Yellow Brick Road, Elton John	*Never Mind the Bollocks...*, The Sex Pistols	*Colour by Numbers*, Culture Club	*Elastica*, Elastica
1972: David Bowie introduces his "Ziggy Stardust" persona	1976: The Sex Pistols and Siouxsie Sioux shock the U.K. in a live TV interview dubbed "The Filth & the Fury!"	Aug. 1, 1981: MTV goes on the air, launching the careers of many New Wave bands	1991–2009: Noel and Liam Gallagher (brother co-founders of Oasis) fight

Liverpool

What at first glance is a down-and-out port city on the River Mersey was once Britain's busiest commercial port, which for several centuries prospered from a lively trade in everything from spices to slaves. This heritage is well preserved in Liverpool's many excellent museums and beautifully restored docklands, but overshadowing the city's impressive landmarks are the four local lads who burst on the scene in the 1960s as the Beatles.

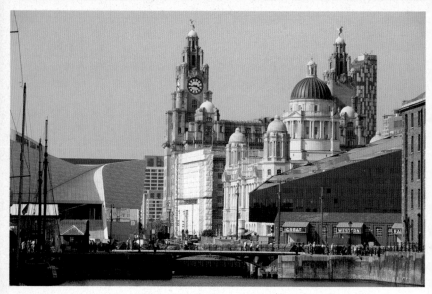

> The "Three Graces"—the Liver Building, Cunard Building, and Port of Liverpool Building—were early 20th-century beacons of the city's prosperity.

START Albert Dock. Liverpool is 215 miles northwest of London.

❶ ★★★ Albert Dock. Wharves along the River Mersey once bustled with commerce that made Liverpool one of the world's most important ports, handling at times as much as 40% of international trade. Albert Dock was the most advanced shipping complex in the world when completed in 1846, with magnificent brick warehouses that rest on iron pillars extending far out into the Mersey, allowing tea, brandy, cotton, and other commodities to be loaded directly on and off ships into cavernous halls for sorting and storage. Albert Dock was soon replaced by more advanced operations, but the vast complex remains intact and has been beautifully restored. With shops, restaurants, and two museums, the Tate Liverpool (❹) and Merseyside Maritime Museum (❷), Albert Dock is the heart of modern Liverpool. ⏱ 45 min. Edward Pavilion. ☎ 0151/708-7334. www.albertdock.com. Shops daily 10am–6pm; restaurants daily 11am–11pm. Albert Dock Shuttle.

❷ ★★★ Merseyside Maritime Museum. Galleries filled with life jackets, photos, and other artifacts tell the stories of three great early-20th-century ocean liners associated with Liverpool, and their catastrophic fates.

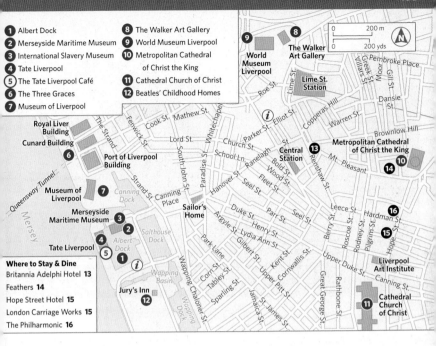

1 Albert Dock
2 Merseyside Maritime Museum
3 International Slavery Museum
4 Tate Liverpool
5 The Tate Liverpool Café
6 The Three Graces
7 Museum of Liverpool

8 The Walker Art Gallery
9 World Museum Liverpool
10 Metropolitan Cathedral of Christ the King
11 Cathedral Church of Christ
12 Beatles' Childhood Homes

Where to Stay & Dine
Britannia Adelphi Hotel 13
Feathers 14
Hope Street Hotel 15
London Carriage Works 15
The Philharmonic 16

The RMS *Titanic* was registered in the city, and Liverpool was a regular port of call for the RMS *Lusitania* and RMS *Empress of Ireland*. The *Titanic* sank when it struck an iceberg on April 14, 1912; the *Empress of Ireland* collided with a Norwegian freighter and sank on May 29, 1914, in Canada's St. Lawrence River; and the *Lusitania* was torpedoed off Ireland by a German U-boat on May 7, 1915. The Battle of the Atlantic exhibit hall traces the role Liverpool played in some of the most decisive events in World War II; several ships can be boarded; and tours explore the Old Dock, where Liverpool's maritime tradition took root in the 1820s. ⏱ 1 hr. Albert Dock. ☎ 0151/478-4499. www.liverpoolmuseums.org.uk. Free admission. Daily 10am–5pm. Albert Dock Shuttle.

3 ★★ **International Slavery Museum.** Liverpool was the center of the Slave Trade Triangle. Ships set out from the Liverpool docks for the west coast of Africa to trade goods for slaves, whom they transported to the Americas, then returned to Liverpool laden with sugar, tobacco, and cotton. Throughout the 18th century, until slave trading was made illegal in the British Empire in 1807, vast profits from this trade made Liverpool into one of the richest cities in the world. The museum chronicles harsh enslavement in the holds of ships on the so-called Middle Passage between Africa and the Americas, as well as other aspects of this brutal legacy. ⏱ 1 hr. Albert Dock. ☎ 0151/478-4499. www.liverpoolmuseums.org.uk. Free admission. Daily 10am–5pm. Albert Dock Shuttle.

4 ★ **Tate Liverpool.** Galleries in a converted warehouse host changing exhibits of works from the Tate Britain (p. 58, 7) and Tate Modern (p. 58, 6) collections in London, as well as works by contemporary artists. Works on view change all the time, but you are likely to encounter Damien Hirst, Rachel Whiteread, or another member of Britain's avant-garde as you tour the sun-filled spaces. ⏱ 45 min. Albert Dock. ☎ 0151/702-7400. www.tate.org.uk/liverpool. Free admission; charge for some special exhibitions. June–Aug daily 10am–5:50pm; Sept–May Thurs–Sun 10am–5:50pm. Albert Dock Shuttle.

5 🍽 **The Tate Liverpool Café.** Enjoy breakfast, lunch, or tea, along with views of Albert Dock, from what is perhaps the most chic eatery in Liverpool. Albert Dock. ☎ 0151/702-7400. Items £3–£8.

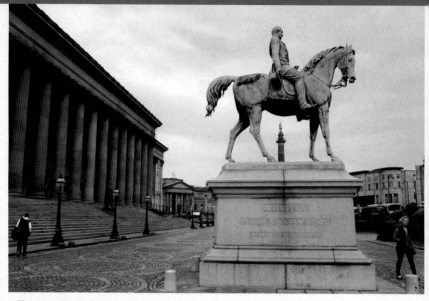

> *The impressive Walker Art Gallery has one of Britain's best art collections outside London.*

6 ★ **The Three Graces.** Well into the early 20th century, Liverpool was even wealthier than London and was often called the "New York of Europe." Symbolic of the city's one-time power are a trio of landmarks that went up along the waterfront between 1900 and 1916: the high-rise **Royal Liver Building** (completed 1911), with two clock towers topped by enormous birds that seem to watch over the city; the **Cunard Building** (completed 1916), one-time headquarters of the famous shipping line; and the domed **Port of Liverpool Building** (completed 1907). ⏱ 15 min. Pier Head.

7 ★ **Museum of Liverpool.** Liverpudlians can take special pride in these galleries devoted to them and their city. The museum pays homage to the huge influx of Irish and other immigrants, the Beatles and other creative artists the city has fostered, and the forces that transformed Liverpool from a small village on an inlet to one of the world's great port cities. ⏱ 1 hr. Pier Head. ☎ 0151/478-4393. www.liverpoolmuseums.org.uk. Free admission. Daily 10am–5pm.

8 ★★★ **The Walker Art Gallery.** The prospect of strolling through these long galleries to find yourself standing in front of Rembrandt's *Self Portrait as a Young Man* or David

Hockney's *Peter Getting Out of Nick's Pool* is reason enough to come to Liverpool. The museum's two strongest collections are the Dutch and Italian works from 1350 to 1550 and the pre-Raphaelite paintings of William Holman Hunt, John Everett Millais, Dante Gabriel Rossetti, and others. Also in the wide-ranging mix are pieces by Thomas Gainsborough and other British artists. ⏱ 1 hr. William Brown St. ☎ 0151/478-4199. www.liverpoolmuseums.org.uk. Free admission. Daily 10am–5pm.

9 ★ **World Museum Liverpool.** Just about anything from the natural world turns up in this wonderful and aptly named collection, based around skulls and other zoological specimens the 13th Earl of Derby bequeathed to the city in 1851 and expanded many, many times since—especially after the museum was gutted during the 1941 Blitz. These days more than 20,000 specimens of flora and fauna line the galleries, tropical fish float through giant tanks in the aquarium, insects crawl through the bug house, and all sorts of other sophisticated exhibits shed light on the precious and fragile natural world around us. ⏱ 1 hr. William Brown St. ☎ 0151/478-4393. www.liverpoolmuseums.org.uk. Free admission. Daily 10am–5pm.

⑩ ★ Metropolitan Cathedral of Christ the King. One of Liverpool's most remarkable landmarks—or most prominent eyesores, depending on the viewer—is known as the "Greatest Building Never Built." In 1933, ground was broken on the site of a former poor house to build a Roman Catholic cathedral designed by Sir Edwin Lutyens (1869–1944), famous for the palatial country houses he built around England. The edifice was meant to overshadow the **Cathedral Church of Christ** (⑪), then being constructed just up the street, and plans called for room for 53 altars and a dome rising 91m (300 ft.). Construction came to a halt with the outbreak of Word War II, and when Liverpool was ready to turn its attention to the new church again, it became clear that the Lutyens design was far too ambitious and costly (the crypt is about all that is true to his original plans). In its place a new, circular cathedral topped with a giant glass cone rose in the 1960s, an attempt at post-World War II modernism that looks much like a space ship. ⏱ 20 min. Hope St., Mount Pleasant. ☎ 0151/709-9222. www.liverpoolmetrocathedral.org.uk. Free admission; £3 to enter crypt and treasury. Daily 7:30am–6pm (until 5pm Sun in winter).

⑪ ★ Cathedral Church of Christ. Liverpool's other cathedral was begun in 1904 and completed in 1978, making it the world's last Gothic cathedral as well as one of the largest churches in the world. Flaunting the notion that pride is one of the seven deadly sins, the Anglican cathedral—designed by Giles Gilbert Scott (1880–1960), grandson of Sir George Gilbert Scott, and ironically a Roman Catholic—boasts the world's highest church tower (100m/330 ft.), the world's highest and heaviest peal of church bells (67m/220 ft. above the ground and 31 tons), and an organ with more pipes than any other in existence (10,000). You can take in the vastness of the cathedral on Great Space audio tours, and enjoy views over Liverpool, the Mersey, and the Welsh Hills from the top of the tower. ⏱ 20 min. St., St. James Mount. ☎ 0151/709-6271. www.liverpoolcathedral.org.uk. Free admission; tower and Great Space tour £5 adults, £3.50 seniors & students, £12 families. Daily 8am–6pm.

⑫ ★★★ Beatles' Childhood Homes. The homes of Paul McCartney (b. 1942) and John Lennon (1940–80) are now in the hands of the National Trust and preserved as shrines. The **McCartney House,** a modest brick row house at 20 Forthlin Rd., has been perfectly restored to look as it did in the 1950s, where the group often met to rehearse and where they wrote some of their first songs. **Mendips** is the solidly middle-class, semi-detached house where John Lennon lived with his Aunt Mimi and Uncle George from 1945 to 1963. The houses can only be visited on organized tours that leave from Jurys Inn Hotel in the city center and from Speke Hall, a half-timbered Tudor house in south Liverpool surrounded by beautiful gardens, also administered by the National Trust. ⏱ 2 hr. ☎ 0151/707-0729, or 0151/427-7231 to reserve tours. www.nationaltrust.org.uk. Tour £20 adults, £3.40 kids 5–15. Mid-Mar to Oct 31 tours leave at 10am & 10:30am from Jurys Inn (31 Keel Wharf) and at 2:30pm & 3:20pm from Speke Hall (8 miles south of city center, off the A561); late Feb to mid-Mar & Nov tours leave from Jurys Inn at 10am, 12:30pm & 3pm.

> *Paul McCartney was raised in a typical terrace house in the suburb of Allerton.*

In Search of the Fab Four

Beatles fans will feel they've died and gone to heaven in Liverpool, where the famous band is remembered around every bend. Aside from visiting the childhood homes above, the best way to trace the most famous Liverpudlians is on a **Magical Mystery Tour** (www.beatlestour.org), a bus trip that takes you past the childhood homes of all four, as well as Strawberry Fields, Penny Lane, and other sights immortalized in the Beatles songbook. Tours leave from Albert Dock Monday to Friday at 2:30pm, Saturday and Sunday at noon and 2:30pm; tickets are £16 and available from the Tourist Information Office at either 08 Place, Whitechapel (☎ 0151/233-2459), or Albert Dock (☎ 0151/709-3350). The **Cavern Club,** 8 Matthew St. (☎ 0151/236-1965; www.cavernclub.org), where the Beatles played from 1961 to 1963, still provides musical entertainment, along with a Cavern City tour map that pinpoints Beatle-related hotspots around town.

Another local group, Gerry and the Pacemakers, also did their part in putting Liverpool on the map with their 1964 hit, *Ferry Cross the Mersey.* You can pay homage by boarding one of the **Mersey Ferries** (www.merseyferries.co.uk) that operate daily from Pier Head to take in waterside views of the Liverpool docks and waterfront; the 50-minute River Explorer Cruises run hourly and cost £3.80 adults, £2.60 kids 5-15.

Where to Stay & Dine

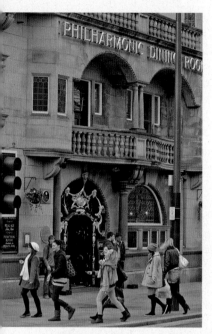

> *The Philharmonic, on Hope Street, an iconic city center pub.*

★★★ Britannia Adelphi Hotel CITY CENTER
You'll be surrounded by character aplenty at Liverpool's largest and most noted hotel, where a recent restoration has brought guest rooms up to snuff with pleasant Edwardian-style furnishings. Three bars and two restaurants have been favorites among Liverpudlians for more than a century. Ranelagh Place. ☎ 0871/222-0029. www.britanniahotels.com/hotels/liverpool. 405 units. Doubles £65–£125. AE, MC, V.

★★★ Feathers CITY CENTER
Conventional, businesslike comfort prevails in this well-managed and pleasant city inn in a row of converted houses near the cathedrals. A casual in-house restaurant and 24-hour room service are especially welcome amenities in Liverpool, where dining options in the city center are fairly sparse. 117-125 Mount Pleasant. ☎ 0151/709-9655. www.feathers. uk.com. 65 units. Doubles £45–£75 w/breakfast. MC, V.

★★ Hope Street Hotel CITY CENTER
A former carriage works is Liverpool's most stylish hotel, restored from cellar to attic with minimalist furnishings, beautiful woods and fabrics, as well as sumptuous soaking tubs, high-tech gadgetry, and many other state-of-the-art amenities. Most rooms enjoy airy views of the city and the Mersey. 40 Hope St. ☎ 0151/709-3000. www.hopestreethotel.co.uk. 48 units. Doubles £85–£150 w/breakfast. AE, MC, V.

★★★ London Carriage Works CITY CENTER
MODERN EUROPEN The dining room of the Hope Street Hotel provides several experiences, from a basement cafe and bar to a stylish ground-floor restaurant. Dishes rely heavily on local beef and seafood, wonderfully prepared and presented in chic, atmospheric surroundings. Sandwiches, salads, and pastas are also on offer. Hope Street Hotel, 40 Hope St. ☎ 0151/705-2222. Entrees £7–£15. AE, MC, V. Lunch & dinner daily.

★★★ The Philharmonic CITY CENTER PUB
John Lennon once said that his only regret about being so famous was that he could no longer slip into the Phil inconspicuously for a pint. You probably won't have any such problems getting in the way of a visit to this Victorian relic. Enjoying a pint at the huge horseshoe-shaped bar or a plate of fish and chips or other pub fare among the mosaics and dark paneling is one of Liverpool's top experiences. 36 Hope St. ☎ 0151/707-2837. Entrees £6–£12. AE, MC, V. Lunch & dinner daily.

Beatlemania

If you're even considering being in Liverpool at the end of August or early September, you'd better reserve a room far in advance and bone up on the Beatles. More than 100,000 fans descend on Liverpool for **International Beatle Week** (http://beatles festival.co.uk), one of the biggest music events in the world, featuring bands from around the world as well as tours, tributes, and other events dedicated to the Fab Four.

Manchester

Manchester fueled the 18th- and 19th-century Industrial Revolution, enjoying enormous prosperity reflected in pompous Victorian and Edwardian landmarks while breeding the soot-choked tenements and horrendous working conditions that Charles Dickens wrote about in *Hard Times*. Today an energetic push to restore the old industrial quays and warehouses as lively commercial and residential quarters, along with a rash of bold new architectural landmarks and a vibrant urban scene, make Manchester one of Britain's most exciting cities.

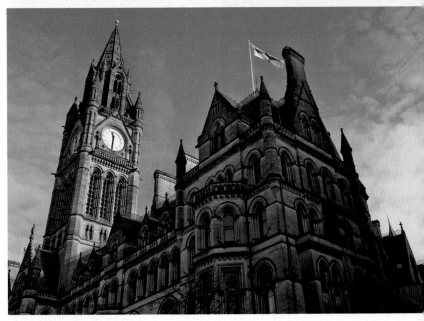

> *Manchester's Town Hall building is an archetypal work of the Victorian Gothic architectural style.*

START Albert Square, in front of Manchester Town Hall. Manchester is 200 miles north of London. **TRIP LENGTH** 2 days.

1 ★★ **Manchester Town Hall.** Many buildings now dwarf the 90m (295-ft.) tower, but this venerable 1877 landmark is still the symbol of Manchester. The stone fortress is, along with the Natural History Museum in London (p. 80, **2**), the crowning achievement of architect Alfred Waterhouse (1830–1905),

a proponent of the Victorian Gothic Revival style. Step inside for a quick course in local history, from the Roman colonization to the Industrial Revolution, as depicted in 12 murals by Pre-Raphaelite contemporary Ford Madox Brown (1821–93). Brown's less than idealized view of history includes a Roman youth kicking an African servant and an inventor of industrial machinery fleeing from an angry mob. ⊕ 30 min. Albert Sq. ☎ 0161/234-5000. Free admission. Mon–Fri 9am–5pm.

- **1** Manchester Town Hall
- **2** Manchester Art Gallery
- **3** The People's History Museum
- **4** Chetham's Library
- **5** Manchester Cathedral
- **6** National Football Museum
- **7** Castlefield
- **8** Museum of Science and Industry

- **9** Whitworth Art Gallery
- **10** John Rylands Library
- **11** The Salford Quays
- **12** Imperial War Museum North
- **13** Old Trafford Museum and Stadium Tour
- **14** Manchester Jewish Museum

Where to Stay & Dine

- Castlefield Hotel **15**
- Dimitri's **16**
- The Lowry Hotel **17**
- Market Restaurant **18**
- Midland Hotel **19**
- The Mitre Hotel **20**
- Palace Hotel **21**
- Peveril Of The Peak **22**
- Yang Sing **23**

2 ★★★ **Manchester Art Gallery.** A neoclassical building in the shadow of Town Hall has housed one of Britain's finest collections of painting and decorative arts since 1882. The Pre-Raphaelites and their associates take center stage, with works by Dante Gabriel Rossetti, John Everett Millais, William Holman Hunt, and Ford Madox Brown. They keep company with such masters as Turner and Modigliani, as well as many lesser-known 20th-century artists. Decorative arts including Greek pottery, 17th-century British silver, and contemporary furniture are housed in dramatic new galleries, while 20,000 items of clothing and fashion accessories from the 17th century to the present day fill the salons of an adjoining mansion of an 18th-century textile merchant. ⏱ 1 hr. Mosely St. at Princess St. ☎ 01612/358-888. www.manchestergalleries.org. Free admission. Tues–Sun 10am–5pm.

3 ★ **The People's History Museum.** While the Town Hall (**1**) and other Manchester monuments show off the riches gained from industry, this collection of union badges, banners, photographs, and other memorabilia pay homage to the labor movement and the working men and women who labored in the factories, dockyards, and warehouses. Even the setting is proletarian—a converted pumping station from the city's 19th-century

> *Chetham's is the world's oldest surviving library.*

> *Manchester United may be the city's most beloved club, but all football fans are welcome in the National Football Museum.*

waterworks. ⏱ 30 min. Left Bank, Spinningfields. ☎ 0161/838-9190. Free admission. Daily 9am–5pm. Metro: St. Peter's Sq.

❹ ★★★ **Chetham's Library.** The oldest library in the English-speaking world, set amid medieval cloisters near the banks of the River Irwell, has served scholarly Mancunians since 1653. As befits the city that helped fuel modern capitalism, Karl Marx and Friedrich Engels formulated communist theory in the reading room, surrounded by rare volumes that are still picturesquely shelved behind 18th-century iron gates. ⏱ 30 min. Long

Millgate. ☎ 0161/834-7961. www.chethams. uk. Free admission. Mon–Fri 9:30am–12:30pm & 1:30–4:30pm.

❺ ★ **Manchester Cathedral.** The medieval church that rose above a 7th-century Saxon church is as solid as its mossy old stones and sturdy wooden roof suggest. The cathedral was ransacked by Cromwell's troops during the Civil War, incurred a direct hit from German firebombs in 1941, and was severely damaged again in an IRA bombing in 1996. A Fire Window, so-called for its inferno-like hues, evokes these calamities, though the ethereal light the colored glass casts across the nave suggests that spirituality might just transcend the folly of humankind. Should the faithful begin to take themselves too seriously, they need only regard the carvings in the choir that depict humorous slices of medieval life in which a woman scolds her husband and men enjoy a forbidden game of backgammon. ⏱ 30 min. Victoria St. ☎ 0161/833-2230. www. manchestercathedral.org. Free admission. Mon–Fri 8am–7pm; Sat 8am–5pm; Sun 8:30am–7:30pm.

❻ ★ **National Football Museum.** Manchester's stunning Urbis complex, a glass shell beneath a sloping copper roof, houses England's National Football Hall of Fame and is filled with images of superstars and a memorabilia-packed collection that ranges from balls used in World Cup finals to historic jerseys. ⏱1 hr. Cathedral Gardens. ☎ 0161/605-8200. www.urbis.org.uk.

SITE GUIDE PAGE 445

7 ★★★ Castlefield. A Roman fort, Mamucium, stood on a grassy knoll above the River Irwell in what would become a grimy 19th-century industrial quarter and gave its name to the present-day city. Castlefield, named in turn for the forgotten, decaying fort that stood in the middle of fields through many centuries, shaped the fate of Manchester, and all Britain, again around 1720, when the Irwell was dredged and quays were built along its banks to facilitate the transfer of goods into Manchester. Within decades a network of canals ran through Castlefield, connecting Manchester with the rest of the Midlands and the North and facilitating the transport of coal and goods that were housed in massive brick warehouses. Railways arrived in the 1830s, making it all the easier to ship goods, and a spider web of tracks crisscrossed the lanes and canals on elaborate viaducts. Castlefield's legacy comes alive on the banks of the canals and massive brick warehouses, preserved as an Urban Heritage Park.

8 ★★ Museum of Science and Industry. The world's first railway station shows off Manchester's prominence as the first major industrial city with such 19th-century innovations as a walk-through Victorian sewer, huge turbines that once powered mills and factories, and massive locomotives. The adjoining Air and Space Gallery, set in an old market hall, shows how the city kept pace with 20th-century innovations as a center of the aviation industry—a 1909 Avro triplane and 1980s Trident passenger jet are parked beneath the glass and steel roof. ⏱1 hr. Liverpool Rd. ☎ 0161/832-2244. www.mosi.org.uk. Free admission. Daily 10am–5pm.

9 ★★ Whitworth Art Gallery. Tucked away on the campus of the University of Manchester, this hidden treasure houses an outstanding collection of watercolors by British artists. You'll discover *Moonlight on Lake Lucerne* and some 50 other pieces by Turner,

> *The Air and Space Gallery, inside the Museum of Science and Industry, is an essential stop on a walk around Castlefield.*

along with works by Gainsborough, Millais, and Constable. A sizable collection of modern art includes pieces by Francis Bacon, Lucian Freud, David Hockney, and just about every other prominent British artist of the 20th century. There's also an exceptional collection of textiles. ⏱1 hr. University of Manchester, Oxford Rd. ☎ 0161/275-7450. www.whitworth.manchester.ac.uk. Free admission. Mon–Sat 10am–5pm; Sun noon–4pm.

10 ★★ John Rylands Library. A neo-Gothic building, opened in 1900 but exuding medieval might, is the suitable home of some of the world's rarest manuscripts. These include a Gutenberg Bible and a fragment of St. John's Gospel from the 2nd century, along with Sumerian clay cuneiform tablets and ancient papyrus scrolls from the Near East. ⏱1 hr. Deansgate. ☎ 0161/275-3751. www.library.manchester.ac.uk. Free admission. Sun–Mon noon–5pm; Tues–Sat 10am–5pm.

Gay Manchester

Manchester has one of Britain's largest gay and lesbian communities outside of London, and the social hub is **Gay Village,** a once-derelict factory district alongside a canal southeast of the city center. More than 25 clubs and bars line the streets, and they come and go as quickly as such venues anywhere do. One of the biggest and busiest is **Churchill's,** 37 Charlton St. (☎ 0161/236-5529; www.churchills manchester.co.uk), with two bar areas and nightly entertainment. **Napoleon's,** 35 Bloom St. (☎ 0161/336-8800; www. napoleons.co.uk), established in 1972 and the first bar in Gay Village, covers three floors with a DJ-hosted dance floor.

Manchester also has several gay hotels and guest houses. **The New Union Hotel,** 111 Princess St. (☎ 0161/228-1492; www. newunionhotel.com), is an old-timer on Manchester's gay scene and one of the city's most popular karaoke bars; upstairs are 12 comfortable guest rooms; doubles run £40 to £55.

> At Manchester's regenerated docks you'll find two of the Northwest's most celebrated venues: the Lowry and the Imperial War Museum North.

⓫ ★★★ **The Salford Quays.** Manchester's docklands began to flourish in the 1890s, when Queen Victoria opened the Manchester Ship Canal, opening a passage for seagoing vessels between Manchester and Liverpool and the Mersey Estuary. Throughout the first part of the 20th century, the Salford docks accommodated as many as 5,000 ships a year, employing more than 75,000 workers loading and offloading ships and working in dockside factories that manufactured textiles and other goods. By the 1980s the docks were abandoned and derelict, but they have recently been reclaimed to house shops, restaurants, and the **Imperial War Museum North** (⓬). The docks are also the setting for the **Lowry,** Pier 8, the Quays (☎ 0843/208-6000; www. thelowry.com; free admission), a stunning performing arts center named for L.S. Lowry (1887–1976), famous for his smokestack-filled landscapes of the industrial North; his works are on view in the galleries. ⏱ 1 hr.

⓬ ★★★ **Imperial War Museum North.** The most striking aspect of this museum is the glass and steel shell that houses it, designed by renowned architect Daniel Libeskind to resemble a globe shattered by war. In galleries with slanted and sloping walls to suggest a world gone mad, exhibits and multimedia presentations trace the World War II bombings that laid waste to much of Manchester,

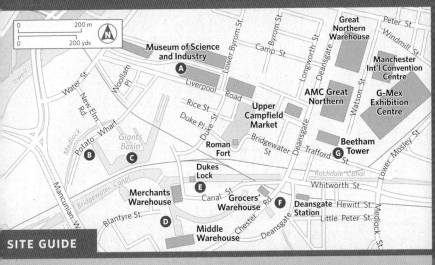

SITE GUIDE

7 Castlefield

A walk along the warehouse-lined canals evokes Castlefield's 19th-century prominence as the hub of the Industrial Revolution. The Liverpool Road Station, modest by comparison to such great railway terminals as London's Victoria Station, was built as a speculative risk in 1830, when railways were just being introduced; the sheds now house the **A Museum of Science and Industry** (p. 443, **8**). The museum's Air and Space Gallery occupies the iron and glass Lower Campfield Market, once crowded with vendors' stalls and later an exhibition hall. **B Potato Wharf,** in front of the old station, is one of many Castlefield locales named for their one-time function; barges here off-loaded potatoes that were shipped from Ireland to Liverpool and from there by rail to Manchester (the line was also the world's first passenger railway). The Bridgewater Canal, connecting Manchester with the coal and factory centers of the Northwest, flowed into the **C Giants Basin,** and from there canals ran directly into the **D Merchants and Middle Warehouses,** allowing goods to be loaded onto carts and taken into cavernous spaces for sorting and storage; cotton and other textiles were loaded back onto barges and trains for transport around England. Next to them is **E Dukes Lock,** part of the elaborate system that ensured the smooth flow of barge traffic through the once-congested waterways.

The **F Grocers Warehouse** was Manchester's first great industrial facility when it opened in 1742 and was equipped with water-driven hoists to lift coal off barges. At 47 stories, **G Beetham Tower** (pictured above) is Manchester's tallest building and the tallest in the U.K. outside of London, a symbol of the city's new prosperity. ⏱ 2 hr. Liverpool Rd. ☎ 0161/834-4026. www.manchester2002 uk.com. Daily 10am–5pm. Castlefield Visitors Centre provides maps and other information and guided tours on Wed & Sun in summer.

> *Wars of the 20th century form the focus of the collection at the Imperial War Museum North.*

the Falklands and Gulf Wars, and other conflicts in which Britain was engaged in the 20th century. ⏱ 1 hr. The Quays, Trafford Wharf Rd., Trafford Park. ☎ 0161/836-4000. www.iwm.org.uk. Free admission. Daily 10am–5pm. Closed Dec 24–26.

⓭ ★ **Old Trafford Museum and Stadium Tour.** One of the world's great soccer clubs, Manchester United, shows off photos, uniforms, and other memorabilia, providing fans with a close-up look at George Best and many of the greatest stars to ever play the game. The trophy room is filled with awards the team has snapped up over the past 130 years. Stadium tours take a look into the players' tunnel, changing rooms, and other areas that are usually off-limits. ⏱ 2 hr., with tour. Sir Matt Busby Way. ☎ 0161/868-8000. www.manutd.com. Museum: £10.50 adults, £8.50 kids, £35–£42.50 families. Tour (includes museum admission): £15 adults, £10 kids, £45–£54 families. Daily 9am–6:30pm; tours every 10 min. Metrolink: Old Trafford.

⓮ ★ **Manchester Jewish Museum.** Manchester has long been home to Britain's largest Jewish community outside London, currently numbering about 27,000. A Victorian-era Moorish-style synagogue in the once predominantly Jewish Cheetham Hill neighborhood is now filled with photographs, audio recordings, religious items, and household objects related to the history of Jews in Manchester, from immigrants who flocked to the city to work in the textile trade to present-day Jewish Mancunians. ⏱ 45 min. Cheetham Hill Rd. ☎ 0161/834-9879. www.manchesterjewishmuseum.com. £3.95 adults; £2.95 seniors, students & kids; £9.50 families. Mon–Thurs 10:30am–4pm; Sun 1–5pm.

A Pint with a View

Cloud23, 303 Deansgate (☎ 0161/870-1600; www.cloud23bar.com), is Manchester's highest bar, on the 23rd floor of the Beetham Tower. A Hilton Hotel occupies the floors below, and Europe's highest residential tower rises 24 floors above. Prices, given the million-dollar views, are relatively down to earth, as is the dizzying look down to ground level through the glass portals in the floor. Manchester's other trendy watering hole is the **River Bar,** 50 Dearmans Place, Chapel Wharf (☎ 0161/827-4000), a sophisticated lounge overlooking the River Irwell from the Lowry Hotel.

Where to Stay & Dine

> *One of many innovative dishes on the menu at the Market Restaurant.*

★★ Castlefield Hotel CASTLEFIELD

An old warehouse surrounded by the canals and buildings that are a relic of Manchester's industrial past has been converted into modern and comfortable accommodations. The historic surroundings are a short walk away from city center attractions, shops, and restaurants. Liverpool Rd. ☎ 0161/832-7073. www.castlefield-hotel. co.uk. 48 units. Doubles £70–£85. AE, MC, V.

★ Dimitri's CASTLEFIELD GREEK

One of Manchester's favorite bastions of exotic cuisine specializes in traditional Greek favorites, including a delicious selection of *meze* (small plates). Campfield Arcade, Deansgate. ☎ 0161/839-3319. Entrees £5–£8. AE, DC, MC, V. Lunch & dinner daily.

★★★ The Lowry Hotel SALFORD QUAYS

Manchester's docklands are being reclaimed as one of the city's trendiest neighborhoods, and the glass-and-steel Lowry rises above the old docks and warehouses along the River Irwell. Guest accommodations are minimalist and stylish, the most luxurious in Manchester, and the restaurants and bars are the city's hot spots. The city center is a short walk away across a stunning modern footbridge. 50 Dearmans Place. ☎ 888/667-9477. www.thelowryhotel.com. 165 units. Doubles £375–£425. AE, DC, MC, V.

★ Market Restaurant CITY CENTER ENGLISH

Old-fashioned ambience prevails in the charmingly dowdy dining room, where the changing menus include innovative preparations of beef and lamb and many vegetarian dishes. 104 High St. ☎ 0161/834-3743. www.market-restaurant.com. Entrees £14–£17. AE, DC, MC, V. Dinner Tues–Sat; lunch Fri–Sat.

★★★ Midland Hotel CITY CENTER

Manchester's grandest hotel was built by the railroads in 1903, and the terra cotta facade is still the emblem of Manchester luxury. Guest rooms are stylish and contemporary, and the vast lobby is the best place in town for tea. Peter St. ☎ 0161/236-3333. www.qhotels.co.uk. 312 units. Doubles £100–£300. AE, MC, V.

★★★ The Mitre Hotel CITY CENTER

Some of the best-value accommodations in central Manchester come with views of the honey-colored cathedral and Tudor houses that surround it. The rooms are no-frills (several share a hall bathroom) but quiet and convenient to anything you want to do in the city. Cathedral Gates. ☎ 0161/834-4128. www.themitrehotel.net. 32 units. Doubles £75–£100. MC, V.

★★★ Palace Hotel CITY CENTER

One of Manchester's first grand hotels has been a local landmark since the city's early-20th-century industrial heyday. Behind the red sandstone facade are stylishly contemporary guest rooms and lounges, restaurants, and bars that are popular gathering spots. Oxford St. ☎ 0161/288-1111. www.palace-hotel-manchester.co.uk. 13 units. Doubles £75–£200. AE, MC, V.

★ Peveril of the Peak CASTLEFIELDS PUB

Manchester's oldest and favorite pub, covered in green glazed tiles, is a triangular landmark alongside the city's old industrial canals. A huge selection of ales and solid pub fare is served in the dark, woody interior. Great Bridgewater St. ☎ 0161/236-6364. Entrees £6–£12. MC, V. Lunch & dinner daily.

★ Yang Sing CITY CENTER CHINESE

Manchester has a large Asian population, and this series of bright dining rooms serving a huge menu of Cantonese dishes has been a city favorite for decades. 34 Princess St. ☎ 0161/236-2200. Entrees £8–£15. AE, MC, V. Lunch & dinner daily.

An Excursion to the East Midlands

The East Midlands are made up of several counties in east-central England. The region encompasses miles of fenland and coastline and is home to Sherwood Forest, perhaps the country's most famous patch of green; it also adjoins Peak District National Park, England's oldest. The two principal cities are Nottingham, once a major industrial center, and Lincoln, famed for its magnificent cathedral. There are also a number of stately homes that offer a unique architectural tour of domestic life for the "upperest" of the upper crust. In short, there's something for everyone in this off-the-beaten-track part of England.

> The Banqueting Hall at medieval Haddon Hall, set as it would have been for the holidays during the 14th century.

START Buxton is about 30 miles southeast of Manchester via the A57, M67, A624, and A6. The drive will take at least an hour. **TRIP LENGTH** 4 days, 287 total miles.

❶ ★ Buxton. This former spa town is the best place to headquarter yourself for exploring Peak District National Park, and you can easily see everything on foot in a couple of hours. It was the Romans in A.D. 79 who first discovered the hot springs where, many centuries later,

Mary, Queen of Scots came to seek relief for her rheumatism. But it wasn't until the late 18th century that Buxton sprang to life as an aspiring spa town when the fifth Duke of Devonshire began building his northern answer to Bath. The

Travel Tip

You'll need a car for this itinerary, which includes areas of the Peak District National Park; rent one in Manchester.

> *The architecture of the Crescent, Buxton, is typical of a spa town that rose to prominence during the Georgian period.*

enterprise failed, but some buildings in compact Lower Buxton remain from that period, most notably the curving **Crescent.** Across the street, you can sample the waters yourself at **St. Anne's Well** and enjoy a stroll in the **Slopes,** a pretty landscaped park that dates from 1818.

The town's former **Pump Room** is now an exhibition space, and the completely restored **Opera House** (☎ 0845/127-2190; www.buxtonoperahouse.org.uk) hosts the popular Buxton Opera Festival every July. Just to the southeast of the opera house, the glass and cast-iron **Pavilion** from 1871 overlooks the manicured **Pavilion Gardens** (☎ 01298/23144; www.paviliongardens. co.uk). East of here is **Cavendish Arcade,** an old bathhouse converted into shops. For a bit of local history, spend a few minutes perusing the exhibits in the **Buxton Museum and Art Gallery,** Terrace Rd. (☎ 01298/24658, free admission). ⏱ 2 hr.

Head 12 miles (25 min.) northeast on the A53 to

❷ ★ **Edale.** Little more than a parish church and a cluster of stone houses, this village is set amidst the most spectacular scenery in the Peak District, between the White Peak and the Dark Peak. The village is a popular departure point for walkers (it marks the start of the Pennine Way) and cyclists. ⏱ 15 min.

Drive 4½ miles (10 min.) southeast on the A6187 to

❸ ★ **Castleton.** This little village of gritstone cottages huddled beneath 517m (1,696-ft.) Mam Tor and the ruins of a Norman castle is famous for its "showcaves." Spend an hour exploring the imposing ruins of **Peveril Castle** (☎ 01433/620-613; admission £4.20 adults, £2.10 kids), built by Henry II in 1176 and one of the earliest Norman fortresses in England. From the tower there are wonderful views over the Hope Valley. Then allot an hour for a guided tour at one of four caves; all of them are easy signposted walks from the village. **Peak Cavern** (☎ 01433/620-285; www.

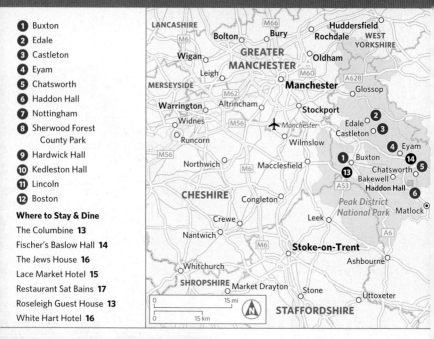

1 Buxton
2 Edale
3 Castleton
4 Eyam
5 Chatsworth
6 Haddon Hall
7 Nottingham
8 Sherwood Forest County Park
9 Hardwick Hall
10 Kedleston Hall
11 Lincoln
12 Boston

Where to Stay & Dine

The Columbine 13
Fischer's Baslow Hall 14
The Jews House 16
Lace Market Hotel 15
Restaurant Sat Bains 17
Roseleigh Guest House 13
White Hart Hotel 16

> Limestone slowly dissolves in water, creating spectacular underground formations such as those in Derbyshire's caverns.

peakcavern.co.uk; £8.25 adults, £6.25 kids) is known locally as the Devil's Arse because it has the largest natural opening of any cave in England. If you suffer from claustrophobia, steer clear of nearby ★ **Speedwell Cavern** (☎ 01433/620-512; www.speedwellcavern. co.uk; £8.75 adults, £6.75 kids), where the tour includes a ride on an enormous subterranean lake. **Treak Cliff Cavern,** Cross St. (☎ 01433/620-571; £7 adults, £4 kids), is noted for its limestone formations and exposed seams of Blue John (fluorite), a locally quarried gemstone. At **Blue John Cavern,** Buxton Rd. (☎ 01433/620-638; www. bluejohn-cavern.co.uk; £9 adults, £4.50 kids), the tour leads through a series of impressive caverns with glittering seams of the precious Blue John Stone. ⏱ At least 2 hr.

Head 9½ miles (20 min.) southeast on the A6187 and B6049 to

4 ★ **Eyam.** A poignant bit of history can be found amidst the gray stone cottages of Eyam (pronounced *eem*), a picture-perfect village set amidst the soft green hills of Derbyshire. When the dreaded bubonic plague arrived in Eyam in 1665, the villagers voluntarily quarantined themselves rather than leave and spread

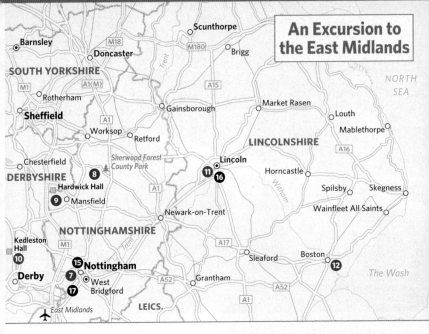

An Excursion to the East Midlands

the disease elsewhere. About a third of Eyam's 800 inhabitants died. The story is recounted in the ancient **Parish Church** (☎ 01433/630-930; free admission) and in the **Eyam Museum,** Hawkhill Rd. (☎ 01433/631-371, £2 adults, £1 kids). Before you leave, take a leisurely stroll through the village and have a look at the **stocks** on the village green. ⏲ 15 min. The nearest Visitor Information Centre is in Castleton; see p. 459.

Return to Buxton for the night. On Day 2, head 16 miles east on the A6 to

❺ ★★★ kids **Chatsworth.** Originally a Renaissance palace built in the mid–16th century by the Earl of Shrewsbury and his wife, the

> Chatsworth's Painted Hall exhibits the lavish baroque tastes of early-19th-century high society.

Over the Hills and Through Edale

Ask at the Edale Tourist Office about the many fine walks that depart from the village and head into the surrounding countryside. Destination points are **Hollins Cross,** on the ridge south of the Edale valley; **Mam Tor,** a high point with spectacular views; the atmospheric **Kinder Scout** plateau; and **Upper Booth,** part of a circular walk that loops back to Edale.

> *Robin Hood may be of dubious historical provenance, but you won't find many in Nottingham's tourism industry doubting his existence.*

legendary Bess of Hardwick, Chatsworth was used as a royal prison for Mary, Queen of Scots. Convinced that her husband had had an affair with Mary, Bess left Chatsworth and returned to her own Hardwick Hall (p. 454, ❾). A century

later the first Duke of Devonshire transformed Chatsworth into a baroque palace that was enlarged again between 1820 and 1827. By the time all this rebuilding was completed, the 327-room palace, sitting on its 40 hectares (100 acres) of parkland, was called "the second Versailles." Dozens of its art- and antiques-filled rooms are open to the public. With its painted ceilings depicting the Triumphs of Caesar, the **Painted Hall** is an exuberant display of Baroque taste and design. Elaborate stone carvings, sculpture, and another painted ceiling adorn the **Grotto.** Art treasures abound in the grand **State Rooms;** above the **grand staircase** is a painting by Tintoretto. Designed in the 18th century by Lancelot "Capability" Brown, the vast park and gardens surrounding Chatsworth are famous for the **Cascade Fountain** and the 19th-century **Great Conservatory** by Joseph Paxton, who designed the Crystal Palace in London. For kids, there's an **Adventure Playground** and **Farmyard.** ⏱ At least 2 hr. Bakewell, Derbyshire. ☎ 01246/565-300. www.chatsworth.org. Admission £17.50 adults, £12.50 seniors, £10 kids, £50 families; 10% discount if booked online; parking £2. Daily mid-Mar to mid-Dec 11am–5:30pm.

A Needle-Sharp Needlewoman

In addition to everything else, Bess of Hardwick was an accomplished needlewoman. When she hosted Mary, Queen of Scots (kept captive by her cousin, Elizabeth I) at Chatsworth in 1569, 1570, and 1571, they worked together on the **Oxburgh Hangings,** some of which are now in the Victoria and Albert Museum in London. In 1601, Bess ordered an inventory of the household furnishings, including textiles, at her Chatsworth and Hardwick Hall estates. In this document, which still survives, she bequeathed these items to her heirs to be preserved in perpetuity. The 400-year-old collection, now known as the **Hardwick Hall textiles,** is the largest collection of tapestry, embroidery, canvaswork, and other textiles to have been preserved by a single family.

Drive 5 miles (10 min.) southwest on the B6012 and A6 to

6 ★★★ **Haddon Hall.** Built in the 12th century as a fortified manor house, Haddon Hall is considered one of the finest (and least altered) medieval houses in England. From its original Norman owners, the hall passed in the 16th century to the Manners family, who have lived in it since 1567. In the 18th and 19th centuries, after many enlargements and additions, the house was virtually abandoned. It wasn't until the early 20th century that the ninth Duke of Rutland embarked on a restoration that preserved this remarkable time-capsule. The house rambles from the medieval **hall** of 1370 to the Tudor **kitchens** and vast **Banqueting Hall** of Henry VIII's time to the remarkable Elizabethan **Long Gallery,** with its wall of windows. Rare wall paintings of plants and animals, painted over during the Reformation, were uncovered in the **Chapel.** Haddon is graced by gorgeous 17th-century terraced **rose gardens** that sweep down to the River Wye and its graceful stone bridge. ☺ At least 1 hr. Bakewell, Derbyshire. ☎ 01629/812-855. www.haddonhall.co.uk. Admission £9.50 adults, £8.50 seniors, £5.50 kids. Daily Apr–Oct noon–5pm.

Nottingham is 32 miles east of Haddon Hall on the A615 and M1, about a 50-min. drive. Check into a hotel for the evening and start Day 3 fresh.

7 **Nottingham.** Founded by a Dane named Snot, Snottingham later became Nottingham and famous throughout the world for its associations with the legendary figure of Robin Hood, whose historical existence is still debated today, though references to him date back to the 13th century (over the years he's managed to evolve from a bandit to mythic English hero and defender of the poor). Medieval Nottingham fostered a renowned school of alabaster carvers and lacemakers, and during the Industrial Revolution the city suffered damage at the hands of the anti-technology Luddites, who rioted in 1811 and 1831.

The central core of the city is compact and easily walkable, and you can see all the main sights in a day. Start your explorations at **Old Market Square.** From here it's a 5-minute walk to the ★ **Castle Museum and Art Gallery,** Castle Rd. (☎ 0115/915-3700; £5.50 adults), with its bronze statue of Robin Hood out front. Only an underground passage survives from the original Norman keep of this once-great fortress; in the museum, have a look at the beautiful medieval alabaster carvings. The same ticket gets you into the **Museum of Nottingham Life at Brewhouse Yard,** Castle Blvd. (☎ 0115/915-3600), a row of 17th-century houses below the castle that present reconstructions of life in Nottingham over the past 300 years. For an unnerving glimpse of the justice system in earlier centuries, pay a visit to the **Galleries of Justice,** High Pavement (☎ 0115/952-0555; www.galleriesofjustice. org.uk; £8.95 adults, £6.95 kids), where you'll see Victorian courtrooms, a grim prison yard,

The Peak District National Park

Britain's first national park (www.peak district.org) was established in 1951, about 20 years after a "mass trespass" act of civil disobedience by a group of ramblers intent on establishing public right of access to this wild and beautiful landscape. The park, which lies mostly in Derbyshire and covers some 555 square miles of protected heathland, dales, craggy hills, caves, and rural villages, is one of the largest in Britain. It's characterized by two very distinct areas. The southern part, called the **White Peak,** has green fields and dales divided by drystone walls. The north, or **Dark Peak,** is wilder, with areas of heather-covered moorland and gritstone cliffs called "edges" that are popular with rock-climbers. Visitor centers are located in Bakewell, Bamford, Castleton, and Edale.

> *Ancient oak trees, like the so-called Major Oak, pictured, are a highlight of Sherwood Forest.*

and cells dating back to the 15th century. A stately Elizabethan manor set in 500 acres of parkland 3 miles west of the city center, **Wollaton Hall** (☎ 0115/915-3900; free admission) features period rooms and houses a Natural History Museum. ⏲ At least 2 hr.

On Day 3, drive 21 miles (40 min.) north on the A616 and B6034 to

❽ Sherwood Forest County Park. If you're a fan of Robin Hood and his Merry Men, you may want to spend a few minutes in the **Sherwood Forest Visitor Centre,** where the somewhat woeful "Robin Hood's Sherwood Forest" attraction uses wooden cut-outs and life-size figures to tell the legendary bandit's story. The major draw is the **Major Oak,** one of Robin's reputed hiding places, found at the end of a 1-mile walk through the forest. ⏲ 15 min. ☎ 0844/980-8080. www.sherwoodforest.org. uk. Free admission; parking £3. Daily 10am–5:30pm (Nov–Mar until 4:30pm).

From the Sherwood Forest Visitor Centre, drive 13 miles west on the A6075 (about 20 min.) to

❾ ★★★ Hardwick Hall. Bess of Hardwick (1527–1608), one of the most resourceful women of the Elizabethan age, is the personality responsible for the remarkable Hardwick Hall, perhaps the most perfectly preserved "pure" Elizabethan house in England. Born Elizabeth Talbot, she grew up in what was then a more modest Hardwick Hall. Widowed three times, she inherited property from each husband, and left her fourth, the Earl of Shrewsbury, after they'd built Chatsworth (❺). Reviling Shrewsbury as a knave and a scoundrel, Bess returned to Hardwick Hall and rebuilt it (at age 70) with the help of architect Robert Smythson (1535–1614). The three-story house is a marvel because of its high ceilings and huge windows (it's said Hardwick Hall is "more glass than wall"), which are larger on each successive floor. The interior, with its enormous Elizabethan fireplaces, is hung with embroideries worked on by Bess and Mary, Queen of Scots. The highlight is the **Long Gallery** on the top floor, flooded with light and with a portrait of the indomitable Bess herself. Some 12 hectares (30 acres) of gardens and orchards surround this monument to Elizabethan domestic architecture. ⏲ At least 1 hr. Doe Lea, Chesterfield, Derbyshire. ☎ 01246/850-430. www.nationaltrust.org.uk. Admission £11 adults, £5.50 kids, £27.45 families. Mid-Feb to Oct Wed–Sun 11am–5pm.

Kedleston Hall is 23 miles southwest of Hardwick Hall, a 40-min. drive on A38.

Sherwood Forest: Robin Hood's 'Hood

Once a royal hunting forest and the legendary home of the celebrated outlaw Robin Hood, Sherwood Forest today is part of a 180-hectare (450-acre) National Nature Reserve with about 900 veteran oak trees, including the famous Major Oak. Much of the ancient and once-vast forest is now scrubby heathland, with birch, gorse, and broom covering grassy clearings. Robin wouldn't recognize his old 'hood today, with its forest rangers, marked nature trails, restaurants, shops, and loads of visitors. To enjoy this legendary broadleaf forest, take one of the trails and find a quiet spot away from the crowds.

> *An exotic collection of Asian artifacts graces the Eastern Museum at Kedleston Hall.*

10 ★★ **Kedleston Hall.** The buildings he saw on his Italian Grand Tour had such a profound effect on the renowned Scottish architect Robert Adam (1728–92) that he sought to create "modern" versions of them at Kedleston Hall. His patron was Sir Nathaniel Curzon (1676–1758), who wanted to replace the family's Tudor manse with a Palladian mansion. The result is a neoclassical paean to the classical fronted by a gigantic six-columned Corinthian portico. The grandly sumptuous **Marble Hall** was designed to suggest the atrium of a Roman villa, while the circular **Saloon** rises 19m (62 ft.) to the top of a dome and has a decorative theme based on the temples of the Roman Forum. The **State bedroom** suite contains fine furniture and paintings, as does the **Drawing Room**; the **Dining Room** has a ceiling based on the Palace of Augustus in Rome's Farnese Gardens. The **Eastern Museum** is a treasure trove of fascinating objects acquired by Lord George Curzon (1859–1925) on his travels in Asia while Viceroy of India (1899–1905). The gardens and grounds, another Adam design, have remained virtually unaltered for over 200 years. ⏱ At least 1 hr. Kedleston Rd., near Quarndon, Derbyshire. ☎ 01332/842-191. www.nationaltrust.org.uk. Admission to hall, gardens,

> *Hardwick Hall is fitted out with the finest Elizabethan furniture and drapery.*

and park £9.90 adults, £4.90 kids, £25 families. Hall: late-Feb to Oct Sat–Wed noon–5pm. Pleasure grounds: late-Feb to Oct daily 10am–6pm.

Lincoln, your overnight stop for Day 3, is 62 miles northeast of Kedleston Hall, a 2-hr. drive on the A46. Check into your hotel and spend the morning of Day 4 exploring Lincoln.

> John Ruskin once called Lincoln Cathedral "the most precious piece of architecture in the British Isles."

11 ★★ **Lincoln.** Perched dramatically atop a high limestone hill that rises from the low wolds and flat fenlands of Lincolnshire, the county's chief city has a history that dates back to Celtic and Roman times and a medieval cathedral and character that makes it a perfect spot to spend your final night. In the Lower Town, have a look at the **High Bridge,** a medieval span across the River Witham lined with a unique assemblage of timber-framed houses; in the Middle Ages, Lincoln prospered as a wool town because the wool could be shipped directly to Flanders from the river's harbor, **Brayford Pool.**

From the High Bridge, make your way up the aptly named Steep Street to the picturesque **Upper Town,** crowned by the massive spires of ★★★ **Lincoln Cathedral** (☎ 01522/544-544; www.lincolncathedral.com; £6 adults, £1 kids), worth at least an hour of your time. Like the neighboring castle, the cathedral was begun by the Normans soon after their successful invasion of 1066, and the central portion of the arcaded **west front** dates from that period. In 1185 the Norman cathedral collapsed in an earthquake and was rebuilt in the 13th and 14th centuries in the Early English Gothic style. The impressive interior is enlivened with carvings in the **nave, Angel Choir,** and the 13th-century **Chapter House** (where the final scene of *The Da Vinci Code* was filmed in 2005).

Lincoln's other memorable attractions are all clustered around the cathedral. Allot half an hour to visit ★ **Lincoln Castle** (☎ 01522/511-068; £5 adults, £3.30 kids), accessible by a ramparts walkway and offering marvelous views of town and countryside. Step into the castle's former ★ **Prison Building** to see one of the four surviving copies of the **Magna Carta,** the 1215 document that is considered the precursor to modern democracy, and have a look at the **Prison Chapel** with its grim wooden cubicles for prisoners. Spend a few minutes visiting the **Bishop's Palace,** Minster Yard (☎ 01522/561-600; £4 adults, £2 kids), ruined in the 17th-century Civil War but still full of intriguing remnants of the days when it was one of the most powerful bishoprics in England. Budget a half-hour to see the nearby ★ **Usher Gallery,** Lindum Rd. (☎ 01522/527-980; free admission), particularly its 19th-century watercolors of Lincoln by Peter de Wint (1784–1849) and the collection of 16th-to-19th-century miniatures. To learn more about Lincoln's long and distinguished history, browse the exhibits at the **Collection,** Danes Terrace (☎ 01522/550-990; free admission), an innovative archaeology museum. ◷ At least 2 hr.

Drive 36 miles (1 hr.) southeast on the A15 and A17 to

12 **Boston.** You can see Lincoln from the tower of ★ **St. Botolph's,** Wormgate (☎ 01205/362-864; free admission to church, tower £2.25), a 15th-century church known as the "Stump" because it has a tower but no spire. In medieval times, Boston was Lincoln's port city until the Withen River silted up and the lucrative wool trade moved elsewhere. Spend an hour exploring the church and the town's Tudor-era maze of streets. America's Pilgrim Fathers were imprisoned in the ★ **Guildhall,** South St. (☎ 01205/365-954; £3 adults, £2 kids) after their attempted escape to the Netherlands in 1607. Later religious dissenters left from Boston and founded Boston in the New World. ◷ 30 min.

Where to Stay & Dine

> *Atmospheric dining at the Jews House restaurant, Lincoln.*

★ **The Columbine** BUXTON *MODERN BRITISH*
Charming and unpretentious, Buxton's best restaurant serves straightforward preparations of Modern British cuisine using fresh local ingredients. 7 Hallbank. ☎ 01298/78752. Entrees £11–£13. MC, V. Dinner Mon–Sat. Closed Tues Nov–Apr.

★★★ **Fischer's Baslow Hall** CHATSWORTH
Located at the edge of the Chatsworth estate, this Edwardian country house is the finest hotel and restaurant in the Peak District. Calver Rd., Baslow. ☎ 01246/583-259. www.fischers-baslowhall.co.uk. 11 units. Doubles £150–£220 w/breakfast. MC, V.

★ **Lace Market Hotel** NOTTINGHAM
This boutique hotel in a restored and modernized Georgian town house is in the trendy and centrally located Lace Market district and has one of the city's better restaurants. High Pavement, Lace Market. ☎ 0115/852-3223. www.lacemarkethotel.co.uk. 42 units. Doubles £150–£230. AE, MC, V.

★ **The Jews House** LINCOLN *CONTINENTAL*
Housed in a beautiful Norman-era house in the Upper Town, this is one of Lincoln's best spots for casual yet sophisticated dining.
15 The Strait. ☎ 01522/524-851. Entrees £15–£18. MC, V. Lunch & dinner Tues–Sat.

★★ **Restaurant Sat Bains** NOTTINGHAM *CONTINENTAL*   Nottingham's best restaurant is known for its intriguing "marriages" of ingredients, such as roast scallops with braised oxtail. There are also seven luxurious bedrooms and special deals for bed, breakfast, and dinner. Lenton Lane. ☎ 0115/986-6566. www.restaurantsatbains.com. Doubles £129–£265. Dinner Tues–Sat. Reservations required. Fixed-price dinners £55–£150. AE, MC, V.

★ **Roseleigh Guest House** BUXTON
This lovingly restored and family-run B&B has views of the Pavilion Gardens and comfortable, nicely decorated rooms. 19 Broad Walk. ☎ 01298/24904. www.roseleighhotel.co.uk. 10 units. Doubles £74–£88 w/breakfast. MC, V.

★ **White Hart Hotel** LINCOLN
Lincoln's oldest and most elegant hotel is an antiques-filled Georgian-era house with rooms looking out over the city; stay in the original part and avoid the annex. Bailgate. ☎ 01522/526-222. www.whitehart-lincoln.co.uk. 48 units. Doubles £110–£130. AE, MC, V.

Fast Facts

Accommodations Booking Services
A good source for character-filled accommodations in the Northwest, including the Lake District, is **National Trust Holiday Cottages,** P.O. Box 536, Melksham, Wiltshire (☎ 0844/ 800-2070; www.nationaltrustcottages.co.uk). The National Trust offers rooms in more than 350 historic properties around Britain. **Sherpa Van Accommodation Service,** 29 The Green, Richmond, North Yorkshire (☎ 0871/5200-124; www.sherpavan.com), is geared to walkers and arranges accommodations in the Lake District, as well as luggage transport from inn to inn, allowing you to walk from one stop to another unencumbered. **Mountain Goat,** Victoria St., Windermere (☎ 015394/45161; www.mountain-goat.com), offers tours of the Lake District, with accommodations, as well as pickup and drop-offs for walkers in the region.

Arriving & Getting Around
Note: For information on getting around the Lake District by steamer, see p. 424. BY PLANE **Manchester Airport** (☎ 08712/710-711; http://www.manchesterairport.co.uk), 15 miles south of the city center, handles direct flights from the United States and the Continent. Airport Link, an above-ground train, runs from the Station (the airport transport hub) to Piccadilly Railway Station in downtown Manchester every 15 minutes, from 5:15am to 10:10pm. Direct rail lines also link the airport to various cities in the region, including Liverpool, Chester, and York. BY TRAIN Extensive train service runs between London and cities and towns throughout the Northwest; Chester, Liverpool, and Manchester are on direct lines from London's Euston Station, and trains run as frequently as every half-hour. The trip from London to Manchester or London to Liverpool takes a little under 3 hours. Trains also run frequently between cities in the region and offer good rail connections to cities in Yorkshire (p. 492) and North Wales (p. 659). For schedules and information, contact **National Rail Enquiries** (☎ 08457/484950; www.nationalrail.co.uk). BY CAR From London, the M1 and M6 motorways head north, with well-marked routes leading off it to Chester, Liverpool, and Manchester; the drive from London to Manchester is about 3 hours (though traffic can lengthen that time). The M6 continues north to Kendal, where you can continue on the A590 and A591 to Windermere, gateway to the Lake District; allow about 5 hours for the trip. Once you're in the region, a car is the best way to get around the Northwest and Lake District if you want to explore the countryside and lakes. BY BUS Buses run hourly between London's Victoria Coach Station and many points in the Northwest, including Chester, Liverpool, Manchester, and Windermere; for schedules and information, contact **National Express** (☎ 0871/781-8181; www.nationalexpress.co.uk). There is a well-run network of bus companies in the Lake District that is geared to getting visitors around without cars, but a car is still a better bet for the time-sensitive traveler. The Lake District Visitor Centre at Brockhole and other visitor information offices can provide bus details (see "Visitor Information," below). For bus service information and schedules for the Northwest, contact **Traveline** (☎ 0871/ 200-2233; www.traveline.org.uk). PUBLIC TRANSPORT Cities and large towns in the region have extensive networks. In **Manchester,** Metrolink trams and buses link all major sights in the city; buses run regularly from 6am to 11pm, with limited night service, and trams operate Monday through Thursday 6am to midnight, Friday and Saturday 6am to 1am, and Sunday 7am to 11pm. Tickets are dispensed from machines at stops. A Travelshop at the Picadilly Gardens Bus Station, Portland St. (☎0161/205-2000), provides information and maps Monday through Saturday 7am to 6pm, and Sunday 10am to 6pm. An extensive bus system operates in **Liverpool,** though you can easily walk to most of the city-center sights. Free shuttle buses run between Lime Street railway station and other city-center sights and Albert Dock; the Tourist Information Centre (see p. 459) provides information and maps.

Emergencies

Call ☎ 999 (free of charge) for police and fire emergencies and to summon an ambulance. Most hotels will be able to refer you to a local doctor or dentist. Manchester, Liverpool, Nottingham, and the region's other cities are well equipped for medical care.

Internet Access

Many hotels are now equipped with Wi-Fi, and many have a public terminal as well. Internet cafes, where you can log on for about £1 an hour, are common in major towns, and public libraries are often Wi-Fi equipped or have terminals you can use for free. In Manchester, a pleasant place to log on while enjoying a cup of tea is **North Tea Power,** 36 Tib St. (☎ 0161/833-3073).

Pharmacies

Pharmacies ("chemists") are usually open 9am to 7pm in the Northwest, though at least one in the region keeps 24 hours on a rotating basis. The most common chain is Boots (www.boots.com), with branches in: MANCHESTER 32 Market St. (☎ 01618/326-533). LIVERPOOL Inside Lime Street Station (☎ 01517/087-699). WINDERMERE 10 Crescent Rd. (☎ 01539/443-093).

Post Office

Post offices are generally open Monday to Friday from 8am to 5pm, and some on Saturday mornings. MANCHESTER A centrally located post office is at 63 Newton St., just off Piccadilly Gardens (☎ 0845/722-3344). NOTTINGHAM The post office is on Queen Street (☎ 0845/722-3344).

Safety

Like the rest of England, the Northwest and the East Midlands are pretty safe, with relatively little crime. You may want to exercise caution in crowded Liverpool and Manchester, where pickpockets are not uncommon. In Nottingham, avoid walking at night in unlit areas.

Visitor Information

You'll find tourist offices in almost any town and village of any size in the Northwest, East Midlands, and Lake District; call ahead as opening times can vary, especially outside of high season. Some major centers include: BOSTON Tourist Information Centre, in Boston Guildhall Museum, South St. (☎ 01205/365-954). BUXTON Buxton Tourist Office, Pavilion Gardens (☎ 01298/25106; www.visitbuxton.co.uk, or www.visitpeakdistrict.com). CASTLETON Castleton Visitor Centre, Castle St. (☎ 01433/620-679). CHESTER Visitor Information Centre, Town Hall, Northgate St. (☎ 01244/402-111; www.visitchester.com). EDALE Edale Tourist Office, Grindsbrook (☎01433/670-207; www.edale-valley.co.uk). LAKE DISTRICT Lake District Visitor Centre, Brockhole (☎ 015394/46601; www.lake-district.gov.uk). LINCOLN Tourist Information Centre, 9 Castle Hill (☎01522/545-458; www.visitlincolnshire.com). LIVERPOOL Liverpool Tourist Information Centre, 08 Place, 36–38 Whitechapel (☎ 0151/233-2459; www.visitliverpool.com). MANCHESTER Manchester Visitor Information Centre, Piccadilly Plaza, Portland St. (☎ 0871/222-8223; www.visitmanchester.com). NOTTINGHAM Nottingham Tourism Centre, 1–4 Smithy Row (☎ 08444/775-678; www.visitnottingham.com).

For general information on the West Midlands, consult **www.visittheartofengland.com**; for the East Midlands, visit **www.eastmidlandstourism.com**. For information on the Peak District, consult **www.visitpeakdistrict.com** (Peak District and Derbyshire) or **www.peakdistrict.gov.uk** (Peak District National Park Authority). For more regional information, visit **www.visitlincolnshire.com** and **www.visitnottingham.com** (covering the city and Nottinghamshire).

Festivals and Events

The **Chester Summer Music Festival** brings classical musicians to town for 2 weeks of concerts in late July (☎ 01244/320-700). Manchester celebrates **Mardi Gras** in late winter/early spring with 3 days of revelry, and **Festival Europa** in late May has street theater, markets, and live music.

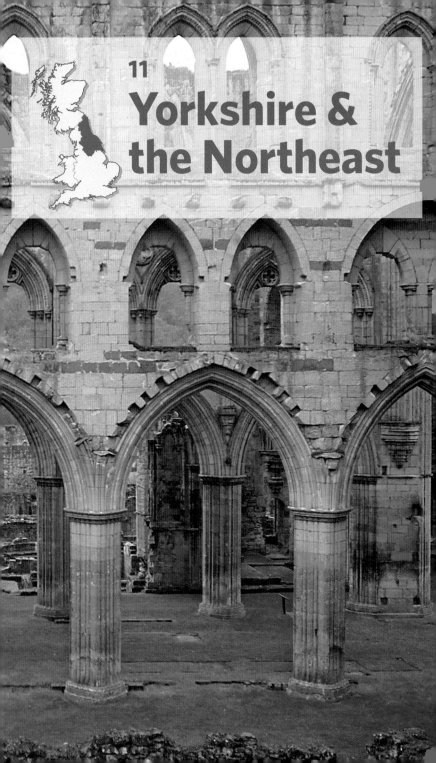

Favorite Yorkshire & the Northeast Moments

The counties of Yorkshire and Northumbria in England's northeastern corner show off their rich heritage in cities like York, with its mighty cathedral and medieval walls; Durham, whose cathedral is a masterpiece of the Romanesque; and Leeds, a former industrial giant that is now home to the fabulous Royal Armouries Museum. Two national parks preserve the region's distinctive landscapes of heather-covered moorland, green dales, and windswept coastline, while the atmospheric ruins of Rievaulx Abbey and the small village of Haworth reveal the turbulent religious past of northeastern England and the inspiration it provided to writers like Charlotte and Emily Brontë.

> PREVIOUS PAGE *Once among England's most powerful monasteries, Rievaulx Abbey now stands romantically in ruins on the edge of a national park.* THIS PAGE *You need to walk right around York Minster to properly appreciate its size and grandeur.*

❶ Admiring York from its medieval walls. York was already an old city when medieval masons built new city walls incorporating parts of the ancient Roman fortifications. Today these walls, unique in England, provide a wonderful walkway for viewing the historic city center. See p. 484.

❷ Roaming the Roman remains of Hadrian's Wall. Erected some 2,000 years ago near what is now the border between England and Scotland, this ancient feat of engineering prowess was an attempt to keep Roman Britain safe from wild northern tribes like the Picts. Well-preserved sections of the ancient defensive bulwark, augmented by museums and viewing areas, provide fascinating insights into life in Roman Britain. See p. 472, ❼.

❸ Gaping at York Minster. The dizzying grandeur of this massive edifice, one of the largest churches in the world and illuminated by

1 York
2 Hadrian's Wall
3 York Minster
4 National Railway Museum
5 Rievaulx Abbey
6 Royal Armouries Museum
7 Brontë Parsonage Museum
8 Yorkshire Dales National Park
9 Durham Cathedral
10 Harewood House

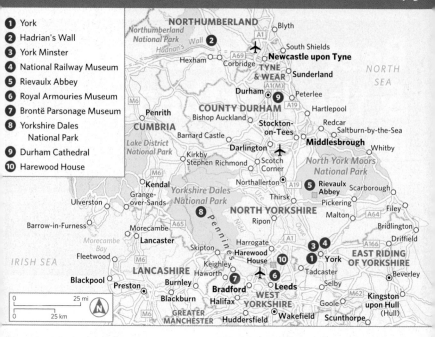

gorgeous stained glass, never fails to awe and inspire. Ascend to the tower for a spectacular bird's-eye view of York, and descend to the undercroft to see the remains of an earlier Roman basilica. See p. 484, 1.

4 **Riding the rails at the National Railway Museum in York.** An amazing assortment of historic trains, ranging from early steam engines of the 1840s to the sleek Eurostar of today, fill the halls of this must-see museum. Treasures include the royal carriages of Queen Victoria and Queen Elizabeth II. See p. 488, 8.

5 **Finding romance in the ruins of Rievaulx Abbey.** The ruins of this once-great abbey in what is now North York Moors National Park are hauntingly romantic and carry the visitor back to a time when Yorkshire was the leading center of Christianity and home to several giant monasteries. See p. 480, 4.

6 **Wondering about war at the Royal Armouries Museum in Leeds.** Aggression in all its forms is the subplot at this exciting new museum dedicated to arms and armor through the ages. It's worth a stop in Leeds just to see it. See p. 490, 1.

7 **Browsing through the Brontë Parsonage Museum in Haworth.** The home of the literary sisters Charlotte, Emily, and Anne, and their debauched brother Branwell, still looks much as it did in their lifetime and contains a museum full of Brontë manuscripts and memorabilia. See p. 472, 9.

8 **Exploring Yorkshire Dales National Park.** Quiet valleys with grazing cows and sheep, high limestone-capped hills and escarpments, cozy villages, and a series of spectacular caves in Ingleton can all be found in this scenically varied and eminently photogenic national park. See p. 474.

9 **Delighting in Durham Cathedral.** Filled with distinctive dog's-tooth carving, England's most glorious example of a Norman-era Romanesque cathedral occupies an imposing site above the River Wear and commands respect however you look at it. See p. 481, 6.

10 **Enjoying the elegance of Harewood House.** Some of the greatest talents of the "Age of Elegance" were involved in the creation of this stately home and its inviting gardens; touring it is a pleasure. See p. 473, 11.

Best of Yorkshire & the Northeast in 3 Days

Yorkshire is the largest county in England and one of the most scenically diverse, a place where hills, dales, moorlands, and North Sea coastline serve as a backdrop to historic towns, bracing vistas, romantic ruins, and amazing cathedrals. Less-visited Northumbria, which includes the counties of Durham and Northumberland, has its share of powerful scenery, too. On this itinerary you'll get a hearty taste of northeast England.

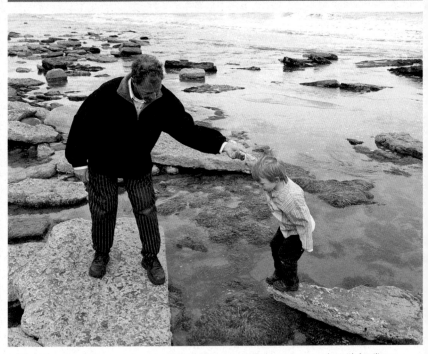

> *Once a favorite spot for coastal smugglers, the coves around Whitby are now popular with families.*

START York is 209 miles north of London, a 4-hr. drive on the M1. Trains from London's King's Cross Station make the journey in 2 hr. TRIP LENGTH 141 total miles.

1 ★★★ **York.** Make "The Queen of the North," as York is called, your first overnight stop, and give yourself at least a day to explore the fascinating nooks and "snickleways"

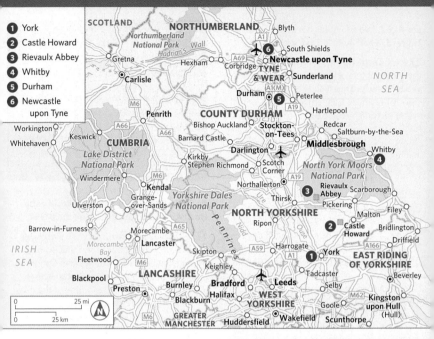

- 1 York
- 2 Castle Howard
- 3 Rievaulx Abbey
- 4 Whitby
- 5 Durham
- 6 Newcastle
  upon Tyne

(alleys) of this proud Yorkshire city. **York Minster** (p. 484, 1), the largest church north of the Alps, is quite literally awesome, and so are the walkable medieval **walls** (p. 466) that encircle York and give you amazing views of the city's architectural treasures, such as the 14th-century **Merchant Adventurers' Hall** (p. 486, 5) and the picturesque medieval street called the **Shambles** (p. 486, 4). **JORVIK Viking Centre** (p. 487, 6) provides an entertaining glimpse of York in the Viking age, and at the marvelous **National Railway Museum** (p. 488, 8), you can see the first trains ever built and those used by Queens Victoria and Elizabeth II. The riches and richness of York and Yorkshire are also on display at **York Castle Museum** (p. 487, 7) and the **Yorkshire Museum** (p. 488, 10). ⏱1 day.

Travel Tip

Driving opens up more of the countryside and makes visiting places like Rievaulx Abbey possible. That said, York is easily accessible by rail, so if you're starting out in London, you can take a train to York and rent a car there.

> The entrance hall, with its Corinthian columns and decorous style, is one of the highlights of Castle Howard.

On Day 2, head 15 miles north to Castle Howard, a half-hour's drive on the A64.

2 ★★★ **Castle Howard.** Anyone who's seen the movie or television series based on Evelyn Waugh's novel *Brideshead Revisited* will instantly recognize Castle Howard, the largest house in Yorkshire and home of the Howard family since the late 17th century. The facade showcases elegant architectural details, including statues, long arched windows, and a beautiful cupola crowning the center of the house. The marble **entrance hall,** lit by the dome, is particularly impressive, as is the **Long Gallery,** but the house has many superb rooms, all filled with fine furniture, statues, and china. The collection of paintings includes works by Rubens, Tintoretto, Van Dyke, Canaletto, and Reynolds, as well as a famous portrait of Henry VIII by Hans Holbein. *Brideshead* memorabilia fills one room. The 400-hectare (1,000-acre) **park** is landscaped with lakes, fountains, rose gardens, and shady woodland gardens. You can choose among three restaurants. ⏱ At least 2 hr. Near Malton. ☎ 01653/648-333. www.castlehoward.co.uk. Admission £13 adults, £11 seniors, £7.50 kids. Daily mid-Mar to Oct & late Nov–early Dec 11am–4pm (grounds 10am–5:30pm). Grounds are also open at select times during the rest of the year; consult the website.

Walking on the Walls

A **path** (daily 8am–dusk) runs along the top of the almost 3 miles of ★★★ **medieval walls** that enclose the center of York, with great views along the way. Stairways up to the top of the walls are found at the four fortified gateways (or "bars") that still serve as entrances into the old part of town. A good place to start a wall walk is Micklegate (p. 488, **11**), the southern entry used by royalty.

Rievaulx Abbey is 16 miles north of Castle Howard, a half-hour's drive on the B1257.

3 ★★ **Rievaulx Abbey.** Yorkshire was fertile ground for the religious fervor that swept through England after the Norman Conquest, and eventually had more monasteries than any other county in England. One of the richest and most powerful of the great abbeys was Rievaulx, founded by the Cistercians in the 12th century. The enormous ruins of this once-thriving monastic complex are both fascinating and picturesque. See p. 480, **4**.

Whitby is 37 miles northeast of Rievaulx Abbey, an hour's drive on the A170 and A169. This segment of the itinerary weaves through North York Moors National Park (p. 474)

> *Though weathered and roofless, the nave at the former Cistercian abbey at Rievalux remains largely intact.*

to the Yorkshire coast and provides a sampling of Yorkshire's dramatically diverse landscapes.

4 ★ **Whitby.** Make this historic harbor town and holiday resort on the wild Yorkshire coast your second overnight stop. Called West Cliff, the Victorian side of Whitby, with its fish-and-chips shops and seaside arcades, sits on the west bank of the River Esk. East Cliff, the older part of the town, is where you'll find, high on a clifftop, the wonderfully atmospheric ruins of ★ **Whitby Abbey,** accessed via the Church Stairs (☎ 01947/603-568; £5 adults, £3 kids), the inspiration for the opening of Bram Stoker's creepy novel *Dracula,* and neighboring **St. Mary's Church,** an architectural hodgepodge that looks like a fortress. If you're interested in Captain James Cook (1728–79), who began his seafaring career in Whitby and whose statue looks out over the harbor, spend a few minutes in the **Captain Cook Memorial Museum,** Grape Lane (☎ 01947/601-900; www.cookmuseumwhitby.co.uk; £4 adults, £3 kids), where you can see a collection of Cook memorabilia. And if the weather is nice, take a beach walk on the great expanse of **Whitby Sands.** ⏲ 2 hr.

On Day 3, head to Durham, 56 miles (1½ hr.) northwest of Whitby via the A174 (trip time.

5 ★★★ **Durham.** This Northumbrian town is proud possessor of the greatest Romanesque cathedral in England. A superb example of 12th-century Norman architecture, design, and craftsmanship, **Durham Cathedral** and the adjacent **Durham Castle** have been named

> *The Millennium Bridge and BALTIC have been symbols of the revival of Newcastle upon Tyne and Gateshead over the last decade.*

a UNESCO World Heritage Site. ⏲ 2 hr. See p. 481, **6**.

Your final stop on Day 3 is Newcastle upon Tyne, 18 miles north of Durham, about a half-hour's drive on the A1.

6 ★ **Newcastle upon Tyne.** The old saying "Like carrying coals to Newcastle" doesn't mean much anymore, since the economy of this old port city on the River Tyne no longer relies on the export of coal. Today, it is culture, not carbon, that fuels Newcastle, and the city has been given new life as a thriving arts center. History buffs can visit the **New Castle** that gave the city its name, pop into the 17th-century **Bessie Surtees house,** and browse the local history exhibits at the **Discovery Museum.** Museum-lovers will also want to stop in at the ★ **Laing Art Gallery** and the ★★ **Great North Museum: Hancock.** But if you want a hint of what's new in Newcastle, simply stroll down regentrified **Grey Street** and the buzzing **Quayside** area. ⏲ At least 2 hr. See p. 470, **6**.

Staying the Night in Whitby

Magpie Café is famous for its fish and chips, and that's what you should order—though you may have to stand in line first. 14 Pier Rd. ☎ 01947/602-058. Entrees £7–£12. MC, V. Lunch & dinner daily.

★ **White Horse & Griffin,** an 18th-century coaching inn, has been transformed into a boutique hotel, with stylish, comfortable rooms and a good restaurant. 87 Church St. ☎ 01947/604-857. www.whitehorseand griffin.co.uk. 20 units. Doubles £85–£100 w/ breakfast. MC, V.

Best of Yorkshire & the Northeast in 1 Week

There's much to see in these two large counties, and a week gives you enough time to do so without rushing. Start your exploration of the major historic sites and scenic splendors of northeast England with York, the region's most beautiful and fascinating city. From there, you'll move on to a diverse array of attractions that ranges from a prisoner-of-war camp from World War II to two beautiful national parks to old industrial cities—Leeds and Newcastle upon Tyne—that have been retooled and refined into surprisingly hip destinations.

> *Yorkshire is dotted with ruined abbeys dissolved during the bloody reign of Henry VIII, like this one at Whitby.*

START York is 209 miles north of London. Trains from London's King's Cross Station make the journey in 2 hr. Check into your hotel for 3 nights. **TRIP LENGTH** 336 total miles.

1 ★★★ **York.** ⏱ 2 days. See p. 484.

Day 3 is taken up by two side trips from York. Head first to Castle Howard, 15 miles north of York, a half-hour's drive on the A64.

2 ★★★ **Castle Howard.** Yorkshire's largest house isn't actually a castle, but it is sumptuous both inside and out. ⏱ 2 hr. See p. 466, **2**.

1 York
2 Castle Howard
3 Eden Camp
4 Whitby
5 Durham
6 Newcastle upon Tyne
7 Corbridge Roman Town, Hadrian's Wall
8 Fountains Abbey and Studley Royal Water Gardens
9 Haworth
10 Leeds
11 Harewood House

Where to Stay
Grey Street Hotel 12
Waterside Hotel 12

Where to Dine
Big Mussel 12
Café 21 12

In the afternoon, head 5 miles east on the A64 to

3 ★ **Eden Camp.** In 1942, Malton became the site of this prisoner-of-war camp, built by its first inmates, 250 Italians captured in North Africa. They were followed by Germans, who remained here until 1948. Eden Camp's huts have now been re-equipped to tell about life in Britain during World War II. Realistic scenes, sounds, and smells have been created to help you imagine life at a time when food was rationed, blackouts were a nightly occurrence, and 80,000 civilians were killed in bombing raids over England. ⏲ At least 1 hr. Old Malton. ☎ 01653/697-777. www.edencamp.co.uk.

Admission: £5.50 adults, £4.50 seniors & kids. Daily 10am–5pm. Closed Dec 23 to mid-Jan.

Return to York for your third overnight. On Day 4, your first stop is Whitby, 49 miles (1 hr. 15 min.) north on the A64 and A169. The drive takes you through a section of North York Moors National Park, one of the largest areas of heather-covered moorland in England.

Travel Tip

To see the countryside stops on this tour, you'll need a car. If you are starting from London, it's most economical to take a train to York and rent a car there.

> *The small university city of Durham boasts a cathedral that is the finest complete Norman building in the country.*

4 ★ **Whitby.** This picturesque harbor town was founded in A.D. 656 on the north Yorkshire coast, though its name arrived care of Norse raiders in the 11th century (Whitby is derived from the Old Norse for "white village."). The fishing industry is a major player here and supplies the many fish-and-chips spots on the west side of town; the older east side is dominated by the spooky ruins of **Whitby Abbey,** which inspired part of Bram Stoker's *Dracula* (some of which is set in the town). The east side is also where you'll find the **Captain Cook Memorial Museum,** filled with memorabilia from the great explorer who apprenticed as a seaman in Whitby. The town is also a great spot to have lunch. ⏱ 2 hr. See p. 467, **4**.

Your next stop on Day 4 is Durham, 56 miles (1½ hr.) north of Whitby on the A174 and A1043. If you want to drive along the Yorkshire coast, with its towering cliffs and rugged beauty, continue north from Whitby via the A174. If you follow this scenic route up to Durham, it will take you at least half a day of driving time.

5 ★★★ **Durham.** Stupendous **Durham Cathedral,** England's greatest example of 12th-century Norman architecture, sits like a fortress high above the River Wear and has been designated a UNESCO World Heritage Site. The adjacent ruins of **Durham Castle** are also worth exploring. ⏱ 2 hr. See p. 481, **6**.

Drive 18 miles (30 min.) north on the A1 to Newcastle upon Tyne and check into a hotel.

6 ★ **Newcastle upon Tyne.** This old coal-mining city on the River Tyne has, like Leeds, undergone a radical transformation in recent years and is now being "rebranded" as NewcastleGateshead, one of northern England's cultural hotspots. You'll get a wonderful view of the city with its seven historic bridges from the top of ★ **Castle Keep** at Castle Garth (☎ 0191/232-7938; £4 adults), all that's left of the 11th-century New Castle that gave the city its name. Another piece of old Newcastle is the ★ **Bessie Surtees House,** 41–44 Sandhill (☎ 0191/269-1200; www.english-heritage.org.uk; free admission), two adjoining merchant houses from the 16th and 17th centuries. You'll get a hint of the hip and happening new Newcastle by strolling down **Grey Street,** with its handsome assortment of neoclassical buildings refashioned into chic shops and restaurants.

Spend an hour at the ★ **Discovery Museum,** Blandford Sq. (☎ 0191/232-6789; www.twmuseums.org.uk; free admission), where fascinating exhibits reveal Newcastle's long and lively history as a port and coal-mining center, and another hour at the ★ **Laing Art Gallery,** New Bridge St. (☎ 0191/232-7734; www.twmuseums.org.uk; free admission), with its intriguing collection of 19th- and 20th-century art, including greats like Yorkshire-born sculptor Henry Moore. Opened in 2009, the ★★ **Great North Museum: Hancock,** Barras Bridge (☎ 0191/222-6765; www.twmuseums.org.uk; free admission), incorporates natural science, archaeology, history, and cultural exhibits that include an interactive model of nearby Hadrian's Wall (**7**) as well as a planetarium. At night, the area called ★★ **Quayside** is a lively spot for strolling, full of pubs, restaurants, and clubs. ⏱ At least 2 hr.

Spend part of the morning on Day 5 exploring Newcastle; then head 19 miles (30 min.) west on the B1307 and B1318 to

> *Ancient and once powerful, Fountains Abbey now sits amid an idyllic Georgian water garden.*

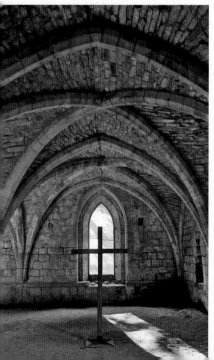

Roamin' Hadrian's Roman Wall

Once patrolled by soldiers from all corners of the Roman Empire, **Hadrian's Wall** is one of the best-known attractions in Yorkshire and Northumbria, and a UNESCO World Heritage Site. Construction of Roman Britain's biggest building project started in A.D. 122 on the order of Emperor Hadrian and was completed 8 years later. Stretches of this 73-mile defensive bulwark are still remarkably intact, dotted with **Roman forts,** milecastles (triangular defensive towers built at 1-mile intervals), temples, and archaeological sites that provide insight into how the Romans lived almost 2,000 years ago. The most striking parts can be found in Northumberland close to the county's western fringes. At **Steel Rigg** you can see the wall wind its way across the countryside. The most dramatic section of the wall is from **Cawfields to Walltown Quarry.** At **Carrawburgh,** just next to the B6318 Military Road, there is a well-preserved **Temple to Mithras.** Costumed re-enactments of Roman battles often take place on summer weekends at places like **Vindolanda, Housesteads, Chesters,** and **Corbridge.** For a map and information on pubs, restaurants, and accommodations along the 84-mile **Hadrian's Wall National Trail,** visit www.nationaltrail.co.uk/hadrianswall.

> *Now a museum, the parsonage in Haworth was for decades home to the Brontë family.*

7 ★★ **Corbridge Roman Town, Hadrian's Wall.** Built by the Romans almost 2,000 years ago as a protective bulwark against the northern tribes, Hadrian's Wall stretches some 73 miles across northern England. From the elevated platform at Corbridge you'll get a good view of the remains of the longest-occupied section of the wall, and exhibits in the small museum provide information on Corstopitum, the Roman town that grew up around it. ⏱ 30 min. ☎ 01434/632-349. www.english-heritage.org.uk. Admission £4.80 adults, £2.40 kids. Nov–Mar Sat–Sun 10am–5:30pm; Apr–Oct daily 10am–5:30pm (Oct until 4pm).

Fountains Abbey is 89 miles south of Corbridge Roman Town, about a 2-hr. drive on the A69 and A1. On the way, you'll pass through Yorkshire Dales National Park (p. 474).

8 ★★★ **Fountains Abbey and Studley Royal Water Gardens.** The ruins of what was once England's largest Cistercian abbey form the centerpiece of a unique 18th-century water garden. ⏱ At least 1 hr. See p. 478, **2**.

Haworth is 36 miles southwest of Fountains Abbey, about an hour's drive on the A59.

9 **Haworth.** All roads in this small West Yorkshire town lead to the ★ **Brontë Parsonage Museum,** Church St. (☎ 01535/642-323; www.bronte.org.uk; £6.80 adults, £3.60 kids), home from 1820 to 1861 of the Brontë sisters, whose novels *Jane Eyre* (by Charlotte) and *Wuthering Heights* (by Emily) have become classics of 19th-century English literature. A fascinating cache of memorabilia, including manuscripts and clothing, fills the attached museum. Also pay a brief visit to **Haworth Parish Church** (free admission), across from the parsonage, where most of the Brontës are buried. Brontë fans can take a walk from the village onto the bleak but beautiful moors that so inspired the novel-writing sisters. ⏱ 1 hr.

Your overnight stop for Day 6 is Leeds, 19 miles east of Haworth, a 50-min. drive on the B6144 and A647.

10 **Leeds.** A city once given over almost entirely to industry, Leeds has brushed itself off and become one of northern England's fastest-growing shopping and cultural hotspots. Be sure to visit the new **Royal Armouries Museum** (p. 490, ❶), a superb collection of historic weapons and weaponry, and spend some time in the **City Art Gallery** (p. 490, ❷), where all the biggies in English art from the 19th and 20th centuries are on view. ⊙ 2 hr. See p. 490.

On the morning of Day 7, head 7 miles north on the A61, about a 20-min. drive, to

⓫ ★★ **Harewood House**. Between 1759 and 1772, the big stars of 18th-century domestic architecture (John Carr), interior design (Robert Adams and Thomas Chippendale), and landscape design (Lancelot "Capability" Brown) worked together to create this superb neoclassical mansion and the grounds surrounding it for Edwin Lascelles, first Baron Harewood (1713–95). In addition to the magnificent **State Rooms,** hung with paintings that include works by Turner, Reynolds, Titian, and El Greco, there is a **Terrace Gallery** for contemporary art exhibitions and a **Below Stairs** area that shows how the staff lived and worked. The gorgeous gardens and parkland can be enjoyed on walks and woodland paths, and there's a wonderful **Bird Garden** with rare and exotic species. ⊙ At least 1 hr. Harewood Village. ☎ 0113/218-1010. www.harewood.org. Admission £11 adults, £10 seniors, £5.50 kids. State Rooms: daily noon–4pm. Below Stairs and Terrace Gallery: daily 10:30am–4pm.

> *Much of the best shopping in Leeds, like the pictured County Arcade, is found under the glass roofs of the Victoria Quarter.*

Where to Stay & Dine

Big Mussel NEWCASTLE UPON TYNE *TRADITIONAL BRITISH/SEAFOOD* Mussels and chips are the big sellers at this informal diner that also has other kinds of shellfish and vegetarian options on the menu. 15 The Side. ☎ 0191/232-1057. Entrees £6–£12. MC, V. Lunch & dinner daily.

★ **Café 21** NEWCASTLE UPON TYNE *MODERN BRITISH* Not-so-radical reinterpretations of favorite Brit dishes make this a nice choice for a "smart-casual" dinner. Trinity Gardens, Quayside. ☎ 0191/222-0755. Entrees £14–£22. MC, V. Lunch & dinner Mon–Sat.

★ **Grey Street Hotel** NEWCASTLE UPON TYNE The best hotel on Newcastle's most elegant street has smallish rooms but loads of contemporary comfort and flair, plus a notable restaurant. 2-12 Grey St. ☎ 0191/230-6777. www.greystreet hotel.com. 49 rooms. Doubles £140–£185 w/breakfast. AE, MC, V.

★ **Waterside Hotel** NEWCASTLE UPON TYNE A great center-of-it-all location and stylishly furnished rooms make this revamped hotel a good choice. 48-52 Sandhill, Quayside. ☎ 0191/230-0111. www.watersidehotel.com. 24 rooms. Doubles £85 w/breakfast. AE, MC, V.

National Parks of Yorkshire

Green dales (valleys) with flat-topped limestone hills characterize Yorkshire Dales National Park, a protected 680-square-mile area located northwest of Leeds and the industrial heartland of Yorkshire. To the east, stretching to the Yorkshire coast, the 553-square-mile North York Moors National Park is England's largest remaining area of heather-covered moorland. This itinerary takes you to an assortment of towns and scenic wonders in both parks.

> *Primula beds in full bloom at the Royal Horticultural Society's Harlow Carr Botanical Gardens, near Harrogate.*

START Harrogate is 22 miles west of York, a 45-min. drive on the A59. **TRIP LENGTH** 4 days; 219 total miles.

① ★ Harrogate. This elegant Victorian spa town in North Yorkshire is a convenient base if you're going to visit the two parks; check into your hotel for 3 nights. With 36 sulphurous hot springs within a half-hectare (1-acre) area, Harrogate became a popular place to "take the waters," a ritual that's explained at the **Royal Pump Room Museum,** Crown Place (☎ 01423/ 556-188; £3 per person), housed in an ornate

building from 1842. You can take the waters yourself at the delightfully old-fashioned **★ Turkish Baths,** Parliament St. (☎ 01423/556-746; £12–£18 per person), which offers steam rooms, plunge baths, and swimming pools. If you're a plant-lover, take time for a stroll through nearby **★ Harlow Carr Botanical Gardens,** Crag Lane, Beckwithshaw (☎ 0142/ 565-418; £6.50 adults, £2.20 kids). ⏲ **2 hr.**

On Day 2, head over to Skipton, 22 miles west of Harrogate, a 45-min. drive on the A59.

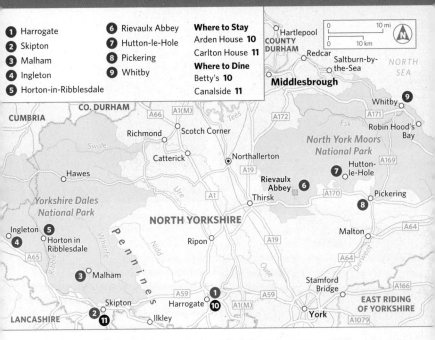

① Harrogate
② Skipton
③ Malham
④ Ingleton
⑤ Horton-in-Ribblesdale
⑥ Rievaulx Abbey
⑦ Hutton-le-Hole
⑧ Pickering
⑨ Whitby

Where to Stay
Arden House 10
Carlton House 11

Where to Dine
Betty's 10
Canalside 11

② **Skipton.** This busy Yorkshire market town grew wealthy in centuries past on sheep farming and now serves as a gateway to the southern part of Yorkshire Dales National Park. Try to visit on a market day (Mon, Wed, Fri & Sat), when broad and bustling **High Street** becomes a hive of activity. A short stroll to the end of High Street brings you to the massive twin towers of 900-year-old ★ **Skipton Castle** (☎ 01756/792-442; £6.20 adults, £3.70 kids), one of England's best-preserved medieval fortresses. **Pennine Boat Trips,** Wharf, Coach St. (☎ 01756/790-829; www.canaltrips.co.uk; £6.50 adults, £3.50 kids), offers pleasant hour-long ★ **boat trips** along the Leeds-Liverpool Canal that runs through the center of town. ⏲ 1 hr.

Continue on to Malham, 10 miles north of Skipton, a 20-min. drive on the A61.

③ **Malham.** Surrounding this pretty little village—popular with walkers—is the largest area of limestone country in England. A half-mile walk from the village brings you to ★★ **Malham Cove,** an enormous rock amphitheater with a steep pathway up the 80m-high (262-ft.) cliffs to a limestone pavement above. Drive or walk another 1½ miles north to reach the glacial lake known as **Malham Tarn.** The remains of an Iron Age settlement can be seen at **Gordale Scar,** a scenic limestone canyon located 1 mile east of Malham. ⏲ 1 hr. Yorkshire Dales National Park Center, Malham. ☎ 01969/652-180.

Return to Harrogate for your second overnight. On Day 3, your first stop is Ingleton, 47 miles (1 hr. 15 min.) west of Harrogate via the A59 and A65.

④ ★ kids **Ingleton.** The craggy limestone landscape around this small village is rich in waterfalls and riddled with caves, making it a favorite destination for hikers, rock climbers, and spelunkers. From Ingleton you can set off on the scenic ★ **Waterfalls Walk,** a 4½-mile circular trail through native oak woodland to waterfalls along the Doe and Twiss rivers. Guided 80-minute tours reveal the natural

Travel Tip

You'll need a car if you want to visit the parks in a short period of time. If you're coming from London, take the train from King's Cross Station to York (2 hr.) and rent a car there.

> *Thornton Force is just one of the cascades you'll see on the Waterfalls Walk from Ingleton.*

> *During peak season, trains on the scenic North Yorkshire Moors Railway depart hourly from Pickering.*

wonders of ★ **White Scar Caves,** 1½ miles northeast on the B6255 (☎ 01524 /241-244; www.whitescarcave.co.uk; £7.95 adults, £4.95 kids, £22 families), a huge limestone cave system with gushing subterranean waterfalls and an Ice Age cavern lined with thousands of stalactites. ⏱ At least 2 hr.

Horton-in-Ribblesdale is 12 miles east of Ingleton, a 20-min. drive on the B6255 and B6479.

5 **Horton-in-Ribblesdale.** Fairly easy gradients and outstanding views make the ★★ **Three Peaks**—Pen-y-ghent (694m/2,277 ft.), Ingleborough (723m/2,372 ft.), and Whernside (736m/2,415 ft.)—a favorite destination for walkers. From this village you can enjoy a classic view of the Three Peaks or set off on the scenic ★★ **Three Peaks Trail** (allow 5 hr.). For information on local walks, check with the **Pen-y-Ghent Café** (☎ 01729/860-333), which serves as an informal tourist office for the area's many hikers. ⏱ 1 hr.

To return to Harrogate, take the B6479 and B6480 43 miles southeast from Horton-in-Ribblesdale. On the morning of Day 4, head to Rievaulx Abbey, 33 miles north of Harrogate, a 1-hr. drive on the A170. This portion of the itinerary takes you into North York Moors National Park.

6 ★★ **Rievaulx Abbey.** Located just outside the village of Helmsley, these atmospheric ruins evoke a time in Yorkshire's past when powerful religious orders built monasteries that grew to be the size of small towns. ⏱ 1 hr. See p. 480, **4**.

From Rievaulx Abbey, head northeast for 13 miles on the A170 to Hutton-le-Hole, a half-hour's drive.

7 **Hutton-le-Hole.** A gurgling beck flows past neat stone cottages and sheep grazing on the village green in this picturesque moorland village. Spend a half-hour visiting **Ryedale Folk Museum** (☎ 01751/417-367; www.ryedale folkmuseum.co.uk; £5.50 adults, £4 kids), a collection of salvaged and reassembled moorland buildings that includes a medieval manor house, blacksmith's forge, and Art Deco village shops; the museum also serves as the local tourist office. If you're visiting in the spring, the 2½-mile **Daffodil Walk** is a circular trail that passes the daffodil-strewn banks of the River Dove. ⏱ 1 hr.

Continue on to Pickering, 8½ miles southeast of Hutton-le-Hole, a half-hour's drive on the A70.

8 Pickering. This town is the starting point for scenic journeys aboard the ★★ **North Yorkshire Moors Railway,** Pickering Station (☎ 01751/472-508; www.nymr.co.uk), a historic steam railroad with period cars that puffs northward along an 18-mile stretch of moorland to Grosmont, an hour away, and from there on to Whitby (**9**). The other tourist attraction in the village is **Pickering Castle** (☎ 01751/474-989; £3.70 adults, £1.70 kids), a 13th-century walled Norman keep. ⏱ 30 min., 2 hr. for train trip.

Your overnight stop for Day 4 is Whitby, 21 miles north of Pickering, about a 40-min. drive on the A169.

9 ★ Whitby. Dramatically situated on the North Sea coast, Whitby was the site of a Saxon monastery in the 7th century and later became a whaling center and industrial port. In Victorian times, the cottages beneath the east cliff were home-workshops where jet, a locally quarried black gemstone, was fashioned into mourning jewelry made fashionable by Queen Victoria. You can see examples of jet carvings and jewelry at the **Whitby Museum and Pannett Art Gallery,** Pannett Park (☎ 01947/602-908; www.whitbymuseum.org.uk; £4 adults, £3.50 seniors, £2.50 students, £1 kids 5–16). Nearby **Robin Hood's Bay,** 5½ miles southeast (a 15-min. drive on the A171 and B1447) is another picturesque seaside village once used by smugglers. ⏱ 2 hr. See p. 467, **4**.

Where to Stay & Dine

★ Arden House HARROGATE
The rooms in this Edwardian-era hotel have been sleekly updated, and the overall ambience, service, and location make it a top choice. 71 Franklin Rd. ☎ 01423/509-224. www.ardenhousehotel.co.uk. 14 rooms. Doubles £80–£85 w/breakfast. AE, MC, V.

★ Betty's HARROGATE *TRADITIONAL BRITISH/TEA ROOM*   Founded in 1919, this old-fashioned restaurant-tea room serves excellent baked goods and quality lunches and afternoon teas. 1 Parliament St. ☎ 01423/502-746. Entrees £8–£10, afternoon tea £15. MC, V. Breakfast, lunch & dinner daily.

Canalside SKIPTON *MODERN BRITISH*
A great canalside location and a menu that includes game pies and local beef and fish dishes make this a worthwhile dining choice. Waterside Court, Coach St. ☎ 01756/795-678. Entrees £7–£17. MC, V. Lunch & dinner Mon–Wed.

Carlton House SKIPTON
Not exactly plain Jane, but a fairly basic B&B with comfortable rooms, a good breakfast, and a warm welcome. 46 Keighley Rd. ☎ 01756/700-921. www.carltonhouse.rapidial.co.uk. 5 units. Doubles £60 w/breakfast. MC, V.

> *Afternoon tea is an event at Betty's, in Harrogate.*

Cathedrals, Monasteries & a Holy Island

After the Norman Conquest of 1066, a new religious fervor swept through England, and especially through Yorkshire, which became home to more monastic orders than any other county in England. This itinerary takes you to majestic cathedrals, beautiful minsters, and the haunting remains of great and powerful abbeys before ending up at the Holy Island of Lindisfarne.

> *Looking down York Minster's towering nave to the Great West Window, a masterpiece of Gothic tracery.*

START York is 209 miles north of London. Trains from London's King's Cross Station make the journey in 2 hr. **TRIP LENGTH** 3 days; 398 total miles.

1 ★★★ **York Minster.** One of the world's largest and most beautiful cathedrals is a must-see attraction. ⏱ At least 1 hr. See p. 484, **1**.

Fountains Abbey is 30 miles northwest of York, about an hour's drive on the A59 and B6265.

2 ★★★ **Fountains Abbey and Studley Royal Water Garden.** Fountains Abbey was founded in 1132 by a group of Benedictine monks unhappy with their abbey in York. The group switched allegiance to the more austere Cistercian order and, within a century, created one of the largest and richest monasteries in England. The abbey fell into ruins after the Dissolution of the Monasteries and eventually became incorporated into a remarkable Georgian-era water garden. Spend a few minutes at the **visitor**

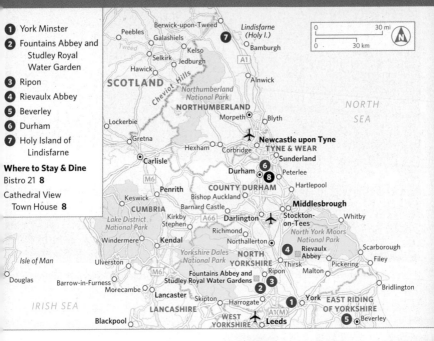

1 York Minster
2 Fountains Abbey and
   Studley Royal
   Water Garden
3 Ripon
4 Rievaulx Abbey
5 Beverley
6 Durham
7 Holy Island of
   Lindisfarne

Where to Stay & Dine
Bistro 21 **8**

Cathedral View
   Town House **8**

center learning more about the fascinating
history of the site before exploring the **abbey
ruins,** with the remarkable 13th-century **Chapel
of the Nine Altars,** copied from a similar chapel
in Durham Cathedral (6). The **water gardens,** created as a picturesque landscape with
neoclassical statues, grottoes, temples, and
surprise views of the abbey ruins, form a spectacular setting for this UNESCO World Heritage
Site. There is an on-site restaurant where you
can have lunch, tea, or a snack. ⊙ At least 2 hr.
Fountains, Ripon, North Yorkshire. ☎ 01765/608-
888. www.fountainsabbey.org.uk. Admission £9
adults, £4.85 kids, £23 families. Daily 10am–5pm
(Nov–Feb until 4pm).

Drive 4 miles (10 min.) east on the B6265 to

3 ★ **Ripon.** The chief reason to stop at this
Yorkshire market town is to pay a visit to
★ **Ripon Cathedral,** Minster Rd. (☎ 1765/603-
462; suggested donation £3). The cathedral
traces its heritage back some 1,350 years to St.
Wilfrid (ca. 634–709), who in 672 constructed
the tiny **Saxon crypt** above which the present
church stands. Construction of the cathedral
with its magnificent Early English **west front** began in the mid-13th century and continued into
the 16th. Worth seeking out are the exquisitely

> The ornate west front of the cathedral is the key
photo stop in the North Yorkshire town of Ripon.

Travel Tip

You'll need a car to visit the abbeys and
Holy Island; take a train to York and rent
a car there. Using York as your base, you
could see everything in the Yorkshire portion of this itinerary in two easy day trips,
and then use Durham as your second overnight base in Northumberland.

> *After the ecclesiastical ruins at Fountains Abbey, take time to soak up the Technicolor beauty of the water gardens.*

carved **choir stalls** and **misericords** created by the medieval master craftsmen of the "Ripon School." Some grimly fascinating social history is on display in the nearby **Ripon Workhouse Museum,** Allhallowgate (☎ 01765/690-799; www.riponmuseums.co.uk; £7 adults), the 19th-century building where the indigent were sent to live and work under the harshest conditions, and the **Prison and Police Museum,** St. Marygate (same phone, website & admission as Workhouse Museum), where exhibits include whipping posts and pillories. If you happen to be in Ripon at 9pm, head to **Market Square,** where every night in an ancient ceremony called "Setting the Watch" a horn is blown in the square's four corners to ensure the safety of the town's citizens at night. ⊕ At least 1 hr.

Return to York, 30 miles (45 min.) southeast on the A1 and A59 for the night. On Day 2, head 28 miles (1 hr.) north on the B1363 to

❹ ★★ **Rievaulx Abbey.** Founded in 1132, Rievaulx (*ree-voh*) was the first Cistercian monastery in England and became the mother church for all the other Cistercian communities. At its height, the community numbered some 140 monks and 500 lay brothers, all of them engaged in farming, fishing, mining, the wool trade, and other money-making activities that made Rievaulx immensely rich. Its power and prestige came to an end in the 16th century with the Dissolution of the Monasteries, at which point the roofs were stripped of their lead and most of the walls were razed. Today Rievaulx stands in ruins—majestic and evocative in a wooded valley. The remains of the triple-arched **nave,** the three-tiered **presbytery,** and the chapter house with its original shrine of William, the first abbot, are most impressive. A good audio tour of the site comes with your admission, and the **visitor center** explains more about the monastic life of the Cistercians and other religious orders in the area. ⊕ 1 hr. Near Helmsley, North Yorkshire. ☎ 01439/798-228. www.english-heritage.org.uk. Admission £5.30 adults, £4.70 seniors, £2.70 kids. Apr–Sept daily 10am–6pm; Oct–Mar Thurs–Mon 10am–4pm.

Head 46 miles east of Rievaulx Abbey, 1½ hr. on the B1257 and B1248 to

❺ ★ **Beverley.** Often overlooked by visitors, this lovely, low-key town full of Georgian and Victorian architecture happens to have one of the greatest "non-cathedral" church buildings in England. ★ **Beverley Minster,** Minster Yard North (☎ 01482/868-540; www.beverley minster.org; free admission) was built in a succession of 13th- to 15th-century Gothic styles—Early English, Decorated, and Perpendicular—and contains famous **stone carvings** of medieval musicians and the **Percy Canopy,** a 14th-century tomb canopy that is considered among the best Gothic stone carvings in England. Constructed over a period of 4 centuries starting in 1120, **St. Mary's,** North Bar Within (☎ 01482/881-437; www.stmarysbeverley.org.uk; free admission) contains a famous 14th-century carving of a "pilgrim rabbit" that is thought to have inspired the character of the White Rabbit in Lewis Carroll's *Alice in Wonderland.* ⏱ 1 hr.

Return to York, 30 miles (45 min.) west on the A1079 for the evening. On Day 3, head to Durham, 75 miles (1 hr. 45 min.) north on the A1 and check into a hotel.

⑥ ★★★ Durham. The spectacular setting of **★★★ Durham Cathedral,** Palace Green (☎ 01913/864-266; www.durhamcathedral.co.uk; admission by donation, tower £3 adults, £1.50 kids), high above the River Wear, enhances the architectural might of the building, a stupendous achievement created in a relatively short time span of 40 years by Norman architects of the 12th century. The towers are later additions, as is the magnificent 13th-century **Chapel of the Nine Altars** (where the Venerable Bede, England's first historian, is buried), but this is otherwise a rare Romanesque cathedral, as you'll see the moment you step inside the nave and marvel at the aesthetic strength and harmony of the piers with their incised zig-zag patterning. The cathedral was built to house the bones of St. Cuthbert, the 7th-century bishop who promoted the spread of Christianity from the Holy Island of Lindisfarne (**⑦**). The cathedral is the main reason to visit Durham,

> *A great Norman edifice, Durham Cathedral towers over England's "third" university city, after Oxford and Cambridge.*

but you may also want to take a guided tour of **★ Durham Castle,** Palace Green (☎ 0191/374-3800; £5 adults, £3.50 kids). Like the cathedral it faces, the castle is Norman in origin, begun in the 11th century not long after William the Conqueror's invasion. For more than 800 years it was the seat of the Prince Bishops, until it became part of Durham University in the 1840s. ⏱ 2 hr.

Drive 78 miles (1½ hr.) north of Durham on the A1 to

⑦ ★★ Holy Island of Lindisfarne. Cross the causeway (accessible only at low tide) to reach this small island where, beginning in the 5th century, the early Christian message was honed and distributed to pagan Northumbria. The story is told at the Lindisfarne Heritage Centre at **Lindisfarne Priory** (☎ 01289/389-200; www.english-heritage.org.uk; £4.50 adults, £2.30 kids), where you can look at an electronic copy of the Lindisfarne Gospels, a remarkable illuminated Latin manuscript (the original is in London's British Library) created by the monks of Lindisfarne in the 8th century. Today, this serene place with its breathtaking views of the Northumberland coast is home to a **national nature reserve** where rare birds and seals from the nearby Farne Islands can be spotted all year round. ⏱ 2 hr. For information on the preserve, contact the Berwick-upon-Tweed Tourist Information Centre (106 Marygate; ☎ 01289/301-780).

Staying the Night in Durham

No saucy sauces or overly clever preparations at **Bistro 21,** just good solid modern British fare prepared from fresh local produce. Aykley Heads House, Aykley Heads. ☎ 0191/384-4354. www.bistrotwentyone.co.uk. Entrees £13–£23. AE, MC, V. Lunch & dinner Mon–Sat.

 Having a view of the stupendous Norman cathedral is the whole point of staying in Durham, and the three back rooms in the comfortable Georgian **Cathedral View Town House** provide just that, in spades. Gilesgate. ☎ 0191/386-9566. www.cathedralview.com. 6 units. Doubles £80–£90 w/breakfast. MC, V.

THEY CAME,
THEY SAW,
THEY CONQUERED

The Romans in Britain BY DONALD OLSON

JULIUS CAESAR'S INVASION of the south coast in 55 B.C. established a Roman presence in Britain, but a full-scale Roman conquest of the island did not occur until A.D. 43 during the reign of Emperor Claudius. For the next 400 years, the Romans remained in power throughout England and Wales. Roman governors were appointed by the emperor to oversee Britannia, and legions of soldiers, drawn from all parts of the Empire, built and manned strategic forts and ports while fighting incursions from fierce northern tribes determined to resist Roman rule. In the countryside, wealthy Roman landowners built luxurious villas decorated with mosaic tiles and wall paintings. All facets of Roman culture and religion were adapted for use in this frontier outpost. The first Christian missionaries arrived in Britain in 167, and by 310, Christianity had become the official religion of Britannia and the rest of the Roman Empire.

Revolts and Resistance

A nation that would eventually go on to create its own global empire had no desire to be part of somebody else's. There was fierce local resistance to the Roman occupation, spurred on by Roman demands for slaves and tribute money, usurpation of land and resources, and the imposition of Roman law and taxation. Caratacus, a native tribal leader, lead the earliest British resistance before being defeated in A.D. 51 (though he sweet-talked Emperor Claudius into sparing his life and ended up living in Rome). Queen Boudicca (p. 697) of the Iceni tribe wasn't as lucky when she led a major rebellion in A.D. 61 that ended in defeat. By A.D. 77, Wales had been subdued and the Roman conquest of Britain was complete—except for Caledonia (Scotland). The fierce Picts of the north posed such a threat that the emperor Hadrian ordered the construction of a defensive wall along the northern frontier in 122. But the locals were not the only people the emperor needed to worry about. During 4 centuries of Roman rule, there were also revolts, uprisings, and power grabs within the Roman ranks. In 287, Carausius, commander of the Roman British fleet, gained enough support to rule Britannia as emperor, but was then murdered by a co-conspirator.

What the Romans Left Behind

Utilizing their skills as engineers and builders, the Romans altered the face and culture of Iron Age Britain by introducing Roman-style religious, civic, domestic, and military architecture into a wild frontier land. Roman forts were small towns, complete with temples, coliseums, shops, and bathhouses such as the famous one at Aquae Sulis (Bath). Many Roman settlements later became important towns and cities. The Romans built paved roads, some of which are still used today as modern streets and highways. Portions of Hadrian's Wall, built as a defensive bulwark along the northern boundary of the Empire, can still be seen in Yorkshire and Northumbria.

Cities and Towns with Roman Origins

The region's Roman legacy lives on in dozens of cities and towns that were originally Roman forts, settlements, or trading posts. The list includes:

BATH Aquae Sulis	YORK Eboracum
CANTERBURY	EXETER
Durovernum	Isca Dumnoniorum
Cantiacorum	LONDON Londinium
CHESTER	MANCHESTER
Deva Victrix	Mamucium
DOVER Portus	WINCHESTER
Dubris	Venta Belgarum

York

One of the most historic cities in England and one of the

best-preserved medieval cities in Europe, York began life as a Roman fort and settlement, became the Saxon capital of Northumbria, and then a thriving Viking settlement called Jorvik. Finally, after the Norman Conquest, the city became a prosperous port and one of Europe's most important trading cities in the Middle Ages. Enormous York Minster dominates the city, and 800-year-old walls and fortified gateways, incorporating parts of the Roman fortifications, still girdle the old town center. You can soak up the city's history while exploring its maze of ancient streets and hidden alleyways, known as snickelways.

> The flying buttress, deployed here at York Minster, was a key weight-distributing innovation of Gothic architects.

START York is 209 miles north of London, a 4-hr. drive on the M1. Trains from London's King's Cross Station make the journey in 2 hr. **TRIP LENGTH** 2 days.

❶ ★★★ **York Minster.** Reputedly the largest Gothic cathedral in Northern Europe, York Minster was begun in 1220 and finally completed in 1472. The name "minster" reflects its status as a missionary teaching church during Anglo-Saxon times. Before entering,

walk around the exterior to take in the massive size of the structure. Light in the cavernous interior is diffused by the medieval stained glass (the cathedral contains half of all the stained glass in England). The **Great East Window** made by artisan John Thornton in the early 15th century is the largest medieval stained-glass window in the world (the size of a tennis court); the **Great West Window,** with stained glass dating from 1338, is called

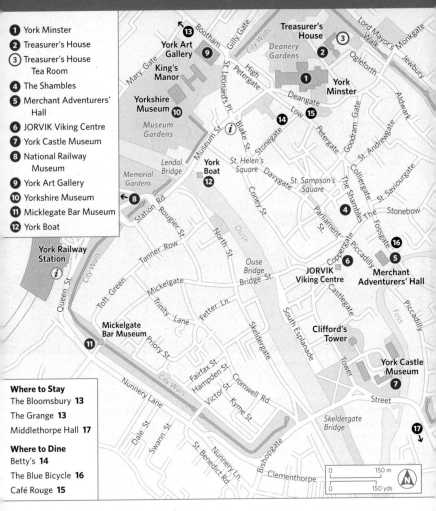

1. York Minster
2. Treasurer's House
3. Treasurer's House Tea Room
4. The Shambles
5. Merchant Adventurers' Hall
6. JORVIK Viking Centre
7. York Castle Museum
8. National Railway Museum
9. York Art Gallery
10. Yorkshire Museum
11. Micklegate Bar Museum
12. York Boat

Where to Stay
The Bloomsbury 13
The Grange 13
Middlethorpe Hall 17

Where to Dine
Betty's 14
The Blue Bicycle 16
Café Rouge 15

the "Heart of Yorkshire." A 15th-century **choir screen** decorated with statues of 15 kings of England separates the nave from the choir. In the south transept, you can descend into the **undercroft,** where excavations have revealed a Roman basilica that stood here nearly 2,000 years ago. From the nave, a separate entrance leads to the 13th-century octagonal **chapter house,** filled with superlative stone carvings and medieval glass. You can ascend the mighty **tower** for a fabulous view of York and the surrounding countryside. ⏱ 45 min. Minster Yard. ☎ 01904/557-216. www.yorkminster.org. Admission (including entrance to tower) £14.50 adults, £12.50 seniors, £3.50 kids 8–16. Mon–Sat 9am–6:30pm; Sun noon–4pm.

Getting Around

The train station is a 5-minute walk from York's pedestrian-friendly historic city center and York Minster, where this itinerary begins.

❷ ★★ **Treasurer's House.** Built in 1620 to house the treasurers of York Minster, the house and its gardens were extensively remodeled during the Victorian era by an eccentric collector. Inside are beautiful period rooms with collections of 17th- and 18th-century furniture, glass, and china; the audio guide

> *Aimed squarely at families, JORVIK recreates the sights, sounds, and smells of Viking York.*

adds fascinating personal anecdotes to your tour, as do the extra-charge basement and roof tours. The lovely walled garden is free to the public—step in and have a look. ⏱ 30 min. Minster Yard. ☎ 01904/624-247. Admission £5.40 adults, £2.70 kids, £15 families. Sat–Thurs Apr–Nov 11am–4:30pm (Nov until 3pm).

③ 🍽 **Treasurer's House Tea Room.** The cozy cafe in the basement—supposedly haunted by Roman soldiers—is a perfect spot for a light lunch or afternoon tea. Minster Yard. ☎ 01904/624-247. Menu items £4–£8.

④ ★ **The Shambles.** Up until 150 years ago, the Shambles was a street where butchers displayed their finest cuts in open windows on wide shelves called *fleshammels* (flesh benches, in Old English). Today, this narrow medieval lane, lined with buildings so close to each other that they nearly shut out the light, is filled with gift shops and specialty stores. ⏱ 5 min. www.insideyork.co.uk/shambles.

⑤ ★ **Merchant Adventurers' Hall.** One of England's largest and best-preserved guildhalls, this 14th-century stone and half-timbered structure, with a great hall on the main floor and a hospital and a chapel below, belonged to York's most powerful guild, the Merchant Adventurers. (Adventurers, in this context, means investors, and members profited from trade into and out of the city.) ⏱ 10 min. Piccadilly. ☎ 01904/654-818. www.theyorkcompany.co.uk. Admission £6 adults, £5 seniors. Apr–Sept Mon–Thurs 9am–5pm, Fri–Sat 9am–3:30pm, Sun noon–4pm; Oct–Mar Mon–Sat 9am–3:30pm.

Sightseeing Tip

If your time in York is very limited, free guided 2-hour city tours depart daily at 10:15am (also 2:15 and 6:45pm in summer) from the York Art Gallery in Exhibition Square. You don't need to make a reservation; just show up.

6 ★ kids **JORVIK Viking Centre.** Hop into a "time car" and be transported back to A.D. 948, when Eric Bloodaxe was king and York was Jorvik, a thriving Viking port and trading town. The scenes you pass—of village life, market stalls, crowded houses, and the wharf—are re-creations based on archaeological finds in this area; even the heads and faces of the animatronic characters were modeled on Viking skulls. It's fun and educational at the same time, but you might find it overpriced for the short spin you get. ⏱ 15 min. Castlegate. ☎ 01904/643-211. www.jorvik-viking-centre.co. uk. Admission £9.25 adults, £7.25 seniors, £6.25 kids. Daily 10am–5pm (Nov–Mar until 4pm).

7 ★ **York Castle Museum.** Using a treasure-trove of now-vanished everyday objects, the exhibitions housed in this former castle and debtors' prison re-create slices of life from the last 400 years. The major collections are divided into Social History, Military History, and Costume History. The cells of the Debtors' Prison paint a grim picture of the fate reserved for those who could not pay their bills. Half Moon Court, in the half-moon-shaped prison yard, is a re-created Yorkshire street from the Edwardian era (1901–10). ⏱ 1 hr. Castlegate. ☎ 01904/653-611. www.yorkcastlemuseum.org. uk. Admission £8.50 adults, £7.50 seniors. Daily 9:30am–5pm.

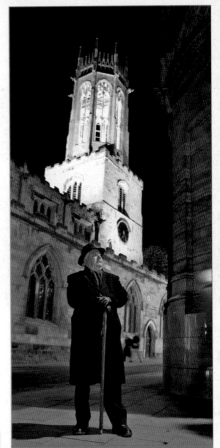

The Saint of the Shambles

Margaret Clitherow (1556–86) lived with her husband John, a butcher, and their three children at no. 10 Shambles. Though raised a Protestant, Margaret converted to Catholicism during a time when the religion was being actively suppressed and its adherents persecuted. Her husband never converted, but Margaret became a fervently devout Catholic, hiding priests in her home and sending her son to France to be educated as a Catholic. Both acts were treasonable offenses, and Margaret was crushed to death for her beliefs. In 1970, she was canonized and became St. Margaret Clitherow. A commemorative plaque at the Micklegate end of the Ouse Bridge marks the site of her martyrdom, and visitors can see the "priest's hole" in her home, now a shop.

Ghost Hunting in York

York lays claim to being England's most haunted city, and several tour companies lead spirited **ghost walks** (£4-£5 adults, £3 kids) to the city's hottest haunt spots. Tours take place nightly year-round (rain or shine) and there's no need to reserve in advance—just show up at the appointed time and location. **Original Ghost Walk of York** (www.theoriginalghostwalkofyork.co.uk) is the oldest of the walks and the one with the best storytelling; it leaves nightly at 8pm from The King's Arms Pub, Ouse Bridge. Two other great options are **Ghost Hunt of York** (www.ghosthunt.co.uk), which leaves nightly at 7:30pm from the Shambles; and the **Ghost Trail** (www.ghosttrail.co.uk), which leaves nightly at 7:30pm from York Minster.

> *Pieces dating from the "golden age of steam" are some of the major draws at the National Railway Museum.*

8 ★★ kids **National Railway Museum.** This museum devoted to Britain's railroads is a bit of a hike from the city center, but it's an absolute must for train buffs. The superlative collection includes dozens of vintage locomotives and railway cars, the earliest of them dating from the 1840s and looking like stagecoaches on tracks. You can peek into the windows of private royal trains, ranging from Queen Victoria's 1869 coach to Queen Elizabeth's streamlined carriage, used until 1977. ⏲ 1 hr. Leeman Rd. ☎ 01904/621-261. www.nrm.org.uk. Free admission. Daily 10am–6pm.

9 **York Art Gallery.** Seven centuries of Western European painting and a collection of 20th-century studio pottery are displayed in newly refurbished galleries inside a 19th-century building. None of the works on display are of major importance; the 17th- and 18th-century portraits by Sir Peter Lely and Sir Joshua Reynolds are the most interesting. ⏲ 15 min. Exhibition Sq. ☎ 01904/551-861. www.yorkartgallery.org.uk. Free admission. Daily 10am–5pm.

10 **Yorkshire Museum.** Set amidst landscaped gardens and the ruins of St. Mary's Abbey, this museum gives a solid presentation of Yorkshire's history from 2 millennia ago up through the 16th century, with displays of elegant Roman jewelry, mosaics, Viking swords and battleaxes, and Anglo-Saxon silver. It relies heavily on text panels, so bring your reading glasses. ⏲ 45 min. Museum Gardens. ☎ 01904/551-800. www.yorkshiremuseum.org.uk. Admission £7.50 adults, £6.50 seniors. Daily 10am–5pm.

11 **Micklegate Bar Museum.** Housed in an 800-year-old fortified tower, this tiny museum looks at the social history of the city's southern entry gate (used by royalty, back in the day) in a quirky, humorous light. ⏲ 10 min. Micklegate Bar. ☎ 01904/634-436. www.micklegatebar.com. Admission £3.50 adults, £2.50 seniors. June–Oct daily 10am–3pm.

12 ★ kids **York Boat.** With live commentary, this excursion boat on the River Ouse nicely complements a walking tour. Buy your ticket on board. ⏲ 45 min. Pier below Lendal Bridge. ☎ 01904/628-324. www.yorkboat.co.uk. Admission £7.50 adults, £6.50 seniors, £3.50 kids, £20 families. Boats depart daily Feb–Nov.

Where to Stay & Dine

> *Stop for afternoon tea or grab some takeaway bakery items at Betty's, close to York Minster.*

★★ **Betty's** *TRADITIONAL BRITISH/SWISS*
Founded in 1919, Betty's is a wonderfully old-fashioned Art Nouveau tea room-patisserie-restaurant. At the shop in front, you can buy specialties such as Yorkshire fat rascals (warm scones with citrus peel, almonds, and cherries). 6–8 St. Helen's Sq. ☎ 01904/659-142. www.bettys.co.uk. Entrees £6.50–£10; cream tea £8–£16. AE, MC, V. Breakfast, lunch & dinner daily.

★ **The Bloomsbury** CITY CENTER
A pleasant house just a 10-minute walk from the Minster provides comfortable and handsomely furnished rooms, accompanied by attentive service. 127 Clifton. ☎ 01904/634-031. www.bloomsburyhotel.co.uk. Doubles £70–£100 w/breakfast. AE, MC, V.

★ **The Blue Bicycle** *MODERN BRITISH*
If you're looking for atmosphere and good brasserie-style food, try this appealing restaurant overlooking the canal-like River Foss. They also rent out six self-contained luxury rooms in the center of York (£165 double). 34 Fossgate. ☎ 01904/673-990. www.theblue bicycle.com. Entrees £15–£22.50. AE, MC, V. Lunch Thurs–Sat; dinner Mon–Sat.

★ **Café Rouge** *FRENCH*
Delicious onion soup, tasty pates and quiches, succulent mussels, great omelets, steaks and frites, Breton chicken, Toulouse sausages, fresh salads, baguette sandwiches–it's all here, as well as reasonably priced house wine and beer. 52 Lower Petergate. ☎ 01904/673-293. www.caferouge.co.uk. Entrees £10–£16. AE, MC, V. Breakfast, lunch & dinner daily.

★★ **The Grange** CITY CENTER
The Grange is an elegant hotel close to the city walls and a few minutes' walk from York Minster, with rooms that convey a comfortable yet stylish English charm. The hotel's restaurant is one of the best in York. 1 Clifton. ☎ 01904/644-744. www.grangehotel.co.uk. 30 units. Doubles £125–£220 w/breakfast. AE, MC, V.

★★★ **Middlethorpe Hall** OUTSIDE CITY
CENTER Built in 1699 and set in a 8-hectare (20-acre) park 1½ miles south of York, this stately red brick country manor house offers a high standard of service and comfort and features beautiful rooms, lovely gardens, a health spa, and an outstanding restaurant. Bishopthorpe Rd. ☎ 01904/641-241. www.middlethorpe.com. 30 units. Doubles £199–£269. AE, MC, V.

Leeds

In the 1990s, after decades of decline, Leeds cast off its reputation as a grim and grimy relic of a vanished industrial past and embarked on a fresh path. Development of new office blocks and redevelopment of Victorian buildings, warehouses, and docks suddenly made Leeds a hip and happening destination and the fastest-growing city in the U.K. England's fourth-largest city has some free cultural treasures that will keep you happily occupied for at least half a day, and is also a good overnight choice.

> The Royal Armouries Museum is home to an impressive collection of weapons and armor native to Britain and the Orient.

START Leeds is 25 miles southwest of York, a 45-min. drive on the A64 or a 25-min. train ride.

① ★★★ kids **Royal Armouries Museum.** There's no denying that everything on display here has to do with aggression or killing, but you will never see the objects of warfare so artfully displayed as in this museum created beside the River Aire to showcase a remarkable collection of historic arms and armor from the Tower of London. In galleries devoted to **War, Hunting,** the **Tournament,** and **Self-defense,** you'll see everything from jousting sticks and elephant armor to medieval helmets, ancient hunting guns, and hand revolvers. And

speaking of jousts—you might be able to see one right here, in the **Tiltyard.** The museum encourages interactivity and boosts the entertainment quotient with videos, demonstrations, and commentary. ⏱ At least 2 hr. Armouries Drive. ☎ 0113/220-1999. www.armouries.org.uk. Free admission. Daily 10am–5pm.

② ★ **City Art Gallery.** Leeds has the best collection of 19th- and 20th-century British art

Getting Around

The central section of Leeds is a 10-minute walk from the train station and easily covered on foot.

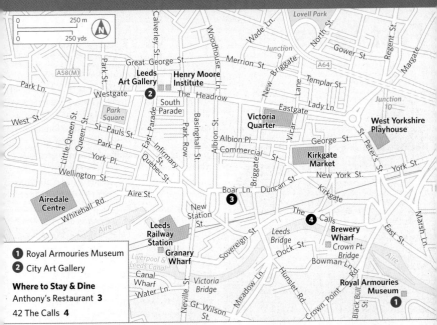

1 Royal Armouries Museum

2 City Art Gallery

Where to Stay & Dine

Anthony's Restaurant **3**

42 The Calls **4**

Another Attraction Near Leeds

Housed in Armley Mills, once the world's largest woolen mill, the **Leeds Industrial Museum** Canal Rd. (☎ 0113/263-7861; £3 adults, £1 kids) focuses on Leeds' unique industrial heritage, with exhibits on textiles, clothing, printing, and engineering that include period machines. To get there, take bus no. 9, or the waterbus from Neville Street bridge.

outside of London, with treasures that include paintings by Stanley Spencer, Francis Bacon, and Graham Sutherland, and sculptures such as Antony Gormley's model for *Leeds Brick Man,* a colossal and controversial statue planned for Leeds city center but never built. From the 19th century there are canvases by Turner and Constable, a slew of Pre-Raphaelite paintings, and Antonio Canova's coolly neoclassical statue called *The Hope Venus.* The works of sculptor Henry Moore (1898–1986), a Yorkshireman who attended the Leeds School of Art, are on display in the museum and adjacent **Henry Moore Institute.** ⏱ 1 hr. The Headrow. ☎ 0113/247-8256. Free admission. Daily 10am–5:30pm (Wed until 9pm).

Staying the Night in Leeds

The Anthony of ★★ **Anthony's Restaurant** in the city center is Anthony James Flinn, one of the best chefs in Yorkshire. The modern British dishes he cooks up are innovative and sometimes provocative in their combinations of taste and texture. 19 Boar Lane. ☎ 0113/245-5922. www.anthonysrestaurant.co.uk. Reservations required. Fixed-price lunch £20–£24, fixed-price dinner £36–£45. AE, MC, V. Lunch & dinner Tues-Sat.

   ★★ **42 The Calls,** an elegant boutique hotel created from an 18th-century grain mill on the River Aire, features riverside views and stylish comfort. 42 The Calls. ☎ 0112/244-0099. www.42thecalls.co.uk. 41 units. Doubles £125–£225. AE, MC, V.

Fast Facts

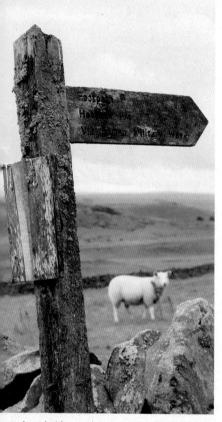

> Armed with a good map, visitors can find miles of moorland walking to enjoy in Yorkshire.

Arriving & Getting Around

BY PLANE The closest airport to Leeds and York is **Leeds Bradford International Airport** (☎ 01132/509-696; www.bradfordairport. co.uk), which handles flights from London Heathrow and Gatwick and serves as a regional hub. **Manchester International Airport** (☎ 08712/710-711; www.manchesterairport. co.uk), convenient if you want to visit the Yorkshire Dales or other places in the north of England, handles international flights (American Airlines flies there from New York) and regional and European carriers. Both airports have car-rental desks. **BY TRAIN** Super-fast

Intercity trains leave London's King's Cross Station for the 2-hour trip to York or Leeds and the 3-hour trip to Durham. For train schedules and information, contact **National Rail Enquiries** (☎ 08457/484-950; www.nationalrail. co.uk). You can explore scenic sections of Yorkshire Dales National Park on the historic **Settle-Carlisle Line** (www.settle-carlisle. co.uk); check the website for up-to-date timetables and fares. The **North Yorkshire Moors Railway** (p. 477, ⑧) runs through North York Moors National Park. **BY CAR** In order to reach smaller towns and villages in the countryside, along the coast, and in the two Yorkshire national parks you'll need a car, making it the first choice for getting around the area efficiently. A good strategy to save time and money is to take the train to York and rent a car there; Alamo, Avis, Hertz, and Dollar all have offices in York. If you drive, you'll need a detailed road atlas; the best are the large-format maps produced by the Automobile Association (AA), Collins, Ordnance Survey, and Royal Automobile Club (RAC). **BY BUS** **National Express** (☎ 0990/808-080; www. nationalexpress.com) serves the major towns and cities in Yorkshire and Northumbria, but if you are traveling from London and on a schedule, taking the bus is not a good idea because of the time involved. Local and regional buses serve all parts of the region, but using them requires researching schedules, and a car is a much better bet; if you still want to use the bus, tourist offices can provide you with local and regional bus information.

Emergencies

To call for emergency, dial ☎ 999 or ☎ 112; these are free calls from public phones. If you have a medical emergency, ask your concierge or B&B proprietor for help in locating a doctor or dentist. **LEEDS** You can get medical assistance at **Leeds General Infirmary**, Great George St. (☎ 0113/243-2799). **YORK** **York District Hospital,** Wiggington Rd. (☎ 01904/ 631-313).

Internet Access

Wi-Fi or dial-up Internet service is available at hotels throughout Yorkshire and Northumbria, either in-room or at a computer reserved for guests; you may not find Internet access at smaller B&Bs. LEEDS You can check e-mail at **Leeds Central Library,** Calverley St. DURHAM At **Durham Public Library,** Millennium Place. YORK At **City Library,** Museum St. Libraries are open Monday to Saturday.

Pharmacies

Cities and larger towns in Yorkshire and Northumberland have at least one pharmacy ("chemist"); Boots (www.boots.com) is the most common. You'll find a Boots in York at 1 Kings Sq. (☎ 01904/671-204).

Post Office

You'll find them in every city and small town, identified by a red box labelled ROYAL MAIL In smaller towns the post office may be in a local store rather than a post office building. LEEDS The main post office is in St. John's Centre, 116 Albion St. DURHAM On Silver Street. YORK At 22 Lendal. They are open Monday to Saturday 9am to 5:30pm.

Safety

If you take common sense precautions, it's unlikely you'll encounter any problems with crime in Yorkshire or Northumberland. If you're driving through the countryside, be aware that some of the local roads are quite narrow and you may have to pull off to the side to let another car or truck pass. If you're leaving your car in a parking lot or visiting a sight in the country, always make sure that your car is locked and your valuables stowed in the trunk.

Visitor Information

The local tourist offices in York, Leeds, Harrogate, Whitby, and Durham are your best sources for up-to-date information and help with accommodations. BEVERLEY Beverley Tourist Information Centre, 34 Butcher Row (☎ 01482/391-672; www.beverley.gov.uk). DURHAM Durham Tourist Office, 2 Millennium Place (☎ 0191/384-3720; www.durham tourism.co.uk). HARROGATE Harrogate Tourist Information Centre, Royal Baths, Crescent Rd. (☎ 0845/389-3223; www.harrogate. gov.uk/tourism). HAWORTH Haworth Tourist

> *A scenic heritage rail route has stops in Yorkshire Dales National Park.*

Information Centre, 2–4 West Lane (☎ 01535/ 642-329; www.bronte-country.com). INGLETON Ingleton Tourist Information Centre, located next to the village car park (☎ 01524/ 241-049; www.visitingleton.co.uk). LEEDS Gateway to Yorkshire/Leeds Visitor Centre, Leeds City Train Station (☎ 0113/242-5242; www.visitleeds.co.uk). NEWCASTLE UPON TYNE Newcastle upon Tyne Tourist Office, 8–9 Central Arcade, Market St. (☎ 0191/277-8000; www.newcastlegateshead.com). PICKERING Pickering Tourist Information Centre, The Ropery (☎ 01751/473-791; www.pickering. uk.net). RIPON Ripon Tourist Information Centre, Minster Rd. (☎ 0845/3890178; www. rippononline.co.uk). SKIPTON Skipton Tourist Office, 35 Coach St. (☎ 01756/792-809; www.skiptononline.co.uk). WHITBY Whitby Tourist Office, Langbourne Rd. (☎ 01947/ 602-674; www.visitwhitby.com). YORK York Tourist Information Centre, 1 Museum St. (☎ 01904/550-099; www.visityork.org); a second office is located in the train station.

For general region-wide information visit the websites for the **Yorkshire Tourist Board** (www.yorkshire.com), and the **Northumbria Tourist Board** (www.visitnortheastengland. com); also check out **www.northumberland. com.** A useful site for planning a trip to North York Moors National Park is **www.northyork moors.org.uk;** for Yorkshire Dales National Park, visit **www.yorkshiredales.org.uk.**

12
Edinburgh

Our Favorite Edinburgh Moments

With the sheer charm of its Old Town and castle, attractions ranging from national galleries to historic palaces, fine world-class food, and lively nighttime entertainment, whether clubbing, pubbing, or theater-going, Edinburgh is one of Europe's foremost metropolises. Robert Louis Stevenson once said: "No situation could be more commanding for the head city of a Kingdom; none better chosen for noble prospects." As you explore its sprawling gardens and majestic cathedrals, you'll be convinced that what he wrote in the 19th century is no less true today.

> *PREVIOUS PAGE Calton Hill provides a memorable panorama over the most photogenic areas of the city.* THIS PAGE *The Water of Leith flows past converted mills and granaries in Dean Village.*

❶ Taking a stroll along the Royal Mile. The most famous boulevard in the city, the historic road that traverses the most ancient part of Edinburgh, runs between the castle and palace of Old Town, a UNESCO World Heritage Site. The best time to do this is at dusk, when the tourist crowds calm down. See p. 502, ❸.

❷ Climbing one of Edinburgh's hills. Bring your camera, of course, as the views can be breathtaking. Your most challenging option is Arthur's Seat in Holyrood Park. Stevenson's favorite vantage point was Calton Hill because he could see Edinburgh Castle, as well as the Old and New Towns. You can cheat a bit by taking the lift to the top of the Museum of Scotland, which has a fine rooftop terrace. See p. 500, ❷.

❸ **Exploring the Palace of Holyroodhouse.** Among several historic attractions in Edinburgh, this one (the Windsors' home away from home) is arguably the best. The palace underwent several periods of construction, from the 15th to the 17th century. The oldest standing wing has the most intriguing sights, such as the room where the top assistant to Mary, Queen of Scots was assassinated. The adjacent ruins are of an abbey that was founded in 1128. See p. 512, ⓬.

❹ **Visiting Dean Village.** A *dean* (alternatively spelled *dene*) is a deep valley, and this one along the Water of Leith has a historic Edinburgh settlement, where the largest of the city's grain mills was established, perhaps as early as the 12th century. Restored and conserved, the settlement is a charming retreat. See p. 507, ❾.

❺ **Getting botanical at the Royal Garden.** This is one of the best traditional parks in all of Great Britain. Begun as a center for studying the beneficial properties of plants, Edinburgh's Royal Botanic Garden now has acres of plush lawns dotted with magnificent trees, sweeping rock gardens, hundreds of flowering rhododendrons, and some impressive Victorian greenhouses with palms threatening to outgrow the towering spaces. See p. 506, ❼.

❻ **Appreciating the National Gallery's collection.** Its holdings are housed in various galleries around town. In the main buildings on Princes Street Gardens, you can admire pieces ranging from Renaissance to Impressionist, as well as excellent examples of Scottish works, whether by the Glasgow Boys or Raeburn. Entry to all of the permanent holdings is free. See p. 502, ❼.

❼ **Shopping for High Fashion.** Between some homegrown boutique outfits in the West End, top labels at Harvey Nichols department store, classic styling at Jenners, groovy vintage clothes in Stockbridge, or the aristocratic shops on New Town's George Street, Edinburgh has advanced in the retail therapy stakes. See p. 518.

> *Shopping in stylish surrounds, at Corniche.*

❽ **Feasting on haute cuisine.** After London and a few other English culinary hotspots, Edinburgh is in the competition for creating fantastic food. The top venues are Restaurant Martin Wishart, the Kitchin, 21212, Plumed Horse, and Number One at the very posh Balmoral Hotel. All capitalize on some of the great ingredients available in Scotland, from hill lamb to sea loch langoustines (Dublin Bay prawns). See p. 523.

❾ **Sampling a dram and a pint.** Edinburgh has a range of places to drop in for a wee whisky and glass of real ale. It can be one of the trendiest "style bars" (bars with a more modern design and a younger and hipper clientele) in New Town or a traditional pub just off the Royal Mile. As for brands, try a peaty Laphroaig whisky from the Isle of Islay and a local beer, such as Deuchars (*dew*-kars) IPA. See p. 531.

❿ **Seeing cutting-edge dramatic performances.** Be it a landmark production by the National Theatre of Scotland at the glorious Corinthian Royal Lyceum Theatre, an edgy dark comedy by one of Scotland's leading contemporary playwrights at ground-breaking Traverse, or a performance by the opera at the Festival Theatre, Edinburgh theater offers many opportunities. See p. 532 & p. 533.

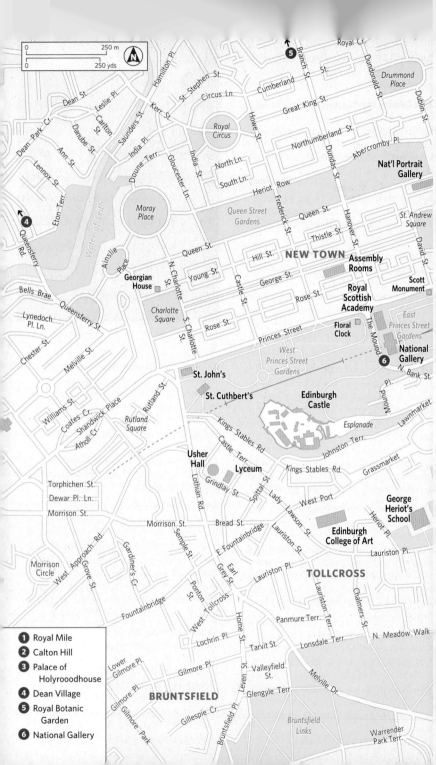

Map scale: 0 — 250 m / 0 — 250 yds

N

Royal Cr.

Branch St.

Dundonald St.

Drummond Place

Dublin St.

Hamilton Pl.

Leslie Pl.

Dean St.

St. Stephen St.

Circus Ln.

Cumberland

Great King St.

Kerr St.

Carlton St.

Saunders St.

India Pl.

Royal Circus

Howe St.

Northumberland St.

Dundas St.

Abercromby Pl.

Carlton St.

Danube St.

Ann St.

Doune Terr.

North Ln.

South Ln.

Nat'l Portrait Gallery

Dean Park Cr.

Lennox St.

Eton Terr.

Gloucester Ln.

India St.

Heriot Row

Frederick St.

Queen Street Gardens

Queen St.

St. Andrew Square

Water of Leith

Moray Place

Ainslie Place

N. Charlotte St.

Young St.

Hill St.

Thistle St.

Hanover St.

David St.

Queensferry Rd.

Queen St.

NEW TOWN

George St.

Rose St.

Assembly Rooms

Bells Brae

Queensferry St.

Georgian House

Charlotte Square

S. Charlotte St.

Castle St.

Royal Scottish Academy

Scott Monument

Lynedoch Pl. Ln.

Chester St.

Melville St.

Rose St.

Princes Street

Floral Clock

The Mound

East Princes Street Gardens

National Gallery

Williams St.

Coates Cr.

Shandwick Place

Rutland St.

Rutland Square

West Princes Street Gardens

N. Bank St.

Athol Cr.

Kings Stables Rd.

St. John's

St. Cuthbert's

Edinburgh Castle

Esplanade

Mound Pl.

Lawnmarket

Torphichen St.

Dewar Pl. Ln.

Morrison St.

Usher Hall

Castle Terr.

Lyceum

Grindlay St.

Spittal St.

Lady Lawson St.

West Port

Johnston Terr.

Grassmarket

George Heriot's School

Morrison St.

Lothian Rd.

Bread St.

E. Fountainbridge

Lauriston St.

Edinburgh College of Art

Heriot Pl.

Morrison Circle

West Approach Rd.

Gardiner's Cr.

Semple St.

Earl Grey St.

Ponton St.

Lauriston Pl.

TOLLCROSS

Lauriston Terr.

Chalmers St.

Lauriston Pl.

N. Meadow Walk

Fountainbridge

West Tollcross

Home St.

Panmure Terr.

Lonsdale Terr.

Lower Gilmore Pl.

Lochrin Pl.

Tarvit St.

Leven St.

Valleyfield St.

Melville Dr.

Gilmore Pl.

BRUNTSFIELD

Gillespie Cr.

Gilmore Park

Bruntsfield Pl.

Glengyle Terr.

Bruntsfield Links

Warrender Park Terr.

1. Royal Mile
2. Calton Hill
3. Palace of Holyrooodhouse
4. Dean Village
5. Royal Botanic Garden
6. National Gallery

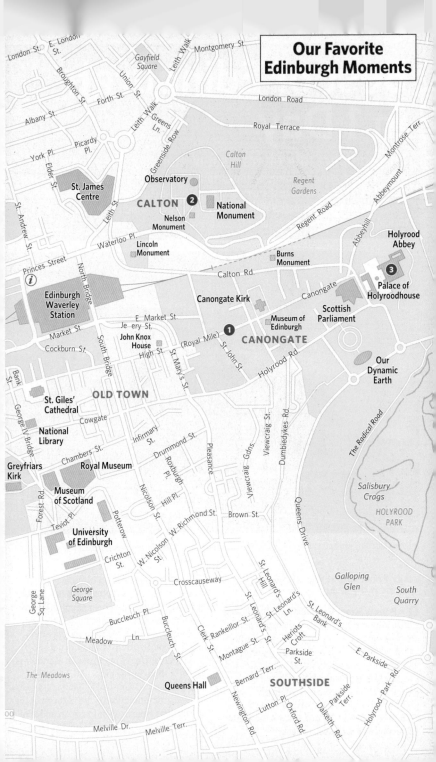

Our Favorite Edinburgh Moments

London St. E. London St.

Gayfield Square

Montgomery St.

Broughton St.

Forth St.

Leith Walk

Union St.

London Road

Albany St.

Picardy Pl.

Royal Terrace

York Pl.

Elder St.

Greenside Row

Greenside Ln.

Calton Hill

Regent Gardens

Montrose Terr.

St. James Centre

St. Andrew's Sq.

Leith St.

Observatory

CALTON ❷

Nelson Monument

National Monument

Regent Road

Abbeymount

Abbeyhill

Holyrood Abbey

Waterloo Pl.

Lincoln Monument

Burns Monument

Calton Rd.

❸ Palace of Holyroodhouse

Princes Street

North Bridge

Edinburgh Waverley Station

Market St.

E. Market St.

Canongate Kirk

Canongate

Scottish Parliament

Je ery St.

John Knox House

Museum of Edinburgh

Cockburn St.

South Bridge

High St.

St. Mary's St.

(Royal Mile) ❶ CANONGATE

St. John St.

Holyrood Rd.

Our Dynamic Earth

Bank St.

St. Giles' Cathedral

Cowgate

OLD TOWN

Viewcraig Gdns.

Dumbiedykes Rd.

The Radical Road

George IV Bridge

National Library

Infirmary St.

Drummond St.

Roxburgh Pl.

Pleasance

Viewcraig St.

Queens Drive

Salisbury Crags

Greyfriars Kirk

Chambers St.

Royal Museum

Forest Rd.

Museum of Scotland

Nicolson St.

Hill Pl.

W. Richmond St.

Brown St.

HOLYROOD PARK

Teviot Pl.

University of Edinburgh

Potterow

W. Nicolson St.

Galloping Glen

South Quarry

Crichton St.

Crosscauseway

St. Leonard's Hill

St. Leonard's Ln.

St. Leonard's Bank

George Sq. Lane

George Square

Buccleuch Pl.

Clerk St.

Rankeillor St.

St. Leonard's St.

Heriots Croft

St. Leonard's

Meadow Ln.

Buccleuch St.

Montague St.

Parkside St.

E. Parkside

The Meadows

Queens Hall

Bernard Terr.

SOUTHSIDE

Newington Rd.

Lutton Pl.

Oxford Rd.

Dalkeith Rd.

Parkside Terr.

Holyrood Park Rd.

Melville Dr.

Melville Terr.

Best of Edinburgh in 1 Day

This compact tour offers a set of stunning sites for a brief visit, concentrating primarily on the historic heart of the metropolis, the Scottish capital's Old Town (where the city first began), with its medieval lanes. Also included are key sites in the 18th-century New Town, which is the largest historical conservation area in all of Great Britain.

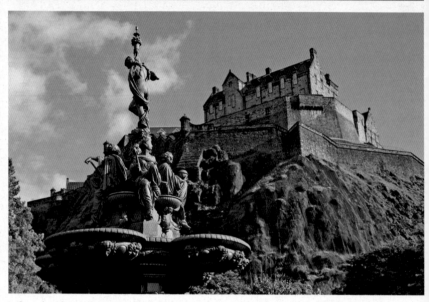

> On a clear day, walk up to Edinburgh Castle, at the high point of the Royal Mile, for great city views.

START Princes St., at Waverley Bridge. Bus: 3, 10, 12, 17, 25, or 44.

❶ ★ Princes Street Gardens. With Edinburgh Castle looming above, this park is one of the most picturesque in Europe. In the early 19th century, the area was a nasty sewage-filled loch set in a valley. Today, the 15 hectares (37 acres) of lawns and formal plantings are a great spot for a picnic or lounging on the grassy slopes. ⏱ 45 min. Princes St., at Waverley Bridge. ☎ 0131/529-4068. www.cac.org.uk. Admission free. Daily dawn–dusk.

❷ ★★ Calton Hill. Get an overview of the city—literally. Rising 106m (348 ft.), Calton Hill offers perhaps the best panoramic views of Edinburgh, and was writer Robert Louis Stevenson's favorite spot for gazing at the city. The hill also boasts a pair of noteworthy monuments. One is the National Monument, an unfinished replica of the Parthenon—meant to honor war dead—that helped garner Edinburgh a reputation as the "Athens of the North." The Nelson Monument, in honor of Admiral Horatio Nelson (1758–1805), was

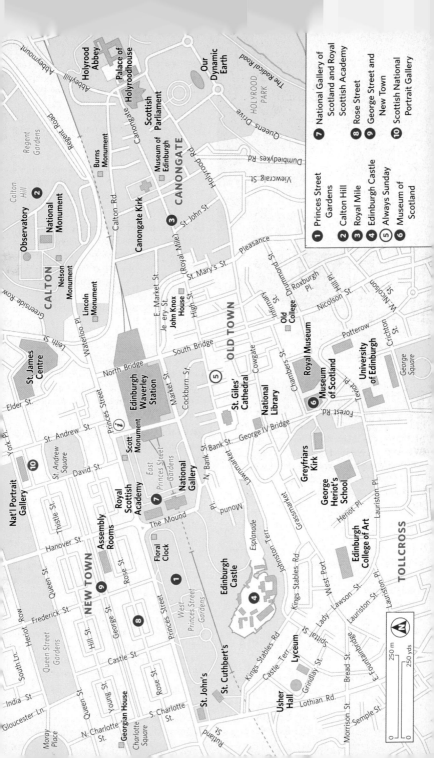

Legend

1. Princes Street Gardens
2. Calton Hill
3. Royal Mile
4. Edinburgh Castle
5. Always Sunday
6. Museum of Scotland
7. National Gallery of Scotland and Royal Scottish Academy
8. Rose Street
9. George Street and New Town
10. Scottish National Portrait Gallery

> *Dolly the sheep, the world's first successfully cloned animal, was stuffed after death and put on display at the Museum of Scotland.*

built in the shape of an inverted telescope. Those interested in the American Civil War should make a point of seeing the Lincoln Memorial in the old Calton Burial Ground off Waterloo Place. ⏲ 1 hr. Waterloo Place, at the Royal High School. Nelson Monument: ☎ 0131/556-2716. www.edinburghmuseums.org.uk. Tickets £3. Summer Mon 1–6pm, Tues-Sat 10am–6pm; winter Mon-Sat 10am–3pm. Bus: X25.

3 ★★★ **Royal Mile.** This is certainly the most famous street in Scotland; it runs east for about 1 mile from Edinburgh Castle down to the new Scottish Parliament building and the royal Palace of Holyroodhouse. Walking is the best way to experience this truly ancient road, and take time to explore some of the narrow alleys that jut off the street. Do note that the Royal Mile takes different names along its length: Castlehill, Lawnmarket, High Street, and Canongate. ⏲ At least 1 hr. High St., at North Bridge. Bus: 28.

4 ★★ **Edinburgh Castle.** In the 11th century, Malcolm III and his Saxon queen, later venerated as St. Margaret, founded a castle on this spot. It eventually began to be used as an ordnance factory, and in 1542, the castle ceased

being a dedicated royal residence. (Instead, the monarchs favored Holyroodhouse when staying in Edinburgh.) If it's not foggy, visit the esplanade for great views of the city. ⏲ 45 min. (2 hr. to tour interiors). See p. 510, **4**.

5 🍽 **Always Sunday.** Come here for good and fresh home cooking in modern surroundings. This cheery cafe is a welcome break from the sometimes overly touristy competition on the Royal Mile. 170 High St. ☎ 0131/622-0667. www.alwayssunday.co.uk. £5.95–£8.75. Bus: 35.

6 ★★ **Museum of Scotland.** Opened in 1998, this impressive sandstone building contains exhibits outlining the story of the country, from Scots geology and archaeology to royalty, technology, and science. The museum's 12,000-item collection ranges from 2.9-billion-year-old stones to a cute Hillman Imp, one of the last 500 automobiles manufactured in Scotland. The roof garden has excellent views, while the recently renovated Royal Museum includes a well-preserved and airy Victorian-era Main Hall and more galleries. ⏲ 2 hr. Chambers St. ☎ 0131/247-4422. www.nms.ac.uk. Free admission. Daily 10am–5pm. Bus: 2, 7, 23, 31, 35, 41, or 42.

7 ★★ **National Gallery of Scotland and Royal Scottish Academy.** On the north side of "the Mound," a hump of earth that forms a land bridge between the Old and New Towns, these Victorian exhibition halls are home to Renaissance, Impressionist, and key Scottish works of art, particularly of the 18th and early 19th centuries. The National Gallery building, designed by William Playfair (1790–1857) and opened to the public in 1859, is connected internally to the Royal Scottish Academy building (by the same architect; opened in 1826). They are superb examples of the Victorian love affair with classical architecture. ⏲ 2 hr. The Mound. ☎ 0131/624-6200. www.nationalgalleries.org. Free admission to permanent collection. Daily 10am–5pm (later on Thurs & during the Edinburgh Festival). Bus: 3, 10, 12, 17, 25, 28, 41, 44, or National Galleries shuttle.

8 ★ **Rose Street.** Many visitors will fondly remember shopping on this pedestrian-only lane in Edinburgh's New Town. Designed originally to provide homes and workshops for artisans,

When the World Comes to Scotland

The cultural highlight of any year in Edinburgh is the famous **Edinburgh Festival** (p. 724). The Scottish capital becomes chock-a-block with gawking visitors and savvy residents, maneuvering amid all sorts of street performers. The Festival (as everyone simply calls it) centers today on the **Festival Fringe.** As the name implies, this was not originally the focus of the event. But the Fringe, with hip comedy and cutting-edge performance, has eclipsed the high art of the International Festival, which focuses on classical music, opera, ballet, and drama.

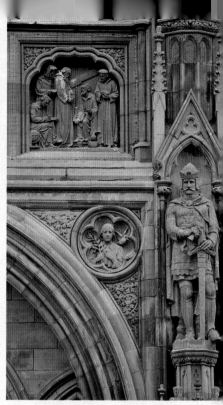

> Many of the city's finest Victorian buildings, like the Scottish National Portrait Gallery, pictured, are hewn from red sandstone.

the road is probably best known as the place in the city center to shop, dine out, and have a compact pub crawl, which can include the classic Abbotsford pub (p. 531) as well as a modern wine bar, Great Grog (☎ 0131/225-1616; www.greatgrog.co.uk). ⏱ 1 hr. Btw. Princes St. & George St. Bus: 19, 23, 27, or 42.

9 ★★ **George Street and New Town.** This broad boulevard is the central street of Edinburgh's New Town, devised during the reign of George III and constructed between 1766 and 1840. Notice how all the names of the main streets refer in some way to Hanoverian royalty, whether it be Frederick Street (George III's son) or Charlotte Street (George III's wife). Once the home of bankers and financiers, George Street is now the most upscale shopping strip in Edinburgh, as well as an avenue with the city's trendiest bars, flashiest restaurants, and dressiest nightclubs. ⏱ 1 hr. George St., at Frederick St. Bus: 13, 24, 36, 41, or 42.

10 ★ **Scottish National Portrait Gallery.** Part of the National Galleries of Scotland (the Scottish national collection of art), this handsome red-stone Gothic-style museum was designed by architect Sir Robert Rowand Anderson (1834–1921). Inside you'll find portraits of many of the country's historic and current luminaries—from Mary, Queen of Scots to the 21st-century composer James MacMillan—done by everyone from Oskar Kokoschka to Raeburn. Renovation work in 2010 has improved access. ⏱ 1 hr. 1 Queen St. ☎ 0131/624-6200. www.nationalgalleries.org. Free admission to permanent collection. Daily 10am–5pm (later on Thurs & during the Edinburgh Festival). Bus: 4, 10, 12, 16, 26, or National Galleries shuttle.

The Best of Edinburgh in 2 Days

Two days reveals a fuller picture of Edinburgh's fairly compact center. A few historic districts are part of the tour, as are more branches of the National Galleries of Art. Use buses to get across town, but when the weather is fine, I suggest that you walk to many of the attractions on this tour and get a feel for the city.

> Lothian-born John Knox was a firebrand Calvinist preacher and leader of the Scottish Protestant Reformation in the 16th century.

START **Waverley Bridge. Bus: 10, 12, 17, 25, or 44.**

1 ★★ **Edinburgh Bus Tours.** These open-top buses offer informative and often entertaining tours with an overview of the city's principal attractions. You will see most of the major sights along the Royal Mile, and also get a gander at the Grassmarket, Princes Street, Holyrood, and more. The Majestic Tour buses—the blue and orange ones—deviate a bit by visiting fewer central Edinburgh landmarks, but include the port of Leith. You can hop off and hop on later if you want to see some place up close. ⏲ 1½ hr. for standard tour. Waverley Bridge. ☎ 0131/220-0770. www.edinburghtour.com. Tickets £12 adults, £5 kids. Daily May–Oct 9:30am–5:30pm, every 15–20 min.; Nov–Apr 9:45am–4pm, every 30 min.

2 kids **John Knox House.** This Royal Mile landmark (built in 1490) is difficult to miss, jutting out into the sidewalk on High Street. There is some doubt whether John Knox (ca. 1505–72), Scotland's most famous 16th-century Reformation preacher, actually lived here, though he may have for a couple of years. Still, the photogenic building is impressive; especially noteworthy is its hand-painted ceiling. ⏲ 30 min. 43 High St. ☎ 0131/556-9575. Tickets £4.25 adults, £1 kids. Mon–Sat 10am–6pm. Bus: 35 or 36.

3 ★ **Palace of Holyroodhouse.** "Rood" is the Scots word for cross, and King David I established the now ruined abbey at Holyrood in 1128. In the 16th century, James IV (1473–1513) started construction on a palatial residence adjacent to the abbey. Most of the

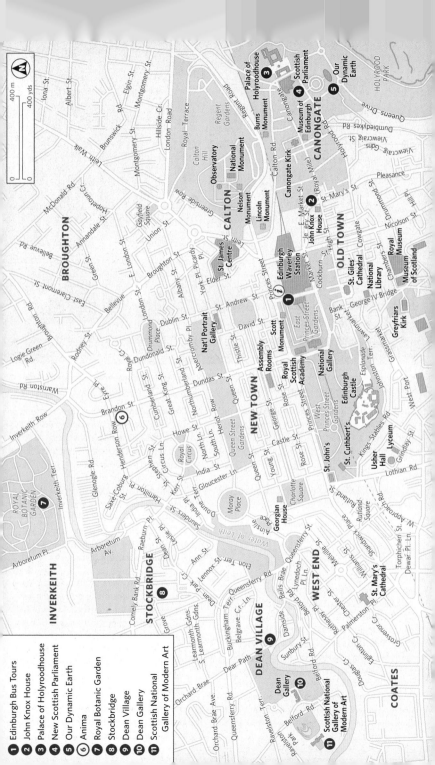

> *Members of the Scottish Parliament (MSPs) govern Scotland in a state of semi-independence from the 21st-century New Scottish Parliament building.*

existing structure you see now dates from the 17th century. A critical episode in the fraught reign of Mary, Queen of Scots (1542–87) was played out at Holyrood: the assassination of her loyal assistant David Rizzio in 1566. The attraction includes landscaped gardens and the Queen's Gallery, which exhibits bits of the royal art collection. ⏱ 1 hr. See p 512, ⑫.

④ ★ New Scottish Parliament. After a right brouhaha over its cost (more than £400 million) and delays in construction, the new Scottish Parliament complex opened in autumn of 2004. Architecture buffs say it was worth the wait and cost. Designed by the late Barcelona-based architect Enric Miralles (1955–2000), the structure is a remarkable bit of design. The full tour explains the mechanics of the Scottish government and affords views of the modern interiors. ⏱ 1 hr. Holyrood Rd., across from the Queen's Gallery. ☎ 0131/348-5000. www. scottish.parliament.uk. Free admission. Tues–Thurs 9am–7pm (when Parliament is in session); Mon–Fri (when Parliament is in recess) Apr–Oct 10am–6pm, Nov–Mar (& Sat–Sun year-round) 10am–4pm. Bus: 35 or 36.

⑤ kids Our Dynamic Earth. Under a big white canopy roof, Dynamic Earth celebrates the evolution and diversity of the planet, with an emphasis on seismic and biological activity. Simulated earthquakes, meteor showers, and views of outer space are part of the display. Skies in a "tropical rainforest" darken every 15 minutes, offering torrents of rain and creepy-crawlies underfoot. ⏱ 2 hr. Holyrood Rd. ☎ 0131/550-7800. www.dynamicearth.co.uk. Admission £11.90 adults, £8 kids 5–15. Daily 10am–5pm (July–Aug until 6pm). Bus 35 or 36.

⑥ 🍴 Anima. A pizza parlor and cafe (everything's available to go), Anima aims to serve "Italian soul food." However humble this operation looks, it offers an extensive wine list to complement the cuisine. For fish and chips, go next door to the sister takeaway. 11 Henderson Row. ☎ 0131/558-2918. www.anima-online. co.uk. Pizza £4.80–£13. Bus: 23 or 27.

⑦ ★★★ Royal Botanic Garden. This is one of the grandest parks in Great Britain. Sprawling across some 28 hectares (69 acres),

Edinburgh's Botanic Garden was inaugurated in the late 17th century as a place for studying plants with medical uses. These days, huge flowering rhododendrons are reason alone to visit here in the spring, but the sheer variety of plants, shrubs, and woods ensure year-round interest. ⏲ 1 hr. 20 Inverleith Row. ☎ 0131/552-7171. www.rbge.org.uk. Free admission (donations accepted). Daily 10am–7pm (Mar & Oct–Dec until 6pm; Jan–Feb until 4pm). Bus: 8, 17, 23, or 27.

8 ★★ **Stockbridge.** No matter how bustling Edinburgh gets during the tourist high season, this neighborhood just northwest of the city center almost always offers a slower, calmer pace. Once a hippie hamlet, and still possessing bohemian vibes, Stockbridge is now one of the more affluent and desirable districts in which to live and play. You can simply stroll around, follow the paths along the Water of Leith, look at the shops, and perhaps take in a cafe or pub, such as the Bailie Bar (p. 531). ⏲ 1 hr. Kerr St., at Hamilton Place. Bus: 24, 29, or 42.

9 ★★ **Dean Village.** Likely as early as the 12th century, a milling village was established on the Water of Leith southwest of Stockbridge. While nothing nearly that old survives in the tiny enclave today, a 20th-century conservation movement preserved the picturesque charm of the town's historic buildings. ⏲ 45 min. Just west of the intersection of Queensferry & Belford rds.

10 ★ **Dean Gallery.** This converted orphanage (built in the 1830s) hosts Edinburgh's best exhibits of 20th-century art and design. Visiting shows have included paintings by Picasso and the architectural plans and drawings of Sir Basil Spence (1907–76). You'll also find permanent exhibits of surrealist art and the re-created London studio of Scots-Italian pop-art pioneer Sir Eduardo Paolozzi (1924–2005). ⏲ 1 hr. 73 Belford Rd. ☎ 0131/624-6200. www.nationalgalleries.org. Free admission to permanent exhibits. Daily 10am–5pm. Bus: 13 or National Galleries shuttle.

11 ★ **Scottish National Gallery of Modern Art.** Highlights of the collection, which occupies two floors of a neoclassical building that once was a school, include works by French post-Impressionists Bonnard and Matisse; European expressionists, such as Kirchner and Nolde; and recent acquisitions from such contemporary Scottish artists as Christine Borland. ⏲ 1 hr. 75 Belford Rd. ☎ 0131/624-6200. www.nationalgalleries.org. Free admission to permanent exhibits. Daily 10am–5pm. Bus: 13 or National Galleries shuttle.

> Plants from the tropics and subtropics thrive in the greenhouses at the Royal Botanic Garden.

Historic & Literary Edinburgh

From Old Town to New Town, there is a veritable slew of historical and literary references across Edinburgh, from a restored 16th-century town house on a traditional "land" or plot; to the Museum of Edinburgh, which tells the story of a city and its rich history; to another museum dedicated to the nation's most significant scribes. The city has done a good job of preserving and promoting both its antiquity and star writers, so this special interest tour covers both.

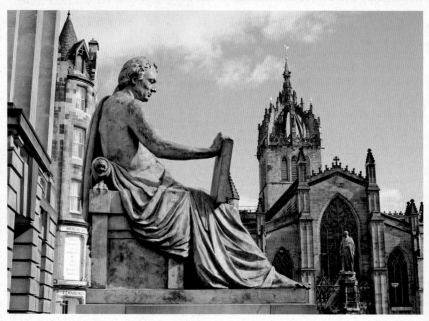

> *The High Kirk of St. Giles, where market trader Jenny Geddes supposedly threw a chair at the minister in a 1637 religious protest.*

START Edinburgh Old College. Bus: 3, 7, 30, or 37.

① ★★ **Old College.** The 1781 exteriors of the University of Edinburgh Old College have been called the greatest public work of neoclassical architect Robert Adam (1728–92). This "Old College" actually replaced an earlier Old College that dated to the 1500s. Construction of the quadrangle of buildings was suspended during the Napoleonic Wars, and William Playfair designed the Quad's interiors in 1819. The Old College is also home to the Talbot Rice Gallery, which has an excellent permanent collection and hosts interesting modern art exhibitions. ⏱ 45 min. Chambers St., at South Bridge. www.ed.ac.uk. Bus: 3, 7, 30, or 37.

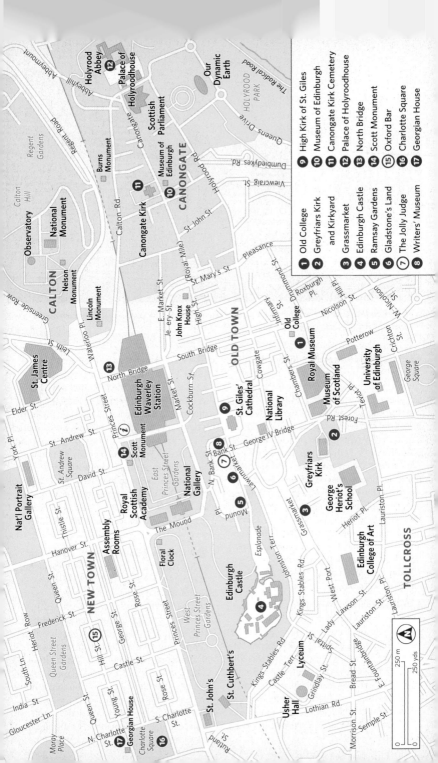

Legend / Points of Interest

1. Old College
2. Greyfriars Kirk and Kirkyard
3. Grassmarket
4. Edinburgh Castle
5. Ramsay Gardens
6. Gladstone's Land
7. The Jolly Judge
8. Writers' Museum
9. High Kirk of St. Giles
10. Museum of Edinburgh
11. Canongate Kirk Cemetery
12. Palace of Holyroodhouse
13. North Bridge
14. Scott Monument
15. Oxford Bar
16. Charlotte Square
17. Georgian House

Map labels:

Abbeyhill · Abbeymount · Holyrood Abbey · Palace of Holyroodhouse · Scottish Parliament · Our Dynamic Earth · HOLYROOD PARK · Queens Drive · The Radical Road · Regent Gardens · Regent Road · Burns Monument · Museum of Edinburgh · CANONGATE · Canongate Kirk · Holyrood Rd · Dumbiedykes Rd. · Viewcraig St. · Pleasance · St. John St. · Calton Hill · Observatory · National Monument · Nelson Monument · Lincoln Monument · CALTON · Calton Rd. · St. Mary's St. · (Royal Mile) · Greenside Row · Leith St. · St. James Centre · Elder St. · York Pl. · Waterloo Pl. · E. Market St. · Jeffrey St. · High St. · John Knox House · Canongate · South Bridge · Cowgate · OLD TOWN · Drummond St. · Roxburgh Pl. · Infirmary St. · Nicolson St. · W. Nicolson St. · Crichton St. · Potterow · University of Edinburgh · George Square · Old College · Royal Museum · Museum of Scotland · Chambers St. · Forest Rd. · North Bridge · Edinburgh Waverley Station · Market St. · Cockburn St. · South Bridge · St. Giles' Cathedral · National Library · George IV Bridge · Greyfriars Kirk · George Heriot's School · Heriot Pl. · Lauriston Pl. · Lauriston St. · Lauriston St. · TOLLCROSS · Nat'l Portrait Gallery · St. Andrew Square · St. Andrew St. · David St. · NEW TOWN · Hanover St. · Queen St. · Thistle St. · Rose St. · George St. · Princes Street · Princes Street · Scott Monument · National Gallery · Royal Scottish Academy · Assembly Rooms · The Mound · Floral Clock · East Princes Street Gardens · West Princes Street Gardens · Esplanade · Edinburgh Castle · Johnston Terr. · Grassmarket · Lawnmarket · N. Bank St. · The Mound · Kings Stables Rd. · Kings Stables Rd. · West Port · Spittal St. · Lady Lawson St. · Edinburgh College of Art · Castle Terr. · Lyceum · Usher Hall · Grindlay St. · Bread St. · E. Fountainbridge · Morrison St. · Semple St. · Lothian Rd. · Rutland St. · St. Cuthbert's · St. John's · Queen Street Gardens · Heriot Row · South Ln. · India St. · Gloucester Ln. · Moray Place · N. Charlotte St. · Georgian House · Charlotte Square · S. Charlotte St. · Castle St. · Frederick St. · Young St. · Hill St. · Queen St. · Rose St. · Charlotte Square

250 m · 250 yds

> *The Flodden Wall, parts of which pass through Greyfriars Kirkyard (pictured above), was built after a disastrous Scottish military defeat in 1513.*

2 ★ **Greyfriars Kirk and** ★★ **Kirkyard.** Dedicated in 1620, this was the first "reformed" church in Edinburgh, where the National Covenant, favoring Scottish Presbyterianism over the English Episcopacy, was signed in 1638 (you can see an original copy here). Among many restorations, one in the 1930s used California Redwood to create the current ceiling. The cemetery in the kirkyard was proposed first by Mary, Queen of Scots. There are bits of the Flodden Wall in the grounds, as well as lots of intriguing (and some creepy) monuments with morbid engravings. ⏱ 45 min. Greyfriars Place. ☎ 0131/225-1900. www.greyfriarskirk.com. Free admission. Apr–Oct Mon–Fri 10:30am–4:30pm, Sat 10:30am–2:30pm; Nov–Mar Thurs 1:30–3:30pm. Bus: 2, 23, 27, 41, 42, or 45.

3 ★ **Grassmarket.** In a city rich with history, the Grassmarket (a rectangle with a short street and a small city park running along it) has more than its share. Convicted criminals were once famously hung here until the 1780s, although the area was first intended as a place for a weekly market. Robert Burns records staying at the Grassmarket's White Hart Inn, and the area still has many hotels, pubs, and restaurants. ⏱ 45 min. Btw. West Port & West Bow. Bus: 2.

4 ★★ **Edinburgh Castle.** The focus of the castle's exhibitions is heavily weighted toward the military: The premises still serve as barracks for current soldiers, and there is the ancient cannon Mons Meg and the halls where captured French soldiers were interred during the Napoleonic Wars. But visitors can also see the Scottish Crown Jewels and the Great Hall (where early Scottish Parliaments convened). ⏱ 2 hr. to tour the interior. Castlehill. ☎ 0131/225-9846. www.historic-scotland.gov.uk. Admission £15 adults, £9 kids 5–15. Daily 9:30am–6pm (Oct–Mar until 5pm). Bus: 23, 27, 41, or 45.

5 ★★ **Ramsay Gardens.** Not a garden but an innovative and charming set of buildings that dates to the end of the 19th century, this bright and cheerful place was the brainchild of Sir Patrick Geddes (1854–1932). A polymath and city planner, Geddes almost single-handedly rid Old Town of squalid living conditions while saving it from total destruction and redevelopment. The architecture is a beautiful mix of Scottish baronial and English cottage, combining corbels (the cantilevered round extensions), conical roofs, crow steps, and half-timber gable construction. ⏱ 30 min. Adjacent to Castle Esplanade, Castlehill. Bus: 23, 27, 41, or 45.

6 ★★ **Gladstone's Land.** This 17th-century merchant's house gives a clear impression of how confined living conditions were some 400 years ago—even for the well-off. On the second level you can see the original exterior facade, and a sensitively restored timber ceiling looks suitably weathered and aged, but still bears the remnants of the originally colorful paintings of flowers and fruit. ⏱ 45 min. 477b Lawnmarket. ☎ 0131/226-5856. www. nts.org.uk. Admission £6 adults, £5 kids, £15.50 families. Daily Apr–Oct 10am–5pm (July–Aug until 6:30pm). Bus: 23, 27, 41, or 45.

⑦ 🍺 **The Jolly Judge** is an unpretentious pub with outdoor space (the only seating section where kids are allowed); it's good for coffee, drinks, and simple lunches. 7 James Court, Lawnmarket. All items under £5. ☎ 0131/225-2669. Bus: 23, 27, 41, or 45.

8 ★ **Writers' Museum.** This 17th-century house contains a treasure-trove of portraits, relics, and manuscripts relating to Scotland's greatest gentlemen of letters: Robert Burns (1759–96), Sir Walter Scott (1771–1832), and Robert Louis Stevenson (1850–94). The museum building, Lady Stair's House, with its narrow passages and low clearances, was originally built in 1622. ⏱ 45 min. Lady Stair's Close, off the Lawnmarket. ☎ 0131/529-4901. Free admission. Mon–Sat 10am–5pm (Aug also Sun noon–5pm). Bus: 23, 27, 41, or 45.

9 ★ **High Kirk of St. Giles.** Its steeple is a key city landmark, visible across central Edinburgh, and this is where Scotland's Martin Luther, John Knox, preached about reform. Also called **St. Giles Cathedral** (the pre-Reformation name), the building combines a dark and brooding stone exterior (the result of a Victorian-era restoration) with surprisingly graceful buttresses. ⏱ 45 min. High St. ☎ 0131/225-9442. www.stgilescathedral.org. uk. £3 donation suggested. May–Sept Mon–Fri 9am–7pm, Sat 9am–5pm, Sun 1–5pm; Oct–Apr Mon–Sat 9am–5pm, Sun 1–5pm. Bus: 23, 27, 28, 35, 41, or 42.

> *Grassmarket has long been a popular gathering place, but now it's pubs rather than public executions that draw the crowds.*

> Edinburgh poet Robert Fergusson, whose statue (pictured) stands in Canongate Kirk Cemetery, was a leading figure of the Scottish Enlightenment.

(1750–74), which bears an inscription by Burns. ⏱ 30 min. Canongate, the Royal Mile. Free admission. Daily dawn–dusk. Bus: 35.

⑫ ★★★ **Palace of Holyroodhouse.** Most of the palace's current structure was built at the behest of King Charles II in the 1670s, although he ironically never stayed here. The reigning monarch, Queen Elizabeth, stays here whenever she's in town, however, and you can see the reception rooms she uses, such as the Throne Room. The real highlight of the tour is in the oldest surviving section of the palace (constructed ca. 1530), where Mary, Queen of Scots lived on the second floor. Be sure to check out some of the queen's needlework, which depicts her cousin (and the woman who had her beheaded), England's Elizabeth I, as a cat and herself as a mouse. The audio tour is good, and the staff is knowledgeable, so don't hesitate to ask questions. ⏱ 1½ hr. East terminus of the Royal Mile, Canongate. ☎ 0131/556-5100. www.royal.gov.uk. Admission £10.50 adults, £6.35 kids, £28 families. Daily 9:30am–6pm (Nov–Mar until 4:30pm). Closed when Royal Family in residence, typically 2 weeks in May–June. Bus: 35.

⑬ ★ **North Bridge.** Most of Edinburgh's many bridges don't necessarily cross waterways but link up ridges and hills. This historic crossing is no different. The first North Bridge took some 9 years to complete from 1763 to 1772, creating a much needed connection between Old and New Towns. The current broad span was built from 1894 to 1897, soaring over the railway lines and Waverley Station. ⏱ 20 min. At Princes St. Bus: 3, 10, 12, 17, 25, 29, 33, 41, or 45.

⑭ ★ **Scott Monument.** In the center of this 61m (200-ft.) tower's Gothic spire (it opened in 1846) is a marble statue of Sir Walter Scott and his dog, Maida, with Scott's fictional heroes carved as small figures in many niches throughout the steeple-like structure. Climb the 287 stairs to the top for worthwhile views: Look east and you can clearly see the Burns Monument, designed by Thomas Hamilton in 1830, on the side of Calton Hill. ⏱ 30 min. East Princes St. Gardens, near Waverley Station. ☎ 0131/529-4068. www.cac.org.uk. Admission £3. Daily Apr–Sept 10am–7pm; Oct–Mar 9am–4pm. Bus: 3, 10, 12, 17, 25, 29, 33, 41, or 45.

⑩ **Museum of Edinburgh.** This museum presents the capital's history via items that represent the city and its traditional industries, such as glassmaking, pottery, wool processing, and cabinetry. The collar of Greyfriars Bobby, a Skye terrier who reportedly kept watch at his deceased owner's grave for 14 years, is in historic Huntly House, actually three small 16th-century houses joined. The house gets its name from a duchess of the Gordons of Huntly, who kept an apartment here in the 1700s. ⏱ 1 hr. 142 Canongate. ☎ 0131/529-4143. www.cac.org.uk. Free admission. Mon–Sat 10am–5pm (Aug also Sun noon–5pm). Bus: 35.

⑪ ★ **Canongate Kirk Cemetery.** Several literary references are here, from the grave of Adam Smith (1723–90), who wrote *The Wealth of Nations*, to that of Robert Burns's paramour Agnes McLehose (his beloved Clarinda). Burns also arranged and paid for the kirkyard's 1789 monument to poet Robert Fergusson

> *The Georgian House lies, appropriately, in Edinburgh's New Town, laid out largely during the Georgian period.*

(15) ⚫ **Oxford Bar** is the occasional real-life hangout of leading crime novelist Ian Rankin (p. 339). Of course, it was also the regular dive for Rankin's most famous fictional character, the world-weary Inspector Rebus. A good place for a pint, but squeeze past the people at the small bar and go into a side room, where there's more space and usually a fire burning in the fireplace. Food is limited to snacks. 8 Young St. ☎ 0131/539-7119. www.oxfordbar.com. Daily noon–midnight. Bus: 13, 19, or 41.

(16) ★ **Charlotte Square.** Charlotte Square, designed by the great Georgian architect Robert Adam, was the final piece of the city's first New Town development. With a charming park at its core, it epitomizes the urbane grace of the area. You can almost imagine 18th-century horse-drawn carriages circumnavigating the place, with gaslights illuminating the sidewalks. Visitors may tour the interior of one property on the square: Georgian House (17) on the north side. ⏱ 30 min. West end of George St. Bus: 10, 19, or 41.

(17) ★ **Georgian House.** This historic town house on the north side of the square displays the furnishings of upper-class 18th-century Edinburgh, including classic Chippendale chairs,

a dining table set with fine Wedgwood china, and the pee pot that the men passed around once their womenfolk had retired to other quarters in the house. ⏱ 1 hr. 7 Charlotte Sq. ☎ 0131/226-3318. www.nts.org.uk. Admission £6 adults, £5 kids, £15.50 families. Daily July–Aug 10am–7pm; Apr–Jun & Sept–Oct 10am–5pm; Mar & Nov 11am–3pm. Bus: 10, 19, or 41.

Following in Authors' Footsteps

The **Literary Pub Tour** retraces the footsteps of Burns, Stevenson, and Scott via the city's more atmospheric taverns, highlighting the tales of Jekyll and Hyde, or the erotic love poetry of Burns. The walking tour costs £10 and departs nightly at 7:30pm (June–Sept) from the Beehive Inn on the Grassmarket (☎ 0131/226-6665; www.edinburghliterarypubtour.co.uk).

Complete with readings and dramatizations, the **Edinburgh Book Lovers' Tour** (☎ 01573/223-888; www.edinburghbookloverstour.com) departs from the Writers' Museum. Its guide is Allan Foster, author of *The Literary Traveller in Edinburgh.* An odyssey around Old Town, this walking tour costs £10 and departs at 10:30am and 1:30pm Saturday and Sunday throughout the year, and daily during the Edinburgh Festival.

Leith

Edinburgh's long-standing port at Leith was established because a natural harbor had formed where the Water of Leith river fed into the massive Firth of Forth estuary. Though it was properly incorporated into Edinburgh's city limits in the 20th century, Leith has long had its own identity, and it was effectively Scotland's capital during the interim rule of Mary of Guise in the 16th century. Her daughter, Mary, Queen of Scots, made a celebrated arrival here in 1561 and dined on a site that is now Lamb's House. While the city keeps close ties with history, it is experiencing fairly rapid recent development and the conversion of former warehouses into destination-worthy venues. In short, Leith is growing up and coming into its own.

START John's Place. Bus: 12, 16, or 35

1 ★ **Leith Links.** Older than the Bruntsfield Links golf course in Edinburgh's Meadows park, Leith Links is by some accounts the birthplace of golf. A version of the sport was first played here in the 1400s, and in 1744, the first rules of the game were laid down at Leith Links. Today no one plays golf here: It's just a pleasant public park, but running adjacent to

John's Place was the fairway of this ancient course's first hole. **East of John's Place, btw. Duke St. & Links Gardens. Free admission. Daily dawn–dusk. Bus: 12, 16, or 35.**

2 **Leith Town Hall.** This neoclassical building was originally constructed as the Leith Sheriff Court in 1828. The designers' firm is emblazoned on the Queen Charlotte Street frontage: R. & R. DICKSON. Today it contains the

> *Trinity House is now a museum displaying memorabilia relating to Leith's seafaring past.*

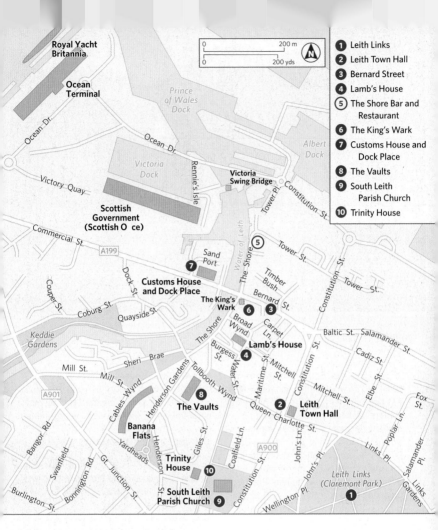

1. Leith Links
2. Leith Town Hall
3. Bernard Street
4. Lamb's House
5. The Shore Bar and Restaurant
6. The King's Wark
7. Customs House and Dock Place
8. The Vaults
9. South Leith Parish Church
10. Trinity House

court house and police office. The adjoining property was incorporated later after the town became a parliamentary burgh in 1833. 75–81 Constitution St. & 29–41 Queen Charlotte St.

3 ★ **Bernard Street.** Bernard Street has been termed Leith's "most formal" architectural space. It's quite short and almost feels more like a square than a street, with a mix of Georgian and 19th-century commercial buildings, such as the former Leith Bank. At its eastern end, where it meets Constitution Street, is another of Scotland's many monuments to poet Robert Burns. This bronze statue was erected in 1898. At this corner, as well, is the **Leith Assembly Rooms,** 37–43 Constitution St. The building includes a merchant's meeting place built in the 1780s, as well as a two-story ballroom.

4 ★★ **Lamb's House.** A detour up Carpet Lane takes you to this handsome four-story red-tile-roofed building. The first thing you might notice is the odd window built into the corner of the facade. Originally a large early-17th-century merchant's house (the finest example of its type in Edinburgh, in fact), it is a masterpiece of architecture, with crow-stepped gables and corbels. I know people who once worked here (it's been converted into offices), and they're convinced that a ghost or two haunt the place. Burgess & Water sts.

> *Leith Links is now a public park, but it's also where the Honourable Company of Edinburgh Golfers first codified golf in 1744.*

⑤ 🍽 ★★ **The Shore Bar and Restaurant,** thanks to its wood paneling, feels as if it has been sitting right here and receiving seafarers for many years. Although it actually opened in the 1980s, it remains one of the best dining venues in Leith. Food is served casually to diners seated on stools at the bar or more formally at tables covered in white linens in the adjoining but separate dining room. The menu still features a number of seafood dishes, but after a recent takeover by new owners (Fishers, next door), more sophisticated dishes are alongside traditional pub favorites. 3-4 The Shore. ☎ 0131/553-5080. Items £6–£12.

⑥ ★ **The King's Wark.** This building dates to the beginning of the 1700s, but its history is richer. The original King's Wark on this site (ca. 1434) was believed to be a palace and arsenal that King James VI had rebuilt during his reign in the 17th century, and which was later given to a tavern-keeping buddy of his, Bernard Lindsay. It currently houses a pub, one of many welcoming options on the Shore, Leith's first main street. 36 The Shore.

⑦ ★ **Customs House and Dock Place.** Designed by Robert Reid in 1810, the Customs House is quite a monumental (if somewhat harsh) building, with sturdy fluted columns.

Award-Winning Dining in Leith

Ten years ago, Edinburgh dining was good, but today it is on the way to becoming nationally recognized as among the best in the U.K. There are five restaurants that boast a Michelin Red Guide star, one of the top honors, and three of these are in Leith. Best among them is Restaurant Martin Wishart, whose chef-owner Martin Wishart is one of the most talented in Europe. The Kitchin restaurant features the cooking of 30-something Tom Kitchin, a certain rising star in Britain, who is becoming something of a TV celebrity. Lastly, but not necessarily least, the Plumed Horse is the most recent restaurant in Edinburgh to join the top ranks (although at his previous restaurant in southern Scotland, chef-owner Tony Borthwick once hit the heights). See "Edinburgh Restaurants A to Z," on p. 523, for more information on these and other standout restaurants.

Look out for the royal arms of King George III in the triangular pediment that rests on the columns. Nearby is the original entrance to the Old East Dock (established at the start of the 19th century and today redeveloped into modern Leith), the Commercial Quay. This area also skirts the remains of the walls of the Leith Citadel, a fortification built on the instruction of Oliver Cromwell, with fragments allegedly now part of Dock Street. **Commercial St., at Dock Place.**

8 ★ **The Vaults.** This handsome and broad stone warehouse dates from 1682, but the vaulted passage and wine cellar underneath may be 100 years older. There was more to Scotland's Auld Alliance with France than simply plotting wars against England. On account of the friendship, Scots merchants had first pick of the latest Bordeaux, and Leith is where bottles and bottles of French wine were shipped. Indeed, the word "claret" is believed by some to be one that Scots gave to red wine from Bordeaux. A link to that history is maintained by the elegant **Vintners Rooms** restaurant (☎ 0131/554-6767; www.vintners rooms.com), which offers an extensive list of fine French wines. The Leith outpost of the members-only Scotch Malt Whisky Society is located on the second floor of the Vaults, but the Vintners serves 1,300 single-malt whiskies by the glass to all comers. **87 Giles St.**

9 **South Leith Parish Church.** A church has been standing at this site since about 1480. The one that is here today was built in 1848, thanks to an Act of Parliament. A plaque in the kirkyard details the intervening history, which includes some very heavy bombardment in 1560 by English troops and Oliver Cromwell's later decision to use the poor, ravaged church as a munitions hold. **6 Henderson St.**

10 ★ **Trinity House.** Trinity House is an early-1800s survivor amid the urban renewal and tall apartment buildings of central Leith. The current building occupies the site of a former 16th-century almshouse. Visitors can explore the museum's collection of seafaring memorabilia accumulated over the past 200 years, with pieces ranging from navigational instruments to nautical paintings. Owned by Historic Scotland, it is home to the Incorporation of Masters and Mariners, an organization that dates to the 14th century. **99 Kirkgate.** ☎ 0131/554-3289. **Group tours by reservation.**

> *The pediment on the Customs House carries the coat of arms of the monarch when it was built, George III.*

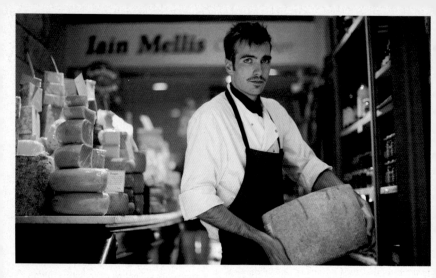

Edinburgh Shopping A to Z

Books

★★ McNaughtan's Bookshop NEW TOWN
In business since 1957, this is one of the city's best antiquarian and secondhand book purveyors. It is a must stop for all book lovers. 3a Haddington Place (Leith Walk, near Gayfield Sq.). ☎ 0131/556-5897. www.mcnaughtans bookshop.com. MC, V. Bus: 7, 12, 16, or 22.

★ Waterstones NEW TOWN
This is a giant Barnes-and-Noble-like operation, with plenty of reading options and soft comfortable seats for lounging and previewing your prospective purchases. If it's in print, it's probably here: Waterstones is the most prominent and best-stocked book retailer in Edinburgh's city center. 128 Princes St. (across from Waverley Station). ☎ 0131/226-2666. www.waterstones.com. AE, MC, V. Bus: 8, 22, 25, 33.

Clothing & Fashions
Arkangel WEST END
William Street, in the city's affluent West End, is home to a host of hot boutique shops. This one specializes in women's designer labels

Edinburgh Shopping Best Bets

Best for a Picnic Basket
Valvona & Crolla 19 Elm Row (p. 522)

Best for Single Malts
Royal Mile Whiskies 379 High St. (p. 522)

Best of Designer Labels
Arkangel 4 William St. (p. 518)

Best Department Store
John Lewis St. James Centre (p. 519)

Best Men's Clothes
Walker Slater 20 Victoria St. (p. 519)

that are exclusive to Scotland. Accessories, jewelry, and bags and shoes are also available. 4 William St. ☎ 0131/226-4466. www.arkangel fashion.co.uk. MC, V. Bus: 4 or 25.

★ Corniche OLD TOWN
One of the more sophisticated boutiques in Edinburgh; if it's the latest in Scottish clothing trends, expect to find it at this fashionable shop, be it women's or men's clothing, or handbags and stilettos. 2 Jeffrey St. (near the

> *I. J. Mellis is the city's finest cheesemonger.*

> *You'll find fashions for both women and men at Corniche.*

Royal Mile). ☎ 0131/556-3707. www.corniche. org.uk. AE, MC, V. Bus: 35.

★ Cruise NEW TOWN

With both a men's and a women's collection, this homegrown fashion outlet began in Edinburgh's Old Town—not generally considered fertile ground for the avant-garde. There is still a branch off the Royal Mile, but the New Town outlet is considered the focus for true couture. 94 George St. ☎ 0131/226-3524. www.cruise clothing.co.uk. MC, V. Bus: 19, 37, or 41.

★★ Walker Slater OLD TOWN

This shop sells well-made and contemporary (if understated) men's clothes, usually made of cotton and dyed in rich, earthy hues. My moleskin suit from here has served me well for years. Walker Slater also carries Mackintosh overcoats and accessories. 20 Victoria St. (near George IV Bridge). ☎ 0131/220-2636. www.walkerslater.com. MC, V. Bus: 35, 41, or 42.

Department Stores

★ Harvey Nichols NEW TOWN

Initially, locals were not quite prepared for this English store's multiple floors of expensive labels and goods by designers such as Jimmy Choo and Alexander McQueen. But they've learned. Expect high-end fashion for both genders as well as a range of merchandise such as accessories and food products. 30–34 St. Andrew Sq. ☎ 0131/524-8388. www.harveynichols. com. AE, MC, V. Bus: 8, 12, 17, or 45.

Jenners NEW TOWN

This neo-Gothic landmark opened in 1838 and was family-run until its 2005 takeover by the department store group, House of Fraser. It continues to sell a variety of local and international merchandise, and the food hall offers a wide array of gift-oriented Scottish products. 48 Princes St. ☎ 0870/607-2841. AE, MC, V. Bus: 8, 22, 25, or 33.

★★ John Lewis NEW TOWN

The largest department store in Scotland, this branch of John Lewis is many people's first choice when it comes to shopping for clothes, appliances, furniture, toys, and everything in between. St. James Centre (at the top of Leith Walk). ☎ 0131/556-9121. www.johnlewis.com. AE, MC, V. Bus: 7, 14, 22, or 25.

Food & Wine

★★★ I. J. Mellis Cheesemongers STOCKBRIDGE

This shop sells an assortment of award-winning British and Irish cheeses, and the

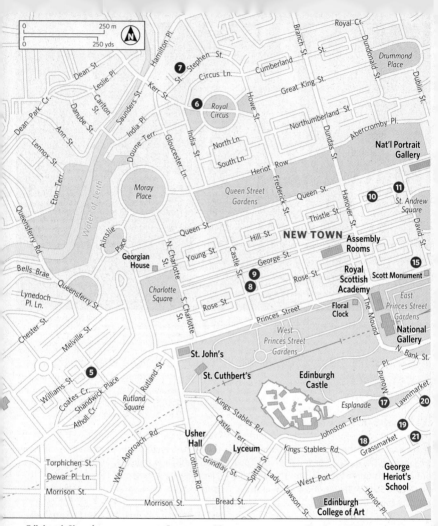

Edinburgh Shopping
Anta **19**
Arkangel **5**
Avalanche **28**
Bill Baber **18**
Corniche **31**
Cruise **9**
Fabhatrix **21**
Harvey Nichols **12**
I.J. Mellis Cheesemongers **6**
Jenners **15**
John Lewis **24**
McNaughtan's
  Bookshop **25**
Ragamu n **32**
Royal Mile Whiskies **16**
Valvona & Crolla **26**
Walker Slater **20**
Waterstones **23**

Edinburgh Restaurants
Barioja **30**
Bell's Diner **7**
Café Royal Oyster Bar **14**
David Bann's Vegetarian
  Restaurant **33**
Dusit **10**
Fishers Bistro **2**
Forth Floor **13**
Henderson's Vegetarian
  Restaurant **11**
Kebab Mahal **35**
The Kitchin **1**
La Garrigue **29**
Number One **22**
Oloroso **8**
Restaurant Martin Wishart **4**
The Shore Bar &
  Restaurant **3**
Spoon Café Bistro **34**
21212 **27**
The Witchery by
  the Castle **17**

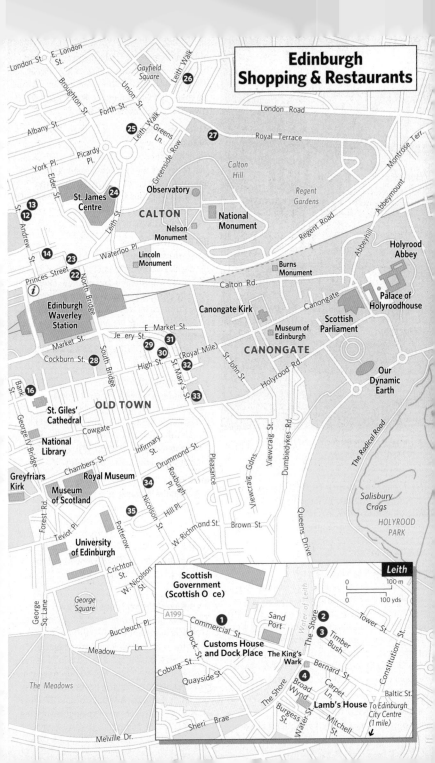

> The staff is knowledgeable and the variety is vast at Royal Mile Whiskies.

staff really knows their stuff. There are similar shops in Old Town on Victoria Street (convenient to the Royal Mile), as well as on Morningside Road on the Southside. 6 **Bakers Place (Kerr St.)**. ☎ 0131/225-6566. www.mellis cheese.co.uk. MC, V. Bus: 24, 29, or 42.

★★ **Valvona & Crolla** NEW TOWN
This Italian deli has an excellent reputation across the United Kingdom thanks to a wonderful range of cheeses and cured meats, fresh fruit and vegetables, plus baked goods ranging from rolls to sourdough loaves. Great for picnics after a hike up 251m-high (823-ft.) Arthur's Seat. 19 **Elm Row (Leith Walk)**. ☎ 0131/556-6066. www. valvonacrolla.co.uk. MC, V. Bus: 7, 14, 22, or 25.

Hats
★★ **Fabhatrix** OLD TOWN
I'm partial to hats, and this shop has hundreds of handmade ones. There are practical and handsome options, as well as a few that are downright frivolous but extremely fun. 13 **Cowgatehead (off Grassmarket)**. ☎ 0131/225-9222. www.fabhatrix.com. MC, V. Bus: 2.

Knits & Woolens
Anta OLD TOWN
Shop here for some of the most stylish Scottish tartans, especially cool minikilts and silk *earasaids* (oversized scarves) for women. Great gifts or souvenirs. **Crocket's Land, 91–93 West Bow**. ☎ 0131/225-4616. www.anta.co.uk. MC, V. Bus: 35, 41, or 42.

Bill Baber OLD TOWN
This workshop and store turns out artfully modernized adaptations of traditional Scottish patterns for both men and women. Each individually designed piece is handmade from an all-natural material, either linen, merino, silk, or cotton. Partners Bill and Helen Baber have also opened a sister shop in York, England. 66 **Grassmarket**. ☎ 0131/225-3249. www.billbaber. com. MC, V. Bus: 2.

★ **Ragamuffin** OLD TOWN
The unique apparel here is considered to be "wearable art" and is created by some 150 designers who herald from all over the U.K. Ragamuffin also has a shop on the Isle of Skye. 276 **Canongate**. ☎ 0131/557-6007. www. ragamuffinonline.co.uk. MC, V. Bus: 35.

Music
★ **Avalanche Records** OLD TOWN
This excellent indie music shop is good for finding new releases of Scottish and U.K. bands and secondhand CDs. Another branch is located on West Nicolson Street. 5 **Grassmarket**. ☎ 0131/659-7708. www.avalanche records.co.uk. MC, V. Bus: 35.

Whisky
★★★ **Royal Mile Whiskies** OLD TOWN
The stock at this rather small shop on the Royal Mile is huge: Some 1,000 different Scotch and other nations' whiskies are available. The staff is very knowledgeable, so don't hesitate to ask for advice. You can also purchase whisky accessories or whisky-flavored sweets—perfect for your friends back home. 379 **High St**. ☎ 0131/622-6255. www.royalmilewhiskies. com. AE, MC, V. Bus: 35.

Edinburgh Restaurants A to Z

★ **Barioja** OLD TOWN *SPANISH*
This casual tapas bar is fun, friendly, and often lively. Portions are substantial for the price. 19 Jeffrey St. ☎ 0131/557-3622. Entrees £6–£10. AE, MC, V. Lunch & dinner Mon–Sat. Bus: 36.

★ **Bell's Diner** STOCKBRIDGE *AMERICAN*
Open for some 30-odd years, this wee diner's burgers are cooked to order with a variety of toppings, from cheese to garlic butter. 17 St. Stephen St. ☎ 0131/225-8116. Entrees £7–£9. Dinner daily; lunch Sat. Bus: 24, 29, or 42.

★ **Café Royal Oyster Bar** NEW TOWN *SEAFOOD/ FISH* Many of this 140-year-old restaurant's splendid Victorian touches remain intact today. The menu offers oysters, salmon, langoustines, and lobsters—as well as beef and rabbit. 17a W. Register St. ☎ 0131/556-4124. Entrees £15–£20. AE, MC, V. Lunch & dinner daily. Bus: 8 or 29.

★★ **David Bann's Vegetarian Restaurant** OLD TOWN *VEGETARIAN* Chef David Bann has been at the forefront of meat-free cooking in Edinburgh for more than a decade, and his meals are tasty and healthy. The dining room is

> *Elegant presentation at the Café Royal Oyster Bar.*

Edinburgh Restaurant Best Bets

Most Atmospheric
The Witchery by the Castle Castlehill (p. 525)

Best Contemporary Scottish Cooking
The Kitchin 78 Commercial Quay (p. 524)

Best for Innovation
21212 3 Royal Terrace (p. 525)

Best for Tapas
Barioja 19 Jeffrey St. (p. 523)

Best Views
Oloroso 33 Castle St. (p. 524)

stylish. 56–58 St. Mary's St. ☎ 0131/556-5888. www.davidbann.com. Entrees £7.50–£10. AE, MC, V. Lunch & dinner daily. Bus: 36.

★ **Dusit** NEW TOWN *THAI*
An unassuming restaurant that serves some of the best Thai in the city. A number of dishes use Scottish produce, such as venison, and the seafood options are plentiful. 49a Thistle St. ☎ 0131/220-6846. www.dusit.co.uk. Entrees £10–£16. AE, MC, V. Lunch & dinner daily. Bus: 24, 29, or 42.

> Tapas at Barioja.

★ Fishers Bistro LEITH FISH
A favorite for its seafood—and views of the harbor at Leith. The chefs here offer such enticing dishes as fresh Loch Fyne oysters or breaded and crispy fish cakes. 1 The Shore. ☎ 0131/554-5666. Entrees £12–£16. AE, MC, V. Lunch & dinner daily. Bus: 16, 22, 35, or 36.

★★ Forth Floor NEW TOWN SCOTTISH/MODERN BRITISH This restaurant and brasserie at the top of the Harvey Nichols department store, with excellent views, dishes out excellent contemporary Scottish cooking. The brasserie food is just as tasty but cheaper. In Harvey Nichols, 30–34 St. Andrew Sq. ☎ 0131/524-8350. www.harveynichols.com. Entrees £15–£25. AE, DC, MC, V. Lunch & dinner daily. Bus: 8, 10, 12, or 45.

Henderson's Vegetarian Restaurant NEW TOWN VEGETARIAN Edinburgh's longtime stalwart of healthy, inexpensive vegetarian cuisine. Dinner features table service and an expanded menu. Wines include organic options. 94 Hanover St. ☎ 0131/225-2131. www.hendersonsofedinburgh.co.uk. Entrees £6–£8. MC, V. Breakfast, lunch & dinner Mon–Sat. Bus: 13, 23, or 27.

★ Kebab Mahal SOUTHSIDE INDIAN
This basic, inexpensive Indian restaurant— where you may share your table with others— is a local landmark. No alcohol is allowed, but it is open late. 7 Nicolson Sq. ☎ 0131/667-5214. Entrees £4–£6. Lunch & dinner daily. No credit cards. Bus: 3, 5, 29, 31, or 35.

★★ The Kitchin LEITH MODERN SCOTTISH/ FRENCH After opening this contemporary restaurant in 2006, chef-owner Tom Kitchin quickly garnered a Michelin star. The 20-something's French-inspired recipes use top seasonal Scottish ingredients. 78 Commercial Quay. ☎ 0131/555-1755. www.thekitchin.com. Entrees £28–£34. MC, V. Lunch & dinner Tues–Sat. Bus: 16, 22, 35, or 36.

★ La Garrigue OLD TOWN FRENCH
Its chef and owner hails from southern France, and he re-creates that region's fresh and rustic cooking in this casual but stylish dining room. 31 Jeffrey St. ☎ 0131/557-3032. www.lagarrigue.co.uk. Set lunch £13; dinner £20. AE, MC, V. Lunch & dinner Mon–Sat. Bus: 36.

★★ Number One NEW TOWN SCOTTISH/ MODERN BRITISH The premier restaurant in the city's premier central hotel has a well-earned Michelin star for its superior cuisine and service. A special treat that's worth the price. In the Balmoral Hotel, 1 Princes St. ☎ 0131/557-6727. www.thebalmoralhotel.com. Set dinner £60. AE, DC, MC, V. Dinner daily. Bus: 3, 8, 19, or 30.

★ Oloroso NEW TOWN SCOTTISH/INTERNATIONAL This rooftop restaurant is contemporary and swanky, and the cooking imaginative. The bar, which mixes a mean cocktail, is usually open until 1am. 33 Castle St. ☎ 0131/226-7614. www.oloroso.co.uk. Entrees £15–£25. MC, V. Lunch & dinner daily. Bus: 24, 29, or 42.

★★★ Restaurant Martin Wishart LEITH MODERN FRENCH Wishart takes his accolades

> *Restaurant Martin Wishart, one of three Leith eateries that hold a Michelin star.*

in stride and constantly strives to improve the quality of this high-priced establishment, where the menu is seasonal and the wine superb. 54 The Shore. ☎ 0131/553-3557. www.martin-wishart.co.uk. Entrees £20–£25, set dinner £60. AE, MC, V. Lunch & dinner Tues–Sat. Bus: 22 or 36.

★ **The Shore Bar & Restaurant** LEITH *FISH*
Whether at the bar (p. 532) or in the dining room, you'll appreciate the simplicity and ease of this operation, dedicated mostly to fresh fish. 3/4 The Shore. ☎ 0131/553-5080. Entrees £12–£18. AE, MC, V. Lunch & dinner daily. Bus: 16, 22, 35, or 36.

★★ kids **Spoon Café Bistro** OLD TOWN *CAFE*
This contemporary place combines a relaxed ambience, first-rate espresso-based coffees, and the sure hand of a classically trained chef on main courses, sandwiches, soups, and cakes. 6a Nicolson St. ☎ 0131/557-4567. http://spooncafe.co.uk. Entrees £7–£15. MC, V. Lunch & dinner Mon–Sat. Bus: 35.

★★ **21212** NEW TOWN *FRENCH*
Gentle, slow cooking is a signature of this highly rated newcomer. Odd but successful combinations of ingredients include beef with tart lemon curd and a bread and butter pudding with cucumber, dried cherries, and sunflower seeds. 3 Royal Terrace, Calton Hill. ☎ 0845/22-21212. Fixed-price lunch £25; fixed-price dinner £65. MC, V. Lunch & dinner Tues–Sat.

★ **The Witchery by the Castle** OLD TOWN
SCOTTISH/MODERN BRITISH In a historic building associated with nearby medieval sites of execution, this restaurant near Edinburgh Castle serves classy Scottish food in even posher surroundings. Great for special occasions. Castlehill, Royal Mile. ☎ 0131/225-5613. Entrees £18–£25. AE, DC, MC, V. Lunch & dinner daily. Bus: 28.

Map Note

All restaurants in this section can be found on the map on p. 520.

Edinburgh Hotels A to Z

Aonach Mor SOUTHSIDE
This well-priced and family-run guesthouse is located in a proud row of three-story Victorian terraced houses, away from the bustle of the city center. Some rooms have views of Arthur's Seat. 14 Kilmaurs Terrace (at Dalkeith Rd.). ☎ 0131/667-8694. www.aonachmor.com. 7 units. Doubles £60–£140. MC, V. Bus: 3, 8, or 29.

★★ Balmoral Hotel NEW TOWN
Opened in 1902, this is one of the grandest hotels in Britain. Kilted doormen supply the Scottish atmosphere; rooms are sumptuously furnished. 1 Princes St. ☎ 800/223-6800 in the U.S. or 0131/556-2414. www.thebalmoralhotel.com. 188 units. Doubles £220–£290. AE, DC, MC, V. Bus: 3, 8, 22, 25, or 30.

★★ The Bonham WEST END
One of Edinburgh's most stylish hotels, the Bonham's individually decorated rooms have plush upholsteries, state-of-the-art bathrooms with expensive toiletries, and high ceilings. 35 Drumsheugh Gardens. ☎ 0131/226-6050. www.thebonham.com. 48 units. Doubles £100–£250. AE, DC, MC, V. Bus: 19 or 37.

Edinburgh Hotel Best Bets

Best Historic Hotel
The Balmoral 1 Princes St. (p. 526)

Best Boutique Hotel
The Bonham 35 Drumsheugh Gardens (p. 526)

Best Guest House
Aonach Mor 14 Kilmaurs Terrace (p. 526)

Best Quiet Retreat
Channings 12–16 S. Learmonth Gardens (p. 527)

Best Converted Landmark
The Scotsman 20 N. Bridge (p. 530)

★ Caledonian Hilton WEST END
This city landmark has commanding views of Edinburgh Castle. An elegant Edwardian atmosphere pervades its public areas and the first-class guest rooms are spacious (except on the fifth floor), but the hotel does lag behind its competitors in its recreational offerings. Princes St. (at Lothian Rd.). ☎ 0131/222-8888. www.

> *Pilrig House has links to Robert Louis Stevenson, author of the* Strange Case of Dr. Jekyll and Mr. Hyde.

> *The Castle Suite Ballroom at the Caledonian Hilton has views of Edinburgh Castle.*

caledonian.hilton.com. 251 units. Doubles £170–£250. AE, DC, MC, V. Bus: 12, 25, or 33.

★★ Channings NEW TOWN

Five Edwardian terrace houses in a tranquil residential area combine to create a hotel with the atmosphere of a Scottish country house. Guest rooms are modern; for the best views, ask for one in the front of the hotel. 12–16 S. Learmonth Gardens (near Queensferry Rd.). ☎ 0131/623-9302. www.channings.co.uk. 46 units. Doubles £100–£150. AE, DC, MC, V. Bus: 37.

The George Hotel NEW TOWN

The buildings that house this elegant inn in the heart of the city were first erected in the 1780s, but a £12-million renovation has updated everything in order to provide modern comfort. 19–21 George St. ☎ 0131/225-1251. 195 units. Doubles £149–£210. AE, DC, MC, V. Bus: 24, 28, or 45.

★ Holyrood Hotel OLD TOWN

This impressive and stylish hotel is close to the new Scottish Parliament, only minutes from the heart of Old Town. Bedrooms are luxurious, with deluxe furnishings and elegant toiletries; the Club Floor is one of the best high-end retreats in town. 81 Holyrood Rd. ☎ 0870/194-2106. www.macdonaldhotels. co.uk/holyrood. 156 units. Doubles £110–£250. AE, DC, MC, V. Bus: 35.

★★ The Howard NEW TOWN

Made up of a set of Georgian houses—with a definite aura of privacy—this has been dubbed one of the most discreet five-star hotels in the city. The guest rooms are individually and rather elegantly decorated, and have some of the best bathrooms in town. 34 Great King St. ☎ 0131/557-3500. www.thehoward.com. 18 units. Doubles £190–£275. AE, DC, MC, V. Bus: 23 or 27.

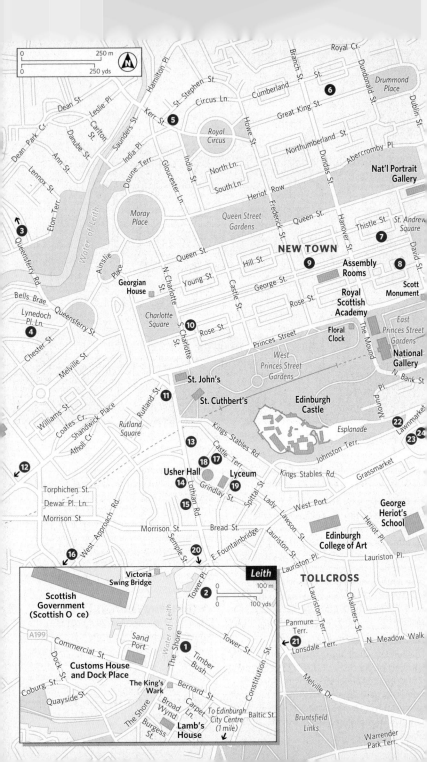

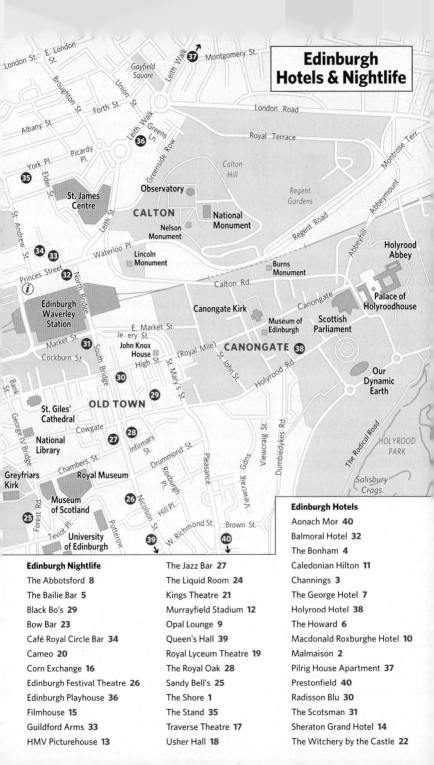

Edinburgh Hotels & Nightlife

Edinburgh Nightlife

The Abbotsford **8**
The Bailie Bar **5**
Black Bo's **29**
Bow Bar **23**
Café Royal Circle Bar **34**
Cameo **20**
Corn Exchange **16**
Edinburgh Festival Theatre **26**
Edinburgh Playhouse **36**
Filmhouse **15**
Guildford Arms **33**
HMV Picturehouse **13**

The Jazz Bar **27**
The Liquid Room **24**
Kings Theatre **21**
Murrayfield Stadium **12**
Opal Lounge **9**
Queen's Hall **39**
Royal Lyceum Theatre **19**
The Royal Oak **28**
Sandy Bell's **25**
The Shore **1**
The Stand **35**
Traverse Theatre **17**
Usher Hall **18**

Edinburgh Hotels

Aonach Mor **40**
Balmoral Hotel **32**
The Bonham **4**
Caledonian Hilton **11**
Channings **3**
The George Hotel **7**
Holyrood Hotel **38**
The Howard **6**
Macdonald Roxburghe Hotel **10**
Malmaison **2**
Pilrig House Apartment **37**
Prestonfield **40**
Radisson Blu **30**
The Scotsman **31**
Sheraton Grand Hotel **14**
The Witchery by the Castle **22**

> *The Editor Suite at the Scotsman.*

★ **Macdonald Roxburghe Hotel** NEW TOWN
Its classy atmosphere starts in the elegant lobby, which has an ornate ceiling and antique furnishings. The largest rooms—in the hotel's original wing—have imposing fireplaces, but rooms in the newer wing have more modern plumbing. 38 Charlotte St. (at George St.). ☎ 0870/194-2108 or from U.S. 888/892-0038. www.macdonaldhotels.co.uk/roxburghe. 197 units. Doubles £110–£180. AE, DC, MC, V. Bus: 13, 19, or 41.

★★ **Malmaison** LEITH
A hip, unpretentious boutique hotel with a minimalist decor. Set in the old harbor district—in the 19th century it served as a seamen's dorm—Malmaison is a quick walk from the Water of Leith. Rooms are average in size but individually designed and well equipped. 1 Tower Place. ☎ 0131/468-5000. www.malmaison.com. 100 units. Doubles £125–£195. AE, DC, MC, V. Bus: 16, 35.

★ **Pilrig House Apartment** LEITH
It was built in 1638, and in the 1800s, Robert Louis Stevenson played in this house's gardens as a child. Today, the self-contained two-bedroom apartment will suit those who want a bit of independence. Pilrig House Close, Bonnington Rd. ☎ 0131/554-4794. www.pilrighouse. com. £80–£250. MC, V. Bus: 36.

★★ **Prestonfield** SOUTHSIDE
Boasting Jacobean splendor amid 5.3 hectares (13 acres) of gardens, pastures, and woodlands, this 17th-century hotel has hosted luminaries ranging from Benjamin Franklin to Sean Connery. The guest rooms hide all their modern conveniences behind velvet-lined walls: Bose sound systems, DVD players, and plasma flatscreen TVs. Priestfield Rd. ☎ 0131/225-7800. www.prestonfield.com. 28 units. Doubles £295–£395. AE, MC, V. Free parking. Bus: 2, 14, or 30.

★ **Radisson Blu** OLD TOWN
The preferred major hotel in central Old Town, this thoroughly modern facility (don't let the baronial exterior fool you) is also one of the best equipped, with a leisure club and an indoor pool. Most bedrooms are spacious and well decorated. 80 High St. ☎ 0131/473-6590. www.radisson.com. 238 units. Doubles £120–£230. AE, DC, MC, V. Bus: 35.

★ **The Scotsman** OLD TOWN
One of the brightest and most stylish hotels in Edinburgh. Traditional decor and cutting-edge design are harmoniously wed in the 1904 baronial building (which was once home to the newspaper that lent the hotel its name), a city landmark since it was first constructed. 20 N. Bridge. ☎ 0131/556-5565. www.thescotsman hotel.co.uk. 68 units. Doubles £200–£350. AE, DC, MC, V. Bus: 3, 8, 14, or 29.

★★ **Sheraton Grand Hotel** WEST END
Elegant, with soaring public rooms and rich carpeting, the Sheraton boasts an enviable location in the proverbial shadow of Edinburgh Castle. The spacious guest rooms are well equipped and the hotel also has the city's best spa and leisure facilities (including a rooftop indoor/outdoor pool). 1 Festival Sq. (at Lothian Rd.). ☎ 800/325-3535 in the U.S. & Canada, or 0131/229-9131. www.sheraton.com. 260 units. Doubles £180–£360. AE, DC, MC, V. Bus: 10, 22, or 30.

★★★ **The Witchery by the Castle** OLD TOWN
Part of the famous restaurant (p. 525), the overnight accommodations in the Witchery include romantic, sumptuous, and theatrically decorated suites with Gothic antiques and elaborate tapestries. The much-lauded property has played host to a long list of celebrity

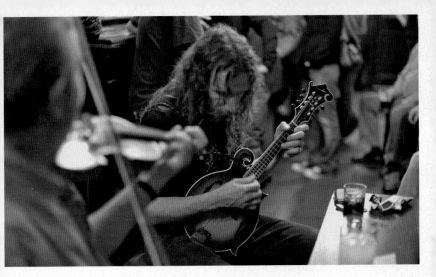

Edinburgh Nightlife & Entertainment A to Z

Bars & Pubs

★ The Abbotsford NEW TOWN

Bartenders have been pulling pints here since around 1900, and the gaslight era is preserved thanks to dark paneling and an ornate plaster ceiling. The array of ales on tap changes about once a week. 3 Rose St. ☎ 0131/225-5276. Bus: 3, 28, or 45.

★ The Bailie Bar STOCKBRIDGE

This traditional pub is in the heart of Stockbridge village and feels as if it could serve as the public meeting hall for the neighborhood, with plenty of banter between the regulars and the staff. 2 St. Stephen St. ☎ 0131/225-4673. Bus: 24, 29, or 42.

★ Black Bo's OLD TOWN

This bar is slightly unconventional and is one of my personal favorites. It is neither a traditional pub nor a particularly stylish place, but it does have an easy air of hipness. 57 Blackfriars St. ☎ 0131/557-6136. Bus: 35.

> You'll find live folk music almost every day at Sandy Bell's.

Edinburgh Nightlife & Entertainment Best Bets

Best for Comedy
The Stand 5 York Place (p. 532)

Best Concert Hall
Usher Hall 71 Lothian Rd. (p. 533)

Best for Folk
Sandy Bell's 25 Forrest Rd. (p. 534)

Best for Jazz
The Jazz Bar 1a Chambers St. (p. 534)

Best Traditional Pub
The Abbotsford 3 Rose St. (p. 531)

★ Bow Bar OLD TOWN

It feels like a classic, time-honored Edinburgh pub, but it's actually just over a dozen years old. Still, it looks the part and features some eight cask-conditioned ales to choose from. 80 West Bow. ☎ 0131/226-7667. Bus: 2 or 35.

★★ Café Royal Circle Bar NEW TOWN

The high Victorian design of Café Royal was nearly demolished in the late 1960s, and thank

> For the best in independent cinema, head to the Cameo.

goodness the wrecking ball wasn't used. Spacious booths and plenty of room around the bar combine to make this a reliably comfortable place to grab a drink. 17 W. Register St. ☎ 0131/556-1884. Bus: 8 or 17.

★ Guildford Arms NEW TOWN
Head through this pub's revolving doors, and you will find seven arched windows with etched glass and exquisite cornices under which to have a heavenly pint. It's reasonably large and bustling, with a good deal of character. 1–5 W. Register St. ☎ 0131/556-4312. www.guildfordarms.com. Bus: 8 or 17.

Opal Lounge NEW TOWN
If you want to experience a Scottish "style bar," this is an excellent example of the genre. After opening in 2001, it became the haunt of Prince William, when the handsome heir to the British throne attended St. Andrew's University. Hence, the Opal draws a predominantly young, well-dressed, and affluent crowd. 51a George St. ☎ 0131/226-2275. www.opallounge.co.uk. Bus: 24, 29, or 42.

★★★ The Shore LEITH
Probably my overall favorite, this pub fits seamlessly into Leith's seaside port ambience, without the usual cork and netting decorations. On 3 nights of the week, you'll find live folk and jazz music; check the website or call for details. 3–4 The Shore. ☎ 0131/553-5080. www.theshore.biz. Bus: 16 or 36.

Cinema

★ Cameo TOLCROSS
This cinema gets occasionally threatened with redevelopment, but it somehow manages to remain one of the best independent film houses in Scotland, showing arts, indie, foreign, and classic cinema to tourists and locals alike. 38 Home St. ☎ 0871-704-2052. Tickets £6.50. Bus: 10, 11, 16, or 24.

★★ Filmhouse WEST END
A must stop for any visiting film buffs, this is Edinburgh's most important movie house. The film genres shown on its three screens include foreign and art house, classic and experimental, and documentaries and shorts. 88 Lothian Rd. ☎ 0131/228-2688. www.filmhousecinema.com. Tickets £6.50. Bus: 10, 22, or 30.

Comedy

★★ The Stand NEW TOWN
Stand-up comedy is taken quite seriously in the Scottish capital. Just down the hill from St. Andrew Square, this is the premier, purpose-built local venue for comedians. Big acts are reserved for weekends, while local talent takes the stage during the week when crowds are smaller. 5 York Place (near Queen St.). ☎ 0131/558-7272. www.thestand.co.uk. Tickets £1.50–£10. Bus: 8 or 17.

Concert Halls

Edinburgh Festival Theatre SOUTHSIDE
This 1,915-seat venue, once known as the Art Deco-style Empire Theatre, dates back to the 1920s, although a theater has stood on this site since 1830. It reopened after major renovations for the 1994 Edinburgh International Festival (which lends it its name). It hosts the national opera and ballet, as well as various touring companies and orchestras. 13–29 Nicolson St. ☎ 0131/529-6000. www.eft.co.uk. Tickets £6–£45. Bus: 5, 7, 8, or 29.

Map Note

All nightlife and entertainment venues in this section can be found on the map on p. 528.

> *A clued-in crowd frequents the Traverse Theatre for the best contemporary drama in Edinburgh.*

Queen's Hall SOUTHSIDE

About a mile south of Old Town, the Queen's Hall began life as the Hope Park Chapel, but was altered in the 1970s (coinciding with Queen Elizabeth's silver jubilee) to accommodate concerts. It's primarily a venue for classical works. Clerk St. (at Hope Park Terrace). ☎ 0131/668-2019. www.thequeenshall.net. Ticket prices vary. Bus: 5, 7, 8, or 29.

★★ Usher Hall WEST END

This Beaux Arts building opened in 1914 and is Edinburgh's equivalent to New York's Carnegie Hall. During the annual Edinburgh International Festival, the 2,900-seat auditorium hosts orchestras such as the London Philharmonic. But top jazz, world music, and pop acts play here, too. 71 Lothian Rd. (at Cambridge St.). ☎ 0131/228-1155. www.usherhall.co.uk. Ticket prices vary. Bus: 1, 10, 15, or 34.

Drama

Edinburgh Playhouse NEW TOWN

Arguably the largest theater in Great Britain (with more than 3,000 seats), this is Edinburgh's best-known venue for popular plays and touring blockbuster/Broadway-style musicals, such as *Miss Saigon* and *Les Miserables.* The Playhouse also hosts other mainstream acts, such as *Lord of the Dance.* 18–22 Greenside Place (top of Leith Walk). ☎ 0131/524-3333. www.edinburgh-playhouse.co.uk. Tickets £6–£40. Bus: 5 or 22.

King's Theatre TOLLCROSS

This Edwardian venue with a domed ceiling and red-stone frontage turned 100 years old in 2006. The 1,300-seat venue offers a wide repertoire, including productions of the Scottish National Theatre, plus classical entertainment, ballet, and opera. 2 Leven St. ☎ 0131/529-6000. www.eft.co.uk. Tickets £6–£30. Bus: 11, 15, or 17.

★ Royal Lyceum Theatre WEST END

The Lyceum, built in 1883, has an enviable reputation thanks to presentations that range from the most famous works of Shakespeare to hot new Scottish playwrights. It is home to the leading theatrical production company in the city, often hiring the best Scottish actors for its shows. Grindlay St. (off Lothian Rd.). ☎ 0131/248-4848 box office; 0131/238-4800 general inquiries. www.lyceum.org. Tickets £8–£30. Bus: 1, 10, 15, or 34.

★★ Traverse Theatre WEST END

This local legend began in the 1960s as an experimental theater company that doubled as a bohemian social club; it still produces contemporary drama at its height. The theater's bar is where you'll find the hippest dramatists and actors in the city. 10 Cambridge St. (off Lothian Rd.). ☎ 0131/228-1404. www.traverse.co.uk. Tickets £5–£16. Bus: 1, 10, 15, or 34.

Folk Music

★ The Royal Oak OLD TOWN

Open normally till about 2am, this pub on the southern fringes of Old Town regularly features a-pickin' and a-singin' (and a-fiddlin') from local musicians. Highlight of the week is the Wee Folk Club every Sunday night. 1 Infirmary St. ☎ 0131/557-2976. www.royal-oak-folk.com. Tickets £3 for Wee Folk Club. Bus: 3, 5, 8, or 29.

> It's usually a sold-out crowd at Murrayfield, the home of Scottish rugby.

★★ Sandy Bell's OLD TOWN

This small pub represents the heart of the traditional Celtic/Gaelic/Highlands & Islands music scene in Edinburgh. Live music is featured practically every night of the week and all day on Saturday and Sunday. 25 Forrest Rd. ☎ 0131/225-2751. Bus: 2 or 42.

Rock and Jazz
Corn Exchange GORGIE

About 2 miles from central Edinburgh, this renovated market hall hosts visiting rock and pop performers (Oasis or Justin Timberlake) and acts with more cultlike followings, such as the Raconteurs, Massive Attack, or the Streets. 11 New Market Rd. ☎ 0131/477-3500. www.ece.uk.com. Bus: 35. Suburban train: Slateford.

HMV Picturehouse OLD TOWN

This venue has had a few incarnations as a nightclub (once called Century 2000), but now it seems well established as a place for gigs by the likes of Dizzee Rascal, Little Boots, or Seth Lakeman. Club nights occupy the space when there's no live music. 31 Lothian Rd. ☎ 0131/221-2280. www.edinburgh-picturehouse.co.uk. Bus: 1, 22, 30, or 34.

★ The Jazz Bar OLD TOWN

Owned and operated by a semi-professional jazz drummer, this is an oasis for lovers of improvisational playing. The basement bar features the best U.K. jazz musicians and occasionally draws international luminaries such as living legend Lee Konitz. 1a Chambers St. ☎ 0131/220-4298. www.thejazzbar.co.uk. Tickets £3–£15. Bus: 3, 5, 8, or 29.

The Liquid Room OLD TOWN

Reopened following a 2-year renovation after a fire in the restaurant upstairs, this busy but smallish space is a dance club when not hosting rock groups or tribute bands. It's popular with guest DJs, too. 9c Victoria St. 0131/225-2564. www.liquidroom.com. Bus: 23, 27, or 48.

Spectator Sports
Murrayfield Stadium

Opened in 1925, this is the country's national home for rugby and the largest stadium in Scotland, with a seating capacity of almost 68,000 visitors. The sport is usually played from autumn to spring, generally on Saturdays. Some of the most celebrated matches are those among teams in the viciously competitive annual Six Nations competition comprising Scotland, Wales, England, Ireland, Italy, and France. About 1¾ miles west of Edinburgh's city center (within walking distance from Haymarket Station). ☎ 0131/346-5000. www.scottishrugby.org. Tickets £25–£45. Bus: 12, 26, or 31.

Fast Facts

Arriving

BY PLANE **Edinburgh International Airport** (☎ 0870/040-0007; www.edinburghairport. com) is about 6 miles west of the city center and has become a growing hub for flights within the British Isles as well as for those going to and from Continental Europe. From the airport to the city, **Airlink Bus** (www.flybybus.com) runs frequent service; the one-way fare is £3.50. **BY TRAIN** The trains that link London to Edinburgh (via Newcastle) on the East Coast Main Line are reasonably fast, efficient, and generally relaxing, with restaurant and bar service as well as air-conditioning. Trains depart throughout the day from London's King's Cross Station; call **National Railway Enquiries** (☎ 08457/484-950) for rail info; from outside the U.K., call ☎ 44-207/278-5240. Trains arrive in Edinburgh at Waverley Station in the heart of the city.

Dentists & Doctors

If you have a dental emergency, go to the **Edinburgh Dental Institute,** 39 Lauriston Place (☎ 0131-536-4900; Bus: 35), open Monday through Friday from 9am to 3pm. Alternatively, call the toll-free **National Health Service Helpline** (☎ 0800-224-488). You can seek medical help from the **Edinburgh Royal Infirmary,** 1 Lauriston Place (☎ 0131/536-1000; Bus: 35). The emergency department is open 24 hours.

Emergencies

Call ☎ 999 in an emergency to summon the police, an ambulance, or firefighters.

Getting Around

Edinburgh's **Lothian Bus** lines (☎ 0131/555-6363; http://lothianbuses.com) are extensive and not terribly pricey. An all-day pass costs £3. A light rail tramway system (Edinburgh Trams) is being built, but disputes and delays make it seem that it may never operate. Fast **black taxis** similar to those in London can be hailed or found at several taxi ranks around central Edinburgh.

Internet Access

E-Corner, at 54 Blackfriars St., between Cowgate and the Royal Mile (☎ 0131/558-7858; http://e-corner.co.uk), is centrally located. Edinburgh public libraries also have computers with Internet connections, and many cafes and hotels now have Wi-Fi.

Pharmacies

Boots has various outlets, including one at 48 Shandwick Place (☎ 0131/225-6757; Mon–Fri 8am–8pm, Sat 8am–6pm, Sun 10:30am–4:30pm.

Post Office

The **Edinburgh Branch Post Office,** St. James Centre, is open Monday through Saturday from 9am to 5:30pm. For general postal information, call ☎ 0845/722-3344.

Safety

Edinburgh poses no particular safety concerns. Late-night robberies are not uncommon, however, so stay alert if walking through a dark street in the wee nighttime.

Telephones

Pay phones are slowly disappearing, but can be found at major tourist attractions and at kiosks on major streets in central Edinburgh.

Toilets

Toilets are found at rail stations, restaurants, hotels, pubs, and department stores. A system of public toilets, often marked **WC,** is in place at strategic corners and squares throughout the city. They're safe and clean but likely to be closed late in the evening.

Visitor Information

Edinburgh's main **Tourist Information Centre** (☎ 0131/473-3800 or 0845/225-5121; www. visitscotland.com) is on Princes Street above Waverley Station. It is one of the best in the country, with lots of literature (travel guides, maps, etc.), staff (for both information and booking hotels), and free brochures. In the summer it has extended evening hours: Monday to Saturday from 9am to 8pm and Sunday from 10am to 8pm (otherwise, closing times vary, so call or go online for details).

Additionally, the **British Hotel Reservation Centre** (☎ 020/7092-3055; www.bhrconline. com) provides free reservation assistance and discounted rates at all the leading hotels.

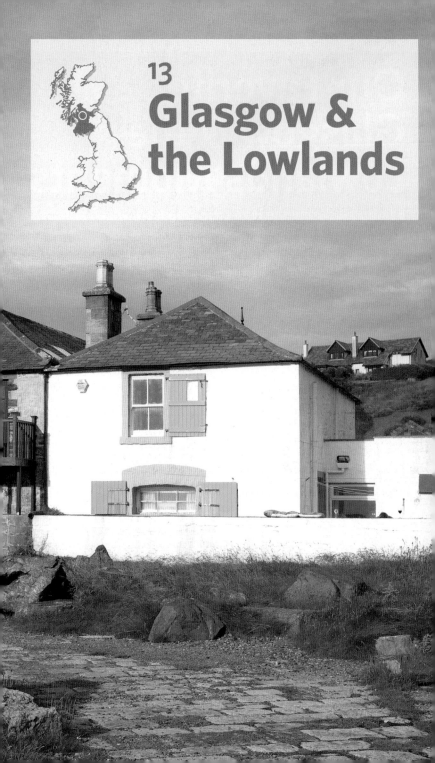

13
Glasgow &
the Lowlands

Our Favorite Glasgow & the Lowlands Moments

Edinburgh during the high tourist season, which now includes most of April and runs well into October, can be a hectic place to visit given that tourists crowd into the central districts of the small city. The Lowland regions offer a break with more relaxed environs, showing off a broad range of Scottish history, scenery, and culture. Glasgow is every bit as ancient as Edinburgh, even if its current layout and architecture belie this fact; it pulses in a manner unlike any other Scottish city.

> PREVIOUS PAGE *Portpatrick lies at the western extremity of the Southern Upland walking trail.* THIS PAGE *There's plenty to keep the kids entertained at Stirling Castle.*

1 Enjoying the energetic city center of Glasgow. While Edinburgh steals most of the headlines in traditional travel guides, tourists in the know recognize that the capital's rival, Glasgow, is the more lively of Scotland's dynamic duo: from the bustling shopping districts of Buchanan Street to cultural corners across the town. See p. 570.

2 Roaming along the West Coast. Graced with placid beaches, dotted by islands, punctuated by sea lochs and with narrow peninsulas, mixing forested glens with craggy hills, the western sea fronts of Lowland Scotland are one of the country's most underrated regions. See p. 552.

3 Surveying the landscape from the ramparts of Caerlaverock Castle. This one-time stronghold of the Maxwell family is among the most interesting castles in the U.K. Its massive ramparts and towers are largely intact in a rare triangular shape along a broad moat, and Caerlaverock historically was passed from Scots to English and back to Scots, such was its attraction as a military goal. See p. 548, **5**.

4 Marveling at the vegetation at Logan Botanic Garden. Visitors can't help but be impressed with the range of plants growing here, from semi-tropical palms to towering pines. Specially designed peat banks create the acid soil necessary for more traditional ornamentals such as rhododendrons. See p. 550, **11**.

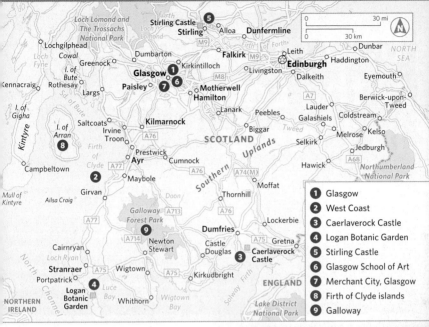

1. Glasgow
2. West Coast
3. Caerlaverock Castle
4. Logan Botanic Garden
5. Stirling Castle
6. Glasgow School of Art
7. Merchant City, Glasgow
8. Firth of Clyde islands
9. Galloway

5 Reliving history at stunning Stirling Castle. Ongoing restoration continues to improve Stirling Castle, as the work brings the various buildings on the grounds of this dramatic and well-fortified hilltop site closer to their original design. See p. 562, **4**.

6 Appreciating the greatness of buildings by Mackintosh and Thomson. Nineteenth-century Glasgow produced two of the greatest architects in Europe in Charles Rennie Mackintosh and Alexander "Greek" Thomson. No trip to the city is complete without seeing an example or two of their works, especially the Glasgow School of Art and Holmwood House. See p. 566, **2** & p. 568, **5**.

7 A night out on the town in Glasgow's Merchant City or West End. Glasgow is the nightlife mecca of the Lowlands, with its combination of brasseries, bars, clubs, and live music venues, such as Mono, which capitalize on the burgeoning band scene in Scotland's biggest city. See p. 583.

8 Ferry trips to the placid islands in the Firth of Clyde. The River Clyde is one defining topographical feature of the entire region; it grows as big as a sea only 25 miles west-southwest of Glasgow. Among the major isles in this firth

> *The Gulf Stream nurtures a microclimate in which subtropical greenery thrives, such as here at Logan Botanic Garden.*

are Arran and Bute, which physically are just short ferry rides from the mainland but are psychologically a million miles away. See p. 554.

9 Relaxing in cute Galloway towns. In Kirkcudbright and Portpatrick, visitors have two charming but quite different ports. The former dates to the 14th century, while the latter was once the key terminus for sea travel between Scotland and Ireland. See p. 549, **8**; p. 550, **10**.

Best of Glasgow & the Lowlands in 1 Week

To properly explore the best of the Scottish Lowlands in a week, start in Glasgow, the country's second and most consistently vibrant city. A metropolis where the city-owned museums, featuring an excellent municipal collection of art that ranges from a Dalí masterpiece to the work of the Glasgow Boys, are free to enter. The range of nightlife—from seasonal opera and classical concerts to the latest in hip indie rock—is consistently engaging. After Glasgow, it's up to the historic city of Stirling with its marvelous and continually restored castle, ancient home to the Stuart dynasty. Next, sweep south of Glasgow, hitting the highlights—including medieval abbeys and isolated, windswept islands.

> Somewhere beneath the romantic ruins of Melrose Abbey lies the heart of beloved Scots king Robert the Bruce—maybe.

START Glasgow, about 45 miles from Edinburgh. **TRIP LENGTH** Total distance traveled is 366 miles.

1 ★★★ **Glasgow.** Scotland's largest city has a very different feel than Edinburgh, but Glasgow (*glaaz*-go) has a growing reputation as a tourist destination, placing it among cities that have seen a revival—such as Berlin. Seeing the best of this vibrant Scottish city in a single day is impossible, but you can take in most of the major highlights in less than two. Begin with the Victorian and Edwardian architectural splendor of the city center, where you'll find the famous **Glasgow School of Art** (p. 566, **2**), designed by Charles Rennie Mackintosh, among the structural highlights. Restaurants, bars, and shops abound in this neighborhood, particularly on Sauchiehall Street. There are several City of Glasgow museums (free admission) to consider, as well as the popular **Merchant City** district. On this area's northeast edge is **St. Mungo's Cathedral** (p. 570, **2**), dating back to the earliest days of the city, on the Clyde River. The salubrious **West End** (p. 576, **14**) is home to Glasgow University and the metropolis's signature art collection: the **Kelvingrove Art Gallery and Museum** (p. 574, **6**)—one of

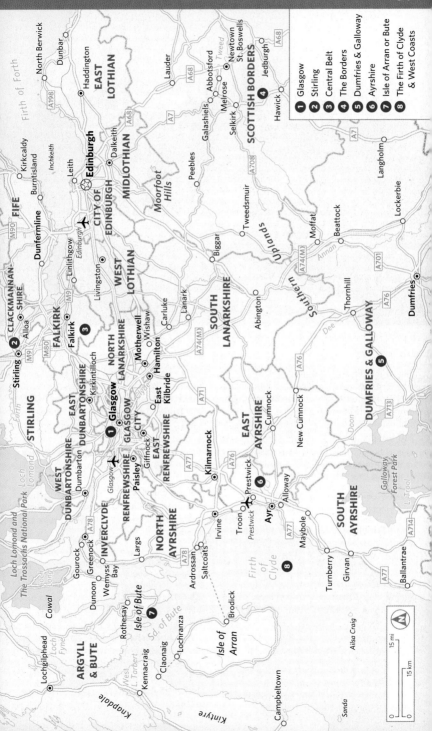

1 Glasgow
2 Stirling
3 Central Belt
4 The Borders
5 Dumfries & Galloway
6 Ayrshire
7 Isle of Arran or Bute
8 The Firth of Clyde & West Coasts

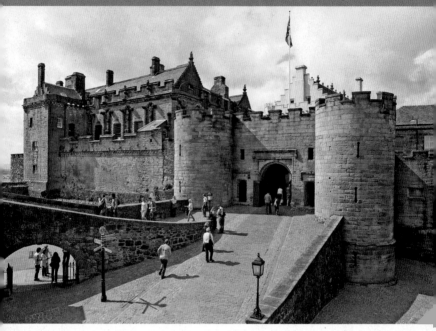

> *Stirling Castle guards a strategic stretch of the central belt that was fought over many times throughout Scottish history.*

the most visited attractions in the U.K. Finally, take an excursion to Glasgow's Southside for another landmark gallery—the **Burrell Collection** (p. 574, **7**)—as well as the works of another architectural great: **Alexander "Greek" Thomson** (p. 574, **8**). At night there is never a shortage of things to do: from clubs to music venues, theaters to cinema. ⏲ 1½ days. See p. 570.

On the afternoon of Day 2, head northeast for 27 miles on the M80 from Glasgow to

2 ★★ **Stirling.** Another ancient seat of royalty, this burgh was a place where Scots often battled English troops more than 500 years ago, whether at Stirling Bridge or at **Bannockburn** (p. 563, **5**) on the southern edge of the city. Stirling's Old Town has its own attractions: Top among them is **Stirling Castle** (p. 562, **4**), a striking Renaissance collection of buildings used by Kings James IV and V as well as Mary, Queen of Scots. ⏲ At least 4 hr. See p. 561, **3**.

On Day 3, first detour north/northwest on the A84 to Doune (9 miles). Then head south/southeast on the M9 from Stirling toward Edinburgh (about 20 miles).

3 ★★ **Central Belt.** In the midsection of Scotland, you'll find many treasures in travel, including **Dunblane Cathedral** (p. 560, **2**) and **Doune Castle** (p. 560, **1**), whose exterior was made famous by scenes from *Monty Python and the Holy Grail.* As you head toward Edinburgh, you will see **Linlithgow Palace** (p. 563, **6**), the first home in Scotland to be called a palace; its well-preserved remains are still a popular spot for more Scottish history, as is **Rosslyn Chapel** (p. 563, **8**), with its ties to the fabled Knights Templar. ⏲ 1 day. See p. 560.

On Day 4, get on the A7 south from the Edinburgh Bypass toward Galashiels (about 32 miles).

4 ★ **The Borders.** The historical ambience of this region includes the remarkable mansion built by famed author Sir Walter Scott, **Abbotsford** (p. 544, **1**), as well as the medieval abbeys that he campaigned to preserve and restore through his writing and lobbying: **Melrose Abbey** (p. 546, **2**) and **Jedburgh Abbey** (p. 547, **3**). ⏲ 1 day. See p. 544.

On Day 5, head southwest on the scenic A701 to Dumfries and Galloway. The distance from Selkirk in the Borders to the town of Dumfries is about 50 miles. To carry on through the Galloway Peninsula (another 70 miles), use the A75.

5 ★★ **Dumfries and Galloway.** Covering the south and southwest area of Scotland, this is arguably the most underrated region of the country. Highlights include **Caerlaverock Castle** (p. 548, **5**), as good as they get with its massive gatehouse, ramparts, and moat, and charming villages and towns, such as the one-time artist colony **Kirkcudbright** (p. 549, **8**). Additionally, there are coastal and inland hikes; the best regional botanic garden in northern Britain, **Logan Botanic Garden** (p. 550, **11**); and an important bird sanctuary on the **Mull of Galloway** (p. 550, **12**). ⏲ 1 day. See p. 544.

On Day 6, rise early because you're heading north on the A77 into South Ayrshire. From Stranraer to Ayr you'll travel 51 miles.

6 ★ **Ayrshire.** This is critical Burns Country, the old stomping grounds of Scotland's most celebrated poet, whose birthplace, **Burns Cottage** (p. 553, **3**), has been well maintained and is well worth a visit. The other major highlight (unless you're a golfer) is **Culzean Castle** (p. 552, **1**), a Georgian pile of exceptional merit. ⏲ 5 hr. See p. 552.

On the afternoon of Day 6, travel on the A78 north to either Saltcoats (19 miles) or Wemyss Bay (38 miles).

7 ★★ **Isle of Arran or Bute.** These two islands in the broad Firth of Clyde are among the easiest to get to from the mainland. The terrain on **Arran** matches all of Scotland, from craggy, steep hills to ambling moorland. **Bute** is probably the most underrated of the Scottish islands. Once a Victorian retreat, after years of decline it is improving and offers plenty to see and the classic calm that island life involves. ⏲ 1 day. See p. 555, **9**; p. 554, **4**.

On Day 7 you are heading back toward Glasgow (33 miles), stopping off en route at

8 ★★★ **The Firth of Clyde and West Coast.** The River Clyde expands into a vast waterway with islands and coastal stretches of beach

> *The fountains at Linlithgow Palace ran with wine to honor the marriage of King James V in the 1530s.*

from the Cowal Peninsula south to the North Channel and Irish Sea. Now we are on the fringes of the ancient kingdom of Dalriada, which linked Western Scotland and Northern Ireland. With a bit of planning (and more time), you can use ferry connections to hop from peninsula to peninsula or peninsula to island and back again. The forested hills run down to deep sea lochs: land and sea in fine partnership. ⏲ 1 day. See p. 552.

The Best of the Borders & Galloway

The ancient abbeys and castles across these two regions remind one of Scotland's ecclesiastical past and turbulent history, as most of these places became ruins after repeated battles with England. It is calm countryside now, pastoral and green. The Borders was favored territory of romantic historical author Sir Walter Scott (1771–1832), while Galloway stretches westward, with rolling hills to the blue Irish sea and some reasonably dramatic coastlines to explore.

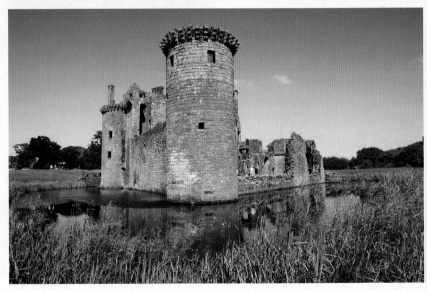

> Centuries of conflict with the English left castles in the borderlands, like Caerlaverock, pictured, in ruins.

START Abbotsford, near Galashiels, about 32 miles from Edinburgh. **TRIP LENGTH** Take 4 days to cover the terrain comfortably, as many of the roads are scenic. Total distance traveled is 165 miles.

❶ ★ Abbotsford. This Scots-baronial mansion was writer Sir Walter Scott's house from 1817 until his death. Remarkable in many ways, the home—the design of which was supervised by

Scott, who called it his "conundrum castle"—and grounds, where he planted thousands of trees, are considered the author's most enduring monument. (Not counting his many books, of course.) He first bought the land here in 1811; the farm was called Cartly Hole, which some have roughly translated to mean dirty place. He decided to rename it in tribute to the 12th-century abbots of nearby Melrose. The

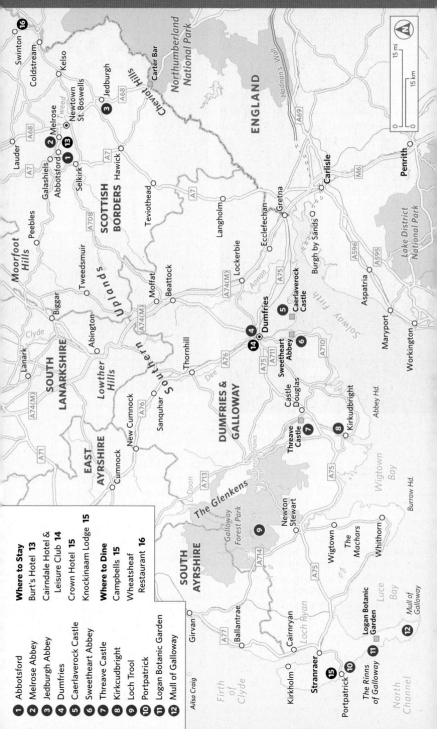

Where to Stay
Burt's Hotel **13**
Cairndale Hotel &
Leisure Club **14**
Crown Hotel **15**
Knockinaam Lodge **15**

Where to Dine
Campbells **15**
Wheatsheaf
Restaurant **16**

1 Abbotsford
2 Melrose Abbey
3 Jedburgh Abbey
4 Dumfries
5 Caerlaverock Castle
6 Sweetheart Abbey
7 Threave Castle
8 Kirkcudbright
9 Loch Trool
10 Portpatrick
11 Logan Botanic Garden
12 Mull of Galloway

> *Abbotsford, the 19th-century home of Walter Scott, houses historical memorabilia collected by the great novelist.*

> *Jedburgh Abbey, like nearby Melrose, suffered repeated sackings at the hands of marauding English noblemen.*

building contains many relics and mementos, from Rob Roy's sporran to a sword given to the Duke of Montrose by King Charles I for his cooperation (some say collaboration). Scott's library contains some 9,000 volumes. Scott died at Abbotsford in 1832. ⏱ 1 hr. Near Galashiels on the B6360 (off the A6091). ☎ 01896/752-043. www.scottsabbotsford. co.uk. Admission £7 adults, £4.50 seniors & students, £3.50 kids. Mar–May Mon–Sat 9:30am–5pm, Sun 11am–4pm; June–Sept Mon–Sun 9:30am–5pm.

Take the A6091 east for 1¼ miles.

② ★★ **Melrose Abbey.** These lichen-covered ruins, among the most evocative in Europe, are all that's left of an ecclesiastical community established in the 12th century. But the location of this abbey is not far from an earlier one established as far back as the 7th century and deserted in the 11th century. While the soaring remains follow the lines of the original abbey on this site, these walls were largely constructed in the 15th century. As with many abbeys in the Borders, the Scottish wars with the English in the 14th century led to Melrose's destruction. England's King Richard II allegedly tore it to the ground in 1385. The heart of the Scottish king Robert the Bruce (1274–1329) is believed to be interred in the abbey, per his wishes. ⏱ 1 hr. Abbey St., Melrose. ☎ 01896/822-562. www.historic-scotland. gov.uk. Admission £5.20 adults, £4.20 seniors, £3.10 kids. Daily 9:30am–5:30pm (Oct–Mar until 4:30pm). Last admission 30 min. prior to closing.

Take the A6091 east a short distance (1 mile) to the A68, then head south to Jedburgh. Total distance is 9⅓ miles.

❸ ★★ **Jedburgh Abbey.** This ruined abbey, founded by King David I in 1138, is one of Scotland's finest. In the 1500s, the English sacked it repeatedly: The Earl of Surrey burned it in 1523, and the Earl of Hertford followed up on his efforts in 1544 and 1545. A few efforts to repair the abbey were made from 1560 until 1875, when teams of Victorian architects set about restoring the structure to its original medieval design. While it remains roofless, most of the exterior stonework is in place. And, while smaller than Melrose, it is arguably more impressive today. ⏱ 1 hr. Jedburgh, on the A68. ☎ 01835/863-925. www.historic-scotland. gov.uk. Admission £5.20 adults, £4.20 seniors & students, £3.10 kids. Daily 9:30am–5:30pm (Oct–Mar until 4:30pm). Last admission 30 min. prior to closing.

Expect this next leg to take nearly 2 hr. Take the A68 and A669 west for 17 miles to Selkirk and the A708 for about 34 miles to Moffat. From there take the A701 south (crossing the M8 motorway) for 21 miles to the roundabouts outside Dumfries, following the signs to the town center. Total distance is 72 miles.

Scott: Inventor of Historical Novels

Today it may be hard to imagine the fame that Sir Walter Scott, poet and novelist, enjoyed as the best-selling author of his day. His works are no longer so widely read, but Scott (1771–1832) was thought to be a master storyteller and today is considered the English-language inventor of the historical novel. Before his novel *Waverley* (1814) and the many works that followed it, no modern author writing in English had spun such tales from actual events, examining the lives of individuals who played a role—large or small—in history.

❹ ★ **Dumfries.** A pleasant market town on the River Nith, Dumfries dates to pre-Roman times although its early origins are not yet known. One of the attractions on the Robert Burns Heritage Trail is here. The **Burns House,** Burns St. (☎ 01387/255-297; free admission), is a modest building where the poet died in 1796. It's a tiny place filled with relics and items such as some original manuscripts. The most impressive feature may be the poet's signature, scrawled with a diamond on an

> *The remains of Threave Castle are marooned on an island in the River Dee.*

> *The colors and quiet of the village of Kirkcudbright have long been an inspiration for Scots artists.*

upstairs window of the sandstone cottage. So-called Burns Walk along the river was one of his favorite perambulations. Nearby, the cemetery at St. Michael's Church has his remains in a purpose-built mausoleum and is also home to the graves of contemporaries. ☺ At least 2 hr.

After spending the night in Dumfries, take the B725 south out of central Dumfries for 8 miles.

⑤ ★★★ Caerlaverock Castle. A favorite target of English armies, Caerlaverock (pronounced Ka-*leh*-ver-ick) is one of Scotland's most impressive medieval castles, home to the Maxwell family for some 400 years. A water-filled moat surrounds the unique triangular-shaped red sandstone ruin. Additionally, the twin-towered gatehouse, serious battlements, and an interior "curtain" wall of the 17th-century Nithsdale Lodging make this one

of the must-see castles in Scotland. On the grounds, there is also an example of the huge siege-engine, or trebuchet, that launched boulders at its fortifications. If the weather cooperates, take the woodland nature trail to see the foundations of the original castle, set nearer to the swampy banks of the Nith River estuary. ☺ At least 1 hr. Southeast of Dumfries on the B725. ☎ 01387/770-224. www.historic-scotland.gov.uk. Admission £5.50 adults, £4.40 seniors & students, £3.30 kids. Daily 9:30am–5:30pm (Oct–Mar until 4:30pm). Last admission 30 min. prior to closing.

Take the B725 back to Dumfries and cross the River Nith, joining the A710 south to New Abbey. Total distance is 7½ miles.

⑥ ★ Sweetheart Abbey. An unusual story explains the name of this towering red sandstone ruin. In 1273, Lady Devorgilla of Galloway founded the abbey in memory of her husband, John de Balliol (the man behind Balliol College at Oxford University; p. 364, ⑪). So attached was she to her husband that she apparently carried his embalmed heart around with her for 22 years until she died in 1289. When she was buried here, in front of the altar, the heart went with her. ☺ 1 hr. A710, at New Abbey village. ☎ 01387/850-397. www.historic-scotland.gov.uk. Admission £4 adults, £3.20 seniors & students, £2.40 kids. Apr–Sept daily 9:30am–5:30pm; Oct–Mar Sat–Wed 9:30am–4:30pm. Last admission 30 min. prior to closing.

The simplest route to your next stop is to return back to Dumfries and take the A75 southwest toward the town of Castle Douglas. Total distance is 27 miles.

⑦ ★ Threave Castle. One of the best things about this massive 14th-century tower house (last used as a 19th-century prison for Napoleonic soldiers) is getting there. Ring a bell to call a boatman, who ferries you in a small boat to the island in the River Dee on which the castle sits. *Note:* Leave your best shoes behind; the path from the parking area can get muddy. ☺ 2 hr. Off the A75, 3 miles west of Castle Douglas. ☎ 07711/223-101. www.historic-scotland.gov.uk. Admission £4.20 adults, £3.40 seniors & students, £2.50 kids. Daily Apr–Oct 9:30am–5pm (Oct until 3:30pm). Last admission 1 hr. prior to closing.

> *One of the most scenic, accessible walks in southern Scotland follows the shores of Loch Trool.*

Return to the A75, taking it west (signs to STRANRAER), then turn left on the A711 and head south. Total distance is 8 miles.

8 ★★ **Kirkcudbright.** Our favorite southern Scottish town, Kirkcudbright (pronounced Kerr-*coo*-bree) was a thriving artist colony in the late 19th and early 20th centuries, drawing many notable artists, such as leading Glasgow Boy E. A. Hornel (1864–1933) and the graphic artist Jessie M. King (1875–1949), a talent who deserves a lot more attention. The appeal of this adorable village remains, although the colony is more of a heritage spot these days, with galleries keeping the artistic history alive. The center of town is full of small, colorful cottages, many with charming wee lanes. From April through October you can visit Hornel's impressive home, studio, and garden, **Broughton House**, High St. (☎ 01557/330-437; www.nts.org; £5.50 adults, £4.50 kids), a Georgian-era mansion with a great yard that the artist adapted for both living and painting. ⏱ At least 2 hr.

After spending the night in Kirkcudbright, on Day 3 take the A755 across the River Dee to the A75, heading west through Creetown (18 miles) to the A714, heading north past Bargrennan, and turning right to Glentrool Village (16 miles). Total distance is 34 miles.

9 ★ **Loch Trool.** This tour doesn't offer too much of the great outdoors, but this stop's an exception. The trail around Loch Trool (moderate to easy) is one of the best short walks in Dumfries and Galloway. On one side of the loch, the army of Robert the Bruce is believed to have defeated a much stronger English force in 1307. The leader of the Scots had been hiding in this region for about a year before King Edward I of England ordered troops to finish him off. The English troops, however, dismounted on difficult, steep ground, and Bruce's men routed the invading force, in part by rolling boulders down the hill. Bruce's Stone is a granite monument commemorating the victory. ⏱ At least 2 hr. Off the A714, 8 miles north of Newton Stewart. Free admission. Daily dawn–dusk.

Take the A714 back 10 miles to the A75 and go west to Stranraer, about 21 miles. Turn at Station St., following the signs to Portpatrick, which takes you to the A77 south out of Stranraer for 2 miles and then west through

Lochans for 7 miles to Portpatrick, where you can spend the night. Total distance is 40 miles.

🔟 ★ Portpatrick. The site of a natural harbor that has been improved over the years, Portpatrick is one of the most picturesque seaside towns in southwest Scotland. There are a few cute shops, a small beach (suitable for kids) in the harbor, and hiking/walking trails that lead away from the village, both up and down the coast. Just south of town, one well-marked path leads to the ruins of 15th-century Dunskey Castle, perched on the edge of a cliff above the sea. A trail north of town takes you to two fine beaches in secluded coves. This path is one end of the Southern Upland Way, which crosses the country. 🕐 At least 2 hr. Terminus of the A77.

On Day 4, take the A77 back out of town, going south for 7 miles on the B7042 to Sandhead, then the A716 for 8 miles, turning onto the B7065 toward Port Logan. Total distance is about 15 miles.

🔟 ★★★ Logan Botanic Garden. Here, in part thanks to the Gulf Stream, a microclimate allows the successful cultivation of palms, tree ferns, and other exotic plants—including towering, flowering columns of *Echium pininanas,* which are native to the Canary Islands. In addition to a more formal walled garden, Logan also has wilder plantings, such as the *Gunnera manicata,* whose leaves are larger than an elephant's ears. Affiliated with Edinburgh's Royal Botanic Garden (p. 506, 7️⃣), this garden is worth the trip if you enjoy plants in the least. 🕐 2 hr. B7065, near Port Logan. ☎ 01776/860-231. www.rbge.org.uk. Admission £5 adults, £4 seniors & students, £1 kids. Mid-Mar to Sept daily 10am–5pm; Feb Sun 10am–4pm.

Return to the B7065 and drive 7 miles south to

🔟 ★ Mull of Galloway. The tip, or mull, of the Galloway Peninsula offers a spectacular seabird sanctuary, with thousands roosting on the cliffs. The **Royal Society for the Protection of Birds** (☎ 01556/670-464) has a good visitor center here, with a cafe. In addition to aviary attractions, you might see dolphins, whales, and on clear days, views across the sea to Ireland, the Isle of Man, and the northwest coast of England. 🕐 2 hr.

> *The pretty little seaport at Portpatrick is one of the best bases for exploring the region.*

Where to Stay & Dine

★ **Burt's Hotel** MELROSE
This family-run inn dates to 1722, offering a taste of small-town Scotland, although the decor is modern. All guest rooms are well furnished. If it's busy, alternative accommodations are offered across the street at its sister, the Townhouse Hotel, where double rooms start at £96. Market Sq. ☎ 01896/822-285. Fax 01896/822-870. www.burtshotel.co.uk. 20 units. Doubles £130 w/breakfast. AE, DC, MC, V.

kids **Cairndale Hotel & Leisure Club** DUMFRIES
This early-20th-century resort with a stone facade offers comfortable rooms, but its best features are in the Barracuda Club (spa, steam room, gym, indoor pool). Twenty-two rooms are suitable for families. 132-136 English St., just off High St. ☎ 01387/254-111. www.cairndalehotel.co.uk. 91 units. Doubles £110 w/breakfast. AE, DC, MC, V.

★ **Campbells** PORTPATRICK *FISH/SEAFOOD*
Facing the harbor, this welcoming family-run restaurant is almost old-fashioned in its unpretentious manner, the decor mixing rustic seaport with modernity. The fresh fish is excellent. 1 S. Crescent. ☎ 01776/810-314. Entrees £12–£20. DC, MC, V. Lunch & dinner Tues–Sun.

Crown Hotel PORTPATRICK
It doesn't offer luxury accommodations, but the unpretentious Crown is right on the harbor, and its guest rooms, with big old-fashioned bathtubs, overlook the sea. You may, however, prefer a unit in the back to avoid noise from the popular hotel pub below. 9 N. Crescent. ☎ 01766/810-261. www.crownportpatrick.com. Doubles £78 w/breakfast. MC, V.

> *The genteel, wood-paneled interiors of Knockinaam Lodge.*

★★ **Knockinaam Lodge** PORTPATRICK
Built in 1869, this small luxury hotel a few miles south of Portpatrick resembles a country manor, with well-manicured gardens and its own private beach. In this tranquil and remote setting, Churchill, Eisenhower, and their staffs met during World War II. Near Portpatrick. ☎ 01776/810-471. www.knockinaamlodge.com. 9 units. Doubles £270–£400 w/breakfast & dinner. AE, MC, V.

★ **Wheatsheaf Restaurant** SWINTON *MODERN BRITISH* Located between Melrose and Eyemouth, from whose harbor the kitchen secures fresh seafood, the Wheatsheaf is an award-winning restaurant that pops up on many "best of" lists. Leave the kids at home at dinnertime. There are also guest bedrooms. Main St. ☎ 01890/860-257. www.wheatsheaf-swinton.co.uk. Entrees £13–£18. MC, V. Lunch & dinner daily.

The Best of the West Coast

Ayrshire, long associated with native son Robert Burns, is also home to one of the greatest Robert Adam-designed Georgian mansions, Culzean Castle. But there's more to the Western Coast than literary and architectural landmarks. You'll also encounter a trio of islands in the Strathclyde region, as well as sights along the Western Scotland peninsulas, which separate deep sea fiords, such as Loch Fyne and Loch Long. Travel here can mean island hopping by ferry, always enjoyable across mostly sheltered seas. Finish up your travels in Argyll, which means the "coast of the Gaels," and is one of our favorite areas of Scotland.

> *Bute is among the most accessible of the Scottish islands for visitors touring by car or public transportation.*

START Culzean Castle and Country Park, near Maybole, 44 miles southwest of Glasgow. **TRIP LENGTH** 5 days. Total distance traveled is about 150 miles

① ★ **Culzean Castle.** In addition to the architectural attributes, such as turrets and ramparts, of this 18th-century "castellated" mansion, it is of special interest to many Americans because General Eisenhower was given an apartment for life here. Fans of the 1973 Scottish cult horror film *The Wicker Man* may recognize the place: Scenes at the home of the devilish character played by Christopher Lee were filmed at Culzean (pronounced *Cull*-ane). ⏱ 1½ hr. A719, 4⅓ miles west of Maybole. ☎ 01655/884-455. www.culzeanexperience. org. Admission (including country park) £15 adults, £10 seniors & kids. Daily Apr–Oct 10:30am–5pm. Last admission 1 hr. prior to closing.

1 Culzean Castle
2 Culzean Country Park
3 Burns Cottage and Museum
4 Isle of Bute
5 Rothesay Castle
6 Cowal Peninsula
7 Kintyre Peninsula
8 Isle of Gigha
9 Isle of Arran

Where to Stay

Abbotsford Hotel 10
Hunters Quay Hotel 11
Lochgreen House Hotel 12
Piersland House Hotel 13
The Royal an Lochan 14
Turnberry 15

Where to Dine

Braidwoods 16
Browne's at Enterkine 17
MacCallums of Troon 18
Russian Tavern at the Port Royal Hotel 19
Seafood Cabin 20

2 ★★ kids **Culzean Country Park.** However grand the house may be, I think the grounds of Culzean are better. The 228-hectare (563-acre) grounds contain a formal walled garden, aviary, swan pond, camellia house, orangery, adventure playground, and a restored 19th-century pagoda. The country park—Scotland's first, opened in 1969—is a real highlight on a fine Ayrshire day. ⏱ At least 2 hr. At Culzean Castle. ☎ 01655/884-400. Admission (park only) £3 adults, £1.50 seniors & kids. Apr-Oct daily 9am-dusk; Nov-Mar Thurs-Sun 11am-4pm.

Take the scenic coastal route up the A719 for 12 miles, turning right on Greenfield Ave. and right again on Alloway St. in the town of Alloway.

3 ★ **Burns Cottage and Museum.** We have always had a soft spot for this National Trust attraction, and it's a must-visit for even the casual Robert Burns fan. A self-guided tour of the cottage shows the kitchen box bed where the poet was born on a stormy January 25, 1759, as well as the room that his family—and livestock—shared. The museum, due to reopen in 2011 after extensive renovation, is a treasure-trove of *Burnsiana,* displaying the best collection of the author's manuscripts and original letters that Burns wrote and received. ⏱ 1½ hr. B7024, in Alloway, 1¾ miles south of Ayr. ☎ 01292/443-700. www.burnsheritagepark.com. Admission £4 adults, £2.50 kids & seniors. Daily 10am-5:30pm (Oct-Mar until 5pm).

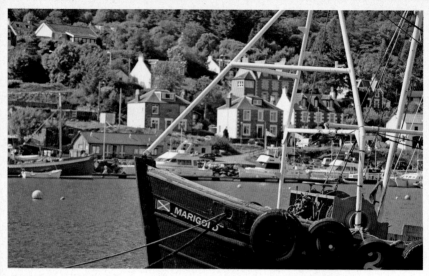

> Tarbert is a great spot to stock up on fresh seafood, landed by the little port's fishing fleet.

On Day 2, after overnighting in the area, take the A719 north about 5 miles to the A78 and the Wemyss Bay ferry terminal. Total distance is nearly 40 miles. Ferries (☎ 08705/650-000; www.calmac.co.uk) to Rothesay on Bute depart every 45 min. from Wemyss Bay.

❹ ★ **Isle of Bute.** Crossing from the rail and ferry terminus in Wemyss Bay, this is among the easiest Scottish islands to reach. Bute officially calls itself Scotland's "unexplored" isle—but "underappreciated" is a more accurate description. Roam a bit and find the ruins of an ancient Christian settlement at St. Blane's

Island Hopscotch Pass

If you want the freedom to hop around a bit from mainland to island and from island to peninsulas west of Glasgow, it is worth buying an "Island Hopscotch" ticket from the ferry operator **Caledonian MacBrayne** (☎ 08705/650-000; www.calmac.co.uk). For example, you can hop from Wymess Bay to the Isle of Bute, and from there onto the Cowal Peninsula. Then carry on to Kintyre, crossing Loch Fyne to Tarbert. In summer, the cost for that excursion is about £8 per passenger and £35 for a car.

near the southern tip of the island. Walk out to the more meager remains of a chapel at St. Ninian's Point on the west coast, and you'll be treated to the company of dozens of seabirds along the wind-swept shoreline. **Rothesay Castle** (❺) is one of the best-preserved medieval castles, which was once sacked by Vikings, while the mansion of **Mount Stuart** (p. 568, ❼), with its red sandstone exteriors and Italian marble interiors, is another fine attraction on this underrated isle. ⏱ At least 4 hr.

❺ ★ **Rothesay Castle.** Located in Bute's principal port, this castle (which dates to the late 12th and early 13th c.) is unusual for its circular plan and exposed site. Interestingly, part of the exhibit here emphasizes the links that ancient Scotland had to Norse rulers—King Haakon IV (1204-63), in particular. If you dare (and if you're thin enough), you can descend from the gatehouse into a small dungeon once reserved for prisoners. ⏱ 1 hr. Rothesay, Isle of Bute. ☎ 01700/502-691. www.historic-scotland.gov. uk. Admission £4.50 adults, £3.60 seniors, £2.70 kids. Daily 9:30am–5:30pm (Oct–Mar until 4:30pm). Last admission 30 min. prior to closing.

Spend the night on the island and on Day 3 drive north of Rothesay 2¾ miles to catch a 5-min. ferry from Rhubodach to Colintraive.

> *Achamore Gardens on the Isle of Gigha is home to species from all over the globe.*

6 ★ **Cowal Peninsula.** For many years, a huge U.S. naval base kept Cowal in business, and when the end of the Cold War terminated the Yankee presence, a large gap in the economy was created. Only now is tourism beginning to fill it. Cowal is easily reached and has nice forested glens and plenty of sea coast to explore. The principal town of Dunoon is ordinary, but coastal villages, such as Tighnabruaich, are charming. ⏱ 4 hr.

From Dunoon, take the A855 north out of town (signposted GLASGOW), and follow the B836 (15 miles) to the A8003 through Tighnabruaich (23 miles). Follow signs to ferry terminal at Portavadie for a 25-min. ferry to Tarbert.

7 ★★ **Kintyre Peninsula.** The westernmost mainland in central Scotland, Kintyre feels as remote as the Highlands. The pretty harbor of **Tarbert** on Loch Fyne is where many local fishing boats land. Indeed, you can purchase fresh scallops, as well as live crabs and lobsters, at the ferry slip. Bird populations abound in this region, too. There is an observatory on the island of Sanda, just off the tip (or mull) of Kintyre. On the peninsula itself, however, a good bird blind is situated near the west-coast village of Machrihanish. ⏱ At least 4 hr.

You can either spend the night on the mainland or carry on to the next spot. From Tarbert take the A83 south for 20 miles to the unmanned ferry terminal at Tayinloan, boarding the 20-min. ferry, which runs hourly.

8 ★★ **Isle of Gigha.** Pronounced *Gee-a*, with a hard "g" (as in gear), this small island gets its name (meaning the good isle) from the ancient Norse ruler King Haakon. Small and placid, Gigha is best known for its **Achamore Gardens**

> *Brodick Castle was a Melrose stronghold for 600 years, but its history stretches further back to the Viking invasions.*

(www.gigha.org.uk/gardens), opened in 1944, with their exceptional springtime display of rhododendrons and azaleas. But it's also a quiet place where you can escape and relax. There are plenty of rural and coastal walks on this compact, community-owned island. ⏱ At least 4 hr. www.gigha.org.uk.

On Day 4, from Tayinloan, return toward Tarbert, taking the B8001 southeast from Kennacraig to the Claonaig ferry terminal near Skipness. The total distance is 18 miles. The ferry (summer only) to Lochranza takes 30 min. In winter, the ferry runs a longer route from Tarbert.

9 ★★ **Isle of Arran.** Sometimes called Scotland in miniature, this island combines pasture-filled lowlands with some reasonably mountainous scenery. Arran also offers **Brodick Castle** (☎ 01770/302-202; www.nts. org.uk; £11 adults, £7.50 kids), stronghold of the Montrose family with some 6 centuries of different architectural alterations. There is excellent hiking (such as trails through Highland-desque Glen Rosa or up the craggy hill Goat Fell) and half a dozen golf courses, including a seaside one—Shiskine (☎ 01770/860-226; www.shiskinegolf.com; £18 per round)—with only 12 holes but plenty of wind and diverting scenery. Arran is also a popular camping and cycling destination, with a growing reputation for producing excellent food, whether harvested from the sea or grown on the land. You can return to the Scottish mainland from Brodick, Arran's main town. ⏱ At least 4 hr.

Where to Stay

> A guest room at the Royal an Lochan.

★ **Abbotsford Hotel** AYR

A small hotel with a popular, civilized pub in a quiet residential neighborhood less than a 10-minute walk from the shoreline. Most of the guest rooms are stylish and comfortable, with flatscreen TVs and modern bathrooms. 14 Corsehill Rd. ☎ 01292/261-506. www.abbotsfordhotel.co.uk. 12 units. Doubles £85 w/breakfast. AE, MC, V.

★ **Hunters Quay Hotel** DUNOON

Right on the water, north of the village center, this up-to-date whitewashed mansion is a very welcoming and comfortable hotel. Guest rooms are of varying size and individually decorated. We think this is your best option in the immediate vicinity. Hunters Quay, Marine Parade. ☎ 01369/707-070. www.huntersquayhotel.co.uk. 10 units. Doubles £80–£100 w/breakfast. AE, MC, V.

Lochgreen House Hotel TROON

This lovely country-house hotel is set on 12 lush hectares (30 acres) of Ayrshire forest and landscaped gardens. The property opens onto views of the Firth of Clyde and the rocky outcropping island of Ailsa Craig. Monktonhill Rd. ☎ 01292/313-343. www.costley-hotels.co.uk. Doubles £150 w/breakfast. AE, MC, V.

★ **Piersland House Hotel** TROON

Opposite Royal Troon Golf Club, this hotel was originally built in 1899 for a member of the Johnnie Walker whisky family. The moderately sized guest rooms have traditional country-house styling; a row of cottages offers more privacy and space. 15 Craigend Rd. ☎ 01292/314-747. www.piersland.co.uk. 30 units. Doubles £145 w/breakfast. AE, MC, V.

★★ **The Royal an Lochan** TIGHNABRUAICH

This hotel overlooking the sea in Tighnabruaich offers some luxurious units. A "superior sea view" room fits the bill, offering super king-size beds, ample bathrooms (with tubs and showers), and comfy leather-upholstered furnishings. Shore Rd. ☎ 01700/811-236. www.hotels-argyll-scotland.co.uk. 11 units. Doubles £100–£200 w/breakfast. AE, MC, V.

★★ **Turnberry** TURNBERRY

The hotel at Turnberry is a remarkable and well-known landmark for golfers and other travelers. The public rooms contain Waterford crystal chandeliers, Ionic columns, molded ceilings, and oak paneling. Spa and health club facilities are exemplary. Maidens Rd., off the A77. ☎ 01655/331-000. www.turnberry.co.uk. Doubles £360 w/breakfast. AE, DC, MC, V.

Where to Dine

> *Local produce, such as the finest smoked salmon, graces the menu at the Seafood Cabin, Skipness.*

★★★ **Braidwoods** DALRY *FRENCH/SCOTTISH*
One of the standout restaurants in Scotland,
the exclusive but not overly formal Braidwoods is housed in a tiny converted cottage.
Holder of a Michelin star and other accolades,
it's expensive but worth the price for such
dishes as roast quail with black pudding, and
baked turbot on a smoked salmon risotto.
Very busy on weekends. Saltcoats Rd., off the
A737. ☎ 01294/833-544. www.braidwoods.
co.uk. Set dinner £40. AE, MC, V. Lunch Wed-
Sun; dinner Tues-Sat.

Browne's at Enterkine NEAR AYR *MODERN
SCOTTISH* Enterkine's menus emphasize local
ingredients, whether seasonal game or fish
landed at nearby Troon. There are also some
five-star-quality overnight rooms (£210 double occupancy). Enterkine Country House Hotel,
Coylton Rd., Annbank. ☎ 01292/520-580. www.
enterkine.com. Set lunch £19; dinner £30. AE,
MC, V. Lunch Sun-Fri; dinner daily.

MacCallums of Troon TROON *FISH/SEAFOOD*
At the harbor, this seaside bistro is adjacent to
a fresh fish market. Oysters, whole sardines,
sole, and combination platters are frequently
on the menu. The Harbour. ☎ 01292/319-339.
Entrees £15. AE, MC, V. Lunch Tues-Sun; dinner
Tues-Sat.

★ **Russian Tavern at the Port Royal Hotel** PORT
BANNATYNE, BUTE *SEAFOOD/RUSSIAN*
This unique (maybe even eccentric) operation offers freshly landed fish and seafood on
most days, as well as rustic Russian dishes
and a great selection of cast ales. The hotel
has modest, affordable overnight rooms (£50
double). Main St. ☎01700/505-073. Entrees
£16- £24. Lunch & dinner Wed-Mon.

★★ **Seafood Cabin** SKIPNESS *FISH/SEAFOOD*
This summer-only operation (also called the
Crab Shack) is worth a detour if you love
seafood. Cooked in a converted 1950s-style
minitrailer, the meals feature langoustines,
queen scallops, mussels, smoked salmon, and
more. It is completely unassuming, and there's
no better place to eat on a sunny day. B8001
off the A83 (at Skipness Castle, 12 miles south
of Tarbert). ☎ 01880/760-207. Entrees £6-£14.
No credit cards. Lunch Sun-Fri.

GOLF
Links to History

FEW THINGS GO TOGETHER MORE NATURALLY THAN SCOTLAND AND GOLF. So quickly did the local population take to the game that in 1457 Scotland's James II banned it because it was interfering with military training for battles with the English. The ban was lifted in 1502 when both sides made peace, and golf's been embraced ever since. Today there are over 400 courses spread throughout the country—including such challenging and iconic courses as St. Andrews, Royal Troon (above), and Muirfield—and the game generally has a less snobby reputation than it does in North America.

A Short Course in Golf History

A form of golf may have first existed elsewhere—some say the Netherlands, others insist China—but history records golfers playing in Scotland at least 6 centuries ago. No certain evidence survives of the sport being played anywhere else at that time. And no one disputes that the first attempt to codify golf's rules was by the Honourable Company of Edinburgh Golfers in 1744. Their home course was Leith Links then, and now the same "honorable company" is located at Muirfield, east of the city. Formal rules were established and are maintained to this day by the Royal and Ancient Golf Club of St. Andrews in Fife. Indeed, the Holy Grail for golfers worldwide remains a round of 18 holes at St. Andrews (p. 608). Host of the Open Championship (a.k.a. the British Open) every 4 years, St. Andrews's Old Course certainly rivals the fame of any other course, be it Augusta or Pebble Beach.

Old Tom

Many greats are associated with the sport, but perhaps none is more important than St. Andrews native Tom Morris, Sr. (1821–1908), better known as "Old Tom." Morris was a pioneer and proponent of the sport who embraced modern developments (such as the new ball that replaced the old "feathery") and eventually set up his own workshop for making balls and clubs. He helped to establish the Open Tournament, which he won four times. Not content, he participated in the designs of some 75 courses, from Prestwick in Ayrshire to Askernish on the Outer Hebrides.

Great Players

HARRY VARDON
Allegedly the first popular golfer to don knickerbocker trousers, Vardon (1870–1937) won a record-holding six Open Championships. His overlapping grip is still used by a majority of players.

NICK FALDO
The best Brit in the modern game, Faldo won 39 tournaments (including six Majors), and was ranked No. 1 in the world for a total of nearly 100 weeks.

COLIN MONTGOMERIE
"Monty" is one of two Scottish greats and has bagged more European tournament victories (40) than any other British golfer.

SANDY LYLE
Representing Scotland, the English-born Lyle was the first British player to win the U.S. Masters and won 27 tournaments, including the Open Championship.

IAN WOOSNAM
The mercurial "Woosie" won 31 tournaments, including the U.S. Masters and British PGA. The Welshman is one of only 15 golfers to achieve the No. 1 world ranking since its inception.

Golf Lingo

ALBATROSS
Three strokes under par for any hole

BEACH
A sand obstacle (a.k.a. "trap" or "bunker")

BIRDIE
One stroke under par for any hole

BOGEY
One stroke over par for any hole

EAGLE
Two strokes under par for any hole

PAR
Number of strokes needed to complete a hole

SNOWMAN
Hitting eight strokes on a single hole

19TH HOLE
The bar at the clubhouse where you go to rehash your round

The Best of the Central Belt

There are fascinating sites and memorable places to visit in Scotland's Central Belt, the general region that surrounds the country's two main cities of Glasgow and Edinburgh. The emphasis of this tour is on critical historic landmarks, whether Stirling Castle, the well-fortified bastion atop a hill and visible for miles, or Hopetoun House, the palatial stately home of the Marquess of Linlithgow. However rooted in history, this tour is diverse, too. You learn about the medieval battle that no one expected Scotland to win (Bannockburn) and see the village (New Lanark) created by the most progressive industrialist of the 19th century.

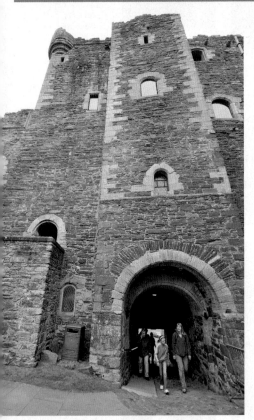

> *Iconic 1975 comedy* Monty Python and the Holy Grail *was filmed at the preserved remains of Doune Castle.*

START Doune, 9 miles northwest of Stirling. TRIP LENGTH 2–3 days. Total distance traveled is about 85 miles.

❶ ★★ **Doune Castle.** Because Historic Scotland's restoration is primarily designed to ensure that this medieval tower house doesn't fall down, Doune Castle feels authentic, and visitors with fit imaginations will get a good notion of 14th-century life (the castle's low doors, narrow spiral stairs, and pervasive damp give more than subtle hints of existence here). At the same time, you can appreciate the grandeur of Doune in the main Lord's Hall with its dual fireplaces. One reason Doune has survived is that it was passed to the Earls of Moray by relatives of Margaret Tudor (1489–1541), wife to King James IV and the sister of England's Henry VIII. ⏱ 1½ hr. Doune, near the A84. ☎ 01786/841-742. www.historic-scotland. gov.uk. Admission £5 adults, £4 seniors, £3 kids. Apr–Sept daily 9:30am–5:30pm; Oct–Mar Sat-Wed 9:30am–4:30pm. Last admission 30 min. prior to closing.

Take the A820 east for 4 miles to Dunblane.

❷ **Dunblane Cathedral.** St. Blane brought Christianity to this region in the 6th century, and this intact church (one of the few medieval churches to survive the Reformation) dates to the 12th and

1. Doune Castle
2. Dunblane Cathedral
3. Stirling
4. Stirling Castle
5. Bannockburn
6. Linlithgow Palace
7. Hopetoun House
8. Rosslyn Chapel
9. Little Sparta
10. New Lanark

Where to Stay
Arden House **11**
Bonsyde House Hotel **11**
Creagan House **12**

Where to Dine
The Boat House **13**
Champany Inn **14**
Monachyle Mhor **15**

13th centuries. The bell tower's 1.5m-thick (5-ft.) walls represent the oldest part (though its top floors are from the 1500s and the roof above the nave dates to a late-19th-c. restoration). ⏱ 45 min. Dunblane, B8033. ☎ 01786/823-388. www.dunblanecathedral.org.uk. Free admission. Apr–Sept Mon–Sat 9:30am–12:30pm & 1:30–5pm, Sun 2–5pm; Oct–Mar Mon–Sat 9:30am–4:30pm, Sun 2–4:30pm.

Take Stirling Rd. (B8033) to M9 south. Total distance is 6 miles.

3 ★ **Stirling.** The settlement of Stirling, assigned royal burgh status by David I in 1124, was preferred over Edinburgh as a base by the royal Stuarts in the 16th century. The Old Town merits a stroll. Stirling Bridge is believed to be the crucial site of a 13th-century battle between English invaders and the ragtag band of Scots led by William "Braveheart" Wallace (1272–1305). You can visit the **Wallace Monument,** Abbey Craig (☎ 01786/472-140; www.nationalwallacemonument.com), a 66m (217-ft.) sandstone tower completed in 1869. If you have kids to entertain, go to the **Old Town Jail,** St. John St. (☎ 01786/450-050; www.oldtownjail.com), where tours feature actors reenacting the conditions. ⏱ At least 2 hr.

> *The Wallace Monument commemorates the life of Sir William Wallace, who defeated the army of English King Edward I.*

❹ ★★★ Stirling Castle. This historic and architectural landmark was the site of Mary, Queen of Scots' coronation in 1543, and the home of several Stuart monarchs. The renovations here are ongoing, and a museum explains how the work is making the castle's many buildings and wings increasingly authentic from a historical point of view. You can see the weavers painstakingly making the tapestries that will hang in one hall. The most recent works have been to restore the palace built for King James V. Even if you don't tour the impressive castle, its ramparts and surrounding grounds are good fun—particularly the cemetery and the "Back Walk" along a wall that once protected Stirling. Admission includes a pass to see Argyll Lodging, a Renaissance mansion at the far end of the castle's esplanade. ⏱ At least 2 hr. Castle Wynd. ☎ 01786/450-000. www.historic-scotland.gov.uk. Admission (including tour of nearby Argyll Lodging) £13 adults, £10 seniors, £6.50 kids. Daily 9:30am–6pm (Oct–Mar until 5pm). Last admission 45 min. prior to closing.

On Day 2 take the A9 south for 3 miles.

> *A grandiose exterior and sumptuous interiors are a feature of Hopetoun House, Scotland's most palatial Georgian stately home.*

5 ★ kids **Bannockburn.** In a land with no shortage of famous, historic battlegrounds, this once boggy site is in the top five for notoriety. It's certainly the one where events turned decisively in Scotland's favor: King Robert the Bruce defeated the English troops of Edward II here in 1314, effectively ensuring Scottish independence. The English army had some 16,000 infantry and 2,500 mounted knights. The Scots had 6,000 spearmen (adept with large spikes) and 500 on horse. The heritage center will tell you everything you need to know about the famous battle. ◷ 2 hr. A872, Glasgow Rd., 1¾ miles south of Stirling. ☎ 0844/493-2139. www.nts.org.uk. Admission £5.50 adults; £4.50 seniors, students & kids. Daily Apr–Sept 10am–5:30pm (Mar & Oct until 5pm). Last admission 45 min. prior to closing.

Take the A9 south to the M9 (toward Edinburgh), then exit at junction 4 onto the A803. Total distance is 17 miles.

6 ★★ **Linlithgow Palace.** Birthplace of Mary, Queen of Scots, this architectural landmark (built primarily between 1425 and 1437) was a favorite residence of Scottish royalty, and is now one of Scotland's most poignant ruins. Enough of the royal rooms are still intact that you can see how grand the palace once was. King James V (Mary's father) was born here in 1512, and when he wed, the palace's impressive fountain ran with wine. ◷ 1½ hr. Linlithgow (A803). ☎ 01506/842-896. www.historic-scotland.gov.uk. Admission £5.50 adults, £4.40 seniors, £3.30 kids. Daily 9:30am–5:30pm (Oct–Mar until 4:30pm). Last admission 45 min. prior to closing.

From Linlithgow, join the M9 east (signposted EDINBURGH) to the B8046 (exit junction 2), following the A904 through Newton Village, and follow signs bearing left toward South Queensferry. Total distance is 5¾ miles.

7 ★ **Hopetoun House.** Amid beautifully landscaped grounds, the home of the earls of Hopetoun is one of Scotland's best examples of 18th-century palatial Georgian architecture. You can wander through splendid reception rooms filled with Renaissance paintings, statuary, and other artwork. The views of the Firth of Forth are panoramic from the rooftop

> *Despite its ruined state, you can still sense the grandeur of Linlithgow Palace, birthplace of Mary, Queen of Scots.*

observation deck. ◷ 1½ hr. South Queensferry, off the A904. ☎ 0131/331-2451. www.hopetounhouse.com. Admission £8 adults, £7 seniors & students, £4.25 kids. Easter–Sept daily 10:30am–5pm. Last admission 1 hr. prior to closing.

Take the A902 and then the A8 (signs for City Bypass) for less than a mile to the A720. Exit on the A702 south to the A703, following signs to Roslin. Total distance is 20 miles.

8 ★ **Rosslyn Chapel.** Thanks to *The Da Vinci Code*, the elaborately carved Rosslyn Chapel is now firmly entrenched on the tourist trail. Visitor numbers apparently doubled thanks to the Tom Hanks movie, part of which was filmed here. The chapel was founded in 1446 by Sir William St. Clair and has long been noted for its architectural and design idiosyncrasies.

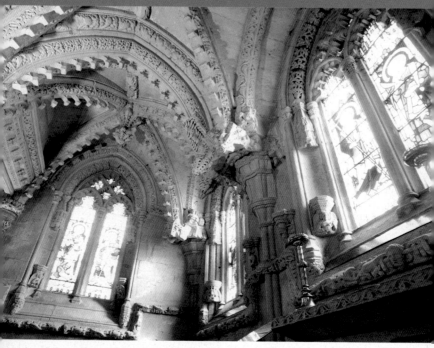

> *Long before it featured in the climax of the* Da Vinci Code, Rosslyn Chapel *was famed for its intricate Gothic stonemasonry.*

🕐 45 min. Roslin, off the A701. ☎ 0131/440-2159. www.rosslynchapel.org.uk. Admission £7.50 adults, £6 seniors & students. Mon–Sat 9:30am–6pm, Sun noon–4:45 pm (Oct–Mar until 4:45pm). Last admission 30 min. before closing.

For Day 3, take the A701 south following signs to Penicuik and then signs to Carlisle (A766), joining the A702 south for about 19 miles.

⑨ ★★ Little Sparta. Little Sparta, called the "only original garden" created in Great Britain since World War II, was devised by one of the most intriguing artists of the 20th century, Ian Hamilton Finlay (1925–2006). It is a surprisingly lush plot of land, given the harsh terrain surrounding it. Dotted throughout the garden are stone sculptures (many with Finlay's pithy sayings and poems) created in collaboration with master stonemasons and other artists. Unique. 🕐 1½ hr. Stonypath, near Dunsyre, off the A702. ☎ 07758/812-263. www.littlesparta.co.uk. Admission £10. Jun 15–Sept Wed, Fri & Sun 2:30–5pm.

From Dunsyre, take Newbigging and Dunsyre rds., turning right on the A721 to A70 (it's 6 miles to the turnoff at Carnwath) and the A743 to Lanark. Total distance is 14 miles.

⑩ kids New Lanark. A UNESCO World Heritage Site, New Lanark was a forward-looking industrial mill and village founded in the late 18th century by industrialist David Dale (1739–1806) and his son-in-law, Welsh social reformer Robert Owen (1771–1858). It offered workers and their families free education, a daycare nursery, a social club, and a co-operative store. Today, the attraction includes a chairlift ride that tells the story of what life here was like, as well as self-guided tours of the principal buildings. 🕐 2 hr. Braxfield Rd., outside Lanark. ☎ 01555/661-345. www.newlanark.org. Admission £6.95 adults; £5.95 seniors, students & kids. Daily April–Sept 10am–5pm; Oct–Mar 11am–5pm.

Where to Stay & Dine

> *A grandstand estuary view from the terrace at the Boat House.*

★ **Arden House** LINLITHGOW

This award-winning Victorian B&B is set on the outskirts of town, amid a country retreat on the Belsyde Estate. Rooms are large, and the beds are famously spacious and plush. Off the A706, 1¼ miles southwest of town. ☎ 01506/670-172. www.ardencountryhouse.com. 3 units. Doubles from £80 w/breakfast. AE, MC, V.

★ **The Boat House** SOUTH QUEENSFERRY *FISH/ SEAFOOD* This restaurant positions diners just above the sea, with views of the marvelous Forth bridges. The typical seafood dishes are creative but not overcomplicated. 19b High St. ☎ 0131/331-5429. www.theboathouse-sq.co.uk. Entrees £12–£18. Lunch & dinner daily.

Bonsyde House Hotel LINLITHGOW

This historic 19th-century country mansion was once home to the man credited with mapping the seven seas: Professor Charles Thomson (1830–82). In addition to the regular guest rooms, there are cabins with their own screened rear patios. Just northwest of Linlithgow, off the A706 on the edge of West Lothian Golf Club. ☎ 01506/842-229. www.bonsydehouse.co.uk. 8 units. Doubles from £68 w/breakfast. MC, V.

★★ **Champany Inn** CHAMPANY CORNER *SCOTTISH* You'll find some of the best steaks in Britain and an award-winning wine list at this converted mill. The meat here is properly hung before butchering, adding to its flavor and texture. Next to the main dining room is the Chop House, offering less expensive cuts. The inn also has overnight rooms (£125 double w/breakfast). A904, 1¾ miles northeast of Linlithgow. ☎ 01506/834-532. www.champany. com. Entrees £25–£50. AE, DC, MC, V. Lunch Mon–Fri; dinner Mon–Sat.

★ **Creagan House** STRATHYRE

There is a clutch of individually decorated rooms at this charming and hospitable inn, including one with a four-poster bed. Dinners here are great, but the baronial dining room is a recent addition to this restored 17th-century farmhouse. A84, 19 miles north of Callander. ☎ 01877/384-638. www.creaganhouse.co.uk. 5 units. Doubles from £120 w/breakfast. AE, MC, V. Closed Feb.

★★ **Monachyle Mhor** BALQUHIDDER *SCOTTISH* Up the highway from Creagan House, this gem serves wonderful food in an 18th-century farmhouse overlooking Loch Voil. The conservatory dining room is modern and so is the cooking. The adjoining inn has guest rooms starting at about £100. Off the A84, 6 miles from turnoff at the Kingshouse Hotel. ☎ 01877/384-622. http:// mhor.net. Set dinner £46. AE, MC, V. Lunch & dinner daily. Closed Jan to mid-Feb.

Glasgow & the Lowlands for Architecture Buffs

Any architectural guide to the Western world will likely highlight Glasgow and the surrounding environs. Two names stand out above all others: Mackintosh and Thomson in the Victorian and Edwardian eras. But there are other architects with fine accomplishments, such as Robert Adam (1728–92), Charles Wilson (1810–63), JT Rochead (1814–78), and John Honeyman (1831–1914). The only sad aside to make is that Glasgow's significant built heritage could have had an even higher reputation. Well-meaning urban renewal schemes have removed essentially all remnants of its medieval past, and any evidence of its reputation as one of the prettiest 17th-century cities in Europe.

START The West End of Glasgow. **TRIP LENGTH** 3 days. Total distance traveled is about 115 miles.

❶ ★★ **Mackintosh House.** Part of the **Hunterian Art Gallery** (p. 576, **13**), this is a literal re-creation of Mackintosh's Glasgow home from 1906 to 1914. It covers three levels, decorated in the original style of the famed architect and his artist wife Margaret Macdonald (1865–1933). All salvageable fittings and fixtures were recovered from the original home before it was demolished in the mid-1960s. It was startling then and little less so today. ☉ 1½ hr. University of Glasgow, 22 Hillhead St. ☎ 0141/330-5431. www.hunterian.gla.ac.uk. Admission £3. Mon–Sat 9:30am–5pm. Underground: Hillhead. Bus: 44.

❷ ★★★ **Glasgow School of Art.** It is difficult not to pile on the superlatives when talking about this edifice. This building, a blend of the Arts and Craft and Art Nouveau movements completed in 1909, is arguably Charles Rennie Mackintosh's finest masterpiece. You must take the tour to see the finer details, such as the sun porch looking back over the city and what I think is the most impressive small library ever devised (plus some original

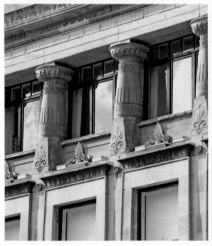

> *Acanthus leaves, used here as a recurring motif on Glasgow's Centre for Contemporary Art, originally decorated Ancient Greece's Corinthian columns.*

watercolor paintings by the great architect). ☉ 1½ hr. 167 Renfrew St. ☎ 0141/353-4526. www.gsa.ac.uk. Tours £8.75 adult, £7 seniors & students, £4 kids. Tours Apr–Sept daily 10am, 11am, noon, 2pm, 4pm & 5pm; Oct–Mar Mon–Sat 11am & 3pm. Underground: Cowcaddens.

❸ ★ Centre for Contemporary Art (CCA).
Originally called the Grecian Building, this leading proponent of conceptual art is a re-worked warehouse done by the city's other great architect, Alexander "Greek" Thomson. Note the exterior stonework and signature acanthus leaves of this great but little known architect. He actually built around an older villa, which can be seen inside the arts center. From Sauchiehall Street, you can glimpse a unique sight by looking up the hill: a Mackintosh and a Thomson in the same view. ⏱ 1 hr. 350 Sauchiehall St. ☎ 0141/352-4900. www. cca-glasgow.com. Free admission. Tues–Sat 11am–6pm.

❹ ★ St. Vincent Street Church. This should be a three-star, must-see attraction, but the congregation that worships here limits public access. Nevertheless, the church remains the most visible landmark attributed to Alexander Thomson. Two classic Greek porticos enclose a clock tower decorated in curiously sympathetic Egyptian, Assyrian, and even Indian-looking motifs and designs. ⏱ 15 min. (unless attending services). 265 St. Vincent St. www.greekthomsonchurch.com. Free admission. Sun services at 11am & 6:30pm. Bus: 62.

On Day 2, head to the Southside of Glasgow using either bus or train.

> *Art Nouveau icon Charles Rennie Mackintosh designed the building housing the Glasgow School of Art, an institution from which he also graduated.*

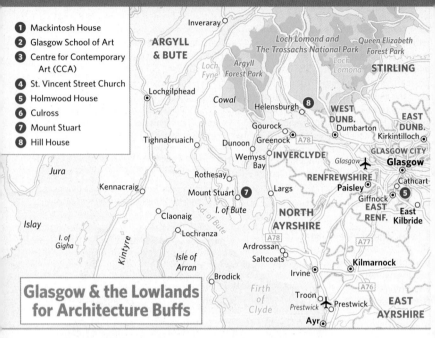

1 Mackintosh House
2 Glasgow School of Art
3 Centre for Contemporary
   Art (CCA)
4 St. Vincent Street Church
5 Holmwood House
6 Culross
7 Mount Stuart
8 Hill House

Glasgow & the Lowlands for Architecture Buffs

5 ★★★ **Holmwood House.** This villa on Glasgow's southern extremities, designed by Thomson and built in 1858, is probably the best example of his innovative style in Victorian homes. Magnificently original, its restoration (which is ongoing) has revealed that the architect concerned himself with every detail, down to the wallpaper. Most impressive is the overall exterior design, as are the interior parlor and the cornices in the dining room. ⏲ 1½ hr. 61–63 Netherlee Rd., Cathcart, about 4 miles south of the city center. ☎ 0141/637-2129. www.nts.org.uk. Admission £6 adults; £5 seniors, students & kids. Apr–Oct Thurs–Mon noon–5pm. Suburban train: Cathcart. Bus: 44 or 66.

Rent a car and take the M80 northeast for about 18 miles to the exit for the Kincardine Bridge (M876). From Kincardine follow the A985 east for 5 miles to

6 ★★ **Culross.** With cobbled streets lined by stout cottages featuring crow-stepped gables, this well-preserved town shows what life was like in a typical village from the 16th to the 18th century. Indeed, it has been called a "a living exemplar" and a "three-dimensional document": the National Trust of Scotland has restored and conserved many of its buildings, including the

1626 Town House. Culross may also have been the birthplace of St. Mungo, who established **Glasgow Cathedral** (p. 570, 2). ⏲ 2 hr. Off the A985, west of Dunfermline. Tourist information, tours ☎ 01383/880-359. www.nts.org.uk.

Head back to Glasgow, from there taking the M8 (A8) west about 25 miles to the A78 south. Continue about 8 miles to the Wemyss Bay ferry terminal and take the ferry to Bute.

7 ★ **Mount Stuart.** This neo-Gothic mansion (built in the 1870s) belongs to the Marquess of Bute's family (descendants of the Stuart royal line). The interiors, including a ceiling covered in constellations, reveal the particular interests of John Crichton-Stuart, the third Marquess (1847–1900) and a fan of astrology. The garden dates back to the early decades of the 18th century. The extensive grounds have a woodlands park, a huge walled area (called the "wee garden"), and a working vegetable plot, too. ⏲ 2 hr. Isle of Bute, the A844 near Scoulag, south of Rothesay. ☎ 01700/503-877. www.mountstuart.com. Admission (house & grounds) £8 adults, £6.50 seniors & students, £4 kids. House: July–Aug noon–4pm (self-guided); May, June & Sept tours noon–3:30pm; Oct tours noon–2:30pm. Gardens: daily May–Sept 10am–6pm (Oct until 5pm).

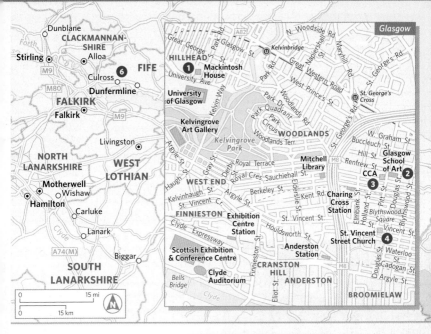

On Day 3, return to the mainland, taking the A78 to the M8 to the Erskine Bridge (20 miles), then crossing the River Clyde to the A82 west to the Helensburgh turnoff (a total of 6 miles) before driving another 9 miles on the A814 to

⑧ ★★★ **Hill House.** Designed by Mackintosh, this timeless house in Helensburgh has been lovingly restored. Inspired by Scottish baronial style, Hill House is still pure Mackintosh, from the asymmetrical juxtaposition of its windows to the sumptuous but uncluttered interior with bespoke details by both the architect and his wife, artist Margaret Macdonald. Though it was completed in 1904, it still looks modern today. A singular and enduring piece of design. ⏱ 2 hr. Upper Colquhoun St., Helensburgh (30 miles west of Glasgow). ☎ 01436/673-900. www.nts.org.uk. Admission £8.50 adults; £5.50 seniors, students & kids. Apr–Oct daily 1:30–5:30pm.

> The building and interiors at Holmwood House were the masterwork of Glasgow architect Alexander "Greek" Thomson.

Glasgow

As Scotland's largest city, Glasgow (pronounced *glaaz-go* by natives) offers a very different feel than Edinburgh, but its reputation as a tourist destination is growing. The city has effectively reinvented itself as a successful example of a post-industrial metropolis. But even during its sooty commercial heyday, it was a cultural capital, too. And for no less than 6 centuries it has been an educational and ecclesiastical mecca. Seeing this vibrant city in a single day is impossible, but you can take in the major highlights over the course of 2 days. Begin with the Victorian splendor of the city center, and finish your full schedule with a foray into the salubrious West End.

> Glasgow Cathedral, the city's grand Gothic edifice, was dedicated during the reign of David I, and is the only intact medieval cathedral in Scotland.

START Buchanan Street underground station.
LENGTH 2 days.

1 ★★ **City Sightseeing Glasgow.** Tours on these brightly colored, open-topped buses hit many of the city's highlights and offer a good orientation. Though some visitors find the live tour guides difficult to follow (due to the Glaswegian accents), their patter is usually as humorous and as entertaining as it is informative. It beats the taped version by miles, so listen carefully. You can hop on and off at some 20-odd stops. ⏰ 1½ hr. George Sq. ☎ 0141/204-0444. www.scotguide.com. Tickets £11 adults, £5 kids. Daily Apr–Oct 9:30am–5pm, every 15–20 min.; Nov–Mar 9:30am–4:30pm, every 30 min. Underground: Buchanan St.

2 ★★ **Glasgow Cathedral.** Mainland Scotland has only one complete medieval cathedral: This is it. Dating at least to the 13th century, this former Roman Catholic cathedral (also known as St. Mungo's) survived the Reformation practically intact. In fact, it was some ill-advised Victorian tampering, not Reformation zeal, that removed one of the earlier towers. The lower church has a vaulted Gothic-style crypt that's among the finest in Europe, and it houses the tomb of St. Mungo (d. 614), patron saint of the city. ⏰ 1½ hr. Castle St. (at High St.). ☎ 0141/552-6891. www.historic-scotland.gov. uk. Free admission. Mon–Sat 9:30am–6pm, Sun 1–5pm (Oct–Mar until 4pm). Sun service 11am. Suburban train: High St. Bus: 11, 36, 37, 38, 42, or 89.

> *Monumental George Square marks the boundary between Glasgow's traditional center and the more offbeat Merchant City.*

❸ ★ Central Necropolis. Built on a proud hill above Glasgow Cathedral and patterned on Paris's Père Lachaise, this graveyard was opened in the 1830s. You won't be able to miss the 62m (203-ft.) monument to John Knox (ca. 1505–72) at the top of the hill; it was erected in 1825. The cemetery's numerous Victorian-style monuments are excellent—as are the views of Glasgow. There is a pamphlet indicating the cemetery's highlights (available at the cathedral or tourist information office on George Sq.). ⏱ 1 hr. Adjacent to Glasgow Cathedral. Free admission. Daily dawn–dusk. Suburban train: High St. Bus: 11, 36, 37, 38, 42, or 89.

❹ ★★ The Merchant City. This district on the eastern edge of the city center is great for a number of reasons. There are cultural venues, from events and music at the **City Halls** (p. 584) to **Trongate 103,** 103 Trongate (☎ 0141/276-8380; www.trongate103.com; free admission), which is the latest in multi-gallery art centers. Additionally, the Merchant City is the closest that central Glasgow gets to offering cafe culture. There are a host

> *The Mackintosh-designed Willow Tea Rooms are a popular stop for a light bite or afternoon tea.*

of places for coffee or something stronger (some with outdoor seating), as well as some of the city's best casual restaurants, such as Café Gandolfi (p. 579). The Merchant City is Glasgow's equivalent of SoHo in Manhattan: warehouses have been converted to loft flats and condos. ⏱ At least 2 hr. www.merchantcity glasgow.com.

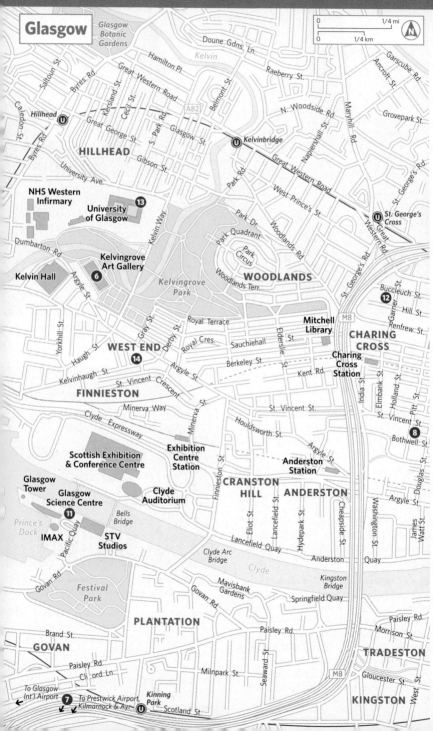

1 City Sightseeing Glasgow
2 Glasgow Cathedral
3 Central Necropolis
4 The Merchant City
5 Mackintosh Trail
6 Kelvingrove Art Gallery and Museum
7 The Burrell Collection
8 "Greek" Thomson Trail
9 Glasgow Green and People's Palace
10 Gallery of Modern Art (GOMA)
11 Science Centre
12 Tenement House
13 Hunterian Art Gallery
14 The West End

Ellesmere St.
Iona Park
Borron St.
Possil Rd.
Craighall Rd.
Garscube Rd.

PORT DUNDAS

North Canal Bank St.

SIGHTHILL

Pinkston St.
Pinkston Dr.
Springburn Rd.

Sighthill Park

M8

New City Rd.
W. Graham St.
Maitland St.
COWCADDENS
Pt. Dundas Rd.
Milton St.
Dobbie's Loan
Calgary St.
Kyle St.
Baird St.
Lister St.
Black St.
Royston Rd.
Castle St.
Rhymer St.
Springburn Rd.

U Cowcaddens
GARNETHILL
Rose St.
McPhater St.
Cowcaddens Rd.
Glasgow Caledonian University
Kennedy St.

5 Glasgow School of Art
Royal Scottish Academy of Music & Drama
Sauchiehall St.
Killermont St.
TOWNHEAD
St. Mungo Ave.
St. James Rd.
Stirling Rd.
Glasgow Royal Infirmary

Blythswood St.
Bath St.
W. Regent St.
W. George St.
Renfield St.
W. Nile St.
N. Hanover St.
Bath St.
Queen Street Station
Montrose St.
Cathedral St.
Castle St.
Wishart St.
Glasgow Cathedral 2
Central Necropolis 3

W. Campbell St.
S. George St.
Wellington St.
CITY CENTRE
Buchanan Street U
George Square
1
Frederick St.
City Chambers
University of Strathclyde
George St.
Drygate
A8

Waterloo St.
Hope St.
Gordon St.
i
Buchanan St.
Cochrane St.
Ingram St.
Duke St.
Cadogan St.
Holm St.
Royal Exchange 10
Miller St.
Virginia St.
Glassford St.
Wilson St.
Candleriggs
MERCHANT CITY
4
High St.
High St. Station

Central Station
Mitchell St.
Union St.
Queen St.
Argyle St.
St. Enoch U
St. Enoch Square
Trongate
MERCHANT SQUARE
King St.
Bell St.
Bell St.
Barrack St.

Broomielaw
"Squiggly" Bridge
King George V Bridge
Jamaica St.
Howard St.
Argyle St. Station
Stockwell St.
Osborne St.
Glasgow Cross
Saltmarket
Gallowgate
EAST END

Oswald St.
Clyde Pl.
Glasgow Bridge
Clyde St.
Footbridge
Bridgegate
Saltmarket
St. Andrew's Square
SALTMARKET
Bain St.
Stevenson St.
Green St.
London Rd.

Kingston St.
Commerce St.
Bridge St.
Carlton Pl.
Oxford St.
Victoria Bridge
Clyde St.
Albert Bridge
Clyde
Greendyke St.
Glasgow Green
9
The Green
The Green

Nelson St.
Wallace St.
Centre St.
Tradeston St.
U Bridge St.
Norfolk St.
Gorbals St.
Ballater St.
Thistle St.
Crown St.
Florence St.
Cook St.
LAURIESTON
GORBALS
Canning St.
The People's Palace
Tobago St.

> *Twenty-two themed galleries at Kelvingrove Art Gallery and Museum display everything from Impressionist paintings to Scottish wildlife exhibits.*

5 ★★★ **Mackintosh Trail.** It might take you most of the day, but if you're a fan, it may be worth visiting as many of the landmarks of famed architect Charles Rennie Mackintosh as you can. There is the great achievement of the **Glasgow School of Art** (p. 566, **2**), or the interiors of **Mackintosh House** (p. 566, **1**). We would also suggest the **Willow Tea Rooms,** 217 Sauchiehall St. (☎ 0141/332-0521; www. willowtearooms.co.uk), the **Mackintosh Church at Queen's Cross,** 870 Garscube Rd. (☎ 0141/946-6600; www.mackintoshchurch. com), or even the **Scotland Street School Museum,** 225 Scotland St. (☎ 0141/287-0500; www.glasgowmuseums.com). ⏱ At least 2 hr. Charles Rennie Mackintosh Society, headquartered in Queen's Cross Church. ☎ 0141/946-6600. www.crmsociety.com.

6 ★★ kids **Kelvingrove Art Gallery and Museum.** The Spanish Baroque-style Kelvingrove (built in 1901 of red sandstone) is the stirring soul of the city's art collection, one of the best amassed by a municipality in Europe. It is the most visited gallery and museum in the U.K. outside of London. The art (ranging from French Impressionists to Spanish surrealists to Scottish modern) is pretty great, but there is more than that to see, with exhibits on Scottish and Glasgow history, armory and war, and natural history, too. There's also some humor: Watch out for the furry haggis animal. ⏱ 2½ hr. Argyle St. ☎ 0141/276-9599. www. glasgowmuseums.com. Free admission, except for some temporary exhibits. Mon–Thurs & Sat 10am–5pm; Fri & Sun 11am–5pm. Underground: Kelvinhall. Bus: 9, 16, 42, or 62.

7 ★★ **The Burrell Collection.** This custom-built modern museum houses close to 9,000 treasures left to Glasgow by wealthy industrialist Sir William Burrell in 1958 (though the building itself didn't open until 1983). His tastes were eclectic: Chinese ceramics, French paintings from the 1800s, stained-glass church windows, medieval stone doorways, and tapestries. One major highlight is an original casting of Rodin's *The Thinker.* ⏱ 2 hr. Pollok Country Park, 2060 Pollokshaws Rd. ☎ 0141/ 287-2550. www.glasgowmuseums.com. Free admission. Mon–Thurs & Sat 10am–5pm; Fri & Sun 11am–5pm.

8 ★★ **"Greek" Thomson Trail.** Perhaps even more important than Mackintosh, Alexander "Greek" Thomson also brought an unrivaled vision of building to Glasgow. While the influence of classical Greece was nothing new to Victorian architects, Thomson honed it to essentials, and then mixed in Egyptian, Assyrian, and other Eastern-influenced motifs. Like Mackintosh, he increasingly found himself out of step with (and well ahead of) others. While a number of his structures have been tragically lost to the wrecker's ball, some key works remain: **St. Vincent Street Church** (p. 567, **④**) is a timeless landmark in Glasgow's Commercial Center, and for domestic dwellings, it doesn't come much better than **Holmwood House** (p. 568, **⑤**). For a virtual pamphlet of the full trail, head online to the Alexander Thomson Society website. ⊙ At least 2 hr. www.greekthomson.org.uk.

⑨ ★ kids Glasgow Green and kids People's Palace. Glasgow Green is the city's oldest park, dating in part to late medieval times (roughly the 15th c.). Its landmarks include the People's Palace museum and adjoining Winter Gardens with a cafe. The museum, first opened in 1898, showcases Glasgow's social history, with displays on how "ordinary people" lived in the city, especially since the Industrial Age. At the Glasgow Green's eastern end, the influence of the Doge's Palace in Venice can be seen in the colorful facade of the old Templeton Carpet Factory (1889). ⊙ At least 1 hr. Greendyke St. (east of Saltmarket). ☎ 0141/287-5098. www.glasgow.gov.uk. Free admission. Park: daily dawn–dusk. Museum: Mon–Thurs & Sat 10am–5pm; Fri & Sun 11am–5pm. Underground: St. Enoch. Bus: 16, 18, 40, 61, 62, or 64.

⑩ Gallery of Modern Art (GOMA). GOMA is housed in a neoclassical building that once served as the Royal Exchange, but was originally built as a mansion for an 18th-century tobacco magnate. Opened in 1996, the gallery focuses on artwork from 1950 onward. The permanent collection has works by Stanley Spencer and John Bellany, as well as art from the 1980s "new Glasgow boys." ⊙ 1 hr. Royal Exchange Sq., Queen St. ☎ 0141/229-1996. www.glasgowmuseums.com. Free admission. Mon–Wed & Sat 10am–5pm; Thurs 10am–8pm; Fri & Sun 11am–5pm. Underground: Buchanan St.

⑪ ★ kids Science Centre. The futuristic-looking edifice of the center's main building is a focal point of Glasgow's drive to redevelop the rundown former docklands. The main themes inside this "Science Mall" are 21st-century challenges and Glasgow's contribution to

> *An original cast for Rodin's* The Thinker *is part of the eclectic Burrell Collection, in Pollok.*

science and technology in the past, present, and future. Many exhibits are of the hands-on variety; kids can even star in their own digital video. The center also has a planetarium, Scotland's only IMAX theater, and an observation tower that's sadly rarely been open due to problems with its construction. ⊙ 2 hr. 50 Pacific Quay. ☎ 0141/420-5010. www.glasgow sciencecentre.org. Admission £9.95 adults; £7.95 seniors, students & kids. Mid-Mar to Oct daily 10am–6pm; Nov to mid-Mar Mon–Sat 10am–5pm. Underground: Cessnock. Suburban train: Exhibition Centre, then walk across the footbridge over the Clyde. Bus: 89 or 90.

⑫ ★ Tenement House. Tenements (or apartment buildings) are what many Glaswegians lived in from the middle of the 19th century onward. This "museum" is a typical tenement flat, preserved with all the old fixtures and fittings: coal fires, box bed in the kitchen, and gas lamps. Its former resident, Miss Agnes Toward, rarely threw anything out from 1911 to 1965, so there are displays of all sorts of

> *The award-winning Science Centre forms the centerpiece of Glasgow's massive Clydeside regeneration project.*

historical memorabilia. ⏱ 1 hr. 145 Buccleuch St. ☎ 0141/333-0183. www.nts.org.uk. Admission £5.50 adults; £4.50 seniors, students & kids. Mar–Oct daily 1–5pm. Underground: Cowcaddens. Bus: 11, 20, 66, 118, or 159.

⑬ ★ **Hunterian Art Gallery.** A part of the University of Glasgow's Hunterian Museum, the oldest public museum in Scotland (opened in 1807). The gallery inherited the artistic estate of Scottish-American James McNeill Whistler (1834–1903), and many of his paintings hang here. You'll also find a selection of Scottish Colourists, as well as a collection of 17th- and 18th-century European masters (from Rembrandt to Rubens). One wing of the building has a re-creation of Charles Rennie Mackintosh's Glasgow home (p. 566, **❶**). ⏱ 1½ hr. University of Glasgow, 22 Hillhead St. ☎ 0141/330-5431. www.hunterian.gla.ac.uk. Free admission. Mon–Sat 9:30am–5pm. Underground: Hillhead. Bus: 44.

SITE GUIDE PAGE 577

⑭ ★★ **The West End.** This is not only the most fashionable of Glasgow districts to live in—it is one of the most fun to visit.

Ahead of Their Time: Thomson & Mackintosh

Although legendary today, Charles Rennie Mackintosh works have not always been recognized as the city's great architectural and design treasures that they are. Mackintosh (1868-1928) was largely forgotten in Scotland at the end of his life. Forms of nature, especially plants, inspired his elegant motifs; designs involved very little clutter—out of step with the predominant fashions of the time. Similarly, Alexander "Greek" Thomson (1817–75) was less appreciated in his day—and while revered now he still awaits the international recognition that his lasting, timeless buildings deserve. He spun the Greek Revival style in a manner that keeps his buildings almost ageless, though at the end of his career the favored style was neo-Gothic. Too bad for him. For more information on all the Mackintosh buildings you can visit, go to the website of the **Charles Rennie Mackintosh Society** at www.crmsociety.com, or call ☎ 0141/946-6600. For more information on "Greek" Thomson, visit the **Alexander Thomson Society** website at www.greekthomson.org.uk.

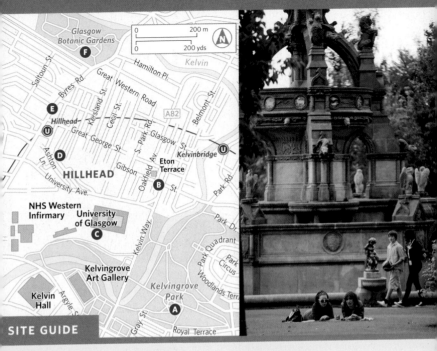

SITE GUIDE

14 The West End

Begin your tour at **A** ★★ **Kelvingrove Park.** Sir Joseph Paxton (1803–65) was commissioned to design a park along the banks of the River Kelvin on land purchased by the city in 1852. The Gothic Stewart Memorial Fountain is a popular gathering spot; it honors Robert Stewart (1810–66), the Lord Provost who helped supply the city with drinking water. Next is **B** ★ **Eton Terrace,** where the hand of architect "Greek" Thomson is unmistakable in this row of eight connected houses, completed in 1864. Note the two temple-like facades serving as bookends; their double porches are fashioned after the Choragic Monument of Thrasyllus in Athens. A short walk will bring you to the central campus of the **C** ★★ **University of Glasgow.** Founded in 1451 (fourth-oldest in the U.K.), the university moved to its current location in 1870. English architect Sir George Gilbert Scott (1811–78), who designed London's Albert Memorial (p. 74, **6**), designed the campus's Gothic Revival main building, punctuated by a 30m (98-ft.) tower. **D** ★ **Ashton Lane** is the

heart of West End nightlife, although it bustles right through the day, too. Its host of bars, cafes, and restaurants includes the venerable **Ubiquitous Chip** (see p. 579), which is housed in a building that once functioned as the stables for an undertaker. A bend in the short cobbled lane leads you right to **E** ★ **Byres Road,** the proverbial Main Street of the West End. If you look up as you approach Downside Road and Byres, note the Victoria Cross sign; it's a remnant of a time when an attempt—derailed by locals—was made to change the name of the street to Victoria Road. At the top of the street, crossing busy Great Western Road (built in 1836 as an impressive road on which to approach Glasgow) is **F** ★ **Glasgow Botanic Gardens.** On dour days, restored Kibble Palace—a domed, cast-iron and glass greenhouse with exotic plants—is a welcome escape. Outdoor plantings include a working vegetable plot, a rose garden, and a 200-year-old weeping ash. ☺ 2 hr.

Glasgow Shopping A to Z

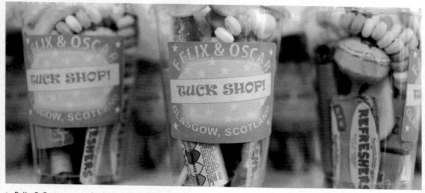

> *Felix & Oscar, great for kids and unique gifts.*

Art

Cyril Gerber Fine Art COMMERCIAL CENTER
One of Glasgow's best small galleries, it veers away from the avant-garde, specializing in British paintings of the 19th and 20th centuries. 148 W. Regent St. ☎ 0141/221-3095. www.gerberfineart.co.uk. Underground: Buchanan St.

★ **Glasgow Print Studio** MERCHANT CITY
The shop of this prestigious collective of artists sells limited-edition etchings, woodblocks, aquatints, and screen prints by Print Studio members, as well as other notable artists. 103 Trongate. ☎ 0141/552-0704. www.gpsart.co.uk. Underground: St. Enoch.

Books

★ **Caledonia Books** WEST END
One of the few remaining secondhand and antiquarian shops in the city of Glasgow. Charming and well run, the stock here tends to favor quality over quantity. 483 Great Western Rd. ☎ 0141/334-9663. www.caledoniabooks.co.uk. Underground: Kelvinbridge.

Edibles

★★ **Heart Buchanan Fine Food and Wine** WEST END Perfect for picnic nosh to take to the nearby Botanic Gardens, this is Glasgow's premier fine food shop. It also has a small cafe. 380 Byres Rd. ☎ 0141/334-7626. heartbuchanan.co.uk. Underground: Hillhead.

★ **I. J. Mellis Cheesemonger** WEST END
The Glasgow branch of this excellent Edinburgh-based cheese specialist offers an outstanding selection of British and Irish cheeses. 492 Great Western Rd. ☎ 0141/339-8998. www.mellischeese.co.uk. Underground: Kelvinbridge.

Gifts & Design

★ **Felix & Oscar** WEST END
An offbeat, fun shop for toys, kitschy accessories, fuzzy bags, and a selection of T-shirts that you're not likely to find anywhere else. 459 Great Western Rd. ☎ 0131/339-8585. www.felixandoscar.co.uk. Underground: Kelvinbridge.

★ **GSA Shop** COMMERCIAL CENTER
This shop in the Glasgow School of Art prides itself on a stock of books, stationery, glassware, and jewelry created from or inspired by the original designs of Charles Rennie Mackintosh. Plus it stocks original, locally produced art. 11 Dalhousie St. ☎ 0141/353-4526. www.gsa.ac.uk. Underground: Cowcaddens.

Music

Avalanche Records COMMERCIAL CENTER
This is the indie music store to beat all others. It's small and cramped (near Queen Street Station), but is the best for the latest releases by everybody from the Decemberists to local stars Belle & Sebastian. 34 Dundas St. ☎ 0141/332-2099. www.avalancheglasgow.co.uk. Underground: Buchanan St.

Glasgow Restaurants A to Z

★★ **Café Gandolfi** MERCHANT CITY *SCOTTISH/ CONTINENTAL* This favorite of local foodies serves up solid cooking at the right price. Particularly recommended are the Stornoway black pudding and creamy Cullen skink (smoked haddock chowder). Bar Gandolfi is up the steel staircase. 64 Albion St. ☎ 0141/552-6813. www.cafegandolfi.com. Entrees £6–£12. MC, V. Breakfast Mon–Sat; lunch & dinner daily. Underground: Buchanan St.

★ kids **Fratelli Sarti** COMMERCIAL CENTER *ITALIAN* The pizza at this cafe-deli is excellent, with a thin, crispy crust and modest amounts of sauce, cheese, and toppings. Pasta dishes, such as "al forno" with sausage, are filling. 133 Wellington St. ☎ 0141/204-0440. www.sarti.co.uk. Reservations recommended. Entrees £7–£10. AE, MC, V. Breakfast Mon–Fri, lunch & dinner daily. Underground: Buchanan St.

★★ **Gamba** COMMERCIAL CENTER *FISH/SEAFOOD* This is the place for a first-rate fish dinner. The basement dining room is modern and stylish without feeling excessively fancy. Main courses may include whole lemon sole in browned butter or delicate pan-seared sea bream. 225a W. George St. ☎ 0141/572-0899. www.gamba.co.uk. Entrees £19–£26. AE, MC, V. Lunch & dinner Mon–Sat. Underground: Buchanan St.

★★ **Mother India** WEST END *INDIAN* In business for more than a decade, this is the most respected Indian restaurant in Glasgow. The menu is not overloaded with hundreds of different dishes, and the staff is professional and courteous. Down the road, a second branch, **Mother India's Café,** offers less expensive, tapas-style dishes. 28 Westminster Terrace (at Kelvingrove St.). ☎ 0141/221-1663. www.motherindia.co.uk. Entrees £7.50–£12. MC, V. Dinner daily; lunch Wed–Sat. Bus: 16, 18, or 42.

Map Note

All of the locations in this section can be found on the map on p. 580.

> *Gamba is known for its refined seafood dishes.*

★ **Stravaigin Café Bar** WEST END *SCOTTISH/ INTERNATIONAL* The motto is "think global, eat local" at this cordial pub-cafe, with a more expensive restaurant in the basement. Scottish produce gets international twists; cheese and herb fritters with sweet chili sauce is just one example. 28 Gibson St. ☎ 0141/334-2665. www.stravaigin.com. Entrees £6–£10. AE, MC, V. Lunch & dinner daily. Underground: Kelvinbridge.

★★ **Ubiquitous Chip** WEST END *MODERN SCOTTISH* Modern Scottish cuisine was essentially created here in 1971. The menus always state the provenance of the produce and may feature Hebridean Soay lamb, Aberdeen Angus fillet steak, or Scrabster-landed lythe. 12 Ashton Lane, off Byres Rd. ☎ 0141/334-5007. www.ubiquitouschip.co.uk. Fixed-price meals £25–£40. AE, DC, MC, V. Lunch & dinner. Underground: Hillhead.

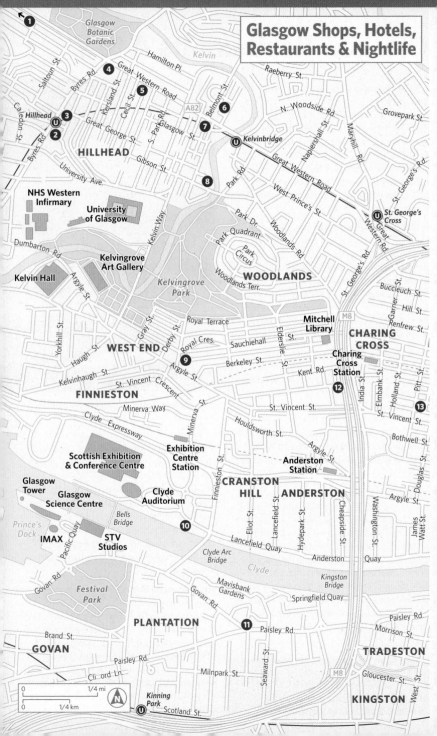

Glasgow Shops, Hotels, Restaurants & Nightlife

Glasgow Botanic Gardens

Kelvin

Saltoun St.

Hamilton Pl.

Raeberry St.

Great Western Road

1

4

Byres Rd.

Kelland Rd.

Cecil St.

5

Grovepark St.

N. Woodside Rd.

A82

Belmont St.

6

Caledon St.

Hillhead

3

Great George St.

Glasgow St.

7

St. George's Rd.

2

U

S. Park Rd.

Kelvinbridge

U

Maryhill Rd.

Napiershall St.

HILLHEAD

Gibson St.

Great Western Road

Byres Rd.

University Ave.

Park Rd.

8

West Prince's St.

St. George's Cross

U

Great Western Rd.

NHS Western Infirmary

Park Dr.

Woodlands Rd.

University of Glasgow

Kelvin Way

Park Quadrant

Park Circus

Dumbarton Rd.

Kelvingrove Art Gallery

WOODLANDS

Woodlands Terr.

Kelvin Hall

Argyle St.

Kelvingrove Park

Woodlands Terr.

Buccleuch St.

Kelvin Hall

Royal Terrace

Gray St.

Derby St.

M8

Garnet Hill St.

Renfrew St.

Yorkhill St.

Haugh Rd.

Royal Cres.

Mitchell Library

CHARING CROSS

WEST END

Sauchiehall St.

Elderslie St.

Charing Cross Station

9

Berkeley St.

Kelvinhaugh St.

St. Vincent Crescent

Kent Rd.

India St.

Elmbank St.

Holland St.

Pitt St.

13

FINNIESTON

Argyle St.

12

St. Vincent St.

Minerva Way

Minerva St.

St. Vincent St.

Clyde Expressway

Houldsworth St.

Bothwell St.

Exhibition Centre Station

Finnieston St.

Argyle St.

Douglas St.

Scottish Exhibition & Conference Centre

Anderston Station

CRANSTON HILL

ANDERSTON

Argyle St.

Glasgow Tower

Clyde Auditorium

Eliot St.

Lancefield St.

Hydepark St.

Cheapside St.

Washington St.

Glasgow Science Centre

Bells Bridge

Eliot St.

Anderston Quay

James Watt St.

Prince's Dock

IMAX

Pacific Quay

STV Studios

10

Lancefield Quay

Anderston

Clyde Arc Bridge

Clyde

Kingston Bridge

Govan Rd.

Festival Park

Mavisbank Gardens

Govan Rd.

Springfield Quay

Paisley Rd.

Brand St.

PLANTATION

11

Paisley Rd.

Morrison St.

TRADESTON

GOVAN

Paisley Rd.

Seaward St.

Milnpark St.

Gloucester St.

West St.

0　　1/4 mi

0　　1/4 km

N

Kinning Park

U

Scotland St.

M8

KINGSTON

SHOPPING

Avalanche Records **21**

Caledonia Books **5**

Cyril Gerber Fine Art **18**

Felix & Oscar **7**

Glasgow Print Studio **28**

GSA Shop **15**

Heart Buchanan Fine
Food and Wine **4**

I.J. Mellis
Cheesemonger **6**

RESTAURANTS

Café Gandolfi **33**

Fratelli Sarti **19**

Gamba **20**

Mother India **9**

Stravaigin Café Bar **8**

Ubiquitous Chip **3**

HOTELS

Blythswood Square **17**

Brunswick Hotel **30**

Hotel du Vin at One
Devonshire Gardens **1**

Mint Inn **10**

Radisson Blu **24**

NIGHTLIFE/ENTERTAINMENT

The Arches **25**

Babbity Bowster **32**

Bar 10 **23**

Barrowland **35**

Bon Accord **12**

Brel **2**

Citizens Theatre **26**

The City Halls **31**

Grand Ole Opry **11**

The Horse Shoe **22**

King Tut's
Wah-Wah Hut **13**

Mono **27**

O2 ABC Glasgow **14**

St. Andrew's in the Square **34**

Theatre Royal **16**

Tron Theatre **29**

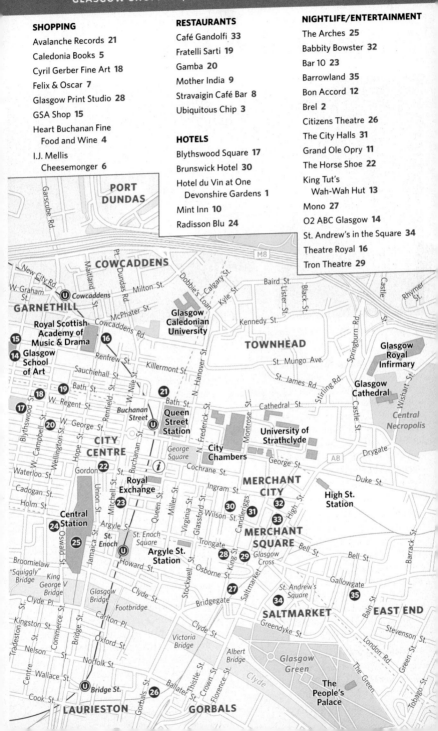

Glasgow Hotels A to Z

> A guest room at One Devonshire Gardens, the city's top hotel.

★★ Blythswood Square COMMERCIAL CENTER
A recent and welcome addition to the scene, this luxury hotel and spa is arguably the best one in the heart of town. The modern guest rooms are comfortable, the spa facilities are extensive, the bar mixes mean cocktails, and the bistro serves excellent meals. 11 Blythswood Sq. ☎ 0141/208-2458. www.townhousecompany.com/blythswoodsquare. 100 units. Doubles £120–£245. AE, MC, V. Underground: Buchanan St.

★ Brunswick Hotel MERCHANT CITY
One of the hippest hotels in town, though it's far from pretentious. The units are generally small but soothing and inviting, with neutral color schemes, comfortable mattresses, and adequate bathrooms (several with both tub and shower). 106–108 Brunswick St. ☎ 0141/552-0001. www.brunswickhotel.co.uk. 18 units. Doubles £100 w/breakfast. AE, DC, MC, V. Underground: Buchanan St.

★★★ Hotel du Vin at One Devonshire Gardens
WEST END This luxurious boutique hotel, spread over five town houses, is the most glamorous the city has to offer—the place where the rich and famous (George Clooney or Tom Jones, anyone?) traditionally stay. The guest rooms have all the necessary modern gadgets, and the hotel's bistro offers first-class dining. 1 Devonshire Gardens. ☎ 0141/339-2001. www.hotelduvin.com. 49 units. Doubles £155–£250 w/breakfast. AE, DC, MC, V. Underground: Hillhead.

★ Mint Inn WEST END
Right on the River Clyde, this smart hotel with a waterside terrace is part of a small chain with other branches in London, Bristol, and Manchester—all of them modern with good facilities (including power showers in the bathrooms). Finnieston Quay. ☎ 0141/240-1002. www.minthotel.com/glasgow. 164 units. Doubles from £60. AE, DC, MC, V. Suburban train: Exhibition Centre.

★ Radisson Blu COMMERCIAL CENTER
Still shiny since its November 2002 opening, the Radisson is just a stone's throw from Central Station. The contemporary guest rooms, with their blond wood details and Scandinavian cool, have all the modern conveniences. 301 Argyle St. ☎ 0141/204-3333. www.radissonblu.co.uk. 250 units. Doubles from £150. AE, DC, MC, V. Underground: St. Enoch.

Glasgow Nightlife & Entertainment A to Z

> For good beer, decent food, and live folk music, stop in at Babbity Bowster.

Bars & Pubs

★ Babbity Bowster MERCHANT CITY

A civilized place for a pint, with no piped-in soundtrack of mindless pop (or indeed any music) to distract from the conversation. The wine selection is good, the food is worth sampling, and there's live folk music on Saturday. 16 Blackfriars St. ☎ 0141/552-5055. Underground: Buchanan St. Suburban train: High St.

Bar 10 COMMERCIAL CENTER

The granddaddy of the Glasgow "style bar" has mellowed into a comfortable place for drinking. The groovy design is still apparent, but more important are the good mix of people and convenient location. The place gets pretty lively when DJs spin on the weekends. 10 Mitchell Lane. ☎ 0141/572-1448. Underground: St. Enoch.

Bon Accord WEST END

This amiable pub is the best in the city for hand-pulled, cask-conditioned real ale. It boasts an array of hand-pumps—a dozen are devoted to real English and Scottish ales. You'll be able to satisfy your taste in malt whisky as well. 153 North St. ☎ 0141/248-4427. Bus: 6, 8, or 16. Train: Charing Cross.

Brel WEST END

Ashton Lane is full of pubs and bars, but this one is possibly the best. It has a Belgian theme—serving up beers and cuisine from that country. 39–43 Ashton Lane. ☎ 0141/342-4966. www.brelbarrestaurant.com. Underground: Hillhead.

★★ The Horse Shoe COMMERCIAL CENTER

If you visit only one pub in Glasgow, make it this one. It's the last remaining "Palace Pub," which opened around the turn of the 20th century. The circular bar is one of the longest in Europe. 17 Drury St. (btw. Renfield & W. Nile sts.). ☎ 0141/229-5711. Underground: Buchanan St.

> *The Theatre Royal, home of the Scottish Opera and the Scottish Ballet.*

Mono MERCHANT CITY

This cafe/restaurant/bar is known for its laid-back vibe, a fantastic CD and LP shop featuring Indie music, and regular performances of live (mostly acoustic) music. The kitchen dishes out dairy-free and meat-free meals, though it may close early on gig nights. 12 Kings Court. ☎ 0141/553-2400. AE, MC, V. Underground: St. Enoch.

Concert Halls & Auditoriums

★ **The City Halls** MERCHANT CITY

Emerging from £8 million in renovations in 2006, these small halls, which date to the 1840s and are the home of the BBC's Scottish Symphony Orchestra and many special events, are acoustically superior to the city's larger auditoriums. Candleriggs. ☎ 0141/353-8000. www.glasgowconcerthalls.com. Ticket prices vary. Underground: Buchanan St.

★★ **Theatre Royal** COMMERCIAL CENTER

This Victorian-style theater is the home of the ambitious Scottish Opera, as well as the recently ascendant Scottish Ballet. London's *Daily Telegraph* has called it (with a trifle of exaggeration) "the most beautiful opera theatre in the kingdom." 282 Hope St. ☎ 0870/060-6647. www.ambassadortickets.com/Theatre-Royal-Glasgow. Ticket prices vary. Underground: Cowcaddens.

Pop, Rock & Folk

★★ **Barrowland** EAST END

There are no seats and it generally stinks of beer, but this former ballroom remains the most exciting place in the city to see touring bands. The hall rocks. 244 Gallowgate. ☎ 0141/552-4601. Bus: 62.

★ **Grand Ole Opry** SOUTH OF CITY CENTER

Glasgow loves its country and western music, and this sprawling sandstone building is the largest club in Europe devoted to the genre. The Opry has a bar, dancing (Texas line-style) on two levels, and a chuck-wagon eatery. Performers are usually from the U.K., but a handful of artists from the States turn up, too. 2–4 Govan Rd., Paisley Toll Rd. ☎ 0141/429-5396. www.glasgowsgrandoleopry.co.uk. Bus: 9 or 54.

★ **King Tut's Wah-Wah Hut** COMMERCIAL CENTER This sweaty, crowded rock bar is a good place to check out the Glasgow music and arts crowd, as well as local bands and the occasional international act. 272 St. Vincent St. ☎ 0141/221-5279. www.kingtuts.co.uk. www.kingtuts.co.uk. Bus: 40, 61, or 62.

★ **O2 ABC Glasgow** COMMERCIAL CENTER

With room for a crowd of about 1,250, this hall is a good place to get a bit closer to the rock and pop bands that play here. 300 Sauchiehall St. ☎ 0870/400-0818. www.o2abcglasgow.co.uk. Underground: Cowcaddens.

St. Andrew's in the Square EAST END

This sympathetically converted early-18th-century church is the city's venue dedicated to folk, Celtic, and traditional Scottish music. 1 St. Andrews Sq. (off Saltmarket). ☎ 0141/559-5902. www.standrewsinthesquare.com. Tickets £4–£8. Bus: 16, 18, 64, or 263.

> *Locals and students pack Barrowland for the latest indie sounds and other touring bands.*

Theater

★ The Arches COMMERCIAL CENTER

A contemporary arts complex that stages edgy new plays, as well as Shakespeare, at inexpensive prices. There's also a fairly full schedule of live music of all description, regular dance clubs, and visual art exhibits. 253 Argyle St. ☎ 0870/240-7528. www.thearches.co.uk. Tickets £4–£10. Underground: St. Enoch.

★ Citizens Theatre SOUTHSIDE

The "Citz," a symbol of the city's democratic approach to theater, is home to a repertory company and has three performance spaces. Prices are always reasonable. 119 Gorbals St. (at Ballater St.). ☎ 0141/429-0022. www.citz.co.uk. Tickets £5–£15. Underground: Bridge St. Bus: 5, 12, 20, or 66.

★★ Tron Theatre MERCHANT CITY

Housed in part of a 15th-century church, this is one of Scotland's leading venues for new drama. It's used often by local companies, such as the acclaimed Vanishing Point, to debut works that end up on the national and international circuit. The bar is a popular hangout. 63 Trongate. ☎ 0141/552-4267. www.tron.co.uk. Tickets £3–£20. Underground: St. Enoch.

> *The bar at the Tron Theatre, in the Merchant City.*

Fast Facts

Arriving

BY PLANE Glasgow International Airport
(☎ 0870/040-0008 or 0141-887-1111; www.
glasgowairport.com) is located at Abbotsinch,
near Paisley, only about 10 miles west of
Glasgow via the M8. Most flights into Glasgow
International Airport from North America
connect via London, but some airlines offer
direct service.

Regular **GlasgowFlyer** bus service (route
no. 500; www.glasgowflyer.co.uk) runs
frequently between the airport and the city
center, terminating at the Buchanan Street
Bus Station. The ride takes only about 20
minutes (though it can be much longer during
rush hour), and it costs £4.50 for a one-way
(single) ticket or £7 for an open return. A taxi
to the city center costs about £17. There are
major car rental desks at the airport.

Some low-budget airlines fly into **Prestwick
International Airport** (☎ 0871/223-0700),
south of Glasgow. Prestwick is on the main
Scotrail line to Ayr, about a 45-minute ride
from Glasgow's Central Station.

BY TRAIN Trains from London arrive in
Glasgow at **Central Station** in the heart of
the city (for rail and fare information, contact
National Rail Enquiries (☎ 08457/48-49-
50; www.nationalrail.co.uk). The trains that
directly link London and Glasgow (via Preston
and Carlisle) run on the so-called West Coast
Main Line. The line has been upgraded once
for faster trains, and there has been some
discussion (but no money) for building a high-
speed line like those in France or Japan, cutting the travel time from London to Glasgow
to about 2 hours. Most of the current trains
still take at least 4 hours to reach the heart
of Scotland's main cities. Glasgow's Central
Station is also the terminus for trains from the
southwest of Scotland.

A 10-minute walk away from Central Station (or via bus no. 398) is **Queen Street Station.** From here, the **ScotRail shuttle service**
to and from Edinburgh runs every 15 minutes
during the day and every 30 minutes in the
evenings until about 11:30 pm. The round-
trip fare during off-peak times (travel from

9:15am–4:30pm and after 6:30 pm) is about
£10, and the trip takes about 50 minutes.
Trains to the north (Stirling) and such Highland destinations as Oban and Inverness also
run frequently through Queen Street Station.

BY BUS The journey from London to Glasgow
by bus or coach can take up to 12 tedious hours,
although express buses can make the trip in as
few as 8 hours. Traffic along the 400-plus mile
journey is impossible to predict. **National Express** (☎ 0870/580-8080; www.national
express.com) runs buses daily from London's
Victoria Coach Station to Glasgow's **Buchanan
Street Bus Station** (☎ 0870/608-2608), north
of the Queen Street Station on North Hanover
Street; they leave London's Victoria Coach
Station at 9am and 11:30pm. Standard fare is
around £35, though Internet and advance purchase discounts are available.

BY CAR If you're driving north to Scotland
from England, it's fastest to take the M1 motorway (freeway or expressway) north from
London.

Emergencies

Call ☎ 999 in an emergency to summon the
police, an ambulance, or firefighters. This is
a free call. For other police inquiries, contact
Strathclyde police headquarters on Pitt Street
in Glasgow at ☎ 0141/532-2000.

Call the toll-free **National Health Service
Helpline** (☎ 0800-224-488) for assistance
with any medical emergency.

The main Glasgow hospital for 24-hour
emergency treatment is the **Royal Infirmary,**
82–86 Castle St. (☎ 0141/211-4000). For dental emergencies, go to the Accident and Emergency Department of Glasgow Dental Hospital, 378 Sauchiehall St. (☎ 0141-211-9600).

Getting Around

Getting full information about traveling
around Glasgow and the Lowlands by public
transportation can be a bit frustrating. **Traveline Scotland** (☎ 0871/200-2233; www.
travelinescotland.com) offers bus and rail
timetable information, but cannot give you
details on fares. For the latter, you will need to
phone individual operators, whose numbers

Traveline can provide. The best way to get around Glasgow itself is on foot, though some attractions will need to be reached by public transport or car. **BY CAR** Aside from Glasgow, the only real way to cover all of the scenic spots in this chapter is by car. Apart from the main roads listed in "Arriving," above, the country is served by many minor routes that crisscross the regions. For regular traffic and weather updates, tune the radio to **BBC Radio Scotland** (92-95 FM and 810 MW). The AA, a leading motoring organization in the UK, provides a free route planner at **www.theaa. com/route-planner**. **BY BUS** Glasgow has an extensive (if somewhat confusing) bus service run by the privately owned **First Group** (www. firstgroup.com). Typically, one-way (single) fares are about £1.80, and for £3.75 you can use the buses (after 9:30am) all day long with few restrictions. The main city bus station is the **Buchanan Street Bus Station. Scottish CityLink** (☎ 0870/550-5050; www.citylink. co.uk) runs frequent bus service between Glasgow and other cities and towns in the Lowlands. **BY TRAIN** Glasgow's Underground, which in a nod to the city's American cousins is officially called the **Subway,** offers a 15-stop circular system linking the city center, West End, and a bit of the Southside. The one-way adult fare is £1.10. Alternatively, you can purchase an all-day Discovery Ticket for £3.50 or a 20-trip ticket booklet for £19. The Underground runs Monday to Saturday 6:30am to about 11:30pm and Sunday 11am to about 6pm. Once you leave the city, stick to roads—trains aren't really suitable for regional exploration.

Internet Access
Wi-Fi is increasingly commonplace in Scotland's major hotels. Usually it is free, sometimes only from the lobbies, other times only in rooms. If you're on the move, public libraries in towns and cities are always safe bets for Internet access.

Pharmacies
In Glasgow, your best bet is Boots at 200 Sauchiehall St. (☎ 0141/332-1925; Mon–Sat 8am–6pm, Sun 11am–5pm).

Post Office
The main Glasgow branch is at 47 St. Vincent's St. (☎ 0141/204-3689; Underground: Buchanan St.). It's open Monday to Friday from 8:30am to 5:45pm and Saturday from 9am to 5:30pm. For general postal information on rural branches, call ☎ 0845/722-3344.

Safety
You're unlikely to encounter any problems. Even Glasgow is relatively safe when compared to cities of its size in the United States. Muggings do occur, however, and drunken violence is random when the bars close on Friday and Saturday nights. Take caution at major railway stations for pickpockets.

Visitor Information
The largest tourist information center in Glasgow is the **Greater Glasgow and Clyde Valley Tourist Board,** 11 George Sq. (☎ 0141/204-4400; www.seeglasgow.com; Underground: Buchanan St.). It has a full range of services, from hotel reservations to currency exchange. In addition to piles of brochures, there is a small bookshop. During peak season it is open Monday to Saturday from 9am to 7pm and Sunday from 10am to 6pm. Hours are more limited during winter months. Additionally, the **British Hotel Reservation Centre** (☎ 020/7092-3055; www.bhrconline.com) provides free reservation assistance and discounted rates at many hotels.

VisitScotland (www.visitscotland.com) runs offices across the region; call for the most up-to-date hours. **COWAL PENINSULA** Tourist Information Centre, 7 Alexandra Parade, Dunoon (☎ 08452/255-121). **DUMFRIES** Visitor Information Centre, 64 White Sands (☎ 01387/245-550). **ISLE OF ARRAN** Tourist Information Centre, The Pier, Brodick (☎ 01770/303-776). **ISLE OF BUTE** Discovery & Information Centre, Winter Garden, Victoria St., Rothesay (☎ 08707/200-619). **KINTYRE PENINSULA** Tourist Information Centre, Harbour St., Tarbert (☎ 08452/255-121; closed in winter). **KIRKCUDBRIGHT** Tourist information is available at Harbour Sq. (☎ 01557/330-494). **STIRLING** Information Centre, 41 Dumbarton Rd. (☎ 08452/255-121).

Scottish Highlands & Islands

Favorite Highlands & Islands Moments

The Highlands and Islands of Scotland inject something into a U.K. visit that no other region in Britain can—in substantial doses, too. The northwesterly regions of the country have by far the highest mountains and deepest waters (in lochs, not lakes). This is just the beginning. The vast area also carries the lion's share of Celtic history and mythology: Scottish Gaelic is a living language in sparsely populated hamlets, tying current communities to an ancient mode of communication, spoken in some form long before the English came here. Some of the oldest monuments made by man are here. Of course, the region's scenery speaks for itself, and the longer summer days mean you can enjoy it for nearly 20 hours per day.

> PREVIOUS PAGE *Majestic Glencoe witnessed the bloody massacre of 38 MacDonald clansmen in 1692. THIS PAGE The ramparts of Duart Castle enclose what is still the headquarters of the Clan Maclean.*

❶ **Easing into island life on the Isle of Mull.** Well served by ferries, the Inner Hebridean Isle of Mull is hilly and photogenic, popular but not overrun with tourists, particularly if you get off the beaten track. A good sampler of island existence. See p. 594, ❺.

❷ **Standing awestruck at the glory of Glencoe.** Adjacent to the prehistorically stunning Rannoch Moor, the hills and mountains on either side of the gorge called Glencoe create a spectacular natural skyline, with the most famous hiking trails in Scotland. See p. 602, ❺.

❸ **Island hopping on the Outer Hebrides.** The dramatic and isolated Western Isles, set on the windswept northwest fringes of Europe, are unlike any other part of the United Kingdom: rich in Gaelic culture, prehistory, wildlife, sandy beaches, rugged moors, and lots and lots of water. Skipping from place to place lets you experience each one's unique brand of island life. See p. 620.

❹ **Rambling up a "Munro" in Western Highlands.** The Munros (named after Scottish mountaineer Sir Hugh Munro; 1856–1919) are those hills that are over 900m (3,000 ft.) tall. And some try to climb (or "bag") every last one. All 238 of them. A good place to ascend one of them is Torridon. See p. 616, ❸.

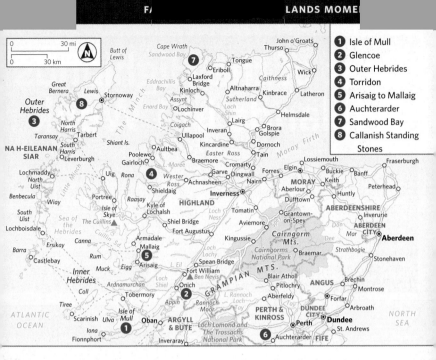

1	Isle of Mull
2	Glencoe
3	Outer Hebrides
4	Torridon
5	Arisaig to Mallaig
6	Auchterarder
7	Sandwood Bay
8	Callanish Standing Stones

5 **Driving along the Arisaig-to-Mallaig coastal route.** This old one-lane shoreline road takes you past some of the finest dunes and sands in the country. Now that commercial traffic is on the new inland artery, this country route is nicer than ever. See p. 604, **9**.

6 **Dining at Restaurant Andrew Fairlie.** There are several fine restaurants in Scotland, but this recipient of two Michelin stars is the best. Combining great Scottish ingredients (such as lobster and lamb) is a signature of Chef Fairlie and other top cooks in the country. See p. 611.

7 **Walking into Sandwood Bay and combing the beach.** The trail across boggy land to this remote, unspoiled cove in the Western Highlands has been much improved by the environmental trust that now owns it. The beach is unparalleled in the U.K. See p. 617, **7**.

8 **Admiring ancient monuments such as the Callanish Standing Stones.** Enigmatic doesn't quite begin to describe the monolithic stones that tower on top of a seaside hill on the Isle of Lewis. Why or how they (and other similar stone circles nearby) got here remains open to debate, but it happened at least 3,000 years ago. See p. 624, **11**.

> Scotland's western coast is blessed with several fine, often deserted beaches; the best among them is Sandwood Bay.

Best of the Highlands & Islands in 1 Week

Any tour of the Highlands and Islands will be a highlight of a visit to the U.K. This excursion will give you only a taste of what's available. To cover the ground, you will need to get an early start each day, but it is possible to go from Loch Lomond over the pass called "Rest and Be Thankful" to Loch Fyne's sheltered shores, then on to the busy harbor at the port of Oban. Next, it's across by ferry to Mull and Iona—the former is considered the best of the Inner Hebridean Islands while the latter has enormous ecclesiastic history. You will still have time for the spectacular, haunting Glencoe as well as the "Road to the Isles" in the region of Lochaber.

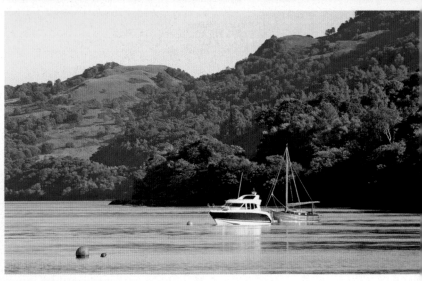

> *The waters of Loch Lomond, and the Trossachs National Park that surrounds it, are under an hour's drive from Glasgow.*

START Loch Lomond, about 32 miles from Glasgow City Centre. **TRIP LENGTH** The total distance is about 300 miles.

1 ★★ **Loch Lomond.** This impressive freshwater loch is Great Britain's largest inland body of water. It is said to contain more water than all the lakes of England combined. You can hike, water ski, cruise in boats (the lake is one of the premier boating destinations in Scotland)—or just sit back and enjoy the scenery. ⏱ At least 2 hr. See p. 606, **1**.

From Alexandria on the western shores of Loch Lomond, take the A82 north for about 10 miles to Tarbet and the A83 west for 23 miles to

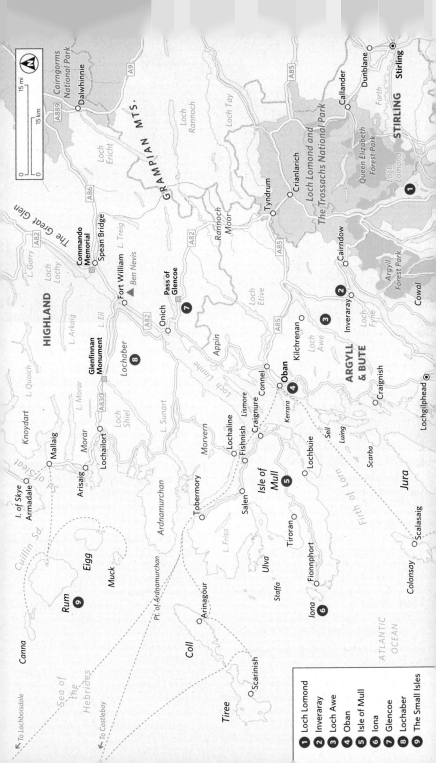

Legend

1. Loch Lomond
2. Inveraray
3. Loch Awe
4. Oban
5. Isle of Mull
6. Iona
7. Glencoe
8. Lochaber
9. The Small Isles

> *Kilchurn Castle, on the shores of Loch Awe, housed Scotland's first purpose-built barracks.*

❷ ★ Inveraray. On the shores of Loch Fyne, this hamlet is the gateway to Argyll and the Scottish Islands. Don't skip **Inveraray Castle** (p. 600, ❷), the seat of Clan Campbell, or the town's **old jail** (☎ 01499/302-381; www.inverarayjail.co.uk; £8.75 adults, £5.75 kids)—the latter will please kids with its portrayal of real life in a 19th-century prison. ⏱ 3 hr.

Take the A819 north for 15 miles and the A85 west for 1 mile to

❸ ★★ Loch Awe. A well-known beauty spot, this large body of water—the third largest freshwater lake in Scotland—also deserves respect: It's deep and cold, so don't go for a swim (though if you like to fish, it's known for its trout). You will notice the terrain turn more wild and remote as you pass the ruins of **Kilchurn Castle** (p. 602, ❸). Follow the road lochside past Lochawe Village, with its quaint railway station that dates back to 1880. ⏱ At least 2 hr.

On Day 2, take the A85 west from Loch Awe for 21 miles to

❹ ★ Oban. This port town was never a particular favorite—the ferry terminal and railway head used to be the main reasons to come here. Not so anymore. The town (pronounced Oh-binn) has spruced up. There are a few good shops and a couple of excellent eating spots, too. Today the "gateway to the isles" is more than a place to catch the ferry. Try fresh shellfish sold on the pier, take a stroll along the waterfront, or watch anglers reel in silvery mackerel. From Oban, you can also take day boat trips to the Isle of Mull (❺). ⏱ At least 2 hr.

Take the Caledonian MacBrayne ("CalMac") ferry to Craignure, Isle of Mull (sail time: 45 min.). There are seven ferries daily in summer from Oban; see www.calmac.co.uk for up-to-date sailing details.

❺ ★★★ Isle of Mull. One of our favorite places in Scotland, Mull (the easiest to reach of the Inner Hebridean Islands) has easily a day's worth of exploration to keep you busy. The cute town of **Tobermory** (p. 622, ❹) is set on a crescent harbor, its buildings painted in pastels. If you're a fan of wildlife, there are sea eagles (year-round) and whales (spring to fall). If you want, you can rent a bike in Salen, in the middle of the island, and ride to the west coast. If you prefer castles, visit **Duart Castle of Clan Maclean,** 3 miles southeast of Craignure (☎ 01680/812-309; www.duartcastle.com), which dates back to the 14th century and has been featured in several films and TV programs. ⏱ 2 days.

On Day 5, take the A849 (35 miles from the Craignure ferry port) to Fionnphort and then the CalMac ferry to Iona (sail time: 10 min.). Frequent ferries (no cars) operate from Fionnphort (www.calmac.co.uk).

6 ★★ **Iona.** This tiny Hebridean island was settled by Christian pilgrims from Ireland, beginning with St. Columba (521–97) in the 6th century. It eventually evolved into a very important Christian pilgrimage site (rumored to be the place where Ireland's famed *Book of Kells* was at least partially produced). Certainly visit **Iona Abbey**—burial site of many Scottish, Norwegian, and Irish kings (☎ 01681/700-512; www.historic-scotland. gov.uk.). But Iona is also great for just getting away from it all. ⏱ At least 3 hr.

Spend the night on Iona. On Day 6, return to Oban via Mull, taking the A85 east for about 50 miles, turning left onto the A82, north through Bridge of Orchy and Rannoch Moor. The total distance is 114 miles. Alternatively, take a more coastal path north on the A828 from Connel for about 34 miles.

7 ★★★ kids **Glencoe.** Whoa, what a sight. But this gorgeous gorge has a bloody event tied to it: the massacre of 40 members of Clan MacDonald in 1692 by the Earl of Argyll's regiment (p. 613). Set aside its grim past, however, as this valley, which extends about 10 miles, is spectacular. The eco- and family-friendly **Glencoe Visitor Centre** (p. 602, **5**) has trail maps and interesting audiovisual presentations that explain the area's social history and geography. ⏱ At least 2 hr.

Take the A82 north to Fort William, joining the A830 (Road to the Isles) west. Total distance is 33 miles.

8 ★★ **Lochaber.** Funny name, perhaps, but one of the truly romantic regions of the Highlands. Stock up in Fort William, the principal town in the shadow of Ben Nevis, but don't look back. Carry on to **Glenfinnan** (p. 603, **8**), where the standard for Bonnie Prince Charlie (1720–88) was raised on the northern tip of Loch Shiel in 1745. Stop at the Glenfinnan visitor center and admire the magnificent railway viaduct (built 1897–1901) that traverses the deep valley—it's played a role in

> *It was through Iona that Christianity spread through Scotland from the 6th century.*

some of the Harry Potter films. From here you may go to the westernmost part of mainland U.K.—the **Ardnamurchan Peninsula** (p. 602, **6**). ⏱ At least 2 hr. See p. 627.

On Day 7, from Glenfinnan, take the A830 west for 19 miles to Arisaig.

9 ★★ **The Small Isles.** The West Coast of Scotland has thousands of islands, only a few of which are inhabited. The so-called Small Isles of Rum, Eigg, Muck, and Canna are pretty easy to reach. One of our favorite sailings is from the coastal hamlet of **Arisaig** (p. 604, **9**), where cruises operate daily trips out to the islands, such as Eigg (www.isleofeigg. net)—a community-owned island with plenty of croft land, sheltered bays, the rugged An Sgurr hill, wildlife, and of course plenty of scenery (as well as a tearoom, shop, post office, and places to stay overnight). ⏱ At least 4 hr. Tours operated by Arisaig Marine, The Harbour, Arisaig. ☎ 01687/450-224. www. arisaig.co.uk.

Best of the Highlands & Islands in 2 Weeks

This tour carries on where the "Best in 1 Week" itinerary ended, taking you further into the beautiful and memorable northern reaches of Scotland, including the magnificent Inner Hebridean island of Skye, and sailing across the Minch to the chain of Outer Hebrides, or Western Isles. Then it's back to the mainland and magnificent mountains of the Western Highlands, as well as the Highland capital, Inverness, and the royal hideaway at Balmoral.

> *Hikes on the Isle of Skye range in difficulty from scenic seaside strolls to the severe test of the Cuillin Ridge.*

START Days 1–7 follow "Best of the Highlands & Islands in 1 Week," p. 592. Start this tour in Mallaig, about 8 miles south of the Small Isles' Arisaig. **TRIP LENGTH** The total distance is 580 miles.

1 ★★ **Isle of Skye.** A 30-minute ferry ride takes you across the Sound of Sleat from Mallaig to Armadale, Skye. This misty isle is many people's favorite. The steep, sharp heights of the Cuillin Hills are dramatic as a backdrop or a place for hiking. In Armadale, the **Clan Donald Skye Center** (☎ 01471/844-305; www.clandonald.com) tells the history of this crucial Scottish family, one time Lords

of the Isles. Portree is Skye's principal town, with some fine gift shops, restaurants, and hotels. Further north, the population is sparse, with crofting settlements dotted over the landscape. The **Skye Museum of Island Life,** A855 (☎ 01470/552-206; www.skyemuseum. co.uk) displays traditional houses of stone and thatch. ⊙ **2 days.**

On Day 9, take the A87 to the northern ferry terminal at Uig, Skye. CalMac ferries run to Lochmaddy, North Uist. From there, take the B888 south (47 miles), crossing the viaduct to Eriskay, and catch the CalMac ferry (sail time: 45 min.) across the Sound of Barra.

1 Isle of Skye
2 Barra
3 The Uists
4 Lewis and Harris
5 Western Highlands
6 Inverness
7 Loch Ness
8 Royal Deeside and
   Highland Perthshire
9 The Trossachs

> *Kisimul Castle on the island of Barra was long the stronghold of Clan MacNeil.*

Grimsay, North Uist). At the **Balranald Nature Reserve,** North Uist, you can spot many types of wading birds and other sea life such as otters (☎ 01463/715-000; www.rspb.org.uk/reserves/guide/b/balranald). The distance from Lochboisdale, South Uist, north to Lochmaddy, North Uist, is just 51 miles. ◷ 1 day.

On Day 11, take the CalMac ferry (45 min.) that links Berneray (North Uist) with Leverburgh to begin your journey across to

❹ ★★★ **Lewis and Harris.** These islands have distinct names, but in fact they form one big isle, third largest in these seas after Great Britain and Ireland. **Harris,** to the south, has amazing azure seas and white beaches (you might think you were in the tropics), plus some towering rocky hills to challenge any of those in the Highlands. **Lewis** has a less celebrated reputation, largely because vast inland stretches are boggy moor, but think of it as a wet desert of desolate beauty. Lewis is diverse; the **Uig area** (p. 624, ⓬) matches the hills of Harris. The **Callanish Standing Stones** (p. 624, ⓫) and other bits of archeology are enduring monuments to the island's early Stone- and Bronze-Age inhabitants. ◷ 2 days.

On Day 13, take the CalMac ferry from Stornoway to Ullapool in the Western Highlands (sail time: 3 hr.).

❺ ★★★ **Western Highlands.** Around Ullapool, the landscape of the vast region known as the Western Highlands is a seemingly never-ending wilderness, with only isolated settlements here and there. Compared to the Alps or the Sierra Nevada, the highest peaks here are comparatively puny. But as they often rise from sea level, with sheer cliffs running up much of the faces, they are undoubtedly dramatic. ◷ At least 2 hr. See p. 614.

Take the A835 south to the A9. Total distance is 57 miles.

❻ ★ **Inverness.** The Highland capital dates back until at least A.D. 500 and is still a growing city. Its **Eden Court,** Bishops Rd. (☎ 01463/234-2340; www.eden-court.co.uk), is an excellent center for the arts, with theater, music, and cinema. There are some fine restaurants, as well. During the day, take a walk on the paths along the River Ness or visit the **Inverness Museum &**

❷ ★★ **Barra.** The southernmost of the major Outer Hebridean Islands, Barra encapsulates the entire chain, with moors, shell-sand dunes, and rocky sea lochs. Castlebay is the main village and port of this compact but beautifully formed isle, and **Kisimul Castle** (p. 622, ❺) is right in the middle of Castlebay. ◷ 4 hr.

On Day 10, return to Eriskay by the ferry, taking the main road (B888) north onto

❸ ★ **The Uists.** This is an archipelago divided North and South, with Benbecula in the middle. Get off the main road (B888) that runs up the spine of the Outer Hebrides and connects these islands via causeways in order to see the western beaches (such as those near Howmore, South Uist) and the rugged inlets in the east (such as those on the small isle of

> *Scotland's rivers, like the Ness, pictured, flowing through Inverness, are world famous for salmon and trout fishing.*

Art Gallery, Castle Wynd (☎ 01463/327-114; http://inverness.highland.museum), which does a good job of explaining both the human and geological history of the Highlands. ⏱ At least 2 hr.

Take the A82 south for 7 miles.

❼ ★★ Loch Ness. Arguably overrated because of the fixation on a mythical monster, Loch Ness is still one magnificent body of fresh water—the largest in Scotland by volume. Dark, brooding, and deep, the loch may well hold a host of beasts. Take one of the boat tours that leave just outside Inverness; **Jacobite Cruises** (☎ 01463/233-999; www.jacobite.co.uk) is a good bet. You can also drive down the western shores to one of the "monster exhibition centers" in the village of **Drumnadrochit** (☎ 01456/450-573; www.lochness.com). ⏱ At least 1 hr.

On Day 14, arise early; the next leg is a bit of a trek through the mountains, so allow about 2 hr. From Inverness, take the A9 south to the A938 east at Carrbridge, the A95, and finally the A939 through Tomintoul and other villages to the A93 at Ballater. Total distance is 72 miles.

❽ ★ Royal Deeside and Highland Perthshire. Crossing the Cairngorm Mountains brings you to Royal Deeside and the forested southern Grampian Mountains. The River Dee's valley was where Queen Victoria and Prince Albert decided to build their summer retreat, **Balmoral Castle** (p. 610, ❾). Heading south from **Braemar** (famous for its annual Highland Games; p. 610, ❽), you enter Highland Perthshire, where the countryside is more hospitable and less rugged. ⏱ At least 3 hr.

Finally, embark on another scenic drive of about 2 hr. From Braemar, take the A93 south to Perth and the A85 toward Crieff and Comrie (73 miles).

❾ ★ The Trossachs. This range of hills and mountains is not as dramatic—nor as threatening—as the hills and mountains of the Highlands. Still, the Trossachs have their own bucolic charms. Along with Loch Lomond, it is part of Scotland's second **National Park** (p. 606, ❶). This region offers forested glens, winding rivers, and gentle scenery that makes a fitting end to this tour of Northern Scotland. ⏱ At least 2 hr. See p. 606.

Best of North Argyll to Lochaber

Argyll is a slightly amorphous region. Though some of the area is situated in the Lowlands, the northern stretches of Argyll are the focus of this particular tour, which brings together mountains (such as the "Arrochar Alps") and sea coasts. From the placid shores of sea lochs, you head further north through the desolate beauty of Rannoch Moor and spectacular Glencoe before venturing into Lochaber, which means the regions west of Fort William on the "Road to the Isles," whose highlights include the romantic castle ruins of Tioram and sandy beaches of Morar.

> *The vast, U-shaped profile of Glencoe is typical of a valley formed by Ice Age glacial erosion.*

START Village of Arrochar on the A83, about 42 miles from Glasgow. **TRIP LENGTH 5 days.** Total distance is about 140 miles.

1 ★★ **Argyll Forest Park.** Its 24,000 hectares (about 60,000 acres) are home to one of our favorite one-day hikes: up the Cobbler (also known as Ben Arthur) in the "Arrochar Alps." If you want some reasonably strenuous hiking, try reaching its craggy peak, which looks down on Loch Long near Succoth. ⏱ 4 hr. A83 at Loch Long. Ardgartan Visitor Centre: ☎ 01301/702-432. www.forestry.gov.uk. Free admission. Daily dawn–dusk.

From Ardgartan, take the A83 west toward Inveraray. Total distance is 20 miles.

2 **Inveraray Castle.** An almost picture-perfect pile (completed in 1789) with fairy-tale spires belonging to the Clan Campbell, whose current 13th Duke (a champion elephant polo player) still lives here. The highlights open to visitors are the armory hall and an elaborately decorated State Dining Room. ⏱ 1½ hr. Off the A83, ⅔ mile northeast of Inveraray. ☎ 01499/302-203. www.inveraray-castle.com. Admission £9.20 adults, £7.60 seniors & students, £6.20 kids. Apr–Oct daily 10am–5:45pm. Last admission 45 min. prior to closing.

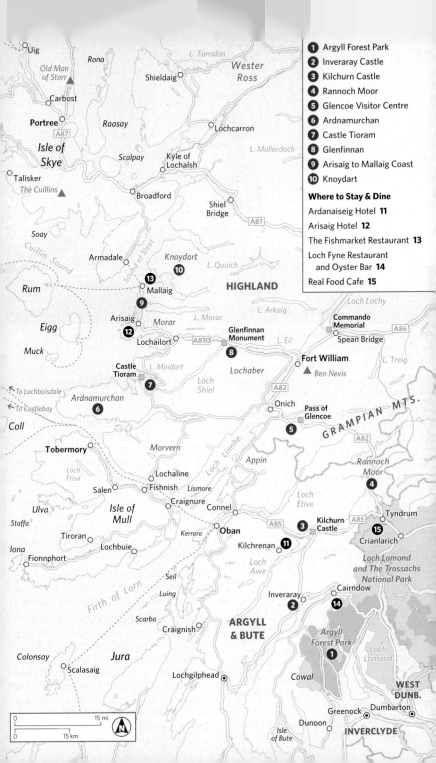

1 Argyll Forest Park
2 Inveraray Castle
3 Kilchurn Castle
4 Rannoch Moor
5 Glencoe Visitor Centre
6 Ardnamurchan
7 Castle Tioram
8 Glenfinnan
9 Arisaig to Mallaig Coast
10 Knoydart

Where to Stay & Dine

Ardanaiseig Hotel 11
Arisaig Hotel 12
The Fishmarket Restaurant 13
Loch Fyne Restaurant
  and Oyster Bar 14
Real Food Cafe 15

> *Castle Tioram is one of many ruined outposts that once guarded strategic points on Highland lochs and mountain passes.*

Take the A819 north, joining the A85 west at Loch Awe. Total distance is 16 miles.

❸ ★ Kilchurn Castle. Part of what we call the tea towel tour of Scottish castles (its image is often on souvenir drying cloths), Kilchurn is quite a sight on the edge of Loch Awe. Well-preserved ruins (it was damaged in 1760 by lightning and subsequently abandoned) date to the 15th century. The footpath from the A85 is prone to flooding—be careful. ⏱ 1½ hr. Off the A85, northeast end of Loch Awe. www. historic-scotland.gov.uk. Free admission.

On Day 2, follow the A85 east from Loch Awe (about 15 miles) to the A82 north. Total distance is 27 miles.

❹ ★ Rannoch Moor. When it comes to beauty defined by desolate wilderness, Rannoch Moor is tops. The 50-square-mile expanse resembles a prehistoric world: Vast stretches of rocky outcrops, scrub heather, streams, peat bogs, and small lochs are often wind- and rain-blasted, some 305m (1,000 ft.) above sea level. Fantastic. ⏱ 30 min (2 hr., if hiking). A82, north of Bridge of Orchy.

Continue on the A82 north and west for 15 miles to

❺ ★★★ kids Glencoe Visitor Centre. Spectacular Glencoe extends about 10 miles from King's House Hotel in the east to the shores of Loch Leven and the village of Glencoe in the west. The National Trust for Scotland's eco-friendly visitor center has area trail maps and audiovisual presentations of local geography. Children receive a free fun guide with admission. Ranger-led walks take place throughout the summer. ⏱ 3 hr. A82 (visitor center 1 mile east of Glencoe Village). ☎ 0844/493-2222. www.glencoe-nts. org.uk. Visitor center admission £6 adults; £5 seniors, students & kids. Daily Apr–Oct 9:30am–5:30pm; Nov–Mar 10am–4pm.

On Day 3, take the A82 west from Glencoe for 8 miles to the Corran ferry (sail time: 15 min.) and then head west on the A861 for 23 miles.

❻ ★★ Ardnamurchan. This peninsula has the most westerly point in the entire British mainland. It has forests, pretty beaches (such as the one at Sanna Bay), tidal pools, lots of hiking trails, salmon fishing, and the **Nàdurra Centre** (☎ 01972/500-209; www.anhc.co.uk; free admission). The lighthouse at the craggy Point of Ardnamurchan can feel like the end of the earth on a windy day. ⏱ At least 2 hr. www. ardnamurchan.com.

World Famous Railroad: The Jacobite Steam Train

The 42-mile ride between Fort William and the port town of Mallaig on this train—named for the 18th-century Jacobite movement to restore the Stuart line of kings, a popular idea in the Highlands—is one of the most picturesque rail journeys in Europe, and perhaps the world. At the route's Glenfinnan station, a small train museum (open seasonally) is worth a look, and you can take a break in the cafe located in an old train car. If you take the round-trip, the schedule allows you to spend 2½ hours in Mallaig. The journey takes 5½ hours round-trip. For information and up-to-date fares, call ☎ 01524/737-751 or head online to www.westcoastrailways.co.uk. Not every train on this route is the historic steam train, so confirm schedules if you want to ride the real thing. Harry Potter fans should note that the train stood in for the Hogwarts Express in several of the movies.

From Salen, take the A861 north 3 miles past Acharacle, following signs for CASTLE TIORAM at Blain.

7 ★★ **Castle Tioram.** The impressive ruins of this classic medieval fortress (pronounced, roughly, *cheer*-rum) sit on a rocky spit of land extending into the picturesque waters of Loch Moidart. Although you can't get inside these days, you can visit at any hour. And it costs nothing. Tioram was a key outpost for Clan MacDonald for hundreds of years and is one

> *The highlanders who fought in the doomed 1745 Jacobite Rising are remembered by the Glenfinnan Monument.*

of our favorite ruined castles: a romantic site that is best accessed at low tide. The castle was sacked and burned during Jacobite uprisings in 1715—in this instance apparently by its own owners in order to keep it from falling into enemy hands. There are good hiking trails near the castle, too. ⊙ At least 1 hr.

From Acharacle, take the A861 north to Lochailort, and then the A830 west. Total distance is 29 miles.

8 ★★ **Glenfinnan.** The monument here marks the hopeful start of the 1745 Jacobite rebellion led by Bonnie Prince Charlie. Be sure to take your camera; this monument (and now slightly sacred historical ground) amid Highland scenery is a great spot for pictures, especially if you're lucky enough to see the steam train (above) cross the arched viaduct behind the visitor center. The Royal Stuart cause captured the Scots' collective imagination, and the small National Trust of Scotland visitor center

> *Between Arisaig and Mallaig, looking out over the Sound of Sleat, lies one of Scotland's most spectacular coastal stretches.*

provides a good primer on the Jacobites and Prince Charlie. ⏱ At least 1 hr. ☎ 01397/722-250. Visitor Centre admission £3 adults; £2 seniors, students & kids. Daily Apr–Jun & Sept–Oct 10am–5pm; July–Aug 9:30am–5:30pm.

On Day 4, from Glenfinnan, take the A830 west for 19 miles.

⑨ ★★★ kids **Arisaig to Mallaig Coast.** Less than 8 miles long, the single-track coastal route from Arisaig to Mallaig is a gem of a drive. Though a new two-lane highway has been built inland linking the scenic natural harbor of Arisaig to the beaches of Morar, you should avoid it and take the old road along the shore. If you golf, try **Traigh,** a beautiful links course 2 miles north of Arisaig (☎ 01687/450-337; www.traighgolf.co.uk). Set against postcard-pretty seas, looking across at the islands Rum and Eigg, the **Sands of Morar** (aka Morar Beach) has been used by filmmakers intent on capturing the quintessential Highland/Island backdrop. Unfortunately, the beach can get

rather crowded—at least by local standards— with sun-seeking locals and tourists in the summer. But that is fine for kids, who can run free and meet new pals. ⏱ 2 hr.

On Day 5, take a boat (☎ 01687/462-320; sail time: 30 min.) from Mallaig to

⑩ ★★ Knoydart. There are only two ways on to the Knoydart Peninsula: a short boat ride from Mallaig or a long walk from Kinloch Hourn. You should do the former. Knoydart is virtually caught between "heaven" and "hell," the traditional translations of Loch Nevis and Loch Hourn, the lochs that surround it. No matter how you arrive, you're rewarded with a mostly roadless landscape, although there is a bunkhouse (run by the Knoydart Foundation) and a famously hospitable pub called the **Old Forge** (☎ 01687/462-267; www.theoldforge. co.uk). If you found Ardnamurchan (⑥) tranquil and liked it, try this place on for size. ⏱ At least 4 hr. ☎ 01687/462-163. www.knoydart-foundation.com.

Where to Stay & Dine

> *Luxury can be found on the banks of Loch Awe at the Ardanaiseig Hotel.*

★★ **Ardanaiseig Hotel** KILCHRENAN
If you seek a bit of luxury in an out-of-the-way corner, this baronial hotel (pronounced *Ard-na-sag*) is a romantic retreat on the shores of Loch Awe. Some of the individually decorated rooms (most with antiques) overlook the gardens; others have views of the loch. A full slate of recreational activities, from tennis to boating, can be arranged. B845, 3 miles north of Kilchrenan, off the A85. ☎ 01866/833-333. www.ardanaiseig.com. 16 units. Doubles £100–£300. AE, MC, V. Closed Jan to mid-Feb.

kids **Arisaig Hotel** ARISAIG
In addition to views of the lovely bay at Arisaig, its small harbor, and the isles beyond, this hotel has two dedicated family rooms. The units are well appointed, if not exceptionally large. The best ones face onto the sea. A restaurant and popular local pub, as well as a playroom for children, are on the premises. Arisaig Harbor. ☎ 01587/450-210. www.arisaighotel.co.uk. 13 units. Doubles £110 w/ breakfast. MC, V.

The Fishmarket Restaurant MALLAIG *FISH/SEAFOOD* Situated right on the harbor and serving dishes that incorporate freshly caught fish, this restaurant is a casual place for a meal. Main courses might include poached haddock with mussels, roasted whole sea bass with fennel and ginger, or traditional fish and chips. Prawns (shrimp) come in by the ton here at Mallaig and are thus one of the restaurant's specialties. Station Rd. ☎ 01687/462-299. Main courses £10–£15. Lunch & dinner daily.

★ **Loch Fyne Restaurant and Oyster Bar** CAIRN-DOW *FISH/SEAFOOD* At the head of Loch Fyne, this well-known casual spot serves oysters and mussels fresh from the clear, cool waters of the loch nearby. Few things are finer than the fish dishes and platters here. Be sure to browse the nice gift shop next door. A83. ☎ 01499/600-263. www.lochfyne.com. Entrees £11–£16. AE, MC, V. Lunch & dinner daily.

★ **Real Food Cafe** TYNDRUM *FISH AND CHIPS* This casual roadside stop has laid claim to the best fish and chips in Scotland. Well, it is among the best, and they offer the option of the eco-friendly fillet of pollock in addition to the heavily fished haddock. A82. ☎ 01838/400-235. www.therealfoodcafe.com. Entrees £6. MC, V. Lunch & dinner daily. Closed Tues–Wed Nov–Dec.

Best of the Trossachs to Balmoral

This tour will take you through some gentle, rolling country-side with brooks and forests, as well as upcountry to the more rugged lands of the Cairngorms National Park—Scotland's first such entity, covering a massive 1,750 square miles. Starting on the proverbial "bonnie banks" of Loch Lomond, you'll traverse central Scotland to see the Trossachs region, and Highland Perthshire, before coming, finally, into the area best known as Royal Deeside, where the British Monarchy invariably spends a portion of every summer.

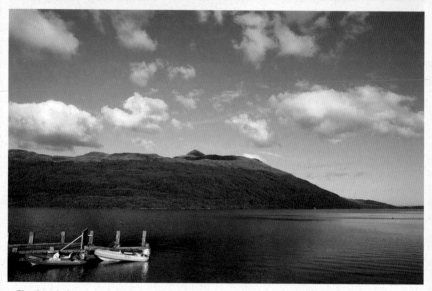

> The "bonnie, bonnie banks o' Loch Lomond" inspired one of Scotland's best known folk songs.

START Balloch, south shore of Loch Lomond, about 32 miles from Glasgow. **TRIP LENGTH** 4 days. Total distance is about 140 miles.

① ★★ **Loch Lomond & the Trossachs National Park.** Loch Lomond is Great Britain's largest inland body of water. Its national park—Scotland's first, established in 2002—comprises some 720 square miles of the surrounding countryside and hills. If you're hiking, the trails up the eastern shoreline are preferable. If you

kayak, the Lomond Shores' visitor center has rentals (☎ 01389/602-576; www.canyou experience.com). Along the western banks, visitors can take loch cruises. ⏰ 2 hr. National Park Gateway Centre, Lomond Shores, Balloch. ☎ 01389/722-199. www.lochlomond-trossachs. org. Free admission. Daily 10am–5pm.

From Balloch take the A811 northeast through Drymen to the A821 north. Total distance is 19 miles.

1. Loch Lomond & the Trossachs National Park
2. Queen Elizabeth Forest Park
3. Callander
4. SS *Sir Walter Scott* Steamship
5. Scone Palace
6. Edradour Distillery
7. Blair Castle
8. Braemar
9. Balmoral Castle and Estate

Where to Stay & Dine
Braemar Lodge Hotel 10
Creagan House 11
Darroch Learg 12
Deans @ Let's Eat 14
Gleneagles 13
Parklands Hotel 14
Restaurant Andrew Fairlie 13

MORAY
Forres
Nairn
Fortrose
Keith
Rothes
Aberlour
Dufftown
A96
Culloden Moor
A95
A9
Tomatin
Grantown-on-Spey
ABERDEENSHIRE
Aviemore
Cairngorm Mts.
Don
Speyside
A9
Kingussie
Newtonmore
Ben Macdui
Cairngorms National Park
Ballater
Braemar
Balmoral Castle
Dee
HIGHLAND
Dalwhinnie
Loch Ericht
L. Treig
Blair Castle
Pass of Killiecrankie
ANGUS
GRAMPIAN MTS.
Blair Atholl
Edradour Distillery
Loch Rannoch
Pitlochry
Forfar
Aberfeldy
Blairgowrie
A90
Rannoch Moor
Loch Tay
Dunkeld
Tay
DUNDEE CITY
Tyndrum
PERTH & KINROSS
A9
Dundee
Crianlarich
Lochearnhead
Scone Palace
A90
Loch Lomond and The Trossachs National Park
A85
Perth
Tay
Strathyre
Creiff
A9
FIFE
Cupar
Loch Lomond & the Trossachs National Park
Callander
Earn
Auchterarder
M90
Queen Elizabeth Forest Park
L. Katrine
Dunblane
Ochil Hills
A91
Loch Leven
Glenrothes
STIRLING
Forth
CLACKMANNAN-SHIRE
Alloa
Stirling
M90
Kirkcaldy
WEST DUNBARTONSHIRE
Dunfermline
EAST DUNBARTONSHIRE
FALKIRK
WEST LOTHIAN
Firth of Forth
Dumbarton
Kirkintilloch
Falkirk
NORTH LANARKSHIRE
Livingston

0   15 mi
0   15 km

3 Callander. Another "gateway" town, though this time to the Trossachs, the figurative foothills of the Highlands. It's not a bad place for a quick rest, a visit to the Trossach tourist information center, shopping for woolens, and a bite to eat. ⏱ 45 min. Rob Roy & Trossachs Visitor Centre, Ancaster Sq. ☎ 08707/200-628.

On Day 2, take the A84 to the A821 west. Total distance is 9 miles.

4 ★ SS *Sir Walter Scott* Steamship. For more than 110 years, this white ship—the last screw-driven steamship to sail in Scotland—has ferried passengers on Loch Katrine (popularized in Sir Walter Scott's poem *The Lady of the Lake*). The views from the ship are stunning. This popular trip can get crowded in summer, so try for a weekday sailing. ⏱ 1 hr. (scenic cruise) or 2 hr. (sailing to Stronachlachar). Trossachs Pier, Loch Katrine (off the A821). ☎ 01877/332-000. www.lochkatrine.com. Tickets for 2-hr. trip £14 adults, £13 seniors, £9 kids. Daily sailings Apr–Oct (weather permitting) 10:30am, 1:30pm & 3pm.

Take the A821 east for 8 miles, going north on the A84 for about 24 miles, and turning east at Lochearnhead on the A85 to Perth. Total distance is 60 miles.

> *There's no shortage of souvenir shopping opportunities in Callander, the main town in the Trossachs.*

2 ★ Queen Elizabeth Forest Park. East of Loch Lomond are thousands of acres of unspoiled nature, set in a park established in 1953 to mark the coronation of the queen. Many trails wind through the woods and hills of the region, managed by the Forestry Commission. The visitor center is a good base for hiking excursions and also offers zip line rides (the biggest in Britain; see www.goape.co.uk) among other recreational options. If nature walks aren't your thing, there are good picnic spots—or you can motor through a part of the park on the scenic Achray Forest Drive (A821). ⏱ At least 2 hr. David Marshall Lodge Visitor Centre, off the A821. ☎ 01877/382-258. www.forestry.gov.uk/qefp. Free admission. Daily 10am–5pm.

Take the A81 east for 11 miles to

Teeing It Up in St. Andrews

Golf fans with extra time should consider stopping in the medieval royal burgh of **St. Andrews** in nearby Fife. Once a revered place of Christian pilgrimage, today the historic college town of cobblestone streets by the sea is best known for golf. It has been played here at least as long ago as the 1600s, though some believe much earlier. The rules of the sport are reviewed, revised, and clarified in St. Andrews by the Royal and Ancient Golf Club (www.standrews.org.uk), and it is currently home to five 18-hole courses (including its Old Course, perhaps the most famous in the world) and a 9-hole course for beginners. For visitor, golfing, and accommodations information, contact the **tourist office** in St. Andrews at 70 Market St. (☎ 01334/472-021; www.standrews.co.uk).

> *Scone, where Scone Palace now stands, was the traditional crowning place for Scottish monarchs, including Shakespeare's fictional Macbeth.*

⑤ ★★ Scone Palace. Scotland's early kings were enthroned at this hallowed place (pronounced "scoon"). The castellated palace dates only to the early 1800s, though parts of much earlier buildings (some dating as far back as the 12th c.) are incorporated. A replica Stone of Scone (where royalty once sat) marks its historical location near a little chapel. Today the palace is loaded with fine furniture, ivory, and a particularly noteworthy porcelain collection. ⏱ 2 hr. A93, 2 miles north of Perth. ☎ 01738/552-300. www.scone-palace.co.uk. Admission £10 adults, £9 seniors & students, £7 kids. Apr–Oct daily 9:30am–5:45pm. Last admission 45 min. before closing.

On Day 3, from Perth, take the A9 north for 28 miles to Pitlochry.

⑥ ★ Edradour Distillery. You get a good primer on the whisky-making process at this distillery, opened in 1825 and pitched as Scotland's smallest. It produces only 12 casks of whisky a week that are matured for 10 years before bottling. It's a cute site, too, with little whitewashed buildings with red doors and a friendly staff using the smallest spirit stills that the law allows. Of course, it's quality, not quantity, that counts. ⏱ 1½ hr. Off the A924,

> *The whisky at Edradour is aged for a decade in specially selected oak casks.*

> Deer antlers lining the hall at Blair Castle provide a clue to the leisure interests of the Dukes of Atholl, who reside there.

just outside Pitlochry. ☎ 01796/472-095. www.edradour.co.uk. Admission £5. Mar–Oct Mon–Sat 9:30am–5pm, Sun noon–4pm; Nov–Feb Mon–Sat 10am–4pm, Sun noon–4pm.

From Pitlochry, take the A9 north for 8 miles.

7 ★ kids **Blair Castle.** This fairy-tale, white castle (begun in 1269) is the home of the Dukes of Atholl and chock-full of antlers and armor. Deer horns decorate one long hall and a ballroom; the weaponry collection spans hundreds of years. This attraction has something (including pony trekking) for nearly everyone. ⏱ 2 hr. Blair Atholl, off the A9. ☎ 01796/481-207. www.blair-castle.co.uk. Admission £9.25 adults, £7.95 seniors & students, £5.65 kids. Apr–Oct daily 9:30am–5:30pm; Nov–Mar Tues & Sat 9:30am–2:30pm. Last tour 1 hr. before closing.

From Pitlochry, take the A924 east and the A93 north. Total distance is 48 miles.

8 ★ **Braemar.** Welcome to the Cairngorms National Park, which envelopes this Highland village. Typically Braemar's population is around 500 people. But when the village holds the Braemar Highland Games (www.braemargathering.org) every September, the population jumps by 20,000 or more. The throngs usually include dignitaries, not to mention Queen Elizabeth and other members of the Royal Family. **Braemar Castle** (www.

braemarcastle.co.uk; £5), once the seat of Clan Farquharson, dates to the 17th century, when it was built as a hunting lodge for the Earl of Mar. The earl lost it to the Hanoverian Crown when he participated in the 1715 Jacobite rebellion—Braemar, a Catholic stronghold in Scotland, was a big supporter of the Stuart line. The antiques-filled castle is allegedly haunted by a variety of ghosts. ⏱ 1 hr.

On Day 4, from Braemar, take the A93 east for 10 miles.

9 ★★ **Balmoral Castle and Estate.** Queen Victoria purchased this estate in 1852, and it remains the personal property of the monarch. Because it is a working residence for the queen and her entourage, visitor access is limited to a few months of the year and only to the ballroom, garden, and grounds. On display are pictures of other rooms as well as clothing and gifts belonging to royalty. You're free to walk the extensive grounds and gardens. Because the castle is closed to tourists when the queen is in town, it's a good idea to call in advance of your visit. In addition to the general opening times, guided tours are sometimes offered one day a week in November and December. ⏱ At least 1 hr. ☎ 013397/42534. www.balmoralcastle.com. Admission £9 adults, £8 seniors & students, £5 kids. Apr–July daily 10am–5pm.

Stone of Scone: Long Strange Trip

Until the late 13th century, Scone Palace (p. 609, **5**) was the home of the Stone of Destiny, aka the Stone of Scone, on which important early Scottish rulers such as David I, Macbeth, and Robert the Bruce were enthroned. According to myth, the hunk of sandstone dates to Biblical times and came through Egypt, Spain, and Italy before landing in Scotland with Celtic pilgrims in the 9th century. So powerful was the lure of the stone that in 1296 English King Edward I stole it and then lodged it in Westminster Abbey, where English kings and queens hoped to get some of its magic during coronations. In 1996, it was returned officially to Scotland with plenty of manufactured fanfare and is now on display in Edinburgh Castle (p. 510, **4**).

Where to Stay & Dine

> One of several Scottish-flavored guest rooms at Darroch Learg, which has been welcoming guests for over 120 years.

Braemar Lodge Hotel BRAEMAR
The rooms here are reasonably spacious and most have views of the mountains at this compact Victorian era country house. Glenshee Rd. ☎ 01339/741-627. www.braemarlodge.co.uk. 7 units. Doubles £70-£120 w/breakfast. MC, V.

★ Creagan House STRATHYRE
There is a clutch of individually decorated rooms at this charming and hospitable inn, including one with a four-poster bed. Fine dining is served in the baronial dining room. A84, 8⅔ miles north of Callander. ☎ 01877/384-638. www.creaganhouse.co.uk. 5 units. Doubles £120 w/breakfast. AE, MC, V. Closed Feb.

★ Darroch Learg BALLATER
Set on a wooded hillside, this highly regarded hotel near Balmoral has 12 overnight rooms in the main lodge, complemented by 5 more in a nearby annex. Braemar Rd. (off the A93), on the west side of town. ☎ 01339/755-443. www.darrochlearg.co.uk. 17 units. Doubles £130-£230 (depending on season) w/breakfast. AE, DC, MC, V. Closed Jan.

★ Deans @ Let's Eat PERTH SCOTTISH/FRENCH
Chef Willie Deans, a member of the Master Chefs of Great Britain, runs this well-established venture. His dishes (most made from local ingredients) include a warm salad of Scottish lobster and prawns. 77-79 Kinnoull St. ☎ 01738/643-377. Entrees £15-£22. MC, V. Lunch & dinner Tues-Sat.

★★ Gleneagles AUCHTERARDER
Scotland's most famous luxury hotel and golf resort, Gleneagles, was built in 1924 in the style of a French château. At the top end, the Whisky Suites have separate sitting rooms and dining spaces for relaxed breakfasts. A823 (off A9), 16 miles southwest of Perth. ☎ 01764/662-231; in the U.S. 866/881-9525. www.gleneagles.com. 250 units. Doubles from £295 w/breakfast. AE, DC, MC, V.

Parklands Hotel PERTH
This award-winning small hotel occupies a stylish Georgian town house once owned by a lord provost (mayor). The spacious rooms at this peaceful oasis are nicely decorated. 2 St. Leonard's Bank. ☎ 01738/622-451. www.theparklandshotel.com. 14 units. Doubles £100-£155. AE, DC, MC, V.

★★★ Restaurant Andrew Fairlie AUCHTERARDER FRENCH/MODERN SCOTTISH
Scotland's only two-Michelin-star restaurant may be the finest dining experience in the country. Meals are seamless but not stuffy. If you have the money, go for the six-course "degustation" menu. Gleneagles Hotel. ☎ 01764/694-267. www.gleneagles.com. Set dinner £75. AE, MC, V. Dinner Mon-Sat.

THE SCOTTISH CLANS

The Backbone of Highland Society

BY BARRY SHELBY

Unraveling the Tartan

Historically, Highland men wore a tartan plaid: a 5 x 12-foot length of heavy wool tweed, which also served as a sleeping bag/tent when stuck out in the elements of the often chilly Highlands. We don't know if every member of a clan wore the same pattern at that time. The association between clan and tartan, however, was strong enough for the latter to be largely banned in 1746 after the failed rebellion of Bonnie Prince Charlie. The modern equivalent—hugely popularized by Queen Victoria—is the kilt. Its checked pattern and colors are distinctly associated with specific clans and families. Wear a Chisholm kilt to a formal dinner dance in Glasgow, or even London, and you're likely to be buttonholed by another Chisholm, complimenting you on your attire.

ACROSS THE WORLD, MILLIONS TRACE THEIR ANCESTRY back to Scottish clans and their associated families, known formally as septs. Clan allegiance—whether to a major, influential family such as MacDonald or to a smaller player such as Cunningham—was once the glue that held much of Scottish society and culture together. Clan chieftains engendered stronger loyalty in their particular regions than monarchs did in many cases. Of course, such strong allegiances led to inter-clan disputes: everything from long-forgotten livestock raids to bloody encounters that echo through history. Part and parcel of the clan system were fortified homes for their chiefs; castles dots the Scottish landscape. Today, the tartan is the item most closely associated with clans and their modern day members dispersed across the world.

The Massacre of Glencoe

The beautiful valley of Glencoe was the site of a dreadfully bloody but momentous event in Scotland's history under British rule: On February 6, 1692, the Campbell Clan's Earl of Argyll's Regiment—on orders approved by England's King William III—slaughtered about 40 members of Clan MacDonald on this picturesque spot, including some women and children. Why? Clan chief Maclain of Glencoe hadn't declared allegiance to the monarch in London, who'd overthrown the last Stuart king 3 years earlier. What made their killings truly distressing in Scotland is the fact that Campbell's troops had been staying as guests,

albeit not especially welcome ones.

So while clan rivalry and conflict were undoubtedly part of this tragedy, events in Glencoe rank right up there with the Battle of Culloden (1746) when it comes to tragic bloodshed at the hands of native forces (Scottish or otherwise) loyal to the central government in England. In fact, Glencoe undoubtedly helped spawn the failed Jacobite Rebellion against English rule in 1745. The patronage system of the clans went into decline after the massacre and succumbed almost entirely after the defeat of Bonnie Prince Charlie (who was trying to restore the Stuart line of Scottish Kings) at Culloden. Although the Highland chieftains didn't uniformly back his rebellion against the Hanoverian monarch of Britain, the Highlanders were generally suspect by the central government, which then put severe restrictions on their culture, such as banning the tartan and trying to eliminate the use of the Gaelic language.

A Clan's Home Is Its Castle

Not every clan chief had a castle, but many did—and some had several. Initially they were for defensive purposes, providing safety from other marauding clans or from outside invaders such as Norse or English troops. Clan Maclean on the Isle of Mull had a string of castles up the narrows of sea between the island and the mainland. The main pile, Duart Castle (p. 620, **1**), is indeed a fortified tower house, dating originally to the 1200s. Another battle-worn Highland castle is picturesque Tioram (p. 603, **7**), belonging to Clan MacDonald. Sometimes a clan castle is more akin to a magnificent palace, such as **Inveraray Castle** (left; p. 600, **2**), home to the Duke of Argyll and head of Clan Campbell.

Best of the Northwest Highlands

Some of the most remarkable sights in the U.K. are found in Scotland's great Northwest Highlands. This tour starts in arguably the most attractive village of the Highlands, Plockton, on a sheltered bay of Loch Carron. From here, the road winds north through the scenic areas of Torridon and up to Gairloch, to the amazing botanic gardens at Inverewe, on to Ullapool, and then via rugged countryside to the northernmost spot in this book: Durness.

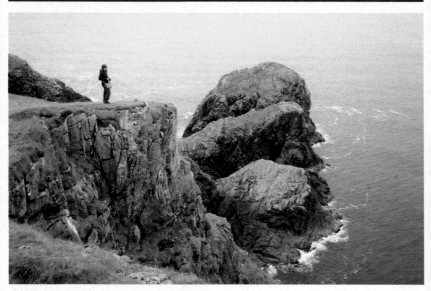

> Due north from the British mainland's highest cliffs, at Cape Wrath, there's nothing until you hit the Arctic.

START Plockton, north of the A87 near Kyle of Lochalsh, about 80 miles southeast of Inverness, the Highland capital. **TRIP LENGTH** 4 days. Total mileage is 185 miles, on single-track and winding roads.

1 ★★ **Plockton.** Palm-like cabbage trees and other nearly tropical plants, as well as cute 18th-and 19th-century cottages, punctuate the crescent-shaped main street of this charming Highland village (pop. 21), arguably the prettiest in Scotland. So picturesque is it that it's often used in BBC films and TV shows, notably *Hamish Macbeth*. On the shores of Loch Carron, you'll find sea cruises (☎ 01599/544-306; www.calums-sealtrips.com) in spring and summer that take in such wildlife as seals and dolphins. Plockton also features some good pub grub and seafood specialties at the Plockton Inn and the Plockton Hotel (p. 619). ⏱ At least 2 hr. www.plockton.com.

Take the road south out of the village to the A87, then head east 11 miles to

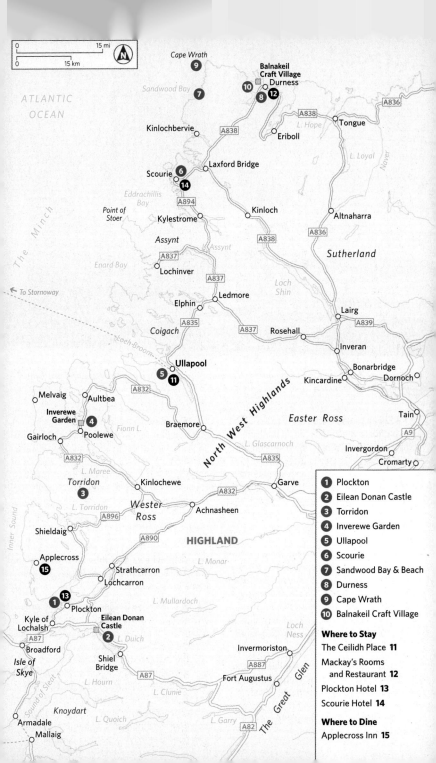

Scale
0 — 15 mi
0 — 15 km

ATLANTIC OCEAN

Cape Wrath **9**
Sandwood Bay **7**
Balnakeil Craft Village **10**
Durness **12** **8**

L. Hope
Tongue

A836

A838

Kinlochbervie
Eriboll

A838

L. Loyal

Laxford Bridge

Scourie **6**
14

Eddrachillis Bay

Point of Stoer

A894

Kinloch

Altnaharra

A836

A838

Kylestrome

Assynt

Assynt

Sutherland

← To Stornoway

Loch Shin

Lochinver

A837

A837

Enard Bay

Coigach

Elphin

Ledmore

A835

A837

Lairg

A839

Rosehall

Inveran

Loch Broom

Ullapool **5** **11**

Bonarbridge

Dornoch

Kincardine

Melvaig
Aultbea

A832

Inverewe Garden **4**
Poolewe

Fionn L.

Braemore

Easter Ross

Tain

A9

Gairloch

A832

Invergordon

Cromarty

L. Maree

Torridon **3**

Kinlochewe

L. Glascarnoch

A835

Garve

North West Highlands

L. Torridon
A896

Achnasheen

A832

Shieldaig

A890

HIGHLAND

Wester Ross

Applecross **15**

Strathcarron
Lochcarron

L. Monar

1 **13** Plockton

L. Mullardoch

Loch Ness

Kyle of Lochalsh

Eilean Donan Castle **2**

L. Duich

Invermoriston

A87

Broadford

Shiel Bridge

A887

Isle of Skye

A87

Fort Augustus

The Great Glen

Sound of Sleat

L. Hourn

L. Clunie

Knoydart

Armadale

L. Quoich

L. Garry

A82

Mallaig

---

1 Plockton
2 Eilean Donan Castle
3 Torridon
4 Inverewe Garden
5 Ullapool
6 Scourie
7 Sandwood Bay & Beach
8 Durness
9 Cape Wrath
10 Balnakeil Craft Village

Where to Stay

The Ceilidh Place **11**

Mackay's Rooms and Restaurant **12**

Plockton Hotel **13**

Scourie Hotel **14**

Where to Dine

Applecross Inn **15**

> *Dramatically sited Eilean Donan, marooned on an islet in Loch Duich, is a favorite location for photographers and movie directors.*

2 ★★ **Eilean Donan Castle.** This could be the most photographed stone pile in the Highlands. On an islet in Loch Duich, this quintessential castle (which lay in utter ruins for 2 centuries) is accessible by an arched bridge. Originally built in the early 1200s by Alexander II to deter Viking invaders, the castle was demolished at the hands of Hanoverian troops during the second Jacobite uprising of 1719 before being restored in the early 20th century by the Clan McRae. Movie fans will be excited by the fact that such films as *Highlander, The World is Not Enough,* and *Elizabeth: The Golden Age* were filmed here. ⏲ 2hr. Near Dornie. ☎ 01599/555-202. www.eileandonancastle. com. Admission £6 adults; £5 seniors, students & kids. Mar–Oct daily 10am–6pm. Last admission 1 hr. before closing.

On Day 2, take the A87 a few miles west to the A890 north to Achnasheen, then head west on the A832 to Kinlochewe. Total distance is 45 miles. Alternatively, you can take the A890 north to the A896 west at New Kelso.

3 ★ **Torridon.** Torridon is the photogenic mountainous region west of Kinlochewe with some of the highest peaks in the U.K., including some of the famed Munros: the 900m-plus (3,000-ft.) mountains of Beinn Alligin (Jeweled Hill, in Gaelic) and Sgorr Ruadh (Red Peak; it's composed of red sandstone). Wildlife abounds, whether eagles or pine martens, though the latter are notoriously shy. ⏲ At least 1 hr.

From Kinlochewe, continue northwest on the A832 through Gairloch and Poolewe. Total distance is 26 miles.

4 ★★★ **Inverewe Garden.** The most impressive garden in the Highlands benefits from shelter planting over decades and the North Atlantic drift, which carries warmer waters up from the Caribbean. In late summer, you can see cabbages the size of basketballs in the large vegetable patch. The 20-hectare (50-acre) garden, however, encompasses much more than just vegetables: There are rhododendron and pine walks, a "bambooselem," two ponds, and a rock garden. Diverse planting means something is in bloom all year round, from azaleas in spring to Kaffir lilies in the autumn. Amazing. ⏱ At least 2 hr. A832, about 6 miles northeast of Gairloch. ☎ 01455/781-200. www.nts.org.uk. Admission £9 adults; £6 seniors, students & kids. Daily Apr–Oct 9:30am–8pm; Nov–Mar 10am–3pm.

Take the A832 north through Gruinard and Dundonnell, then head north on the A835. Total distance is 50 miles.

5 ★ **Ullapool.** On the shores of Loch Broom, this is the busiest fishing port on the northwest coast of Scotland. Established in 1788, the town has become a popular resort—the last outpost before the sparsely populated regions further north. If you need to stock up at a supermarket, stop here. It also has some good casual restaurants that feature freshly landed fish and seafood, such as crabs, while the hotel and bar **Ceilidh Place** (p. 619) is a hub of cultural activity with frequent music and dance events through the summer season. ⏱ At least 2 hr.

On Day 3, take the A837 and the A894 north through Kylesku. Total distance is 42 miles.

6 ★★ **Scourie.** After some inland roads, the highway finds its way back to the sea at Badcall, just south of Scourie Bay and this remote village. You'll probably notice how sparsely populated this part of Great Britain is: Settlements marked on your road map are little more than clusters of small-holding farms and houses. Sometimes there is a shop, often there is not. This is the greater area of Lochinver, north of Assynt, famous for hiking and fishing—and relaxing. Enjoy the calm and peace. ⏱ 2 hr.

Take the A894 north to Laxford Bridge, joining the A838 north to a left turn on the B801 toward Kinlochbervie. Total distance is 19 miles.

7 ★★★ **Sandwood Bay & Beach.** Purchased in the early 1990s by the John Muir Trust, the 4,700-hectare (11,600-acre) Sandwood Estate has *the* most beautiful and unsullied beach on the British mainland. Yes, getting there and back from the nearest road requires a 9-mile hike on a peat-and-stone trail. But then why do you think the sand at Sandwood Bay is so pristine? The rugged bay itself is bordered by dunes and a freshwater loch;

> *Skillful planting at Inverewe Garden ensures that pretty much any month is a good time to visit.*

> *The remote, dune-backed sands at Sandwood Bay are arguably the most scenic beach in the British Isles.*

local legends have everyone from ghosts to mermaids paying a visit here. The entire estate covers many thousands of acres and encompasses crofts and peat bogs as well as dunes and craggy coastline. From here, the ambitious can also hike to **Cape Wrath** (❾). ⏱ At least 3 hr. www.jmt.org. Blairmore carpark. Free admission.

Take the A838 north for 22 miles.

❽ ★★ **Durness.** This village in the northwest corner of the British mainland features a small memorial for the late Beatle John Lennon, who took vacations in this part of Scotland. If you're camping, here's another place to pitch a tent right on the sea, but up atop cliffs that look down on the boulder-strewn beach of Sango Bay below. Another attraction, about 1½ miles east of the village, is **Smoo Sea Cave** (www.smoocave.org), a one-time smugglers' hideaway (its name is thought to come from the Norse word for "hideout") with a waterfall that is easily accessible by foot at low tides; there's boat access in summer (☎ 01971/511-259). ⏱ 2hr.

On Day 4, from Durness , drive about 2 miles south, turning right at the sign reading KEODALE/CAPE WRATH to the pier at the Kyle of Durness, where a ferry will take you across a narrow inlet. From there you either hike 9 miles or use the minibus service (suspended in bad weather) to

❾ ★★ **Cape Wrath.** A Stevenson lighthouse dating to 1828 stands proud on this north-westerly windswept promontory, whose name isn't as ominous as it seems—the cape was a navigation marker for Vikings, and its name is derived from the old Norse for "turning point." The moors (on land called the Parph) were once home to several families, and there was even a school. The Clo Mor cliffs are the highest in the British mainland, towering about 190m (620 ft.) above the ocean. In addition to lots of wildlife, you may see a bomb or two burst: This area is still a Ministry of Defense test site. ⏱ At least 2½ hr. For ferry information ☎ 01971/511-376.

Just west of Durness, take the Balnakeil Rd. for 1 mile to

❿ ★ **Balnakeil Craft Village.** This artist community, on the outskirts of Durness near Cape Wrath, has plenty of galleries selling local artwork. The craft village is housed in a former military communications installation with lots of flat-roofed institutional-looking buildings. Still, the place is friendly, communal, and vaguely hippy-esque. The cafe serves tasty natural foods, a chocolatier sells hot drinks and cool cacao confections, and the bookshop is well stocked with local titles. If you've come this far, carry on to the end of Balnakeil Road and Balnakeil Bay, where there are the old ruins of a 17th-century church and a lovely beach. ⏱ 2 hr.

Where to Stay & Dine

> *From the guest rooms to the public areas, you'll find a high level of comfort at the Scourie Hotel.*

★★ **Applecross Inn** APPLECROSS *SEAFOOD/ SCOTTISH* This may not be the easiest place to reach, but many visitors feel the twists and turns of the road to Applecross are well worth a meal at the inn. This one-time fisherman's cottage sits right on the shores of the Inner Sound of Raasay, looking out toward the mountains on the Isle of Skye. Naturally, seafood dishes make up the majority of the menu, but you can expect local venison or sausages, too. There are 6 overnight rooms with sea views. Off the A896 from Loch Kishorn. ☎ 01520/744-262. www.applecross.uk.com. Doubles £100 w/breakfast. Lunch & dinner daily. Entrees £8–£16. MC, V.

The Ceilidh Place ULLAPOOL

How many hotel rooms are themed according to the minilibrary they contain? Fair to say, not many. But here at the Ceilidh Place, which has its own acclaimed bookshop on the premises, each overnight room features a set of books selected by a Scottish writer or luminary. 14 W. Argyle St. ☎ 01854/612-103. www.theceilidh place.com. 11 units. Doubles £90–£130 w/breakfast. MC, V.

Mackay's Rooms and Restaurant DURNESS

This small hotel is almost universally well regarded. It is 150 years old but fully restored, with just over a dozen simply decorated rooms. The restaurant menu changes daily, usually emphasizing local fish and seafood. ☎ 01971/511-202. www.visitmackays.com. 7 units. Doubles £100–110 w/breakfast. Easter-Oct. MC, V.

Plockton Hotel PLOCKTON

The village of Plockton (p. 614, **1**) is one of the prettiest you'll find in the Highlands, and this is the only hotel on the waterfront, looking onto a sheltered bay in Loch Carron. The guest rooms in the hotel include two that work for families and a half-dozen that offer sea views. Plus, there's a cottage annex nearby with four smaller rooms (one without en suite facilities). Harbour St. ☎ 01599/544-274. www.plockton hotel.co.uk. 15 units. Doubles £110 w/breakfast. AE, MC, V.

Scourie Hotel SCOURIE

This one-time coaching inn way up north in Sutherland is a hotel that believes guests have better things to do than sit in their rooms and watch television. (There are no TVs here, although they provide you with a radio if asked.) Rooms are quite homey and spacious. Some of them overlook Scourie Bay, while others have vistas toward the inland mountains, such as Ben Stack. Off the A894. ☎ 01971/502-423. www.scourie-hotel.co.uk. 20 units. Doubles £90 w/breakfast. MC, V.

Best of the Hebrides

The allure of Scotland's Western Islands isn't difficult to understand: The history and culture of the Hebrides (*Heb-ri-dees*)—combined with the beauty of the seascape—are captivating. Travelers have been exploring the Hebrides for eons, whether Vikings looking for loot in the Bronze Age, or Boswell and Johnson seeing sights in the 1700s that Georgian-era Britons in England could hardly imagine. Getting to the islands is half the fun, and when you arrive, you can be almost guaranteed to have a peaceful retreat from the mainland, particularly on places such as Barra, Harris, Iona, or Lewis.

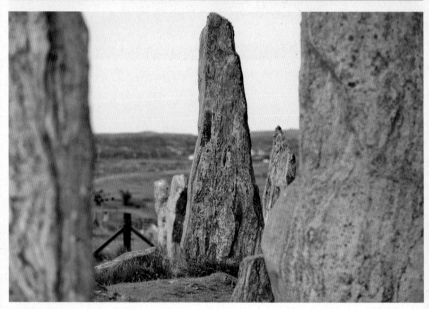

> Unlike Stonehenge, Callanish Standing Stones allows visitors to get up close with the mysterious ancient monument.

START Isle of Mull, about 110 miles from Glasgow. **TRIP LENGTH** 8 days. The total distance is 280 miles on land.

❶ ★★ Duart Castle. Clearly seen from the Oban-Mull ferry, Duart was built in the 13th century but abandoned in 1751. Thanks to the efforts of Sir Fitzroy Maclean (1835–1936), it was completely restored from ruins in 1911. As the ancestral home of the Clan Maclean (it still serves as home of the clan chief), one floor is devoted to clan history, with various references to the 17th-century battle cry: "Another for Hector!" ⏱ 1½ hr. Off the A849, 3 miles from Craignure, Mull. ☎ 01680/812-309. www.duartcastle.com. Admission £5.50 adults, £4.90 seniors & students, £4 kids. Apr–Oct daily 10am–5pm.

From Craignure, take the A849 35 miles to the ferry terminal at Fionnphort, crossing to Iona (sail time: 10 min.). For ferry information, see www.calmac.co.uk.

Map legend:

1. Duart Castle
2. Iona Abbey
3. Staffa
4. Tobermory
5. Kisimul Castle
6. Machair Plains
7. Scarista Beach
8. Stornoway
9. The Black House
10. Dun Carloway
11. Callanish Standing Stones
12. Bernera and Uig
13. Dunvegan Castle
14. The Cuillins
15. Armadale Castle

Where to Stay & Dine

Argyll Hotel 18
Cabarfeidh Hotel 20
Kinloch Lodge 16
Langass Lodge 19
The Three Chimneys 17

Map labels: Butt of Lewis, Port Nis, Laxford Bridge, The Black House, Eddrachillis Bay, Lewis, Dun Carloway, Gt. Bernera, Broad Bay, Pt. of Stoer, Gallan Hd., Stornoway, Assynt, Uig, Eye Pen., Enard Bay, Lochinver, Callanish Standing Stones, Outer Hebrides, ATLANTIC OCEAN, Coigach, Scarp, North Harris, Shiant Is., L. Broom, Ullapool, Taransay, Tarbert, Aultbea, NA H-EILEANAN SIAR, Scarista Beach, South Harris, Scalpay, Poolewe, Braemore, Boreray, Pabbay, Leverburgh, Gairloch, Fionn L., St. Kilda, Berneray, North Uist, Lochmaddy, Uig, Rona, L. Maree, Wester Ross, Torridon, Old Man of Storr, Monach Is., Shieldaig, Achnasheen, Dunvegan Castle, Carbost, Benbecula, Portree, Raasay, Lochcarron, Wiay, Isle of Skye, Scalpay, Kyle of Lochalsh, L. Mullardoch, South Uist, Talisker, HIGHLAND, Sea of the Hebrides, The Cuillins, Broadford, Shiel Bridge, Lochboisdale, Soay, Cuillin Sd., Armadale Castle, Ersikay, Canna, Knoydart, L. Quoich, Barra, Rum, Mallaig, Castlebay, Kisimul Castle, Eigg, Arisaig, Morar L. Morar, L. Eil, Mingulay, Muck, Lochailort, Fort William, Berneray, Inner Hebrides, Ardnamurchan, Lochaber, Onich, Coll, Tobermory, Morvern, Appin, Arinagour, Tiree, Craignure, Scarinish, Ulva, Isle of Mull, Oban, Staffa, Fionnphort, Duart Castle, Iona Abbey, ARGYLL & BUTE

---

2 ★★ Iona Abbey. This spiritual landmark is a significant shrine to the early days of Christianity in Scotland. The settlement was first established in 563 A.D. by St. Columba, a Celtic pilgrim from Ireland who almost single-handedly brought established religion to a pagan land. Crosses laid into the abbey floor mark the graves of several monks, while there are impressive medieval crosses on the grounds. ⏱ 2 hr. ½ mile from Iona pier. ☎ 01681/700-512. www.historic-scotland.gov.uk. Admission £5.50 adults, £4.40 seniors & students, £3.30 kids. Daily 9:30am–5:30pm (Oct–Mar until 4:30pm).

Spend the rest of day relaxing on Iona, and on Day 2 take a cruise boat (1 hr.) from Iona or Mull to

3 ★★ Staffa. The uninhabited 32-hectare (80-acre) Isle of Staffa is a unique attraction in Scotland. Its volcanic origins have left dramatic, vertical rock formations, especially the cathedral-like columns of **Fingal's Cave.** Made of black basalt, the cave is one of the natural wonders of the world and is famous for being the inspiration for Mendelssohn's *Hebrides Overture*. ⏱ At least 2 hr. Staffa cruises: *MB Io-laire* ☎ 01681/700-358. www.staffatrips.co.uk.

> *A boat trip is the only way to view the famous polygonal basalt columns of Fingal's Cave, Staffa.*

> *Colorful Tobermory, where you'll find the only whisky distillery on the Isle of Mull.*

Turus Mara ☎ 088/858-786. www.turus mara.com. Tickets £25 adults, £10–£23 kids. Easter–Sept.

Follow the A848 on Mull past the Craignure ferry port, going north 21 miles to

❹ ★★ kids Tobermory. Brightly painted houses and storefronts in pastel shades of blue, red, and yellow give the largest town on Mull the look of a little Copenhagen and the feel of an Italian fishing village. Tobermory boasts a malt whisky distillery (☎ 01688/302-647 for tours; www.tobermorymalt.com), a great bakery (☎ 01688/302-225), and an excellent fish 'n' chip stall (no phone). Just a mile outside of town the Mull Theatre Company performs (☎ 01688/302-828; www.mulltheatre.com). ⏱ At least 2 hr.

On Day 3, it's back to Oban on the mainland to catch the ferry (sail time: 5 hr.) to Castlebay on the Isle of Barra.

❺ ★ Kisimul Castle. This is the only substantially intact medieval castle in the Western Isles, and is the stronghold of the MacNeils of Barra, whose clan chief in recent years has resided part-time in the U.S. You take a boat to get to the ruins, which are set in the middle of the bay. There are a few rooms reserved for clan business, but you otherwise have freedom to roam through this compact castle. ⏱ 1 hr. ☎ 01871/810-313. www.historic-scotland. gov.uk. Admission £4.70 adults, £3.80 seniors & students, £2.80 kids. Apr–Sept daily.

On Day 4, drive around Barra to the ferry terminal for the 45-min. crossing to Eriskay and South Uist.

❻ ★ Machair Plains. Spend any time on the Western Isles and you'll hear references to the Machair (mac-har). But what is it? This is the flat coastal land amid the dunes. You see it up and down the western fringes of the Outer Hebrides (particularly the Uists), where shell sand has been windblown inland for eons. In the spring, these plains are a riot of wildflowers. Additionally, these fertile lands are often repositories of archaeological finds. ⏱ 1 day.

On Day 5, cross the Uists (p. 598, ❸) for the Berneray to Leverburgh, Harris, ferry (sail time: 1 hr.). About 3 miles northwest of Leverburgh on the A859 is

❼ ★★★ kids Scarista Beach. The hard part is picking the best of the West Harris beaches. This one narrowly edges out nearby Traigh

> *Spring and summer, when a plethora of wildflowers bloom, are the best seasons to visit the machair grasslands of the Uists.*

lar, though others may insist it's the dunes at Hushinish. What makes Scarista the winner? The combination of fine, brilliant sands with equally dazzling clear seas when the sun shines, which may be more often than you think. It may never get hot, but island beaches rarely come any better than this one. ⏲ 2 hr. Btw. Leverburgh & Luskentyre, Harris.

Follow the main Harris–Lewis (A859) road north 53 miles to

❽ **Stornoway.** The capital of the Outer Hebrides is not going to win any top awards for being picturesque, but neither is it as rough and ready as some guides insist. It is a working harbor and active ferry terminal, with good hotels and restaurants, such as **Digby Chick,** 5 Bank St. (☎ 01851/700-026; www.digbychick.co.uk). The cultural center, called **An Lanntair** (the Lighthouse), Kenneth St. (☎ 01851/703-307; www.lanntair.com), has a cafe-bar, art exhibitions, live music shows (there is a lively local scene), and cinema screenings. Additionally, there is the **Western Isles Museum** on Francis St. (☎ 01851/709-266), which is small but free. ⏲ At least 2 hr. Tourist information: 26 Cromwell St., Stornoway, Lewis. ☎ 01851/703-088.

On Day 6, take the A857 north out of Stornoway for 11 miles, then head west on the A858 for about 4 miles to Arnol.

❾ ★★ **The Black House.** Step back a hundred years and see traditional island living. Built in 1885 and occupied until 1964, this "black house" is a classic Hebridean stone, turf, and thatched-roof structure, which served as both home and byre. In the middle of the main room, an open peat fire glows and smolders as smoke drifts up through the thatch. Visitors are free to poke around, and the information center gives more background on a lost way of life. Across the road is the "white house," the more modern cottage built of stone and proper mortar that replaced black houses across Lewis and the Hebrides after 1900. ⏲ 1 hr. Off the A858, Arnol. ☎ 01851/710-395. www.historicscotland.gov.uk. Admission £2.50 adults, £2 seniors & students, £1.50 kids. Mon–Sat 9:30am–6:30pm (Oct–Mar until 4:30pm).

Another 10 miles south on the A858 is

❿ ★★ **Dun Carloway.** This intriguing Iron Age stone ruin is also known as Doune Broch. (A broch (*brok*) was a tower used for defensive purposes and/or as a home.) It is in remarkably sound condition—good enough for you to walk into, at least. Dun Carloway provides some insight into prehistory and was likely a Norse-built structure. ⏲ 1 hr. Off the A858, Carloway. ☎ 01851/643-338. Free admission. Broch: year-round. Visitor Centre: Apr–Sept Mon–Sat 10am–6 pm.

> *Peat was the key Hebridean fuel for centuries, as a visit to the Arnol Black House explains.*

Another 7 miles south on the A858 are the

⑪ ★★★ Callanish Standing Stones. This circle-and cross-shaped formation of large standing stones atop a flat hill by the sea is the most significant archaeological find of its kind in the region—and among the most important in Europe. There's no charge to see the impressive and ragged stones, which were erected sometime around 3000 to 2500 B.C. and were—until the mid–1800s—buried much deeper in the bog on top of the hill. And you can walk right up next to them. There are other sets of standing stones in all directions from Callanish, all part of some prehistoric community. The visitor center has a cafe. ◷ 1 hr. Off the A858, Callanish. ☎ 01851/621-422. Exhibition £2.50 adults, £1.90 seniors & students, £1.20 kids. Visitor Centre: Mon–Sat 10am–9pm (Oct–Mar until 4pm).

On Day 7, from Stornoway, take the A859 south 7 miles, turning west on the A858 for another 7 miles to Garynahine and the B8011 south for 9 miles into

⑫ ★★ Bernera and Uig. The "wild" west side of Lewis merits a detour. This scenic area combines rocky cliffs, steep hills, peatlands, sandy beaches, and a few archaeological attractions. Best of the beaches are probably those at Valtos, in Uig, and Bosta, on the island of Great Bernera. But for tidal sweep, the big beach near Crowlista, Uig, where the famous Lewis (or Norse) Chessmen were found, is tops. Crofting (small holdings) communities are dotted here and there in this region, and many abandoned villages with their black-house ruins can be found. Also at Bosta is a replica Iron Age house based on foundations uncovered at the beach. ◷ At least 2 hr.

Return to the A859, taking it south for 30 miles to Tarbert, Harris. Take the CalMac ferry from Tarbert on Harris to Uig, Isle of Skye. From Uig, follow the A87 10 miles south to the A850 west for 16 miles.

⑬ ★ Dunvegan Castle. The seat of the Macleod of Macleod (chief of the Clan MacLeod of Harris), this is said to be Scotland's oldest castle continually owned and occupied by the same family—going on 800 years now. In addition to antiques, oil paintings, rare books, and clan heirlooms (some dating to the Middle Ages), the legendary Fairy Flag is a relic thought to bring "miraculous powers" to the clan. Also displayed are personal items belonging to Bonnie Prince Charlie, and there's a reasonably creepy dungeon. ◷ 2 hr. Off the A850. ☎ 01470/521-206. www.dunvegancastle.com.

com. Admission £9 adults, £7 seniors & students, £4.50 kids. Apr to mid-Oct daily 10am–5:30pm. Last admission 30 min before closing.

On Day 8, return to A87, going south about 25 miles.

⓮ ★★ **The Cuillins.** These brooding, massive hills—craggy enough to pass for mountains—are a point of pride for the residents of Skye. Considered some of the best climbing and hiking in Scotland, the 900m (3,000-ft.) peaks rise in the south of the island. You might consider spending an afternoon walking amid the spectacular scenery, but if you're inexperienced, inquire about professional guides at the tourist office in Portree (p. 627). ◷ At least 2 hr. South of the A87, btw. Broadford and Sligachan. Trail heads at Glen Brittle, south of Merkadale. For tour information, contact Walkabout Scotland: ☎ 0845/686-1344. www.walkaboutscotland.com.

From Broadford, take the A851 south for about 16 miles.

⓯ ★★ kids **Armadale Castle.** The Armadale estate, on the Sound of Sleat in southern Skye, covers more than 8,000 hectares (20,000 acres). It traditionally belonged to the Clan Donald or Macdonald, known as the Lords of Isles, but is now held in a family trust. The old castle is in ruins, but it still occupies a magnificent spot, with 19th-century woodland gardens, nature trails, and sea views. It isn't difficult to understand the allure of this place. A museum, opened in 2002, is full of information about the historically significant clan, at one time as powerful as Scottish royalty. ◷ 2 hr. Off the A851, north of the ferry terminal. ☎ 01471/844-305. www.clandonald.com. Admission £6.95 adults; £4.95 seniors, students & kids. Apr–Oct daily 9:30am–5:30pm; Nov & Mar Fri 11am–3pm.

Where to Stay & Dine

★ **Argyll Hotel** IONA
This environmentally aware hotel, dedicated to minimizing its impact on the fragile island ecology, was originally built in 1868. Dinner is recommended—not least because the ingredients in your meal are actually grown in the hotel's own organic garden. Near the pier. ☎ 01681/700-334. www.argyllhoteliona.co.uk. 16 units. Doubles from £50 w/breakfast. MC, V. Closed Dec–Feb.

Cabarfeidh Hotel STORNOWAY
This hotel on the fringe of Stornoway's town center has the best, most reliable accommodations in town. After refurbishment, the rooms are excellent, even if the exterior looks rather dated in a late-'60s/early-'70s way. Good meals can be had at the in-house restaurant, Solas. Manor Park, Perceval Rd. S. ☎ 01851/702-604. www.cabarfeidh-hotel.co.uk. 46 units. Doubles £165 w/breakfast. AE, DC, MC, V.

★ **Kinloch Lodge** SKYE SCOTTISH
The matriarch of the house, Lady Claire Macdonald, has become famous in Scottish culinary circles. Expect dishes such as halibut with spinach gnocchi or Scotch beef filet with

port peppercorn sauce. There are bedrooms, too. Off the A851. ☎ 01471/833-333. www.kinloch-lodge.co.uk. 15 units. Doubles from £160 w/dinner & breakfast. Lunch & dinner daily. Set dinner £55. MC, V.

★ **Langass Lodge** NORTH UIST
The Langass is a traditional hunting lodge with a few modern additions such as the bright lounge off the bar, new dining room, and a wing of contemporary accommodations: the "Hillside Rooms," which are larger than those in the main building. Off the A867. ☎ 01876/580-385. langasslodge.co.uk. 11 units. Doubles from £90 w/breakfast. MC, V.

★★ **The Three Chimneys** SKYE MODERN SCOTTISH
This whitewashed shoreside restaurant (with six luxury overnight rooms; £285 double w/breakfast) is arguably the most popular on Skye—and probably the most famous in the Hebrides. Using superb Scottish produce, owners Eddie and Shirley Spear offer top-quality seafood and Highland game dishes from menus that change seasonally. Off the B884, near Dunvegan. ☎ 01470/511-258. www.threechimneys.co.uk. Set dinner £55. Dinner daily. AE, MC, V.

Fast Facts

Arriving & Getting Around

BY PLANE From Edinburgh or Glasgow, franchise carrier **Flybe** (☎ 01871/700-2000, or from outside the U.K. 1392/268-529; www.flybe.com) offers daily flights to Inverness, the Highland "capital." The trip takes about 1 hour. Flybe has flights to Inverness only from Manchester (p. 458), Birmingham (p. 372), and Belfast, Northern Ireland. Flybe also has flights within the Highlands and Islands, linking Inverness, Benbecula (the Uists), and Barra, the southern most of the major outer Hebridean Islands. As yet, there are no commercial flights to the Isle of Skye. For local airport information in Inverness, call ☎ 01667/464-000, or check out www.hial.co.uk. Budget airline **EasyJet** (www.easyjet.com) has flights to Inverness from London and Bristol (p. 288). There are car rental desks at all of the airports. **BY TRAIN** From England, two main rail lines link London (p. 137) to Scotland. One departs King's Cross Station in London to Edinburgh's Waverley Station by way of Newcastle. The others leave Euston Station in London for Glasgow's Central Station. **Scotrail** (☎ 0845/601-5929; www.scotrail.co.uk) has daily service from both Edinburgh and Glasgow to Inverness. Train service within the region varies from frequent to sporadic, which means some branch lines will only have a couple trains per day. There is good access by train to Fort William, Glenfinnan, and Mallaig in the Western Highlands. If you're going to Mull, take the train from Glasgow to Oban. You can also get to the Northwestern Highlands from Inverness, as limited service goes to Plockton and the Kyle of Lochalsh, near Skye. There are no railways on the Hebridean Islands. For more detailed information on rail travel in Scotland, consult Scotrail. **BY BUS** The primary service from Edinburgh and Glasgow north is run by **Scottish CityLink** (☎ 0870/550-5050; www.citylink.co.uk). Stagecoach (☎ 01463/233-371; www.stagecoachbus.com) also runs buses to the Highlands. Small bus companies have contracts for local service on the Highlands and Islands. **Traveline** (☎ 0871/200-2233) offers local bus and rail timetable information, but cannot tell you the costs involved. You will need to phone individual operators for your selected route, whose numbers Traveline can provide. Do note, however, that bus service in the region is only adequate, increasingly expensive, and not really geared to tourists. **BY CAR** Most of the tours in this chapter require a car to complete. If you're driving north to the Highlands, it's fastest to take the A9 via Perth. There are stretches of the A9 that allow passing, but use caution as every year there are many accidents on this road. The slower but more scenic route is via the A82 along Loch Lomond and up through Glencoe, Fort William, and Loch Ness. Note that road signs in the North may be bilingual or sometimes only in Scottish Gaelic when giving names of towns and settlements. Like rural roads anywhere, most will not be lit at night, except within towns. When driving, you will encounter many single-lane roads; use passing places to allow oncoming traffic past and to allow local traffic to overtake you. Local drivers will know every twist and turn, so don't be lured into keeping up with them. **BY FERRY** For boats to the Hebrides, the main points of departure from the mainland are Oban (p. 594, ❹), Mallaig (p. 604, ❾), and Ullapool (p. 617, ❺). Contact **Caledonian MacBrayne** (☎ 0800/066-5000; www.calmac.co.uk) for a full schedule of ferries and up-to-date fare information.

ATMs

Cash machines are not widely available. Expect them only at banks in the towns with ferry terminals.

Emergencies

Call ☎ 999 in an emergency to summon the police, an ambulance, or firefighters. This is a free call. **Western Isles NHS** operates two small hospitals in Castlebay, Barra, and Balavanich, Benbecula. The principal accident and emergency department is at the Western Isles Hospital, Macaulay Road, Stornoway (☎ 01851/704-704). On Skye, the hospital is in Portree (☎ 01470/582-262). **NHS 24** is a telephone service that dispense health information and advice at ☎ 08454/242-424.

Internet Access

High-speed access to the Web is more hit and miss on the islands, though some hotels have good Wi-Fi connections. In Stornoway, Lewis, the public library has several computers with Internet access; the cultural center, An Lanntair, has free Wi-Fi.

Pharmacies

In Stornoway, you'll find a Boots pharmacy at 4 Cromwell St. (☎ 01851/701-769).

Safety

There is very little crime on the islands. Only in Stornoway, Lewis, when the bars close, are there any incidents, and they virtually never involve visitors.

Visitor Information

VisitScotland (www.visitscotland.com) has offices across the region. Some are quite small and only open in the summer (call before you go for opening hours, especially outside of the summer high season). Their local knowledge varies, however, and the organization puts an emphasis on booking accommodations for a £4 fee. **BARRA** The tourist information office is on Main St., Castlebay (☎ 01871/810-336). **DURNESS** The tourist information office is at Village Sq. (☎ 0845/225-5121). **HIGHLAND PERTHSHIRE** The tourist information office in Ballater is at Station Sq. (☎ 01339/755-548); in Braemar, it's on Mar Rd. (☎ 01339/741-600). **INVERARAY** Tourist information is dispensed on Front St. (☎ 018452/255-121). **INVERNESS** Visitor information is available at Castle Wynd (☎ 0145/225-5121). **ISLE OF MULL** Tourist information is available at Craignure ferry pier (☎ 08452/255-121). **ISLE OF SKYE** Touring advice is available on Bayfield Rd. in Portree (☎ 08452/225-121; www.skye.co.uk). **LEWIS AND HARRIS** In Harris, go to Pier Rd., Tarbert (☎ 01859/502-011); in Lewis, you can get visitor information at 26 Cromwell St. (☎ 01851/703-088). **LOCHABER** Tourism information is available at 15 High St., Fort William (☎ 0845/225-5121). **OBAN** The tourist information office is on Argyll Sq. (☎ 01631/563-122; www.oban.org.uk). **TOBERMORY** Tourist

> The "CalMac" car ferry links the Hebrides to the mainland, and many of Scotland's islands with each other.

information is dispensed at the Pier (☎ 0845/225-5121). **THE TROSSACHS** You can get visitor information either on High St. in Crieff (☎ 01764/652-578), or Ancaster Sq. in Callander (☎ 08707/200-628). **THE UISTS** The tourist information office for South Uist is at Pier Rd., Lochboisdale (☎ 01878/700-286); for North Uist, it's on Pier Rd., Lochmaddy, (☎ 01876/500-321). **ULLAPOOL** The tourist information office is at 20 Argyll St. (☎ 0845/225-5121).

Our Favorite South Wales Moments

No people in the islands of Britain keep the Celtic spirit alive as effectively as the Welsh. Centuries as a political and administrative adjunct to England have done nothing to alter the fact that theirs is a country apart, whose jagged coast, harmonious tongue, and bleak, romantic hills seem to reflect its inhabitants' hardy but idealistic nature. The southern half is Wales's heartland, with a redefined, cosmopolitan capital; endless rural and coastal walks; and a growing reputation for delivering the finest produce to the tables in its informal restaurants.

> PREVIOUS PAGE *Even a short walk is rewarded with a dramatic panorama at Three Cliffs Bay, on the Gower Peninsula.* THIS PAGE *Burges's allegorical Victorian Gothic detailing is found throughout Cardiff Castle.*

① **Standing on the 886m (2,907-ft.) peak of Pen y Fan.** The flat-topped summit of South Wales's most varied national park is accessible to anyone with a reasonable degree of fitness and a half-day to spare. The savage beauty of the surrounding moorland is also a great place to spy soaring birds of prey. See p. 650, **③**.

② **Hiking the clifftop trails.** Thanks to the U.K.'s first official Area of Outstanding Natural Beauty (Gower) and its only coastal national park (Pembrokeshire), southwest Wales has some of Britain's best seaside walking. See p. 652; p. 654.

③ **Getting acquainted with William Burges's Victorian Gothic.** Architect Burges was hired

1. Pen y Fan
2. Pembrokeshire coastal path
3. Cardiff Castle
4. Nantyffin Cider Mill Inn
5. Black Mountain
6. Felin Fach Griffin
7. Llanthony Priory
8. St. David's Hotel
9. Pembrokeshire beaches

by the third Marquess of Bute to renovate his private apartments at Cardiff Castle and Castell Coch. Both Bute—who had grown rich on coal and cargo transport—and Burges were intelligent, complex men, and their designs are rich in hidden meaning. See p. 642, **1**; p. 638, **4**.

4 Dining on saltmarsh lamb or Brecon venison. The south's rural restaurants and gastropubs are rapidly establishing Wales as a premier foodie destination—and few better represent that trend than Fairyhill and the Nantyffin Cider Mill Inn. See p. 653; p. 651.

5 Surveying the vast, remote tracts of the Black Mountain. From their 100m (325-ft.) crag southeast of Llandeilo, the lonely ruins of Carreg Cennen overlook mile after mile of empty emerald pasture. It's one of Southern Wales's great panoramas, and there's history in those hills, too. See p. 638, **7**.

6 Swapping walking tales as you browse the evening menu at the Felin Fach Griffin. All sorts prop up the bar here: gastro-tourists on a pilgrimage to one of the Beacons' lauded eateries, long-time locals frequenting their village pub, even literary types who can't find a room any closer to Hay during Festival time. Order a pint and join in. See p. 651.

7 Contemplating the silence and serenity of Llanthony Priory. Nestled in a valley well suited to the quiet religious life, this favorite abbey of 12th-century chronicler Gerald of Wales is the starting point these days for miles of country walks and horseback treks. See p. 648, **1**.

8 Scanning Cardiff Bay from the comfort of the St. David's Hotel. Every room in the capital's flagship spa hotel comes with a view—decide whether you want to look out to Penarth and the sea, or back to the daring bayside architecture. See p. 645.

9 Swapping hiking boots for swimming trunks. Pembrokeshire has the south's best sandy beaches, notably at dramatic, sheltered Barafundle Bay and along the sweeping, surfer-friendly arc of St. Bride's Bay. See p. 655, **3**; p. 656, **5**.

10 Grinning and bearing it as wind and rain sweep through your well-planned hike. No matter when you arrive, it's unlikely you'll escape a sharp shower during your time here. Experienced hands stay safe and warm, but appreciate the thrill of donning waterproofs and boots to plow on through the best the heavens can conjure.

The Best of South Wales in 3 Days

The economic, cultural, and industrial heartland of Wales is both the most populous and most varied part of this country. With such a short time to experience the region, plan (and pack) to spend most of that time outdoors. The hiking in the uplands of the Brecon Beacons and the coastal paths of the Gower can be adapted to fit any ability, age, or stamina level. Cosmopolitan Cardiff could hardly be more different, and offers Gothic Revival architecture and French Impressionism as a cultural counterpoint. Make the city your base and sample the best of the south as day trips from there.

> *The glorious walk out to Worms Head is only possible at low tide.*

START Cardiff. **TRIP LENGTH** 214 miles.

1 ★★ **Cardiff.** Start your morning with a guided tour around the private Bute apartments inside **Cardiff Castle** (p. 642, **1**)—the 45-minute visit is the only way you can enjoy the flair, craftsmanship, and spirituality of the fantastical Gothic Revival renovations designed in the 1870s by architect William Burges. The history of the rest of the castle is told in a short film, after which you're free to wander the fortifications that have been left by multiple generations of inhabitants, including Roman and Norman invaders. Highlights of the **National Museum** (p. 642, **2**), a short walk away, include some of Britain's most significant portrait and landscape painters, as well as one of the world's most important collections of French Impressionism. Bute Park should be your next stop for the Aquabus

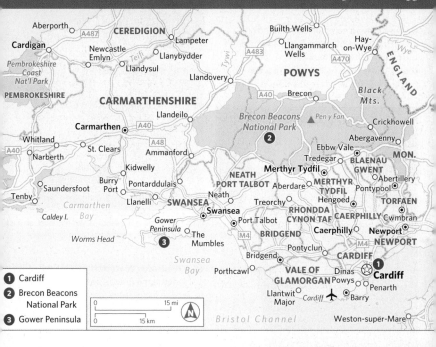

1 Cardiff
2 Brecon Beacons National Park
3 Gower Peninsula

0 ———— 15 mi
0 ———— 15 km

down the River Taff to **Cardiff Bay** (p. 644, **4**). Cardiff was once the most important coal port on the planet—a third of the world's exports started their journey here. The dockside neighborhood, once known as Tiger Bay, fell into disrepair as the industry declined, but was rescued and re-instilled with vibrancy (and, more controversially, renamed) thanks to a massive boardwalk redevelopment. The restaurants and cafes are largely cookie-cutter chain joints, but the architecture is quite the opposite—notably the Senedd building, designed by Lord Richard Rogers, where Wales's devolved government sits. For a cultural end to the evening bayside, buy tickets in advance for the Millennium Centre. The performance could be anything from a children's classic to a top-ranked comedian or a well-known opera. ⏱ 1 day. See p. 642.

More Information

For detailed coverage of sights and recommended hotels and restaurants in **Cardiff,** see p. 645; for the **Brecon Beacons,** see p. 651; for the **Gower Peninsula,** see p. 653.

> *Any external view of Cardiff Castle takes in buildings and architectural elements from a mishmash of styles and eras.*

On Day 2, head north on the A470 from Cardiff, passing Merthyr Tydfil and through the heart of the National Park. A round-trip by car to Brecon and returning via Crickhowell to Cardiff is 95 miles.

> *You'll find the very best of Wales outdoors, so pack your walking gear and some sturdy footwear.*

Drink your Brains

Ask anyone to name a famous Welsh brewer and you'll get the same answer: Brains (www.sabrain.com). This Cardiff institution opened in 1882 and now produces a range of five traditional ales sold in tied pubs, free houses, and bottle shops across Wales. Our favorite is their rich, fruity Rev. James ale, named after the clergyman founder of a brewery Brains bought in the 1990s. Other independent brewers to look out for include Carmarthenshire's Evan Evans (www.evan-evans.com); Felinfoel (www.felinfoel-brewery.com), based in Llanelli; Otley (www.otleybrewing.co.uk) from Pontypridd; and Breconshire (www.breconshirebrewery.co.uk). For a taste of local or seasonal niche ales and microbrews, never be afraid to ask a barman to recommend something or to guide you through what's available on tap.

❷ ★★★ Brecon Beacons National Park. With just a day in the Brecon Beacons you're going to need to make some compromises—you can't see it all. The Park is split into four distinct terrains: the Black Mountain, in the far west, is a verdant, rolling agricultural expanse, while the **Black Mountains** (note the difference of that one crucial letter; p. 648, ❶), closest to England in the east, is a peaceful, rural idyll of narrow valleys and gentle, scenic walks. Sandwiched in between are the Fforest Fawr, designated as a European geopark for its unique geology and waterfall woods; and the jewel of the Park, the Beacons themselves. As long as you're reasonably fit, the moorland peaks of **Corn Du** and **Pen y Fan** (p. 650, ❸) are both accessible in a morning's energetic yomp; park beside the A470 a mile north of the junction with the A4059. These distinctive flat-headed sandstone outcrops form the roof of South Wales—in fact, they are the highest points in southern Britain and favored terrain for birds of prey such as the buzzard, peregrine falcon, and red kite (pack your binoculars). If you've already tackled the classic Beacons walks, contact the Brecon Beacons Park Society (www.breconbeaconsparksociety.org); volunteer enthusiasts guide a varied program of weekend hikes at various locations within the park in return for a £5 per person donation to the Society. All are welcome.

Aside from the outdoors, your other essential appointment in the Beacons is with a plate of food. The distance from field to fork is minimal for Brecon pork, lamb, and venison, and seasonal vegetables populate plates year-round. Reserve your table at either the **Griffin,** in Felin Fach, or the **White Swan,** in Llanfrynach (p. 651), and fill your bellies with creative Welsh dishes before your evening return to Cardiff. ⏱ **1 day.**

On Day 3, take the M4 westbound as far as Swansea, and then follow signs for Gower. The Cardiff–Rhossili–Cardiff round-trip is 121 miles.

⑧ ★★ The Gower Peninsula. There's fine coastal walking along much of the southern edge of this scenic peninsula that hangs from South Wales like a rocky tear. Limited time, however, means you'll have to arrive early, eschew the villages and paths around **Three Cliffs Bay** (p. 652, ❷) and Oxwich Bay, and continue to **Rhossili** (p. 653, ❸). Shod in a decent pair of walking boots, you can head north for the stranded headland known as Burry Holms, across the vast, flat expanse of Rhossili Sands and past the skeletal remains of the Norwegian bark *Helvetia,* sunk in 1887; or alternatively out to Worms Head. The latter is a sphinx-shaped headland that gets its name from the Old English word for dragon, "wyrm," and is home to nesting kittiwakes and a year-round colony of playful seals. For sound advice and a selection of detailed maps and local walking guides, make the National Trust Visitor Centre at Rhossili your first stop. Head back to Cardiff via Reynoldston, stopping at **Cefn Bryn** (p. 653, ❹) to admire the view from the Gower's highest point. ⏱ **1 day.**

What about Pembrokeshire?

With just 3 days to see the best that southern Wales has to offer, you want to spend as little time as possible in transit. Covering Wales's most famous stretch of coastline would involve too much time in the car, and Pembrokeshire requires at least 2 days to cover properly. The coastal walks and noble crags of the Gower Peninsula are both equally spectacular and closer to Cardiff. If you have a week to spend in Wales, see p. 640, ❾; for a longer visit focusing on just Pembrokeshire, see the 3-day tour starting on p. 654.

Welsh: A Language as Well as a People

Like the other Celtic peoples of the British Isles, the Welsh have their own language (known in its native tongue as *Cymraeg*), which you'll see emblazoned on bilingual road signs, written down on visitor information leaflets and websites, and spoken on TV. Unlike many other Celtic languages, Welsh is very much alive: About a fifth of the population speaks Welsh, and it's compulsory to be taught Welsh (although not necessarily *in* Welsh) in state schools. The language's heartland lies along the western half of the country from Carmarthenshire in the south to Anglesey in the north (largely excluding southern Pembrokeshire, "Little England"); the county of Gwynedd has the largest proportion of inhabitants able to speak Welsh, 69 percent at last count.

Although there is no need for you to speak any Welsh as you travel around, the odd word of greeting or thanks when you're in an obviously Cymrophone establishment will certainly elicit a grateful smile, even if you mangle the pronunciation...which you almost certainly will! Watch out, too, when you're navigating for places with different names in the two national languages, some straightforward (Cardiff/*Caerdydd*) and some frankly mystifying to the first-time visitor (Brecon/*Aberhonddu*). Below are a few common words to get you started.

WELSH	PRONUNCIATION	ENGLISH
Bore da	bor-EH dah	Good morning
Nos da	noss dah	Good night
Diolch	dee-OLK	Thank you
Croeso	CROY-so	Welcome
Gorsaf	gor-SAF	Station
Cymru	COME-ree	Wales

The Best of South Wales in 1 Week

Most of the great currents that swept through British history were felt most strongly in the southern half of Wales. The Roman occupation, the rise and dissolution of Roman Catholic religious orders, and centuries of dispute with the English all left behind architectural remnants. The age of iron, the coming of the railways in the 1840s, the coal boom, and the rise of working class consciousness each stamped their more modern mark in the Valleys and along the southern coast. A week crossing the country from England to Pembrokeshire gives you time to sample all this, and leaves enough space in your itinerary to enjoy what Wales does best: the great outdoors.

> Aim to arrive at Tintern Abbey early or late in the day to avoid high-season tour buses.

START Enter Wales from England via the M48 Severn Bridge, 12 miles north of Bristol. Turn north on the A466 immediately after the bridge, and follow the Wye Valley north. **TRIP LENGTH** 388 miles.

1 ★ **Tintern Abbey.** The mini tourism industry that's grown up around Wales's most imposing religious ruin has detracted only slightly from the romance that painter J. M. W. Turner (1775–1851) captured on canvas in the 1790s. The country's first Cistercian abbey was founded by the banks of the River Wye in 1131, and by the early 1300s had grown into a vast monastic complex. Early architectural simplicity was abandoned in favor of the English Gothic or Decorated style, as evidenced by the vast church's skillful tracery. The abbey was suppressed during the Dissolution in 1536, and quickly fell into ruin. However, the Cistercians left a long-lasting impression on their host country: They introduced sheep farming to Wales and are therefore responsible for the best-known 21st-century Welsh export, lamb. ⏱ 1½ hr. Tintern. ☎ 01291/689-251. Admission £3.60 ages 6 & up. Apr–Oct daily 9am–5pm; Nov–Mar Mon–Sat 9:30am–4pm, Sun 11am–4pm.

1. Tintern Abbey
2. Caerleon
3. Brecon Beacons
   National Park
4. Castell Coch
5. Cardiff
6. Gower Peninsula
7. Carreg Cennen Castle
8. Carmarthenshire
9. Pembrokeshire

Where to Stay & Dine

Hurst House on
   the Marsh **10**
Y Polyn **11**

Return to the M48 and follow it and the M4 west as far as Newport, then follow signs to nearby

2 Caerleon. Wales's most important Roman site focuses on the twin delights of the average inhabitant of a garrison town: bathing and savagery. The home of the Second Augustan Legion was once known as Isca, and had 5,000 inhabitants. All would have frequented the **baths,** now excavated and given over to an exposed dig and engaging indoor exhibition about the town. The open-air **amphitheater** once seated 4,000 spectators for the bloody sports of which Romans were so fond. Built in A.D. 90, it measures 56m by 41m (184 ft. x 135

ft.) and was used until the Romans left Britain for good at the beginning of the 5th century. ⏱ 1 hr. Nr. Newport. ☎ 01633/422-518. Free admission. Apr–Oct daily 9:30am–5pm; Nov–Mar Mon–Sat 9:30am–5pm, Sun 11am–4pm.

Proceed to one of our recommended hotels in the Brecon Beacons for a 2-night stay (see p. 651). Trip time is less than 1 hr.

3 ★★★ Brecon Beacons National Park. An extra half-day in South Wales's most extensive national park supplies you with more options than you'd have in a single day (see p. 634, **2**). You have time to combine an assault on the peaks of **Corn Du** and **Pen y Fan** (p. 650, **3**) with some more gentle walking in the remarkable **Waterfall Woods** around Pontneddfechan (p. 650, ⑤) or the rural idyll of the **Black Mountain** around the ruins of Llanthony Priory (p. 648, ①). Alternatively, you could combine two of those walks with your first half-day exploring the preserved industrial heritage around **Blaenavon** (p. 649, ②), en route to the national park's uplands. The small Valleys town is recognized as a UNESCO World Heritage Site for the role it played at the forefront of the Industrial Revolution—first as an iron-producing town and later at the heart of one of the most productive areas of the South Wales coalfield. The scars of centuries of extraction still pepper this unique landscape, but it's 90m (295 ft.) below ground at Big Pit (not, in fact, that deep for a South Wales coal seam) that you really get a sense of the hardships of the Welsh miner's working life. ⏱ 1½ days.

On Day 3, on your way to Cardiff for a 1-night stay, head south down the A470. The distance from Brecon to Castell Coch is 37 miles; central Cardiff is 6 miles further.

④ ★ **Castell Coch.** This turreted neo-Gothic fantasy castle was a collaboration between John Crichton-Stuart (1847–1900), the third Marquess of Bute and a Cardiff coal baron, and his favorite architect and Pugin protégé, William Burges (1827–81). The original "Red Castle" dated to the 13th century, but Burges indulged his own (and his wealthy patron's) peculiarly Victorian tastes in his 1870s "medieval"

restoration. The gilded interior of Lady Bute's bedroom, in particular, owes as much to Moorish influence and playful imagination as to any "Gothic" reality. Despite the magnificent, meticulously-researched decoration of the grand Banqueting Hall and Drawing Room, both patron and guests were rarely ever here. ⏱ 1 hr. Tongwynlais. ☎ 029/2081-0101. Admission £3.60 ages 5 & up. Apr–Oct daily 9am–5pm; Nov–Mar Mon–Sat 9:30am–4pm, Sun 11am–4pm.

⑤ ★★ **Cardiff.** See p. 632, ①.

On Day 4, leave Cardiff via the M4, heading for the Gower Peninsula (62 miles). Check into a Gower hotel (p. 653) for 1 night.

⑥ ★★ **Gower Peninsula.** See p. 635, ③.

On Day 5, return to the M4, then follow it to its western end, where it becomes the A48. Make for Carmarthenshire for the night (about 1 hr. away), stopping en route at

⑦ ★★ kids **Carreg Cennen Castle.** The dramatic setting atop a limestone crag might look impenetrable, but one of the few certain things about Carreg Cennen's history is that it was breached and subsequently torn apart in 1462 during the Wars of the Roses. The Yorkist conquerors left a beautiful ruin, standing like a sentinel over the western fringes of the Black Mountains. Much of what's left today was likely built and used during Edward I's reign in the late 1200s—including the "caves" below ground level that you are free to explore (bring a flashlight). There's a steep 10-minute walk up to the castle from the parking lot, which can get very muddy

> The unique industrial landscape around Blaenavon and Big Pit was designated a UNESCO World Heritage Site in 2000.

> *The gates into and out of the gladiatorial arena are still clearly visible at Caerleon's amphitheater.*

after rainfall. ⏱1 hr. Near Trapp. ☎ 01558/822-291. Admission £3.60. Daily 9:30am–6:30pm (Nov–Mar until 4pm).

8 ★ **Carmarthenshire.** Two very different Carmarthenshire gardens can fill a delightfully greenery-filled afternoon. At **Aberglasney Gardens,** Llangathen (☎ 01558/668-998; www.aberglasney.org; £7), ancient lawns and planting schemes—the gardens date to at least 1477—are arranged formally around historic cloisters and a magnificent house. The technology-filled 200 hectares (500 acres) that make up the **National Botanic Garden of Wales,** Llanarthne (☎ 01558/668-768; www.gardenofwales.org.uk; £8.50) include the Great Glasshouse, a Lord Norman Foster–designed protected environment where thousands of rare plants thrive in a Mediterranean climate. ⏱3½ hr.

Rise early on Day 6 to get a jump start on your final 2 days in southwest Wales. The distance from Carmarthen to St. David's is 46 miles.

> *Plants from six different world zones, including California and Australia, grow inside the Great Glasshouse at the National Botanic Garden.*

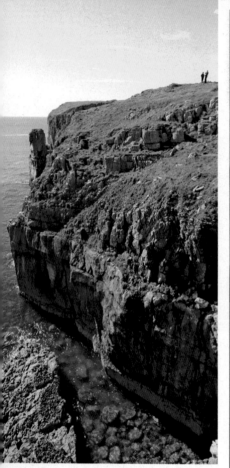

> *The southwest coast of Wales has the best coastal walking in the British Isles.*

Staying the Night in Carmarthenshire

Rolling agricultural plains, birds chirruping in the hedgerows, and relatively few visitors all combine to make Carmarthenshire a peaceful stopover between the more popular attractions of central South Wales and the Pembrokeshire coast. At ★ **Hurst House on the Marsh,** East Marsh (☎ 01994/427-417; www.hurst-house.co.uk), expect a stylish, boutique welcome in converted ancient premises and an idyllic location close to languid, literary Laugharne. Rooms range from £175 to £265, including a hearty Welsh breakfast. Dishes such as filet of organic salmon with sauce vierge and saltmarsh lamb hotpot lift cooking to another level at the wonderfully remote ★ **Y Polyn,** Capel Dewi (☎ 01267/290-000; www.ypolyn restaurant.co.uk). Dine in traditional pub surroundings or on a small summer terrace; entrees cost £11 to £16.

⑨ ★★★ Pembrokeshire. The 258 miles that make up Wales's most famous coast demand at least 2 days of your time. It's not easy to choose the most beautiful stretch, but at **Stackpole** (p. 655, **③**) you'll find classic cliff-top walking around St. Govan's Head plus one of Pembrokeshire's most picturesque beaches, Barafundle Bay. On your second day, visit sites associated with the patron saint of Wales, David, in the tiny cathedral city to which he gave his name (p. 657, **⑥**), leaving time to visit the mysterious stones and landscapes of the **Mynydd Preseli** (p. 658, **⑦**) that overlook Pembrokeshire's northern coast and Cardigan Bay beyond. Leave time to dine at either the **Shed,** in Porthgain (for sublime seafood) or **Cwtch,** in St. David's, for creative, contemporary Welsh fusion cooking; see p. 654. ⏱ 2 days.

Rugby: A National Obsession

In what's probably an apocryphal tale, Wales's national pastime and sporting passion was in fact invented in 1823 by a Lancastrian clergyman, William Webb Ellis (1806–72). He supposedly picked up the ball during a game of "football" (soccer) being played at Rugby School in the English Midlands, and so the sport of "rugby football," more commonly called plain "rugby," was born. Perhaps more credible is the idea that rugby evolved from an obscure medieval sport played in western Wales known as *cnapan*. Whatever its origins, by the end of the 1800s, the sport had become ingrained in the recreational lives of working class communities across the southern half of the country. There's still no more authentic a slice of South Wales life than a trip to watch a match. Rugby union games—there is another code, "rugby league," whose heartland is northern England—involve two teams of 15 players engaged in a seemingly chaotic but in fact highly organized attempt to carry an oval-shaped ball across each other's line, or kick it over and between the opponent's H-shaped posts. The most important rule for the newbie to grasp is that the ball may not be passed (by hand) in a forward direction. It can be kicked or run forward, but must only be passed backward.

The most atmospheric place to see a game is Cardiff's cavernous **Millennium Stadium,** home of the Welsh national team (see p. 643, ❸). The regular "Autumn internationals" series (November) and home matches in the Six Nations tournament in February and March are generally sold out, so purchase well ahead of time. Perhaps more realistic is catching one of the country's professional club teams, who play in a league contested by Celtic sides from Wales, Scotland, and Ireland, as well as two Italian clubs. This 12-team Magners League (www.magnersleague.com) runs from September to May (with a break in November), and matches are usually played on Fridays and Saturdays. The league's most successful team is the **Ospreys** (www.ospreysrugby.com), who play home games at Swansea's Liberty Stadium (☎ 08700/400-004). The **Cardiff Blues** (www.cardiffblues.com) have their HQ in the capital at the Cardiff City Stadium (ticket office ☎ 0845/345-1400). The **Newport Gwent Dragons** (www.newport gwentdragons.com) play at Rodney Parade in Newport (☎ 01633/674-990), and the **Llanelli Scarlets** (www.scarlets.co.uk) at Park y Scarlets on the outskirts of Llanelli (☎ 0871/871-8088). Expect to pay around £20 for an adult ticket, children a little less. Games are split into two 40-minute halves with a break at halftime.

For more on Welsh rugby, visit the Welsh Rugby Union website at www.wru.co.uk.

Cardiff

Two hundred years ago no town in Wales had more than 10,000 inhabitants, but times have changed. This university city steadily grew rich on industry and philanthropy, and in 1955, became the British Isles' youngest capital. Docks that once transported more coal than any on the planet now host a bayside boardwalk. A city center once a byword for decline is home to a thriving Cafe Quarter. In a country famed for its hills and coasts, this is one urban center worth an overnight stay.

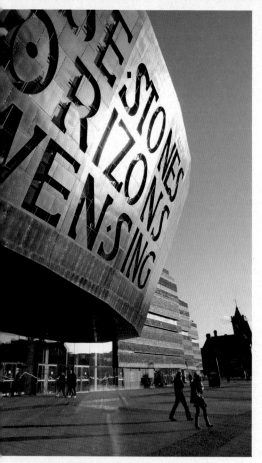

> Opened in 2004, the Millennium Centre is Wales's leading arts venue.

START **Cardiff Castle.** TRIP LENGTH 2 days.

① ★★★ **Cardiff Castle.** There's been a castle on this site since Roman times—the city's name translates as "fort by the Taff"—though the oldest standing part is a moated Norman keep from the 12th century. In the 19th century, the third Marquess of Bute commissioned major figures from the Gothic Revival movement—notably architect William Burges—to transform the interiors into a fairytale medieval masterpiece rich in meaning and symbolism. Many highlights, including Burges's Winter Smoking Room, decorated on a theme of time and the Zodiac; his Arab Room, inspired by the Cappella Palatina of Sicily's Palazzo Reale; and an extraordinary nursery handpainted by H. W. Lonsdale (1844–1919), can only be viewed on the must-do 45-minute premium tour. ⏱ 2 hr. Castle St. ☎ 029/2087-8100. www.cardiffcastle.com. Admission £11 adults (£14 with premium tour); £8.50 kids 5–16. Daily 9am–5pm (Nov–Feb until 4pm). Bus: 6, 27, 28, 52, or 58.

② ★★ **National Museum Cardiff.** Founded in 1907, the country's national collection showcases some of Britain's most significant painters, as well as art from the workshops of grand Europeans (El Greco and Botticelli included). The dignified

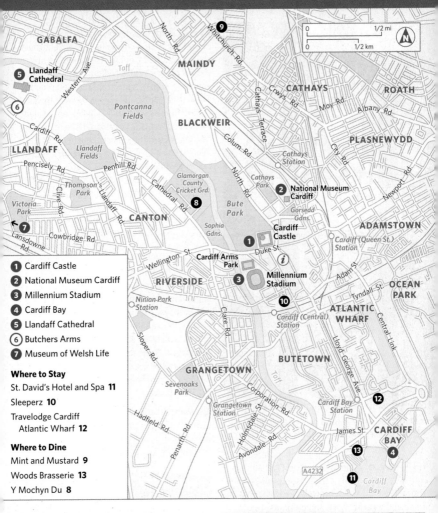

1. Cardiff Castle
2. National Museum Cardiff
3. Millennium Stadium
4. Cardiff Bay
5. Llandaff Cathedral
6. Butchers Arms
7. Museum of Welsh Life

Where to Stay

St. David's Hotel and Spa **11**

Sleeperz **10**

Travelodge Cardiff
   Atlantic Wharf **12**

Where to Dine

Mint and Mustard **9**

Woods Brasserie **13**

Y Mochyn Du **8**

18th-century portraits of Sir Joshua Reynolds and Thomas Gainsborough share wall space with Pre-Raphaelites Dante Gabriel Rossetti, Edward Burne-Jones, and Ford Madox Brown. L. S. Lowry's *Abertillery* industrial landscape from the 1960s is a notable modern work. The museum is also home to one of the world's great Impressionism collections, which includes works by Degas, Monet, and Renoir. ⏱1 hr. Cathays Park. ☎ 029/2039-7951. www.museumwales.ac.uk/cardiff. Free admission. Tues–Sun 10am–5pm. Bus: 6, 27, 35, 53, or 86.

③ ★ Millennium Stadium. No need to check whether it's match day at the home of Welsh

> The vivid detailing designed by William Burges for both Cardiff Castle and Castell Coch mix Christian and pagan symbolism.

> *Behind the ornate stained glass of Llandaff Cathedral lies one of Britain's oldest places of Christian worship.*

4 ★★ **Cardiff Bay.** The Aquabus docks at a boardwalk lined with quality if unadventurous chain restaurants, but it's the sweeping bronze shell of the ★★ **Wales Millennium Centre** that anchors Cardiff's waterfront redevelopment. The "Armadillo" is the engine room of the city's high-culture scene, hosting ballet, opera, dance, popular shows, and occasional free recitals in the lobby. Cardiff Bay is also the home of the Welsh Assembly, or the ★★ **Senedd,** a glass building with an undulating canopy designed by Lord Richard Rogers and inaugurated in 2006. To see Welsh democracy in action, you can usually turn up unannounced and take a seat in the Siambr (debating chamber) public gallery. When parliament isn't sitting (Fri–Mon usually), free all-access tours run three times daily. School-age children might prefer **Techniquest** (☎ 029/2047-5475; www.techniquest.org; £7 adults, £5 kids 4–16), a discovery center where hands-on science exhibits are supplemented by fun shows and demonstrations. ⏱ At least 1 hr. www.visitcardiffbay.info. Wales Millennium Centre: Bute Place. ☎ 029/2063-6464. www.wmc.org.uk. Senedd: ☎ 0845/010-5678. www.assemblywales.org/sen-home. Check the website for most current hours. Train: Cardiff Bay. Bus: 8, 35, 36, or Baycar.

5 **Llandaff Cathedral.** This former village of Llandaff still has a rural feel, despite having been wholly swallowed by Cardiff's suburbs. Its cathedral occupies one of Britain's oldest

rugby—the city becomes a sea of red jerseys and a cacophony of patriotic songs a few Saturdays each year. (Book well ahead if you want to attend a game: www.millenniumstadium.com/tickets.) On non-match days, you can tour this impressive stadium (opened in 1999) known for its canyon-like acoustics. A behind-the-scenes guided tour includes the dressing rooms and royal box, and best of all, takes you out to the pitch via the player's tunnel accompanied by the recorded sound of 74,500 hollering fans. ⏱ 1 hr. Westgate St. ☎ 029/2082-2228. www.millenniumstadium.com/tours. Tour £6.50. Mon–Sat 10am–5pm; Sun 10am–4pm. Bus: 11, 27, 28, 52, or 58.

From Bute Park, ride the Aquabus (www.aquabus.co.uk; £5 round-trip; hourly) to Mermaid Quay.

Cardiff After Dark

It's nothing special to look at, but the **Cayo Arms,** 36 Cathedral Rd. (☎ 029/2039-1910; www.cayoarmspub.co.uk), has quality real ales on tap. Funkier **Gwdihŵ,** 6 Guildford Crescent (☎ 029/2039-7933; www.gwdihw.co.uk), has shabby chic done just-so, with a young clientele and a decent cocktail list. You'll find the city's best high culture courtesy of the **Welsh National Opera,** headquartered at Cardiff Bay's Millennium Centre (☎ 029/2063-6464; www.wmc.org.uk). **Clwb Ifor Bach,** 11 Womanby St. (☎ 029/2023-2199; www.clwb.net), is the legendary home of Wales's mighty alt-rock scene, and stages something musical (often live) most nights on its three floors.

Christian sites and sports a 13th-century Lady Chapel that's largely escaped the remodeling and wartime destruction that befell the rest of the building. The *Seed of David* triptych (1858–64) by Pre-Raphaelite painter Dante Gabriel Rossetti (1828–82), no longer used as an altarpiece, is housed on the left of the main door. ⏱ 1 hr. Cathedral Close, Llandaff. No phone. Free admission. Mon–Sat 10am–4pm. Bus: 25, 33, or 62.

⑥ 🍺 **Butchers Arms.** For nearby sustenance, this pub remains a proper "local," where friendly residents chew over neighborhood news and enjoy authentic real ales. 16 High St. ☎ 029/2055-1000. Items £2–£7.

⑦ ★ kids **Museum of Welsh Life.** Laid out in the style of an "open-air museum," this popular family attraction features such former staples of rural Welsh life as a cockpit built for the (now illegal) sport of cockfighting, a roadside tollhouse built in the 1770s, and a Workmen's Institute of a kind that used to be the focal point of working class communities across the U.K. Each structure was dismantled and rebuilt in this 40-hectare (100-acre) parkland site presided over by **St. Fagan's Castle,** an Elizabethan manor dating from 1580. You're free to picnic, but avoid summer weekends if you prefer peace and quiet. ⏱ At least 2 hr. St. Fagan's. ☎ 029/2057-3500. www.museum wales.ac.uk/stfagans. Free admission. Daily 10am–5pm. Bus: 32.

Where to Stay & Dine

★★ **Mint and Mustard** CATHAYS *KERALAN INDIAN* Skillful combinations of southern Indian spices have won this neighborhood joint countless cooking awards. Monkfish, prawns, and bream are specialties, but there's plenty of choice for meat-lovers and vegetarians. 134 Whitchurch Rd. ☎ 029/2062-0333. www.mintandmustard.com. Reservations essential. Entrees £5.95–£13. AE, MC, V. Dinner daily.

★★ **St. David's Hotel and Spa** CARDIFF BAY A soaring Guggenheim-style lobby is the prelude to sleek, Scandinavian-influenced guestrooms at Cardiff Bay's flagship hotel. Rooms, especially bathrooms, aren't large, but each comes with a balcony and an unimpeded bay view. Havannah St. ☎ 029/2045-4045. www.thestdavidshotel.com. 132 units. Doubles £99–£219 w/breakfast. AE, MC, V.

★★ **Sleeperz** CITY CENTER Industrial-boutique chic comes with an affordable price tag at this fresh arrival smack in Cardiff's Cafe Quarter. Double rooms are compact, designer wood and glass affairs with ensuite wetrooms (has open showers); twin rooms are cabin-bunk style with top-floor skyline views. Station Approach, Saunders Rd. ☎ 029/2047-8747. www.sleeperz.com. 74 units. Doubles £55–£85. AE, MC, V.

Travelodge Cardiff Atlantic Wharf CARDIFF BAY Where fashionable designer budget joints in town disappoint, this reliable chain offers knockout quality and value. Decor is plain and boxy, but rooms are spacious, spotless, and, if you book online at least 21 days ahead, available at incredible discount rates. Atlantic Wharf Leisure Park. ☎ 0871/984-6424. www.travelodge.co.uk. 112 units. Doubles £19–£99. AE, MC, V.

★ **Woods Brasserie** CARDIFF BAY *MODERN EUROPEAN* Crisp, modern decor complements clean flavors at the Bay's most refined dining experience. There's always plenty of fish, and in the evening a grill that specializes in cuts of local grass-fed beef. Pilotage Building, Stuart St. ☎ 029/2049-2400. www.woods-brasserie.com. Entrees £12–£27. MC, V. Lunch daily; dinner Mon–Sat.

Y Mochyn Du PONTCANNA *TRADITIONAL WELSH* Stick to the home-cooked light bites at this no-frills, sports-themed pub-restaurant with garden seating. Welsh rarebit (cheese, onion, and bacon on toast) or cawl (lamb and vegetable soup-stew) make filling lunches for under £5. Sophia Close. ☎ 029/2037-1599. Entrees £6.25–£13. MC, V. Lunch & dinner daily.

BRITISH CASTLES

Landmarks of Medieval Life **BY STEPHEN BREWER**

POPULARIZED BY THE NORMANS IN THE EARLY MIDDLE AGES, castles have been a fixture on the British landscape for nearly a thousand years. These walled compounds were home to nobles and knights and defended borders, towns, trade routes, and parcels of land. A moat (either dry or filled with water), a bailey (an enclosure surrounded by walls), and a keep (a fortified tower) helped ensure the safety of residents, who launched counterattacks against assailants from battlements and towers equipped with arrow slits and crenellations. By the 16th century, advanced artillery rendered most castles defenseless and obsolete, but hundreds of these walled and turreted landmarks still stand today. Some have crumbled into romantic ruin; others house royalty and the gentry. Many evoke storybook romance, while others illustrate the harsh realities of warfare and feudal life. All are beloved emblems of British history and culture.

Medieval Castle Life

Heating a mammoth castle was no easy feat, and the need to provide warmth often dictated a castle's structure. In the early Middle Ages, castle life centered around the Great Hall, where the lord, lady, and a retinue of servants and retainers ate and slept around a central hearth beneath a hole in the ceiling. Fireplaces eventually replaced the central hearth, providing greater warmth and allowing inhabitants to branch out into private quarters that became more elaborate with the passing centuries.

WARWICK CASTLE

Saxon Princess Aethelflaed built a rampart high above the River Avon in 914 to repel invading Danes, and over the next 10 centuries, it morphed into a castle that has served the Earls of Warwick as a prison, fortification, and lavish country house. Today, the Great Hall, dungeons, towers, and gardens are enlivened by jousting tournaments, ghost hunts, and other events. See p. 342, ➋.

WINDSOR CASTLE

Built by William the Conqueror to protect a stretch of the Thames near London, this imposing palace-fortress is the oldest continuously occupied castle in Europe, and the favorite retreat of Queen Elizabeth II The staterooms are spectacular, and St. George's Chapel is the resting place of 10 monarchs. See p. 134, ➋.

CAERLAVEROCK CASTLE

Britain's only triangular castle, built in Scotland around 1270, is surrounded by two moats, thick walls, and sturdy towers. But these defenses were not enough to stave off frequent English attacks, and much of the castle today is an evocative ruin. See p. 548, ➎.

DOVER CASTLE

Set atop the strategically important White Cliffs, this mostly medieval castle is England's largest. Henry II added the rings of formidable walls and a massive keep that since the 12th century have made Dover the mightiest in the land. And Dover hasn't lost its luster over the years—it served Britain as recently as World War II as a military command center and underground hospital. See p. 162, ➊.

CONWY CASTLE

Edward I built Conwy in the late 13th century atop a rocky Welsh promontory to help defend his newly acquired Principality of Wales. The king introduced arrow slits and other innovations he came across during the Crusades and employed more than 1,500 laborers on what remains one of Britain's most imposing fortifications. See p. 686, ➊.

The Brecon Beacons

The 520 square miles of Brecon Beacons National Park enclose a landscape of glacier-hewn sandstone uplands, hidden waterfalls, vast limestone caves, and timeworn historic ruins. Sandwiched between the industrial heartland of the Valleys and the emptiness of Mid-Wales, it's varied terrain for hikers, cyclists, and anyone who loves rural peace, scenic drives, and well-kept market towns—as well as home to some of Wales's best dining opportunities. The most efficient accommodation strategy is to pick a base and then see the park on a series of day trips.

> *The woods around Ystradfellte are great for quiet walks—or even some wild swimming in the waterfall plunge pools.*

START Brecon, 43 miles north of Cardiff.
TRIP LENGTH 3 days.

1 ★★ **The Black Mountains.** The easternmost valley of these agricultural hills is the setting for the 12th-century ruins of **Llanthony Priory.** Although the Augustinian priory has been a roofless ruin for centuries, the great Gothic nave arcades and solid stones of the transepts and chapterhouse are intact, giving the site a sense of noble, romantic disrepair. Llanthony is also a jumping-off point for walking or horseback riding (☎ 01873/890-359;

www.llanthony.co.uk) in an idyllic rural setting. There are more fine walks beyond the village of **Llanbedr,** north of Crickhowell. Follow a road from Llanthony lined with towering hedgerows that leads past **Partrishow Church.** This ancient and isolated parish church has one of the few carved-oak rood screens to escape the iconoclasm of the Protestant Reformation and English Civil War years. ⏱ 3 hr. Llanthony Priory: Free admission. Daily 10am–4pm. Partrishow Church: Free admission. Daily during daylight hours.

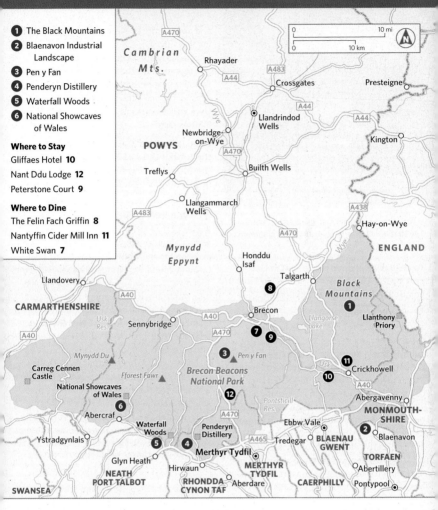

1. The Black Mountains
2. Blaenavon Industrial Landscape
3. Pen y Fan
4. Penderyn Distillery
5. Waterfall Woods
6. National Showcase of Wales

Where to Stay

Gliffaes Hotel **10**
Nant Ddu Lodge **12**
Peterstone Court **9**

Where to Dine

The Felin Fach Griffin **8**
Nantyffin Cider Mill Inn **11**
White Swan **7**

Rejoin the A40 at Crickhowell, and then make for Blaenavon via the A4077 and B4246. Total distance is 11 miles.

2 ★ kids Blaenavon Industrial Landscape. By the height of the Industrial Revolution, when a third of the world's coal exports were dug from the ground under South Wales, this former hamlet had become an economic powerhouse. At Big Pit, now the **National Coal Museum,** you can don hard hat and headlamp and descend in original cage lifts to the mine 90m (295 ft.) below, as part of a 1-hr. underground guided tour led by former miners. Built in 1788, **Blaenavon Ironworks** dates to the era before coal became king. This uniquely preserved complex includes Stack Square, tiny terrace houses where key ironworkers were housed…almost close enough to the blast furnaces to burn their toast. The traditional Valleys town and mine-scarred surrounds is now a UNESCO World Heritage Site. ⏱ 2 hr. Heritage Information Centre: ☎ 01495/742-333. www.visitblaenavon.co.uk. Free admission. Big Pit: Daily Feb–Nov 10am–3:30pm; Dec–Jan shorter hours. Ironworks: Apr–Oct daily 10am–5pm; Nov–Mar Fri–Sat 9:30am–4pm, Sun 11am–4pm.

> *The Morgan brothers first explored the weird formations of Dan-yr-Ogof by candlelight in 1912.*

To begin Day 2, drive to the Pont ar Daf parking lot, 1 mile north of the A470/A4059 junction and 9 miles south of Brecon.

③ ★★★ Pen y Fan. The Park's most famous summit marks the peak of some fine hiking. The sandstone crags, or "Beacons," were carved out by glaciers during the last Ice Age and lend the park their name. The classic ascent heads across open moor to flat-topped Corn Du (873m/2,864 ft.) and from there along a well-worn ridge to Pen y Fan, at 886m (2,907 ft.) the highest point of the Beacons, with sweeping panoramas that stretch to Snowdonia and into England. Bird-watchers should look out for such moorland residents as the once almost extinct red kite or the peregrine falcon, Britain's fastest bird, which can reach speeds of 200 mph while in a dive. With a good map or guide, you can hike these highlands for hours—one alternate, comfortable route back heads from Corn Du down to the Storey Arms just north of the parking lot. ⏱ At least 3 hr.

On Day 3 head for Penderyn, 17 miles southwest of Brecon via the A470 and A4059.

④ Penderyn Distillery. The unmistakable aroma of malt permeates the roadside headquarters and shop of Wales's only whisky distiller. The long history of whisky in Wales (which includes Welshmen helping to establish a similar industry in Kentucky) ended in the 1900s, and domestic Welsh whisky was no more. Penderyn revived traditions in 2004 and now produces three prized malts, including their flagship Aur Cymru (Welsh gold), finished in Madeira barrels. The informative tour includes the chance to sample two Penderyn expressions. Book ahead in high season. ⏱ 1 hr. Penderyn. ☎ 01685/810-651. www.welsh-whisky.co.uk. Tour £5 adults. Daily 9.30am–5pm.

Head to Pontneddfechan, 8 miles away via the A4059 and A465. Park when you see the Angel Inn. The Waterfalls Centre, which dispenses advice and maps (£1), is opposite the pub.

⑤ ★ Waterfall Woods. The lush ash and oak woods of the Fforest Fawr grow on top of some unique geology that makes the area rich in cascades and waterfalls. The **Elidir Trail** (around 2 hr.) links Pontneddfechan with Pont Melin-fach, following the Nedd Fechan past four waterfalls; if you're more time-pressed, a 90-minute round-trip veers off at the confluence with the Pyrddin to **Sgwd Gwladys,** an impressive, high-shelved fall that plunges into an accessible pool deep enough to swim in. Longer walks, from further up the valley toward Ystradfellte, take in **Sgwd yr Eira,** which has an overhang so pronounced that you can walk behind it. Each walk follows a well-trodden trail but still requires sturdy waterproof footwear that grips; don't attempt any walk here with kids under 8. ⏱ At least 1½ hr. Waterfalls Centre: ☎ 01639/721-796. www.fforestfawrgeopark.org.uk. Free admission.

Head back to Glyn-Neath and follow the A4109 north. Total distance is 10 miles.

⑥ ★ kids National Showcaves of Wales. Despite some tacky commercialism bolted on, it's impossible not to be astounded by the contorted formations that populate this vast underground cave complex. Meandering, magnificent **Dan-yr-Ogof** was built by millennia of water dripping through porous limestone, but remained undiscovered until the Morgan

Living It Up

Brecon and its environs are home to some of Wales's, and Britain's, best loved **festivals.** For more information on the annual offerings, see p. 661.

brothers spelunked here in 1912. **Cathedral Cave** is shorter on surreal rocks but impressive in scale, with indoor waterfalls and the so-called Dome of St. Paul's (also a licensed wedding venue). We could have lived without the scale-model plastic dinosaurs schmaltzing about the place, but our 9-year-old companion didn't concur. The onsite cafe is expensive, so pack a picnic. ⏱ 2 hr. Near Glyntawe. ☎ 01639/730-284. www.showcaves.co.uk. Admission £14 adults, £7 kids 3–16. Apr–Oct daily 10am–3pm.

Travel Tip

If you're a Beacons novice, head first to the **Mountain Centre,** Libanus (☎ 01874/623-366), signposted off the A470, 5 miles south of Brecon. The staff dispenses valuable advice, and the shop sells Ordnance Survey maps OL12 and OL13, which provide a good basis for exploring the Beacons in more depth. Daily hours are 9:30am to 4:30pm (until 5pm in summer).

Where to Stay & Dine

★★★ **The Felin Fach Griffin** BRECON *CREATIVE WELSH* Serious cooking without the dress code is the hallmark of this local gastronomic phenomenon. The changing daily menu always includes cuts of local meat and produce from the organic garden, combined with flair. Felin Fach. ☎ 01874/620-111. www.felinfach griffin.co.uk. Entrees £9.50–£18. MC, V. Lunch & dinner daily.

★ **Gliffaes Hotel** USK VALLEY
This genteel country manor deep in the woods delivers old-fashioned grandeur, total seclusion, and only slightly (yet nobly) faded luxury. Trout fishing packages on the adjacent River Usk are recommended. Near Crickhowell. ☎ 01874/730-371. www.gliffaeshotel.com. 23 units. Doubles £99–£238 w/breakfast. MC, V.

Nant Ddu Lodge BEACONS
A modernized roadside hotel with an indoor pool and spa in the heart of walking country. Superior rooms (ask for a river view) with queen beds and more space are easily worth the extra £10. Cwm Taf, near Merthyr Tydfil. ☎ 01685/379-111. www.nant-ddu-lodge.co.uk. 31 units. Doubles £90–£125 w/breakfast. MC, V.

★★ **Nantyffin Cider Mill Inn** USK VALLEY *MODERN WELSH* The bar at this pink-brick former drover's inn is open every day; weekends and holidays see the opening of a more formal barn restaurant annex. Menus in both change every month but usually include fish smoked in-house and sensational pork and gammon. Brecon Rd., near Crickhowell. ☎ 01873/810-775. www.cidermill.co.uk. Entrees £10–£19. AE, MC, V. Lunch & dinner Tues–Sun.

> *The refined public rooms at Peterstone Court.*

★★ **Peterstone Court** USK VALLEY
Large Georgian rooms and public areas retain the decor and feel of this rural hotel's former life as a country manor. Rooms at the back have dramatic views of the national park. Llanhamlach, near Brecon. ☎ 01874/665-387. www.peterstone-court.com. 12 units. Doubles £110–£220 w/breakfast. AE, MC, V.

★★ **White Swan** NEAR BRECON *MODERN WELSH*
Traditional beamed ceilings, flagstone floors, and a menu stuffed with local ingredients like Brecon venison. Lunchtime dishes are a quality twist on pub favorites, and the cooking refinement heads up a notch at dinner. No kids on Friday or Saturday night. Llanfrynach. ☎ 01874/665-276. www.the-white-swan.com. Entrees £15–£17. AE, MC, V. Lunch & dinner Wed–Sun.

The Gower Peninsula

Designated Britain's first official Area of Outstanding

Natural Beauty in 1956, the Gower (Gŵyr in Welsh) is famed for its spectacular coastal paths and expansive horseshoe bays. The sea-facing southern fringe is a land of bleak cliffs, hidden coves, and ruined castles—and made a superb smuggling base in centuries past. Avoid summer weekends, when traffic along the A4118 can be busy.

> Although not as extensive as those in Pembrokeshire, the clifftop trails of the Gower are easier to reach from Cardiff or Swansea.

START Swansea, 41 miles west of Cardiff.
TRIP LENGTH 37 miles round-trip from Swansea.

1 Swansea. Wartime bombing scarred much of Wales's second city, but the revamped Marina Quarter rewards a short visit. Fans of the city's great poet, Dylan Thomas (1914–53), shouldn't miss the **Dylan Thomas Centre** for an exhibition that explains what makes his verse so special. Wales historically looked seaward for riches, and a highlight of the nearby **National Waterfront Museum** are scale models of various great ships that have graced its docks. ⏲ 2 hr. Dylan Thomas Centre: Somerset Place. ☎ 01792/463-980. Free admission. Tues–Sun 10am–4:30pm. National Waterfront Museum: Oystermouth Rd. ☎ 01792/638-950. www.museumwales. ac.uk. Free admission. Daily 10am–5pm.

Leave the city via Mumbles Rd. before turning west on the B4336 toward the village of Southgate.

2 ★★ Three Cliffs Bay. A gentle walk along the clifftop from the village parking lot ends in a view of this sweeping stretch of flat sand, as well as Oxwich beyond and England's Devon coast on a good day. It's a great vantage point from which to snap the rock monoliths that gave the bay its name. Look out for a chough, a red-orange beaked member of the crow family driven close to extinction and now being reintroduced to Pennard Cliffs. The walk toward Penmaen is a pretty way to extend a hike. ⏲ At least 1 hr.

Head back to the B4436, then west on the A4118; follow the B4247 as far as it goes.

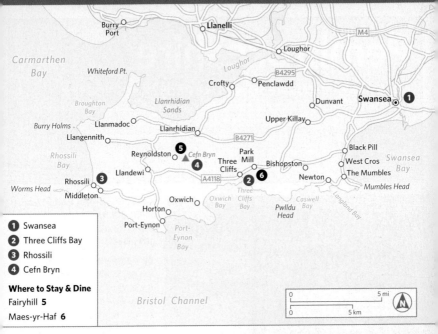

Map legend:

1. Swansea
2. Three Cliffs Bay
3. Rhossili
4. Cefn Bryn

Where to Stay & Dine

Fairyhill **5**

Maes-yr-Haf **6**

3 ★★★ **Rhossili.** The furthest reach of Gower is this rugged place, where the few trees still standing are bowed by the prevailing south-westerly wind. The most rewarding walk takes you to Worms Head, a 3-hour round-trip that passes a seal colony of 30 or so (pups appear in October). Check tide times at the Visitor Centre, because the Head is only accessible around low tide and requires sturdy footwear. An alternative trek heads north on Rhos-sili Sands to Burry Holms, with photogenic views back to the sphinx-shaped headland and an outside chance of spotting bottlenose dolphins in the bay. A full day-hike takes the southern path to the cove at Port Eynon. Essentially, you can cover as much or as little terrain as you like. ☉ At least 1 hr. National Trust Visitor Centre: ☎ 01792/390-707. www.nationaltrust.org.uk. Free admission (parking £2).

Head back with a detour to Reynoldston, 4 miles northeast of Rhossili.

4 ★ **Cefn Bryn.** Gower's highest point—and site of a giant boulder known as "King Arthur's Stone"—looks over the Llanrhidian salt marshes and Carmarthenshire beyond the estuary. ☉ 30 min.

Staying the Night in the Gower

You'll be able to plan longer walks if you stay here overnight. From the snug bar and piano lounge to the individually decorated guest rooms, everything at ★★ **Fairyhill,** Reynoldston (☎ 01992/390-139; www.fairyhill.net), screams understated exclusivity. Doubles cost £175 to £275 including breakfast. A 3-course set lunch costs £20 in its award-winning creative Welsh restaurant. The kitchen at ★ **Maes-yr-Haf,** Parkmill (☎ 01792/371-000; www.maes-yr-haf.com), also keeps faithful to a local, seasonal, creative mantra. Entrees range from £11 to £25.

Pembrokeshire

Millennia of exposure to wild westerly winds and the currents of the Atlantic Ocean have cut the southwestern fringe of Wales into a jagged, scenic silhouette. As a result, Pembrokeshire has Britain's only coastal national park and its most famous coastal path—as well as sandy coves and surf to rival anything in the British Isles. It's also the place most associated with the country's spiritual patron, St. David.

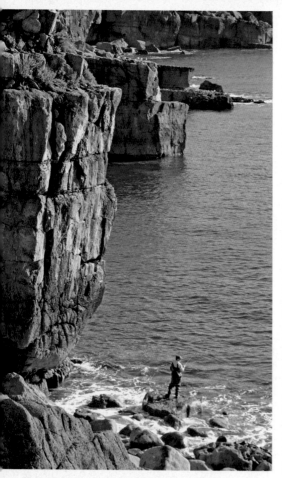

> The Pembrokeshire coastal path stretches for 186 miles along one of Europe's most dramatic coastlines.

START Pembroke, 97 miles west of Cardiff. **TRIP LENGTH** 3–4 days. Total distance traveled is 101 miles.

❶ ★ kids Pembroke Castle. Since the day it was erected in 1093, the mighty Norman fortress of successive Earls of Pembroke has proven impregnable. The intact ring of walls encloses a Norman keep constructed around 1200 with a unique domed roof, and withstood two separate sieges during the Civil Wars (in 1644 by Royalists and in 1648 by Parliamentarians) before being put beyond use by Cromwell's victorious government forces. Most illustrious of the sons born here was Henry Tudor, later King Henry VII (1457–1509), who landed at nearby Dale Beach on his way to decisive victory at the Battle of Bosworth Field in 1485. The vast sands at **Freshwater West,** 8 miles west, are a favorite of Hollywood producers (*Robin Hood* and *Harry Potter* were recent visitors) and surfers. ⏱ 1½ hr. Pembroke. ☎ 01646/684-585. www.pembrokecastle.co.uk. Admission £5.25 adults, £4.25 kids (guided tour additional £1). Daily Apr–Sep 9:30am–6pm; Mar & Oct 10am–5pm; Nov–Feb 10am–4pm.

Head 4 miles northwest to Angle.

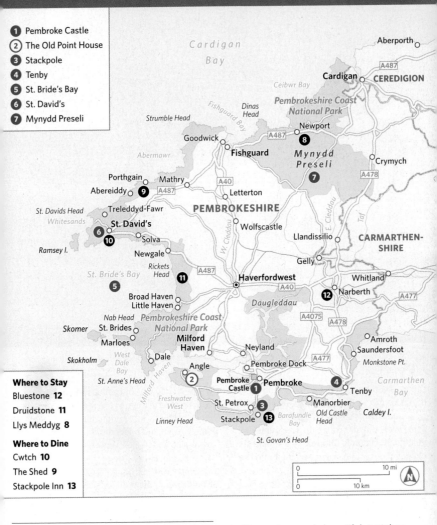

1 Pembroke Castle
2 The Old Point House
3 Stackpole
4 Tenby
5 St. Bride's Bay
6 St. David's
7 Mynydd Preseli

Where to Stay
Bluestone **12**
Druidstone **11**
Llys Meddyg **8**

Where to Dine
Cwtch **10**
The Shed **9**
Stackpole Inn **13**

---

② 🍽 ★ **The Old Point House.** Pub classics such as fish chowder and pints of prawns with Marie Rose sauce are prepared freshly on the premises and delivered in hearty portions at this headland lifeboatmen's inn. East Angle Bay. ☎ 01646/641-205. Items £2–£9. MC, V. Lunch & dinner daily. Closed Tues in winter.

Return to Freshwater West, then take the B4319 past Castlemartin to the turning for Bosherston. Total distance is 11 miles.

③ ★★★ **Stackpole.** The former estates of the Cawdor family provide access to one of the coast's most savagely beautiful stretches. Backed by dunes and rolling gently into turquoise water, **Barafundle Bay** is perhaps Pembrokeshire's most idyllic beach. Reach it by a well-trodden 15-minute walk from Stackpole Quay. Lakes created from a tidal creek as part of Stackpole Estate's landscaping between 1782 and 1850 are now known as the **Bosherston Lily Ponds.** The interconnected pools are carpeted with thousands of water lily pads (that flower in early summer), and are home to wild sea otters. From here it's an easy ¾-mile walk through lakeside woods to **Broadhaven South Beach,** another glorious cove with flat

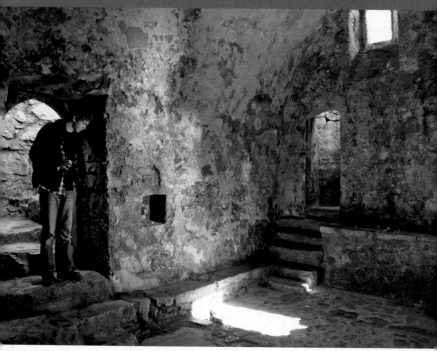

> Eerie St. Govan's Chapel, wedged into the cliff near Stackpole, is reached by a path accessible to any sure-footed visitor.

sands. Another easy hike (1 mile) from here brings you to St. Govan's Head, where winds howl and sheer sea cliffs drop into boiling seas. Walk down through an accessible cliff gully to **St. Govan's Chapel.** This simple stone chapel of uncertain origin was built into the cliffs sometime during the medieval period. If you don't fancy the walk, you can drive round and park right above. ☉ At least 3 hr. ☎ 01646/661-359. Free admission.

Return to Pembroke, then follow the A4139 east. Total distance is 16 miles.

④ ★ **Tenby.** With its undistinguished B&B accommodation, rock-and-fudge shops and peak-season crowds, this seaside town initially seems miles away from the place that inspired George Eliot (1819–80) to pick up a quill. However, a stroll inside the ring of 13th-century walls and down Georgian **St. Julian Street** to the pastel-painted harborside facades soon transports you back to an earlier era in the life of a once-genteel Victorian resort. The **Tudor Merchant's House,** Quay Hill (☎ 01834/842-279), is preserved in a 15th-century time

warp—Tenby was once a busy trading port with links as distant as the Iberian Peninsula—when business was conducted downstairs and dining room and bedchamber were above. The town also has two expansive sandy beaches arranged on either side of the outcrop known as **Castle Hill**—although the nearby cove at **Manorbier** beats both for scenery. ☉ 1½ hr. Tudor Merchant's House: Admission £3 adults, £1.50 kids. Apr–Oct Sun–Fri 11am–5pm.

Follow signs for the A40/Haverfordwest, then out to St. Bride's Bay. The distance from Tenby to Newgale is 28 miles.

⑤ ★ kids **St. Bride's Bay.** There's sands galore along this sweeping bay. The pretty little tumbledown cove at ★★ **Little Haven** has a seductive, but small, sandy beach and the Bay's liveliest and best-located pub, the ★ **White Swan** (☎ 01437/781-880; www.theswanlittlehaven.co.uk). The beach further north at **Druidston Haven** is more dramatic, but you'll need to take a cab (parking is impossible). The best family fun is the 2-mile strip of flat sand at ★ **Newgale.** The northern end has

Market Day

Inland Pembrokeshire, the barren Preseli Hills apart, is an agricultural region dotted with occasional small settlements. The best places to buy produce are the farmers' markets at **Fishguard** (alternate Sat, weekly Jun–Aug) and **Haverfordwest** (alternate Fri). See **www.pembrokeshire farmersmarkets.co.uk** for a schedule. Cheese-lovers should plan a stop at **Pant Mawr Cheeses**, Rosebush (☎ 01437/532-627; www.pantmawrcheeses.co.uk), for delicious young, aged, and smoked varieties made with both cow's and goat's milk.

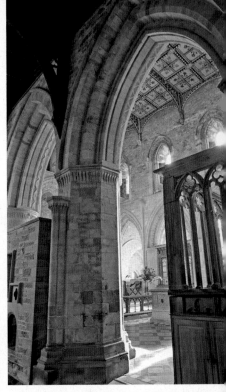

> *Painted wooden ceilings and pointed Gothic arches are part of the architectural mix at St. David's Cathedral.*

exposed rock-pools full of miniature life at low tide. When surf's up, rent boards, wetsuits, and sea kayaks opposite the sands at **Newsurf** (☎ 01437/721-398; www.newsurf.co.uk). ⏱ At least 2 hr.

Follow the A487 for 8 miles to St. David's.

❻ ★★ St. David's. Britain's smallest official city is, in size, barely more than a bustling village. It's been a place of Christian pilgrimage since 1120, when Dewi Sant (St. David in English) was recognized by the Roman Catholic

Church. Building of **St. David's Cathedral** began in the 1180s, and produced a dignified architectural mishmash of Norman, Romanesque, and Gothic styles, including a magnificent painted wooden ceiling carved to resemble a fan-vault above the Choir. St. David's was the most powerful bishopric in medieval Wales, with power over half the country—and the **Bishop's Palace** built for Bishop Henry Gower in the 1330s and 1340s became the finest ecclesiastical lodgings in the Isles. It's now an evocative but roofless ruin in Caerbwdy stone, although much of the first floor is intact, including the vast Great Hall with its circular "wheel window" in the gable. When the sun is shining, the bay and flat strand at **Whitesands** just outside town are a delight. ⏱ At least 2 hr. Cathedral: ☎ 01437/720-199. www.stdavidscathedral.org.uk. Suggested donation £3. Mon–Sat

8:30am–5:30pm; Sun 12:45–5:30pm. Bishop's Palace: ☎ 01437/720-517. £3 adults, £2.60 kids. Mar–Oct daily 9:30am–5pm (July–Aug until 6pm); Nov–Feb Mon–Sat 10am–4pm, Sun 11am–4pm.

Follow the A487 past Fishguard to Newport. Total distance is 23 miles.

7 ★★ **Mynydd Preseli.** The curvaceous moorland of the Preseli Hills seems to reflect the more distinctly Welsh, northern side of Pembrokeshire. The mysterious megaliths at **Pentre Ifan** mark a dolmen (burial chamber) that dates to the Neolithic age and frame **Carn Ingli,** the "Mountain of the Angels," beyond. This sacred outcrop stands 347m (1,138 ft.) over the little town of **Newport,** known for its fine-dining restaurants, and can be hiked from there in around 2½ hours for magical views along a much less-visited stretch of the coastal path. In nearby Nevern, the church-yard of **St. Brynach's Church** (free admission) houses a weathered but still beautifully intri-cate Celtic cross that dates to the 10th cen-tury, and the legendary "bleeding yew" that seeps red sap. ⏱ At least 3 hr.

Where to Stay & Dine

★ **Bluestone** NARBERTH
Luxury, country club-style woodland vacation resort with individual lodges and cottages, sleeping up to eight, designed to blend in with the rural surroundings. Three-night minimum in all units except studios. Carnaston Wood. ☎ 01834/862-400. www.bluestonewales.com. 225 units. Lodges £99–£480. MC, V.

★★ **Cwtch** ST. DAVID'S WELSH FUSION
Contemporary dining room that specializes in local ingredients prepped with a dash of Medi-terranean flair—think sea trout and cockles with a sauce vierge, or sea bass and laver-bread risotto. 22 High St. ☎ 01437/720-491. www.cwtchrestaurant.co.uk. Set menu £30. MC, V. Dinner daily (call ahead in winter).

Druidstone ST. BRIDE'S BAY
This legendary clifftop hotel is a love-it or hate-it place. It looks like the chaotic kind of joint a bohemian aunt might open, and could do with a revamp, but there's no disputing the staggering location and come-as-you-please atmosphere. Druidston Haven. ☎ 01437/781-221. www.druidstone.co.uk. 11 units. Doubles £75–£150 w/breakfast. MC, V.

★★ **Llys Meddyg** NEWPORT
This freestanding, stone-built Georgian town house has a stylish selection of rooms deco-rated in muted, contemporary tones. Units differ in size, but most are compact. Fine din-ing on-site. East St. ☎ 01239/820-008. www. llysmeddyg.com. 8 units. Doubles £100–£150 w/breakfast. MC, V.

> *Contemporary dining at Cwtch, whose name is a Welsh word that translates approximately as "hug."*

★★ **The Shed** PORTHGAIN SEAFOOD
You'll find stripped wood, whitewashed walls, and plenty of harborside informality at this tiny seafood restaurant with a big reputa-tion—reservations are essential. The menu depends on the day's catch but always fea-tures simply-cooked dishes bursting with fla-vor. ☎ 01348/831-518. www.theshedporthgain. co.uk. Entrees £8.50–£16. MC, V. Lunch & dinner daily (call ahead out of season).

★ **Stackpole Inn** STACKPOLE GASTROPUB
Lunchtime light bites like homemade fishcakes or local mussels, plus a daily specials board offering full-sized fresh fish and meat dishes. Or just enjoy a pint in the idyllic garden. Jasons Corner. ☎ 01646/672-324. www.stackpoleinn. co.uk. Entrees £7–£17. MC, V. Lunch daily; dinner Mon–Sat.

Fast Facts

Accommodation Booking Services
The best way to get immersed in Wales is to stay in a cottage or rural house. Agencies with fine portfolios include **English Country Cottages** (www.english-country-cottages.co.uk), **Coastal Cottages of Pembrokeshire** (www.coastalcottages.co.uk), **Under the Thatch** (www.underthethatch.co.uk), **Sheepskin** (www.sheepskinlife.com), and **Cottages 4 You** (www.cottages4you.co.uk).

Arriving
BY PLANE Wales's only international hub is **Cardiff Airport** (☎ 01446/711-111; www.tbicardiffairport.com), 12 miles southwest of the center, with scheduled flights to European cities including daily to Glasgow and Edinburgh on Flybe (www.flybe.com) and bmibaby (www.bmibaby.com). To reach the city center, take the hourly train (£3.30; 35 min.) to Cardiff Central. Your ticket also entitles you to free travel on the Baycar, linking the center with Cardiff Bay. Bus route X91 also connects the airport with Cardiff Central Station (35 min.), every 2 hours. A single costs £3.40; if you're planning to tour the city that day, ask for a "Day to Go Plus" ticket—it allows unlimited travel on city buses as well and costs £4.20. The airport also has car rental desks operated by Avis (☎ 08445/446-006), Europcar (☎ 01446/711-924), Hertz (☎ 01446/711-722), and National Alamo (☎ 01446/719-528), but you won't need a car in the city itself. For intercontinental connections to Wales, the airports at Bristol (for South Wales; www.bristolairport.co.uk; p. 288), Birmingham (www.birminghamairport.co.uk; p. 372), and Manchester (for North Wales; www.manchesterairport.co.uk; p. 458) have direct connections to North America. BY TRAIN Cardiff has a quick rail link with London's Paddington Station (trip time: 2¼ hr.). Trains for North Wales depart from London Euston and usually require a change in Chester to the coast line that links Rhyl, Llandudno Junction, Conwy, Bangor, and Holyhead; London to Conwy takes just over 3 hours. Contact **National Rail Enquiries** (☎ 08457/484-950; www.nationalrail.co.uk) for rail schedules. Non-U.K. residents planning to cover serious miles by rail can find details about the **BritRail** train pass at www.britrail.com. BY CAR South Wales is connected to London and the south of England by the M4 motorway, which enters the country via the **Second Severn Crossing** toll bridge (£5.50; www.severnbridge.co.uk). This connects all the principal cities of South Wales before terminating between Swansea and Carmarthen. London is 150 miles from Cardiff, but expect a drive to take at least 3 hours on this busy route. North Wales is best reached via Shrewsbury and the A5 or from the A55/A487 north coast road that connects Chester with Conwy, Bangor, and Caernarfon.

Emergencies
In any emergency, dial ☎ 999. To report a lost or stolen item, such as a wallet or passport, visit the local police station. Your insurance provider may require a Crime Number, which only the police can issue.

In a medical emergency, ask to be taken to the nearest hospital with an Accident and Emergency department. For non-urgent care, your hotel should be able to direct you to a doctor or dentist, though be aware that dentists charge and doctors may charge anyone without a European Health Identity Card, or "EHIC." Alternatively, call ☎ 111 for non-emergency advice.

> ## Travel Tip
> Many of Wales's historic buildings, castles, landscapes, and monuments are looked after by a state heritage organization called **Cadw** (pronounced "ka-doo"). There's a list of properties on the organization's website (www.cadw.wales.gov.uk). If you're planning to visit several during your stay, purchase a 3- or 7-day Explorer Pass from any staffed Cadw site. Prices are £11 and £18, respectively (£26 and £36 for family passes).

Getting Around

BY CAR The only real way to cover all of the scenic corners of Wales is by car. Apart from the main roads listed in "Arriving," above, the country is served by well-maintained minor routes that repay patience and regular refreshment stops. The journey should be as enjoyable as the arriving when you're touring Wales. For regular traffic and weather updates, tune the radio to **BBC Radio Wales** (93–104 FM, 657 & 882 MW). The AA, Britain's leading motoring organization, provides a free route planner at **www.theaa.com/route-planner/index.jsp**. East–west journeys tend to be quicker than north–south travel, and snow can shut down just about any rural route. **BY HISTORIC TRAIN** Riding one of the country's narrow-gauge or steam railways is a great way to enjoy the scenery. For details on the Welsh Highland and Ffestiniog Railways see p. 682, ②, and p. 680, ④; several more routes countrywide are promoted by **Great Little Trains of Wales** (www.greatlittletrains ofwales.co.uk). Rail enthusiasts should consider a Discount Card: It costs £10 and entitles you to 20% off all heritage train rides for a year. **BY PUBLIC TRANSPORT** Wales is crisscrossed by a network of rail and bus links, and as long as you have a little slack built into your schedule, public transport is a magical way to travel. Some of Wales's most scenic rail lines are detailed at www.scenicwales.co.uk. The **Freedom of Wales Flexi Pass** (www.walesflexipass.co.uk) buys 4 days' unlimited free train travel and 8 days' free bus travel anywhere in Wales for £78. Also included are free journeys on the Ffestiniog and Welsh Highland lines, 2-for-1 entry into Cadw historic monuments, and other discounts. Geographically-restricted passes covering South or Mid/North Wales are £54. Passes are available on the spot at any British railway station. There's a downloadable map of the Welsh rail network at www.arrivatrainswales.co.uk/routemap. **Traveline Cymru** (☎ 0871/200-2233; www.traveline-cymru.info) is the best source of integrated bus and rail scheduling. Their live bus schedule service (http://nextbuses.mobi) works on all smartphones, and there's a NextBuses app available from Apple's iTunes Store. **WITHIN CARDIFF** Traveling within Cardiff is easy on the extensive bus network.

Buses run between 6:15am (8am Sunday) and around 11:30pm all week. A single journey costs £1.50; if you intend to spend the day hopping about town, an unlimited-use "Day to Go" ticket costs £3, or £7 for a family of five. Buy tickets from the driver. Journeys between the center and Cardiff Bay are quickest on the Baycar bendy bus; day tickets are valid, and the journey is free for anyone with a ticket to any Cardiff rail station. For more information on bus travel within Cardiff, and to download a route map for the center, see www.cardiffbus.com.

Internet Access

Wi-Fi is a commonplace—and often free—amenity in Welsh hotels. If you're on the move, branches of McDonald's and Starbucks are good bets for Wi-Fi, as are any public library and many bar-cafes. You may also find the Global Hotspot Finder at www.jiwire.com useful. Though erratically updated, the Wiki map at www.wifi-in-cardiff.co.uk is a fallback. For anyone traveling with an unlocked GSM cellphone, every high street has at least one phone shop selling pay-as-you-go SIM cards that allow access to 3G networks at reasonable rates. Not all SIM-only deals are available to buyers without a U.K. credit card, but both **Tesco Mobile** (www.tescomobile.com) and **Three** (www.three.co.uk) SIMs are. There's a Three store in Cardiff inside the St. David's Centre, 36–44 St. David's Way (☎ 029/2023-6862).

Pharmacies

In theory, wherever you are in Wales should have a 24-hour pharmacy (or "chemist"). Look for the all-hours roster posted in the window. Large supermarkets also dispense prescriptions. Boots (www.boots.com) is the largest pharmaceutical chain, with branches nationwide, including inside the Capitol Shopping Centre, Queen St., Cardiff (☎ 029/2066-4506); hours are Monday to Saturday 8.30am to 6pm, Sunday 11am to 5pm.

Post Office

Main city post offices (www.postoffice.co.uk) are generally open Monday to Saturday 9am to 5:30pm, although shorter hours and lunch breaks are common in rural offices. For domestic mail, books of stamps are also sold by some newsagents and supermarkets. Cardiff's central post office is at 45–46 Queens Arcade, Queen St.

Safety

Rural Wales is one of the safest parts of the U.K.—though, as in any location, you should never leave valuables on display in a parked car. Parts of inner Cardiff and some of the depressed former industrial towns of South Wales can be occasionally edgy late at night, but as long as you avoid ostentatious displays of wealth and take care using ATMs, you're unlikely to encounter trouble. If you're hiking or climbing, it's essential to pack for every season (even in summer); let your hotel know if you plan to stay away overnight, and heed local advice on weather conditions. Also, see "Mountain Do's & Mountain Don'ts" on p. 668.

Visitor Information

Online headquarters of **Wales Tourism** is www.visitwales.co.uk (www.usa.visitwales.com in the U.S., and www.visitwales.ca in Canada). The regions of Wales are also represented by informative visitor websites. BRECON BEACONS NATIONAL PARK See www.brecon beacons.org. CARDIFF Go to www.visitcardiff.com. NORTH WALES An excellent accommodation directory can be found at www.visit anglesey.co.uk. PEMBROKESHIRE Visit www.visitpembrokeshire.com. SNOWDONIA Covered by www.visitsnowdonia.info. SOUTH WALES The wider area is covered by www.visitsouthwales.com. THE VALLEYS The former industrial heartland is covered by www.thevalleys.co.uk. Dedicated gastro-tourists should bookmark www.walesthetruetaste.co.uk, www.madeinmonmouthshire.com, and www.pembrokeshire.gov.uk/foodanddrink.

There's a comprehensive list of street addresses, telephone numbers, and e-mail contact details for Wales's 50-plus **Tourist Information Centres** at www.visitwales.co.uk/contact-visit-wales/tic's-tourist-information-centres. The **Cardiff Visitor Centre** is inside the Old Library, The Hayes (☎ 029/2087-3573; Mon–Sat 9:30am–5:30pm, Sun 10am–4pm).

The Beacons' Famous Festivals

Four of Wales's most soul-nourishing summer festivals take place within Brecon Beacons National Park (p. 648). The **Hay Festival of Literature and Arts** (www.hayfestival.com) fills late May with literary talks, comedy, and a sideshow dedicated to little readers. "The town of cooks" hosts Wales's premier gastronomic event, the **Abergavenny Food Festival** (www.abergavennyfoodfestival.com). There are live demonstrations, celeb-chef events and produce on sale over one busy mid-September weekend. A fast-expanding festival for eclectic indie-folk music fans, **Green Man** (www.greenman.net) runs over a long weekend in August. Recent headline acts have included the Flaming Lips, Doves, and Bon Iver. Also in August, **Brecon Jazz** (www.breconjazz.org) sees the sleepy town swaying to the sound of blue notes.

Our Favorite North Wales Moments

Remembering a youth spent wandering Wales, author Thomas De Quincey (1785–1859) wrote: "Happier life I cannot imagine...if the weather were but tolerable." It's a thought that pretty much sums up a trip to the majestic empty spaces of the mountainous North—where every bend in the way reveals views of glacier-hewn valleys or idyllic pastures flanking a gushing torrent. These are lands that have been fought over for centuries, by the English armies of Edward "Longshanks," Welsh freedom fighters under Llywelyn ap Gruffydd and Owain Glyndŵr, slate and copper barons of the Industrial Age, and even King Arthur and his mythical knights. The landscape and history left behind is not to be missed—but do pack your raincoat.

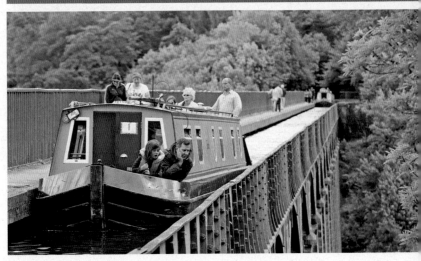

> PREVIOUS PAGE One of many breathtaking views of Snowdonia National Park. THIS PAGE Look down from the 38m (126-ft.) heights of the Pontcysyllte Aqueduct—if you dare.

① **Standing on Yr Wyddfa, Mount Snowdon's 1,085m (3,560-ft.) peak.** Whether you've arrived on the rack railway or hiked any of the marked trails to the summit, the view over the Snowdonia range and into the five countries of the British Isles is equally spectacular. See p. 678, **①**.

② **Walking out to the midpoint of Thomas Telford's Pontcysyllte Aqueduct and looking down.** There's 38m (126 ft.) of thin air below you and the suspended canal you're standing on before your gaze hits the River Dee. See p. 673, **③**.

③ **Exploring Edward's "Iron Ring."** The tyrannical "Longshanks," King of England between 1272 and 1307, constructed several fortresses across the ancient kingdom of Gwynedd designed to keep the rebellious Welsh at bay.

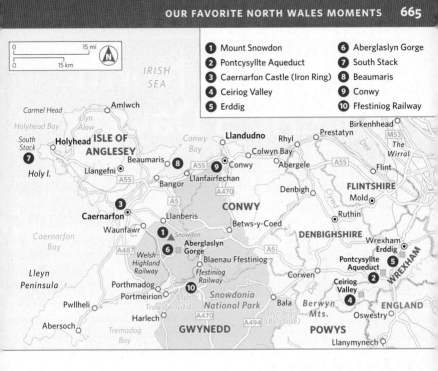

1. Mount Snowdon
2. Pontcysyllte Aqueduct
3. Caernarfon Castle (Iron Ring)
4. Ceiriog Valley
5. Erddig
6. Aberglaslyn Gorge
7. South Stack
8. Beaumaris
9. Conwy
10. Ffestiniog Railway

Mighty, relatively intact ruins at Conwy, Harlech, Beaumaris, and Caernarfon show that his masons knew how to build for posterity. See "Edward's Iron Ring," p. 669.

4 Driving and dining by the Ceiriog. This little-visited valley twists an idyllic, 15-mile path from rolling terrain around Chirk to the Berwyn Mountains on the fringes of Snowdonia. The most beautiful stretch, around Llanarmon, is also home to one of Denbighshire's best dining experiences. See p. 672.

5 Exploring "below stairs" at Erddig, outside Wrexham. The noble Yorke family hit hard times at the start of the 20th century, so modernity barely took hold at their fine Georgian country house, which now appears frozen in time. See p. 670, ❶.

6 Hiking up the Aberglaslyn Gorge as the Welsh Highland Railway puffs past. Between Beddgelert and Pont Croesor, the most famous stretch of this recently rebuilt narrow-gauge line cuts through terrain that's been a beauty spot since the 1800s. See p. 680, ❸.

7 Heading out to the heath and cliffs around South Stack, the far northwest point of Wales's Holy Island. On a sunny morning, the peaks of Snowdonia and the Lleyn pepper a hazy horizon beyond Caernarfon Bay. See p. 684, ❺.

8 Enjoying the tranquil comforts of 21st-century Beaumaris. The more you encounter fragments of life in centuries past here, the more you discover that it wasn't always so genteel—although the skillful, contemporary cuisine at the Loft drags you right back to the present. See p. 683, ❸; p. 685.

9 Striding the streets and walls of historic Conwy. The town was built together with its castle in the 1280s and now houses some of the best preserved ancient property in Wales. See p. 686.

10 Riding the little steam trains. Originally built to carry slate and copper from mine to port, these restored historic railways now rattle through some of Snowdonia's most breathtaking scenery. See p. 682, ❷; p. 680, ❹.

Fast Facts

The Fast Facts for both North and South Wales can be found on p. 659.

The Best of North Wales in 3 Days

If the South is Wales's heart, the North keeps watch over its soul. It was in the North that many of the key battles for Welsh independence were fought—and lost. It's in the far northwest that "Welshness" is guarded most vigilantly—around 80 percent of the population of the Lleyn Peninsula can speak the native language. But there's more than just Celtic pride and culture here. The North is home to Wales's most dramatic crags and mightiest castles, to a coastline that's perfect for leisure but that equally can turn wild and windswept at a moment's notice. With walking boots and a good map, you could spend 3 weeks here...but these are your best 3 days.

> *The llyn, or lake, is a common geographical feature around the high peaks of Snowdonia.*

START Caernarfon, 105 miles west of Manchester (p. 440).

1 ★★★ Snowdonia. As long as the weather's in your favor, set out from your accommodation to make an attempt on **Mount Snowdon**'s summit (p. 678, **1**). The peak so loved by such English Romantic poets as Wordsworth and Shelley remains quite literally the high-point of any trip to North Wales. On a clear day, you'll see every country of the British Isles, and every wrinkle and fold in the national park below. Although there are trails that, given the wrong conditions,

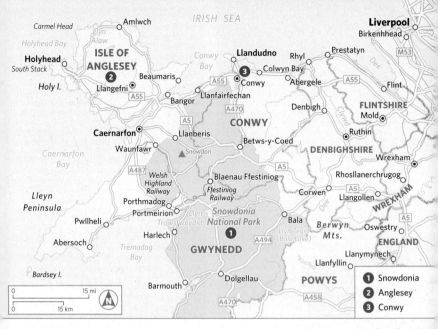

IRISH SEA

Carmel Head — Amlwch — Liverpool
Birkenhead
Holyhead Bay — Llyn Alaw — Conwy Bay — M53
ISLE OF ANGLESEY — **Llandudno** — Rhyl — Prestatyn
Holyhead — ❸ — Colwyn Bay
South Stack — Beaumaris — **Conwy** — Abergele — A55 — Flint
Holy I. — Llangefni ❷ — A55 — **FLINTSHIRE**
Bangor — Llanfairfechan — Denbigh — Mold
Caernarfon — Llanberis — A470 — **CONWY** — Ruthin
Waunfawr — ▲ Snowdon — Betws-y-Coed — **DENBIGHSHIRE**
Caernarfon Bay — A487 — Welsh Highland Railway — A5 — Wrexham
Lleyn Peninsula — Porthmadog — Blaenau Ffestiniog — Rhosllanerchrugog
Pwllheli — Portmeirion — Ffestiniog Railway — Corwen — A5 — Llangollen — WREXHAM
Abersoch — Harlech — Llyn Trawsfynydd — **Snowdonia National Park** — Bala — Berwyn Mts. — Oswestry — A5
Bardsey I. — Tremadog Bay — ❶ — A494 — Llyn Tegid (Bala Lake) — **ENGLAND**
GWYNEDD — Llanymynech
Barmouth — Dolgellau — Llanfyllin — A458 — **POWYS**
A470

0 — 15 mi
0 — 15 km

❶ Snowdonia
❷ Anglesey
❸ Conwy

would challenge an experienced alpine hiker, the summer months offer tracks that any fit traveler can attempt. The most popular route is the Llanberis Path, which slowly winds its way from Llanberis past cascades, across open sheep grazing moorland, and then finally up to the peak, with a dizzying view down into the Llanberis Pass. A fit child of 10 could handle the trail. The same goes for the Rhyd Ddu Path that rides Snowdon's western flank to the top. The best way to reach the trailhead from Caernarfon is to take the first train of the day on the **Welsh Highland Railway** (p. 682, ❷). Alight at Rhyd Ddu Station, just after one of the most glorious stretches of the line along the shore of Llyn Cwellyn, and then walk to the trailhead. Check the timetable before setting off to confirm the time of the day's last return train. Both of these paths require about 5 hours round-trip. Of course, the view from the top is the same if you prefer to ascend via the **Snowdon Mountain Railway** (2½-hr. round-trip; p. 678, ❶); aim to get an early start so there are fewer people at the summit and a slightly cheaper ticket price.

Either way, make time back in Llanberis to visit the **National Slate Museum** (p. 679, ❷). Snowdonia was once the source of almost all of Britain's slate and exported its precious rock across the planet—the area even exported its quarrymen to work in the New World. This mightily impressive industrial museum manages to re-create the sounds, smells, and even the feelings associated with the industrial past without ever becoming mawkish about the hardships that working families endured in these slate-rich hills. ⏱1 day.

On Day 2, take the A487 northeast to the Britannia Bridge, and then follow the signs for Beaumaris. Total distance from Caernarfon is 12 miles.

Where to Stay

For detailed coverage of sights and recommended hotels and restaurants in **Snowdonia**, see p. 681; for **Anglesey**, see p. 685; for **Conwy**, see p. 687. Distances between destinations on your 3-day tour aren't great, however. Stay at **Bishopsgate House** (p. 685) or **Gwesty Portmeirion** (p. 674) to cover the first two stops without changing hotels; choose **Tan-y-Foel** (p. 681), and you can see all three stops without the need to check out.

> *The Snowdon Mountain Railway basically follows the Llanberis Path to the summit, which is known in Welsh as Yr Wyddfa.*

❷ ★★ **Anglesey.** A full day gives you plenty of time to enjoy the best of the remote Isle of Anglesey, known as "Ynys Môn" in Welsh. Its "capital," the quaint little town of **Beaumaris** (p. 683, ❸; named from a distinctly un-Welsh corruption of the French for "beautiful marsh") is the natural first stop. Visit the castle, then the court and gaol, to glimpse some unsavory but fascinating snapshots of life for those who got on the wrong side of this frontier town over the centuries—most of which were spent cut off from the rest of Wales by the narrow stretch of tidal water known as the Menai Strait (see "A Tale of Two Engineers," p. 675). More remote still is **Holy Island** (p. 684, ❺) and Anglesey's westernmost point, South Stack. Admire views back to Snowdonia and the Lleyn from the paths that cut through this barren coastal heath, and coastal precipices that birds such as the rare chough, puffin, and razorbill call home. Summer is the best season for bird-watching. ⏱ **1 day.**

Mountain Do's and Mountain Don'ts

"How often do people fall off the mountain?" asks a local joke with a serious edge. The answer: "Usually just once." The highest peaks of northern Wales shouldn't be taken lightly. These are mountains, not hills, and anyone tackling them needs to observe the rules to stay safe.

- Come wearing or carrying the **proper equipment.** That means hiking boots, clothing layers that can be added or removed as you go, a raincoat, emergency food and water, a mobile phone, and some basic first aid supplies.

- **Plan** your route thoroughly. If you're ascending Mount Snowdon, the Snowdonia National Park website (www.eryri-npa.gov.uk) has the best summary of the right routes for different abilities. Snowdonia is well served by a network of village information offices. Never be afraid to ask a local for advice.

- Carry a **specialist walking map and compass.** We use and recommend the Ordnance Survey 1:25,000 *Explorer* maps (OL17 covers Snowdon), available at any local bookstore. Heading out with a map designed for driving or a piece of paper with scribbled directions is just asking for trouble.

- Once up high, **never leave a marked trail** unless you know the terrain.

- Watch the **weather forecast,** and even on a fine-looking day, make sure you're equipped for a turnaround. Conditions can become *very* different when you hit an exposed ridge.

- Always **let your hotel know** where you're heading, and if you expect to be back late—particularly if you're tackling one of the high peaks.

- **Never be embarrassed to turn back** or admit you're not up to a particular hike. There are plenty of stunning walks that ascend barely an inch (for example, around **Beddgelert,** p. 680, ❸).

Edward's Iron Ring

Although Edward I (1239–1307) was one of medieval England's most powerful kings, he had more than his share of problems with the Celts. Trouble flared up in the early 1280s when Llywelyn ap Gruffydd (1223–82)—still the only native prince a united Welsh nation has ever had—occupied Caernarfon. The Welsh appeared to have abandoned a tradition of fighting each other in order to mount an effective insurrection again the English. However, Llywelyn was betrayed and killed in 1282 at the Battle of Orewin Bridge, near Builth Wells, and Edward moved quickly to eradicate his line and to establish an Iron Ring of castles designed to keep the locals in check forever. Flint and Rhuddlan, erected after lesser troubles in the 1270s, were strengthened. Progress at Caernarfon (p. 682, ❶) was so rapid that by 1284, Edward I's son, later Edward II, was born inside its Eagle Tower (a "native prince!" his father proclaimed). Coastal castles at Conwy (p. 686, ❶) and Harlech (p. 681, ❻) were designed to be equally impregnable, and when the Welsh revolted again, in 1294, Edward ordered Caernarfon's walls to be built even taller. The final link in his imperious chain, Beaumaris (p. 683, ❸), is the most elegant of royal master mason James of St. George's constructions. All have survived the centuries remarkably intact and represent the pinnacle of medieval castle building in Europe.

On Day 3, head northeast on the coastal A55. The distance from Caernarfon to Conwy is 23 miles.

❸ ★★ **Conwy.** This tiny market town and former trading port, with its ¾ mile of medieval walls, 21 towers and three gates, is so uniquely preserved and historically important that it has been recognized by UNESCO as a World Heritage Site. The castle and street-plan were built simultaneously for Edward I over the site of a 12th-century Cistercian abbey—St. Mary's Church at the town's center is all that remains from the period before Wales's wars of independence were won by England's king. Despite years when the town has been under almost constant siege, and long spells of neglect and squalor, architectural relics such as the **castle** (p. 686, ❶) and Elizabethan house **Plas Mawr** (p. 686, ❷) have survived remarkably intact. Of more recent architectural vintage are the town's iconic bridges, feats of impressive 19th-century engineering that span the Conwy Estuary. This little town is easily manageable in a day; follow the tour on p. 686. ◷ 1 day.

> James of St. George was the Savoyard architect responsible for North Wales's great castles, including Conwy, pictured.

The Best of North Wales in 1 Week

With the very best of North Wales spread out across dramatic hills and plunging river gorges, along scenic seaside paths and empty coastal tracts, you really need a week to appreciate it. The peaks of Snowdonia, historic streets of Conwy, and pastures and wild coastline of Anglesey are deserved highlights. Our week-long tour also leads you through Denbighshire and the best of the borderlands, where you'll find some of North Wales's finest dining.

> If you do your research, you'll find walks to suit all ages, abilities, and schedules across North Wales.

START Wrexham, 40 miles south of Liverpool. Total distance traveled is 270 miles.

1 ★★ **Erddig.** A chance to glimpse the lives of the servant class is the principal attraction of this stately Georgian home. Built in the 1680s, Erddig was the understated residence of the Yorke family for 2½ centuries starting in the 1720s, before being rescued from (literally) the brink of collapse by the National Trust. The restored outbuildings house the Yorkes' 19th-century carriages, their 1907 family Rover motor-car and a smithy, sawmill, and even working Shire-horse stables—all of which were put to use during a massive restoration project in the 1970s that stuck to traditional materials and processes. Electricity never arrived at Erddig; it's as if the 20th century didn't happen in the house's "below stairs" servants' area, with intact kitchen, pantry,

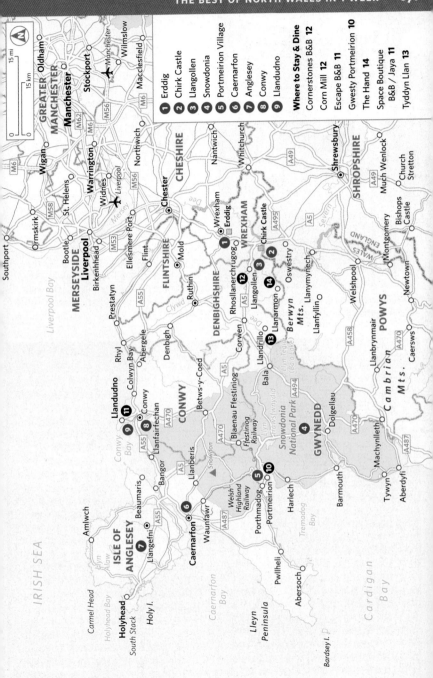

1 Erddig
2 Chirk Castle
3 Llangollen
4 Snowdonia
5 Portmeirion Village
6 Caernarfon
7 Anglesey
8 Conwy
9 Llandudno

Where to Stay & Dine

Cornerstones B&B 12
Corn Mill 12
Escape B&B 11
Gwesty Portmeirion 10
The Hand 14
Space Boutique
B&B / Jaya 11
Tyddyn Llan 13

> The interiors at Erddig, like the wood-paneled library, are typical of a Georgian stately home.

scullery, and social rooms. More unusual are portraits commissioned by the Yorke family (first paintings, later photographs) of the staff, each eulogized with its own substantial poem and hung proudly in the Servants' Hall. ⊙ 2 hr. Wrexham. ☎ 01978/355-314. Admission £9.35 adults, £4.70 kids. Mid-Mar to Oct Sat–Wed 11am–5pm (July–Aug also Thurs); Nov–Dec Sat–Sun 11am–4pm.

Head south for 8 miles on the A483, then the A5, to Chirk, and follow signs to

❷ ★ **Chirk Castle.** Perched majestically and strategically on a knoll overlooking the lower Ceiriog Valley, the marcher (border) fortress of Chirk was built around 1300 by Roger Mortimer (1287–1330) under the patronage (like so many castles in North Wales) of English King Edward I. Mortimer was a key player in the betrayal and killing of Llywelyn ap Gruffydd (see p. 669), still the only native "Prince of Wales," in 1282, and Chirk was one

Staying the Night in Denbighshire

The historic county of Denbighshire is a terrain of rolling, lush pastures, misty hills, and wooded slopes. It's also the best part of North Wales to tuck yourself away in an inn or restaurant with rooms. You'd be hard-pressed to find a more peaceful setting than the tiny village of Llanarmon Dyffryn Ceiriog in the upper reaches of the unspoilt Ceiriog Valley, where the ★★ **Hand** (☎ 01691/600-666; www.thehandhotel.co.uk) has established itself as a food destination. The menu sticks largely to gastropub classics, but delivers them with panache using the best local ingredients, such as Ceiriog trout; entrees range from £9 to £20. The hotel's Character Rooms, with bigger beds and decor more in keeping with the traditions of this former coaching inn, are worth the extra £20 over standard rooms; a double with breakfast costs £125.

At ★★ **Tyddyn Llan,** Llandrillo (☎ 01490/440-264; www.tyddynllan.co.uk), an elegant manor with private grounds has been converted into a restaurant with rooms that successfully combines Georgian exclusivity with modern hospitality. Rooms are traditionally

and individually decorated, with leather seating; doubles cost £140 to £220 with breakfast. The fine-dining restaurant usually features an inventive menu stuffed with local ingredients such as Welsh Black beef or foraged ceps; the two-course menu costs £39 and is open to non-residents (reservations essential).

In Llangollen itself, **Cornerstones B&B,** 15 Bridge St. (☎ 01978/861-569; www.corner stones-guesthouse.co.uk), has bags of character crammed into its riverside terrace premises. There's plenty of exposed stone and wood beams on show, but the decor manages to retain a contemporary edge. To secure the prized River Room (with a view), call or e-mail direct; doubles run £80 to £100. On a sunny day there are few better nearby spots for an informal lunch than the weirside terrace of the **Corn Mill,** Dee Lane (☎ 01978/869-930; www.brunningand price.co.uk/cornmill). The mill was built in 1786, but the food is a more modern vintage: a wide-ranging menu of reliable gastropub fare that usually includes everything from crab linguine to a rib-eye with hand-cut fries. Entrees cost £8.75 to £17.

of his rewards. The dungeon and Adam Tower date to this period, although the rest of the castle and courtyard has the genteel feel of an Oxford quadrangle, converted as it was to serve as the Myddleton family home for 400 years. The servants' intact laundry dates back a century or so. Views back to the castle from the manicured formal gardens, with their box-cut yews, are sublime. ⏱ 2 hr. Chirk, near Wrexham. ☎ 01691/777-701. Admission £9 adults, £4.50 kids. Mar–Oct Wed–Sun 10am–5pm (July–Aug also Tues). Gardens: Sat–Sun Feb & Nov–Dec.

Head for your accommodation in Denbighshire for 1 night (see below). In the morning, begin Day 2 in

❸ ★ **Llangollen.** Despite its popularity with visitors, this attractive little market town straddling the River Dee has managed to retain much of its original Victorian character, and the high street remains a pleasant place to stroll. It's easy to see why the so-called "Ladies of Llangollen," Miss Sarah Ponsonby (1755–1832) and Lady Eleanor Butler (1739–1829), loved their house and gardens at **Plas Newydd,** perched on a hill above the town. The enviable location is complemented by the eccentric Tudor-Gothic house, rich in stained glass and carved oak, in which they lived for nearly 50 years from 1778—all an appropriate reflection of two remarkable characters who were "civil partners" and celebrities long before either term was invented.

The canal boat was the air freight of the Industrial Revolution, and 3½ miles east of Llangollen at Trevor, engineer Thomas Telford built the spectacular **Pontcysyllte Aqueduct** between 1795 and 1805 to carry the Ellesmere (now Llangollen) Canal across the Dee Valley. Standing 39m (126 ft.) above the river, it's the tallest navigable aqueduct ever constructed; walk across it to get a sense of the dizzying height of its 18 piers, and drive the road below armed with a good camera. The aqueduct is still used to carry drinking water to Cheshire, over the border in England.

West of Llangollen stand the noble remains of **Valle Crucis Abbey.** Founded in 1201 by Cistercian monks, by the 16th century it had risen to almost match Tintern Abbey (p. 636, ❶ in temporal power. The atmospheric site is only

> *The International Musical Eisteddfod, held each year in Plas Newydd, is a first-rate spot to experience Welsh music and dance.*

slightly marred by the proximity of a busy campsite. Llangollen is also home to an annual **International Musical Eisteddfod** (☎ 01978/862-001; www.international-eisteddfod.co.uk), a 6-day festival of choral music, dance, and song each July. ⏱ 4 hr. Plas Newydd: ☎ 01978/862-834. Admission £5.50 adults, £4.50 kids. Apr–Oct

More Information

For the best hotels and restaurants in **Snowdonia National Park,** see p. 681. For lodgings near **Caernarfon** and on the **Isle of Anglesey,** see p. 685; for **Conwy,** see p. 687.

> *Caernarfon Castle guards a strategic point overlooking the Menai Strait and adjacent to a natural harbor formed by the River Seiont.*

daily 10am–5pm. Valle Crucis Abbey: ☎ 01978/ 860-326. Admission £3.60 adults, £2.25 kids. Apr–Oct daily 10am–5pm.

From Llangollen, continue on the A5 to Capel Curig, then follow the A4086 to Llanberis. Total distance is 48 miles. Begin Day 3 in

4 ★★★ **Snowdonia.** Allow 2 days to explore North Wales's national park along with nearby Portmeirion Village (**5**). If you can check a weather forecast, choose the better of your two to attack the summit of **Mount Snowdon** (1,085m/3,560 ft.; p. 678, **1**). On your second day, make for the southern end of the National Park. **Harlech Castle** (p. 681, **6**) was another mighty stronghold built by Edward I, but between 1404 and 1409 it served as the headquarters for Owain Glyndŵr's ultimately failed attempt to retake Wales from the English. Its formidable walls and coastal views have been hardly touched by the passing of time. Return to the heart of the park via the A496, and enjoy spectacular panoramas

along the Mawddach Estuary before stopping at Blaenau Ffestiniog's **Llechwedd Slate Caverns** (p. 680, **5**). On a rainy day, do the route backwards: The underground (and more importantly indoor) trains and caverns become increasingly busy on wet summer days.

On the afternoon of your non-summit day, head 23 miles south to Porthmadog via spectacular roads through the Llanberis Pass (A4086), Nant Gwynant, and the

Spending the Night in Portmeirion

Stay at ★★ **Gwesty Portmeirion** (☎ 01766/ 770-000; www.portmeirion-village.com) and you can choose between the original 1850 manor house with luxury rooms by the estuary or full-service hotel "cottage-suites" scattered about the Italianate Village. Each is meticulously decorated in Williams-Ellis inspired style. Check the website for (very) special offers. Doubles cost £170 to £235 with breakfast.

Aberglaslyn Pass (A498). Then take the A487 1½ miles east to

5 ★ Portmeirion Village. There's more than a whiff of Disney about this magical multi-colored village by the sea. It took architect Clough Williams-Ellis (1883–1978) over half a century to turn what was an original 1850 manor house and its abandoned estate into a "resort" like no other. His elaborate pastiche, with eclectic architectural influences both in-digenous and foreign, wrapped in an Italianate sugar-coating and transplanted onto a wild Welsh estuary, probably shouldn't work… but Williams-Ellis's understanding of how archi-tecture and nature can work in harmony en-sures that it just does. Wander buildings that veer between Arts and Crafts and neoclassical styles, or lose yourself in acres of sub-tropical garden walks and soak up a place that made a suitably surreal setting for the cult 1960s TV show *The Prisoner*. ◷ 2 hr. ☎ 01766/770-000. www.portmeirion-village.com. Admission £9 adults, £6 kids (£4.50/£3 after 3:30pm). Daily 9:30am–7:30pm.

Return to Porthmadog, then follow the A487 north for 19 miles to spend Day 5 in

6 ★★ Caernarfon. A town that was once so important to the Romans and English King Ed-ward I became for centuries a sleepy outpost of a forgotten corner of Wales. First the riches and infrastructure needs of the slate industry, then the investiture of two 20th-century Prin-ces of Wales at **Caernarfon Castle** (p. 682, **1**) changed all that. The mighty curtain walls erected by Edward's Savoyard master mason James of St. George (1230–1309) were described as "an edifice of stupendous mag-nitude and strength" by Dr. Samuel Johnson in the 1770s, and still bear barely a scratch 7 centuries after their completion. When you've toured the castle, spend the remainder of the day on Wales's newest and most scenic narrow-gauge line, the **Welsh Highland Rail-way** (p. 682, **2**). Reinstating the historic link between Carenarfon and Porthmadog, via the Aberglaslyn Gorge, has been something of a local *cause celèbre* in recent years, and bit by bit the task has been completed, with the final stretch between Pont Croesor and Porth-madog opening in 2011. Either ride the historic carriages there and back (a 6-hr. round-trip)

or, with careful planning, get out along the way to hike the fells before catching the last train back to Caernarfon. ◷ 1 day.

On Day 6, follow the A487 northeast and over the Britannia Bridge to

7 ★★ Anglesey. See p. 668, **2**.

Return to the Britannia Bridge, then follow the A55 northeast for 17 miles.

8 ★★ Conwy. For the best way to spend a day in Conwy, see p. 669, **3**. Restrict your roam-ing to just the **castle** (p. 686, **1**) and Elizabe-than house **Plas Mawr** (p. 686, **2**) to leave time for one final, nearby stop.

Cross the road bridge over the Conwy Estuary, then follow signs for Llandudno, 5 miles north. We recommend you spend your final night in North Wales here.

9 ★ kids Llandudno. This once-fashionable, purpose-built Victorian resort may have lost a little of its luster in the past half-century or so, but a sweeping seaside promenade of white stucco hotels and a setting wedged between the giant limestone headlands of Great Orme

A Tale of Two Engineers

Thomas Telford (1757–1834) and Robert Stephenson (1803–59) brought the world to North Wales. Telford's first major com-mission was the Ellesmere (now Llangol-len) Canal, and its spectacular Pontcysyllte Aqueduct (p. 673, **3**). He's now best remembered for building the Holyhead to London road (the current A5) through Snowdonia. It carried mail coaches to the shortest sea crossing to Ireland and earned him the nickname "Colossus of Roads" from poet Robert Southey. The photogenic Menai Suspension Bridge, opened in 1826, is the most photographed stretch of his route. Stephenson was a railway engineer and bridge builder whose Chester–Holyhead line opened the North Wales coast up to rail travelers. The Conwy Railway Bridge (1849) and Britannia Bridge (1850) over the Menai Strait both employed a revolutionary tubular design, though the latter was destroyed by fire in 1970 (and later rebuilt to carry cars, too).

> *It's easy to miss the unobtrusive entrance to Plas Mawr, Conwy's only surviving Elizabethan house.*

and Little Orme make it a fun end to a week in North Wales. The only part of town to predate the 1850s, a few streets hugging the flanks of the Great Orme, was all that existed prior to the Mostyn family laying down grand plans to transform farms and common land into the town you see today. A ride up the 1902 **Great Orme Tramway** ends in expansive views along the North Wales coast and is the best place to appreciate Llandudno's elliptical grid of planned streets. Coastal views are equally spectacular from **Marine Drive,** a toll road (£2.50) that starts from the Happy Valley pleasure gardens and 1877 iron pier, then circumnavigates the Orme. ⏱ At least 3 hr. Great Orme Tramway: Church Walks. ☎ 01492/879-306. www.greatormetramway.co.uk. Tickets £5.80 adults, £4 kids 3–16. Daily late Mar–late Oct 10am–6pm (until 5pm Mar & Oct).

Staying the Night in Llandudno

Conwy and Llandudno are so close together, and so well served by local bus connections (see www.travelinecymru.info for timetables), that you can comfortably lodge in one and dine in the other. At design-savvy ★★ **Space Boutique B&B,** 36 Church Walks (☎ 01492/818-198; www.spaceboutique.co.uk), the vibe is relaxed and personal, with the clean decor and bespoke contemporary furnishings of the 11 rooms based subtly on traditional Indian elements. The small onsite restaurant **Jaya** (entrees £15–£18; Wed–Sun only) is open to nonresidents and serves home-cooked dishes based on authentic Punjabi recipes. Double rooms run £95 to £115, including a la carte breakfast. An equally stylish alternative, almost across the road, is ★ **Escape B&B,** 48 Church Walks (☎ 01492/877-776; www.escapebandb.co.uk); doubles run £85–£135, with breakfast.

> Llandudno's pier, the longest in Wales, was the focus of seaside fun for Victorian vacationers.

Snowdonia

Not just the roof of Wales and the tallest British peaks south of Scotland, the giant mountains of Snowdonia National Park have also long been places of myth. Legend has it that dragons, faithful hounds, and even (in the original tales) King Arthur have all lived round here, but the principal attraction for visitors is the endless miles of hiking trails and epic scenery.

> *Quarrymen and farmers have for centuries eked out a hard living in the foothills of Mount Snowdon.*

START Llanberis, 11 miles south of Bangor.

TRIP LENGTH 3–4 days.

❶ ★★★ Mount Snowdon. Depending on your energy level and mountain proficiency, there are several options for scaling Britain's tallest peak south of the Highlands. The **Snowdon Mountain Railway** has been in operation since 1896—outdoor tourism isn't new around here—and is the Isles' only passenger rack railway. The 5-mile track at first climbs gently away from Llanberis, passing plenty of evidence of human activity on Snowdon's flanks: sheep pens, slate and copper works, even hideouts used by Welsh rebels in 14th-century uprisings against English rule. The steep

final stretch affords views over classic glacial landscape features like U-shaped troughs and hanging valleys, as well as a frightening look down into the Llanberis Pass with the Glyderau peaks beyond. On foot, the easiest route outside winter months is the scenic **Llanberis Path** (5 hr.), which more or less follows the Mountain Railway. The **Rhyd Ddu Path** (5 hr.), originating from the Welsh Highland Railway (p. 682, ❷) station with the same name, is another *relatively* gentle way to the summit. More experienced hikers should consider the **Pyg Track** (5 hr.), starting from the Pen-y-Pass parking lot on the A4086. Whichever route you attempt (there are three other maintained trails), be sure to plan properly: The Web

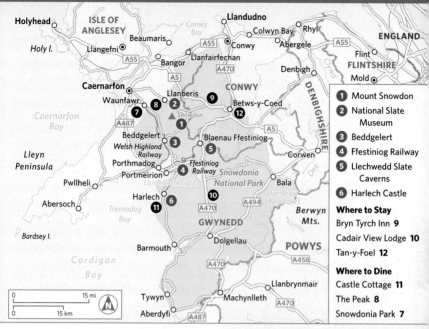

Map legend:
1. Mount Snowdon
2. National Slate Museum
3. Beddgelert
4. Ffestiniog Railway
5. Llechwedd Slate Caverns
6. Harlech Castle

Where to Stay
Bryn Tyrch Inn 9
Cadair View Lodge 10
Tan-y-Foel 12

Where to Dine
Castle Cottage 11
The Peak 8
Snowdonia Park 7

page "Walking on Snowdon" (http://www.eryri-npa.gov.uk/visiting/walking/snowdon) should be your first stop. ☺ At least 2½ hr. Snowdon Mountain Railway: Llanberis. ☎ 0844/493-8120. www.snowdonrailway.co.uk. Round-trip ticket £25 adults, £18 kids (9am departure booked at least one day in advance £18/£12). Late Mar–Oct daily from 9am, up to half-hourly in peak period; Mar–May trains normally terminate short of the summit.

❷ ★★ **National Slate Museum.** While surrounded by so much tranquility and natural beauty, it's easy to forget that Snowdonia was until recently a place of toil and hardship. The courtyard here once echoed the industrial din of crushing, hammering, and splitting—this great gray building housed the workshops that kept Dinorwic Quarry running. The impressive museum chronicles the methods, machinery, and men that dug 90,000 tons of slate a year from the mountainside. Particularly poignant are the relocated quarrymen's cottages, each dressed authentically at important moments in Snowdonia's industrial past, including 1969—when Dinorwic closed. ☺ 1½ hr. Llanberis. ☎ 01286/870-630. www.museumwales.ac.uk/en/slate. Free admission. Easter–Oct daily 10am–5pm.

> The leaden gray of Dinorwic slate is the predominant color at the National Slate Museum, just outside Llanberis.

> The Ffestiniog heritage railway runs on a narrow-gauge line once used to transport Blaenau slate to the nearest port.

Follow the A4086 south through the Llanberis Pass, then take a right turn on the A498 to

❸ ★★ Beddgelert. This well-kept little mountain village is the jumping-off point for some of Snowdonia's best gentle walks. Its name (literally, Gelert's grave) comes from the faithful dog of 13th-century Prince Llywelyn, slain by his master after having been falsely suspected of killing his child. The classic local trek heads past

Gelert's Grave (mythical rather than genuine) into the **Aberglaslyn Gorge,** a stunning, steep-sided trail constantly soundtracked with the rushing water of the River Glaslyn. The area was a favorite of well-to-do Victorians who first popularized Snowdonia as a leisure destination. Alternatively, a 2-hour circuit takes you northeast along the shores of **Llyn Dinas** and back to the village. With a little more time, you can link the two into a half-day hike by looping around Cwm Bychan. It's all relatively easy walking, but as with everywhere in Snowdonia, you need to be fit and sure-footed. ⊕ At least 2 hr.

Take the A4085, then A498 south for 8 miles to Porthmadog.

❹ ★★ kids Ffestiniog Railway. Ride near the front, with the window wedged down, for the full "age of steam" ambience (and odor) on Wales's most famous narrow-gauge heritage railway. The tiny steam engine pulls its wood-paneled carriages with antique booth seating the majestic 14 miles from Portmadog to Blaenau Ffestiniog several times a day for most of the year. The route climbs quickly away from the Traeth Bach estuary, clinging to the hillside and winding through forests of pine and oak, past waterfalls and over expansive uplands to the slate mining community of Blaenau Ffestiniog; the railway was originally completed in 1836 to carry Blaenau's slate down to the port. ⊕ At least 3 hr. Harbour Station, Porthmadog. ☎ 01766/516-024. www.festrail.co.uk. Day ticket £19, half-way round-trip £11; kids 3–15 one free fare with each paying adult. See website for current timetable.

❺ ★ kids Llechwedd Slate Caverns. There are 25 miles of tunnels and mine chambers buried in the great gray hill above Blaenau, many of them still part of a working slate mine that opened in 1846. At Llechwedd, you can don hard hats to make two separate but complementary half-hour visits underground. The **Deep Mine** takes you 122m (400 ft.) below ground on a self-guided visit helped by eerie audio commentaries emanating from the darkness, and ends at a giant subterranean lake. The **Miners' Tramway** starts with a half-mile ride into the slate mountain and continues with a more didactic talk on the geology of the mine and the working life of the

19th-century miner. On a wet day in high season, arrive early to minimize waiting times. ⊕ At least 1½ hr. Blaenau Ffestiniog. ☎ 01766/830-306. www.llechwedd-slate-caverns.co.uk. One tour £10 adults, £7.90 kids; two tours £16.30 adults, £12.10 kids. Daily 10am–5:15pm (Oct–Mar until 4:15pm).

Follow the A487 east, then the A496 southwest to Harlech, a distance of 10 miles.

❻ ★ kids **Harlech Castle.** If you were selecting a castle to live in, you'd be hard-pressed to find one with a view to match Edward I's great coastal pile. Built in the 1280s as one of the English king's imperial fortresses (see p. 669), and despite brief occupation during Owain Glyndŵr's rebellion in 1404–9, its shell and gatehouse in particular are remarkably intact. ⊕ 45 min. Castle Square, Harlech. ☎ 01766/780-552. Admission £3.60 adults, £3.20 kids. Mar–Oct daily 9:30am–5pm (July–Aug until 6pm); Nov–Feb Mon–Sat 10am–4pm, Sun 11am–4pm.

Where to Stay & Dine

★ **Bryn Tyrch Inn** CAPEL CURIG
A renovation completed in 2011 upgraded this cozy, informal roadside inn to create an ideal base for discerning hikers. Rooms are compact to midsized and have a slightly luxurious, Scandinavian feel. Capel Curig. ☎ 01690/720223. www.bryntyrchinn.co.uk. 12 units. Doubles £75–£85. MC, V.

kids **Cadair View Lodge** TRAWSFYNYDD
These basic but comfortable log cabins sleep two to six people. The location next to the renowned mountain biking forest at Coed y Brenin, with southern Snowdonia on the doorstep, is a big plus for outdoors types. Bronaber. ☎ 01978/759-603. www.cadairviewlodge.co.uk. 22 units. Cabins £90–£135. MC, V.

★★ **Castle Cottage** HARLECH *CONTEMPORARY EUROPEAN* There's a determined focus on local ingredients at this refined boutique restaurant (that also rents rooms; £120–£160 double). Expect Welsh lamb and shellfish to appear on the menu—but bring an open mind to creative combinations from farther afield. Y Lech, Harlech. ☎ 01766/780479. www.castlecottageharlech.co.uk. Set menu £38. MC, V. Dinner daily.

★ **The Peak** LLANBERIS *MODERN EUROPEAN*
This reliable, informal dining room remains the best place to eat in Snowdon's shadow. The part traditional, part Mediterranean–inspired menu includes beef and lamb dishes, and everything is assembled using local ingredients. 86 High St. ☎ 01286/872-777. www.peakrestaurant.co.uk. Entrees £13–£17. MC, V. Dinner Wed–Sun.

> One of the contemporary guest rooms at Tan-y-Foel.

Snowdonia Park WAUNFAWR *PUB FOOD*
This no-frills roadside brewpub could do with a refurbishment, but you can't go wrong with one of their filling homemade pies after a day on the hills. The bar sells microbrews crafted on-site. ☎ 01286/650-409. www.snowdonia-park.co.uk. Entrees £7–£14. MC, V. Lunch & dinner daily.

★★ **Tan-y-Foel** BETWS-Y-COED
A secluded country house with stylish, themed rooms, a creative kitchen, and jaw-dropping views over the Conwy Valley. Boutique luxury, attention to detail, and personal service are the watchwords. No children under 12. Capel Garmon. ☎ 01690/710-507. www.tyfhotel.co.uk. 6 units. Double £110–£240 w/breakfast. MC, V.

Anglesey & the Northwest Coast

Wales has almost 1,700 miles of coastline, some of the best of it wrapped around the cliffs and coves of its far northwest. Low-rise farmhouses and villages are the only man-made structures disrupting the gentle, green panoramas of inland Anglesey, while the Lleyn Peninsula across Caernarfon Bay offers more serene, empty terrain ideal for walkers and anyone seeking time and space to breathe deep. There's history here, too, with the grandest and most elegant castles of Edward's Iron Ring.

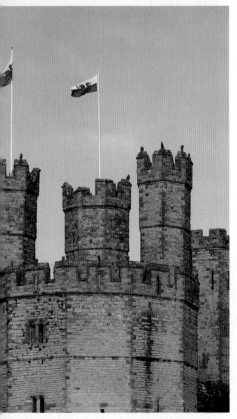

> So skillfully built were the curtain walls of Caernarfon Castle that they have survived over 700 years virtually unscathed.

START Caernarfon, 8 miles southwest of Bangor. TRIP LENGTH 3 days.

① ★ **Caernarfon Castle.** Edward I's Welsh castles (p. 669) have certainly stood the test of time: Caernarfon's is yet another well-preserved, intact ring of 13th-century walls that affords plenty of opportunities for visitors to climb on and inside the mightiest structure ever built in Wales and learn about the castle's role in the investiture of Princes of Wales. The walls between the Chamberlain Tower and Queen's Tower also house the **Museum of the Royal Welch Fusiliers** (www.rwfmuseum.org.uk), which traces the history of the regiment's role in wars across the globe since 1659. ⏱ 1½ hr. Pen Deitsh, Caernarfon. ☎ 01286/677-617. Admission (includes museum) £5.25 adults, £4.85 kids. Apr–Oct daily 9:30am–5pm (July–Aug until 6pm); Nov–Mar Mon–Sat 10am–4pm, Sun 11am–4pm.

② ★★★ **Welsh Highland Railway.** Wales's most spectacular little steam railway plies a course from regal Caernarfon right into the heart of Snowdonia—and since early 2011, out the other side to Porthmadog. Historic carriages creak, rattle, and cough their way along the Gwyrfai Valley and the shores of Llyn Cwellyn before striking out into undiluted uplands suited only to sightseers, sheep, and the occasional hardy drover. A few trains a day make the return journey, so if you plan it right you

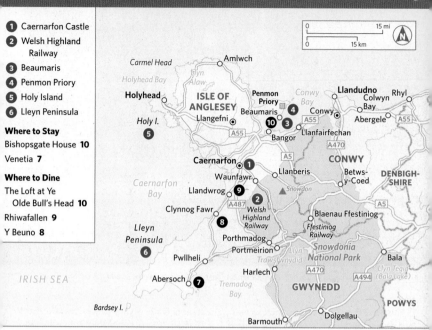

1 Caernarfon Castle
2 Welsh Highland Railway
3 Beaumaris
4 Penmon Priory
5 Holy Island
6 Lleyn Peninsula

Where to Stay
Bishopsgate House 10
Venetia 7

Where to Dine
The Loft at Ye Olde Bull's Head 10
Rhiwafallen 9
Y Beuno 8

can combine the train with some superlative hill walking: Alight at Rhyd Ddu or Snowdon Ranger for major paths up **Mount Snowdon** (p. 678, 1) or **Beddgelert** for the Aberglaslyn Gorge (p. 680, 3), also the most memorable stretch of the rail line. ☺ At least 4 hr. St. Helens Rd., Caernarfon. ☎ 01286/677-018. www. festrail.co.uk. Round-trip tickets £10–£28; kids 3–15 one free fare with each paying adult. Apr-Oct two to four trains daily; see website for timetable.

On Day 2, take the A487 northeast toward Bangor, cross the Menai Strait via the Britannia Bridge, and then follow signs along the A545 to Beaumaris. Total distance is 12 miles.

3 ★★ **Beaumaris.** This prosperous little town is the best place to get acquainted with some of Anglesey's occasionally checkered history, or just stroll along the Strait admiring Snowdonia in the distance. Low-rise turrets and circumnavigating ducks give moated **Beaumaris Castle** a rather twee appearance. However, in the 14th century the last and most elegant of Edward I's maritime fortresses was a feared outpost of English might. Its formidable and largely intact concentric defenses give you an immediate sense of what it was used

for—you'll quickly lose count of how many firing berths there are for defenders. Preserved just as it was in 1614, **Beaumaris Court** hosts a fascinating if somewhat grim exhibition that highlights the arbitrary and brutal nature of justice in centuries past. Although, timbered interior aside, it looks little different from a modern British courtroom, stories of "burning in the hand," hanging, and penal transportation thankfully belong to another era. The town's squat Victorian **gaol** continues the penitentiary theme. You're completely free to explore its gloomy corridors and cells, many enhanced with detailed explanations of the prison's harsh regime. Grisly highlights include the prisoner-powered treadwheel (a punishment) and the "luxury" condemned man's cell. Two public executions were staged at the gaol in the 1800s. ☺ 3 hr. Castle: ☎ 01248/810-361. www.beaumaris.com. Admission £3.80. Apr-Oct daily 9am-5pm; Nov-Mar Mon-Sat 9:30am-4pm, Sun 11am-4pm. Court: Castle St. ☎ 01248/811-681. Admission £3. Apr-Sep Mon-Thurs, Sat-Sun 10:30am-5pm; Oct weekends only. Gaol: Steeple Lane. ☎ 01248/810-921. Admission £3.50. Same hours as Court.

Follow the B5109 and well-signed minor roads to Penmon Point, 3 miles northeast.

> *Beaumaris occasionally hosts live reenactments of historic trials in its preserved 17th-century Court.*

④ Penmon Priory. This semi-ruined former Augustinian priory is one of Wales's ancient Christian places, long connected with St. Seiriol, who reportedly inhabited a hermitage here in the 6th century. Much of what's standing dates to the 13th century, including the church that houses two badly weathered 10th-century Celtic crosses. More remarkable still is an intact dome-shaped dovecote, built just after the priory's dissolution in the 1530s. One mile's easy walk from here is Penmon Point, the easterly tip of Anglesey, where a coastal ramble is rewarded with views of uninhabited Puffin Island and Llandudno's Great Orme. ⊙ 1½ hr. No phone. Free admission (parking/road toll £2.50). Daily during daylight hours.

Return to the Britannia Bridge, but instead of crossing it, head northwest on the A55. Total distance to Holyhead is 28 miles.

⑤ ★ Holy Island. At once lonely, spiritual, and uplifting, Holy Island is the end of the road. Telford's A5 (p. 675), which begins its 269-mile journey at London's Marble Arch, terminates at **Admiralty Arch** in Holyhead—the only way to continue west is by ferry to Ireland (a doable day trip). For magnificent coastal views from gorse and heather moorland paths, follow signs for **South Stack;** you can reach its lighthouse if you wish (beware lots of steps). The cliffs are part of a protected birdlife reserve (with viewing tower open Apr–Sept 10am–5:30pm); the seabird colony includes the puffin, guillemot, and chough among its residents. ⊙ 2 hr. www.rspb.org.uk/southstack. Ferry: ☎ 08447/707-070. www.stenaline.co.uk/days. Round-trip ticket £26 adults, £13 kids.

Return to Caernarfon, then take the A499 past Pwllheli into the Lleyn, where you'll spend Day 3. The distance to Abersoch is 57 miles.

⑥ ★ Lleyn Peninsula. Sticking out into the Irish Sea like a giant claw, this empty and mysterious finger of land is the heartland of Welsh feeling: Plaid Cymru, Wales's nationalist political party, was formed in Pwllheli in 1925. The northern Lleyn has some of North Wales's emptiest walking terrain. The coastal path between Clynnog Fawr over Yr Eifl to Nefyn, following an ancient pilgrims' route, is our favorite spot. **Llŷn Adventures** (☎ 07751/826-714; www.llynadventures.com) runs half-day organized outdoor activities, with a program that includes kayaking, rock climbing, and coasteering—a mixture of scrambling, coastal swimming, and exhilarating leaps first organized as a "sport" in Wales. Any half-day guided activity costs £30. Surfers might prefer to make straight for **Porth Neigwl**, "Hell's Mouth" beach (for a surf report, check www.westcoastsurf.co.uk/surfreport.htm). At the

> *The cliffs around South Stack lighthouse are a protected reserve managed by the Royal Society for the Protection of Birds (RSPB).*

Oriel Plas Glyn-y-Weddw, prints and original works by Welsh artists are displayed and sold inside an extraordinary neo-Gothic mansion surrounded by woodland. There's also a delightful garden tearoom. ⏲ At least 4 hr. Oriel Plas Glyn-y-Weddw: Llanbedrog. ☎ 01758/740-763. www.oriel.org.uk. Free admission. Feb–Dec Wed–Mon 10am–5pm.

Where to Stay & Dine

Bishopsgate House ANGLESEY
Traditional and slightly old-fashioned but friendly, this good value hotel occupies a historic town house in central Beaumaris. Castle St., Beaumaris. ☎ 01248/810-302. www.bishopsgatehotel.co.uk. 9 units. Doubles £90–£102 w/ breakfast. MC, V.

★★ **The Loft at Ye Olde Bull's Head** ANGLESEY
MODERN WELSH Anglesey's most creative contemporary cooking in exclusive surroundings under the eaves of Beaumaris's famous old coaching inn. Castle St., Beaumaris. ☎ 01248/810-329. www.bullsheadinn.co.uk. Set menu £40. MC, V. Dinner Tues–Sat.

★★ **Rhiwafallen** LLEYN *CREATIVE WELSH*
Chic wallpaper and light-wood furniture set off a stylish, intimate dining room at this farmhouse restaurant. The contemporary menu changes regularly but often includes local specialties like Welsh Black beef and wild sea bass. Advance reservations are essential. Llandwrog. ☎ 01286/830-172. www.rhiwafallen.co.uk. Set menu £35. MC, V. Dinner Tues–Sat; lunch Sun.

★★ **Venetia** LLEYN
A chic seaside hideaway close to the center of a pretty resort. Rooms inside the modernized Victorian villa are midsized and stylish, decorated in muted tones with flashes of exuberance, and dressed with Italian furniture. Lon Sarn Bach, Abersoch. ☎ 01758/713-354. www.venetiawales.com. 5 units. Doubles £80–£148 w/breakfast. AE, MC, V.

★ **Y Beuno** LLEYN *GASTROPUB*
Hearty homemade dishes for hungry hikers are injected with a touch of class at this cozy traditional inn. Think locally reared gammon steaks or beef 'n' ale pies enjoyed in nook seating. Clynnog Fawr. ☎ 01286/660-785. www.ybeuno.com. Entrees £9–£15. MC, V. Lunch & dinner daily.

Conwy

Pint-sized and atmospheric, the market town of Conwy has a historical importance that punches well above the weight of its population of 15,000. The castle, walls, and enclosed street plan were laid down by English King Edward I in the 1200s, when Conwy was a crucial garrison town. Later history almost forgot this little trading port, until the 19th century, when great bridges spanning the estuary brought roads and the railway to its ancient town gates.

> *Conwy was an important mercantile town in Tudor times, as the grandeur of Plas Mawr testifies.*

START Conwy Castle. Conwy is 55 miles west of Liverpool.

1 ★★ kids **Conwy Castle.** More than any other fortress built for Edward I, Conwy Castle provides insight into the clever military architecture of the king's master mason, James of St. George. Separated from the town by a massive ditch, with one entrance through two gates followed by the protection of Outer and Inner Wards, the castle would have been practically impossible to assault head-on—in fact, it was only ever taken by ruse or negotiation in its 700-year history. The wall-walk above the East Barbican is the place to head for the best view of more recent architectural wonders: Telford's **Menai Suspension Bridge** (1826) and Stephenson's tubular **Conwy Railway Bridge** (1849) cross the estuary and end right by the walls (p. 675). ⏱ 45 min. Castle St. ☎ 01492/592-358. Admission £4.60 adults, £4.10 kids. Mar–Oct daily 9am–5pm (July–Aug until 6pm); Feb–Mar Mon–Sat 10am–4pm, Sun 11am–4pm.

Spend a half-hour walking the town walls (free admission), as far as their apex above **Mount Pleasant.** Then stroll into the center to

2 ★★ **Plas Mawr.** From its modest entrance, you get no sense of the scale of this immaculately preserved Elizabethan town house. The mansion and courtyard garden were built in

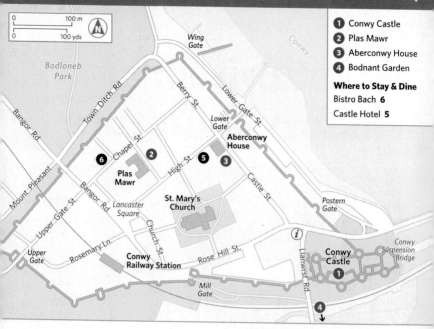

1 Conwy Castle
2 Plas Mawr
3 Aberconwy House
4 Bodnant Garden

Where to Stay & Dine
Bistro Bach **6**
Castle Hotel **5**

the 1580s for Robert Wynn, a Tudor nobleman who fathered seven children in his seventies while simultaneously serving as the Member of Parliament for Caernarvonshire and as County sheriff. The kitchen, pantry, and dining hall are dressed as if the owner and staff have just stepped out to the hunt and the market, respectively. ⏲ 1 hr. High St. ☎ 01492/580-167. Admission £4.95 adults, £4.60 kids. Tues-Sun Apr-Sep 9am-5pm; Oct 9:30am-4pm.

3 **Aberconwy House.** The town's only medieval house still standing (and the oldest in Conwy), was completed sometime during the 14th century in the half-timbered English style—although it owes its survival to the stone construction of the first story. Rooms are dressed according to the house's various guises over 6 centuries: as a working base for a Tudor merchant placed strategically close to the quay, as the sometime home of an 18th-century sea captain, and as a temperance (i.e. alcohol-free) hotel in the 1890s. ⏲ 30 min. Castle St. ☎ 01492/592-246. Admission £3. Mid-Mar to Oct Wed-Mon 11am-5pm (July-Aug also Tues).

Ride bus 25 from Llandudno Junction (20 min.) to

4 ★ **Bodnant Garden.** The 32-hectare (80-acre) hillside grounds of Bodnant Hall have been transformed into a charming mix of multi-tiered, labyrinthine formal gardens and managed wild spaces. Perfumed rose terraces have been carefully designed to afford views over the River Conwy to Snowdonia's foothills beyond. ⏲ 2 hr. Bodnant Rd. ☎ 01492/650-460. www.bodnantgarden.co.uk. Admission £7.72 adults, £3.86 kids. Late Feb-Oct daily 10am-5pm (early Nov until 4pm).

Staying the Night in Conwy

A traditional inn smack on Conwy's High Street, **Castle Hotel** has recently renovated rooms decorated in comfortable Edwardian style. High St. ☎ 01492/582-800. www.castlewales. co.uk. Doubles £130-£170. MC, V.

The backstreet ★ **Bistro Bach** has an unshakable commitment to local ingredients and a creative take on combining them. The short, modern menu always includes vegetarian options alongside Llandudno-smoked fish and prize-winning meats. 26 Chapel St. ☎ 01492/596-326. Entrees £13-£21. MC, V. Dinner Tues-Sun.

Great Britain's History & Culture

> Afternoon tea, like the one served in this Chipping Campden tearoom, is an English institution.

Britain's 10 Greatest Cultural Hits

1 Whisky. Its name means "water of life," but forget the hype: The malted barley the Scots have been distilling for more than 500 years is just plain tasty. What non-Brits call scotch (an esteemed tribute to its originators) is smoky and earthy—and whether you're sipping a glass in a London pub or a New York sports bar, each drop whisks you off to the Highlands.

2 Henry VIII. His penchant for dispatching wives and tearing down monasteries has made him a perennial bad boy, even in a monarchy riddled with royal scandals over the centuries. But egotism, corpulence, and lust aside, the second monarch of the House of Tudor was educated and charismatic, and 500 years after his death, Henry still has rock star status; he's the one English king everyone knows.

3 A stiff upper lip. The British are famous for remaining calm in the face of adversity. Think of James Bond, who never breaks a sweat,

even when he's about to be cut in half by a blade saw. (One could say he's shaken but not stirred.) The same quality helped Londoners through the Blitz and other scrapes, too, and the rest of us would do well to follow suit.

4 The pub. France has cafes, Germany has ratskellers, America has bars, but there's nothing like a British pub (short for public house). Some are character-filled, half-timbered old piles, others are modest holes in the wall, and they all show us just how much more pleasant it is to drink in good company than alone.

5 Bagpipes. When Roman emperor Nero wasn't fiddling, he was blowing into his *tibia utricularis,* the first known bagpipe. The Scots, with a plethora of sheepskins to fashion into airbags, became especially attached to the contraption in the Middle Ages, and ever since no solemn occasion has been complete without a band of kilted Scottish pipers.

6 **London's double decker buses.** The bright red, lumbering vehicles are as iconic of London as Big Ben and put a whole new spin on bus riding. Not only do they look great, but they're fun to ride, too. Elbow your way to the front row of the upper deck, take a seat, and watch the spectacle of one of the most exciting cities on earth pass before your eyes.

7 **The Beatles.** The world changed forever the night of February 9, 1964—at least, the world of modern music. Four million viewers heard the Beatles, already a success in England, sing "I Want to Hold Your Hand" and other hits on their first appearance on *The Ed Sullivan Show.* As their host would have said, "They were a really big shooow." In Liverpool (p. 434), you can see where these modern legends got their start.

8 **Shakespeare.** His name is synonymous with England, and the greatest playwright of the Elizabethan Age—of any age, for that matter—still speaks to everyone everywhere with his sumptuous language and universal truths. Millions come to pay homage to him at Stratford-upon-Avon (p. 366), where the Bard was born, lived, and is buried.

9 **Tea.** The Chinese were the first to cultivate tea, the Japanese create entire ceremonies around pouring it, the Americans name political movements after it, and just about every culture in the world drinks it. But over the centuries the British have truly made the beverage their own—a ritual, a pastime, and one of life's great pleasures.

10 **Monty Python.** They pushed the envelope, showed us that the British really do have a sense of humor, and have inspired comedians ever since we began rolling on the floor watching their crazy antics in 1969. The plain and simple truth is, cross-dressing or wearing chain mail, the brilliantly clever comedy team just makes us laugh.

BOMBS AND BLACKOUTS

The London Blitz **BY DONALD OLSON**

THE BLITZ was one of the most traumatic and character-shaping events in London's history. From September 1940 to May 1941, and then sporadically until the end of World War II, Nazi bombers dropped thousands of bombs on cities, towns, and industrial sites throughout England. At the height of the Blitz, London endured 76 consecutive nights of bombing, including a devastating attack on the City of London that caused a firestorm called the Second Great Fire of London. More than 22,000 London civilians were killed during the Blitz, and more than a million houses and buildings, including some of the city's most venerable churches, landmarks, and monuments, were damaged or destroyed. Instead of undermining civilian morale, as Hitler had hoped, the Blitz brought besieged Londoners closer together as they shared the crisis with bravery and resilience.

London During the Blitz

Daily bombing raids took a huge toll on the fabric of the city and disrupted lives. At night, the city went into blackout mode. As bombs exploded, bringing death and destruction to people and places they held dear, Londoners bravely stuck together and carried on. Civilians joined organizations such as the Home Guard, the Air Raid Precautions service, and the Auxiliary Fire Service. Boy Scouts guided fire engines to where they were most needed. During air raids, people took shelter in Tube stations and in backyard Anderson bomb shelters. About 13% of the population left London in the days following the declaration of war, and thousands of children were evacuated to the country. Many Londoners slept far from their homes and travelled several hours to and from work every day.

Winston Churchill: Wartime Prime Minister

During "England's darkest hour," the British looked to Winston Churchill (1874–1965) for leadership. Appointed Prime Minister and Minister of Defense in 1940, he set the tone for the nation in his first speech: "You ask, what is our aim? I can answer in one word: It is victory, victory at all costs, victory in spite of all terror, victory, however long and hard the road may be." London's Cabinet War Rooms and Churchill Museum (p. 100, **②**) is located in the underground bunker that served as Churchill's office during the Blitz.

London Blitz Timeline

1939
3 SEPTEMBER War is declared. Children begin evacuating to the countryside, and 1,500,000 Anderson shelters are distributed to poor families

1940
25 AUGUST The first bomb drops on London

7 SEPTEMBER The first air raid bombs the East End, the City, and Central London, killing 430 people, injuring 1,600, and causing over a 1,000 fires

15 OCTOBER Bombs kill 430 people; 250,000 people are left homeless

14 NOVEMBER End of nighttime raids on London

15 NOVEMBER Luftwaffe hits almost every borough with new high-explosive bombs

29 DECEMBER Incendiaries cause over 1,400 fires, destroy eight Wren churches, and damage five

railway stations, nine hospitals, 16 Tube stations, and St. Paul's

1941
11 JANUARY Direct hit on Bank Underground station kills 117 people

19 MARCH A raid on the docks and East End kills 750 people, injures over 1,000

16 APRIL A raid kills more than 1,000 people, causes over 2,000 fires

19 APRIL The biggest bombing raid of the London Blitz with more high-explosives and incendiaries dropped than any other night

10 MAY In the last and worst of the major raids, bombers drop more than 700 tons of bombs and thousands of incendiaries, killing 1,500, injuring 1,800, destroying the Chamber of the House of Commons, and damaging the House of Lords, Westminster Abbey, and other historic buildings

1941–1945
Sporadic raids on London begin again in June 1944

A Timeline of British History

B.C.

5000 B.C. Neolithic civilizations erect Stonehenge (left) and other stone circles across Britain.

3000–100 B.C. Celts settle in Scotland and Wales.

A.D. 43–410 The Romans conquer and occupy England and Wales, building roads, villas, walls, and baths; they fail, however, to conquer the Scots to the North.

500–1066 Anglo-Saxon kingdoms fight off invading Vikings, who finally gain a stronghold in Jorvik (York) in the 11th century.

1066 William, Duke of Normandy, defeats Saxon King Harold at the Battle of Hastings and is crowned King in Westminster Abbey.

1154 Henry II comes to power, initiating 250 years of Plantagenet rule.

1200

1215 King John signs the Magna Carta (left) at Runnymede, granting more rights to nobles and setting the foundations of parliamentary democracy.

1282 Welsh prince Llywelyn ap Gruffydd dies in battle, and England assumes control of Wales; in 1301, Edward I's heir is named the first English Prince of Wales.

1314 The Scots defeat the English at the Battle of Bannockburn; the defeat results in the 1328 Treaty of Northampton, wherein England recognizes Scottish independence.

1337 Hundred Years' War between France and England begins; its most famous skirmish, the Battle of Agincourt, is won by Henry V and the English in 1415.

1348 The Black Death ravages Scotland and England, significantly reducing their populations.

1400

1485 Henry VII wins the Battle of Bosworth; Tudor dynasty begins.

1534–1536 Henry VIII launches the English Reformation and dissolves England's monasteries; the Act of Union seals Wales to England.

1558 Elizabeth I (left) ascends the throne and ushers in an age of exploration and a renaissance in science and learning.

1603 James VI of Scotland becomes James I of England, uniting the crowns of Scotland and England.

1649 Charles I is beheaded, and England becomes a republic under Oliver Cromwell.

1660 Charles II is restored to the throne.

1665–1666 The plague and the Great Fire devastate London.

1700

1707 Act of Union makes Scotland part of the United Kingdom of Great Britain.

1746 Bonnie Prince Charlie is defeated at the Battle of Culloden; the Stuart line officially ends.

1750-1850 The Clearances in Scotland force many crofters off their farms, creating new migration patterns.

1763 Britain wins Canada from France.

1775-1783 Britain loses its American colonies.

1815 Britain defeats Napoleon at the Battle of Waterloo (left).

1837 Victoria ascends the throne for a 64-year-long reign during which Britain expands its empire around the globe.

1900

1901 Edward VII ushers in the Edwardian era.

1914-1918 England fights Germany in World War I, emerging victorious but suffering a devastating loss of life.

1936 Edward VIII abdicates to marry American divorcee Wallis Simpson.

1939-1945 In what Winston Churchill (left) calls the nation's "finest hour," Britain withstands 6 years of war with Germany.

1948 India gains independence, marking the slow dissolution of the British Empire.

1952 Queen Elizabeth II ascends the throne.

1982 Britain defeats Argentina in the Falklands War.

1988 Terrorists blow up Pan Am flight 103 over Lockerbie, Scotland.

1990

1994 The Channel Tunnel links England to the Continent.

1996 An IRA bomb rips through London's Docklands; mad cow disease puts a dent in the British beef industry.

1997 Labour's Tony Blair (left) wins a landslide victory to become prime minister; Princess Diana is killed in a car crash in Paris.

1999 Scottish Parliament sits for the first time; Welsh National Assembly convenes for first time in 600 years.

2005 Terrorist bombs explode on the London Underground and in a bus, killing 52.

2010 David Cameron, leader of the Conservative Party, becomes prime minister.

A Brief History of Great Britain

> Hadrian's Wall originally spanned the width of England, from the River Tyne in the east to the Solway Firth in the west.

The Earliest Britons & the Roman Invasion

Britain was probably split off from the continent of Europe some 8 millennia ago by continental drift and other natural forces. The earliest inhabitants, the **Iberians,** are the people whose ingenuity and enterprise are believed to have created **Stonehenge** (p. 199, ❷), but despite that great and mysterious monument, little is known about them. They were replaced by the iron-wielding **Celts,** whose massive invasions around 500 B.C. drove the Iberians back to the Scottish Highlands and Welsh mountains, where some of their descendants still live today.

In 54 B.C., Julius Caesar invaded England, but the Romans did not become established there and in Wales until A.D. 43. They went as far as Caledonia (now Scotland), where they gave up, leaving that land to "the painted ones," or the warring Picts. In Wales, the Romans stuck to the lowlands and did not set out to subdue the natives of this wild country who took to the hills and mountains. **Hadrian's Wall** (p. 472, ❼), built by the emperor across the north of England, marked the northernmost reaches of the Roman Empire. They also built a fort called Londinium that the historian Tacitus was soon describing as "famed for commerce and crowded with merchants." Queen Boudicca of the Iceni tribe (p. 697) led some violent revolts against the settlers, but the Romans remained until the empire began to wane in the 5th century. During almost 4 centuries of occupation, the Romans built roads, villas, towns, walls, and fortresses; they farmed the land and introduced first their pagan religions, then Christianity.

The Saxons & the Scots

The Saxons, a confederation of old Germanic tribes, sailed across the North Sea and arrived in England around A.D. 450. They spent the next 6 centuries fending off Vikings and other invaders. Little remains of their presence except for a few Saxon churches, such as St. Mary in Castro within the walls of Dover Castle (p. 162; ❶) and St. Martin's in Canterbury (p. 170; ❺). The Anglo-Saxons also played a large part in settling Wales—splitting it into various small kingdoms that subsequently spent centuries fighting internal turf wars (and a few with some occasionally bellicose neighbors). Only one man has ever ruled an independent Wales as sole king: **Gruffydd ap Llywelyn** (1007–64). Danish Vikings finally conquered England in the 11th century, converting the Roman settlement of Eboracum into Jorvik, which eventually became York; the city re-creates its Viking past in a well-done exhibit at the JORVIK Viking Centre (p. 487; ❻).

Meanwhile, in Scotland, in A.D. 500, the Picts were successfully subdued by invaders called Scots. They established themselves on the Argyll Peninsula and battled and intermarried with the Picts. Britons emigrated from the south and Norsemen from the east, creating new bloodlines and migratory patterns (and quite a melting pot of languages and dialects, notably Celtic

> Treasures found at Sutton Hoo, displayed at London's British Museum, date to the Anglo-Saxon period.

> Norman conquerors built castles and cathedrals, including Winchester.

and Norse). Under **Malcolm II** (reigned 1005–34), the British and the Angles, who occupied the southwest and southeast of the Scottish mainland, merged with the Scots and the Picts. Malcolm's grandson and heir, Duncan, was murdered by Macbeth of Moray, and this event fueled the plotline of Shakespeare's famous "Scottish play."

The Normans

In 1066, at the Battle of Hastings, a Norman army led by William of Normandy (1028–87) conquered the last of the Saxon armies led by the Saxon King Harold (1022–66); the **battleground** (p. 180) is one of England's most venerable pieces of turf. William proved to be a capable leader, and he left behind the White Tower, the tallest structure within the Tower of London (p. 56, ❶) and the famed Domesday Book, or "Book of Doom," a survey of all the land he had conquered and an invaluable resource for historians (and William's pockets—he used it to assess taxes). William also managed to seize much of Wales, touching off a struggle between the English and Welsh for several centuries. Normans took control of estates, built castles and cathedrals (including Windsor Castle, p. 134, ❷; and Winchester Cathedral, p. 214, ❶), and became the nobility—the feudal system became firmly entrenched. French was the language of the court well into the Middle Ages (yep, Richard the Lionheart, 1157–99, probably didn't know a word of English).

In Scotland, **Malcolm III's** (d. 1093) marriage to an English princess, **St. Margaret** (ca. 1045–93), helped

Boudicca: A Warrior Queen

One of England's most storied queens was born 13 years before the Romans invaded Britain, and Boudicca (A.D. 30–60) spent her short adult life trying to vanquish them. At age 18 she married Prasutagus, king of the Iceni tribe, who soon died. When Roman soldiers confiscated the property Prasutagus had left his family, whipped Boudicca, and raped her two daughters, the young queen sprang into action. She raised an army among warring local tribes and launched a series of fierce attacks on Roman forts. Celtic women painted their faces blue and fought alongside their men in battle, and they allegedly terrified the Roman soldiers—but not so much that legionnaires under Suetonius Paulinus didn't eventually put down Boudicca and her Celtic uprising, on a battlefield in the Midlands in A.D. 61.

anglicize the Scottish Lowlands. She carried out church reforms that soon replaced the local Gaelic form of Christianity and laid important groundwork for making Scotland into a potential English kingdom. Cultural assimilation with England continued under **David I** (1083–1153), who made land grants to many Anglo-Norman families and embarked on one of the most lavish building sprees in Scottish history (bankrupting the country), erecting many abbeys, including Jedburgh (p. 547, ❸) and Melrose (p. 546, ❷).

> The Battle of Crécy, won by England's Edward III, was one of the most important battles in the Hundred Years' War.

The Plantagenets

Henry II (1133–89), the first of the Plantagenets, was crowned in 1154. The charismatic and powerful Henry proved himself to be a capable ruler, infamous for the murder by his knights of Thomas Becket (1118–70) and famous for introducing a system of common law that formed the basis of the British and American legal systems. At Runnymede in 1215, his son **John** (1166–1216) signed into law Britain's most influential legal document, the **Magna Carta,** making the monarch subject to the law of the land, establishing certain rights for subjects, and setting forth the policies that gave birth to the parliamentary democracy practiced in England today (and by extension the principles of western democracy).

Another Plantagenet monarch also had a considerable influence on Britain. **Edward I** (1239–1307), the Hammer of the Scots, wasn't content just to rule England—he sought

domination over Scotland and Wales as well. For a while he succeeded. Wales fell to him when their last prince, **Llywelyn ap Gruffydd** (1223–82), died in battle (Edward then began the tradition of investing the English heir as Prince of Wales). But the Scots didn't take too kindly to English rule, and the clan system rose to prominence. Many of Scotland's legendary heroes lived during this period: **Sir William Wallace** (1270–1305), who drove the English out of Perth and Stirling; **Sir James Douglas,** the Black Douglas (1286–1330), who terrorized the English borders; and **Robert the Bruce** (1274–1329), who finally succeeded in freeing Scotland from England at the 1314 Battle of Bannockburn. Scotland's independence was formally recognized in the 1328 Treaty of Northampton, inaugurating a heady but short-lived separation from England.

In 1348, the **Black Death** began to ravage Britain,

reducing the population of the region by half. Wales promptly rebelled against English rule in the late 14th century, but resistance proved futile. The **Hundred Years' War** with France proved quite the distraction for a while (and turned **Henry V** 1387–1422 into a hero of mythic proportions when he emerged victorious at the Battle of Agincourt), but also marked the end of medieval chivalry. Society slowly revived, and the introduction of the printing press in 1476 helped spread literacy among the middle and upper classes.

The Tudors & the Stuarts

The **Wars of the Roses** between the houses of York and Lancaster ended at the Battle of Bosworth and brought the first Tudor, the wily **Henry VII** (1457–1509), to the throne. His son, **Henry VIII** (1491–1547; p. 160), proved to be the most flamboyant member of the line, best known for his many unfortunate wives and his reformation of the Church

Sir Walter Raleigh and Sir Francis Drake, who plied the world's seas from Plymouth and other ports, returning with spices, coffee, tobacco, and other riches. Sir Thomas Gresham founded the Royal Exchange, making London into the important financial center it remains. William Shakespeare came to London in 1586, joining Ben Jonson, Christopher Marlowe, John Donne, and others in what would become the boon years of English drama and poetry.

It was Elizabeth's death, however, that finally let England do in peace what it hadn't been able to do in war. Her heir was **James VI of Scotland** (1566-1625), who promptly united the kingdoms of Scotland, England, and

> The casualties of the Black Death in Britain were so numerous that large "plague pits" were dug to bury them.

in England. He broke with Rome, destroyed many of the country's magnificent monasteries (such as St. Augustine's Abbey in Canterbury, p. 168, ❹), and established the Church of England. England's Reformation was mirrored in Scotland as clergyman **John Knox** (1510-72) championed the fervently anti-Catholic Church of Scotland. Henry's daughter, **Mary I** (1516-58), took the throne and turned the tables, earning the name Bloody Mary for her persecution of the Protestants. Her half-sister, **Elizabeth I** (1533-1603), succeeded her, returning England to Protestantism and, to forestall an overthrow by Catholic forces, had her cousin **Mary, Queen of Scots** (1542-87) executed.

Elizabeth was a great monarch who earned her moniker "Good Queen Bess." Her reign, the Elizabethan Age, saw the exploits of

Mary, Queen of Scots

The fascinating Mary Stuart (1542-87), who stood almost 6 feet tall, was crowned Queen of the Scots when she was 9 months old. She was sent off to the French court as a child to marry Francis II (1544-60), much to the anger of Henry VIII, who'd tried to force the Scots to marry her to his son, Edward, by invading the country (known to the Scottish as "the Rough Wooing.") At age 17, Mary became queen of France—for one year, as she was soon widowed. Mary returned to Scotland, where her marital career was no less tumultuous—one husband was murdered, and Mary next married his alleged assassin, the Earl of Bothwell. Scottish nobility looked askance at these events and forced Mary to abdicate the throne in favor of her son, James VI. When she fled to England and sought the protection and assistance of her cousin, Elizabeth I, Elizabeth was not all that hospitable—Catholics claimed Elizabeth illegitimate and Mary the true queen of England (a claim Mary didn't go out of her way to dispute). Elizabeth had Mary arrested and held prisoner in various castles for the next 19 years. A court eventually found Mary guilty of sanctioning the assassination of Elizabeth, and she was beheaded.

> *London's Great Exhibition in 1851 showed off Britain's prominence in both culture and industry.*

> *George III lost the American colonies to revolution and his mind to porphyria.*

Wales when he ascended the throne of England as James I of the Stuart line (though officially the United Kingdom of Britain wouldn't be declared until 1707).

Roundheads, the Plague, and Fire

The 17th century was not kind to England. **Charles I** (1600–49) started a civil war when he insisted on the divine right of kings and dissolved Parliament. **Oliver Cromwell** (1599–1658), leading the Roundheads, had Charles beheaded and ushered in 18 years of harsh Puritan rule. **Charles II** (1630–85) then returned from exile in France and avenged the execution of his father by publicly beheading Cromwell's corpse. The plague emerged again in 1665, decimating the

population of London and villages alike. No sooner had the worst of the crises subsided than, on September 2, 1666, sparks from a baker's oven in Pudding Lane started a conflagration that all but leveled London, which slowly began to rise from the ashes, with Sir Christopher Wren (1632–1723) rebuilding 51 churches, including St. Paul's Cathedral (p. 54, ❾).

The Hanoverians

By 1714, the Protestant Stuart line had ended with Queen Anne (1665–1714). Britain (having outlawed Catholics as rulers) was looking for a Protestant monarch, and turned to a German grandson of James I, **George of Hanover** (1660–1727), ushering in 174 years of Hanoverian rule (much to the consternation of the Scots—the Jacobite Rebellion attempted to put the exiled descendants of Catholic James II back on the throne, but it was crushed by the English, who also came

down hard on Scotland's clans). Hanoverians included mad **George III** (1738–1820) and his dissipated son **George IV** (1762–1830), but any vacuum they created was filled by an increasingly powerful Parliament. Under the Hanoverians, Britain lost the American colonies but gained Canada; laid claim to Australia, New Zealand, and India; and defeated Napoleon at Trafalgar and Waterloo. The Hanoverian era was the great age of British writers, thinkers, and artists: William Hogarth, Sir Joshua Reynolds, Thomas Gainsborough (painting); Jonathan Swift, Henry Fielding, Oliver Goldsmith (literature); David Garrick (theater); Alexander Pope (poetry); John Nash and Robert Adams (architecture); Edward Gibbon (history); David Hume (philosophy); Captain James Cook (exploration); Adam Smith (economics); and James Watt (technology).

The Victorians

Victoria (1819–1901) was only 18 years old when she became queen in 1837. Her 64-year-long reign coincided with enormous changes in Britain. The Industrial Revolution transformed the kingdom from a rural, agricultural society into an industrial power. London, Manchester, Leeds, and other cities grew at an amazing rate as people moved from the countryside looking for work. Conditions in the tenements and factories were appalling; children as young as six were put to work. Railroads began crisscrossing the countryside (you can see some of the first trains at the National Railway Museum in York, p. 488, **8**), shipping canals were dug, and trade unions were formed. Prince Albert, Victoria's husband, organized the Great Exhibition of 1851 to show the world that England was at the vanguard of progress. While the industrialized cities were growing ever more filthy and crowded, William Wordsworth and the other Romantic poets were extolling the beauties of nature. And socially, conservative middle-class values, embodied by the queen, spread throughout the empire.

The Edwardians and the World Wars

Victoria's playboy son, Edward VII (1841–1910), was a relatively undistinguished monarch, but the last to have an age named after him. Edwardian England saw peace, prosperity, and the introduction of telephones and motorcars—that is, the modern era, leading novelist Virginia Woolf to famously comment, "In or about December 1910, human character changed."

Soon, however, German zeppelins were floating over London, and Britain was plunged into a war that wiped out an entire generation of young men. The war was won, but peace, progress, and prosperity came to an end. In the 1920s and 1930s, England was beset by economic depression, unemployment, and the terrible residues of World War I. Bright spots were a glamorous Jazz Age social scene and the riveting, gossip-fueled drama surrounding the abdication of **King Edward VIII** (1894–1972) in 1936 to marry the "woman he loved," American divorcee Wallis Simpson. Not only did the event create a constitutional crisis, but it set in motion a new national pastime that thrives to this day: royal watching.

Soon, though, attention was turned to the threat of another war with Germany. On September 7, 1940, German planes raced up the Thames to London and dropped bombs on docks, gas works, and power stations. The war was on. The Blitz continued for 76 consecutive nights, and the Luftwaffe dropped bombs on Coventry, Plymouth, and other cities as well. The British rose to the challenge of Prime Minister **Winston Churchill** (1874–1965): "Let us therefore brace ourselves to our duties, and so bear ourselves that, if the British Empire and its Commonwealth last for a thousand years, men will still say, 'This was their finest hour.'" To this day, the World War II era is remembered by many with pride and nostalgia for a time when Britain was still a great world power.

> World War I was fought largely in the dirty, disease-ridden trenches of northern France and Belgium.

Enter Elizabeth, Exit Empire

England spent the 1950s rebuilding and living under strict food rationing. When wartime king **George VI** (1895–1952) died, his daughter **Elizabeth II** (b. 1926) ascended the throne. The amiable, hard-working queen has seen England through the ups and downs of the postwar years. Indian independence in 1948 marked the beginning of the dismantling of the British Empire, England slowly lost much of its industrial might, and a new "welfare system" introduced profound social change. Almost as if to fill a void, London became the epicenter of the swinging '60s: the Beatles, Twiggy, Carnaby Street, Kings Road, the Rolling Stones—anything British became the height of fashion.

Margaret Thatcher's (b. 1925) ascendancy to the prime ministership in 1979 threw a pail of cold water on all but the wealthiest Britons,

> The nation came to a virtual standstill for the wedding of Charles and "Di" in 1981.

> Britain's first female prime minister, Conservative Margaret Thatcher, served from 1979 until she was ousted by her own party in 1990.

The 1990s onward

The 1990s were marked by a series of royal scandals and break-ups as three of Queen Elizabeth's children (including Charles) split from their spouses; Princess Diana was later tragically killed in a car accident in Paris in 1997, resulting in a major outpouring of national grief. In 1997, 44-year-old Tony Blair won a landslide victory to become Britain's youngest prime minister in 185 years. His election coincided with a renaissance—"Cool Britannia"—in which being British, whether you were a Spice Girl or a fashion designer, implied that you were hip. It also gave a lift to Scottish and Welsh nationalists—both countries began to convene their own parliaments (under British auspices) as part of his reform package.

On July 7, 2005, Britain became the victim of radical Islamic terrorism as explosions in the London Underground and on a bus killed 52 and wounded 700. Londoners, in typical fashion, made a point of returning to business as usual. In 2010, David Cameron, leader of the Conservative Party, became prime minister as Britain eyed recovery from a pervasive economic slowdown. But British spirits remained upbeat despite the downturn. The entire country rejoiced when London was awarded the 2012 Olympic Games, which will coincide with the Queen's Diamond Jubilee. And in 2011, the country buzzed with excitement as Prince William, the future king, married Kate Middleton in Westminster Abbey.

seriously eroding the welfare state. Homelessness soared, race riots broke out in Brixton, civil workers went on strike. Spirits brightened briefly in 1981, when Prince Charles married Lady Diana Spencer and when Britain triumphed over Argentina in the Falklands War in 1982.

Britain's Architectural Evolution

The Romans
The Romans who occupied Britain from A.D. 43 left behind walls, mosaics, and other remnants of their 400-year-long presence; for information on their architectural contributions, see p. 482.

The Normans
The Norman Conquest of 1066 brought the Romanesque style to Britain and began an era of cathedral and castle building. These somber, even oppressive structures had thick walls to support their weight, pierced by infrequent small windows, and large arches to open up the spaces. **Chichester Cathedral** (p. 182, **1**) is a magnificent assemblage of Norman architecture in which the arches and vaulting work in perfect harmony. Other good examples include Scotland's **Jedburgh Abbey** (p. 547, **3**), Wales's mighty **Pembroke Castle** (p. 654, **1**), and one of William the Conqueror's great landmarks, the Tower of London's **White Tower** (p. 59, **1**).

Gothic
The French Gothic style invaded England in the late 12th century, and heavy, thick walls and rounded arches were replaced by an engineering marvel, the pointed arch. This innovation could carry more weight, allowing walls to thin, windows to proliferate, and ceilings to soar. Gothic can be divided into three periods in Britain: **Early English** (1150–1300), **Decorated** (1250–1370), and **Perpendicular** (1350–1550). Common to all periods are huge circular rose windows, spires, gargoyles, and elaborately carved choir screens.

Salisbury Cathedral (p. 212, **9**), with its tall, pointy lancet windows, is a fine example of pure Early English style, as is Wells Cathedral (p. 261, **5**), the first structure in Britain to use the pointed arch. **York Minster** (p. 484, **1**) and **Exeter Cathedral** (p. 276, **1**), with their lacy spider webs of carved stone and great expanses of stained glass, were fashioned in what has come to be known as the Decorated style. Fan vaulting (side-by-side, cone-shaped, concave vaults springing from the same point) is the trademark of the Perpendicular style, and you'll see an elaborate use of this technique in Cambridge's **King's College Chapel** (p. 400, **4**) and **Henry VII's Lady Chapel** in Westminster Abbey (p. 53, **1**).

The Renaissance
As Renaissance principles of proportion, order, and classical ideals swept across the Continent, Britain was slow to catch on, sticking to the Tudor and Elizabethan versions of the Perpendicular style, as seen at **Hampton Court Palace** (p. 76), **Plas Mawr** (p. 686, **2**), and **Longleat**

> *Intricate stained-glass panels at York Minster.*

> *The Palladian Bridge at Wilton House.*

> *William the Conqueror's mostly intact White Tower.*

(p. 204, **3**). By the 17th century, however, the architect and landscape designer Inigo Jones (1573–1652) ushered in the Renaissance era when he returned from Italy full of the theories of **Palladianism,** which emphasized symmetry, proportion, and the use of classical columns. He applied those theories to his many designs, an excellent example of which is **Wilton House** (p. 203, **2**).

The Baroque

A more decorative version of Renaissance style began to emerge in the mid-17th century, adding curves and an overall lightness to classical design. Britain's greatest architect of the baroque was **Sir Christopher Wren** (1632–1723), who was entrusted with the task of rebuilding London after the fire of 1666 (p. 90). His crowning achievement was **St. Paul's Cathedral** (p. 54, **9**), though another good example of his work is Oxford's Sheldonian

Theatre (p. 363, **9**). Other proponents of baroque architecture were **John Vanbrugh** (1664–1726) and his mentor **Nicholas Hawksmoor** (1661–1731). Yorkshire's **Castle Howard** (p. 466, **2**) is one of their many collaborations, and Vanbrugh also designed stunning **Blenheim Palace** (p. 340, **1**).

Neoclassical and Greek Revival

The ornate frippery of the baroque was not universally admired, and architecture began to turn back to classical ideals (symmetry, crescent structure, classical orders, and restrained but elegant simplicity), giving rise to the neoclassical, or Greek revival, as practiced by England's **Sir John Soane** (1753–1857) and Scotland's **Robert Adam** (1728–92). **Bath** (p. 266) was largely redone in neoclassical style between 1727 and 1775, and the stunning effect of the attention to classical order and symmetry comes

powerfully to light in the **Royal Crescent** (p. 269; **9**). Edinburgh's **New Town** (p. 503, **9**) is similarly structured. Perhaps the most famous example of the style, however, is London's **British Museum** (p. 68).

Victorian Gothic Revival

As the Industrial Age began to envelope English landscapes, creative spirits harked back to the good ol' days of the Middle Ages—not to the harsh realities of the Dark Ages, but to fairy tales of chivalrous knights and idealized scenes of simple, agrarian life. Architects picked and plucked from the Gothic repertoire, favoring the grand scale, arches, and elaborate stonework seen on such landmarks as London's **Palace of Westminster** (p. 52, **3**) and **Albert Memorial** (p. 74, **6**), as well as Cardiff's **Castell Coch** (p. 638, **4**) and **Cardiff Castle** (p. 642, **1**). Scotland's fantastic **Inveraray Castle** (p. 600, **2**) took

> *"If you seek his monument, look around you"—so reads Wren's commemorative plaque beneath the dome of St. Paul's Cathedral.*

> *Bath's Royal Crescent is perhaps the most instantly recognizable work of Georgian architecture in England.*

> *The Albert Memorial is distinctly Victorian, with many ornate embellishments.*

> *The "Gherkin" is just one of many daring new skyscrapers changing the City of London's skyline.*

so long to complete that it started off baroque, has elements of the neoclassical, and then was completed in Gothic revival.

The 20th and 21st centuries
Proponents of the late-19th-century and early-20th-century Arts and Crafts Movement placed a great emphasis on the revival of craftsmanship. You can see the beautiful workmanship of the period at **Owlpen** (p. 312, ❺) and **Rodmarton** (p. 313, ❻). Architecture-wise, however, it was Scotland that dominated the early 20th century, thanks to the Art Nouveau style popularized by Glasgow's **Charles Rennie Mackintosh**

(1868–1928), which emphasized asymmetrical, curvaceous designs based on the organic inspiration of plants and flowers. A prime example is the **Glasgow School of Art** (p. 566, ❷).

In general, however, British architecture took a few wrong turns in the 20th century, first with the ungainly urban sprawl of the pre-World War II years, then with the massive postwar building that in many cases wreaked as much havoc with its concrete banality as the Blitz did. Much of late-20th-century architecture, such as London's **Barbican Centre** (p. 130), can best be described as Brutalism. But British postmodern

architecture, usually combining the skyscraper motif with a reliance on historical details, has produced a few winners, including the graceful **Lloyd's Building** in London (1986) and Cardiff's **Senedd building** (p. 644, ❹), both by Lord Richard Rogers (b. 1933). The work of his contemporary Lord Norman Foster (b. 1935) is equally renowned, including the innovative **30 St. Mary Axe** (the **"Gherkin"**), a pickle-shaped London City office tower (2003); the **Greater London Authority building** (**London City Hall,** 2002); and one of his early commissions, the **Sainsbury Centre for Visual Arts** in Norwich (p. 397, ⓬).

British Art

> *The Gothic* Wilton Diptych, *painted for King Richard II.*

The Celts left behind some early traces of an artistic heritage, including the famed 7th-century illuminated **Lindisfarne Gospels** and the **Wilton Diptych** (p. 63, ❼), crafted in the late 1390s for Richard II. But British art wasn't much of a factor on the world scene until more modern times. **Joshua Reynolds** (1723–92) and rival **Thomas Gainsborough** (1727–88) both produced colorful, classically inspired works (often featuring the aristocracy). Romantic **John Constable** (1776–1837) created idealized bucolic rural scenes, while **J.M.W. Turner** (1775–1851) is often called the First Impressionist for his moody cityscapes and influence on the work of Claude Monet. Even more unabashedly romantic were the Pre-Raphaelites, who took their inspiration from Shakespeare, mythology, and the Bible; major proponents were **Dante Gabriel Rossetti** (1828–82) and **John Everett Millais** (1829–96).

Many British painters and sculptors gained international acclaim in the 20th century, as **Henry Moore** (1898–1986) became renowned for his abstract surrealistic figures while **Francis Bacon** (1909–92) and **Lucian Freud** (b. 1922) plumbed human frailty and despair in their masterful, colorful canvases. **David Hockney** (b. 1937) totters on the edge of pop art with his bold and enticing work, while **Damien Hirst** (b. 1965) flaunts convention with a death theme and gimmicks that are probably more shocking than they are timeless.

British Music

> *Sir Arthur Sullivan, the composing half of the comic-opera partnership of Gilbert and Sullivan.*

British music can easily be divided into two categories—timeless classics and the pop/rock sensations that began to make waves starting in the 1960s (for details on the latter, see p. 432). The division is not actually that clear-cut—the late-19th-century comic opera team of **Gilbert and Sullivan,** creators of *The Pirates of Penzance* and *H.M.S. Pinafore,* are a delightful cross between the two.

Also make it a point in your travels to slip into a cathedral at Evensong to hear classic English church music by **William Byrd** (1543–1623) and others; recordings of the **Choir of King's College,** Cambridge (p. 400, ❹), and many other fine choirs, will also introduce you to the genre. Britain's classical canon includes the masterpieces of **Henry Purcell** (1659–95), a baroque composer whose work even influenced the Who; **Edward Elgar** (1857–1934), whose *Pomp and Circumstance* is *de rigueur* at many graduations; **Ralph Vaughan Williams** (1872–1958), who edited *The English Hymnal*; **Gustav Holst** (1874–1934), famed composer of *The Planets*; and **Benjamin Britten** (1913–76), whose *Young Person's Guide to the Orchestra* is a mainstay of musical education.

Great British Fiction

> Jane Austen hit the headlines again in 2011 when an unfinished manuscript by the novelist sold for almost £1 million.

The British have mastered the art of storytelling since **Geoffrey Chaucer** (ca. 1343–1400) wove his accounts of pilgrims wending their way across the English countryside in the 14th-century *Canterbury Tales,* and the realm that gave us Shakespeare still sets the gold standard when it comes to mastering the English language. There are a quite a number of fictional works that evoke many of the places and cultures you will encounter in your travels. Britain's literary heritage is so vast that it's hard to select particular titles, but here are a few favorites.

Master storyteller **Charles Dickens** (1812–70) captured Victorian England in *David Copperfield, Oliver Twist, A Christmas Carol,* and other novels, all of them classics. Not only did Dickens create some of the greatest characters ever to populate fiction, but his depictions of factories, slums, and London streets have shaped the way readers ever since have perceived 19th-century England. To evoke England at its wittiest

and romantic best, you can't beat *Pride and Prejudice* or *Sense and Sensibility* by **Jane Austen** (1775–1817). The countryside of Dorset and Devon is called to mind by Thomas Hardy's *Tess of the D'Urbervilles* and *The Mayor of Casterbridge.* The **Brontë sisters,** meanwhile, immortalized the windswept moors of Yorkshire in such classics as Charlotte's *Jane Eyre* and Emily's *Wuthering Heights.* And the narrow cobblestone streets of Rye are wonderfully captured in **E.F. Benson's** (1867–1940) delightful Mapp and Lucia series.

Fantasy and children's authors also were inspired by various British landscapes. Famed author **J.R.R. Tolkien** (1892–1973) took inspiration for some of the locations in his legendary *Lord of the Rings* trilogy from the region around Birmingham where he grew up. And for the Lake District at its most childlike and charming, the classic *Tale of Peter Rabbit* by **Beatrix Potter** (1866–1943) delights both young and old.

Ushering in the 19th century, Scottish writer **Sir Walter Scott** (1771–1832), novelist and poet, was known for his Medieval Romanticism (*Ivanhoe*) and perceptive description of character and locales (*The Heart of Midlothian*). Edwardian London and the '20s and '30s is captured wonderfully in any of **Evelyn Waugh's** (1903–66) social satires and comedies; any work from the Bloomsbury

Group will also prove enlightening, such as **Virginia Woolf's** (1882-1941) *Mrs. Dalloway,* which peers beneath the surface of the London scene. **Robert Louis Stevenson's** (1850-94) tour de force, *The Strange Case of Dr. Jekyll and Mr. Hyde,* has often been interpreted as a representation of Scotland's character in its relationship with Britain. *How Green Was My Valley,* by **Richard Llewellyn** (1906-83), is a 1939 classic about growing up in a Welsh coal-mining village that is endearing but not overly sentimental.

Contemporary writers have ably carried on England's literary traditions. **Zadie Smith** (b. 1975) captured the racial complexity of modern Britain in *White Teeth,* her story of two immigrant families in North London, and **Martin Amis** (b. 1949), son of novelist Sir Kingsley Amis, explores the ragged edges of modern Britain in *London Fields* and other novels. Sir Kingsley's wife, **Elizabeth Jane Howard** (b. 1923), turned her attention to life in England before, during, and after World War II in her highly engaging *Cazalet Chronicles.* **Ian McEwan** (b. 1948) cuts a broad swath of British life during the same period in his novel *Atonement,* in which he portrays a dramatic single day in the life of an upper-middle-class London family. And perhaps no British writer has captured the modern imagination (or launched as many book sales) as **J.K. Rowling** (b. 1965), whose Harry Potter books have entertained millions even as they offer some occasionally biting social commentary on the British class system and prejudice.

If you prefer poetry, then peruse the best works of Scottish Romanticist **Robert Burns** (1759-96), perhaps the most famous Scot of all and writer of that New Year's staple, "Auld Lang Syne." Burns was a major influence on the legendary English poet **William Wordsworth** (1770-1850), whose popular appeal has never waned thanks to his *Lyrical Ballads, The Prelude,* and other works extolling nature and emotion. **Dylan Thomas** (1914-53) often recorded his works ("Under Milk Wood," "Do Not Go Gentle into that Good Night," "Fern Hill," and "A Child's Christmas in Wales"), and the sound of his sonorous voice reciting those magnificent words should entice anyone to Wales.

British Theater

> *Shakespeare has had more influence over English drama than any other playwright.*

The legacy of British theater dates back for centuries, and it's a vital part of the region's cultural landscape. To do it justice would take more pages than this book has, but here's a primer on some of its major movers and shakers.

Christopher Marlowe (1564-93). A master of the tragedy (who suffered his own tragic end when he was stabbed to death) and blank verse, this much-admired dramatist is known for protagonists whose reach always exceeds their grasp. Top works include *The Jew of Malta* and *Dr. Faustus.*

William Shakespeare (1564-1616). The Bard of Avon is the greatest dramatist the English language has ever known, deft in comedy, history, and tragedy. His plays, from *Macbeth* to *Henry V* to *Much Ado About Nothing,* are performed more often than those of any other playwright, and have been translated into nearly every language.

Noël Coward (1899-1973). A playwright whose dapper sense of personal style was matched by his talent for capturing British high society at its wittiest, in both drama and musical theater. Some of his best works include *Private Lives* and *Blithe Spirit.*

Joe Orton (1933-67). His life tragically ended in murder, but this master of the macabre black comedy ushered British theater into the second half of the 20th century with such plays as *Entertaining Mr. Sloane* and *Loot*.

Harold Pinter (1930–2008). This Nobel Laureate was one of modern Britain's most influential dramatists, and his work is often marked by conflict and issues of identity. Notable plays include *The Birthday Party, The Caretaker,* and *The Homecoming*.

Peter Shaffer (b. 1926). An expert at mixing philosophical drama with a hint of comedy, Shaffer wrote such standouts as *Equus* and *Amadeus*.

Tom Stoppard (b. 1937). An influential playwright with a penchant for social commentary on personal and political freedom. Some of his best known works include *Rosencrantz and Guildenstern are Dead, Travesties,* and *The Real Thing*.

Andrew Lloyd Webber (b. 1948). A composer who's the king of the modern British musical and the man (often in collaboration with lyricist Tim Rice) behind such megahits as *Jesus Christ Superstar, Evita, Cats,* and *The Phantom of the Opera*.

British Television

> *During the 1990s, everyone set their VCRs for an episode of* Absolutely Fabulous, *starring Jennifer Saunders and Joanna Lumley.*

America's Hollywood may have the greatest global cache when it comes to television nowadays, but Britain deserves a lot of credit for being quite the influence on its neighbor across the Atlantic, thanks to seminal BBC productions and groundbreaking series. Many of the following provide insight into British character and humor, as well as offering a look at a lot of the region's landscape; they're highly recommended as a prelude to a trip there

Brits have an often outrageous sense of humor and have had exceptional success in creating landmark comedy series that have influenced broadcasters around the world. Classic British comedies include *The Benny Hill Show* (1951–91), *Monty Python's Flying Circus* (1969–74), *Blackadder* (1983–89), *Fawlty Towers* (1975–79), and *Absolutely Fabulous* (1992–96, 2001-4). Sitcoms with a slightly more good-natured bent include *Keeping Up Appearances* (1990–95) and *The Vicar of Dibley* (1994–2007). In some cases, the British originals have been so good that they have inspired copies elsewhere (*The Office,* for example).

Until recently, British TV had a reputation for creating far tonier television than Hollywood (though not always as slick and mindlessly entertaining). That reputation rests largely on the laurels of the **BBC,** the world's largest broadcasting corporation, and its competitor **ITV;** many of their programs have aired in the United States as part

of the latter's famous *Masterpiece Theatre* and *Mystery!* series.

The BBC has produced and aired such classics as *Upstairs, Downstairs* (1971–75), *The Forsyte Saga* (two versions of the John Galsworthy novels, one in 1967 and another in 2002), and the *Duchess of Duke Street* (1976–77), as well as at least a dozen dramatizations of Jane Austen novels (its 1995 production of *Pride and Prejudice* is often regarded as the definitive version of that classic). It's also responsible for the longest-running sci-fi show in TV history, the legendary *Dr. Who*.

ITV has been responsible for the spy classic *The Avengers* (1961–69); *Brideshead Revisited* (1981); the internationally acclaimed *Prime Suspect* (1991–2006); a long string of successful adaptations of mystery classics (its *Adventures of Sherlock Holmes* and *Agatha Christie's Poirot* being standouts); and the world's longest-running soap opera, *Coronation Street* (1960–present).

British Film

> *Lawrence of Arabia is a romantic retelling of the life of Welshman T. E. Lawrence, army officer and former student at Jesus College, Oxford.*

The British are artful filmmakers and have produced a long list of classics that feature talented actors and directors who've gone on to become household names. To whet your cinematic appetite, here are just a few options (representing a number of genres) that get our thumbs up.

The 39 Steps (1935). A justly-lauded classic by the king of the cinematic thriller, Alfred Hitchcock, during his British heyday.

Hamlet (1948). This Sir Laurence Olivier classic interpretation of Shakespeare was the first British film to score an Oscar, vaulting Britain into the international cinematic limelight.

Lawrence of Arabia (1962). David Lean's epic study of T.E. Lawrence and British involvement in the Middle East is historically questionable, but still one of the best films ever made.

A Hard Day's Night (1964). A lauded "mockumentary" that was the forerunner of today's modern music video... and helped spread the gospel of the Fab Four.

Goldfinger (1964). *Dr. No* introduced the quintessential British spy to the world, but this is the best Bond film of them all.

My Beautiful Laundrette (1985). This noteworthy dramedy focuses on the immigrant experience during the Thatcher years in England.

Hope & Glory (1987). John Boorman's autobiographical film vibrantly mixes both comedy and drama as a family tries to survive London during the Blitz.

The Madness of King George (1994). Nobody does historical costume dramas like the Brits, and this Nicholas Hytner film has the added bonus of a stellar cast and script.

Four Weddings and a Funeral (1994). An endearing film that kicked off the era of the modern British rom-com and made a star of Hugh Grant.

Trainspotting (1996). Often cited as the best Scottish film of all time, Danny Boyle's acclaimed drama tackles drug use and urban poverty in late '80s Edinburgh.

The Queen (2006). Helen Mirren won a deserved Oscar for her uncanny portrayal of Elizabeth II in this modern examination of the monarchy.

British Food & Drink

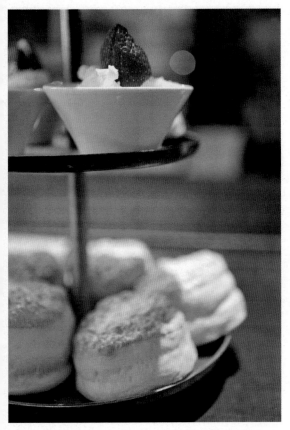

> *Some of the best afternoon teas are served in the grand hotels of London's West End.*

British food—boiled meat, boiled potatoes, and boiled Brussels sprouts—has been the butt of jokes for centuries. "Continentals have good food, the British have good table manners," is one tried-and-true quip. Well, let's put those worn-out notions to rest. British food is getting better all the time, and an emphasis on fresh ingredients in exciting preparations is sweeping the land. Good,

old-fashioned British cuisine (reinvented as "Modern British") is taken seriously these days, and holds its own against the Indian, South Asian, French, and Italian fare that is also a common fixture on the British dining scene. Even pubs are reinventing pub grub and touting themselves as "gastropubs."

Despite these trends, you can still look forward to four staunchly British culinary

traditions. At least once during your visit, you'll want to throw concerns about cholesterol to the winds and start the day with a traditional **English breakfast** (also called a "fry up"), consisting of bacon, eggs, grilled tomato, fried bread, baked beans, and maybe some kippers (smoked herring) and braised kidneys. A traditional **Welsh breakfast** is laverbread—boiled seaweed rolled with oatmeal, formed into a patty, fried, and served with eggs, bacon, and cockles. A traditional **ploughman's lunch** consists of a hefty piece of cheese, a hunk of crusty bread, and pickled onion and butter; some pubs dress these basics up with pâté, chutney, tomatoes, and other extras. And, finally, the ritual of **afternoon tea** is still a permanent fixture of British life. You can sit down to enjoy tea, or a "cuppa," often accompanied by crustless sandwiches and cakes, just about anywhere you go. Especially in the West Country, you can enjoy a cream tea, a treat of homemade scones topped with fresh Devonshire clotted cream and strawberry jam. In Wales, your tea might come with Welsh cakes, made with currants (also known as griddle scones), and in Scotland with bannocks, or oat biscuits.

Old British Favorites

These traditional favorites often make an appearance in even the trendiest restaurants, and when done well, they are simply delicious.

PIES

These are not sweet, as in North America, but savory. **Shepherd's pie** and cottage pie are, respectively, casseroles of lamb and chopped beef sautéed with onions, carrots, and other vegetables, topped with a layer of mashed potatoes, and baked. **Stargazy pie** is a Cornish invention, a creamy concoction of herring and vegetables topped with a crust. **Poacher's pie** is a Welsh favorite, in which rabbit, steak, and sausages are baked under a thick crust. Variations abound: **Steak and kidney pie** is a pastry-topped mixture of steak, kidney, and mushrooms in gravy; **bubble and squeak** is a fried mixture of mashed potatoes and cabbage; **Cornish pasties** are thick pastry shells filled with meat, onions, and vegetables.

ROAST BEEF

Legend has it that James I once addressed a leg of beef, the longtime favorite dish of kings, as "Sir Loin," giving a name to this favorite of carnivores. British beef, especially **Angus beef** reared in the Scottish highlands, is excellent; the best way to enjoy any beef in England is roasted the classic way, with **Yorkshire pudding**, a floury rue into which the fat drips as the beef cooks.

SEAFOOD

The trout and salmon caught in the lakes and streams of Scotland and Wales are so fresh that you'll think they swam right into the kitchen. Fresh **Dover sole** is probably the most prized fish in

> *Fish and chips is traditionally taken away in yesterday's newspaper, but these days you're as likely to find it in a trendy restaurant.*

England. And you can't visit the area without indulging at least once in **fish and chips** (thick French fries or fried potatoes); the best renditions are made with cod and haddock.

INDIAN FOOD

That's right, as in **curry** and **korma.** As a legacy of the Empire, Indian cooking is a national cuisine in Britain, served in thousands of restaurants all over the realm.

HAGGIS

One wit described Scotland's national dish as a "castrated bagpipe." It's actually made of lamb offal (lungs, liver, and heart) mixed with onions and suet and baked in a lamb's stomach—and usually washed down with whisky.

> *It's a little known fact that Britain produces more different cheeses than France.*

PUDDING

This is Britspeak for dessert, and it's usually a homey concoction, often with a coy name: **Eton mess** is a gooey glob of strawberries, meringue, and cream; **figgy dowdy** is a fruit cake with raisins and figs; **spotted dick,** a near cousin, uses currants and rum; **trifle** is a sponge cake soaked in sherry, layered with raspberry preserves, covered with custard sauce, and capped with whipped cream; a **fool** is a light cream dessert whipped up from seasonal fruits; and **treacle tart** is a pastry topped with syrup and ginger.

CHEESE

Britain claims to produce 700 varieties. You'll find cheese served on sandwiches or in Welsh rarebit (cheese melted over toast), and a selection of cheese is often served at the end of a meal, sometimes accompanied by port. Some distinctly British cheeses are **Cheddar,** made all over the world but originating in England and best in the West Country, where it has Protected Designation of Origin (PDO) status; **Cheshire cheese,** from around Chester and popular with the Roman legions who settled that ancient city; **Stilton,** a blue-veined crumbly cheese that has PDO status and must be made in the counties of Nottinghamshire, Derbyshire, or Leicestershire to a precise recipe; and **Wensleydale,** from Yorkshire.

Beer and Other Libations

Every town, village, and neighborhood has at least one pub, or public house, and you won't find a better place to rub shoulders with the locals. You can have a Cosmo, or a glass of chardonnay, but why would you? **Beer** is the national drink of Britain, and a pub is the place to enjoy a pint, or two, in whatever variety—brown (or bitter), blond (lager), or very dark (stout). Whatever you order, it will come from the tap and be served as a half pint (10 oz.) or a pint (20 oz.). Lager is chilled, as is stout sometimes, and ale, contrary to what's often reported, isn't served warm, but rather at cellar temperature (i.e. cool).

Britons are becoming increasingly enamored of the

> *Brains is Wales's best known, and best loved, major brewer.*

grape. Excellent wines from Continental vineyards, including many small production operations that don't export outside of Europe, are widely available, especially in better restaurants and in the wine bars that are a new craze across the country.

But Britain's most famous beverage is arguably the one

most outside the region call scotch (known here as whisky, without the "e"), which Sir Walter Scott labeled "the only liquor fit for a gentleman to drink." Order a whisky and you'll usually be served a smoky, earthy single malt, from a distiller in Scotland, that's been aged for at least 3 years.

The Best Special Interest Trips

> *PREVIOUS PAGE Pack an Ordnance Survey map, and you'll find Britain's countryside easy to navigate. THIS PAGE Rural Britain is ideal for cycling, as long as you steer clear of busy roads.*

Short Jaunts

If you're basing yourself in London, you may want to take advantage of one of the many day tours that operate out of the capital. Prices for these usually include admission fees as well as pickup at your hotel or some other central London location, so you won't have to bother with train schedules, admission hours, and other details. For a complete list, visit the **Britain and London Visitor Centre (BLVC),** 1 Lower Regent St., Piccadilly Circus, London, or Tourist Information Centres elsewhere around the country, or check online at **VisitBritain** (www.visitbritain.com).

  Golden Tours offers sight-filled full-day tours that usually include stops in several places of interest. Some typical itineraries are: Stratford-upon-Avon, the Cotswolds, and Oxford; Bath, Stonehenge, and Salisbury; Leeds Castle, Canterbury, and Dover; and Royal Windsor and Hampton Court Palace. Prices run about £70. **Visitor Centre Victoria,** 4 Fountain Sq., 123-151 Buckingham Palace Rd., London. ☎ 0207/233-7030. www.goldentours.com.

Multi-Activity Outfitters

Great Britain is one of the most popular destinations for **Road Scholar** (formerly Elderhostel), the not-for-profit organization for mature adults that combines travel and educational opportunities. Two-week programs in London and Edinburgh and tours showing off the highlights of the U.K. have been among recent offerings. 11 Avenue de Lafayette, Boston, MA. ☎ 800/454-5768. www.roadscholar.org.

  Specializing in trips for the 18-to-35 set, **Contiki Tours** has a number of itineraries that primarily appeal to young professionals. Some focus on cities only (London and Edinburgh), but others take in the coast and Scottish Highlands. c/o Vacations To Go, 5851 San Felipe, Ste. 500, Houston, TX. ☎ 800/680-2858 or 713/974-2121. www.contikivacations.com.

Outdoor Activities A to Z

The **Great Outdoor Recreation Pages (GORP;** www.gorp.com) offer the best and most up-to-date information on camping and otherwise getting the most out of the English countryside.

Cycling

A **National Cycle Network** covers about 10,000 miles throughout the U.K., from Dover in southeast England to Inverness in the Highlands. Most routes cross old railway lines, canal towpaths, and riversides. Among the more popular routes are the **Sea to Sea (C2C) Cycle Route,** a 140-mile path linking the Irish Sea with the North Sea across the Pennine Hills and into the north Lake District and the Durham Dales. The **Essex Cycle Route** covers 250 miles of countryside, going through some of England's most charming villages; the **Devon Coast to Coast Route** runs for 90 miles in southwest England, skirting the edge of Dartmoor; the **West Country Way** for 248 miles, linking the Cornish coast to Bath and Bristol; and the **Severn and Thames Route** for 100 miles, linking two of Britain's major rivers. Go to **www.sustrans.org.uk** for route maps. *Britain for Cyclists,* a booklet with information on these routes, is available from tourist offices throughout Britain.

  Ten-day bike tours through the Cotswolds and other scenic regions of Britain with

Wildlife photography and bird-watching are popular weekend activities in this nation of animal-lovers.

Escorted Tours

Escorted tours, including transportation, accommodations, and sightseeing are a popular way to see Britain. They usually hit the major highlights and make touring the region a breeze. On the downside, there is usually not much opportunity to get off the beaten path or for leisure time—you won't be able to linger on the lawns at Leeds Castle or pause in front of a painting at Hampton Court if your coach is ready to pull out of the parking lot.

Upscale options that include top-notch accommodations and other high-class perks include **Abercrombie & Kent** (☎ 800/554-7016; www.abercrombiekent.com); **Maupintour** (☎ 800/255-4266; www.maupintour.com); and **Tauck World Discovery** (☎ 800/788-7885; www.tauck.com).

Tours run by **Wallace Arnold Worldchoice** (☎ 0845/365-6747; www.waworldchoice.com), the U.K.'s largest operator, are less extravagant than the above options, but are reasonably priced, generally of excellent quality, and offer decent accommodations.

Among the many U.S.-based operators offering packages in Britain are **Trafalgar** (☎ 866/544-4434; www.trafalgartours.com), with various 7-day itineraries that take in such must-sees as Stratford-upon-Avon and Bath. **Globus and Cosmos Tours** (☎ 866/755-8581; www.globusandcosmos.com) offer similar packages and are generally well regarded for the level of their accommodations and quality of the guides.

Hindriks include guided rides, hotel accommodations, and entrance fees to historic homes and other sights. P.O. Box 222, Peru, IN. ☎ 866-605-0289. www.hindrikstours.com.

Lynott Tours arranges self-guided and group tours for cyclists in Scotland; itineraries are geared to terrain that is suitable for various fitness levels. 205 Mineola Blvd., Suite 1B, Mineola, NY. ☎ 800/221-2474 or 516/248-2042. www.lynotttours.com.

Fishing

Go Fly Fishing UK arranges fishing excursions throughout Britain, offering instruction, guides, and equipment rental on many of the most scenic rivers and lakes. The organization can also make recommendations for accommodation in prime fishing spots. ☎ 01252/851-397 in southern England; 01756/748-378 in northern England. www.goflyfishing.co.uk.

Golf

Stops at the best courses in England, Scotland, and Wales (including St. Andrews, Carnoustie, and Turnberry) are included on itineraries from **Best of Scotland Holidays;** trips are self-guided, but escorted tours are also available, as is instruction. 6A Main St., Upper Largo, Fife, Scotland. ☎ 888/678-1567 in North America or 01333/360-395 in the U.K. www.golfvacations.co.uk.

Golf International arranges golf packages for anywhere from 7 to 14 days on courses around Britain. Courses include St. Andrews and Gleneagles, as well as the Belfry (near Birmingham). 260 Fifth Avenue, New York, NY. ☎ 800/833-1389 or 212/986-9176. www.golfinternational.com.

> *Garden tours may include the famous Chelsea Flower Show.*

Horseback Riding

With **Equitour,** riding enthusiasts can enjoy instruction in jumping and dressage or a 7-day trek through Wales, with stops at atmospheric inns. P.O. Box 807, 10 Stalnaker St., Dubois, WY. ☎ 800/545-0019 or 307/455-3363. www.riding tours.com.

Natural Interest

Guided bird-watching excursions along the coast of Cornwall are among the tours conducted by the **American Museum of Natural History Expeditions,** which offers a changing roster of trips that often include a natural and archaeological focus on Britain. Central Park West at 79th St., New York, NY. ☎ 800/462-8687. www.amnhexpeditions.org.

Bird-watching is a main focus of **Naturetrek,** whose naturalists lead walks through the New Forest, along the Dorset coast, and in other U.K. bird habitats; the group also offers trips geared to travelers interested in wildflowers, gardens, and other natural attractions. Cheriton Mill, Hampshire. ☎ 01962/733-051. www.naturetrek.co.uk.

Walking

One of the most sustainable ways to explore England is on foot, and doing so was made easier in 2000 when the country passed the **Rights of Way Act,** granting countryside ramblers access to open land even if it is held by a private owner. Of course, all walkers must leave the land as they find it, including carrying out all trash and personal belongings.

Britain's venerable **Ramblers** offers guided walks in the Lake District, Cotswolds, and other scenic regions, and nonmembers are welcome to participate. Most last a day, but others are longer treks that include basic accommodations en route. Second floor, Camelford House, 87–90 Albert Embankment, London. ☎ 0207/339-8500. www.ramblers.org.uk.

The coast of Northumberland, the Yorkshire Moors and Dales, the Hebrides, and the Scottish Highlands are among the landscapes covered in walks led by **Inntravel;** most are hotel-to-hotel walks and many are as short as 4 days. Whitewell Grange, near Castle Howard, York. ☎ 01653/617-001. www.inntravel.co.uk.

The Wayfarers leads walks in Britain through such regions as the Cotswolds, the Lake District, and Cornwall. 174 Bellevue Ave., Newport, RI. ☎ 800/249-4620 or 401/849-5087. www.thewayfarers.com.

Special Interest Trips A to Z

Barging

Barge cruises up the Thames into the heart of England can be arranged through the **Barge Company;** trips make stops at such storied places as Oxford and Eton, include fine meals, and are geared to special interests, such as antiques, gardens, architecture, and history. A tour of Scotland along the Caledonian Canal is also available. 501 Chemin Lacoste, 82710, Grisolles, France. ☎ 800/688-0245 in U.S. & Canada, or 33/0563-028-704. www.barge company.com.

Gardens

Brightwater Holidays leads small groups through the gardens of Kent and Sussex, to the Chelsea Flower Show, and to other famous British horticultural venues; trips last 3 days to a week and often include visits to private gardens hat are not generally open to the public. **Eden Park House, Cupar, Fife, Scotland. ☎ 01334/657-55. www.brightwaterholidays.com.**

The great gardens of Yorkshire, Cornwall, Devon, and East Anglia are often on the itinerary of the **American Horticultural Society Travel Study Program Garden Tours,** led by experts and usually including meetings with noted horticulturalists. **7931 E. Boulevard Dr., Alexandria, VA. ☎ 866-627-6621. www.ahs.org.**

Lynott Tours visits some of England's most spectacular gardens, often with a focus on Devon and Cornwall, as well as some gardens often not included on organized tours—such as those in the Lake District, Wales, and Scottish Highlands. **Lynott Tours, 205 Mineola Blvd., Suite 1B, Mineola, NY. ☎ 800/221-2474 or 516/248-2042. www.lynotttours.com.**

A good source for other garden tours in Britain is the website www.gardenvisit.com, which provides information on recommended garden tours in England, Scotland, and Wales.

History & Culture

Experience some of Britain's best architecture, museums, cultural offerings, and historical sites on one of several expert-led tours by **Smithsonian Journeys.** Tours might include a cultural study of London, an exploration of major Tudor sites in England, or a hike through some of the stunning countryside of North Wales. **P.O. Box 23182, Washington, DC. ☎ 877/338-8687. www.smithsonianjourneys.org.**

Literary Trips

Travel2Books immerses readers in the works and worlds of writers they love, with itineraries that follow Jane Austen around Bath, Shakespeare from Stratford-upon-Avon to London, or Agatha Christie from Devon to Harrogate. Lectures, visits to homes and locales, and guided itineraries are included. **☎ 404/373-1420. www.travel2books.com.**

"Literary Cotswolds" and "The Brontës Literature and Countryside" are among the escorted excursions from **Lynott Tours;** the group also sets up self-guided tours, with a car, accommodations at inns and castles, and itineraries that include stops at Haworth (the Yorkshire home of the Brontë sisters) and other literary sites throughout Britain. **205 Mineola Blvd., Ste. 1B, Mineola, NY. ☎ 800/221-2474. www.lynotttours.com.**

Tennis

Centre Court seats, five-star hotel accommodations, theater tickets, and other perks are included in **Steve Furgal's International Tennis Tours,** whose main focus in England is on Wimbledon. **11305 Rancho Bernardo Road, Suite 108, San Diego, CA. ☎ 800-258-3664 or 858-675-3555. www.tours4tennis.com.**

Whisky Tasting

Distillery Destinations conducts 3- to 5-day tours of Scotland's leading whisky distilleries (Macallan and Glenfiddich are just some of the more famous names), often with an expert guide to lead you through tastings. Some tours also include sightseeing in such locations as Edinburgh, Glasgow, and the Orkney Isles. **304 Albert Dr., Glasgow. ☎ 0141/429-0762 or 01531/670-333. www.whisky-tours.com.**

More Tour Sources

An excellent overall resource to special interest travel is **ShawGuides,** an online listing of workshops, nature treks, and much more. Browse through the offerings at www.shawguides.com.

A good overall introduction to London, Bath, Edinburgh, and other cities is a tour with **City Sightseeing** (www.city-sightseeing.com), the hop-off/hop-on bus tour company that allows 24 hours' worth of transport to major sights around a city, allowing you to get on and off the bus as you wish. The canned, multilingual commentary is not going to enlighten you greatly, but rolling through a strange city is a delight. The best approach is to stay aboard once for the whole route, then redo the circuit making the stops that interest you. For routes and prices for the city you are visiting, check the website.

Wherever your travels take you, check with the local tourist information office (see our listings throughout this guide) and ask what guided walking tours might be available. Most are led by in-the-flesh guides, and others are conducted via MP3 player; in either form, they are usually an informative and pleasant way to get to know a place.

19
The Savvy
Traveler

> Cellphones have almost killed off the traditional red public phone box... but not quite.

Before You Go

Government Tourist Offices

Visit Britain (www.visitbritain.com) operates offices in North America, 551 Fifth Ave., 7th floor, New York, NY (☎ 800/462-2748 or 212/986-2266); and in Australia, Level 2, 15 Blue St., North Sydney (☎ 02/1300-858-589). For information in Canada, call ☎ 888/847-4885; in New Zealand, call ☎ 0800/700-741; and in Ireland, call ☎ 0845/644-3010.

For information on London, contact **Visit London,** 1 Regent St., London (☎ 0870/242-9988; www.visitlondon.com). For information on Wales, contact **Visit Wales Centre,** Burnel House, 2 Firzalan Rd., Cardiff (☎ 0870/211-255; www.visitwales.com). For information on Scotland, contact **Visit Scotland,** Level 3, Ocean Point 1, 94 Ocean Dr., Edinburgh (☎ 0845/225-5121; www.visitscotland.com).

Best Times to Go

Though Britain is essentially an all-year destination, the period from Easter to October is the best time to visit (though you'll pay top dollar for the privilege). Gardens are at their peak in spring, and the countryside is at its greenest. The sky stays light well into the evening, so you'll have extra time to get the most out of your touring. In summer, all of Britain seems to move outdoors, and you can enjoy long walks and other outdoor activities. Many cities host lively summer festivals. In early fall, parks and gardens can be especially alluring when the air is crisp and forested hillsides are a carpet of color. And the tourist hordes tend to thin in early September.

You can avoid crowds by planning trips for November or January through March (also the cheapest time to visit, except for New Year's in Scotland when Hogmanay celebrations attract throngs). British towns are often especially welcoming in the winter, and wherever you go you're likely to find yourself sitting in front of a roaring fire. Museums, chapels, cathedrals, and other attractions will provide a wealth of indoor activities to get you out of the winter chill. And hotel rates and airfares often drop significantly. Keep in mind, though, that many castles and country houses close in November and don't open again until April.

A note about the weather: Yes, it rains in Britain, just about any time of the year. That shouldn't dampen your enthusiasm, however, because rain tends to fall gently, and heavy downpours are not the norm. Temperatures are generally moderate in most of Britain. In **England,** temps rarely drop below 35°F (2°C) or go above 78°F (26°C). Evenings are cool, even in summer. **Scotland** is a bit cooler: The Lowlands average between 38°F (3°C) in winter and 65°F (18°C) in summer. Temperatures in the north of Scotland are lower, especially in winter, and you should dress accordingly. **Wales** enjoys a temperate climate, though there are variations in the time the seasons change. Spring comes a week or two earlier to Anglesey in the far northwest than in Snowdonia to its east. In winter, mild sea breezes blow around the southern and western coastal areas; winter can be hard in the mountains, and the peaks may be snow-capped until spring. It rains a lot in the hills and mountains, but, then, Wales has lots of bright, sunny days.

Festivals & Special Events

If your visit to Britain coincides with one of the following events, you may well want to go out of your way to take part in the festivities. For more about events throughout Britain, go to www.visitbritain.com and http://events.frommers.com.

JANUARY

On January 1, the **London New Year's Day Parade** features marching bands, floats, and the Lord Mayor of Westminster traipsing in a procession from Parliament Square to Berkeley Square. At the **Charles I Commemoration,** London, held the last Sunday in January, hundreds of cavaliers march through London in 17th-century dress "in the name of freedom and democracy." On January 25, **Burns Night celebrations** all over Scotland honor beloved poet Robert Burns with much whisky toasting and haggis eating.

FEBRUARY

During the **Jorvik Festival,** York (☎ 01904/643-211; jorvik@yorkarchaeology.co.uk), held over 2 weeks from mid- to late February, Vikings retake the medieval city, with costumed parades, mock battles, storytelling, song fests, food fairs, and more.

MARCH

Cardiff comes to a standstill on March 1, the Welsh national day, when the **St. David's Day Parade (http://stdavidsday.org),** the country's showiest spectacle, honors the country's patron saint. Some of the world's most acclaimed authors are on hand for readings and discussions of their works at the **Bath Literature Festival** (☎ 01225/463-231; www.bathfestivals.org.uk), held in early March. Stars of the canine variety (23,000 of them, representing 209 breeds), meanwhile, head to Birmingham's National Exhibition Centre for the **Crufts Dog Show** (☎ 0870/606-6750; www.crufts.org.uk).

APRIL

The **Shakespeare Season** in Stratford-upon-Avon opens in early April, and performances by the Royal Shakespeare Company (RSC) run through October, presenting works by the Bard on the stages of the Swan Theatre, Royal Shakespeare Theatre, and Courtyard Theatre. Contact the RSC (☎ 01789/403-444; www.rsc.org.uk) for information and schedules.

MAY

One of London's most famous spring events, the **Chelsea Flower Show,** draws tens of thousands of visitors from around the world; get your tickets well in advance. For information, contact the Royal Horticultural Society (☎ 020/7834-4333; www.rhs.org.uk). The **Brighton Festival** (☎ 01273/709-709; www.brightonfestival.org), held through most of May, is the largest performing arts festival in Britain and stages more than 400 events, bringing theater, dance, classical music, opera, film, and other programs to venues around the city. If you're an opera fan, the **Glynde-bourne Festival** (☎ 01273/813-813; www.glyndebourne.com), in Lewes, kicks off in May; it's one of the world's most acclaimed opera festivals and stages six productions, attracting the world's leading voices and legions of ardent fans to a stunning hall. For classical music, the **Bath International Music Festival** (☎ 01225/462-231; www.bathmusicfest.org.uk), which runs mid-May to early June, attracts classical and popular musicians from around the world to perform in theaters and churches throughout the city.

JUNE

Men wear top hats and women, including the queen, put on silly millinery creations for the **Derby Stakes** (☎ 01372/726-311; www.epsomderby.co.uk), a famous horse race at Epsom Downs, Epsom, Surrey. But the most prestigious horse racing event (and a very tough ticket) in Britain is **Royal Ascot** (☎ 01344/876-876; www.ascot.co.uk), held at the Ascot Racecourse (near Windsor) in the presence of the Royal Family. **Trooping the Colour** (☎ 020/7414-2479; www.trooping-the-colour.co.uk) is the queen's official birthday parade, which features exquisite pageantry and pomp as she inspects her regiments and takes their salute as they parade their colors before her at the Horse Guards Parade, Whitehall. Tickets for the parade and two reviews, held on preceding Saturdays, are allocated by ballot.

The world's top tennis players whack their rackets at the **Wimbledon Lawn Tennis Championships** (www.wimbledon.com) from late June to early July; tickets are exceedingly hard to come by. Two outfits that book both hotel accommodations and tickets to the event are Steve Furgal's International Tennis Tours, 11305 Rancho Bernardo Rd., Ste. 108, San Diego, CA (☎ 800/258-3664 or 858/675-3555; www.tours4tennis.com); and Championship Tennis Tours, 13951 N. Scottsdale Rd., Ste. 133, Scottsdale, AZ (☎ 800/468-3664 or 480/429-7700; www.tennistours.com).

During the **Exeter Summer Festival** (☎ 01392/277-888; www.exeter.gov.uk.), late June to mid-July, Exeter hosts more than 150 events celebrating classical music, ranging from concerts and opera to lectures. The **Ludlow Festival** (☎ 01584/872-150; www.ludlowfestival.co.uk), late June to early July, is one of England's major arts festivals, complete with an open-air Shakespeare performance within the Inner Bailey of Ludlow Castle. The **Cardiff Festival** (☎ 029/2087-2087; www.cardiff-festival.com) features pop, jazz, theater, street performances, fairs, opera, comedies, and children's events for 3 weeks across the Welsh capital from late June into July.

JULY

The **Hampton Court Flower Show** (☎ 0870/906-3791; www.rhs.org.uk), is the world's largest horticultural show, featuring magnificent floral displays and show gardens. The **Winchester Festival** (☎ 01962/877-977; www.musicatwinchester.co.uk), in early July, presents choral concerts in the city's famous cathedral, plays at the Theatre Royal, and other musical and theatrical events. For the late-July **Southern Cathedrals Festival** (☎ 01722/555-125; www.southerncathedralsfestival.org.uk), which rotates among Chichester, Salisbury, and Winchester in alternating years, choirs from the cathedrals of these three cities gather for concerts, candlelight recitals, and other events. The **Cambridge Folk Festival** (☎ 01223/357-851; www.cambridgefolkfestival.co.uk), in late July, is one of Europe's largest and most acclaimed celebrations of folk music and brings together performers from around the world.

The **Henley Royal Regatta** (☎ 01491/572-153; www.hrr.co.uk), an international rowing competition in Oxfordshire in early July, is the premier event on the English social calendar. The **Proms** (☎ 020/7589-8212; www.bbc.co.uk/proms), the annual BBC Henry Wood Promenade Concerts at London's Royal Albert Hall from mid-July to mid-September, attract music aficionados from around the world. And **Musicfest Aberystwyth** (☎ 01970/623-232; www.aberystwythartscentre.co.uk), at the end of July, is a pageant of cultural and sporting events in the cultural center of the western section of middle Wales.

AUGUST

Pride in Brighton & Hove (☎ 01273/775-939; www.brightonpride.org), held the first week in August, is one of Europe's largest gay pride celebrations, with a big parade and lively street parties. In Wales, the **Pontardawe International Music Festival** (☎ 01792/830-200; www.pontardawefestival.com), in the little Welsh village of Pontardawe, attracts some of the world's leading folk and rock musicians for its annual summer concert series in mid-August.

One of the largest annual street festivals in Europe, **Notting Hill Carnival** (☎ 020/7727-0072; www.nottinghillcarnival.biz) in London, attracts more than half a million people in late August for live reggae and soul music, plus great Caribbean food. Tens of thousands of fans gather in Liverpool in late August to celebrate the music of the Fab Four at **International Beatle Week** (☎ 0151/233-2008; http://beatlesfestival.co.uk), with concerts by international cover bands, plus tributes, auctions, and tours.

The major player when it comes to August events in Britain, however, is Edinburgh. Orchestras, dance troupes, and soloists gather in Scotland for the 3-week **Edinburgh International Festival (www.eif.co.uk)**; the concurrent Edinburgh Festival Fringe adds an avant-garde element, with some of Europe's edgiest theatrical and musical performances. The **Edinburgh Jazz Festival** brings some of the world's finest jazz and blues artists to Scotland for 10 days. For information on all the Edinburgh festivals, visit **www.edinburghfestivals.co.uk**. Finally, more than 200,000 onlookers gather at Edinburgh Castle for the **Royal Edinburgh Military Tattoo** (☎ 0131/225-1188; www.edintattoo.co.uk), when Scottish regiments and military bands and drums corps from around the world gather to parade, play the bagpipes, and in other ways put on an impressive show.

SEPTEMBER

For the **Horse of the Year Show** (☎ 01582/711-411; www.hoys.co.uk), held in Birmingham in late September to early October, riders fly in from every continent to join in this festive display of horsemanship (much appreciated by the queen). Held the first weekend in September, the **Braemar Gathering** (☎ 01339/755-377; www.braemargathering.org) is probably the best known of the annual Highland Games, regularly attended by members of the Royal Family, whose Balmoral Castle is nearby. Spectators take in piping, dancing, and strength competitions.

OCTOBER

The **Cheltenham Festival of Literature** (☎ 01242/227-979; www.cheltenhamfestivals.co.uk) in early to mid-October features readings, book exhibitions, and theatrical performances in the famed spa town.

NOVEMBER

On the second Saturday in November, the

BRITAIN'S AVERAGE DAYTIME TEMPERATURES & RAINFALL

LONDON	JAN	FEB	MAR	APR	MAY	JUNE	JULY	AUG	SEPT	OCT	NOV	DEC
TEMP °F	40	40	44	49	55	61	64	64	59	52	46	42
TEMP °C	4	4	7	9	13	16	18	18	15	11	8	6
RAINFALL (IN.)	2.1	1.6	1.5	1.5	1.8	1.8	2.2	2.3	1.9	2.2	2.5	1.9

EDINBURGH	JAN	FEB	MAR	APR	MAY	JUNE	JULY	AUG	SEPT	OCT	NOV	DEC
TEMP °F	38	38	42	44	50	55	59	58	54	48	43	40
TEMP °C	3	3	6	7	10	13	15	14	12	9	6	4
RAINFALL (IN.)	2.2	1.6	1.9	1.5	2.0	2.0	2.5	2.7	2.5	2.4	2.5	2.4

CARDIFF	JAN	FEB	MAR	APR	MAY	JUNE	JULY	AUG	SEPT	OCT	NOV	DEC
TEMP °F	40	40	43	46	52	57	61	61	57	52	44	42
TEMP °C	4	4	6	8	11	14	16	16	14	11	7	6
RAINFALL (IN.)	4.2	3.0	2.9	2.5	2.7	2.6	3.1	4.0	3.8	4.6	4.3	4.6

Lord Mayor of London goes on the grand **Lord Mayor's Procession** (☎ 020/7222-4345; www.lordmayorshow.org) through the City in London from Guildhall to the Royal Courts of Justice in a gilded coach; festivities include a carnival and fireworks on the Thames. For the **Opening of Parliament** (☎ 020/7219-3107; www.parliament.uk), usually held some time in November, Queen Elizabeth II rides from Buckingham Palace to Westminster in a royal coach accompanied by the Yeoman of the Guard and the Household Cavalry to address the assembled houses in the House of Lords; the public galleries are open on a first-come, first-served basis.

Towns and cities throughout England celebrate **Guy Fawkes Night** on November 5, to commemorate the failed 1605 attempt by Guy Fawkes and members of the Gunpowder Plot to blow up Parliament in retaliation for anti-Catholic legislation. **St. Andrew's Day** celebrates Scotland's patron saint, and events surrounding November 30 include exhibits, concerts, and fireworks.

DECEMBER
Christ Church Cathedral, Oxford, is the setting for the annual **Christmas Concert** (☎ 01865/305-305; www.cathedralsingers.org.uk), in which the Cathedral Singers are joined by singers from around the world. That said, it's the **Festival of Nine Lessons and Nine Carols** (☎ 01223/331-313; www.kings.cam.ac.uk), held in Cambridge on December 24, that is England's most noted Christmas service; broadcast around the world, it features the voices of the King's Chapel Choir. Edinburgh is the place to be on **Hogmanay,** which begins on New Year's Eve and merges into New Year's Day festivities. Events include a torchlight procession, a fire festival along Princes Street, a carnival, and a street theater spectacular.

Useful Websites
In addition to the official tourist information websites, two excellent online resources are the websites of **English Heritage** (www.english-heritage.org.uk) and the **National Trust** (www.nationaltrust.org.uk), the two preservation agencies that maintain most of Britain's historic properties. **Welcome to the British Isles** (www.the-british-isles.com) provides hundreds of links to town and tourism websites in England, Wales, and Scotland, taking you on a clickable tour around the realm. On **www.knowhere.co.uk**, local residents give the inside scoop on cities and towns, providing plenty of juicy tidbits.

Ecotourism
Brits in general are an eco-aware bunch—but don't always practice what they preach. And even the concept of taking a "responsible," "green," or "environmentally friendly" trip here isn't without controversy, particularly if you're coming by plane. However, there are

everyday things you can do to minimize the impact—and especially the carbon footprint—of your travels. Remove chargers from cellphones, PSPs, laptops, and anything else that draws from the mains, once the gadget is fully charged. If you're shopping, buy seasonal fruit and vegetables or local cheeses from farmers' markets rather than produce sourced by supermarkets from the far side of the globe. Most important, use public transportation to get around.

Britain does put in effort to preserving landscapes. Of interest to visitors are 15 **national parks** (www.nationalparks.gov.uk) in England, Wales, and Scotland, as well as many miles of protected coastlines. You will also find national trails, areas of natural beauty, and parks wherever you travel.

The **Green Tourism Business Scheme** (www.green-business.co.uk), a national sustainability program approved by Visit Britain, rates over 2,000 British attractions and places to stay on their commitment to sustainability and to the environment. A general ecotourism organization is **Tourism Concern** (www.tourismconcern.org.uk), which works to reduce social and environmental problems linked to tourism in Britain. The **Association of Independent Tour Operators** (www.aito.co.uk) is a group of specialist operators leading the field in making U.K. vacations sustainable.

Getting There

By Plane

Britain's major overseas gateways are London's Heathrow (LHR) and Gatwick (LGW) airports (p. 137), which are usually the cheapest airports to fly into out of North America. Manchester (MAN; p. 458), Birmingham (BHX; p. 372), and Edinburgh (EDI; p. 535) airports also handle overseas flights, and Manchester and Edinburgh are served by nonstop flights from North America. In Wales, there are airports in the capital of Cardiff (CWL; p. 659) and in the second city of Swansea (SWS), but you'll need to connect to them through London.

FROM THE UNITED STATES

British Airways (☎ 800/247-9297; www.britishairways.com) offers flights from 19 U.S. cities to Heathrow and Gatwick airports, as well as many others to Manchester; many of the flights are nonstop. **Virgin Atlantic Airways** (☎ 800/821-5438; www.virgin-atlantic.com) flies daily to either Heathrow or Gatwick from Boston, Newark, New York's JFK, Los Angeles, San Francisco, Washington's Dulles, Miami, Orlando, and Las Vegas; Virgin also operates nonstop flights (the frequency varies seasonally) from Manchester to Orlando and Las Vegas. **American Airlines** (☎ 800/433-7300; www.aa.com) offers daily flights to Heathrow from half a dozen U.S. gateways—New York's JFK,

Discounts on Heritage Travel

One of the joys of traveling through Britain is the chance to see many of its historic attractions and gardens. Many of these places are administered by a select number of preservation agencies—and also carry some hefty admission fees. If your touring plans hit enough of these places, buying a membership (good for one calendar year) at one of these organizations can save you some money. In addition to free admission to the locations administered by the organization (and sometimes for your kids as well), you'll often get discounts at other attractions, free guides and magazines, shopping discounts, and more. Some agencies also offer explorer passes of shorter duration geared to visitors; see the websites listed below for up-to-date offerings and prices.

National Trust (www.nationaltrust.org.uk) and **National Trust Scotland** (www.nts.org.uk) oversee over 300 properties throughout Britain, including St. Michael's Mount and Monk's House in England, and Glencoe in Scotland.

English Heritage (www.english-heritage.org.uk) oversees 400 historic attractions in England, including Stonehenge, Rievaulx Abbey, and Tintagel. Its Scottish counterpart, **Historic Scotland** (www.historic-scotland.gov.uk), looks after more than 300 attractions, including Edinburgh Castle, Glasgow Cathedral, and Iona Abbey. And their Welsh equivalent, **Cadw** (www.cadw.wales.gov.uk), oversees such historic sites as Tintern Abbey and Castell Coch.

Chicago, Boston, Miami, Los Angeles, and Dallas. Depending on the day and season, **Delta Air Lines** (☎ 800/221-1212; www.delta.com) operates several nonstop flights daily between New York JFK and London Heathrow, as well as many others with connections in Amsterdam or Paris; Delta also runs either one or two daily nonstop flights between Atlanta and Gatwick, and offers nonstop daily service from Cincinnati. Depending on the season, Delta also operates several flights a week to Edinburgh. **United Airlines** (☎ 800/864-8331; www.united.com) flies nonstop from New York's JFK and Chicago to Heathrow two or three times daily, depending on the season. United also offers nonstop service from Washington's Dulles, Cleveland, Houston, Newark, Los Angeles, and San Francisco.

FROM CANADA

Air Canada (☎ 888/247-2262; www.air canada.com) flies daily to London's Heathrow nonstop from Vancouver, Montreal, and Toronto. There are also frequent direct flights from Calgary, Ottawa, and St. John's. **British Airways** (☎ 800/247-9297) has direct flights from Toronto, Montreal, and Vancouver.

FROM AUSTRALIA

British Airways (☎ 1300/767-177) has flights to London from Sydney, Melbourne, Perth, and Brisbane. **Qantas** (☎ 612/131-313; www. qantas.com) offers flights from Australia to London's Heathrow. Direct flights depart from Sydney and Melbourne.

FROM NEW ZEALAND

Air New Zealand (☎ 800/262-1234 in the U.S., or 0800/737-000 in New Zealand; www.airnewzealand.co.nz) has daily direct flights to London from Auckland.

FROM IRELAND

British Airways (☎ 0844/493-0787) schedules four flights daily from Dublin into London's Gatwick airport, and **Aer Lingus** (☎ 0818/365000; www.aerlingus.com) flies from Dublin into Heathrow, as well as to Edinburgh and Glasgow. Flights from Dublin to London and Edinburgh and Glasgow are also available through **Ryanair** (☎ 0818/303030; www.ryanair.com). **British Midland** (☎ 0870/6070555; www.flybmi.com) also flies between Dublin and London.

By Train

One of the great engineering feats of all time, the Channel Tunnel, or Chunnel, is the first link between Britain and the Continent since the Ice Age. It's also one of the best (and most comfortable) ways to get from the Continent to London. **Eurostar** (☎ 800/387-6782 in the U.S., or ☎ 08705/186-186 in London; www.eurostar. com) express passenger train service makes the trip between Paris and London in 2 hours and 15 minutes. Train fares vary widely depending on date and time of travel, and how far in advance you reserve; check with Eurostar for up-to-date prices. Generally, the earlier you buy your ticket, the more leeway you'll get with the price. Eurostar trains arrive and depart from London's St. Pancras International Terminal, Paris's Gare du Nord, and Brussels' Central Station. Remember that if you're traveling through the Continent on a Eurailpass, it won't be valid when you reach the Chunnel—you will receive a discount on a Chunnel ticket, and once in England, you must use a separate BritRail pass or purchase individual tickets to continue onward by train.

By Car

If you plan to transport a rented car between Britain and France, check in advance with the car rental company about license and insurance requirements and additional drop-off charges before you begin. From a price and convenience standpoint, you're almost always better off dropping off your car in France, taking the train into Britain, and then renting a car there.

Should you still wish to take your car across the Channel, call ☎ 0870/535-3535, or go online to **www.eurotunnel.com** for information about car-rail service through the Chunnel. The English Channel is also crisscrossed with "drive-on, drive-off" car-ferry services. **P&O Ferries** (☎ 08716/645-645; www.poferries. com) operates car and passenger ferries between Dover and Calais, France (25 sailings a day; 75 min. each way).

By Bus

Bus connections between Britain and the Continent are available on **Eurolines,** 52 Grosvenor Gardens, SW1W 0AU (☎ 0871/781-8181; www. eurolines.com), but though bus travel is relatively cheap, it's definitely not the most convenient or comfortable way to get to Britain.

Getting Around

By Train

Train travel on Britain's extensive network is getting faster and more reliable. For instance, from London, 24 trains a day run to Cardiff (2 hr.); 20 travel to Edinburgh (4½ hr.); 16 run to Manchester (2½ hr.); and 27 run to York (just under 2 hr.). We recommend it whenever possible on the tours in this book.

There is, however, no single unified British Rail system. The system was privatized many years ago, and various train companies now service different routes and cities. For one-stop shopping for rail information, routes, times, and fares (of which there can be many), consult **National Rail Enquiries** (☎ 08457/484-950 in the U.K. or 020/7278-5240; www.nationalrail.co.uk). Though the website doesn't actually sell tickets, it will connect you to one that does; sometimes it's just easier to buy tickets at a station, especially if it's not a route where an advance reservation is a must (such as the Edinburgh–London run during the height of summer). If you are able to book in advance, **Trainline** (www.thetrainline.com) can bring significant savings on long-distance travel. You can collect tickets from your departure station. If you're fortunate, **MegaTrain** (www.megatrain.com) may have a seat on your route at a big discount.

The sleek, high-speed intercity (IC) trains that run along the heavily traveled, main-line routes in Britain are the most dependable and the most comfortable trains you can take. For shorter trips, you often take commuter trains. Local trains connect larger towns to smaller ones and are very basic, without toilets or food service. These trains are sometimes not even staffed with ticket takers, so be sure you have all the information you need before you board. Local stations are often small, one-person operations. Sometimes (particularly on Sun) no one is available to help with information or ticket sales, or a station closes down in the afternoon. You will always find train schedules posted in or just outside the station, but don't expect much in the way of services. In these small local stations there are often only two tracks with an overpass to get from one side to the other.

Different train lines use slightly different terminology and impose different restrictions, but generally speaking, in Britain, a one-way train ticket is called a "single" and a round-trip ticket is a "return." Note that buying two single (one-way) tickets is sometimes cheaper than buying a round-trip (return) ticket, so compare your options. When you buy your ticket, you must choose between first and standard (second) class. First-class tickets cost about one-third more than standard class. The first-class cars have roomier seats, but you can travel quite comfortably in standard class, and some commuter trains have no first-class cars. If you want a first-class ticket, you must request one—otherwise the agent will sell you a standard-class ticket. First-class service on some intercity train routes includes free beverages and snacks served at your seat, plus a free newspaper and a higher standard of personal service. Standard-class passengers can buy sandwiches and drinks in a cafe car. Local trains do not offer first-class service or food service. Smoking is not permitted on local trains, and is confined to strictly designated areas on commuter and intercity trains.

USING BRITRAIL PASSES

If you plan to travel around extensively by train, consider purchasing a BritRail pass, which allows unlimited travel in England, Scotland, and Wales on any British Rail scheduled train over the whole of the network during the validity of the pass, without restrictions. They offer a good bit of convenience and potentially a fair bit of savings. The passes are not available in Britain; you must buy them before you arrive. Many kinds of passes are available, allowing you to travel for a certain number of consecutive days or for a certain number of days within a set period, and throughout Britain or only within certain regions. Consult **BritRail** (☎ 866/BRIT-RAIL [274-8724]) in the U.S. and Canada; www.britrail.com) for the pass that will work best for you. Discounts are available for seniors and children.

Note: Though a BritRail Pass allows you to hop on and off trains at will during the pass's validity, it does not guarantee you a seat. If you have a firm itinerary and will be traveling on crowded or popular routes (such as

London–Edinburgh in summer), reserve a seat in advance to avoid derailing your travel plans.

By Bus

In Britain, a long-distance bus is called a "coach," and they are generally the cheapest way to get around the country, but also the slowest (if you're time-strapped, forget them as an option). Most sizable towns have a coach link with the capital, either direct or via a connection, most run by **National Express** (☎ 0871/781-8181; www.nationalexpress. com), which uses coaches equipped with reclining seats and toilets. A good alternative is super-budget **MegaBus** (☎ 0871/266-3333; www.megabus.com). Tickets cost as little as a pound, plus £1 booking fee.

In Wales, **Arriva Buses Wales** (☎ 0844/ 800-4411; www.arrivabus.co.uk) is one of the main operators, with local buses in the north and faster services down to the south. The area around Cardiff is covered by **Cardiff Bus** (☎ 029/2066-6444; www.cardiffbus.com). For a full list of bus companies, see **www. traveline-cymru.info**.

By Car

If you want to see the British countryside at its best, or tour rural areas not served by trains, you're going to need a car (and some of our itineraries require this), but it's a cost-effective option only if you plan to venture outside of towns and cities. And if you're not familiar with British traffic rules, driving here is not for the faint of heart. Before you even consider renting a car, ask yourself if you'd be comfortable driving with a steering wheel on the right-hand side of the vehicle while shifting with your left hand (you can get a car with automatic transmission, but it will cost considerably more.) **Remember, you must drive on the left and pass on the right.** Two essential rules for drivers are: Always look to the right, the direction from which oncoming traffic will approach; and, to ensure you're on the left side of the road, make certain that the center of the road is to your right.

If you plan to drive in Britain, before you leave on your car journey, find and purchase a good-quality, large-scale road map with a scale of 3 miles to 1 inch. Though we give general directions from place to place on the tours in this book, we simply don't have the room

to detail every twist and turn—a good map or road atlas is a must!

HITTING THE ROAD

What is commonly known as a freeway in some countries, the Brits call a motorway (indicated as "M" plus a number on maps). A two-way road is a single carriageway, and a four-lane divided highway (two lanes in each direction) is a dual carriageway. Country roads, some of them paved-over tracks dating back centuries, are full of twists and turns and are often barely wide enough for two cars to pass.

Motorways and other main roads have a 70 mph speed limit. On certain sections of the motorway, where speeding is especially dangerous, speed cameras have been installed. The cameras take a photograph of any car exceeding the speed limit so the police can trace the culprit. You will see a camera symbol upon entering these areas. Surveillance cameras have also been installed at some traffic lights to catch anyone who runs a red. The limit decreases depending on size of road, conditions, and locality. Built-up areas generally have a 30 mph limit, although a number of towns are now introducing a 20 mph limit on main streets. Road signs are clear and use international symbols. Seat belts are required for all car occupants. The Highway Code gives full details of signs and driving requirements. It is an essential read and is available at most service stations and many newsstands and bookshops (it costs about £1); it can also be read online at **www.direct.gov.uk**.

One element of British roads that invariably throws non-native drivers is the roundabout—a traffic junction where several roads meet at one traffic circle. On a roundabout, the cars to your right (that is, those already on the roundabout) always have the right of way.

Once you do make it to your intended destination, note that parking in the center of most towns and cities is difficult to find and expensive; before you park anywhere, make sure you read all posted restrictions or you may find yourself ticketed and/or towed. And be advised that you must stop for pedestrians in crosswalks marked by striped lines (called zebra crossings) on the road. Pedestrians have the right of way.

CAR RENTALS

Do yourself a favor: Forget about renting a car while in Edinburgh or London. Driving in the latter especially is an endurance test, and given the fact that drivers are now assessed a daily £8 "congestion charge" to use a car in central London, it can be incredibly expensive as well. Add, too, the hassle and cost of parking, which can be upwards of £30 a day. Instead, rent a car before you depart those cities (in London, you're best off renting at one of the airports and then heading out from there).

Americans, Canadians, Australians, the Irish, and New Zealanders renting a car in England need a valid driver's license from their home country that they've had for at least 1 year. In most cases, depending on the agency, you must be at least 23 years old (21 in some instances, 25 in others) and no older than 70. (Some companies have raised the maximum age to 75.)

The price of renting a car depends on a host of factors, including the size of the car, the length of time you keep it, where and when you pick it up and drop it off, and how far you drive it. Don't go for a big car unless you need it because gas prices in Britain are exceptionally high (almost three times as expensive as in the U.S., for example). There are a number of price comparison websites such as **CarRentals.co.uk** and **travelsupermarket. com**, which can help you find a good deal if you are here and are planning a short trip. There are often good weekend offers, especially away from high season.

Although not as common a practice as in the United States, some companies in the U.K. also offer refueling packages, in which you pay for an entire tank of gas upfront. The price is usually fairly competitive with local gas prices, but you don't get credit for any gas remaining in the tank. If you reject this option, you pay only for the gas you use, but you have to return the car with a full tank or face costly per-gallon charges for any shortfall. If you think that a stop at a gas station on the way back to the airport will make you miss your plane, then by all means take advantage of the fuel purchase option. Otherwise, skip it.

The main rental companies can be found at almost any British airport, but you'll find it cheaper to book a car before you arrive.

Rentals are available through **Alamo** (☎ 800/462-5266; www.alamo.com), **Avis** (☎ 800/331-1212; www.avis.com), **Budget** (☎ 800/527-0700; www.budget.com), **Dollar** (☎ 800/800-4000 in U.S., 800/848-8268 in Canada, 080/8234-7524 in U.K.; www.dollar.com), **Enterprise** (☎ 800/261-7331 in U.S., 514/355-4028 in Canada, 012/9360-9090 in U.K.; www.enterprise.com), and **Hertz** (☎ 800/654-3001; www.hertz.com). **Kemwel Drive Europe** (☎ 877/820-0668; www.kemwel.com) is among the cheapest and most reliable of the rental agencies. **AutoEurope** (☎ 888/223-5555 in the U.S., or 0800/223-5555 in London; www.autoeurope.com) acts as a wholesale company for rental agencies in Europe.

INSURANCE

On top of the standard rental prices, other optional charges apply to most car rentals. The Collision Damage Waiver (CDW), which limits your liability for damages caused by a collision, is covered by many credit card companies if you pay with their credit card. Check with your credit card company before you go so you can avoid paying this fee (as much as £10 per day). The car rental companies also offer additional liability insurance (if you harm others in an accident), personal accident insurance (if you harm yourself or your passengers), and personal effects insurance (if your property is stolen from your car). If you have insurance on your car at home, you're probably covered for most of these unlikelihoods; check before you leave home—it's not unheard of for rental agencies to try and pressure renters into buying insurance they don't need. If your own insurance doesn't cover you for rentals, or if you don't have auto insurance, you should consider these additional types of coverage (liability coverage is mandatory in Britain).

EMERGENCIES ON THE ROAD

All motorways have emergency telephones stationed about a mile apart; if you don't see one, walk down the road for a bit to the blue-and-white marker with an arrow that points to the nearest box. The phone operator will obtain emergency or automotive services if you require them. If you must pull over to the side of the motorway, park as close to the far edge of the shoulder as possible. Motorway service stations are usually about 25 miles apart and occasionally as far as 50 miles apart.

Membership in the **Automobile Association (AA)** (☎ 0161/333-0004; www.theaa.com) comes with roadside assistance should you break down. Its 24-hour service hotline is ☎ 0800/887-766. You can join the club through your car rental agent. (Members of AAA in the U.S. can enjoy reciprocity overseas.)

GAS (PETROL)

Petrol (gasoline) stations are self-service. The green filler pipe is for unleaded petrol, the red filler pipe is for leaded petrol, and the black filler pipe is for diesel fuel. Petrol is often cheapest at supermarkets, but going to a motorway service station is more convenient. Petrol is purchased by the liter (3.78L = 1 U.S. gal.) and is very expensive; at press time, gas cost around £1.37 a liter (1 U.S. gal.= 3.785L). Do note, though, that any gallon prices mentioned in Britain are imperial gallons (4.546L).

Tips on Accommodations

British hotels are graded using a star-rating system by VisitEngland, the national tourism organization. They are judged on standards, quality, and hospitality, and are rated "approved," "commended," "highly commended," and "deluxe." Five stars (deluxe) is the highest rating. A classification of "listed" refers to places that are, for the most part, very modest. All establishments from two stars upward must have 100% en suite (private bathroom) facilities. In a one-star hotel, buildings are required to have hot and cold running water in all rooms, but in "listed" hotels, hot and cold running water in each room is not mandatory. Star ratings are posted outside the buildings, but the system is voluntary, and many hotels do not participate.

Breakfast is often included in quoted rates, and this can range from a full breakfast of bacon and eggs to a continental breakfast of tea or coffee and toast. This is on a bed and breakfast (B&B) basis; ask when booking, as sometimes it's not always clear whether breakfast is part of the deal, and in some big, upscale hotels you can find yourself paying a goodly extra sum if you sit down without checking.

Bed & Breakfasts

In towns, cities, and villages throughout Britain, homeowners take in paying guests. Watch for the familiar bed-and-breakfast (B&B) signs. Generally, these are modest family homes, but sometimes they may be built like small hotels, with as many as 15 rooms. B&Bs are some of the cheapest places you can stay in England and are often extremely comfortable. Nowadays, many are run with the sensibility of a small hotel and some might be quite stylish. **Bed & Breakfast Nationwide** (☎ 01255/672-377; www.bedandbreakfast nationwide.com) is an agency dealing in almost 700 privately-owned bed-and-breakfasts across Great Britain, from cottages to castles.

Farmhouses

Farms across Britain often have rooms set aside for paying guests, sometimes in the main house, but increasingly in converted barns, outhouses, or cottages. You might still find some that offer a visitor a simple room for the night, but more and more they are expanding into full B&B territory, with breakfasts often sourced from the farm and its surroundings. Many farms are geared toward children, who can participate in light chores—gathering eggs or just tagging along—for an authentic farm experience. Sometimes, also, you will find self-catering options. A growing number also offer evening meals, sometimes around a big kitchen table in front of a warming stove. The settings are often wonderful, deep in the countryside.

Farm Stay UK (☎ 024/7669-6909; www.farmstay.co.uk), set up in part by the Royal Agricultural Society of England, and still owned by a consortium of farmers, features more than 1,200 rural retreats including farms, B&Bs, and campsites. Most are open year-round.

Historic Properties

National Trust Holiday Cottages (☎ 0844/800-2070; www.nationaltrustcottages.co.uk) is part of Britain's leading conservation group and rents out 370 houses and cottages in some of the most beautiful parts of England and Wales. They sleep 2–12, are self-catering, and are mostly available year-round, for weekends, short breaks, and longer. National Trust properties are also bookable from the Trust's U.S. affiliate, the **Royal Oak Foundation** (☎ 800/913-6565 or 212/480-2889; www.royal-oak.org). Annual membership is $55 (families $90), which gives admission to all National Trust sites and properties, plus discounts on air travel, train tickets, and bookings at NT cottages and houses.

The **Landmark Trust** (☎ 01628/825-925; www.landmarktrust.org.uk) is a charity that rescues historic buildings and turns them into places to stay. As well as cottages, you'll find castles, country houses, towers, and other odd buildings. **Welsh Rarebits: Hotels of Distinction** (☎ 01686/668-030; www.rarebits.co.uk) is a collection of 52 historic hotels across Wales, from Georgian country houses to the Italianate village of Portmeirion, all of them luxury, most of them small and personally run. In Scotland, a good source of options is the website of the **Association of Scotland's Self-Caterers** (www.assc.co.uk), whose properties range from cottages to castles.

Holiday Cottages

Throughout Britain, fully furnished studios, houses, cottages, "flats" (apartments), and even trailers suitable for families or groups can be rented by the week or month. From October to March, rents are sometimes reduced by 50%. **English Country Cottages** (☎ 0845/268-0785; www.english-country-cottages.co.uk) focuses on 4- and 5-star properties across the breadth of England and Wales. **Cottages 4 You** (☎ 0845/268-0760; www.cottages4you.co.uk), part of the same company, deals in more modest options, and has 10,000 properties in the United Kingdom. In Wales, **Coastal Cottages of Pembrokeshire** (☎ 01437/765-765; www.coastalcottages.co.uk) is a specialist in the busy southwestern getaway spot. Visit Britain is also a good source of information on vacation rentals.

Chain Hotels

Many American chains, such as Best Western, Hilton, Sheraton, and Travelodge, are found throughout Britain. In addition, Britain has a number of leading chains. **Thistle Hotels** (☎ 0871/376-9099 in U.K., or 0845/305-8379; www.thistle.com) is a decent chain of moderate to upscale hotels. There are, increasingly, small chains of boutique hotels such as the discreetly stylish **Hotel du Vin** (☎ 0845/365-4438; www.hotelduvin.com) and the more outrageously stylish **Malmaison** (☎ 0845/365-4247; www.malmaison.com), whose properties include a former church and prison. Both are part of the same group. At the other end of the scale, **Premier Inn** (www.premierinn.com; ☎ 0870/242-8000) is now Britain's largest hotel chain, offering simple quality at low prices.

House Swapping

HomeLink International (www.homelink.org; ☎ 800/638-3841 or 954/566-2687), which costs $119 for a year's membership, is the oldest, largest, and best home-exchange holiday group in the world. A competitor is **Intervac International** (www.intervac-homeexchange.com; ☎ 800/756-HOME 4663), which costs $99.99 annually.

Youth Hostels

The **Youth Hostels Association** (☎ 01629/592-700; www.yha.org.uk) and **Scottish Youth Hostels** (☎ 01786/891-400; www.syha.org.uk) operate more than 300 hostels in cities, in the countryside, and along the coast. Hostels used to be known for their stark surroundings, dormitory rooms, and clientele of hardened hikers. However, in recent years, they have widened their scope with new, purpose-built properties, family rooms, good food, and warm welcomes. What haven't changed are the locations, many of which 5-star hotels would kill for, not least in Snowdonia.

Fast Facts

ATMs

Often referred to as "cash machines" or "cashpoints," ATMs are the easiest way to get cash away from home. The **Cirrus** (☎ 800/424-7787; www.mastercard.com) and **PLUS** (☎ 800/843-7587; www.visa.com) networks span the globe, and you'll find ATMs almost everywhere you go in Britain (they might be scarce in some of the tiniest villages in the countryside and national parks). Note that U.K. machines use **4-digit PINs,** so if your bank issues a 6-digit number, contact them before you leave home.

Bike Rentals

England is a wonderful country for cycling, and rentals are widely available. An excellent source for cycling in the U.K. is the **National Cyclists Organization,** CTC, Parklands, Railton Rd., Guildford, Surrey (☎ 0844/736-8450; www.ctc.org.uk).

Business Hours

With many exceptions, business hours are Monday to Friday 9am to 5pm. In general, retail stores are open Monday to Saturday 9am to 6pm, Sunday 11am to 5pm (sometimes noon to 6pm). In country towns, there is usually an early closing day (often Wed or Thurs), when the shops close at 1pm.

Standard British banking hours are 9 or 9:30am to 3:30 or 4pm; in London and other large cities, some banks remain open until 5pm.

Customs

Non-E.U. nationals aged 17 and over can bring in, duty-free, 200 cigarettes or 100 cigarillos or 50 cigars or 250 grams of smoking tobacco. You can also bring in 4 liters of wine and 16 liters of beer, plus either 1 liter of alcohol more than 22% ("spirits") or 2 liters of "fortified" wine at less than 22%. Visitors may also bring in other goods, including perfume, gifts, and souvenirs, totaling £390 in value. (Customs officials tend to be lenient about these general merchandise regulations, realizing the limits are unrealistically low.) For **arrivals from within the E.U.,** there are no limits as long as goods are for your own personal use, or are gifts.

Dining

In general, you will find decent, and often excellent, meals wherever you travel. In addition to restaurants and cafes, many pubs serve lunch and dinner, and tea shops are open during the day, usually from about 8am to 5pm, for breakfast, lunch, and tea. Wine bars, serving light fare, are becoming increasingly common around Britain. Excellent options for snacks and lunches are the cafeterias (buffets) at many cathedrals, manor houses, and other historic sights; these can be extremely atmospheric, and they usually serve a very decent assortment of food at reasonable prices. For more information on British cuisine, see p. 711.

Electricity

British mains electricity operates at 240 volts AC (50 cycles), and most overseas plugs don't fit Britain's unique three-pronged wall outlets. Always bring suitable transformers and/or adapters such as world multiplugs—if you plug some American appliances directly into a European electrical outlet without a transformer, you'll destroy your appliance and possibly start a fire.

Embassies & Consulates

The **U.S. Embassy** is at 24 Grosvenor Square, London (☎ 020/7499-9000; www.usembassy.org.uk; Tube: Marble Arch or Bond St.). Standard hours are Monday to Friday 8am to 5:30pm. However, for passport and visa services relating to U.S. citizens, contact the **Passport and Citizenship Unit,** 55–56 Upper Brook St., London, close to the Embassy (same phone number as above). Most non-emergency enquiries require an appointment.

The **High Commission of Canada,** Macdonald House, 1 Grosvenor Square, London (☎ 020/7258-6600; www.canadainternational.gc.ca/united_kingdom-royaume_uni/index.aspx; Tube: Bond St.), handles passport and consular services for Canadians. Hours are Monday to Friday 9:30am to 1pm. (*Please note:* This is a temporary location that has been set up while Canada House, home of the Canadian High Commission on Trafalgar Square, undergoes renovations before reopening in summer 2012. Macdonald House is just a short walk from Trafalgar Square.)

The **Australian High Commission** is at Australia House, Strand, London (☎ 020/7379-4334; www.australia.org.uk; Tube: Charing Cross, Covent Garden, or Temple). Hours are Monday to Friday 9am to 5pm.

The **New Zealand High Commission** is at New Zealand House, 80 Haymarket (at Pall Mall), London (☎ 020/7930-8422; www.nzembassy.com/uk; Tube: Charing Cross or Piccadilly Circus). Hours are Monday to Friday 9am to 5pm.

The **Irish Embassy** is at 17 Grosvenor Place, London (☎ 020/7235-2171; www.embassyofireland.co.uk; Tube: Hyde Park Corner). Hours are Monday to Friday 9:30am to 5pm.

Emergencies

Dial ☎ 999 or ☎ 112 for police, fire, or ambulance, free of charge, anywhere in Britain. Give your name, address, and telephone number and state the nature of the emergency.

Family Travel

Britain is well geared to young travelers. Most hotels will let kids under 16 or so stay in their parents' room for free, many restaurants have kids' menus, just about all attractions charge less for children 16 and under, and admission is often free for children under 5. You'll also find babysitting available at most hotels; enquire at the concierge or reception desk. If London is on your itinerary, help your kids check out the family page on **Visit London** at www.visitlondon.com/attractions/family/. The **London Tourism Guide** also has a page for kids, www.londontourist.org/kids.html.

If you're renting a car, children under 12 and under 1.35m (4½ ft.) in height must ride in an appropriate car seat. Consult your car rental company in advance of arrival, but it's the driver's legal responsibility to ensure that all child passengers comply (see **www.childcar seats.org.uk/law** for details).

Some Frommer's guides were written specifically for families and are worth consulting, including *Frommer's London with Kids*, *Frommer's England with Your Family*, *Frommer's Devon & Cornwall with Your Family*, *Frommer's Scotland with Your Family*, and *Frommer's Wales with Your Family*.

LGBT Travelers

Britain has one of the most active gay and lesbian scenes in Europe, most evident in London and Brighton; in fact, London has been chosen to host World Pride 2012. **Gay News** (www.gayuknews.com) has a comprehensive database of the scene around the country. The **LGBT Tourist Information Office** (www. gaytouristoffice.co.uk) is another good place to find out what's on, or to seek advice on gay-friendly hotels and hostels. The **Lesbian and Gay Switchboard** (☎ 020/7837-7324; www. llgs.org.uk) is open 10am to 11pm daily, providing information about activities in London and general advice. Their searchable online database (www.turingnetwork.org.uk) lists gay bars, clubs, and other services countrywide. London's best gay-oriented bookstore is **Gay's the Word,** 66 Marchmont St. (☎ 020/7278-7654; www. gaystheword.co.uk; Tube: Russell Sq.).

July's annual **Pride London** march and festival (☎ 0844/884-2439; www.pridelondon. org) is the highlight of London's LGBT calendar, while Pride in Brighton & Hove (☎ 01273/

775-939; www.brightonpride.org) and Manchester Pride (☎ 0161/831-7700; www. manchesterpride.com) are the main events outside London, on different weekends in August. Manchester-based **Gaydio** (www. gaydio.co.uk) was the U.K.'s first radio station dedicated to lesbian, gay, bisexual, and trans listeners.

If you're planning to visit from the U.S., the **International Gay and Lesbian Travel Association** (IGLTA; ☎ 800/448-8550 or 954/630-1637; www.iglta.org) is the trade association for the gay and lesbian travel industry, and offers an online directory of gay- and lesbian-friendly travel businesses.

Health

Traveling to Britain poses no health risk. The tap water is safe to drink, the milk is pasteurized, and mad cow disease and foot-and-mouth disease are no longer epidemic.

If you need a doctor, your hotel can recommend one, or you can contact your embassy or consulate. Or dial ☎ 100 and ask the operator for the local police, who will give you the name, address, and telephone number of a doctor in your area. *Note:* Visitors who become ill while they're in Britain are eligible only for free emergency care. For other treatment, including follow-up care, you'll be asked to pay (though your existing insurance policy may cover you; check before you leave home).

Holidays

Britain observes New Year's Day, Good Friday, Easter Monday, May Day (first Mon in May), spring and summer bank holidays (the last Mon in May and Aug, respectively), Christmas Day, and Boxing Day (Dec 26).

Insurance

For information on traveler's insurance, trip cancellation insurance, and medical insurance while traveling, please visit www.frommers. com/tips.

Internet Access

The availability of the Internet across the U.K. is in a constant state of development. How you access it depends on whether you've brought your own computer or smartphone, or if you're searching for a public terminal. Many hotels have computers for guest use, although pricing can vary from gratis to extortionate.

To find a local Internet cafe, start by checking **www.cybercaptive.com**. Although such places have suffered due to the spread of smartphones and free Wi-Fi (see below), they do tend to be prevalent close to popular tourist spots. Aside from formal cybercafes, some **public libraries** allow nonresidents to use terminals.

If you have your own computer or smartphone, **Wi-Fi** makes access much easier. Always check before using your hotel's network—many charge exorbitant rates, and free or cheap Wi-Fi isn't hard to find elsewhere, in urban locations at least. Ask locally, or even Google "free Wi-Fi + (town)" before you arrive. You may also find the Global Hotspot Finder at www.jiwire. com useful. National chains like **Welcome Break** motorway service stations (www. welcomebreak.co.uk) and **Wetherspoon** pubs (www.jdwetherspoon.co.uk), among many others, offer free Wi-Fi. There are also **BT Openzone** (www.btopenzone.com) hotspots in many cafes, hotels, and public places across the country (see http://btopenzone.hotspot-directory.com for a searchable directory and map).

Legal Aid

If you're visiting from overseas and find yourself in legal trouble, contact your consulate or embassy. They can advise you of your rights and will usually provide a list of local attorneys (for which you'll have to pay if services are used), but they cannot interfere on your behalf in the English legal process. For questions about American citizens who are arrested abroad, including ways of getting money to them, telephone the **Citizens Emergency Center** of the Office of Overseas Citizens Services in Washington, D.C. (☎ 202/647-5225). Citizens of other nations should go to their consulate for advice.

Mail

The British postal system (www.royalmail. com) is among the most reliable in the world, so you shouldn't need to depend on FedEx or some other courier service unless you're in a hurry. An airmail letter to anywhere outside Europe costs 67p for up to 10g (⅓ oz.) and generally takes 5 to 7 working days to arrive; postcards also require a 67p stamp. Within

the E.U., letters or postcards under 20g (⅔ oz.) cost 60p. Within the U.K, First Class mail ought to arrive the following working day; Second Class mail takes around 3 days.

Post offices can be found in every city and small town, identified by a red box labelled ROYAL MAIL. In smaller towns the post office may be in a local store rather than a post office building. Most are open 9am to 5pm on weekdays, and some might be open on Saturday mornings.

Money

Frommer's lists exact prices in the local currency, the British pound (also called "quid"). For up-to-the-minute conversion rates, check a currency exchange website such as **www.oanda.com/currency/converter**.

If you plan on using a credit card, note that Britain is moving from magnetic strip credit cards to the new system of **Chip and PIN** ("smartcards" with chips embedded in them). If you are visiting from a country where Chip and PIN is less prevalent (like the U.S.), it's possible that some retailers will be reluctant to accept your (to Brits, old-fashioned) swipe cards. Swipe cards are still legal, and the same machines that read the smartcard chips can also read your magnetic strip. However, do carry some cash with you too, just in case.

If you're leaving your home country to visit Britain, also beware of hidden **credit- or debit-card fees.** Check with your card issuer to see what fees, if any, will be charged for overseas transactions. Recent reform legislation in the U.S., for example, has curbed some exploitative lending practices. But many banks have responded by increasing fees in other areas, including fees for customers who use credit and debit cards while out of the country—even if those charges were made in U.S. dollars. Fees can amount to 3% or more of the purchase price. Check with your bank before departing to avoid any surprise charges on your statement.

Passports

To enter the United Kingdom, all U.S. citizens, Canadians, Australians, New Zealanders, and South Africans must have a passport valid through their length of stay. No visa is required.

FOR RESIDENTS OF THE UNITED STATES

Download passport applications from the U.S. Department of State website at http://travel.state.gov. To find your regional passport office, either check the U.S. Department of State website or call the toll-free number of the National Passport Information Center (☎ 877/487-2778) for automated information.

FOR RESIDENTS OF CANADA

Passport applications are available at Passport Canada offices and Canada Post outlets across the country, or from the central Passport Office, Department of Foreign Affairs and International Trade, Ottawa, ON (☎ 800/567-6868; www.passportcanada.gc.ca). Forms can also be downloaded from the Passport Canada website. **Note:** Canadian children who travel must have their own passport.

FOR RESIDENTS OF IRELAND

You can apply for a 10-year passport at the Passport Office, Setanta Centre, Molesworth Street, Dublin (☎ 01/671-1633; www.irlgov.ie/iveagh). Those under age 18 and over 65 must apply for a 3-year passport. You can also apply at 1A South Mall, Cork (☎ 021/494-4700) or at most main post offices.

FOR RESIDENTS OF AUSTRALIA

You can pick up an application from your local post office or any branch of Passports Australia, but you must schedule an interview at the passport office to present your application materials. Call the Australian Passport Information Service at ☎ 131-232, or visit the government website at www.smarttraveler.gov.au.

Pharmacies

In Britain, they're called "chemists." Most are open from about 9am to 5pm Monday to Saturday, though in cities and larger towns one or two will keep late hours and open on Sunday as well. Every police station in the country has a list of emergency chemists and can give you the name of one nearest you; you can also ask at your hotel's front desk. If you take medications, note that British pharmacies can't honor prescriptions written by doctors outside the U.K. This means you will have to see a physician in the U.K. to obtain a prescription if you get ill or lose your medicine. Options are to go to a National Health clinic, or to go to a private clinic such as **Medicentre** (visit www.medicentre.co.uk for locations) and pay the out-of-pocket expense.

Safety

Britain is one of the safer destinations in the world, but the sensible precautions you would heed anywhere prevail, of course. As elsewhere, London, Manchester, Edinburgh, Cardiff, and other large British cities have their share of crime, but in general they are among the safer destinations of Europe. Pickpockets are a major concern, so conceal your wallet or hold onto your purse and don't flaunt jewelry or cash. When driving, try to avoid leaving valuables in your car and always make sure the doors are locked. Women traveling alone encounter less aggressive, or so-called macho, behavior than they will find in such countries as Spain and Italy. Of course, discretion is always advised—that is, don't get into unlicensed cabs within cities, and avoid walking in deserted areas after dark.

Senior Travelers

Residents of Britain are entitled to many senior discounts, and some apply to travelers as well. Notably, most attractions, including those operated by **English Heritage** and the **National Trust** (p. 726), offer reduced entrance fees to seniors, as do many museums. Even if discounts aren't posted, ask if they're available and make sure you carry some kind of identification that shows your date of birth. **BritRail** (p. 728) offers overseas seniors discounted rates on some rail passes around Britain. Many British hotels offer discounts to seniors as well.

Smoking

Brtiain has banned smoking in enclosed public spaces, including hotels, restaurants, and pubs. Many pubs and bars provide covered outdoor smoking areas, and many hotels set aside rooms for smokers.

Taxes

A national value-added tax (**VAT**) of 20% is included in all hotel and restaurant bills, and in the price of most items you purchase in Britain. If you permanently reside outside the E.U., VAT on goods can be refunded if you shop at stores that participate in the **Retail Export Scheme**—look for the window sticker or ask the staff. You need to fill out form VAT 407 in the store, which the retailer will supply, and show your passport when you make the purchase. Show your receipt and form 407 to customs officials when you leave Britain and you then qualify for your refund. Details of the scheme are posted online at **www.hmrc. gov.uk/vat/sectors/consumers/overseas-visitors.htm**.

Telephones

MOBILE PHONES

The three letters that define much of the world's wireless capabilities are **GSM** (Global System for Mobiles), a seamless satellite network that makes for easy cross-border cellphone use throughout most of the planet, including Britain. If you own an unlocked GSM phone, simply pack it in your hand luggage and pick up a contract-free **SIM-only card** when you arrive in Britain. The SIM card will cost very little, but you will need to load it up with credit to start making calls. Prices change constantly in response to the market, but in general expect call charges of around 20p per minute, 10p for a text message, and a deal on data that might cap daily usage charges at about £2. There are phone and SIM card retailers on practically every major street in most cities, but not every retailer will sell SIM-only deals to nonresidents. **Tesco Mobile** (www.tescomobile.com) sells SIMs for 99p that you can top up in-store with cash or an overseas credit card. Find a convenient branch at **www.tesco.com/storelocator**. **Three** (www.three.co.uk) sells SIMs for £1.99 that you can top up at Three stores, supermarkets, and newsagents across the country. Three SIMs work only in 3G-compatible phones.

For a short visit, **renting** a phone may be a good idea, and we suggest renting the handset before you leave home. North Americans can rent from **InTouch USA** (☎ 800/872-7626 or 703/222-7161; www.intouchglobal.com) or **BrightRoam** (☎ 888/622-3393; www.bright roam.com). However, handset purchase prices have fallen to a level where you can probably **buy a basic U.K. pay-as-you-go (PAYG) phone** for less than one week's handset rental. Prices at many cellphone retailers start from under £20 for an inexpensive model; there are now basic smartphones costing around £50. Expect outgoing call charges of approximately 25p per minute to anywhere in the U.K., 10p for text messages (SMS); receiving calls on your local number is free. **Carphone Ware-house** (www.carphonewarehouse.com) has retail branches across the country and stocks a reliable range of cheap PAYG phones. If you plan to do a lot of calling home, you might want to use a VoIP service like **Skype** (www.skype.com) or **Truphone** (www.truphone.com) in conjunction with a Web connection.

Mobile phone coverage is usually very good, although there are still areas where you can't get a signal, and it's as likely to be in an unpopulated area of Suffolk as on a Welsh mountain.

CALLING INFO

To call Britain from abroad, dial 011 from the U.S. or Canada, 00 from Ireland or New Zealand, or 0011 from Australia; then 44 (Britain's country code); then the local area code (given throughout this book); and finally the local phone number. The area codes listed in this book begin with a "0"; you do not need to dial the "0" when calling from outside the U.K., but you do need to include it when calling from within the U.K. For calls within the same city or town, the local number is all you need, minus the area code. Dial just the **6- to 8-digit number.** Calling from a mobile phone, you need to dial the full number including area code, *no matter where you're calling from.*

To make an **international call** from Britain, dial the international access code (**00**)**,** then the country code, then the area code, and finally the local number. Common country codes are: U.S. and Canada, **1**; Australia, **61**; Ireland, **353**; and New Zealand, **64**. For example, if you wanted to call the British Embassy in Washington, D.C., you would dial 00-1-202-588-7800.

Phone cards are often the most economical method for visitors from overseas to make both international and national calls. They are available in several values and are reusable until the total value has expired. Cards can be purchased from newsstands and small retailers nationwide, and offer call rates of a few pence per minute to English-speaking countries like Australia and the United States. Follow the instructions on the card to make a call from a public pay phone. Most pay phones now also take **credit cards,** but if your card doesn't have Chip and PIN technology embedded (see "Money," above), you may encounter problems.

For directory assistance, dial ☎ **142** in London; for the rest of Britain, ☎ **192.** For operator assistance, dial ☎ **155.**

Numbers beginning with 0800 within Britain are toll-free, but calling a 1-800 number in the States from Britain is not toll-free—it costs the same as an overseas call.

Time

Britain follows **Greenwich Mean Time** (GMT) between late October and late March. Daylight-saving **British Summer Time** (BST), one hour ahead of GMT, is in operation for the rest of the year. London is generally 5 hours ahead of U.S. Eastern Standard Time (EST), although because of different daylight saving time practices in the two nations, there's a brief period in autumn when Britain is only 4 hours ahead of New York or Toronto, and a brief period in spring when it's 6 hours ahead. Sydney is 10 or 11 hours ahead of U.K. time; Auckland 12 or 13 hours ahead.

Tipping

For minicab drivers, add about 10% to 15% to the fare on the meter. In hotels, porters receive £1 per bag, even if you have only one small suitcase. Hall porters are tipped only for special services. Maids receive £1 per day.

In restaurants and nightclubs, a 15% service charge is added to the bill, which is distributed among all the help. Tipping in pubs isn't common, but in wine bars, the server usually gets about £1 per round of drinks.

Barbers and hairdressers expect 10%. Tour guides expect £2 ($4), though it's not mandatory. Theater ushers don't expect tips.

For help with tip calculations, and more, download our convenient Travel Tools app for your mobile device. Go to **www.frommers. com/go/mobile** and click on the Travel Tools icon.

Toilets

Also known as "loos" or "public conveniences," these are marked by PUBLIC TOILET signs in streets, parks, and Tube stations; many are automatically sterilized after each use. You can also find well-maintained lavatories in all larger public buildings, such as museums and art galleries, large department stores, and railway stations. It's not always acceptable to use the lavatories in hotels, restaurants, and pubs if you're not a customer. Public lavatories are usually free, but you may need a small coin to get in or to use a proper washroom.

Travelers with Disabilities

Britain is better adapted to persons with disabilities than many other countries; at least in the major cities, you'll find that many hotels and attractions have dedicated wheelchair entries, and persons with disabilities are often granted admission discounts. In rural areas and in historic buildings and older inns, you might have a bit more difficulty getting around.

The best local organization to consult for trip-planning advice is **Tourism for All UK,** Shap Road Industrial Estate, Shap Road, Kendal, Cumbria (☎ 0845/124-9971, from overseas 01539/814-683; www.tourismforall. org.uk). The website also has an invaluable list of relevant organizations to contact for advice relating to specific chronic complaints. The **Royal Association for Disability Rights (RADAR),** 12 City Forum, 250 City Road, London (☎ 020/7250-3222; www.radar.org.uk), publishes a number of handy written resources and, for a small fee, sells a key that opens over 8,000 locked public disabled toilets countrywide (£3.50 including U.K. shipping and handling; £5.40 to anywhere in the world). **Holiday Care** (☎ 0845/124-9971 in U.K.; www.holidaycare.org.uk) also provides a wide range of travel information and resources for disabled and elderly people. In London, your first stop should be the "Accessible London" section of the **Visit London** website: **www. visitlondon.com/access.** You'll find links to details of accessible hotels and information about which parts of the transport network are adapted to your needs.

Index

A

Abbotsbury Swannery, 188, 197
Abbotsford (near Galashiels), 542, 544, 546
Aberconwy House (Conwy), 687
Abergavenny Food Festival, 661
Aberglaslyn Gorge, 665, 675, 680, 683
Aberglasney Gardens (Llangathen), 639
Accommodations, 731–32. See also specific hotels/areas; Fast Facts for specific areas
    favorite hotels and inns, 18
    London services for, 137
    romantic, 17
Achamore Gardens (Isle of Gigha), 555
Acton Scott Historic Working Farm (near Church Stretton), 356
Addison's Walk (Magdalen College, Oxford), 363
Admiralty Arch (Holyhead), 684
Admiralty Arch (London), 100
A5 (Holyhead to London), 675, 684
Agatha Christie Memorial Room (Torquay), 238, 338
Aira Force waterfall (near Ullswater), 415, 426
Albany (Mayfair), 95
Albert Bridge (Chelsea), 99
Albert Dock (Liverpool), 11, 407, 413, 434
Albert Memorial (Kensington Gardens, London), 66, 74, 577, 704
Alcester, 358
Alexander Keiller Museum (Avebury), 200
All Saints Church (Hereford), 351
American Museum (Bath), 270
Ancient House (Ipswich), 391
Anglesey, Isle of, 668, 683–84
Anglesey and the Northwest Coast of Wales, 682–85
An Lanntair (Stornoway), 623
Anne Boleyn, 6, 42, 57, 59, 76, 149, 158, 160
Anne Hathaway's Cottage (Stratford-upon-Avon), 27, 327, 331, 370
Anne of Cleves, 6, 42, 149, 158, 160, 168
Anne of Cleves House (Lewes), 150, 175
Apsley House (London), 61, 84
Aquarium/Sea life/Marine attractions. See also specific attractions/museums
    London, 83
    South-Central England, 188–89, 192, 193, 194–96
    West Country, 8, 223, 233, 239, 272–73, 274
    Northwest and the Lake District, 8, 407, 413, 414, 418, 434–35

Yorkshire, 467, 470
Archaeological attractions, 10, 696–97, 703. See also Avebury; British Museum; Roman Britain; Stonehenge; specific attractions
    Cotswolds, 302–3
    Northwest and the Lake District, 35, 415, 426, 456
    Oxford and the Heart of England, 30, 326, 330, 356–57, 364
    Scottish Highlands and Islands, 10, 591, 598, 623–24
    South-Central England 10, 16, 28, 189, 191, 192, 193, 196, 198–201, 211, 212–13
    West Country, 230, 258, 286
    Yorkshire and Northeast, 31, 465, 471, 475, 487, 696
Architecture, 703–5. See also Bridges, famous; Cathedrals and abbeys; Houses, historic; specific architects
    Bath, 29, 227, 260, 268–70, 704
    Cardiff Bay, 11, 30, 631, 633, 644, 705
    Glasgow/Scottish Lowlands, 566–69
    Liverpool, 413, 436
    New Scottish Parliament (Edinburgh), 506
    Norwich, 396
Ardnamurchan Peninsula, 595, 602, 604
Argyll, northern, 594, 600-2. See also North Argyll to Lochaber, tour of
Argyll Forest Park (Cowal Peninsula), 600
Arisaig, 595
    coastal route to Mallaig, 591, 604
Arlington Mill (Bibury), 308
Arlington Row (Bibury), 300, 308
Armadale Castle (Isle of Skye), 625
Arran, Isle of (Firth of Clyde), 539, 543, 555, 587
Art, 706. See also specific artists
Art collections, 9. See also specific museums and galleries
Arundells (Salisbury), 212
Ashmolean Museum (Oxford), 30, 326, 330, 364
Ashton Lane (Glasgow), 577
Asia Galleries (British Museum), 71
Assembly Rooms (Bath), 29, 227, 269. See also Fashion Museum
At-Bristol, 274
ATMs/Cashpoints, 732. See also Fast Facts for specific areas
Audley End House and Gardens (Saffron Walden), 386–87
Augustus John's Studio (Chelsea), 98

Austen, Jane, 53, 202, 248–49, 707, 709, 719. See also Jane Austen Centre and entries following
    as Bath resident, 29, 227, 270
    grave (Winchester Cathedral), 214, 216
Avebury, 10, 188, 199–200
Avon River boat cruises (Stratford-upon-Avon), 370
Ayrshire, 543, 552–53

B

Ballet, 21, 131, 503, 532, 533, 584, 644
Balliol College (Oxford), 364, 548
Balmoral Castle and Estate (near Braemar), 599, 610, 724
Balnakeil Craft Village (near Durness), 618
Balranald Nature Reserve (North Uist), 598
Bannockburn, and battle of, 542, 563, 694, 698
Banqueting House (London), 101
Barafundle Bay, 631, 640, 655
Barbara Hepworth Museum and Sculpture Garden (St. Ives), 9, 32, 222–23, 226, 234–35, 285
Barber Institute of Fine Arts (Birmingham), 332–33
The Barbican (Plymouth), 238–39
Barbican Centre (London), 130, 705
Barge cruises, 718
Barra, Isle of (Outer Hebrides), 598, 622, 627
Barrie, J.M., 47, 82, 87, 305
Bars. See also Pubs; Nightlife
    Brighton, 177
    Cardiff, 644
    Edinburgh, 497, 531–32
    Glasgow, 583–84
    London, 95, 127, 130
    Manchester, 446
Bath, 5, 29–30, 227, 228, 260, 266–71, 288–89, 296, 483, 704
    architecture, 29, 227, 260, 268–70, 704
    bathing in, 268
    staying/dining in, 271
Bath Abbey, 227, 266
Batsford Arboretum (near Moreton-in-Marsh), 295, 296, 299, 304
Battle (near Rye)/Battle of Hastings, site of, 42, 142, 150, 180, 694, 697
Beaches
    East Anglia, 392, 393
    Kent/Sussex, 146, 149, 172
    North Wales, 684
    Northwest, 417, 418
    Scottish Highlands and Islands, 2, 590, 591, 598, 602, 604, 617–18, 622–23, 624
    Scottish Lowlands, 538, 543, 550

South-Central England, 192, 196, 197
South Wales, 631, 640, 655–57
West Country, 222, 234, 238, 241–42, 284
Yorkshire, 467
Beasts of Dacre (V&A), 66
Beatles, 265, 432, 436, 691, 701
childhood homes of, 414, 437
International Beatle Week, 439, 724
tours, 407, 414, 437, 438
Beatrix Potter Gallery (near Hawkshead), 415
Beaumaris (Anglesey), 668, 683
Beaumaris Castle, 665, 668, 669, 683
Beddgelert, 668, 680, 683
Beer and ale, 497, 634, 713. See also Pubs
Beetham Tower (Manchester), 445
Bell, Vanessa, 37, 150, 157–58. See also Charleston
Benbecula (The Uists), 598, 626
Benson, E.F., 13, 178, 707
Berkeley Square (Mayfair), 92
Bernard Street (Leith), 515
Bernera (Isle of Lewis), 624
Bessie Surtees House (Newcastle upon Tyne), 467, 470
Bess of Hardwick, 451–52, 454
Beverley, 480–81, 493
Beverley Minster, 480–81
Bibury, 4, 292, 300, 308
Bicycling, 324, 555, 594, 648, 716–17, 732–33
Big Ben (London), 24, 47, 50, 52
Birdland (Bourton-on-the-Water), 297, 307
Bird-watching, 718. See also specific sites
Cotswolds, 297, 307
East Anglia, 393
Kent, 16, 146, 163
North Wales, 668, 684
Northwest and the Lake District, 419
Scottish Islands, 598
Scottish Lowlands, 543, 550, 554, 555
South-Central England, 188, 197
South Wales, 630, 634, 650
Yorkshire and the Northeast, 473, 481
Birmingham, 332–33, 373
Birmingham Museum and Art Gallery, 332
Bishop's Castle, 356
Bishop's Palace (St. David's), 657
Bishop's Palace (Wells), 262
The Black House (Isle of Lewis), 623
Black Mountain (Brecon Beacons National Park), 631, 634, 638

Black Mountains (Brecon Beacons National Park), 34, 351, 634, 638, 648
Blackpool, 406, 414–15, 417–18
Blackwell (Bowness-on-Windermere), 421
Blaenavon Industrial Landscape, 638, 649
Blair, Tony, 695, 702
Blair Castle (near Pitlochry), 610
Blenheim Palace (near Oxford), 30, 209, 324, 326, 330, 340–41, 704
Blickling Hall (near Norwich), 377, 384, 389
Blists Hill Victorian Town (Ironbridge Gorge), 328, 335
The Blitz, World War II, 55, 99, 436, 690, 692–93, 701, 705, 710
Bloomsbury Group, 133, 150, 157–58, 707–8. See also Charleston; Monk's House
Blue John Cavern (near Castleton), 450
Blue Reef Aquarium (Portsmouth), 192, 195–96
Blue Reef Bristol Aquarium and IMAX, 274
Boadicea Statue (London), 100. See also Boudicca
Boat cruises/tours
Cambridge and East Anglia, 380, 385, 392, 393
Kent/Sussex, 164,168
London, 26, 58, 88, 136, 718
Northwest and the Lake District, 2, 411, 415, 423, 424, 426, 438
Oxford and the Heart of England, 333, 370
Scottish Highlands and Islands, 592, 594, 595, 599, 606, 608, 614, 621
South-Central England, 195
West Country, 233, 238, 239, 282
Yorkshire, 475, 488
Boating Lake (Regent's Park, London), 89
Bodleian Library (Oxford), 363
Bodnant Garden (Conwy), 687
Bond, James, 15, 95, 690
Bonnie Prince Charlie, 595, 603–4, 613, 624, 695
The Borders and Galloway, 542–43, 544–51
Boscombe Artificial Pier (Bournemouth), 192
Bosherston Lily Ponds (Stackpole), 655
Bosta (Great Bernera, Isle of Lewis), 624
Boston, 456, 459
Botanical gardens. See also Gardens, historic; specific gardens

Cotswolds, 295, 296, 299, 304
Edinburgh, 497, 506–7, 550
Glasgow and the Scottish Lowlands, 538, 543, 550, 555, 577
Oxford, 362, 363
Scottish Highlands, 616–17
South-Central England, 209
South Wales, 639
West Country, 38, 233, 251–52, 253–54
Yorkshire, 474
Botanic Garden (Oxford University), 209, 362
Boudicca (Boadicea), 100, 390, 483, 696, 697
Bournemouth, 192–93, 196, 219
Bourton Model Railway (Bourton-on-the-Water), 307
Bourton-on-the-Hill, 295, 296, 299
Bourton-on-the-Water, 293, 296, 297, 299, 306, 307
Bowness-on-Windermere, 35, 411, 415, 420–21, 424
Bradford-on-Avon, 260–61, 289
Braemar (Cairngorms National Park), 599, 610, 627
Braemar Castle, 610
Braemar Gathering (Highland Games), 599, 610, 724
Brains (Welsh beer), 634
Brantwood (Coniston), 415
Brecon Beacons National Park, 34, 634, 637–38, 648–51, 661
famous mountains of, 630, 634, 637, 650
festivals in, 650, 661
staying/dining in/near, 651
visitor information, 651
Brecon Jazz, 661
Bridewell Museum (Norwich), 396
Bridge of Sighs (Oxford), 363
Bridges, famous
Bristol, 223, 272, 275
Cambridge, 398
Conwy, 675, 686
Ironbridge Gorge, 328, 335
London, 2, 24, 25, 47, 52, 54, 57
Oxford, 363
Brighton, 37, 143, 146, 149, 172–77, 185
for gay/lesbian travelers, 146, 149, 177, 724, 734
nightlife/entertainment, 177
staying/dining in, 176–77
Brighton Fringe Festival, 185
Brighton Museum and Art Gallery, 174
Brighton Pier, 146, 149, 172
Bristol, 223, 261, 272–75, 289
Bristol Cathedral, 274
Britain & London Visitor Centre (London), 137, 139
The British Galleries (V&A), 64, 66
British Museum (London), 8, 13, 25,

47, 55, 68–71, 109, 417, 704. *See also specific attractions/exhibits, identified as* "British Museum"

British Open, 558, 559

BritRail train passes, 727, 728–29

Broadhaven South Beach, 655–56

Broad Walk (Kensington Gardens, London), 87

Broadway, 4, 296, 300, 305, 321

Broadway Tower, 296, 300, 305

Brodick Castle (Isle of Arran), 555

Brontë, Charlotte and Emily, and family of, 13, 281, 419, 463, 472, 707

Brontë Parsonage Museum (Haworth), 13, 419, 463, 472

Broughton House (Kirkcudbright), 549

Brown, Lancelot "Capability," 207, 209, 345, 387, 388, 452. *See also* Blenheim Palace; Harewood House; Longleat; Warwick Castle

Brownsea Island Nature Preserve (near Poole), 197

Brunel, Isambard Kingdom, 223, 272, 275. *See also* Clifton Suspension Bridge; SS *Great Britain*

Buckingham Palace (London), 7, 26, 40, 61, 72–73, 100

Buckland Abbey (near Plymouth), 232, 239, 246–47, 259

Building of Bath Collection (Bath), 270

Burford, 307–8, 321

Burford Church, 307

Burford House & Gardens (Tenbury Wells), 345

Burges, William, 67, 630–31. *See also* Cardiff Castle; Castell Coch

Burns, Robert, 510, 511, 513, 552, 708
    Burns Night celebrations, 722
    monuments to (Edinburgh), 512, 515

Burns Cottage and Museum (near Ayr), 543, 553

Burns House (Dumfries), 547–48

Burrell Collection (Glasgow), 31, 542, 574

Burton, Richard, 15, 365

Bury Ditches (near Clun), 356

Bury St. Edmunds, 377, 378–79, 384, 403

Buses, double decker, 83, 192, 691

Bus tours, 719. *See also* City Sightseeing
    Edinburgh, 504
    Glasgow, 31, 570
    Stonehenge, 29, 192

Bus travel, 729. *See also* Fast Facts *for specific areas*

Business hours, 733

Bute, Isle of (Firth of Clyde), 539, 543, 554, 587

Buxton, 39, 448–49, 459

Buxton Museum and Art Gallery, 449

Buxton Opera House, 449

Bygones Museum (Holkham Hall), 389

Byres Road (Glasgow), 577

C

Caerlaverock Castle (near Dumfries), 538, 543, 548, 647

Caerleon, 637

Caernarfon, 675

Caernarfon Castle, 665, 669, 675, 682

Cairngorms National Park, 610

Caledonian MacBrayne ("CalMac") ferries, 554, 626

Callander (Trossachs), 608

Callanish Standing Stones (Isle of Lewis), 10, 591, 598, 624

Calton Hill (Edinburgh), 2, 496, 500, 502

Cam, River, 376, 383, 402

Cambridge, 27, 378, 382–83, 398–402

Cambridge and East Anglia, 376–403. *See also* Cambridge; East Anglia; Norwich
    staying/dining in, 381, 385, 397, 402
    visitor information, 401, 403

Cambridge University, 376, 398–402. *See also specific colleges*
    the Backs, 376, 383, 402
    visitor information, 401

Cameron, David, 695, 702

Canal boat tours, 88, 333, 475, 718

Canongate Kirk Cemetery (Edinburgh), 512

Canterbury, 26–27, 144–45, 151, 166–71, 185, 483
    markets in, 167
    staying/dining in, 171
    walking tours/boat trips, 168

Canterbury Cathedral, 12, 27, 144, 166–68, 169, 170, 209. *See also* Thomas Becket, Saint
    Evensong at, 27, 143, 145, 151

The Canterbury Tales (attraction), 170

Cape Wrath (Northwest Highlands), 618

Captain Cook Memorial Museum (Whitby), 467, 470

Cardiff, 30, 632–33, 642–45, 661

Cardiff and South Wales, 630–61. *See also* Brecon Beacons National Park; Gower Peninsula; Pembrokeshire
    Cadw Explorer Pass, 659
    staying/dining in, 640, 645, 651, 653, 658, 732
    visitor information, 651, 659–61

Cardiff Bay, 11, 30, 633, 644

Cardiff Castle, 30, 631, 632, 642, 704

Carfax Tower (Oxford), 360

Carlyle Mansions (Chelsea), 99

Carmarthenshire, 639, 640

Carnforth, 415, 418

Carreg Cennen Castle (Brecon Beacons National Park), 631, 638

Car travel, 729–31. *See also* Fast Facts *for specific areas*

Cast Courts (V&A), 66, 67

Castell Coch (near Cardiff), 631, 638, 704

Castle Drogo (Dartmoor National Park), 232, 244, 246, 256

Castlefield (Manchester), 2, 407, 410, 443, 445

Castle Garth (Newcastle upon Tyne), 467, 470

Castle Howard (near York), 6, 31, 466, 468, 704

Castle Museum and Art Gallery (Nottingham), 453

Castlerigg Stone Circle (near Keswick), 35, 415, 426

Castles, 646–47. *See also* Palaces; *specific castles*
    Edward's "Iron Ring" of, 664–65, 669, 682
    Scottish clans, 613

Castle Tioram (Loch Moidart), 603, 613

Castleton, 449–50, 453, 459

Castleton showcaves, 449–50

Cathedral Church of Christ (Liverpool), 414, 437

Cathedrals and abbeys, 12, 703–4. *See also specific cathedrals and abbeys*

Catherine of Aragon, 42, 151, 154, 160, 344, 357

Catherine Parr, 78, 297, 311, 312

Cave exploring (spelunking)
    Castleton showcaves, 449–50
    Cheddar Gorge Caves, 223, 230, 261
    National Showcaves of Wales, 650–51
    White Scar Caves (near Ingleton), 475–76

Cavendish Arcade (Buxton), 449

Cavern Club (Liverpool), 414, 438

Cefn Bryn (Gower Peninsula), 635, 653

Ceiriog Valley, 665, 672

Central Belt of Scotland, 542, 560–65
    Central Necropolis (Glasgow), 571

Centre for Contemporary Art (Glasgow), 567

The Ceramic Staircase (V&A), 66

Cerne Abbas (near Dorchester), 201

Chagford (Dartmoor National Park), 258, 259

Changing of the Guard, 26, 61, 100, 135

Channel Tunnel ("Chunnel"), 138, 695, 727

Chapel Street (Penzance), 234, 280–81

Charlecote Park (near Stratford-upon-Avon), 344–45

Charleston (near Lewes), 37, 150, 157–58

Charlotte Square (Edinburgh), 513

Chartwell (near Edenbridge), 152–53

Chatsworth (Peak District), 6, 39, 451–52, 454

Chaucer, Geoffrey, 53, 170, 362, 707

Cheddar Gorge, 34, 223, 230, 261

Chedworth Roman Villa (near Cirencester), 10, 292, 301, 316

Chelsea (London), 96–99. *See also specific attractions identified as "Chelsea"*
   authors'/artists' homes in, 98, 99

Chelsea Flower Show, 98, 209, 723

Chelsea Old Church, 99

Chelsea Physic Garden, 98

Cheltenham, 293, 300, 318–19, 321

Cheltenham Art Gallery and Museum, 300, 318

Chesil Beach, 16, 188, 196, 197

Chester, 30–31, 408–9, 412, 428–31, 459, 483
   pubs, 430
   Roman Walls walk, 406, 408–9, 430
   staying/dining in, 431

Chester Cathedral, 31, 408, 429–30

Chesterfield Street (Mayfair), 93

Chester Summer Music Festival, 459

Chetham's Library (Manchester), 410, 442

Cheyney Court (Winchester Cathedral), 215

Chichester, 142, 150, 182–83, 185

Chichester Cathedral, 182, 703
   sacred music festival, 185, 724

Chichester Festival Theatre, 21, 150, 183

Chiddingstone (near Edenbridge), 159

Chihuly Glass Chandelier (V&A), 46, 64

Children, traveling with, 734. *See also* Aquariums/Sea life attractions; Beaches; Cave exploring; Marine attractions/ museums; Roman Britain; Science and technology attractions; Zoos and wildlife attractions; *specific castles; attractions with the KIDS icon*
   London, 80–83
   Cotswolds, 307
   Blackpool, 418

Chipping Campden, 34, 296, 297, 298, 304–5, 321

Chipping Norton, 299, 302–3

Chirk Castle, 672–73

Christ Church Cathedral (Oxford), 362, 725

Christ Church College (Oxford), 362

Christchurch Mansion (Ipswich), 391

Christie, Agatha, 238, 338

Christmas concerts/services (Cambridge and Oxford), 725

Churchill, Sir Winston, 55, 92, 146, 551, 693, 695, 701
   Blenheim Palace, 30, 324, 326, 330, 340–41, 704
   Chartwell, 152–53
   Churchill Museum/Cabinet War Rooms, 100, 693
   London Blitz, 693, 701
   Memorial (Westminster Abbey), 53

Churchill Museum/Cabinet War Rooms (London), 100, 693

Church Stretton, 325, 348, 356, 373

Chysauster (near St. Ives), 286

Cider Museum and King Offa's Brandy Distillery (Hereford), 358

Cinque Ports (Kent/Sussex towns), 146, 181

Circus (Bath), 29, 227, 268–69

Cirencester, 300–1, 314–17, 321

Cirencester Park, 315

City Art Gallery (Leeds), 473, 490–91

City Bridge (Winchester), 216

City Museum (Winchester), 217

City Museum and Art Gallery (Bristol), 274–75

City Sightseeing, 719
   Bath, 267
   Bristol, 273
   Glasgow, 31, 570
   Oxford, 363
   Stratford-upon-Avon, 366
   Windsor and Eton, 135

Clan Donald Skye Centre (Isle of Skye), 596

Clans, Scottish, 612–13

Clapper Bridge (Dartmoor National Park), 258

Clarence House (London), 73–74

Claridge's (Mayfair), 118, 119

Clifton Suspension Bridge (Bristol), 223, 272, 275

Clitheroe, 414, 416

Clitherow, Saint Margaret, 487

Clocks and Watches collection (British Museum), 71

Clothing. *See also* Fashion; Woolens and tartans
   Edinburgh, 497, 518–19
   London, 102, 106

Clovelly, 4, 34, 235, 242

Clun, 356

Coalbrookdale Museum of Iron (Ironbridge Gorge), 328, 334

Coalport China Museum (Ironbridge Gorge), 335

Colchester, 390, 403

Coleridge, Samuel Taylor, 410, 411, 425–26

Collection (Lincoln), 456

Commandery (Worcester), 329, 354

Concert halls, 21
   Blackpool, 417
   Cardiff Bay, 633, 644
   Edinburgh, 21, 531, 532–34
   Glasgow, 584
   London, 21, 130

Coniston, 35, 415, 423

Constable, John, 63, 312, 332, 376, 377, 391, 443, 491, 706

Contiki Tours, 716

Conwy, 5, 665, 675, 686–87

Conwy Castle, 647, 665, 669, 675, 686

Conwy Railway Bridge, 675, 686

Corbridge Roman Town (Hadrian's Wall), 471, 472

Corinium Dobunnorum (now Cirencester), 10, 314, 316

Corinium Museum (Cirencester), 293, 300–1, 315

Corn Du (Brecon Beacons National Park), 634, 637, 650

Cornwall, Duchy of, 226

Corpus Christi Guildhall (Lavenham), 383

Corsham Court (near Lacock), 207

Cotehele (near Plymouth), 6, 38, 223, 247

Cotswolds, 34, 292–321. *See also* Cheltenham; Cirencester
   Arts and Crafts Movement, 301
   gardens/great houses, 292, 293, 310–13
   hiking/walking, 292, 293, 296
   inns, 2, 293
   kids' attractions, 307
   Roman heritage, 10, 292, 294, 299, 300–1, 303, 306, 314–17
   staying/dining in, 309, 317, 319
   transportation, 295, 297, 300, 303, 320
   wool villages of, 302–8

Cotswolds Motoring Museum and Toy Collection (Bourton-on-the-Water), 297, 307

Cotswold Way, 293, 296

Coughton Court (near Alcester), 343–44, 358

Covent Garden (London), 26, 62

Coventry, 332, 373, 701

Cowal Peninsula, 543, 554, 555, 587
   Argyll Forest Park, 600

Craven Arms, 348, 357

Crime, 736

The Cuillins (Isle of Skye), 16, 596, 625

Culross, 568

Culture, 690–91, 703–13

Culzean Castle, 543, 552

Culzean Country Park, 553

Cumberland Pencil Museum (Keswick), 426

Cunard Building (Liverpool), 436
Curfew Tower (Moreton-in-Marsh), 294-95, 304
Currency/Currency exchange, 735
Custom House (King's Lynn), 381
Customs and duties, 733
Customs House and Dock Place (Leith), 516-17

D

Daffodil Walk (Hutton-le-Hole), 476
Dante Gabriel Rossetti's Home (Chelsea), 99
Daphne du Maurier Festival of Arts and Literature (Penzance), 281
Darby, Abraham, 328, 334, 347, 352
Dartmoor National Park, 16, 33-34, 256-59, 289
Dean Gallery (Edinburgh), 507
Dean Village (Edinburgh), 497, 507
Denbighshire (North Wales), 672. See also North Wales
Dentists. See Fast Facts for specific areas
Diana, Princess of Wales, 40-41, 74, 75, 82, 86, 695, 702
Dickens, Charles, 53, 68, 95, 99, 133, 410, 440, 707
Digby Chick (Stornoway), 623
Dinosaurland Fossil Museum (Lyme Regis), 197
Disabilities, travelers with, 738
Discovery Museum (Newcastle upon Tyne), 467, 471
Dissolution of the Monasteries, 160, 207, 215, 232, 262, 266, 311, 377, 684, 694
    churches destroyed/in ruins, 144, 150, 168, 169, 180, 315, 478, 480, 636, 699
Distillery tours. See Whisky
Doctors, 734. See Fast Facts for specific areas
The Dome (Brighton), 177
Dorchester, 193, 196, 200, 219. See also Hardy, Thomas
Dorset, 196-97, 200-1. See also Dorchester
Dorset County Museum (Dorchester), 193
Doune Castle, 542, 560
Dove Cottage (Grasmere), 13, 407, 411, 415, 425
Dover, 145-46, 151, 162-65, 185, 483
    ferry to Calais, 727
    Cinque Ports, 146
Dover Castle, 42, 145, 147, 151, 162-63, 165, 647, 696
Dover Museum, 164
Dragon Hall (Norwich), 396
Druidston Haven (St. Bride's Bay), 656
Drumnadrochit (Loch Ness), 599

Duart Castle (Isle of Mull), 594, 613, 620
Du Maurier, Daphne, 233, 281
Dumfries, 547-48, 587
Dumfries and Galloway, 543. See also The Borders and Galloway
Dun Carloway (Isle of Lewis), 623
Dunskey Castle ruins (near Portpatrick), 550
Dunvegan Castle (Isle of Skye), 624-25
Durham, 467, 470, 481, 493
Durham Cathedral, 12, 463, 467, 470, 479, 481
Durness (Northwest Highlands), 618, 627

E

East Anglia. See also Cambridge; Cambridge and East Anglia; Norwich
    broads and fens, 380, 390-93
    historic homes, 386-89
Eastbridge Hospital (Canterbury), 26, 166
Eastgate Clock (Chester), 430
East Midlands, 448-57, 459
Ecotourism, 725-76
Edale, 449, 451, 453, 459
Eden Camp (Malton), 469
Eden Court (Inverness), 598
Eden Project (St. Austell Bay), 251, 252
Edinburgh, 31, 43, 496-535. See also Leith
    bars/pubs, 497, 511, 531-34
    bus tours of, 504
    festivals/events, 503, 724, 725
    hilltop views, 2, 496-97, 500
    historic/literary, 508-13
    hotels, 526-27, 530
    literary tours, 513
    New Town, 502-3, 512, 513, 704
    nightlife/entertainment, 531-34
    Old Town, 2, 31, 496, 502, 510, 512, 513
    performing arts, 497
    restaurants, 497, 502, 506, 516, 523-25
    shopping, 497, 518-19, 522
Edinburgh Book Lovers' Tour, 513
Edinburgh Bus Tours, 504
Edinburgh Castle, 7, 31, 43, 496, 502, 510, 610, 724
Edinburgh International Festival, 21, 503, 513, 532, 533, 724
    Festival Fringe, 503
Edradour Distillery (near Pitlochry), 609-10
Edward Elgar Birthplace Museum (Worcester), 329
Edward I, 42, 151, 154, 549, 610, 638, 672, 694, 698
    "Iron Ring," 664-65, 669, 682

Egyptian House (Penzance), 281
Egyptian Room (British Museum), 71
Eilean Donan Castle (Northwest Highlands), 616
Electricity, 733
Elgar, Edward, 305, 329, 350, 706
Elgin Marbles (British Museum), 8, 47, 70, 71, 84
Elizabeth I, 53, 266, 273-74, 342, 382, 386, 418, 694, 699
    and Mary, Queen of Scots, 53, 452, 512, 699
Elizabeth II, 43, 226, 647, 695, 701, 702, 710, 725
Elm Hill (Norwich), 377, 384, 396
Ely, 377, 385, 393, 403
Embassies and consulates, 733
Emergencies, 733. See also Fast Facts for specific areas
Enlightenment Gallery (British Museum), 71
Erddig (near Wrexham), 665, 670, 672
Escorted tours, 717
Eton College, 42, 136
Eton Terrace (Glasgow), 577
Evensong (Evening Prayer service), 400, 706
    Canterbury Cathedral, 27, 143, 145, 151
    Jesus College (Cambridge), 401
    King's College (Cambridge), 2, 27, 376, 382, 400, 706
    Wells Cathedral, 262
    Worcester Cathedral, 329
Exeter, 224-25, 231, 244, 276-79, 289, 483
Exeter Cathedral, 12, 222, 224, 231, 256, 276, 703
Exeter Guildhall, 231, 276, 278
Exeter Summer Festival, 723
Eyam, 450-51

F

Falmouth, 252, 255
Fashion, 264-65, 701
    Edinburgh shops, 497, 518-19, 522
    London shops, 102, 106
Fashion attractions
    Fashion Gallery (V&A), 66
    Fashion Museum (Bath), 227, 228, 269
    Manchester Art Gallery, 441
Fashion Museum (Bath), 227, 228, 269
Fawkes, Guy, 57
    Guy Fawkes Night, 175, 185, 725
Festivals/Special events, 722-25. See also specific areas; festivals
    Edinburgh, 503
    Kent/Sussex, 185
    Northwest, 439, 459
    South Wales, 650, 661
    West Country, 231, 281

Ffestiniog Railway, 665, 680
Film, 14-15, 710
Fingal's Cave (Isle of Staffa), 621
Firth of Clyde, 539, 543, 554 . *See also* Arran, Isle of; Bute, Isle of
Fishbourne Roman Palace (Chichester), 10, 142, 150, 183, 209
Fishguard, 657
Fishing, 717
Fish Street and Grope Lane (Shrewsbury), 336, 355
Fitzwilliam Museum (Cambridge), 27, 383, 402
Flatford Mill and Bridge Cottage (near Ipswich), 377, 391-92
Fleming, Ian, 95. *See also* Bond, James
Food and drink, 711-13, 733
    beer and ale, 634, 713
    best pubs, 20
    most memorable dining, 19
Forest of Dean (Gloucestershire), 352
    Dean Heritage Centre (Sudley), 353
Fortnum & Mason (Mayfair), 94-95, 107
The Forum (Norwich), 395
Fosse Way (ancient Roman road), 294, 299, 303, 306, 316
Foster, Lord Norman, 68, 391, 397, 639, 705
Fountains Abbey and Studley Royal Water Gardens (near Ripon), 472, 478-79
Four Shires Stone (Moreton-in-Marsh), 304
Fowey, 232, 233, 235, 239, 249, 250, 281, 289
Fox Talbot Museum of Photography (Lacock Abbey), 207
Freshwater West (near Pembroke), 654

G
Gaelic, Scottish, 590, 613, 626
Galleries of Justice (Nottingham), 453-54
Gallery of Modern Art (GOMA, Glasgow), 575
Gardens, historic, 36-39, 208-9. *See also* Botanical gardens; Houses, historic
    Cotswolds, 310-13
    Kent/Sussex, 152-57
    West Country, 250-55
    West Midlands, 340-45
    Wiltshire, 202-7
Garden tours, 718-19
Gay and lesbian travelers, 734
    Brighton, 146, 149, 177, 724, 734
    London, 126, 130, 131, 133
    Manchester, 409, 444
    pride festivals, 724, 734
Geo. F. Trumper (Mayfair), 94, 103

George Eliot's Home (Chelsea), 99
George III, 40, 71, 72, 147, 161, 172, 270, 503, 517, 700
George IV, 72, 135, 147, 177, 700
    as Prince Regent, 7, 37, 43, 143, 147, 149, 172-73
George Street and New Town (Edinburgh), 497, 503
Georgian House (Bristol), 274
Georgian House (Edinburgh), 513
Gigha, Isle of, 555
Gilbert Bayes Sculpture Gallery (V&A), 67
Gilbert Collection (V&A), 67
Gladstone Pottery Museum (Stoke-on-Trent), 349
Gladstone's Land (Edinburgh), 511
Glasgow, 31, 538, 540, 542, 570-87
    City Sightseeing tours of, 31, 570
    hotels, 582
    Merchant City district, 539, 540, 571
    nightlife/entertainment, 583-85
    restaurants, 579
    shopping, 578
    West End, 539, 540, 576, 577
Glasgow and the Scottish Lowlands, 538-87. *See also* Borders and Galloway; Central Belt of Scotland; West Coast of Scotland
    architecture, 566-69
    staying/dining in, 551, 556-57, 565, 579, 582
Glasgow Botanic Gardens, 577
Glasgow Cathedral (formerly St. Mungo's Cathedral), 12, 540, 568, 570
Glasgow Green and People's Palace/Winter Gardens, 575
Glasgow School of Art, 539, 540, 566, 574, 578, 705
Glastonbury, 223, 231, 262, 289
Glastonbury Festival of Contemporary Performing Arts, 223, 231
Glencoe, 590, 595, 602
    Massacre of, 595, 613
Glendurgan Garden (near Falmouth), 253
Glenfinnan, 595, 603-4
Glyndebourne Festival (opera), 175, 185, 723
Golf, history of, 558-59
    Leith Links, 514, 558
Golf courses
    Gleneagles (Auchterarder), 18, 611
    Muirfield (near Edinburgh), 558
    Royal Troon (Troon), 558
    St. Andrews (Fife), 558, 608
    Shiskine (Isle of Arran), 555
    Traigh (near Arisaig), 604
Golf tours, 717

Gondola (Coniston Water steam yacht), 415, 423
Goodrich Castle, 352-53
Gordale Scar (near Malham), 475
Gordon Russell Museum (Broadway), 305
Gower Peninsula, 16, 630, 635, 652-53
Grand Union Canal/Regent's Canal (Regent's Park, London), 88-89
Grant, Duncan, 150, 157-58. *See also* Charleston
Grasmere, 35, 407, 411, 424-25. *See also* Wordsworth, William
Grassmarket (Edinburgh), 510
Great Bernera (Isle of Lewis), 624
Greater London Authority building, 705
Great Fire of London, 55,57-58, 90-91, 694, 700
Great Hall (Winchester), 190, 217
Great Malvern, 34, 350, 351. *See also* Malvern Hills
Great North Museum: Hancock (Newcastle upon Tyne), 467, 471
Great Orme Tramway (Llandudno), 676
Great Outdoor Recreation Pages (GORP), 716
"Greek" Thomson Trail (Glasgow), 574-75
Greene King Brewery (Bury St. Edmunds), 379, 384
Green Man indie-folk music festival (Brecon Beacons National Park), 661
Greyfriars (Worcester), 329, 355
Greyfriars Kirk and Kirkyard (Edinburgh), 510
Grey Street (Newcastle upon Tyne), 467, 470
Grosvenor Museum (Chester), 409, 428-29
Gruffydd ap Llywelyn, 430, 696
Guildhalls
    Boston, 456
    Corpus Christi (Lavenham), 383
    Exeter, 231, 276, 278
    Merchant Adventurers' Hall (York), 486
    Much Wenlock, 348
    Norwich, 395
    St. George's (King's Lynn), 381, 384
    Worcester, 329

H
Haddon Hall (Peak District), 453
Hadrian's Wall (Yorkshire/Northumbria), 2, 462, 471, 483, 696
    Corbridge Roman Town, 471, 472
Hall's Croft (Stratford-upon-Avon), 27, 327, 331, 368, 369

The Halls (Norwich), 396

Hampshire and Dorset Coast, 188–89, 192–93, 194–97. *See also* Dorset

Hampton Court Flower Show, 724

Hampton Court Palace (near London), 7, 41, 76–79, 703
  guided tours of, 77
  South Gardens, 78, 208–9
  visitor information, 77

Hanse House (King's Lynn), 380, 384

Hardwick Hall (near Chesterfield), 39, 452, 454

Hardy, Thomas, 13, 53, 193, 200, 365, 707

Harewood House (near Leeds), 6, 463, 473

Hark to Bounty Inn (Slaidburn), 416–17

Harlow Carr Botanical Gardens (near Harrogate), 474

Harris, Isle of (Outer Hebrides), 598, 622–23, 624–25, 627

Harrods (London), 102, 106, 107

Harrogate, 474, 493

Hatfield House (near Hertford), 382, 386

Hathaway, Anne, cottage of (Stratford-upon-Avon), 27, 327, 331, 370

Haverfordwest, 657

Hawkshead, 4, 415, 422

Haworth, 472, 493

Hay Festival of Literature and Arts (Brecon Beacons National Park), 631, 661

Hay's Mews (Mayfair), 93

Health issues, 734

Heart of England Way, 358

Hebrides, 2, 620–25, 626–27. *See also specific islands/attractions*
  ferries to, 554, 626
  Inner, 590, 594–95, 596, 604, 620–22, 624–25
  Outer, 590, 591, 598, 622–24
  staying/dining on, 625

Henry II, 161, 449, 694. *See also* Thomas Becket, Saint
  Dover Castle, 42, 145, 147, 165, 647

Henry VIII, 84, 88, 96, 99, 135, 153, 160, 162, 175, 195, 217, 352, 690, 698. *See also* Anne Boleyn; Anne of Cleves; Catherine of Aragon; Catherine Parr; Dissolution of the Monasteries; Jane Seymour
  Hampton Court Palace, 7, 41, 76–79
  The King's School (Canterbury), 169
  Leeds Castle, 42, 151, 154
  Trinity College (Cambridge), 400

Henry Moore Institute (Leeds), 491

Hereford, 34, 337, 350–51, 353, 357–58, 373

Hereford Cathedral, 325, 337, 351, 357–58
  Mappa Mundi, 325, 337, 358

Hever Castle (near Edenbridge), 6, 42, 143, 149, 158–59, 168, 184, 185

Heritage travel, 726
  accommodations, 731–32
  special-interest trips, 719

Hidcote Manor Garden (near Chipping Campden), 34, 39, 156, 292–93, 297, 298–99, 305, 310

Highland Perthshire, 599, 627. *See also* Balmoral Castle and Estate; Braemar *and entries following*

Highlands, Scottish. *See* Scottish Highlands and Islands

Hiking, 718
  Borders/Galloway, 549–50
  Church Stretton/Shropshire Hills, 325, 348, 350
  Cotswolds, 292, 293, 296
  Dartmoor National Park, 258
  Lake District, 34, 418, 423, 424, 426, 458
  Malvern Hills, 16, 34, 350, 351
  North Wales/Snowdonia, 665, 666–67, 668, 678–80, 683, 684
  Peak District National Park, 16, 449, 453
  Ridgeway National Trail (Wiltshire), 200
  Scottish Highlands/Islands, 2, 555, 590, 596, 600, 602, 606, 608, 617, 625
  South Wales/Brecon Beacons, 34, 630, 631, 632, 635, 637–38, 640, 648, 650
  West Midlands, 348, 352, 353, 358
  Yorkshire, 475, 476

Hill House (Helensburgh), 569

Hill Top (near Hawkshead), 415

History, 694–702

History and culture tours, 719

History of Farming Exhibition (Holkham Hall), 389

Hitchcock, Alfred, 15, 710

HMS *Victory* (Portsmouth), 189, 192, 194–95

The Hoe (Plymouth), 233, 239

Holburne Museum (Bath), 270

Holidays, 734

Holkham, 392

Holkham Hall, 6, 384, 389, 392

Hollins Cross (near Edale), 451

Hollytrees Museum (Colchester), 390

Holmwood House (near Glasgow), 539, 568, 575

Holyhead (Anglesey), 675, 684

Holy Island (Anglesey), 665, 668, 684

Holyroodhouse, Palace of (Edinburgh), 7, 43, 497, 502, 504, 506, 512

Holy Trinity Church (Long Melford), 392

Holy Trinity Church (Stratford-upon-Avon), 27, 327, 331, 368, 369

Hopetoun House (near South Queensferry), 563

Horseback riding, 718
  in Hyde Park (London), 86

Horse Guards Parade (London), 61, 100
  Trooping the Colour, 723
  Whitehall Entrance to, 101

Horse racing, 723

Horton-in-Ribblesdale, 476

Hospital of Saint Cross (Winchester), 216

Hotels and inns, favorite, 18. *See also* Accommodations

Houses, historic, 6, 36–39. *See also* Gardens, historic; Heritage travel; *specific houses*
  Cotswolds, 310–13
  Kent/Sussex, 152–57, 159
  West Country, 244–49
  West Midlands, 340–45
  Wiltshire, 202–7

Houses of Parliament (London), 24, 52
  Opening of Parliament, 725

Hunterian Art Gallery (Glasgow), 566, 576
  Mackintosh House, 566, 574, 576

Hutton-le-Hole, 476

Hyde Park (London), 84–87

Hyde Park Corner (London), 60

Hyde Park Corner Screen (London), 84

I

Ickworth House, Park and Gardens (near Bury St. Edmunds), 388

Ightham Mote (Kent), 6, 153–54

Imperial Gardens (Cheltenham), 293, 318

Imperial War Museum North (Manchester), 11, 414, 444, 446

Industrial attractions/exhibits
  North Wales, 8, 667, 674, 679, 680–81
  Northwest and the Lake District, 2, 407, 410, 441–42, 443, 445
  Oxford and the Heart of England, 8, 325, 328, 333, 334–35, 347, 349
  Scottish Lowlands, 564
  South Wales, 638, 649
  Yorkshire and the Northeast, 467, 471, 491

Ingleton, 475–76, 493

Insurance, traveler's, 734

International Beatle Week (Liverpool), 439, 724

International Musical Eisteddfod (Llangollen), 673
International Slavery Museum (Liverpool), 413, 435
Internet access, 734–35. See also Fast Facts for specific areas
Inveraray, 35, 594, 627
Inveraray Castle, 594, 600, 613, 704–5
Inverewe Garden (Northwest Highlands), 209, 616–17
Inverness, 598–99, 627
Iona, Isle of (Inner Hebrides), 35, 595
Iona Abbey, 35, 595, 621
Ipswich, 391, 403
Ireland's Mansion (Shrewsbury), 355
Ironbridge Gorge, 8, 325, 328, 333, 334–35, 347, 373
Ironwork Gallery (V&A), 66
Italian Gardens (Kensington Gardens, London), 87

J

Jacobite Cruises (Loch Ness), 599
Jacobite Rebellions, 603–4, 610, 612–13, 616, 700. See also Bonnie Prince Charlie
Jacobite Steam Train (Fort William to Mallaig), 603
James, Henry, 4, 99, 296, 305
Lamb House (Rye), 13, 146, 150, 178
James VI of Scotland (James I of England), 53, 155, 161, 175, 212, 516, 694, 699–700, 712
Jane Austen Centre (Bath), 227, 268, 269
Jane Austen House (Winchester), 190, 216
Jane Austen's House Museum (Chawton), 13, 188, 190, 217
Jane Seymour, 99, 135, 160
Jedburgh Abbey, 542, 547, 698, 703
Jekyll, Gertrude, 156, 209
Jesus College (Cambridge), 401
Jewel Tower (London), 52
Jewel Tower (Tower of London), 59
John I, 161. See also Magna Carta
John Knox House (Edinburgh), 504
John Rylands Library (Manchester), 414, 443
John Singer Sargent's Home (Chelsea), 98
JORVIK Viking Centre (York), 31, 465, 487, 696
Jubilee Market (Covent Garden, London), 62
Jubilee Pool (Penzance), 282
Jurassic Coast (Dorset), 16, 189, 193, 196

K

Kedleston Hall (near Derby), 455
Kelvingrove Art Gallery and Museum (Glasgow), 540, 542, 574
Kelvingrove Park (Glasgow), 577
Kenilworth Castle, 332, 342
Kensington Gardens (London), 82, 86, 87
Kensington Palace (London), 40–41, 74, 75
Kent and Sussex, 142–85. See also Battle of Hastings, and site of; Brighton; Canterbury; Chichester; Dover; Rye
Cinque Ports, 146, 181
festivals/events, 185
great houses/gardens, 152–57
nightlife, 177
staying/dining in, 164, 171, 176, 181, 183
Keswick, 415, 425–26
Keswick Rambles, 426
Kettle's Yard (Cambridge), 27, 383, 401–2
Kids. See Children, traveling with
Kilchurn Castle (Loch Awe), 35, 594, 602
Kilpeck, 325, 351
Kinder Scout plateau (near Edale), 451
King Alfred's Tower (near Salisbury), 206
King Alfred the Great, Statue of (Winchester), 216–17
King's College (Cambridge), 400
King's College Chapel (Cambridge), 400
Christmas service, 725
Evensong, 2, 27, 376, 382, 400, 706
fan vaulting, 703
King's Lynn, 380–81, 384, 392, 403
King's Road (Chelsea), 96
The King's School (Canterbury), 169
The King's Wark (Leith), 516
Kintyre Peninsula, 554, 555, 587
Kirkby Lonsdale, 407, 415, 419
Kirkcudbright, 4, 539, 543, 549, 587
Kisimul Castle (Isle of Barra), 622
Knole (Sevenoaks), 36, 142, 148–49, 150, 153, 155, 156
Knoydart Peninsula, 604

L

Lacock, 206, 207
Lacock Abbey, 205, 206–7
Fox Talbot Museum of Photography, 207
Laing Art Gallery (Newcastle upon Tyne), 467, 471
Lake District, 2, 16, 35, 410–11, 415, 420–27, 459. See also Northwest England and the Lake District
Lake District National Park, 415. See also Lake District (above)
Lake Village Museum (Glastonbury), 262
Lamb House (Rye), 13, 150, 178
Lamb's House (Leith), 515
Lancaster, 415, 418
Land's End, 32, 234, 239, 241
The Lanes (Brighton), 174
Lanhydrock (near Fowey), 38, 249
Lanyon Quoit (near St. Ives), 286
Lavenham, 4, 377, 383–84, 392, 403
Lean, David, 15, 415, 418, 710
Leeds, 472–73, 490–91, 492–93
Leeds Castle (Kent), 42, 151, 154, 156, 185
Leeds Industrial Museum, 491
Leeds-Liverpool Canal boat tours (Skipton), 475
Legal aid, 735
Leighton Hall (near Warton), 419
Leighton Moss (near Carnforth), 419
Leith, 514–17
Leith Assembly Rooms, 515
Leith Links, 514, 558
Leith Town Hall, 514–15
Lennon, John, 20, 414, 437, 439, 618. See also Beatles
Lewes, 150, 175
Lewis, Isle of (Outer Hebrides), 598, 623–24, 627
Libraries
Bodleian (Oxford), 363
British Museum Reading Room, 13, 47, 68
Chetham's (Manchester), 410, 442
Hereford Cathedral, 325, 337, 358
John Rylands (Manchester), 414, 443
Wren (Cambridge), 401
Lichfield, 346–47, 373
Lincoln, 456, 459
Lindisfarne, Holy Island of, 481
Lindisfarne Gospels, 481, 706
Lindow Man (British Museum), 71
Linlithgow Palace, 542, 563
Literary attractions/tours. See also specific authors
best literary experiences, 13
Chelsea homes of famous authors, 98–99
Edinburgh, 512–13
Poets' Corner (Westminster Abbey), 53
special-interest trips, 719
Literary festivals
Bath Literature Festival, 723
Cheltenham Festival of Literature, 724
Daphne du Maurier Festival of Arts and Literature (Penzance), 281

Hay Festival of Literature and Arts (Brecon Beacons), 631, 661
Literary Pub Tour (Edinburgh), 513
Literature and fiction, 707–8. See also specific authors
mystery writers, 338–39
Little Hall (Lavenham), 383–84
Little Haven (St. Bride's Bay), 656
Little Sparta (near Dunsyre), 564
Liverpool, 413–14, 434–39, 459. See also Beatles
Llanarmon Dyffryn Ceiriog, 665, 672
Llanbedr (Black Mountains), 648
Llandaff Cathedral (Cardiff), 644–45
Llandudno, 675–76
Llanfair Hill (Clun), 356
Llangollen, 672, 673
Llanthony Priory (Black Mountains), 631, 638, 648
Llechwedd Slate Caverns (Blaenau Ffestiniog), 674, 680–81
Lleyn Peninsula, 684–85
Lloyd's Building (London), 705
LlÐn Adventures (Lleyn Peninsula), 684
Llywelyn ap Gruffydd, 669, 672, 694, 698
Lochaber, 595, 602–4, 627. See also North Argyll to Lochaber, tour of
Loch Awe, 35, 594
Loch Lomond, 35, 592, 606
Loch Lomond & the Trossachs National Park, 599, 606, 608
Loch Ness, 599
Loch Trool, 549
Logan Botanic Garden (near Portpatrick), 538, 543, 550
London, 24–27, 28, 40–41, 46–139, 483. See also British Museum; Chelsea; Mayfair; Windsor and Eton
accommodation services, 137
with children, 54–59, 61–62, 64–66, 73–75, 77, 79, 80–89, 100, 109
fashion, 264–65
festivals/parades in, 722–25
getting around, 24, 138–39
Great Fire, 55, 57, 90–91, 694, 700
Hampton Court Palace, 76–79
hotels, 118–25
Hyde Park, 84–87
nightlife/entertainment, 126–33
Regent's Park, 88–89
restaurants, 110–17
royal tour, 40–41, 72–75
shopping, 102–9
tour operators, 716
traveling to, 137–38
V&A Museum, 64–67
visitor information, 137, 139
wartime Blitz, 692–93, 701
Whitehall, 100–1

London Brass Rubbing Centre, 82
London Coliseum, 21, 130
London Eye, 11, 24, 46, 54, 58, 83
London's Transport Museum, 83
London Zoo (Regent's Park), 88, 89
Longleat (near Salisbury), 37–38, 204–5, 703–4
Long Melford, 392
Lost Gardens of Heligan (near Fowey), 38, 233, 251–52
Lowlands, Scottish. See Glasgow and the Scottish Lowlands
The Lowry (Manchester), 414, 444
Ludlow, 5, 35, 325, 336–37, 357, 373, 723
Lutyens, Sir Edwin, 135, 156, 307, 437. See also Castle Drogo
Lydford (Dartmoor National Park), 259
Lyme Regis, 189, 196, 197, 219

M

Machair Plains (South Uist), 622
Mackintosh, Charles Rennie, 539, 574, 576, 705. See also Glasgow School of Art; Hill House; Scotland Street School Museum; Willow Tea Rooms; entries below
Mackintosh Church at Queen's Cross (Glasgow), 566
Mackintosh House (Glasgow), 566, 574, 576
Mackintosh Trail (Glasgow), 31, 574
Madame Tussauds (London), 83
Magdalen College (Oxford), 363
water meadows, 2, 324, 363
Magical Mystery Tour (Liverpool), 438. See also Beatles
Magna Carta, 136, 161, 212, 329, 456, 694, 698
Maiden Castle (near Dorchester), 201
Mail/Post offices, 735. See also Fast Facts for specific areas
Major Oak (Sherwood Forest County Park), 454
Malham, 475
The Mall (London), 100
Mallaig, 591, 603, 604, 626
Malvern Hills, 16, 34, 350, 351, 373
Malvern Museum of Local History (Great Malvern), 350
Mam Tor (near Castleton), 449, 451
Manchester, 409–10, 414, 440–47, 459, 483. See also Castlefield
canal walks, 407, 443, 445
festivals, 459
Gay Village, 409, 444
industrial history, 409, 410, 440–45
staying/dining in, 447
trendy bars, 446
Manchester Art Gallery, 9, 410, 441

Manchester Cathedral, 410, 442
Manchester Jewish Museum, 446
Manchester Town Hall, 409, 440, 441
Manchester United football club, 414, 446
The Manege and Children's Playground (Hyde Park, London), 86
Mappa Mundi (Hereford Cathedral library), 325, 337, 358
Marine attractions. See Aquarium/Sea life/Marine attractions
Marine Drive (Llandudno), 676
Maritime Heritage Centre (Bristol), 273
Maritime Museum (Southampton), 196
Markets
Cambridge, 27, 398
Canterbury, 167
Cirencester, 314, 317
London, 26, 47, 62, 93–94, 102, 109
Moreton-in-Marsh, 294, 299, 303
Norwich, 394, 396
Oxford, 360
Pembrokeshire, 657
Salisbury, 210
Skipton, 475
Stow-on-the-Wold, 293, 299, 306, 317
Wells, 262
Market Square (Cambridge), 27, 398
Mary, Queen of Scots, 39, 53, 344, 448, 503, 510, 514, 699
birthplace (Linlithgow Palace), 563
needlework, 389, 452, 454, 512
Palace of Holyroodhouse, 7, 43, 497, 506, 512
Stirling Castle, 542, 562
Mary I ("Bloody Mary"), 53, 160, 161, 175, 216, 364, 699
Mary Arden's House & Shakespeare Countryside Museum (Stratford-upon-Avon), 370
Mausoleum of Halikarnassos (British Museum), 70
Max Gate (Dorchester), 13, 193, 200
Mayfair (London), 92–95. See also specific attractions, identified as "Mayfair"
Mayflower Steps (Plymouth), 233, 239
McCartney, Paul, 414, 437. See also Beatles
Melrose Abbey, 542, 546, 698
Menai Suspension Bridge, 675, 686
Mendips (Liverpool), 437. See also Beatles; Lennon, John
Merchant Adventurers' Hall (York), 31, 465, 486
Merchant City district (Glasgow), 539, 540, 571
Mermaid Pleasure Trips (Penzance/Mount's Bay), 282

Mersey Ferries, 438
Merseyside Maritime Museum
    (Liverpool), 8, 407, 413, 434–35
Merton College (Oxford), 362
Metropolitan Cathedral of Christ the
    King (Liverpool), 414, 437
Micklegate Bar Museum (York), 488
Millennium Bridge (London), 2, 47, 54
Millennium Seed Bank Project
    (Wakehurst Place, West Sussex),
    209
Millennium Stadium (Cardiff), 641,
    643–44
The Minack Theatre (near Land's
    End), 21, 241
Model Village (Bourton-on-the-
    Water), 297, 306
Modern Art Oxford, 364
Mompesson House (Salisbury), 28,
    37, 191, 202–3, 211
Monarchs, notorious/memorable,
    147, 160–61. See also specific
    monarchs; History
Money, 735
Monk's House (Rodmell), 13, 37, 143,
    150, 157, 158
Montpellier Parade (Cheltenham),
    293, 318
Monty Python, 14, 542, 691, 709
The Monument (London), 57–58, 91
Moorcroft Pottery (Stoke-on-Trent),
    349
Morar, Sands of (beach), 604
More, Sir Thomas, Statue of
    (Chelsea), 99
Moreton-in-Marsh, 294–95, 296,
    299, 303–4
    as travel hub, 295, 297
Mountain climbing/hiking. See also
    Snowdon, Mount
    Black Mountains (Brecon
        Beacons National Park), 34,
        351, 634, 638, 648
    The Cuillins (Isle of Skye), 16,
        596, 625
    Malvern Hills, 16, 34, 350, 351
    Northwest Scottish Highlands,
        590, 616
    Peak District National Park, 16, 453
Mount Stuart (Isle of Bute), 554, 568
Mousehole (near Newlyn), 240
Much Wenlock, 348, 373
Mull, Isle of (Inner Hebrides), 35,
    590, 594, 613, 620–22, 627
Mull of Galloway, 543, 550
Multi-activity tours, 716
Munros (Northwest Scottish
    Highlands), 590, 616
Museum of Edinburgh, 512
Museum of Liverpool, 436
Museum of Nottingham Life at
    Brewhouse Yard, 453

Museum of Prehistory (Cheddar
    Gorge Caves), 230
Museum of Science and Industry
    (Manchester), 410, 443, 445
Museum of Scotland (Edinburgh), 31,
    497, 502
Museum of the Gorge (Ironbridge
    Gorge), 328, 334
Museum of the History of Science
    (Oxford), 364
Museum of the Royal Welch Fusiliers
    (Caernarfon Castle), 682
Museum of Welsh Life (Cardiff), 645
Museums, 8. See also specific
    museums
Music, classical, 706
    festivals, 126, 130, 723, 724
Music, live, venues
    Edinburgh, 531, 533–34
    Glasgow, 584
    London, 46, 66, 126, 131–32
Music, pop/rock, 432–33. See also
    Beatles
Music, sacred, 185, 400, 706, 724.
    See also Evensong
Music festivals, 722–25. See also
    Festivals/Special events;
    Performing arts festivals
    Brecon Jazz, 661
    Buxton Opera Festival, 449
    Chester Summer Music Festival,
        459
    Glastonbury Festival, 223, 231
    Glyndebourne Festival, 175, 185,
        723
    Green Man (Brecon Beacons), 661
    International Beatle Week
        (Liverpool), 439, 724
    International Musical Eisteddfod
        (Llangollen), 673
    The Proms (London), 126, 130, 724
    Southern Cathedrals Festival,
        185, 724
Mustard Shop (Norwich), 396
Mynydd Preseli, 640, 658

N
National Army Museum (Chelsea),
    98
National Botanic Garden of Wales
    (Llanarthne), 209, 639
National Coal Museum (Blaenavon),
    649
National Football Museum
    (Manchester), 410, 442–43
National Gallery (London), 9, 26, 62,
    63
National Gallery of Scotland and
    Royal Scottish Academy
    (Edinburgh), 9, 31, 497, 502
National Marine Aquarium
    (Plymouth), 233, 239

National Monument (Edinburgh),
    500
National Museum Cardiff, 30, 632,
    642–43
National Portrait Gallery (London),
    26, 62
National Railway Museum (York), 8,
    31, 463, 465, 488, 701
National Showcaves of Wales (near
    Glyntawe), 650–51
National Slate Museum (near
    Llanberis), 8, 667, 679
Natural History Museum (London),
    8, 80, 82, 440
Nature preserves. See also Parks,
    national
    Balranald Nature Reserve (North
        Uist), 598
    Brownsea Island (near Poole),
        197
    Holy Island (Anglesey), 668, 684
    Lindisfarne Priory, 481
    Mull of Galloway, 543, 550
    Rye Harbour, 180–81
    Sherwood Forest, 454
    Titchwell Marsh Bird Preserve
        (near Hunstanton), 393
    Wicken Fen (near Ely), 16, 377, 393
Nelson Monument (Edinburgh), 500,
    502
Newcastle upon Tyne, 467, 470–71,
    473, 493
Newgale beach (St. Bride's Bay),
    656–57
New Lanark (near Lanark), 564
Newlyn (near Penzance), 240
Newport (near Fishguard), 658
New Scottish Parliament (Edin-
    burgh), 506
Newsurf (St. Bride's Bay), 657
New Place/Nash's House (Stratford-
    upon-Avon), 27, 327, 331, 366,
    368, 369
Nicolson, Harold, 36, 143, 150, 156,
    297. See also Sissinghurst
Nightlife, 20
    Brighton, 177
    Cardiff, 644
    Edinburgh, 497, 531–34
    Glasgow, 583–85
    London, 126–33
    Manchester, 444, 446
Norfolk Broads (East Anglia), 380,
    392
North Argyll to Lochaber, tour of,
    600–5
North Bridge (Edinburgh), 512
North Uist, 598, 627
North Wales, 664–87. See also
    Anglesey and the Northwest
    Coast of Wales; Conwy;
    Snowdonia

staying/dining in, 667, 672, 674, 676, 681, 685, 687, 732
steam railways, 660, 665, 667, 675, 678, 680, 682–83
Northwest England and the Lake District, 406–59. See also Chester; East Midlands; Lake District; Liverpool; Manchester
off the beaten path, 416–19
staying/dining in, 427, 431, 439, 447, 457
Northwest Scottish Highlands, 590, 598, 614–19
North York Moors National Park, 463, 476–77, 492, 493
North Yorkshire Moors Railway, 477, 492
Norwich, 5, 380, 384, 387, 392, 394–97, 403
Norwich 12 (historic buildings), 396
Norwich Castle, 380, 384, 392, 396
Norwich Cathedral, 377, 380, 384, 392, 394
Norwich Market, 394
Nottingham, 453–54, 459

O

Oban, 35, 594, 626, 627
Oceanarium (Bournemouth), 193, 196
Offa's Dyke, 356
Old College (Edinburgh), 508
Old Custom House (Penzance), 281
Old Forge (Knoydart Peninsula), 604
Old Gaol House (King's Lynn), 381, 384
Old Grammar School (Hawkshead), 415, 422
Old Sarum (Salisbury), 10, 28, 191, 192, 198, 211, 212–13
Old Town (Edinburgh), 2, 31, 496, 510
Old Town Jail (Stirling), 561
Old Trafford Museum and Stadium Tour (Manchester), 414, 446
Oliver Cromwell House (Ely), 385, 393
Olivier, Sir Laurence, 15, 133, 710
Chichester Festival Theatre, 150, 183
Open Air Theatre (Regent's Park, London), 126, 133
Opera
Blackpool Opera House, 417
Buxton Opera House, 449
Edinburgh Festival Theatre, 532
Glyndebourne Festival, 175, 185, 723
London Coliseum, 21, 130
Royal Opera House (London), 21, 38, 126, 130
Theatre Royal (Glasgow), 584
Welsh National Opera, 644

Oriel Plas Glyn-y-Weddw (Lleyn Peninsula), 685
Oscar Wilde's Home (Chelsea), 98
Our Dynamic Earth (Edinburgh), 506
Outdoor activity trips, 716–18. See also specific activities
Owlpen Manor (near Painswick), 6, 39, 301, 312–13, 705
Oxburgh Hall (near King's Lynn), 389
Oxford, 30, 326, 330, 360–65, 373
covered market, 360
river walks/punting, 330, 333
staying/dining in, 365
walking/bus tours, 362, 363
water meadows, 2, 324, 326, 330, 333, 363
Oxford and the Heart of England, 324–73. See also Stratford-upon-Avon; West Midlands
staying/dining in, 337, 353, 359, 365, 371
Oxford Cathedral (Christ Church College), 362, 725
Oxford University, 30, 326, 330, 360–65. See also specific colleges
Botanic Garden, 209, 362
visitor information, 362
walking tours, 362
Oyster Cards and Travelcards (London), 138

P

Painswick, 301, 308, 321
Painswick Rococo Garden, 301, 308, 312
Palace of Holyroodhouse (Edinburgh), 7, 43, 497, 502, 504, 506, 512
Palace of Westminster (London), 704
Big Ben, 24, 47, 50, 52
Houses of Parliament, 24, 52
Palaces, 7. See also Castles; specific palaces
Pallant House Gallery (Chichester), 9, 150, 182
Parks, national. See also Nature preserves; specific parks
Brecon Beacons, 34, 634, 637–38, 648–51, 661
Cairngorms, 610
Dartmoor, 16, 33–34, 256–59
Lake District, 415
Loch Lomond & the Trossachs, 599, 606, 608
North York Moors, 476–77, 492, 493
Peak District, 16, 453
Pembrokeshire Coast, 630, 654
Snowdonia, 16, 666–67, 674, 678–81
Yorkshire Dales, 463, 475–76, 493

Parthenon Sculptures (British Museum), 8, 47, 70, 71, 84
Partrishow Church (Black Mountains), 648
Passports, 735–36
Pavilion and Pavilion Gardens (Buxton), 449
Peak Cavern (near Castleton), 449–50
Peak District National Park (East Midlands), 16, 448–53, 459
Pembroke Castle, 654, 703
Pembrokeshire, 635, 640, 654–58, 661
beaches, 631, 640, 655–57
farmers' markets, 657
staying/dining in, 655, 658
Pembrokeshire Coast National Park, 630, 654
Penderyn Distillery, 650
Penlee House Gallery & Museum (Penzance), 282
Penmon Priory (near Beaumaris), 684
Penshurst Place, 159
Penwith Peninsula, 239, 286
Pen y Fan (Brecon Beacons National Park), 630, 634, 637, 650
Penzance, 234, 239, 249, 255, 280–83, 289
The People's History Museum (Manchester), 441–42
People's Palace and Winter Gardens (Glasgow), 575
Performing arts, 21. See also Ballet; Concert halls; Music entries; Opera; Symphony orchestras; Theater entries
Performing arts festivals. 722–25. See also Festivals/Special events; Music festivals
Brighton Fringe Festival, 185
Edinburgh International Festival/ Festival Fringe, 503, 724
Glastonbury Festival, 223, 231
Rye Arts Festival, 185
Peter Pan, 47, 82, 87
Peveril Castle (Castleton), 449
Pharmacies, 736. See also Fast Facts for specific areas
Photography Gallery (V&A), 67
Piccadilly (Mayfair), 94
Piccadilly Circus (Mayfair), 95
Pickering, 477, 493
Pilchard Works Museum and Factory (Newlyn), 240
Pitt Rivers Museum (Oxford), 324, 364
Pittville Pump Room (Cheltenham), 300, 319
Plague, outbreaks of, 91, 352, 369, 450–51, 694, 700

Plas Mawr (Conwy), 669, 675, 686–87, 703

Plas Newydd (Llangollen), 673

Pleasure Beach Amusement Park (Blackpool), 418

Pleasure Gardens (Bournemouth), 192, 196

Plockton (Northwest Highlands), 4, 614, 619

Plymouth, 233, 238–39, 289, 701

Police, 733

Pontcysyllte Aqueduct (near Llangollen), 664, 673, 675

Poole, 197, 219

Porth Neigwl beach (Lleyn Peninsula), 684

Portmeirion Village, 4, 675
  staying in, 667, 674, 732

Portobello Road Market (London), 47, 102, 109

Port of Liverpool Building, 436

Portpatrick, 539, 550

Portsmouth, 188–89, 192, 194–96

Post offices, 735. See also Fast Facts for specific areas

Potter, Beatrix, 415, 421, 422

The Potteries (Stoke-on-Trent and area), 349

Potteries Museum and Art Gallery (Stoke-on-Trent), 349

Poultry Cross (Salisbury), 210

Preston Manor (Brighton), 174

Pride in Brighton & Hove, 724, 734

Princess Diana Memorial (Hyde Park, London), 86

Princess Diana Memorial Playground (Kensington Gardens, London), 82

Princes Street Gardens (Edinburgh), 31, 500

Prison and Police Museum (Ripon), 480

The Proms (London), 126, 130, 724

The Prospect (Ross-on-Wye), 352

Pubs, 20, 690. See also Bars; Nightlife
  Brighton, 177
  Cardiff, 644
  Chester, 430
  Edinburgh, 497, 531–32
  Glasgow, 583
  London, 132–33
  Manchester, 446

Pulteney Bridge (Bath), 29, 227, 268

Punting (pole-boating)
  Avon River, 370
  Cambridge, 383, 402
  Canterbury, 168
  Oxford, 330, 333

Q

Quay House Visitor Centre (Exeter), 224, 231, 244, 278

Quayside (Newcastle upon Tyne), 467, 471

Queen Elizabeth Forest Park (near Loch Lomond), 608

Queen Mary's Gardens (Regent's Park, London), 89

Queens' College (Cambridge), 398

Queen's Gallery (outside Buckingham Palace), 40, 72–73

R

Radcliffe Camera (Bodleian Library, Oxford), 363

Ragley Hall (near Alcester), 343, 358

Railways, steam
  Scottish Highlands, 603
  Wales (North/South), 660, 665, 667, 675, 678, 680, 682–83
  Yorkshire, 477

Ramsay Gardens (Edinburgh), 510

Ramblers (walkers' group), 426

Ranelagh Gardens (Chelsea), 98

Rankin, Ian, 339, 513

Rannoch Moor, 590, 602

Raphael's Cartoons (V&A), 66

Redesdale Market Hall (Moreton-in-Marsh), 294, 304

Regent's Park (London), 88–89, 126, 133

Renaissance Galleries (V&A), 67

Rhossili (Gower Peninsula), 635, 653

Ribchester, 414, 417

Richard III, 57, 59, 161, 312, 339

Ridgeway National Trail (near Avebury), 200

Rievaulx Abbey (near Thirsk), 12, 463, 466, 476, 480

Ripon, 479–80, 493

Road Scholar (educational trips), 716

Robert the Bruce, 546, 549, 563, 610, 698

Robin Hood, 453, 454

Robin Hood's Bay (near Whitby), 477

Rodmarton Manor (near Cirencester), 6, 39, 292, 301, 313, 705

Rogers, Lord Richard, 633, 644, 705

Rollright Stones (near Chipping Norton), 302–3

Roman Alcester Heritage Centre, 358

Roman amphitheater (Cirencester), 315–16

Roman Baths Museum and Pump Room (Bath), 8, 29–30, 223, 227, 228, 266–68

Roman Britain, 482–83, 696. See also specific attractions and cities/towns; entries starting with "Roman"
  Cotswolds 10, 292, 294, 299, 300–1, 303, 306, 314–17
  Kent/Sussex, 10, 142, 150, 183, 209
  Northwest, 417
  South-Central England, 10, 28,
    191, 192, 198, 212–13
  Yorkshire and the Northeast, 2, 462, 471, 472, 483, 696

Roman Museum (Canterbury), 26–27, 144, 151, 170

Roman Painted House (Dover), 164

Roman Walls and amphitheater (Chester), 10, 30–31, 406, 408–9, 412, 430–31

Rose Garden (Hyde Park, London), 84

Rose Street (Edinburgh), 502–3

Rosetta Stone (British Museum), 8, 47, 68, 70

Rosslyn Chapel (Roslin), 542, 563–64

Ross-on-Wye, 352, 373

Rothesay Castle (Isle of Bute), 554

Rotten Row (Hyde Park, London), 84, 86

Round Pond (Kensington Gardens, London), 87

The Rows (Chester), 31, 408, 428

Royal Academy of Arts (Mayfair), 94

Royal Albert Hall (London), 74, 130
  The Proms, 126, 130, 724

Royal Albert Memorial Museum (Exeter), 224, 231, 244, 278

Royal Armouries Museum (Leeds), 8, 463, 473, 490

Royal Avenue (Chelsea), 97

Royal Botanic Garden (Edinburgh), 497, 506–7, 550

Royal Britain, 40–43. See also specific monarchs
  notorious/memorable monarchs, 147, 160–61

Royal Court Theatre (Chelsea), 96

Royal Crescent (Bath), 29, 227, 269–70, 704

Royal Deeside and Highland Perthshire, 599, 627. See also Balmoral Castle and Estate; Braemar and entries following

Royal Hospital Chelsea, 97–98

Royal Liver Building (Liverpool), 436

Royal Lyceum Theatre (Edinburgh), 497, 533

Royal Mews (outside Buckingham Palace), 40, 73

Royal Mile (Edinburgh), 2, 31, 43, 496, 502

Royal National Theatre (London), 21, 133

Royal Opera House (London), 21, 38, 62, 126, 130, 131

Royal Pavilion (Brighton), 7, 37, 43, 143, 146, 147, 172–73, 174

Royal Pump Room Museum (Harrogate), 474

Royal Scottish Academy. See National Gallery of Scotland and Royal Scottish Academy

Royal Shakespeare Theatre (Stratford-upon-Avon), 2, 21, 27, 324, 328, 368, 370, 723

Royal Society for the Protection of Birds, 550, 684

Royal Sudeley Castle and Gardens (near Winchcombe), 300, 312

Royal Worcester Porcelain Works (Worcester), museum at, 329, 337, 354

Rugby, 534, 641, 643–44

Runnymede, 136, 694, 698

Ruskin, John, 407, 415, 419, 423

Russell, Sir Gordon, 301, 305

Russell-Cotes Art Gallery & Museum (Bournemouth), 192, 196

Rydal Mount (near Grasmere), 411, 415, 424

Rye, 5, 146, 150, 178–81, 185, 707

Rye Arts Festival, 185

Rye Bonfire Weekend, 185

Ryedale Folk Museum (Hutton-le-Hole), 476

Rye Harbour Nature Preserve, 180–81

S

Saatchi Gallery (Chelsea), 97

Sackville-West, Vita, 36, 143, 148, 150, 153, 156, 297, 310. *See also* Knole; Sissinghurst

Safety, 736

Sainsbury Centre for Visual Arts (Norwich), 9, 397, 705

St. Andrew, Church of (Slaidburn), 416

St. Andrews, Royal and Ancient Golf Club of (Fife), 558, 608

St. Anne's Well (Buxton), 449

St. Anne's Well (Great Malvern), 350

St. Augustine's Abbey (Canterbury), 26, 144, 151, 167, 168, 170, 699

St. Botolph's Church (Boston), 456

St. Bride's Bay, 631, 656–57

St. Brynach's Church (Nevern), 658

St. David's, 640, 657–58

St. David's Cathedral, 657

St. Edmundsbury Cathedral (Bury St. Edmunds), 379, 384

St. Fagan's Castle (Cardiff), 645

St. George's Chapel (Windsor Castle), 135–36

St. George's Guildhall (King's Lynn), 381, 384

St. Giles, High Kirk of (Edinburgh), 511

St. Govan's Chapel (near Stackpole), 656

St. Ives, 4, 32, 226, 234–35, 241–42, 284–87, 289

getting around, 285

prehistoric sites around, 286

St. Ives Museum, 286

St. Ives Parish Church, 286

St. James, Church of (Chipping Campden), 297, 298, 304

St. James's Church and Market (Mayfair), 95, 126, 130

St. James's Park (London), 26, 61

St. John the Baptist, Parish Church of (Cirencester), 314–15

St. John's Church (Bishop's Castle), 356

St. John's College (Cambridge), 401

St. Laurence, Church of (Bradford-on-Avon), 260–61

St. Laurence's Church (Ludlow), 336, 357

St. Margaret's Church (Canterbury), 170

St. Margaret's Church (King's Lynn), 380, 384

St. Martin-in-the-Fields Church (London), 82, 126, 130

St. Martin's Church (Canterbury), 170, 696

St. Mary in Castro, Church of (Dover Castle), 165, 696

St. Mary Redcliffe (Bristol), 273–74

St. John the Baptist Chapel, 274

St. Mary's Church (Beverley), 481

St. Mary's Church (Chipping Norton), 299, 302

St. Mary's Church (Painswick), 308

St. Mary's Church (Penzance), 281

St. Mary's Church (Ross-on-Wye), 352

St. Mary's Church (Rye), 179

St. Mary's Church (Shrewsbury), 336, 348, 356

St. Mary's Church (Whitby), 467

St. Michael's Church (Southampton), 196

St. Michael's Mount (near Penzance), 33, 222, 225–26, 234, 239, 240, 249

St. Mungo's Cathedral. *See* Glasgow Cathedral

St. Nicholas' Church (Alcester), 358

St. Nicholas Priory (Exeter), 278

St. Oswald's Church (Warton), 419

St. Paul's Cathedral (London), 2, 24–25, 47, 54–55, 91, 363, 693, 700, 704

St. Peter and St. Paul, Church of (Lavenham), 384

St. Peter Mancroft, Church of (Norwich), 395

St. Thomas Church (Salisbury), 210

St. Vincent Street Church (Glasgow), 567, 575

Saint's Way (Padstow to Fowey), 232

Salford Quays (Manchester), 414, 444

Salisbury, 28, 191, 198, 210–13, 219

Salisbury and South Wiltshire Museum, 212

Salisbury Cathedral, 28, 191, 198, 202, 212, 213, 703

Cathedral Close, 28, 191, 202, 211, 213

sacred music festival at, 185, 724

tower tours of, 212

Saltram House (near Plymouth), 6, 239, 247–49

Samuel Johnson Birthplace Museum (Lichfield), 346

Sandringham House (near King's Lynn), 381

Sandwood Bay & Beach (Northwest Highlands), 591, 617–18

Scarista Beach (Isle of Harris), 622–23

Science and technology attractions. *See also specific attractions/ museums*

Bristol, 274

Cardiff, 644

Edinburgh, 502

Glasgow, 575

London, 8, 71, 80, 82, 440

Northwest, 410, 414, 436, 443, 445

Oxford, 364

Yorkshire and the Northeast, 8, 31, 463, 465, 471, 488, 701

Science Centre (Glasgow), 575

Science Museum (London), 80

Scone Palace (near Perth), 7, 609, 610

Scorhill Stone Circle (Dartmoor National Park), 258

Scotland. *See also* Edinburgh; Glasgow; Glasgow and the Scottish Lowlands; Golf *entries;* Scottish Highlands and Islands

bagpipes, 690

clans, 612–13

golf, 558–59

tartans, 612

Scotland Street School Museum (Glasgow), 574

Scott, Sir Walter, 511, 512, 513, 547, 707, 713. *See also* Abbotsford

Scott Monument (Edinburgh), 512

Scott Polar Research Institute (Cambridge), 402

Scottish Highlands and Islands, 2, 35, 590–627. *See also* Hebrides; North Argyll to Lochaber, tour of; Northwest Scottish Highlands; Trossachs to Balmoral, tour of

staying/dining in, 605, 611, 619, 625

Scottish Lowlands. *See* Glasgow and the Scottish Lowlands

Scottish National Gallery of Modern Art (Edinburgh), 507

Scottish National Portrait Gallery (Edinburgh), 503

Scourie (Northwest Highlands), 619

Sculpture Gallery (V&A), 66

SEA LIFE London Aquarium, 83
Selfridges (London), 102, 107
Senedd (Welsh National Assembly, Cardiff Bay), 11, 30, 633, 644, 705
Senior travelers, 736
The Serpentine (Hyde Park, London), 47, 82, 86
Shakespeare, William, 2, 344, 369, 691, 699, 706, 707, 708
Shakespeare attractions (Stratford-upon-Avon), 368
    Anne Hathaway's Cottage, 27, 327, 331, 370
    Hall's Cröft, 27, 327, 331, 368, 369
    Holy Trinity Church, 27, 327, 331, 368, 369
    Mary Arden's House/Shakespeare Countryside Museum, 370
    New Place/Nash's House, 27, 327, 331, 366, 368, 369
    Royal Shakespeare Theatre, 2, 21, 27, 324, 328, 368, 370, 723
    Shakespeare Centre, 366
    Shakespeare's Birthplace, 13, 27, 327, 331, 366
Shakespeare's Globe Theatre (London), 21, 25, 58, 133
The Shambles (York), 465, 486, 487
ShawGuides (online resource), 719
Sheldonian Theatre (Oxford), 30, 363-64, 704
Shepherd Market (Mayfair), 93-94
Sherborne Wharf Heritage Narrowboats (Birmingham), 333
Sherwood Forest County Park (near Nottingham), 454
Shrewsbury, 35, 336, 348, 355-56, 373
Shropshire Hills Discovery Centre (Craven Arms), 357
Silbury Hill (near Avebury), 200
Silver Gallery (V&A), 67
Sissinghurst (Kent), 2, 36, 143, 150, 156, 209, 297
Skipton, 475, 493
Skye, Isle of (Inner Hebrides), 16, 596, 624-25, 626, 627
Slaidburn, 414, 416-17
The Slaughters, 293, 296, 297, 299, 307
Sloane, Sir Hans, 68, 96
Sloane Square (Chelsea), 96
Smallhythe Place (near Winchelsea), 181
Small Isles (Inner Hebrides), 595, 604
Smith, Maggie, 15, 133
Smoking, 736
Smoo Sea Cave (near Durness), 618
Snowdon, Mount (Yr Wyddfa), 2, 16, 664, 666, 674, 678, 683
    advice for climbers, 668, 678-79
    hiking paths, 678-79, 683

Snowdonia National Park, 16, 661, 666-67, 674, 678-81
Snowdon Mountain Railway, 667, 678
Snowshill Manor and Garden (near Broadway), 297, 300, 305, 311
Somerset, 260-63
Southampton, 196, 219
South-Central England, 188-219. See also Dorset; Hampshire and Dorset Coast; Salisbury; Wiltshire; Winchester
    staying/dining in, 193, 197, 201, 207, 213, 217
Southern Cathedrals Festival, 185, 724
Southern Upland Way starting point (Portpatrick), 550
Southey, Robert, 425, 675
South Foreland Lighthouse (Dover), 163
South Leith Parish Church, 517
South Stack (Anglesey), 665, 668, 684
South Uist, 598, 622, 627
South Wales. See Cardiff and South Wales
Spa towns. See Bath; Buxton; Cheltenham; Great Malvern; Harrogate
Speakers' Corner (Hyde Park, London), 84
Special-interest trips, 716-19. See also Tours
Speedwell Cavern (near Castleton), 450
Spinnaker Tower (Portsmouth), 192, 195
Spode pottery, 349
Sports attractions and venues
    Cardiff, 641, 643-44
    Edinburgh, 534
    Fife, 558, 608
    Manchester, 410, 414, 442-43, 446
Sports events. 722-25. See also Festivals/Special events
    British Open, 558, 559
SS Great Britain (Bristol), 8, 223, 272-73
SS Sir Walter Scott Steamship (Loch Katrine), 608
Stackpole, 640, 655-56
Staffa, Isle of, 621-22
Statues of the Nereid Monument (British Museum), 70
Stephenson, Robert, 675. See also Conwy Railway Bridge
Stevenson, Robert Louis, 2, 496, 500, 511, 513, 530, 708
Stirling, 542, 561, 587, 698
Stirling Castle, 539, 542, 561-62
Stockbridge (Edinburgh), 497, 507

Stoke-on-Trent, 349
Stokesay Castle (near Craven Arms), 357
Stonehenge (near Salisbury), 2, 10, 29, 188, 191, 192, 199, 200, 212, 694, 696
Stone of Scone (Edinburgh Castle), 7, 43, 610
Stornoway (Isle of Lewis), 623
The Story of Rye, 181
Stourhead (near Salisbury), 38, 189, 205-6
Stow-on-the-Wold, 293, 297, 299, 306, 317, 321
Stratford-upon-Avon, 2, 13, 27, 30, 366-71, 373, 691. See also Shakespeare, William; Shakespeare attractions
    Avon River boat cruises, 370
    bus/walking tours of, 366
    Shakespeare season in, 723
    staying/dining in, 371
    tips for visitors, 368
Sunken Garden (Kensington Gardens, London), 87
Surfing, 192, 631, 654, 657, 684
Sussex Downs, 150
Sutton Hoo, Treasures of (British Museum), 71
Sweetheart Abbey (near Dumfries), 548
Symonds Yat Rock (near Goodrich), 353
Symphony orchestras, 130, 173, 177, 584

T
Talbot, William Henry Fox, 205, 207
Tarbert (Kintyre Peninsula), 554, 555
Tartans, 612. See also Woolens and tartans
Tate Britain (London), 9, 26, 58, 401, 435
Tate Liverpool, 413, 435
Tate Modern (London), 2, 11, 25-26, 47, 58, 435
Tate St. Ives, 32, 226, 234, 284, 285
"Tate to Tate" boat ferry (London), 26, 58
Taxes, 736-37
Tea, 691, 711
Techniquest (Cardiff Bay), 644
Telephones, 737-38. See also Fast Facts for specific areas
Telford, Thomas, 675. See also A5; Menai Suspension Bridge; Pontcysyllte Aqueduct
Television, 709
Tenby, 656
10 Downing Street (London), 101
Tenement House (Glasgow), 575-76
Tennis, 719, 723

Tewkesbury, 308, 321

Thatcher, Margaret, 701-2

Theater, 21, 708-9. *See also* Festivals/Special events; Shakespeare, William; Stratford-upon-Avon; *and specific playwrights*
Edinburgh, 533
Glasgow, 585
London, 21, 58, 96, 126, 132, 133

Theater houses/companies. *See also* Royal Shakespeare Theatre
Chichester Festival Theatre, 21, 150, 183
The Minack Theatre (near Land's End), 21, 241
Mull Theatre Company (near Tobermory), 622
Royal Court Theatre (Chelsea), 96
Royal Lyceum Theatre (Edinburgh), 497, 533
Theatre Royal (Brighton), 177
Theatre Royal Bath, 21, 268

Theatre Royal (Brighton), 177

Theatre Royal Bath, 21, 268

Thermae Bath Spa (Bath), 11, 268

30 St. Mary Axe (London), 705

Thomas Becket, Saint, 12, 26, 144, 147, 165, 168, 169, 698

Thomas Carlyle's House (Chelsea), 99

Thomas Hardy's Cottage (near Dorchester), 13, 193, 200

Thomson, Alexander "Greek," 539, 542, 574-75, 576. *See also* Centre for Contemporary Art; Eton Terrace; "Greek" Thomson Trail; Holmwood House; St. Vincent Street Church

Threave Castle (near Castle Douglas), 548

Three Cliffs Bay (Gower Peninsula), 635, 652

The Three Graces (Liverpool waterfront landmarks), 413, 436

Three Peaks (Horton-in-Ribblesdale), 476

Time, 738

Tintagel, 33, 223, 226-27, 235, 242

Tintern Abbey, 636, 673

Tipping, 738

Titchwell Marsh Bird Preserve (near Hunstanton), 393

Tobermory (Isle of Mull), 35, 594, 622, 627

Toilets, public, 738. *See also* Fast Facts *for specific areas*

Tolmen Stone (Dartmoor National Park), 258

Torquay, 236, 238, 289

Torre Abbey (Torquay), 238
Agatha Christie Memorial Room, 238, 338

Torridon (Northwest Highlands), 616

Tourist/Visitor information, 722, 725. *See also* Fast Facts *for specific areas*

Tours, 716-19. *See also* Boat cruises

Tower Bridge (London), 25, 57

Tower of London, 25, 40, 46, 56, 57, 59, 490, 697, 703

Town Hall (King's Lynn), 381

Town House Museum (King's Lynn), 381, 384

Trafalgar Square (London), 26, 62, 100

Traigh golf course (near Arisaig), 604

Traveling to Great Britain, 726-27. *See also* Fast Facts *for specific areas*

Treak Cliff Cavern (near Castleton), 450

Treasurer's House (York), 485-86

Treasures of Sutton Hoo (British Museum), 71

Trebah Garden (near Falmouth), 253-54

Trelissick (near Falmouth), 252

Trengwainton Garden (near Penzance), 234, 239, 255

Trewithen (near Truro), 254

Trinity College (Cambridge), 400-1

Trinity House (Leith), 517

The Trossachs, 599, 606, 608, 627. *See also* Loch Lomond & the Trossachs National Park

Trossachs to Balmoral, tour of, 606-11
national parks, 599, 606, 608, 610

Tudor Merchant's House (Tenby), 656

Turkish Baths (Harrogate), 474

The Turks Head (Penzance), 281, 283

Turner, J.M.W., 9, 26, 55, 58, 407, 419, 423, 636, 706

Tymperleys Clock Museum (Colchester), 390

Uig (Isle of Lewis), 598, 624

The Uists (Outer Hebrides), 598, 622, 627

Ullapool (Northwest Highlands), 598, 617, 626, 627

Ullswater, 415, 426

Underground Passages (Exeter), 225, 231, 278

Union Hotel (Penzance), 280

University Museum of Natural History (Oxford), 364

University of Glasgow, 577

Upper Booth (near Edale), 451

Upton House & Gardens (near Banbury), 345

Usher Gallery (Lincoln), 456

Usher Hall (Edinburgh), 21, 531, 533

Valle Crucis Abbey (near Llangollen), 673

The Valleys (South Wales), 636, 661. *See also* Blaenavon Industrial Landscape

Value-added tax (VAT), 736-37

The Vaults (Leith), 517

Victoria, 43, 66, 72, 173, 381, 444, 477, 612, 695, 701
Balmoral Castle, 599, 610
Kensington Palace, 41, 74, 75
memorials to Albert, 74, 136
statue (London), 61, 100

Victoria & Albert Museum ("V&A," London), 8, 64-67. *See also* *specific attractions/exhibits, identified as "V&A"*
Late View, 46, 66
V&A Shop, 102, 109
visitor information, 66

Villages, most picturesque, 4

Volk's Electric Railway (Brighton), 174

Wade, Charles Paget, 297, 300, 305, 311

Wales. *See* Cardiff and South Wales; North Wales

Wales Millennium Centre (Cardiff Bay), 11, 633, 644

Walker Art Gallery (Liverpool), 9, 413, 436

Walking, 426, 718. *See also* Hiking; Wall walks

Wallace, Sir William, 561, 698

Wallace Monument (Stirling), 561

Wall walks (medieval/Roman)
York, 462, 465, 466
Chester, 406, 408-9, 430

Warton (near Carnforth), 419

Warwick Castle, 27, 209, 325, 327, 328, 332, 342, 647

Waterfalls Walk (Ingleton), 475

Waterfall Woods (Brecon Beacons National Park), 634, 638, 650

Weather, 722, 725

Websites, useful, 725

Wedgwood Visitor Centre (Stoke-on-Trent), 349

Wellington Arch (London), 60, 84

Wells, 5, 223, 230, 261-62, 289

Wells Cathedral, 12, 223, 230, 261-62, 703

Welsh, 635

Welsh Highland Railway, 660, 665, 667, 675, 678, 680, 682-83

Welsh National Opera (Cardiff Bay), 644

Wenlock Edge (Much Wenlock to Craven Arms), 348

Wenlock Priory (Much Wenlock), 348

Werburgh, Saint, 429, 430

Wesleyan Chapel (Penzance), 281

West Coast of Scotland, 538, 552–57
ferry trips along, 539, 543, 554

West Country, 222–89. See also
Bath; Bristol; Dartmoor
National Park; Exeter;
Penzance; Somerset; St. Ives
great gardens, 250–55
great houses, 244–49
Penwith Peninsula, 239–41
southwest coast, 236–43
staying/dining in, 235, 243, 255,
259, 263, 271, 275, 279, 283,
287

West End (Glasgow), 539, 540, 576,
577

West End (London), seeing plays in,
46, 132

Western Isles Museum (Stornoway),
623

Western Scottish Highlands, 590,
591, 598. See also Northwest
Scottish Highlands

West Gate (Canterbury), 166

West Kennet Long Barrow (near
Avebury), 200

West Midlands, 340–45, 346–53,
354–58, 459. See also Oxford
and the Heart of England;
Stratford-upon-Avon

Westminster. See Palace of
Westminster

Westminster Abbey (London), 12,
24, 50, 53, 188
Henry VII's Lady Chapel, 53, 703
historical events, 53, 610, 693,
694, 702

Westminster Bridge (London), 24, 52

Westwood, Vivienne, 62, 66, 265

Whisky, 293, 497, 517, 690, 713
Distillery Destinations tours, 719
Edradour Distillery (near Pit-
lochry), 609–10
Penderyn Distillery, 650
Royal Mile Whiskies (Edinburgh),
518, 522
Tobermory distillery tours (Isle of
Mull), 622

Whitby, 467, 470, 477, 493

White Cliffs of Dover, 16, 42, 143,
145, 146, 151, 163, 164

Whitehall (London), 100–1

White Hart Hotel (Lewes), 150, 175

White Hart Royal (Moreton-in-
Marsh), 304

Whitesands beach (near St. David's),
657

White Scar Caves (near Ingleton),
475–76

White Tower (Tower of London), 59,
697, 703

Whitworth Art Gallery (Liverpool),
414, 443

Wicken Fen Nature Preserve (near
Ely), 16, 377, 393

Willis Corroon Building (Ipswich), 391

Wilton Diptych (National Gallery),
63, 706

Wilton House (near Salisbury), 37,
192, 203–4, 704

Wiltshire, 198–200, 202–7. See also
Stonehenge

Winchelsea, 181

Winchester, 5, 188, 190, 214–17, 219,
483
Austen's grave, 214, 216
Cathedral, 12, 190, 214, 697
Cheyney Court, 215
Deanery, 215
sacred music festival, 185, 724

Winchester City Mill, 216

Winchester College, 216

Winchester Military Museums, 217

Windermere, 35, 411, 415, 420–21,
424

Windmill Hill (near Avebury), 200

Windsor and Eton, 134–36

Windsor Castle, 41–42, 134–36, 647,
697
Changing of the Guard, 135
St. George's Chapel, 135–36, 647

Winfield House (Regent's Park,
London), 89

Winged Victory (Wellington Arch,
London), 60, 84

Woburn Abbey and Safari Park,
387–88

Wollaton Hall (Nottingham), 454

Wolvesey Castle (Winchester), 190,
216

Woolens and tartans, 102, 109, 522,
608, 612

Woolf, Leonard, 13, 37, 143, 157. See
also Monk's House

Woolf, Virginia, 13, 37, 143, 157, 701,
707–8. See also Monk's House
Knole, 142, 148–49, 153

Woolstaplers Hall (Chipping
Campden), 297, 298, 304

Worcester, 329, 337, 354–55, 373
Elgar Trail, 329

Wordsworth, William, 2, 4, 35, 410,
420, 427, 666, 701, 708. See
also Dove Cottage; Old
Grammar School; Rydal
Mount; below
grave (Grasmere), 13, 425

Wordsworth Museum (Grasmere),
411, 415, 425

World Museum Liverpool, 414, 436

The World of Beatrix Potter
(Bowness-on-Windermere), 421

World War II sites/attractions
Churchill Museum/Cabinet War
Rooms (London), 100, 693
Dover Castle, 162–63, 165, 647
Eden Camp (Malton), 469
Imperial War Museum North
(Manchester), 11, 414, 444,
446

Wren, Sir Christopher, 30, 57–58, 78,
79, 91, 95, 130, 97–98, 363–64,
401, 593, 704. See also St. Paul's
Cathedral

Writers' Museum (Edinburgh), 511

Wroxham, 380, 392

Wye Valley Walk (West Midlands/
Wales), 352

Y

York, 2, 5, 31, 464–65, 483, 484–89,
493
ghost walks, 487
medieval wall walk, 462, 465,
466
sightseeing tours, 486
staying/dining in, 489

York Art Gallery, 486, 488

York Boat excursions, 488

York Castle Museum, 465, 487

York Minster, 5, 12, 31, 462–63, 465,
478, 484–85, 703

Yorkshire and Northeast England,
462–93. See also Leeds; York
national parks, 474–77, 493
religious sites, 478–81
staying/dining in, 467, 473, 477,
481, 489, 491

Yorkshire Dales National Park, 463,
475–76, 493

Yorkshire Museum (York), 465, 488

Youth hostels, 732

Ypres Tower (Rye), 179–80

Yr Wyddfa. See Snowdon, Mount

Photo Credits

Note: l= left; r= right; t= top; b= bottom; c= center

p565; Caledonian Hilton: p527; © Alice Carfare: p238, p258, p271; © Thornton Cohen: p v(c), p vi(b), p vii(

p19, p35, p219, pp404-05, p406, p408, p409, p411, p412, p413, p415, p420, p421, p422, p423, p424, p425, ⌐

p428, p430, p431, p434, p437, pp536-37, p538, p539, p540, p542, p543, p544, p546(l and r), p547, p548, p⌐

p550, p551, p552, p554, p555(l and r), p556, p557, p560, p562(t and b), p563, p566, p567, p569, p570, p571(t an

b), p574, p575, p576(t and b), p577, p578, p579, p582, 583, p584, p585(t and b), pp588-89, p590, p591, p⌐

p594, p595, p596, p598, p599, p600, p602, p603(l and r), p604, p605, p606, p608, p609(t and b), p610, p⌐⌐

p614, p616, p617, p618, p619, p620, p622(l and r), p623, p624, p635, p647(c and b), p661, p664, p668, p669,

p670, p674, p676, p678, p680, p681, p682, p684, p685, p686, p690(l), p691(bc), pp720-21; Corbis: © Ted

Spiegel/CORBIS: p673; Covent Garden Hotel: p123; © Amanda Dawes/frommers.com: p106(l); © KIERAN

DODDS/Panos: p31, pp494-95, p496, p497, p500, p502, p503(r), p504, p506, p507, p508, p510, p511, p512,

p513, p514, p516, p517, p518, p519, p522, p523, p524, p525, p531, p532, p533, p712(r); Getty: David Cannon/Getty

Images: pp558-59; Popperfoto/Getty Images: p264; Sasha/Getty Images: p339(tl); © Jenny Hardy: p ii(c), p viii

(c), p5, p24, p42, p146, p148, p158, p166(r), p169, p179, p228, p252, p260, p262, p272, p275, p279, p333(t),

p712(l); © Paul Harris: p iii(b), p10, p20, p28, p32, p144, p151, p154, p166(l), p167, p168, p171, pp186-87, p190, p194,

p196, p198, p210, p212, p213(b), p218, pp220-21, p222, p224, p225, p231(r), p232, p233, p234, p236, p241, p242,

p246(l), p256, p276, p278(t and b), p280, p284, p286(r), p694(t); Haymarket Hotel: p119; Hazlitt's: p118;

© Nic Holman: p v(b), p456; Jeake's House: p181; Jew's House Restaurant: p457; Kensington Palace: p75(t); Kobal:

DANJAQ/EON/UA /THE KOBAL COLLECTION: p95; EON/DANJAQ/SONY/THE KOBAL COLLECTION: p15(bl);

ITV Global/THE KOBAL COLLECTION: p15(tr); SEE-SAW FILMS/THE KOBAL COLLECTION: pp14-15(tl); The

Lanesborough: p122; Lebrecht: © Mirrorpix/Lebrecht Authors: p338(2nd from tl); © The Times, London/Lebrecht:

p338(3rd from tl); Montague on the Gardens: p124; National Theatre, © Stephen Cummiskey: p133; National Trust:

©NTPL/Mark Bolton: p248; ©NTPL/Jonathan Buckley: pp140-41; ©NTPL/Andrew Butler: p259; ©NTPL/Eric

Crichton: p156; ©NTPL/Rod Edwards: p390; ©NTPL/Andreas von Einsiedel: p vii(b), p155(b), p204, p246(r),

p344, p672; ©NTPL/John Hammond: p239; ©NTPL/Jerry Harpur: 253; ©NTPL/Andrew Lawson: p310; ©NTPL/

Nadia Mackenzie: p203, p213(t), pp322-23, p340, p455(b); ©NTPL/Nick Meers: p247; ©NTPL/John Miller: p153,

p155(t); ©NTPL/Robert Morris: p152, p455(t); ©NTPL/Stephen Robson: p39; ©NTPL/David Sellman: p157; New

Inn Hotel: p235, p243; © Gavin Parsons: p226, p240, p282, p287, p690(tr); Pilrig House: p526; San Domenico

House: p125; The Scotsman Hotel: p530; © Tim Smith/PANOS: p vi(t), p12, p30, p410, p414, p436, p439, p440,

p442(t and b), p443(l and r), p444(l and r), p445, p446, p447, pp460-61, p462, p464, p465, p466, p471(l),

p472, p473, p476(r), p477, p478, p479, p480, p484, p486, p487, p488, p489, p490, p491, p703(c); © Jon Stroud:

p4, pp290-91, p292, p294, p295, p298, p305, p306, p309, p319, p321, p329, p332, pp688-89; Superstock: © age

fotostock/SuperStock: p68, p178; © Art Archive, The/SuperStock: p147, p690(tc); © Axiom Photographic

Limited/SuperStock: p209(tr); © Peter Barritt/SuperStock: p286(l); © Bridgeman Art Library, London/SuperStock:

p467; © Everett Collection/SuperStock: p698, p701; © Robert Harding Picture Library/SuperStock: p208, p230,

p418(r), p454; © Image Asset Management Ltd./SuperStock: p694(c and b), p695(c), p700(l); © JTB Photo/

SuperStock: p170; © Marka/SuperStock: p695(b); © Picture Colour Library/SuperStock: p91(b), p265(t);

© Science and Society/SuperStock: p205(l), p699(l), 700(r); © Stock Montage/SuperStock: p699(r);

© SuperStock/SuperStock: p15(bc), p702(t); © Yoshio Tomii/SuperStock: p690(br); © Travel Library Limited/

SuperStock: p 214, p360; © Steve Vidler/SuperStock: p134, p691(tl); © View Pictures Ltd/SuperStock: p691(tc);

© Visual & Written/SuperStock: p viii(l), p708; © Chris Warren/SuperStock: p467; The Swan Hotel: p263;

© Chiara Tocci: p630, p643; © Anthony Woods: p ii(b), p iii(t), p8, p62(r), p67, p70(t and b), p71, p72,

p80, p83, p86(t and b), p87(t and b), p92, p94, p96, p98, p99(t and b), p100, p101, p111, p114, p137, p697(l).